HANDBOOK OF POSITIVE PSYCHOLOGY IN SCHOOLS

The *Handbook of Positive Psychology in Schools* offers the most current and comprehensive insights into how positive psychology principles provide a framework for young people to become active agents in their own learning. The third edition of this groundbreaking volume assembles the latest global research identifying fundamental assets—hope, optimism, gratitude, self-efficacy, emotional regulation, among others—that support students' learning and well-being. Chapters examining social-ecological perspectives on classroom quality and school climate provide best practice guidance on schoolwide policies and practices. These 35 new chapters explore positive psychology's ongoing influence and advances on prevention, intervention, and assessment practices in schools.

Kelly-Ann Allen is Senior Lecturer in the Faculty of Education, Monash University, Australia, and Honorary Senior Fellow of the Centre for Wellbeing Science in the Melbourne Graduate School of Education at the University of Melbourne, Australia. She is a Fellow for the Australian Psychological Society and the College of Educational and Developmental Psychologists and is currently Editor-in-Chief of the *Educational and Developmental Psychologist* as well as Co-Founder and Co-Editor-in-Chief of the *Journal of Belonging and Human Connection*. In 2020, Dr Allen was recognized by the The Australian as one of Australia's top 40 early career researchers, listed within the top five for her discipline.

Michael J. Furlong is Distinguished Professor Emeritus and Research Professor in the International Center for School-Based Youth Development at the University of California Santa Barbara, USA. There, he is also Principal Investigator of Project Covitality, which supports schools' efforts to foster social-emotional development for all students. He is currently Associate Editor of the *Educational and Developmental Psychologist*. He was awarded a 2021–2022 University of California Edward A. Dickson Emeritus Professorship.

Dianne Vella-Brodrick is Professor and Gerry Higgins Chair in Positive Psychology at the Melbourne Graduate School of Education and Deputy Director and Research Director at the Centre for Wellbeing Science at the University of Melbourne, Australia. She founded the Australian Positive Psychology Network and directed the inaugural Master of Applied Positive Psychology program at the University of Melbourne. She is a Fellow and serves on the Council of Advisors of the International Positive Psychology Association. Dianne is also the founder of the innovative

Bio-Dash wellbeing program which aims to make learning about well-being engaging for students through the use of biofeedback.

Shannon M. Suldo is Professor and Director of Clinical Training in the School Psychology Program at the University of South Florida, USA. There, she is Principal Investigator of a federally funded study to evaluate the efficacy of the Well-Being Promotion Program, a manualized small group positive psychology intervention for middle school students with low life satisfaction. She is a Licensed Psychologist and provides school-based mental health services to youth in the Tampa area. She is currently Associate Editor of *School Mental Health* and President of the Society for the Study of School Psychology.

"An expert team of editors and contributors from around the globe has joined forces to produce a comprehensive, scientific, cross-cultural snapshot of contemporary positive psychology in schools. This book offers a refreshing array of perspectives, processes, and practices that can transform schools into places that intentionally promote wellness and success for students of all ages and levels."

—*John J. Murphy, Professor of Psychology at
the University of Central Arkansas, USA*

"The *Handbook of Positive Psychology in Schools, Third Edition*, is a major accomplishment and an immense body of knowledge for anyone interested in children's well-being and positive development. Since its initial study by a small group of devoted experts, positive psychology has grown and developed into a scientific movement. These thirty-five chapters, sorted into five sections, presents a thoughtful effort to better understand not only the positive psychology of children, especially in schools, but also how the COVID-19 pandemic has caused significant changes in schools and learning as well as in children's lives."

—*Asher Ben-Arieh, Full Professor in the Paul Baerwald School of
Social Work and Social Welfare at the Hebrew University of Jerusalem, Israel*

EDUCATIONAL PSYCHOLOGY HANDBOOK SERIES
Series Editor: Patricia A. Alexander

HANDBOOK OF MOTIVATION AT SCHOOL
Edited by Kathryn Wentzel and Allan Wigfield

HANDBOOK OF MORAL AND CHARACTER EDUCATION
Edited by Larry P. Nucci and Darcia Narvaez

HANDBOOK OF SELF-REGULATION OF LEARNING AND PERFORMANCE
Edited by Barry J. Zimmerman and Dale H. Schunk

HANDBOOK OF RESEARCH ON LEARNING AND INSTRUCTION
Edited by Patricia A. Alexander and Richard E. Mayer

THE INTERNATIONAL GUIDE TO STUDENT ACHIEVEMENT
Edited by John Hattie and Eric M. Anderman

THE INTERNATIONAL HANDBOOK OF COLLABORATIVE LEARNING
Edited by Cindy E. Hmelo-Silver, Clark A. Chinn, Carol Chan, and Angela M. O'Donnell

INTERNATIONAL HANDBOOK OF RESEARCH ON CONCEPTUAL CHANGE, 2ND EDITION
Edited by Stella Vosniadou

HANDBOOK OF POSITIVE PSYCHOLOGY IN SCHOOLS, 2ND EDITION
Edited by Michael J. Furlong, Rich Gilman, and E. Scott Huebner

HANDBOOK OF MORAL AND CHARACTER EDUCATION, 2ND EDITION
Edited by Larry Nucci, Tobias Krettenauer, and Darcia Narvaez

HANDBOOK OF POSITIVE PSYCHOLOGY IN SCHOOLS, 3RD EDITION
Edited by Kelly-Ann Allen, Michael J. Furlong, Dianne Vella-Brodrick, and Shannon M. Suldo

HANDBOOK OF POSITIVE PSYCHOLOGY IN SCHOOLS

Supporting Process and Practice

THIRD EDITION

Edited by Kelly-Ann Allen, Michael J. Furlong,
Dianne Vella-Brodrick and Shannon M. Suldo

Routledge
Taylor & Francis Group

NEW YORK AND LONDON

Cover image: Emma Cleine, www.emmacleine.com

Third edition published 2022
by Routledge
605 Third Avenue, New York, NY 10158

and by Routledge
2 Park Square, Milton Park, Abingdon, Oxon, OX14 4RN

Routledge is an imprint of the Taylor & Francis Group, an informa business

First edition published by Routledge 2009

Second edition published by Routledge 2014

Library of Congress Cataloging-in-Publication Data
Names: Allen, Kelly-Ann (Educational psychologist), editor. |
Furlong, Michael J., 1951– editor. | Vella-Brodrick, Dianne, editor. |
Suldo, Shannon M., editor.
Title: Handbook of positive psychology in schools: supporting process and
practice / edited by Kelly-Ann Allen, Michael J. Furlong, Dianne
Vella-Brodrick, Shannon M. Suldo.
Description: Third edition. | New York, NY: Routledge, 2022. |
Includes bibliographical references and index. | Identifiers: LCCN 2021036097 (print) |
LCCN 2021036098 (ebook) | ISBN 9780367420826 (hardback) |
ISBN 9780367855864 (paperback) | ISBN 9781003013778 (ebook)
Subjects: LCSH: School psychology—Handbooks, manuals, etc. |
Positive psychology—Handbooks, manuals, etc.
Classification: LCC LB1027.55 .H363 2022 (print) | LCC LB1027.55 (ebook) |
DDC 370.15—dc23
LC record available at https://lccn.loc.gov/2021036097
LC ebook record available at https://lccn.loc.gov/2021036098

ISBN: 978-0-367-42082-6 (hbk)
ISBN: 978-0-367-85586-4 (pbk)
ISBN: 978-1-003-01377-8 (ebk)

DOI: 10.4324/9781003013778

Typeset in Bembo
by codeMantra

Access the Support Material: www.routledge.com/9780367855864

CONTENTS

Contents

FOREWORD

We face an extraordinary moment in education. The social and economic fallout of the pandemic and the global reckoning around race relations have provided us with a long-overdue opportunity to rethink and redo how we educate young people. Do we continue along a path that perpetuates a transactional view of students, focusing on college and career readiness in service of economic outcomes? Or do we shift this paradigm by recognizing each child's full humanity and boundless potential to create a flourishing life for themselves and help build a better world?

The scientists and practitioners who have contributed to this book and the entire field of Positive Psychology make a clear case for the latter. At the Greater Good Science Center at UC Berkeley, we, too, make this argument. For 20 years, we have been translating science into practical ways people can foster well-being in their lives in service of building a more compassionate and resilient world. Again and again, as the Center's education director, I meet education professionals from all over the world who share this vision. Most of us who enter the field of education do so because we want to make a difference in the world and the lives of children—it is a gnawing drive that sustains us in the face of overwhelming challenges and inequities within our school systems and society itself. Teachers know there is more to education than academic success because they interact at a profound level with human beings, each with their unique experiences, struggles, and dreams, and who are so much more than a test score. Indeed, many educators tell me that when they started helping students cultivate empathy, compassion, gratitude, mindfulness, emotional skills, and other tenets of Positive Psychology, they felt that "this is why I got into education!"

We are fortunate to have volumes such as this one to make a case for bringing human flourishing into classrooms and to deepen our understanding of *how* to do it. Schools worldwide are adopting social-emotional learning, mindfulness, character education, and other forms of Positive Education. However, to do this work effectively, educators need to have the vision to work toward. In other words, what is our individual and collective potential as human beings, and how do we achieve it?

At Greater Good, we start with the premise that our capacity for connection, kindness, and compassion far outweighs our proclivity for selfishness, greed, and violence—a premise that science not only corroborates but also makes imperative for personal and societal well-being. Cultivating this side of ourselves and our communities takes effort, with schools assuming a significant role. However, as principals and educators quickly learn, 30-minute, weekly lessons that teach a social or emotional or ethical skill are insufficient. To truly make an impact requires a whole school effort: school leaders, teachers, staff, students, parents, and the greater community must work together to foster a learning environment where *all* stakeholders thrive.

Communicating the importance of well-being along with what is possible is the first step. The opening chapters offer several models that school leaders can use to frame their vision, including the well-known PERMAH framework, which now includes the sixth pillar, physical *Health* (Chapter 2). Leaders then need to put their words into action. As years of testing have taught us, we measure what matters. If well-being matters, leaders need instruments such as the Social-Emotional Health Survey (Chapter 4) to understand how their school community members are faring and whether their efforts to cultivate well-being are working. Nevertheless, I challenge schools to do more than just surveys. To truly create a school culture where everyone thrives, leaders need to deeply listen to their students, staff, and community members—and then encourage everyone to do the same for each other. If Greater Good has only one message from science to communicate to the world, it is this: we thrive in healthy, positive relationships. One of the most powerful experiences we can have as human beings is to be seen, heard, and valued in our full humanity.

United under a shared vision of well-being for everyone, the next step is to teach the skills that lead to thriving. Over 20 years of research in positive psychology has shown us that human beings are very complex, and a "one-size-fits-all" approach does not exist. This is "rocket science," as one human development expert has described. However, we must start somewhere, and helping students to *experience and feel* the benefits of practicing prosocial qualities such as optimism (Chapter 8), gratitude (Chapter 9), mindfulness (Chapter 10), and empathy (Chapter 15) can help motivate them and provide them with the agency to continue this lifelong work. Beyond the individual benefits of skills such as these are the social ones. Students thrive in a safe learning environment where everyone belongs (Chapter 17), and these skills help create that kind of climate. However, it is not just the youth who can benefit. Adults, too, thrive when they express and receive gratitude from their colleagues or use empathy to understand a child from a different background than their own or practice mindfulness when their work becomes overwhelming. It is breathtaking to consider the kinds of schools we can create when the adults and students work in tandem to foster their well-being and support each other in these efforts.

For those in education who worry about time—how will they fit this into their already over-full schedules—I challenge you to think differently. Educators capably see learning through a cognitive lens. We now need to add the lens of positive human development. To give an example, scientists have discovered that emotions play a crucial role in learning (Chapter 22), influencing where students focus their attention, helping them to remember and retrieve information, and motivating them to learn. Perhaps most importantly, when educators take the time to make academic content relevant and meaningful to students' lives (the M in PERMAH), learning becomes enjoyable, resulting in higher academic achievement, creativity (Chapter 23), and growth orientation (Chapter 21). This recognition of the inner experience of the learning process is a profound shift in how we view and shape education. It puts to rest all industrial school models and honors the wisdom and humanity of each student.

Lastly, one of the most exciting aspects of this work is its universal appeal. As the book highlights, schools worldwide adopt Positive Education practices with great success (Chapters 29–33). At Greater Good, we, too, have experienced the outpouring of global interest, hosting educators from over 40 countries at our annual Summer Institute for Educators. While the joy of bringing together people representing many different racial, cultural, and religious backgrounds is palpable, we are ultimately humbled by how much we have to learn from them. Gratitude, as science defines it, does not mean the same thing for everyone. In certain cultures, saying "thank you" is considered an insult when helping another person is seen as a duty. Our emotional displays are culture-specific, as well. Some cultures value external displays of excitement, while others prefer a calm demeanor. For our increasingly diverse schools, these differences offer an extraordinary opportunity to grow our understanding and respect for one another as we delight in the variety of approaches to life.

Years ago, I interviewed Paul Tough about his bestseller book *How Children Succeed*. At one point, he said to me, "When I asked parents what they wanted most for their children when they grow up, they all said the same thing: I just want my child to be happy. *But no one agreed on how to make that a reality*." It is a great gift to humankind to even consider the possibility of such an outcome. It is a greater gift that scientists and practitioners alike are working hard to deepen our understanding of how to achieve it. May this book offer guidance and hope along the way.

Vicki Zakrzewski, PhD
Education Director
Greater Good Science Center at University of California Berkeley

ACKNOWLEDGMENTS

Thank you to all the contributors of the book who have so carefully prepared exceptional work. The chapters build a comprehensive compendium of contemporary scientific understandings of positive psychology in schools and the many ways in which positive educational processes can be supported.

The editorial team, on behalf of Taylor and Francis, wish to share our heartfelt appreciation and thanks for the work of cover artist, Emma Cleine who has so generously provided her artwork for the *Handbook of Positive Psychology in Schools*.

Sincere thanks to the Higgins family (especially John and the late Gerry Higgins) for supporting scientific work advancing the promotion and practice of well-being in schools—such as this handbook—by funding the Gerry Higgins Chair in Positive Psychology held by Professor Dianne Vella-Brodrick.

Dianne also wishes to thank all the educators out there who are receptive to creating a school culture that actively and authentically promotes student well-being. Dianne extends her love and gratitude to her family, particularly to her children Joshua and Sarah who, along with their student peers, provide the incentive for this important work.

Michael recognizes the many youths who inspired the development of this handbook and, as sentinels, provide hope for the future, particularly Indigo, Onyx, and Raven.

Kelly-Ann wishes to thank her three children, Henry, Florence, and Georgie, and hope they grow rich with the positive psychological assets emphasized throughout this handbook.

Shannon thanks her graduate student and faculty colleagues at the University of South Florida, and school partners throughout the Tampa Bay area, for their collaboration in identifying, developing, implementing, and evaluating programs and practices that boost youth and educator well-being. She is grateful that her children Emma and Blake can thrive in public schools that nurture academic and emotional health.

All Editors would like to send a special thanks and acknowledgment to two extraordinary dedicated teachers, Jill Young and Kylie Allen who through lockdowns and other challenges, contributed their time to help prepare this handbook for publication with their exceptional proof-reading skills. Your support and dedication to the field of positive psychology in schools is greatly appreciated by the many contributors to this book.

ABOUT THE CONTRIBUTORS

Dr Kelly-Ann Allen, PhD FAPS, FCEDP, is an Educational and Developmental Psychologist, a Senior Lecturer in the Faculty of Education, Monash University, and an Honorary Senior Fellow at the Centre for Wellbeing Science, The University of Melbourne. She is also the co-director and founder of the Global Belonging Collaborative and Editor-in-Chief for both the *Educational and Developmental Psychologist* and *Journal of Belonging and Human Connection*.

Mark Ammermann is a teaching associate and PhD student at Monash University. He is also a practicing artist and has a background as a secondary school teacher and an IT consultant in the Insurance industry. He is interested in how the creative practices and approaches within the art classroom can be effective in broadening the accessibility and participation of students in computer programming.

Gökmen Arslan, PhD, is an Associate Professor of counseling psychology at Mehmet Akif Ersoy University in Burdur, Turkey and also a honorary senior fellow at Centre for Wellbeing Science, University of Melbourne, Australia. His research interests are centered on measuring and improving youths' positive psychological functioning, mental health, and well-being. His research aims to explore how best to provide meaningful programs and resources that promote positive youth development and well-being.

Lisa M. Baker BEd (EC), MAPP, is a PhD candidate at the Centre for Wellbeing Science, The University of Melbourne. She is currently researching how Well-being Literacy can be conceptualized in early education. Lisa is also an early childhood educator and mentor whose practice and pedagogy centers around learning, development, and well-being in the early years.

John D. Barr, BS, is a doctoral student in the School Psychology Program at Utah State University. He is interested in mindfulness and psychological flexibility as mechanisms of change for effective school-based mental health services and youth psychotherapy.

Dr Geetanjali Basarkod is a Postdoctoral Researcher at the Institute for Positive Psychology and Education, Australian Catholic University. Her current work explores the impact of gender and immigrant status on educational and well-being outcomes, using cross-national data. She was awarded her PhD in Psychology in 2019 from the same institute.

George G. Bear, PhD, is a Professor in the School of Education at the University of Delaware. His research focuses on school climate, classroom management, and children's social, emotional, and moral development. He has authored over 100 journal articles and book chapters and eight books, including *Improving School Climate* (2020).

Ronald A. Beghetto, PhD, is the Pinnacle West Presidential Chair and Professor in the Mary Lou Fulton Teachers College at Arizona State University. His research focuses on creative thought and action in educational settings. Beghetto is a Fellow of the American Psychological Association (Division 10), Editor of the *Journal of Creative Behavior*, and a creativity advisor for the LEGO Foundation. He has received numerous awards for his research and teaching (e.g., APA's Berlyne and Arheim Awards for research and teaching awards from the University of Connecticut and the University of Oregon, including the highest teaching award for early career faculty the Ersted Crystal Apple Award).

Peter Boman, PhD, is both a qualified psychologist and secondary teacher. He has been teaching and researching in the higher education sector since 2001. His interests are broad and cross the boundaries of education, psychology, and counseling. His main areas of research are optimism, well-being, resilience, and covitality.

Giacomo Bono, PhD, is a Professor of psychology at California State University, Dominguez Hills. He researches forgiveness, gratitude, well-being, health promotion, and youth development and directs the Youth Gratitude Project, which examines youths' social-emotional skills and well-being and provides resources and research support to promote student success and wellness.

Keiko C. P. Bostwick, PhD, is a postgraduate research officer in the School of Education at the University of New South Wales, Sydney. Her current research focuses on students' and teachers' growth-focused motivation. Her other research interests include applied educational psychology, STEM education, and quantitative research methods.

Christopher Boyle, PhD, is an Associate Professor in Inclusive Education and Psychology at the University of Exeter. He is a Fellow of the British Psychological Society. He is co-editor (with Kelly Allen) of the new journal *Belonging and Human Connection* which will be launched in 2022. He is an internationally recognized and respected academic and author on the subjects of inclusive education and psychology.

Philip M. Brown, PhD, is a Senior Consultant for the National School Climate Center and a Fellow, Center for Applied Psychology at Rutgers University where he founded and led the Center for Social and Character Development. He co-edited and contributed to the two volumes, *Handbook of Prosocial Education* (2012) and *School Discipline: A Prosocial Perspective* (2016).

Tan-Chyuan Chin, PhD, is a Senior Research Fellow and Director of the Wellbeing Profiler at the Centre for Wellbeing Science, The University of Melbourne. Her research examines the enablers and contextual factors of what contributes to improved and sustained well-being over the lifespan. Tan-Chyuan leads several local government communities and youth well-being projects.

Jonathan Cohen, PhD, ABPP, is the co-president of the International Observatory for School Climate and Violence Prevention; University of Seville, Spain; Adjunct Professor in Psychology and Education, Teachers College, Columbia University; and, a practicing child/adult clinical psychologist and psychoanalyst. He is the author of many papers, chapters, and books.

Rebecca J. Collie, PhD, is a Scientia Senior Lecturer in Educational Psychology at the University of New South Wales, Australia. Rebecca conducts research in the broad areas of well-being, motivation, and social-emotional development using quantitative research methods. Previously, Rebecca worked as a primary school teacher in Melbourne.

Adam Cooper is the Coordinator of Youth and Children's Services at Maroondah City Council in Victoria, Australia and has worked in various roles in local government for over 20 years. He holds a Master of Applied Positive Psychology from the University of Melbourne and is passionate about raising well-being individually and within systems.

Tegan Cruwys, PhD, is an Associate Professor and Clinical Psychologist at the Australian National University. She is an Emerging Leadership Fellow of the National Health and Medical Research Council, Australia. Her research focuses on how social relationships affect mental and physical health, including both advancing theoretical understanding of the social determinants of health, and the translational impact that improves outcomes for vulnerable communities.

Maria K. DiBenedetto's research is focused on self-regulated learning, motivation, self-efficacy, and assessment. She currently works at the Bryan School of Business, University of North Carolina at Greensboro as a Lecturer and Director of Assessment and Reporting. In addition to several chapters and articles, she has published two books and does consulting for schools, testing services, and publishers of books focused on student learning throughout the country.

Dr Theresa Dicke is a Senior Lecturer at the Institute for Positive Psychology and Education, Australian Catholic University. Her research interests lie in the realm of organizational, health, and educational psychology. Applying complex quantitative methods, she has extensively studied the role of (occupational) well-being, performance, and their interrelationship in organizations, mostly focusing on schools and educational settings.

Beth Doll is Professor of School Psychology, University of Nebraska Lincoln. Her research interest is the promotion of youth mental health, the psychological well-being of children, and aspects of school/classroom systems that strengthen students' resilience. Her investigations of students' psychological well-being challenge existing mental health policies and practices.

Erin Dowdy, PhD, is a Professor in the Department of Counseling, Clinical, and School Psychology at the University of California Santa Barbara. She is a licensed psychologist and a nationally certified school psychologist. Her research career and scholarly publications have focused on behavioral assessment, particularly universal assessment for social and emotional health and risk. She is involved in grant-funded research projects including measurement work funded by the Institute of Education Sciences investigating universal screening in schools.

Andrea Downie is an educator, action researcher, and facilitator who has worked with over 200 schools and organizations in Australia and overseas on education redesign, systems leadership, and well-being science. She is a proven change-maker and effective learning and well-being designer. Andrea is the founding director at Project Thrive.

Taylor Duffy is currently a graduate student and is working to obtain her Master's degree in Clinical Psychology from California State University, Dominguez Hills. She plans to obtain a Developmental Psychology PhD and she has goals to teach on the university level as a psychology professor and to conduct research.

Tracy L. Durksen, PhD, is a Lecturer of Educational Psychology in the School of Education at the University of New South Wales, Australia. She conducts research in teacher education and professional development. Her interests include non-academic approaches to teacher recruitment and selection. Previously, Tracy worked as a primary school teacher in Canada.

Denise Dussert has a BA in psychology from Universidad de Chile, and a MA in Applied Positive Psychology from the University of Melbourne. She is the founder of Centro Pinda, a psychotherapy Centre for Latin Americans. Her professional and academic interests are in well-being, positive education, and narrative research.

Raquel Falcó, PhD, student (Health Psychology department, Miguel Hernández University, Elche, Spain), received Master's degree in Psychological Therapy with Children and Adolescents and in General Health Psychology. Research interests include the assessment of stressful life events, social-emotional competencies, bidimensional mental health, and suicidality in adolescents and college students.

Caleb D. Farley, BS, is a doctoral student in the School Psychology Program at Utah State University. He is interested in idiographic approaches to measuring and implementing mindfulness-based interventions with youth and their caregivers.

Jacqueline J. Francis, MEd, BTech (Hons), BBSc, is a PhD candidate at the University of Melbourne Graduate School of Education. Her studies inquire into planning for, developing and measuring effective online positive psychology interventions. She teaches into the breadth and postgraduate subjects and is research assistant for the Well-being Language and Literacy research team.

Jessica Frisina, MEd Psych, is a Psychologist with a keen interest in emotional intelligence, mindfulness, and trauma. Jessica has worked across research and practice in the area of positive education applied to primary and high school-aged children in the hope of bettering their lives.

Erica Frydenberg, Associate Professor, is a Principal Research Fellow in psychology in the Melbourne Graduate School of Education at the University of Melbourne. She has authored and co-authored over 150 academic journal articles and chapters in the field of coping, 25 books on topics ranging from early years through to adolescence and parenting and developed psychological instruments to measure coping.

Dr Aileen Fullchange is a multilingual Licensed Psychologist and a Nationally Certified School Psychologist. She received her PhD in Counseling, Clinical, and School Psychology from the University of California, Santa Barbara and now works at the intersection of mental health and education, as a clinician, assessor, supervisor, and presenter.

Michael Furlong, PhD, is a Distinguished Professor Emeritus of School Psychology and Research Professor at the International Center for School Based Youth Development, University of California Santa Barbara. He co-edited the *Handbook of Positive Psychology in Schools* (2009, 2014, 2021) and served as a past editor of the *Journal of School Violence* (2008–2015). He currently serves as an associate editor of *Educational and Developmental Psychology* and the *Journal of Positive School Psychology*. He collaborates with colleagues on Project Covitality (www.covitalityucsb.info), supporting schools' efforts to foster all students' social-emotional development.

Hannah L. Gilfix, MA, is a doctoral candidate in the School Psychology Program at the University of South Florida. Her current research focuses on the impact of various coping strategies on youth subjective well-being. She is also interested in factors that contribute to greater well-being and sense of purpose in youth adults.

Richard Gilman, PhD, is a licensed child and clinical psychologist president of Terrace Metrics, Inc. Formerly on the faculties of Georgia State University (1999–2002), the University of Kentucky (2002–2007), and the University of Cincinnati Medical School (2007–2018), he served as Director of Psychology and Special Education and Director of School-Based Mental Health Programming (Cincinnati Children's Hospital Medical Center) and Director of the PTSD program (UC Medical School). Dr Gilman is a Fellow of the American Psychological Association and the International Society of Quality of Life Studies. He has published over 100 peer-reviewed papers on factors that best predict optimal mental health, academic and behavioral outcomes across the lifespan. He is an International Research Fellow at Harvard Medical School; Dr Gilman received his MBA in 2018 from Oxford University (Kellogg College).

Regina Giraldo-García is an Assistant Professor at Ball State University. Her research, grounded in critical theories and social justice in education, examines factors that influence disenfranchised students' academic performance. She has published her work in peer-reviewed journals such as *Urban Education*, *Psychology in the Schools*, and *School Psychology International*.

Annie Gowing, PhD, leads the Student Wellbeing Specialization in the Master of Education at The University of Melbourne. How student well-being is understood, implemented, monitored, and evaluated in schools is a longstanding practice, policy, and research focus, along with school connectedness, and the concepts of helping and caring in schools.

Dr Jiesi Guo is a senior lecturer at the Institute for Positive Psychology and Education. He was awarded the Rising Star by American Psychological Society (APS) in 2020. His major research interests include how cultural, social, and motivational development of youth shape individual and gender difference in achievement choice.

Timothy Hsi, PhD, is both a qualified psychotherapist and career development practitioner. He established the counseling service at Singapore Management University and was the Centre Director of the Student Wellness Centre (2003–2015) and is still on the advisory board. He is also the Founding President of the Career Development Association of Singapore.

Lanxi Huang is a PhD candidate at the Centre for Wellbeing Science, Melbourne Graduate School of Education, the University of Melbourne, Australia. Her current research focuses on well-being, lay concept, language, international education, and tertiary education, with specific emphasis on exploring Chinese international students' conceptualization and language used about well-being.

E. Scott Huebner, PhD, is a Professor in the Department of Psychology at the University of South Carolina. His research interests include children's subjective well-being, school climate, positive psychology applications to schools.

Hanchao Hou is a PhD student at the Centre for Wellbeing Science at the University of Melbourne. He was also a research assistant in the Centre for Program Evaluation at the University of

Melbourne. His research interests include Positive Psychology, Wellbeing, Wellbeing literacy, and Computational Social Science.

Rowan Jacques-Hamilton is a Research Assistant at the Centre for Wellbeing Science, The University of Melbourne. His research investigates how personality traits and daily behavior relate to well-being. He has a particular interest in quantitative analyses and using diverse methodological approaches.

Mohsen Joshanloo is an Associate Professor of Psychology at Keimyung University, South Korea. His research focuses on well-being, culture, and measurement. Mohsen completed his PhD in 2013 at Victoria University of Wellington, New Zealand.

Avi Kaplan is a Professor of educational psychology in the College of Education and Human Development at Temple University, USA. His research focuses on identity, motivation, and the role of the environment in these processes.

James C. Kaufman, PhD, is a Professor of Educational Psychology at the University of Connecticut. He is the author/editor of more than 45 books and 300 papers. He is a past president of Division 10 (Society for Psychology of Aesthetics, Creativity, & the Arts) of the American Psychological Association (APA). James has won many awards, including Mensa's research award, the Torrance Award from the National Association for Gifted Children, and APA's Berlyne, Arnheim, and Farnsworth awards. He wrote the book and lyrics to Discovering Magenta, which had its NYC premiere in 2015, and co-authored a book on bad baseball pitchers with his father. His current research interests include creativity and meaning and creativity assessment.

Margaret (Peggy) L. Kern is an Associate Professor at the University of Melbourne's Centre for Wellbeing Science. Her research focuses on understanding, measuring, and supporting well-being across the lifespan for individuals, schools, organizations, and communities. You can find out more about her work at www.peggykern.org

Dr Eui Kyung Kim (She/Her) is an Assistant Professor in the School Psychology Program at the University of California, Riverside. Her research interests focus on understanding the pathways to risk and resilience among children and adolescents. She has been conducting research on universal mental health screening, early identification, and prevention services for children's social and emotional health. Dr Kim is currently conducting grant-funded research on a mentorship program (Check, Connect, & Respect) where undergraduate mentors are trained and supervised to provide one-on-one mentorship to struggling youth in local schools. She also conducts research internationally, examining the social and emotional development of children and adolescents from diverse cultural and linguistic backgrounds.

Fiona H. Lachman is an Education Specialist student in the School Psychology Program at the University of Delaware, with interests in the areas of social and emotional learning, trauma-informed practices, and equity.

Erin Leif, PhD, is a Board Certified Behavior Analyst and senior lecturer at Monash University. In this role, she coordinates the Master of Applied Behavior Analysis program. Dr Leif's research interests include functional behavior assessment and strengths-based, skill-based positive behavior support. She is interested in helping educators adopt and use prevention-focused, evidence-based behavior support practices that facilitate the inclusion of all students.

Michelle H Lim, PhD, is a Research Fellow at the Iverson Health Innovation Research Institute, and Centre for Mental Health at Swinburne University of Technology. Dr Lim is the head of the Social Health and Wellbeing (SHAW) Laboratory and her research is focused on understanding the impact of loneliness and mental health outcomes across the lifespan.

Dr Daniel Loton, PhD, Educational Research Advisor, Connected Learning Department, Victoria University, Honorary Fellow, Centre for Wellbeing Science, The University of Melbourne and Editor of the *International Journal of Applied Positive Psychology*. Dr Loton's research interests include internet gaming disorder, positive psychology and learning, and well-being in higher education.

Professor Herbert Marsh, PhD, DSc, HonDoc, is an "ISI highly cited researcher" (700+ publications, 125,000+ citations, H-index = 180) and is recognized as a leading researcher in both Psychology and Education. He founded and directs the International SELF Research Centre and co-edits the SELF monograph series. He coined the phrase substantive-methodological research synergy which underpins his research interests—including multilevel and structural equation modeling in relation to self-concept, students' evaluations of teaching, and gender issues.

Andrew J. Martin, PhD, is Scientia Professor, Professor of Educational Psychology, and Co-Chair of the Educational Psychology Research Group in the School of Education at the University of New South Wales, Australia. He specializes in motivation, engagement, achievement, and quantitative research methods.

Syed Marwan, PhD IBF, is an Assistant Professor at the Institute of Islamic Banking and Finance (IIiBF), International Islamic University Malaysia (IIUM). Dr Marwan is also a Fellow at the Institute for Research & Development of Policy (IRDP), a think-tank based in Kuala Lumpur. His research interests are in SRI, social finance, and social impact.

Juan C. Marzo is an Associate Professor (Health Psychology department, Miguel Hernández University, Elche, Spain). He is the author of 40 articles published in high-impact journals (Publons H-index = 10). Research interests include Organizational Psychology and Psychological Assessment especially on social-emotional learning and validation of measures. Co-principal Investigator of the Project Covitality-Spain.

Vicki McKenzie is an Associate Professor at the University of Melbourne and is Coordinator of the Master of Educational Psychology, and Master of Educational Psychology/PhD programs. Dr McKenzie has experience as a leader of a multidisciplinary team of school support personnel working with schools on systemic intervention in the areas of student and community well-being.

Stephanie A. Moore, PhD, is an Assistant Professor of School Psychology at the University of California Riverside. Her work focuses on promoting youth wellness by advancing comprehensive and multitiered school mental health support systems. Her expertise includes mental health screening, school and mental health service systems, and implementation science.

Selena Moreno acquired a bachelor's degree in Psychology from California State University Dominguez Hills in Spring 2020. She is interested in exploring the benefits of gratitude intervention in at-risk youth populations. In the future, Selena hopes to pursue her passion for therapy by obtaining her PsyD in Clinical Psychology.

Beatriz Moreno-Amador, PhD student (Health Psychology department, Miguel Hernández University, Elche, Spain), received Master's degree in Psychological Therapy with Children and Adolescents. Research interests include symptomatology of the OCD Spectrum (especially body-focused repetitive behaviors), transdiagnostic and assessment of social-emotional competencies in teenagers and youth population.

Myesha M. Morgan, MA, is a doctoral student in the School Psychology Program at the University of South Florida. She earned a BA in Psychology from the University of South Carolina. Her research interests include the implementation of positive psychology interventions in different cultural contexts and pediatric school psychology.

Lara Mossman developed an online training program for youth football coaches as part of her PhD research. Lara holds a BSc (hons) in Philosophy with Computing, a Master of Arts in Philosophy with Historical Studies, and a Master of Applied Positive Psychology (MAPP). She is a Lecturer at the University of Melbourne.

Christopher P. Niemiec, PhD, is an Associate Professor in Psychology at the University of Rochester. His program of research has extended principles from self-determination theory in social, personality, and developmental psychology, and has applied those principles to the domains of education, health, and organizational behavior. His primary research interests include the nature and function of basic psychological needs, human wellness, health behavior change and its maintenance, life goals, and cross-cultural issues. Also, Dr Niemiec is an award-winning teacher at the University of Rochester, having been named Professor of the Year in the Social Sciences in 2012–2013, among other honors.

Lindsay Oades, PhD, is a Professor and Director of the Centre for Wellbeing Science, at the Melbourne Graduate School of Education, The University of Melbourne, Australia. With over 130 publications, Lindsay's research and scholarship in well-being science spans the health, organizational, and education sectors. He is currently a coordinating lead author on a UNESCO Education Assessment examining the relationship between education and flourishing. He has consulted to the NSW Department of Education and Training and the Australian Mental Health Commission. His current research interests include well-being literacy, Thriveability Theory, and personalized well-being coaching and planning.

Meagan O'Malley, Associate Professor in the School Psychology graduate program at California State University, Sacramento, concentrates on building assets in school environments that support the psychological well-being of youth. Her research has been featured in a variety of outlets, including the *Journal of School Psychology* and *Educational Administration Quarterly*.

Professor Philip D. Parker, PhD is the Deputy Director of the Institute for Positive Psychology and Education at the Australian Catholic University. He received his doctorate in Educational Psychology from the University of Sydney. His major research interest includes educational inequality, developmental transitions, and educational attainment.

Helen Patrick is a Professor of educational psychology in the College of Education at Purdue University, USA. Her research includes associations of classroom contexts and teacher practices with student motivation, engagement, and achievement.

Kent Patrick, PhD, is a Research Fellow at the Centre for Wellbeing Science, The University of Melbourne. He is passionate about research promoting the health and well-being of young people.

Jennica Paz, PhD, is an Assistant Professor in the Department of Counseling and School Psychology at the San Diego State University. Passionate about ensuring high-quality service delivery, her work focuses on positive youth development, strengths-based assessment, resiliency among foster youth, school-based mental health, school violence/safety, psychometrics, assessment, and intervention among CLD students.

Reinhard Pekrun is Professor for Psychology at the University of Essex, United Kingdom, and Professorial Fellow at the Institute of Positive Psychology and Education, Australian Catholic University, Sydney, Australia. He is a highly cited scientist who pioneered research on emotions in education, originated the Control-Value Theory of Achievement Emotions, and authored more than 350 books, articles, and chapters.

Mary L. Phan, BA, is a doctoral student in the School Psychology Program at Utah State University. She is interested in implementing mindfulness-based interventions with underserved youth in public schools.

José A. Piqueras is an Associate Professor (Health Psychology department, Miguel Hernández University, Elche, Spain), Chief of the Applied Psychology Center, member of AITANA research group, and principal Investigator of the Project Covitality-Spain. Publons H-index = 19. Research interests include ICT for assessment and intervention in bidimensional mental health of children and adolescents.

Carmel Proctor, PhD, is a chartered psychologist and accredited psychotherapist. She is the author of research papers and book chapters on youth life satisfaction, character strengths, well-being, and happiness. Her interests are primarily in the areas of positive psychology, applied positive psychology, values, character, virtue, personality, existential psychology, and well-being.

Tyler L. Renshaw, PhD, is an Associate Professor in the School Psychology Program within the Department of Psychology at Utah State University, where he directs research and practicum labs focused on advancing school mental health services. He is interested in both measurement and intervention issues regarding using mindfulness to promote youth and caregiver well-being.

Edwina Ricci has taught in Secondary Schools in Melbourne for 25 years and is passionate about creating environments that enable schools to flourish individually and collectively. She is the Project Manager of the Maroondah Positive Education Network, 27 schools collaborating with the council and community to raise well-being and resilience.

Mark Richardson, PhD, is a freelance industrial designer and learning facilitator with a career spanning industry practice, academic research, and tertiary/postgraduate teaching and learning. His practice investigates how we might transition from current design and production methods to more sustainable, participatory, resilient and accessible systems of creating, making, sharing, and learning.

Kathryn Riley, PhD, is Professor of Urban Education at UCL, Institute of Education and an international scholar whose work bridges policy and practice. She has taught in inner-city schools, held political office, been a local authority Director and World Bank Officer. With DancePoet TioMolina she co-leads The Art of Possibilities http://www.theartofpossibilities.org.uk

Maria Rivera-Riquelme is an Adjunct Professor (Health Psychology Department, Miguel Hernández University, Elche, Spain) and received Master's degree in psychological therapy with children and adolescents. Research interests include psychological assessment of bidimensional mental health, as well as promotion of well-being and mental health by social-emotional skills programs for children, adolescents, and college students.

Anthony J. Roberson, PhD, is currently a practicing school psychologist with Cypress-Fairbanks Independent School District. His research interests broadly concern improving well-being-oriented measurement practices and the use of data in school-based mental health service delivery.

Anne M. Roberts, MEd, is a doctoral candidate in the Department of Educational Psychology at the University of Connecticut. Her research focuses on teachers' perceptions of student curiosity and creativity. Anne has presented regionally, nationally, and internationally on creativity, gifted education, and STEM topics. In addition, she has been published in a few versions of *The Cambridge Handbook of Creativity*.

Tíscar Rodríguez-Jiménez is an Assistant Professor (UCAM Catholic University of Murcia, Murcia, Spain). She is the author of 14 articles published in high-impact journals (Publons H-index = 7). Research interests include Obsessive-Compulsive Symptomatology and suicide in children and adolescents.

Lisa S. Romero is an Associate Professor in the College of Education at California State University Sacramento. Her scholarship on student trust, discipline, and school climate is published in leading peer-reviewed journals. Her work on Latinx student perceptions of school climate is supported by the Spencer Foundation.

Guadalupe Sánchez Martínez has a BA in psychology from University of Valencia and a MA in Applied Positive Psychology from Jaume I University. She is currently a Professor at the FPT University in Vietnam. She has international experience as a psychologist and therapist in the United States, México, Spain, Australia, and Vietnam.

Dale H. Schunk is Professor of Education at the University of North Carolina at Greensboro. His research and teaching interests focus on student learning, motivation, and self-regulation. He has published empirical articles and chapters on these topics and is the author of textbooks on learning and motivation.

David J. Shernoff, PhD, is Director of the Center for Mathematics, Science and Computer Education (CMSCE) and Associate Professor in the Department of School Psychology at the Graduate School of Applied and Professional Psychology at Rutgers University. His research interests include student engagement and flow, STEM, and teacher professional development.

Angela B. Soltys is a doctoral candidate in the School Psychology Program at the University of Delaware, with research interests in the areas of school climate, social and emotional competence, and classroom management and disciplinary techniques.

Victoria Soto-Sanz is an Adjunct Professor (Health Psychology department, Miguel Hernández University, Elche, Spain), received Master's degree in General Health Psychology, and is a member of AITANA research group. Research interest includes psychological factors related to mental health and suicide in adolescents and university students.

Mark Stevens, PhD, is a Postdoctoral Research Fellow at the Australian National University. His research focuses on social-psychological influences on health and health behaviors (particularly physical activity) and draws heavily on the Social Identity Approach.

Shannon M. Suldo, PhD, is Professor and Director of Clinical Training in the School Psychology Program at the University of South Florida. She studies youth mental health in a dual-factor model that considers psychopathology and subjective well-being; and evidence-based positive psychology interventions for promoting positive indicators of student and educator well-being.

Shalva L. Twersky is a doctoral candidate in the Department of School Psychology at the Graduate School of Applied and Professional Psychology (GSAPP) at Rutgers University. Her research interests include classroom climate and engagement, and the connection between pediatric gastrointestinal conditions and mental health.

Shelley R. Upton, PhD, is a postdoctoral fellow in the Psychology Department and Sorenson Center for Clinical Excellence at Utah State University. She received her PhD in school psychology from Louisiana State University in 2020. Her research focuses on the utilization of mindfulness-based interventions and Acceptance and Commitment Therapy.

Rick van der Zwan, PhD, is a neuroscientist, and leader of the Research and Innovation team at Sydney Catholic Schools. He is known internationally for his research and for articulating neuroscience into practice. Rick leads the development and implementation of innovative, research-based educational strategies across Sydney Catholic Schools.

Dianne Vella-Brodrick, PhD, holds the Gerry Higgins Chair in Positive Psychology and is Deputy Director and Head of Research at the Centre for Wellbeing Science, The University of Melbourne. Dianne's research interests include the development and evaluation of well-being programs using innovative quantitative and qualitative methods. She specializes in working with young people in learning environments.

Duyen Vo is a PhD, candidate at Monash University where she is investigating positive psychology interventions to foster the well-being of educators. Her extensive teaching and leadership roles, particularly in disadvantaged schools, in Australia, Italy, and Japan inspired her research interest.

Adam Voight is an Associate Professor in the College of Education and Human Services at Cleveland State University. He works in partnership with schools, communities, and youth to create environments more conducive to the learning and well-being of young people, particularly those marginalized by structural forces like poverty and racism.

Roby Michelangelo Vota, BSc mathematics, BSc & MSc design, is a PhD candidate investigating the psychological concept of collective social intelligence, adopting design research methods. As a researcher, lecturer, and consultant, he aims to support the understanding and presence of social well-being in a variety of social contexts, through a creative combination of experience design, phenomenology, and action research.

Allison Rae Ward-Seidel, EdM, directs research at Rutgers University, evaluating school-wide restorative practices and racial equity. Her scholarship focuses on education reform for social justice, reducing disproportionate discipline, and school-wide social-emotional skill development for staff and students. Ms. Ward-Seidel's elementary teaching experience drives her dedication to equitable school improvement.

Professor Lea Waters AM, PhD, is the Founding Director of the Centre for Wellbeing Science, The University of Melbourne, where she has held an academic position for 24 years. Lea sits on the Science Board, University of California Berkeley's Greater Good Science Center and has published over 110 scientific publications.

Sean N. Weeks, MS, is a doctoral student in the School Psychology Program at Utah State University. He is interested in the relationship of mindfulness and psychological flexibility to youth mental health, especially for individuals identifying as gender and sexual minorities.

Monique West is a PhD candidate and Research Assistant at the Centre for Wellbeing Science, The University of Melbourne. Her PhD investigates the implications of social media on young people's well-being. Monique's research interests include exploration into factors that contribute to optimal and sustained well-being for young people.

Dr Melissa Joy Wolfe is a teacher educator in Visual Art and Media Education at Monash University. Her research in schools applies a creative filmic research methodology. Melissa's feminist research interests and publications in education encompass a filmic synthesis of aesthetics, affect, gender, and belonging through participatory creative methods.

Marissa Yi-Hsuan Wu is a MPsych (Ed&Dev)/PhD candidate at the University of Melbourne. She has a strong interest in social-emotional learning and cross-cultural studies. Marissa completed a Master's in Educational Psychology in both Taiwan and the United States. She is currently a registered psychologist in Melbourne, Victoria, Australia.

Chunyan Yang, PhD, is an Assistant Professor of school psychology in the Graduate School of Education at the University of California, Berkeley. Her research interests focus on understanding how school members (e.g., students, teachers, parents) interact with their living contexts (e.g., school, family, community, culture) to find their resilience in face of a variety of risk factors in school settings such as bullying, teacher-targeted violence, and mental health challenges.

SECTION I

Conceptual and Theoretical Foundations

1

A SELECTED INTRODUCTION TO THE SCIENCE AND PRACTICE OF POSITIVE PSYCHOLOGY IN SCHOOLS

E. Scott Huebner, Michael J. Furlong, Kelly-Ann Allen,
Dianne Vella-Brodrick, Shannon M. Suldo and Rich Gilman

What is positive psychology? Among various definitions, Seligman and Csikszentmihalyi's (2000) seminal article in the *American Psychologist* defined positive psychology as the "...science of positive subjective experiences, positive individual traits, and positive institutions" (p. 5). Peterson further (2006) defined positive psychology as "...those things in life that make life most worth living" (p. 4). These definitions contrasted with the traditional view of positive psychological functioning (i.e., mental health) as merely the absence of psychological problems, focusing on the personal strengths and environmental assets expected to alleviate or prevent psychological problems and promote optimal psychological functioning. Early research based on the positive psychology perspective mostly involved adults, with considerably less attention devoted to children and adolescents.

The potential for applying positive psychology to children and youth, particularly in the context of schools, was highlighted in special issues of *School Psychology Quarterly* (2003) and *Psychology in the Schools* (2004). These efforts were followed by an increase in research attention. Following this increased interest, Huebner and Hills (2011) wrote a commentary for a special issue of *The Journal of Positive Psychology*, which was devoted to research on positive psychology with children and youth. This commentary focused primarily on an article in *Psychological Inquiry* by Richard Lazarus (2003). In his article, Lazarus questioned whether positive psychology "had legs," suggesting that it was likely to become just another of the many psychology fads that come and go. Huebner and Hills concluded that although positive psychology research with youth might be preliminary, the extant work suggested that positive psychology "had legs," offering findings likely to generate additional research and subsequent applications.

Huebner and Hills (2011) also addressed the as-yet relatively neglected literature on positive psychology in schools. For example, it was not until the release of the second edition of the *Handbook of Positive Psychology* (Lopez & Snyder, 2011) that a positive education chapter was included. Given the small literature base at the time, Huebner and Hills concluded that although positive psychology "had legs," it was unlikely at that time to be having more than a modest impact on educational thinking and practices in the United States and elsewhere.

The relative lack of research attention to positive psychology in schools was surprising, given that most children spend substantial portions of their everyday lives in the school setting.

DOI: 10.4324/9781003013778-2

Furthermore, students spend considerable time interacting with teachers and peers in the school setting and their parents regarding schooling matters. However, by 2009, Gilman, Huebner, and Furlong had authored the first edition of the *Handbook of Positive Psychology in Schools*, highlighting the increasing attention to the topic. A second edition appeared in 2014 reflecting the growth of the research and its emerging international scope. Other publications followed, such as Proctor and Linley's (2013) book on positive psychology and children and adolescents, which was aimed at various professions, but included a major section on positive education.

In 2009, Seligman et al. authored a seminal article entitled "Positive education: Positive psychology and classroom interventions." In this article, they argued that positive psychology could have a considerable impact in the school setting, given that nearly all children attend schools. Furthermore, they specifically argued that positive psychology or positive well-being should be infused directly into school curricula to provide "...an antidote to depression, as a vehicle for increasing life satisfaction, and as an aid to better learning and more creative thinking" (Seligman et al., 2009, p. 294).

In 2011, Froh et al. reported on the status of empirical research on positive psychology in school psychology. To do so, they analyzed the articles published in the major school psychology journals over five decades, calculating the frequencies and proportions of that literature devoted to positive psychology topics. That is, they addressed the levels of attention to positive psychology research and practice in the literature, comparing the 2000s to previous historical levels of interest to assess whether the frequencies and proportion of publications had increased, decreased, or remained unchanged across the earlier four decades. In the first edition of the *Handbook of Positive Psychology*, Huebner et al. (2009) proposed a conceptual framework to organize the positive psychology literature. The model was portrayed as a $3 \times 3 \times 4$ matrix that included three personal well-being indicators, four ecosystemic indicators, and three research foci. In line with the research focus portion of the conceptual model, Froh et al. also examined the specific content of the literature to determine the nature and degree of attention to the various research foci. The three foci were basic science, measurement, and interventions. The data from Froh et al.'s study showed that approximately 27% of articles examined focused on positive constructs, with relative stability across the decades: 33% in the 1960s, 27% in the 1970s, 28% in the 1980s, 25% in the 1990s, and 27% in the 2000s. This finding suggested that positive psychology constructs have been of consistent interest to psychologists in schools. However, it could be argued that research focused on positive psychology constructs and practices could have been greater. Furthermore, the authors noted the greater attention paid in the literature to the measurement and intervention domains than the basic science domain. Perhaps this should not have been surprising given the applied focus of school psychology. Whatever the case, positive psychology appeared to be consistently relevant to psychologists who practiced in schools.

The emergence of this third edition of the *Handbook of Positive Psychology in Schools* demonstrates the growing impact of positive psychology research and practice in schools. Compared to the previous editions, this edition provides new information about how research and applications of positive psychology principles and practices are now influencing schooling in many places worldwide as illustrated in Chapter 29. Following the publication of the first and second editions, considerable additional research has appeared in the literature. This research increased the knowledge base concerning how positive psychology can be applied to school settings to emphasize and implement more comprehensive assessment and intervention programs that include positive psychology principles and constructs and the more traditional deficit-focused emphasis. Furthermore, international and national positive psychology associations such as the International Positive Psychology Association (IPPA, which includes a Positive Education Division), International Positive Education Network (IPEN), and Positive Education Schools Association (PESA) have emerged, further demonstrating the impact of positive psychology in general and in the schools in particular. In the following pages, we provide a selective introduction to current positive psychological practices in the schools to provide illustrations of advances in the field, first concerning assessment and then emphasizing the growing intervention literature and increasing systems focus.

Positive Psychology Assessment

Historically, large-scale efforts to monitor mental health and quality of life have focused on base rates of problems and risk factors, and objective indicators of income, health status, and educational attainment (Diener & Seligman, 2004). Given the subjective nature of emotional experiences, feelings and overall judgments of one's quality of life are arguably best assessed using self-report measures. Measures of life satisfaction ask respondents to rate satisfaction with their life as a whole (i.e., global life satisfaction) or satisfaction with domain-specific areas of life that are considered central to overall appraisals of happiness (e.g., school/work, family, and friends). As societal interest in well-being has expanded beyond disease and economic conditions to include perceived quality of life, the past couple of decades have ushered in impressive initiatives to monitor happiness and life satisfaction through direct assessment of individuals' subjective well-being. Since 2012, the annual World Happiness Report has summarized adults' average life satisfaction in approximately 150 countries (Helliwell et al., 2020). The World Happiness Report uses data from the Gallop World Poll, and the primary indicator of subjective well-being is the single-item Cantril ladder question assessing global life satisfaction. Specifically, respondents imagine a ladder with steps numbered from the bottom (0 = *worst possible life*) to the top (10 = *best possible life*) and indicate their current position on the ladder. The annual World Happiness Report rank orders nations by their citizens' happiness reports and draws attention to cross-time changes in average happiness ratings within a given country. Keeping abreast of trends in adults' subjective well-being is critical given the role of teachers, administrators, and other adults in schoolwide positive educative initiatives and the strong relationship between parent and youth happiness.

Children's Worlds is an international project to monitor *youth* well-being. The International Survey of Children's Well-Being (ISCWeB) assessed life satisfaction, happiness, and quality of life among representative samples of 8-, 10-, and 12-year-olds (about 1,000 children per age group, per country) in up to 40 countries (https://isciweb.org/). Data from three waves collected in 2011–2012 (Wave 1), 2013–2014 (Wave 2), and 2016–2020 (Wave 3) permit identification of developmental and national trends in youth subjective well-being. The questionnaire used in Children's Worlds includes items from multiple well-validated measures of global and domain-specific life satisfaction, namely the Students' Life Satisfaction Scale (SLSS; Huebner, 1991) and the Brief Multidimensional Students' Life Satisfaction Scale (BMSLSS; Seligson et al., 2005). The seven-item SLSS and six-item BMSLSS are among the most commonly used global and domain-specific life satisfaction measures, respectively, for children and adolescents in Grades 3–12.

Comprehensive assessment of subjective well-being can also include measures of daily affective experiences. Measures of affect can ask about one's mood at the moment (e.g., "how do you feel right now?") or how often—from *not at all* too *frequently*—one has felt various positive emotions (e.g., interested and delighted) and negative emotions (e.g., lonely and mad) during a specified period of time (e.g., the past day or few weeks). The 27-item Positive and Negative Affect Schedule for Children (PANAS-C; Laurent et al., 1999) is a commonly used self-report measure of youth affect; children and adolescents estimate their frequency of positive and negative emotional experiences over the past few weeks. The Children's World questionnaire includes a short version of Russell's Core Affect scale (Russell, 2003) to assess the frequency of experiences of positive emotions, specifically active, calm, full of energy, happy, relaxed, and satisfied.

As conceptualizations of positive mental health status have evolved to include more than subjective well-being, broader measures of youth and adult flourishing have been advanced. One example is the 20-item EPOCH Measure of Adolescent Well-Being that assesses Engagement,

Perseverance, Optimism, Connectedness, and Happiness (Kern et al., 2016). The EPOCH Measure is theoretically grounded in and is a variation of Seligman's (2011) PERMA model and therefore measures characteristics in youth that are believed to influence the PERMA domains later in life. Another example is the Flourishing Scale (Diener et al., 2010) which is an eight-item measure that assesses one's functioning in the areas of relationships, self-esteem, purpose, and optimism.

Some positive psychology measures assess the promotive factors underlying well-being. For example, the Social Emotional Health Survey-Primary (SEHS-P; Furlong et al., 2013) is a 20-item self-report measure that assesses elementary school students' psychological strengths (i.e., gratitude, optimism, zest, and persistence), which collectively indicate *covitality*. Adolescents can complete the 36-item secondary version (SEHS-S; Furlong, You et al., 2014) or the 36-item version for college students (Furlong et al., 2017). In sum, a growing number of self-report measures can be used to conduct a comprehensive assessment of positive emotional outcomes and associated assets (protective and promotive factors) in both youth and adults. Chapter 7 in this volume illustrates how to assess student subjective well-being in schoolwide mental health screening and integrate data from measures of well-being and ill-being (psychopathology) in line with a dual-factor model of mental health.

Positive Psychology Interventions

Positive psychology is a rapidly growing field of scientific inquiry aimed at helping individuals, groups, and communities feel good, function well, and help others. A key benefit of positive psychology is its highly applied nature and the broad scope of practical activities and formal interventions designed to enhance well-being. Positive psychology interventions have a common aim of improving well-being by increasing positive feelings, behaviors, and thoughts (Hendriks et al., 2020; Sin & Lyubomirsky, 2009) and can help cope with life adversities as well as to thrive and make the most of life. These interventions have been applied in many contexts such as schools (Quinlan et al., 2019; Vella-Brodrick et al., 2020), workplaces, and communities (Page & Vella-Brodrick, 2013). Positive psychology interventions in schools—often referred to as positive education—involve the delivery of well-being interventions through explicit well-being programs and implicit processes and ideally should incorporate best practices in education. Positive psychology interventions can be applied at the individual level, such as with students or teachers, and/or can target the broader systems, including the school culture and community. This breadth of applications is evident from the diverse range of studies described within this handbook. Furthermore, throughout this handbook, the interventions demonstrate that positive psychology interventions are theory-driven and based on empirical research.

Core Considerations of Positive Psychology Interventions

Recent research has identified the core qualities of successful, positive psychology programs in school settings. Specifically, interventions with clear aims and objectives that respond to predetermined needs in a school and have demonstrated desirable long-term outcomes are usually evaluated as being the most desirable in schools (Waters & Loton, 2019). In addition, positive psychology interventions that are effective in school settings foster opportunities for agency, student voice, and student engagement and, in doing so, involve all members of a school community (Vella-Brodrick et al., 2020). As illustrated in Chapter 24, new studies have demonstrated that researcher-based interventions can be codesigned with implementers to offer new and exciting opportunities for engagement and efficacy. Such researcher–implementer collaborations provide the potential to narrow the widely acclaimed gap between research and practice. Finally, effective positive psychology interventions are also sustainable. Although an intervention's sustainability may be at the mercy of the implementer, suitable interventions offer staff training and resources, evaluation, and future planning (Vella-Brodrick et al., 2020). As positive psychology has grown, practitioners have demonstrated that deliberate training can enhance well-being; indeed, professional training is central to the successful implementation of positive psychology interventions (Vella-Brodrick et al., 2017).

The Importance of Individual Fit

Lyubomirsky and Layous (2013) emphasize the importance of purpose and fit for successful, positive psychology interventions, and school-based interventions are no exception. For specific examples, the dosage of positive psychology activities, the variety of activities, the participants' motivations, person-activity fit, and school climate are critical features to consider when delivering well-being interventions (Vella-Brodrick, 2013, 2016). Lyubomirsky and Layous' model also stresses the importance of positive thoughts, behaviors, emotions, and psychological need satisfaction as mediators between successful interventions and enhanced well-being. Furthermore, enforcing or mandating positive psychology interventions for any group within a school setting is unlikely to be effective. Finally, Revord et al. (2018) emphasized that the goal of positive psychology interventions should focus on the individuals or organizations initiating the intervention and the target of the intervention, which could be the initiators themselves.

Nevertheless, there are some limits to the research to date. For example, schools report that whole-school universal approaches involving all stakeholders are rarely a priority compared to standalone programs or activities (e.g., Vella-Brodrick et al., 2020). For another example, empirical validation is lagging, possibly due to the complexity in testing such dynamic and ephemeral environments (Slemp et al., 2017). Fortunately, more scientific attention to systems thinking is starting to emerge within positive psychology (Kern et al., 2019).

Using a Systems Lens to Examine Positive Psychology Interventions and Practices

One example of a valuable systems lens is Bronfenbrenner's (1979) ecological systems theory, which eloquently posits that children's development is substantially influenced by their environments and their interactions across the layers of systems surrounding them. Children's learning opportunities (e.g., cognitive, social, and moral) occur within this context of human development. As such, all children and adolescents are at the center of the school system's layers that can significantly affect their development, including their well-being.

Given the universal and diverse interpretations of positive psychology interventions in schools, systems approaches to examining positive psychology pay homage to existing theoretical frameworks, described in this book (e.g., PERMA, Chapter 2). They also represent the dynamic and multifaceted environments that best represent life in school.

Systems Perspectives

Many fields that undergo a rapid increase in growth experience requisite problems. Exaggerated expectations about the field's potential can emerge, resulting in hyperbole, misrepresentation, disillusionment, and dismissiveness. Unfortunately, interventions in positive psychology have also experienced these growing pains.

To prevent these problems from occurring in this field and the modern world, Kern et al. (2019) suggested a new system of informed positive psychology. This new multidisciplinary system incorporates the individual beliefs, communications, and methodologies involved in these interventions to consolidate and improve the smaller systems embedded in the field. Therefore, Kern et al. outlined the ethics, politics, and epistemology that have been involved in this field thus far, suggesting the necessity to first take the time to understand the bigger picture. This understanding includes researching past mistakes and successes, reviewing multiple perspectives, and identifying all possible consequences before planning the next steps. In this way, educators can make better-informed and more effective decisions, interventions, and strategies.

Lomas et al. (2015) extended this one step further with the LIFE model, a multidimensional framework approach to promoting well-being. The LIFE model includes various levels within the four domains of the subjective mind, objective body/brain, intersubjective culture, and interobjective society. A systems perspective emphasizes the importance of social relationships and includes tangible environmental, physical, and ecological variables, accounting for schools' unique features such as classrooms and resources (Bronfenbrenner, 1979). In general, systems perspectives offer flexibility in how they can be applied and hence have become popular (e.g., Vella-Brodrick et al., 2017) and applied to school systems (e.g., Waters, 2011). A systems approach provides structure yet flexibility for schools to implement whole-school approaches (Weare, 2001).

Systems approaches also offer a critical lens from which schools can implement positive psychology interventions. While various theoretical constructs describe positive psychology, the research described in this handbook demonstrates that positive psychology interventions and strategies fall across multiple domains in a school system (i.e., parents, teachers, peer group, policy, practice, and environment; Lomas et al., 2015). Frameworks and approaches that focus on the methods and mechanisms underlying a school's systems provide a fertile foundation for efficacy.

Summary

The chapters that follow go beyond this selective introduction, highlighting critical assessment, intervention, and systems-level approaches that have expanded positive psychology's reach to broader education audiences. This edition also calls attention to the enormous growth of the field internationally, reminding us that the value of positive experiences, traits, and institutions in student's lives is universal. However, their expression may differ by cultural background. Although researchers began exploring cross-national applications during previous editions, this current edition highlights fundamental advances in assessment and intervention science that education researchers in a short period have embraced.

This third edition also hearkens back to concerns expressed almost two decades ago regarding the long-term appeal of positive psychology in general. The information in this edition exemplifies the rapid growth of positive psychology in schools, particularly transitioning from its roots in assessment to a framework that embraces individually focused and systems interventions. The field of positive psychology in the schools continues to "have legs" to stand on, but much work needs to be done before it reaches cruising altitude.

Given this foundation, the question becomes: What's next? Lomas et al. (2020) offer an interesting analysis of the development and future of positive psychology in general, which provides a valuable framework to synthesize the extant research as well as generate new research in the field of positive psychology in the schools in particular. Their paper argues that three central waves characterize the development of positive psychology. The first wave focused on studying positive phenomena (e.g., emotions, traits, and organizations) in contrast to the more traditional focus on negative phenomena (e.g., psychological symptoms and institutional problems). The second wave critiqued distinctions in the meaning and relative importance of positive and negative phenomena. As an alternative, multidimensional conceptualizations were offered (e.g., integrated models of ill-being and well-being). Although research in the second wave represented an increase in complexity, it remained focused on individual persons as did the first wave. As a next step, Lomas et al. suggested that research is entering into a necessary third wave beyond the individual person as the primary focus and locus of inquiry. This wave involves a shift in focus to groups, organizations, and broader systems. It examines the various sociocultural factors and processes that impact the well-being of people and institutions. This shift requires a movement toward more sophisticated theories and studies, going beyond psychology's boundaries to fully include other disciplines, methods, and cultures to capture this area of inquiry's complexities fully. Such third-wave research should provide the impetus for even greater gains in knowledge, skills, and psychology applications in the schools. In concert with emerging areas in neuroscience (Luetz et al., 2020), systems intervention research (Kern et al., 2020), and social network science (Montgomery et al., 2020), we anticipate that such third-wave research will generate important implications for research, practice, and policy (and new editions of this book) for years to come.

References

Bronfenbrenner, U. (1979). *The ecology of human development: Experiments by nature and design.* Harvard University Press.

Diener, E., & Seligman, M. E. P. (2004). Beyond money: Toward an economy of well-being. *Psychological Science in the Public Interest, 5,* 1–31. http://dx.doi.org.ezproxy.lib.usf.edu/10.1111/j.0963-7214.2004.00501001.x

Diener, E., Wirtz, D., Tov, W., Kim-Prieto, C., Choi, D., Oishi, S., & Biswas-Diener, R. (2010). New well-being measures: Short scales to assess flourishing and positive and negative feelings. *Social Indicators Research, 97*(2), 143–156. https://doi.org/10.1007/s11205-009-9493-y

Froh, J. J., Huebner, E. S., Youseef, A., & Conte, V. (2011). Acknowledging and appreciating the full spectrum of the human condition: School psychology's (limited) focus on positive psychological functioning. *Psychology in the Schools, 48,* 110–123. https://psycnet.apa.org/doi/10.1002/pits.20530

Furlong, M. J., Gilman, R., & Huebner, E. S. (2014). *Handbook of positive psychology in schools* (2nd ed.). Routledge.

Furlong, M. J., You, S., Renshaw, T. L., O'Malley, M. D., & Rebelez, J. (2013). Preliminary development of the Positive Experiences at School Scale for elementary school children. *Child Indicators Research, 6,* 753–775. https://doi.org/10.1007/s12187-013-9193-7

Furlong, M. J., You, S., Renshaw, T. L., Smith, D. C., & O'Malley, M. D. (2014). Preliminary development and validation of the Social and Emotional Health Survey for secondary students. *Social Indicators Research, 117,* 1011–1032. https://doi.org/10.1007/s11205-013-0373-0

Furlong, M. J., You, S., Shishim, M., & Dowdy, E. (2017). Development and validation of the Social Emotional Health Survey–Higher Education version. *Applied Research in Quality of Life, 12,* 343–367. https://doi.org/10.1007/s11482-016-9464-9

Gilman, R., Huebner, E. S., & Furlong, M. J. (2009). *Handbook of positive psychology in schools.* Routledge.

Helliwell, J. F., Layard, R., Sachs, J. D., & De Neve, J. E. (Eds.) (2020). *World Happiness Report 2020.* Sustainable Development Solutions Network.

Hendriks, T., Schotanus-Dijkstra, M., Hassankhan, A., de Jong, J., & Bohlmeijer, E. (2020). The efficacy of multi-component positive psychology interventions: A systematic review and meta-analysis of randomized controlled trials. *Journal of Happiness Studies, 21,* 357–390, 1–34. https://doi.org/10.1007/s10902-019-00082-1

Huebner, E. S. (1991). Initial development of the Students' Life Satisfaction Scale. *School Psychology International, 12,* 231–243. https://doi.org/10.1177/0143034391123010

Huebner, E. S., Gilman, R., & Furlong, M. J. (2009). A conceptual model of positive psychology research and application. In R. Gilman, E. S. Huebner, & M. J. Furlong (Eds.), *The handbook of positive psychology in schools* (pp. 3–9). Routledge.

Huebner, E. S., & Hills, K. J. (2011). Does the positive psychology movement have legs for children in schools? *The Journal of Positive Psychology, 6*(1), 88–94. https://doi.org/10.1080/17439760.2010.536778

Kern, M. L., Benson, L., Steinberg, E. A., & Steinberg, L. (2016). The EPOCH measure of adolescent well-being. *Psychological Assessment, 28*(5), 586–597. https://doi.org/10.1037/pas0000201

Kern, M. L., Williams, P., Spong, C., Colla, R., Sharma, K., Downie, A., Taylor, J. A., Sharp, S., Siokou, C., & Oades, L. G. (2019). Systems informed positive psychology. *The Journal of Positive Psychology, 15*(6), 705–715. doi:10.1080/17439760.2019.1639799

Laurent, J., Catanzaro, S. J., Joiner, T. E., Jr., Rudolph, K. D., Potter, K. I., Lambert, S., Osborne, L., & Gathright, T. (1999). A measure of positive and negative affect for children: Scale development and preliminary validation. *Psychological Assessment, 11*(3), 326–338. https://doi.org/10.1037/1040-3590.11.3.326

Lazarus, R. S. (2003). Does the positive psychology movement have legs? *Psychological Inquiry, 14*, 93–109. https://psycnet.apa.org/doi/10.1207/S15327965PLI1402_02

Lomas, T., Hefferon, K., & Ivtzan, I. (2015). The LIFE model: A meta-theoretical conceptual map for applied positive psychology. *Journal of Happiness Studies, 16*(5), 1347–1364. https://doi.org/10.1007/s10902-014-9563-y

Lomas, T., Walters, L., Williams, P., Oades, L.G., & Kern, M.L. (2020). Third wave positive psychology: Broadening towards complexity. *The Journal of Positive Psychology,16,* 660–674. https://doi.org/ 10.1080/17439760.2020.1805501

Lopez, S. L., & Snyder, C. R. (2011). *The Oxford handbook of positive psychology* (2nd ed.). Oxford University Press.

Luetz, J. M., Margus, R., & Prickett, B. (2020). Human behavior changes for sustainable development: Perspectives informed by psychology and neuroscience. In F. W. Leal., A. M. Azul, L. Brandli, P. G. Özuyar, & T. Wall (Eds.), *Quality education. Encyclopedia of the UN sustainable development goals.* Springer. https://doi.org/10.1007/978-3-319-95870-5_12

Lyubomirsky, S., & Layous, K. (2013). How do simple positive activities increase well-being? *Current Directions in Psychological Science, 22*(1), 57–62. https://doi.org/10.1177%2F0963721412469809

Montgomery, S. C., Donnelly, M., Bhatnagar, P., Carlin, A., Kee, F., & Hunter, R. F. (2020). Peer social network processes and adolescent health behaviors: A systematic review. *Preventive Medicine, 130*, 105900. doi.org/10.1016/j.ypmed.2019.105900

Page, K. M., & Vella-Brodrick, D. A. (2013). The working for wellness program: RCT of an employee well-being intervention. *Journal of Happiness Studies, 14*(3), 1007–1031. https://doi.org/10.1007/s10902-012-9366-y

Peterson, C. (2006). *A primer in positive psychology.* Oxford University Press.

Proctor, C., & Linley, A. (2013). *Research, applications, and interventions for children and adolescents: A positive psychology perspective.* Springer.

Quinlan, D., Vella-Brodrick, D. A., Gray, A., & Swain, N. (2019). Teachers matter: Student outcomes following a strengths intervention are mediated by teacher strengths spotting. *Journal of Happiness Studies, 20*(8), 2507–2523. https://doi.org/10.1007/s10902-018-0051-7

Revord, J., Walsh, L. C., & Lyubomirsky, S. (2018). Positive activity interventions to enhance well-being: Looking through a social psychological lens. In J. E. Maddux (Ed.), *Frontiers of social psychology. Subjective well-being and life satisfaction* (pp. 451–471). Routledge/Taylor & Francis.

Russell, J. A. (2003). Core affect and the psychological construction of emotion. *Psychological Review, 110*, 145–172. doi:10.1037/0033-295X.110.1.145

Seligman, M. E. P. (2011). *Flourish: A visionary new understanding of happiness and well-being.* Simon & Schuster.

Seligman, M. E. P., & Csikszentmihalyi, M. (2000). Positive psychology: An introduction. *American Psychologist, 55*, 5–14. https://psycnet.apa.org/doi/10.1037/0003-066X.55.1.5

Seligman, M. E. P., Ernst, R. M., Gillham, J., Reivich, K., & Linkins, M. (2009). Positive education: Positive psychology and classroom interventions. *Oxford Review of Education, 35*, 293–311. https://doi.org/10.1080/03054980902934563

Seligson, J. L., Huebner, E. S., & Valois, R. F. (2005). An investigation of a brief life satisfaction scale with elementary school children. *Social Indicators Research, 73*, 355–374. doi:10.1007/s11205-004-2011-3

Sin, N. L., & Lyubomirsky, S. (2009). Enhancing well-being and alleviating depressive symptoms with positive psychology interventions: A practice-friendly meta-analysis. *Journal of Clinical Psychology, 65*(5), 467–487. https://doi.org/10.1002/jclp.20593

Slemp, G. R., Chin, T. C., Kern, M. L., Siokou, C., Loton, D., Oades, L. G., Vella-Brodrick, D., & Waters, L. (2017). Positive education in Australia: Practice, measurement, and future directions. In E. Frydenberg, A. Martin, & R. J. Collie (Eds.), *Social and emotional learning in Australia and the Asia-Pacific* (pp. 101–122). Springer.

Vella-Brodrick, D. A. (2013). Positive psychology interventions – Research evidence, practical utility and future steps. In C. Keyes (Ed.), *Mental well-being: International contributions to the study of positive mental health* (pp. 331–353). Springer.

Vella-Brodrick, D. A. (2016). Positive interventions that erode the hedonic and eudaimonic divide to promote lasting happiness. In J. Vitterso (Ed.), *Handbook of eudaimonic well-being. International handbooks of quality-of-life* (pp. 395–406). Springer.

Vella-Brodrick, D. A., Chin, T. C., & Rickard, N. S. (2020). Examining the processes and effects of an exemplar school-based well-being approach on student competency, autonomy and relatedness. *Health Promotion International, 35*(5), 1190–1198. https://doi.org/10.1093/heapro/daz115

Vella-Brodrick, D. A., Rickard, N. S., & Chin, T. C. (2017). Evaluating positive education: A framework and case study. In N. J. L. Brown, T. Lomas, & F. J. Eiroa-Orosa (Eds.), *The Routledge international handbook of critical positive psychology* (pp. 488–502). Routledge/Taylor & Francis.

Waters, L. (2011). A review of school-based positive psychology interventions. *The Educational and Developmental Psychologist, 28*(2), 75–90. https://psycnet.apa.org/doi/10.1375/aedp.28.2.75

Waters, L., & Loton, D. (2019). SEARCH: A meta-framework and review of the field of positive education. *International Journal of Applied Positive Psychology, 4*(1–2), 1–46. https://doi.org/10.1007/s41042-019-00017-4

Weare, K. (2001). The health promoting school: An overview of concept, principles, and strategies and the evidence for their effectiveness. In K. Weare (Ed.), *Second workshop on practice of evaluation of the health promoting school: Models, experiences and perspectives* (pp. 9–18). European Network of Health Promoting Schools.

2

PERMAH

A Useful Model for Focusing on Well-Being in Schools

Margaret L. Kern

The application of Positive Psychology within schools contends that the purpose of education should be about academic development and performance *and* well-being (Seligman et al., 2009). Most parents want their children to be happy. However, in many cultures around the world, modern conceptualizations of happiness are embedded within societal paradigms that – at least in part - equate happiness with success, evidenced by high academic marks, high scores on standardized exams, entry into elite universities, and the pursuit of profitable, socially valued careers. A multibillion-dollar industry centered around academic testing has emerged, combined with social norms that reinforce academic and economic advancement as the road to happiness. Many of the educational systems worldwide have developed and enforce policies and practices so that (a) students receive a "standard" education, (b) their abilities can be directly compared, (c) high performance is rewarded, and (d) students who fail to conform to expectations are corrected or excluded. However, this has also brought a number of unintended consequences, including student disengagement with learning, high rates of depression, anxiety, attention deficiencies, school violence, self-harm, and suicide, and many teachers leaving the profession within their first few years of practice (e.g., Jones et al., 2003; Ryan & Weinstein, 2009; Wyn et al., 2014). Humanity is sacrificed for performance, and it is the children who suffer.

Well-being needs to become a priority within our schools -- embedded in the schools' values, policies, procedures, and behaviors -- to change the dominant paradigms that drive education today. Before this can occur, there is an immediate barrier: what is well-being? Well-being is abstract—people have a general sense of what it is and that it matters, and yet lack consensus on what it explicitly is. Most simply, well-being refers to feeling and functioning well (Huppert & So, 2013; McQuaid & Kern, 2017), but bringing well-being into school requires concrete, practical ways to understand it, measure it, and improve it. After all, measurement matters because it prioritizes accountability efforts (Stiglitz et al., 2009). Academic performance expectations promise that standardized tests can theoretically remove bias and subjectivity and place students on an even playing field. An unfortunate shortcoming of academic performance expectations, however, is that they primarily evaluate how well students regurgitate the information that teachers have emphasized while disconnecting from the rationale and relevance of that information.

DOI: 10.4324/9781003013778-3

Positive Psychology has developed several frameworks and models that attempt to turn the ephemeral well-being construct into something relatable, tangible, accessible, and measurable. Numerous proposed definitions have corresponding measures and implications for practice. For instance, the World Health Organization includes physical, mental, and social dimensions. Theories within Positive Psychology tend to focus on the mental and social aspects, with a primary focus on subjective perceptions rather than objective conditions (Chia et al., 2020), incorporating a mixture of hedonic and eudaimonic dimensions (Ryan & Deci, 2001).

Well-being models offer a form of simplexity, simplifying the real world's complexity in simpler, meaningful ways (Kern et al., 2019). There is no one right model, but some can be useful at different times (Box, 1976). Seligman's (2011) PERMA model is one such model. Seligman suggests that flourishing arises from five pillars: Positive emotion, Engagement, positive Relationships, a sense of Meaning, and Accomplishment, summarized by the acronym PERMA. Goodman and colleagues (2018) found a latent correlation of $r = 0.98$ between PERMA and Diener's (1984) subjective well-being, suggesting that the PERMA factors together contribute to one's overall sense of well-being.

Returning to the World Health Organization's inclusion of physical, mental, and social domains, a sixth dimension—physical Health—is often added. Although the model has received some criticism, some schools have found it to be a useful model for integrating Positive Psychology principles within their schools (e.g., Kern et al., 2015; Norrish et al., 2013). This chapter unpacks the PERMAH model, by focusing on four Ps: pillars, profilers, practices, and perspectives.

PERMAH Pillars

The following section describes the six domains. Throughout this chapter, I use PERMA when referring to Seligman's original model, and PERMAH when referring to applications of the model by myself and others.

The Roots of the PERMA Model

The PERMA model is a theoretical model of well-being, based upon Seligman's extensive understanding and thinking around various areas of scholarship, combined with his own perceptions about and interpretations of people's experiences. Models are based on knowledge and scholarship at a specific time, which can evolve over time as empirical knowledge develops (Box, 1976). This evolution is evident in Seligman's thinking. His original model included positive emotion, engagement, and meaning and primarily emphasized hedonic well-being (Seligman, 2002). Aligned with the field's increased focus on eudaimonic well-being, eudaimonic components take precedence in the revised PERMA model.

Positive Emotion

How often do you feel pleasure, joy, calmness, peace, excitement, gratitude, or hope, versus feeling sad, anxious, angry, or bored? Positive emotion refers to "the pleasant life" (Seligman, 2011, p.11). Positive emotions capture hedonic aspects of well-being, reflecting the felt benefit of pursuing pleasure and escaping pain. The emphasis on positive emotions does not negate negative emotions and what is painful. Indeed, some of the most exceptional pleasurable experiences occur by persevering through pain and suffering (Kashdan & Biswas-Diener, 2014). Negative emotions signal that something is wrong, either within or without, which requires attention and care. However, numerous studies, meta-analyses, and reviews find that experiencing more frequent positive emotions than negative emotions relate to many good outcomes, including good social relationships, success at work, good physical health, faster recovery from illness, and even longer life (e.g., Howell et al., 2007; Lyubomirsky et al., 2005; Pressman & Cohen, 2005).

Importantly, this does not mean that positive emotions *cause* good outcomes. There are many things that people could do to feel happy, but they would be detrimental to longer-term outcomes. The positive emotionality that correlates with good life outcomes arises from thinking and behaving in health-promoting ways, living aligned to our values, and meeting our basic needs for competence, relatedness, and autonomy (Friedman & Kern, 2014). Emotions provide feedback as to what is working and what is not working; by tuning into our emotions, we can better navigate the opportunities and challenges that life brings.

Engagement

Engagement has long been a paramount concern for schools. The 2019 Gallup student poll estimates that only 49% of students in Australia and New Zealand were actively engaged with their learning, with 19% reporting active disengagement. Considering the high rates of burnout and attrition for the teaching profession, teachers, school leaders, and other school staff are also at high risk for disengagement.

Engagement is a multidimensional construct defined and conceptualized in several ways (Appleton et al., 2008; Fredricks et al., 2011). For students, major dimensions include:

1   *behavioral engagement* (e.g., attendance, participation in activities, persisting with tasks, being prepared for class, listening, following classroom rules);
2   *emotional or psychological engagement* (e.g., interest and enjoyment of learning, feeling safe, sense of belonging to and valuing school); and
3   *cognitive engagement* (e.g., concentration, paying full attention, focused, self-regulation, use of different learning strategies, willingness to exert effort).

Meaningful engagement in learning is more likely to occur when the teacher knows their content well and is passionate about what they do, the student and teacher have a good relationship, and students can see the relevance of the content.

For adults, workplace engagement involves being dedicated and committed to the organization (emotional engagement), vigor and energy for the work one does (physical or behavioral engagement), and absorption and focus on one's work (cognitive engagement) (Schaufeli, 2013). For older adults, engagement involves ongoing activity (behavioral engagement) and interactions with other people (social engagement) (Rowe & Kahn, 1987).

Seligman's conception of engagement is more limited than these multidimensional conceptions of engagement, focusing specifically on very high levels of psychological engagement, represented by Csikszentmihalyi's (1990) concept of flow. Flow is a state of deep focus, where cognition and emotion merge, time seems to stop, the individual becomes lost within an absorbing activity, and action and awareness come together. Flow is more likely to occur for intrinsically motivating activities when the challenge of situation meets the individual's skill and ability to meet the challenge, and attention is completely focused (Bakker, 2005; Beard & Hoy, 2010).

I suggest that broader definitions of engagement, including student and workplace engagement, are most useful within a school context. Numerous studies point to the benefits of engagement (e.g., Appleton et al., 2008; Fredericks et al., 2004; Newmann et al., 1992) with the focus on the broader dimensions rather than the flow experience. Realistically, students will find some subjects more interesting and motivating than others. There are many distractions in the classroom, disrupting the intense concentration that makes flow possible. Further, the intensity of a flow experience can deplete cognitive energy—it is time-limited while engaged in a specific challenge. Students need to be present consistently, pay attention, and feel connected to their learning.

Relationships

Human beings need to connect with, relate to, and be accepted by others (Allen et al., 2018; Baumeister & Leary, 1995; Deci & Ryan, 2000). With the fulfillment of this need, people experience positive relationships with others. Conversely, loneliness can increase the risk of both mental and physical illness, including the risk of premature mortality (Cacioppo et al., 2003). However, relationships are not inherently positive—conflict, hostility, and incivility can be one of the biggest threats to well-being.

In defining relationships, Seligman (2011) points to the words of Chris Peterson, who contended that Positive Psychology is about recognizing that other people matter. Objectively, relationships include the number of social ties and the frequency of social interactions, such as the number of friends on social media and the frequency of spending time with others. Notably, studies find that the quality and perception of one's relationships matter more than quantity (Taylor, 2011). Indeed, some of the loneliest people have many social interactions but feel disconnected. Quality speaks more to satisfaction with one's relationships with other people—feeling heard, cared for, and accepted, as. Relationships also reflect the interdependent nature of connections— the balance between giving and receiving, including feeling supported by others, receiving help when needed, and providing support for others. Relational satisfaction tends to occur when there is a balance between giving and receiving from others. People need to know that others are there for them, but well-being becomes increasingly challenged when they must be dependent completely upon others, or others are dependent completely on them.

Meaning

Meaning has been defined in several ways. Isaksen (2000) suggested that meaning can be understood across four levels:

1 *cosmic level* (the existential question of what the meaning of life truly is);
2 *subjective level* (the meaning of my life, within that broader cosmic perspective);
3 *local level* (the meaning of the things we do); and
4 *situational level* (the meaning of the situations that we encounter).

Across these levels, meaning involves making sense of our experiences, cognitions, behaviors, thoughts, and seeking purpose and coherence within a broader life story.

Steger (2012) points to two primary dimensions of meaning: *comprehension* (being able to make sense of one's life) and *purpose* (having one or more personally relevant goals that motivate one's behavior). King and colleagues (2016) add *significance* as a third dimension, such that one perceives that their life is valuable and important. Seligman (2011) focuses on a subjective sense of purpose, combined with self-transcendence or spirituality—serving something or other people beyond ourselves. He suggests that while there is a subjective aspect to meaning, it is not solely subjective, such that others can define a person's life as full of meaning (based on their contributions to others and the world around them), regardless of whether the person sees their contributions as meaningful.

Accomplishment

Accomplishment similarly can be defined objectively or subjectively. Objectively, this includes winning competitions or awards, acts of greatness, and other socially created recognitions of success. Within schools, objective accomplishment includes high performance and achievement across various areas (e.g., academics, sports, music, and arts). Subjectively, accomplishment reflects a personal sense of achievement, perceived competence, mastery, and setting, pursuing, and achieving goals. From a well-being perspective, I prefer to focus on subjective aspects; however, this focus does not diminish the value of pursuing high-performance levels. Winning and succeeding require passion, perseverance, and hard work to achieve. However, accomplishment defined narrowly as high achievement can privilege those with unique talents, resources, and time for those pursuits. It also places the focus on specific outcomes, rather than the process of accomplishment that occurs as one develops a sense of mastery and competence within everyday tasks and experiences.

Health

Seligman (2011) did not include physical health in the PERMA model, yet it arguably meets his criteria of contributing to well-being—people pursue it for its own sake—and it can be defined and measured separately from the other dimensions. Objectively, health includes one's ability to complete a range of daily activities; diagnosis of organic conditions such as heart disease, cancer, or influenza; disabilities that physically limit one or more aspects of functioning; and measured physical fitness and strength (Friedman & Kern, 2014). Subjectively, health refers to a person's perception of their health, feeling physically healthy, having a subjective sense of physical vitality, and having sufficient strength and energy for their daily activities.

While some children's conceptions of health focus on biomedical aspects such as not having illness or infections, others are holistic in nature, including feeling happy, strong, and connected with others (e.g., Piko & Bak, 2006; Pridmore & Bendelow, 1995). Past experiences with illness and infection appear to play a role in how children conceptualize and think about health (Piko & Bak, 2006). Some children focus on environmental aspects that contribute to feeling healthy, such as spending time outside and the lack of smoke and other contaminants, and healthy lifestyles are perceived to be the main pathway toward staying healthy and preventing diseases.

PERMAH Profilers

Seligman (2011) contends that these pillars are distinctive and can be measured, which I have found to be accurate, with some caveats, as discussed below in the PERMAH in perspective section. My colleague, Julie Butler, and I developed the PERMA-Profiler, a 23-item self-report measure. The measure includes three items capturing each of the six PERMAH components, and five additional items assessing negative emotions, loneliness, and overall well-being. Through a series of 11 studies with nearly 39,000 participants, we developed and tested the psychometric properties of the measure, finding adequate model fit, internal and cross-time reliability, and evidence supporting the convergent and divergent validity of the factors (Butler & Kern, 2016).

Extending the original measure, I developed a workplace version that adjusted the context of the questions to the work context. To make the measure practically useful, Michelle McQuaid created an online version (see www.permahsurvey.com). Over time we have tested and refined the questions to reflect the workplace context better. Although a peer-reviewed paper testing the workplace version's psychometrics is lacking, [1] we have found the measure to be practically useful.

A third measure focuses on late childhood and adolescence. In developing the measure, my colleagues and I were concerned about directly translating the PERMA model to younger ages. PERMA, as conceptualized by Seligman, is an outcome or state that we try to achieve. Further, some of the PERMA dimensions manifest differently in childhood. For instance, the ability to comprehend and find one's place in the world is still developing, such that older teenagers often have a very different understanding of meaning than preadolescents. As such, we chose to focus on the process of living life well, choosing five positive psychological characteristics, which numerous longitudinal studies suggest make PERMAH more likely in adulthood: Engagement, Perseverance, Optimism, Connectedness, and Happiness (EPOCH). We developed a 20-item measure that captures these five domains. Across the United States, Australian, and Chinese samples, the measure has demonstrated adequate psychometric properties (Kern et al., 2016, 2019; Zeng & Kern, 2019).

These measures each produce a score profile, with the PERMAH measures on a 0–10 scale and the EPOCH measure on a 1–5 scale. The advantage of the profile is that it allows people to see how they are functioning across multiple areas. Seligman (2018) describes PERMA as a dashboard on a vehicle. How does one know whether their vehicle is functioning well or not? They might have a sense that something is wrong, but it is more helpful to have separate gauges that can quickly identify that the oil needs a top-up or the battery is dead. The profilers similarly provide a sense of how a person is functioning across a range of dimensions.

The measures are freely available for research and noncommercial purposes (www.peggykern. org/questionnaires.html). In practice, I find it useful to combine these measures with other questions to capture other domains of interest. For instance, I commonly combine the EPOCH measure with subscales from the Healthy Pathways Scales (Bevans et al., 2010) or the Kessler-6 measure of psychological distress (Kessler et al., 2003) to provide a broader understanding of how a young person is functioning, along with measures of socioeconomic status, demographics, and personality (although see Kern, Cahill, et al., 2020 for consideration of ethical concerns and challenges that can arise with assessing sensitive information, including mental health and well-being measurement).

These measures provide brief snapshots of well-being, but the dimensions may not all be relevant to the intended purpose. In such cases, I recommend using all of the questions within a dimension (e.g., the three meaning items in the PERMA-Profiler or the four connectedness questions in the EPOCH measure), removing unneeded dimensions. Further, the measures focus on general functioning, rather than functioning over a specific period. When studying change over time, it is necessary to adjust the questions to reflect the relevant time period of interest (e.g., changing "in general" to "in the past week").

The measures are descriptive, not prescriptive. There are no precise cutoffs as to what is low, average, or high functioning. Thresholds can lead to labels (e.g., a person is flourishing or not), suggesting a fixed state, when well-being is fluid, shifting based on our experiences, perceptions, and situations. Thresholds perpetuate a push toward constant improvement, which should not necessarily be the goal. While it is generally preferable to score above the midpoint, it may be maladaptive to be a 10 out of 10 on all dimensions all of the time. Instead, an individual might consider what is optimal for them, and aim to stay within their optimal zone. Different profiles will be best for different people, based on their values, interests, and experiences. For a highly social person, relationships may be particularly important. Another person might particularly value good physical health or high accomplishment. Others prefer a balance across the dimensions.

PERMAH in Practice

How can PERMAH practically be applied within schools? There is no one right approach or formula, as what is right depends upon the context and intentions of the school. PERMAH can be a useful way to help teachers and students develop well-being skills. Each pillar aligns with specific activities that support the pillar. Begin by choosing and focusing on one pillar. Get to know what the pillar means, consider some of the research and strategies that support that pillar. Table 2.1 provides some ideas to get started (see McQuaid & Kern [2017] for additional details and examples). Different activities will fit different people, so it is useful to experiment with different activities, seeing which activities work best for different students and staff.

Table 2.1 Example Activities for the Classroom that Support the PERMAH Pillars

Pillar	Strategy	Example Activities
Positive emotion	Promote positivity	Write down a list of small actions that bring a smile to your face and help you feel good. When you start to feel down, select something from the list that you can do to give yourself a pick-me-up.
	Decrease negativity	We are often our own worst critics. For a week, write down your thoughts, without editing. At the end of the week, read through your statements. How much was negative versus positive? Would you say those negative things to a friend? Are the negative beliefs really true? Challenge your thinking.
	Grow gratitude	Take a bowl and create scraps of paper. During the week, look for things that you can be grateful for, write it on the scrap and add the scrap to the bowl. At the end of the week, read through and appreciate the positive things that you experienced during the week.
Engagement	Discover and use your strengths	What are your talents and strengths? What energizes you and gives you a sense of life? What are your flaws and weaknesses? Complete a survey, such as the Values in Action (www.viacharacter.org) to help get to know your strengths. Then consider how you can use your strengths in everyday life, drawing on your strengths to bring out the best in yourself and others.
	Reduce distractions	How often do you and your students give full attention to things? Create a classroom environment that reduces distraction, creates a sense of calmness, and allows focus.
	Engage in mindful actions	Mindfulness involves being present in the moment, not dwelling on the past or worrying about the future. Engaging in simple, mindful activities can help focus attention, helping students be grounded and centered. Explore a variety of ways to cultivate mindfulness in the classroom, such as taking a few minutes to breathe deeply, doing a rhythmic activity, or listening to a recorded meditation.
Relationships	Approach interactions with a strength lens	In your interactions with others, put on "strength goggles"—intentionally look for the strengths of others. Observe how the strength manifests. If you have the opportunity, share with the person the strength they demonstrated and why you valued it.
	Cultivate deep friendships	We need at least one good friend—someone who we can be real with, supports us, and cares about us. But good friends take time and commitment. Identify one or two people with whom you will commit to cultivating a deep friendship. Schedule regular times to connect. Listen deeply to them, be willing to be open and vulnerable with them, and readily forgive wrongs.
	Be available	Make yourself available to others. This may mean leaving your classroom/office door open, showing up early or staying late from meetings, spending time in the lunchroom, or walking around the school and observing how people are going. Ask others how they are *really* going and be willing to listen if they are not ok.
Meaning	Find your story	Investigate your life like a journalist. What are the defining events in your life? What are your strengths and weaknesses? How did you get to where you are at today? Take time to write your story, celebrating the successes, mourning the failures, and considering what lessons you might have learned along the way.

Pillar	Strategy	Example Activities
	Make the mundane meaningful	Everyday tasks can seem meaningless—we do them because we should, but they deplete us. Create a meaning map. Take a piece of paper. On the left side, write down tasks that seem meaningless—you feel you have to do them, but they drain your energy. Draw an arrow to the right and write the purpose of the task or the outcome it helps achieve. Reflect on that purpose. If that feels unimportant, draw another arrow to the right, and ask again the purpose or potential outcomes of the task. Can you find a clear purpose for the task? Moving forward, spend more time on the things that have purpose, and limit the meaningless tasks.
	Gain perspective	We can get lost within the worries and activities of everyday life. Step away and spend time in nature. Sit on a beach and watch the waves, walk among forests, spend time in a garden, go to a dark place and see the stars. Be present in the moment, using your senses to notice all around you. Breathe deeply and acknowledge the much bigger world around you.
Accomplishment	Create a hope map	Take a sheet of paper horizontally and fold it into thirds. In the right column, write "Goals" and write down a goal you want to achieve over a specific time period. In the left column, write "Pathways" and list at least three actions that could help you to reach your goal. In the middle, write "Obstacles." For each pathway you listed, note obstacles or challenges you might encounter. At the bottom of the page, add the things you can do to maintain motivation, people who can support you, and ways you can celebrate your efforts.
	Take one small step	When things seem impossible, it is helpful to take one small step, and then another. Consider something you are trying to accomplish that seems overwhelming. What is a small step that you are willing to take? Write the step-down, give it a go. Record how it went. Then take another step, step again. Every so often, look back at where you were—you might be surprised at how far you have come.
	Learn from failures	Think about a situation that went really wrong. What happened? Think through the details of the situation. What did you do? What were your actions? Do not judge what you did, simply write about your actions. What were the outcomes or costs of your actions? What did you learn from the situation, and what would you do differently in the future? By processing our failures, we can learn and improve.
Health	Sleep well	Good sleep is more likely to occur if we create the right conditions. Set clear bed and wake times. Try to maintain a consistent schedule, even on weekends. Begin winding down 30–60 minutes before bedtime, with cues that help the body relax, avoiding vigorous exercise, caffeine, and alcohol. Dim the lights, lower the temperature. If possible, turn off electronics. Keep a notepad by your bed. If your mind is spinning, write down what is on your mind, clearing your thoughts.
	Eat wisely	There is conflicting dietary advice about specific foods to eat or not eat. In general, some foods are healthier than others. When we feel stressed, high fat, sugary foods can be calming in the short-term, but not so good for how we feel and function. Proactively plan out your meals, making decisions before you are hungry and stressed. Identify healthy snacks that will fuel your mind during the day, avoiding the tendency to binge eat all of your calories in the evening.
	Move regularly	Humans are made to move. If you enjoy sport, working out at the gym, running, walking, yoga, etc., plan this into your diary, scheduling the time as if it was a class or meeting. Short bits of movement add up to have a big impact on how we feel and function.

Beyond drawing on the pillars to shape activities and interventions, some schools use PER-MAH as a guiding framework for embedding well-being within the school's culture. This choice begins with determining whether the PERMAH model is appropriate to the context of the school. To what extent does PERMAH align with these values and interests? Are all of the dimensions relevant? Are other dimensions missing? For example, schools might incorporate spirituality, strengths, and coping dimensions (see, for instance, Waters, 2019).

Second, consider how each dimension is specifically defined and what concepts are included within each dimension. Practically, schools have taken considerable liberty in identifying what concepts are relevant to the different dimensions.

Third, establish a well-being baseline. Use the freely available measures described above (or modified versions of them), along with other scales capturing important areas of functioning, considering patterns and trends across different year levels and classes. Measurement sends a message that well-being matters, and it helps identify where people are doing well, and areas that could benefit from additional focus. It also allows change, growth, and development to be tracked over time, pointing to what is helpful and what is a waste of time and resources.

Fourth, align activities with the pillars, identifying and communicating a clear purpose and intention for those activities. Carefully planned activities identify which skills are being developed, their underlying intentions, and communicate the purpose, rationale, and process to students. Activities should focus on quality rather than quantity, emphasizing pedagogical aspects (White & Kern, 2018).

Fifth, provide professional development, resources, and support for teachers. It is helpful for teachers to get to know the ideas underlying PERMAH, try activities in their own life, and consider what resonates with them (Norrish et al., 2013). Various resources and curricula supporting the PERMAH elements are readily available, through organizations such as the Positive Education Schools Association (http://www.pesa.edu.au/) and the education division of the International Positive Psychology Association (www.ippanetwork.org).

Sixth, encourage teachers to incorporate PERMAH into the taught and caught curriculum (White & Kern, 2018). The taught curriculum reflects explicit lessons, activities, and teachings on the PERMAH pillars. The caught curriculum reflects how PERMAH appears through the norms, practices, and culture of the classroom and school, including the language that teachers use, the school's appearance, and behaviors that are modeled by adults.

Finally, embed PERMAH within the strategies, policies, and structures of the school. These broader elements impact the extent to which PERMAH is simply a fad versus a more permanent part of the school's culture. Educators can commit to activities for a while, but only by embedding well-being within a school's culture will they be sustained beyond the tenure of a single person or across multiple years.

PERMAH in Perspective

Seligman's claims are straightforward. The model makes it possible to turn the abstract notion of well-being into a simple five- or six-dimensional framework, identifying specific focal areas. Still, the model has received some criticisms. Still, all models are imperfect (Box, 1976), and it is helpful to consider some strengths and weaknesses so that the model can be thoughtfully and purposefully informed.

A Compelling Acronym

From my observations, the PERMAH model appears to resonate well with people. The acronym is easy to remember. The dimensions resonate with many people's everyday experiences. Having positive emotions, interest in life, a sense of purpose, good relationships with others, achieving things—most people can connect with at least one of these domains. Indeed, self-determination theory suggests that we have a basic need for relatedness (experienced through positive relationships) and competence (leading to a sense of accomplishment), and autonomy underlies meaningful and engagement pursuits (Deci & Ryan, 2000).

The included dimensions arise from the theorists' working model of the world, which is influenced by their own experiences, perspectives, and values in life. Seligman was trained in clinical psychology; thus, his model primarily focuses on psychological dimensions. He was close friends with Chris Peterson, who consistently emphasized the importance of social Relationships, and Mihaly Csikszentmihalyi, who illustrated the value of flow (Engagement), and Seligman greatly values objective Accomplishment. My background is in health psychology, and too often, there is an unhelpful split between psychological and physical dimensions of functioning, and so I include Health in the model. People also identify the importance of a spiritual dimension. Seligman includes spirituality within Meaning, but arguably it could be a missing dimension.

Flourishing and Permaculture

Seligman suggests that the five PERMA elements represent the flourishing life, which is a useful choice of words, providing a compelling visual representation of the good life. The word flourish arises from the Latin word flor, or "flower." One can look at a garden and identify flourishing plants and flowers versus those that are struggling to survive. It is a general universal hope that children and families are vibrant and alive, not dying and decrepit.

There is also a fascinating parallel with the acronym itself. Permaculture refers to sustainable ecological approaches toward agriculture (and culture more generally), which aim to work with the land rather than against it, creating a sustainable ecosystem that is respectful of both the natural and social influences upon the land (Mollison, 1991). Seligman primarily applies PERMA at the individual level. Permaculture suggests that achieving well-being for an individual at the expense of other people or the environment is not flourishing, as it is not sustainable. Especially within schools, a system-informed perspective is necessary, striving for optimal functioning not only at the individual level but also at the human social system level (Kern, Williams, et al., 2020; Kern & Taylor, 2021). We need to consider the system as a whole—people, environment, and other aspects—that make our classrooms and schools more or less physically, mentally, socially, ecologically, and economically sustainable.

Statistically Problematic but Practically Useful

One of the main critiques of the PERMA model is that Seligman claims that its five elements are distinctive and that people choose to pursue each dimension as a valuable outcome in and of itself, not as a means for achieving another dimension. For instance, flow (which represents high levels of psychological engagement) is often reported as devoid of emotion or even negative during the experience, even as it is retrospectively perceived as positive (Csikszentmihalyi, 1990). The pursuit of accomplishment can be a stressful, intense, and lonely journey. A meaningful life is not necessarily a happy life (Baumeister et al., 2013).

However, evidence of the distinctiveness of the five dimensions is mixed at best. While confirmatory analyses across multiple populations and languages repeatedly support the five factors, exploratory analyses do not. Analyses typically result in one or two factors (e.g., Goodman et al., 2018), with an additional factor appearing if health is included. This is perhaps not surprising. The elements are mutually supportive and interconnected. Activities are often pursued because they are meaningful. Positive interactions with others evoke positive emotions. Many people find a sense of meaning in their relationships with other people. When one feels and functions well in one area, they often feel and function well in other areas (Kern, Williams, et al., 2020). As such, the factors tend to be strongly correlated with one another. Indeed, Seligman (2011) notes that when one feels joy, they have a sense of purpose, and feel proud about accomplishments with other people, suggesting that these dimensions are interconnected even at the definitional level. Based on many studies across multiple ways of collecting data, I sense that from a statistical lens, any argument of the distinctiveness of the factors is tenable at best.

Still, the PERMAH model is practically useful, offering concrete strategies for building well-being, which are more useful than focusing on the more global, abstract well-being construct (Kern et al., 2015; McQuaid & Kern, 2017; Seligman, 2018). This perspective should make sense to an educator. An average grade point average hides the specific profile of the student. One student might excel in math and struggle in literacy, while another earns top marks in art and music but achieves poorly in science and math. A parallel appears with the Values in Action (VIA) character strengths inventory (Peterson & Seligman, 2004). The VIA proposes six different "virtues," which translate into 24 strengths, measured by a range of items. Factor analytic models find that items cluster into three to five factors, which differ from the proposed six virtues (McGrath, 2014). However, the VIA was never intended to be a statistical model (Peterson & Seligman, 2004). It was assumed that the strengths and virtues were correlated and complementary. While statistically the model is questionable, practically VIA is useful. Similarly, PERMAH may not be a definitive well-being model, but it can still be a useful model.

Conclusion

There is growing recognition that there is a need to focus on well-being in schools. Nevertheless, well-being is abstract, value-laden, and less tangible than academic outcomes. Well-being frameworks can be useful for cutting through complexity. To that end, PERMAH has emerged over the past decade as a useful model. The pillars are accessible to people, reflecting many lay notions of well-being. The pillars can be measured, and various practices can help build and support each pillar. As a whole, PERMAH contributes to educators' ability to incorporate Positive Psychology within schools, supporting the well-being of students, staff, leaders, and others within the educational community.

Note

1 I have not published a psychometric paper on the refined Workplace Well-being measure, but other researchers have published psychometric studies on various translations and versions of the original workplace measure of other variants (see for instance Watanabe et al., 2018).

References

Allen, K. A., Kern, M. L., Vella-Brodrick, D., Hattie, J., & Waters, L. (2018). What schools need to know about fostering school belonging: A meta-analysis. *Educational Psychology Review, 30*, 1–34. http://dx.doi.org/10.1007/s10648-016-9389-8

Appleton, J. J., Christenson, S. L., & Furlong, M. J. (2008). Student engagement with school: Critical conceptual and methodological issues of the construct. *Psychology in the Schools, 45*, 379–386. https://doi.org/10.1002/pits.20303

Bakker, A. B. (2005). Flow among music teachers and their students: The crossover of peak experiences. *Journal of Vocational Behavior, 66*, 26–44. https://doi.org/10.1016/j.jvb.2003.11.001

Baumeister, R. F., & Leary, M. R. (1995). The need to belong: Desire for interpersonal attachments as a fundamental human motivation. *Psychological Bulletin, 117*, 497–529. https://doi.org/10.1037/0033-2909.117.3.497

Baumeister, R. F. Vohs, K. D., Aasker, J. L., & Garbinsky, E. N. (2013). Some key differences between a happy life and a meaningful life. *The Journal of Positive Psychology, 8*, 505–516. http://dx.doi.org/10.1080/17439760.2013.830764

Beard, K. S., & Hoy, W. K. (2010). The nature, meaning, and measure of teacher flow in elementary schools: A test of rival hypotheses. *Educational Administration Quarterly, 46*, 426–458. https://doi.org/10.1177/0013161X10375294

Bevans, K. B., Riley, A. W., & Forrest, C. B. (2010). Development of the healthy pathways child report scales. *Quality of Life Research, 19*, 1195–1214. https://doi.org/10.1007/s11136-010-9687-4

Box, G. E. P. (1976). Science and statistics. *Journal of the American Statistical Association, 71*, 791–799. https://doi.org/10.1080/01621459.1976.10480949

Butler, J., & Kern, M. L. (2016). The PERMA-Profiler: A brief multidimensional measure of flourishing. *International Journal of Wellbeing, 6*, 1–48. https://doi.org/10.5502/ijw.v6i3.526

Cacioppo, J. T., Hawkley, L. C., & Berntson, G. G. (2003). The anatomy of loneliness. *Current Directions in Psychological Science, 12*, 71–74. https://doi.org/10.1111/1467-8721.01232

Chia, A., Kern, M. L., & Neville, B. A. (2020). CSR for happiness: Corporate determinants of societal happiness as social responsibility. *Business Ethics, 29*, 422–437. https://doi.org/10.1111/beer.12274

Csikszentmihalyi, M. (1990). *Flow: The psychology of optimal experience.* HarperCollins.

Deci, E. L., & Ryan, R. M. (2000). The "what" and "why" of goal pursuits: Human needs and the self-determination of behavior. *Psychological Inquiry, 11*, 227–268. https://doi.org/10.1207/S15327965PLI1104_01

Diener, E. (1984). Subjective well-being. *Psychological Bulletin, 95*, 542–575. https://doi.org/10.1037/0033-2909.95.3.542

Fredricks, J. A., Blumenfeld, P. C., & Paris, A. H. (2004). School engagement: Potential of the concept, state of the evidence. *Review of Educational Research, 74*, 59–109. https://doi.org/10.3102/00346543074001059

Fredricks, J., McColskey, W., Meli, J., Montrosse, B., Mordica, J., & Mooney, K. (2011). *Measuring student engagement in upper elementary through high school: A description of 21 instruments.* Regional Educational Laboratory, 98. Retrieved from http://ies.ed.gov/ncee/edlabs/regions/southeast/pdf/REL_2011098.pdf

Friedman, H. S., & Kern, M. L. (2014). Personality, well-being, and health. *Annual Review of Psychology, 65*, 719–742. http://dx.doi.org/10.1146/annurev-psych-010213-115123

Goodman, F. R., Disabato, D. J., Kashdan, T. B., & Kauffman, S. B. (2018). Measuring well-being: A comparison of subjective well-being and PERMA. *The Journal of Positive Psychology, 13*, 321–332. https://doi.org/10.1080/17439760.2017.1388434

Howell, R., Kern, M. L., & Lyubomirsky, S. (2007). Health benefits: Meta-analytically determining the impact of well-being on objective health outcomes. *Health Psychology Review, 1*, 83–136. http://dx.doi.org/10.1080/17437190701492486

Huppert, F. A., & So, T. T. C. (2013). Flourishing across Europe: Application of a new conceptual framework for defining well-being. *Social Indicators Research, 110*, 837–861. https://doi.org/10.1007/s11205-011-9966-7

Isaksen, J. (2000). Constructing meaning despite the drudgery of repetitive work. *Journal of Humanistic Psychology, 40*, 84–107. https://doi.org/10.1177/0022167800403008

Jones, M. G., Jones, B. D., & Hargrove, T. (2003). *The unintended consequences of high stakes testing.* Rowman & Littlefield Publishers.

Kashdan, T. B., & Biswas-Diener, R. (2014). *The upside of your dark side.* Hudson Street Press.

Kern, M. L., Benson, L., Steinberg, E. A., & Steinberg, L. (2016). The EPOCH measure of adolescent well-being. *Psychological Assessment, 28*, 586–597. https://doi.org/10.1037/pas0000201

Kern, M. L., Cahill, H., Morrish, L., Farrelly, A., Shlezinger, K., & Jach, H. (2020). The responsibility of knowledge: Identifying and reporting students with evidence of psychological distress in large-scale school-based studies. *Research Ethics, 17*(2), 193–216. https://doi.org/10.1177/1747016120952511

Kern, M. L., & Taylor, J. A. (2021). Systems informed positive education. In M. L. Kern & M. L. Wehmeyer (Eds.), *Palgrave handbook on positive education.* Palgrave Macmillan.

Kern, M. L., Waters, L. E., Adler, A., & White, M. A. (2015). A multidimensional approach to measuring well-being in students: Application of the PERMA framework. *Journal of Positive Psychology, 10*, 262–271. http://dx.doi.org/10.1080/17439760.2014.936962

Kern, M. L., Williams, P., Spong, C., Colla, R., Sharma, K., Downie, A., Taylor, J. A., Sharp, S., Siokou, C., & Oades, L. G. (2020). Systems informed positive psychology. *Journal of Positive Psychology, 15*, 705-715. https://doi.org/10.1080/17439760.2019.1639799

Kern, M. L., Zeng, G., Hou, H., & Peng, K. (2019). The Chinese version of the EPOCH Measure of Adolescent Wellbeing: Testing cross-cultural measurement invariance. *Journal of Psychoeducational Assessment, 37*, 757–769. https://doi.org/10.1177/0734282918789561

Kessler, R. C., Barker, P. R., Colpe, L. J., Epstein, J. F., Gfroerer, J. C., Hiripi, E., Howes, M. J., Normand, S. L. T., Manderscheid, R. W., Walters, E. E., & Zaslavsky, A. M. (2003). Screening for serious mental illness in the general population. *Archives of General Psychiatry, 60*, 184–189. https://doi.org/10.1001/archpsyc.60.2.184

King, L. A., Heintzelman, S. J., & Ward, S. J. (2016). Beyond the search for meaning: A contemporary science of the experience of meaning in life. *Current Directions in Psychological Science, 25*, 211–216. https://doi.org/10.1177/0963721416656354

Lyubomirsky, S., King, L. A., & Diener, E. (2005). The benefits of frequent positive affect: Does happiness lead to success? *Psychological Bulletin, 131*, 803–855. https://doi.org/10.1037/0033-2909.131.6.803

McGrath, R. E. (2014). Scale- and item-level factor analyses of the VIA inventory of strengths. *Assessment, 21*, 4–14. https://doi.org/10.1177/1073191112450612

McQuaid, M., & Kern, M. L. (2017). *Your wellbeing blueprint: Feeling good and doing well at work.* McQuaid Ltd.

Mollison, B. (1991). *Introduction to permaculture.* Tagari.

Newmann, F. M., Wehlage, G. G., & Lamborn, S. D. (1992). The significance and sources of student engagement. In F. M. Newmann (Ed.), *Student engagement and achievement in American secondary schools* (pp. 11–39). Teachers College Press.

Norrish, J. M., Williams, P., O'Connor, M., & Robinson, J. (2013). An applied framework for positive education. *International Journal of Wellbeing, 3*, 147–161. https://doi.org/10.5502/ijw.v3i2.2

Peterson, C., & Seligman, M. E. P. (2004). *Character strengths and virtues.* Oxford University Press.

Piko, B. F., & Bak, J. (2006). Children's perceptions of health and illness: Images and lay concepts in preadolescence. *Health Education Research, 21*, 643–653. https://doi.org/10.1093/her/cyl034

Pressman, S. D., & Cohen, S. (2005). Does positive affect influence health? *Psychological Bulletin, 131*, 925–971. https://doi.org/10.1037/0033-2909.131.6.925

Pridmore, P., & Bendelow, G. (1995). Images of health: Exploring beliefs of children using the 'draw-and-write' technique. *Health Education Journal, 54*, 473–488. https://doi.org/10.1177/001789699505400410

Rowe, J. W., & Kahn, R. L. (1987). Human aging: Usual and successful. *Science, 237*, 143–149. https://doi.org/10.1126/science.3299702

Ryan, R. M., & Deci, E. L. (2001). On happiness and human potentials: A review of research on hedonic and eudaimonic well-being. *Annual Review of Psychology, 52*, 141–166. https://doi.org/10.1146/annurev.psych.52.1.141

Ryan, R. M., & Weinstein, N. (2009). Undermining quality teaching and learning: A self-determination theory perspective on high-stakes testing. *Theory and Research in Education, 7*, 224–233. https://doi.org/10.1177/1477878509104327

Schaufeli, W. B. (2013). What is engagement? In C. Truss, K. Alfes, R. Delbridge, A. Shantz, & E. Soane (Eds.), *Employee engagement in theory and practice* (pp. 15–35). Routledge.

Seligman, M. E. P. (2002). *Authentic happiness.* Free Press.

Seligman, M. E. P. (2011). *Flourish.* Simon & Schuster.

Seligman, M. (2018). PERMA and the building blocks of well-being. *The Journal of Positive Psychology, 13*, 333–335. https://doi.org/10.1080/17439760.2018.1437466

Seligman, M. E. P., Ernst, R. M., Gillham, J., Reivich, K., & Linkins, M. (2009). Positive education: Positive psychology and classroom interventions. *Oxford Review of Education, 35*, 293–311. https://doi.org/10.1080/03054980902934563

Steger, M. F. (2012). Making meaning in life. *Psychological Inquiry, 23*, 381–385. https://doi.org/10.1080/1047840X.2012.720832

Stiglitz, J., Sen, A., & Fitoussi, J. P. (2009). *Report by the commission on the measurement of economic performance and social progress.* Retrieved from www.stiglitz-sen-fitoussi.fr/documents/rapport_anglais.pdf

Taylor, S. E. (2011). Social support: A review. In H. S. Friedman (Ed.), *The Oxford handbook of health psychology* (pp. 189–214). Oxford University Press.

Waters, L. (2019). Searching for wellbeing in schools: A new framework to guide the science of positive education. *Journal of Educational and Psychological Research, 1*:2. Retrieved from https://opastonline.com/wp-content/uploads/2019/11/searching-for-wellbeing-in-schools-a-new-framework-to-guide-the-science-of-positive-education-jepr-19.pdf

White, M., & Kern, M. L. (2018). Positive education: Learning and teaching for wellbeing and academic mastery. *International Journal of Wellbeing, 8*(1), 1–17. http://dx.doi.org/10.5502/ijw.v8i1.588

Wyn, J., Turnbull, M., & Grimshaw, L. (2014). *The experience of education: The impacts of high stakes testing on school students and their families.* The Whitlam Institute. Retrieved from http://citeseerx.ist.psu.edu/viewdoc/download?doi=10.1.1.737.8428&rep=rep1&type=pdf

Zeng, G., & Kern, M. L. (2019). The Chinese EPOCH measure of adolescent wellbeing: Further testing of the psychometrics of the measure. *Frontiers in Psychology, 10*, 1457. https://doi.org/10.3389/fpsyg.2019.01457

3

CAPACITIES AND VULNERABILITIES IN THE CLASSROOM

Self-Determination Theory and the Promotion of Proactive Human Nature among Students

Christopher P. Niemiec

Introduction

By their nature, humans are active and proactive organisms. In other words, humans are naturally oriented toward acting on their environment and self-regulating with regard to internal and external events and/or experiences, rather than passively receiving and responding to inputs after they have occurred. Even casual observation of children's behavior affords the opportunity to witness this proactive nature. From a very early age, young children explore their environment visually and through motor movements; they reach, grab, mimic, and smile. Importantly, these behaviors need not be understood as instincts (Watson, 1924), as random (Skinner, 1953), or as controlled by contingencies of reinforcement in the environment (Skinner, 1971). Rather, these behaviors can be understood as children's proactive, intentional efforts to understand themselves, their environment, and themselves in relation to their environment, as this understanding enables the formation of a more coherent, unified, and organized sense of self (Piaget, 1971).

Such organismic theorizing can be found in psychological theories of personality, as well. For instance, Loevinger (1976) posited that the ego is a process of synthesis whose critical role is to manage intrapsychic and interpersonal conflicts, and Rogers (1963) posited a natural tendency toward self-actualization and realization of one's full potential. In each of these perspectives, this proactive human nature forms the basis for growth, integration, and healthy functioning. Indeed, similar views have been used to characterize the nature of life itself by developmental theorists (Gottlieb, 2003) and organismic biologists (Kauffman & Clayton, 2006). Organismic theorists in psychology, most notably Ryan and Deci (2002), have proposed that this proactive human nature is oriented toward seeking out opportunities for choice, mastery, and connection with important others. Such opportunities are aligned with the psychological content of human nature (Niemiec et al., 2014) and are conducive to personal (autonomy) and interpersonal (homonomy) integration (Angyal, 1965), full functioning, and organismic wellness (cf. Niemiec & Ryan, 2013). Given the centrality of choice, mastery, and connection in optimal approaches to pedagogic practice (cf. Niemiec & Ryan, 2009), this proactive human

DOI: 10.4324/9781003013778-4

nature would seem to be worth harnessing as educators guide their students' discovery, understanding, and development.

To be sure, humans possess a natural love of learning and actively seek to "make sense" of their surroundings through the internalization and integration of abiding values, knowledge, beliefs, and practices. Indeed, this proactive human nature commonly takes the form of curiosity (Loewenstein, 1994), interest (Silvia, 2008) and interest taking (Deci et al., 2015), passion (Vallerand, 2010), and synthesis (Ryan, 1995)—experiences among students that can be cultivated to promote flourishing in the classroom. It is unfortunate, therefore, that amid a confluence of personal beliefs and outside pressures (Ryan & Brown, 2005), some teachers apply external factors such as reward and punishment contingencies, close surveillance, evaluation, and competition to their pedagogic practice in an attempt to "make" their students learn. Indeed, such controlling elements not only detract from conceptual understanding and personal growth but can also undermine the very foundation upon which a positive psychology in schools can be built—namely, students' proactive nature. It is important to consider how teachers can align pedagogic practice with students' proactive nature. Therefore, in this chapter, I present an application of self-determination theory to educational practice with a particular focus on the concept of basic psychological needs, how those needs can be supported by educators, and the student outcomes that are associated with such support. Also, I discuss several recent lines of research using self-determination theory that can be applied to educational practice to facilitate thriving among students.

Self-Determination Theory and the Concept of Basic Psychological Needs

Self-determination theory (Deci & Ryan, 2008; Niemiec et al., 2010; Ryan & Deci, 2017; Vansteenkiste et al., 2010) is a macro-theory of human motivation that has received empirical validation in numerous life domains, including education (Niemiec & Ryan, 2009; Ryan & Niemiec, 2009). Informed by an organismic-dialectic meta-theory (Ryan & Deci, 2002), self-determination theory assumes a proactive human nature that is oriented toward internal coherence and adaptation to the environment. Yet, there is a dialectic between capacities and vulnerabilities that can describe the human experience more fully (Vansteenkiste & Ryan, 2013). That is, though proactive, humans remain vulnerable to experiences of control, passivity, psychological fragmentation, and alienation, particularly when conditions within and around the individual are not supportive of their proactive human nature. Oftentimes, this dialectic between capacities and vulnerabilities is readily apparent among students in educational contexts. Hence, it is important to consider factors that can have a proximal impact on this dialectic and, in turn, affect important student outcomes in the classroom.

Aligned with the psychological content of human nature (see Niemiec et al., 2014), the concept of basic psychological needs is a unifying principle within self-determination theory that represents "innate psychological nutriments that are essential for ongoing psychological growth, integrity, and well-being" (Deci & Ryan, 2000, p. 229). As a plant needs sunlight, water, and soil to grow, so too individuals require support for satisfaction of basic psychological needs to thrive and flourish (cf. Ryan, 1995). The need for autonomy (de Charms, 1968) refers to the experience of behavior as owned and reflectively endorsed, rather than pressured and coerced. The need for competence (White, 1959) refers to the experience of capability and mastery in behavior, rather than the inability to attain important outcomes. The need for relatedness (Baumeister & Leary, 1995) refers to the experience of connection, care, and respect vis-à-vis valued others. Indeed, research has shown that satisfaction of autonomy, competence, and relatedness is associated with wellness among both men and women (Ryan et al., 2005); among children (Joussemet et al., 2005), adolescents (Curran et al.,

2013), and adults (Vansteenkiste et al., 2007); among residents of various cultures and regardless of individual differences in need strength (Chen et al., 2015); and in a sample of primarily poor, working-class individuals (Williams et al., 2009). This set of findings highlights the *universality* of these needs for optimal functioning and wellness. Therefore, within self-determination theory, the concept of basic psychological needs represents the factor that has the most proximal impact on the dialectic between capacities and vulnerabilities (Vansteenkiste & Ryan, 2013).

Engendering Student Vulnerabilities: Need Thwarting and Frustration in Education

Parents and teachers represent important sources of influence on students' motivation and experience in the classroom. It is unfortunate, therefore, that both parents and teachers often face various pressures that can leave those socializers less likely to support students' proactive human nature. For instance, Wuyts et al. (2015) reported that parents who experience social pressure (from partners, grandparents, other parents, the school, and the media) to be an achievement-promoting parent and who have unfulfilled personal dreams not only invest contingent self-esteem in their children's achievements but also are psychologically controlling around those achievements. As another example, Pelletier et al. (2002) reported that pressures that teachers face "from above" (i.e., accountability standards; see Deci et al., 1982; Flink et al., 1990), as well as "from below" (e.g., disengaged students), can undermine the support for basic psychological needs that teachers communicate to their students. Such pressures often can translate into need thwarting behaviors that parents and teachers exhibit toward students.

In the home, one manifestation of need thwarting occurs when parents provide more (or less) attention and affection to their children based on how well the children do academically—a practice known as parental conditional positive regard and parental conditional negative regard, respectively (Roth et al., 2009). This type of parental control pits one content of human nature (support for autonomy and competence) against another (relatedness), essentially communicating (often implicitly) that parents will love their children more (or less) if children live up to their parents' values and standards (or not). In the classroom, need thwarting occurs when teachers make demands of and issue directives toward their students, do not provide ample opportunity for their students to engage in independent problem solving, and control the flow of interpersonal communication, among other teacher behaviors (see Reeve & Jang, 2006). In need-thwarting contexts, students are at risk of experiencing pressure to comply with others' decisions (autonomy frustration), rather than pursuing personal interests and values; receiving negative feedback (competence frustration), rather than constructive and positive feedback; and feeling rejected by parents and teachers (relatedness frustration), rather than supported by those socializers. To be sure, research has shown that parental conditional positive regard is associated with grade-focused engagement among students and that parental conditional negative regard is associated with academic disengagement among students (Roth et al., 2009). As well, controlling teacher behaviors not only are experienced by students as controlling (Reeve & Jang, 2006) but also impede effective self-regulation strategies among students (Soenens et al., 2012).

The adverse consequences of need thwarting and frustration in the education domain are readily apparent. Indeed, as Albert Einstein (as quoted in Schilpp, 1949) asserted:

> It is, in fact, nothing short of a miracle that the modern methods of instruction have not yet entirely strangled the holy curiosity of inquiry; for this delicate little plant, aside from stimulation, stands mainly in need of freedom; without this it goes to wreck and ruin without fail. It is a very grave mistake to think that the enjoyment of seeing and searching can be promoted by means of coercion and a sense of duty.

Einstein's perspective on education is wholly compatible with research from self-determination theory on engendering student vulnerabilities. Bearing this in mind, it is useful also to consider research from self-determination theory on engendering student capacities to offer a blueprint for teachers to align their pedagogic practice with students' proactive nature. Indeed, in the words of Plutarch (trans. 1927):

> For the mind does not require filling like a bottle, but rather, like wood, it only requires kindling to create in it an impulse to think independently and an ardent desire for the truth.

Perhaps this "kindling" to which Plutarch referred can be understood as support for satisfaction of the basic psychological needs for autonomy, competence, and relatedness in the classroom.

Engendering Student Capacities: Need Support and Satisfaction in Education

Within self-determination theory, basic psychological need frustration is not thought to be the antipode of basic psychological need satisfaction (cf. Olafsen et al., 2017; see also Vansteenkiste & Ryan, 2013), and thus it is not sufficient for teachers simply to refrain from the use of need-thwarting behaviors in their pedagogic practice. In need-dissatisfying contexts, students are at risk of experiencing little (if any) voice and choice in their learning endeavors, recognition for their skill development and accomplishments, and connection with their teachers and classmates. Recent research has shown that students can distinguish their experiences of autonomy dissatisfaction from autonomy satisfaction and autonomy frustration. It is perhaps more important, though, that at the zero-order level autonomy dissatisfaction predicted lower levels of engagement along with higher levels of disengagement among students (Cheon et al., 2019). Thus, it is important to consider ways that teachers can actively support the autonomy, competence, and relatedness of their students in the classroom.

In the classroom, autonomy support occurs when teachers afford their students a sense of "voice," listen to their students and acknowledge their students' perspectives and feelings, offer ample opportunity for their students to engage in independent problem solving, encourage their students' effort, provide hints (rather than answers/solutions) to promote their students' progress, communicate positive feedback around their students' skill development and/or mastery, and are responsive to their students' needs and points of view (see Reeve & Jang, 2006). Importantly, Reeve and Jang found that such behaviors are predictive of perceived autonomy among students, which, in turn, yielded higher levels of interest-enjoyment, engagement, and performance. More broadly, autonomy support is an interpersonal style and set of behaviors that is consistent with students' interests, preferences, and values (inner motivational resources) and involves teachers' being student-centered and choice-promoting; offering meaningful rationales for limits that are set, and requests that are made, in the classroom; using informational (rather than controlling) language; and accepting expressions of unpleasant affect from students (see Reeve, 2002, 2006, 2009). As detailed by Haerens and colleagues (2013), competence support occurs when teachers provide clear instructions for learning tasks and materials, offer meaningful rationales for what students are asked to do (or not do), and convey positive feedback, whereas relatedness support occurs when teachers are eager, express enthusiasm, and put energy into their lessons. In need-supportive contexts, students are likely to experience volition (autonomy satisfaction), effectance (competence satisfaction), and closeness with important others (relatedness satisfaction).

As such, it seems that a need-supportive pedagogic practice can be aligned with students' proactive nature, and faculty are rated more favorably by their university students when teachers provide opportunities for autonomy, competence, and relatedness in education (Filak & Sheldon,

2003). It is unfortunate, therefore, that many teachers report not only being unfamiliar with the concept of autonomy (Boggiano et al., 1987) but also having a preference for (Barrett & Boggiano, 1988) and tendency to use (Newby, 1991; Sarrazin et al., 2006) rewards and other forms of control to motivate students. Importantly, though, individuals in positions of responsibility—including healthcare providers (Ntoumanis et al., 2020), managers (Hardré & Reeve, 2009), and parents (Joussemet et al., 2014)—can be trained through intervention to support the autonomy of others. Su and Reeve (2011) reported that this "teachability" of need support is particularly salient for teachers. Most of the interventions in the education domain that are informed by self-determination theory have been examined in the context of physical education (Chatzisarantis & Hagger, 2009; Cheon & Moon, 2010; Cheon & Reeve, 2013; Cheon et al., 2012; Moustaka et al., 2012), and these interventions investigated the facilitation of optimal motivation in students.

Nevertheless, several interventions have focused on teachers of academic subjects other than physical education. For instance, among preservice teachers, Reeve (1998) found that receipt of autonomy-supportive training engendered an endorsement of such a style, relative to teachers who received training in controlling and neutral motivational strategies. Subsequent to this early work, Reeve et al. (2004) found not only that high school teachers who received training in autonomy-supportive methods were rated as more autonomy supportive by observers but also that students of teachers who received this training were rated objectively as more engaged. Among university tutors in the United Kingdom, McLachlan and Hagger (2010) reported that training in autonomy-supportive instructional methods produced somewhat higher levels of autonomy support toward students. Moreover, this training was associated with tutors' issuing fewer directives and comments toward their students, along with students' spending more time speaking in their class. Among second-grade teachers in Quebec, Guay et al. (2016) reported that a professional development program based on the principles of self-determination theory produced more use of collaboration, authentic activities, involvement, and autonomy support, along with higher levels of intrinsic motivation and writing achievement among students. Hence, not only are the principles of need support "teachable" as a motivational strategy in the classroom but also the benefits associated with this interpersonal style are observable and radiate to students.

Previous research using self-determination theory has shown that the positive correlates associated with need support in the classroom are manifold. Students who are in need-supportive classrooms are more likely to report experiences of intrinsic motivation, perceived competence, and self-esteem, regardless of whether perceptions of need support are provided by the teachers (Deci, Nezlek, et al., 1981; Deci, Schwartz, et al., 1981) or by the students (Ryan & Grolnick, 1986). Also, perceptions of need support are associated with higher levels of interest (Tsai et al., 2008), conceptual understanding (Benware & Deci, 1984; Grolnick & Ryan, 1987), engagement (Jang et al., 2010), performance in school, and intention to stay in school (Hardre & Reeve, 2003), along with lower levels of school dropout (Vallerand et al., 1997). Finally, at both phenomenological and physiological levels, perceptions of need support are associated with more vitality and positive affect (Niemiec & Muñoz, 2019) and less anxiety (Black & Deci, 2000), as well as higher levels of heart rate and emotional arousal (Streb et al., 2015) and lower levels of cortisol (Reeve & Tseng, 2011).

As such, need-supportive educational contexts can engender student capacities. From the perspective of self-determination theory, support for autonomy, competence, and relatedness in the classroom can also facilitate students' coming to endorse the value associated with behaviors that are important yet not inherently satisfying—a process known as internalization (Ryan, 1993; see also Deci & Ryan, 2000). As previous research using experimental (Deci et al., 1994) and nonexperimental (Niemiec et al., 2006) methods has confirmed this postulate, it is important to specify different reasons for enacting behavior that vary along a continuum of relative autonomy and describe different degrees of internalization. With external regulation, the behavior is performed to satisfy an external contingency, whereas with introjected regulation the behavior is performed to satisfy an internal contingency. Both external regulation and introjected regulation are relatively controlled types of motivation. As the process of internalization moves toward completion, identified regulation characterizes behavior that is performed for reasons of personal relevance and importance, whereas integrated regulation characterizes behavior that is coherent with endorsed values and aspects of the self. Both identified and integrated regulation are relatively autonomous types of motivation.

To be sure, research has shown that controlled motivation (i.e., to be coerced into action by external and/or internal forces) is associated with maladaptive educational outcomes, whereas autonomous motivation (i.e., to endorse one's action fully) is associated with adaptive outcomes among students (De Naeghel et al., 2012). For instance, Niemiec and colleagues (2006) found that autonomous motivation for pursuing collegiate studies predicts higher levels of well-being and lower levels of ill-being among high school students. In a similar regard, autonomous motivation is associated with higher levels of optimal learning behavior and academic functioning (Vansteen-kiste et al., 2009), effort to learn (Reeve et al., 2002), perceived academic performance (Jeno & Diseth, 2014), and final grades in STEM courses (Botnaru et al., 2021). It is quite interesting to note, as well, that having examined Chinese university students' reasons for doing their tasks, course work, and reading, Yu et al. (2021) reported that daily fluctuations in autonomous motivation covary (positively) with daily fluctuations in state vitality, which in turn predict (positively) daily fluctuations in everyday creativity—that is, an expression of proactive human nature (see Maslow, 1968/1999). Accordingly, support for and satisfaction of the basic psychological needs for autonomy, competence, and relatedness—along with autonomous motivation—appear to be *sine qua non* for flourishing among students in the classroom.

Mitigating Student Vulnerabilities and Promoting Student Capacities

So far in this chapter, one primary area of focus has been on the myriad ways that parents and teachers can thwart satisfaction of the basic psychological needs for autonomy, competence, and relatedness among their students. Amid this confluence of pressures, negative feedback, and rejection, it might be easy to overlook another student vulnerability—namely, loneliness among peers at school. Loneliness among peers is experienced when students perceive a deficit in social integration and friendship quality at school (Frostad et al., 2015; Russell et al., 1984). There are serious and adverse consequences associated with loneliness (Holt-Lunstad et al., 2015), and thus it is prudent to examine both the developmental trajectory and longitudinal correlates of loneliness among peers at school. It is notable, then, that Tvedt et al. (2021) found an average increase in loneliness among peers during a 13-month period in upper secondary school. Of concern as well, the rate of change in loneliness among peers at school predicted an increase in intentions to quit school over time. Although alarming, Tvedt and colleagues also reported that the rate of change in perceived emotional support from teachers predicted a decrease in intentions to quit school over time, and this finding highlights the importance of building educational climates in which teachers convey trust, care, and concern to their students (Pianta et al., 2012). Hence, a strong support for relatedness might help to mitigate the development of students' intentions to quit school.

Need thwarting and frustration are pervasive experiences in the education domain, where factors—such as external control—that are antithetical to proactive human nature are commonly introduced. Accordingly, it is important to consider inner psychological resources that might help to mitigate the adverse impact that such factors can have on student outcomes. One such resource is mindfulness (Brown & Ryan, 2003)—a form of open attention to present experiences in which the ego is "quieted" (Niemiec et al., 2008) and internal/external events are "allowed" to occur (Deci et al., 2015) without distortion (Brown et al., 2008). It is interesting to note, then, that mindfulness is associated with less defensive responding to threat (Niemiec et al., 2010). Also in the workplace, individuals who are more mindful are less likely to (a) experience need frustration in response to a lack of need support from their manager (Schultz et al., 2015) and (b) convert need frustration into adverse physical and psychological outcomes (Olafsen et al., 2021). Although this research has been conducted outside the education domain, it is reasonable to suggest that the enhanced capacities for choice, authenticity (Ryan et al., 2012), cognitive flexibility, and executive function (Zeidan et al., 2010) that mindfulness confers might help to support students' proactive nature. Hence, additional research is warranted and encouraged.

A second primary area of focus in this chapter has been on the many specific ways that educators can support satisfaction of the basic psychological needs for autonomy, competence, and relatedness among their students. Yet, it is also interesting to reflect on emerging ways that teachers might promote student capacities further. Bru et al. (2021), for instance, examined the behavioral engagement and emotional engagement of eighth- to tenth-grade students in Norway. Although, as anticipated, no gender differences emerged in the strength of association between perceived emotional support from teachers and student engagement, results revealed stronger associations between structuring of learning activities and student engagement for males than females. By contrast, the results revealed a stronger association between learning process support and emotional engagement for females than males. In other words, even though both structuring of learning activities and learning process support are consistent with the provision of support for competence, it seems that males tend to derive more benefit from receiving clarity around academic tasks whereas females tend to derive more benefit from receiving guidance on metacognitive strategies and deep processing of learning activities. To be sure, more research is needed to replicate and extend these intriguing findings of gender differences in the classroom.

Other recent research has examined the effect of self-tracking (Ajana, 2018) in effortful activities on perceived competence, task enjoyment, and state vitality. Jin et al. (2021), for instance, presented a set of three experiments in which participants in a self-tracking condition received numerical feedback about their performance on riddle-solving, math-solving, and word-scramble tasks. Interestingly, across these experiments gender moderated the effect of self-tracking (versus a control condition) on task experience, such that females derived more perceived competence, task enjoyment, and subjective vitality from receipt of self-tracking feedback, relative to males. Indeed, it seems that self-tracking feedback can help females develop a more accurate assessment of their abilities and capacities, from which a sense of competence is derived. Still, other recent research has shown that incidental curiosity can prompt the intention to obtain curiosity-irrelevant, unknown information via a "spillover" process (Jin et al., in press). Of course, the implications of this finding for educational practice are quite remarkable, as it suggests that by stimulating curiosity in the classroom teachers might be able to "ready" their students for engagement with new conceptual material. Though encouraging, these lines of research await translation in the classroom.

Concluding Comments

Proactive human nature is, at once, replete with capacities and vulnerabilities, which have implications for full functioning and organismic wellness. In the classroom, this proactive nature commonly manifests as curiosity, interest, passion, and synthesis in students, which can form the bedrock for thriving in the education domain. Yet all too often, some teachers introduce external factors to their pedagogic practice in an attempt to ensure that learning occurs according to some "predefined" schedule. In this chapter, I discussed self-determination theory and the concept of basic psychological needs to offer a blueprint for how teachers can align their pedagogic practice with their students' proactive nature via support for satisfaction of autonomy, competence, and relatedness. It is my hope that by doing so, teachers can work to mitigate student vulnerabilities, promote student capacities, and develop the firm foundation for a positive psychology in schools.

References

Ajana, B. (2018). Introduction: Metric culture and the over-examined life. In B. Ajana (Ed.), *Metric culture: Ontologies of self-tracking practices* (pp. 1–9). Emerald.

Angyal, A. (1965). *Neurosis and treatment: A holistic theory.* Wiley.

Barrett, M., & Boggiano, A. K. (1988). Fostering extrinsic orientations: Use of reward strategies to motivate children. *Journal of Social and Clinical Psychology, 6,* 293–309. https://doi.org/10.1521/jscp.1988.6.3-4.293

Baumeister, R. F., & Leary, M. R. (1995). The need to belong: Desire for interpersonal attachments as a fundamental human motivation. *Psychological Bulletin, 117,* 497–529. http://dx.doi.org/10.1037/0033-2909.117.3.497

Benware, C. A., & Deci, E. L. (1984). Quality of learning with an active versus passive motivational set. *American Educational Research Journal, 21,* 755–765. http://dx.doi.org/10.3102/00028312021004755

Black, A. E., & Deci, E. L. (2000). The effects of instructors' autonomy support and students' autonomous motivation on learning organic chemistry: A self-determination theory perspective. *Science Education, 84,* 740–756. http://dx.doi.org/10.1002/1098-237X(200011)84:6%3C740::AID-SCE4%3E3.0.CO;2-3

Boggiano, A. K., Barrett, M., Weiher, A. W., McClelland, G. H., & Lusk, C. M. (1987). Use of the maximal-operant principle to motivate children's intrinsic interest. *Journal of Personality and Social Psychology, 53,* 866–879. https://doi.org/10.1037/0022-3514.53.5.866

Botnaru, D., Orvis, J., Langdon, J., Niemiec, C. P., & Landge, S. M. (2021). Predicting final grades in STEM courses: A path analysis of academic motivation and course-related behavior using self-determination theory. *Learning and Motivation, 74,* 101723. https://doi.org/10.1016/j.lmot.2021.101723

Brown, K. W., & Ryan, R. M. (2003). The benefits of being present: Mindfulness and its role in psychological well-being. *Journal of Personality and Social Psychology, 84,* 822–848. https://doi.org/10.1037/0022-3514.84.4.822

Brown, K. W., Ryan, R. M., Creswell, J. D., & Niemiec, C. P. (2008). Beyond me: Mindful responses to social threat. In H. A. Wayment & J. J. Bauer (Eds.), *Transcending self-interest: Psychological explorations of the quiet ego* (pp. 75–84). APA Books. https://doi.org/10.1037/11771-007

Bru, E., Virtanen, T., Kjetilstad, V., & Niemiec, C. P. (2021). Gender differences in the strength of association between perceived support from teachers and student engagement. *Scandinavian Journal of Educational Research, 65,* 153–168. https://doi.org/10.1080/00313831.2019.1659404

Chatzisarantis, N. L., & Hagger, M. S. (2009). Effects of an intervention based on self-determination theory on self-reported leisure-time physical activity participation. *Psychology and Health, 24,* 29–48. http://dx.doi.org/10.1080/08870440701809533

Chen, B., Vansteenkiste, M., Beyers, W., Boone, L., Deci, E. L., Van der Kaap-Deeder, J., Duriez, B., Lens, W., Matos, L., Mouratidis, A., Ryan, R. M., Sheldon, K. M., Soenens, B., Van Petegem, S., & Verstuyf, J. (2015). Basic psychological need satisfaction, need frustration, and need strength across four cultures. *Motivation and Emotion, 39,* 216–236. https://doi.org/10.1007/s11031-014-9450-1

Cheon, S. H., & Moon, I. S. (2010). Implementing an autonomy-supportive fitness program to facilitate students' autonomy and engagement. *Korean Journal of Sport Psychology, 21,* 175–195.

Cheon, S. H., & Reeve, J. (2013). Do the benefits from autonomy-supportive PE teacher training programs endure?: A one-year follow-up investigation. *Psychology of Sport and Exercise, 14,* 508–518. http://dx.doi.org/10.1016/j.psychsport.2013.02.002

Cheon, S. H., Reeve, J., Lee, Y., Ntoumanis, N., Gillet, N., Kim, B. R., & Song, Y. G. (2019). Expanding autonomy psychological need states from two (satisfaction, frustration) to three (dissatisfaction): A classroom-based intervention study. *Journal of Educational Psychology, 111,* 685–702. https://doi.org/10.1037/edu0000306

Cheon, S. H., Reeve, J., & Moon, I. S. (2012). Experimentally based, longitudinally designed, teacher-focused intervention to help physical education teachers be more autonomy supportive toward their students. *Journal of Sport & Exercise Psychology, 34,* 365–396. http://dx.doi.org/10.1123/jsep.34.3.365

Curran, T., Hill, A. P., & Niemiec, C. P. (2013). A conditional process model of children's behavioural engagement and behavioural disaffection in sport based on self-determination theory. *Journal of Sport & Exercise Psychology, 35,* 30–43.

de Charms, R. (1968). *Personal causation.* Academic Press.

Deci, E. L., Eghrari, H., Patrick, B. C., & Leone, D. (1994). Facilitating internalization: The self-determination theory perspective. *Journal of Personality, 62,* 119–142. http://dx.doi.org/10.1111/j.1467-6494.1994.tb00797.x

Deci, E. L., Nezlek, J., & Sheinman, L. (1981). Characteristics of the rewarder and intrinsic motivation of the rewardee. *Journal of Personality and Social Psychology, 40,* 1–10. https://doi.org/10.1037/0022-3514.40.1.1

Deci, E. L., & Ryan, R. M. (2000). The "what" and "why" of goal pursuits: Human needs and the self-determination of behavior. *Psychological Inquiry, 11*, 227–268. http://dx.doi.org/10.1207/S15327965PLI1104_01

Deci, E. L., & Ryan, R. M. (2008). Facilitating optimal motivation and psychological well-being across life's domains. *Canadian Psychology, 49*, 14–23. http://dx.doi.org/10.1037/0708-5591.49.1.14

Deci, E. L., Ryan, R. M., Schultz, P. P., & Niemiec, C. P. (2015). Being aware and functioning fully: Mindfulness and interest taking within self-determination theory. In K. W. Brown, J. D. Creswell, & R. M. Ryan (Eds.), *Handbook of mindfulness: Theory, research, and practice* (pp. 112–129). Guilford.

Deci, E. L., Schwartz, A. J., Sheinman, L., & Ryan, R. M. (1981). An instrument to assess adults' orientations toward control versus autonomy with children: Reflections on intrinsic motivation and perceived competence. *Journal of Educational Psychology, 73*, 642–650. http://dx.doi.org/10.1037/0022-0663.73.5.642

Deci, E. L., Spiegel, N. H., Ryan, R. M., Koestner, R., & Kauffman, M. (1982). Effects of performance standards on teaching styles: Behavior of controlling teachers. *Journal of Educational Psychology, 74*, 852–859. https://doi.org/10.1037/0022-0663.74.6.852

De Naeghel, J., Van Keer, H., Vansteenkiste, M., & Rosseel, Y. (2012). The relation between elementary students' recreational and academic reading motivation, reading frequency, engagement, and comprehension: A self-determination theory perspective. *Journal of Educational Psychology, 104*, 1006–1021. http://dx.doi.org/10.1037/a0027800

Filak, V. F., & Sheldon, K. M. (2003). Student psychological need satisfaction and college teacher-course evaluations. *Educational Psychology, 23*, 235–247. https://doi.org/10.1080/0144341032000060084

Flink, C., Boggiano, A. K., & Barrett, M. (1990). Controlling teaching strategies: Undermining children's self-determination and performance. *Journal of Personality and Social Psychology, 59*, 916–924. https://doi.org/10.1037/0022-3514.59.5.916

Frostad, P., Pijl, S. J., & Mjaavatn, P. E. (2015). Losing all interest in school: Social participation as a predictor of the intention to leave upper secondary school early. *Scandinavian Journal of Educational Research, 59*, 110–122. https://doi.org/10.1080/00313831.2014.904420

Gottlieb, G. (2003). Probabilistic epigenesis of development. In J. Valsiner & K. J. Connolly (Eds.), *Handbook of developmental psychology* (pp. 3–17). Sage. http://doi.org/10.1111/j.1467-7687.2007.00556

Grolnick, W. S., & Ryan, R. M. (1987). Autonomy in children's learning: An experimental and individual difference investigation. *Journal of Personality and Social Psychology, 52*, 890–898. https://doi.org/10.1037/0022-3514.52.5.890

Guay, F., Valois, P., Falardeau, É., & Lessard, V. (2016). Examining the effects of a professional development program on teachers' pedagogical practices and students' motivational resources and achievement in written French. *Learning and Individual Differences, 45*, 291–298. http://dx.doi.org/10.1016/j.lindif.2015.11.014

Haerens, L., Aelterman, N., Van den Berghe, L., De Meyer, J., Soenens, B., & Vansteenkiste, M. (2013). Observing physical education teachers' need-supportive interactions in classroom settings. *Journal of Sport & Exercise Psychology, 35*, 3–17. https://doi.org/10.1123/jsep.35.1.3

Hardre, P. L., & Reeve, J. (2003). A motivational model of rural students' intentions to persist in, versus drop out of, high school. *Journal of Educational Psychology, 95*, 347–356. http://dx.doi.org/10.1037/0022-0663.95.2.347

Hardré, P. L., & Reeve, J. (2009). Training corporate managers to adopt a more autonomy-supportive motivating style toward employees: An intervention study. *International Journal of Training and Development, 13*, 165–184. https://doi.org/10.1111/j.1468-2419.2009.00325.x

Holt-Lunstad, J., Smith, T. B., Baker, M., Harris, T., & Stephenson, D. (2015). Loneliness and social isolation as risk factors for mortality: A meta-analytic review. *Perspectives on Psychological Science, 10*, 227–237. http://doi.org/10.1177/1745691614568352

Jang, H., Reeve, J., & Deci, E. L. (2010). Engaging students in learning activities: It is not autonomy support or structure but autonomy support and structure. *Journal of Educational Psychology, 102*, 588–600. http://dx.doi.org/10.1037/a0019682

Jeno, L. M., & Diseth, Å. (2014). A self-determination theory perspective on autonomy support, autonomous self-regulation, and perceived school performance. *Reflecting Education, 9*, 1–20.

Jin, D., Halvari, H., Mæhle, N., & Niemiec, C. P. (2021). Self-tracking in effortful activities: Gender differences in consumers' task experience. *Journal of Consumer Behaviour, 20*, 173–185. https://doi.org/10.1002/cb.1865

Jin, D., Halvari, H., Mæhle, N., & Niemiec, C. P. (in press). Incidental curiosity and consumer intention to obtain unknown information: Implications for new product adoption and self-tracking behavior. *Journal of Customer Behaviour.*

Joussemet, M., Koestner, R., Lekes, N., & Landry, R. (2005). A longitudinal study of the relationship of maternal autonomy support to children's adjustment and achievement in school. *Journal of Personality, 73*, 1215–1235. https://doi.org/10.1111/j.1467-6494.2005.00347.x

Joussemet, M., Mageau, G. A., & Koestner, R. (2014). Promoting optimal parenting and children's mental health: A preliminary evaluation of the How-to Parenting Program. *Journal of Child and Family Studies, 23*, 949–964. https://doi.org/10.1007/s10826-013-9751-0

Kauffman, S., & Clayton, P. (2006). On emergence, agency, and organization. *Biology and Philosophy, 21*, 501–521. https://doi.org/10.1007/s10539-005-9003-9

Loevinger, J. (1976). *Ego development.* Jossey-Bass.

Loewenstein, G. (1994). The psychology of curiosity: A review and reinterpretation. *Psychological Bulletin, 116*, 75–98. http://dx.doi.org/10.1037/0033-2909.116.1.75

Maslow, A. H. (1968/1999). *Toward a psychology of being.* Wiley.

McLachlan, S., & Hagger, M. S. (2010). Effects of an autonomy-supportive intervention on tutor behaviors in a higher education context. *Teaching and Teacher Education, 26*, 1204–1210. http://dx.doi.org/10.1016/j.tate.2010.01.006

Moustaka, F. C., Vlachopoulos, S. P., Kabitsis, C., & Theodorakis, Y. (2012). Effects of an autonomy-supportive exercise instructing style on exercise motivation, psychological well-being, and exercise attendance in middle-age women. *Journal of Physical Activity and Health, 9*, 138–150. http://dx.doi.org/10.1123/jpah.9.1.138

Newby, T. J. (1991). Classroom motivation: Strategies of first-year teachers. *Journal of Educational Psychology, 83*, 195–200. https://doi.org/10.1037/0022-0663.83.2.195

Niemiec, C. P., Brown, K. W., Kashdan, T. B., Cozzolino, P. J., Breen, W. E., Levesque-Bristol, C., & Ryan, R. M. (2010). Being present in the face of existential threat: The role of trait mindfulness in reducing defensive responses to mortality salience. *Journal of Personality and Social Psychology, 99*, 344–365. https://doi.org/10.1037/a0019388

Niemiec, C. P., Lynch, M. F., Vansteenkiste, M., Bernstein, J., Deci, E. L., & Ryan, R. M. (2006). The antecedents and consequences of autonomous self-regulation for college: A self-determination theory perspective on socialization. *Journal of Adolescence, 29*, 761–775. http://dx.doi.org/10.1016/j.adolescence.2007.02.002

Niemiec, C. P., & Muñoz, A. (2019). A need-supportive intervention delivered to English language teachers in Colombia: A pilot investigation based on self-determination theory. *Psychology, 10*, 1025–1042. http://doi.org/10.4236/psych.2019.107067

Niemiec, C. P., & Ryan, R. M. (2009). Autonomy, competence, and relatedness in the classroom: Applying self-determination theory to educational practice. *Theory and Research in Education, 7*, 133–144. http://dx.doi.org/10.1177/1477878509104318

Niemiec, C. P., & Ryan, R. M. (2013). What makes for a life well lived? Autonomy and its relation to full functioning and organismic wellness. In S. A. David, I. Boniwell, & A. C. Ayers (Eds.), *The Oxford handbook of happiness* (pp. 214–226). Oxford University Press. http://dx.doi.org/10.1093/oxfordhb/9780199557257.013.0016

Niemiec, C. P., Ryan, R. M., & Brown, K. W. (2008). The role of awareness and autonomy in quieting the ego: A self-determination theory perspective. In H. A. Wayment & J. J. Bauer (Eds.), *Transcending self-interest: Psychological explorations of the quiet ego* (pp. 107–115). APA Books. https://doi.org/10.1037/11771-010

Niemiec, C. P., Ryan, R. M., & Deci, E. L. (2010). Self-determination theory and the relation of autonomy to self-regulatory processes and personality development. In R. H. Hoyle (Ed.), *Handbook of personality and self-regulation* (pp. 169–191). Blackwell. http://dx.doi.org/10.1002/9781444318111.ch8

Niemiec, C. P., Soenens, B., & Vansteenkiste, M. (2014). Is relatedness enough? On the importance of need support in different types of social experiences. In N. Weinstein (Ed.), *Human motivation and interpersonal relationships: Theory, research and applications* (pp. 77–96). Springer. http://dx.doi.org/10.1007/978-94-017-8542-6_4

Ntoumanis, N., Ng, J. Y. Y., Prestwich, A., Quested, E., Hancox, J. E., Thøgersen-Ntoumani, C., Deci, E. L., Ryan, R. M., Lonsdale, C., & Williams, G. C. (2020). A meta-analysis of self-determination theory-informed intervention studies in the health domain: Effects on motivation, health behavior, physical, and psychological health. *Health Psychology Review, 3*, 1–31. http://doi.org/10.1080/17437199.2020.1718529

Olafsen, A. H., Niemiec, C. P., Deci, E. L., Halvari, H., Nilsen, E. R., & Williams, G. C. (2021). Mindfulness buffers the adverse impact of need frustration on employee outcomes: A self-determination theory perspective. *Journal of Theoretical Social Psychology, 5*, 283–296. https://doi.org/10.1002/jts5.93

Olafsen, A. H., Niemiec, C. P., Halvari, H., Deci, E. L., & Williams, G. C. (2017). On the dark side of work: A longitudinal analysis using self-determination theory. *European Journal of Work & Organizational Psychology, 26*, 275–285. https://doi.org/10.1080/1359432X.2016.1257611

Pelletier, L. G., Séguin-Lévesque, C., & Legault, L. (2002). Pressure from above and pressure from below as determinants of teachers' motivation and teaching behaviors. *Journal of Educational Psychology, 94,* 186–196. https://doi.org/10.1037/0022-0663.94.1.186

Piaget, J. (1971). *Biology and knowledge.* University of Chicago Press.

Pianta, R. C., Hamre, B. K., & Allen, J. P. (2012). Teacher-student relationships and engagement: Conceptualizing, measuring, and improving the capacity of classroom interactions. In S. L. Christenson, A. L. Reschly, & C. Wylie (Eds.), *Handbook of research on student engagement* (pp. 365–386). Springer. https://doi.org/10.1007/978-1-4614-2018-7_17

Plutarch (1927). *Moralia, Volume 1.* (F. C. Babbitt, Trans.). Harvard University Press.

Reeve, J. (1998). Autonomy support as an interpersonal motivating style: Is it teachable? *Contemporary Educational Psychology, 23,* 312–330. http://dx.doi.org/10.1006/ceps.1997.0975

Reeve, J. (2002). Self-determination theory applied to educational settings. In E. L. Deci & R. M. Ryan (Eds.), *Handbook of self-determination research* (pp. 183–203). University of Rochester Press.

Reeve, J. (2006). Teachers as facilitators: What autonomy-supportive teachers do and why their students benefit. *The Elementary School Journal, 106,* 225–236. http://dx.doi.org/10.1086/501484

Reeve, J. (2009). Why teachers adopt a controlling motivating style toward students and how they can become more autonomy supportive. *Educational Psychologist, 44,* 159–175. http://dx.doi.org/10.1080/00461520903028990

Reeve, J., & Jang, H. (2006). What teachers say and do to support students' autonomy during a learning activity. *Journal of Educational Psychology, 98,* 209–218. http://dx.doi.org/10.1037/0022-0663.98.1.209

Reeve, J., Jang, H., Carrell, D., Jeon, S., & Barch, J. (2004). Enhancing students' engagement by increasing teachers' autonomy support. *Motivation and Emotion, 28,* 147–169. http://dx.doi.org/10.1023/B:MOEM.0000032312.95499.6f

Reeve, J., Jang, H., Hardre, P., & Omura, M. (2002). Providing a rationale in an autonomy-supportive way as a strategy to motivate others during an uninteresting activity. *Motivation and Emotion, 26,* 183–207. https://doi.org/10.1023/A:1021711629417

Reeve, J., & Tseng, C. M. (2011). Cortisol reactivity to a teacher's motivating style: The biology of being controlled versus supporting autonomy. *Motivation and Emotion, 35,* 63–74. https://doi.org/10.1007/s11031-011-9204-2

Rogers, C. R. (1963). The actualizing tendency in relation to "motives" and to consciousness. In M. R. Jones (Ed.), *Nebraska symposium on motivation* (Vol. 11, pp. 1–24). University of Nebraska Press.

Roth, G., Assor, A., Niemiec, C. P., Ryan, R. M., & Deci, E. L. (2009). The emotional and academic consequences of parental conditional regard: Comparing conditional positive regard, conditional negative regard, and autonomy support as parenting practices. *Developmental Psychology, 45,* 1119–1142. https://doi.org/10.1037/a0015272

Russell, D., Cutrona, C. E., Rose, J., & Yurko, K. (1984). Social and emotional loneliness: An examination of Weiss's typology of loneliness. *Journal of Personality and Social Psychology, 46,* 1313–1321. https://doi.org/10.1037/0022-3514.46.6.1313

Ryan, R. M. (1993). Agency and organization: Intrinsic motivation, autonomy and the self in psychological development. In J. Jacobs (Ed.), *Nebraska symposium on motivation: Developmental perspectives on motivation* (Vol. 40, pp. 1–56). University of Nebraska Press.

Ryan, R. M. (1995). Psychological needs and the facilitation of integrative processes. *Journal of Personality, 63,* 397–427. http://dx.doi.org/10.1111/j.1467-6494.1995.tb00501.x

Ryan, R. M., & Brown, K. W. (2005). Legislating competence: High-stakes testing policies and their relations with psychological theories and research. In A. J. Elliot & C. S. Dweck (Eds.), *Handbook of competence and motivation* (pp. 354–372). Guilford.

Ryan, R. M., & Deci, E. L. (2002). Overview of self-determination theory: An organismic dialectical perspective. In E. L. Deci & R. M. Ryan (Eds.), *Handbook of self-determination research* (pp. 3–33). University of Rochester Press.

Ryan, R. M., & Deci, E. L. (2017). *Self-determination theory: Basic psychological needs in motivation, development, and wellness.* Guilford.

Ryan, R. M., & Grolnick, W. S. (1986). Origins and pawns in the classroom: Self-report and projective assessments of individual differences in children's perceptions. *Journal of Personality and Social Psychology, 50,* 550–558. http://dx.doi.org/10.1037/0022-3514.50.3.550

Ryan, R. M., La Guardia, J. G., Solky-Butzel, J., Chirkov, V., & Kim, Y. (2005). On the interpersonal regulation of emotions: Emotional reliance across gender, relationships, and cultures. *Personal Relationships, 12,* 145–163. https://doi.org/10.1111/j.1350-4126.2005.00106.x

Ryan, R. M., Legate, N., Niemiec, C. P., & Deci, E. L. (2012). Beyond illusions and defense: Exploring the possibilities and limits of human autonomy and responsibility through self-determination theory. In P. R. Shaver & M. Mikulincer (Eds.), *Meaning, mortality, and choice: The social psychology of existential concerns* (pp. 215–233). APA Books. https://doi.org/10.1037/13748-012

Ryan, R. M., & Niemiec, C. P. (2009). Self-determination theory in schools of education: Can an empirically supported framework also be critical and liberating? *Theory and Research in Education, 7*, 263–272. http://dx.doi.org/10.1177/1477878509104331

Sarrazin, P. G., Tessier, D. P., Pelletier, L. G., Trouilloud, D. O., & Chanal, J. P. (2006). The effects of teachers' expectations about students' motivation on teachers' autonomy-supportive and controlling behaviors. *International Journal of Sport and Exercise Psychology, 4*, 283–301. https://doi.org/10.1080/1612197X.2006.9671799

Schilpp, P. A. (1949). *Albert Einstein: Philosopher-scientist*. Open Court.

Schultz, P. P., Ryan, R. M., Niemiec, C. P., Legate, N., & Williams, G. C. (2015). Mindfulness, work climate, and psychological need satisfaction in employee well-being. *Mindfulness, 6*, 971–985. https://doi.org/10.1007/s12671-014-0338-7

Silvia, P. J. (2008). Interest—The curious emotion. *Current Directions in Psychological Science, 17*, 57–60. http://dx.doi.org/10.1111/j.1467-8721.2008.00548.x

Skinner, B. F. (1953). *Science and human behavior*. Macmillan.

Skinner, B. F. (1971). *Beyond freedom and dignity*. Alfred A. Knopf.

Soenens, B., Sierens, E., Vansteenkiste, M., Dochy, F., & Goossens, L. (2012). Psychologically controlling teaching: Examining outcomes, antecedents, and mediators. *Journal of Educational Psychology, 104*, 108–120. https://doi.org/10.1037/a0025742

Streb, J., Keis, O., Lau, M., Hille, K., Spitzer, M., & Sosic-Vasic, Z. (2015). Emotional engagement in kindergarten and school children: A self-determination theory perspective. *Trends in Neuroscience and Education, 4*, 102–107. http://dx.doi.org/10.1016/j.tine.2015.11.001

Su, Y. L., & Reeve, J. (2011). A meta-analysis of the effectiveness of intervention programs designed to support autonomy. *Educational Psychology Review, 23*, 159–188. http://dx.doi.org/10.1007/s10648-010-9142-7

Tsai, Y., Kunter, M., Lüdtke, O., Trautwein, U., & Ryan, R. M. (2008). What makes lessons interesting? The role of situational and individual factors in three school subjects. *Journal of Educational Psychology, 100*, 460–472. https://doi.org/10.1037/0022-0663.100.2.460

Tvedt, M. S., Bru, E., Idsoe, T., & Niemiec, C. P. (2021). Intentions to quit, emotional support from teachers, and loneliness among peers: Developmental trajectories and longitudinal associations in upper secondary school. *Educational Psychology, 41*, 967–984. https://doi.org/10.1080/01443410.2021.1948505

Vallerand, R. J. (2010). On passion for life activities: The dualistic model of passion. *Advances in Experimental Social Psychology, 42*, 97–193. http://dx.doi.org/10.1016/S0065-2601(10)42003-1

Vallerand, R. J., Fortier, M. S., & Guay, F. (1997). Self-determination and persistence in a real-life setting: Toward a motivational model of high school dropout. *Journal of Personality and Social Psychology, 72*, 1161–1176. http://dx.doi.org/10.1037/0022-3514.72.5.1161

Vansteenkiste, M., Neyrinck, B., Niemiec, C. P., Soenens, B., de Witte, H., & Van den Broeck, A. (2007). On the relations among work value orientations, psychological need satisfaction and job outcomes: A self-determination theory approach. *Journal of Occupational and Organizational Psychology, 80*, 251–277. https://doi.org/10.1348/096317906X111024

Vansteenkiste, M., Niemiec, C. P., & Soenens, B. (2010). The development of the five mini-theories of self-determination theory: An historical overview, emerging trends, and future directions. In T. C. Urdan & S. A. Karabenick (Eds.), *Advances in motivation and achievement, v. 16A—The decade ahead: Theoretical perspectives on motivation and achievement* (pp. 105–165). Emerald Group. http://dx.doi.org/10.1108/S0749-7423(2010)000016A007

Vansteenkiste, M., & Ryan, R. M. (2013). On psychological growth and vulnerability: Basic psychological need satisfaction and need frustration as a unifying principle. *Journal of Psychotherapy Integration, 23*, 263–280. https://doi.org/10.1037/a0032359

Vansteenkiste, M., Sierens, E., Soenens, B., Luyckx, K., & Lens, W. (2009). Motivational profiles from a self-determination perspective: The quality of motivation matters. *Journal of Educational Psychology, 101*, 671–688. https://doi.org/10.1037/a0015083

Watson, J. B. (1924). *Behaviorism*. University of Chicago Press.

White, R. W. (1959). Motivation reconsidered: The concept of competence. *Psychological Review, 66*, 297–333. https://doi.org/10.1037/h0040934

Williams, G. C., Niemiec, C. P., Patrick, H., Ryan, R. M., & Deci, E. L. (2009). The importance of supporting autonomy and perceived competence in facilitating long-term tobacco abstinence. *Annals of Behavioral Medicine, 37*, 315–324. http://doi.org/10.1007/s12160-009-9090-y

Wuyts, D., Chen, B., Vansteenkiste, M., & Soenens, B. (2015). Social pressure and unfulfilled dreams among Chinese and Belgian parents: Two roads to controlling parenting via child-invested contingent self-esteem. *Journal of Cross-Cultural Psychology, 46*, 1150–1168. https://doi.org/10.1177/0022022115603125

Yu, H., Zuo, S., Liu, Y., & Niemiec, C. P. (2021). Toward a personality integration perspective on creativity: Between- and within-persons associations among autonomy, vitality, and everyday creativity. *The Journal of Positive Psychology, 16*, 789–801. https://doi.org/10.1080/17439760.2020.1818810

Zeidan, F., Johnson, S. K., Diamond, B. J., David, Z., & Goolkasian, P. (2010). Mindfulness meditation improves cognition: Evidence of brief mental training. *Consciousness and Cognition, 19*, 597–605. https://doi.org/10.1016/j.concog.2010.03.014

4

COVITALITY

Cultivating Psychosocial Strengths and Well-Being

Jennica Lee Paz and Eui Kyung Kim

Review of Theoretical Foundations

Conceptualizations of Student Wellness

Educators' duty to enhance students' capacity to thrive is imperative as they face a world with moral and sociopolitical upheavals, publicized school shootings, a global pandemic, and unapologetic activism calling to mobilize minoritized voices. School systems serve as a critical protective factor for youth. They offer a sense of safety in which to learn, provide opportunities for meaningful social-emotional development, and help youth become productive global citizens in the future. School ecosystems have an ethical and legal duty to promote educational success and ensure well-being among their students. To adequately foster the social-emotional development of their students, educational agencies need reliable tools and methods for prevention and intervention systems to promote students' complete mental wellness. Conceptualized as, "not merely the absence of psychopathology, but also the presence of sufficient levels of emotional, psychological, and social well-being [flourishing]" (Keyes & Michalec, 2010, p. 126), complete mental wellness assessment involves the measurement of two distinct continua among the population. The public health field advocates assessing mental health from a multidimensional framework, aligning well with population-based frameworks of school-based mental health screenings (Dowdy et al., 2010). Positive psychological researchers continue to advance the paradigm shift by highlighting the need to refine mental wellness classification. One such effort is the Dual Factor Model (DFM) that integrates adaptive and maladaptive dimensions to assist with the early identification of psychological and behavioral challenges (Greenspoon & Saklofske, 2001; Keyes, 2003; Suldo & Shaffer, 2008).

Specifically, the potential benefits of simultaneously considering the integrative effects of distress and personal strengths have been proposed to better understand student wellness (Kim et al., 2019; Moore et al., 2019a; Smith et al., 2020). These holistic approaches assess core, combinatorial strengths associated with positive psychosocial development, rather than isolated constructs (e.g., hope or gratitude; Lenzi et al., 2015). Holistic assessment practices, such as DFM (Greenspoon & Saklofske, 2001) and two-continua (Westerhof & Keyes, 2010) models, place positive (e.g., psychosocial strengths) and negative (e.g., psychosocial distress) mental wellness indicators on distinct yet interrelated continua. Attending to positive and negative indicators of mental wellness shows additive

38

DOI: 10.4324/9781003013778-5

value in predicting students' attendance and academic achievement over time (Dougherty & Sharkey, 2017; Suldo et al., 2011).

We propose that indicators of psychosocial distress and strengths be considered in combination, aligned with a whole-child paradigm (Alford & White, 2015) when attending to student wellness. Inspecting both continua simultaneously unveils comprehensive psychosocial strengths, and provides a more thorough depiction of important quality-of-life (QOL) indicators (e.g., positive life functioning, psychological well-being, mental well-being, and life satisfaction) among students. Expanding upon and complementing mental health assessment approaches, which traditionally focus on identifying problems and deficits among students, strengths-based assessments highlight the importance of internal assets, strengths, and mindsets involved in thriving developmental trajectories (Nickerson, 2007). Several seminal positive youth development (PYD; Bowers et al., 2010) and cumulative risk and resilience scholars (Benson et al., 2011; Leffert et al., 1998; Scales, 1999) have paved the way for this contemporary wave of positive psychological assessment research.

Though beyond the scope of this chapter, some exemplars include:

1   Five Cs framework of positive development (Lerner et al., 2005),
2   Search Institute's 40 Developmental Assets framework (Benson et al., 2011),
3   Kern et al.'s (2016) Engagement, Perseverance, Optimism, Connectedness, and Happiness (EPOCH) framework which is rooted in Seligman's (2011) Positive emotion, Engagement, Relationships, Meaning and purpose, and Accomplishment (PERMA) model (*see Chapter 2 in this handbook for recent advancements*), and
4   Furlong et al.'s (2014) Covitality framework.

The PYD perspective emphasizes the importance of creating conditions that empower youth to make things happen proactively. Rooted in prevention science, these best practice models of integrative, cumulative strengths-based assessments are of great utility to incorporate within DFM or complete mental health screenings, especially among culturally and linguistically diverse students, globally. Importantly, these models are predictive of increased school achievement and positive QOL outcomes for youth (Paz et al., 2020; Scales, 1999).

Previous DFM studies used various single-construct (e.g., multidimensional student life satisfaction), and multifaceted tools (e.g., Social-Emotional Health Survey [SEHS]), paired with broadband distress measures (e.g., Behavioral Assessment System for Children [BASC]). Several approaches to date (e.g., use of cut-scores for high and low ratings vs. latent profile analyses) have examined how to efficiently and practically cross-tabulate wellness and distress scores to identify profiles of complete mental health functioning in youth (Moore et al., 2019a; Smith et al., 2020).

Advances in Covitality Theoretical Framework

There are continuous efforts to validate practices that can be integrated into multitiered systems of supports and promote, "psychologically healthy educational environments for [all] children" (Huebner et al., 2009, p. 565). The current wave of positive psychological research has continued to investigate multiasset measures (Furlong et al., 2013, 2014), and interventions (Suldo, 2016). As with several of the positive psychological assessment and intervention models reviewed elsewhere in this handbook, advances have been made to the Covitality construct (Furlong et al., 2014; Renshaw et al., 2014) and applications, which have been supported through a practice informed by refined research.

Originally conceptualized as a counterpart to comorbidity, Furlong and colleagues (2014) hypothesized youth psychosocial strengths as linked to a higher-order trait, called Covitality, defined as, "the synergistic effect of positive mental health resulting from the interplay among multiple positive psychological building blocks" (Furlong et al., 2013, p. 3). The Covitality psychosocial strengths matter more than any individual strength when considering the QOL among youth.[1] This model's conceptual underpinnings are in social psychology (e.g., Lips, 1995), self-concept theory (Chi-Hung, 2005), and cognitive therapy (e.g., Dozois et al., 2012; Young et al., 2003) research. The framework posits a developmental process from childhood through adolescence and beyond in which a person forms, sustains, nurtures, and enhances cognitive schemas that organize life experiences and give them meaning. Thus, this original cognitive-based framework understands adolescents as actively constructing worldviews of who they are, and arrive at conclusions about their fit within their social ecosystems. Shifting from a focus on understanding maladaptive self-schemata (i.e., "cognitive generalizations about the self, derived from experience, that organize and guide the processing of self-related information contained in the individual's social experiences"; Markus, 1977, p. 64), the 12 mindsets embedded in the Covitality model focus on adaptive self-schemas associated with resilience and their relation to adaptive and thriving developmental outcomes. For a review of operational definitions for each of the 12 positive psychological assets, see Table 2.1 in Renshaw et al. (2014).

More recently, a transactional development lens described Covitality conceptual framework refinements (Furlong et al., 2020a). The development of core psychosocial strengths (e.g., gratitude, empathy, and persistence) promotes positive interpersonal transactions within a child's socio-ecological system, which, in turn, contributes to better developmental outcomes. Youth are understood to be thriving and flourishing when developing these cumulative psychosocial strengths that promote positive, supportive everyday interactions with individuals (e.g., family, teachers, and peers) within their immediate microsystem. When emphasizing these critical positive psychological dispositions in schools, educators support students' ability to engage meaningfully in, "interpersonal transactions that facilitate their near- and long-term development across their bio-psycho-social developmental domains" (Furlong et al., 2020a, p. 6). Further, the odds of students achieving positive developmental outcomes increase when they have internal dispositions and skills to influence the quality of their daily interpersonal interactions proactively.

The Covitality framework has been translated onto a robust measurement system, the SEHS, described in the next section of this chapter. The SEHS is a social-emotional health model that includes the measurement of a range of social and emotional skills and psychological dispositions that are empirically associated with positive youth development. Further, the SEHS system has been widely applied in DFM and complete mental health screening approaches with a Multitiered Systems of Supports (MTSS) framework.

Covitality Measurement Model: The Social-Emotional-Health Survey System

As a measurement model, the SEHS system comprises structured surveys that operationalize and measure Covitality and offers a method for assessing complete mental health among primary school through higher education students. There are three self-report versions of the SEHS: Primary (SEHS-P; Furlong et al., 2013) for students ages 9–12, Secondary (SEHS-S; Furlong et al., 2014) for students ages 13–18, and Higher Education (SEHS-HE; Furlong et al., 2017) for college students. Given this chapter's focus, it reviews school-aged students, the SEHS-P (Furlong et al., 2013) and SEHS-S (Furlong et al., 2014). Recently, psychometric refinements were made to the SEHS-S, and there is an available SEHS-S 2020 version (Furlong, Dowdy, et al., 2020). Refer to the Project Covitality website for administration and interpretive information (https://www.covitalityucsb.info/sehs-measures/index.html).

The SEHS-P (previously known as Positive Experience at School Survey [PEASS]) was developed as a self-report behavior rating scale to measure school-specific well-being among primary school students in Grade 4–5. The SEHS-P has four subscales: Gratitude (e.g., *I am lucky to go to my school*); Zest (e.g., *I wake up in the morning excited to go to school*); Optimism (e.g., *When I have problems at school, I know they will get better in the future*); and Persistence (e.g., *When I get a bad grade, I try even harder the next time*). The PEASS had 20 items hypothesized to measure these four subscales above (five items each subscale). The SEHS-P (Furlong et al., 2013) has 16 items (four items each subscale), and its four subscales load onto a higher-order latent trait, *Covitality,* and fifth Prosocial Behavior subscale, which is not calculated in the overall total Covitality score.

The SEHS-S is a 36-item measure that assesses 12 psychosocial strengths derived from the social-emotional learning (SEL) and PYD literature (e.g., Bandura et al., 1996; Furlong et al., 2014; Masten et al., 2009; Zins et al., 2007). These 12 psychosocial strengths are associated with four second-order positive social-emotional constructs:

1 *Belief-in-self* (self-awareness, self-efficacy, and persistence);
2 *Belief-in-others* (family coherence, peer support, and school support);
3 *Emotional competence* (emotion regulation, self-control, and empathy); and
4 *Engaged living* (optimism, zest, and gratitude).

These four domains load onto a higher-order latent trait, *Covitality* (see Figure 4.1 for illustration of conceptual to measurement mapping for the SEHS). The SEHS system is continually evolving to reflect valid and parsimonious psychometric properties, sensitivity to developmental considerations, and affirming cultural and demographic qualities. While the conceptual model has remained the same, in the latest SEHS-S 2020 version, adaptations and refinements were implemented to present items in a more developmentally appropriate way (Furlong, Dowdy, et al., 2020). For example, a change reflected in the SEHS-S 2020 version includes items reframed as questions rather than statements in order to make items easier for students to respond.

Recognizing the importance of internal strengths for youth QOL, school psychology scholars have adapted the SEHS within their countries to identify students' psychosocial strengths and their relations with various school-specific outcomes. For example, the SEHS-S is administered to U.S. middle and high school students (Carnazzo et al., 2019; Dougherty & Sharkey, 2017), Australia (Boman et al., 2017), South Korea (Kim et al., 2019; Lee et al., 2016), Japan (Ito et al., 2015), and Turkey (Telef & Furlong, 2017). The SEHS identified positive psychological factors associated with improving academic achievement (Dougherty & Sharkey, 2017) and school connectedness (Kim et al., 2019), and reduced behavioral concerns such as truancy (Wroblewski et al., 2019). These results suggest that the SEHS measurement system can inform and promote mental health prevention, intervention, and or MTSS efforts within schools across the globe.

Advances in National and International Covitality Psychometric Research

The SEHS system has strong national and international validity for its use within schools as a strengths-based assessment tool. Table 4.1 summarizes relevant national and international studies examining the psychometric properties of the SEHS-P and SEHS-S. Psychometric results of the SEHS-P supported its validity, internal consistency, and invariance across sociocultural and gender groups. Specifically, there are SEHS-P validation studies from Australia (Wilkins et al., 2015), China (Liu et al., 2016; Wang et al., 2018; Xie et al., 2018), South Korea (Kim et al., 2019), Spain (Pineda et al., 2017), Turkey (Telef, 2016), and the USA (Renshaw, 2017). The SEHS-P Covitality score had a positive relationship with the Psychological Sense of School Membership (PSSM) Acceptance and Caring Relationship subscales and was negatively related to the PSSM Rejection subscale (Furlong et al., 2013). Furthermore, it was positively correlated with school engagement, prosocial behavior, and final exams six months later (Wang et al., 2018; Wilkins et al., 2015).

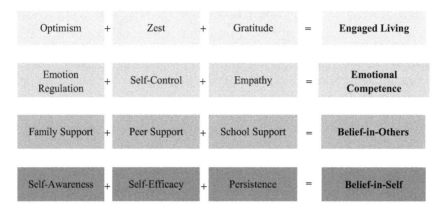

Figure 4.1 Covitality Conceptual Framework and Social-Emotional Health Survey Measurement Model

Note: Figure adapted from Furlong et al (2020a). Covitality Framework for successful and thriving students.

However, it was negatively associated with depressive symptoms, bullying victimization, and bullying perpetration (Wang et al., 2018). Recently, the SEHS-P was adapted by Wang et al.'s (2018) study that modified the items into questions, rather than statements, to increase the understanding and engagement of primary school students. The adapted version of the SEHS-P has also been applied in schools across countries including the USA, China, England, and Japan (e.g., Castro et al., 2019; Chan et al., 2019; Iida et al., 2020; Moffa et al., 2019). Internal reliabilities of Covitality and domain scores were in acceptable and excellent ranges (0.60–0.97) and associated with emotional and behavioral difficulties, school membership, and satisfaction with classroom life.

Similarly, an increasing number of studies provide evidence for the psychometric properties of the SEHS-S, including reliability and validity of the higher-order model, internal consistency, construct and predictive validity, and invariance across sociocultural and gender groups. Full measurement invariance has also been recently established for both anonymous (i.e., surveillance) and self-identified (i.e., screening) versions of the SEHS-S 2020 (Wagle et al., 2020). SEHS-S validation studies were conducted in Japan (Ito et al., 2015), South Korea (Lee et al., 2016), Spain (Piqueras et al., 2019), Turkey (Telef & Furlong, 2017), and the USA (You et al., 2014, 2015). More recently, Hinton and colleagues (2020) examined the SEHS-S with Latinx youth in the USA to reflect its validity and reliability with more diverse subgroup youth populations. The SEHS-S total Covitality index has evidence of convergent validity with measures of youth global psychosocial strengths. For example, the Covitality score had a significant positive relation with the Strengths and Difficulties Questionnaire's (SDQ; Goodman, 1997) prosocial behavior subscale, and a negative relation with the SDQ total difficulties scale among Turkish youths (Telef & Furlong, 2017). Significant positive correlations have also been found with other QOL outcomes such as subjective well-being among Korean youth (Kim et al., 2019; Lee et al., 2016) and depression, anxiety, and stress in Chinese youth (Xie et al., 2018).

The U.S. Department of Education Institute of Education Sciences (IES) funded Project Covitality, a four-year grant to enhance and standardize the SEHS-S. In particular, the preliminary SEHS-S version (Furlong et al., 2013) lacked psychometric evidence and normative characteristics derived from large samples. Thus, Furlong, Dowdy et al. (2020) aimed to refine and standardize its content and build evidence supporting its psychometric properties using substantial samples of California high school students. Furthermore, the researchers attempted to standardize the response format of the SEHS-S to enhance the standardized application across various contexts. Specifically, structural validity analyses using 72,740 students' responses supported an excellent model fit for the second-order factor structure and measurement invariance across gender, grade,

Table 4.1 Summary of Key Social-Emotional Health Survey-Primary (SEHS-P) and Social-Emotional Health Survey-Secondary (SEHS-S) Psychometric Studies

Study	Grade	Gender	Sample		Reliability[a]		Validity[b]
SEHS-P							
Furlong et al. (2013) N = 1,995	4–6	52% F 48% M	USA Latin Amer. White Amer. Other	78% 16% 5%	Gratitude Zest Optimism Persistence Covitality	0.70 0.75 0.66 0.76 0.88	*Structural*: Acceptable fit second-order model, invariance gender *Convergent*[c]: Prosocial behavior (male 0.65, female 0.64), PSSM Acceptance (male 0.55, female 0.48), Caring relationships (male 0.59, female 0.39), Rejection (male−0.34, female −0.27)
Wilkins (2015) N = 112	Ages 8–12	59% F 41% M	Australian	100%	Gratitude Zest Optimism Persistence Covitality	0.69 0.61 0.68 0.76 0.88	*Convergent*: School engagement (0.69), prosocial behavior (0.64)
Wang et al. (2018) N = 662	4–6	51% F 49% M	China	100%	Gratitude Zest Optimism Persistence Covitality	0.84 0.82 0.80 0.83 0.93	*Structural*: Acceptable fit second-order model, invariance gender *Convergent*: Prosocial behavior (0.65), depressive symptoms (−0.32), victimization (−0.15~−0.18), perpetration (−0.25), final exams six months later (0.13~0.18)
Wagle et al. (2018) N = 2,482	Ages 8–13	46% F 54% M	USA China UK	32% 47% 21%	Gratitude	0.68~0.69	*Convergent*: School membership (0.51~0.62)
Chan et al. (2019) N = 1,756	Ages 9–11	46% F 54% M	China USA	57% 43%	Scales (China) Scales (USA) Covi (China) Covi (USA)	0.60~0.76 0.65~0.85 0.85 0.89	*Convergent*: School membership in USA sample (0.19~0.72) and in Chinese sample (0.34~0.57).
Castro et al. (2019) N = 522	Ages 8–11	51% F 49% M	UK	100%	Gratitude Optimism Zest Persistence	0.70 0.69 0.64 0.60	

(Continued)

Table 4.1 (*Continued*)

Study	Grade	Gender	Sample		Reliability[a]		Validity[b]
Moffa et al. (2019) *N* = 1,322	Ages 8–12	54% F 46% M	USA UK	59% 41%	Gratitude Zest Optimism	0.70 0.78 0.77	*Structural*: Acceptable fit second-order model, invariance gender *Convergent*: Emotional and behavioral difficulties (0.10~0.27)
Iida et al. (2020) *N* = 955	4–6	49% F 51% M	Japan	100%	Gratitude Optimism Zest Persistence Covitality 2-wk test-retest	0.83 0.84 0.91 0.88 0.95 0.70~.77	*Structural*: Acceptable fit second-order model, invariance gender and grade *Convergent*: Emotional difficulties in M&MS (−0.32~−0.47), behavioral difficulties (−0.20~−0.27), QU Security (−0.22~−0.42), QU Approval (0.32~0.41)

SEHS-S—2015

Study	Grade	Gender	Sample		Reliability[a]		Validity[b]
Furlong et al. (2014) *N* = 4,189	8,10, 12	50% F 50% M	USA Latin Amer.	72%	Belief in self Belief in others Emotion comp. Engaged living Covitality	n/a n/a n/a n/a .92	*Structural*: Acceptable fit second-order model, invariance gender *Convergent*[c]: SWB (0.89), academic (0.08), school safety (0.12)
You et al. (2014) *N* = 2,240	9–12	47% F 53% M	USA Latin Amer.	72%	Belief in self Belief in others Emotion comp. Engaged living Covitality	0.76 0.81 0.78 0.87 0.91	*Structural*: Acceptable fit second-order model, invariance gender and age *Convergent*: BESS (−0.63)
Kim et al. (2014) *N* = 118	10	56% F 44% M	USA Other European Amer. Latin Amer.	50% 24% 12%	Belief in self Belief in others Emotion comp. Engaged living Covitality	n/a n/a n/a 0.90	*Structural*: n/a *Convergent*: SWB (0.57)

Study	Grade	Gender	Sample		Reliability[a]		Validity[b]
You et al. (2015) N = 14,171	9–12	51% F 49% M	USA Latin Amer. White Amer. African Amer. Asian Amer.	51% 17% 7% 8%	Belief in self Belief in others Emotion comp. Engaged living Covitality	n/a n/a n/a n/a .95	Structural: Acceptable fit second-order model, invariance gender and race/ ethnicity
Ito et al. (2015) N = 975	7–9	52% F 48% M	Japan	100%	Belief in self Belief in others Emotion comp. Engaged living Covitality	0.78 0.87 0.82 0.88 0.93	*Structural*: Acceptable fit second-order model, invariance gender
Lee et al. (2016) N = 686	7–12	56% F 44% M	Korea	100%	Belief in self Belief in others Emotion comp. Engaged living Covitality	0.84 0.85 0.82 0.88 0.94	*Structural*: Acceptable fit second-order model, invariance gender *Convergent*: SWB (0.56)
Telef and Furlong (2017) N = 2,242	9–12	55% F 45% M	Turkey USA	50% 50%	Belief in self Belief in others Emotion comp. Engaged living Covitality	0.76 0.77 0.74 0.80 0.89	*Structural*: Latent mean differences on belief-in-self domain (ES = 0.16) *Convergent*: SWB (0.66)
Xie et al. (2018) N = 3,750	7–12	52% F 48% M	China	100%	Belief in self Belief in others Emotion comp. Engaged living Covitality	0.77 0.81 0.80 0.88 0.92 0.89	*Structural*: Acceptable fit second-order model, invariance gender and grade *Convergent*: LS (0.46), PANAS-P (0.46), DASS-D (−0.36), DASS-A (−0.25), DASS-S (−0.22)
Piqueras et al. (2019) N = 1,042	Ages 12–18	42% F 58% M	Spain	100%	Belief in self Belief in others Emotion comp. Engaged living Covitality	0.82~0.88 0.77~0.89 0.80~0.86 0.89~0.92 0.87~0.94	*Structural*: Adequate fit second-order model, invariance gender

(Continued)

Table 4.1 (Continued)

Study	Grade	Gender	Sample		Reliability[a]		Validity[b]

SEHS-S-2020

Study	Grade	Gender	Sample		Reliability[a]		Validity[b]
Furling et al. (2020a) *Three samples (Ns = 72,740, 10,757, 707) were used. Refer to the manuscript for further information on the samples			USA Latin Amer. White Amer. African Amer. Asian Amer.		Belief in self Belief in others Emotion comp. Engaged living Covitality 1-yr test-retest	0.88 0.87 0.87 0.94 0.95 0.59~0.68	Structural: Excellent fit second-order model, invariance gender, grade, Latinx status, and ethnic group Convergent: distress (−0.41), school connectedness (0.52), self-report grades (0.25), cigarette use (−0.10), vaping (−0.10), binge drinking (−0.10), marijuana use (−0.17), and suicidal ideation (−0.34)
Hinton et al. (2020) N = 1,404	7–12		USA Latinx	100%	Belief in self Belief in others Emotion comp. Engaged living Covitality	0.77 0.81 0.80 0.88 0.92	*Structural*: Acceptable fit second-order model, invariance language
Wagle et al. (2020) N = 3,367	9–12	46% M 52% F 2% Other	USA Latin Amer. White Amer. African Amer. Asian Amer. Native Amer. Pacific Islander	45% 40% 1% 3% 1% 1%	Belief in self Belief in others Emotion comp. Engaged living Covitality	0.77 0.81 0.80 0.88 0.92	*Structural*: Acceptable fit second-order model, invariance self-reported vs. anonymous response format

Note: BESS = Behavioral and Emotional Screening Scale; DASS-D = Depression Anxiety and Stress 21-Depression; DASS-A = Depression Anxiety and Stress 21-Anxiety; DASS-S = Depression Anxiety and Stress 21-Stress; Emotion comp. = Emotional competence domain; PSSM-A = Psychological Sense of School Membership-Acceptance; PANAS-P = Positive and Negative Affect Scale-Positive; PANAS-N = Positive and Negative Affect Scale-Negative; PSSM-R = Psychological Sense of School Membership-Rejection; SEHS = Social-Emotional Health Survey, Covitality = SEHS-S and SEHS-P total score; SWB = subjective well-being.

a All reliabilities are alpha coefficients unless otherwise indicated.

b All validity coefficients are Pearson correlation coefficients or structural equation model path coefficients.

c Covitality scores are the sum of all SEHS-S and SEHS-P items.

Latinx status, and ethnic group identification. Internal consistencies of the SEHS-S-2020 Covitality score and domains scores were excellent, ranging from 0.87 to 0.95. Criterion validity analyses were then conducted using 11,217 students' responses and indicated that Covitality predicted student distress, school connectedness, self-report grades, cigarette use, vaping, binge drinking, marijuana use, and suicidal ideation, supporting the measure's convergent validity. Lastly, stability analysis conducted using a sample of 707 students reported the one-year test-retest stability coefficients of 0.48–0.68, which indicate stable, trait-like positive psychological orientations. Another recent study with a sample of 3,367 California high school students found that the SEHS-S-2020 measures the same construct across self-identified and anonymous groups (Wagle et al., 2020). Furthermore, Hinton et al. (2020) found that the factor structure was invariant across language (Hispanic vs. English speaking) groups among Latinx youths.

Another goal of Project Covitality included providing updated information on the stability of complete mental health across time and its ability to predict a wide range of educational and psychosocial outcomes. Moore et al. (2019b) examined the stability of the four mental health classes identified by using the SEHS-S-2013 and the SDQ: *complete mental health* ("high well-being and low distress"), *moderately mentally healthy* ("high-average well-being and low distress"), *symptomatic but content* ("average to high-average well-being and average to above-average distress), and *troubled* ("average to low-average well-being and above-average distress"; Moore et al., 2019b, p. 64). It was found that the *complete mental health* class exhibited the most stability, followed by *moderately mentally healthy* and *symptomatic, but content* classes, while *the troubled* class exhibited the least stability. Only less than 24% of participants remained in the same mental health class across the high school years, and few students remained in the complete mental health class each year. These results suggested that mental health screening once during the high school period would be insufficient. School professionals should engage in regular (i.e., annual or biannual) and systematic monitoring of students' complete mental health to accurately provide MTSS supports and interventions that appropriately match the present social-emotional functioning levels exhibited by individual students.

Applications among Diverse School Systems

In addition to understanding the theoretical underpinnings and psychometric support for the Covitality construct and SEHS measurement system, practitioners and researchers need to understand how this comprehensive strength-based model can be applied in school-based practice. From a public health approach to assessment (Dowdy et al., 2010), information obtained from the SEHS may be used in an MTSS framework to assess and monitor the psychosocial strengths of individual students or an entire population, to identify students at risk who require more tier II or III levels of support to prevent further risk by cultivating their strengths (Furlong et al., 2019). At the universal or tier I level, wellness surveillance data can be used to help school-based practitioners direct resources appropriately for students within individual schools or entire school systems (e.g., districts, Special Education Local Planning Areas). For example, surveillance data for an 11th-grade cohort of females might reveal low ratings on the belief-in self domain, suggesting that targeted interventions to increase self-efficacy, self-awareness, and persistence among these students would be warranted.

Traditional approaches to school-wide mental health screenings employ screeners designed to assess risk factors or clinical symptoms (e.g., BASC, BESS, SEDS, and CHKS), which identify no more than approximately 20% of students in need of mental health supports. Thus, further refinement of approaches to identify the smaller groups of needful or students with troubles is warranted, and the SEHS as a component in a DFM to mental health assessment is one suggestion to remedy this problem while providing relevant feedback for all students. In this approach, a screener that assesses positive aspects of youths' psychological development helps complement the traditional distress-focused screening process. High and low SEHS scores provide meaningful information—all students, regardless of their level of impairment or risk, have strengths that should be fostered to promote optimal developmental outcomes. School-based stakeholders can use the data obtained from the SEHS in conjunction with traditional mental health screening data to gain a more comprehensive understanding of youths' complete mental health profile, which, in turn, may help school teams provide more targeted services aimed at improving the academic performance and other QOL outcomes for all students. For a detailed description of how to conduct universal complete mental health screening within a school system utilizing the SEHS, please see Moore et al. (2016) for a full step-by-step implementation guide with specific guidelines for practitioners seeking to implement complete mental health screening.

To better understand SEHS applications, the following sections of this chapter provide examples of its use within an MTSS framework: (a) tier I complete mental health screening and (b) tiers II and III individual applications.

Tier I School-Wide Complete Mental Health Screening Examples

To date, there are several examples of national and international school-wide applications utilizing the SEHS to gather data on complete mental health among students (e.g., Dowdy et al., 2015; Fullchange & Furlong, 2016; Lee & Ahn, 2018; Moore, Mayworm et al., 2019; Wagle et al., 2020). To illustrate, two brief overviews from recent applications of the SEHS-S across two unique school-based contexts, one in the USA and the other in Spain, are summarized (see Paz et al. 2020, for more detailed descriptions). These selected case examples demonstrate how strength-based assessments may be integrated within school-based service delivery models to improve data-based decision making and effectively plan for the delivery of related positive psychological interventions.

Case Example 1: Local Education Agency in Southern California

In 2017, a unified school district in Southern California launched an MTSS to address student behavioral and mental health concerns and improve psychosocial strengths. The educational agency had an enrollment of over 13,000 students across 20 diverse schools. The district's mental health framework centered around three goals:

1   Tier I universal services and supports to build a positive school climate and promote students' well-being and psychosocial resilience;
2   Tier II targeted selected and brief evidenced-based supports for approximately 15% of students displaying, or at-risk of mild mental health challenges; and
3   Tier III intensive, ongoing strategies to support targeted students (approximately 5%) in need of significant coping mechanisms, functioning, and recovery needs, including referrals for school-based mental health providers.

Beginning in the 2018–2019 academic year, parents provided consent for students in Grades 7, 9, and 10 (N = 2,912). At the tier I level of screening, all students completed a secure online social-emotional screening assessment, comprised of the SEHS-S, the Student Emotional Distress Scale (SEDS; Dowdy et al., 2018), and brief measures of life satisfaction and school belonging. The SEHS-S and the SEDS were used to obtain students' psychosocial wellness from a complete mental health model that synthesizes indicators of distress and strengths. A total of 14 school and community-based team professionals (i.e., school counselors, school psychologists, and community mental health therapists) supported the administration of the complete mental health screening and monitored the needs of students who participated in the screening. Students with high distress ratings on the SEDS and low levels on the SEHS-S (highest and lowest 15% from each measure, respectively) were identified for tier II school support services. The percentage of students identified for tier II services ranged from 3% to 10% across the eight secondary schools in the school district. For the students who displayed elevated risk profiles (e.g., highest and lowest 3%–5%, respectively, across the dual-factor measures), a follow-up structured interview occurred within a few days of the screening. Interviews were conducted by school-based administrators and professionals to document areas of concern and discuss available resources (at the tier III level) and barriers. Following the initial screening efforts, several debriefing meetings were held with school team members, district office administrators, and leadership teams to discuss successes and challenges and create timelines for achieving tiered mental health support goals based on a school wellness action plan. School-community, mental health organizations collaborated on the development and implementation of parent workshops and tier II student support groups.

Case Example 2: Diverse School Ecosystem in Spain

In an ongoing international collaboration with scholars in Spain beginning in 2016, the Covitality-Spain team began implementing strengths-based psychological assessment practices across children, adolescents, and university students to inform detection, identification, and early intervention for mental health. The Covitality team administered school-wide screening measures (i.e., distress and strength variables) to students online to gather youth complete mental health surveillance data and collect additional psychometric evidence for the use of the SEHS-S with Spanish students.

The initial screening consisted of 1,042 adolescents, and results indicated that the total Covitality index was negatively associated with internalizing and externalizing symptoms, as well as with peer and parent relationship challenges. Further, data from this implementation revealed strong and positive associations with the measures of positive covariates (i.e., well-being, health-related QOL, and prosocial behaviors). Subsequent longitudinal studies with 5,172 high school students specifically explored patterns between well-being, health-related QOL, psychopathology/distress, and relationships with parents. Data from these longitudinal analyses indicated that social-emotional competencies predicted psychosocial adjustment and mediated the influence of stressful events on psychosocial adjustment. The Covitality-Spain team also utilized SEHS-S data to create customized reports to illustrate feedback regarding groups of adolescents and specific individuals who presented with increased risk for suicide or low mental health. Together, the comprehensive assessment of Spanish students' strengths and distress supported the validity of the SEHS-S with the population and its use to inform prevention and intervention services for all students.

Individual Assessments at Tier II and Tier III

In addition to serving as a school-wide or district-wide surveillance screener, the SEHS is administered to assess a student's present levels of psychosocial functioning as part of a comprehensive evaluation for determining the student's eligibility for special education services. Scholars have long identified increased benefits when including strengths-based questionnaires within psychoeducational evaluations as this not only provides a broader perspective on students' functioning but also may yield increased satisfaction with the testing process and intervention supported (Cox, 2006; Epstein et al., 2001).

Further research is still needed to determine the relative sensitivity of the SEHS concerning sensitivity and specificity (e.g., progress monitoring) to changes in response to interventions. Given the brevity of this measure, it would also serve as a helpful progress-monitoring tool to evaluate the effects of mental health interventions. The SEHS can also serve clinical utility within group-counseling interventions designed to increase students' psychosocial assets and gather data regarding intervention effectiveness. Importantly, the SEHS has been implemented successfully within populations of students receiving special education services due to underlying learning disabilities, suggesting that this measure can be reliability administered across students receiving either general or special education educational programming (Carnazzo et al., 2019). Whether population-based screening efforts or individual assessments and progress monitoring for evaluation of interventions, the SEHS may be an effective system to include at varying tiers within a comprehensive service delivery model. See Figure 4.2 for an infographic summarizing steps for implementing mental wellness surveillance or screening measures.

Diversity and Developmental Considerations and Conclusions

As global citizens, educators all play important roles in ensuring the well-being of future generations. As change agents, educators have the responsibility to engage in conflict resolution and policy change so that youth can thrive. Educators must begin to shed layers of privileged ways of thinking and shift from biased views of purely assessing deficits and risk factors, toward a commitment to honoring and cultivating positive psychological well-being and complete mental health for *all* generations to come. For questions regarding the Covitality framework's applications with diverse youth, the SEHS system offers a means of capturing well-being among a broad range of students manifesting individual differences concerning age, gender, cultural background, and other relevant factors. This chapter reviewed fundamental advances that support its use as a unifying construct for understanding the dynamic interplay of a range of internal and external assets that work synergistically to enhance overall well-being among youth from a range of cultural and linguistically diverse youth across the globe. The Covitality framework is also making meaningful relations and unifying connections across different countries and contexts and has the potential to integrate research and practice across sociocultural dimensions. One such example is the emerging relations and school-based applications between Covitality and psychological Suzhi—a Chinese cultural construct comprised of a hierarchical, integrated set of positive psychological qualities, and represents a traditional Chinese approach to integrating positive constructs (Qian et al., 2020).

Across the three SEHS measures, advances have been made for structural invariance according to age, gender, and nationality, as well as to determine the predictive utility of such scales for youth in primary grades through higher education. There remains a continued need to examine the SEHS's factorial invariance across diverse samples of students who differ in socioeconomic circumstances, cognitive dimensions, language skills, and broader distinctions related to culture and ethnicity. Specifically, more work is needed to examine the utility and applicability of the SEHS as a supportive tool to assess strengths and resilience, and link with culturally affirming positive psychological interventions among our African-American/Black identified youth, as groups from historically minoritized communities of color. Efforts are underway to continue addressing questions regarding the applicability of the SEHS among specific groups, including foster youth from various ethnic and cultural backgrounds, youth with histories of complex trauma receiving residential and nonpublic school supports (i.e., students in more restrictive educational settings), among others.

In closing, there is still a need to continue exploring other iterations of the Covitality framework and SESH system, including additional correlations of psychosocial strengths associated with positive youth development as informed explicitly by cultural and linguistic differences. Specifically, there may well be specific combinations of psychological assets that differentially predict a variety of positive outcomes for youth, and cultural and ethnic factors may further influence these differences.

As researchers and practitioners continue to place importance on further understanding student psychosocial strengths, there will likely be continued developments toward a standard of practice for

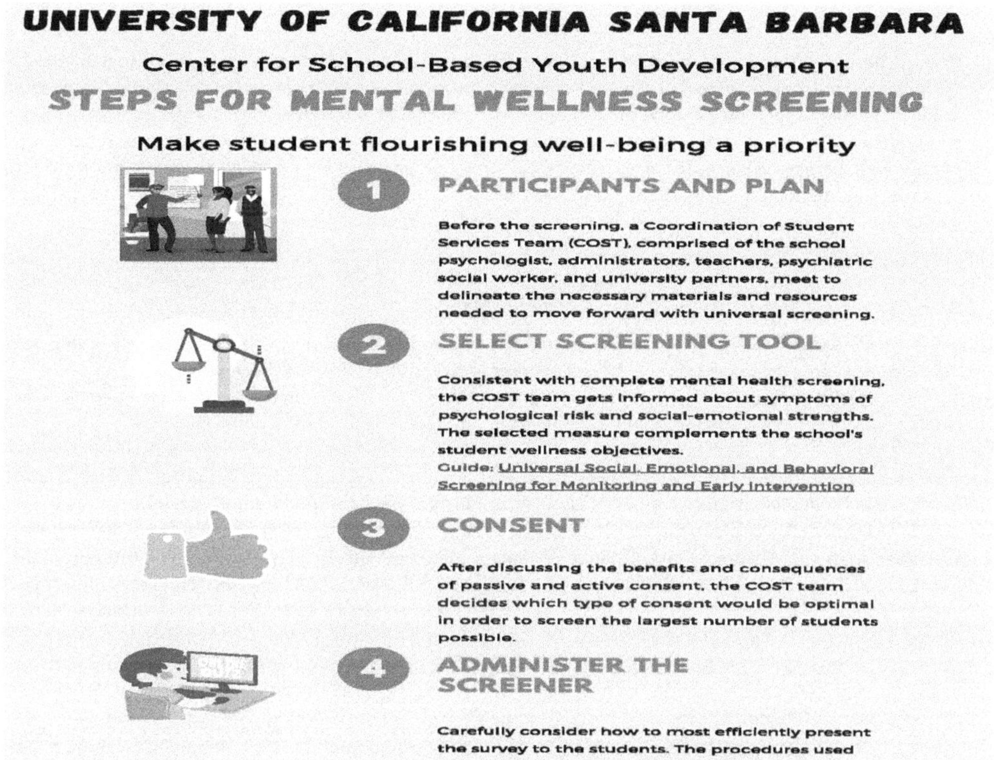

UNIVERSITY OF CALIFORNIA SANTA BARBARA

Center for School-Based Youth Development

STEPS FOR MENTAL WELLNESS SCREENING

Make student flourishing well-being a priority

1 PARTICIPANTS AND PLAN

Before the screening, a Coordination of Student Services Team (COST), comprised of the school psychologist, administrators, teachers, psychiatric social worker, and university partners, meet to delineate the necessary materials and resources needed to move forward with universal screening.

2 SELECT SCREENING TOOL

Consistent with complete mental health screening, the COST team gets informed about symptoms of psychological risk and social-emotional strengths. The selected measure complements the school's student wellness objectives.
Guide: Universal Social, Emotional, and Behavioral Screening for Monitoring and Early Intervention

3 CONSENT

After discussing the benefits and consequences of passive and active consent, the COST team decides which type of consent would be optimal in order to screen the largest number of students possible.

4 ADMINISTER THE SCREENER

Carefully consider how to most efficiently present the survey to the students. The procedures used are influenced by available resources. However, given the efficiency of online administration, scoring, and report generation, it will be most effective and cost efficient over time.

5 FOLLOW-UP

Infographics are visual representations of data, making complex info easier to share and digest. When making your own, simply organize your images, charts, and text. Finally, cite your sources.
Infographic examples: Safety and Wellness Building Student Strengths

6 RECYCLE

Universal mental wellness screening and monitoring is a process. Student growth and development is maximized by sustained assessment and caring support across K-12.

SEE MORE, LEARN MORE

Dowdy, E., Furlong, M. J., Raines, T. C., Price, M., Murdock, J., ... Bovery, B. (2014). Enhancing school-based mental health services with a preventive and promotive approach to universal screening for complete mental health. *Journal of Educational and Psychological Consultation*, 25, 1-20. https://www.tandfonline.com/doi/full/10.1080/10474412.2014.929951

Dowdy, E., Harrel-Williams, L., Dever, B., Furlong, M. J., Moore, S., Raines, T., & Kamphus, R. (2016). Universal self-report screening in high school to predict internalizing symptoms. *School Psychology Review*, 45, 458-476. https://www.tandfonline.com/doi/abs/10.17105/SPR45-4.458-476

Moore, S. A., & Widales-Benitez, O., & Carrazco, K. W., Kim, E. K., Moffa, K., & Dowdy, E. (2016). Conducting universal complete mental health screening via student self-report. *Contemporary School Psychology*, 19, 253-267. http://link.springer.com/article/10.1007/s40688-015-0062-x

Bertone, A., Moffa, K, Wagle R, et al. (2019). Considerations for mental health screening with Latinx dual language learners. *Contemporary School Psychology*, 23, 20-30 (2019). https://doi.org/10.1007/s40688-018-0205-v

Moore, S., Mayworm, A. M., Stein, R., Sharkey, J. D., & Dowdy, E. (2019). Languishing students: Linking complete mental health screening in schools to Tier II intervention. *Journal of Applied School Psychology*, 35, 257-289. https://doi.org/10.1080/15377903.2019.1577780

Romer, N., von der Embse, N. Eklund, K, Kilgus, S, Perales, K., Splett, J. W., Sudlo, S, Wheeler, D. (2020). Best practices in social, emotional, and behavioral screening: An implementation guide. Version 2.0. Retrieved from smhcollaborative.org/universalscreening. https://smhcollaborative.org/universalscreening/

Verlenden, J., Naser, S., & Brown, J. (2020). Steps in the implementation of Universal Screening for Behavioral and Emotional Risk to Support Multi-Tiered Systems of Support: Two Case Studies. *Journal of Applied School Psychology*, 1-39. First online 24 June, 2020. https://doi.org/10.1080/15377903.2020.1780440

HTTPS://WWW.COVITALITYUCSB.INFO/SCREENING.HTML

Figure 4.2   SEHS Mental wellness screening implementation infographic

the universal assessment of child and adolescent psychosocial strengths. As with any contemporary approach to assessment, Covitality researchers look forward to not only continued advancements in the comprehensive assessment of youths' psychosocial strengths, mainly as it helps students and school systems across the globe to take a more preventive approach and cultivate strengths and look forward to continuing to evolve the model to support the resilience within capable youth.

Note

1   While the Covitality framework uses 12 positive constructs in combination, the authors recognize the great value of assessing other isolated personal emotional strengths (e.g., courage, self-compassion, hope). The Covitality framework aims to identify exemplary strengths, and highlights the idea that when these 12 psychosocial strengths develop in harmony and synergy, the outcome is reflective of overall well-being. Other positive psychological strengths can also be a part of fostering any individual's complete mental health, and the continued interest and importance of investigating other personal strength-based constructs are highly beneficial in SBA approaches.

References

Alford, Z., & White, M. (2015). Positive school psychology. In M. White & A. Murray (Eds.), *Evidence-based approaches in positive education* (pp. 93–109). Springer. doi:10.1007/978-94-017-9667-5_5

Bandura, A., Barbaranelli, C., Caprara, G. V., & Pastorelli, C. (1996). Multifaceted impact of self-efficacy beliefs on academic functioning. *Child Development, 67,* 1206–1222. doi:10.2307/1131888

Benson, P. L., Scales, P. C., & Syvertsen, A. K. (2011). The contribution of the developmental assets framework to positive youth development theory and practice. In R. M. Lerner, J. V. Lerner, & J. B. Benson (Eds.), *Advances in child development and behavior* (vol. 41, pp. 197–230). Academic Press.

Boman, P., Mergler, A., & Pennell, D. (2017). The effects of covitality on well-being and depression in Australian high school adolescents. *Clinical Psychiatry, 3*(2), 1–4. doi:10.21767/2471-9854.100046

Bowers, E. P., Li, Y., Kiely, M. K., Brittian, A., Lerner, J. V., & Lerner, R. M. (2010). The Five Cs model of positive youth development: A longitudinal analysis of confirmatory factor structure and measurement invariance. *Journal of Youth and Adolescence, 39,* 720–735. doi:10.1007/s10964-010-9530-9

Carnazzo, K., Dowdy, E., Furlong, M. J., & Quirk, M. P. (2019). An evaluation of the Social Emotional Health Survey–Secondary for use with students with learning disabilities. *Psychology in the Schools, 56,* 433–446. doi:10.1002/pits.22199

Castro, S., Palikara, O. Gaona, C., Eirinaki, V. & Furlong, M. J. (2019). Psychological sense of school membership predicts patterns of socio-emotional health. *School Mental Health.* First online, 11 November 2019. https://doi.org/10.1007/s12310- 019-09349-7

Chan, M., Yang, C., Furlong, M. J., Dowdy, E., & Xie, J-S. (2019). Association between social-emotional strengths and school membership: A cross-cultural comparison. International *Journal of School and Educational Psychology.* First online Nov 2019. https://doi.org/10.1080/21683603.2019.1677539

Chi-Hung, N. (2005). Academic self-schemas and their self-congruent learning patterns: Findings verified with culturally different samples. *Social Psychology of Education, 8,* 303–328. doi:10.1007/s11218-005-4015-5

Cox, K. (2006). Investigating the impact of strength-based assessment on youth with emotional or behavioral disorders. *Journal of Child and Family Studies, 15,* 287–301. doi:10.1007/s10826-006-9021-5

Dougherty, D., & Sharkey, J. D. (2017). Reconnecting youth: Promoting emotional competence and social support to improve academic achievement. *Children and Youth Services Review, 74,* 28–34. doi:10.1016/j.childyouth.2017.01.021

Dowdy, E., Furlong, M. J., Nylund-Gibson, K., Moore, S., & Moffa, K. (2018). Initial validation of the Social Emotional Distress Scale to support complete mental health screening. *Assessment for Effective Intervention, 43,* 241–248. doi:10.1177/1534508417749871

Dowdy, E., Furlong, M. J., Raines, T. C., Bovery, B., Kauffman, B., Kamphaus, R., Dever, B. V., Price, M., & Murdock, J. (2015). Enhancing school-based mental health services with a preventive and promotive approach to universal screening for complete mental health. *Journal of Educational and Psychological Consultation, 25,* 178–197. doi:10.1080/10474412.2014.929951

Dowdy, E., Ritchey, K., & Kamphaus, R. W. (2010). School-based screening: A population-based approach to inform and monitor children's mental health needs. *School Mental Health, 2,* 166–176. doi:10.1007/s12310-010-9036-3

Dozois, D. J. A., Eichstedt, J. A., Collins, K. A., Phoenix, E., & Harris, K. (2012). Core beliefs, self-perception, and cognitive organization in depressed adolescents. *International Journal of Cognitive Therapy, 5,* 99–112. doi:10.1521/ijct.2012.5.1.99

Epstein, M., Hertzog, M., & Reid, R. (2001). The Behavioral and Emotional Rating Scale: Long term test-retest reliability. *Behavioral Disorders, 26,* 314–320. https://doi.org/10.1177/019874290102600403

Fullchange, A., & Furlong, M. J. (2016). An exploration of effects of bullying victimization from a complete mental health perspective. *Sage Open* (January-March), 1–12. Retrieved from http://sgo.sagepub.com/content/6/1/2158244015623593

Furlong, M. J., Coats, S., & Leung, B. (2019, October 24). *Monitoring students' complete mental wellness: Tier 1 and tier 2 best practices* [Conference presentation]. Annual Meeting of the California Association of School Psychologists, Long Beach, CA. Retrieved from https://www.covitalityucsb.info/ewExternalFiles/CASP%202019%20Workshop%20Covitality%20Furlong%20Coats%20Leung%20copy.pdf

Furlong, M. J., Dowdy, E., Nylund-Gibson, K., Wagle, R., Carter, D., & Hinton, T. (2020). *Enhancement and standardization of a universal social-emotional health measure for students' psychological strengths.* Manuscript under review.

Furlong, M. J., Gilman, R., & Huebner, E. S. (Eds.). (2014). *Handbook of positive psychology in schools* (2nd ed.). Routledge/Taylor & Francis.

Furlong, M. J., Nylund-Gibson, K., Dowdy, E., Wagle, R., Hinton, T., & Carter, D. (2020a). *Modification and standardization of Social Emotional Health Survey-Secondary— 2020 edition.* Santa Barbara, CA, University of California Santa Barbara, International Center for School Based Youth Development.

Furlong, M. J., Nylund-Gibson, K., Dowdy, E., Wagle, R., Hinton, T., & Carter, D. (2020b). Social Emotional Health Survey-Secondary— 2020. Poster. U.S. Department of Education, Institute of Education Science. Principal Investigator Meeting. January 8, 2020, Washington, DC. Retrieved from https://indd.adobe.com/view/47e58539-b092-4393-a9cec9a689a62105

Furlong, M. J., You, S., Renshaw, T. L., O'Malley, M. D., & Rebelez, J. (2013). Preliminary development of the Positive Experiences at School Scale for elementary school children. *Child Indicators Research, 6*, 753–775. Retrieved from http://link.springer.com/article/10.1007/s12187-013-9193-7

Furlong, M. J., You, S., Renshaw, T. L., Smith, D. C., & O'Malley, M. D. (2014). Preliminary development and validation of the Social and Emotional Health Survey for secondary students. *Social Indicators Research, 117*, 1011–1032. doi:10.1007/s11205-013-0373-0

Furlong, M. J., You, S., Shishim, M., & Dowdy, E. (2017). Development and validation of the Social Emotional Health Survey–Higher Education version. *Applied Research in Quality of Life, 12*, 343–367. Retrieved from http://link.springer.com/article/10.1007/s11482-016-9464-9

Goodman, R. (1997). The Strengths and Difficulties Questionnaire: A research note. *Child Psychology & Psychiatry & Allied Disciplines, 38*(5), 581–586. https://doi.org/10.1111/j.1469-7610.1997.tb01545.x

Greenspoon, P. J., & Saklofske, D. H. (2001). Toward an integration of subjective well-being and psychopathology. *Social Indicators Research, 54*, 81–108. doi:10.1023/A:1007219227883

Hinton, T., Dowdy, E., Nylund-Gibson, K., Furlong, M. J., & Carter, D. (2020). *Examining the Social Emotional Health Survey-Secondary for use with Latinx youth.* Manuscript under review.

Huebner, E. S., Gilman, R., Reschly, A. L., & Hall, R. (2009). Positive schools. In S. J. Lopez & C. R. Synder (Eds.), *The Oxford handbook of positive psychology* (2nd ed., pp. 561–568). Oxford University Press.

Iida, J., Ito, A., Aoyama, I., Sugimoto, K., Endo, H., & Furlong, M. J. (2020). Development of Japanese version of Social Emotional Health Survey. *The Japanese Journal of Psychology. 90*, 32–41. https://doi.org/10.4992/jjpsy.90.17222

Ito, A., Smith, D. C., You, S., Shimoda, Y., & Furlong, M. J. (2015). Validation of the Social Emotional Health Survey–Secondary for Japanese students. *Contemporary School Psychology, 19*, 243–252. doi:10.1007/s40688-015-0068-4

Kern, M. L., Benson, L., Steinberg, E. A., & Steinberg, L. (2016). The EPOCH measure of adolescent well-being. *Psychological Assessment, 28*, 586–597. doi:10.1037/pas0000201

Keyes, C. L. M. (2003). Complete mental health: An agenda for the 21st century. In C. L. M. Keyes (Ed.), *Flourishing, positive psychology, and the life well-lived* (pp. 293–312). American Psychological Association.

Keyes, C. L. M., & Michalec, B. (2010). Viewing mental health from the complete state paradigm. In T. L. Scheid & T. N. Brown (Eds.), *A handbook for the study of mental health: Social contexts, theories, and systems* (pp. 125–134). Cambridge University Press.

Kim, E. K., Dowdy, E., & Furlong, M. J. (2014). Exploring the relative contributions of the strength and distress components of dual-factor complete mental health screening. *Canadian Journal of School Psychology, 29*, 127–140. http://cjs.sagepub.com/content/29/2/127.abstract

Kim, E., Dowdy, E., Furlong, M. J., & You, S. (2019). Complete mental health screening: Psychological strengths and life satisfaction in Korean students. *Child Indicators Research, 12*, 901–915. doi:10.1007/s12187-018-9561-4

Lee, S., & Ahn, S. (2018). Complete mental health screening based on a dual-factor model of mental health: Differences among mental health groups and implications on intervention. *The Korean Journal of School Psychology, 15*(2), 197–219. 이승연, & 안소현. (2018). 정신건강 2 요인 모델에 따른 완전정신건강 선별검사. 한국심리학회지: 학교, *15*(2), 197–219.

Lee, S., You, S., & Furlong, M. J. (2016). Validation of the Social Emotional Health Survey for Korean school students. *Child Indicators Research, 9*, 73–92. doi:10.1007/s12187-0149294-y

Leffert, N., Benson, P. L., Scales, P. C., Sharma, A., Drake, D., & Blyth, D. A. (1998). Developmental assets: Measurement and prediction of risk behaviors among adolescents. *Applied Developmental Science, 2,* 209–230. doi:10.1207/s1532480xads0204_4

Lenzi, M., Dougherty, D., Furlong, M. J., Dowdy, E., & Sharkey, J. D. (2015). The configuration protective model: Factors associated with adolescent behavioral and emotional problems. *Journal of Applied Developmental Psychology, 38,* 49–59. http://www.sciencedirect.com/science/article/pii/S0193397315000179

Lerner, R. M., Lerner, J. V., Almerigi, J. B., Theokas, C., Phelps, E., Gestsdottir, S., Naudeau, S., Jelicic, H., Alberts, A., Ma, L., Smith, L. M., Bobek, D. L., Richman-Raphael, D., Simpson, I., Christiansen, E. D., & Von Eye, A. (2005). Positive youth development, participation in community youth development programs, and community contributions of fifth-grade adolescents: Findings from the first wave of the 4-H Study of Positive Youth Development. *Journal of Early Adolescence, 25,* 17–71. doi:10.1177/0272431604272461

Liu Hai-ning, Han Bu-xin, LI Xiao-min, Wang Lu-yao, & Xiao Qiao-ling. (2016). Reliability and validity of Social Emotional Health Survey-Elementary in Chinese children. *Chinese Journal of Clinical Psychology, 24,* 450–457. https://doi.org/10.16128/j.cnki.1005-3611.2016.03.015

Lips, H. M. (1995). Through the lens of mathematical/scientific self-schemas: Images of students' current and possible selves. *Journal of Applied Social Psychology, 25,* 1671–1699. Retrieved from http://search.proquest.com/docview/618915232?accountid=14522

Markus, H. (1977). Self-schemata and processing information about the self. *Journal of Personality Social Psychology, 35,* 63–78. doi:10.1037/0022-3514.35.2.63

Masten, A. S., Cutuli, J. J., Herbers, J. E., & Reed, M. G. J. (2009). Resilience in development. In S. J. Lopez & C. R. Snyder (Eds.), *Oxford handbook of positive psychology* (2nd ed., pp. 117–131). Oxford University Press.

Moffa, K., Wagle, R., Dowdy, E., Pailkara, O., Castro, S., Dougherty, D., & Furlong, M. J. (2019). The Me and My School Questionnaire: Examining the cross-cultural validity of a children's self-report mental health measure. *International Journal of School and Educational Psychology.* First online Aug-2019. https://doi.org/10.1080/21683603.2019.1650858Moore, S., Dowdy, E., Nylund-Gibson, K., & Furlong, M. J. (2019a). *An empirical approach to complete mental health classification in adolescents. School Mental Health.* First Online 23 Jan 2019. https://doi.org/10.1007/s12310-019-09311-7

Moore, S., Dowdy, E., Nylund-Gibson, K., & Furlong, M. J. (2019b). A latent transition analysis of the longitudinal stability of dual-factor mental health in adolescence. *Journal of School Psychology, 73,* 56–73. doi:10.1016/j.jsp.2019.03.003

Moore, S., Mayworm, A. M., Stein, R., Sharkey, J. D., & Dowdy, E. (2019). Languishing students: Linking complete mental health screening in schools to Tier II intervention. *Journal of Applied School Psychology,* First online, 27 March, 2019. doi:10.1080/15377903.2019.1577780

Moore, S. A., & Widales-Benitez, O., & Carnazzo, K. W., Kim, E. K., Moffa, K., & Dowdy, E. (2016). Conducting universal complete mental health screening via student self-report. *Contemporary School Psychology, 19,* 253–267. Retrieved from http://link.springer.com/article/10.1007/s40688-015-0062-x

Nickerson, A. B. (2007). The use and importance of strength-based assessment. *School Psychology Forum, 2*(1), 15–25. Retrieved from https://www.nasponline.org/publications/periodicals/spf/volume-2/volume-2-issue-1-(fall-2007)/the-use-and-importance-of-strength-based-assessment

Paz, J. L., Kim, E. K., Dowdy, E., Furlong, M. J., Hinton, T., Piqueras, J. A., Rodríguez-Jiménez, T., Marzo, J. C., & Coats, S. (in press). Contemporary assessment of youth comprehensive psychosocial assets: School-based approaches and applications. In W. Ruch, A. Bakker, L. Tay, & F. Gander (Eds.), *Handbook of Positive Psychology Assessment Psychological Assessment – Science and Practice.* European Association of Psychological Assessment.

Pineda, D., Piqueras, J. A., Martinez, A., Rodriguez-Jimenez, T., Martínez Gonzalez, A. E., Santamaria, P., & Furlong, M. J. (2017). *A new instrument for covitality: The revised Social Emotional Health Survey–Primary in a Spanish sample of children.* 14th European Conference on Psychological Assessment, Lisbon, Portugal, July.

Piqueras, J. A., Rodriguez-Jimenez, T., Marzo, J. C., Rivera-Riquelme, M., Martinez-Gonzalez, A. E., Falco, R., & Furlong, M. J. (2019). Social Emotional Health Survey-Secondary (SEHS-S): A universal screening measure of Social-Emotional strengths for Spanish speaking adolescents. *International Journal of Environment Research Public Health, 16,* 4982. doi:10.3390/ijerph16244982

Qian, N., Yang, C., Teng, Z., Furlong, M. J., Pan, Y., Guo, C., & Zhang, D. (2020). Psychological Suzhi mediates the longitudinal association between perceived school climate and depressive symptoms. School Psychology, 35(4), 267–276. https://doi.org/10.1037/spq0000374 Renshaw, T. R. (2017). Technical adequacy of the Positive Experiences at School Scale with adolescents. *Journal of Psychoeducational Assessment, 35,* 323–335. https://doi.org/10.1177/0734282915627920

Renshaw, T. L., Furlong, M. J., Dowdy, E., Rebelez, J., Smith, D. C., O'Malley, Lee., S., & Strom, I. F. (2014). Covitality: A synergistic conception of adolescents' mental health. In M. J. Furlong, R. Gilman, & E. S. Huebner (Eds.), *Handbook of positive psychology in the schools* (2nd ed., pp. 12–32). Routledge/Taylor & Francis. Retrieved from www.tandfebooks.com/isbn/9780203106525

Scales, P. C. (1999). Reducing risks and building developmental assets: Essential actions for promoting adolescent health. *Journal of School Health, 69*, 113–119. doi:10.1111/j.1746-1561.1999.tb07219.x

Seligman, M. E. P. (2011). *Flourish: A visionary new understanding of happiness and well-being.* Simon and Schuster.

Smith, N. D. W., Suldo, S. M., Hearon, B. V., & Ferron, J. M. (2020). An application of the dual-factor model of mental health in elementary school children: examining academic engagement and social outcomes. *Journal of Positive Psychology and Wellbeing, 4*, 49–68. Retrieved from https://www.researchgate.net/publication/340681785

Suldo, S. M. (2016). *Promoting student happiness: Positive psychological interventions in schools.* Guildford.

Suldo, S. M., & Shaffer, E. J. (2008). Looking beyond psychopathology: The dual-factor model of mental health in youth. *School Psychology Review, 37*, 52–68.

Suldo, S. M., Thalji, A., & Ferron, J. (2011). Longitudinal academic outcomes predicted by early adolescents' subjective well-being, psychopathology, and mental health status yielded from a dual-factor model. *The Journal of Positive Psychology, 6*, 17–30. doi:10.1080/17439760.2010.536774

Telef, B. B. (2016). Validity and reliability study of Positive Experiences at School Scale (Okulda Pozitif Yaşantılar Ölçeği geçerlik ve güvenirlik çalışması). *Journal of Human Sciences, 13*(2), 2475–2487.

Telef, B. B., & Furlong, M. J. (2017). Adaptation and validation of the Social Emotional Health Survey-Secondary into Turkish culture. *International Journal of School & Educational Psychology, 5*, 255–265. doi: 10.1080/21683603.2016.1234988

Wagle, R., Dowdy, E., Furlong, M. J., Nylund-Gibson K., Carter, D., & Hinton, T. (2020). Anonymous vs. self-identified response formats: Implications for mental health screening in schools. *Assessment for Effective Intervention.* First online 30 September 2020. https://doi.org/10.1177/1534508420959439

Wagle, R., Dowdy, E., Yang, C., Pailkara, O., Castro, S., Nylund-Gibson, K., & Furlong, M. J. (2018). Preliminary investigation of the Psychological Sense of School Membership Scale with primary school students in a cross-cultural context. School Psychology International, 39, 568–586. doi:10.1177/0143034318803670

Wang, C., Yang, C., Jiang, X., & Furlong, M. J. (2018). Validation of the Chinese version of the Social Emotional Health Survey-Primary. *International Journal of School & Educational Psychology, 6*, 62–74. http://dx.doi.org/10.1080/21683603.2016.1272026

Wilkins, B., Boman, P., & Mergler, A. (2015). Positive psychological strengths and school engagement in primary school children. *Cogent Education, 2*(1), 1–11. Retrieved from http://www.tandfonline.com/doi/full/10.1080/2331186X.2015.1095680

Westerhof, G. J., & Keyes, C. L. M. (2010). Mental illness and mental health: The two continua model across the lifespan. *Journal of Adult Development, 17*(2), 110–119. doi:10.1007/s10804-009-9082-y

Wroblewski, A. P., Dowdy, E., Sharkey, J. D., & Kim, E. K. (2019). Social-emotional screening to predict truancy severity: Recommendations for educators. *Journal of Positive Behavior Interventions, 21*, 19–29. doi:10.1177/1098300718768773

Xie, J., Liu, S., Yang, C., & Furlong, M. J. (2018). Chinese version of Social and Emotional Health Survey–Primary. *Chinese Journal of Clinical Psychology, 25*(6), 1012–1016. doi:10.16128/j.cnki.1005-3611.2017.06.004

You, S., Dowdy, E., Furlong, M. J., Renshaw, T., Smith, D. C., & O'Malley, M. D. (2014). Further validation of the Social and Emotional Health Survey for high school students. *Applied Quality of Life Research, 9*, 997–1015. doi:10.1007/s11482-013-9282-2

You, S., Furlong, M. J., Felix, E., & O'Malley, M. D. (2015). Validation of the Social and Emotional Health Survey for five sociocultural groups: Multigroup invariance and latent mean analyses. *Psychology in the Schools, 52*, 349–362. doi:10.1002/pits.21828

Young, J. E., Klosko, J. S., & Weishaar, M. E. (2003). *Schema therapy: A practitioner's guide.* Guilford.

Zins, J. E., Bloodworth, M. R., Weissberg, R. P., & Walberg, H. J. (2007). The scientific base linking social and emotional learning to school success. *Journal of Educational & Psychological Consultation, 17*(2–3), 191–210. doi:10.1080/10474410701413145

5

ADAPTING THE DUAL-FACTOR MODEL FOR UNIVERSAL SCHOOL-BASED MENTAL HEALTH SCREENING

Bridging the Research to Practice Divide[1,2]

Michael J. Furlong, Erin Dowdy, Stephanie Moore
and Eui Kyung Kim

The perspective that mental health encompasses a balance of wellness–health and distress–illness has deep historical roots in applied psychology. Jahoda (1958), widely cited, made prescient observations more than 60 years ago discussing *positive psychology* and noting that mental health is a human value and right. Some 40 years ago, Veit and Ware (1983) operationalized this concept in the *Mental Health Inventory*, as a measure of psychological distress and well-being intended for use with general, not clinical populations. Ryff's (1989) vital contributions formulated a subjective well-being (SWB) model that incorporated hedonic (emotional) and eudemonic (psychological and social) dimensions. Following these pioneering efforts and building on Seligman and Csikszentmihalyi's (2000) positive psychology resurgence in the late 1990s, Greenspoon and Saklofske (2001) contributed the paper, *Toward an Integration of Subjective Well-Being and Psychopathology*, that inspired essential, meaningful research under the mental health *dual-factor system* concept. Building on this research, Suldo and Shaffer (2008) further explored the dual-factor system and contributed the paper, *Looking Beyond Psychopathology: The Dual-Factor Model of Mental Health in Youth*. This research specialization is uniquely pertinent to school practices grounded in positive psychology (Seligman et al., 2009) and positive education principles (Waters & Loton, 2019). It recognizes the value of a balanced mental health conceptualization and, at its inception, considered school-aged children's perspectives.

Despite its intuitive appeal and a body of research examining the dual-factor mental health model, it is not yet validated as a practical application for applied school mental health practice—this is a pressing need. It is crucial because there are increasing calls for the standardization of easures and procedures for educational research. As exemplified by the United States Institute of Education Sciences requirement, all grant submissions must include common measures to support cross-study comparisons (Schneider, 2020). The current chapter proposes and presents evidence

DOI: 10.4324/9781003013778-6

validating a practical dual-factor approach for universal school-based mental health screening and monitoring, an unrealized aspiration, and a critical social and educational imperative (Catalano & Kellogg, 2020).

School Mental Health Context and Need

Informal psychosocial screening occurs in all schools every day. When a school staff member notices a child looking down, or not playing or interacting with their schoolmates, they check-in with the student. Moreover, even if a child is not visibly down, scared, or anxious, school staff often check-in with students: "How are you doing?" "Is everything okay?" In such circumstances, the school staff focuses on, monitors, and attends to each student's needs. They informally assess whether the child feels well or is generally getting along with their schoolmates and their school work is progressing. In general, they are concerned about whether the child is doing "well." This watch, care, response sentiment happens informally on school campuses every day. Reflective of the overall reasoning behind informal screening and check-ins at school, the purpose of universal screening is to offer a way to more formally, carefully, and systematically conduct check-ins for all students. The emphasis on checking in on *all* students is further emphasized due to the known systematic biases in schools and the cultural mismatch between school staff and students (Raines et al., 2009). Specific subgroups of students may be more or less likely to be attended to when relying solely on school staff to randomly check in on students, further highlighting the need for a systematic approach to asking all students how they are doing. Such an effort should include a way to assess whether each child has experienced recent distress. It should also advance a way to monitor positive psychosocial development (Is a student's life going well?) while limiting potential referral biases (Weathers, 2019).

A formal school-based screening and monitoring process grounded in positive psychology principles is not designed to recognize distinct types of psychological and social problems. Instead, its primary purpose is to alert school staff about the need to follow up with vulnerable students and find out more about their experiences than is readily available via direct observation (Dowdy et al., 2015). Moreover, a secondary purpose is to provide information that helps school staff support youth who are generally doing well and help them thrive and reach their optimal development levels (Kim et al., 2014). Universal monitoring is ideally implemented within a multitiered comprehensive student health and wellness plan (Moore et al., 2019).

Balanced Mental Health Models

In designing and executing comprehensive school mental wellness programs and services that include universal wellness screening and monitoring, educators require validated measures that produce information relevant to all students' social and emotional well-being. Various scholars have advocated incorporating strength-based measures (e.g., Nickerson & Fishman, 2013) in a balanced mental health screening approach that considers emotional distress indicators and optimal well-being (e.g., Keyes, 2013). This approach takes a whole child, whole-school approach, identifying personal assets and social resources that foster positive youth development. Screening optimally should provide information about all youth who could benefit from specialized services. It is also vital to support all youths' growth toward higher well-being levels. The dual-factor mental health approach fits this balanced, complete mental health perspective (Antaramian et al., 2010).

The dual-factor approach is related to and influenced by complementary balanced mental health frameworks. For instance, the Diagnostic and Statistical Manual for Mental Disorders (DSM; American Psychiatric Association, 2013) includes mental health disorder symptom lists. However, the DSM also evaluates symptomatology juxtaposed with global functioning. An individual would not necessarily be given a diagnosable disorder if the associated symptoms did not have a corresponding adverse impact on an individual's capacity to live life to a reasonable capacity. Similarly, Keyes (2005, 2006) proposed the dual continua model (DCM) grounded in Ryff's robust multidimensional well-being framework (Ryff & Keyes, 1995), as a way to examine the balance across affective, psychological, and social well-being. In the DCM, an individual has complete mental health when their well-being profile suggests frequent weekly or daily experiences of positive affect and favorable judgments of experiencing their personal and social life.

Dual-Factor Mental Health

As Seligman and Csikszentmihalyi (2000) called to expand positive psychology research and practice, efforts to evaluate balanced mental health paradigms advanced. Greenspoon and Saklofske (2001) articulated a mental health approach that simultaneously considered co-distributions of well-being levels and psychopathology symptoms. In their model, full or complete mental health is the balance of high life satisfaction and low mental ill-health symptoms. In adapting what Greenspoon and Saklofske named a *dual-factor system*, Suldo and Shaffer (2008) used the term *dual-factor model* (DFM), which has been used in most subsequent research (Antaramian et al., 2010; Grych et al., 2020; Kelly et al., 2012; Lim et al., 2021; Lyons et al., 2012, 2013; Zhou et al., 2020). For presentation convenience, we use DFM in the remainder of this chapter.

Greenspoon and Saklofske's Dual-Factor Model Prototype

Greenspoon and Saklofske's (2001) main premise was that if a dual-factor conceptualization had promise, then groups logically formed by crossing scores on both factors should present significantly different psychosocial profiles. Their goal was to create representative groups of students with varying levels of life satisfaction and pathology. Figure 5.1 shows Greenspoon and Saklofske's prototype dual-factor framework. One group had high life satisfaction with low psychopathology, exemplars of positive mental health (Group 1). A second group included students with low life satisfaction and high internalizing distress, exemplars of students with mental health challenges (Group 2). A third group had students with low life satisfaction and low psychological distress (Group 3), and the last group in this prototypic model comprised students who counterintuitively reported high levels of life satisfaction while also reporting elevated distress symptoms (Group 4).

Group 3 Low Subjective Well-Being Low Pathology	Group 2 Low Subjective Well-Being High Pathology
Group 1 High Subjective Well-Being Low Pathology	Group 4 High Subjective Well-Being High Pathology

Figure 5.1 Greenspoon and Saklofske (2001) Prototypic Dual-Factor Model Groups

Greenspoon and Saklofske's (2001) prototypical DFM intimates that the data analyses contrasted all four DFM groups. However, this was not the case. Figure 5.2 represents their two central analyses. For Analyses A and B, the 40-item *Multidimensional Life Satisfaction Scale* (MSLSS; Huebner, 1994) total score assessed a wellness satisfaction factor. The analyses employed different sample-specific cut-scores to create three life satisfaction levels (low, mid, and high) to maximize cross-group differentiation and to produce the group sizes needed for the analysis. Analysis A compared DFM Groups 1, 2, and 3, as shown in Figure 5.1. Group 2 included children's self-report of internalizing distress using the internalizing problems composite score of the *Behavior Assessment System for Children Self-Report of Personality* (BASC SRP; Reynolds & Kamphaus, 1992). Group 3 students (low internalizing distress and low life satisfaction) served as a comparison. This analysis included only the subset of students who reported *low or high life satisfaction* and *low or high internalizing symptoms*—it excluded 42% of the sample in the middle. Analysis B was conceptually similar but used a behavioral disorder measure to form Group 3; in this instance, the *Behavior Assessment System for Children Teacher Rating Scales* (BASC TRS; Reynolds & Kamphaus, 1992) hyperactivity subscale rating was used. Different BASC cut-scores identified *low* (bottom 35%) and *high* (top 35%) *hyperactivity*. This analysis excluded the middle 30% of children's BASC responses. Students with *high hyperactivity* ratings and *high life satisfaction* (Group 4) were the Analysis B comparison group. Psychopathology was defined differently in each analysis using gender *t*-scores, published, or sample-specific distributions.

Analysis A		BASC Student Self-Report Internalizing (PTH)		
		retained 40%	dropped 20%	retained 40%
MSLSS	Low retained 40%	Group 3 Low LS–Low PTH *n* = 30	Sample Omitted	Group 2 Low LS–High PTH *n* = 104
	dropped 20%	*n* = 170 (42%) excluded "…to offer the best balance between retaining cases and highlighting group differences (Greenspoon & Saklofske, 2001; p. 87)		
	High retained 40%	Group 1 High LS–Low PTH *n* = 103		

Analysis B		BASC Teacher Report Hyperactivity (PTH)		
		retained 35%	dropped 30%	retained 35%
MSLSS	Low retained 35%	Sample Omitted		Group 2 Low LS–High PTH *n* = 65
	dropped 30%	*n* = 345 (68%) excluded, "…the 35/30/35 split appeared superior while retaining a sufficient number of cases." (Greenspoon & Saklofske, 2001; p. 92)		
	High retained 35%	Group 1 High LS–Low PTH *n* = 53		Group 4 High LS–High PTH *n* = 44

Figure 5.2 Representation of the Greenspoon Saklofske (2001) Primary Data Analyses

The Greenspoon and Saklofske (2001) article contributed substantially to research by stressing the importance of considering positive mental health indicators and symptomatology indicators. Their two analyses showed that prototypic well and unwell mental health groups differed on a range of characteristics, including locus of control and quality of interpersonal relationships. Having stated this, Greenspoon and Saklofske's exploratory study used (a) measures selected post facto from a more extensive assessment battery and (b) sample-specific distribution cut-score values to optimize group differences. This study did not specifically test a full DFM framework inclusive of the entire sample. Furthermore, it would be challenging to replicate this study. The students were young, Grades 3–5, and responded to a research questionnaire that took 150 minutes over two days to complete. As a proof of concept exploratory study, this study had a substantial impact. However, it had limited implications for school practice and did not inform universal school mental health screening or monitoring in practical ways.

Suldo and Shaffer (2008) Dual-Factor Model Adaptation

Suldo and Shaffer (2008) provided meaningful, substantial contributions by expanding on Greenspoon and Saklofske's (2001) pioneering work. They proposed and tested an integrated DFM that simultaneously created and contrasted all four prototypic groups. Figure 5.3 shows the Suldo and Shaffer DFM adaptation. An SWB index comprised the wellness factor (*Student Life Satisfaction Scale* [SLSS; Huebner, 1991] and *Positive and Negative Affect Scale* [PANAS; Laurent et al., 1999]). An SWB composite was created by generating sample-specific *z*-scores for the SLSS,

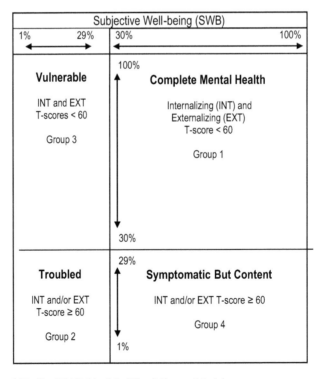

Figure 5.3   Suldo and Shaffer (2008) Modified Dual-Factor Model

PANAS positive, and PANAS negative ([zSLSS–zPANAS-P]—[zPANAS-N]). As in Greenspoon and Saklofske (2001), the sample-specific SWB distribution was used to select a cut-score that produced cell sizes sufficient to allow for the chosen data analysis.

The *Achenbach scales* (Child Self-Report of internalizing symptoms and the Teacher Report of externalizing symptoms; Achenbach & Rescorla, 2001) measured psychopathology. Published norms established cut-scores for internalizing and externalizing disorders. Here, students with *t*-scores of 60 or higher (top 15%) on either the internalizing (student self-report) or externalizing (teacher report) measures were assigned into the high symptom category. Across both measures, about 30% of students were symptom positive. Referencing this symptom proportion, low and high SWB groups were formed by designating the approximate bottom 30% on the sample SWB distribution to *low SWB*, and the top 70% to *average/high SWB*. As shown in Figure 5.3, the DFM groups' arrangement differed from Greenspoon and Saklofske (2001), and Suldo and Shaffer contributed the descriptive labels for each group employed in most subsequent DFM studies: Complete Mental Health, Troubled, Vulnerable, and Symptomatic but Content.

Dual-Factor Model Proof of Concept

Following from the Suldo and Shaffer (2008) analysis, an impressive research body has further examined the DFM (e.g., Antaramian et al., 2010; Grych et al., 2020; Kelly et al., 2012; Lyons et al., 2012, 2013; Zhou et al., 2020). These studies contribute to the proof of concept of the value of considering symptoms and wellness, which provide researchers and practitioners with a richer understanding of youth's psychosocial development. Differences among dual-factor mental health groups have been identified across developmental periods (e.g., children [Smith et al., 2020], adolescents in middle [e.g., Antaramian et al., 2010] and high school [Suldo et al., 2016], and adults [e.g., Renshaw & Cohen, 2014]) and quality of life indicators. Across investigations, individuals with high well-being and low psychopathology (complete mental health) experience the most favorable outcomes. For example, adolescents with complete mental health had superior engagement (Antaramian et al., 2010; Lyons et al., 2013; Smith et al., 2020), academic achievement (Antaramian et al., 2010; Lyons et al., 2013), social skills (Suldo et al., 2016), physical health (Suldo & Shaffer, 2008; Suldo et al., 2016), identity development (Suldo et al., 2016), and social support (Smith et al., 2020). That youth with complete mental health experience more positive outcomes than vulnerable youth indicates that the absence of psychopathology is insufficient in realizing positive outcomes (e.g., Antaramian et al., 2010). Further, in the presence of distress, research has indicated that well-being can protect against negative outcomes—individuals with symptomatic but content mental health experience more favorable outcomes than youth with troubled mental health (e.g., Grych et al., 2020; Lyons et al., 2013; Smith et al., 2020; Suldo et al., 2016).

Overall, these various DFM studies show robust differences in outcomes between groups with similar pathology levels, but different levels of SWB. Additionally, this approach's prototypical complete mental health and troubled groups are significantly different on numerous quality of life indicators. As proof of concept, there is a sufficient body of knowledge to support the core DFM principle that an optimal assessment of youth mental health is ground by considering distress and wellness factors simultaneously.

Dual-Factor Model Limitations for Universal School Mental Health Screening

Notwithstanding DFM's substantial contributions, research has not yet developed a standard procedure that facilitates the measurement of its factors simultaneously. Even more pressing, it has not bridged the science to practice gap. The DFM, as examined in research studies, is not readily accessible by school mental health professionals. Research-employed measures and algorithms are not easily translated for use in individual student case assessment or universal school-wide screening and monitoring. Among DFM's limitations are:

1   the measures have too many items for universal screening applications,
2   studies rely on sample-specific distribution procedures that practitioners could not readily replicate,
3   studies have not examined the joint distribution of co-normed wellness and distress factors,
4   a consensus is not established on the cut-scores to create groups, and
5   the approach is not yet tested and validated in the context of actual tier 1 school-wide wellness screening.

Another critical limitation is that previous DFM research has adopted Greenspoon and Saklofske's (2001) 2 × 2 prototypic model. This practice seems to have been driven by the need for studies with modest sample sizes to have large enough cell sizes for analyses. Consequently, positive well-being or life satisfaction has typically included students in the upper 70%–75% of the sample's distribution (e.g., Suldo & Shaffer, 2008, Suldo et al., 2016) meaning that some study participants on the positive end of the wellness factor actually had below-average, but not low, SWB.

A Step toward Bridging the Science to Practice Gap

The remainder of the chapter contributes to research by addressing the DFM limitations mentioned above. We first describe the dataset we draw upon for this purpose. We then propose and test a modified 3 × 3 DFM that expands understanding of students whose emotional distress experiences and wellness declarations fall in between what Suldo and Shaffer (2008) prototypically named *Troubled* and *Complete Mental Health* groups. An overall goal is to offer a standardized DFM approach that provides increased uniformity across research efforts. Simultaneously, the approach should be practical enough for psychologists to use it in their work with individual students (case studies) and to monitor students' well-being in the whole-school context.

Data Source

The current chapter's analyses used the responses of 8,017 high school students. They attended one of 15 high schools located in nine counties randomly selected from California high schools. The students completed the *California Healthy Kids Survey* (CHKS), a biennial state-wide survey that anonymously monitors student risk behaviors and resilience factors, and a supplementary module that included DFM measures. Students were enrolled in Grades 9–12 and most identified as female (51.6%) and non-Latinx (51.4%). This sample was diverse for traditional racial group identification: White (36.0%), multiple group identity (34.6%), Asian (10.7%), American Indian-Alaskan Native (5.5%), Black (3.8%), Native Hawaiian-Pacific Islander (2.1%), and declined to respond (7.2%). Most of these students reported that they resided with their parents/guardians (91.3%) whose modal educational degree attainment was a four-year college degree (36.0%); 13.8% of parents did not complete high school.

Measures

Consistent with a DFM approach, measures simultaneously assessed symptoms of wellness and distress. Scores on these DFM measures were then plotted and combined to create a 3 × 3 DFM to provide a system easily used by practitioners to classify all students. To examine and provide validity information in support of this approach, several additional measures were co-administered. Specifically, we aimed to evaluate how students in the various 3 × 3 groups differed with respect to behavioral functioning, perceived school safety, sense of school belonging, and social emotional strengths.

Dual-Factor Measures

WELLNESS FACTOR

In principle, DFM does not require the use of any specific wellness factor measure. Past DFM research with adolescents used Huebner's (1991) SLSS (e.g., Antaramian et al., 2010; Lyons et al., 2012; Suldo & Shaffer, 2008; Suldo et al., 2016) and Diener et al.'s (1985) *Satisfaction with Life Scale* (e.g., Grych et al., 2020; Xiong et al., 2017). In the context of universal DFM monitoring, we followed Greenspoon and Saklofske's (2001) original approach and used the multidimensional life satisfaction measure, in this instance the *Brief Multidimensional Students' Life Satisfaction Scale* (BMSLSS; Huebner et al., 2006). Our rationale is that it (a) is brief (six items) and (b) touches on multiple life domains, not just global life satisfaction. The BMSLSS assesses satisfaction for five general life domains: *friends, family, self, living environment*, and most relevant to universal screening, *school*. Research evidence supports its internal consistency among high school students ($\alpha = 0.81$; Zullig et al., 2001). Convergent validity is documented with the Multidimensional Students' Life Satisfaction Scale ($r = 0.69$, Seligson et al., 2003, 2005; $r = 0.62$). Factor analyses support a single factor structure (Seligson et al., 2003, 2005). In the current application, the responses options were: 0 = *strongly dissatisfied*, 1 = *moderately satisfied*, 2 = *mildly dissatisfied*, 3 = *mildly satisfied*, 4 = *moderately satisfied*, and 5 = *strongly satisfied* (see Table 5.1). Sum scores range from 0 to 25, with higher scores indicating greater life satisfaction.

SYMPTOM OR DISTRESS FACTOR

Most dual-factor studies use comprehensive symptom measures, including the Youth Self-Report of the Self-Report of Personality form from the *Behavior Assessment System for Children, Second Edition* (BASC-2; Reynolds & Kamphaus, 2004; used by Suldo et al., 2016) and the *Child Behavior Checklist* (CBCL; Achenbach, 1991; used by Lyons et al., 2012). Although well-validated, these measures are inefficient and impractical for universal screening applications due to the costs and the high number of items. Hence, to evaluate a DFM approach applicable to universal screening, we recognized the need to develop and validate a brief, unidimensional distress measure complementing the BMSLSS. With this aim, we previously developed the *Social-Emotional Distress Survey-Secondary* (SEDS-S).

The SEDS-S asks students to rate internal psychological experiences related to sad (e.g., *in the past month, I felt sad and down*) and anxious (e.g., *I was scared for no good reason*) emotional experiences (see Table 5.1). Consonant with a screening efficiency principle, SEDS-S assesses overall emotional distress to prioritize and identify students for follow-up assessment and support services. To develop the tool, we examined the clinical literature and longer measures of distress (e.g., Depression, Anxiety, and Stress Scales-21; Lovibond & Lovibond, 1995) with the goal of capturing internalizing, as opposed to externalizing behaviors (Dowdy et al., 2018), as they are often more difficult to detect within school settings (Kamphaus et al., 2014). We intentionally sought fewer items than existing pathology-focused screening measures and adopted language appropriate for adolescent students. Additionally, we designed the tool to ask about recent (i.e., past month) emotional experiences, as opposed to general life experiences, to support progress monitoring of functioning throughout a given school year. An initial study supported a unidimensional factor structure. Convergent validity was documented with significant positive

Table 5.1 Items, Response Format, and Psychometric Properties for the SEDS-S and BMSLSS

	Female (n = 4154)		Male (n = 3853)			
	M	SD	M	SD	t	d
Social Emotional Distress Scale [a] (response range = 0–3)						
I had a hard time breathing because I was anxious.	1.13	1.14	0.55	0.96	24.48	**0.55**
I worried that I would embarrass myself in front of others.	1.47	1.16	1.00	1.09	18.50	0.42
I was tense and uptight.	1.26	1.10	0.82	1.02	18.99	0.41
I had a hard time relaxing.	1.44	1.14	0.98	1.10	18.48	0.41
I felt sad and down.	1.50	1.16	1.00	1.11	20.26	0.44
I was easily irritated.	1.71	1.10	1.16	1.09	22.25	0.50
It was hard for me to cope and I thought I would panic.	1.10	1.15	0.59	0.95	21.88	0.48
It was hard for me to get excited about anything.	0.97	1.05	0.76	1.00	9.14	0.20
I was easily annoyed and sensitive.	1.66	1.11	0.99	1.07	27.36	**0.61**
I was scared for no good reason.	0.96	1.10	0.54	0.93	18.32	0.41
Total (0–30)	13.21	8.67	8.38	7.62	26.38	**0.59**
Brief Multidimensional Life Satisfaction Scale [b] (response range = 0–5)						
Family	3.57	1.45	3.74	1.38	5.59	0.12
Friendships	3.82	1.23	3.88	1.22	2.43	0.05
School experience	2.98	1.36	2.99	1.43	0.32	0.01
Myself	3.13	1.49	3.44	1.47	9.68	0.21
Where I live	3.61	1.38	3.69	1.39	2.76	0.06
Total (0–25)	17.01	5.15	17.74	5.22	5.56	0.14

Note: Males: SEDS-S skewness = 0.92, kurtosis = 0.86, α = 0.91. Females: skewness = 0.28, kurtosis = −1.02, α = 0.93. For total sample, BMSLSS α = 0.81. $r_{SEDS-BMSLSS}$ = −0.52 (females). $r_{SEDS-BMSLSS}$ = −0.47 (males).
a "In the past month…" Response options: 0 = not like me, 1 = a little like me, 2 = pretty much like me, and 3 = very much like me.
b "These questions ask about your satisfaction with different areas of your life." Response options: 0 = strongly dissatisfied, 1 = moderately dissatisfied, 2 = mildly dissatisfied, 3 = mildly satisfied, 4 = moderately satisfied, and 5 = strongly satisfied.

relations between the overall SEDS-S score and anxiety and depression symptoms as measured by the Generalized Anxiety Disorder −7 scale (Spitzer et al., 2006) and the Patient Health Questionnaire-9 (Kroenke et al., 2001), respectively (Dowdy et al., 2018). A second study with a diverse sample of California high school students (N = 72,740) replicated a one-factor structure with strong reliability (α = 0.93 and Ω = 0.95; Furlong et al., 2021). Sum scores for the SEDS-S range from 0 to 30, with higher scores indicating greater distress.

DFM Validation Measures

California Healthy Kids Survey
The California Healthy Kids Survey (CHKS, 2017; https://calschls.org) is a surveillance survey of school climate and safety, student wellness, and youth resiliency administered biennially in California high school students. Behavioral risk, school safety, and school belonging items from

the CHKS were used to assess DFM group differences (see Table 5.2 or 5.3 note for items used in this chapter's analyses).

Social-Emotional Health Survey-Secondary

The Social-Emotional Health Survey-Secondary-2020 (SEHS-S-2020; Furlong et al., 2021) was used to explore how students' perceptions of their internal assets and external resources differed across DFM categories. Research supports a three-level model: one general factor model with four domains and 12 subscales (three items per subscale) that load onto the four domains: *belief in self* (self-awareness, persistence, and self-efficacy), *belief in others* (school support, family coherence, and peer support), *emotional competence* (empathy, self-control, and behavioral self-control), and *engaged living* (gratitude, zest, and optimism). The response options were: 0 = *not at all true*, 1 = *a little true*, 2 = *pretty much true,* and 3 = *very much true*. Confirmatory factor analysis (CFA) and measurement invariance (Furlong et al., 2021; You et al. 2014, 2015) provide validity and reliability evidence. Internal response consistency evidence is favorable for the SEHS-S-2020 domains (α_{range} = 0.87–0.94, Ω_{range} = 0.87–0.94; Furlong et al., 2021).

A Proposed 3 × 3 Dual-Factor Model for Universal Screening

In this section, we propose and evaluate a modification of Suldo and Shaffer's (2008) DFM with a large sample using jointly administered measures of distress and life satisfaction and applying a common cut-score strategy. This consideration is extended to explore more deeply a matter that has been underexamined in the DFM research. Harkening back to the original study conducted by Greenspoon and Saklofske (2001), their analysis excluded students in the middle ranges between what they defined as low and high symptomatology and low and high life satisfaction. When applied in most other DFM studies, these middle groups were unexamined. This chapter contributes to DFM research by exploring whether and how the quality of life indicators of students who fall in middle distress and middle life satisfaction ranges compared to their lower and higher student counterparts. The following sections describe the sequential steps we took to refine, standardize, examine, and provide validity evidence for a 3 × 3 DFM for school-wide, universal mental wellness screening and monitoring.

Evaluate DFM Measures' Validity

Recognizing that any DFM classification approach initially hinges on the psychometric properties of the measures used to create the classification system, it is critical to first evaluate the validity evidence supporting score inferences to be made from the DFM measures. For use with universal monitoring, DFM measures should optimally have several characteristics. Measuring DFM factors and creating mental health categories should be a standardized, uniform procedure in which any sample's responses can be compared directly to any other sample. This procedure should also facilitate the comparison of individual students' responses over time. Such an approach should be brief to facilitate screening and provide an efficient, easy to calculate and interpret index. The measures should be unidimensional with strong psychometric properties, and the distress and wellness factors should be validated together (i.e., co-administered to the same large, norming population) so that their joint distribution is known. For maximum utility, the DFM measures should have invariance across gender and ethnic groups.

As an example, in this illustration, we used the BMSLSS and SEDS-S. However, we recognize that other measures that meet similar standards can also create a DFM classification. Previous research has demonstrated that both the BMSLSS (Seligson et al., 2003, 2005) and the SEDS-S are unidimensional (Dowdy et al., 2018; Furlong et al., 2021). For this illustration, these two measures were

Table 5.2 Dual-Factor Category Differences on Quality of Life Indicators for Females

	Brief Multidimensional Student Life Satisfaction Scale (BMSLSS)									
	(A) High			(B) Mid			(C) Low			
	SEDS Distress			SEDS Distress			SEDS Distress			
	(A) Low	(B) Mid	(C) High	(A) Low	(B) Mid	(C) High	(A) Low	(B) Mid	(C) High	V
	AA	AB	AC	BA	BB	BC	CA	CB	CC	
	1442	328	169	440	367	256	233	382	537	
Dual-Factor Model 3 x 3 Group ID N%	34.7%	7.9%	4.1%	10.6%	8.8%	6.2%	5.6%	9.2%	12.9%	V
Quality of Life Indicators (N)										
Demographics										
[a]Youth of color (non-White) (4059)	54.2%	55.2%	61.5%	56.7%	58.4%	50.4%	64.8%	55.9%	51.1%	0.020
Odds ratio 95% CI compared with AA	—	0.67–1.11	0.95–1.83	1.08–1.60	1.01–1.52	0.69–1.09	1.66–3.19	1.13–2.03	0.88–1.39	
[b]Identifies other than straight (3826)	7.2%	14.1%	24.5%	11.3%	25.2%	29.9%	18.9%	32.7%	41.4%	**0.292**
Odds ratio 95% CI compared with AA	—	1.38–3.19	2.70–6.43	1.15–2.31	3.17–5.87	3.95–7.61	1.92–4.63	4.29–9.03	6.65–12.40	
Emotional Risk										
[c]YRBS sadness item (4134)	12.1%	46.5%	67.3%	31.0%	59.0%	86.3%	43.5%	75.2%	91.6%	**0.604**
Odds ratio 95% CI compared with AA	—	3.9–6.9	11.6–23.9	2.0–3.2	10.3–16.5	30.3–57.8	3.6–7.2	13.0–24.7	58.2–129.3	
[d]YRBS suicide item (4143)	3.8%	17.1%	30.4%	10.5%	26.2%	45.7%	21.9%	36.9%	64.2%	**0.487**
Odds ratio 95% CI compared with AA	—	2.1–5.0	6.9–16.0	2.0–4.2	7.6–14.5	16.7–32.7	3.8–9.1	12.4–26.1	35.2–69.4	
Behavioral Risk										
[e]30-day marijuana use (3516)	5.2%	10.4%	10.1%	12.5%	15.7%	15.8%	22.2%	24.2%	25.2%	**0.224**
Odds ratio 95% CI compared with AA	—	1.23–3.21	1.01–3.40	1.51–3.12	2.26–4.56	2.60–5.54	2.28–5.62	3.67–8.19	4.37–8.69	
[f]30-day alcohol use (3505)	10.5%	18.2%	19.6%	12.3%	19.9%	19.0%	27.4%	27.2%	24.0%	0.164
Odds ratio 95% CI compared with AA	—	1.35–2.85	1.28–3.21	1.13–2.05	1.89–3.35	1.80–3.42	1.37–3.09	2.30–4.68	1.99–3.67	

Safety, Victimization

[g] Feels safe at school (4142)	73.5%	67.7%	63.9%	52.6%	48.4%	44.1%	39.4%	38.8%	28.5%	**0.334**
Odds ratio 95% CI compared with AA	—	0.50–0.86	0.43–0.82	0.34–0.50	0.26–0.39	0.23–0.36	0.15–0.27	0.14–0.25	0.08–0.14	
[h] Made fun of teased (4151)	10.5%	22.9%	30.8%	17.3%	25.6%	41.2%	18.9%	34.0%	49.8%	**0.318**
Odds ratio 95% CI compared with AA		1.64–3.06	2.56–5.19	1.09–1.84	2.33–3.79	4.67–7.79	0.69–1.64	2.58–4.82	5.12–8.47	

School Belonging

[i] Feel I am part school (4117)	70.0%	62.4%	59.2%	43.3%	41.6%	45.3%	26.6%	26.3%	20.1%	**0.382**
Odds ratio 95% CI compared with AA	—	0.54–0.91	0.49–0.96	0.23–0.34	0.20–0.31	0.20–0.31	0.14–0.25	0.08–0.15	0.06–0.10	
[j] Enjoy work with classmates (4397)	68.4%	60.6%	57.1%	44.6%	46.7%	38.4%	30.8%	26.0%	26.4%	**0.331**
Odds ratio 95% CI compared with AA		0.59–1.00	0.50–0.97	0.30–0.43	0.26–039	0.19–0.30	0.10–0.20	0.11–0.20	0.10–0.17	

Note: The AA group reporting high life satisfaction and low emotional distress corresponds with the "complete mental health" label used in previous dual-factor model studies. BMSLSS = Brief Multidimensional Student Life Satisfaction Scale (Using the combined male and female sample: A = highest 50.2% [approximately 50%–100%] of combined sample, B = middle 24.3% [approximately 26%–49%], and C = lowest 25.5% [approximately 1%–25%]). SEDS = Social Emotional Distress Scale for the female sample: (Low = bottom 50.2%, Mid = middle 24.3%, and High = top 25.5%, and most distress). Crammer's V moderate to relatively strong effect sizes in bold. V effect size ranges = weak (0.10–0.19), moderate (0.20–0.39), relatively strong (0.40–0.59), strong (0.60–0.79), and very strong (0.80–1.0). Items shown in this table are from the California Healthy Kids Survey. Student responses collected during the 2017–2018 academic year.

a "What is your race?" (44.7% reported White; youth of color identified as American Indian, Alaskan Native, Asian, Black, Native Hawaiian, Pacific Islander, or a multiple group identity).

b Which of the following best describes you? (Other than straight youth identified as: gay or lesbian, bisexual, I am not sure yet, something else, or declined to respond).

c During the past 12 months, did you ever seriously consider attempting suicide? (Percent responding yes).

d During the past 12 months, did you ever feel so sad or hopeless almost every day for two weeks or more that you stopped doing some usual activities? (Percent responding yes).

e During the past 30 days, on how many days did you use marijuana (smoke, vape, eat, or drink)? (Percent responding one or more days).

f During the past 30 days, on how many days did you use one or more drinks of alcohol? (Percent responding one or more days).

g How safe do you feel when you are at school? (Percent responding safe or very safe).

h During the past 12 months, how many times on school property have you been made fun of, insulted, or called names? (Percent responding one or more times).

i How strongly do you agree or disagree with the following statements? I feel I am part of this school. (Percent responding agree or strongly agree).

j I enjoy working together with other students on class activities. (Percent responding pretty much true or very much true).

Table 5.3 Dual-Factor Category Differences on Quality of Life Indicators for Males

	Brief Multidimensional Student Life Satisfaction Scale (BMSLSS)									
	(A) High			(B) Middle			(C) Low			
	SEDS Distress			SEDS Distress			SEDS Distress			
	(A) Low	(B) Mid	(C) High	(A) Low	(B) Mid	(C) High	(A) Low	(B) Mid	(C) High	
	AA	AB	AC	BA	BB	BC	CA	CB	CC	V
Dual-Factor Model 3 × 3 Group ID	1384	440	259	354	288	242	196	261	429	
N %	35.9%	11.4%	6.7%	9.2%	7.5%	6.3%	5.1%	6.8%	11.1%	
Quality of Life Indicators										
Demographics										
[a] Youth of color (3601)	56.2%	56.1%	62.2%	58.1%	60.0%	55.9%	67.9%	64.4%	54.7%	0.071
Odds ratio 95% CI compared with AA	—	0.77–1.23	0.63–1.07	0.66–1.01	0.96–1.55	0.93–1.47	1.64–3.28	1.47–3.00	0.80–1.29	
[b] Identifies other than straight (3197)	2.8%	7.6%	9.8%	3.8%	8.7%	20.5%	6.7%	10.5%	18.2%	**0.214**
Odds ratio 95% CI compared with AAQ	—	1.47–4.08	1.95–5.39	0.54–1.77	1.56–4.34	3.20–7.64	0.70–3.35	1.20–4.83	4.86–11.41	
Emotional Risk										
[c] YRBS sadness item (3833)	5.2%	20.6%	39.5%	11.4%	31.9%	62.9%	17.0%	38.5%	70.9%	**0.521**
Odds ratio 95% CI compared with AA	—	3.39–6.58	8.41–16.75	1.55–3.50	6.05–12.01	21.63–43.85	2.39–5.78	8.04–16.00	32.23–60.65	
[d] YRBS suicide Item (3843)	1.3%	9.2%	19.0%	4.8%	14.6%	35.5%	8.8%	22.0%	45.2%	**0.426**
Odds ratio 95% CI compared with AA	—	4.55–14.04	10.15–31.06	1.55–5.38	7.35–22.92	24.46–71.23	3.68–14.23	12.33–37.04	37.83–103.31	
Behavior Risk										
[e] Marijuana use (3680)	7.2%	9.2%	9.8%	15.1%	18.0%	20.6%	16.3%	21.9%	23.2%	0.141
Odds ratio 95% CI compared with AA	—	0.87–1.97	0.86–2.28	1.57–3.39	1.73–3.86	1.88–4.28	1.57–4.02	2.46–5.36	2.82–5.42	

									V
^f Alcohol use (3312)	8.1%	12.1%	17.5%	17.4%	21.4%	14.4%	15.5%	22.9%	0.131
Odds ratio 95% CI compared with AA	—	0.99–2.43	1.66–3.44	1.61–3.50	2.08–4.53	1.17–3.06	1.36–3.16	2.43–4.61	
School Safety, Victimization									
^g Feels safe at school (3831)	76.0%	63.4%	58.4%	52.3%	47.9%	44.1%	43.7%	35.1%	**0.302**
Odds ratio 95% CI compared with AA	—	0.41–0.73	0.35–0.56	0.27–0.45	0.20–0.39	0.18–0.34	0.19–0.32	0.14–0.22	
^h Made fun of teased (3852)	8.4%	28.6%	12.7%	22.2%	33.1%	14.3%	28.4%	38.9%	**0.272**
Odds ratio 95% CI compared with AA	—	3.14–6.08	1.10–2.29	2.23–4.37	3.88–7.49	1.17–2.83	3.11–6.01	5.31–9.14	
School Belonging									
^i Feel I am part school (3824)	69.4%	63.7%	42.7%	42.0%	41.4%	25.1%	30.6%	26.5%	**0.341**
Odds ratio 95% CI compared with AA	—	0.59–1.02	0.26–0.42	0.25–0.42	0.24–0.41	0.15–0.26	0.15–0.26	0.13–0.20	
^j Enjoy work with classmates (3837)	74.1%	76.7%	46.5%	47.9%	41.4%	36.4%	40.0%	35.9%	**0.326**
Odds ratio 95% CI compared with AA	—	0.84–1.58	0.24–0.39	0.28–0.47	0.24–0.43	0.15–0.27	0.16–0.25	0.16–0.25	

Note: The AA group reporting high life satisfaction and low emotional distress corresponds with the "complete mental health" label used in previous dual-factor model studies. BMSLSS = Brief Multidimensional Student Life Satisfaction Scale (Using the combined male and female sample: A = highest 50.2% to [approximately 50%–100%] of combined sample, B = middle 24.3% [approximately 26%–49%], and C = lowest 25.5% [approximately 1%–25%]). Social Emotional Distress Scale for the male sample: (Low = bottom 50.9%, Mid = middle 25.9%, High = top 23.2%, and most distress). Crammer's V moderate to relatively strong effect sizes in bold. V effect size ranges = weak (0.10–0.19), moderate (0.20–0.39), relatively strong (0.40–0.59), strong (0.60–0.79), and very strong (0.80–1.0). Items shown in this table are from the California Healthy Kids Survey. Student responses collected during the 2017–2018 academic year.

a   "What is your race?" (42.0% reported White; youth of color identified as American Indian, Alaskan Native, Asian, Black, Native Hawaiian, Pacific Islander, or a blended racial heritage).

b   Which of the following best describes you? (Other than straight youth identified as: gay or lesbian, bisexual, I am not sure yet, something else, or declined to respond).

c   During the past 12 months, did you ever seriously consider attempting suicide? (Percent responding yes).

d   During the past 12 months, did you ever feel so sad or hopeless almost every day for two weeks or more that you stopped doing some usual activities? (Percent responding yes).

e   During the past 30 days, on how many days did you use marijuana (smoke, vape, eat, or drink)? (Percent responding one or more days).

f   During the past 30 days, on how many days did you use one or more drinks of alcohol? (Percent responding one or more days).

g   How safe do you feel when you are at school? (Percent responding safe or very safe).

h   During the past 12 months, how many times on school property have you been made fun of, insulted, or called names? (Percent responding one or more times).

i   How strongly do you agree or disagree with the following statements? I feel I am part of this school. (Percent responding agree or strongly agree).

j   I enjoy working together with other students on class activities. (Percent responding pretty much true or very much true).

co-administered to the same youth in our large sample so that we could examine their joint distribution. For the sample examined in this chapter's analyses, females and males reported comparable mean responses on the BMSLSS ($0.01 \leq d \leq 0.21$), with average item means ranging from 2.98 to 3.88 on the 0–5 response scale (see Table 5.1 for the BMSLSS items, response format, and psychometric properties). Internal consistency reliability for the BMSLSS was satisfactory ($\alpha = 0.81$). However, as expected on a measure of internalizing symptoms, females reported higher scores on the SEDS-S than males ($0.20 \leq d \leq 0.61$), with average total distress being significantly higher for females than males. Average item scores ranged from 0.55 to 1.16 for males and 0.96 to 1.71 for females on the 0–3 response scale (see Table 5.1 for SEDS-S items, response format, and psychometric properties). Internal consistency reliability for the SEDS-S was satisfactory for males ($\alpha = 0.91$) and females ($\alpha = 0.93$). In this large sample, the BMSLSS and SEDS-S total scores were correlated at -0.52 for females and -0.47 for males. Overall, we found that the SEDS-S and BMSLSS met the requirements needed to create a 3×3 DFM.

Determine Cut-Scores for Use in DFM

After examining the psychometrics of the measures used to create a 3×3 DFM, the next logical step was to determine cut-scores. Recognizing the myriad of limitations associated with cut-scores (Moore et al., 2019), we decided to examine cut-scores as a heuristic rather than a precise cut-point. This process is not considered a traditional cut-score obtained through receiver operating characteristic curve analyses with specific attention to sensitivity and specificity. Instead, the use of a cut-score heuristic recognizes that with these skewed distributions, many students are surrounding those cut-points. Hence, there is no clear binary indicator and no exact cut-score provided. This approach recognizes the overarching goal of universal screening, which does not aim to provide information sensitive enough for a discrete diagnosis. Instead, it aims to provide information that helps the school team take the next and look more in-depth into students' concerns. This approach recognizes that there are many reasons why a student might report relatively high distress, low life satisfaction, or both. A universal screener cannot be sensitive to the range of possible precipitating experiences and conditions. Nevertheless, it is not crucial in the universal screening context. The knowledge that a youth's life is not going well and that their responses place them in a zone indicative of distress is sufficient information to provoke follow-up action.

Cut-Scores in Previous DFM Research

Many previous DFM studies have relied on predetermined values as a decision point to assign students into DFM groups (e.g., raw scores, sample means, standard deviations, or *T*-scores; Antaramian et al., 2010; Kelly et al., 2012; Lyons et al., 2012; Suldo & Shaffer, 2008). Examples of frequently used risk measures include the *Child Behavior Checklist-Youth Self-Report* (CBCL-YSR, Achenbach & Ruffle, 2000; e.g., Antaramian et al., 2010; Lyons et al., 2012; Suldo & Shaffer, 2008), *Strength and Difficulties Questionnaire* (SDQ, Goodman, 1997; e.g., Thayer et al., 2021), and *Behavior Assessment System for Children-2 Self-Report of Personality* or *Teacher Rating Scales* (BASC-2 SRP and TRS; e.g., McMahan, 2012; Thalji, 2013). Students were classified into a high pathology (PTH) group if they had a *t*-score of 60 or higher on internalizing, externalizing, or both scales or their percentile rank was at or above the normed 70th percentile (high) or below (low). Studies have classified roughly 25%–30% of participants as having high PTH.

Concerning the life satisfaction factor, there is even less uniformity because there are no large-sample standardization norms for the measures employed (Grych et al., 2020; Suldo et al., 2016). Examples of strength-based instruments included in DFM studies are the combination of the SLSS and the *Positive Affect and Negative Affect Scale for Children* (e.g., Antaramian et al., 2010; McMahan, 2012; Suldo & Shaffer, 2008; Thalji, 2013), the SLSS alone (e.g., Lyons et al., 2012), and the *Satisfaction With Life Scale* (SWLS; e.g., Grych et al., 2020). Previous DFM studies classified students as having either high or low SWB using a cut-point such as a mean item score of 4 on the SWB measure (e.g., 30% in low SWB; Suldo & Shaffer, 2008) or a score of 15 on the SWLS measure (e.g., 41% in low and 59% in high; Grych et al., 2020).

Many recent DFM studies have used a raw score that corresponds to the proportion of students classified as having high or low PTH or to the selected percentile of the distribution (e.g., 23.5%–27.5% in low SWB; McMahan, 2012; Smith et al., 2020; Thalji, 2013). Smith et al. (2020) used an SWB composite score corresponding to the 27.5th percentile as the cut-score; students with scores below the 27.5th percentile were categorized as having low SWB, while those at or above were categorized as having average to high SWB (72.5%). Gilman and Huebner (2006) also grouped students into low (bottom 20%), average (middle 50%; 25%–75%), and high (top 20%) using the SLSS global mean score distribution. In other studies (e.g., Antaramian et al., 2010; Lyons et al., 2012), the lowest 1 *SD* (bottom 15%) were designated as having low SWB, and the top 85% were designated as having high SWB. This same algorithm has been employed in subsequent DFM studies (Suldo et al., 2011; Xiong et al., 2017).

DFM 3 × 3 Cut-Scores

The selection of cut-scores in past DFM research has not been arbitrary; however, they have not been uniformly applied. Some consensus with regards to cut-scores is needed to facilitate the integration of DFM research across samples. Furthermore, within applied contexts, schools need a reasonable standard that they can use to evaluate the two DFM factors meaningfully, which does not fluctuate by the idiosyncratic variance in a given school context.

We propose a 25-25-50 cut-score approach using the known distributions of scores based on their distress (i.e., SEDS-S) and life satisfaction scores (i.e., BMSLSS) to categorize students into high (top 50%), medium (middle 25%), and low (lowest 25%) categories for a 3 × 3 DFM. SEDS-S scores between 0 and 9 are indicative of the lowest levels of distress (lowest 50%). Students with SEDS-S scores between 10 and 16 comprise about the next 25% of students and are placed in a middle range. The remaining about 25% of students report experiencing the highest levels of distress with scores on the SEDS-S between 17 and 30.[3] The same logic is applied to create the 25-25-50 cut-score approach for life satisfaction. The largest group of students (approximately the top 50%) reported the highest levels of life satisfaction on the BMSLSS with scores in the 19–25 range. The middle 25% of students scored in the 15–18 range and were placed in a middle category, whereas the bottom 25% of students scored in the 0–14 range and reported the lowest levels of life satisfaction. Figures 5.4 and 5.5 provide cut-scores and the number of students placed in each of these categories based on responses by females and males, respectively. Specifically, the cell shading indicates cell size density. The numbers in each of the cells represent the number of students who had that exact score combination based on their distress and life satisfaction scores. Note also that the lines on Figures 5.4 and 5.5 show the cut-scores used to form the 3 × 3 DFM categories discussed in this chapter's previous sections.

This proposed 25-25-50 approach matches closely to past research (e.g., Suldo & Shaffer, 2008) with additionally providing information about youth in the middle ranges on indicators of distress and life satisfaction. Instead of removing students within the middle ranges to create a simplified 2 × 2, all students are included within this 3 × 3 DFM. This approach is compatible with the mission of schools to help all children learn and thrive and is also consistent with the aim of universal screening to provide actionable information for all students (Furlong et al., 2014). The 3 × 3 DFM supports efforts to understand and foster all students' positive development, including those experiencing nonoptimal health in the middle ranges. Recognizing that the 2 × 2 approach may be too simplistic to consider all youth, it is equally essential that any procedure not be overly

Social Emotional Distress Scale

Brief Multidimensional Students Life Satisfaction Scale (BMSLSS) by Social Emotional Distress Scale (SEDS-S) — Females

Column groups of SEDS-S: Low (A) (50.9%) = scores 0–12; Middle (B) (25.9%) = scores 13–20; High (C) (23.2%) = scores 21–30.

Row groups of BMSLSS: High (A) (50.2%); Middle (B) (24.3%); Low (C) (25.5%).

BMSLSS	0	1	2	3	4	5	6	7	8	9	10	11	12	13	14	15	16	17	18	19	20	21	22	23	24	25	26	27	28	29	30	N
25	45	14	11	10	14	9	12	4	8	4	4	3	3	2	2	2	1	1	1	1	1		1		1	2	3	1	1	1		9	172
24	31	16	22	16	22	10	13	5	6	2	6	3	4	2	1	1	1	2	2	2	1		5		1		1	2	1	1		2	173
23	21	16	20	17	18	22	14	10	8	11	8	3	9			3	4	2	2	2		5		3	3	4	2	2	2	1	1	2	211
22	16	12	20	26	20	14	22	18	14	16	15	11	9	7	9	6	4	4	4	4	5	2	5	4	4	1	4	1	1	2	2	1	269
21	24	15	19	24	26	29	23	16	23	18	19	14	8	14	8	10	7	5	5	7	5	5	3	3	3	2	4	2	4	2	2	2	337
20	29	19	21	26	27	20	28	23	21	18	17	15	18	16	14	18	7	10	8	8	9	10	10	4	2	6	4	2	2	3	1	1	418
19	9	21	16	10	15	18	20	16	12	18	15	16	18	13	18	15	16	13	14	11	9	11	11	4	12	4	4	3	3	1	7	359
18	6	4	7	4	11	9	18	15	12	18	15	13	15	12	15	15	9	9	20	10	9	8	7	6	12	4	10	3	2	6	7	2	309
17	3	3	8	7	6	13	14	9	14	13	18	17	10	11	14	13	11	7	12	9	5	4	6	6	9	6	6	4	6	6	4	271
16	2	2	3	2	8	10	18	17	10	8	8	7	11	11	10	10	9	8	9	5	15	8	10	4	5	2	5	5	9	1	4	240
15	4	1	4	4	6	8	12	17	10	6	8	9	9	4	11	14	13	13	11	13	13	11	10	4	2	7	6	10	10	8	7	243
14		1	1	2		5	6	7	2	7	7	5	11	9	11	6	10	7	6	14	10	7	7	6	6	5	6	6	8	7	2	191
13		1		1	1	5	3	5	8	7	3	3	7	5		12	11	4	3	9	12	14	3	6	13	1	5	6	4	4	5	181
12			1		2	1	2	1	1	6	1	5	5	8	2	5	10	8	7	5	8	3	12	5	10	5	5	7	8	7	8	154
11		1		1		2	1	4	4	2	7	9	1	5	5	6	4	9	6	4	5	4	7	5	6	6	5	3	6	3	5	135
10	2		1				1		5		2	2	3	4	5	3	11	6	3	6	4	4	5	8	6	8	2	6	5	8	10	121
9	1			1		1	1		3		3			1		2		4		6	2	6	3	3	5	3	4	2	2	5	8	90
8							1		1		1				4	4				4	1	2	2	2	3	5	2	3	5	5	5	58
7	1				2	1	1					1	2	2			4		1		5	5	5	1	9	1	1	2	1	6	8	62
6							1			1	1								1		2	2	2		1	1	6	1	2		6	31
5	1	1	1	1			1				1			1			1		1		1	1	3	1	1	1	6	1	1		8	49
4								1				1	1				1				1	1			1	2		4	1	1	4	24
3			1		1											1		1		1	1	1			1	1	2	3	3	5		21
2												1	1	1						1	1					2	1	1	4			13
1		1			1																			1							1	4
0	6	6	1							1			1	1				1			1		1			1			1	6	6	18
Total N	204	124	155	152	179	165	178	157	161	155	170	164	151	126	148	150	121	128	157	121	126	104	106	73	107	92	101	87	85	82	125	4154

Figure 5.4 BMSLSS by SEDS-S Array Distribution Density for Females

Social Emotional Distress Scale (SEDS-S)

Brief Multidimensional Students Life Satisfaction Scale (BMSLSS), Male — High (A) (50.2%), Middle (B) (24.3%), Low (C) (25.5%)

SEDS-S groups: Low (A) (50.2%), Middle (B) (25.7%), High (C) (24.1%)

BMSLSS	0	1	2	3	4	5	6	7	8	9	10	11	12	13	14	15	16	17	18	19	20	21	22	23	24	25	26	27	28	29	30	N
25	97	19	21	17	11	5	8	7	8	1	3	1	2	1	3	6	3	1	0	1	2	1	0	0	0	0	5	2	1	0	17	239
24	58	23	18	12	10	8	9	4	9	4	5	6	2	2	3	1	0	2	0	1	1	1	0	0	0	1	0	0	0	0	2	174
23	68		20	19	13	15	9	8	9	12	3	3	2	1	2	2	2	2	0	1	1	1	0	1	0	0	1	0	1	0	0	235
22	56	24	24	17	23	16	22	13	9	7	13	17	3	4	8	3	4	5	2	3	2	1	1	1	1	0	0	0	1	0	0	261
21	56	35	34	19	32	26	20	17	22	21	14	14	7	3	6	6	4	2	12	2	3	1	1	0	1	1	2	3	1	0	1	351
20	90	39	51	40	32	30	22	22	22	24	23	15	14	9	8	6	7	6	5	6	11	4	3	2	3	2	0	0	0	2	2	501
19	36	27	41	17	26	22	18	15	15	15	15	15	14	6	8	5	6	2	3	4	4	2	1	2	0	2	1	2	0	0	1	322
18	23	22	12	23	25	16	15	22	15	22	11	8	9	7	7	4	4	5	5	1	3	2	2	2	1	2	3	2	1	1	1	264
17	16	13	12	12	17	12	12	9	17	13	9	9	8	5	11	6	3	3	8	5	6	5	5	2	2	3	4	1	1		1	231
16	11	5	12	11	10	8	17	11	13	16	13	8	13	7	6	6	8	4	7	7	5	5	3	4	2		1	1	2	1	1	196
15	10	4	11	5	7	9	13	10	9	11	9	3	6	6	16	8	8	5	5	4	8	3	3	2	3		3	2	2		2	193
14	4	3	4	7	6	11	6	4	6	8	7	5	8	6	9	9	9	7	5	5	6	7	6	1	1	1			2	2	1	152
13	7	2	7	5	5	2	6	5	4	8	6	7	2	6	7	6	6	5	5	1	6	1	1	1	2	2	1	4	2	2	2	127
12	2	2	2	2	4	4	4	8	10	7	6	5	6	3	6	7	2	4	7	4	1	1		4	3	3		3	3	2	2	114
11	2	2	2	4	3	3	6	5	6	3	3	3	3	7	5	4	4	2	1	2	3	4	2	1	1	1	3	2	1	1	2	84
10	5	2		3	4	3	4	5		7	4	6	3	5	5	4	3	2	2	4	2	4	5	3		1	1	1	1		2	85
9	1		2		2	4	1	2	2	4	4	6	3	3	3	4	3	3	5	2	2	4	1	1	1		1	1	1		4	71
8	1	1		2	1	2	2		1	3	2	1	1		5	3	4	2	3		2	2	2	1	1	3					1	53
7	1	1	1	1	1	2		1		2	1		5	2	5	5	2	3	5	3	2		5	1	2	3	1	1	2	2	1	54
6	3		1	1			1			1			1	1	5	3	4	4	3		2	4	1	1	3	1		2	3	2	2	26
5	3	1	2		2	1		1		3	2	1		1	1	3	3	2	3	2	2	1		1	1		2	1	1	1	1	37
4	3		2	1	1	1	1		1	2			1		1			2	1		2	1	2	1	1	1	1	1	1	1	1	22
3	2		1	1	1		1	1		1	1		1		1		1	1		1		1	1						1	2	4	12
2	2	1	1			1	1					1		1			1	1		1		1	1	1	1	1		1		1	1	10
1						1																					2					5
0	11	2	2	3	4	2	6	2	6	2	7	5	9	7	14	15	16	17	18	19	20	21	22	23	24	25	26	27	28	29	30	34
Total N	568	256	264	222	234	204	186	166	177	168	154	123	108	93	123	98	79	81	84	65	72	48	37	32	34	34	26	27	23	17	50	3853

Figure 5.5 BMSLSS by SEDS-S Array Distribution Density for Males

cumbersome or too restrictive to direct resources appropriately. This 25-25-50 approach to cut-scores is offered as a balanced way to consider and categorize all students within a 3 × 3 DFM.

Applying this perspective creates nine logical array zones; however, this is not a constrained categorization system. We do not use or suggest descriptive labels, although it is clear that array areas represent positive wellness (upper left) and deficient wellness (lower right). As a convention to facilitate review and discussion, encourage "zonal" DFM universal wellness monitoring thinking, and given DFM's use primarily in educational contexts, we use low, middle, and high to label array zones. Additionally, consistent with "grades" that are often offered in schools, we use the "ABCs" to label array zones and to provide a mnemonic to facilitate conversation. For each factor, an *A-grade* or *high* represents a positive wellness indicator (top 50% BMSLSS and lowest 50% SEDS), and a *C-grade* or *low* represents an adverse wellness indicator (lowest 25% BMSLSS and highest 25% SEDS). Middle-range values designate a *B-grade* or *middle*. Figures 5.4 (females) and 5.5 (males) show the resulting DFM joint arrays with the associated ABC designation zone along with descriptors of high, middle, and low. Instead of relying on precise cut points, we recommend that scores on the two measures used to examine the DFM be plotted in a logical array. Graphing a student's score in the distribution array provides information on possible areas or zones related to different symptoms and wellness profiles' covariates, as opposed to an exact score.

Considering DFM as an array has potential advantages because it naturally and logically depicts a response space that retains complete information about students' response patterns. As a result, the interpretation deemphasizes where the child falls on each DFM factor and emphasizes each student's jointly defined response distribution zone. Amending the prototypic DFM structure (Greenspoon & Saklofske, 2001), we propose an array representation that merges with and complements universal school-based mental wellness monitoring aims. The next logical step is to propose wellness by distress response patterns representing meaningful joint distribution zones. Here, cut-scores are not intended, as usual, to make diagnostic or placement decisions; they are a heuristic to provide school personnel an added datum, which, when integrated with other information, inform care teams' evaluation of students' needs.

Reframing DFM as a Joint Distribution Array

Following an examination of the measures' psychometrics and creating cut-scores for the 3 × 3 DFM, we examined the joint distribution of scores across the two DFM measures used in this example. Using the BMSLSS and SEDS-S for DFM screening assessment produces 806 (31 × 16, note 0 is a valid score) unique, directly scrutinized response combinations. Because males and females had significantly different SEDS-S responses, we ascertained the wellness × distress response distributions for females (Figure 5.4) and males (Figure 5.5) individually. Previous DFM research has inconsistently organized the x and y axes; hence, we propose and use the traditional 0,0 array coordinate origin as a convention for DFM 3 × 3 research and screening applications.

A core observation is that even with a large sample, the two DFM measures' joint distribution had many response patterns with empty cells for females and males. The BMSLSS and SEDS-S had skewed distributions, with most joint responses falling in the array's upper left quadrant. This array location reflects higher life satisfaction and lower distress, or balanced, positive mental health. Figures 5.4 and 5.5 show the number of students, out of 8,008 (4,154 females and 3,854 males, respectively) that have each unique joint DFM response. For example, the most upper-left cell of Figure 5.4 shows that 45 females had a BMSLSS maximum score of 25 and a SEDS-S score of zero.

Evaluate Dual-Factor Category Differences

After establishing the validity of the measures used and reframing the DFM as a joint distribution array, we sought to evaluate the differences among the various DFM categories based on their life satisfaction (obtained from the BMSLSS) and distress (obtained from the SEDS-S). Specifically, we examined how students in the nine logical array zones differed on critical quality of life indicators, including emotional and behavioral risks; school safety, victimization, and belonging; and psychological assets and social resources (see Tables 5.2–5.5). For ease of presentation, we describe levels of life satisfaction (from high to low A, B, and C) followed by distress levels (from high to low C, B, and A) with nine resulting combinations.

Emotional and Behavioral Risks

The high life satisfaction/low distress (AA) group had the lowest percentage of students reporting emotional risk, including past 12-month chronic sadness and suicidal thoughts. The low life satisfaction/high distress group (CC) had the highest percentage of students reporting emotional risk. Both distress and life satisfaction levels were significant predictors of emotional risk—a positive predictor and a negative predictor, respectively. Hence, the combination of lower life satisfaction and higher distress predicted less emotional risk in both female (see Table 5.2) and male (see Table 5.3) students.

Among female students (see Table 5.2), we identified dual-factor group differences in only one of the behavioral risk indicators (30-day marijuana use) but not in the other indicator (30-day alcohol use). Differences in 30-day marijuana use across distress groups did not seem significant, especially between mid and high distress groups. However, differences in 30-day marijuana use between life satisfaction groups were noticeable when combined with any distress group. For example, the percentage of students reporting marijuana use in the past 30 days was 5.2% for the high life satisfaction/low distress (AA) group, 12.5% for the middle life satisfaction/low distress (BA) group, and 22.2% for the low life satisfaction/low distress (CA) group (see Table 5.2). Among male students, there were no significant dual-factor group differences in behavioral risk (see Table 5.3).

School Safety, Victimization, and Belonging

Among both male and female students, dual-factor group differences were found in feeling safe at school and reporting victimization experience (see Table 5.2 for females and Table 5.3 for males). Students with higher life satisfaction and lower distress were more likely to report higher school safety and less likely to report victimization. Although both life satisfaction and distress were significant predictors, life satisfaction was a stronger predictor of school safety than distress level. Specifically, regardless of distress levels, students with high life satisfaction (A) were more likely to report higher school safety than students with middle (B) and low (C) life satisfaction. Those with middle life satisfaction (B) were more likely to report higher school safety than those with low life satisfaction (C). For example, students in the high life satisfaction and high distress (AC) group still reported higher school safety levels than those in the middle life satisfaction and low distress (BA) group, suggesting the significant role of life satisfaction in feeling safe at school.

Among both female (see Table 5.2) and male (see Table 5.3) students, dual-factor group differences were reported in both school belonging indicators—feeling part of the school and enjoying work with classmates. Distress level was not a significant predictor of school belonging, having no clear positive or negative relationship. Conversely, life satisfaction level was a significant predictor of both school belonging indicators. Regardless of distress level, students with high life satisfaction

Michael J. Furlong et al.

Table 5.4 Female Mean Item Response Values for Personal Assets by Dual-Factor Model 3 × 3 Group Classification Groups

	Brief Multidimensional Student Life Satisfaction Scale									
	(A) High			(B) Middle			(C) Low			
	SEDS-S distress			SEDS-S distress			SEDS-S distress			
	(A) Low	(B) Mid	(C) High	(A) Low	(B) Mid [9] [10] [18]	(C) High	(A) Low	(B) Mid	(C) High	F
Dual-Factor Model 3 × 3 Group ID	(AA)	(AB)	(AC)	(BA)	(BB)	(BC)	(CA)	(CB)	(CC)	
Resource and Asset Indicators										
SEHS-S Belief in Self (0–3) M	2.05_{a}	1.83_{b}	1.96_{a}	1.61_{c}	1.58_{cd}	1.47_{de}	1.36_{ef}	1.29_{f}	1.13_{g}	231.68***
SD	(0.48)	(0.49)	(0.59)	(0.49)	(0.50)	(0.55)	(0.62)	(0.48)	(0.54)	
SEHS-S Belief in Others (0–3) M	2.43_{a}	2.32_{a}	2.37_{a}	1.88_{b}	1.96_{b}	1.98_{b}	1.46_{c}	1.53_{c}	1.45_{c}	306.28***
SD	(0.44)	(0.44)	(0.48)	(0.53)	(0.48)	(0.53)	(0.64)	(0.56)	(0.60)	
SEHS-S Emotional Competence (0–3) M	2.20_{a}	2.08_{bc}	2.27_{a}	1.92_{de}	2.03_{cd}	2.16_{ab}	1.77_{e}	1.87_{de}	2.00_{cd}	42.33***
SD	(0.51)	(0.50)	(0.45)	(0.51)	(0.47)	(0.45)	(0.62)	(0.51)	(0.52)	
SEHS-S Engaged Living (0–3) M	2.10_{a}	1.80_{b}	1.88_{b}	1.55_{c}	1.51_{c}	1.33_{d}	1.23_{de}	1.14_{e}	0.91_{f}	331.93***
SD	(0.53)	(0.52)	(0.63)	(0.51)	(0.49)	(0.56)	(0.63)	(0.54)	(0.56)	
School Connectedness (0–4) M	2.84_{a}	2.72_{a}	2.73_{a}	2.38_{b}	2.36_{b}	2.33_{b}	1.93_{cd}	2.00_{c}	1.82_{d}	157.48***
SD	(0.66)	(0.65)	(0.75)	(0.61)	(0.66)	(0.75)	(0.80)	(0.72)	(0.79)	
MHC-SF Social Well-being (0–5) M	3.51_{a}	2.94_{b}	2.98_{b}	2.29_{c}	2.09_{d}	2.00_{d}	1.55_{e}	1.56_{e}	1.10_{e}	208.47***
SD	1.26	1.27	1.42	1.26	1.12	1.24	1.30	1.12	1.01	1.01

Note: The AA group reporting high life satisfaction and low emotional distress corresponds with the "complete mental health" label used in previous dual-factor model studies. SEDS-S = Social Emotional Distress Scale (Low = bottom 50.9%, Mid = middle 25.9%, High = top 23.2%, and most distress). BMSLSS = Brief Multidimensional Student Life Satisfaction Scale (Using the combined male and female sample: A = highest 50.2% to [approximately 50%–100%] of combined sample, B = middle 24.3% [approximately 26%–49%], and C = lowest 25.5% [approximately 1%–25%]). SEHS-S = Social Emotional Health Survey-Secondary. MHC-SF = Mental Health Continuum-Short Form. Significant pairwise comparisons (Turkey's) shown by different letter subscripts for each measure.
*** p < 0.001.

76

Table 5.5 Male Mean Item Response Values for Personal Assets by Dual-Factor Model 3 × 3 Group Classification Groups

Brief Multidimensional Student Life Satisfaction Scale

Resource and Asset Indicators	Stat	(A) High — SEDS‑S distress			(B) Middle — SEDS‑S distress			(C) Low — SEDS‑S distress			F
Dual-Factor Model 3 × 3 Group ID		(AA) (B) Mid *(see note)*	(AB)	(AC)	(BA) (A) Low	(BB) (B) Mid	(BC) (C) High	(CA) (A) Low	(CB) (B) Mid	(CC) (C) High	
SEHS-S Belief in Self (0–3)	M	2.11_a	2.00_a	2.10_a	1.74_b	1.63_b	1.67_b	1.40_c	1.42_c	1.32_c	158.60***
	SD	(0.52)	(0.47)	(0.54)	(0.49)	(0.47)	(0.51)	(0.69)	(0.56)	(0.60)	
SEHS-S Belief in Others (0–3)	M	2.26_a	2.21_a	2.32_a	1.71_c	1.80_{bc}	1.93_b	1.32_c	1.48_d	1.47_{de}	190.23***
	SD	(0.53)	(0.50)	(0.53)	(0.53)	(0.52)	(0.54)	(0.70)	(0.59)	(0.60)	
SEHS-S Emotional Competence (0–3)	M	2.08_{ab}	2.06_b	2.21_a	1.80_{de}	1.84_c	2.01_{bc}	1.54_f	1.73_c	1.89_{cd}	46.09***
	SD	(0.53)	(0.48)	(0.48)	(0.54)	(0.51)	(0.50)	(0.71)	(0.56)	(0.54)	
SEHS-S Engaged Living (0–3)	M	2.56_a	1.89_b	1.95_b	1.58_c	1.43_d	1.42_d	1.20_e	1.17_{ef}	1.02_f	243.67***
	SD	(0.57)	(0.53)	(0.63)	(0.55)	(0.57)	(0.59)	(0.70)	(0.59)	(0.63)	
School Connectedness (0–4)	M	2.90_a	2.81_a	2.75_a	2.32_b	2.43_b	2.38_b	2.02_c	2.10_c	1.94_c	115.01***
	SD	(0.68)	(0.67)	(0.79)	(0.67)	(0.67)	(0.76)	(0.88)	(0.76)	(0.87)	
MHC-SF Social Well-being (0–5)	M	3.59_a	3.19_b	3.21_b	2.37_c	2.18_c	2.05_c	1.74_d	1.52_{de}	1.37_e	200.06***
	SD	(1.31)	(1.30)	(1.49)	(1.34)	(1.23)	(1.27)	(1.54)	(1.25)	(1.24)	

Note: The AA group reporting high life satisfaction and low emotional distress corresponds with the "complete mental health" label used in previous dual-factor model studies. BMSLSS = Brief Multidimensional Student Life Satisfaction Scale (Using the combined male and female sample: A = highest 50.2% to [approximately 50.9%–100%] of combined sample, B = middle 24.3% [approximately 26%–49%], and C = lowest 25.5% [approximately 1%–25%]). Social Emotional Distress Scale (approximately 26%–49%], and C = lowest 25.5% [approximately 1%–25%]). SEHS-S = Social Emotional Health Survey-Secondary. MHC-SF = Mental Health Continuum–Short Form. Significant pairwise comparisons (Turkey's) shown by different letter subscripts for each measure. *** $p < 0.001$.

(A) showed higher levels of school belonging than students with middle (B) and low (C) levels of life satisfaction, and students with middle (B) levels of life satisfaction showed higher levels of school belonging than students with low (C) levels of life satisfaction groups. For example, students with high life satisfaction and high distress (AC) still reported higher school belonging levels than those with middle life satisfaction and low distress (BA), suggesting the importance of life satisfaction in feeling of belonging to the school.

Psychological Assets and Social Resources

Among both male and female students, there were dual-factor group differences in all psychological assets and social resources indicators, including Belief in Self, Belief in Others, Emotional Competence, Engaged Living, School Connectedness, and MHC-SF Social Well-being (see Table 5.4 for females and Table 5.5 for males). Distress level was not a significant predictor of psychological assets and social resources, having no clear positive or negative relationship with psychological assets and social resources. Conversely, life satisfaction was found to be a significant predictor of all indicators. Regardless of distress level, students with high (A) life satisfaction reported higher levels of psychological assets and social resources than student with middle (B) and low (C) levels of life satisfaction, and middle life satisfaction (B) groups showed higher levels of psychological assets and social resources than low life satisfaction (C) groups. For example, students with high life satisfaction and high distress (AC) still reported higher levels of psychological assets and social resources than those with middle life satisfaction and low distress (BA), once again suggesting the significant role of life satisfaction in reporting psychological assets and resources.

Summary of the 3 × 3 DFM Validation Analyses

Is this proposed 3 × 3 DFM approach the only way to address and measure DFM? Certainly not. A DFM application should include general well-being or life satisfaction measures; however, the distress or symptomatology assessments could vary depending on the interests of a school's care team. We used a general distress measure that focused on sad or worried emotions during the past month. Such assessments are generally useful in numerous educational contexts and represent the students' most common emotional distress experiences. Other DFM approaches could focus on other concerns, such as behavioral problems. A caveat is that the measures need to be validated for a wellness screening and have a known joint distribution, as was demonstrated in this chapter. One other requirement is a standardized interpretation protocol that produces the same arrangement across the two DFM factors, regardless of who administers and scores responses and the sample employed. One final observation is that although the DFM conceptual frame has been applied in a non-Western cultural context (e.g., Xiong et al., 2017), the 3 × 3 approach might not provide an optimal fit in all contexts. For example, DFM might include constructs such as Psychological Suzhi applicable to Chinese cultural contexts (Qian et al., 2020; Wang & Zhang, 2012).

Applying the 3 × 3 Model: Implications for Universal School Wellness Screening

Using the joint distribution array, combined with the cut-scores created and described above, practitioners may efficiently plot students' complete mental health functioning, inclusive of positive and negative indicators of mental health. Consistent with previously recommended dual-factor approaches, this proposed approach's initial steps involve administering measures that assess distress and wellness. If a practitioner uses both the BMSLSS and the SEDS-S, students' scores can be plotted on the separate joint distribution arrays for females (see Figure 5.4) and males (see Figure 5.5). Scores on the BMSLSS range from 0 to 25 and can be plotted on the y axis. Using the cut-scores as denoted by the bold vertical lines and determined based on the large, diverse sample described above, a practitioner can determine if the student's life satisfaction is in the low (C), middle (B), or high (A) range. Scores on the SEDS-S range from 0 to 30 and can be plotted on the x axis. Similarly, using the cut-scores for the SEDS-S as denoted by the bold horizontal lines in the graph, a practitioner can readily see if the student's level of distress is in the low (A), middle (B), or high (C) range. Using the combination of both scores will lead to an *x, y* coordinate within the graph. Considering the 3 × 3 nature of this graph, a student will then be placed into one of the nine DFM categories to describe their complete mental health functioning, inclusive of distress and life satisfaction. A female student (use Figure 5.4) who obtains a score of 13 on the BMSLSS and a score of 15 on the SEDS would be plotted precisely in the middle of the graph (BB). Visual examination of the array distributions compared to the plotted *x, y* coordinate for each student provides useful information about how common that student's score profile is. More importantly, the plotted *x, y* coordinate provides information describing the student's functioning, which can be useful for prevention and intervention planning. Figures 5.6 (for females) and 5.7 (for males) are provided as blank joint distribution arrays that can be used to plot the *x, y* coordinates for students. Although additional research is needed to determine if the distribution of scores will remain across other samples, these arrays based on a large sample are provided to assist practitioners and researchers seeking a simplified approach to DFM assessment.

This proposed approach to implementing DFM has the advantage of being efficient and brief—it also supports school mental health screening multiple times per year. We also recognize that this approach requires the need to plot each student's score before interpretation. Additional technology would help automate further the process of plotting multiple students' scores simultaneously; this will be especially needed when all students complete measures within a universal screening context. The use of an emotional distress measure that asks about students' past-month experiences has the added advantage of allowing practitioners and others to assess student changes across one academic year and beyond. A student's *x, y* coordinate score and resulting category could be easily graphed across multiple administrations to monitor progress or set intervention targets. Future research is needed to establish practical suggestions and resources for students within each of the nine categories. Additionally, as this is a proposed approach for screening instead of comprehensive assessment, practitioners are encouraged to combine this DFM information with other information available to them (i.e., attendance, grades, and teacher reports) to determine the best path forward. For example, additional assessment with more comprehensive tools may be necessary for students, particularly in the lowest balanced wellness zones (i.e., low life satisfaction, high distress CC category), to determine how to best support these students. However, with a uniform approach to DFM assessment, researchers and practitioners can begin to make progress in determining how to best support students within each of these nine DFM zones.

Connecting the 2 × 2 and 3 × 3 DFMs

Unsurprisingly, there was substantial overlap between the 2 × 2 and 3 × 3 DFM approaches. In the 2 × 2 DFM construction, the two most intriguing groups are Suldo and Shaffer's (2008) *languishing* and the *symptomatic but content* groups because traditional school-based mental health screening already identifies *troubled* students. For this chapter's 3 × 3 categories, 47% of the students were in the highest balanced wellness (AA; high life satisfaction and low distress) and lowest balanced wellness (CC; low life satisfaction and high distress) zones. In the 2 × 2 model, these students would have been placed in the *complete mental health* (i.e., highest balanced wellness) or *troubled* (i.e., lowest balanced wellness) zones. In this chapter's analyses, these two groups had large effect size differences on nearly all covariates—these students' needs and support are reasonably well understood. This

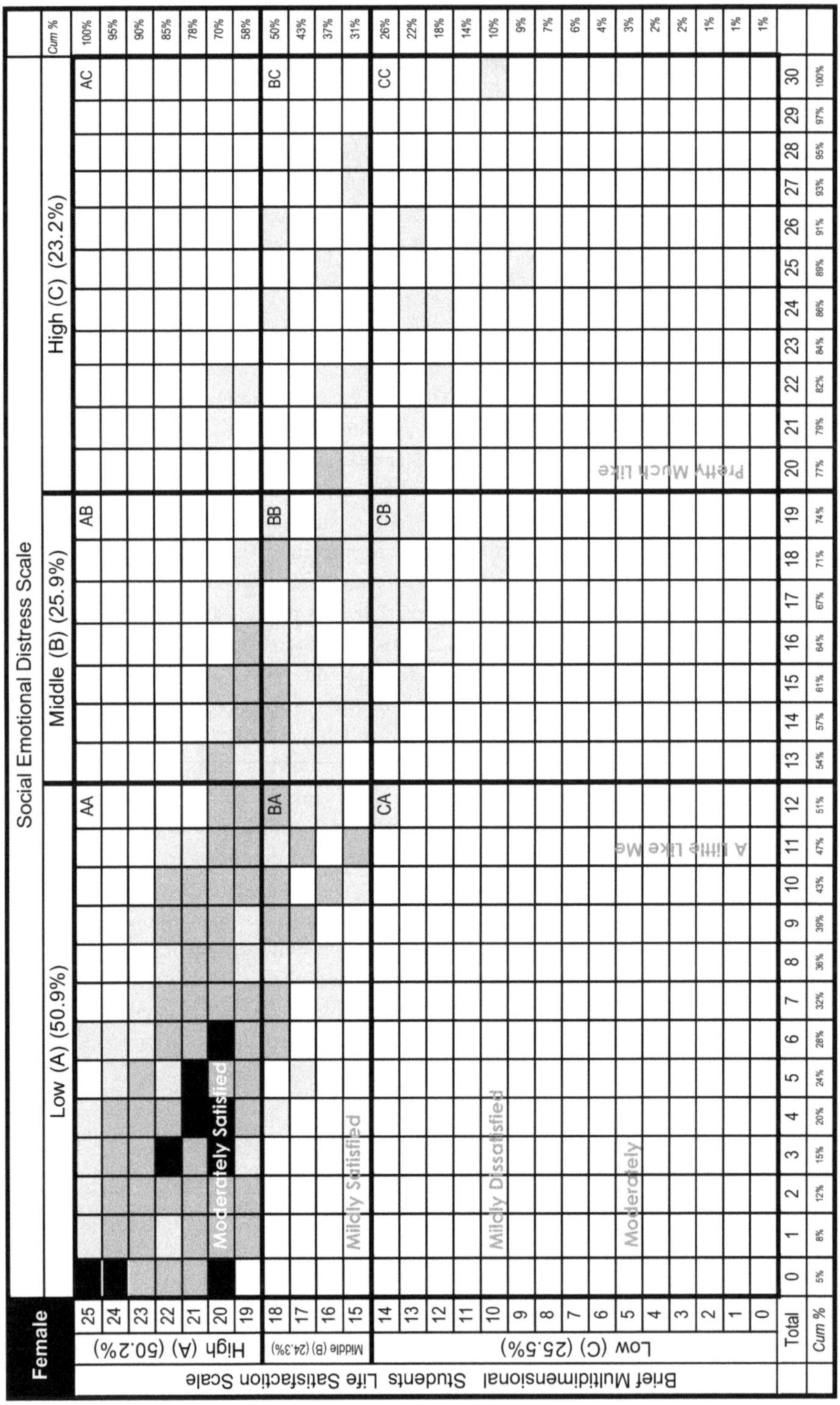
Female
Social Emotional Distress Scale
Low (A) (50.9%)
Middle (B) (25.9%)
High (C) (23.2%)
Brief Multidimensional Students Life Satisfaction Scale
High (A) (50.2%)
Middle (B) (24.3%)
Low (C) (25.5%)
AA
AB
AC
BA
BB
BC
CA
CB
CC
Moderately Satisfied
Mildly Satisfied
Mildly Dissatisfied
Moderately
A Little Like Me
Pretty Much Like
Total
Cum %

Figure 5.6 BMSLSS by SEDS-S Distribution Density for Females Monitoring Array

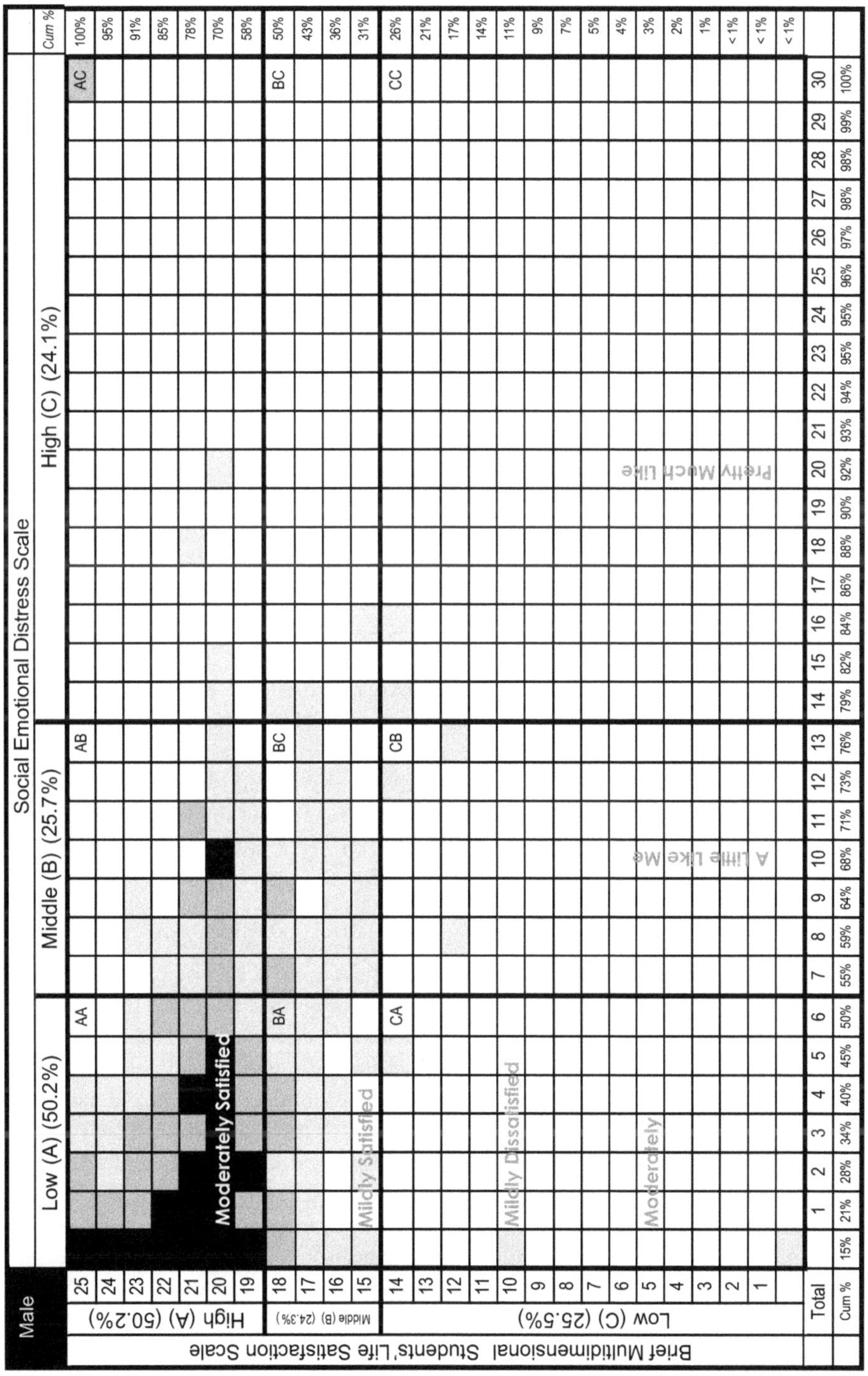

Figure 5.7 BMSLSS by SEDS-S Distribution Density for Males Monitoring Array

finding further validates the 2 × 2 DFM approach, particularly when used for school-wide student wellness screening.

Moreover, when used for universal monitoring, a school's coordinated care service response explores ways to nurture, foster, and support students' continued positive development. Students in the low life satisfaction coupled with high distress (CC) zone would benefit from follow-up, tier 2 assessment, and support services. Conversely, students in the high life satisfaction and low distress (AA) zone report thriving mental health and will likely benefit from tier 1 services and will not need additional individualized services.

The finding that students in the highest (AA) and lowest (CC) balanced wellness zones differed in the current analyses is not especially informative. A traditional symptom universal screener sets cut-scores at 15%–25% of cases and targets those youth for follow-up check-ins. One DFM proof of concept test examines how the *symptomatic but content* zones (AC and BC) compare with the *troubled* zone (CC). If they are not different, it would indicate that accounting for life satisfaction does not add useful information beyond that gleaned from emotional distress alone. Likewise, the *symptomatic but content* (AC and BC) versus *languishing* (CA) zones comparison helps evaluate the relative impacts of low life satisfaction. Indeed, in this instance, life satisfaction was essential in differentiating mental health zones—students in zones with higher levels of life satisfaction, regardless of distress level, tended to report greater feelings of safety and belonging at school as well as more psychological assets and resources. *Symptomatic but content* zones (AC and BC) reported more assets and fewer emotional risks than the *troubled* zone (CC).

Higher life satisfaction was beneficial for the *symptomatic but content* (AC and BC) zones, as students in these zones were more likely to report positive outcomes despite having mid or high distress compared to those in the *languishing* zone (CA). This critical role of life satisfaction on positive student outcomes is also well-presented in the results for the *languishing* (CA) zone. The *languishing* zone (CA) consistently differed from *complete mental health* (AA and BA) and *symptomatic but content* (AC and BC) zones on positive outcomes, including school safety and belonging and psychological assets and resources. Specifically, students in the *languishing* (CA) zone consistently reported more frequent positive outcomes compared to *complete mental health* (AA and BA) and *symptomatic but content* (AC and BC) zones. The absence of distress was not sufficient in supporting similarly positive outcomes for the *languishing* zone compared to *complete mental health* zones (AA and BA).

What is gained from a 3 × 3 model is additional information on the students caught in the middle zones (i.e., middle wellness and middle distress)? In this example, students in these zones significantly differed from youth in the higher and lower balanced wellness zones across several outcomes, including feelings of safety, connection, and belonging at school, psychological assets, and social well-being. This variation tended to be more pronounced for youth in the middle (B) life satisfaction zone, regardless of distress level, when compared to youth in the high (A) or low (C) life satisfaction zones. Youth in middle life satisfaction and distress zones generally enjoyed a happier, healthier quality of life than youth with lower levels of life satisfaction and more distress, but not as well as youth with the highest levels of life satisfaction and lowest levels of distress. These findings underscore the benefits of DFM examining how students in the middle distress and well-being zones fair in their psychosocial development. Even though students in these middle zones may not be a target for immediate follow-up, school care providers must understand that these students may be experiencing nonoptimal life experiences and are at risk for more negative experiences. Overall, there is potential value in looking at students in the middle DFM zones when the penultimate goal is to help as many students as possible thrive and reach higher wellness levels, autonomy, and competence and make meaningful community contributions.

The analyses suggested an intriguing new perspective on students scoring in the zones corresponding to high or middle life satisfaction and high distress (AC and BC). Students in these zones generally resembled Suldo and Shaffer's (2008) *symptomatic but content* group. Researchers have previously suggested that the symptomatic but content group could be behaviorally maladjusted (e.g., Greenspoon's & Saklofske, 2001; Analysis B, Figure 5.2). The information reviewed in this chapter, however, suggests another hypothesis. The students in these zones (high or middle life satisfaction and high distress; AC and BC) reported several traditional mental health concerns; for example, they reported high levels of sadness and suicidal ideation (Tables 5.2 and 5.3). However, they also reported having more social resources and personal assets (Tables 5.4 and 5.5). Rather than presenting as a confounding or counterintuitive classification, youth in these DFM zones might be better understood and further considered through a resilience, theoretical competence lens (see Lenzi et al., 2015).

Grych et al. (2020) examined a resilience hypothesis in a survey study of 466 adolescents residing in the Appalachia region of the United States. This study's primary goal was to investigate which factors might play a protective, resilience-boosting influence on youth. Diener's well-being measure and a trauma checklist created the prototypic DFM groups. Instead, it assessed if protective resilience factors (e.g., internal = self-control, emotional regulation, and external = parental and peer support) were associated differentially with DFM groups. Consistent with typical DFM research, a complete mental health group differed from a troubled group on all life quality indicators. Of interest, the symptomatic but content and languishing groups had different strength patterns. Compared to each other, the symptomatic but content group reported more positive social supports, emotional awareness, and a sense of purpose. The languishing group reported relative resilience strengths of emotional regulation and optimism. Hence, both the languishing and symptomatic but content youths reported resilience-promoting characteristics that might help understand how they have not declined into the troubled group. Both groups have access to interpersonal and intrapersonal resilience promoters.

More information is needed to explore the role that resilience plays and students' zonal placements in the DFM array. But to do this, DFM research must adopt a standard method to form the groups; otherwise, it is futile to compare across studies when the DFM measures and cut-points are essentially unique to each study. This chapter provided one possibility for a uniformed 3 × 3 DFM approach that could be adopted to further scientific research and applied practice within schools.

Discussion and Contributions

We proposed a DFM protocol using co-normed measures across a large, diverse sample, simultaneously linked with other quality of life indicators and measures. The current chapter offered these contributions to the broader DFM research line:

1   This chapter proposed and validated a 3 × 3 DFM approach that is easily adaptable for individual practitioners and scalable to the school, district, and regional levels.
2   A large-sample, wellness-distress joint distribution was presented for the first time.
3   The modified DFM approach de-emphasized traditional cut-scores and labels, emphasizing DFM joint response zones.
4   Practitioners can integrate this information with other known information accessible by school personnel and care coordination teams.

The following sections discuss essential considerations for the chapter's information and subsequent use of the 3 × 3 DFM for research and universal school wellness monitoring.

Importance of Life Satisfaction

Life satisfaction was strongly related to a range of quality of life indicators, more so than emotional distress. The finding is consistent with previous research on life satisfaction's positive associations with various quality of life indicators (self-esteem, hope, gratitude, and positive social relationships) and negative associations with adverse development indicators (anxiety, depression, and social stress; Gilman & Huebner, 2006, Proctor et al., 2009a). In the current study, youth fared more favorably when reporting higher life satisfaction, even when distress was present. This compelling finding showed that students with higher life satisfaction levels reported substantially higher quality of life indicators than students with similar distress. Moreover, even more dramatically, students with high life satisfaction in the presence of high distress had healthier quality of life indicators than students with middle life satisfaction combined with low distress.

The overwhelming majority of all comparisons across the nine DFM groups favored those students in the highest life satisfaction range. This finding is consistent with research revealing the overall benefits of facilitating students' realistic and grounded life satisfaction mindsets (Gilman & Huebner, 2006; Proctor et al., 2009b). Students reporting the highest level of life satisfaction had more favorable status on positive and adverse wellness indicators, regardless of their reported level of recent emotional distress. It was more indispensable to know the students' overall life satisfaction level in evaluating students' overall well-being than ascertaining their recent emotional distress experience.

Students reporting higher life satisfaction levels may be in virtuous developmental cycles that lead to upwardly improving life circumstances (Zhou et al., 2020). This pattern is consistent with Fredrickson's *broaden and build* theory (Stiglbauer et al., 2013). It is not just that students experience positive emotions. These positive experiences could facilitate the growth of a global mindset that a student's "life is going well." These students experience more favorable longer-term developmental outcomes. Suldo and Huebner (2004) found that students with positive life satisfaction were less likely to develop later externalizing behaviors in the presence of stressful life events. Life satisfaction, thus, is not a simple by-product of positive life experiences, but it actively promotes resilience and wellness among youth as a fundamental psychological construct (Huebner et al., 2006).

This current sample's life satisfaction levels revealed a positively skewed distribution; however, this alone is not a cause for celebration for educators. Even for the highest life satisfaction groups (AA, AB, and AC), regardless of the level of distress, only two of three or three out of four students reported feeling they felt they were part of the school. About one of two students in middle life satisfaction groups reported that they felt part of the school (BA, BB, and BC). Furthermore, for the lowest life satisfaction group of students (CA, CB, and CC), only one out of four to one out of three felt they were a part of their school. This observation highlights the value of employing a universal DFM mental health screening and monitoring approach. It has an expansive focus, including efforts to improve the whole school context. It links efforts to improve the school climate in ways that impact and benefit all students, emphasizing building their well-being.

Limitations and Cautions

The current chapter's sample included students from randomly selected schools, which is a strength of the methodology used. However, a possible selection bias was that the schools volunteered to participate in the study; hence the students were from schools with positive valence toward monitoring students' well-being. The survey procedures employed in this chapter were well developed and used in California for more than 25 years. Nonetheless, many students did not respond to a gender identity item, excluding them from the DFM analyses. This limitation diminished the sample size and introduced indiscernible bias into the study. We investigated which students did not respond to the gender items and examined their social-emotional distress item means. We found that the mean scores fell between the means of students identifying as male or female. So, we suspect that this was a random, not systematic, bias. Future research must also employ nonbinary gender identification items. Of course, this needs to be evaluated in future research and can be further assessed by researchers who agree to combine dataset samples that employ the BMSLSS and SEDS-S in future research. In any case, the current sample provides a DFM origin or baseline sample. Researchers can use its means, standard deviations, and joint distribution to evaluate possible sample bias or sample differences in their future studies.

It is crucial in our view that school-wide universal screening has contextual and practical validity. All DFM indicators should provide information relevant to considering and understanding all students' mental health. Hence the approach proposed here was not to single out just the lowest or highest students in terms of the distribution of mental health and well-being but to understand better where all students fall within the distress by life satisfaction zone. Recognizing the life satisfaction and distress skewed distribution found in this study, DFM zones can readily fluctuate as the numerous students at the zonal boundaries experience multiple life and developmental challenges as they traverse the critical adolescent years.

Conclusion

In closing, we emphasize that the DFM approach presented in this chapter is just one circumscribed source of information about students' balanced mental health. A full assessment of youth well-being is more intricate (e.g., physical, social, spiritual, and cultural) than can be included in a universal DFM monitoring procedure. Hence, the 3 × 3 modified DFM is not appropriate for a high-stakes assessment context. DFM information should not be used to make definitive diagnostic or programmatic decisions about any particular student. Responsible use of universal DFM procedures incorporates it with other measures and indicators known to the school staff, community counselors, and others; information that is otherwise unobtainable via school-wide universal screening surveys. We look forward to continued progress in the field of DFM research to ultimately help students thrive both within the school context and throughout their lives.

Notes

1 The research reported in this chapter was supported in part by the Institute of Education Sciences, U.S. Department of Education, through Grant # R305A160157 to the University of California, Santa Barbara. The opinions expressed are those of the authors and do not represent views of the Institute of Education Sciences or the U.S. Department of Education.

2 Furlong, M. J., Dowdy, E., Moore, S., & Kim, E. (2022). Adapting the dual-factor model for universal school-based mental health screening: Bridging the research to practice divide. In K. A. Allen, M. J. Furlong, S. Suldo, & D. Vella-Brodrick (Eds.), *Handbook of positive psychology in schools: Supporting process and practice* (3rd ed.). Routledge, Taylor and Francis.

3 The cut-scores divided the responses into the low, middle, and high groups as close as possible into the 25-25-50 groups. Figures 5.6 and 5.7 show the cumulative percent of students for each SEDS-S and BMSLSS value.

References

Achenbach, T. M. (1991). *Integrative guide to the 1991 CBCL/4–18, YSR, and TRF profiles*. University of Vermont.

Achenbach, T. M., & Rescorla, L. A. (2001). *Manual for the ASEBA school-age forms and profiles*. University of Vermont, Research Center for Children, Youth, and Families.

Achenbach, T. M., & Ruffle, T. M. (2000). The child behavior checklist and related forms for assessing behavioral/emotional problems and competencies. *Pediatrics in Review, 21*(8), 265–271. https://doi.org/10.1542/pir.21-8-265

American Psychiatric Association. (2013). *Diagnostic and statistical manual of mental disorders* (5th ed.). Publisher.

Antaramian, S. P., Huebner, E. S., Hills, K. J., & Valois, R. F. (2010). A dual-factor model of mental health: Toward a more comprehensive understanding of youth functioning. *American Journal of Orthopsychiatry, 80*(4), 462–472. https://doi.org/10.1111/j.1939-0025.2010.01049.x

California Healthy Kids Survey. (2017). *California School Climate, Health, and Learning Surveys.* Retrieved from http://chks.wested.org

Catalano, R. F., & Kellogg, E. (2020). Fostering healthy mental, emotional, and behavioral development in children and youth: A national agenda. *Journal of Adolescent Health, 66*(3), 265–267. https://doi.org/10.1016/j.jadohealth.2019.12.003

Diener, E., Emmons, R. A., Larsen, R. J., & Griffin, S. (1985). The satisfaction with life scale. *Journal of Personality Assessment, 49*, 71–75. http://dx.doi.org/10.1207/s15327752jpa4901_13

Dowdy, E., Furlong, M. J., Nylund-Gibson, K., Moore, S., & Moffa, K. (2018). Initial validation of the Social Emotional Distress Scale to support complete mental health screening. *Assessment for Effective Intervention, 43*(4), 241–248. https://doi.org/10.1177/1534508417749871

Dowdy, E., Furlong, M. J., Raines, T. C., Bovery, B., Kauffman, B., Kamphaus, R., Dever, B. V., Price, M., & Murdock, J. (2015). Enhancing school-based mental health services with a preventive and promotive approach to universal screening for complete mental health. *Journal of Educational and Psychological Consultation, 25*, 178–197. https://doi.org/10.1080/10474412.2014.929951

Furlong, M. J., You, S., Renshaw, T. L., Smith, D. C., & O'Malley, M. D. (2014). Preliminary development and validation of the Social and Emotional Health Survey for secondary students. *Social Indicators Research, 117*, 1011–1032. doi:10.1007/s11205-013-0373-0

Furlong, M. J., Dowdy, E., Nylund-Gibson, K., Wagle, R., Carter, D., & Hinton, T. (2021). Enhancement and standardization of a universal social-emotional health measure for students' psychological strengths. *Journal of Well-Being Assessment.* https://doi.org/10.1007/s41543-020-00032-2

Gilman, R., & Huebner, E. S. (2006). Characteristics of adolescents who report very high life satisfaction. *Journal of Youth and Adolescence, 35*, 293–301. https://doi.org/10.1007/s10964-006-9036-7

Goodman, R. (1997). The Strengths and Difficulties Questionnaire: A research note. *Journal of Child Psychology and Psychiatry, 38*, 581–586. https://doi.org/10.1111/j.1469-7610.1997.tb01545.x

Greenspoon, P. J., & Saklofske, D. H. (2001). Toward an integration of subjective well-being and psychopathology. *Social Indicators Research, 54*, 81–108. https://doi.org/10.1023/A:1007219227883

Grych, J., Taylor, E., Banyard, V., & Hamby, S. (2020). Applying the dual factor model of mental health to understanding protective factors in adolescence. *American Journal of Orthopsychiatry, 9*(4), 458–467. http://dx.doi.org/10.1037/ort0000449

Huebner, E. S. (1991). Initial development of the Students' Life Satisfaction Scale. *School Psychology International, 12*, 231–240. https://doi.org/10.1177/0143034391123010

Huebner, E. S. (1994). Preliminary development and validation of a multidimensional life satisfaction scale for children. *Psychological Assessment, 6*(2), 149–158. https://doi.org/10.1037/1040-3590.6.2.149

Huebner, E. S., Seligson, J. L., Valois, R. F., & Suldo, S. M. (2006). A review of the brief Multidimensional Students' Life Satisfaction Scale. *Social Indicators Research, 79*(3), 477–484. Retrieved from https://www.jstor.org/stable/27522650

Huebner, E. S., Suldo, S. M., & Gilman, R. (2006). Life satisfaction. In G. G. Bear & K. M. Minke (Eds.), *Children's needs III: Development, prevention, and intervention* (pp. 357–368). National Association of School Psychologists.

Huebner, E. S., Suldo, S. M., Valois, R. F., & Drane, J. W. (2006). The brief multidimensional students' life satisfaction scale: Sex, race, and grade effects for applications with middle school students. *Applied Research in Quality of Life, 1*, 211. https://doi.org/10.1007/s11482-006-9016-9

Jahoda, M. (1958). *Joint commission on mental health and illness monograph series: Vol. 1. Current concepts of positive mental health.* Basic Books. https://doi.org/10.1037/11258-000

Kamphaus, R. W., Reynolds, C. R., & Dever, B. V. (2014). Behavioral and mental health screening. In R. J. Kettler, T. A. Glover, C. A. Albers, & K. A. Feeney-Kettler (Eds.), *Universal screening in educational settings: Evidence-based decision making for schools* (pp. 249–273). American Psychological Association.

Kelly, R. M., Hills, K. J., Huebner, E. S., & McQuillin, S. D. (2012). The longitudinal stability and dynamics of group membership in the dual-factor model of mental health: Psychosocial predictors of mental health. *Canadian Journal of School Psychology, 27*(4), 337–355. https://doi.org/10.1177/0829573512458505

Keyes, C. L. M. (2005). The subjective well-being of America's youth: Toward a comprehensive assessment. *Adolescent and Family Health, 4*, 3–11. https://doi.org/10.1037/0002-9432.76.3.395

Keyes, C. L. M. (2006). Mental health in adolescence: Is America's youth flourishing? *American Journal of Orthopsychiatry, 76*, 395–402. https://doi.org/10.1037/0002-9432.76.3.395

Keyes, C. L. (2013). Promoting and protecting positive mental health: Early and often throughout the lifespan. In C. L. Keyes (Ed.), *Mental well-being* (pp. 3–28). Springer.

Kim, E. K., Dowdy, E., & Furlong, M. J. (2014). Exploring the relative contributions of the strength and distress components of dual-factor complete mental health screening. *Canadian Journal of School Psychology, 29*, 127–140. Retrieved from http://cjs.sagepub.com/content/29/2/127.abstract

Kroenke, K., Spitzer, R. L., & Williams, J. B. W. (2001). The PHQ-9: Validity of a brief depression severity measure. *Journal of General Internal Medicine, 16*, 606–613. doi:10.1046/j.1525-1497.2001.016009606.x

Laurent, J., Catanzaro, J., Joiner, T. E., Rudolph, K., Potter, K. I., Lambert, S., Osborne, L., & Gathright, T. (1999). A measure of positive and negative affect for children: Scale development and preliminary validation. *Psychological Assessment, 11*(3), 326–338. https://doi.org/10.1037/1040-3590.11.3.326

Lenzi, M., Dougherty, D., Furlong, M. J., Dowdy, E., & Sharkey, J. D. (2015). The configuration protective model: Factors associated with adolescent behavioral and emotional problems. *Journal of Applied Developmental Psychology, 38*, 49–59. https://doi.org/10.1016/j.appdev.2015.03.003

Lim, M., Allen, K., Craig, H., Smith, D., & Furlong, M. J. (2021). Feeling lonely and a need to belong: What is shared and distinct? *Australian Journal of Psychology*. doi:10.1080/00049530.2021.1883411

Lovibond, S. H., & Lovibond, P. F. (1995). *Manual for the depression anxiety stress scales*. Psychology Foundation.

Lyons, M. D., Huebner, E. S., & Hills, K. J. (2013). The dual-factor model of mental health: A short-term longitudinal study of school-related outcomes. *Social Indicators Research, 114*(2), 549–565. https://doi.org/10.1007/s11205-012-0161-2

Lyons, M. D., Huebner, E. S., Hills, K. J., & Shinkareva, S. V. (2012). The dual-factor model of mental health: Further study of the determinants of group differences. *Canadian Journal of School Psychology, 27*, 183–196. https://doi.org/10.1177/0829573512443669

McMahan, M. M. (2012). *A longitudinal examination of high school students' group membership in a dual-factor model of mental health: Stability of mental health status and predictors of change* (Doctoral Dissertation). Retrieved from University of South Florida Scholar Commons (4369).

Moore, S. A., Mayworm, A. M., Stein, R., Sharkey, J. D., & Dowdy, E. (2019). Languishing students: Linking complete mental health screening in schools to Tier 2 intervention. *Journal of Applied School Psychology, 35*(3), 257–289. https://doi.org/10.1080/15377903.2019.1577780

Nickerson, A. B., & Fishman, C. E. (2013). Promoting mental health and resilience through strength-based assessment in US schools. *Educational and Child Psychology, 30*(4), 7–17. Retrieved from https://psycnet.apa.org/record/2014-01610-002

Proctor, C. L., Linley, P. A., & Maltby, J. (2009a). Youth life satisfaction: A review of the literature. *Journal of Happiness Studies, 10*(5), 583–630. https://doi.org/10.1007/s10902-008-9110-9

Proctor, C., Alex Linley, P., & Maltby, J. (2009b). Youth life satisfaction measures: A review. *The Journal of Positive Psychology, 4*(2), 128–144. https://doi.org/10.1080/17439760802650816

Qian, N., Yang, C., Teng, Z., Furlong, M. J., Pan, Y., Guo, C., & Zhang, D. (2020). Psychological Suzhi mediates the longitudinal association between perceived school climate and depressive symptoms. *School Psychology, 35*(4), 267–276. https://doi.org/10.1037/spq0000374

Raines, T. C., Dever, B. V., Kamphaus, R. W., & Roach, A. T. (2009). Universal screening for behavioral and emotional risk: A promising method for reducing disproportionate placement in special education. *The Journal of Negro Education, 81*(3), 283–296.

Renshaw, T. L., & Cohen, A. S. (2014). Life satisfaction as a distinguishing indicator of college student functioning: Further validation of the two-continua model of mental health. *Social Indicators Research, 117*, 319–334. doi:10.1007/s11205-013-0342-7

Reynolds, C. R., & Kamphaus, R. W. (1992). *Behavior Assessment System for Children*. Pearson.

Reynolds, C. R., & Kamphaus, R. W. (2004). *Behavior Assessment System for Children* (2nd ed.). Pearson.

Ryff, C. D. (1989). Happiness is everything, or is it? Explorations on the meaning of psychological well-being. *Journal of Personality and Social Psychology, 57*(6), 1069–1081. doi:10.1037/0022-3514.57.6.1069

Ryff, C. D., & Keyes, C. L. M. (1995). The structure of psychological well-being revisited. *Journal of Personality and Social Psychology, 69*, 719–727. https://doi.org/10.1037/0022-3514.69.4.719

Schneider, M. (2020). *Making common measures more common*. Institute of Education Sciences (May 5). Retrieved from https://ies.ed.gov/director/remarks/5-05-2020.asp

Seligman, M. E. P., & Csikszentmihalyi, M. (2000). Positive psychology: An introduction. *American Psychologist, 55*(1), 5–14. https://doi.org/10.1037/0003-066X.55.1.5

Seligman, M. E. P., Ernst, R. M., Gillham, J., Reivich, K., & Linkins, M. (2009). Positive education: Positive psychology and classroom interventions. *Oxford Review of Education, 35*(3), 293–311. https://doi.org/10.1080/03054980902934563

Seligson, J., Huebner, E. S., & Valois, R. F. (2003). Preliminary validation of the Brief Multidimensional Students' Life Satisfaction Scale (BMSLSS). *Social Indicators Research, 61*(2), 121–145. https://doi.org/10.1023/A:1021326822957

Seligson, J. L., Huebner, E. S., & Valois, R. F. (2005). An investigation of a brief life satisfaction scale with elementary school children. *Social Indicators Research, 73*, 355–374. https://doi.org/10.1007/s11205-004-2011-3

Smith, N. D. W., Suldo, S. M., Hearon, B. V., & Ferron, J. M. (2020). An application of the dual-factor model of mental health in elementary school children: Examining academic engagement and social outcomes. *Journal of Positive Psychology & Wellbeing, 4*(1), 49–68.

Spitzer, R. L., Kroenke, K., Williams, J. B. W., & Löwe, B. (2006). A brief measure for assessing generalized anxiety disorder: The GAD-7. *Archives of Internal Medicine, 166*, 1092–1097. doi:10.1001/archinte.166.10.1092

Stiglbauer, B., Gnambs, T., Gamsjäger, M., & Batinic, B. (2013). The upward spiral of adolescents' positive school experiences and happiness: Investigating reciprocal effects over time. *Journal of Positive School Psychology, 51*(2), 231–242. Retrieved from https://www.journalppw.com/index.php/JPPW/article/view/186

Suldo, S. M., & Huebner, E. S. (2004). Does life satisfaction moderate the effects of stressful life events on psychopathological behavior during adolescence? *School Psychology Quarterly, 19*, 93–105. doi:10.1521/scpq.19.2.93.33313

Suldo, S. M., & Shaffer, E. J. (2008). Looking beyond psychopathology: The dual-factor model of mental health in youth. *School Psychology Review, 37*, 52–68. https://doi.org/10.1080/02796015.2008.12087908

Suldo, S., Thalji, A., & Ferron, J. (2011). Longitudinal academic outcomes predicted by early adolescents' subjective well-being, psychopathology, and mental health status yielded from a dual factor model. *Journal of Positive Psychology, 6*, 17–30. doi:10.1080/17439760.2010.536774

Suldo, S. M., Thalji-Raitano, A., Kiefer, S. M., & Ferron, J. M. (2016). Conceptualizing high school students' mental health through a dual-factor model. *School Psychology Review, 45*(4), 434–457. doi:10.17105/SPR45-4.434-457

Thalji, A. L. (2013). *A dual-factor model of mental health in high school students: Group characteristics and social functioning* (Order No. AAI3519079). Available from PsycINFO. (1426228741; 2013-99120-186). Retrieved from http://search.proquest.com/docview/1426228741?accountid=14522

Thayer, A. J., Weeks, M. R., & Cook, C. R. (2021). Dual factor mental health model: Validation through mixture modeling and cut scores. *Psychology in the Schools, 58*(2), 286–306. https://doi.org/10.1002/pits.22447

Veit, C. T., & Ware, J. E. (1983). The structure of psychological distress and well-being in general populations. *Journal of Consulting and Clinical Psychology, 51*(5), 30–742. https://doi.org/10.1037/0022-006X.51.5.730

Wang, X., & Zhang, D. (2012). The criticism and amendment for the dual-factor model of mental health: From Chinese psychological Suzhi research perspectives. *International Journal of Clinical Medicine, 3*, 319–327. http://dx.doi.org/10.4236/ijcm.2012.35063

Waters, L., & Loton, D. (2019). SEARCH: A meta-framework and review of the field of positive education. *International Journal of Applied Positive Psychology, 4*, 1–46. https://doi.org/10.1007/s41042-019-00017-4

Weathers, E. S. (2019). Bias or empathy in universal screening? The effect of teacher–student racial matching on teacher perceptions of student behavior. *Urban Education*, 0042085919873691. https://doi.org/10.1177/0042085919873691

Xiong, J., Qin, Y., Gao, M., & Hai, M. (2017). Longitudinal study of a dual-factor model of mental health in Chinese youth. *School Psychology International, 38*(3), 287–303. https://doi.org/10.1177/0143034317689970

You, S., Furlong, M. J., Dowdy, E., Renshaw, T., Smith, D. C., & O'Malley, M. D. (2014). Further validation of the Social and Emotional Health Survey for high school students. *Applied Quality of Life Research, 9*, 997–1015. doi:10.1007/s11482-013-9282-2

You, S., Furlong, M. J., Felix, E., & O'Malley, M. (2015). Validation of the Social and Emotional Health Survey for five sociocultural groups: Multigroup invariance and latent mean analyses. *Psychology in the Schools, 54*(2), 349–362. https://doi.org/ 10.1002/pits.21828

Zhou, J., Jiang, S., Zhu, X., Huebner, E. S., & Tian, L. (2020). Profiles and transitions of dual-factor mental health among Chinese early adolescents: The predictive roles of perceived psychological need satisfaction and stress in school. *Journal of Youth Adolescence*. First online 22 May 2020. https://doi.org/10.1007/s10964-020-01253-7

Zullig, K. J., Valois, R. F., Huebner, E. S., Oeltmann, J. E., & Drane, J. W. (2001). Relationship between perceived life satisfaction and adolescents' substance abuse. *Journal of Adolescent Health, 29*(4), 279–288. doi:10.1016/s1054-139x(01)0026

SECTION II

Individual Psychological Assets

PART A

Emotional and Physical Development

6

WELL-BEING LITERACY

Language Use as a Way to Contextualize the Process of Positive Education

Lindsay G. Oades, Hanchao Hou, Jacqueline J. Francis, Lisa M. Baker, and Lanxi Huang

Introduction

The integration of positive psychology with education over the past two decades has resulted in the proliferation of positive education research and rapid changes to positive education itself (Norrish et al., 2013). However, this merge has brought to light several unanswered questions: What exactly is a positive educational process? What should be the outcome of a positive educational process? In response to these questions, we introduce the language-use capability of *wellbeing literacy* (WL). A capability is defined briefly as *what people can be and do* (Sen, 1993). Therefore, WL as a language-use capability is what *people can be and do with well-being language* to foster well-being.

We argue that at its humanistic core, education is relational—it cannot exist without the activity of human relations (Rutyer et al., 2020). This argument is consistent with positive psychology's humanistic origins (Rich, 2018; Robbins, 2008; Taylor, 2001). Within schools, relationships exist between teachers, learners, and the knowledge shared between the parties. Positive education, broadly defined as positive psychology applications within educational contexts, is also an important relational process. By necessity, language mediates positive education and the component enterprises of education itself (e.g., teaching, learning, and assessment; Rutyer et al., 2020). Additionally, positive educational processes, defined as those focused on well-being outcomes through prevention, intervention, and assessment practices, are relational and language-dependent. Relational and language capabilities are, therefore, crucial. Understanding well-being, defined herein as "feeling good and functioning effectively" (Huppert & So, 2013, p. 838), is fundamental to positive education processes and outcomes.

Communicating about and for well-being is key to WL. WL, a language-use capability, is inherently relational and thereby necessitates reframing positive education in educational discourse (Oades & Johnston, 2017). This chapter outlines WL as a five-component capability model, how it may exist in action in schools, and why it is crucial. Implications for schools in measuring positive education gains, framing positive educational practices, and providing a shared well-being language are discussed. We conclude that WL is a necessary aspect of achieving and sustaining positive well-being outcomes in education. Moreover, we assert that it contributes to understanding the nascent conceptualization of positive educational processes, more than mechanistically transplanting positive psychology interventions (PPIs) from psychology into educational contexts.

DOI: 10.4324/9781003013778-9

Table 6.1 Five Component Model of Wellbeing Literacy

Component	Description
1 Vocabulary and knowledge *about* well-being	Words and basic facts about well-being (i.e., content that is signified).
2 Comprehension of multimodal text related to well-being	Reading, listening, and viewing about and for well-being.
3 Composition of multimodal text related to well-being	Writing, speaking, and creating about and for well-being.
4 Context awareness and adaptability	Awareness of differences across contexts and adapt use of language to fit the relevant context.
5 Intentionality *for* well-being	Habit of intentionally using language to maintain or improve well-being of self or others.

What Is Wellbeing Literacy?

Language is a lever for influencing well-being as a natural, universal, and constant tool that is never put down (Brothers, 2005; Oades et al., 2020). Consistent with a conceptualization of literacy as a form of language use (Perry, 2012; Snow, 1983), WL is the purposeful, mindful language used about and for well-being (Oades, 2017; Oades & Johnston, 2017). Specifically, WL is the capability (e.g., incorporating knowledge, vocabulary, and language skills) of comprehending and composing well-being languages, sensitivity to contexts, and being used intentionally to maintain or improve one's or others' well-being (see Table 6.1).

The Five-Component Model of Wellbeing Literacy

WL is a capability consisting of five components: (a) vocabulary and knowledge, (b) comprehension of multimodal texts, (c) composition of multimodal texts, (d) context-sensitivity, and (e) intentionality (see Table 6.1). The following sections discuss these capabilities in more detail.

Vocabulary and Knowledge

Well-being vocabulary includes language associated with the well-being of oneself and others. Well-being knowledge includes declarative knowledge about and for well-being (refer to Tables 6.1 and 6.2). One example may be a university student who recently moved away from home and feels lonely but knows that well-being is related to a positive relationship and social support. In this instance, the student could articulate words associated with the problem and express how this made them feel, such as "isolated," "I feel lonely because I am isolated," and "I know it is good to be connected because then I have support."

Multimodal Comprehension

Communicating about and for well-being includes both receiving (comprehension) and producing (composition) aspects of literacy (see Table 6.2). WL is multimodal, reflecting a real-world, societal view of literacy (Perry, 2012). Comprehension of well-being communication occurs through reading, listening, and viewing (Australian Curriculum, Assessment and Reporting Authority [ACARA], 2020a, 2020b). For example, reading about well-being could include older students reading the novel *How It Feels to Float* by Helena Fox, discussing perspective and building student empathy for people who have experienced mental illness. Listening about or for well-being could involve intentionally listening to music to boost student and teacher mood in the classroom or online. Viewing about or for well-being could involve viewing a portrait, which generates positive feelings such as awe or inspiration.

Multimodal Composition

The *composition* of well-being communication is also multimodal and occurs through writing, speaking, and creating (ACARA, 2020b) (See Table 6.2). Literacy is understood here as pivotal for relationships and well-being, as a sociocultural phenomenon, and as occurring between people (Gee, 1998). Well-being experiences are likely composed in congruence with values and the sociocultural context. Examples of intentionally composing for well-being could include sending regular text messages to a sibling, who lives interstate, to strengthen their sense of family connection. Speaking for well-being could involve deliberately singing personally favorite songs in the shower to get ready for the day, exercising one's strength of playfulness, and boosting positive emotion. Creating about well-being, could involve painting or choreographing a dance, representing the joys and sorrows of life.

Context Sensitivity

The meaning of language varies with context. WL requires context identification and appropriately adaptive language use. For example, words and communication modes differ across a person's life domains, such as home, school, the workplace, and with grandparents, friends, or work colleagues. Sensitivity to context is demonstrated when an individual can select language and communication modes that meet different situations and their contexts' communication needs. Therefore, a well-being-literate person can adapt their comprehension and composition of language to be context-appropriate (see Table 6.2).

Intentionality

Relevant to both context sensitivity and intentionality, Malle and Knobe (1997) provide a folk model of intentionality that involves belief, desire, intention, and awareness. Intentionality relates to the component of WL; that is not just what language is about or signifies, but why it is being used. Does the sender or receiver of communication aim for the positive well-being of self, others, or the world? Intentionality is more than a single good intention. Rather it involves the ongoing habit of those intentions, or more specifically the capability to keep having good intentions regarding language use for well-being. Paradoxically, by becoming a habit it may become more automatic, less conscious. The paradox is that we mean that we become unaware that we have good intentions with our language use. This forms a key aspect of the capability of WL.

   In everyday communication, the terms skillful or mindful language use are relevant to intentionality awareness. A nonautonomous view of language provides the basis for WL (Street, 2003). Language does not use itself; it has the user's intentions and awareness of contexts in which they use the language. Intentionality in this context refers to an ongoing mental state, rather than a solitary instance or action. A single act of intervention for the well-being of self or others is simply a well-being activity and does not assume or create literacy. Rather, WL denotes awareness, values, and goals, which motivate a habit of intention.

Table 6.2 A Broad Overview of the Wellbeing Literacy Model within the School Context

	Wellbeing Literacy Component and Description	Capabilities	Capabilities Demonstrated as Individual Psychological Assets by Students.	How This Capability Might Be Demonstrated within the Whole School—School Climate and Culture?
The what of wellbeing literacy— about well-being.	1. Well-being vocabulary and knowledge. Words and information about well-being— possessing words (vocabulary) and knowledge about well-being that is consistent with our values and social context.	I have the words that I can use, and that other people understand, to help myself and/or others, feel good, and function well.	Early years. Children learn that mindfulness can help them feel calm. They learn and use the word mindfulness. Primary. Children learn that our beliefs, attitudes, and behaviors are linked. They learn the vocabulary of perspective taking. Secondary. Children learn that humans have the fundamental psychological needs of competence, autonomy, and relatedness. They learn the vocabulary associated with these needs including belonging.	Teachers purposefully use conversation to connect with students, and to understand the whole child. Family/wider community. Communication, with teachers and leadership including conversations and emails, are considered, calm, and respectful. Leadership. School leaders are open, honest, and kind in communication with students, teachers, and community.
The how of wellbeing literacy.	2. Well-being comprehension. Being able to comprehend texts relevant to well-being in multiple modalities, including viewing, listening, and reading about and for well-being.	I can hear, see, read and understand ways to feel good, function well, and contribute to others' well-being.	Early years. Students listen to a story about mindfulness and understand that mindfulness can help them feel calm. Students listen to music and talk about how the music makes them feel. Primary. Students watch and understand a movie illustrating two different perspectives of the same situation. Students notice the film score, and the role of music in setting the scene, telling the story, and conveying perspectives. Secondary. Students listen to a range of musical pieces, to determine which piece to perform for the music festival, students consider which piece will allow the strengths of everyone in the group to be showcased.	Teachers. A classroom teacher plays music, wrapping up the day with a class dance. She understands different music suits different people, so the play list is collaboratively created by the teacher and her students. The music and dancing encourage students (and the teacher) to reflect positively on the day, and to look forward to school the following day. Family/ community. Parents/carers talk to their children about music, what music the child enjoys, how the music make them feel. Parents share times listening to music, understanding which types of music they and their child prefer. School leadership and community leaders come together, to hold a community music festival.

Wellbeing Literacy Component and Description	Capabilities	Capabilities Demonstrated as Individual Psychological Assets by Students.	How This Capability Might Be Demonstrated within the Whole School—School Climate and Culture?
3. Well-being composition. Students compose texts relevant to well-being in multiple modalities, including writing, creating and speaking about and for well-being.	I can write, draw, make, create and talk about things that make me happy and that promote happiness in others.	Early years. Students create a yoga zone in their room, for free play with yoga poses and music. They learn a yoga sequence for stretching the body and focusing the mind. Primary. Students collaborate to present a debate on well-being activities, presenting the benefits and limitations of yoga. Secondary. Students analyze and explain the language of belonging in the novel and compare this to language use in social media, and how this impacts a sense of belonging and relatedness.	Teachers. A teacher with expertise in yoga creates and runs a weekly yoga class for staff and past students. Purposefully developing the language and skills of yoga and associated well-being and belonging. Family/wider community. Parents from the community participate in the class, talking to others who may be interested in joining. Leadership provides a room within the school to be used for the class, and provides the teacher with an extra hour of planning time, to support her role as teacher and yoga leader.
The who, when, and where of wellbeing literacy.	Sensitivity to context. Awareness of adapting and changing language according to a specific context. Understanding the composition and comprehension of language can be adapted to different contexts.	I know that receiving and expressing language can be different in different places, with different people and different circumstances.	Early years. Students collaboratively decide on an ideal place to undertake daily mindfulness practice and also ask parents about ways to do this at home. Primary. Students consider an appropriate audience to watch their debate, based on the topic. Secondary. Students compare the language of belonging in different life domains, such as home, school, club, work.	Teachers, family and leadership hold a shared understanding that context effects well-being language use and meaning. A variety of life experiences, in a variety of contexts, are collaboratively planned for students, such as school camps, fetes, or participation in valued community events. Well-being language is used purposefully adapted to suit the context.
The why of wellbeing literacy.	Habit of Intention. The habit of intentionally communicating for the purpose of intention. A mindful or skillful use of language with an intention, desire, and awareness about and for well-being.	I can purposefully use language (by listening, reading, viewing, writing, creating, and speaking) for and about my own well-being and that of others.	Early years. Students routinely engage with mindfulness practice during transition times, for the purpose of calming their minds and bodies. Primary. Students use the skill of perspective taking, during conflict resolution. Secondary. Students use the language of belonging to purposefully create cohort connection.	Teachers, family and leadership value well-being and the use of language to promote well-being within the whole system. Language about and for well-being is used by all, regularly and consistently, and is maintained over time. It is a natural and integrated part of life. Well-being language is visible in the artifacts, values, and culture of the system.

Wellbeing Literacy as a Model of Capability

WL is a capability about and for well-being. In educational discourse, the terms capability, *capacity, competence, skill,* and *ability* are often used interchangeably; however, they are distinct concepts (Scheffler, 1985; von Tunzelmann, 2009). Within this chapter's context, we define a *capability* as the fluid, dynamic, and interwoven formation of skills, knowledge, opportunities, choice, and behavior that emerge as an interaction between a person and the environment (Nussbaum, 2011; Scheffler, 1985; Sen, 1993). Capability is the autonomous skill within the students' minds, the behaviors they demonstrate, and the opportunities and freedom to flourish created by education experience and environment.

As a capability about and for well-being, WL is a relational process between a person and their environment, such as students and their school, possessing multiple interacting components. First, one must possess the words and knowledge *about* well-being. In other words, does the person have a word for describing well-being that helps them understand their experience (see Table 6.2)? Following this is one's ability to engage with words and knowledge in both receptive and productive aspects. People move toward comprehension and composition opportunities for language as a relational process between others and one's environment. Building upon comprehension and composition of one's language is an ability to demonstrate awareness of the contexts within which they use this knowledge and skills in adapting language for specific contexts. Lastly, in regard to literacy for well-being and literacy *for* well-being, one demonstrates behaviors that embrace choice and intentionality for using these words, skills, and knowledge for the intent of well-being *for* oneself and others (see Table 6.1). As one can see from these necessary components about and for, WL as a capability model is, therefore, more than merely a fixed skill, competence, or ability. The term capability becomes a distinct, dynamic core organizing concept, possessing multiple components that interact between people and their environments to create one's capability.

Wellbeing Literacy Capability Model in Action

Overall, the five-component WL model contains WL capability components and shows how they are related. The WL model applies to individuals and the systems within which they reside (see Table 6.2). To further understand the elements of Table 6.2, it is useful to consider a vignette of WL in an educational context to illustrate the capability model.

Sharing a book on mindfulness, a classroom teacher asks what the students think mindfulness means, and they respond: *being happy, looking at the stars, being quiet.* She writes the word "mindfulness" on the whiteboard and reads, "Mindfulness is about connecting with the world around us and the present moment. It helps to balance our minds and our bodies." The students listen, periodically answering questions and sharing ideas. Reading about mindful listening and mindful tasting, the teacher asks, "If we stop and listen now, what do we notice? What can we hear? What is your favorite food? How does it taste? (hot, salty, sweet, or sour)?" Children then use art materials to create giant-sized cakes and fruit, labeling their work with words about taste, savoring, feeling happy, and mindful. The artwork is displayed and used as a stimulus for future discussion and writing about ways bodies can be balanced in the present moment and feel well. Photographs are taken of the artworks and sent home. When children eat their lunch, the teacher roves between small groups and asks,

> If you stop and think mindfully, how does your food taste (hot, salty, sweet, or sour)? Can you remind yourself to stay in this moment of nourishing your body? How do your body and mind feel after you have eaten?

Later in the week, other sensory examples of mindfulness are explored (e.g., touching and smelling), and the teacher introduces a formal practice of mindfulness to the class. The Art teacher presents clay and other materials to represent what mindfulness may look like sculpturally. Music is played at the start of math class to encourage the students to reconnect with their bodies and focus on the present moment and cognitive challenges.

Through these cross-curricular activities and interactions, teachers in this scenario allow students opportunities to view, listen, read, write, speak, and create about mindfulness (as an area related to well-being). Through conversations and experiences regarding nutrition, presence, physicality, and senses, the teacher exposes the students to relevant language and knowledge about well-being (see Table 6.1). This learning experience delivered intentionally to build students' well-being, and sensitivity to their educational context exhibits the teacher's WL (see Table 6.2). In turn, students develop their WL as they explore the language, knowledge, and skills of well-being by reading, writing, listening, speaking, creating, and experiencing mindfulness. This vignette illustrates building capabilities about and for well-being within and through the simultaneous meeting of essential curriculum learning requirements. Additionally, this example could be viewed equally through the lens of early childhood education or the primary and secondary grades, with activities and experiences adapted to students' age and developmental stage.

Further, WL may be more compelling when taking action within multiple levels of a system. Consider the shared language of music in one well-being-literate school system. In a junior primary class, the teacher plays the audio of *Peter and the Wolf*, narrated along with The Melbourne Symphony Orchestra music. She asks her students: "Can you hear the bird? What does it sound like? How do you feel when you hear the bird? How do you think the bird feels?" Later, students work in small collaborative groups to put their own stories to percussive music; their stories' narratives and emotions are communicated through language and sound.

In an upper primary class, students are studying belonging and loneliness and how these impact well-being. The teacher shares the Vimeo clip of *The Orchestra* (https://www.featherfilms.com.au/portfolio/the-orchestra/) in which a band of tiny musicians follows a shy, older adult, Vernon, playing the soundtrack of his life. The teacher asks the students to think about an older person in their lives and how a day of belonging and connection might look for them. Students create a stop-motion animation about connection and belonging, as if through an older person's eyes. They accompany their stop motion animation with music that reflects the experiences and feelings of their character. Each stop motion movie includes a descriptive synopsis, using the language of music, belonging, connection, and well-being. The stop motion movies are shared with parents via digital learning portfolios.

Meanwhile, school leadership and the parent community representatives are planning for an upcoming school fair. Music is central to the day; students and parents perform musically to lift their well-being and others' well-being. The music teachers have worked with the student choir to perform. Songs have words deliberately chosen to uplift those singing and those listening. The music teachers know that this experience of being seen and performing well affords their students a mastery goal achievement experience and fosters self-efficacy. The leadership group knows that the music teachers needed extra time to work with the choir to prepare for the fair and scheduled an additional hour for rehearsal each week, releasing them from other duties at that time. When the multiple and diverse levels of a system, in this case, a school, engage in a shared and interconnected approach to WL, interventions and strategies become robust and sustainable capability-building opportunities.

Why Is Wellbeing Literacy Important to Positive Psychology in Schools?

Instead of viewing positive education as applying positive psychology into the existing education system, WL realizes an education system that equally includes promoting well-being capabilities alongside academic capabilities. Possessing the language, knowledge, and skills of well-being makes it possible to intentionally communicate for oneself and others as individuals, groups, and systems (including those within educational contexts). From this view, positive education is reconceptualized as more than the ad hoc implementation of PPIs. Positive education is conceptualized as building students' WL capabilities by habitually and intentionally communicating culturally aligned values, beliefs, and behaviors that facilitate well-being maintenance and enhancement. WL is discussed here as a fundamental tool for understanding PPIs and processes in schools and as a model for integrating positive psychology into the fabric of an education system.

One way to think of positive education is the delivery of PPIs. Paradoxically, the term intervention frames PPIs as illness oriented. In contrast, WL is rooted in a capability model, leaning toward a reorientation of PPIs, perhaps better termed PPPs (positive psychology practices), intended to build the capability of language use about and for well-being. Moreover, by nesting this approach within a humanistic view of education, which is necessarily a relationship between a teacher and learner, we have a more sophisticated understanding of positive educational processes. It is helpful to note here that WL is an umbrella term that encompasses multiple well-being domains. For example, emotional literacy (Sharp, 2000) should not be confused with WL per se; instead, conceptually, emotional literacy is a specific domain of WL. Health literacy (Nutbeam, 2000), and mental health literacy (Jorm, 2000), are also conceptually different from WL. Health literacy intends to improve safety and quality in health and mental health literacy concerns understanding mental disorders. WL is concerned with the flourishing end of the mental health continuum.

Positive education or PPIs are often evaluated and utilized based on well-being-related outcome measures, such as those derived from randomized controlled trials (RCT). However, PPI's effectiveness to enhance well-being and/or relieve distress has been recently challenged, with meta-analytic studies revealing relatively small effect sizes (White et al., 2019). Additionally, this well-being product focus leaves several important process questions unanswered. What was actually learned during the PPI? Do students apply learnings in the future? How did learning and teaching occur? What was the mechanism for change? Moreover, many PPIs are intended to foster "positive feelings, behaviors, or cognitions" (Sin & Lyubomirsky, 2009, p. 468), rather than being directed toward building well-being capabilities (i.e., the knowledge and skills available to impact their well-being positively). WL may be the intermediate construct that mediates (enables) or moderates (modifies) what is experienced in intervention and the well-being outcomes. We propose WL as necessary to optimize PPI effectiveness.

Wellbeing Literacy Implications for Schools

WL is proposed as a capability for students and is core to positive psychology in schools. However, schools may well ask, so what? What impacts, practical, useful, or not, does WL have on schools' core business—education? What does it provide for students, educators, or the school as a whole? These questions are rightly asked by institutions whose fundamental purpose is, arguably, education, not positive psychology.

However, schools are increasingly being called upon to respond to students' well-being. Alongside well-being as a subject to be taught, evidence suggests that school communities' relationships are essential to fostering students' well-being. Students' well-being has an interrelationship with school connectedness (Frydenberg et al., 2009), school climate and culture (Gray & Hackling, 2009; Zullig et al., 2011), teachers' well-being (Waters, 2011), and positive school relationships (Graham et al., 2016). In this case, a school setting can be viewed as an ecosystem, combining interactions with/between students and teachers, such as how they feel at school, the relationship they experience, and the participation and engagement with learning and socializing. For positive psychology to be applied effectively in schools, incorporating advances in knowledge and interventions from well-being science and contemporary positive education practices, new models such as WL must be explored.

We argue WL presents a model that not only engages educators but is practical, understandable, and does not add to an already crowded curriculum and workload. With these factors in mind, WL is proposed as a measurement tool, a frame for educational practices, and a language system bridge for schools and their stakeholders (e.g., students, teachers, and families).

Wellbeing Literacy as a Way to Measure the Proximal Gains of Positive Education

Importantly, positive education must be measured to evaluate program effectiveness and determine whether targeted constructs are nurtured (Waters & Loton, 2019). Measurement is needed to safeguard legitimacy, provide the evidence base for training and PPIs (White, 2016), and confirm the link between well-being and academic mastery (Adler & Seligman, 2016). If we value and promote positive education, we must endeavor to measure its constructs and effects (White & Kern, 2018). Ongoing and rigorous assessment of positive educational processes and well-being programs is necessary for the longevity of positive education and positive psychology applied to education (Seligman & Adler, 2018; Waters & Loton, 2019). Within schools, educators pursue evaluation of the effectiveness of pedagogical and well-being practices. Evaluation is critical as teachers are increasingly asked to combine positive educational practices and interventions with existing pedagogical practices (Adler & Seligman, 2016). Schools and educators need to know about expected outcomes and their attainment.

Previous literature has supported the contention that PPIs correlate to well-being gains (Bolier et al., 2013; Seligman & Adler, 2018; Sin & Lyubomirsky, 2009; Waters, 2011). However, more recent meta-analytic studies suggest small effect sizes (White et al., 2019). For positive education to endure (White, 2016), schools need reassurance that PPIs (or PPPs) work. For example, under what conditions are well-being skills of resilience, growth mindset, or character strengths being gained by students, if at all? As a capability model that measures positive educational practices' proximal outcomes, WL illuminates these obscure positive psychology areas in schools.

WL is measurable, either via self-report measures such as the WL Six-item Self-Report Scale (Well-Lit 6) (Hou et al., 2021) or via tracking skill acquisition (representing latent WL through developmental stages). Oades (2017) argues WL is an essential conduit between well-being interventions and student outcomes. Insight on well-being gains is possible when students are viewed as developing language skills, knowledge, and intentionality, related to well-being, enabling them to continue improving well-being over time. Instead of imposing an external intervention on students (Oades & Johnston, 2017), their capability is built. As students increase their capability to engage with PPIs and positive education, increased benefit from such interventions is available (Oades et al., 2020). Improved capabilities to comprehend and compose well-being language may increase students' likelihood of engaging with positive educational practices. Thus, more significant gains and insight are likely visible across the educational context and school system.

Questions about how students receive and effectively use (or not use) positive education can be posed in terms of WL. A student with high capability in well-being knowledge, skills, and language (i.e., high WL) may broadly and sustainably utilize the PPIs delivered in the classroom. Hence, arguably facilitating more robust well-being outcomes for a student for whom WL capabilities are low. In this way, WL is not only a conduit between interventions and outcomes (mediator) but a potential relationship influencer of the strength (moderator) of positive education (Oades et al., 2020).

Wellbeing Literacy Frames Positive Educational Processes

WL offers a frame for schools to engage educators in positive educational practices. Teachers should involve and inform parents about well-being and positive psychology through familiar and tangible literacy references. WL provides an avenue to integrate positive education into the fabric of the education system. The link between well-being and other disciplines' specific learning and teaching may not be immediately obvious (White & McCallum, 2020). However, WL draws on existing learning and teaching capacities to redesign the curriculum of positive psychology following the multiliteracies' pedagogy (Cope & Kalantzis, 2009; The New London Group, 1996), hence, encouraging multimodal learning and well-being (as demonstrated above in the section on WL in action). Additionally, WL learning and teaching can occur while simultaneously addressing existing curriculum requirements (ACARA, Australian Curriculum, 2020a, 2020b). WL reframes positive education as a purposeful and compelling direction for well-being education to navigate crowded curriculum barriers to prioritize and integrate well-being.

As a capability model, WL presents a frame for schools to view and deliver existing and/or new positive education practices rather than individual interventions or programs. The WL concept offers teachers and leaders a frame to select, convey, and connect specific interventions. Previous disparate practices, such as gratitude journaling in an English course, breathing exercises in Physical Education, reflective self-portraits in Art, charity collections, and buddy activities, are connected as comprehension and composition of well-being capabilities. Existing curricula of various labels (pastoral care, social-emotional learning, health, relationships, personal identity, positive education, and programs such as Mind Matters or MoodGYM) might not formally link to discrete curriculum outcomes under the higher-order frame of WL capabilities. Thus, the intangible and diverse definitions and dimensions of student well-being (Fraillon, 2004), along with voluminous and fragmented PPIs, have the potential to be operationalized and articulated through a WL frame.

The application of positive psychology in schools is growing globally and rapidly (Rusk & Waters, 2013; Seligman & Adler, 2018), offering a broad terrain of positive educational practices and processes for schools to consider. However, the conceptualization of well-being lacks clarity in schools and policy, leading to fragmentation and inconsistent implementation (Thomas, 2016; Thomas et al., 2016). Concerning the selection and application of PPIs, context, time, relevance, efficacy, and practicality need to be weighed by busy educators and schools as a whole. Ad hoc, one-off, inconsistent, and/or disconnected interventions are at risk of being utilized as practices are added enthusiastically or involuntarily to the curriculum. Within one school, PPI usage varies depending on teacher uptake or expertise, whole-school curriculum approaches, and philosophy. Arguments exist that, despite practices being well-meaning, ineffective or harmful effects can result (White, 2016; White & Kern, 2018; White & Murray, 2015).

Wellbeing Literacy Enables Us to Understand a School Community as a Language System

Finally, we assert that WL enables educators to understand a school community as a language system. A criticism of positive psychology is that it overemphasizes the individual within its approaches and interventions (Kern et al., 2020). So too could positive educational practices if they fail to view well-being as a complex and adaptive system beyond the individual student. Positive psychology in schools requires a system approach and interconnected view for effectiveness, sustainability, and longevity. Schools are a mesosystem consisting of inseparable and interdependent relationships, primarily of students (or peers), teachers, and parents (or families). Student well-being is vital to all parties in the system; however, communication about this complex and intangible construct is challenging. More so, explaining the teaching process for well-being and its relationship to academic outcomes is vital for those adept in pedagogy over psychology.

The pervasive role of contextual language use is an underutilized tool, particularly within positive education. Positive education exists within systems. Individual students are nested within multiple school systems, including teacher/student, student/student, student/parent, and parent/

teacher. These microsystems are then nested within larger school mesosystems, such as parent/ teacher/student. These interrelated parts and systems are mediated necessarily by language. Individual well-being, systemic well-being, and language are thus inseparable and interdependent. WL helps us use language to traverse all dimensions of well-being within the education system, as educators and students interact with language and with each other.

If WL assists the use of language to traverse all dimensions of well-being, it also bridges participants' educational landscape. A school leader and/or educator's task is arguably more manageable when all parties share a common language and expectations for well-being in education. Advantages exist for students (and teachers) when parents can "speak the language of schooling" (Clinton et al., 2007, p. 71), and parental expectations and ambitions for their child are both shared and realistic. WL offers a language of well-being that can belong to the system, forming a bridge of understanding and expectation from home to school. PPIs such as mindfulness, breathing, and gratitude more readily fit curricula and expectations of an academic system when bridged by the language of WL knowledge, skills, and capabilities.

We argue that, by weaving WL into the fabric of education, positive education may become more broadly accessible, acceptable, and sustainable at multiple system levels (e.g., students, parents, teachers, the wider community, and governing bodies). Synergistic commitment to positive education (both top-down and bottom-up), and thus sustained practice, may be achieved through the shared understandings and practices (overtime, across year levels, and contexts) achieved through WL. As a language system, WL supports the repositioning and reframing of communication interactions within education, becoming a systemic approach to understanding, building, and generating well-being. Understanding these language systems helps effective and sustained learning about and for well-being. This language system can generate well-being for the entire system, arguably advancing beyond the simple application and outcome evaluation of isolated well-being programs or PPIs.

Conclusion

Twenty-first-century learning and teaching require multiliterate, multimodal, and inclusive well-being education. To date, positive education processes have been underdeveloped conceptually, often associated with disparate understandings and practices within and between education contexts. WL, as a language-use capability, is a way to contextualize positive educational processes. Understanding and communicating WL capabilities, including the use of well-being language shared by educators, families, and students, holds promise for the systemic, sustainable adoption of positive psychology principles and practices in schools. Importantly, education, including positive psychology in schools, is relational. With this in mind, the role of educators in positive education is essential. Teaching students the vocabulary, knowledge, and language skills to positively affect their well-being and others' well-being may be the catalyst for a lifetime of well-being gains and generational change to individual and societal well-being.

References

Adler, A., & Seligman, M. E. P. (2016). Using wellbeing for public policy: Theory, measurement, and recommendations. *International Journal of Wellbeing, 6*(1), 1–35. https://doi.org/10.5502/ijw.v6i1.429

Australian Curriculum, Assessment and Reporting Authority. (2020a, June 16). *General capabilities.* https://www.australiancurriculum.edu.au/f-10-curriculum/general-capabilities/

Australian Curriculum, Assessment and Reporting Authority. (2020b, June 16). *Literacy.* https://www.australiancurriculum.edu.au/f-10-curriculum/general-capabilities/literacy/

Bolier, L., Haverman, M., Westerhof, G. J., Riper, H., Smit, F., & Bohlmeijer, E. (2013). Positive psychology interventions: A meta-analysis of randomized controlled studies. *BMC Public Health, 13*(1), 119. https://doi.org/10.1186/1471-2458-13-119

Brothers, C. (2005). *Language and the pursuit of happiness: A new foundation for designing your life, your relationships & your results.* New Possibilities Press.

Clinton, J., Hattie, J., & Dixon, R. (2007). *Evaluation of the Flaxmere Project: When families learn the language of school.* Ministry of Education New Zealand. https://www.educationcounts.govt.nz/publications/schooling/10001

Cope, B., & Kalantzis, M. (2009). "Multiliteracies": New literacies, new learning. *Pedagogies: An International Journal, 4*(3), 164–195. https://doi.org/10.1080/15544800903076044

Fraillon, J. (2004). *Measuring student well-being in the context of Australian schooling: Discussion paper.* Curriculum Corporation. https://research.acer.edu.au/well_being/8

Frydenberg, E., Care, E., Chan, E., & Freeman, E. (2009). Interrelationships between coping, school connectedness and wellbeing Erica Frydenberg. *Australian Journal of Education, 53*(3), 261–276. https://doi.org/10.1177/000494410905300305

Gee, J. P. (1998). What is literacy? In V. Zamel & R. Spack (Eds.), *Negotiating academic literacies: Teaching and learning across languages and cultures* (pp. 51–59). Lawrence Erlbaum.

Graham, A., Powell, M. A., & Truscott, J. (2016). Facilitating student well-being: Relationships do matter. *Educational Research, 58*(4), 366–383. https://doi.org/10.1080/00131881.2016.1228841

Gray, J., & Hackling, M. (2009). Wellbeing and retention: A senior secondary student perspective. *The Australian Educational Researcher, 36*(2), 119–145. https://doi.org/10.1007/BF03216902

Hou, H., Chin, T.-C., Slemp, G. R., & Oades, L. G. (2021). Wellbeing Literacy: Conceptualization, measurement, and preliminary empirical findings from students, parents and school staff. *International Journal of Environmental Research and Public Health, 18*(4), 1485. https://doi.org/10.3390/ijerph18041485

Huppert, F. A., & So, T. T. (2013). Flourishing across Europe: Application of a new conceptual framework for defining well-being. *Social Indicators Research, 110*(3), 837–861. https://doi.org/10.1007/s11205-011-9966-7

Jorm, A. F. (2000). Mental health literacy: Public knowledge and beliefs about mental disorders. *The British Journal of Psychiatry, 177*(5), 396–401. https://doi.org/10.1192/bjp.177.5.396

Kern, M. L., Williams, P., Spong, C., Colla, R., Sharma, K., Downie, A., Taylor, J. A., Sharp, S., Siokou, C., & Oades, L. G. (2020). Systems informed positive psychology. *The Journal of Positive Psychology, 15*(6), 705–715. https://doi.org/10.1080/17439760.2019.1639799

Malle, B.F., & Knobe, J. (1997). The folk concept of intentionality. *Journal of Experimental and Social Psychology, 33*, 101–121. https://doi.org/10.1006/jesp.1996.1314

Norrish, J. M., Williams, P., O'Connor, M., & Robinson, J. (2013). An applied framework for positive education. *International Journal of Wellbeing, 3*(2), 147–161. https://doi.org/10.5502/ijw.v3i2.2

Nussbaum, M. C. (2011). *Creating capabilities: The human development approach.* Harvard University Press.

Nutbeam, D. (2000). Health literacy as a public health goal: A challenge for contemporary health education and communication strategies into the 21st century. *Health Promotion International, 15*(3), 259–267. https://doi.org/10.1093/heapro/15.3.259

Oades, L. G. (2017). Wellbeing literacy: The missing link in positive education. In M. A. White, G. R. Slemp, & A. S. Murray (Eds.), *Future directions in well-being: Education, organizations and policy.* (pp. 169–173). Springer. https://doi.org/10.1007/978-3-319-56889-8_29

Oades, L. G., & Johnston, A. L. (2017). Wellbeing literacy: The necessary ingredient in positive education. *Psychology and Behavioural Science International Journal, 3*(5), 555621. https://doi.org/10.19080/PBSIJ.2017.03.555621

Oades, L. G., Ozturk, C., Hou, H., & Slemp, G. R. (2020). Wellbeing literacy: A Language-use capability relevant to wellbeing outcomes of positive psychology intervention. *The Journal of Positive Psychology, 15*(5), 696–700. https://doi.org/10.1080/17439760.2020.1789711

Perry, K. H. (2012). What is literacy? — A critical overview of sociocultural perspectives. *Journal of Language and Literacy Education, 8*(1), 50–71. https://files.eric.ed.gov/fulltext/EJ1008156.pdf

Rich, G. J. (2018, 2018/05//). Positive psychology and humanistic psychology: Evil twins, sibling rivals, distant cousins, or something else? *Journal of Humanistic Psychology, 58*(3), 262–283. https://doi.org/10.1177/0022167817698820

Robbins, B. D. (2008). What is the good life? Positive psychology and the renaissance of humanistic psychology. *The Humanistic Psychologist, 36*(2), 96–112. https://doi.org/10.1080/08873260802110988

Rusk, R. D., & Waters, L. E. (2013). Tracing the size, reach, impact, and breadth of positive psychology. *The Journal of Positive Psychology, 8*(3), 207–221. https://doi.org/10.1080/17439760.2013.777766

Rutyer, D., Oades, L., & Waghid, Y. (2020). *Meaning(s) of human flourishing and education* [Research brief]. International Science and Evidence Based Education Assessment. UNESCO MGIEP. https://

d1c337161ud3pr.cloudfront.net/files%2Fa8cd2349-650b-4312-8950-750fe87497e0_Flourishing%20 and%20Education.pdf

Scheffler, I. (1985). *Of human potential. An essay in the philosophy of education.* Routledge.

Seligman, M. E. P., & Adler, A. (2018). Positive education. In J. F. Helliwell, R. Layard, & J. Sachs (Eds.), *Global happiness policy report: 2018* (pp. 52–73). Global Happiness Council. http://www.happinesscouncil.org/

Sen, A. (1993). Capability and well-being. In M. C. Nussbaum & A. Sen (Eds.), *The quality of life* (pp. 30–53). Clarendon Press.

Sharp, P. (2000). Promoting emotional literacy: Emotional literacy improves and increases your life chances. *Pastoral Care in Education, 18*(3), 8–10. https://doi.org/10.1111/1468-0122.00165

Sin, N. L., & Lyubomirsky, S. (2009). Enhancing well-being and alleviating depressive symptoms with positive psychology interventions: A practice-friendly meta-analysis. *Journal of Clinical Psychology, 65*(5), 467–487. https://doi.org/10.1002/jclp.20593

Snow, C. (1983). Literacy and language: Relationships during the preschool years. *Harvard Educational Review, 53*(2), 165–189. https://doi.org/10.17763/haer.53.2.t6177w39817w2861

Street, B. (2003). What's "new" in new literacy studies? Critical approaches to literacy in theory and practice. *Current Issues in Comparative Education, 5*(2), 77–91.

Taylor, E. (2001, 2001/01//). Positive psychology and humanistic psychology: A reply to Seligman. *Journal of Humanistic Psychology, 41*(1), 13–29. https://doi.org/10.1177/0022167801411003

The New London Group. (1996). A pedagogy of multiliteracies: Designing social futures. *Harvard Educational Review, 66*(1), 60–93. https://doi.org/10.17763/haer.66.1.17370n67v22j160u

Thomas, I. (2016). Challenges for implementation of education for sustainable development in higher education institutions. In M. Barth, G. Michelsen, M. Rieckmann, & I. Thomas (Eds.), *Routledge handbook of higher education for sustainable development* (pp. 56–71). Routledge. https://doi.org/10.4324/9781315852249

Thomas, N., Graham, A., Powell, M. A., & Fitzgerald, R. (2016). Conceptualisations of children's well-being at school: The contribution of recognition theory. *Childhood, 23*(4), 506–520. https://doi.org/10.1177/0907568215622802

von Tunzelmann, N. (2009). Competencies versus capabilities: A reassessment. *Economia Politica, 26*(3), 435–464. https://doi.org/10.1428/30999

Waters, L. (2011). A review of school-based positive psychology interventions. *The Australian Educational and Developmental Psychologist, 28*(2), 75–90. https://doi.org/10.1375/aedp.28.2.75

Waters, L., & Loton, D. (2019, 2019/09/01). SEARCH: A meta-framework and review of the field of positive education. *International Journal of Applied Positive Psychology, 4*, 1–46. https://doi.org/10.1007/s41042-019-00017-4

White, C. A., Uttl, B., & Holder, M. D. (2019). Meta-analyses of positive psychology interventions: The effects are much smaller than previously reported. *PloS one, 14*(5), e0216588. https://doi.org/10.1371/journal.pone.0216588

White, M. A. (2016). Why won't it stick? Positive psychology and positive education. *Psychology of Well-Being, 6*(1), 2. https://doi.org/10.1186/s13612-016-0039-1

White, M. A., & Kern, M. L. (2018). Positive education: Learning and teaching for wellbeing and academic mastery. *International Journal of Wellbeing, 8*(1), 1–17. https://doi.org/10.5502/ijw.v8i1.588

White, M. A., & McCallum, F. (2020). Responding to teacher quality through an evidence-informed well-being framework for initial teacher education. In J. Fox, C. Alexander, & T. Aspland (Eds.), *Teacher education in globalised times* (pp. 115–137). Springer. https://doi.org/10.1007/978-981-15-4124-7_7

White, M. A., & Murray, A. S. (2015). Building a positive institution. In M. A. White & A. S. Murray (Eds.), *Evidence-based approaches in positive education* (pp. 1–26). Springer. https://doi.org/10.1007/978-94-017-9667-5_1

Zullig, K. J., Huebner, E. S., & Patton, J. M. (2011). Relationships among school climate domains and school satisfaction. *Psychology in the Schools, 48*(2), 133–145. https://doi.org/10.1002/pits.20532

7

OPTIMISM IN THE CLASSROOM AND BEYOND

Peter Boman and Timothy Hsi

Introduction

A pessimist sees the difficulty in every opportunity; an optimist sees the opportunity in every difficulty.

— *Winston Churchill*

Optimism has its modern roots in philosophy, dating back to the 17th century in the writings of philosophers such as Descartes and Voltaire (Domino & Conway, 2001). The word optimism can be traced back to the Modern Latin word *optimum* and essentially meant "the greatest good" or the Latin word *optimus* meaning "the best" (see https://www.etymonline.com/word/optimism). Previous to these philosophical writings, the teachings of many great spiritual traditions such as Buddhism and Christianity revealed the concept of optimism (Miller et al., 2001). In the 20th century, optimism became defined in juxtaposition to pessimism, sometimes conceptualized as a bipolar unidimensional construct and by others as two related, but separate constructs (Garber, 2000). Contemporary models of optimism have generally studied optimism as a general dispositional orientation, described by expectancy theory and as an explanatory process, described by explanatory style theory (Scheier & Carver, 1994; Seligman, 2011).

Optimism Theoretical Perspectives

Optimism as an expectancy is having the "confidence that the goal can be obtained" (Carver et al., 2010, p. 2). From the expectancy perspective, optimism and pessimism are forward-looking, proactive dispositional tendencies. In explanatory style theory, optimism and pessimism are immediate, reactive tendencies, used to explain the cause of events, associated with a general coping response. In these views, expectancy is a generalized belief about goal attainment, and explanatory style describes a predominant process of cognitive mediation.

Optimism and Pessimism as Generalized Expectancy

There are no universally agreed-upon definitions for dispositional optimism and pessimism (Chang et al., 2009). However, researchers have offered related definitions that involve biases in

DOI: 10.4324/9781003013778-10

generalized positive or negative expectations for future events (Peterson & Chang, 2003). Optimism has been defined as (a) the tendency to expect positive outcomes (Hmieleski & Baron, 2009), (b) the belief that positive events exceed negative ones (Sharot, 2011), or a tendency to look on the bright side of things (Silva et al., 2004). Conversely, pessimism has been defined as (a) failure expectancy (Schueller & Seligman, 2008), (b) anticipating adverse outcomes, or (c) a tendency to take a gloomy view of things (Carver et al., 2010).

Both optimism and pessimism have been associated with the coping strategies that individuals use (Carver et al., 2008; Chang et al., 2009; Helton et al., 2005). Optimism is linked with adaptive strategies such as problem-solving, obtaining social support, and looking for any positive aspects in stressful situations. On the other hand, pessimism is related to maladaptive strategies, namely, problem avoidance, denial, withdrawal, and the failure to complete goals when a stressor intrudes. Concerning the school environment, in their study with 102 year 8 students, Boman and Yates (2001) found that optimistic children were more successful in transitioning from primary school to high school revealed through lower levels of depression, anxiety, and school hostility. In another study with 199 children with cancer aged 7–18, Williams et al. (2010) found that children who had higher levels of optimism experienced less pain and had better emotional coping. Overall, optimism and pessimism can be expected to play an essential role in generalized outcomes or in situations where the individual has no previous experience.

Optimism and Pessimism as a Cognitive Explanatory Style

Seligman (2011) advanced another influential theory that incorporated the constructs of optimism and pessimism. This perspective emphasized the role of cognitive explanatory style and emerged from learned helplessness research that focused on individuals with depression (Seligman, 1975). Learned helplessness refers to expectations that lead depressed persons to conclude that there is nothing they can do to help or control future outcomes. This expectation develops from a person's experiences with uncontrollable events where attempted coping strategies did not help. The belief that one lacks control leads to lowered response initiation and persistence (motivational deficits), an inability to perceive new opportunities for control (cognitive deficits), and lowered self-esteem and increased sadness (emotional deficits) (Seligman, 1975).

However, the theory of learned helplessness was critiqued on several grounds (Miller, 2008; Seligman, 2006). First, not all vulnerable people became helpless and, of those who did, some never recovered while others responded positively almost immediately. Second, some people only gave up in the immediate situation they faced, whereas others gave up in new situations. Third, some people blamed themselves for their circumstances, and others blamed someone or something in the surrounding environment. Seligman and other researchers turned to attribution theory (Weiner et al., 1971) to address outcomes that learned helplessness theory did not predict (Seligman, 2006).

Weiner et al.'s (1971) attribution theory posited that certain causal interpretations of other individuals' behaviors or events largely determine both emotional and behavioral reactions to achievement or failure. These include whether the cause is (a) viewed as internal or external to the person, (b) its perception as stable or permanent over time, and (c) the degree to which the other views it as controllable or uncontrollable.

Seligman and others drew from Weiner's theory, but their application differed in several ways (Abramson et al., 1978; Seligman, 2011). This modified theory stated that individuals have a habitual explanation style, not just a single explanation for each discrete failure experience. To this end, they added the third dimension of pervasiveness to Weiner's permanent and personal dimensions (Seligman et al., 1984, 1988). Finally, they shifted the focus from achievement to mental illness and therapy (e.g., Reivich et al., 2005). This perception shift became the basis of explanatory style theory operationalized for children and adolescents (Gillham et al., 2001).

In essence, children and adolescents can differ in their manner of personal attributions; that is, their style of explanation. Those with pessimistic explanatory styles are more inclined to use *permanent* ("It always happens this way"), *personal* ("It's my fault"), and *pervasive* ("It affects everything I do") causal attribution dimensions when facing hardship, setbacks, challenges, or stressful circumstances. Those with optimistic explanatory styles are more inclined to perceive setbacks as only temporary, not being their fault, and limited to the immediate incident. When faced with good events, these styles of explanation are reversed. Those with a pessimistic explanatory style would see a good event as temporary, not their fault, and only an isolated incident. Conversely, children and adolescents with an optimistic explanatory style see the same event as permanent, being caused by them, and as all-encompassing. These explanatory styles are formed when the youth models the behavior of parents and other significant adults (Seligman et al., 1995).

Comparing Expectancy and Explanatory Style Perspectives

Scheier and Carver (1992) reported several studies where explanatory style did not correlate strongly with dispositional optimism and pessimism. Overall, correlations have tended not to be more than .20. In a study with Grade 8 students, Boman (2002) found a nonsignificant relation between dispositional optimism and explanatory style. Scheier and Carver believe the limited amount of conceptual overlap is due to the different foci of the two theories; that is, causal explanations for specific events as opposed to generalized expectations for the future. Garber (2000) suggests that "there is a clear conceptual and empirical difference between attributions and expectancies" (p. 303) but also that attributions may predict expectations. Once a person explains the cause of an event, expectations maintain the positive or negative affect associated with that event.

Measurement of Optimism

Assessing Optimism and Pessimism as Generalized Expectancy

Despite the generally accepted view that optimism and pessimism play a role in coping and adjustment, there are two opposing views about how they should be measured (Chang et al., 2009; Fischer & Leitenberg, 1986; Myers & Steed, 1999; Olason & Roger, 2001). Some researchers consider optimism and pessimism to be a single bipolar continuum. Therefore, a person is either optimistic or pessimistic, but cannot be both. Conversely, the partially dependent view sees both as capable of existing within a person. Scheier and Carver's (1992) unidimensional view of optimism and pessimism has tended to be the dominant view, but not all researchers see an optimist as being devoid of pessimism.

Other researchers have suggested that optimism and pessimism are partially dependent dimensions (Chang et al., 2009; Fischer & Leitenberg, 1986). All of these studies reveal optimism and pessimism as yielding two separable, but correlated factors. In a 2007 German study, Pinquart et al., (2007) also found that optimism and pessimism are interrelated but independent dimensions. Interestingly, Pais-Ribeiro et al. (2012), in two studies with over 900 participants, found support for seeing optimism and pessimism as both one-dimensional or bidimensional depending on the purpose of the study.

Chang et al. (2009) suggest that when defining optimism and pessimism as positive or negative outcome expectancies, the partially dependent model appears to be more appropriate. Chang and Bridewell's (1998) study of undergraduate students reported those who more often endorsed irrational beliefs (e.g., "I absolutely should not have made obvious mistakes in my life") were significantly more pessimistic. However, they were not found to be less optimistic. This finding supports the partially dependent view of optimism and pessimism, which states a pessimist is not considered absent of optimism but has higher numbers of irrational beliefs than an optimist.

Assessing Optimism and Pessimism as Expectancy

The Life Orientation Test (LOT; Scheier & Carver, 1985) and the Revised Life Orientation Test (LOT-R; Scheier et al., 1994) are the most widely used assessments of dispositional optimism and pessimism. The LOT and LOT-R were designed to be a unidimensional measure of optimism in that the pessimism scores are reversed and added to the optimism scores. The LOT has 12 items, four of which are fillers. Four items are positively worded (e.g., "I always look on the bright side of things"), and four are negatively worded ("If something can go wrong for me it will"). The LOT-R has 10 items with three positively and three negatively worded items plus four fillers. There was some LOT item content overlap, so some original items were removed (Chang, 2001). Three other scales, the Expanded Life Orientation Test (ELOT; Chang et al., 1997), the Generalized Expectancy for Success Scale (Fibel & Hale, 1978), and the Optimism and Pessimism Scale (Dember et al., 1989), have been developed, but have not been used as extensively in research.

Research with adolescents uses the ELOT (Boman & Yates, 2001; Boman et al., 2003) but more recently, the Youth Life Orientation Test (YLOT) was developed specifically for children and adolescents (Ey et al., 2005; Taylor et al., 2004). The YLOT is a 16-item self-report measure created to better evaluate optimism and pessimism in school-age children. LOT-R item wording is developmentally appropriate for children. Additional items that reflect positive and negative expectations were added to the scale yielding a total of seven optimism items, seven pessimism items, and two filler items, all on a 4-point Likert scale—children respond using on a scale of 0–3 (0 = *not true for me* to 3 = *true for me*). The scale produces three scores: optimism, pessimism, and a total optimism score in response to the long-standing question of whether optimism and pessimism represent two separate constructs or opposite ends of a bipolar continuum. The initial administration of the instrument reported internal consistencies in the acceptable range through Cronbach alpha coefficients (optimism = 0.70, pessimism = 0.78, and total optimism = 0.83). However, this only applied to Grades 3–6 because Cronbach alphas for the first and second graders were unacceptable. After the original study, Williams et al. (2010), in a study with 199 children (mean age of 11) with cancer, used confirmatory factor analysis to validate the structure of the YLOT. More recently, a 2018 study with Spanish children (aged between 8 and 11) also replicated the factor structure of the YLOT (Gonzálvez et al., 2018).

Assessing Optimism and Pessimism as an Explanatory Style

According to Seligman (2006), explanatory style is a cognitive personality variable that plays a role in adjustment to various life situations. A person's response as explanatory style can be assessed by a specially designed instrument, the Attributional Style Questionnaire (Peterson et al., 1988). The instrument measured personal, permanent, and pervasive dimensions concerning specific events after initially asking to state a cause for that event. Seligman (2006) suggested removing the personal dimension due to the concern over the possible lessening of the sense of personal responsibility through the optimist's use of blaming others (externality) for failures. Although developed initially to incorporate positive and negative events, research has revealed that causal explanations about bad events reflect stronger correlations than good events (Peterson & Steen, 2009). This relationship is not surprising, as memories for adverse events are more likely to persist than good events (Kensinger, 2007).

The Attributional Style Questionnaire (ASQ) is the most commonly used measure associated with evaluating explanatory style (Peterson & Steen, 2009). Several new versions of the ASQ have been designed to target specific audiences or settings (Chang & Sanna, 2007;

Dykema et al., 1996; Furnham et al., 1992; Lieber, 1997; Mayerson, 1991; Norman, 1988; Peterson & Villanova, 1988; Whitley, 1991). This is in line with Peterson's (2009) development of various forms of the ASQ that use the original format but adjust the stimulus events to be relevant to the target population. The ASQ generally has a series of events to which a person initially responds to a possible cause and then follows with items that measure permanent and pervasive explanatory style dimensions. For example, Boman et al. (2003) developed a version for use with high school students that utilized 12 hypothetical negative events, which reflected situations likely to occur within the school context (e.g., "You fail a test or an examination"). Students wrote a main cause for the event, recording *permanent* ("How likely is it that this cause will continue to affect you?") and *pervasive* ("Is this cause something that just affects failing a test or does it affect other areas of your life?") responses. The Cronbach alphas were strong at 0.90 and 0.93, respectively.

Children's Attributional Style Questionnaire

The Children's Attributional Style Questionnaire (CASQ; Kaslow et al., 1978) is the most widely used measure of explanatory style for children (Reivich & Gillham, 2003). This 48-item forced-choice questionnaire has the same structure as the ASQ but was altered to be developmentally appropriate for children as young as eight years old. Each item consists of a hypothetical scenario (24 positive and 24 negative) followed by two statements explaining why the event happened. Children choose the statement that best explains why the event took place. For example, one item is, "you get an 'A' on a test." The child chooses between "I am smart" or because "I am good in the subject that the test was in." Items measure the child's attributional or explanatory style (internal versus external, global versus specific, and stable versus unstable).

The CASQ yields three scores: positive composite score, negative composite score, and overall composite score. Psychometric examinations of the CASQ show moderate internal consistency for all three scores: (0.47–0.73) for positive scores, (0.42–0.67) for negative scores, and 0.62 for the overall composite scores. Also, there was moderate stability with test-retest reliability of 0.71 for positive scores and 0.66 for negative scores at six months, and 0.35 for the overall composite score at 12 months (Thompson et al., 1998). More recently, a study found partial substantiation for the validity of the CASQ (Reijntjes et al., 2008). Overall, the CASQ is a widely used instrument that offers valuable information. However, the lengthy nature is not always ideal for limited administration time or when assessing children with short attention spans.

In response to this concern, Kaslow and Nolen-Hoeksema (1991) developed the Children's Attributional Style Questionnaire-Revised (CASQ-R) is a 24-item forced-choice measure adapted from the original CASQ. The measure was designed to be a more user-friendly assessment, catering to children's short attention spans. To create this new revised measure, the original CASQ was administered to 449 elementary school children. The responses were analyzed. The items with the weakest item-total correlations were dropped, leaving 12 positive composite items with a correlation of 0.14 or higher, and 12 negative composite items with a correlation of 0.08 or higher.

Thompson and colleagues evaluated the psychometric structure of the revised measure to compare reliability and validity to the original CASQ (Thompson et al., 1998). The CASQ-R was then administered to 1085 (515 boys and 570 girls) students aged 9–12 years old. Internal consistency of the CASQ-R using Fisher's r-to-z transformation showed no age or gender differences; however, the CASQ-R was more internally consistent for European American students than African American students. The stability of the CASQ-R over six months showed no gender, race, or age differences (Thompson et al., 1998). Overall, results comparing the CASQ-R and the CASQ show that the CASQ-R is psychometrically sound and is appropriate when time constraints are an issue. However, if time allows, the CASQ would be the measure of choice.

Can Optimism Be Changed?

In recent years, schools' vital role in developing students' strengths and positive values has been identified (Lovat et al., 2010). The positive psychology movement has focused on facilitating individuals to lead flourishing lives centered on well-being (Seligman et al., 1995). This focus stimulated the development of programs aimed at enhancing all students' well-being, not just those facing difficulties (Kibe & Boniwell, 2015; McGrath & Noble, 2010). Many of these programs take a holistic approach by exploring a range of areas including individual factors (optimism, personal responsibility, and problem-solving), social factors (developing friendships, prosocial behavior, and bullying), and school-based factors (e.g., student engagement/ connection, relationships between teachers and students).

Before moving to some of the programs that are available to schools, there is something essential to consider concerning optimism. As Fredrickson (2011) says, "Whether we seek it or not, negativity has a way of finding us" (p. 136). That is, life will not be positive all the time, so it is also about coping when considering optimism. Fredrickson describes the positivity ratio, which suggests that a minimum for an optimistic life is three positive events to one negative. In essence, children need challenges with which to cope in their lives and not just the absence of anything negative. For example, debating ideas and being asked to support them is a challenge worth having for a child. Being challenged to meet higher levels of attainment, for example, reading 10 pages of a book instead of five before bedtime, while being positively supported helps breed optimism. As she says: Without negativity, you become Pollyanna, with a forced clown smile painted on your face. You lose touch with reality. You're not genuine. In time, you drive others away (Fredrickson, 2011, p. 136). So as we review several optimism programs, it is essential to remember that life is not all positivity. However, those with higher levels of optimism learn to cope with life's difficulties better and not just try to ignore them.

In general, school-based programs to promote optimism, well-being and, mental health have produced mixed results. Seligman and others developed the Penn Prevention Program to change the explanatory style (how one explains positive and negative events) and prevent depressive symptoms in at-risk 10- to 13-year-old children in America (Seligman et al., 1995; Shatte et al., 1999). The program included training in developing an optimistic explanatory style (feeling able to positively impact negative events that affect us and taking appropriate ownership of our role in the positive events we experience) and positive social skills. It was effective in reducing depressive symptoms and improving classroom behavior. A two-year follow-up study by Gillham et al. (1995) confirmed the effectiveness of the prevention program. Overall, these children had a positive change in explanatory style and used more optimistic thinking (Shatte et al., 1999). More recently, this program has been called the Penn Resiliency Program (PRP) and subsequent studies have all reported successful results (see Gillham et al., 2001; Reivich et al., 2005). These studies have shown improved explanatory styles and lower levels of depressive tendencies across cultures.

Several similar programs have undergone school-based trials based on the successful evaluations of PRP in America. There have been a limited number of random controlled trials conducted for these programs with varying results, ranging from positive and significant outcomes to inconclusive and insignificant results. These equivocal findings may be due to the small sample sizes employed in some studies, high attrition rates, and poor design (as per criteria published by the Society for Prevention Research), as opposed to the effectiveness of the programs themselves (Horowitz & Garber, 2006; Spence & Shortt, 2007).

An initiative occurring in Australia that uses a range of school-based programs to support well-being and mental health is the Be You program. This program integrates five existing programs (KidsMatter Early Childhood, KidsMatter Primary, MindMatters, Response Ability, and Headspace School Support) into one single national initiative across Australia. This initiative, funded by the Australian Government and led by Beyond Blue with Early Childhood Australia and Headspace as delivery partners, supports schools and children from early childhood (including extended childcare) to primary school (aged 4–18; Be You, n.d.). The initiative centers on four overarching components, including a positive school community, social and emotional learning for students, parenting support and education, and early intervention for students experiencing mental health difficulties. Within each component, a range of school-based programs are available, and schools are encouraged to select programs that they feel would most benefit their school and the broader community. While this initiative focuses on and develops many personal characteristics that support students, particular attention is paid to optimism as a protective factor for an individual child's mental health (Beyond Blue, 2020). The Australian Government's investment in the Be You initiative demonstrates the growing belief that schools play a fundamental role in developing a range of strengths and skills in students, including their social and emotional competence.

One program designed to prevent internalizing problems and enhance optimism in upper primary school students (i.e., Grades 6 and 7), and listed as a resource within the Be You framework, is the Aussie Optimism Program. This program was based directly on the Penn Resiliency Program, although modified to suit the Australian school system timetable and culture (Bishop & Roberts, 2005; Roberts et al., 2011; Roberts & Rudge, 2015). The program has two components: the Optimistic Thinking Skills Program (Roberts et al., 2002), and the Social Life Skills Program (Roberts et al., 2002). The optimism component explores children's beliefs about themselves, their life circumstances, and their futures and teaches them to identify and challenge those beliefs that are negative. Children are then encouraged to consider explanations for their lives that may be more optimistic and realistic. Importantly, children are taught strategies and techniques to assist them with identifying, labeling, and monitoring their feelings (Roberts, 2006). The social component of the program involves teaching children listening skills, assertiveness, negotiation, social problem-solving skills, decision-making, perspective-taking, and coping skills (Roberts, 2006).

The Aussie Optimism Program (AOP) has been used extensively in Western Australia, where it was initially developed and implemented in schools across Australia. Quayle et al. (2001) implemented the program with seventh-grade girls (11 and 12 years old) using a random control trial. Results revealed no significant difference in symptoms of depression, pessimism, or global self-worth between the control and intervention groups at posttest. A significant difference was found between these groups at the six-month follow-up; however, girls in the intervention group reported significantly fewer depressive symptoms than control group girls. Further evaluation of the program involved a larger random controlled trial of preadolescents with elevated levels of depression (Roberts et al., 2003, 2004) with no significant effect size differences for depression on any of the follow-up tests. There was a small intervention effect for anxiety at posttest, and the six-month and 30-month follow-ups. However, a study by Swannell et al. (2009) showed that Grade 8 students in Queensland who exhibited high levels of depression and emotional/behavioral difficulties before undertaking the program demonstrated significantly lower levels in these areas after completing the intervention. Roberts et al. (2011) used the AOP intervention with 3,288 students, aged 10–13 years, to see its effect on substance use. At a 12-month follow-up, they found that higher levels of optimism were associated with lower levels of alcohol and tobacco use.

Another program with varied results is the Problem Solving for Life Program (PSFL) directed at secondary school students (Grades 8–10). This preadolescent depression prevention program promotes optimistic thinking by teaching better problem-solving skills. There have been two major randomized controlled trial studies conducted for the PSFL program, which employed larger sample sizes compared to the majority of other program evaluations. The first study's initial results found a significant decrease in depressive symptoms among the participants in the high risk for the depression intervention group compared with the high-risk control group (Spence et al., 2003).

Likewise, the low risk for depression intervention group also showed fewer depressive symptoms than the low-risk control group, although the effect size was smaller. These results were not maintained at the 12-month follow-up. Subsequent follow-up studies conducted at two-, three-, and four-year intervals again showed no significant intervention effects (Spence et al., 2005). In the second random controlled trial study, the results were even less effective with interventions showing no effect at any of the time points (Sheffield et al., 2006).

Overall, while school-based prevention programs for promoting optimism and changing depressive cognitions have yielded some promising and varying results, more research is needed to establish their long-term effectiveness (Merry et al., 2004). Meta-analyses suggest that specific (as opposed to universal) approaches appear to have more consistent results, but routine screening would render these approaches less sustainable over time. Most of the successful outcomes for promoting optimism, in particular, have been with the preadolescent age group. Limited longitudinal data are available to assess the long-term effects of increasing optimism and resilience in children concerning many areas other than protection against some mental health problems.

Despite these limitations, support for school-based programs that promote positive emotions and values, individual strengths, positive character traits, and meaningful connections between students and schools is growing (Noble & McGrath, 2008). Research is beginning to show that school-based programs, and whole-school approaches, that develop positive values and character traits in students, result in positive outcomes for students, teachers, and school communities (Benninga et al., 2006; DEST, 2008; Lovat et al., 2010). Many teachers choose teaching as their profession as they wish to shape, support, and care for students (Krečič & Grmek, 2005; Watt & Richardson, 2007). Adopting programs that focus on optimism, life skills, and other supportive factors is one way that teachers can impact students' lives. Complementary efforts involve additional everyday classroom practices that can positively influence students' optimism.

Building Optimism in the Classroom

Teachers and other significant people, such as coaches, influence children. One could also presume optimistic teachers would be better able to cope with life and school-related stress. A recent study by Tyson et al. (2009) investigated whether the Aussie Optimism Program provided mental health-related benefits to teachers who teach it. The researchers argued that teachers trained to implement the program to support their students might use the strategies learned in their professional lives. The results revealed that teachers who received program training and additional coaching support from school psychologists reported significantly lower levels of job-related anxiety and depression than teachers in training only and control groups. This study shows that while teaching mental health programs may provide related benefits to teachers, this only occurs when teachers are appropriately trained and receive on-going coaching support. To promote optimism and coping in students, teachers need to have experiences that support the development and maintenance of optimism in their own teaching experiences.

According to Jensen et al. (2004), teachers seem to think they are positive and see themselves as using positive techniques to manage classroom behaviors. However, these self-reports of positiveness are in contrast to observations of teachers in their classrooms. For example, Boman and Yates (2001) found that although optimism was the single most critical predictor of a student's successful transition to high school, the teachers' views of a successful transition were only predicted by gender. That is, if the teacher knew the student was female, then they were more likely to predict a successful transition while if they knew the student was male an unsuccessful transition was predicted. In general, although a student may have an optimistic disposition, teachers were not necessarily likely to recognize and develop this asset. In another study that analyzed differences between teachers' beliefs and behavior, Russo and Boman (2007) found that although teachers reported a very sound knowledge of resilience, they were not as successful in recognizing which children were resilient. That is, teachers may not be as aware of children's strengths or weaknesses as they might suggest. Some teachers may need more professional development in these areas to help them move beyond the theoretical knowledge and develop the necessary practical skills to help children develop their optimism and other positive attributes.

Nevertheless, teachers can generally promote optimism by their attributions about students' successes or failures in the classroom (Dweck et al., 1978). By attributing success to effort, or failure to lack of effort, teachers can help promote a sense of optimism in their students. They can also help students learn to solve problems and look for alternatives in addressing troubling issues (Seligman, 2011; Seligman et al., 1995). The role modeling that teachers do in the classroom is very powerful. Teachers need to demonstrate a positive explanatory style where they focus on things that are going well and discuss the effort they are committing to a task (Noble & McGrath, 2007). Teachers should model problem-solving in the classroom and show students there is always something they can do rather than giving up.

It is integral that teachers make social and emotional learning a regular occurrence in the classroom, and offer students many opportunities to explicitly learn and practice these skills (Be You, n.d.b). Providing group work activities and engaging students in explicit discussions around emotional awareness and prosocial behaviors are meaningful ways for teachers to help develop optimism and competency in students (Noble & McGrath, 2007). Being realistic in feedback to students is also crucial in helping to develop optimism. Students know when they have not put their best effort into something. Giving students honest, constructive feedback rather than trying to protect their feelings helps them learn that their effort or behavior may be the problem and not them personally.

Sagor (2008) argues that there are two key variables that teachers need to nurture in students in order for students to develop optimism: faith in the future and personal efficacy. Faith in the future requires students to believe that the work and energy they invest today will pay off for them in the future. He argues that while some students can see the benefits of hard work in their environment, other students may not. These students are in most need of teachers who believe in them and offer them insight into how their effort can be rewarded. Personal efficacy is the deep-seated belief that individuals have in their ability. Students will develop and maintain optimistic thinking when they see that they are capable of achieving what they want to achieve. Teachers can demonstrate to students that effort and hard work will pay off, and encourage students to continue with challenging tasks to experience success. Sagor (2008) encourages all teachers to ponder whether their students will leave the classroom each day feeling more or less confident that their futures are bright.

Conclusion

It is important to understand that optimists' lives are not perfect, and they do experience adverse events in their lives. Their ability to use problem-focused coping to recover from these events sets them apart. Building children's levels of optimism will not prevent them from encountering problems and trauma in their lives. However, it will help ensure that they cope with them positively and adjust psychologically in the best possible way. What more could we ask for our children?

Chapter Summary: Optimism

- Optimism has two forms and can be measured as a general dispositional orientation, as described by expectancy theory, and as an explanatory process, described by explanatory style theory.
- Optimism, in expectancy theory, has been defined as (a) the tendency to expect positive outcomes and (b) the belief that positive events exceed negative ones, or a tendency to look on the bright side of things.

- In explanatory style theory, individuals are believed to have a habitual explanation style, not just a single explanation for each discrete failure experience. Children and adolescents with an optimistic explanatory style see the good events as permanent and pervasive. Those with optimistic explanatory styles are more inclined to perceive setbacks as only temporary and limited to the immediate incident.

- The Life Orientation Test and the Revised Life Orientation Test are the most widely used assessments of dispositional optimism and pessimism. The Youth Life Orientation Test (YLOT) has been developed more specifically for use with children and adolescents.

- Explanatory style is assessed by a person's responses to a specially designed instrument, the Attributional Style Questionnaire. The instrument measures the permanent and pervasive dimensions in relation to specific events after initially asking to state a cause for that event. The Children's Attributional Style Questionnaire is the most widely used measure of explanatory style for children.

- In recent years, the important role schools have in developing strengths and positive values in students has been identified. In general, school-based programs to promote optimism, well-being, and mental health have produced mixed results.

- Seligman and others specifically developed the Penn Prevention Program to help change the explanatory style (the way in which we explain the positive and negative events that happen to us) and prevent depressive symptoms developing in at-risk 10- to 13-year-old children in America. More recently, this program has been called the PRP and subsequent studies have all reported successful results.

- The Aussie Optimism Program has been used extensively in Western Australia and other Australian states. Although original studies produced inconsistent results, in the most recent study Grade 8 students in Queensland who exhibited high levels of depression and emotional/behavioral difficulties before undertaking the program demonstrated significantly lower levels in these areas after completing the intervention.

References

Abramson, L. Y., Seligman, M. E. P., & Teasdale, J. D. (1978). Learned helplessness in humans: Critique and reformulation. *Journal of Abnormal Psychology, 87*, 49–74. http://psycnet.apa.org/index.cfm?fa=buy.optionToBuy&id=1979-00305-001

Benninga, J. S., Berkowitz, M. W., Kuehn, P., & Smith, K. (2006). Character and academics: What good schools do. *Phi Delta Kappan, 87*, 448–452.

Be You. (n.d.a). *Organisations involved.* https://beyou.edu.au/organisations-involved

Be You (n.d.b). *Educators handbook: Early learning services.* https://beyou.edu.au/-/media/pdfs/handbooks/educators_handbook_early_learning_services_pdf_9mb.pdf?la=en&hash=F6ADAD627A7A13A921 BFBE15771CF8DC5E7FE170

Beyond Blue. (2020). *Educators.* http:// https://beyou.edu.au/get-started/educators

Bishop, B., & Roberts, C. (2005). The process of embedding and sustaining a mental health promotion program in social contexts. *Community Psychologist, 38*(1), 14–16.

Boman, P. (2002). *Optimism, pessimism, anger, and adjustment in adolescents.* [Unpublished Doctoral thesis]. University of South Australia.

Boman, P., Smith, D. C., & Curtis, D. (2003). Effects of pessimism and explanatory style on the development of anger in children. *School Psychology International, 24*(1), 80–94. https://doi.org/10.1177/0143034303024001581

Boman, P., & Yates, G. C. R. (2001). Optimism, hostility, and adjustment in the first-year of high school. *British Journal of Educational Psychology, 71*(3), 401–411. https://doi.org/10.1348/000709901158587

Carver, C. S., Scheier, M. F., & Fulford, D. (2008). Self-regulatory processes, stress, and coping. In O. P. John, R. W. Robins, & L. A. Pervin (Eds.), *Handbook of personality: Theory and research* (pp. 725–742). Guilford.

Carver, C. S., Scheier, M. F., & Segerstrom, S. C. (2010). Optimism. *Clinical Psychology Review, 30*(7), 879–889. https://doi.org/10.1016/j.cpr.2010.01.006

Chang, E. C. (2001). Introduction: Optimism and pessimism and moving beyond the more fundamental question. In E. C. Chang (Ed.), *Optimism & pessimism: Implications for theory, research, and practice* (pp. 3–12). American Psychological Association.

Chang, E. C., & Bridewell, W. B. (1998). Irrational beliefs, optimism, pessimism, and psychological distress: A preliminary examination of differential effects in a college population. *Journal of Clinical Psychology, 54*(2), 137–142. https://doi.org/10.1002/(SICI)1097-4679(199802)54:2<137::AID-JCLP2>3.0.CO;2-P

Chang, E. C., Chang, R., & Sanna, L. J. (2009). Optimism, pessimism, and motivation: Relations to adjustment. *Social and Personality Psychology Compass, 3*(4), 494–506. https://doi.org/10.1111/j.1751-9004.2009.00190.x

Chang, E. C., & Maydeu-Olivares, A., & D'Zurilla, T. J. (1997). Optimism and pessimism as partially independent constructs: Relationships to positive and negative affectivity and psychological well-being. *Personality and Individual Differences, 23*(3), 433–440. https://doi.org/10.1016/S0191-8869(97)80009-8

Chang, E. C., & Sanna, L. J. (2007). Affectivity and psychological adjustment across two adult generations: Does pessimistic explanatory style still matter? *Personality and Individual Differences, 43*(5), 1149–1159.

Dember, W. N., Martin, S., Hummer, M. K., Howe, S., & Melton, R. (1989). The measurement of optimism and pessimism. *Current Psychology: Research and Reviews, 8*(2), 102–119. https://doi.org/10.1007/BF02686675

DEST. (2008). *At the heart of what we do: Values education at the centre of schooling – The final report of the values education good practice schools project – Stage 2 August 2008.* Retrieved from http://www.curriculum.edu.au/verve/_resources/VEGPSP-2_final_3.pdf

Domino, B., & Conway, D. W. (2001). Optimism and pessimism from a historical perspective. In E. C. Chang (Ed.), *Optimism & pessimism: Implications for theory, research, and practice* (pp. 3–12). American Psychological Association.

Dweck, C. S., Davidson, W., Nelson, S., & Enna, B. (1978). Sex differences in learned helplessness: II. The contingencies of evaluative feedback in the classroom and III. An experimental analysis. *Developmental Psychology, 14*(3), 268–276. https://doi.org/10.1037/0012-1649.14.3.268

Dykema, J., Berbbower, K., Doctora, J. D., & Peterson, C. (1996). An attributional style questionnaire for general use. *Journal of Psychoeducational Assessment, 14*(2), 100–108. https://doi.org/10.1177/073428299601400201

Ey, S., Hadley, W., Allen, D., Palmer, S., Klosky, J., Deptula, D., & Cohen, R. (2005). A new measure of children's optimism and pessimism: The Youth Life Orientation Test. *Journal of Child Psychology and Psychiatry, 46*(5), 548–558. https://doi.org/10.1111/j.1469-7610.2004.00372.x

Fibel, B., & Hale, W. D. (1978). The generalised expectancy for success scale: A new measure. *Journal of Consulting and Clinical Psychology, 46*(5), 924–931. https://doi.org/10.1037/0022-006X.46.5.924

Fischer, M., & Leitenberg, H. (1986). Optimism and pessimism in elementary school aged children. *Child Development, 57*(1), 241–248. https://doi.org/10.1111/1467-8624.ep7251052

Fredrickson, B. (2011). *Positivity: Groundbreaking research to release your inner optimist and thrive.* Oneworld.

Furnham, A., Sadka, V., & Brewin, C. (1992). The development of an occupational attributional style questionnaire. *Journal of Organizational Behavior, 13*(1), 27–39. https://doi.org/10.1002/job.4030130104

Garber, J. (2000). Optimism: Definitions and origins. In J. E. Gillham (Ed.), *The science of optimism and hope: Research essays in honor of Martin E. P. Seligman* (pp. 299–314). Templeton Foundation Press.

Gillham, J. E., Reivich, K. J., Jaycox, L. H., & Seligman, M. E. P. (1995). Prevention of depressive symptoms in school children: Two-year follow up. *Psychological Science, 6*(6), 343–351. https://doi.org/10.1111/j.1467-9280.1995.tb00524.x

Gillham, J. E., Shatté, A. J., Reivich, K. J., & Seligman, M. E. P. (2001). *Optimism, pessimism, and explanatory style.* In E. C. Chang (Ed.), *Optimism & pessimism: Implications for theory, research, and practice* (pp. 53–75). American Psychological Association. https://doi.org/10.1037/10385-003

Gonzálvez, C., Inglés, C. J., Sanmartín, R., Vicent, M., Gisbert, B., & García-Fernández, J. M. (2018). Youth life orientation test-Spanish version: Factorial invariance, latent mean differences and effects on school refusal. *School Mental Health, 10*(4), 477–487. https://doi.org/10.1007/s12310-018-9266-3

Helton, W. S., Matthews, G., Warm, J. S., & Dember, W. N. (2005). Being optimistic may not always be advantageous: The relationship between dispositional optimism, coping, and performance. *Proceedings of the Human Factors and Ergonomics Society, 49*(13), 1224–1228.

Hmieleski, K. M., & Baron, R. A. (2009). Entrepreneurs' optimism and new venture performance: A social cognitive perspective. *Academy of Management Journal, 52*(3), 473–488. https://doi.org/10.5465/amj.2009.41330755

Horowitz, J., & Garber, J. (2006). The prevention of depressive symptoms in children and adolescents: A meta-analytic review. *Journal of Consulting and Clinical Psychology, 74*(3), 401–415. https://doi.org/10.1037/0022-006X.74.3.401

Jensen, W. R., Olympia, D., Farley, M., & Clark, E. (2004). Positive psychology and externalizing students in a sea of negativity. *Psychology in the Schools, 41*(1), 67–79. https://doi.org/10.1002/pits.10139

Krečič, M., & Grmek, M. (2005). The reasons students choose teaching professions. *Educational Studies, 31,* 265–274. https://doi.org/10.1080/03055690500236449.

Kaslow, N. J., & Nolen-Hoeksema, S. (1991). *Children's Attributional Style Questionnaire-Revised (CASQ-R).* Unpublished manuscript, Emory University.

Kaslow, N. J., Tannenbaum, R. L., & Seligman, M. E. P. (1978). *The Kastan: A Children's Attributional Style Questionnaire.* Unpublished manuscript, University of Pennsylvania, Philadelphia.

Kensinger, E. A. (2007). Negative emotion enhances memory accuracy: Behavioral and neuroimaging evidence. *Current Directions in Psychological Science, 16*(4), 213–218. https://doi.org/10.1111/j.1467-8721.2007.00506.x

Kibe, C., & Boniwell, I. (2015). Teaching well-being and resilience in primary and secondary school. In J. Stephen (Ed.), *Positive psychology in practice: Promoting human flourishing in work, health, education, and everyday life* (pp 297–312). Wiley.

Lieber, E. (1997). *The Teenage Attributional Style Questionnaire.* (Doctoral dissertation, University of Illinois at Urbana-Champaign, 1997) Dissertation Abstracts International, 57(11-B), 7271.

Lovat, T., Clement, N., Dally, K., & Toomey, R. (2010). Values education as holistic development for all sectors: Researching for effective pedagogy. *Oxford Review of Education, 36*(6), 713–729. https://doi.org/10.1080/03054985.2010.501141

Mayerson, D. (1991). *The Parenting Attributional Style Questionnaire.* Dissertation abstracts international. B, The Sciences and Engineering, 51(11-A), 36–76.

McGrath, H., & Noble, T. (2010). Supporting positive pupil relationships: research to practice. *Educational and Child Psychology, 27*(1), 79–90.

Merry, S., McDowell, H., Wild, C. J., Bir, J., & Cunliffe, R. (2004). A randomized placebo-controlled trial of a school-based depression prevention program. *Journal of the American Academy of Child and Adolescent Psychiatry, 43*(5), 538–547. https://doi.org/10.1097/01.chi.0000117063.63530.68

Miller, A. (2008). A critique of positive psychology—or 'the new science of happiness'. *Journal of Philosophy of Education, 42*(3-4), 591–608. http://doi.org/ 10.1111/j.1467-9752.2008.00646.x

Miller, L., Richards, P. S., & Keller, R. R. (2001). Foreword. In E. C. Chang (Ed.), *Optimism & pessimism: Implications for theory, research, and practice* (pp. xiii–xvii). American Psychological Association.

Myers, L. B., & Steed, L. (1999). The relationship between dispositional optimism, dispositional pessimism, repressive coping, and trait anxiety. *Personality and Individual Differences, 27*(6), 1261–1272. https://doi.org/10.1016/S0191-8869(99)00071-9

Noble, T., & McGrath, H. (2007, October). *The positive educational practices framework: Leadership transforming schools through optimism.* [Paper presentation]. ACEL/ASCD Conference: New Imagery for Schools and Schooling: Challenging, Creating, and Connecting, Sydney, Australia. Retrieved from http://www.acel.org.au/conf07/papers/Noble%20McGrath%20postive%20education.pdf

Noble, T., & McGrath, H. (2008). The positive educational practices framework: A tool for facilitating the work of educational psychologists in promoting pupil wellbeing. *Educational & Child Psychology, 25,* 119–134. http://hdl.handle.net/10536/DRO/DU:30018015

Norman, P. (1988). Real events attributional style questionnaire. *Journal of Social and Clinical Psychology, 7*(2-3), 97–100. https://doi.org/10.1521/jscp.1988.7.2-3.97

Olason, D. T., & Roger, D. (2001). Optimism, pessimism, and 'fighting spirit': A new approach to assessing expectancy and adaptation. *Personality and Individual Differences, 31*(5), 755–768. https://doi.org/10.1016/S0191-8869(00)00176-8

Pais-Ribeiro, J., Pedro, L., & Marques, S. (2012). Dispositional optimism is unidimensional or bidimensional? The Portuguese revised life orientation test. *The Spanish Journal of Psychology, 15*(3), 1259–1271. https://doi.org/10.5209/rev_SJOP.2012.v15.n3.39412

Peterson, C., & Chang, E. C. (2003). Optimism and flourishing. In C. L. M. Keyes & J. Haidt (Eds.), *Flourishing: Positive psychology and the life well-lived* (pp. 55–79). American Psychological Association. https://doi.org/10.1037/10594-003

Peterson, C., & Steen, T. A. (2009). Optimistic explanatory style. In C. R. Snyder & S. J. Lopez (Eds.), *Oxford handbook of positive psychology* (2nd ed., pp. 313–321). Oxford University Press.

Peterson, C., & Villanova, P. (1988). An expanded attributional style questionnaire. *Journal of Abnormal Psychology, 97*(1), 87–89. https://doi.org/10.1037/0021-843X.97.1.87

Pinquart, M., Fröhlich, C., & Silbereisen, R. (2007). Optimism, pessimism, and change of psychological well-being in cancer patients. *Psychology, Health & Medicine, 12*(4), 421–432. https://doi.org/10.1080/13548500601084271

Quayle, D., Dziurawiec, S., Roberts, C., Kane, R., & Ebsworthy, G. (2001). The effect of an optimism and life skills program on depressive symptoms in preadolescence. *Behaviour Change, 18*(4), 194–203. https://doi.org/10.1375/bech.18.4.194

Reijntjes, A., Dekovic, M., Vermande, M., & Telch, M. J. (2008). Predictive validity of the Children's Attributional Styles Questionnaire: Linkages with reactions to an in vivo peer evaluation manipulation. *Cognitive Therapy and Research, 32*(2), 247–260. https://doi.org/10.1007/s10608-007-9124-3

Reivich, K., & Gillham, J. (2003). Learned optimism: The measurement of explanatory style. In S. J. Lopez & C. R. Snyder (Eds.), *Positive psychological assessment: A handbook of models and measures* (pp. 57–74). American Psychological Association.

Reivich, K., Gillham, J. E., Chaplin, T. M., & Seligman, M. E. P. (2005). From helplessness to optimism: The role of resilience in treating and preventing depression in youth. In S. Goldstein & R. B. Brooks (Eds.), *Handbook of resilience in children* (pp. 223–237). Kluwer Academic/Plenum.

Roberts, C. (2006). Embedding mental health promotion programs in school contexts: The Aussie Optimism Program. *International Society for the Study of Behavior Newsletter, 2*(50), 1–4.

Roberts, C., Ballantyne, F., & van der Klift, P. (2002). *Aussie optimism: Social life skills program. Teacher resource.* Curtin University of Technology.

Roberts, C., Kane, R., Bishop, B., Matthews, H., & Thomson, H. (2004). The prevention of depressive symptoms in rural school children: A follow-up study. *International Journal of Mental Health Promotion, 6*(3), 4–16. https://doi.org/10.1080/14623730.2004.9721934

Roberts, C., Kane, R., Thomson, H., Bishop, B., & Hart, B. (2003). The prevention of depressive symptoms in rural school children: A randomized controlled trial. *Journal of Consulting and Clinical Psychology, 71*(3), 622–628. https://doi.org/10.1037/0022-006X.71.3.622

Roberts, R., Roberts, C., Cosgrove, S., Houston, K., Ludlow, T., Mar, D., & van der Klift, P. (2002). *Aussie optimism: Optimistic thinking skills program. Teacher resource.* Curtin University of Technology.

Roberts, C., & Rudge, L. (2015). *Aussie optimism social life skills trainer's manual.* Curtin University of Technology.

Roberts, C., Williams, R., Kane, R., Pintabona, Y., Cross, D., Zubrick, S., & Silburn, S. (2011). Impact of a mental health promotion program on substance use in young adolescents. *Advances in Mental Health, 10*(1), 72–82. https://doi.org/10.5172/jamh.2011.10.1.72

Russo, R., & Boman, P. (2007). Primary school teachers' ability to recognise resilience in their students. *The Australian Educational Researcher, 34*(1), 17–31. http://www.eric.ed.gov/PDFS/EJ766602.pdf

Sagor, R. (2008). Cultivating optimism in the classroom. *Educational Leadership, 65*(6), 26–31. http://www.ascd.org/publications/educational-leadership/mar08/vol65/num06/Cultivating-Optimism-in-the-Classroom.aspx

Scheier, M. F., & Carver, C. S. (1985). Optimism, coping and health: Assessment and implications of generalized outcome expectancies. *Health Psychology, 4*(3), 219–247. https://doi.org/10.1037/0278-6133.4.3.219

Scheier, M. F., & Carver, C. S. (1992). Effects of optimism on psychological and physical well-being: Theoretical overview and empirical update. *Cognitive Therapy and Research, 16*(2), 201–228. https://doi.org/10.1007/BF01173489

Scheier, M. F., Carver, C. S., & Bridges, M. W. (1994). Distinguishing optimism from neuroticism (and trait anxiety, self-mastery, and self-esteem): A re-evaluation of the Life Orientation Test. *Journal of Personality and Social Psychology, 67*(6), 1063–1078. https://doi.org/10.1037/0022-3514.67.6.1063

Schueller, S. M., & Seligman, M. E. P. (2008). Optimism and pessimism. In K. S. Dobson & D. J. A. Dozois (Eds.), *Risk factors in depression* (pp. 171–194). Elsevier.

Seligman, M. E. P. (1975). *Helplessness: On depression, development, and death.* Reffman.

Seligman, M. E. P. (2006). *Learned optimism.* Vintage.

Seligman, M. E. P. (2011). *Learned optimism: How to change your mind and your life.* Vintage.

Seligman, M. E. P., Kamen, L. P., & Nolen-Hoeksema, S. (1988). *Explanatory style across the life-span: Achievement and health.* Erlbaum.

Seligman, M. E. P., Peterson, C., Kaslow, N. J., Tanenbaum, R. L., Alloy, L. B., & Abramson, L. Y. (1984). Attributional style and depressive symptoms among children. *Journal of Abnormal Psychology, 93*(2), 235–238. https://doi.org/10.1037/0021-843X.93.2.235

Seligman, M. E. P., Reivich, K., Jaycox, L., & Gillham, J. (1995). *The optimistic child.* Houghton Mifflin.

Sharot, T. (2011). The optimism bias. *Current Biology, 21*(23), R941–R945. https://doi.org/10.1016/j.cub.2011.10.030.

Shatte, A. J., Reivich, K. J., Gillham, J. E., & Seligman, M. E. P. (1999). Learned optimism in children. In C. R. Snyder (Ed.), *Coping: The psychology of what works* (pp. 165–181). Oxford University Press.

Sheffield, J. K., Spence, S. H., Rapee, R. M., Kowalenko, N., Wignall, A., Davis, A., & McLoone, J. (2006). Evaluation of universal, indicated, and combined cognitive-behavioral approaches to the prevention of depression among adolescents. *Journal of Consulting and Clinical Psychology, 74*(1), 66–79. https://doi.org/10.1037/0022-006X.74.1.66

Silva, I., Pais-Ribeiro, J., & Cardoso, H. (2004). Dificuldade em perceber o lado positivo davida? stresse em doentes diabéticos com e sem complicações crónicas da doença / difficultyin seeing the bright side of life: Stresses in diabetes patients with and without chronic complications from the disease. *Análise Psicológica, 22*(3), 597–605.

Spence, S., Sheffield, J., & Donovan, C. (2003). Preventing adolescent depression: An evaluation of the problem solving for life program. *Journal of Consulting and Clinical Psychology, 71*(1), 3–13. https://doi.org/10.1037/0022-006X.71.1.3

Spence, S., Sheffield, J., & Donovan, C. (2005). Long-term outcome of a school-based, universal approach to prevention of depression in adolescents. *Journal of Consulting and Clinical Psychology, 73*(1), 160–167. https://doi.org/10.1037/0022-006X.73.1.160

Spence, S., & Shortt, A. (2007). Research review: Can we justify the wide spread dissemination of universal, school-based interventions for the prevention of depression among children and adolescents? *Journal of Child Psychology and Psychiatry, 48*(6), 526–542. https://doi.org/10.1111/j.1469-7610.2007.01738.x

Swannell, S., Hand, M., & Martin, G. (2009). The effects of a universal mental health promotion programme on depressive symptoms and other difficulties in year eight high school students in Queensland, Australia. *School Mental Health, 1*(4), 229–239.

Taylor, W. C., Baranowski, T., Klesges, L. M., Ey, S., Pratt, C., Rochon, J., & Zhou, A. (2004). Psychometric properties of optimism and pessimism: Results from the Girls' Health Enrichment Multisite Studies. *Preventive Medicine, 38*, S69–S77. https:// doi.org/10.1016/j.ypmed.2003.10.015

Thompson, M., Kaslow, N., Weiss, B., & Nolen-Hoeksema, S. (1998). Children's attributional style questionnaire–Revised: Psychometric examination. *Psychological Assessment, 10*(2), 166–170. https://doi.org/10.1037/1040-3590.10.2.166

Tyson, O., Roberts, C. M., & Kane, R. (2009). Can implementation of a resilience program for primary school children enhance the mental health of teachers? *Australian Journal of Guidance and Counselling, 19*(2), 116–130. https://doi.org/10.1375/ajgc.19.2.116

Watt, H.M.G., & Richardson, P.W. (2007). Motivational factors influencing teaching as a career choice: Development and validation of the FIT-Choice Scale. *The Journal of Experimental Education, 75*(3), 167–202. https://doi.org/10.3200/JEXE.75.3.167-202

Weiner, B., Frieze, I., Kukla, A., Reed, L., Rest, S., & Rosenbaum, R. M. (1971). *Perceiving the courses of success and failure.* General Learning Press.

Whitley, B. (1991). A short form of the expanded attributional style questionnaire. *Journal of Personality Assessment, 56*(2), 365–369. https://doi.org/10.1207/s15327752jpa5602_14

Williams, N. A., Davis, G., Hancock, M., & Phipps, S. (2010). Optimism and pessimism in children with cancer and healthy children: Confirmatory factor analysis of the Youth Life Orientation Test and relations with health-related quality of life. *Journal of Pediatric Psychology, 35*(6), 672–682. https://doi.org/10.1093/jpepsy/jsp084

Suggested Readings

Boman, P., Smith, D. C., & Curtis, D. (2003). Effects of pessimism and explanatory style on the development of anger in children. *School Psychology International, 24*, 80–94. https://doi.org/10.1177/0143034303024001581
One of the small number of studies that assesses both expectancy and explanatory style in children.

Quayle, D., Dziurawiec, S., Roberts, C., Kane, R., & Ebsworthy, G. (2001). The effect of an optimism and life skills program on depressive symptoms in preadolescence. *Behavior Change, 18*, 194–203. https://doi.org/10.1375/bech.18.4.194
Discusses and presents the development of the Aussie Optimism Program.

Sagor, R. (2008). Cultivating optimism in the classroom. *Educational Leadership, 65*, 26–31.
Argues the case that there are two key variables that teachers need to nurture in students in order for students to develop optimism: faith in the future and personal efficacy.

Scheier, M. F., & Carver, C. S. (1985). Optimism, coping and health: Assessment and implications of generalized outcome expectancies. *Health Psychology, 4*, 219–247. https://doi.org/10.1037/0278-6133.4.3.219
This study describes the initial development of the Life Orientation Test and gives a sound overview of expectancy theory.

Seligman, M. E. P. (2011). *Learned optimism: How to change your mind and your life.* Vintage.

8

GRATITUDE IN SCHOOL
Benefits to Students and Schools

Giacomo Bono, Taylor Duffy, and Selena Moreno

Introduction

Contemporary society presents many challenges for youth. They face many choices for what to do, value, and be, and the path to adulthood is longer, more competitive, and more uncertain than ever (Twenge, 2017). Schools struggle to tailor teaching and support mental health for more diverse populations with increasingly constrained budgets. Families are busier than ever, with more dual-income households confronting greater financial and time management challenges (Fisher & Johnson, 2019). Additionally, individuals' attentional resources are being taxed by more media, information, and communications than ever (Serrano-Puche, 2017). Achieving a positive and purposeful identity has become more challenging than ever for adolescents, and schools must support students' academic growth despite such difficult conditions.

In this chapter, we contend that promoting gratitude more effectively in students can help alleviate the challenges schools face in supporting their students in academic and personal development. Indeed, beyond promoting academic growth, schools today are helping students develop character and well-being using techniques such as gratitude promotion (Trask-Kerr et al., 2019). Unfortunately, mental illness disproportionately affects youth worldwide, and, for many countries, school-based resources are not enough to meet these needs (Gil-Rivas et al., 2019). In the last decade, research has uncovered many ways that gratitude benefits youth. Much has been learned about advantages to school-related processes and outcomes since the second edition of this Handbook (Furlong et al., 2014). Thus, gratitude may help bridge the resource gap schools face and enhance their efforts to support social-emotional learning (SEL).

Developmentally, adolescence is a vital period for establishing positive habits for thriving into adulthood. However, researchers point to a discouraging trend in the United States; between 2008 and 2017, adolescents are becoming more bored across and within secondary school grades by an increase of 1.65% per year (Weybright et al., 2020). These findings coincide with another national survey, which finds that over 70% of students report feeling stressed out or bored at their high school most or some of the time (DePaoli et al., 2018). The trends are consistent with psychopathology trends, which have been rising among college students and high school students for several decades (Twenge et al., 2010). These researchers argue that cultural shifts toward extrinsic goals (e.g., materialism and status) and away from intrinsic goals (e.g., community, affiliation, and meaning in life) underlie these trends.

118

DOI: 10.4324/9781003013778-11

Throughout life, supportive social networks help buffer individuals from adversity and pathology and enhance health and well-being (Feeney & Collins, 2015). Thus, establishing strong, positive social ties with peers, teachers, staff, and support groups and communities is essential for students' mental health and functioning and can provide a bedrock for many positive outcomes in their lives. Gratitude is not only uniquely suited to developing such social resources; it is widely valued and cost-effective. Unfortunately, meta-analytic research concludes that it is unclear whether gratitude interventions conducted in schools are generally effective or useful for students or schools (Renshaw & Olinger Steeves, 2016). However, two recent studies show that sharing gratitude genuinely with others and providing opportunities to reflect on behavior helps improve interventions' impact on students' gratitude and well-being (Armenta et al., 2020; Bono et al., 2020). Nonetheless, determining best practices is still needed in this fledgling field.

This chapter covers research on gratitude, with an emphasis on its relevance to students and schools. After a brief introduction of the concept of gratitude, its measurement in youth, and its implications for academic development, we turn to the literature on the consequences of gratitude—its links to prosociality and supportive relationships, motivation and goal striving, and well-being and resilience. We then cover research on interventions with youth and moderators of gratitude. Finally, we close by touching on the potential benefits of gratitude for schools as organizations and future research suggestions.

What Is Gratitude?

Gratitude is a distinct character strength for its reliably strong link to life satisfaction among youth and adults (Park & Peterson, 2006). It is a transcendence strength because of its potential to provide a sense of meaning and connection to the universe. Park and Peterson (2006) also found that the strength of gratitude is linked with better social skills and grades among youth. Research conceptualizes gratitude at the trait and state level (McCullough et al., 2002), with both linked to higher psychological health among adults (Wood et al., 2010). As a moral emotion, gratitude supports altruistic interactions by helping people recognize those who intentionally augment their welfare, reinforcing others' beneficial actions, and motivating beneficiaries to reciprocate kindness or extend it to others (McCullough et al., 2001). Gratitude falls under the broader multidimensional concept of appreciation, but both create meaning, well-being, and coherence in one's life (Adler & Fagley, 2005; Rusk et al., 2016).

Behaviorally, gratitude can be personal or interpersonal and involves thoughts, emotions, and behaviors about positive things, events, circumstances, and people one has in life. Beyond differing in positive feelings for benefits received (e.g., receiving help from a friend or being recognized with an award), people differ in how they focus on and think about such benefits or whether and how much they respond positively or constructively. Interpersonally, gratitude helps recipients of kind acts respond positively by reciprocating kindness or extending kindness to others (McCullough et al., 2001). Finally, researchers also distinguish between general gratitude (i.e., felt when broadly appreciating what is important or meaningful in life) and benefit-triggered gratitude (i.e., felt in response to others' specific actions) (Lambert et al., 2009).

Thus, there are many ways to experience gratitude. While various forms may be beneficial, evidence finds interpersonal gratitude to be more potent, especially when shown and shared in a meaningful way with significant benefactors (Seligman et al., 2005) or relationship partners (Algoe, 2012; Lambert et al., 2013). Scholars also argue that interpersonal gratitude is virtue-promoting for youth and society because it helps build social capital intergenerationally (Bono & Odudu, 2016) and resilience (Bono & Sender, 2018).

Research on the Benefits of Gratitude for Youth

Meta-analyses with adults show that gratitude interventions yield significant but small effects on psychological well-being (i.e., happiness, positive affect, and life satisfaction) compared to neutral control conditions (Davis et al., 2016; Dickens, 2017). Importantly, results showed negligible effects on trait gratitude, and overall, suggest that interventions may be no better than placebos. Other meta-analyses have made similar conclusions about gratitude's effects on depression and anxiety (Cregg & Cheavens, 2021). A meta-analysis of research with youth was consistent with these findings overall (Renshaw & Olinger Steeves, 2016). It is also possible that gratitude mostly improves well-being if baseline levels of well-being are low (Cummins, 2013). However, how to personalize inductions so that practices are genuine and habit-forming remains unsettled (see Interventions section below). Thus, for now, correlational and longitudinal research provides a clearer picture of gratitude's benefits for youth and schools.

Benefits to Well-Being and Prosociality

Grateful people tend to be more helpful, supportive, forgiving, and empathic toward others, and they tend to have personalities that are more agreeable, less narcissistic, and less materialistic (McCullough et al., 2002). The experience of gratitude motivates people to reciprocate to bene-factors (Bartlett & DeSteno, 2006; Tsang, 2006) and respond prosocially to others (Bartlett & DeSteno, 2006). It appears to be an evolutionary adaptation that acknowledges the value of when others benefit our welfare, reinforcing others' kindness toward us and spurring mutually cooperative relationships (Forster et al., 2017; Smith et al., 2017).

Evidence supports these notions among youth too. For instance, adolescents reporting higher gratitude levels also report more relational satisfaction and support (Froh, Yurkewicz et al., 2009). Further, trait gratitude was negatively associated with materialism, envy, and depression, positively associated with life satisfaction, self-reported grade-point average, flow or engrossment in valued activities, and social integration (Froh et al., 2011). Other studies corroborate and extend these findings. For instance, among South Korean children (ages 10–12), trait gratitude was associated with prosocial behavior, internalizing problems, and externalizing problems. Social support from family, teachers, and peers partially and fully mediated these links, respectively (You et al., 2020). Another study found that trait gratitude was associated with less depression and more well-being among Taiwanese youth (ages 20–22); self-esteem fully mediated these associations (Lin, 2015).

Gratitude predicts increases in life satisfaction and prosocial behavior prospectively (i.e., three months later). In turn, these associations predict increases in motivation to help others and contribute to society six months later (Froh et al., 2010). Further analyses showed that gratitude and social integration mutually increased each other, partly due to increases in life satisfaction at three months. This finding supports the notion that gratitude may promote upward spirals of emotional and social well-being. Other longitudinal research with adolescents has found that gratitude and prosocial behavior mutually influence each other over four years and that changes in gratitude, not prosocial behavior, were associated with greater empathy and intentional self-regulation, or the ability to identify and strive toward major goals (Bono et al., 2019). This latter research suggests that, beyond fostering well-being and prosociality, gratitude energizes self-improvement in development—a notion recently supported by intervention research (Armenta et al., 2020).

Finally, in an experimental study to further investigate the gratitude-prosocial link, adolescents who kept a gratitude journal for two weeks were more generous in the amount of money they donated than those who kept a control journal for two weeks (Chaplin et al., 2019). Notably, the intervention significantly reduced materialism among adolescents and attenuated materialism's negative effect on generosity. Using real money and donations as a behavioral measure, these researchers found that adolescents who kept a gratitude journal donated 60% more of their earnings to charity than those in the control condition. Therefore, taken together, research indicates that gratitude's myriad benefits to personal and social well-being appear transformative for youth, serving to protect them from the trappings of consumerist culture and mental health problems and helping them to consolidate a positive identity.

Does Gratitude Promote Resilience?

There is evidence that gratitude buffers people from psychiatric disorders like depression, anxiety, and substance abuse (Kendler et al., 2003) and protects people from debilitating emotions and distress. For example, an archival study of newspaper accounts about what children were thankful for before and after the September 11 event found that themes of gratitude for basic human needs (e.g., family, friends, and teachers) increased (Gordon et al., 2004). This phenomenon suggests that gratitude fosters coping and adjustment in youth, but whether children who expressed such gratitude were coping and adjusting better than the children who expressed gratitude for other less prominent themes was unknown.

More direct evidence shows that gratitude supports coping and resilience in youth. One study found that parent and teacher support were robust environmental antecedents of early adolescents' gratitude, and further, gratitude buffered students from stress (Reckart et al., 2017). Other research examined the link between moral affect gratitude (expressing thanks and appreciation to others) and life-orientation gratitude (deep, broad sense of appreciation in life) to risk and protective factors among African-American adolescents (Ma et al., 2013). Both moral affect and life-orientation gratitude correlated with positive family ties. Further, moral affect gratitude correlated with more protective factors (i.e., academic interest and performance and engagement in extracurricular activity), and life-orientation gratitude correlated with lower risk factors (i.e., related to sexual intimacy and intercourse and drug/alcohol use).

Another study examined older adolescents' functioning in response to parental illness and whether gratitude protected them from adversity (Stoeckel et al., 2015). Though there were no differences in depression or anxiety between the ill-parent group and the healthy parent group, family quality of life was lower for the ill-parent than the healthy parent group. Importantly, dispositional gratitude moderated the association between parental health status and participants' anxiety and depression. Two studies found protective properties in terms of body image; one found that among young adult females, gratitude moderated the effect of viewing thin models on body dissatisfaction, with decreases being more robust for higher body mass index scores (Homan et al., 2014). Another pair of studies found that a gratitude letter writing induction helped facilitate healthy eating behavior in adolescents and young adults (Fritz et al., 2019). Research in a school context has found that gratitude has protective properties for bullying victims. Specifically, researchers found that gratitude was negatively related to victimization and suicide risk among high schoolers (ages 12–17). For girls, who reported higher levels of suicide risk than boys, higher gratitude was associated with a lower risk of suicide (Rey et al., 2019). These studies suggest that gratitude helps buffer youth from adversity at home and school.

Finally, research also has found protective effects of gratitude for victims of severe trauma. One study investigated whether gratitude contributed to resilience among adolescents who survived the devastating 2008 earthquake in Wenchuan, China. Examining adolescent survivors 3.5, 4.5, and 5.5 years after the earthquake, Zhou and Wu (2016) found that gratitude predicted posttraumatic growth (PTG) from T1 to T3 and that gratitude predicted deliberate rumination from T1 to T2, related to increases in PTG from T2 to T3. A second study examined if gratitude had a protective role for Israeli adolescents traumatized by nearby missile attacks (Israel-Cohen et al., 2015). These researchers found that gratitude predicted fewer PTSD symptoms in adolescents 2.5

months after the attack and that life satisfaction and negative affect, but not positive affect, mediated this effect. Thus, gratitude may be a stable factor for developing PTG in the aftermath of serious traumatic events.

The above findings indicate that gratitude serves as a distinct protective factor from other positive emotions that facilitate psychological growth and community connection. At the individual level, gratitude seems to protect youth from materialistic motivations, risky behaviors, and the mental health consequences of adverse events and trauma. At the social level, gratitude's links with a sense of connection to family and others, positive reappraisals of adverse and traumatic events, achievement, and engagement in extracurricular activity seem to help gratitude's contribution to resilience in development.

Social-Emotional Learning (SEL) and Gratitude

High school is a critical time to support youths' mental health because they face many developmental challenges (e.g., pubertal changes, meeting higher academic demands, and changes in family and social relationships). Developmentally, adolescents must strive to meet many demands at once. They must endorse a coherent set of values and beliefs, and they must internalize norms and practices to develop their academic and social identities (LaGuardia & Ryan, 2002). It is critical for adolescents to meet social and academic demands simultaneously and for schools to effectively support both social and academic development in students. Indeed, evidence from two longitudinal studies using large representative samples indicates that adolescents' well-being predicts positive outcomes in young adulthood. For instance, Hoyt et al. (2012) found that well-being—broadly construed as happiness, enjoyment of life, feeling just as good as others, hopefulness about the future, and different self-esteem aspects—predicted better self-reported health (e.g., physical activity and nutritional eating) and fewer health risk behaviors (e.g., binge drinking, alcohol, marijuana, and drug use) four years later among U.S. adolescents. Among Australian adolescents, O'Connor et al. (2017) found that positive mental health—a latent factor comprised of emotions, engagement, relationships, purpose, and accomplishment—predicted higher education levels, greater job competence, citizenship behavior, and volunteering civic engagement up to a decade later. Thus, promoting high school students' motivation across life domains and strengthening their social ties with peers, teachers, and other adults at school are valuable endeavors.

In middle school, adolescents face other difficulties in establishing social belonging. Transitioning from a more intimate elementary school setting, they must form and manage relationships with multiple teachers and classmates while adjusting to higher academic expectations (Eccles et al., 1993). With awareness of diverse social and racial groups emerging and teachers seeking greater disciplinary control, middle schoolers desire more autonomy and respect socially but may see disciplinary decisions as unfair (Yeager et al., 2018). Further, Yeager et al. found that this can imperil students' academic identity development, especially for Black and Hispanic boys. Other research found that when teachers adopt an empathic rather than punitive mindset about misbehavior with diverse middle schoolers, suspension rates were cut in half a year later (Okonofua et al., 2016).

Supporting both academic success and well-being in elementary school is important too. Elementary school students with greater life satisfaction have greater self-worth, regardless of psychopathology level, and they have better relationships with parents, teachers, and peers than troubled students (Greenspoon & Saklofske, 2001). Thus, subjective well-being (SWB) is important throughout primary and secondary school and is linked to better academic attitudes, physical health, social support, satisfaction with romantic relationships, and identity development, even if students have some psychopathology (Suldo et al., 2016). For these reasons, promoting behaviors that broadly support mental health, well-being, and prosociality in students—like gratitude—is valuable for primary and secondary schools.

Opportunities to cooperate and help others abound in school and afterschool settings. Cooperative learning is positively associated with academic achievement, motivation, and social belonging across all grade levels and school subjects (Johnson et al., 2014). More broadly, gratitude practices may help enhance SEL programs. High-quality SEL programs in K–12 schools significantly improve social and emotional skills, attitudes, behavior, and academic performance (Durlak et al., 2011; Jeynes, 2019). Indeed, schools may support students' moral education and foster caring social relationships better by emphasizing a few "master virtues"—like self-control, humility, and gratitude (Meindl et al., 2018). Evidence supports these notions.

Does Gratitude Support School-Related Factors and SEL?

Only recently has research begun focusing on gratitude and SWB at school. Tian et al. (2015), examining trait gratitude among elementary school students (ages 8–14) in southern China, found that gratitude was significantly related to school-specific SWB. Prosocial behavior partially mediated gratitude's associations with school satisfaction and positive affect in school, and gender moderated the association between gratitude and school satisfaction—with boys benefitting more. Later research further explains gratitude's link to SWB in school. In a follow-up study of adolescents in northern China (ages 11–15), Tian et al. (2016) found that satisfaction of basic psychological needs entirely mediated gratitude's association with SWB in school. Specifically, gratitude indirectly predicted SWB through greater satisfaction of relatedness and competence needs, followed by autonomy needs. Another study found that lower materialism also accounted for gratitude's association with school SWB among late adolescent college students in southern China (Jiang et al., 2016).

Research shows links between gratitude and learning outcomes, as well. In three studies using cross-sectional, longitudinal, and experimental methods, King and Datu (2018) found that gratitude contributed to academic motivation and self- and teacher-reported engagement among Filipino high school and university students. They also found that trait gratitude was associated with improvements in academic grades with high schoolers. Other research with elementary and middle school students (ages 8–13) in China found that improvements in teacher-student relationships helped account for gratitude's positive impacts on academic self-efficacy and engagement (Zhen et al., 2019). Qualitative research by Howells (2014) on practicing gratitude in school during a professional development workshop supported such effects. The Australian high school teachers in the study noted that gratitude practices lead to more active engagement among students, improved relationships with them, and helped nurture more school community in general. Therefore, evidence supports the importance of promoting gratitude in school to improve students' school behaviors and social experiences. The above research, focused on learning and school-related processes and outcomes, emerged after the last edition of this Handbook. More work on gratitude is needed in this area that focuses on other learning factors, dyads, and social networks.

Gratitude Interventions with Youth

Jeffrey Froh and his colleagues conducted the earliest empirical gratitude interventions with youth. In one study, 11 classrooms were randomly assigned to gratitude, hassles, or no-treatment control groups. Students completed measures daily during a two-week intervention period and then again after three weeks (Froh et al., 2008). The gratitude condition involved "counting blessings" or considering up to five things in their lives for which students were grateful, and the hassles condition involved focusing on irritants. The intervention was associated with increased optimism and life satisfaction, fewer physical complaints, and less negative affect. Students who reported grateful feelings in response to aid also had a more positive affect, and this association became stronger by the three-week follow-up. Students in the gratitude condition reported greater school satisfaction at the immediate posttest and three-week follow-up, compared to students in the hassles or control group. The non-neutral nature of the control group, however, may have contributed to the results.

Another study, employing the "gratitude visit," examined whether affect moderated the effects of gratitude interventions on youth aged 8–19 (Froh, Kashdan et al., 2009). Students were randomly assigned to write and then read a thank you letter to a benefactor or to a control condition (i.e., writing about daily mundane events). Students in the gratitude condition who were low in positive affect reported more gratitude and positive affect at posttest and more positive affect at a two-month follow-up. Finally, a third study employed a gratitude curriculum designed to train elementary school students (ages 8–11) in interpersonal gratitude (Froh et al., 2014). Using a quasi-experimental design, classrooms were randomly assigned to a gratitude or a neutral control condition. Experimenters delivered five lessons daily in one study and weekly in a second study. Lessons included classroom discussions, writing assignments, and role-playing activities. The gratitude condition involved a "benefit appraisal" curriculum (i.e., training students to appreciate the personal value of kindness or gifts, the altruistic intentions of benefactors, and the costs to benefactors in time or effort). The control condition was structured similarly with five lessons but had students focus on daily mundane events.

In both of Froh et al.'s (2014) studies, students in the gratitude condition reported stronger benefit appraisals and more grateful affect by the end of the intervention than students in the control condition. Notably, the daily-curricular students wrote 80% more thank you cards to their parent–teacher association, exhibiting gratitude behaviorally. The weekly curricular students reported increases in positive affect five months after the intervention. An advantage of this benefit appraisal curriculum for younger participants (i.e., in elementary or middle school) is that it scaffolds how to respond when one receives help or gifts from another, which makes it more practical than a gratitude journal. Another advantage is that benefit appraisals can be used anytime cooperating, helping, or giving occurs during the school day to reinforce gratitude naturally.

Other interventions using broader techniques show advantages for students and schools. For example, a four-week intervention combining gratitude visualizations with meditation produced medium to large effects on middle school students' life satisfaction, school satisfaction, and trait gratitude, compared to the waitlist or no-treatment control groups (Duthely et al., 2017). Another study examined a 12-week mindfulness-kindness curriculum for preschoolers (Flook et al., 2015). Intervention students improved in social competence, executive functioning, and report card grades, whereas the control students exhibited more selfish behavior (i.e., less sharing) over time. Small to medium intervention effects were found on cognitive flexibility and delay of gratification too. Finally, Suldo et al. (2015) developed and tested an 11-session positive psychology intervention with fourth graders that trained students in the novel use of character strengths, gratitude, kindness, and relationships in the classroom. Afterward, children experienced a greater frequency of positive emotions, global life satisfaction, and contentment with themselves, their friends, and their living environment. These improvements held a few months later when a significant increase in school satisfaction also emerged. However, whether gratitude specifically was the influential component cannot be discerned in these broader interventions.

Challenges and Progress in Interventions

The above studies indicate that engagement in genuine practices that elicit positive appraisals of one's daily life is critical for effectively promoting gratitude and well-being. As noted earlier, research with adults has found the interpersonal practice of gratitude to be a powerful way to promote gratitude. Two studies mentioned earlier corroborate this with youth (i.e., Fritz et al., 2019; King & Datu, 2018), as they involved interventions of writing gratitude letters to significant people. However, overall, gratitude interventions with youth have yet to identify best practices for promoting interpersonal gratitude sustainably in schools.

There are two significant challenges in the field. One concerns a significant barrier to the practice of interpersonal gratitude. Kumar and Epley (2018) found that people have egocentric biases that prevent them from expressing thanks to recipients (with gratitude letters). Expressers underestimated the surprise and positive feelings recipients experienced, and they overestimated the awkwardness recipients would feel—expectations that, in turn, hindered their intentions to express gratitude. Thus, to foster interpersonal gratitude effectively, these egocentric biases must be overcome. Another major challenge in the field is effectively applying person × activity fit in gratitude intervention designs. To counter hedonic adaptation and achieve profound, sustainable effects with interventions, activities must be novel and varied. People must select practices that they enjoy, be intrinsically motivated to do them, and be willing to exert effort on them (Lyubomirsky et al., 2011). These qualities improve positive psychology interventions, but their application to gratitude interventions so far has been scant. They are crucial for adolescents because interventions that are unresponsive to their needs and the daily context of their lives can provoke reactance (Yeager et al., 2015).

Two recent intervention studies directly addressed the two significant challenges posed above. One study randomly assigned 1,017 students (in ninth and tenth grades) in four high schools located in metropolitan areas (Los Angeles and New York) to a gratitude or control condition for four weeks (Armenta et al., 2020). Students in the gratitude condition were instructed to spend 10 minutes each week writing gratitude letters to their parents, teachers, coaches, or friends and reflecting on the costs and benefits to these benefactors and the impacts of this activity. Students in the control condition were instructed to spend 10 minutes each week trying to be more organized by listing their daily activities and reflecting on obstacles and benefits. Compared to controls, students in the gratitude condition reported more life satisfaction and motivation to improve themselves throughout the semester.

The above effects were partially mediated by increases in feelings of connectedness, elevation, and indebtedness; and gratitude's effect on life satisfaction was partially mediated by negative affect. Thus, expressing gratitude and reflecting on benefactors' actions and the effects of such incidents sustained students' motivation and satisfaction with their lives throughout the semester. This shows that sharing thanks with benefactors and having opportunities to appreciate the meaning of the exchange of kindness and gratitude is particularly powerful for adolescents. Further, the study's intervention practices are brief (10 minutes, four times weekly) and easy to incorporate in classes.

A second intervention study that engaged adolescents in sharing genuine gratitude with others used a technology-based approach. Bono et al. (2020) tested a gratitude intervention lasting six weeks in two urban high schools. They used a research-based curriculum (Bono, 2018) and a web-app for practicing grateful behavior (Fauteux, 2017). This study used a quasi-experimental pretest-posttest design with classes assigned either to an intervention or a control group (waitlist or pure control condition). The curriculum included teacher slides on the science of gratitude and assignments and activities employing various practice strategies—thanking, journaling, letter writing, and reflection—that teachers deliver to students. The app lets students and staff establish a personal practice routine in the same way: they pick a recipient to send a digital "thx" note to, select a hashtag reason from among school-determined competencies (e.g., listening, help, and courage), and make meaning of their exchanged notes in a journal. Most students use laptops, but any device with a browser can be used. Thx notes, stored online, can be graphed in the app. Users can reflect gratefully in the journal on who they are thankful for and why and how their actions impact others. Therefore, the app lets students discover patterns inherent in the natural exchange of kindness and gratitude at school that would otherwise remain less visible. See Table 8.1 for descriptions of the app's different gratitude practices and Figure 8.1 for illustrations of how the app is used.

Table 8.1 Give and Reflect Exercises/Practices of the GiveThx App

Practice Title	Time	Grade-Level	Type of Exercise	Practice Description
Give Functions				
Group gratitude	5 min	All grades	Process check	Write individual thx notes recognizing productive behaviors.
Partner gratitude	4 min	All grades	Process check	Write a partner a thx note recognizing a productive behavior of theirs.
L/R/Pick gratitude	7 min	All grades	Kinesthetic	Form a circle. Write thx notes to the people at left and right and a 3rd.
Gratitude wave	4 min	All grades	Intervention	Everyone sends a thx note to one person.
Behavior challenge	6 min	All grades	Challenge	Everyone sends thx notes only for one behavior.
Peer gratitude	4 min	2nd and up	Choice	Send thx notes to peers of your choice.
New gratitude	4 min	2nd and up	Intervention	Send thx notes to peers you have not sent to (or sent few to).
Write and shoutout	5 min	All grades	Modeling	Send thx notes and then share.
Thank, pair, share	7 min	All grades	Dialogue	Send thx note, discuss with partner, share out with class.
Grateful moment	5 min	All grades	Public sharing	Form a circle and share grateful moments from the day.
Gratitude letter	10 min	All grades	Community	Create a handwritten thank you letter. Give it to the person. Reflect.
Face-to-face gratitude	10 min	All grades	Interpersonal	Write a thx note to someone. Read it to them, face-to-face. Reflect.
Secret agent thx	5 min	2nd and up	Observation	Observe a peer all day and thank them at the end for something.
Reflect Functions				
Check-in	5 min	2nd and up	Check-in	Students share one thing they want their teacher to know.
General thx	5 min	All grades	Journaling	Write about something general you are thankful for.
3 Good things	10 min	All grades	Challenge	Write down three things that went well that day and associated feelings.
Grateful by subtraction	10 min	3rd and up	Perspective	Think of the difference if an event or relationship did not happen.
Message received	8 min	2nd and up	Self-awareness	Pick a favorite thx note received and explain why.
Message given	8 min	2nd and up	Social awareness	Pick a favorite thx note given and explain why.
Strengths inventory	15 min	2nd and up	Self-awareness	Analyze data & thx notes to identify personal character strengths.
Giving inventory	10 min	2nd and up	Social awareness	Analyze data & thx notes to identify trends in gratitude to others.
Class trends	5 min	2nd and up	Class data	Review class gratitude trends and consider the reasons behind them.
Gratitude letter	15 min	All grades	Community	Create a handwritten thank you letter. Give it to the person. Reflect.
Face-to-face gratitude	10 min	All grades	Interpersonal	Write a thx note to someone. Read it to them, face-to-face. Reflect.
Gratitude interview	20 min	3rd and up	Reporting	Interview an adult about something they are grateful for. Reflect.

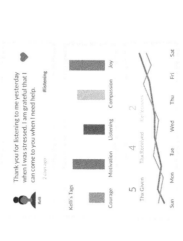

Illustrations of the GiveThx app thank and reflect functions, from teachers' perspective (first page) and students' perspective (second page)

Note. Illustrations of thanking and grateful reflection functions provided by www.GiveThx.org (Fauteux, 2017). First page shows a teacher's perspective of classroom gratitude activities, first in terms of students' reasons for thanking (i.e., tags) and then in terms of number of thx notes received and given as well as number of grateful reflections completed. Second page shows two different student's perspectives. The first student is doing 1 of 3 grateful reflection tasks assigned by the teacher. The second student is acknowledging a thx note received (by having clicked on the heart), graphing a strengths inventory based on reasons for thx notes received, and graphing the number of thx notes given and received as well as of grateful reflections completed during a particular week.

Figure 8.1 Illustrations of the GiveThx App Thank and Reflect Functions from a Teacher's Perspective

Bono et al. (2020) found that, compared to the control group, the intervention group exhibited significant increases from baseline in trait gratitude ($d = 0.55$), positive affect ($d = 0.31$), life satisfaction ($d = 0.46$), and friendship satisfaction ($d = 0.33$). Further, the intervention group showed significant decreases from baseline in mental health outcomes, including anxiety ($d = 0.42$), negative affect ($d = 0.49$), depression for boys ($d = 0.45$), and perceived stress for girls ($d = 0.40$), compared to the control group. They argued that combining a top-down psychoeducational approach (curriculum) and a bottom-up user-centered approach (such as a social-media-like web app) helps improve interventions' effectiveness in school settings. Therefore, the intervention provides users opportunities for positive digital and face-to-face interactions in school to better support their personal development, social belonging, and mental health. Another advantage of the intervention is that schools can integrate the practice everywhere (e.g., classes, advisories, and faculty meetings). Staff can review gratitude exchanges to understand, coach, and connect with students or with each other better, enabling schools to infuse gratitude practices into their culture.

Moderator Variables to Consider in Interventions

When testing the efficacy of gratitude interventions, it is critical to consider moderators, as some subgroups may be more responsive to the intervention than others. For example, there is evidence that gratitude benefits boys' SWB (Froh, Yurkewicz et al., 2009) and school SWB (Tian et al., 2015) more than girls. Research examining distinct mechanisms through which gratitude benefits males and females on different outcomes will help improve interventions. For example, Bono et al.'s (2020) intervention found stronger effects on females' perceived stress and depression for males. This dovetails with other findings. Besides being female, people who have higher curiosity, utility beliefs about gratitude interventions, self-control beliefs, and social norms favoring gratitude intervention, and less depression are more prone to initiate gratitude intervention (Kaczmarek et al., 2014). For example, while males may be more challenging to engage than females, researchers should attend to these factors to make individuals more open to engaging in interventions genuinely. For example, while males may be tougher to engage overall, compared to females, emphasizing how interventions can improve social connections may help engage males more; emphasizing how interventions can improve personal management may help engage females more. Indeed, individuals are more likely to "own" and commit to interventions when the exercises are tailored to different genders (Kashdan et al., 2009), thus improving the person × activity fit.

Considering other moderators, such as positive affect, could improve person × activity fit. That gratitude benefits personal SWB more in youth with lower positive affect suggests that cultural, personality, and attitudinal factors may moderate the effects of gratitude on well-being (Froh, Kashdan et al., 2009). For instance, evidence shows that ambivalence over emotional expression is another moderator; it decreased the effect of gratitude on Taiwanese college students' subjective happiness, loneliness, and depression (Chen et al., 2012). Recent research suggests that attachment insecurity and responsive relationship partners are other important moderators that can decrease or increase, respectively, gratitude's beneficial effects (Park et al., 2019). Importantly, in achievement situations, where outcomes tend to be self-relevant, people's sense of personal responsibility for their success moderates whether they feel grateful for the help received (Chow & Lowery, 2010). Thus, when students receive help from a teacher, staff, or peer at school, they will be more grateful if they feel responsible for their success. Indeed, different people experience different amounts of gratitude for help or gifts they receive, depending on the amount of help or size of gifts they are accustomed to receiving (Wood et al., 2011).

Finally, research is needed in terms of environmental and cultural factors. For instance, Li et al. (2012) found that the mediating effect of self-esteem between gratitude and suicidality was weaker among adolescents who experienced more stressful life events than those who experienced fewer stressful life events. This finding suggests that gratitude interventions' stress-buffering effects may be limited in high trauma or disabled students. Despite high levels of trait gratitude, these students may have less opportunity to experience gratitude or be less likely to express thanks to benefactors or seek help in the future out of concerns of feeling dependent or incapable. Therefore, a better understanding of how gratitude is experienced and expressed in different cultures and groups will improve schools' ability to foster gratitude and maximize its potential benefits. Cross-cultural research by Tudge and colleagues finds that the most virtuous form of gratitude, connective gratitude (i.e., when one's gratitude motivates them to repay benefactors with something of value), was higher for Chinese children ages 7–14 years than among U.S. children (Wang et al., 2015). Another study with children of the same age found that gratitude was expressed differently across countries. South Korea joined China as the highest in connective gratitude, with Russia and Turkey having moderate levels and Guatemala and the United States having lower levels (Mendonça et al., 2018). However, a better understanding of how different expression forms are linked to well-being cross-culturally would help yield more culturally appropriate interventions.

Applying Gratitude to Schools

Bono et al. (2020) found support for the notion that gratitude's interpersonal practice is essential for broadly supporting SEL. High school students who reported expressing thanks to others more also exhibited improvements in indicators of all five competencies outlined in the Collaborative for Social and Emotional Learning (CASEL) framework (i.e., self-awareness, self-management, social awareness, relationship skills, and responsible decision-making). This finding suggests that promoting gratitude in schools, especially interpersonal gratitude, is worthwhile.

Simmel (1950) argued that gratitude is the moral glue that bonds people together into a functioning society. His logic of gratitude as the "moral memory of mankind" can be applied to school communities. For example, school psychologists, counselors, teachers, and staff can be more effective as a team by helping students appreciate the resources and support provided by:

- school boards (e.g., funding for new programs, extracurricular activities, or buildings),
- school-level administration (e.g., dedicated support of student and teacher success),
- teachers (e.g., using engaging learning strategies, always making time for students),
- support staff (e.g., making events memorable for students and families feel valued), and
- community volunteers (e.g., commitment to organizing/creating enrichment events).

Most importantly, recognizing the contributions and investments others make toward their welfare would focus students on concrete ways that they, their progress, and their goals are valued. Knowing that others believe in and care to bring out the best in them could engage students' motivation to better themselves.

Gratitude felt and expressed by students and the improved behaviors that could ensue would likely spread to teachers and staff, encouraging them to work harder on students' behalf and prevent burnout. Though there is no direct evidence for this, there is evidence that a gratitude intervention helped reduce burnout and increase life satisfaction and a sense of personal accomplishment among Chinese schoolteachers (Chan, 2011). Therefore, developing attitudes and routines around genuine gratitude not just in students but also in school may foster stronger bonds to schools *and* communities, helping both students and schools thrive.

Social exchange is necessary for most organizations in society to function properly. One experiment showed that beneficiaries' appreciation of help depends on how they perceive helpers' actions to facilitate active goals (Converse & Fishbach, 2012), indicating that helpful exchanges prompt individuals to complete tasks and feel good. Research on gratitude in the workplace shows that gratitude promotes social cohesion, relational and job satisfaction, and even enhanced organizational functioning (Ford et al., 2018). Thus, gratitude and the valuing of benefits seem to spread across groups and positively impact organizational culture. Research examining these phenomena directly in school contexts, however, is needed.

Conclusion

This chapter reviewed the literature on gratitude in youth to focus on its advantages for students and schools. Gratitude leads to many positive outcomes of central importance to youth in schools, including satisfaction with school and other domains, supportive social relationships, psychological well-being, and resilience. Gratitude also supports engagement in the classroom, academic self-efficacy, improved motivation, and not just a readiness to learn but a greater focus on priorities and future planning among students. Thus, gratitude applications in schools have much promise for advancing students' learning and engagement with school. This chapter also reviewed recent interventions and emphasized critical areas for improving students' mental health and well-being. In particular, interventions should improve person × activity fit. The practice of gratitude is more genuine and meaningful to students and teachers, and interventions achieve broader, more sustained impacts on school cultures.

Much progress has been made in SEL programs in K-12 schools since the last edition of this Handbook. Evidence shows that such programs significantly improve social and emotional skills, attitudes, behavior, and even academic success (Durlak et al., 2011). This chapter has provided a broad survey of the field to highlight gratitude as a critical element for enhancing such programs and character education more generally. However, gratitude's impacts could likely generalize beyond individual students to improve schools' organizational effectiveness. Such individual-system interactions portend promise that gratitude could help transform schools into places that value youth and their potential above all else and where people (and communities) thrive.

References

Adler, M. G., & Fagley, N. S. (2005). Appreciation: Individual differences in finding value and meaning as a unique predictor of subjective well-being. *Journal of Personality, 73*, 79–114. https://doi.org/10.1111/j.1467-6494.2004.00305.x

Algoe, S. B. (2012). Find, remind, and bind: The functions of gratitude in everyday relationships. *Social and Personality Psychology Compass, 6*(6), 455–469. https://doi.org/10.1111/j.1751-9004.2012.00439.x

Armenta, C. N., Fritz, M. M., Walsh, L. C., & Lyubomirsky, S. (2020). Satisfied yet striving: Gratitude fosters life satisfaction and improvement motivation in youth. *Emotion.* https://doi.apa.org/doi/10.1037/emo0000896

Bartlett, M. Y., & DeSteno, D. (2006). Gratitude and prosocial behavior: Helping when it costs you. *Psychological Science, 17*, 319–325. https://doi.org/10.1111/j.1467-9280.2006.01705.x

Bono, G. (2018). Thanks! A strengths-based gratitude curriculum for tweens and teens: Four lessons to help students understand the meaning of gratitude and how to cultivate it in their everyday lives. https://ggsc.berkeley.edu/images/uploads/GGSC_Gratitude_Curriculum_MS_HS.pdf

Bono, G., Froh, J. J., Disabato, D., Blalock, D., McKnight, P., & Bausert, S. (2019). Gratitude's role in adolescent antisocial and prosocial behavior: A 4-year longitudinal investigation. *The Journal of Positive Psychology, 14*(2), 230–243. https://doi.org/10.1080/17439760.2017.1402078

Bono, G., Mangan, S., Fauteux, M., & Sender, J. (2020). A new approach to gratitude interventions in high schools that supports student wellbeing. *The Journal of Positive Psychology, 15*(5), 657–665. https://doi.org/10.1080/17439760.2020.1789712

Bono, G., & Odudu, C. (2016). Promoting the development of gratitude to build character and improve society. In D. Carr (Ed.), *Perspectives on gratitude: An interdisciplinary approach* (pp. 185–198). Routledge.

Bono, G., & Sender, J. T. (2018). How gratitude connects humans to the best in themselves and in others. *Research in Human Development, 15*(3–4), 224–237. https://doi.org/10.1080/15427609.2018.1499350

Chan, D. W. (2011). Burnout and life satisfaction: Does gratitude intervention make a difference among Chinese school teachers in Hong Kong? *Educational Psychology, 31*, 809–823. https://doi.org/10.1080/01 443410.2011.608525

Chaplin, L. N., John, D. R., Rindfleisch, A., & Froh, J. J. (2019). The impact of gratitude on adolescent materialism and generosity. *The Journal of Positive Psychology, 14*(4), 502–511. https://doi.org/10.1080/17 439760.2018.1497688

Chen, L. H., Chen, M. Y., & Tsai, Y. M. (2012). Does gratitude always work? Ambivalence over emotional expression inhibits the beneficial effect of gratitude on well-being. *International Journal of Psychology, 47*(5), 381–392. https://doi.org/10.1080/00207594.2011.632009

Chow, R. M., & Lowery, B. S. (2010). Thanks, but no thanks: The role of personal responsibility in the experience of gratitude. *Journal of Experimental Social Psychology, 46*(3), 487–493. https://doi.org/10.1016/j. jesp.2009.12.018

Converse, B. A., & Fishbach, A. (2012). Instrumentality boosts gratitude: Helpers are more appreciated while they are useful. *Psychological Science, 23*, 560–566. https://doi.org/10.1177/0956797611433334

Cregg, D. R., & Cheavens, J. S. (2021). Gratitude interventions: Effective self-help? A meta-analysis of the impact on symptoms of depression and anxiety. *Journal of Happiness Studies, 22*, 413–445. https://doi. org/10.1007/s10902-020-00236-6

Cummins, R. A. (2013). Limitations to positive psychology predicted by subjective well-being homeostasis. In Michael L. Wehmeyer (Ed.), *The Oxford handbook of positive psychology and disability* (pp. 509–526). Oxford University Press.

Davis, D. E., Choe, E., Meyers, J., Wade, N., Varjas, K., Gifford, A., Quinn, A., Hook, J. N., Van Tongeren, D. R., Griffin, B. J., & Worthington, E. L., Jr. (2016). Thankful for the little things: A meta-analysis of gratitude interventions. *Journal of Counseling Psychology, 63*(1), 20–31. https://doi.org/10.1037/cou0000107

DePaoli, J. L., Atwell, M. N., Bridgeland, J. M., & Shriver, T. P. (2018). *Respected: Perspectives of youth on high school and social and emotional learning.* Civic with Hart Research Associates. https://eric. ed.gov/?id=ED593319

Dickens, L. R. (2017). Using gratitude to promote positive change: A series of meta-analyses investigating the effectiveness of gratitude interventions. *Basic and Applied Social Psychology, 39*(4), 193–208. https://doi. org/10.1080/01973533.2017.1323638

Durlak, J. A., Weissberg, R. P., Dymnicki, A. B., Taylor, R. D., & Schellinger, K. B. (2011). The impact of enhancing students' social and emotional learning: A meta-analysis of school-based universal interventions. *Child Development, 82*(1), 405–432. https://doi.org/10.1111/j.1467-8624.2010.01564.x

Duthely, L. M., Nunn, S. G., & Avella, J. T. (2017). A novel heart-centered, gratitude-meditation intervention to increase well-being among adolescents. *Education Research International*, 1–12. https://doi. org/10.1155/2017/4891892

Eccles, J. S., Wigfield, A., Midgley, C., Reuman, D., Iver, D. M., & Feldlaufer, H. (1993). Negative effects of traditional middle schools on students' motivation. *The Elementary School Journal, 93*(5), 553–574. http:// www.jstor.com/stable/1001828

Fauteux, M. (2017). *Build community one thank you at a time.* http://www.givethx.org/

Feeney, B. C., & Collins, N. L. (2015). A new look at social support: A theoretical perspective on thriving through relationships. *Personality and Social Psychology Review, 19*(2), 113– 147. https://doi. org/10.1177/1088868314544222

Fisher, J., & Johnson, N. (2019). *The two-income trap: Are two-earner households more financially vulnerable?* (Working Papers 19-19). Center for Economic Studies, U.S. Census Bureau.

Flook, L., Goldberg, S. B., Pinger, L., & Davidson, R. J. (2015). Promoting prosocial behavior and self-regulatory skills in preschool children through a mindfulness-based kindness curriculum. *Developmental Psychology, 51*(1), 44–51. https://doi.org/10.1037/a0038256

Ford, M. T., Wang, Y., Jin, J., & Eisenberger, R. (2018). Chronic and episodic anger and gratitude toward the organization: Relationships with organizational and supervisor supportiveness and extrarole behavior. *Journal of Occupational Health Psychology, 23*(2), 175–187. https://doi.org/10.1037/ocp0000075

Forster, D. E., Pedersen, E. J., Smith, A., McCullough, M. E., & Lieberman, D. (2017). Benefit valuation predicts gratitude. *Evolution and Human Behavior, 38*(1), 18–26. https://doi.org/10.1016/j. evolhumbehav.2016.06.003

Fritz, M. M., Armenta, C. N., Walsh, L. C., & Lyubomirsky, S. (2019). Gratitude facilitates healthy eating behavior in adolescents and young adults. *Journal of Experimental Social Psychology, 81*, 4–14. https://doi. org/10.1016/j.jesp.2018.08.011

Froh, J. J., Bono, G., & Emmons, R. A. (2010). Being grateful is beyond good manners: Gratitude and motivation to contribute to society among early adolescents. *Motivation & Emotion, 34*, 144–157. https://doi. org/10.1007/s11031-010-9163-z

Froh, J. J., Bono, G., Fan, J., Emmons, R. A., Henderson, K., Harris, C., Leggio, H., & Wood, A. M. (2014). Nice thinking! An educational intervention that teaches children to think gratefully. *School Psychology Review, 43*(2), 132–152. https://doi.org/10.1080/02796015.2014.12087440

Froh, J. J., Emmons, R. A., Card, N. A., Bono, G., & Wilson, J. (2011). Gratitude and the reduced costs of materialism in adolescents. *Journal of Happiness Studies, 12*, 289–302. https://doi.org/10.1007/s10902-010-9195-9

Froh, J. J., Kashdan, T. B., Ozimkowski, K. M., & Miller, N. (2009). Who benefits the most from a gratitude intervention in children and adolescents? Examining positive affect as a moderator. *The Journal of Positive Psychology, 4*, 408–422. https://doi.org/10.1080/17439760902992464

Froh, J. J., Sefick, W. J., & Emmons, R. A. (2008). Counting blessings in early adolescents. An experimental study of gratitude and subjective well-being. *Journal of School Psychology, 46*, 213–233. https://doi.org/10.1016/j.jsp.2007.03.005

Froh, J. J., Yurkewicz, C., & Kashdan, T. B. (2009). Gratitude and subjective well-being in early adolescence: Examining gender differences. *Journal of Adolescence, 32*, 633–650. https://doi.org/10.1016/j.adolescence.2008.06.006

Furlong, M. J., You, S., Renshaw, T. L., Smith, D. C., & O'Malley, M. (2014). Preliminary development and validation of the Social and Emotional Health Survey for Secondary school students. *Social Indicators Research, 117*, 1011–1032. https://doi.org/10.1007/s11205-013-0373-0

Gil-Rivas, V., Handrup, C. T., Tanner, E., & Walker, D. K. (2019). Global mental health: A call to action. *American Journal of Orthopsychiatry, 89*(4), 420–425. https://doi.org/10.1037/ort0000373

Gordon, A. K., Musher-Eizenman, D. R., Holub, S. C., & Dalrymple, J. (2004). What are children thankful for? An archival analysis of gratitude before and after the attacks of September 11. *Journal of Applied Developmental Psychology, 25*, 541–553. https://doi.org/10.1016/j.appdev.2004.08.004

Greenspoon, P. J., & Saklofske, D. H. (2001). Toward an integration of subjective well-being and psychopathology. *Social Indicators Research, 54*, 81–108. https://doi.org/10.1023/A:1007219227883

Homan, K. J., Sedlak, B. L., & Boyd, E. A. (2014). Gratitude buffers the adverse effect of viewing the thin ideal on body dissatisfaction. *Body Image, 11*(3), 245–250. https://doi.org/10.1016/j.bodyim.2014.03.005

Howells, K. (2014). An exploration of the role of gratitude in enhancing teacher–student relationships. *Teaching and Teacher Education, 42*, 58–67. https://doi.org/10.1016/j.tate.2014.04.004

Hoyt, L. T., Chase-Lansdale, P. L., McDade, T. W., & Adam E. K. (2012). Positive youth, healthy adults: Does positive well-being in adolescence predict better perceived health and fewer risky health behaviors in young adulthood? *Journal of Adolescent Health, 50*(1), 66–73. https://doi.org/10.1016/j.jadohealth.2011.05.002

Israel-Cohen, Uzefovsky, Y. F., Kashy-Rosenbaum, G., & Kaplan, O. (2015) Gratitude and PTSD symptoms among Israeli youth exposed to missile attacks: Examining the mediation of positive and negative affect and life satisfaction. *The Journal of Positive Psychology, 10*(2), 99–106. https://doi.org/10.1080/17439760.2014.927910

Jeynes, W. H. (2019). A meta-analysis on the relationship between character education and student achievement and behavioral outcomes. *Education and Urban Society, 51*(1), 33–71. https://doi.org/10.1177/0013124517747681

Jiang, H., Sun, P., Liu, Y., & Pan, M. (2015). Gratitude and late adolescents' school well-being: The mediating role of materialism. *Social Indicators Research, 127*, 1363–1376. https://doi.org/10.1007/s11205-015-1007-5

Johnson, D. W., Johnson, R. T., Roseth, C. J., & Shin, T.-S. (2014). The relationship between motivation and achievement in interdependent situations. *Journal of Applied Social Psychology, 44*, 622–633. https://doi.org/10.1111/jasp.12280

Kaczmarek, L. D., Kashdan, T. B., Drążkowski, D., Bujacz, A., & Goodman, F. R. (2014). Why do greater curiosity and fewer depressive symptoms predict gratitude intervention use? Utility beliefs, social norm, and self-control beliefs. *Personality and Individual Differences, 66*, 165–170. http://dx.doi.org/10.1016/j.paid.2014.03.032

Kashdan, T. B., Mishra, A., Breen, W. E., & Froh, J. J. (2009). Gender differences in gratitude: Examining appraisals, narratives, the willingness to express emotions, and changes in psychological needs. *Journal of Personality, 77*, 691–730. https://doi.org/10.1111/j.1467–6494.2009.00562.x

Kendler, K. S., Liu, X., Gardner, C. O., McCullough, M. E., Larson, D., & Prescott, C. A. (2003). Dimensions of religiosity and their relationship to lifetime psychiatric and substance use disorders. *American Journal of Psychiatry, 160*, 496–503. https://doi.org/10.1176/appi.ajp.160.3.496

King, R. B., & Datu, J. A. D. (2018). Grateful students are motivated, engaged, and successful in school: Cross-sectional, longitudinal, and experimental evidence. *Journal of School Psychology, 70*, 105–122. https://doi.org/10.1016/j.jsp.2018.08.001

Kumar, A., & Epley, N. (2018). Undervaluing gratitude: Expressers misunderstand the consequences of showing appreciation. *Psychological Science, 29*, 1423–1435. https://doi.org/10.1177/0956797618772506

LaGuardia, J. G., & Ryan, R. M. (2002). What adolescents need: A self-determination theory perspective on development within families, school, and society. In F. Pajares & T. Urdan (Eds.), *Academic motivation of adolescents* (pp. 193–220). Information Age.

Lambert, N. M., Graham, S. M., & Fincham, F. D. (2009). A prototype analysis of gratitude: Varieties of gratitude experiences. *Personality and Social Psychology Bulletin, 35*, 1193–1207. https://doi.org/10.1177/0146167209338071

Lambert, N. M., Gwinn, A. M., Baumeister, R. F., Fincham, F. D., Gable, S. L., Strachman, A., & Washburn, I. J. (2013). A boost of positive affect: The perks of sharing positive experiences and grateful experiences. *Journal of Social and Personal Relationships, 30*, 24–43. https://doi.org/10.1177/0265407512449400

Li, D., Zhang, W., Li, X., Li, N., & Ye, B. (2012). Gratitude and suicidal ideation and suicide attempts among Chinese adolescents: Direct, mediated, and moderated effects. *Journal of Adolescence, 35*(1), 55–66. https://doi.org/10.1016/j.adolescence.2011.06.005

Lin, C. C. (2015). Gratitude and depression in young adults: The mediating role of self-esteem and well-being. *Personality and Individual Differences, 87*, 30–34. https://doi.org/10.1016/j.paid.2015.07.017

Lyubomirsky, S., Dickerhoof, R., Boehm, J. K., & Sheldon, K. M. (2011). Becoming happier takes both a will and a proper way: An experimental longitudinal intervention to boost well-being. *Emotion, 11*(2), 391–402. https://doi.org/10.1037/a0022575

Ma, M., Kibler, J. L., & Sly, K. (2013). Gratitude is associated with greater levels of protective factors and lower levels of risks in African American adolescents. *Journal of Adolescence, 36*(5), 983–991. https://doi.org/10.1016/j.adolescence.2013.07.012

McCullough, M. E., Emmons, R. A., & Tsang, J. (2002). The grateful disposition: A conceptual and empirical topography. *Journal of Personality and Social Psychology, 82*, 112–127. https://doi.org/10.1037/0022–3514.82.1.112

McCullough, M. E., Kilpatrick, S. D., & Emmons, R. A., & Larson, D. B. (2001). Is gratitude a moral affect? *Psychological Bulletin, 127*, 249–266. https://doi.org/10.1037/0033–2909.127.2.249

Meindl, P., Quirk, A., & Graham, J. (2018). Best practices for school-based moral education. *Policy Insights from the Behavioral and Brain Sciences, 5*(1), 3–10. https://doi.org/10.1177/2372732217747087

Mendonça, S. E., Merçon-Vargas, E. A., Payir, A., & Tudge, J. R. (2018). The development of gratitude in seven societies: Cross-cultural highlights. *Cross-Cultural Research, 52*(1), 135–150. https://doi.org/10.1177/1069397117737245

O'Connor, M., Sanson, A. V., Toumbourou, J. W., Norrish, J., & Olsson, C. A. (2017). Does positive mental health in adolescence longitudinally predict healthy transitions in young adulthood? *Journal of Happiness Studies, 18*(1), 177–198. https://doi.org/10.1007/s10902-016-9723-3

Okonofua, J. A., Paunesku, D., & Walton, G. M. (2016). Brief intervention to encourage empathic discipline cuts suspension rates in half among adolescents. *PNAS, 113*(19), 5221–5226. https://doi.org/10.1073/pnas.1523698113

Park, N., & Peterson, C. (2006). Moral competence and character strengths among adolescents: The development and validation of the values in action inventory of strengths for youth. *Journal of Adolescence, 29*(6), 891–909. https://doi.org/10.1016/j.adolescence.2006.04.011

Park, Y., Impett, E. A., MacDonald, G., & Lemay Jr, E. P. (2019). Saying "thank you": Partners' expressions of gratitude protect relationship satisfaction and commitment from the harmful effects of attachment insecurity. *Journal of Personality and Social Psychology, 117*(4), 773–806. https://doi.org/10.1037/pspi0000178

Reckart, H., Huebner, E. S., Hills, K. J., & Valois, R. F. (2017). A preliminary study of the origins of early adolescents' gratitude differences. *Personality and Individual Differences, 116*, 44–50. https://doi.org/10.1016/j.paid.2017.04.020

Renshaw, T. L., & Olinger Steeves, R. M. (2016). What good is gratitude in youth and schools? A systematic review and meta-analysis of correlates and intervention outcomes. *Psychology in the Schools, 53*(3), 286–305. https://doi.org/10.1002/pits.21903

Rey, L., Quintana, C., Merida-Lopez, S., & Extremera, N. (2019). Being bullied at school: Gratitude as potential protective factor for suicide risk in adolescents. *Frontier Psychology.* https://doi.org/10.3389/fpsyg.2019.00662

Rusk, R. D., Vella-Brodrick, D. A., & Waters, L. (2016). Gratitude or gratefulness? A conceptual review and proposal of the system of appreciative functioning. *Journal of Happiness Studies, 17*(5), 2191–2212. https://doi.org/10.1007/s10902-015-9675-z

Seligman, M. E. P., Steen, T. A., Park, N., & Peterson, C. (2005). Positive psychology progress: Empirical validation of interventions. *American Psychologist, 60*, 410–421. https://doi.org/10.1037/0003–066X.60.5.410

Serrano-Puche, J. (2017). Developing health habits in media consumption: A proposal for dealing with information overload. In R. P. Figueiredo Marques & J. C. L. Batista (Eds.), *Information and communication overload in the digital age* (pp. 202–222). IGI Global. https://doi.org/10.4018/978-1-5225-2061-0.ch009

Simmel, G. (1950). *The sociology of Georg Simmel.* Free Press.

Smith, A., Pedersen, E. J., Forster, D. E., McCullough, M. E., & Lieberman, D. (2017). Cooperation: The roles of interpersonal value and gratitude. *Evolution and Human Behavior, 38*(6), 695–703. https://doi.org/10.1016/j.evolhumbehav.2017.08.003

Stoeckel, M., Weissbrod, C., & Ahrens, A. (2015). The adolescent response to parental illness: The influence of dispositional gratitude. *Journal of Child and Family Studies, 24*, 1501–1509. https://doi.org/10.1007/s10826-014-9955-y

Suldo, S. M., Hearon, B. V., Bander, B., McCullough, M., Garofano, J., Roth, R. A., & Tan, S. Y. (2015). Increasing elementary school students' subjective well-being through a classwide positive psychology intervention: Results of a pilot study. *Contemporary School Psychology, 19*(4), 300–311. https://doi.org/10.1007/s40688-015-0061-y

Suldo, S. M., Thalji-Raitano, A., Kiefer, S. M., & Ferron, J. M. (2016). Conceptualizing high school students' mental health through a dual-factor model. *School Psychology Review, 45*, 434–457. https://doi.org/10.17105/SPR45-4.434–457

Tian, L., Du, M., & Huebner, E. S. (2015). The effect of gratitude on elementary school students' subjective well-being in schools: The mediating role of prosocial behavior. *Social Indicators Research, 122*(3), 887–904. https://doi.org/10.1007/s11205-014-0712-9

Tian, L., Pi, L., Huebner, E. S., & Du, M. (2016). Gratitude and adolescents' subjective well-being in school: The multiple mediating roles of basic psychological needs satisfaction at school. *Frontiers in Psychology, 7*, 1409. https://doi.org/10.3389/fpsyg.2016.01409

Trask-Kerr, K. M., Chin, T-C., & Vella-Brodrick, D. A. (2019). Positive education and the new prosperity: Exploring young people's conceptions of prosperity and success. *Australian Journal of Education, 63*,190–208. https://doi.org/10.1177/0004944119860600

Tsang, J. (2006). Gratitude and prosocial behaviour: An experimental test of gratitude. *Cognition and Emotion, 20*, 138–148. https://doi.org/10.1080/02699930500172341

Twenge, J. M. (2017). *iGen: Why today's super-connected kids are growing up less rebellious, more tolerant, less happy—and completely unprepared for adulthood–and what that means for the rest of us.* Simon and Schuster.

Twenge, J. M., Gentile, B., DeWall, C. N., Ma, D., Lacefield, K., & Schurtz, D. R. (2010). Birth cohort increases in psychopathology among young Americans, 1938–2007: A cross-temporal meta-analysis of the MMPI. *Clinical Psychology Review, 30*(2), 145–154. https://doi.org/10.1016/j.cpr.2009.10.005

Wang, D., Wang, Y. C., & Tudge, J. R. (2015). Expressions of gratitude in children and adolescents: Insights from China and the United States. *Journal of Cross-Cultural Psychology, 46*(8), 1039–1058. https://doi.org/10.1177/1069397117737245

Weybright, E. H., Schulenberg, J., & Caldwell, L. L. (2020). More bored today than yesterday? National trends in adolescent boredom from 2008 to 2017. *Journal of Adolescent Health, 66*(3), 360–365. https://doi.org/10.1016/j.jadohealth.2019.09.021

Wood, A. M., Brown, G. D. A., & Maltby, J. (2011). Thanks, but I'm used to better: A relative rank model of gratitude. *Emotion, 11*, 175–180. https://doi.org/10.1037/a0021553

Wood, A. M., Froh, J. J., & Geraghty, A. W. (2010). Gratitude and well-being: A review and theoretical integration. *Clinical Psychology Review, 30*, 890–905. https://doi.org/10.1016/j.cpr.2010.03.005

Yeager, D. S., Dahl, R. E., & Dweck, C. S. (2018). Why interventions to influence adolescent behavior often fail but could succeed. *Perspectives on Psychological Science, 13*(1), 101–122. https://doi.org/10.1177/1745691617722620

Yeager, D. S., Fong, C. J., Lee, H. Y., Espelage, D. L. (2015). Declines in efficacy of anti-bullying programs among older adolescents: Theory and a three-level meta-analysis. *Journal of Applied Developmental Psychology, 37*, 36–51. https://doi.org/10.1016/j.appdev.2014.11.005

You, S., Lee, J., & Lee, Y. (2020). Relationships between gratitude, social support, and prosocial and problem behaviors. *Current Psychology,* 1–8. https://doi.org/10.1007/s12144-020-00775-4

Zhen, R., Liu, R. D., Ding, Y., Jiang, R., Jiang, S., & Hong, W. (2019). Gratitude and academic engagement among primary students: Examining a multiple mediating model. *Current Psychology,* 1–9. https://doi.org/10.1007/s12144-019-00202-3

Zhou, X., & Wu, X. (2016). Understanding the roles of gratitude and social support in posttraumatic growth among adolescents after Ya'an earthquake: A longitudinal study. *Personality and Individual Differences, 101*, 4–8. https://doi.org/10.1016/j.paid.2016.05.033

9

CULTIVATING MINDFULNESS IN SCHOOLS TO PROMOTE WELL-BEING

Tyler L. Renshaw, Sean N. Weeks, Anthony J. Roberson, Shelley R. Upton, John D. Barr, Mary L. Phan and Caleb D. Farley

Mindfulness is a contemporary psychological construct that has origins in Buddhism's ancient traditions and other Eastern worldviews. It was not until the late 1970s that mindfulness transitioned from Eastern philosophy to Western science. This secularizing shift was spurred by the work of Jon Kabat-Zinn (1990), who claimed that mindfulness "can be learned or practiced ... without appealing to [Eastern] culture or Buddhist authority to enrich or authenticate it" (p. 12). Kabat-Zinn and colleagues initiated the mindfulness-as-intervention movement by testing the effects of mindfulness-based practices for reducing stress with medical patients experiencing chronic pain. The success of these early studies led, over time, to the eventual generalization of mindfulness-based intervention (MBI) as an evidence-based practice for reducing suffering and promoting well-being with diverse individuals across a variety of service settings. This chapter focuses specifically on the application of mindfulness and MBI within school settings to promote desirable psychological functioning among students and their caregivers. This chapter's previous version focused on cultivating mindfulness with *students* (Renshaw & O'Malley, 2014). The present work expands the reach of MBI to *teachers* and *parents*, as schools are becoming increasingly common hubs for intervening with caregivers—both for their own sake (i.e., direct benefit) and for the sake of the youth they care for (i.e., indirect benefit).

To set the stage for mindfulness in schools, definitions and key concepts are discussed. Following, we highlight the landscape of evidence-based practice related to MBI and measuring mindfulness, pointing out key considerations and directions for future research. Practical applications of mindfulness and MBI in schools are then discussed, emphasizing its potential within a multitiered system of supports (MTSS) for promoting mental health and social-emotional well-being as well as its promise as an indirect service delivery approach with caregivers. Finally, essential diversity and developmental considerations are identified when using mindfulness in schools to address health disparities and optimize the potential benefit of MBI for all students.

Definitions and Key Concepts

The most common definition of mindfulness is likely that provided by Kabat-Zinn (1994), who described it as "paying attention in a particular way: on purpose, in the present moment, and

DOI: 10.4324/9781003013778-11

nonjudgmentally" (p. 4). Smalley and Winston (2010) offered a similar definition of mindfulness, describing it as a state of consciousness wherein one "observ[es] physical, emotional, and mental experiences with deliberate, open, and curious attention" (p. 11). Brown et al. (2007) have defined mindfulness along the same lines as "receptive attention to and awareness of present events and experience" (p. 212). To consolidate the essence of these similar definitions, a few different distillations of the *core components* of mindfulness have been offered in other works (e.g., Renshaw, 2012; Renshaw & Cook, 2017; Renshaw et al., 2017). Yet, this chapter prefers the consensus definition from a renowned group of mindfulness scholars (Bishop et al., 2004), who describe the construct as "the self-regulation of attention so that it is maintained on immediate experience," which is accompanied by "a particular orientation towards one experience in the present moment" (p. 232). Throughout this chapter, we refer to these two core components of mindfulness as *present moment awareness* (PMA) and *responding with acceptance* (RWA). Instead of thinking of PMA and RWA as states of mind or qualities of consciousness, we suggest that it is more useful to think of them as *actions, behaviors,* or *skills,* which can be learned and therefore trained in schools like any other social-emotional skill (Renshaw, 2020).

The first core component of mindfulness, PMA, is the action or skill of orienting one's attention to experiences in the *here and now.* Noticing what one is thinking in the moment—whether helpful or unhelpful—and tuning in to one's feelings—whether desirable or undesirable—are common, everyday applications of PMA. Nonapplications or opposites of PMA include the just as common, everyday experiences of ruminating about one's past mistakes or forecasting about one's future (but not yet actual) missteps. Examples of proper PMA include an adolescent noticing the "heartbreak" they experience following a romantic break-up, the "butterflies in their stomach" before taking a math test, and the encouraging self-talk running through their mind while succeeding at a well-rehearsed task (e.g., "Wow! I'm really good at this!"). Nonexamples of PMA, then, include the same adolescent retracing the events leading up to the romantic break-up, planning ways to effectively avoid the math test to relieve the "butterflies in their stomach," and becoming completed absorbed in—or lost in *flow* with (see Chapter 19 of this volume)—the familiar task at hand. These nonexamples of PMA are not necessarily unhelpful actions, as these same experiences can sometimes be useful for problem-solving or even enjoyable for their own sake. The point is simply that these examples are *not* mindfulness, as PMA requires being directly in touch with one's experiences in the here and now, as opposed to planning around or being absorbed in these experiences.

The second core component of mindfulness, RWA, is the behavior or skill of engaging in one's experiences in a welcoming and open way. As Renshaw (2020) puts it,

> the core features of RWA are being curious about the nature of one's experiences in the present moment while either (a) intentionally staying in contact with whatever one is experiencing for however long it happens to last or (b) persisting in accomplishing a valued activity with which the experience may potentially interfere.
>
> *(p. 146)*

The opposite of RWA is an *avoidant response,* which functions to change the content of one's experiences or reduce the amount of time one is in contact with such experiences. To continue the scenarios from earlier, examples of proper RWA include an adolescent staying in touch with the "butterflies in their stomach" while persisting and engaging with the math test, or mundanely noticing the onset and offset of their "heartbreak" throughout the school day. Nonexamples of RWA, then, might include this same adolescent complaining to the teacher that they are "sick" and requesting to visit the nurse's office (to escape the math test), or picking up one's phone to check notifications or cruise social media for a quick distraction whenever feelings of "heartbreak" arise.

Again, these nonexamples or RWA are not inherently or always harmful. Rather, the point is that they are *not* mindfulness, as they involve actions that are antithetical to staying in touch with one's experiences in a welcoming and open way.

With these two core components of mindfulness—PMA and RWA—in hand, we can now move to define the notion of mindfulness-as-intervention or MBI. In short, MBI refers to any approach or procedure that aims to train PMA and RWA to reduce suffering or improve well-being. As Renshaw (2020) puts it, the critical feature of MBI "is not necessarily the structure of the intervention [per se] but rather the functions of the intervention" (p. 147). Thus, any intervention that improves PMA and RWA might be considered an MBI. Various techniques and treatment packages have been developed toward this end. MBI is currently a broad umbrella category of interventions, accounting for a variety of approaches ranging from relatively standardized and narrow treatment approaches (e.g., mindfulness-based stress reduction [MBSR]; Kabat-Zinn, 1994) to more flexible and integrative treatment approaches (e.g., acceptance and commitment therapy [ACT]; Hayes et al., 1999). MBI also includes prevention-oriented social-emotional learning (SEL) curricula for educational use (e.g., Learning to Breathe; Broderick, 2013), and even brief, focused procedures targeting specific problems and populations (e.g., Soles of the Feet; Felver & Singh, 2020). Despite their differences, MBIs tend to share common elements, such as formal mindfulness meditations (e.g., mindful breathing and mindful body scan) and applied or everyday mindfulness exercises (e.g., mindful eating and mindful movement). Other common elements of MBIs include metaphorical exercises to help with intuiting mindfulness (e.g., leaves on the stream, taking your mind for a walk) and formal psychoeducation about how mindfulness works to affect emotional regulation and positive behavior change. What is becoming increasingly apparent throughout the last decade is that—despite their composition or complexity—MBIs demonstrate empirical support for uses that are relevant to schools. The next section overviews what is known, so far, about the effectiveness of MBI with youth and caregivers, with a specific focus on students, teachers, and parents.

Empirical Support for Mindfulness-Based Interventions

MBI with Children and Adolescents

Over the past 20 years, the literature on MBI with children and adolescents has proliferated (Black, 2015). While many scholars suggest that the research base is still relatively young, several recent meta-analyses synthesizing effect sizes from primary studies provide a reliable estimate of the overall effectiveness of MBI with students and youth. This section of the chapter reviews evidence gathered from eight meta-analytic reviews, which have been discussed by Klingbeil et al. (2020) and others (Borquist-Conlon et al., 2019; Carsley et al., 2017; Dunning et al., 2019; Kallapiran et al., 2015; Klingbeil, Fischer et al., 2017; Klingbeil, Renshaw et al., 2017; Zenner et al., 2014; Zoogman et al., 2015). Taken together, we believe the outcomes of these eight meta-analytic reviews suggest that the use of MBIs in schools and with youth is generally safe and effective for improving various desirable psychological outcomes. Nevertheless, much work remains to optimize MBI for efficient, acceptable, and sustainable use in schools.

According to these several available meta-analyses, the majority of MBIs currently used in schools are modeled after the following approaches: MBSR (Kabat-Zinn, 1994), mindfulness-based cognitive therapy (MBCT; Segal et al., 2002), ACT (Hayes et al., 1999), dialectical behavior therapy (DBT; Linehan et al., 1991), and mindfulness-based yoga programs (MY; e.g., Dariotis et al., 2017). Most school-based MBI used formalized interventions through third-party providers or research staff, although some included programs explicitly designed for implementation by teachers or other staff at the school. Interestingly, Klingbeil, Renshaw et al. (2017) found no difference in average effect sizes from studies conducted in schools versus those carried out in community or clinical settings—suggesting that school-based MBI is just as effective as MBI with youths in other settings.

Perhaps the most striking conclusion drawn from the several available meta-analyses of MBI with children and adolescents is how broad the range of outcomes is that have been positively affected by mindfulness training (Borquist-Conlon et al., 2019; Carsley et al., 2017; Dunning et al., 2019; Kallapiran et al., 2015; Klingbeil, Fischer et al., 2017; Klingbeil, Renshaw et al., 2017; Zenner et al., 2014; Zoogman et al., 2015). To start with, when measuring the mechanism of mindfulness itself, MBI effect sizes have ranged from small to medium, are positive, and have moderated the effects of mental health outcomes. In terms of reducing stress, negative emotions, and internalizing problems, MBI effect sizes were positive and ranged from small to moderate. Furthermore, MBI has been shown to have small to moderate effect sizes for increasing subjective well-being and related positive psychological variables, including positive emotions, coping strategies in response to stress, self-esteem, and self-concept. Although research is less robust in terms of MBI effects on undesirable behavioral outcomes—with far fewer studies targeting this domain—available evidence indicates small to moderate effect sizes for reducing externalizing and disruptive behaviors, with small effects on reducing aggression and hostility. Maybe the most inconsistent findings, so far, are in the area of MBI effects on prosocial behavior and social skills, with some reviews yielding nonsignificant outcomes while others showed small positive effects. Furthermore, multiple meta-analyses indicate that school functioning and academic achievement are improved by MBI, with small positive effects. Ultimately, it seems safe to say that MBI is useful in schools for improving a variety of psychological and educational outcomes for children and adolescents. However, given the variability in effect sizes observed across meta-analyses, it also seems wise to conclude that these effects are likely small, especially for classroom-based MBI implemented as universal supports (Renshaw, 2020).

Beyond indicating generally positive effects, the available literature on MBI with children and adolescents also suggests several limitations. For example, barriers to MBI provision within schools have been identified, including scheduling conflicts, lack of resources or available spaces, coordinating student schedules, and securing buy-in from parents and teachers (Dariotis et al., 2017). Interestingly, youths' age has not significantly moderated the overall effect sizes of MBI in meta-analyses. However, some studies have found differences by age, suggesting the need to explore further demographic moderators. For example, MBIs produced stronger effects on executive functioning with older youths and reduced externalizing behaviors with larger effect sizes with younger youths. Moreover, effect sizes for mental health outcomes were generally larger for participants in late adolescence, with effects reducing to nonsignificant levels with younger children. Furthermore, some primary studies within the meta-analyses found that MBIs may be more effective for females and that they worked equally well across youth with varying clinical diagnoses, and with and without educational disabilities. We, therefore, echo the calls made elsewhere, recommending that further rigorous research is warranted to understand potential moderators that might inform the precise use of MBI in schools (Renshaw, 2020; Renshaw & Cook, 2017; Renshaw et al., 2017).

MBI with Teachers and Parents

As the research base for youth-focused MBI has grown in recent years, so too has the evidence for using MBI with teachers and parents. Much of the investigations with this population have honed-in on the effectiveness of mindfulness training for positively altering mental health outcomes centered around psychological well-being and distress. Thus far, the evidence suggests that MBI offers some improved outcomes for both parents and teachers. Yet, this conclusion should be held more tentatively than the upshot of MBI with children and adolescents, which we believe indicates broader and more consistently positive effects compared to MBI with caregivers. It is noteworthy that much of the theory underlying providing MBI with caregivers focuses on their potential indirect benefits to youth. However, evaluation studies have focused almost entirely on the direct benefit of MBI for caregivers themselves—recognizing that caregiving can have substantial psychological costs.

Teachers are crucial contributors to society, and their occupation is often demanding and stressful (Kyriacou, 2001). Teachers experience high burnout and job transition (Markow & Pieters, 2012), with recent data suggesting that 50% of new teachers will not be teaching within five years (Markow & Cooper, 2008). Clearly, then, stress management skills and psychological support are germane considerations for these caregivers. MBI has been developed as one potential means toward this end. To date, recent syntheses of relevant research with teachers suggest that MBIs produce improvements in stress levels and psychological health, including higher resiliency levels, which may help address teacher burnout (Thayer et al., 2020). A recent meta-analysis on this topic by Klingbeil and Renshaw (2018) indicated that MBI produced moderate improvements in teacher psychological well-being, mindfulness skills, and classroom practices. Overall, this emerging evidence suggests that MBI may help enhance teachers' stress management skills and improve their psychological health. Yet, the evidence base does not provide any information about how MBI might indirectly benefit students in the classroom.

In addition to serving as a setting for intervening with educators, schools are also common hubs for targeting youths' primary caregivers: parents and guardians. Tasked with the vital responsibility of raising youths, parents, and caregivers often experience emotional adversity and may benefit from direct training in coping skills to overcome these challenges. It is well-understood that the parent–child relationship within the home environment is one of the most critical factors for healthy child development and well-being. Specifically, insufficient or neglectful parental care is a common predictor of youths' future problems (Felitti et al., 1998). In response to these realities, a large number of parent training programs have been created. However, research suggests that these programs are less effective for caregivers who struggle with mental health issues or significant stress, primarily because they are less likely to complete the program and implement these practices at home (van den Hoofdakker et al., 2010). MBI with parents has been offered as a potential solution to address this concern.

Recent syntheses of the research suggest that MBI with parents has produced significant decreases in parental stress, depression, anxiety, and significant increases in self-reported mindfulness skills, with effect sizes ranging from small to medium (Frantz et al., 2018; Taylor et al., 2016). Other nonexperimental studies investigating the value of mindful parenting have demonstrated that caregivers reporting higher levels of mindfulness employ more helpful and less problematic parenting practices than those with lower levels of mindfulness (de Bruin et al., 2014; Williams & Wahler, 2010). Congruent with the evidence base with teachers, the available research supporting the use of MBI with parents suggests that this approach to intervention may be useful for addressing parental psychological health and cultivating nurturing familial environments. Yet, it has revealed little about how MBI with this population might indirectly improve youth outcomes. We, therefore, reiterate the calls of others to both strengthen and expand research in this area, with the goal of understanding both MBI's potential direct and indirect impacts with caregivers (Klingbeil & Renshaw, 2018).

Empirical Support for Measuring Mindfulness

In addition to evidence-based intervention, another—often overlooked—consideration when applying mindfulness in schools is the available empirical support for mindfulness measures. Using appropriate assessment tools is a critical component in effectively implementing and evaluating interventions, and MBIs are no exception. The use of strong measures allows for validating the purported mechanisms of change driving MBI and reveals if changes in mindfulness proceed observed changes in outcomes of interest, strengthening the evidence for causation (see Nock, 2007). The development and study of mindfulness assessment tools intended for youths have recently expanded considerably. Although these measures vary in a variety of important theoretical ways, most share a common self-report rating format with respondents indicating the relative frequency of—or degrees of agreement with—statements focusing on measuring trait (or dispositional) mindfulness.

Given the mindfulness core components model presented earlier in this chapter, youths' trait mindfulness might be best understood as the regularity with which one experiences PMA and RWA during everyday life. In other words, not only may people be considered more or less mindful at a particular moment in time (i.e., *state* mindfulness) but they might also be described as more or less mindful individuals most of the time (i.e., *trait* mindfulness). Similar to other survey instruments measuring state-trait distinctions, mindfulness measures were originally developed with university students and adult-aged samples. In recent years, however, trait mindfulness surveys have been successfully tested with youth samples and shown to co-vary with valued outcomes (Goodman et al., 2017). However, with few exceptions, such as the State Mindfulness Scale for Physical Activity (Ullrich-French et al., 2017), trait mindfulness surveys outnumber state measures (Goodman et al., 2017). We suggest this discrepancy in measurement approaches is far from trivial, as the primary focus of MBI is developing PMA and RWA *right now*, which relates more closely to state views of mindfulness than trait views. Yet, because trait mindfulness measures are the primary tools available, mindfulness research with youth and in schools has relied almost exclusively on trait measurements (Goodman et al., 2017). The present understanding of the evidence supporting the processes underlying MBI is thus based on a construct indirectly related to its purported mechanism of change (Thompson & Waltz, 2007).

The concerns with the current measurement paradigm are less about the strength of traditional reliability and validity evidence of particular scales and more about the lack of theoretical coherence between what these instruments measure and how they are used. To understand the true strength of MBI evidence with youth, it is important to recognize how mindfulness is typically measured and how conclusions from mindfulness studies depend, in part, on the particular instrument chosen to assess the construct. Although an in-depth analysis of available instruments is beyond this chapter's scope, we highlight features of several trait mindfulness measures to provide interested readers a starting point to seek information about their theoretical and psychometric strengths and weaknesses (see Eklund et al., 2017; Goodman et al., 2017; Grossman, 2011). The previous edition of this chapter (Renshaw & O'Malley, 2014) identified and discussed two primary trait mindfulness surveys: the adolescent version of the Mindful Attention Awareness Scale (MAAS-A) and the Child and Adolescent Mindfulness Measure (CAMM). The MAAS-A and CAMM remain the most frequently studied instruments and are commonly used as convergent validity measures of youth mindfulness in the research of other mindfulness tools (e.g., Johnson et al., 2017; Levinson et al., 2014; West, 2008). These two measures are reviewed below first, followed by an expanded review of several other trait mindfulness scales developed in recent years.

Trait Mindfulness Assessment Tools

The CAMM is a 10-item, self-report mindfulness measure for youth ages 10–17 years (Greco et al., 2011) based on a multidimensional conceptualization of mindfulness—*acting with awareness*, *accepting without judgment*, and *observing*—used by the adult Kentucky Inventory of Mindfulness Scale (KIMS). All items are reverse coded to produce a global mindfulness score. Two other commonly used youth mindfulness measures are adapted from the MAAS (Brown & Ryan, 2003) and reflect a single facet of mindfulness—*being present*. These are the MAAS-A (for adolescents) and the MAAS-C (for children). The MAAS-A is a 14-item measure for ages 14–18 years (Brown et al., 2011), whereas the MAAS-C is a 15-item measure for ages 9–13 years (Lawlor et al., 2014). Item content is nearly identical, with the MAAS-A excluding an item related to driving (i.e., "I drive places on 'automatic pilot'…") and the MAAS-C changing the language of that same item to "I walk into a room, and then wonder why I went there." Like the CAMM, all MAAS items are reverse-coded and summed to produce a single total score representing mindfulness.

Newer and less commonly studied self-report measures feature multidimensional factor structures and produce multiple scores. These include the Mindful Thinking and Action Scale for Adolescents (MTASA), the Comprehensive Inventory of Mindfulness Experiences-Adolescents (CHIME-A), the Adolescent and Adult Mindfulness Scale (AAMS), and the Mindfulness Inventory for Children and Adolescents (MICA). The MTASA (West et al., 2005) is a 32-item measure appropriate for ages 11–19 years, which uses a mix of positively and negatively worded items. The negative items are reverse-coded to produce an overall mindfulness total score and four subscale scores. The CHIME-A is a 25-item measure for adolescents that uses both positively and negatively worded items derived from the adult version of the CHIME (Johnson et al., 2017). Total scores are calculated for each of the eight specific domains, but the authors recommend against calculating a global total mindfulness score.

The AAMS, on the other hand, is a 19-item measure that has been investigated with individuals from ages 9 to 25 years and recommended for use with individuals 11 years and older (Droutman, 2018). Item content covers four domains and has mixed valence. The authors recommend averaging items within each subdomain to obtain subscale scores, followed by summing the averages to obtain a higher-order overall mindfulness score. Furthermore, the MICA is a 25-item measure appropriate for youth ages 8–18 (Briere, 2011). Items are both positively and negatively worded and cover five subdomains. Importantly, in contrast with the other measures described above, the MICA's structural characteristics and construct validity have not been formally evaluated in an empirical study. Finally, to our knowledge, only one measure—the Mindful Student Questionnaire (MSQ)—uses all positive wording, tapping the presence of mindful experience rather than the lack thereof (cf. CAMM and MAAS). The MSQ is also the only instrument developed explicitly for use within educational contexts to measure school-specific mindfulness experiences, yielding both PMA and RWA scores that have been validated for use with students in Grades 6–8 (Renshaw, 2017).

Future Directions and Alterative Assessment Approaches

As stated earlier, the measures described above share a common self-report format. However, they differ significantly in underlying theory, psychometric qualities of scores, and contexts in which their use is justified. It is critical, then, that these instruments are not considered interchangeable but rather as unique tools producing related yet distinct scores. These differences across measures create challenges for evaluating MBI evidence, as the meaning of change in process or mechanism scores will depend on what tools were used. Instead of relying on unidimensional mindfulness measures, we recommend multidimensional measurements to identify the mechanisms for changing or mediating responses to MBI. We also recommend that future research should focus on investigating the interrelationships among these trait measures and the value-added effects of these measures for predicting valued outcomes. Such findings may inform an evidence-based approach for matching the most useful mindfulness assessment tools with desired MBI outcomes. Additionally, given the development of competing mindfulness frameworks vying for attention in schools, such as psychological flexibility (Greco et al., 2008) and self-compassion (Neff et al., 2021), more empirical attention should be paid to exploring the differences (or lack thereof) among these seemingly synonymous constructs.

Although self-report rating scales administered before and after an intervention (summatively or as progress monitors) is the dominant modality for assessing youth mindfulness at present, some other measurement approaches from the adult literature have also been proposed for youth. One suggested method involves experiential reports sampled throughout a given period (Moore et al., 2016), such as a school day. This approach maintains self-report ratings but allows for data to be collected outside the immediate context of an MBI to give more detail about the stability of mindful experience over time. Moreover, the wording of items within an experience-sampling measurement approach might be tailored to tap trait or state mindfulness constructs, increasing potential application for targeted assessment.

Some other proposed methods for assessing mindfulness break from self-reports entirely. One promising nonsurvey method is the objective breath counting tasks (BCT), which may have utility as both an assessment of PMA and a mindfulness skill-building exercise (Levinson et al., 2014). Research shows BCT scores have small to moderate correlations with mindfulness survey scores, suggesting potential incremental validity beyond traditional rating scales. BCT scores have also shown some discriminate validity with similar constructs as well as predictive validity with more objective measures, such as discerning between individuals that have and have not received MBI (Levinson et al., 2014; Wong et al., 2018). Notably, the direct construct representation of BCT is narrowly focused on PMA and only indirectly associates with the other core mindfulness component, RWA. Translational research is still needed to investigate to what degree and for what applications nonsurvey methods, like the BCT, are defensible for use with youth and in schools. Yet these approaches offer the possibility of expanding the variety of mindfulness assessment tools available for informing and evaluating school-based MBI. Given that strong validation evidence supporting these alternative methods is likely a ways off, we strongly recommend that current applications of nonsurvey methods in schools be considered adjuncts to—not replacements for—traditional (albeit limited) trait mindfulness measures.

Key Consideration for Using Mindfulness in Schools

So far in this chapter, mindfulness and MBI have been defined and readers have been oriented to the landscape of evidence-based practice related to MBI and mindfulness measures. Moreover, mindfulness has been conceptualized as a positive psychological disposition or skillset that is amenable to empirical measurement and effective intervention, similar to other constructs covered in this volume (e.g., optimism, Chapter 9; empathy, Chapter 13; and growth orientations, Chapter 21). Although the research to date is promising, much is still unknown; thus, much work remains to be done. Readers interested in discussion of future directions for mindfulness and MBI in schools are encouraged to consult other works on this topic, which offer directions toward this end (e.g., Klingbeil & Renshaw, 2018; Klinbgeil, Renshaw et al., 2017; Renshaw, 2020; Renshaw & Cook, 2017; Renshaw et al., 2017). To round out this chapter, we highlight key considerations for using mindfulness and MBI in schools. Although much could be considered, two areas of practice are emphasized that we believe are especially beneficial for progressing mindfulness applications in schools: integrating MBI within MTSS, and diversity and developmental considerations for informing equitable and acceptable use of MBI in schools.

Integrating MBI within MTSS

Schools using SEL or positive behavior interventions and supports (PBIS) are likely familiar with MTSS as an organizing framework for prevention and intervention. The standard MTSS model consists of three tiers—universal, targeted, and intensive levels—that function to calibrate preventative and proactive supports with student needs based on the intensity of the presenting problem, responsiveness to intervention, and resource availability. Other works have suggested that an MTSS framework could provide a viable means for implementing and distributing MBI in schools (e.g., Felver et al., 2013; Renshaw et al., 2017). A few guidelines for educators and school-based practitioners are provided below toward this end.

Foremostly, most mindfulness-based programs are designed for universal (or classwide) implementation, focusing on training basic mindfulness skills to promote well-being and improve all students' academic success. There are currently several available schoolwide mindfulness programs offering semistandardized classroom curricula (e.g., MindUp; https://mindup.org) and consultancy services to train educators and support implementation (e.g., Mindful Schools; https://www.mindfulschools.org). One example of an evidence-based MBI commonly used at this tier is *Learning to BREATHE* (L2B; Broderick, 2013), which uses the BREATHE acronym (i.e., body, reflections, emotions, attention, tenderness, and health habits) as an implementation framework. Given that the bulk of evidence for MBI exists at the universal level (Klingbeil, Renshaw et al., 2017), educators and other school-based practitioners integrating MBI within MTSS can do so with relative confidence at this tier, as long as they select a program that has demonstrated empirical support. Readers are referred back to the several meta-analyses mentioned above, which provide detailed information about the available evidence for specific approaches and curricula for universal MBI. To prevent redundancy among school programming approaches, universal MBI can be conceptualized as an SEL approach, with PMA and RWA considered core social-emotional competencies (Lawlor, 2016).

When it comes to integrating MBI within the other tiers of MTSS, there is, unfortunately, substantially less evidence available to guide educators and school-based practitioners. At the targeted level, mental health or SEL-type interventions are usually provided in small group settings that address a common dilemma or shared problems among students with identified risk. Although mindfulness curricula, such as L2B, may be effectively implemented at the targeted level with a subset of students, there are fewer evidence-based options at this tier. Theoretically, this tier within MTSS provides a good avenue for more specific and intensive mindfulness training and psychoeducation. Practitioners may consider a few emerging options in this area, including (a) the *DNA-V* model of ACT for SEL (Rayner et al., 2017), (b) more intensive applications of MBSR (e.g., Biegel et al., 2009), and (c) the group-based version of MBCT with youth (Semple et al., 2010). At the intensive level within MTSS, students typically receive individualized supports and specific interventions to target severe problems that cannot be precisely addressed within group or classroom settings. Although individualized MBI has been thoroughly researched in clinical settings with adults, the evidence base still lacks for guiding applications with youths in schools. Generalizing from the best available evidence in clinical settings, however, we suggest practitioners consider using MBSR, ACT, MBCT, or DBT as MBI at the intensive level. Sufficient practical guidance for applying these approaches with youths has been provided elsewhere (e.g., Greco & Hayes, 2008). Yet practitioners taking this route should proceed with appropriate caution, recognizing that MBI is best considered an adjunct to—rather than a replacement for—other well-validated interventions at this level (Renshaw, 2020).

Diversity and Developmental Considerations

As described earlier, a growing body of intervention research supports the effectiveness of MBI with youth and their caregivers in both school and nonschool settings. However, there is less evidence regarding the effectiveness of MBI with individuals who are economically disadvantaged and/or racially-/ethnically-minoritized (DeLuca et al., 2018). This is especially true with youths and in schools (Black & Fernando, 2014; Semple et al., 2010). One explanation from the National Health Interview Survey suggested that underrepresented populations were less likely to engage in MBI; however, the reasons are unclear (Olano et al., 2015). Similarly, DeLuca et al. (2018) indicated that the evidence for using MBI with this population is underdeveloped, which might limit the baseline frequency with which practitioners recommended it. That said, there is evidence to suggest that MBI are acceptable for underrepresented and marginalized populations, reporting higher program completion rates than other evidence-based treatments, along with high rates of continued use even after study termination (Dutton et al., 2013; Roth & Robbins, 2004). MBI may also reduce the risk for health disparities among underserved populations, by empowering individuals with effective social-emotional competencies that address these disparities (Woods-Giscombé & Black, 2010). Given that school-based interventions are considered key for reducing disparities among undeserved youths (Fung et al., 2016), MBI integration in schools might be a pivotal strategy for reducing mental healthcare disparities for this population (Phan & Renshaw, 2021).

To effectively adapt MBI with diverse populations in schools, it is crucial to make MBI culturally responsive to optimize intervention effects (Chu & Leino, 2017; Proulx et al., 2018). Elements of MBI should include addressing stress and its influence on health by incorporating techniques to encourage health promotion and self-care through the development of self-awareness and self-compassion (Woods-Giscombé & Black, 2010). Incorporating these elements addresses psychological stress within its social context, which is especially important when supporting underrepresented populations' social-emotional needs. Moreover, practitioners implementing MBI in schools should consider that diverse youths may have different experiences with mind–body interventions depending on their gender identity, sexual identity, socioeconomic circumstances, and personal histories (Proulx et al., 2018). Becoming aware of how these identities and intersectionality may affect students and their caregivers is a touchstone for developing and implementing culturally responsive MBIs in schools.

Beyond general developmental considerations, appropriate use of MBI in schools may also require openness to cultural perspectives and adaptation for those with different cultural backgrounds or those presenting with specific disabling conditions. Since mindfulness originated in ancient Eastern Buddhist traditions, those with different cultural backgrounds might be cautious with mindfulness training and its perceived religious implications. Woods-Giscombé and Gaylord (2014) suggest adapting mindfulness training in ways that are viewed as compatible with the individual's values to handle such situations sensitively. For instance, practices such as benevolence and loving-kindness promoted through the practice of mindfulness are harmonious with the notion that loving one's neighbor is the most important directive in the Christian tradition (Proulx et al., 2018). Those presenting with specific disabling conditions might also have difficulties with mindfulness training. Using techniques tailored to an individual's cognitive level may therefore be critical for facilitating the success of MBI in schools (Felver & Singh, 2020). Given MBI exercises can use complex language, Neece et al. (2019) recommended that practitioners make their language less cognitively demanding. Finally, when considering mindfulness practices with special populations, we cannot overstate the importance of responding empathetically and transparently to their particular needs when developing adaptations to MBI. Compassionate responding may serve an important function of rapport building, which is likely to encourage subsequent engagement with the intervention. Ultimately, diversity and developmental considerations should be actively attended to when implementing MBI in schools, not just passively acknowledged.

References

Biegel, G. M., Brown, K. W., Shapiro, S. L., & Schubert, C. M. (2009). Mindfulness-based stress reduction for the treatment of adolescent psychiatric outpatients: A randomized clinical trial. *Journal of Consulting and Clinical Psychology*, 77(5), 855–866.

Bishop, S. R., Lau, M., Shapiro, S., Carlson, L., Anderson, N. D., Carmody, J., et al. (2004). Mindfulness: A proposed operational definition. *Clinical Psychology: Science and Practice*, 11(3), 230–241. https://doi.org/10.1093/clipsy.bph077

Black, D. S. (2015). Mindfulness training for children and adolescents: A state-of-the-science review. In K. W. Brown, J. D. Creswell, & R. M. Ryan (Eds.), *Handbook of mindfulness: Theory, research, and practice* (pp. 283–310). Guilford.

Black, D. S., & Fernando, R. (2014). Mindfulness training and classroom behavior among lower-income and ethnic minority elementary school children. *Journal of Child and Family Studies, 23*, 1242–1246. https://doi.org/10.1007/s10826-013-9784-4

Borquist-Conlon, D. S., Maynard, B. R., Brendel, K. E., & Jarina, A.S. (2019). Mindfulness-based interventions for youth with anxiety: A systematic review and meta-analysis. *Research on Social Work Practice, 29*, 195–205. https://doi.org/10.1177/1049731516684961

Briere, J. (2011). *Mindfulness inventory for children and adolescents.* Unpublished measure. University of Southern California. https://mindfulscience.usc.edu/?usc_research=psychometric-validation-of-the-mindfulness-inventory-for-children-and-adolescents

Broderick, P. (2013). *Learning to BREATHE: A mindfulness curriculum for adolescents to cultivate emotion regulation, attention, and performance.* New Harbinger.

Brown, K. W., Ryan, R. M., & Creswell, J. D. (2007). Mindfulness: Theoretical foundations and evidence for its salutary effects. *Psychological Inquiry, 18*(4), 211–237. https://doi.org/10.1080/10478400701598298

Brown, K. W., & Ryan, R. M. (2003). The benefits of being present: Mindfulness and its role in psychological well-being. *Journal of Personality and Social Psychology*, 84, 822–848. https://doi.org/10.1037/0022-3514.84.4.822

Brown, K. W., West, A. M., Loverich, T. M., & Biegel, G. M. (2011). Assessing adolescent mindfulness: Validation of an adapted Mindful Attention Awareness Scale in adolescent normative and psychiatric populations. *Psychological Assessment, 23*, 1023–1033. https://doi.org/10.1037/a0021338

Carsley, D., Khoury, B., & Heath, N. L. (2018). Effectiveness of mindfulness interventions for mental health in schools: A comprehensive meta-analysis. *Mindfulness, 9*, 693–707. https://doi.org/10.1007/s12671-017-0839-2

Chu, J., & Leino, A. (2017). Advancement in the maturing science of cultural adaptations of evidence-based interventions. *Journal of Consulting and Clinical Psychology, 85*, 45–57. https://doi.org/10.1037/ccp0000145

Dariotis, J. K., Mirabal-Beltran, R., Cluxton-Keller, F., Gould, L. F., Greenberg, M. T., & Mendelson, T. (2017). A qualitative exploration of implementation factors in a school-based mindfulness and yoga program: Lessons learned from students and teachers. *Psychology in the Schools, 54*, 53–69. https://doi.org/10.1002/pits.21979

de Bruin, E. I., Zijlstra, B. J., Geurtzen, N., van Zundert, R. M., van de Weijer-Bergsma, E., Hartman, E. E., Nieuwesteeg, A. M, Dunca, L. G., & Bögels, S. M. (2014). Mindful parenting assessed further: Psychometric properties of the Dutch version of the Interpersonal Mindfulness in Parenting Scale (IM-P). *Mindfulness, 5*, 200–212. https://doi.org/10.1007/s12671-012-0168-4

DeLuca, S. M., Kelman, A. R., & Waelde, L. C. (2018). A systematic review of ethnoracial representation and cultural adaptation of mindfulness-and meditation-based interventions. *Psychological Studies, 63*, 117–129. https://doi.org/10.1007/s12646-018-0452-z

Droutman, V., Golub, I., Oganesyan, A., & Read, S. (2018). Development and initial validation of the Adolescent and Adult Mindfulness Scale (AAMS). *Personality and Individual Differences, 123*, 34–43. https://doi.org/10.1016/j.paid.2017.10.037

Dunning, D. L., Griffiths, K., Kuyken, W., Crane, C., Foulkes, L., Parker, J., & Dalgleish, T. (2019). The effects of mindfulness-based interventions on cognition and mental health in children and adolescents–A meta-analysis of randomized controlled trials. *The Journal of Child Psychology and Psychiatry, 60*, 244–258. https://doi.org/10.1111/jcpp.12980

Dutton, M. A., Bermudez, D., Matas, A., Majid, H., & Myers, N. L. (2013). Mindfulness-based stress reduction for low-income, predominantly African American women with PTSD and a history of intimate partner violence. *Cognitive and Behavioral Practice, 20*, 23–32. https://doi.org/10.1016/j.cbpra.2011.08.003

Eklund, K., O'Malley, M., & Meyer, L. (2017). Gauging mindfulness in children and youth: School-based applications. *Psychology in the Schools, 54*, 101–114. https://doi.org/10.1002/pits.21983

Felitti, V. J., Anda, R. F., Nordenberg, D., Williamson, D. F., Spitz, A. M., Edwards, V., & Marks, J. S. (1998). Relationship of childhood abuse and household dysfunction to many of the leading causes of death in adults: The Adverse Childhood Experiences (ACE) Study. *American Journal of Preventive Medicine, 14*, 245–258. https://doi.org/10.1016/S0749-3797(98)00017-8

Felver, J. C., Doerner, E., Jones, J., Kaye, N. C., & Merrell, K. W. (2013). Mindfulness in school psychology: Applications for intervention and professional practice. *Psychology in the Schools, 50*, 531–547. https://doi.org/10.1002/pits.21695

Felver, J. C., & Singh, N. N. (2020). *Mindfulness in the classroom: An evidence-based program to reduce disruptive behavior and increase academic engagement.* New Harbinger.

Frantz, R., Hansen, S. G., & Machalicek, W. (2018). Interventions to promote well-being in parents of children with autism: A systematic review. *Review Journal of Autism and Developmental Disorders, 5*, 58–77. https://doi.org/10.1007/s40489-017-0123-3

Fung, J., Kim, J. J., Jin, J., Chen, G., Bear, L., & Lau, A. S. (2019). A randomized trial evaluating school-based mindfulness intervention for ethnic minority youth: Exploring mediators and moderators of intervention effects. *Journal of Abnormal Child Psychology, 47*, 1–19. https://doi.org/10.1007/s10802-018-0425-7

Goodman, M. S., Madni, L. A., & Semple, R. J. (2017). Measuring mindfulness in youth: Review of current assessments, challenges, and future directions. *Mindfulness, 8*, 1409–1420. https://doi.org/10.1007/s12671-017-0719-9

Greco, L. A., & Hayes, S. C. (Eds.). (2008). *Acceptance & mindfulness treatments for children and adolescents: A practitioner's guide*. New Harbinger.

Greco, L. A., Baer, R. A., & Smith, G. T. (2011). Assessing mindfulness in children and adolescents: Development and validation of the Child and Adolescent Mindfulness Measure (CAMM). *Psychological Assessment, 23*, 606–614. https://doi.org/10.1037/a0022819

Greco, L. A., Lambert, W., & Baer, R. A. (2008). Psychological inflexibility in childhood and adolescence: Development and evaluation of the Avoidance and Fusion Questionnaire for Youth. *Psychological Assessment, 20*, 93–102. https://doi.org/10.1037/1040-3590.20.2.93

Grossman, P. (2011). Defining mindfulness by how poorly I think I pay attention during everyday awareness and other intractable problems for psychology's (re)invention of mindfulness: Comment on Brown et al. (2011). *Psychological Assessment, 23*, 1034–1040. https://doi.org/10.1037/a0022713

Hayes, S. C., Strosahl, K. D., & Wilson, K. G. (1999). *Acceptance and commitment therapy: An experiential approach to behavior change*. Guilford.

Johnson, C., Burke, C., Brinkman, S., & Wade, T. (2017). Development and validation of a multifactor mindfulness scale in youth: The Comprehensive Inventory of Mindfulness Experiences–Adolescents (CHIME-A). *Psychological Assessment, 29*, 264–281. https://doi.org/10.1037/pas0000342

Kabat-Zinn, J. (1994). *Wherever you go, there you are: Mindfulness meditation in everyday life*. Hyperion.

Kallapiran, K., Koo, S., Kirubakaran, R., & Hancock, K. (2015). Effectiveness of mindfulness in improving mental health symptoms of children and adolescents: A meta-analysis. *Child and Adolescent Mental Health, 20*, 182–194. https://doi.org/10.1111/camh.12113

Klingbeil, D. A., Fischer, A. J., Renshaw, T. L., Bloomfield, B. S., Polakoff, B., Willenbrink, J. B., Copek, R. A., & Chan, K. T. (2017). Effects of mindfulness-based interventions on disruptive behaviors: A meta-analysis of single-case research. *Psychology in the Schools, 54*, 70–87. https://doi.org/10.1002/pits.21982

Klingbeil, D. A., Fischer, A. J., & Silberman, M. (2020). Overview of mindfulness-based intervention research with youth and students. Unpublished manuscript.

Klingbeil, D. A., & Renshaw, T. L. (2018). Mindfulness-based interventions for teachers: A meta-analysis of the emerging evidence base. *School Psychology Quarterly, 33*, 501–511. https://doi.org/10.1037/spq0000291

Klingbeil, D. A., Renshaw, T. L., Willenbrink, J. B., Copek, R. A., Chan, K. T., Haddock, A., Yassine, J., & Clifton, J. (2017). Mindfulness-based interventions with youth: A comprehensive meta-analysis of group design studies. *Journal of School Psychology, 63*, 77–103. https://doi.org/10.1016/j.jsp.2017.03.006

Kyriacou, C. (2001). Teacher stress: Directions for future research. *Educational Review, 53*, 27–35. https://doi.org/10.1080/00131910120033628

Lawlor, M. S. (2016). Mindfulness and social emotional learning (SEL): A conceptual framework. In K. A. Schonert-Reichl & R. W. Roeser (Eds.), *Handbook of mindfulness in education* (pp. 65–80). Springer.

Lawlor, M. S., Schonert-Reichl, K. A., Gadermann, A. M., & Zumbo, B. D. (2014). A validation study of the Mindful Attention Awareness Scale adapted for children. *Mindfulness, 5*, 730–741. https://doi.org/10.1007/s12671-013-0228-4

Levinson, D. B., Stoll, E. L., Kindy, S. D., Merry, H. L., & Davidson, R. J. (2014). A mind you can count on: Validating breath counting as a behavioral measure of mindfulness. *Frontiers in Psychology, 5*, Article 1202, 1–10. https://doi.org/10.3389/fpsyg.2014.01202

Linehan, M. M., Armstrong, H. E., Suarez, A., Allmon, D., & Heard, H. L. (1991). Cognitive-behavioral treatment of chronically parasuicidal borderline patients. *Archives of General Psychiatry, 48*, 1060–1064. https://doi.org/10.1001/archpsyc.1991.01810360024003

Markow, D., & Pieters, A. (2012). *The MetLife survey of the American teacher: Teachers, parents and the economy*. MetLife.

Moore, R. C., Depp, C. A., Wetherell, J. L., & Lenze, E. J. (2016). Ecological momentary assessment versus standard assessment instruments for measuring mindfulness, depressed mood, and anxiety among older adults. *Journal of Psychiatric Research, 75*, 116–123. https://doi.org/10.1016/j.jpsychires.2016.01.011

Neece, C. L., Chan, N., Klein, K., Roberts, L., & Fenning, R. M. (2019). Mindfulness-based stress reduction for parents of children with developmental delays: Understanding the experiences of Latino families. *Mindfulness, 10*, 1017–1030. https://doi.org/10.1007/s12671-018-1011-3

Neff, K. D., Bluth, K., Tóth-Király, I., Davidson, O., Knox, M. C., Williamson, Z., & Costigan, A. (2021). Development and validation of the Self-Compassion Scale for Youth. *Journal of Personality Assessment, 103*, 92–105. https://doi.org/10.1080/00223891.2020.1729774

Nock, M. K. (2007). Conceptual and design essentials for evaluating mechanisms of change. *Alcoholism: Clinical and Experimental Research, 31*, 4s–12s. https://doi.org/10.1111/j.1530-0277.2007.00488.x

Olano, H. A., Kachan, D., Tannenbaum, S. L., Mehta, A., Annane, D., & Lee, D. J. (2015). Engagement in mindfulness practices by US adults: Sociodemographic barriers. *The Journal of Alternative and Complementary Medicine, 21*, 100–102. https://doi.org/10.1089/acm.2014.0269

Phan, M. L., & Renshaw, T. L. (2021). *Guidelines for adapting mindfulness-based school interventions with underserved youth.* OSF preprint. https://doi.org/10.31234/osf.io/rt65b

Proulx, J., Croff, R., Oken, B., Aldwin, C. M., Fleming, C., Bergen-Cico, D., Le T., & Noorani, M. (2018). Considerations for research and development of culturally relevant mindfulness interventions in American minority communities. *Mindfulness, 9*, 361–370. https://doi.org/10.1007/s12671-017-0785-z

Rayner, M., Hayes, L. L., & Ciarrochi, J. (2017). *Write your own DNA: A group program to help young people live with vitality and strength.* https://thrivingadolescent.com

Renshaw, T. L. (2020). Mindfulness-based intervention in schools. In M. Bray & C. Maykel (Eds.), *Promoting mind–body health in schools: Interventions for mental health professionals* (pp. 145–160). American Psychological Association.

Renshaw, T. L. (2012). Mindfulness-based practices for crisis prevention and intervention. In S. E. Brock & S. R. Jimerson (Eds.), *Handbook of school crisis prevention and intervention* (2nd ed., pp. 401–422). National Association of School Psychologists.

Renshaw, T. L. (2017). Preliminary development and validation of the Mindful Student Questionnaire. *Assessment for Effective Intervention, 42*, 168–175. https://doi.org/10.1177/1534508416678971

Renshaw, T. L., & Cook, C. R. (2017). Mindfulness in the schools—Historical roots, current trends, and future directions. *Psychology in the Schools, 54*(1), 5–12. https://doi.org/10.1002/pits.21978

Renshaw, T. L., Fischer, A. J., & Klingbeil, D. A. (2017). Mindfulness-based interventions in school psychology. *Contemporary School Psychology, 21*, 299–303. https://doi.org/10.1007/s40688-017-0166-6

Renshaw, T. L., & O'Malley, M. D. (2014). Cultivating mindfulness in students. In M. J. Furlong, R. Gilman, & E. S. Huebner (Eds.), *Handbook of positive psychology in the schools* (2nd ed., pp. 245–259). Routledge.

Roth, B., & Robbins, D. (2004). Mindfulness-based stress reduction and health-related quality of life: Findings from a bilingual inner-city patient population. *Psychosomatic Medicine, 66*, 113–123. https://doi.org/10.1007/s40688-017-0166-6

Segal, Z. V., Williams, J. M. G., & Teasdale, J. D. (2002). *Mindfulness-based cognitive therapy for depression: A new approach to preventing relapse.* Guilford.

Semple, R. J., Lee, J., Rosa, D., & Miller, L. F. (2010). A randomized trial of mindfulness-based cognitive therapy for children: Promoting mindful attention to enhance social-emotional resiliency in children. *Journal of Child and Family Studies, 19*, 218–229. https://doi.org/10.1007/s10826-009-9301-y

Smalley, S. L., & Winston, D. (2010). *Fully present: The science, art, and practice of mindfulness.* Da Capo Press.

Taylor, B. L., Cavanagh, K., & Strauss, C. (2016). The effectiveness of mindfulness-based interventions in the perinatal period: a systematic review and meta-analysis. *PLoS ONE, 11*(5), e0155720. https://doi.org/10.1371/journal.pone.0155720

Thayer, A. J., Sullivan, M., Larson, M., & Cook, C. R. (2020). Overview of mindfulness-based intervention research with parents and educators. Unpublished manuscript.

Thompson, B. L., & Waltz, J. (2007). Everyday mindfulness and mindfulness meditation: Overlapping constructs or not? *Personality and Individual Differences, 43*, 1875–1885. https://doi.org/10.1016/j.paid.2007.06.017

Ullrich-French, S., Cox, A., Cole, A., Rhoades Cooper, B., & Gotch, C. (2017). Initial validity evidence for the State Mindfulness Scale for Physical Activity with youth. *Measurement in Physical Education and Exercise Science, 21*, 177–189. https://doi.org/10.1080/1091367X.2017.1321543

van den Hoofdakker, B. J., Nauta, M. H., Veen-Mulders, L. V. D., Sytema, S., Emmelkamp, P. M., Minderaa, R. B., & Hoekstra, P. J. (2010). Behavioral parent training as an adjunct to routine care in children with attention-deficit/hyperactivity disorder: moderators of treatment response. *Journal of Pediatric Psychology, 35*(3), 317–326. https://doi.org/10.1093/jpepsy/jsp060

West, A. M., Sbraga, T. P., & Poole, D. A. (2005). *Measuring mindfulness in youth: Development of the mindful thinking and action scale for adolescents.* Unpublished manuscript. Central Michigan University.

West, A. M. (2008). *Mindfulness and well-being in adolescence: An exploration of four mindfulness measures with an adolescent sample.* Unpublished doctoral dissertation. Central Michigan University.

Williams, K. L., & Wahler, R. G. (2010). Are mindful parents more authoritative and less authoritarian? An analysis of clinic-referred mothers. *Journal of Child and Family Studies, 19*(2), 230–235. https://doi.org/10.1007/s10826-009-9309-3

Wong, K. F., Massar, S. A., Chee, M. W., & Lim, J. (2018). Towards an objective measure of mindfulness: Replicating and extending the features of the breath-counting task. *Mindfulness, 9*, 1402–1410. https://doi.org/10.1007/s12671-017-0880-1

Woods-Giscombé, C. L., & Black, A. R. (2010). Mind-body interventions to reduce risk for health disparities related to stress and strength among African American women: The potential of mindfulness-based stress reduction, loving-kindness, and the NTU therapeutic framework. *Complementary Health Practice Review, 15*, 115–131. https://doi.org/10.1177/1533210110386776

Woods-Giscombé, C. L., & Gaylord, S. A. (2014). The cultural relevance of mindfulness meditation as a health intervention for African Americans: Implications for reducing stress-related health disparities. *Journal of Holistic Nursing, 32*, 147–160. https://doi.org/10.1177/0898010113519010

Zenner, C., Hermleben-Kurz, S., & & Walach, H. (2014). Mindfulness-based interventions in schools—a systematic review and meta-analysis. *Frontiers in Psychology, 5*, 1–20. https://doi.org/10.3389/fpsyg.2014.00603

Zoogman, S., Goldberg, S. B., Hoyt, W. T., & Miller, L. (2015). Mindfulness interventions with youth: A meta-analysis. *Mindfulness, 6*, 290–302. https://doi.org/10.1007/s12671-013-0260-4

10

SOCIAL-EMOTIONAL LEARNING

What Are the Learning Outcomes from a Preschool SEL Program (COPE-Resilience) in Taiwan and Australia

Marissa Yi-Hsuan Wu, Erica Frydenberg, and Vicki McKenzie

The Challenge: Developing Well-Being in Early Childhood

Early childhood was once considered to be a period that is joyful and trouble-free for children. It is only in recent years that there has been a realization that young children, like adolescents and adults, reflect the prevalence of internalizing problems that can be evidenced through neuroimaging. According to researchers such as Whalen et al. (2017), the prevalence of mental health problems in preschool children is increasing. Studies in the USA have shown that between 10% and 30% of preschool children are not behaviorally and emotionally ready to succeed in school (Brauner & Stephens, 2006; Hemmeter et al., 2007), and around 16%–18% of preschool-age children experience mental health difficulties (von Klitzing et al., 2015). Many preschool-age children who have behavioral problems or low social and emotional capacity may experience long-term complications, including difficulties in school, trouble in social situations and personal relationships, engaging in risky behaviors, and even having suicidal tendencies. Indeed, the management of anxiety, including general self-regulation, plays an important role in school readiness.

The preschool years are a significant time of development and transition. In the context of education, it is a challenging period with new relationships being built, achieving independence from parents, and engagement with teachers and significant others in the educational context. In that sense, the period provides unique opportunities for skill development, particularly in the social and emotional domains and the fostering of well-being.

The World Health Organization defines well-being as a state "in which an individual realizes his or her own abilities, can cope with normal stresses of life, can work productively, and is able to make a contribution to his or her community" (World Health Organization, 2018). Well-being here is defined as more than the absence of mental health issues; it incorporates both aspects of "feeling good and functioning well" (Huppert, 2014). However, considerable research into social and emotional development has focused on ameliorating skill deficits or problem behaviors. Positive psychological approaches to well-being provide an opportunity for a paradigm shift from framing mental health as reactive and illness-focused toward fostering a primary preventative approach. In simple terms—positive psychology is a philosophical, theoretical, and psychological

DOI: 10.4324/9781003013778-13

orientation that focuses on the health and well-being aspects of human endeavor rather than the pathology and incapacity of individuals.

Social-Emotional Learning in the Early Years

Social-emotional learning (SEL) in the early years is focused on the development of social-emotional skills, including emotional awareness relationship building and the management of emotions, also known as self-regulation. Skill-building is an inherent aspect of the early learning environment where the skills are being nurtured both intentionally and indirectly. For example, children with weak social skills are at risk for early academic problems (McClelland et al., 2000) and peer victimization (Crawford & Manassis, 2011). Individuals with low emotional literacy similarly present with higher levels of stress and anxiety, as well as problem behaviors such as aggression and delinquency (Liau et al., 2003). It is, therefore, crucial to consider how SEL programs can both overcome skill-based deficits, as well as provide opportunities for all children to develop skills that lead to optimal functioning and well-being. Levels of emotional literacy have also been shown to predict positive emotion regulation in preschoolers (Miller et al., 2006).

Social and emotional competence is the capacity to get along with others and is crucial for supporting children's emotional, social, and cognitive development (Carman & Chapparo, 2012). The most commonly cited definition for SEL comes from the Collaborative for Academic, Social and Emotional Learning (CASEL). It is described as:

> The process through which children and adults acquire the knowledge, attitudes, and skills to recognize and manage their emotions, set and achieve positive goals, demonstrate caring and concern for others, establish and maintain positive relationships, make responsible decisions [and] handle interpersonal situations effectively.
>
> *(Payton et al., 2008, pp. 5–6)*

CASEL (2019) offers five core competencies: self-awareness, social awareness, self-management, relationship skills, and responsible decision-making that should be addressed in social and emotional educational practices. Research has demonstrated that nurturing social and emotional learning in preschoolers can help protect against current and future stresses and challenges (Bornstein et al., 2010; Rose-Krasnor & Denham, 2009). For example, a lack of social and emotional competence can increase the risk for poor social functioning, difficulties with peers (including rejection and withdrawal), emotional and behavioral problems, and academic difficulties (Denham, 2006; Eisenberg et al., 2001; Fantuzzo et al., 2003). These core competencies, while articulated by CASEL, are also mirrored in documents that are associated with curriculum requirements in other jurisdictions. Table 10.1, for example, compares and contrasts the competencies in three communities, namely, the USA, Australia, and Taiwan.

Social and Emotional Development in Early Childhood

Children reach several social and emotional milestones during their preschool years. For example, from ages three to five years, children are learning important skills such as self-awareness, self-regulation, and social awareness including empathy (Kostelnik et al., 2009). Research has found that assisting children with their emotional awareness and regulation can help them acquire empathy (Shipman et al., 2003). Empathy is the ability to "conceptualize other people's inner world and to reflect on their thoughts and feelings" (Gillberg, 1992, p. 835). It plays an important role in prosocial behaviors, developing friendships, and concern for others (Decety et al., 2012). As such,

Table 10.1 SEL in Australia, USA and Taiwan

	Australia	USA	Taiwan
ACARA (2012)	Four interrelated elements of the personal and social capability learning continuum	CASEL (2013) Area — Five interrelated sets of cognitive, affective, and behavioral competencies	Competency Framework of the Twelve-year Curriculum (2014) — The competency framework emphasizes the three core competencies (spontaneity, communicative interaction, and social participation) that one needs to respond to the complexity of life. Early Childhood Education & Care Curriculum Framework (2016) — Although the 12-year curriculum did not explicitly draw from any SEL framework, the essentialness of foundational SEL skills are highlighted in the early childhood curriculum.
Self-awareness	Developing personal and social capacities to: • recognize emotions • recognize personal qualities and achievements • understand themselves as learners • develop reflective practice	Self-awareness — The ability to accurately recognize one's emotions and their thoughts and their influence on behavior (strengths and limitations). To develop a sense of confidence and optimism.	Early Childhood Framework Emotional Principle Component 1–3 (Awareness, Recognition, Expression, and Understanding) • Aware and recognize one's emotions • Appropriately express one's emotion • Understand one's emotion and why it occurs Social Principles Component 1–3 (Exploration, Awareness, Negotiating, Regulating, Care, and Respect) • Self-awareness • Develop self-concept • Self-appreciation, self-valuing • Self-protection Twelve-year Curriculum Spontaneity (self-directed action) • A sound body and mind and self-improvement

(Continued)

Table 10.1 (Continued)

	Australia	USA	Taiwan
ACARA (2012)	Four interrelated elements of the personal and social capability learning continuum	CASEL (2013) Five interrelated sets of cognitive, affective and behavioral competencies	Competency Framework of the Twelve-year Curriculum (2014) Early Childhood Education & Care Curriculum Framework (2016)	The competency framework emphasizes on the three core competencies (spontaneity, communicative interaction, and social participation), that one needs to respond to the complexity of life. Although the 12-year curriculum did not explicitly draw from any SEL framework, the essentialness of foundational SEL skills is highlighted in the early childhood curriculum.
Self-management	Regulating emotional responses and to work independently. Students are to: • express emotions appropriately • develop self-discipline and set goals • work independently and show initiative • become confident, resilient, and adaptable	Self-management — The ability to regulate one's emotions, thoughts, and behaviors effectively in different situations and work toward achieving personal and academic goals.	Early Childhood Framework Emotional Principle Component 4: Regulating Social Principles Component 1: Exploration and Awareness Component 2: Negotiation and Regulating	• Use strategies to regulate one's emotions Aware of rules and regulation • Regulate one's action and follow rule and regulation

	Australia	USA	Taiwan
ACARA (2012)	Four interrelated elements of the personal and social capability learning continuum	CASEL (2013) — Five interrelated sets of cognitive, affective and behavioral competencies	Competency Framework of the Twelve-year Curriculum (2014) — The competency framework emphasizes on the three core competencies (spontaneity, communicative interaction, and social participation), that one needs to respond to the complexity of life. Early Childhood Education & Care Curriculum Framework (2016) — Although the 12-year curriculum did not explicitly draw from any SEL framework, the essentialness of foundational SEL skills are highlighted in the early childhood curriculum.
Social awareness	Social awareness — Learning to show respect for and understand others' perspectives, emotional states, and needs: • appreciate diverse perspectives • contribute to civil society • understand relationships	Social awareness — Being able to recognize social support and take the perspective of and empathize with others from diverse backgrounds and cultures.	Early Childhood Framework Emotional Principle Component 1–3 • Being able to observe, identify, express, and understand emotions of others and personification objects in the living environment. • Aware of the differences between thoughts Social Principles Component 1–3 • Empathies and interact with others • Care for and respect others in the environment • Aware of importance of family • Explore, understand, and respect multiculturalism Twelve-year Curriculum Social participation • Multicultural and international understanding

(Continued)

153

Marissa Yi-Hsuan Wu et al.

Table 10.1 (Continued)

Australia	USA	Taiwan	
ACARA (2012) Four interrelated elements of the personal and social capability learning continuum	CASEL (2013) Five interrelated sets of cognitive, affective and behavioral competencies	Competency Framework of the Twelve-year Curriculum (2014)	The competency framework emphasizes on the three core competencies (spontaneity, communicative interaction, and social participation), that one needs to respond to the complexity of life.
		Early Childhood Education & Care Curriculum Framework (2016)	Although the 12-year curriculum did not explicitly draw from any SEL framework, the essentialness of foundational SEL skills are highlighted in the early childhood curriculum.
Social management Learning to interact effectively and respectfully with a range of adults and peers; Developing the ability to initiate and manage successful personal relationships, and participate in social and communal activities: • communicate effectively • work collaboratively • make decisions • negotiate and resolve conflict • develop leadership skills	Relationship skills Building communication, negotiation, and conflict management skills. Able to seek and offer help to others.	Twelve-year Curriculum Communicative Interaction	• Communicate effectively by using symbols, communicative expression, technology, information, media literacy, arts, and aesthetic skills.
		Social Participation	• Interpersonal relations and teamwork

154

Australia	USA	Taiwan
ACARA (2012)	CASEL (2013)	Competency Framework of the Twelve-year Curriculum (2014)
Four interrelated elements of the personal and social capability learning continuum	Five interrelated sets of cognitive, affective and behavioral competencies	Early Childhood Education & Care Curriculum Framework (2016)
Responsible decision making	Learning to evaluate the consequences of one's behavior—to make constructive and respectful choices about personal behavior and social interactions. Being considerate to the well-being of self and others.	Twelve-year Curriculum
		Spontaneity (self-directed action)
		Social Participation

The competency framework emphasizes on the three core competencies (spontaneity, communicative interaction, and social participation), that one needs to respond to the complexity of life. Although the 12-year curriculum did not explicitly draw from any SEL framework, the essentialness of foundational SEL skills is highlighted in the early childhood curriculum.

- Planning, implementing, and creating flexibility
- Systemic thinking and problem solving
- Moral practice and civic consciousness

it is an important skill to support during the early years (Eisenberg et al., 2006), particularly given a lack of empathy can lead to aggression and antisocial behavior in children (Belacchi & Farina, 2012). Moreover, early childhood presents a period of malleable neurobiology and SEL can assist to overcome early adversity (Fox et al., 2010).

SEL takes into account the developmental milestones at the same time infusing the learning environment with educational goals as outlined in key documents that are reflected in Table 10.1. Resilience, like well-being, is an outcome of healthy social-emotional development and good coping skills. As such it is the underlying objective guiding SEL curriculum development. In their forward-looking article, Kalisch et al. (2019) attempt to deconstruct and reconstruct the concept of resilience. They debunk the myth that resilience is a unitary construct that protects against mental illness. Rather they consider several protective factors in the interconnected networks that are biological, psychological, and sociological. They include genetic predisposition, gene expression, volitional appraisal, and self-regulation processes. They go on to develop a network that takes account of the multiple factors at play, at the same time critiquing the extensive "naïve" use of resilience questionnaires as predictors of mental health under adversity (Kalisch et al., 2019). While well-being and resilience are outcomes that everyone desires or aspires to, coping is a substantive process by which it is achieved. Coping is a significant component of how individuals achieve health, well-being, and resilience through their thoughts, feelings, and actions. Coping is the process and resilience is the outcome.

What Is Coping?

There are numerous definitions of coping. One widely cited description of coping is, "the conscious and volitional efforts to regulate emotion, cognition, behavior, physiology and the environment in response to stressful events or circumstances" (Compas et al., 2001, p. 89). The definition confirms the importance of both emotion regulation and actions in response to demands. Lazarus and Folkman (1984) defined coping as cognitive and behavioral efforts to manage specific external or internal demands that are appraised as exceeding the resources of the individual. Eisenberg and colleagues (1997) defined coping as a subset of the broader category of self-regulation in response to stress. Substantial research in child and adolescent coping has revealed that coping is similar to adaptation with situations in which temperament, developmental, and environmental factors all play a part. Coping is the process through which well-being and resilience can be achieved. There is no right or wrong coping, but the situation determines what is likely to achieve the desired outcomes. Coping can be construed as a dichotomous dimension with both productive and nonproductive coping strategies utilized in situations that individuals encounter (Frydenberg & Lewis, 2011). In simple terms, coping can be described as the thoughts, feelings, and actions in response to the demands of our everyday lives.

It is widely acknowledged that a child's developmental level may also both contribute to, and limit, the type of coping responses employed and hence it influences the types of coping strategies that a child utilizes (Compas et al., 2001; Compas, 2009; Rudolph et al., 1995). In general, as children develop and with the increase in cortical functioning, their coping repertoire increases and shifts from primarily behavioral to more cognitive actions (Skinner & Zimmer-Gembeck, 2007). This enhances both the child's self-control when facing a stressful situation and the ability to plan effective coping options (Derryberry et al., 2003).

Self-Regulation in the Context of SEL

Overall emotional competence is about having well-developed emotional understandings and skills. It is about understanding one's own emotions and those of others. It is also about the capacity to cope with negative emotions, often termed self-regulation. Thus, in the early learning setting, whether it be in the home, school, or community, both primary and secondary emotions are at play and opportunities for awareness and development need to be offered to advance the best outcomes.

Self-regulation underlies the management of thoughts, feelings, and emotions. That requires a capacity to calm oneself when angry, make friends, resolve conflicts, and make safe choices. One neurobiological theory of self-regulation likens the brain to a highly tuned, highly trained orchestra in which the performers or parts of the brain have their roles and functions, but the performance is built to a crescendo by the interplay of the performers. Blair and Raver (2015) call it a *holistic connectionist* model, which is explained in a hierarchical way starting from the base of the structure, the genes, to stress physiology, emotional reactivity and regulation, attention, and executive functioning. The hierarchy moves from the automatic to the volitional and genes play a part. The influences are both bottom-up and top-down so there is both maturation and development that moves in both directions. It is commonly accepted that neither nature nor nurture acts alone, but rather in concert. When it comes to the teaching of SEL the general principle of neural activity is that "neurons that fire together, wire together," a phrase coined by neuropsychologist Donald Hebb in 1949. Studies have found that the correlation between self-discipline and achievement is twice as large as the correlation between IQ and achievement. The basis of determination and self-regulation is developed very early as children start to play—with toys and with each other. Using play as an all-important foundation provides opportunities to teach and cultivate grit and self-regulation.

Teaching SEL

Numerous programs have been designed to teach and develop social-emotional competence in the preschool years and beyond. The programs themselves are diverse in focus and content. Some require extensive cost, training, and the allocation of curriculum time. For example, in the USA where the leadership in this field has dominated, there are programs such as *I Can Problem Solve* (Boyle & Haslett-Walker, 2008), which focuses on developing prosocial behaviors and the reduction of aggressive behaviors with 83 twice-weekly lessons introduced over three months. The *Pre-school Promoting Alternative Thinking Strategies* (Hamre et al., 2012) focuses on prosocial and friendship, self-control, and problem-solving skills with 36 lessons delivered during circle time with resource materials available and associated training costs. The *RULER* program (Brackett, 2019), which has followed successful implementation in pre-K–12 settings, focuses on understanding and expressing emotions as well as learning to regulate them. The scripted program is integrated with the curriculum for the relevant year level and is implemented after extensive training of teachers.

In Australia, there is the *Fun Friends Program* (Barrett, 2007), which targets feelings and relaxation with five sessions of 2–2.5 hours each with a trained teacher and facilitator. Also, in Australia, the *COPE-Resilience* program has been developed at the Early Learning Centre at the University of Melbourne and evaluated on numerous occasions. It aims to promote preschoolers' social-emotional competencies using an explicit, teacher-led approach (Cornell et al., 2017).

COPE-Resilience

The COPE-Resilience program underpins and aligns with several theoretical approaches, including Piaget's Theory of Cognitive Development (1952), Vygotsky's Socio-cultural Theory of Development (1962), Bronfenbrenner's Ecological Systems Theory (1979), Salovey and Mayer's Emotional Intelligence (1990), and Frydenberg's Coping Theory (Frydenberg, 2017).

The program objectives are to build children's emotional knowledge, empathy, and prosocial and coping skills (Cornell et al., 2017; Deans et al., 2017).

Piaget (1953) viewed children as active learners in which their development and knowledge are based on their interactions with the world. Through exploring and interacting children create mental representations, which he called *schema,* that they use to respond to and understand situations. These schemas, in turn, are linked to discrete stages of child development. Four years of age, according to Piaget, is in the preoperational stage of development where children understand symbolic meanings as opposed to physical and concrete meanings. Vygotsky's (1962) theorizing overcame the limitations of Piaget by emphasizing culture and context, arguing that language and thought worked together as they morphed into skills of communication and understanding in a cultural context. These approaches are complemented by Bronfenbrenner's (1979) sophisticated ecological approach, which takes into account time and context. For example, time is an important feature of youth development, as is socioeconomic circumstances and person-related characteristics such as ability and personality. Together, these "classic" theories provide an understanding of how children learn.

More recent theorizing of emotional intelligence (Salovey & Mayer, 1990) and coping theory (Frydenberg, 2017) also underpin the program. Emotional intelligence is the way individuals understand their own emotions and that of others. Emotion language and labeling of emotions are considered to be important features of the learning experience and these have an impact on self-regulation. That is if you can "name" it then it is possible to "tame" or control the emotions. Similarly, coping theory, which focuses on the thoughts, feelings, and actions of the individual, underscores the content of the social-emotional program with an emphasis on skill-building both in the emotional sense and the positive action sense, and are reflected in acts of empathy and kindness.

The COPE-Resilience Program comprises activities on Caring for Others (C); Open communication (O); Polite/Respectful behaviors (P); Empathies/Sharing behaviors (E) and a Review (R). The Program incorporates the Early Years Coping Cards, as a way of teaching coping skills, including empathy and prosocial skills, to children aged four to eight years of age. The Early Years Coping Cards are a teaching and learning tool that depicts a range of visual representations of challenging situations used to stimulate children's verbal responses about the coping strategies used to help children explore their feelings, that of others, and what they might do in the different situations presented. Children are asked to become a "Feelings Detective." The program uses drawings, puppetry, and role-plays.

Early evaluations of the teacher-led program have reported significant reductions in emotional problems postprogram. Qualitative responses from parents indicated that they noticed positive differences in their children postprogram. A thematic analysis of parents' responses was conducted, revealing two major themes in the differences parents noticed in their children, "an increase in prosocial behavior" and "enhanced communication skills." Drawings and comments made by preschool participants provide support for the benefit of the program (Cornell et al., 2017; Deans et al., 2017; Pang et al., 2018). One interesting finding in a classroom with four-year-old's receiving the COPE-Resilience program from an experienced teacher (in contrast to one who was teaching it for the first time and a nonintervention group), was that the experienced teacher-led classroom reported the greatest gains in teacher-reported prosocial behavior, empathy, inhibitory control, and positive coping (such as working with others or helping them), as well as reductions in problem behavior and negative coping behaviors (such as crying screaming, fighting, and getting angry with others; Wu et al., 2020). The significant increase in empathy scores had a large effect size ($d = 2.53$). Large effect sizes were also found in children's positive and negative coping behavior ($d = 1.70$ and $d = 0.87$, respectively), with an increase of positive coping behavior and reduction of negative coping behavior. Moreover, in regard to the children's inhibitory control and externalizing and internalizing problem behavior, medium effect sizes were found ($d = 0.78$ for both). Overall, it was demonstrated that the program is beneficial to children's social and emotional well-being.

Moving Beyond a Western Cultural Context

While the benefits of implementing SEL programs to increase behavioral change and positive adaptations in children are well researched and recognized in Western countries, little attention has been given in the Eastern part of Asia. One major reason may be the social values inherent in how individualist and collectivist communities make decisions about how they educate their young people to prepare for the workforce and life. In Asian countries, attitudes toward education have been heavily influenced by traditional Chinese culture and the Confucian paradigm. Traditionally, educators in Confucian heritage countries spend a considerable amount of time on academic training, in comparison to personal skills development. The value of education as Confucius put it is a means to improve one's socioeconomic position; competitive examinations and meritocracy are highly valued by Confucius. This philosophy has influenced the Confucian heritage countries, believing that the pursuit of theory and knowledge will entitle them to a higher status in the society, whereas the learning of practical skills is for those of the lower class (Yao, 2000). As a result, while ranking highly on international test scores, Asian contexts such as Taiwan, have long been criticized for promoting a highly competitive and pressurized environment for students (Huang, 2019). Such values and environment are believed to be ineffective in facing the demand of the 21st century, resulting in an ossified education system and a gap between school education and societal development (Chen & Huang, 2017). In fact, in the recent global student well-being survey, Taiwan was ranked one of the lowest in students' well-being among Programme for International Student Assessment (PISA) participating countries and economies (Organisation for Economic Co-operation and Development [OECD], 2019). In response to these contemporary problems, the Taiwanese government launched a series of education reforms in an attempt to stress the importance of self-development, embracing SEL, and competency-based assessments.

The New Curriculum in Taiwan

In Taiwan, it is now required by law for preschools and kindergartens to implement the relatively new national curriculum guidelines (Ministry of Education [MOE], 2016). The Early Childhood Education & Care Curriculum Framework (ECECCF) was created as a result of the unification of the early childhood education (ECE) and the early childhood care (ECC) systems in Taiwan. Before the system integration, the preschool curriculum in Taiwan was relatively unregulated. It was legislated in 1987 and unrevised until 2012. Shing et al. (2015) explored the shortcomings of the 1987 preschool curriculum, stating that not only were the contents outdated, but teacher training programs rarely reference it, and it was infrequently practiced in the ECE field. Drawing from the traditional Confucian value of Jen (benevolence), the aim of the current preschool curriculum is to teach young children to "love themselves and others, environmental stewardship, facing challenges, practicing cultural values, and establishing a foundation for life-long learning practices" (Cheng, 2018, p. 177). Moreover, under the premise of the new preschool curriculum, ECE teachers and care providers are expected to cultivate the six core learning domains, including: (a) physical education and health, (b) literacy and language development, (c) cognitive development, (d) social development, (e) emotional development, and (f) aesthetics (MOE, 2016). Two examples of learning goals in the emotional domain are: "aware and recognize emotion in self and others" and "use strategies to regulate one's emotions." As noted earlier, these two outcomes are essential for helping young children cope effectively in life.

Challenges in Teaching Social-Emotional Skills

Although the current curriculum stresses the importance of social-emotional development and skills, the teaching of such skills has become a major issue in Taiwan. Prior to 2012, both the ECE and the ECC systems required early childhood educators and care providers to design a segmented, subject-oriented curriculum. Social and emotional skills were not seen as a "subject" at that time; thus, it was rarely taught in teacher training programs. Consequently, the professional understanding of SEL along with the initiative to teach SEL skills is fairly vague in Taiwan. Following the implementation of the current preschool curriculum, teachers have been experiencing enormous pressure; designing an integrated curriculum to foster or intentionally teach social-emotional skills continues to be problematic. Moreover, constrained emotion is regarded as essential in Confucian ideology (Fu, 2012) making it even harder to teach children to express "emotions" when the society and teachers themselves were taught to "hide" emotions. One major challenge identified was the teacher's lack of familiarity with the concept and content of emotions. In addition to this lack of familiarity, teachers also have trouble identifying the right time in classrooms to teach emotions, as well as designing activities related to the teaching of emotions (Shing & Zhou, 2017).

Although some aspects of the SEL framework seem to clash with Confucian ideology, the importance of emotions in interpersonal relationships and mental health has become increasingly valued in Taiwan. In November 2019, a special edition on SEL was published in a widely circulated publication, the *Global Family Monthly,* for family and school teachers in Taiwan (Gao, 2019). Not only did it indicate that social and emotional education is the current zeitgeist in global education, but it also stressed that emotional competence is the cornerstone of learning power and is the most valuable intangible asset of a child's life, consequently, placing considerable emphasis on the importance of early SEL in children's lives.

The Chinese COPE-Resilience Project

The Chinese COPE-Resilience project established and implemented a coping-based SEL program that considers the context and culture of its implementers; it aims to evaluate the COPE-Resilience program in Asian culture. The studies reported below are part of a four-year PhD project (Wu, 2020) conducted by the first author of this chapter. The adapted program was trialed in sequential phases in three different preschools/kindergartens. Each phase was built upon the previous one, in the following phases:

Phase 1: cultural adaptation and translation of the program
Phase 2: pilot study design, instruments, and adapted program with a small sample
Phase 3: examine the effectiveness of the Chinese COPE-Resilience program in relation to children's gender and year level
Phase 4: extend the study to explore sustained effects on children
Phase 5: assess teachers' personal change and growth through implementing the program

Phase 1: Cultural Adaptation and Translation

Given that the COPE-Resilience program was originally designed for preschool children in Australia and is generally delivered to preschool children in English-speaking environments, the precursor for undertaking the study in an Asian context was for the manual to be translated into a suitable Chinese dialect for localization and to culturally adapt the program's manual. In general, while making cultural adaptations to existing programs, experts in the field of cultural adaptations suggested two important procedures: (a) know your target population and (b) adapt delivery methods to best reach the target population (Bernal et al., 1995; Castro et al., 2004). Details of this translation process are included below to provide sufficient context for the English reader as to how the localization process affected implementation as well as provide the reader with an overview of the critical parts of program implementation for context.

Traditional Chinese character is the standardized character sets used in writing in Taiwan. The cultural adaptation of the COPE-Resilience manual began with the translation of the manual. The program was first translated into traditional Chinese by a local translation service in Taiwan. It was then evaluated for semantic equivalence by a bilingual psychologist with a degree in ECE. The Chinese COPE-Resilience manual was then culturally amended by a native Mandarin-speaking school counselor in Taiwan, who was recruited to check for culturally sensitive wordings. The school counselor also examined the suitability and appropriateness of the Chinese language used in the manual for everyday Taiwanese classroom settings. To ensure the social validity of the newly adapted manual and for it to match the Taiwanese community, before trial the program, the Chinese COPE-Resilience manual was also reviewed by three early childhood professionals, including a kindergarten director and two preschool teachers.

Although the cultural contexts of Australia and Taiwan are different, according to Hecht and Shin (2015) all humans are born into a social world, and to one degree or another, they must learn to interact and handle interpersonal challenges. Hence, while culture impacts the values, beliefs, and skills learned in school, all humans have emotions and need to learn how to manage and regulate them. Moreover, research on cross-cultural program adaptations has indicated that the majority of programs adapted to another cultural setting are often adapted superficially (Gonzale et al., 2016; Kam et al., 2011) with the core curriculum remaining fairly consistent. To avoid this shortcoming, there were no major adaptations or modifications to the content of the COPE-Resilience program. Additionally, cultural adaptation of the COPE-Resilience program was kept to a minimum. Adaptation mainly focused on language translation, use of familiar analogies, and changing certain text to reflect cultural norms, with the core curriculum remaining fairly consistent.

Phase 2: Piloting the Study Design, Instruments, and Adapted Program with a Small Sample

Jones et al. (2018) identified two common characteristics that foster the successful implementation of SEL programs: (1) the presence of a supportive SEL culture and contexts and (2) building teachers' understanding of SEL. How the program is perceived and delivered is influenced by the cultural context and values, attitudes, and abilities of the teachers. As teachers are often the ones charged with implementing SEL programs, their beliefs about SEL play an important part in the adoption and implementation of an SEL program. The support of schools and teacher buy-in is crucial for the adoption and sustainability of SEL concepts and programs in a new community.

Through self-selection sampling, a public kindergarten in Taiwan (preschool A) volunteered to take part in the study. This sampling method ensured that the school leadership was committed to taking part in the study, which supported teacher buy-in and increased the school and teachers' willingness to provide insight into the phenomenon being studied. The Chinese COPE-Resilience program was piloted first in preschool A before moving on to phases 3 and 4. Thabane et al. (2010) indicated that pilot studies are a crucial element of good study design; conducting a pilot study increases the likelihood of program success. A one-group pre and posttest mixed-method design was used to collect both quantitative and qualitative data that were used to determine whether the program was appropriate in Taiwan. A total of 10 children were recruited via stratified random sampling from a class of 30 children. Children's age at the commencement of the program ranged between 5 and 5.6 years, with an equal gender ratio.

The program ran as six modules over six weeks. All modules were delivered by the children's classroom teacher(s) as part of their curriculum to further enhance children's social and emotional competencies. The six modules were embedded in daily teaching and/or run as stand-alone 20- to 45-minute sessions. Teachers were provided with the Chinese version of the COPE-Resilience program manual two weeks before the start of the intervention. Teachers were encouraged to modify and pick any activities in the manual to match the interests, needs, and developmental stage of the children. Teachers were advised to deliver a minimum of two activities per week from an average of five to six activities in each module of the COPE-Resilience program manual. Before the commencement of the program, teachers attended a one-hour workshop on SEL and COPE-Resilience program implementation and participated in ongoing consultation with the researcher during the six-week program.

Assessments of children's empathy, inhibition, and coping were collected from their classroom teachers at two time points of baseline (T1) and postintervention (T2). Children were also interviewed one-on-one by the researcher to assess their skills in emotional labeling and empathetic responses. In addition to the child measures, teachers were also invited to complete a questionnaire to ascertain the level of experience and confidence in SEL and COPE-Resilience program facilitation. To ensure that all modules were delivered as intended over six weeks, teachers in the intervention condition were asked to complete a structured implementation checklist for each of the weekly modules. The researcher also observed three of the six sessions.

Even with only 10 children, children in preschool A showed significant improvement in their ability to label emotions, with a statistically significant increase of emotional knowledge (large effect size, $d = 2.56$). Large effect sizes were also found in children's empathetic responses, empathy scores, and positive coping behavior (ES ranged from $d = 1.30–1.55$). Likewise, there were no identifiable complications during the recruitment process, data collection strategies, and instruments used. In general, teachers found it easy to administer and implement the program.

Phase 3: Effectiveness of the Chinese COPE-Resilience Program in Relation to Gender and Year Level

Phase 3 study adopted similar research recruitment, data collection procedures, and measurements as phase 1. A total of 60 children from a privately managed public preschool (preschool B) were recruited; 30 in the prekindergarten (ages four to five) and 30 in the kindergarten class (ages five to six). The children's mean age (in months) was 63.8 months.

Following the completion of the six-week program, a similar trend was also observed in preschool B, with large effect sizes found in children's improvements of emotional labeling ($d = 1.39$) and reduction of negative coping ($d = 1.04$). Small and medium effect sizes were found in children's inhibitory control, empathetic responses, and empathy scores. These significant changes were also equally beneficial across gender and year level (prekindergarten and kindergarten).

Phase 4: Sustained Effects of the Chinese COPE-Resilience Program

Children recruited in this phase were from a private preschool in Taiwan (preschool C). Unlike previous phases where class sizes were more substantial (30 children in each class), this preschool had smaller class sizes (10–15 children in each class). A total of seven classes were recruited. There were 98 children in total—57 in the COPE-Resilience intervention group (four classes) and 41 in the nonintervention group (three classes). Children's age at the commencement of the program ranged between 4.2 and 6.1 years. Instead of assessing children before and after the intervention, children were assessed at three time points of baseline (T1), postintervention (T2), and six-month follow-up (T3) for preschool C.

Results indicated that when compared with a nonintervention comparison group, children in the COPE-Resilience group showed significantly greater improvements in measures of emotional labeling, empathetic responses, empathy, and lower inhibitory difficulties at T2 even after controlling for T1 differences. Although there was no difference in children's positive coping behavior between the two groups at T2, children's negative coping behavior was significantly lower in the intervention group when measured six months after the intervention. Furthermore, children's scores on the teacher-rated empathy, inhibitory control, and positive and negative coping measures remained relatively constant for children in the COPE-Resilience group. There were no substantial changes from T2 to T3. This indicated that the effect of the COPE-Resilience was still measurable in the intervention group six months after the intervention.

In general, teachers in the intervention group felt that the Chinese COPE-Resilience program had helped improve children's social-emotional competencies. Teachers' responses were predominantly positive, showing similar results as the direct child and teacher-rated measurements. For example, one teacher reported that after the program, children were "*better equipped to understand the feelings of others*," while another teacher acknowledged that children in her class "*are using more caring words*." Another teacher found that children were "*more expressive and are beginning to show and talk about their emotions, especially the negative ones*," while another said, "*they became more observant, paid more attention to others' emotions in class or at playtime*." One teacher also reported that children in her class "*became more caring, patient, resilient and are more inclusive towards those that are different*." This informal feedback from teachers in the intervention groups suggests that the program had a positive effect on preschoolers' ability to recognize, understand, label, and express emotions.

Overall, some clear insights were found from phases 2 to 4. Specifically, results showed that children undertaking the program demonstrated the greatest improvements in social-emotional functioning, namely, emotional labeling, empathy, empathetic response, positive coping behavior, and inhibitory control. There was also a significant decrease in children's negative coping behavior. These findings are consistent with the work in Australia (Cornell et al., 2017; Pang et al., 2018), indicating that the adapted COPE-Resilience program can improve social-emotional skills and positive adaptation in preschool-aged children.

Phase 5: Teachers' Personal Change and Growth through Implementing the Program

Teacher participants were composed of preschool teachers from preschools B and C. A total of 10 teachers were interviewed in phase 5, seven of whom took part in the COPE-Resilience program. These teachers delivered lessons from the Chinese COPE-Resilience program for six weeks during the 2018–2019 school year. The remaining teachers ($n = 3$) did not deliver the Chinese COPE-Resilience program nor did they attend the preprogram workshop on SEL or the COPE-Resilience program. Teachers who participated in the Taiwanese studies were experienced working in the early childhood sector (eight to 20+ years of experience). The teachers had no prior knowledge of the COPE-Resilience program prior to the intervention. They also indicated that they had never heard of the term "social-emotional learning" but were fairly familiar with the term "social-emotional development." Of the 10 teachers interviewed, teachers strongly believed SEL to be highly important and considered that there was a need for it to be introduced in teacher training programs and children's daily learning.

A thematic analysis of teachers' responses between seven intervention teachers and three nonintervention teachers six months after implementing the COPE-Resilience program suggested that there were some differences between the intervention and nonintervention group. When asked to define what SEL is, the majority of teachers in the intervention group identified it as a process of learning about emotions, or planning activities or programs to support children's social-emotional development. In contrast, teachers in the nonintervention group defined it as *"understanding of feelings"* and *"social skills"*; the terms "learning process" and "teaching or planning" were barely mentioned. Moreover, regarding the responsibility of teaching and socializing children early in social-emotional skills, consistent with past literature, all teachers in the nonintervention group believed that family is the dominant socializing unit for children's early learning (Wilkinson & Kao, 2019) and therefore, *"Parents have a greater responsibility for teaching children social-emotional skills...if parents refuse to cooperate or change their home environment there is nothing we can do."* In contrast, the majority (71%) of teachers in the intervention group indicated that preschool/kindergarten is a primary place for children to learn about social-emotional skills, *"We can teach them, and we can also support parents, in case of behavioural problems at home we can teach parents strategies, like introduce new ideas."*

In regards to increasing teachers' understanding of SEL through the Chinese COPE-Resilience program, all teachers (100%) in the COPE-Resilience group believed that the program has helped improve their understanding of SEL. Moreover, interviews with teachers in the intervention group indicated that they noticed an increase in their emotional skills and knowledge after implementing the Chinese COPE-Resilience program. Teachers identified change occurring in three areas consequent to their engagement in the program, namely, social-emotional skills and self-efficacy, ways to approach and teach SEL, and knowledge of emotions. For example, one teacher noted,

> *"I've learnt that there are different dimensions of emotions"*, while another teacher found that she *"learnt a lot from COPE-R. I will tell myself that I can relax my emotions a little bit more, then I am able to be more calmer at handeling things, by becoming calmer, I am able to be more patient and observant"*. Likewise, another teacher reported that she now learnt that *"there are different ways of teaching emotions and feelings, through teaching this program. I began to remind myself to be aware of children's emotions constantly. Emotions come before Actions. Before this program, I rarely dealt with children's emotions, usually only focusing on their actions. Now, instead of firmly believing what I thought he/she is feeling, or disciplining his or her action, I am more willing to observe and do more homework, searching for more ways to make myself a better teacher."*

These findings suggest that the program had some effect on teachers' understanding of the term SEL and supports previous research that implementation of SEL programs can impact and change both students and the adults who work with them (Kimber et al., 2013; Zakrzewski, 2014).

Conclusion

The importance of cultivating SEL in schools and its association with 21st-century skills, namely, critical thinking, collaboration, creativity, and communication (Pellegrino & Hilton, 2012), has gained momentum throughout the world. This growing interest is not limited to Westernized or individualist cultures. Many collectivist cultures, particularly countries where Confucianism is endorsed, are starting to lead educational reforms, stressing the importance of SEL in education. What may be surprising for these countries is the degree to which they are transforming from traditional academically driven focus to self-development, embracing SEL and competency-based assessments. While in Australia the COPE-Resilience program has provided preliminary evidence of increasing SEL skills and positive adaptation in preschool-aged children (Cornell et al., 2017; Pang et al., 2018), in countries such as Taiwan, where there have been no formal SEL programs in place in preschools, it is important to consider the cross-culture utility of the SEL programs when implementing from one cultural context into another. This chapter provides insights into the benefits of implementing SEL programs in both individualistic and collectivistic societies.

Additionally, various behavioral outcomes, namely, emotional labeling, problem behavior, positive and negative coping, and behavioral inhibition and regulations have been reported in various studies (Cornell et al., 2017; Pang et al., 2018). Also, it was found in one study that when teacher experience was taken into account, the outcomes for the experienced instructor were demonstrable different to that of the first-time classroom teacher (Wu et al., 2020). Similarly, in the Taiwanese context, improvements in children's behavioral outcomes have also been demonstrated (Wu et al., 2019).

While culture and context are all important, it is clear that SEL is informing curriculum in the early years in diverse communities across the globe. This chapter provides an example demonstrating that it is possible to apply learning from a Western cultural context to an Eastern one. SEL programs have grown in number and focus over the past two decades, particularly since the founding of CASEL. Whilst the intent and focus of the programs may not have been closely linked with Positive Psychology and Positive Education, they each have, in various ways, focused on the well-being of children and the development of social-emotional skills. What is somewhat different in COPE-Resilience is the emphasis on the development of language and concepts associated with helpful and unhelpful coping. Additionally, the early years' school experience has afforded an opportunity to develop empathy, gratitude, and sharing and caring for all living things, including the environment. These unique elements make COPE-Resilience a useful resource for healthy child development. If programs have universal positive psychological elements such as COPE-Resilience, it is possible to adapt from one context to another if it is executed cautiously, taking into account the needs of the community and bringing them along the journey.

References

Barrett, P. M. (2007). *Fun friends. The teaching and training manual for group leaders*. Fun Friends Publishing.

Belacchi, C., & Farina, E. (2012). Feeling and thinking of others: Affective and cognitive empathy and emotion comprehension in prosocial/hostile preschoolers. *Aggressive Behavior, 38*(2), 150–165. https://doi.org/10.1002/ab.21415

Bernal, G., Bonilla, J., & Bellido, C. (1995). Ecological validity and cultural sensitivity for outcome research: Issues for cultural adaptation and development of psychosocial treatments with Hispanics. *Journal of Abnormal Child Psychology, 23*(1), 67–82. https://doi.org/10.1007/bf01447045

Blair, C., & Raver, C. C. (2015). School readiness and self-regulation: A developmental psychobiological approach. *Annual Review of Psychology, 66*, 711–731. https://doi.org/10.1146/annurev-psych-010814-015221

Bornstein, M., Hahn, C., & Haynes, O. (2010). Social competence, externalizing, and internalizing behavioural adjustment from early childhood through early adolescence: Developmental cascades. *Development and Psychopathology, 22*(4), 717–735. http://doi.org/10.1017/s0954579410000416

Boyle, D., & Haslett-Walker, C. (2008). Reducing overt and relational aggression among young children: The results from a two-year outcome evaluation. *Journal of School Violence, 7*(1), 27–42. http://doi.org/10.1300/J202v07n01_03

Brackett, M. (2019). *Permission to feel*. Celadon Books.

Brauner, C. B., & Stephens, C. B. (2006). Estimating the prevalence of early childhood serious emotional/behavioral disorders: Challenges and recommendations. *Public Health Reports, 121*(3), 303–310. http://doi.org/10.1177/003335490612100314

Bronfenbrenner, U. (1979). Contexts of child rearing: Problems and prospects. *American Psychologist, 34*, 844–850. http://doi.org/10.1037/0003-066x.34.10.844

Carman, S., & Chapparo, C. (2012). Children who experience difficulties with learning: Mother and child perceptions of social competence. *Australian Occupational Therapy Journal, 59*(5), 339–346. http://doi.org/10.1111/j.1440-1630.2012.01034.x

CASEL. (2019). *What is SEL*. Retrieved on February 19, 2020 from https://casel.org/what-is-sel/

Castro, F. G., Barrera, J. M., & Martinez, J. C. R. (2004). The cultural adaptation of prevention interventions: Resolving tensions between fidelity and fit. *Prevention Science, 5*(1), 41–45. http://doi.org/10.1023/b:prev.0000013980.12412.cd

Chen, H. L. S., & Huang, H. Y. (2017). *Advancing 21st century competencies in Taiwan*. Asia Society, Center for Global Education.

Cheng, M. F. (2018). The new integrated early childhood education and care system in Taiwan. In J. L. Roopnarine, J. E. Johnson, S. F. Quinn, & M. M. Patte (Eds.), *Handbook of international perspectives on early childhood education* (pp. 175–186). Taylor & Francis. https://doi.org/10.4324/9781315562193

Compas, B. (2009). Coping, regulation, and development during childhood and adolescence: Coping and the development of regulation. *New Directions for Child and Adolescent Development, 124*, 87–99. http://doi.org/10.1002/cd.245

Compas, B. E., Connor-Smith, J. K., Saltzman, H., Thomsen, A. H., & Wadsworth, M. E. (2001). Coping with stress during childhood and adolescence: Problems, progress, and potential in theory and research. *Psychological Bulletin, 127*(1), 87–127. http://doi.org/10.1037/0033-2909.127.1.87

Cornell C., Kiernan N., Kaufman D., Dobee P., Frydenberg, E., & Deans, J. (2017). Developing social emotional competence in the early years. In E. Frydenberg, A. Martin, R. Collie (Eds.), *Social and emotional learning in Australia and the Asia-Pacific: Perspectives, programs and approaches* (pp. 391–412). Springer.

Crawford, A. M., & Manassis, K. (2011). Anxiety, social skills, friendship quality, and peer victimization: An integrated model. *Journal of Anxiety Disorders, 25*(7), 924–931. http://doi.org/10.1016/j.janxdis.2011.05.005

Deans, J., Klarin, S., Liang, R., & Frydenberg, E. (2017). All children have the best start in life to create a better future for themselves and for the nation. *Australian Journal of Early Childhood, 42*(4), 78–86. http://doi.org/ 10.23965/ajec.42.4.09

Decety, J., Michalska, K. J., & Kinzler, K. D. (2012). The contribution of emotion and cognition to moral sensitivity: A neurodevelopmental study. *Cerebral Cortex, 22(1)*, 209–220. http://doi.org/10.1093/cercor/bhr111

Denham, S. (2006). Emotional competence: Implications for social functioning. In J. L. Luby (Ed.), *Handbook of preschool mental health: development, disorders, and treatment* (pp. 23–44). Guilford Press.

Derryberry, D., Reed, M. A., & Pilkenton–Taylor, C. (2003). Temperament and coping: Advantages of an individual differences perspective. *Development and Psychopathology, 15*(4), 1049–1066. http://doi.org/10.1017/s0954579403000439

Eisenberg, N., Cumberland, A., Spinrad, T. L., Fabes, R. A., Shepard, S. A., Reiser, M., Murphy, B. C., Losoya, S. H., & Guthrie, I. K. (2001). The relations of regulation and emotionality to children's externalizing and internalizing problem behavior. *Child Development, 72*(4), 1112–1134. http://doi.org/10.1111/1467-8624.00337

Eisenberg, N., Fabes, R. A., & Guthrie, I. K. (1997). Coping with stress: The roles of regulation and development. In S. A. Wolchik & I. Sandler (Eds.), *Handbook of children's coping: Linking theory and intervention* (pp. 41–70). Plenum.

Eisenberg, N., Fabes, R. A., & Spinrad, T. L. (2006). Prosocial development. In W. Damon & R. Lerner (Eds.), *Handbook of child psychology, social, emotional, and personality development* (Vol. 3, pp. 646–702). Wiley.

Fantuzzo, J., Bulotsky, R., McDermott, P., Mosca, S., & Lutz, M. N. (2003). A multivariate analysis of emotional and behavioral adjustment and preschool educational outcomes. *School Psychology Review, 32*, 185–203.

Fox, S., Levitt, P., & Nelson, C. (2010). How the timing and quality of early experiences influence the development of brain architecture. *Child Development, 81*(1), 28–40. https://doi.org/10.1111/j.1467-8624.2009.01380.x

Frydenberg, E. (2017). *Coping and the challenge of resilience.* Palgrave Macmillan.

Frydenberg, E., & Lewis, R. (2011). *Adolescent Coping Scale-2.* Australian Council for Educational Research.

Fu, C. S. (2012). What are emotions in Chinese Confucianism. *Linguistics, Culture & Education, 1*(1), 78–93.

Gao, C. C., (2019). 7 Dà zhòngyào guānjiàn fāxiàn: Jìnxíng `shèhuì/qíngxù xuéxí', chéngjī tígāo 13 gèbǎifēndiǎn. [7 important key findings: Social/Emotional learning increases grades by 13 percent]. *Global Family Monthly, 48*. Retrieved from https://times.hinet.net/magazineCp/cp119

Gillberg, C. (1992). Autism and autistic-like conditions: Subclasses among disorders of empathy. *Journal of Child Psychology & Psychiatry & Allied Disciplines, 33*(5), 813–842. https://doi.org/10.1111/j.1469-7610.1992.tb01959.x

Gonzales, N. A., Lau, A. S., Murry, V. M., Pina, A. A., & Barrera, M., Jr. (2016). Culturally adapted preventive interventions for children and adolescents. In D. Cicchetti (Ed.), *Developmental psychopathology: Risk, resilience, and intervention* (pp. 874–933). Wiley.

Hamre, B. K., Pianta, R. C., Mashburn, A. J., & Downer, J. T. (2012). Promoting young children's social competence through the preschool PATHS curriculum and MyTeachingPartner professional development resources. *Early Education and Development, 23*(6), 809–832. https://doi.org/10.1080/10409289.2011.607360

Hebb, D. O. (1949). *The organization of behavior: A neuropsychological theory.* Wiley.

Hecht, M. L., & Shin, Y. (2015). Culture and social and emotional competencies In J. A. Durlak, C. E. Domitrovich, R. P. Weissberg, & T. P. Gullotta (Eds.), *Handbook of social and emotional learning: Research and practice* (pp. 50–64). Guildford.

Hemmeter, M. L., Fox, L., Jack, S., & Broyles, L. (2007). A program-wide model of positive be-havior support in early childhood settings. *Journal of Early Intervention, 29*, 337–355. http://doi.org/10.1177/105381510702900405

Huang, K. (2019). Taiwan's Department of Education must limit the number of tests students take. *Taipei Teen Tribune.* Retrieved from https://taipeiteentribune.com/taiwan-must-limit-tests-students-take/

Huppert, F. A. (2014). *The state of wellbeing science: Concepts, measures, interventions, and policies. Wellbeing: Volume 6: Interventions and policies to enhance wellbeing.* https://doi.org/10.1002/9781118539415.wbwell036

Jones, S., Bailey, R., Brush, K., & Kahn, J. (2018). *Preparing for effective SEL implementation.* Retrieved from https://www.wallacefoundation.org/knowledge-center/Documents/Preparing-for-Effective-SEL-Implementation.pdf

Kalisch, R., Cramer, A. O. J., Binder, H., Fritz, J., Leertouwer, Ij., Lunansky, G., Meyer, B., Timmer, J., Veer, I. M., & van Harmelen, A.-L. (2019). Deconstructing and reconstructing resilience: A dynamic network approach. *Perspectives on Psychological Science, 14*(5), 765–777. https://doi.org/10.1177/1745691619855637

Kam, C., Wong, L. W., & Fung, K. M. (2011). Promoting social-emotional learning in Chinese schools: A feasi-bility study of PATHS implementation in Hong Kong. *International Journal of Emotional Education, 3*(1), 30–47.

Kimber, B., Skoog, T., & Sandell, R. (2013). Teacher change and development during training in social and emotional learning programs in Sweden. *The International Journal of Emotional Education, 5*(1), 17–35.

Kostelnik, M. J., Whiren, A. R., Soderman, A. K., Stein, L. C., & Gregory, K. (2006) *Guiding children's social development. Theory to practice* (5th ed.). Thomson Learning.

Lazarus, R. S., & Folkman, S. (1984). *Stress, appraisal, and coping.* Springer.

Liau, A. K., Liau, A. W. L., Teoh, G. B. S., & Liau, M. T. L. (2003). The case for emotional literacy: The in-fluence of emotional intelligence on problem behaviours in Malaysian secondary school students. *Journal of Moral Education, 32*(1), 51–66. http://doi.org/10.1080/0305724022000073338

McClelland, M. M., Morrison, F. J., & Holmes, D. L. (2000). Children at risk for early academic problems: The role of learning-related social skills. *Early Childhood Research Quarterly, 15*(3), 307–329. http://doi.org/ 10.1016/s0885–2006(00)00069-7

Miller, A. L., Fine, S. E., Gouley, K. K., Seifer, R., Dickstein, S., & Shields, A. (2006). Showing and telling about emotions: Interrelations between facets of emotional competence and associations with classroom adjustment in Head Start preschoolers. *Cognition and Emotion, 20*(8), 1170–1192. http://doi.org/10.1080/02699930500405691

Ministry of Education. (2016). *Yòu'éryuán jiào bǎo huódòng kèchéng dàgāng* [Early childhood education and care curriculum framework]. Taipei: MoE. Retrieved from https://www.ece.moe.edu.tw/?p=5432

OECD. (2019). *PISA 2018 results (Volume III): What school life means for students' lives.* PISA OECD Publishing. https://doi.org/10.1787/acd78851-en

Pang, D., Frydenberg, E., Liang, R., Deans, J., & Su, L. (2018). Improving coping skills & promoting social and emotional competence in pre-schoolers: A 5-week COPE-R programme. *Journal of Early Childhood Education Research, 7*(2), 1–31

Payton, J. W., Weissberg, R. P., Durlak, J. A., Dymnicki, A. B., Taylor, R. D., Schellinger, K. B., & Pachan, M. (2008). *The positive impact of social and emotional learning for kindergarten to eighth-grade students: Findings from three scientific reviews.* Chicago, IL: Collaborative for Academic, Social, and Emotional Learning.

Pellegrino, J. W., & Hilton, M. L. (2012). *Education for life and work: Developing transferable knowledge and skills in the 21st century.* The National Academies Press.

Piaget, J. (1952). *The origins of intelligence in children.* W.W. Norton.

Rose-Krasnor, L., & Denham, S. (2009). Social-emotional competence in early childhood. In K. H. Rubin, W. M. Bukowski, & B. Laursen (Eds.), *Social, emotional, and personality development in context: Handbook of peer interactions, relationships, and groups* (pp. 162–179). Guilford.

Rudolph, K., Dennig, M., & Weisz, J. (1995). Determinants and consequences of children coping in a med-ical setting: Conceptualisation, review and critique. *Psychological Bulletin, 118*(3), 328–357. http://doi.org/10.1037/0033-2909.118.3.328

Salovey, P., & Mayer, J. D. (1990). Emotional intelligence. *Imagination, Cognition, and Personality, 9*, 185–211. http://doi.org/0.2190/DUGG-P24E-52WK-6CDG

Shing, M. L., Yang, K. B., Chiu, C. H., Ko, H. W., Tsai, M. L., Chin, J. C., Kuo-Li, T. W., Chien, S. C., & Lin, M. C. (2015). *Xīn kè gāng xiǎng shuō de shì: Yòu'éryuán jiào bǎo huódòng kèchéng dàgāng de lǐniàn yǔ fāzhǎn* [What We Want to Say: The Rationale and Development of Curriculum Guidelines for Early Childhood Education and Care (ECEC)]. Psychological Publishing Co.

Shing, M. L., & Zhou, Y. (2017). *Yòu'éryuán jiào bǎo huódòng kèchéng dàgāng de shíjiàn-yī wèi fǔdǎo fǎng shì rényuán de guānchá* [Practice of early childhood education and care curriculum- an officer's observation]. *Journal of Textbook Research, 3*(10), 101–131.

Shipman, K., Zeman, J., Fitzgerald, M., & Swisher, L. M. (2003). Regulating emotion in parent-child and peer relationships: A comparison of sexually maltreated and nonmaltreated girls. *Child Maltreatment, 8*(3), 163–172. https://doi.org/10.1177/1077559503254144

Skinner, E. A., & Zimmer-Gembeck, J. (2007). The development of coping. *Annual Review of Clinical Psychology, 58*, 119–144. http://doi.org/10.1146/annurev.psych.58.110405

Thabane, L., Ma, J., Chu, R., Cheng, J., Ismaila, A., Rios, L. P., Robson, R., Thabane, M., Giangregorio, L., & Goldsmith, C. H. (2010). A tutorial on pilot studies: the what, why and how. *BMC Medical Research Methodology, 10*(1). https://doi.org/10.1186/1471-2288-10-1

von Klitzing, K., Dohnert, M., Kroll, M., & Grube, M. (2015). Mental disorders in early childhood. *Deutsches Arzteblatt International, 112*(21–22), 375–386. https://doi.org/10.3238/arztebl.2015.0375

Vygotsky, L. S. (1962). *Thought and language.* MIT Press.

Whalen, D. J., Sylvester, C. M., & Luby, J. L. (2017). Depression and anxiety in preschoolers: A review of the past 7 years. *Child and Adolescent Psychiatric Clinics of North America, 26*(3), 503–522. https://doi.org/10.1016/j.chc.2017.02.006

Wilkinson, J. E., & Kao, C.-P. (2019). Aspects of socio-emotional learning in Taiwan's preschools: An exploratory study of teachers' perspectives. *International Journal of Child Care and Education Policy, 13*(1). http://doi.org/10.1186/s40723-019-0057-6

Wu, M. Y. (2020). *Social emotional learning (SEL) in practice in early childhood: translating and applying the COPE-resilience program in Taiwan.* [Doctoral thesis, University of Melbourne]. Minerva Access. https://minerva-access.unimelb.edu.au/handle/11343/274631#file_3532916

Wu, M. Y., Alexander, M. A., Frydenberg, E. & Deans, J. (2020). Early childhood social-emotional learning based on the Cope-Resilience program: Impact of teacher experience. *Issues in Educational Research, 30*(2), 782–807. http://www.iier.org.au/iier30/wu.pdf

Wu, M. Y., McKenzie, V. L., & Frydenberg, E. (2019). *Early years social emotional learning – What, why, how? The success of cross-culture adaptation of the COPE-Resilience preschool SEL program.* Paper presented at the 2019 College of Educational and Developmental Psychologist Biennial Conference, Hobart, Australia.

Yao, X.-Z. (2000) *An introduction to confucianism.* Cambridge University Press. https://doi.org/10.1017/CBO9780511800887

Zakrzewski, V. (2014). How social-emotional learning transforms classrooms. *Greater Good Science Center.* Retrieved from https://greatergood.berkeley.edu/article/item/how_social_emotional_learning_transforms_classrooms

11

PHYSICAL ACTIVITY AND SPORT

Lara H. Mossman and Lindsay G. Oades

Physical inactivity has raised global concerns as it is identified as a significant risk factor to noncommunicable diseases. In response to these concerns, schools have been urged to introduce policies and initiatives to promote physical activity (World Health Organization [WHO], 2007, 2008, 2009). Guidelines recommend a minimum of 60 minutes of moderate-intensity physical activity per day for children aged 5–17 (Janssen & LeBlanc, 2010). To meet these recommendations, schools are encouraged to implement a range of strategies including running enjoyable sport classes (WHO, 2008). This is because enjoyment is a crucial factor in developing ongoing physical activity habits; the principal reason for dropout in sport has been attributed to a lack of enjoyment (Butcher et al., 2002; Crane & Temple, 2015). While theoretical and empirical research looking at sport enjoyment aligns with positive psychology's (Seligman & Csikszentmihalyi, 2000) and positive education's (Seligman et al., 2009) intended focus, there is a scarcity of literature on this topic stemming from these bodies of work. However, self-determination theory (SDT) offers an extensive body of research on enjoyment, motivation, and well-being in a range of contexts, including sport, physical education (PE), and physical activity (Ryan & Deci, 2000, 2017). Indeed, SDT's contribution to positive psychological science is acknowledged in the seminal work on positive psychology (Seligman & Csikszentmihalyi, 2000). The SDT literature highlights the key role teachers and coaches play in creating enjoyable environments (e.g., Haerens et al., 2018; Leptokaridou et al., 2016; Vlachopoulos et al., 2011). Notably, the SDT literature provides insights for those wishing to address the criticism that positive education has somewhat overlooked context (e.g., interpersonal climate) in its drive to embed well-being content (Allison et al., 2020). Therefore, this chapter looks at the SDT literature and interventions targeting coach and teacher interpersonal behaviors. It also draws on a complementary body of research on creating positive climates and achievement goal theory (AGT; Elliot, 1999; Elliot & McGregor, 2001). Physical literacy and *wellbeing literacy* are described as contemporary examples of the role of language use in influencing well-being, in this case, physical activity and sport-related behaviors. Ultimately, it is argued that there is a body of existing and emerging literature that can guide positive psychology and positive education in physical activity and sport.

Needs Supportive Coaching

SDT is a key research area that offers insights into creating enjoyable and highly motivating climates (Ryan & Deci, 2000, 2017). The past two decades have seen considerable growth in

SDT literature, focusing on the impact PE teachers and coaches have on the youth sport experiences (Ryan & Deci, 2017). Originating from motivation research, SDT has since evolved into a meta-theory that is principally concerned with conditions that foster or thwart flourishing (Ryan & Deci, 2017). SDT identifies basic psychological human needs it contends are essential nutriments for facilitating human tendencies for growth, optimal functioning, and well-being (Deci & Ryan, 2008). Furthermore, SDT argues that the interpersonal climate created by motivators (e.g., PE teachers, coaches, leaders, parents, and peers) is a significant factor in either supporting or thwarting these needs (Ryan & Deci, 2017). Therefore, in this section, we briefly outline SDT, provide evidence for the benefits of need support in youth sport settings, and discuss the effectiveness of interventions designed to increase PE teacher and coach need support.

The three basic psychological needs identified in SDT are *autonomy* (an individual's sense of volition), *competence* (mastery and an individual's belief that they can attain desired outcomes), and *relatedness* (feeling cared for and connected to others and a sense of belongingness). These needs are conducive to well-being (Vansteenkiste & Ryan, 2013) and, in particular, they are favorable to eudaimonic well-being (Ryan et al., 2008). Eudaimonic well-being involves carrying out one's life in accordance with one's "true self" while striving to reach one's potential, which encompasses human growth and excellence (Waterman, 1993). Conversely, SDT argues that thwarting these three needs predicts diminished human growth, lower quality motivation, ill-being, and poor functioning (Ryan & Deci, 2017; Vansteenkiste & Ryan, 2013). Research into numerous settings such as schools (Niemiec & Ryan, 2009) and workplaces (Slemp et al., 2018) demonstrates the benefits of autonomy, competence, and relatedness satisfaction to a range of well-being, motivation, and performance outcomes (Ryan & Deci, 2017). Variations in need satisfaction can occur across different domains (Ryan & Deci, 2017). For example, a child can experience need satisfaction in their sport in a club setting but not during an activity in the same sport in a PE lesson. Variations can also occur over time (Ryan & Deci, 2017), such that a child may experience need satisfaction in their PE lessons during their primary years of schooling, but not in secondary school. Importantly, the support of the three basic psychological needs is crucial for nurturing and sustaining higher quality motivation (Ryan & Deci, 2019). The distinctions between motivational quality as outlined in SDT are shown in Table 11.1.

SDT places motivation on a continuum (see Table 11.1). The continuum differentiates between three types of motivation: *amotivation* that involves a lack of intent to act and unwillingness to engage in an activity, *extrinsic motivation* that involves engaging in activities in order to attain outcomes external to the self, such as rewards, and *intrinsic motivation* that entails engaging in activities because they are inherently satisfying in themselves (Deci, 1975; Ryan & Deci, 2000). Intrinsic motivation arises from our inbuilt tendency "to seek out novelty and challenges, to extend and exercise one's capacities, to explore, and to learn" (Ryan & Deci, 2000, p. 70). It is considered essential to human development. It represents a principal source of enjoyment and vitality throughout life (Ryan, 1995). Thus, extrinsic motivation and intrinsic motivation make up the two types of motivation on the SDT continuum along with amotivation; however, the theory offers a more nuanced perspective on these distinctions.

An essential feature of SDT is that it categorizes extrinsic motivation into four regulatory styles ranging from more controlled to more autonomous forms of motivation (Deci & Ryan, 1985; Ryan & Deci, 2000, 2017). The most controlled form of extrinsic motivation is known as *external regulation*. It involves engaging in activities that are conditional upon rewards or punishments. Next to external regulation on the continuum is *introjected regulation* that involves engaging in activities because of self-induced internal pressure (e.g., anxiety, guilt, and pride). Both external and introjected regulations are considered controlled forms of motivation. *Identified regulation* is next on the continuum and is present where activities are engaged in due to the value or meaning. Although identified regulation is an extrinsic form of motivation, it is considered to arise more

Table 11.1 The SDT Continuum of Motivation, Regulatory Styles, and Applied Examples

Non-self-determined					*Self-determined*
Amotivation	*Extrinsic Motivation*				*Intrinsic Motivation*
	Most Controlled (Lower Quality)				*Most Autonomous (Higher Quality)*
Nonregulation	*External Regulation*	*Introjected Regulation*	*Identified Regulation*	*Integrated Regulation*	*Intrinsic Regulation*
Young person has no motivation to engage in a sporting activity because they do not value it (e.g., it's not worth the effort) or they feel incompetent at it (e.g., believe they lack the coordination to do it).	Young person engages in a sporting activity to gain rewards (e.g., to receive money for scoring goals) or avoid punishment (e.g., avoid being banned from playing on electronic devices).	Young person engages in a sporting activity as they enjoy showing off their skills relative to their peers (e.g., out of pride) or out of guilt (e.g., avoiding letting a coach or parent down).	Young person engages in a sporting activity because it is personally important to them or they value the activity in itself (e.g., for the physical fitness or social benefits the activity affords).	Young person engages in a sporting activity because it feels like part of their identity (e.g., they may say, "I am an athlete") and is congruent with their life value more broadly.	Young person engages in a sporting activity because they are interested in it (e.g., they are curious about developing skills) or enjoy the activity (e.g., it leads to positive emotions).

Note: This table shows the regulatory styles on the SDT continuum of motivation with corresponding applied examples indicating how each of the regulatory styles may present in the context of a sporting activity.

from within the self and is therefore regarded as an autonomous form of motivation. However, the most autonomous form of extrinsic motivation is *integrated regulation*. It is present where behaviors are congruent with a person's identity. While identified regulation and integrated regulation are considered autonomous forms of motivation, only intrinsic motivation is considered entirely self-determined because it emanates wholly from within (Ryan & Deci, 2000). Autonomous motivation is important because it is where individuals feel a sense of volition over their actions rather than feeling controlled in what they do (Ryan & Deci, 2000).

SDT is cognizant that not all human actions can, or indeed should, be regulated entirely from within (Ryan & Deci, 2017). However, the theory does argue that extrinsic motivational regulations can change over time such that they become more autonomous and internalized (Ryan & Deci, 2000, 2017). In SDT, this process, whereby values, beliefs, or behavioral regulations are integrated with the self, is known as *internalization* (Ryan & Deci, 2017). The internalization process can be promoted by significant others, especially through support of the three basic psychological needs (Ryan & Deci, 2017, 2019). For example, a young person may not value walks outdoors; however, their parents may espouse the health benefits of physical activity and an appreciation of nature's beauty, such that the child comes to value the activity themselves. Hence, while not all actions emanate from within, the internalization process illustrates that controlled forms of motivation can turn into more autonomous forms of motivation over time, a process that can be facilitated by important agents such as motivators (Ryan & Deci, 2000, 2017, 2019).

The mechanisms by which key agents facilitate the internalization process are autonomy support, competence support, and relatedness support, collectively known as need support (Ryan & Deci, 2017). *Autonomy support* involves motivators recognizing the need for people to volitionally undertake activities, thereby supporting others' curiosities, views, and feelings (Delrue et al., 2019). Recent advances in SDT research have viewed autotomy support through two lenses: participative and attuning (Aelterman et al., 2019; Delrue et al., 2019). *Participative* autonomy-supportive behaviors entail the provision of meaningful choices and allow for contributions and ideas from young people (e.g., Delrue et al., 2019; Mageau & Vallerand, 2003; Stroet et al., 2015). *Attuning* autonomy-supportive behaviors involve (a) finding ways to make activities more interesting and enjoyable (Aelterman et al., 2019; Delrue et al., 2019; Jang et al., 2010); (b) acknowledging and accepting others' perspectives and emotions, especially feelings of negative affect (e.g., Aelterman et al., 2019; Delrue et al., 2019; Mageau & Vallerand, 2003; Stroet et al., 2015); (c) fostering meaning by offering a rationale for tasks and limits congruent with the values of others (e.g., Delrue et al., 2019; Mageau & Vallerand, 2003; Stroet et al., 2015); and (d) inhibiting ego involvement (e.g., Mageau & Vallerand, 2003). While autonomy support is the most widely researched form of need support (Ryan & Deci, 2017), the simultaneous support of all three basic psychological needs is said to lead to the most thriving (Jang et al., 2010). Therefore, competence and relatedness supportive behaviors must also be considered when facilitating optimal well-being and motivational environments.

The provision of competence support can be attained through providing structure (Aelterman et al., 2019; Jang et al., 2010). Structure can be afforded either through guiding or clarifying behaviors (Aelterman et al., 2019; Delrue et al., 2019). *Guiding* entails demonstrating steps involved in completing tasks, enabling independent work, and allowing questioning (Aelterman et al., 2019; Delrue et al., 2019). It entails collaboratively and constructively reflecting on mistakes in such a way that enables others to identify their areas for development and ways to improve (Aelterman et al., 2019; Delrue et al., 2019). *Clarifying* involves being clear and transparent when outlining what is required of others. It encompasses the outlining of expectations regarding learning outcomes for lessons or sessions. Finally, clarifying includes monitoring others' development regarding attaining the set levels (Aelterman et al., 2019; Delrue et al., 2019) and providing non-controlling competence feedback (Mageau & Vallerand, 2003). SDT argues that while autonomy and competence supports are crucial for enhancing and sustaining intrinsic motivation, relatedness support is also an essential aspect of motivational climates (Ryan & Deci, 2017).

Relatedness support entails interpersonal involvement with others, such as being warm, friendly, and providing social support (Sparks et al., 2015). Motivators demonstrate relatedness support when they are attentive, caring, responding to subtle details about others, expressing concern, and initiating personalized conversations (Sparks et al., 2015). They build trusting environments and promote teamwork and cooperation (Sparks et al., 2015). While relatedness support is not required in all contexts, such as solitary activities, it should be considered advantageous in fostering relatedness and autonomy (Costa et al., 2015). Furthermore, those who provide autonomy support can be viewed as more caring because they allow for others' viewpoints (Ryan & Deci, 2017). Thus, in interpersonal settings, autonomy and relatedness support tend to occur and function together (Deci et al., 2006; La Guardia et al., 2000).

While need support addresses the behaviors that should be amplified to foster necessary need satisfaction, it does not account for the behaviors that can actively frustrate the basic psychological needs. Thus, the past decade has witnessed a focus on needs thwarting behaviors that are controlling in nature (Bartholomew, Ntoumanis, Ryan, Bosch et al., 2011; Vansteenkiste & Ryan, 2013). These behaviors can occur through (a) overt control, such as using rewards or punishments in a controlling way; (b) negative conditional regard; (c) intimidation; (d) excessive use of control (Bartholomew, Ntoumanis, Ryan, & Thøpersen-Ntoumani, 2011), (e) controlling praise

(Deci & Ryan, 1985); (f) surveillance (Ryan et al., 1991); and (g) controlling language (Reeve & Jang, 2006).

Within sport settings, PE teachers and coaches are key agents who can support (Ntoumanis, 2005; Mageau and Vallerand, 2003) or thwart (Haerens et al., 2015; Tilga et al., 2018) the basic psychological needs of young people in their care. Burgeoning research in youth sport settings highlights the benefits of autonomy-supportive behaviors. Autonomy support predicts athletes' basic psychological needs satisfaction (e.g., Curran et al., 2014; Garn et al., 2012; Ntoumanis, 2005; Reinboth et al., 2004) as well as factors related to subjective well-being such as positive affect (Bartholomew, Ntoumanis, Ryan, Bosch et al., 2011; Cronin et al., 2018; Garn et al., 2019) and higher satisfaction with life (Cronin et al., 2018). It is also related to subjective vitality (López-Walle et al., 2012; Vlachopoulos et al., 2011; Vlachopoulos, Katartzi, & Kontou, 2013), physical activity enjoyment (Fin et al., 2019), and leisure-time physical exercise (Hagger et al., 2009). Autonomy support predicts autonomous motivation in sport (Fenton et al., 2014; Ntoumanis, 2005; Vlachopoulos et al., 2011, 2013), engagement (Curran et al., 2014; Meng & Keng, 2016), team cohesion (García-Calvo et al., 2014), and is negatively related to needs thwarting (e.g., Curran et al., 2016; Haerens et al., 2015; Tilga et al., 2018) and athlete burnout (Adie et al., 2012; Balaguer et al., 2012). Thus, autonomy support predicts higher well-being and lower ill-being; however, it should be noted that the literature is largely cross-sectional.

In contrast to autonomy support, controlling behaviors predict (a) need thwarting (Balaguer et al., 2012; Curran et al., 2014, 2016; Healy et al., 2014; Tilga et al., 2018); (b) extrinsic and intro-jected forms of motivation (Fenton et al., 2014; Healy et al., 2014), (c) negative affect and burnout (Balaguer et al., 2012); (d) sport disaffection (Curran et al., 2014, 2016); (e) dropout (Sarrazin et al., 2002); and (f) physical symptoms (Healy et al., 2014). Controlling behaviors are also neg-atively related to engagement (Curran et al., 2014, 2016) and autonomy support (Balaguer et al., 2012; Fenton et al., 2014). Hence, controlling behaviors predict ill-being and are negatively related to well-being. It should be noted that autonomy-supportive and controlling behaviors are not on a continuum but two discernible dimensions. Therefore, coaches can be high in both di-mensions, low in both, or high in one dimension and low in the other (Haerens et al., 2018). High autonomy support and low control are identified as the optimal profile even in more competitive contexts (Haerens et al., 2018). Given the benefits associated with need-supportive behaviors, there has been a growing interest in interventions designed to increase these behaviors in sports settings. The efficacy of such interventions can inform future research into positive education.

Need Support Interventions

Need support interventions amongst PE teachers cover theoretical components of motivation, basic psychological needs, and autonomy support (e.g., Aelterman et al., 2013; Chatzisarantis & Hagger, 2009; Cheon et al., 2012; Escriva-Boulley et al., 2018; Sánchez-Oliva et al., 2017; Tessier et al., 2008). Most interventions cover competence support (e.g., Aelterman et al., 2013; Amado et al., 2014; Meng & Keng, 2016; Sánchez-Oliva et al., 2017) and controlling teaching (e.g., Cheon et al., 2012; Cheon & Reeve 2013; Meng & Keng, 2016; Sánchez-Oliva et al., 2017; Tessier et al., 2008), however, few interventions explicitly cover relatedness support (e.g., Amado et al., 2014; Sánchez-Oliva et al., 2017). Training is predominantly face-to-face (Aelterman et al., 2013; Cheon et al., 2012; Meng & Keng, 2016) and incorporates a combination of (a) slide presenta-tions (Cheon et al., 2012; Reeve & Cheon, 2016); (b) interactive videos (Aelterman et al., 2013; Sánchez-Oliva et al., 2017); (c) guest speakers (Cheon et al., 2012; Reeve & Cheon, 2016); (d) applied examples (Aelterman et al., 2013); (e) video analysis (Reeve & Cheon, 2016; Tessier et al., 2008); (f) benefits of need supportive approaches (Reeve & Cheon, 2016); (g) reflective vi-gnettes (Cheon et al., 2012; Meng & Keng, 2016; Reeve & Cheon, 2016); (h) group discussions

(Cheon et al., 2012, 2016); (i) sample session plans (Meng & Keng, 2016); (j) sharing of tips after implementing the espoused strategies; (k) role play (Chatzisarantis & Hagger, 2009); and (l) handouts (Aelterman et al., 2013). Interventions are generally tested using control groups (e.g., Amado et al., 2014; Cheon & Reeve, 2013) and randomized groups (Aelterman et al., 2014; Cheon et al., 2012, 2016).

Intervention study designs seek to detect change proximally at the source of the training (e.g., teacher self-reports) and more distally by others not directly receiving the training (e.g., students' perceptions of the teaching environment and trained observers). Proximally, need support interventions have detected changes in teacher beliefs around autonomy support and structure (Aelterman et al., 2014) as well as increases in teacher autonomy-supportive behaviors (Aelterman et al., 2014; Perlman, 2015). Structure (Aelterman et al., 2014) also increases teacher efficacy (Cheon et al., 2018) and intrinsic instructional goals focused on the promotion of relationships and individual growth (Cheon et al., 2018). More distally, increases in perceived autonomy support have been observed by students (e.g., Aelterman et al., 2014; Chatzisarantis & Hagger, 2009; Cheon & Reeve, 2013; Perlman, 2015; Sánchez-Oliva et al., 2017) including one year later (Cheon & Reeve, 2013), and by trained observers (Aelterman et al., 2014; Perlman, 2015). Students have also reported increased relatedness support from PE teachers (Sánchez-Oliva et al., 2017).

In addition to changes in teachers, many studies also seek to detect changes in student outcomes such as motivation and well-being. Students of teachers who received interventions have reported

1 increased autonomous motivation (Amado, 2014; Chatzisarantis & Hagger, 2009; Perlman, 2015; Sánchez-Oliva et al., 2017);
2 decreased controlled motivation (Sánchez-Oliva et al., 2017);
3 increased autonomy satisfaction (Sánchez-Oliva et al., 2017);
4 increased overall basic need satisfaction (Cheon et al., 2016);
5 decreased need frustration (Cheon et al., 2016);
6 increased self-reported physical activity during leisure time (Chatzisarantis & Hagger, 2009);
7 increased intent to be physically active (Sánchez-Oliva et al., 2017); and
8 increased moderate-to-vigorous activity (MVPA; Escriva-Boulley et al., 2018).

Furthermore, Cheon et al. (2019) found autonomy support and intrinsic goals training to be more effective at increasing student need satisfaction and physical self-concept and decreasing problematic peer relationships to a greater extent than autonomy support training alone.

While there is a growing body of literature in PE settings, intervention research into youth sport contexts has been less widely addressed (Raabe et al., 2020). Findings are varied regarding intervention effectiveness in affecting coach autonomy support. Some research has reported increases in coach autonomy support (Langan et al., 2015; Langdon et al., 2015) while others (Mahoney et al., 2016) did not report any change. Findings have also been varied with regards to changes in controlling coaching behaviors, with some studies indicating a reduction in these behaviors (Langdon et al., 2015; Reynders et al., 2019) and others not reporting a significant change (Langan et al., 2015; Mahoney et al., 2016). One reason for this may be due to these interventions focusing on autonomy-supportive behaviors while omitting specific, explicit content on controlling coaching behaviors. Training should cover both autonomy support and controlling behaviors to encourage coaches to facilitate optimal sporting environments. Athletes of coaches who have received autonomy support training have reported increased need satisfaction (Langdon et al., 2015; Pulido et al., 2017), increased autonomous motivation (Reynders et al., 2019), engagement (Reynders et al., 2019), and sport commitment (Pulido et al., 2017). Moreover, athletes have reported decreases in need thwarting (Pulido et al., 2017) and the exhaustion facet of burnout (Langan et al., 2015). Whether such interventions can impact player subjective well-being or subject vitality is yet to be established.

Taken together, the intervention research into PE and youth sport settings suggests that behaviors of coaches and PE teachers can be affected through relatively short training programs. Furthermore, there is some evidence that these changes may affect young people in sport settings, although more research is needed to establish how long these effects last. Nonetheless, need support interventions that incorporate controlling behavior content provide essential insights for positive education researchers; however, moving beyond the SDT literature will afford a deeper understanding of well-being in sport settings.

Achievement Goal Theory (AGT)

Meta-analytical research has suggested that multicomponent interventions may be more effective than single-component interventions (Hendriks et al., 2019). Indeed, the SDT literature has found more benefits by broadening its focus from predominantly autonomy support to encompass all three need supports (Amado et al., 2014), controlling coaching (Cheon et al. 2016), and more recently, intrinsic goals (Cheon et al., 2019). A further component of interest is AGT, which encompasses the distinction between mastery and ego goals. Mastery goals are self-referenced. For example, they can be focused on attaining a personal best, whereas ego (or performance) goals are other-referenced, for example, focused on not getting beaten by a particular opponent. Both mastery and ego goals are theorized to take either approach or avoidance forms (Elliot, 1999; Elliot & McGregor, 2001). For example, trying to avoid getting a worse result than in a previous competition or trying to approach doing better than a race competitor. These four dimensions make up the 2 × 2 achievement goal framework (Elliot, 1999; Elliot & McGregor, 2001). Developments over the past decade have seen the addition of approach and avoidance task-referenced goals into a new 3 × 2 goal model (Elliot et al., 2011). Task-referenced goals can involve getting as many answers right on a test as possible rather than trying to beat a past performance. Self- and task-focused goals are theorized to lead to favorable outcomes compared to other-focused goals (Elliot et al., 2011). Applied examples of each of these dimensions are shown in Table 11.2.

PE teachers and coaches can facilitate climates that favor particular AGT goals leading to different outcomes. Mastery-approach goals, hypothesized to be the optimal 2 × 2 goal dimension, are associated with higher sport well-being (Adie et al., 2010). Mastery-based PE teaching is predictive of increased class-time physical activity (Wadsworth et al., 2013). Furthermore, mastery climates,

Table 11.2 The Distinctions Between Different Goal Types in the 3 × 2 Achievement Goal Model

| | *Performance/Ego* | *Mastery Goals* | |
	Other-Focused	*Self-Focused*	*Task-Focused*
Approach	Focused on approaching other-based competence, e.g., "to perform better in the finals than the previous winner."	Focused on approaching self-based competence, e.g., "to perform faster in an upcoming competition than before."	Focused on approaching task-based competence, e.g., "to make as many passes as possible in the next drill."
Avoidance	Focused on avoiding other-based incompetence, e.g., "not to be slower than my competitor in the upcoming race."	Focused on avoiding self-based incompetence, e.g., "to avoid being slower in an upcoming competition than in my previous race."	Focused on avoiding task-based incompetence, e.g., "to avoid turning over possession to the opposition as much as possible in the next drill."

Note: This table highlights the distinctions between other-focused, self-focused, and task-focused goals and provides corresponding applied examples.

defined as climates that emphasize mastery goals (Blumenfeld, 1992), and autonomy-supportive climates, are associated (Ntoumanis, 2005; Reinboth et al., 2004). Together they are positively related to athlete-reported positive affect, self-esteem, vitality, and perceived competence (e.g., Kipp & Weiss, 2013, 2015; Quested & Duda, 2010). Jaitner et al. (2019) meta-analyzed data on AGT in PE settings and found that mastery goals and climates support psychological well-being, sports participation, prosocial behavior, and healthy living. Therefore, the combination of interventions drawing on both AGT and SDT may provide several benefits to young athletes.

Physical and Wellbeing Literacy

The promotion of physical activity and sport usually resides within a health and well-being discourse. It is useful to explore contemporary literacy concepts, particularly as they relate to school education, community sport, and young people's participation. How do young people use language about physical activity and well-being? How might this affect their activity and participation? It is useful for educators and coaches to conceptualize these as literacies. This perspective provides broad and well-established curricula and pedagogical frameworks—for example, physical literacy continua for state education departments. The concepts of physical literacy and well-being literacy from existing literature are now described and discussed. Almond and Whitehead (2012) describe physical literacy as a human capability that encompasses motivation, confidence, physical competence, understanding, and knowledge to establish purposeful physical pursuits as an integral part of one's lifestyle.

With the rise of awareness about well-being as being more than the absence of illness, combined with integrated physical and mental health approaches, wellbeing literacy provides promise in this context. Wellbeing literacy is intentional language use about well-being and the well-being of self, others, and the world (Oades et al., 2020, 2021) and has a close relationship to positive education. Conceptualized as a language use capability, it constitutes what we *can be* and what we *can do,* with language to build well-being. The capability model of wellbeing literacy (Oades et al., 2020, 2021) involves necessary conditions: (a) knowledge and vocabulary about well-being; (b) skills of composing well-being language (i.e., writing, speaking, and creating); (3) skills of comprehending well-being language (i.e., reading, listening, and viewing); (d) sensitivity to context; and (e) intentionality (i.e., the habit of intention to use language for the well-being of self, others, and the world).

Table 11.3 provides an illustrative list of questions relevant to assessing wellbeing literacy, emphasizing physical activity in a sports club. Wellbeing literacy is more than knowing words. It involves how people intentionally communicate about physical or mental well-being. A sports club may examine its wellbeing literacy by exploring how its members, coaches, athletes, and parents interact and communicate well-being. This interaction includes physical activity and sport

Table 11.3 Questions Relevant to Physical and Wellbeing Literacy in a Sports Club

Do the coaches and athletes have language to communicate about physical activity?
What is the extent and quality of written material about physical activity?
Are coaches and athletes encouraged to read about physical activity?
Do the coaches and athletes listen to communication about physical activity?
Do coaches and athletes speak about physical activity in addition to doing it?
Are there stories, performances, or images (e.g., logos) created about physical activity?
How well do athletes and coaches view or take notice of these images?
Are these different types of language use about physical activity adapted to the age and culture of the athlete?
Do coaches and athletes intentionally use language to improve their physical activity and well-being?

in multiple writing modes, speaking, creating, reading, listening, and viewing. The club may be examined as a language system, where its components (coaches, athletes, and parents) interact through language; this may be a more tangible way of examining "club culture." It relates directly to how coaches communicate with athletes, how athletes communicate with each other.

Conclusion

This chapter examined SDT literature and interventions targeting coach and teacher interpersonal behaviors, including the complementary body of research on creating positive climates, AGT. Physical literacy and wellbeing literacy are described as contemporary examples of the role of language use in influencing well-being, in this case, physical activity and sport-related behaviors. Readers are encouraged to explore further these existing and emerging literatures, which include a developing evidence base, that can guide the application of positive psychology and positive education in physical activity and sport.

References

Adie, J., Duda, J., & Ntoumanis, N. (2010). Achievement goals, competition appraisals, and the well- and ill-being of elite youth soccer players over two competitive seasons. *Journal of Sport and Exercise Psychology, 32*(4), 555–579.

Adie, J. W., Duda, J. L., & Ntoumanis, N. (2012). Perceived coach-autonomy support, basic need satisfaction and the well- and ill-being of elite youth soccer players: A longitudinal investigation. *Psychology of Sport and Exercise, 13*(1), 51–59. https://doi.org/10.1016/j.psychsport.2011.07.008

Aelterman, N., Vansteenkiste, M., Haerens, L., Soenens, B., Fontaine, J. R., & Reeve, J. (2019). Toward an integrative and fine-grained insight in motivating and demotivating teaching styles: The merits of a circumplex approach. *Journal of Educational Psychology, 111*(3), 497–521. http://dx.doi.org/10.1037/edu0000293

Aelterman, N., Vansteenkiste, M., Van den Berghe, L., De Meyer, J., & Haerens, L. (2014). Fostering a need-supportive teaching style: Intervention effects on physical education teachers' beliefs and teaching behaviors. *Journal of Sport and Exercise Psychology, 36*(6), 595–609. http://dx.doi.org/10.1123/jsep.2013-0229

Aelterman, N., Vansteenkiste, M., Van Keer, H., De Meyer, J., Van den Berghe, L., & Haerens, L. (2013). Development and evaluation of a training on need-supportive teaching in physical education: Qualitative and quantitative findings. *Teaching and Teacher Education, 29*, 64–75. https://doi.org/10.1016/j.tate.2012.09.001

Allison, L., Waters, L., & Kern, M. L. (2020). Flourishing classrooms: Applying a systems-informed approach to positive education. *Contemporary School Psychology,* First online 10 June 2020. 1–11. https://doi.org/10.1007/s40688-019-00267-8

Almond, L., & Whitehead, M. (2012). Physical literacy: Clarifying the nature of the concept. *Physical Education Matters, 7*(1), 68–71. http://blogs.ubc.ca/ubcpe/files/2014/09/PL-Clarifying-the-nature-of-the-concept-SPRING12.pdf

Amado, D., Del Villar, F., Leo, F. M., Sánchez-Oliva, D., Sánchez-Miguel, P. A., & García-Calvo, T. (2014). Effect of a multi-dimensional intervention programme on the motivation of physical education students. *PLOS One, 9*(1). https://doi.org/10.1371/journal.pone.0085275

Balaguer, I., González, L., Fabra, P., Castillo, I., Mercé, J., & Duda, J. L. (2012). Coaches' interpersonal style, basic psychological needs and the well-and ill-being of young soccer players: A longitudinal analysis. *Journal of Sports Sciences, 30*(15), 1619–1629. http://dx.doi.org/10.1080/02640414.2012.731517

Bartholomew, K., Ntoumanis, N., Ryan, R. M., Bosch, J. A., & Thøgersen-Ntoumani, C. (2011). Self-Determination Theory and diminished functioning: The role of interpersonal control and psychological need thwarting. *Personality and Social Psychology Bulletin, 37*(11), 1459–1473. https://doi.org/10.1177/0146167211413125

Bartholomew, K., Ntoumanis, N., Ryan, R. M., & Thøpersen-Ntoumani, C. (2011). Psychological need thwarting in the sport context: Assessing the darker side of athletic experience. *Journal of Sport & Exercise Psychology, 33*(1), 75–102. https://doi.org/10.1123/jsep.33.1.75

Blumenfeld, P. C. (1992). Classroom learning and motivation: Clarifying and expanding goal theory. *Journal of Educational Psychology, 84*(3), 272–281. https://doi.org/10.1037/0022-0663.84.3.272

Butcher, J., Lindner, K. J., & Johns, D. P. (2002). Withdrawal from competitive youth sport: A retrospective ten-year study. *Journal of Sport Behavior, 25*(2), 145–163. http://static1.1.sqspcdn.com/static/f/1109123/24906774/1400507345587/Withdrawal+from+Competitive+Youth+Sport.pdf?token=5hQ0gpDpIVwZezKC8ZKzCzlgNc8%3D

Chatzisarantis, N. L., & Hagger, M. S. (2009). Effects of an intervention based on self-determination theory on self-reported leisure-time physical activity participation. *Psychology and Health, 24*(1), 29–48. https://doi.org/10.1080/08870440701809533

Cheon, S. H., & Reeve, J. (2013). Do the benefits from autonomy-supportive PE teacher training programs endure?: A one-year follow-up investigation. *Psychology of Sport and Exercise, 14*(4), 508–518. https://doi.org/10.1016/j.psychsport.2013.02.002

Cheon, S. H., Reeve, J., Lee, Y., & Lee, J. (2018). Why autonomy-supportive interventions work: Explaining the professional development of teachers' motivating style. *Teaching and Teacher Education, 69*, 43–51. https://doi.org/10.1016/j.tate.2017.09.022

Cheon, S. H., Reeve, J., & Moon, I. S. (2012). Experimentally based, longitudinally designed, teacher-focused intervention to help physical education teachers be more autonomy supportive toward their students. *Journal of Sport & Exercise Psychology, 34*(3), 365–396. https://doi.org/10.1123/jsep.34.3.365

Cheon, S. H., Reeve, J., & Song, Y. G. (2016). A teacher-focused intervention to decrease PE students' amotivation by increasing need satisfaction and decreasing need frustration. *Journal of Sport & Exercise Psychology, 38*(3), 217–235. http://dx.doi.org/10.1123/jsep.2015-0236

Cheon, S. H., Reeve, J., & Song, Y. G. (2019). Recommending goals and supporting needs: An intervention to help physical education teachers communicate their expectations while supporting students' psychological needs. *Psychology of Sport and Exercise, 41*, 107–118. https://doi.org/10.1016/j.psychsport.2018.12.008

Costa, S., Ntoumanis, N., & Bartholomew, K. J. (2015). Predicting the brighter and darker sides of interpersonal relationships: Does psychological need thwarting matter? *Motivation and Emotion, 39*(1), 11–24. https://doi.org/10.1007/s11031-014-9427-0

Crane, J., & Temple, V. (2015). A systematic review of dropout from organized sport among children and youth. *European Physical Education Review, 21*(1), 114–131. https://doi.org/10.1007/s11031-014-9427-0

Cronin, L. D., Allen, J., Mulvenna, C., & Russell, P. (2018). An investigation of the relationships between the teaching climate, students' perceived life skills development and well-being within physical education. *Physical Education and Sport Pedagogy, 23*(2), 181–196. https://doi.org/10.1080/17408989.2017.1371684

Curran, T., Hill, A. P., Hall, H. K., & Jowett, G. E. (2014). Perceived coach behaviors and athletes' engagement and disaffection in youth sport: The mediating role of the psychological needs. *International Journal of Sport Psychology, 45*(6), 559–580. https://doi.org/10.7352/IJSP 2014.45.559

Curran, T., Hill, A. P., Ntoumanis, N., Hall, H. K., & Jowett, G. E. (2016). A three-wave longitudinal test of self-determination theory's mediation model of engagement and disaffection in youth sport. *Journal of Sport and Exercise Psychology, 38*(1), 15–29. http://dx.doi.org/10.1123/jsep.2015-0016

Deci, E. L. (1975). *Intrinsic motivation.* [electronic resource]. Springer.

Deci, E. L., La Guardia, J. G., Moller, A. C., Scheiner, M. J., & Ryan, R. M. (2006). On the benefits of giving as well as receiving autonomy support: Mutuality in close friendships. *Personality and Social Psychology Bulletin, 32*(3), 313–327. https://doi.org/10.1177/0146167205282148

Deci, E. L., & Ryan, R. M. (1985). *Intrinsic motivation and self-determination in human behavior.* Plenum Press.

Deci, E. L., & Ryan, R. M., (2008). Facilitating optimal motivation and psychological wellbeing across life's domains. *Canadian Psychology/Psychologie Canadienne, 49*(1), 14–23. https://psycnet.apa.org/doi/10.1037/0708-5591.49.1.14

Delrue, J., Reynders, B., Broek, G. V., Aelterman, N., De Backer, M., Decroos, S., ... Haerens, L. (2019). Adopting a helicopter-perspective towards motivating and demotivating coaching: A circumplex approach. *Psychology of Sport and Exercise, 40*, 110–126. https://doi.org/10.1016/j.psychsport.2018.08.008

Elliot, A. J. (1999). Approach and avoidance motivation and achievement goals. *Educational Psychologist, 34*(3), 169–189. https://doi.org/10.1207/s15326985ep3403_3

Elliot, A. J., & McGregor, H. A. (2001). A 2 x 2 achievement goal framework. *Journal of Personality and Social Psychology, 80*, 501–519. https://doi.org/10.1037/0022-3514.80.3.501

Elliot, A. J., Murayama, K., & Pekrun, R. (2011). A 3 x 2 achievement goal model. *Journal of Educational Psychology, 103*(3), 632–648. https://doi.org/10.1037/a0023952

Escriva-Boulley, G., Tessier, D., Ntoumanis, N., & Sarrazin, P. (2018). Need-supportive professional development in elementary school physical education: Effects of a cluster-randomized control trial on teachers' motivating style and student physical activity. *Sport Exercise and Performance Psychology, 7*(2), 218–234. https://doi.org/10.1037/spy0000119

Fenton, S. A. M., Duda, J. L., Quested, E., & Barrett, T. (2014). Coach autonomy support predicts autonomous motivation and daily moderate-to-vigorous physical activity and sedentary time in youth sport participants. *Psychology of Sport & Exercise, 15*(5), 453–463. https://doi.org/10.1016/j.psychsport.2014.04.005

Fin, G., Moreno-Murcia, J. A., León, J., Baretta, E., & Nodari Júnior, R. J. (2019). Teachers' interpersonal style in physical education: Exploring patterns of students' self-determined motivation and enjoyment of physical activity in a longitudinal study. *Frontiers in Psychology, 9.* https://doi.org/10.3389/fpsyg.2018.02721

García-Calvo, T., Leo, F. M., Gonzalez-Ponce, I., Sánchez-Miguel, P. A., Mouratidis, A., & Ntoumanis, N. (2014). Perceived coach-created and peer-created motivational climates and their associations with team cohesion and athlete satisfaction: Evidence from a longitudinal study. *Journal of Sports Sciences, 32*(18), 1738–1750. http://dx.doi.org/10.1080/02640414.2014.918641

Garn, A. C., McCaughtry, N., Martin, J., Shen, B., & Fahlman, M. (2012). A basic needs theory investigation of adolescents' physical self-concept and global self-esteem. *International Journal of Sport and Exercise Psychology, 10*(4), 314–328. https://doi.org/10.1080/1612197X.2012.705521

Garn, A. C., Morin, A. J., & Lonsdale, C. (2019). Basic psychological need satisfaction toward learning: A longitudinal test of mediation using bifactor exploratory structural equation modeling. *Journal of Educational Psychology, 111*(2), 354–372. http://dx.doi.org/10.1037/edu0000283

Haerens, L., Aelterman, N., Vansteenkiste, M., Soenens, B., & Van Petegem, S. (2015). Do perceived autonomy-supportive and controlling teaching relate to physical education students' motivational experiences through unique pathways? Distinguishing between the bright and dark side of motivation. *Psychology of Sport & Exercise, 16*, 26–36. https://doi.org/10.1016/j.psychsport.2014.08.013

Haerens, L., Vansteenkiste, M., De Meester, A., Delrue, J., Tallir, I., Vande Broek, G., … & Aelterman, N. (2018). Different combinations of perceived autonomy support and control: Identifying the most optimal motivating style. *Physical Education and Sport Pedagogy, 23*(1), 16–36. http://dx.doi.org/10.1080/17408989.2017.1346070

Hagger, M., Chatzisarantis, N., Hein, V., Soos, I., Karsai, I., Lintunen, T., & Leemans, S. (2009). Teacher, peer and parent autonomy support in physical education and leisure-time physical activity: A trans-contextual model of motivation in four nations. *Psychology and Health, 6*, 689–711. http://dx.doi.org/10.1080/08870440801956192

Healy, L. C., Ntoumanis, N., Veldhuijzen van Zanten, J. J., & Paine, N. (2014). Goal striving and well-being in sport: The role of contextual and personal motivation. *Journal of Sport & Exercise Psychology, 36*(5), 446–459. http://dx.doi.org/10.1123/jsep.2013-0261

Hendriks, T., Schotanus-Dijkstra, M., Hassankhan, A., de Jong, J., & Bohlmeijer, E. (2019). The efficacy of multi-component positive psychology interventions: A systematic review and meta-analysis of randomized controlled trials. *Journal of Happiness Studies, 21*, 357–390. https://doi.org/10.1007/s10902-019-00082-1

Jaitner, D., Rinas, R. S. L., Becker, C., Niermann, C., Breithecker, J., & Mess, F. (2019). Supporting subject justification by educational psychology: A systematic review of achievement goal motivation in school physical education. *Frontiers in Education, 4*(70), 1–25. https://doi.org/10.3389/feduc.2019.00070

Jang, H., Reeve, J., & Deci, E. L. (2010). Engaging students in learning activities: It is not autonomy support or structure but autonomy support and structure. *Journal of Educational Psychology, 102*(3), 588–600. https://doi.org/10.1037/a0019682

Janssen, I., & LeBlanc, A. G. (2010). Systematic review of the health benefits of physical activity and fitness in school-aged children and youth. *International Journal of Behavioral Nutrition and Physical Activity, 7*(1), 40–55. https://doi.org/10.1186/1479-5868-7-40

Kipp, L. E., & Weiss, M. R. (2015). Social predictors of psychological need satisfaction and well-being among female adolescent gymnasts: A longitudinal analysis. *Sport, Exercise, and Performance Psychology, 4*(3), 153–169. https://doi.org/10.1037/spy0000034

La Guardia, J. G., Ryan, R. M., Couchman, C. E., & Deci, E. L. (2000). Within-person variation in security of attachment: A self-determination theory perspective on attachment, need fulfillment, and well-being. *Journal of Personality and Social Psychology, 79*(3), 367–384. https://doi.org/10.1037//0022-3514.79.3.367

Langan, E., Toner, J., Blake, C., & Lonsdale, C. (2015). Testing the effects of a self-determination theory-based intervention with youth Gaelic football coaches on athlete motivation and burnout. *The Sport Psychologist, 29*(4), 293–301. http://dx.doi.org/10.1123/tsp.2013-0107

Langdon, J., Schlote, R., Harris, B., Burdette, G., & Rothberger, S. (2015). Effects of a training program to enhance autonomy supportive behaviors among youth soccer coaches. *Journal of Human Sport & Exercise, 10*(1), 1–14. https://doi.org/10.14198/jhse.2015.101.01

Leptokaridou, E. T., Vlachopoulos, S. P., & Papaioannou, A. G. (2016). Experimental longitudinal test of the influence of autonomy-supportive teaching on motivation for participation in elementary school physical education. *Educational Psychology, 36*(7), 1135–1156. https://doi.org/10.1080/01443410.2014.950195

López-Walle, J., Balaguer, I., Castillo, I., & Tristan, J. (2012). Autonomy support, basic psychological needs and well-being in Mexican athletes. *Spanish Journal of Psychology, 15*(3), 1283–1295. https://doi.org/10.5209/rev_SJOP.2012.vl5.n3.39414

Mageau, G. A., & Vallerand, R. J. (2003). The coach–athlete relationship: A motivational model. *Journal of Sports Science, 21*(11), 883–904. http://dx.doi.org/10.1080/0264041031000140374

Mahoney, J. W., Ntoumanis, N., Gucciardi, D. F., Mallett, C. J., & Stebbings, J. (2016). Implementing an autonomy-supportive intervention to develop mental toughness in adolescent rowers. *Journal of Applied Sport Psychology, 28*(2), 199–215. http://dx.doi.org/10.1080/10413200.2015.1101030

Meng, H. Y., & Keng, J. W. C. (2016). The effectiveness of an autonomy-supportive teaching structure in physical education. *RICYDE: Revista Internacional de Ciencias del Deporte, 12*(43), 5–28. https://doi.org/10.5232/ricyde2016.04312

Niemiec, C. P., & Ryan, R. M. (2009). Autonomy, competence, and relatedness in the classroom: Applying self-determination theory to educational practice. *Theory and Research in Education, 7*(2), 133–144. https://doi.org/10.1177/1477878509104318

Ntoumanis, N. (2005). A prospective study of participation in optional school physical education using a self-determination theory framework. *Journal of Educational Psychology, 97*(3), 444–453. https://doi.org/10.1037/0022–0663.97.3.448

Oades, L. G., Jarden, A., Hou, H., Ozturk, C., Williams, P., Slemp, G. R. & Huang, L. (2021). Wellbeing literacy: A capability model for wellbeing science and practice. *International Journal of Environmental Research and Public Health, 18*(2), 719. https://doi.org/10.3390/ijerph18020719

Oades, L. G., Ozturk, C., Hou, H., & Slemp, G. R. (2020). Wellbeing literacy: A language use capability relevant to wellbeing outcomes of positive psychology interventions. The *Journal of Positive Psychology, 15*, 696–700. https://doi.org/10.1080/17439760.2020.1789711

Perlman, D. (2015). Assisting preservice teachers toward more motivationally supportive instruction. *Journal of Teaching in Physical Education, 34*(1), 119–130. https://doi.org/10.1123/jtpe.2013-0208

Pulido, J. J., Sánchez-Oliva, D., Leo, F. M., Matos, S., & García-Calvo, T. (2017). Effects of an interpersonal style intervention for coaches on young soccer players' motivational processes. *Journal of Human Kinetics, 59*(1), 107–120. https://doi.org/10.1515/hukin-2017–0151

Quested, E., & Duda, J. L. (2010). Exploring the social-environmental determinants of well- and ill-being in dancers: A test of basic needs theory. *Journal of Sport & Exercise Psychology, 32*(1), 39–60. https://doi.org/10.1123/jsep.32.1.39

Raabe, J., Schmidt, K., Carl, J., & Höner, O. (2020). The effectiveness of autonomy support interventions with physical education teachers and youth sport coaches: A systematic review. *Journal of Sport & Exercise Psychology, 41*(6), 345–355. https://doi.org/10.1123/jsep.2019-0026

Reeve, J., & Cheon, S. H. (2016). Teachers become more autonomy supportive after they believe it is easy to do. *Psychology of Sport & Exercise, 22*, 178–189. https://doi.org/10.1016/j.psychsport.2015.08.001

Reeve, J., & Jang, H. (2006). What teachers say and do to support students' autonomy during a learning activity. *Journal of Educational Psychology, 98*(1), 209–218. https://doi.org/10.1177/1477878509104318

Reinboth, M., Duda, J. L., & Ntoumanis, N. (2004). Dimensions of coaching behavior, need satisfaction, and the psychological and physical welfare of young athletes. *Motivation and Emotion, 28*(3), 297–313. https://doi.org/10.1023/B:MOEM.0000040156.81924.b8

Reynders, B., Vansteenkiste, M., Van Puyenbroeck, S., Aelterman, N., De Backer, M., Delrue, J., ... & Broek, G. V. (2019). Coaching the coach: Intervention effects on need-supportive coaching behavior and athlete motivation and engagement. *Psychology of Sport and Exercise, 43*, 288–300. https://doi.org/10.1016/j.psychsport.2019.04.002

Ryan, R. M. (1995). Psychological needs and the facilitation of integrative processes. *Journal of Personality, 63*(3), 397–427. https://doi.org/10.1111/j.1467-6494.1995.tb00501.x

Ryan, R. M., & Deci, E. L. (2000). Self-determination theory and the facilitation of intrinsic motivation, social development, and well-being. *American Psychologist, 55*(1), 68–78. https://psycnet.apa.org/doi/10.1037/0003-066X.55.1.68

Ryan, R. M., & Deci, E. L. (2017). *Self-determination theory: Basic psychological needs in motivation, development, and wellness.* Guilford.

Ryan, R. M., & Deci, E. L. (2019). Brick by brick: The origins, development, and future of self-determination theory. *Advances in Motivation Science, 6*, 111–156. https://doi.org/10.1016/bs.adms.2019.01.001

Ryan, R. M., Huta, V., & Deci, E. L. (2008). Living well: A self-determination theory perspective on eudaimonia. *Journal of Happiness Studies, 9*(1), 139–170. https://doi.org/10.1007/s10902-006-9023-4

Ryan, R. M., Koestner, R., & Deci, E. L. (1991). Ego-involved persistence: When free-choice behavior is not intrinsically motivated. *Motivation and Emotion, 15*(3), 185–205. https://doi.org/10.1007/BF00995170

Sánchez-Oliva, D., Pulido-González, J. J., Leo, F. M., González-Ponce, I., & García-Calvo, T. (2017). Effects of an intervention with teachers in the physical education context: A self-determination theory approach. *PLOS One, 12*(12), e0189986. 1–17. https://doi.org/10.1371/journal.pone.0189986

Sarrazin, P., Vallerand, R., Guillet, E., Pelletier, L., & Cury, F. (2002). Motivation and dropout in female handballers: A 21-month prospective study. *European Journal of Social Psychology, 32*(3), 395–418. https://doi.org/10.1002/ejsp.98

Seligman, M. E. P., & Csikszentmihalyi, M. (2000). Positive psychology: An introduction. *American Psychologist, 55*(1), 5–14. https://doi.org/10.1037//0003-066x.55.1.5

Seligman, M. E. P., Ernst, R., Gillham, J., Reivich, K., & Linkins, M. (2009). Positive education: Positive psychology and classroom interventions. *Oxford Review of Education, 35*(3), 293–311. https://doi.org/10.1080/03054980902934563

Slemp, G. R., Kern, M. L., Patrick, K. J., & Ryan, R. M. (2018). Leader autonomy support in the workplace: A meta-analytic review. *Motivation and Emotion, 42*(5), 706–724. https://doi.org/10.1007/s11031-018-9698-y

Sparks, C., Dimmock, J., Whipp, P., Lonsdale, C., & Jackson, B. (2015). "Getting connected": High school physical education teacher behaviors that facilitate students' relatedness support perceptions. *Sport, Exercise, and Performance Psychology, 4*(3), 219–236. http://dx.doi.org/10.1037/spy0000039

Stroet, K., Opdenakker, M. C., & Minnaert, A. (2015). Need supportive teaching in practice: A narrative analysis in schools with contrasting educational approaches. *Social Psychology of Education, 18*(3), 585–613. https://doi.org/10.1007/s11218-015-9290-1

Tessier, D., Sarrazin, P., & Ntoumanis, N. (2008). The effects of an experimental programme to support students' autonomy on the overt behaviours of physical education teachers. *European Journal of Psychology of Education, 23*(3), 239–253. https://doi.org/10.1007/BF03172998

Tilga, H., Hein, V., Koka, A., Hamilton, K., & Hagger, M. S. (2018). The role of teachers' controlling behaviour in physical education on adolescents' health-related quality of life: Test of a conditional process model. *Educational Psychology, 39*(7), 862–880 https://doi.org/10.1080/01443410.2018.1546830

Vansteenkiste, M., & Ryan, R. M. (2013). On psychological growth and vulnerability: Basic psychological need satisfaction and need frustration as a unifying principle. *Journal of Psychotherapy Integration, 23*(3), 263–280. https://doi.org/10.1037/a0032359

Vlachopoulos, S. P., Katartzi, E. S., & Kontou, M. G. (2013). Fitting multidimensional amotivation into the self-determination theory nomological network: Application in school physical education. *Measurement in Physical Education and Exercise Science, 17*(1), 40–61. https://doi.org/10.1080/1091367X.2013.741366

Vlachopoulos, S. P., Katartzi, E. S., Kontou, M. G., Moustaka, F. C., & Goudas, M. (2011). The revised perceived locus of causality in physical education scale: Psychometric evaluation among youth. *Psychology of Sport and Exercise, 12*(6), 583–592. https://doi.org/10.1016/j.psychsport.2011.07.003

Wadsworth, D. D., Robinson, L. E., Rudisill, M. E., & Gell, N. (2013). The effect of physical education climates on elementary students' physical activity behaviors. *Journal of School Health, 83*(5), 306–313. https://doi.org/10.1111/josh.12032

Waterman, A. S. (1993). Two conceptions of happiness: Contrasts of personal expressiveness (eudaimonia) and hedonic enjoyment. *Journal of Personality and Social Psychology, 64*(4), 678–691. https://psycnet.apa.org/doi/10.1037/0022-3514.64.4.678

World Health Organization. (2007). *Promoting physical activity in schools: An important element of a health-promoting school*. Retrieved from https://apps.who.int/iris/bitstream/handle/10665/43733/9789241595995_eng.pdf?sequence=1&isAllowed=y

World Health Organization. (2008). *School policy framework: Implementation of the WHO global strategy on diet, physical activity and health*. Retrieved from https://www.who.int/dietphysicalactivity/SPF-en-2008.pdf

World Health Organization. (2009). *Global health risks: mortality and burden of disease attributable to selected major risks*. Retrieved from https://www.who.int/healthinfo/global_burden_disease/GlobalHealthRisks_report_full.pdf?ua=1&ua=1

12

CONCEPTUALIZATIONS OF WELL-BEING DURING MIDDLE CHILDHOOD

Investigating Developmental Shifts through Visual Narrative Analysis

Lea Waters, Denise Dussert, Daniel Loton,
and Guadalupe Sánchez Martínez

Research into Youth Well-Being

The last three decades have seen considerable research on the mental health of young people (Greenberg et al., 2017; Kazdin, 1993), and well-being is a guiding principle of the UN Convention on the Rights of the Child (Ruck et al., 2014). Youth mental health research can be split into two approaches: (1) *investigations into youth ill-being*—triggers, risks, consequences, and prevention of ill-being (Catalano et al., 2004) and (2) *inquiry into youth well-being*—sources, assets, benefits, and promotion of well-being (Lerner et al., 2011). While the study of how to prevent and/or reduce youth ill-being was predominant before the 2000s (Durlak et al., 2011), fields such as Positive Education (Slemp et al., 2017), positive youth development (Lerner et al., 2012), and social-emotional learning (Weissberg et al., 2015) have prompted research seeking to understand well-being as more than the absence of ill-being. Well-being promotion research has been conducted in schools (Shankland & Rosset, 2017), community settings (Catalano et al., 2004), and families (Waters & Sun, 2017). The current study seeks to examine developmental shifts in well-being literacy through middle childhood and, thus, is situated within the well-being promotion approach.

Research has consistently found that well-being is a bedrock that leads to a myriad of positive outcomes for young people, including adaptability and receptiveness to change (van Eeden et al., 2008), coping capacity (Frydenberg et al., 2004), physical health (Lubans et al., 2016), prosocial behavior (Quinlan et al., 2015), higher satisfaction with life (Proctor et al., 2011), better grades (MacCann et al., 2020), successful school adjustment (Shoshani & Aviv, 2012), and positive classroom behavior (Wagner & Ruch, 2015). This has prompted researchers to investigate the steps young people can take to increase their well-being. While research has shown that, generally, Positive Education has a beneficial impact on the life of a young person at school, the question still remains as to how well-being changes as a student grows older, and thus, how to target Positive Psychology Interventions (PPIs) developmentally.

DOI: 10.4324/9781003013778-15

How Does Well-Being Change as Children Grow Older?

Research on "developmental psychopathology" (Larson, 2000, p. 170) has been studied for more than two decades and much is known about the risks of psychological illness at each developmental stage of childhood and adolescence (Stavropoulos et al., 2017; Uchida et al., 2018). In contrast, comparatively little research has looked at "developmental Positive Psychology" and Positive Education has not adequately studied if and how well-being differs through each developmental stage. The absence of developmental research in Positive Education was noted by Froh et al. (2011), who asserted that "[l]ittle research has addressed the development of gratitude in children and adolescents" (p. 312). Shin et al. (2011) lamented, "[t]he absence of developmental studies in positive psychology" (p. 356).

In a review of the literature for the purposes of this chapter, a small number of papers were found that had studied the influence of age, developmental stage, and/or school level on well-being. These studies examined developmental differences in happiness, interpersonal strengths, social competence, emotional knowledge, empathy, and moral reasoning. For example, Borland et al. (1998), Park and Peterson (2006), and Holder et al. (2016) found that sources of happiness change as young people grow older. Borland et al. (1998) found that the happiness of five- and six-year-old children were mostly concerned with short-term, hedonic, rewards (e.g., sweets, toys, and trips to McDonald's). At age 7, happiness was tied to relationships (e.g., family holidays and having friends over to play). By the age of 11–12, significant aspects of happiness were group identity, relationships, and achievements.

Holder et al. (2016) asked students from kindergarten, elementary, and junior high school to write single-sentence responses to describe what made them happy on "Walls of Well-being" (WOWs). Kindergarten and elementary school students listed relationships (e.g., friends and pets) and other-orientation (e.g., sharing and helping someone), whereas junior high students listed personal feelings (e.g., feeling proud and feeling inspired) and activities (e.g., reading, eating, gaming, and music). Holder et al. suggested developmental stages should be taken into account when designing PPIs for schools.

Research has also shown that aspects of emotional and social well-being mature with age. For example, examining emotional knowledge (i.e., understanding one's own and others' emotions) and social competence (i.e., skills associated with successful interactions with peers), Denham et al. (2015) found that both aspects of well-being were higher in four- and five-year-olds compared to three-year-olds. Similarly, Shoshani (2019) found that interpersonal strengths (e.g., kindness, fairness, social intelligence, and teamwork) increased in children aged 5–6 years compared to children who were 3–4 years old.

Regarding moral aspects of well-being, Schwenck et al. (2014) found that cognitive empathy (i.e., emotion recognition and perspective taking) improved with age. Benish-Weisman et al. (2019) suggested that "[s]tarting at the age of 6, children develop a more advanced perspective-taking ability and a more nuanced understanding of moral reasoning and moral emotions" (p. 242). Malti et al. (2016) found that the moral emotions of sympathy and guilt-sadness had a stronger relationship with helping, cooperation, and sharing behaviors as children went through middle childhood (6–12 years).

The findings from developmental psychology showing cognitive, social, emotional, and moral milestones reached at different development stages have much to offer Positive Education when designing age-appropriate well-being curricula.

Well-Being during Middle Childhood

According to Eccles (1999), all developmental theories point to middle childhood (defined as ages 6–10)[1] as a significant period of cognitive, emotional, social, and moral growth. This may be why "[a]ll cultures that provide formal schooling for their children begin it between ages five and seven" (p. 32).

One aspect of rapid growth in middle childhood is the notable shifts that occur in cognition (Cooper et al., 2005). For example, around the age of 6, problem-solving, reasoning, and perspective-taking skills become more effective and continue to develop. By 10–12, most children have the capacity for systematic problem solving, complex reasoning, and generalizing knowledge across instances and environments, enabling more competence, resourcefulness, and independence. The cognitive growth that occurs during middle childhood is also linked to developing a "theory of mind," that is, the ability to attribute mental states to oneself and others (Imuta et al., 2016), which requires a greater cognitive capacity for perspective-taking.

Growth in cognitive capacity and theory of mind expands empathy and emotional functioning capacity during middle childhood. Regarding emotional functioning, Charlesworth et al. (2010) stated, "As most children move from early childhood into and through middle childhood, they experience significant gains in their ability to identify and articulate their own emotions as well as the emotions of others" (p. 194). As children move through middle childhood, research has documented gains in emotional awareness and a stronger link between thoughts and emotions. For example, research by Harris et al. (1981) showed that six-year-old children tended to link their emotions to situational cues or events (e.g., "I was upset because I banged my head on the table"). In contrast, 11-year-olds referred to mental cues ("I know that I am happy when I think 'everything is fine'"). Greater awareness of the cause of one's emotions also leads to an increased capacity to regulate one's emotions. The development of emotion regulation is a key milestone developed in middle childhood, with children learning to predict their own and others' emotional reactions and regulate them accordingly (Stegge & Meerum Terwogt, 2011).

Middle childhood is a time of exciting change and growth for children. However, it is also "exacerbated by an increase in risks and stressors for children, relative to early childhood" (Collins et al., 2012, p. 77). According to Eccles (1999), problems with anxiety, low self-esteem, and withdrawal in the face of challenges begin to emerge during this life stage as (1) children respond to the new demands placed upon them; (2) the complex social institutions they now belong to; and (3) the greater risks and adversities to which they are exposed.

Middle childhood is a critical life stage for Positive Education researchers to study when considering the rapid development (cognitive, emotional, social, and moral), the unique aspects of distress that arise during middle childhood, and the shifts in happiness, gratitude, social skills, and moral emotions. The qualitative study presented in this chapter examines how students in this developmental stage understand and conceptualize well-being.

Well-Being Literacy in Middle Childhood

An important yet overlooked factor in youth well-being is the child's own understanding of what well-being is. Oades and Johnston (2017) coined the term "well-being literacy" (p. 1) as one's knowledge of and vocabulary about well-being. Several other scholars have argued that a young person's *understanding* of well-being is a fundamental ingredient shaping their *experience* of well-being (Woodman, 2003).

Well-being literacy is an essential aspect of how a student engages with, or benefits from, Positive Education interventions. For example, students who understand that well-being is closely tied to emotions may gain much from PPIs that target the cultivation of emotions (e.g., gratitude letter or hope mapping). However, they may take longer to engage with cognitively focused interventions (e.g., cognitive re-framing) or identity-based interventions (e.g., strength identification). Similarly, the students who view well-being as a private, internal experience may find much benefit in interventions that help to change an internal state (e.g., mindfulness). However, they may be less likely to see the benefit in participating in relational PPIs at school (e.g., reciprocity rings).

Knowing the understanding that students have about well-being can help researchers design tailored interventions that support teachers' efforts to explicitly and intentionally teach well-being—what it is, why it is important, and how to bolster it. Nevertheless, according to Fattore et al. (2009), "[l]ittle is known about what children and young people identify as well-being" (p. 58). According to Ben-Arieh (2010) children's daily life "is something that children know the most about" (p. 135), and, as such, they should be the primary source of information. Oades (2017) argues that well-being literacy is a "missing link" (p. 169) in Positive Education.

Why is well-being literacy a missing link in Positive Education, and why have student-based understandings of well-being and co-design principles not featured in topical research? We suggest that one reason for this is that Positive Education is conducted primarily as a top-down endeavor where much of the "research on children's well-being has relied on adult perspectives" (Kosher & Ben-Arieh, 2017, p. 256). While Positive Education is *youth-focused* (i.e., young people are the focus of inquiry), it may, in truth, be seen as an *adult-centric* field (Holder et al. 2016), as found in Waters and Loton (2019) where child-generated definitions and understandings of well-being were largely absent.

Directly accessing young people's understanding and voice as legitimate sources of data in Positive Education is a way to empower students in the research process. It can yield scientific insights not seen when we overlay adult definitions of well-being or use data collection methods that restrict child participant input by using predefined well-being models. The current study allows students to be the experts on their perceptions of well-being by studying well-being literacy during middle childhood.

Method

Narrative Analysis

Many researchers agree that children can construct and communicate valid meanings about aspects of their own life (Lawthom & Tindal, 2011; Qvortrup, 2014). Rather than imposing a pre-existing theory, definition, or measure of well-being, the current study utilizes an open-ended, inductive approach to engender the students' well-being narratives. Specifically, the "draw-and-write" technique, which combines visual narratives with verbal narratives, was used (Clark-Ibañez, 2008; Sixsmith et al., 2007). Visual narrative analysis (VNA) is especially useful because drawings and visual creations play a significant role in children's natural exploration and expression of their inner world (Carlberg et al., 2009; Driessnack, 2006). Drawing has proven effective in highlighting cognitive states that are difficult for children to express in words (Capella et al., 2015; Pace et al., 2015). The "draw-and-write" technique was chosen in line with Oades' (2017) idea that well-being literacy can be communicated via *drawing*.

Study Participants

Primary school children in Years 1–4 (ages 6–10)[2] were recruited from a coeducational, private school located in the capital city of Northern Territory, Australia. The school has three primary campuses located in three different geographic areas across the city. Students from all three campuses participated in the study and all students in the class participated.

A total of 430 students took part in the exercise, with roughly equal sample sizes across the four-year levels from the three campuses. Given that the teachers were using the draw-and-write exercise as a learning tool (see section "Procedure" below), it was possible to collect data from all students. However, a sample size of 430 is excessive for the needs of qualitative analysis and, thus, a smaller sample of the drawings was analyzed (20%).

Qualitative studies are different from quantitative studies in that they aim to unearth patterns rather than quantify magnitudes. Qualitative research favors smaller sample sizes and aims to achieve confirmability (i.e., results are credible, defensible, and warranted) rather than generalizability (Miles & Huberman, 1994). As such, Sandelowski (1995) recommends that qualitative sample sizes need to be *large enough* to allow the unfolding of a new understanding but *small enough* so that the in-depth, rich, time-consuming analysis can occur.

We used two guiding principles to determine the appropriate sample size for the current study: (1) informational comprehensiveness and (2) informational redundancy. The principle of informational comprehensiveness means that sample size can be determined, in part, by the richness of information obtained from each participant. Where the type of data collected encompasses much information (e.g., rich data such as in-depth interviews), a smaller sample size is needed to produce core themes compared to data that contain a lesser amount of information (e.g., brief data such as sentence completion) (Malterud et al., 2015). The current data are on the higher end of informational comprehensiveness for young children. The visual and verbal data were analyzed against three key dimensions (subject, elements, and context), each of which had many subelements (see section "Analytical Steps" below).

The second criterion we used to determine sample size was the principle of "informational redundancy" (Lincoln & Guba, 1985), which is the point in the dataset when continued analysis of cases extracts no new themes and renders the addition of more cases redundant. Ritchie et al. (2003) maintain that informational redundancy often occurs with sample sizes of around 50–60 participants. We erred on the side of having too much data (Fugard & Potts, 2015). We randomly selected 20% of the drawings from each year level across all three campuses, which gave us a total of 86 drawings. If informational redundancy did not occur with a sample size of 86, we planned to randomly select more students from the larger dataset to analyze—this was unnecessary because informational redundancy was met.

Procedure

After receiving approval from the University of Melbourne Human Ethics Research Committee, the researchers sent worksheets to the three campuses. Students from Years 1–4 completed a drawing exercise in class that asked them to "Draw a picture showing your idea of well-being." Students were provided with colored pencils and were encouraged to draw any image they liked. Afterward, they wrote a brief description of their pictures in a text box at the bottom of the page. The inclusion of verbal data follows Riessman's (2008) suggestion that the presence of words can give meaning to images and, thus, provides valuable data to investigators seeking to make interpretations of the drawings. Researchers such as Capella et al. (2015) and Esin and Squire (2013) have supplemented visual materials with verbal or written narratives to reduce interpretative gaps.

Teachers delivered this exercise in class both as a learning tool (i.e., working on drawing skills and vocabulary) and also for research collection purposes—all drawings were collected by a research assistant at the school, scanned, and sent to researchers at the University of Melbourne (note that drawings were also sent via postal mail).

Analytical Steps

Analysis of the themes of well-being examined three broad dimensions of the drawings: (1) subject; (2) elements; and (3) context. Regarding dimension one—subject—the researchers recorded the main subject in the picture (e.g., a person [or people], a pet, a toy, an object, and so on). If the main subject was a person/people, researchers recorded details of facial expressions, the direction of gaze, body language, detail of clothing, and so on. The second analytical dimension, elements, included: (a) the use of color; (b) width of outlines; (c) use of movement; (d) location of the main subject (e.g., in the center and to the right or left); (e) the proportion of the main subject to other picture elements (e.g., Was the child larger than their friend?); and (f) any included objects (e.g., food). The third analytical dimension was context, and researchers noted background elements in the drawing, such as being in nature, a family home, a park/playground, or a school.

To demonstrate the credibility of the three steps of data analysis, the process of "referential adequacy" (Lincoln & Guba, 1985) was employed. The first three authors independently analyzed a subset of the same images from the larger data and individually generated key codes. The three authors then met to complete an intercase analysis. This process produced an agreement on codes for analysis and the rest of the analyses proceeded from there.

Results

Analysis of the visual and verbal data revealed five main themes: agency, emotions, mind, relationships, and positive identity. Well-being literacy was more sophisticated, multidimensional, and interconnected for children at the end of their middle childhood than at the start. Table 12.1 summarizes themes and subthemes in each year level. The remainder of this section explores the themes in more detail. All students' names are pseudonyms.

Table 12.1 Narrative Analysis Themes of Well-Being Identified across Age Groups

Themes	Year 1 (6–7-year-olds)	Year 2 (7–8-year-olds)	Year 3 (8–9-year-olds)	Year 4 (9–10-year-olds)
Agency	Physical self-care (body self-care and exercising)	Physical self-care (body self-care and exercising)	Physical self-care (body self-care and exercising)	Physical self-care (body self-care and exercising)
	Hedonic activities	Hedonic activities Eudemonic activities	Hedonic activities Eudemonic activities	Hedonic activities Eudemonic activities
Emotions	Positive affect only	Affect duality	Affect duality	Affect duality
	Primary emotions	Primary and secondary emotions High-intensity emotions	Primary and secondary emotions High- and low-intensity emotions Emotional granularity	Primary and secondary emotions High- and low-intensity emotions Emotional granularity Emotional self-care
Mind		Mental self-care Thought–emotion link	Mental self-care Thought–emotion link Mindfulness/Meditation	Mental self-care Thought–emotion link Mindfulness/Meditation
Relationships		Prosocial behavior	Prosocial behavior Connections Friendships	Connections Friendships Social traits
Positive identity			Physical appearance Personality traits	Physical appearance Personality traits Social traits

Year 1: 6–7-Year-Olds

Students in Year 1 depicted well-being in simple ways, often focusing on one activity or simple emotions that occur in daily life. Half the drawings in this year level focused on the theme of "agency," representing how students can enact and boost their own well-being by performing simple actions in their daily lives. Within the subtheme of physical self-care, children identified different activities they do to take care of their physical body, such as eating healthy food, drinking water, having a shower, or brushing their teeth. Some children also depicted well-being as the physical exercise they do in their daily lives, such as running and riding bicycles. Figure 12.1 illustrates these ideas. Here Adam divided the exercise sheet, drawing a person running in the upper part and two people eating healthy food below, showing how physically caring for himself is his main idea of well-being.

Emotions were the second theme featured by Year 1 students. Students typically wrote about the emotional state of feeling "*good*," thus describing their emotions in a generalized, diffuse way rather than with emotional granularity/specificity (Smidt & Suvak, 2015). Where specific emotions were mentioned, they were primary emotions, defined by Damasio (1994) as neurologically typical and pan-cultural emotions, experienced as innate responses to the context, such as surprise, happiness, and anger. These emotions contrast with secondary emotions, which are acquired through the learning process in the social context and, presumably, arise from higher cognitive processes, like hope or relief (Damasio, 1994). In Year 1 students, the primary emotions of happiness (62%) and love (25%) were the two most commonly mentioned.

The narratives illustrate the vital role that doing a preferred, intrinsically motivated activity plays in children's experiences of well-being. For instance, in Figure 12.2, Carla pictures herself playing on a rainbow-shaped slide. This slide is higher than the trees, colorful, and big. She has

Figure 12.1 Example of the Theme of Physical Self-Care in Student Drawings of Well-Being

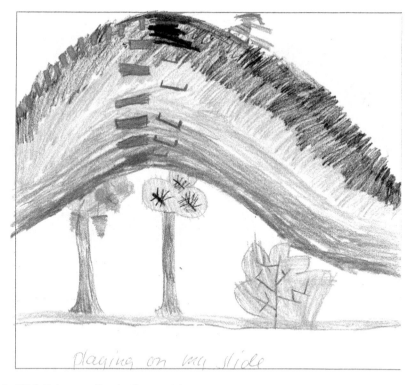

Playing on my slide

Figure 12.2 Well-Being as a Simple, Present-Moment Activity

used all the space on the sheet from left to right, suggesting that her simple activity can have a "big" impact on well-being. Drawing herself at the top (suggesting agency), Carla's use of movement in her picture suggests excitement. This picture, like many in the Year 1 dataset, shows that well-being at this age is understood to be simple, activity-based, pleasurable, and within the child's control.

Year 2: 7–8-Year-Olds

Year 2 students showed that well-being begins to become a more complex and multidimensional concept at this age, comprising diverse aspects rather than a simple activity or emotion.

Within the first theme of agency, physical self-care remained a present, but less common, subtheme in this age group, with body self-care behaviors (e.g., eating healthy food) and physical activities (e.g., doing exercise) present in 25% of the drawings. Although fewer than Year 1, hedonic activities that gave simple pleasure were also present in this dataset, with children mentioning well-being as playing, eating delicious food, patting their pets, or having fun.

Happiness and love again were the most mentioned emotions, but this age group also depicted and wrote about secondary emotions such as pride, self-love, and feeling encouraged. Children in Year 2 referred to a broader range of emotions, both positive and negative, suggesting an understanding of the duality of emotions and the idea that well-being is more than the experience of positive emotion. Examples of negative emotions drawn were sadness, anger, and fear.

Amongst this age group, the theme of mind emerged. Agency over well-being was shown within this theme by "controlling actions and thoughts." Two main subthemes emerged under the theme of mind. First was the idea of taking care of a "*healthy brain*" through getting enough sleep, relaxing the mind, and resting. We labeled this "mental self-care." The second aspect of psychological

Figure 12.3 Mind as an Aspect of Shaping Well-Being

well-being was the awareness of the thought–emotion link and the awareness of the mind as a "resource" that helps a child develop well-being. This idea is clearly illustrated in Figure 12.3, in which Tom drew a large, red brain with "thought bubbles" showing us that the brain is deciding which pathway to choose—life or death (*"Which way should I go?"*, *"I know, it should be for life!"*). Tom then writes *"I choose the right path"* as his verbal narrative. Here, by controlling his brain, Tom is enacting his agency and recognizes that his well-being is linked to his thought processes. Being able to make a decision as meaningful as choosing life over death also shows that well-being has eudemonic aspects in addition to the hedonic pleasures mentioned at this age.

Year 2 introduces the theme of "relationships" and its subtheme of prosocial behavior. This aspect of well-being is seen in acts of kindness drawn by children, where they aim to turn a negative emotion into a positive one for their friends. For example, some students drew themselves helping other children who were hurt or sad, and others pictured the acts of saying sorry and of forgiving. Figure 12.4 shows an example of this where Mairi drew herself thinking, *"I should stop"* after saying, *"I hate you"* to a friend, and then saying sorry. Her friend reacts with forgiveness—*"That's ok"*—so the relationship is fixed and social well-being is re-established. This example of prosocial behavior again is connected with the children's agency. Being prosocial is the child's option; they have power to take care of others' well-being and manage their friendships when things go wrong.

Year 3: 8–9-Year-Olds

As shown in Table 12.1, there are several developmental shifts in the understanding of well-being from Year 2 to Year 3—most notably, the notion of how one's own identity (physical identity and personality traits) influences well-being, the demonstration of emotional granularity, and

Figure 12.4 Depicting Prosocial Behaviors as a Key Aspect of Well-Being

a growth in social well-being to recognize that connections with others are crucial ingredients for well-being. Overall, the pictures and descriptions of the Year 3 students had a broader range of subjects, elements, and backgrounds than children in the younger ages. Aspects of well-being were interconnected. More children were able to describe well-being as the opposite of ill-being—talking about "not being angry" and "choosing to be happy instead." Well-being shifted from being located in the body to be more about the mind and one's identity.

Within the theme of agency, subthemes of physical self-care became less dominant but were still present. Hedonic behaviors remained a key element of well-being, with a range of diverse activities that children enjoyed doing such as swimming, singing, playing, sunbathing, and drawing. The activities described by children were not only about simple pleasures; they can also be seen as pursuing more eudemonic angles of well-being, such as self-discovery and being connected to something larger than oneself (e.g., reading poems, art, and hobbies). Figure 12.5 illustrates this point, where James depicts four different scenarios that represent well-being for him: "*telling jokes*," "*reading poems*," "*loving*," and "*working in groups*." Like the younger year levels, agency over one's well-being through the activities of daily life was a present theme among Year 3 students.

By this age, more students depicted secondary emotions and a higher degree of emotional granularity, drawing and writing about detailed and specific emotions. Emotional duality becomes a stronger theme, with negative emotions such as anger, sadness, and fear represented. A distinct trend in Year 3 students was the more frequent inclusion of low-intensity emotions such as feeling calm, peaceful, and relaxed as key aspects of well-being, showing an evolution from the earlier year levels where children aged 6–8 typically focused on higher-intensity emotions such as happiness and excitement. It is noteworthy that while emotions become more complex and mature, this theme did not make up as high a proportion in the narratives as it did in earlier years, possibly because well-being was understood as more multidimensional, and there were new aspects/themes depicted, thus reducing/dissipating the dominance of emotions.

Figure 12.5   Well-Being as a Multidimensional Agentic Experience

The theme of "mind" continued to grow in Year 3. Children drew and wrote about "mental self-care" and the "thought–emotion link" subthemes by depicting themselves being aware of their positive thoughts, taking responsibility for having a "healthy brain," and showing how thoughts influence emotions and actions. The subtheme of "mindfulness" as an action to better "see" one's thoughts was introduced in this age group—some children referred to the possibility of *"cooling down"* by relaxing the mind with mindfulness/meditation exercises.

Prosocial behaviors were represented through depictions of children giving or receiving gifts and receiving help or helping others.

Two new subthemes within relationships emerged in Year 3: those of "connections" and "friendship." Children began depicting positive connections with others through their relationships, such as laughing and joking, loving others, or working in groups. Friendship began to be named as a particular relationship form that was part of one's well-being. Figure 12.5 shows examples of these subthemes, where James connects "love" and "jokes" and "working in groups" as a part of his well-being idea. Also, in Figure 12.6, Elizabeth wears a friendship bracelet, indicating how this element is embodied and directly connected with her idea of well-being.

Within this year group, the theme of "positive identity" emerged. Analysis revealed two main subthemes: "physical appearance" and "personality traits." Positive physical aspects began to be an element that constitutes well-being and is integrated within the self-image. Year 3 students started to draw self-portraits, mentioning different elements of the body as their well-being idea, such as having *"strong biceps," "nice smile," "the correct uniform,"* or *"cool hair."*

For the first time, children focused on something that is within the self, showing unique aspects of their personality as distinctive elements of their well-being (e.g., *"risk-taker," "love of learning,"* and *"kindness"*). Figure 12.6 is illustrative of this point, where Elizabeth depicts her

Figure 12.6   Well-Being Is More than Just the Absence of Ill-Being

different personality traits such as "*smart brain*," "*happy*," and "*humor*." Elizabeth's picture also shows how she sees well-being as an interconnection between her body (eating good food and lifting weights), her brain (smart brain), her personality (humor), and her emotions (happy). Her picture also shows that well-being is not simply the absence of a negative state, but the active presence of a positive state, as shown by the red circle and cross over the state of sleepiness *together* with a green circle and tick over happiness.

Year 4: 9–10-Year-Olds

Year 4 students typically had the "self" as the central subject of the drawing, with several aspects interconnected to form a multidimensional and integrated understanding of well-being. A small number of children also presented abstract, higher-level concepts to represent well-being, such as "*hygiene*," "*nutrition*," or "*balance*." In Figure 12.7, Nina shows herself with a big, open smile, thinking of a range of physical activities that promote well-being (singing, gymnastics), linking well-being to relationships (family, friends), and showing that she understands that certain contexts and environments (the beach) can promote well-being.

Regarding the theme of "agency," physical self-care was not an evident theme in the Year 4 students' narratives. However, physical activities and body self-care behaviors still featured as a source of well-being in this age group, including actions depicted in previous year groups such as exercising and eating healthy food. Although fewer in number, children still mentioned hedonic (e.g., "*sleeping like a sloth*" and "*go-karting makes me happy*") and eudemonic activities (e.g., "*cooperating with your feelings*" and "*reuse, recycle*").

Within the theme of "emotions," subthemes of Year 4 were similar to the previous year, but the analysis revealed a new subtheme—emotional self-care behavior. Students related well-being

Figure 12.7   Well-Being as a Self-referential, Multidimensional Phenomenon Involving Activities, Relationships, and Contexts

with taking responsibility for their emotional state when negative emotions were present. Some of them narrated it as "*coping with your feelings,*" "*cooperating with my emotions,*" or "*moving on.*" Children depicted examples where meditating, listening to music, or saying sorry to a friend helped them to move from a negative to a positive emotional state, re-establishing well-being.

The mind became a more frequently mentioned theme among Year 4 students than in other years. Students highlighted the idea of using the mind for their well-being and a commonly mentioned way to do this was "*having happy thoughts.*" Meditating and mindfulness were more frequently drawn than in previous years. Figure 12.8 shows an example of this where Maggie pictured herself and a friend meditating. She wrote the verbal narrative, "*Well-being is meditating.*" She and her friend are elevated from the ground in a colorful, open space, perhaps suggesting an understanding that meditation helps to "elevate" her well-being.

Interestingly, prosocial behaviors did not emerge as a subtheme, yet the subthemes of connections and friendship featured as a usual form of well-being. Figure 12.8 is an example of this, where Maggie pictures herself meditating with a friend who is also happy and elevated. Well-being here is an experience that, even though it is internal, can be externally shared. At the same time, in Figure 12.7, Nina does not draw specific friends and family, but names these relationships with a heart beneath them, representing how her well-being is also composed of these.

A new subtheme of "social abilities" emerged for the Year 4 cohort. Ten-year-old children identified that having good social abilities played a significant role in their well-being, with children's narratives mentioning "*making friends,*" "*leadership,*" "*co-operation,*" and "*teamwork.*"

Regarding the final theme of "positive identity," the subtheme of physical appearance was notably exceeded by personality traits, which became a more frequent theme by this age. Children showed that well-being was as much about one's inner world (mind, emotions, and personality) than one's outer world (body, physical activities, and social relationships). This self-referential element of well-being included elements such as "*being brave,*" "*coping with emotions,*" and "*respectful,*" "*kind,*" and "*honest.*"

Discussion

Positive Education will benefit from a greater focus on the principles of developmental psychology to gain a clearer understanding of the potentially different sources, understandings, and outcomes of well-being in each developmental stage. Yet, despite its benefits to Positive Education, research into "positive developmental psychology" is still underdeveloped (Shin et al., 2011). A second way to move the field forward is through the use of student's voice to avoid an overreliance on top-down approaches (Holder et al., 2016). We believe that a young person's *understanding* of well-being is a fundamental ingredient that shapes their *experience* of well-being.

We focused the current study on the relatively new construct put forward by Oades and colleagues (Oades, 2017; Oades & Johnston, 2017; Oades et al., in press) of well-being literacy, defined as one's knowledge of, and vocabulary about, well-being. Specifically, we examined developmental shifts in well-being literacy during the middle childhood years (ages 6–10).

Piaget's theory of learning (1964) provides a developmental psychology lens through which to consider this study's results. Piaget put forward the "principle of organization," wherein he theorized that children organize their thinking into psychological structures called schemas, a cognitive framework that helps a child to organize and interpret information. The current study's visual and verbal data suggest that, by the stage of middle childhood, children have an explicit well-being schema that is a multidimensional, multilayered, and agentic phenomenon. Within this schema, children have slotted in both external aspects of well-being (e.g., playing with friends) and internal features of well-being (e.g., thoughts and emotions).

Student drawings depicted the following five dimensions of well-being: agency, emotions, mind, relationships, and positive identity. This multidimensionality of the students' understanding of well-being aligns with that of many adult scholars in the field. Tongue in cheek, we might reorient the student dimensions to form the acronym PERMA (Positive identity, Emotions, Relationships, Mind, and Agency). However, as the dimensions from the bottom-up make clear, student-generated versions of PERMA are different from Seligman's top-down, adult-centric approach (Positive emotion, Engagement, Relationships, Meaning, and Achievement; Seligman, 2018). While emotions and relationships are the same, children in the middle childhood stage did not illustrate engagement, meaning, and achievement.

This fact might be a function of our study methodology, as concepts like engagement and meaning are reasonably abstract and could be challenging to draw. However, these ideas were also absent in the students' verbal descriptions of their drawings. Additionally, achievement, which could arguably be drawn (e.g., learning at school or winning a race) was absent. Relatedly, in Borland et al.'s (1998) study, achievement was not mentioned as a source of happiness until the age of 11. This finding suggests that schools applying Seligman's PERMA model to children in middle childhood may be missing the mark. They superimpose "engagement, meaning, and achievement" on these children and assume this is how they see and want to build their well-being. Contrasting the results of this study to adult models of well-being shows that there is some correspondence between young people and adult versions of well-being *and* that there are important differences to consider.

The provision of student agency requires thoughtful attention when aiming to build well-being in students in this developmental stage. Agency was a core element in the well-being schemas of this sample, and the drawings showed that children see well-being as something they can influence through their own volition and actions. In this way, students saw themselves as agents of their well-being (Bandura, 1993).

These findings support the contention of the authors mentioned in the introduction that children are agentic in their worlds (e.g., Ben-Arieh, 2010; Fattore et al., 2009). Agency gives children opportunities to have influence over their experiences and create meaning from their social contexts. The theme of agency can be considered when designing PPIs for students in middle childhood so that they are active participants in the design of the program itself—they choose what parts of the intervention to engage with. The aim is to help students feel that Positive Education is something done *with* and *for* them, not something that is done *to* them.

The schema of well-being as a multilayered construct expanded with age, showing further evidence of the developmental process of assimilation (Piaget, 1964). Year 1 students focused on hedonic activities in terms of agency; students in Years 2–4 added eudemonic activities into their well-being conceptualizations, aligning with Borland et al. (1998), who found that the happiness of five- and six-year-olds was mostly concerned with short-term, hedonic, rewards (e.g., sweets, toys, and trips to McDonald's), whereas at age 7 and older, more eudemonic sources came into play (e.g., taking care of the environment and reading poetry).

Emotions were an aspect of well-being literacy across all ages in this study but became more layered and nuanced with age through the process of assimilation. For example, younger students in this study identified well-being as states of high-intensity emotions such as feeling happy and excited. These students drew more high-intensity emotions and pictures with bright colors and lots of movement compared to their older peers. Perhaps, at this age, high-intensity emotions are more evident as they are easier to see and feel. In children aged 7 onward, there was a recognition that well-being consists of low-intensity emotions such as feeling calm and peaceful. The frequency of low-intensity emotions in drawings grew at the older age levels. In this way, we speculate that children in the middle years have an understanding (i.e., a literacy) that emotions are a core part of well-being and that, with age, they use the process of assimilation to expand the repertoire of *types* of emotions that make up well-being.

The theme of emotional duality emerged over the course of middle childhood. The idea that well-being consists of both positive and negative emotions was not presented by Year 1 students but featured increasingly with each higher year level as children drew and wrote about being both happy and unhappy. In this way, with increasing age, we see children adopting Russell's (1980) circumplex model of emotions as they narrated both the positive and negative dimensions of emotion (i.e., valence) and also the intensity levels (i.e., arousal).

Another dimension of well-being literacy that grew during middle childhood, presumably through developmental assimilation, was that of the "mind" as a core aspect of one's well-being. The theme of "mind" featured prominently in the well-being literacy of students was understood from age 7 upward. Children drew and wrote about "mental self-care," as well as taking responsibility for having a "healthy brain" and the link between thoughts and emotions. The subtheme of "mindfulness" as an action to better "see" one's thoughts was also present in Years 3 and 4 students. Year 4 students also included the theme of emotional self-care, narrating their drawings with text such as *"cooperating with my emotions"* or *"moving on"* from negative emotions. This trend suggests that at around 9–10, children develop greater awareness of the effects of emotions on their well-being. They also develop deeper understandings about their agency to change and care for their emotions. This finding is in keeping with research by Harris et al. (1981), who found six-year-olds tended to link their emotions to external situations, while 11-year-olds tended to prefer to connect their emotions to their thoughts. These results support the use of mindfulness programs that teach internal awareness, and resilience programs that teach students in middle childhood the skills of cognitive reframing.

Figure 12.8   The Importance of Meditation for Well-Being

Limitations and Strengths

The findings of this study must be considered within its limitations. The sample includes students from a middle-class school, and this may circumscribe the generalizability of the results. It could be that students from lower socioeconomic backgrounds identify different dimensions of well-being, and this suggests that further research with more diverse samples is needed. However, it is also worth stating that "generalizability" is not the core principle or goal of qualitative research. Instead, external validity is assessed based upon the "confirmability" of the findings. Miles and Huberman (1994) argue that qualitative analysis is "confirmable" if it is credible, defensible, warranted, and able to withstand alternative explanations. Given how the findings from our data support and extend past research together with the child-centric way in which we obtained student's voice, we are confident that the current study meets these criteria. Additionally, the use of Riessman's (2008) steps for narrative analysis and the "referential adequacy" process (Lincoln & Guba, 1985) undertaken ensured the data were analyzed rigorously and is a further strength of the study.

VNA is especially useful in research with children, given the significant role that drawings play in children's natural exploration and expression of their inner world (Carlberg et al., 2009; Pace et al., 2015). We consider this methodology a strength of the current study in that it allowed for in-depth and nuanced examinations of the well-being literacy of students in middle childhood and allowed us to see how literacy evolved with age. However, the limitations of this methodology must also be recognized in that there may be some abstract aspects of well-being literacy that are difficult to draw (e.g., meaning); this may have affected the study's results. The addition of "write" in the method—asking students to write about their drawing briefly—should offset this criticism somewhat, but this limitation remains.

Conclusions

Students during middle childhood have an explicit well-being schema that differs from adult-derived definitions. Moreover, a child's understanding of well-being expands and adapts through this stage. This finding provides an exciting opportunity for teachers to boost children's understanding of well-being and paves the way for researchers to develop age-tailored PPIs. Beyond the current study, we call for a deeper dedication from the field to more intentionally incorporate student voice and agency in the design, study, and delivery of Positive Education.

Notes

1 The age bracket for middle childhood is typically 6–10 but there are small variations across researchers. Eccles (1999) defines middle childhood as 6–10 years old. According to Charlesworth et al. (2010), "it is most often defined as the period beginning at approximate ages 5 or 6 and ending at approximate ages 10 to 12" (p. 182). Collins et al. (2001) classify it as 5–12 years.
2 In Australia, year 1 students are typically six or seven years of age, year 2 students are typically seven to eight, year 3 students are typically eight to nine, and year 4 students are typically 9–10 years old.

References

Bandura, A. (1993). Perceived self-efficacy in cognitive development and functioning. *Educational Psychologist, 28*, 117–148. https://doi.org/10.1207/ s15326985ep2802_3.

Ben-Arieh, A. (2010). Developing indicators for child-well-being in a changing context. In C. McAuley and W. Rose (Eds.), *Child well-being: Understanding children's lives* (pp. 129–142). Jessica Kingsley.

Benish-Weisman, M., Daniel, E., Sneddon, J., & Lee, J. (2019). The relations between values and prosocial behavior among children: The moderating role of age. *Personality and Individual Differences, 141*, 241–247. https://doi.org/10.1016/j.paid.2019.01.019

Borland, M., Laybourn, A., Hill, M., & Brown, J. (1998). *Middle childhood: The perspective of children and parents.* Jessica Kingsley.

Capella, C., Rodrìguez, L., Aguila, D., Dussert, D., Lama, X., Gutierrez, C., & Beiza, G. (2015). Storied images of psychotherapeutic change: Approaching children's voices through drawings. *Research in Psychotherapy, 18*(2), 141–151. https://doi.org/10.4081/ripppo.2015.188

Carlberg, G., Thorén, A., Billström, S., & Odhammar, F. (2009). Children's expectations and experiences of psychodynamic child psychotherapy. *Journal of Child Psychotherapy, 35*(2), 175–193. https://doi.org/10.1080/00754170902996130

Catalano, R. F., Berglund, M. L., Ryan, J. A., Lonczak, H. S., & Hawkins, J. D. (2004). Positive youth development in the United States: Research findings on evaluations of positive youth development programs. *The Annals of the American Academy of Political and Social Science, 591*(1), 98–124. https://doi.org/10.1177%2F0002716203260102

Charlesworth, L., Wood, J., & Viggiani, P. (2008). Middle childhood. In E. D. Hutchison (Ed.), *Dimensions of human behavior: The changing life course* (pp. 175–226). SAGE.

Clark-Ibañez, M. (2008). Gender and being "bad": Inner-city students' photographs. In P. Thomson (Ed.), *Doing visual research with children and young people* (pp. 95–113). Routledge.

Collins, W., Madsen, S., & Susman-Stillman, A. (2012). Parenting during middle childhood. In M. H. Bornstein (Ed.), *Handbook of parenting: Volume I: Children and parenting* (2nd ed., pp. 73–101). Lawrence Erlbaum.

Cooper, C. R., Coll, C. T. G., Bartko, W. T., Davis, H., & Chatman, C. (Ed.) (2005). *Developmental pathways through middle childhood: Rethinking contexts and diversity as resources.* Lawrence Erlbaum.

Damasio, A. R. (1994). *Descartes' error: Emotion, reason and the human brain.* Putnam.

Denham, S. A., Bassett, H. H., Brown, C., Way, E., & Steed, J. (2015). "I know how you feel": Preschoolers' emotion knowledge contributes to early school success. *Journal of Early Childhood Research, 13*(3), 252–262. https://doi.org/10.1177%2F1476718X13497354

Driessnack, M. (2006). Draw-and-tell conversations with children about fear. *Qualitative Health Research, 16*(10), 1414–1435. https://doi.org/10.1177%2F1049732306294127

Durlak, J. A., Weissberg, R. P., Dymnicki, A. B., Taylor, R. D., & Schellinger, K. B. (2011). The impact of enhancing students' social and emotional learning: A meta-analysis of school-based universal interventions. *Child Development, 82*(1), 405–432. https://doi.org/10.1111/j.1467–8624.2010.01564.x

Eccles, J. (1999). The development of children ages 6 to 14. *The Future of Children, 9*(2), 30–44. https://doi.org/10.2307/1602703

Esin, C., & Squire, C. (2013). Visual autobiographies in East London: Narratives of still images, interpersonal exchanges, and intrapersonal dialogues. *Forum: Qualitative Social Research, 14*(2), article 1. http://doi.org/10.17169/fqs-14.2.1971

Fattore, T., Mason, J., & Watson, E. (2009). When children are asked about their well-being: Towards a framework for guiding policy. *Child Indicators Research, 2*(1), 57–77. https://doi.org/10.1007/s12187-008-9025-3

Froh, J. J., Fan, J., Emmons, R. A., Bono, G., Huebner, E. S., & Watkins, P. (2011). Measuring gratitude in youth: Assessing the psychometric properties of adult gratitude scales in children and adolescents. *Psychological Assessment, 23*(2), 311–324. https://doi.org/10.1037/a0021590

Frydenberg, E., Lewis, R., Bugalski, K., Cotta, A., McCarthy, C., Luscombe-Smith, N., & Poole, C. (2004). Prevention is better than cure: Coping skills training for adolescents at school. *Educational Psychology in Practice, 20*(2), 117–134. https://doi.org/10.1080/02667360410001691053

Fugard, A. J. B., & Potts, H. W. W. (2015). Supporting thinking on sample sizes for thematic analyses: A quantitative tool. *International Journal of Social Research Methodology, 18*(6), 669–684. https://doi.org/10.1080/13645579.2015.1005453

Greenberg, M. T., Domitrovich, C. E., Weissberg, R. P., & Durlak, J. A. (2017). Social and emotional learning as a public health approach to education. *The Future of Children, 27*(1), 13–32. https://doi.org/10.1353/foc.2017.0001

Harris, P. L., Olthof, T., & Meerum Terwogt, M. (1981). Children's knowledge of emotion. *Journal of Child Psychology and Psychiatry, 22*(3), 247–261. https://doi.org/10.1111/j.1469–7610.1981.tb00550.x

Holder, M. D., Passmore, H.-A., Broom, C., Berg, S., Li, E., Hickey, R., & Martin, C. (2016). Walls of Well-being (WOWs): A pilot study of a new methodology to explore children's and adolescents' perceived sources of happiness. *International Journal of Applied Positive Psychology, 1*(1–3), 91–106. https://doi.org/10.1007/s41042-017-0008-9

Imuta, K., Henry, J. D., Slaughter, V., Selcuk, B., & Ruffman, T. (2016). Theory of mind and prosocial behavior in childhood: A meta-analytic review. *Developmental Psychology, 52*(8), 1192–1205. https://doi.org/10.1037/dev0000140

Kazdin, A. E. (1993). Adolescent mental health: Prevention and treatment programs. *American Psychologist, 48*(2), 127–141. https://doi.org/10.1037/0003–066X.48.2.127

Kosher, H., & Ben-Arieh, A. (2017). What children think about their rights and their well-being: A cross-national comparison. *American Journal of Orthopsychiatry, 87*(3), 256–273. https://doi.org/10.1037/ort0000222

Larson, R. W. (2000). Toward a psychology of positive youth development. *American Psychologist, 55*(1), 170–183. https://doi.org/10.1037/0003–066X.55.1.170

Lawthom, R., & Tindall, C. (2011). Phenomenology. In P. Banister, G. Bunn, E. Burman, J. Daniels, P. Duckett, D. Goodley, R. Lawthom, I. Parker, K. Runswick-Cole, J. Sixsmith, S. Smailes, C. Tindall, & P. Whelan (Eds.), *Qualitative methods in psychology: A research guide* (2nd ed., 175–206). Open University Press.

Lerner, R. M., Lerner, J. V., & Benson, J. B. (2011). Positive youth development: Research and applications for promoting thriving in adolescence. In R. M. Lerner, J. V. Lerner & J. B. Benson (Eds.), *Advances in child development and behavior* (Vol. 41, pp. 1–17). JAI Press. https://doi.org/10.1016/B978-0-12-386492-5.00001-4

Lincoln, Y. S., & Guba, E. G. (1985). *Naturalistic inquiry*. Beverly Hills, CA: SAGE.

Lubans, D., Richards, J., Hillman, C., Faulkner, G., Beauchamp, M., Nilsson, M., Kelly, P., Smith, J., Raine, L., & Biddle, S. (2016). Physical activity for cognitive and mental health in youth: A systematic review of mechanisms. *Pediatrics, 138*(3), article e20161642. https://doi.org/10.1542/peds.2016-1642

MacCann, C., Jiang, Y., Brown, L. E., Double, K. S., Bucich, M., & Minbashian, A. (2020). Emotional intelligence predicts academic performance: A meta-analysis. *Psychological Bulletin, 146*(2), 150–186. https://doi.org/10.1037/bul0000219

Malterud, K., Siersma, V. D., & Guassora, A. D. (2016). Sample size in qualitative interview studies: Guided by information power. *Qualitative Health Research, 26*(13), 1753–1760. https://doi.org/10.1177/1049732315617444

Malti, T., Ongley, S. F., Peplak, J., Chaparro, M. P., Buchmann, M., Zuffianò, A., & Cui, L. (2016). Children's sympathy, guilt, and moral reasoning in helping, cooperation, and sharing: A 6-year longitudinal study. *Child Development, 87*(6), 1783–1795. https://doi.org/10.1111/cdev.12632

Miles, M. B., & Huberman, A. M. (1994). *Qualitative data analysis: An expanded sourcebook.* SAGE.

Oades, L. G. (2017). Wellbeing literacy: The missing link in positive education. In M. A. White, G. R. Slemp & A. S. Murray (Eds.), *Future directions in well-being* (pp. 169–173). Springer.

Oades, L. G., & Johnston, A. L. (2017). Wellbeing literacy: The necessary ingredient in positive education. *Child Development*, 3, article 555621. https://doi.org/10.19080/PBSIJ.2017.03.555621

Oades, L., Ozturk, C., Hou, H., & Slemp, G. (in press). Wellbeing literacy: A language use capability relevant to wellbeing outcomes of positive psychology interventions. *Journal of Positive Psychology.* https://www.tandfonline.com/toc/rpos20/current

Pace, C. S., Zavattini, G. C., & Tambelli, R. (2015). Does family drawing assess attachment representations of late-adopted children? A preliminary report. *Child and Adolescent Mental Health, 20*(1), 26–33. https://doi.org/10.1111/camh.12042

Park, N., & Peterson, C. (2006). Character strengths and happiness among young children: Content analysis of parental descriptions. *Journal of Happiness Studies, 7*(3), 323–341. https://doi.org/10.1007/s10902-005-3648-6

Piaget, J. (1964). Cognitive development in children: Piaget development and learning. *Journal of Research in Science Teaching, 2*, 176–186. https://doi.org/10.1002/tea.3660020306

Proctor, C., Tsukayama, E., Wood, A. M., Maltby, J., Eades, J. F., & Linley, P. A. (2011). Strengths Gym: The impact of a character strengths-based intervention on the life satisfaction and well-being of adolescents. *The Journal of Positive Psychology, 6*(5), 377–388. https://doi.org/10.1080/17439760.2011.594079

Quinlan, D. M., Swain, N., Cameron, C., & Vella-Brodrick, D. A. (2015). How "other people matter" in a classroom-based strengths intervention: Exploring interpersonal strategies and classroom outcomes. *The Journal of Positive Psychology, 10*(1), 77–89. https://doi.org/10.1080/17439760.2014.920407

Qvortrup, J. (2014). Sociology: Societal structure, development of childhood, and the well-being of children. In A. Ben-Arieh, F. Casas, I. Frønes, & J. E. Korbin (Eds.), *Handbook of child well-being: Theories, methods and policies in global perspective* (pp. 663–707). Springer.

Riessman, C. K. (2008). *Narrative methods for the human sciences.* SAGE.

Ritchie, J., Lewis, J., & Elam, G. (2003). Designing and selecting samples. In J. Ritchie & J. Lewis (Eds.), *Qualitative research practice: A guide for social science students and researchers* (pp. 77–108). SAGE.

Ruck, M. D., Peterson-Badali, M., & Helwig, C. C. (2014). Children's perspectives on nurturance and self-determination rights: Implications for development and well-being. In A. Ben-Arieh, F. Casas, I. Frønes & J. E. Corbin (Eds.), *Handbook of child well-being* (pp. 2537–2559). Springer.

Russell, J. A. (1980). A circumplex model of affect. *Journal of Personality and Social Psychology, 39*(6), 1161–1178. https://doi.org/10.1037/h0077714

Sandelowski, M. (1995). Sample size in qualitative research. *Research in Nursing & Health, 18*(2), 179–183. https://doi.org/10.1002/nur.4770180211

Schwenck, C., Göhle, B., Hauf, J., Warnke, A., Freitag, C. M., & Schneider, W. (2014). Cognitive and emotional empathy in typically developing children: The influence of age, gender, and intelligence. *European Journal of Developmental Psychology, 11*(1), 63–76. https://doi.org/10.1080/17405629.2013.808994

Seligman, M. E. P. (2018). PERMA and the building blocks of wellbeing. *Journal of Positive Psychology, 13*, 333–335. https://doi.org/10.1080/17439760.2018.1437466

Shankland, R., & Rosset, E. (2017). Review of brief school-based positive psychological interventions: A taster for teachers and educators. *Educational Psychology Review, 29*(2), 363–392. https://doi.org/10.1007/s10648-016-9357-3

Shin, N., Vaughn, B. E., Akers, V., Kim, M., Stevens, S., Krzysik, L., Coppola, G., Bost, K. K., McBride, B. A., & Korth, B. (2011). Are happy children socially successful? Testing a central premise of positive psychology in a sample of preschool children. *The Journal of Positive Psychology, 6*(5), 355–367. https://doi.org/10.1080/17439760.2011.584549

Shoshani, A. (2019). Young children's character strengths and emotional well-being: Development of the Character Strengths Inventory for Early Childhood (CSI-EC). *The Journal of Positive Psychology, 14*(1), 86–102. https://doi.org/10.1080/17439760.2018.1424925

Shoshani, A., & Aviv, I. (2012). The pillars of strength for first-grade adjustment—parental and children's character strengths and the transition to elementary school. *The Journal of Positive Psychology, 7*(4), 315–326. https://doi.org/10.1080/17439760.2012.691981

Sixsmith, J., Nic Gabhainn, S., Fleming, C., & O'Higgins, S. (2007). Childrens', parents' and teachers' perceptions of child wellbeing. *Health Education, 107*(6), 511–523. https://doi.org/10.1108/09654280710827911

Slemp, G. R., Chin, T.-C., Kern, M. L., Siokou, C., Loton, D., Oades, L. G., Vella-Brodrick, D., & Waters, L. (2017). Positive education in Australia: Practice, measurement, and future directions. In E. Frydenberg, A. Martin & R.J. Collie (Eds.), *Social and emotional learning in Australia and the Asia-Pacific* (pp. 101–122). Springer.

Smidt, K., & Suvak, M. (2015). A brief, but nuanced, review of emotional granularity and emotion differentiation research. *Current Opinion in Psychology, 3*, 48–51. http://doi.org/10.1016/j.copsyc.2015.02.007

Stavropoulos, V., Moore, K. A., Lazaratou, H., Dikeos, D., & Gomez, R. (2017). A multilevel longitudinal study of obsessive compulsive symptoms in adolescence: Male gender and emotional stability as protective factors. *Annals of General Psychiatry, 16*(1), article 42. https://doi.org/10.1186/s12991-017-0165-z

Stegge, H., & Meerum Terwogt, M. (2011). Awareness and regulation of emotion in typical and atypical development. In J. J. Gross (Ed.), *Handbook of emotion regulation* (1st ed., pp. 269–286). Guilford Press.

Uchida, M., Fitzgerald, M., Woodworth, H., Carrellas, N., Kelberman, C., & Biederman, J. (2018). Subsyndromal manifestations of depression in children predict the development of major depression. *The Journal of Pediatrics, 201*, 252–258. https://doi.org/10.1016/j.jpeds.2018.05.049

van Eeden, C., Wissing, M. P., Dreyer, J., Park, N., & Peterson, C. (2008). Validation of the values in action inventory of strengths for youth (VIA-Youth) among South African learners. *Journal of Psychology in Africa, 18*(1), 143–154. https://doi.org/10.1080/14330237.2008.10820181

Wagner, L., & Ruch, W. (2015). Good character at school: Positive classroom behavior mediates the link between character strengths and school achievement. *Frontiers in Psychology, 6*(610), 1–13. https://doi.org/10.3389/fpsyg.2015.00610

Waters, L., & Loton, D. (2019). SEARCH: A meta-framework and review of the field of positive education. *International Journal of Applied Positive Psychology, 4*(1–2), 1–46. https://doi.org/10.1007/s41042-019-00017-4

Waters, L., & Sun, J. (2016). Can a brief strength-based parenting intervention boost self-efficacy and positive emotions in parents? *International Journal of Applied Positive Psychology, 1*, 41–56. https://doi.org/10.1007/s41042-017-0007-x

Weissberg, R. P., Durlak, J. A., Domitrovich, C. E., & Gullotta, T. P. (2015). Social and emotional learning: Past, present, and future. In J. A. Durlak, C. E. Domitrovich, R. P. Weissberg & T. P. Gullotta (Eds.), *Handbook of social and emotional learning* (pp. 3–19). Guilford Press.

Woodman, D. (2003). Responsibility and time for escape: The meaning of wellbeing to young Australians. *Melbourne Journal of Politics, 29*, 82–95. https://doi.org/10.1080/13676260600805713

13

ACADEMIC SELF-CONCEPT

A Key Construct for Positive Psychology

Geetanjali Basarkod, Herbert W. Marsh, Theresa Dicke,
Jiesi Guo, and Philip D. Parker

Over the past few decades, there has been an increased effort to identify and understand the strengths and skills that enable individuals and communities to thrive. This scientific study of optimal functioning, called positive psychology, emphasizes how healthy individuals can get the most from life (e.g., Bruner, 1996; Marsh & Craven, 2006; Seligman & Csikszentmihalyi, 2000). In this chapter, we argue that positive self-concepts and related self-belief constructs are crucial elements of this positive psychology movement. The phenomenon of the self is widely accepted as an essential universal aspect of being human and central to understanding the quality of human existence (Bandura, 2006; Bruner, 1996; Harter, 1990; Marsh & Craven, 2006; Pajares & Schunk, 2005). Indeed, a positive self-concept is a desirable outcome in many disciplines of psychology, such as educational, developmental, sport/exercise, health, social, and personality psychology, as well as in a broad array of other social science disciplines. It represents

> a basic psychological need that has a pervasive impact on daily life, cognition and behavior, across age and culture…an ideal cornerstone on which to rest the achievement motivation literature but also a foundational building block for any theory of personality, development and well-being.
>
> *(Elliot & Dweck, 2005, p. 8)*

In the seminal review of self-concept theory and research by Shavelson and colleagues (Shavelson et al., 1976; also see Marsh & Shavelson, 1985), self-concepts were defined to be individuals' perceptions of themselves, formed through their experiences with and interpretations of their environment, and impacted by others' evaluations of them. Self-concepts include feelings of self-confidence, self-worth, self-acceptance, and perceptions of one's competence and ability; they affect how we act, feel, and adjust to a changing environment. A theme emphasized here is that the most powerful effects of self-concept are based on specific components of self-concept (e.g., social, academic, physical, and emotional) most logically related to specific outcomes considered in a particular study (a multidimensional perspective), rather than on the global component of self-concept represented in global measures of self-esteem (a unidimensional perspective).

Indeed, much of the theoretical and empirical research on this multidimensional perspective of self-concept has been conducted in the field of education. For instance, a positive academic self-concept (ASC) is both a desirable goal and a means of facilitating subsequent academic

DOI: 10.4324/9781003013778-16

accomplishments and long-term educational attainment (Marsh & Craven, 2006; Marsh, Parker, Guo, Pekrun, & Basarkod, 2020). By focusing on the field of education, the aim of this chapter is to provide an overview of why self-concept is important, how it is formed through temporal, social, and dimensional comparison processes, and how it is differentiated from the related construct of self-efficacy.

Why Is Self-Concept Important?

There is abundant evidence for the impact of self-concept on important outcomes such as social and emotional health (Harter, 2012; Marsh et al., 2004) and academic functioning (Chen et al., 2013; Marsh & Craven, 2006; Marsh & Yeung, 1997). Self-concept has been associated with the social and personal adjustment of children and adolescents (Harter, 1990; Parker et al., 2020), approaches to learning (Burnett et al., 2003), emotional adjustment and socialization (Donahue et al., 1993), bullying (Marsh et al., 2004), elite athlete success (Marsh & Perry, 2005), and parent–adolescent relations (Barber et al., 2003). In a large longitudinal birth cohort study, Trzesniewski et al. (2006) reported that adolescents with low levels of global self-concept tended to have poorer mental and physical health, worse economic prospects (e.g., more likely to leave school early and to have money problems), and higher levels of criminal behavior, 10 years later. This was observed even after controlling for adolescent depression, gender, socioeconomic status, intelligence quotient (IQ), and body mass index. Several other longitudinal studies have highlighted the importance of self-concept in specific domains. For instance, Luszczynska and Abraham (2012) showed that, in a sample of 551 late adolescents, higher levels of perceived physical activity competence at baseline predicted greater vigorous physical activity two months later, which in turn predicted better lung functioning 12 months later.

In terms of education, studies have consistently shown ASC to positively impact academic achievement (Marsh & Craven, 2006), interest and satisfaction in school (Marsh, Trautwein et al., 2005), course selection (Marsh et al., 2019; Marsh & Yeung, 1997; Parker et al., 2014), persistence, and long-term attainment (Guo, Marsh et al., 2015; Guo, Parker et al., 2015; Marsh & O'Mara, 2008), above and beyond the effects of prior achievement and IQ. This evidence has been gathered not only through cross-sectional regional data but also using cross-national and longitudinal datasets (e.g., Marsh, 2006). The Organisation for Economic Co-operation and Development (OECD) has previously noted that self-concepts are also "closely tied to students' economic success and long-term health and wellbeing" (OECD, 2003, p. 9), further highlighting the broad-scoped and long-term impact of ASC.

The Structure of Self-Concept

Before we describe how self-concept is formed, it is crucial to understand the structure of self-concept. Self-concept is multifaceted and hierarchically organized, with perceptions of personal behavior in specific situations at the base of the hierarchy, inferences about the self in broader domains (e.g., social, physical, and academic) in the middle of the hierarchy, and a global, general self-concept (also known as self-esteem) at the apex (Shavelson et al., 1976; Figure 13.1). Furthermore, a person's self-concept in a specific domain not only leads to a range of positive outcomes in that domain but may also influence their competence perceptions in other domains. The assessment of the overall structure of self-concept was made possible with the development of the Self-Description Questionnaire (SDQ; Marsh, Relich, & Smith, 1983). Based on SDQ instruments, Marsh and Shavelson (1985) provided empirical support for the multidimensionality of self-concept. The two main points of note are that self-concept is hierarchical and multidimensional, and that self-concept gets increasingly multifaceted with age.

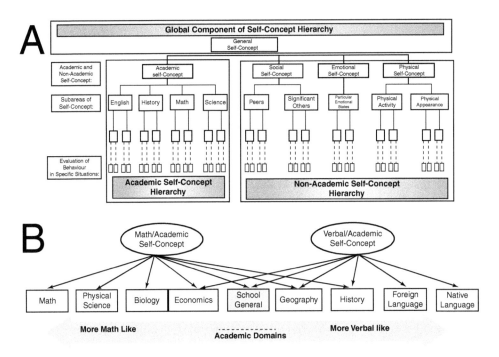

Figure 13.1 (a) Structure of self-concept (Shavelson et al., 1976). (b) Structure of academic self-concept (Marsh et al., 1998)

For older adolescents, Marsh and Shavelson (1985) provided evidence from two studies based on the 13-factor SDQ-III (general, same-sex, opposite sex, parent relationship, emotional stability, problem-solving, religion/spirituality, honesty/dependability, physical ability, physical appearance, reading, math, and overall school subjects). In both studies, there was good support for the 13-factor a priori model, and correlations between factors were small (mean *r* < 0.10 in both studies). In support of convergent and discriminant validity, there was also high agreement between the self-ratings and inferred self-concept ratings by significant others (*r* range = 0.42–0.79, median *r* = 0.52). In both studies, a single "academic self-concept" was insufficient to explain the subject-specific SCs below it, as was posited by the Shavelson et al. (1976) model. Instead, two higher-order factors—math and verbal—were required to explain the lower order subject-specific SCs (see Figure 13.1 for the structure of ASC).

For preadolescent children, Marsh and Shavelson (1985) reported good support for the a priori seven-factor structure (physical appearance, physical abilities, peer relationships, parent relationships, reading, mathematics, and school subjects). In the sample of primary school students (Year levels 2–5), there was good support for the invariance of factor loadings over year levels. However, the factors became more distinct (less correlated) for the older students, in line with the Shavelson et al. (1976) model. Marsh and Shavelson (1985) concluded that for preadolescent children, self-concept was best represented by a multidimensional and hierarchical model with seven first-order factors and three second-order factors (reading, math, and nonacademic) that were all correlated with each other.

Developmental and early childhood researchers are interested in ASC development, but problems in the measurement of self-concept at early ages have caused a hindrance. Addressing this issue, Marsh and colleagues (Marsh, Debus et al., 2005; Marsh et al., 2002) developed an individually administered version of the SDQ for preschool children aged four and five years of age.

Using this novel measurement approach in combination with factor analysis, they found that children were able to distinguish between multiple dimensions of self-concept at a younger age than suggested by previous research. Nevertheless, verbal and math self-concepts (MSCs) for these four- and five-year-old children were highly correlated ($r = 0.73$) in comparison to the typical small correlations observed with older children and adolescents.

It is important to note how the multidimensionality of self-concept impacts research decisions on global versus domain-specific measures of self-concept and related constructs. While global self-concept (also referred to as self-esteem) measures have stronger associations with global outcomes than with domain-specific outcomes, the opposite is true for domain-specific measures of self-concept. Therefore, using self-esteem measures in studies with a focus on broad, global outcomes would be suitable. However, ASC is more relevant to academic outcomes, and specific components of ASC are more relevant to outcomes concerning specific school subjects. For instance, Valentine et al. (2004) showed that stronger effects of self-belief measures are found when assessing self-beliefs specific to the academic domain and when measures of self-beliefs and achievement are matched by domain (e.g., same subject area).

We now discuss the psychological processes that underlie self-concept formation. Arguably, the three most important comparison processes are temporal, social, and dimensional comparisons. Models that involved these processes include the reciprocal effects model (REM), the big-fish-little-pond effect (BFLPE) model, and the internal/external frame-of-reference effects (I/E) model.

The Reciprocal Effects Model: Does A Positive Self-Concept "Cause" Better School Performance or Is It the Other Way Around?

There is ample evidence for the positive association between academic achievement and ASC (see Marsh, 2007). However, a critical question with important theoretical and policy/practice implications is the temporal ordering of these constructs. Does a positive self-concept lead to better school performance, or is it the other way around? Traditional approaches to this issue (Calsyn & Kenny, 1977) have taken an "either-or" approach; the "skill development model" posits that prior achievement leads to subsequent ASC, while the "skill-enhancement model" postulates that prior ASC leads to subsequent achievement. However, research has shown that it might be best to amalgamate these two perspectives. Indeed, integrating theoretical and statistical perspectives, Marsh (1990) argued for a dynamic REM that incorporates both the skill development and the self-enhancement models. That is, they theorized both ASC and achievement to be causes and also effects of each other. The REM, therefore, is a longitudinal model of self-concept that involves temporal comparisons based on the juxtaposition of ASC and achievement for at least two waves of data. It is important to note that the REM is a domain-specific model. Thus, for instance, MSC at time one positively predicts math achievement at time two, while math achievement at time one also positively predicts MSC at time two (Marsh, 1990; see Figure 13.2a).

The first empirical examination of the REM used data from the large and nationally representative American Youth in Transition Study, based on four waves of data from Year 10 through one year after typical high school graduation (Marsh, 1990). The data comprised three different constructs: academic ability, ASC, and school grades. Results were in line with the hypothesized relationships. Specifically, (a) ASC in one wave had a significant effect on subsequent achievement, controlling for prior ASC and achievement, and (b) achievement in one wave had a significant effect on subsequent ASC, controlling for prior ASC and achievement. Importantly, the results were replicated across two different intervals, providing strong support for the reciprocal relationship between achievement and self-concept.

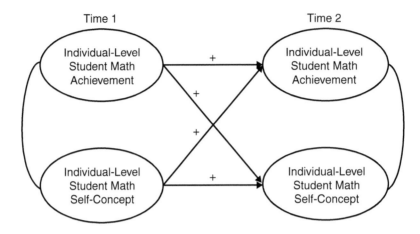

Figure 13.2a The Reciprocal Effects Model (REM)

Generalizability

Since the Marsh (1990) seminal study, there have been plenty of empirical studies, cross-cultural studies, as well as meta-analyses that lend support to the REM predictions (Huang, 2011; Marsh & Martin, 2011; Marsh, Pekrun et al., 2018; Valentine et al., 2004). While these studies have primarily focused on math achievement and self-concept, research focusing on reading and science domains has also found similar results (e.g., Chiu, 2012; Sewasew, & Koester, 2019). In a meta-analysis, Valentine et al. (2004) found consistent support for the REM. They reported that the effect of prior self-beliefs on subsequent achievement, after controlling for the effects of prior achievement, was highly significant overall and positive in 90% of the studies they considered. Furthermore, and consistent with a multidimensional perspective, the effects of prior self-beliefs were significantly stronger when the measure of self-belief was domain-specific and in the same domain as the achievement measure (e.g., MSC and math achievement). In contrast, they reported little evidence of the effects of generalized self-beliefs, such as self-esteem, on academic achievement. They concluded that the REM relating academic self-beliefs and achievement is consistent with theories of learning and human development that view the self as a causal agent (e.g., Bandura, 2008b; Carver & Scheier, 2002; Deci & Ryan, 2012; Ryan & Deci, 2017). Based on similar findings in a subsequent meta-analysis, Huang (2011) concluded that "as high self-concept is related to high academic performance and vice versa, intervention programs that combine self-enhancement and skill development should be integrated" (p. 505). It is important to note, however, that while there is ample evidence for paths in both directions to be positive and significant, the path from achievement to self-concept is generally stronger than the path from self-concept to achievement.

The Big-Fish-Little-Pond Effect: How Does the Peer Group Impact a Student's Self-Concept?

Context is important for self-concept formation; judgment about one's ability is affected by comparisons with those around them. The centrality of the social comparison processes follows from work done by William James (1890/1963), Festinger (1954), and Davis (1966). In an educational setting, one of the most important comparisons is the one students make with their peer groups. This comparison is most commonly known as the big-fish-little-pond effect (BFLPE; Marsh & Parker, 1984). In it, students compare their own achievement in a specific domain with the achievement of their classmates in the same domain. For instance, if they outrank their peers in mathematics, they will have higher levels of MSC, but if they perform below-average compared to their peers in math, they will have lower MSC. It follows then, that a student in a class with high-achieving students will have low MSC, while a student with similar levels of achievement who attends a class with low or moderately achieving students will have high MSC. Research has shown these findings to be true at the school (Dicke et al., 2018) and country-level as well (Marsh, Parker, Guo, Basarkod et al., 2020). Thus, individual achievement has a positive effect on ASC, but the effect of class-, school-, or country-average achievement is negative (Figure 13.2b).

Marsh and Parker (1984) conducted the initial BFLPE study in Australia, with a sample of 305 sixth-grade students in five schools (48% female; three high-SES and two low-SES schools). Not only did they show that individual-level achievement was positively associated with ASC and that school-average achievement was negatively associated with ASC, but they also showed a similar pattern of results for individual- and school-level SES. That is, within a given level of school SES, the higher the family SES, the higher the ASC. However, at a given level of family SES, the higher the school SES, the lower the ASC.

The BFLPE also has effects beyond just impacting self-concept. Marsh (1991) demonstrated that students attending higher-ability high schools were likely to have lower GPAs, lower educational aspirations, lower occupational aspirations, and lower standardized test scores. They were also more likely to select less demanding coursework than their equally able peers attending schools with lower average abilities (Marsh, 1991). Studies have also shown that participating in gifted and talented programs has similar negative effects on the individual (Marsh et al., 1995). Predictions based on BFLPE research also imply that academically disadvantaged students will have higher self-concepts when grouped with other academically disadvantaged students (compared to similarly disadvantaged students in classes with students of a variety of academic skill levels). Thus, while high-achieving students may be disadvantaged by being segregated, low-achieving students might benefit from being grouped. These findings have important consequences for parents and policymakers, concerning which types of schools and programs children should be enrolled in, as these decisions may have long-term consequences for the students attending them.

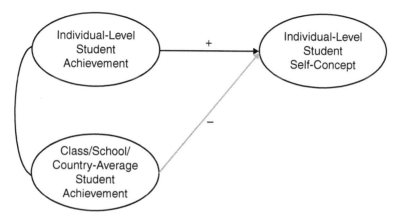

Figure 13.2b   The Big-Fish-Little-Pond Effect (BFLPE)

Generalizability

Since the initial BFLPE study (Marsh & Parker, 1984), a wealth of studies has supported BFLPE predictions by employing differing experimental and analytical approaches (Alicke et al., 2010; Marsh, 1987; Marsh & Seaton, 2015; Marsh et al., 2008; Marsh et al., 2012). It is one of the most robust psychological findings, with evidence traversing cross-sectional, longitudinal, and cross-cultural studies (Marsh & Seaton, 2015; Marsh et al., 2008). Results from four Programme for International Student Assessment (PISA) data collections (Marsh & Hau, 2004: 103,558 students from 26 countries; Marsh, Parker, & Pekrun, 2018: 485,490 from 68 countries/regions; Nagengast & Marsh, 2012: 397,500 students from 57 countries; and Seaton et al., 2010: 265,180 students from 41 countries) have shown that the effect of school-average achievement on ASC was negative in all but one of the 191 samples, and significantly so in 181 samples. Guo et al. (2018) used combined data from Trends in International Mathematics and Science Study (TIMSS) and Progress in International Reading Literacy Study (PIRLS) from 2011 to further test the cross-cultural generalizability of the BFLPE. In this nationally representative sample of fourth-grade students from 15 OECD countries (67,386 students in 3,808 classes and 2,564 schools), Guo et al. found evidence for the BFLPE for reading, math, and science self-concepts. In the only meta-analysis on the BFLPE to date, which included 33 studies with 56 effect sizes (total $N = 1,276,838$), Fang et al. (2018) found the mean effect of class/school average-achievement on student ASC to be significant and negative ($\beta = -0.28$). Providing further evidence for the multidimensionality of self-concept, the BFLPE was stronger in studies using domain-specific measures of achievement and self-concept ($\beta = -0.30$ to -0.31) than those using general measures ($\beta = -0.22$).

The Internal/External Frame of Reference Model: Why Do People Think of Themselves as "Math" or "Verbal" Persons?

The I/E model involves cross-dimensional comparisons across multiple self-concept factors and helps further explain the domain-specificity of ASC. Marsh (1986) developed this model (see Figure 13.2c) to explain why math and verbal self-concepts are so distinct—almost uncorrelated even—though corresponding areas of academic achievement are substantially correlated (Möller & Marsh, 2013). According to the I/E model, students use both internal and external comparison processes to evaluate their accomplishments in a specific subject. In terms of the external comparison process, students base their judgment about their performance in a given subject on objective indicators, such as test scores, grades, and feedback from their teachers. For instance, if they perform well on a math test, they will have a high MSC. With regard to the internal process, however, students compare their achievement in this subject with their achievement in another subject (e.g., English)—a cross-dimensional comparison process. If they score higher in Math than they do in English, they will have higher levels of MSC and lower levels of English self-concept. In other words, not only do students use their achievement in a given domain to form their self-concept in the same domain but they also use their own achievement in a different domain as a frame of reference for the formation of their self-concept in the first domain.

In the original presentation of the I/E model, Marsh (1986) reanalyzed results from 13 studies that considered students of different ages and different academic achievement indicators. He found that the correlations between indicators of verbal and math achievement were substantial ($r = 0.42 - 0.94$) but that the correlations between measures of verbal and MSCs were much smaller ($r = -0.10 - 0.19$). Further, the path coefficients from verbal achievement to verbal self-concept, and from math achievement to MSC were all significantly positive. In contrast, the path coefficients from math achievement to verbal self-concept, and from verbal achievement to MSC, were significantly negative.

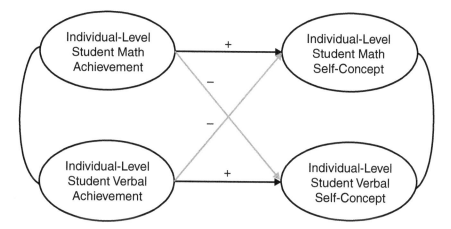

Figure 13.2c The Internal/External Frame-of-Reference Effect Model (I/E)

Generalizability

Since this original study, there has been broad support for the I/E model in samples from different countries, age groups, and using different measures and methodology. For example, Marsh et al. (2015) studied the I/E model using the TIMSS data. This study contained matched samples of fourth- and eighth-grade students (N = 117,321) from culturally and religiously diverse countries such as the Middle East (e.g., Iran and Kuwait), Western countries (e.g., Italy and the United States), and Asian countries (e.g., Japan and Singapore). Results indicated that the I/E model generalized across the domains of math and science, but also age and nationality. Another large-scale cross-cultural study was conducted using the PISA 2000 data (Marsh & Hau, 2004). Marsh and Hau showed that the results from the I/E model generalized over 26 countries. Specifically, the path relating math achievement to MSC (β = 0.44) and the path relating reading achievement to verbal self-concept (β = 0.47) were substantial and positive. In contrast, the paths leading from reading achievement to MSC (β = −0.20) and mathematics achievement to verbal self-concept (β = −0.26) were negative. Further, the zero-order correlation between math and verbal achievement factors was very large (r = 0.78), whereas the correlation between the two self-concept factors was very small (r = 0.10).

Evidence for the I/E model has also been obtained through meta-analyses. For example, using 69 datasets (N = 125,308), Möller and colleagues (2009) confirmed predictions from the I/E model that generalized across age, gender, and nationality. They found that although math and verbal achievements were highly correlated (r = 0.67), math and verbal self-concepts were nearly uncorrelated (r = 0.10) across all studies. Moreover, as the I/E model predicts, the paths leading from achievement in one domain to its matching ASC were positive (β = 0.61 for math and β = 0.49 for verbal). In contrast, the paths to nonmatching domains were negative (math achievement to verbal self-concept: β = −0.21 and verbal achievement to MSC: β = −0.27).

Frame-of-Reference Effects: What Is the Difference between Self-Concept and Self-Efficacy?

Positive self-beliefs are a central construct in educational psychology, and self-concept and self-efficacy are the most widely used and theoretically important representations of positive self-beliefs. The focus of our chapter has been on ASC, but it is also relevant to discuss how the results and theoretical models relate to self-efficacy responses. There are many similarities between self-efficacy and self-concept, such as an emphasis on perceived competence, content specificity, and the prediction of future performance, emotion, and motivation (Bong & Skaalvik, 2003; Marsh et al., 2019). Although reviews of these constructs point to important distinctions, in practice and theory, the distinction remains murky. Marsh et al. (2019) critiqued previous conceptual attempts to distinguish the two constructs, arguing against some distinctions offered in the past, and offering some new theoretical distinctions and new empirical approaches to testing these distinctions.

On the one hand, as emphasized in this chapter, ASC formation relies heavily on social and dimensional comparison information. For example, MSC is a function of the social comparisons (one's own math accomplishments in relation to the math accomplishments of classmates) and dimensional comparisons (comparison of one's own math performance with one's own performance in other school subjects). On the other hand, Bandura (1994, p. 71) suggests that "perceived self-efficacy is defined as people's beliefs about their capabilities to produce designated levels of performance that exercise influence over events that affect their lives." Thus, appropriately constructed ("pure") self-efficacy items should "solicit goal referenced evaluations and do not directly ask students to compare their abilities to those of others" (Bong & Skaalvik, 2003, p. 9) and "provide respondents with a specific description of the required referent against which to judge their competence" (p. 9). Similarly, Bandura (1986) argued that self-esteem and self-concept—but not self-efficacy—are partly determined by "how well one's behavior matches personal standards of worthiness" (p. 410). Thus, appropriate ("pure") self-efficacy measures provide an explicit criterion of success that is not based on social or dimensional comparison processes (e.g., "how many seconds would it take you to run 100 meters"). In educational settings, for example, a pure measure of math self-efficacy might be to show students examples of math problems of varying degrees of difficulty and asking them the likelihood of being able to answer each of them correctly. Responses to these items do not require students to make comparisons with other students or their own performances in other school subjects. In this way, pure self-efficacy measures minimize frame-of-reference effects considered here.

However, the distinction is murky because many so-called measures of self-efficacy implicitly (or explicitly) invoke social comparison processes so that they behave more like self-concept measures (see Marsh et al., 2019 for a discussion on jingle-jangle fallacies). One such example is the use of self-concept and self-efficacy measures used by PISA (note: in the 2000 cohort, both measures were in relation to general academics, while those used in 2003 and 2012 were math domain-specific). PISA 2000 used a self-efficacy measure that was more like a general self-concept measure, in terms of not involving the criterion for successful performance (e.g., "I'm confident I can do an excellent job on assignments and tests"). These self-efficacy items were also similar to the self-concept items used (e.g., "I learn things quickly in most school subjects"). In contrast, the self-efficacy measure in PISA 2003 and 2012 was a purer measure of math self-efficacy that minimized social comparison processes and involved explicit criteria (e.g., "calculating how much cheaper a TV would be after a 30% discount"). These self-efficacy items were different from the self-concept items used in these cohorts (e.g., "I learn mathematics quickly"). From this perspective, it is reasonable that frame-of-reference effects for self-concept and self-efficacy were similar, based on PISA 2000, but that frame-of-reference effects were systematically weaker for the math self-efficacy responses than for MSC in PISA 2003 and 2012 (Marsh, Parker, & Pekrun, 2018; also see Marsh, Pekrun et al., 2018). Thus, what might appear to be a failure to replicate results in relation to self-efficacy is really due to inappropriate labeling of the self-efficacy measure used in PISA 2000.

Indeed, using a four-year longitudinal study based on a representative sample of 3,350 students from math classes in 43 German schools, Marsh et al. (2019) demonstrated the importance of these distinctions. Consistent with the research reviewed in the present chapter, Marsh et al. (2019) found negative frame-of-reference effects in relation to social (big-fish-little-pond effect) and dimensional (internal/external frame-of-reference effect) comparisons for three self-concept-like constructs (MSC, math outcome expectancy, and generalized math self-efficacy) in each of the first four years of secondary school. In contrast, none of the frame-of-reference effects were significantly negative for either of the two pure self-efficacy constructs (math test-related self-efficacy and math functional self-efficacy) in any of the four years of testing. These results suggest that self-efficacy measures might be useful in terms of minimizing frame-of-reference effects that complicate interpretations. However, Marsh et al. (2019) noted that after controlling for pretest variables, each of the three self-concept-like constructs in each year of secondary school was more strongly related to posttest outcomes (school grades, test scores, and future aspirations) than were the corresponding two pure measures of self-efficacy. The problem, they noted, was that self-efficacy did not predict future performance as well as self-concept after controlling for prior achievement. Indeed, Marsh (2007) argued that much of the power of self-belief to motivate and predict future behavior depends on the evaluation one makes of a pure performance expectation—something that is explicitly absent in pure self-efficacy measures that are designed to be entirely descriptive (i.e., assessing what one can do rather than assessing an evaluation of how good one thinks their performance is).

Summary and Conclusion

Self-concept is crucial for positive psychology (and psychology generally). It is developed via three main psychological comparison processes: temporal (REM), social (BFLPE), and dimensional (I/E model). Self-concept is conceptually and empirically distinct from self-efficacy. We focused on ASC, drawing examples from the educational psychology literature while highlighting numerous meta-analyses and cross-cultural studies. The arguments and evidence posed in this chapter have highlighted the importance of ASC not only as a predictor of other crucial outcomes but also as an essential construct in its own right.

It is important to note that the comparison processes mentioned in this chapter are cumulative. Temporal, social, and dimensional processes will all work collectively to inform one's self-concept. For instance, a student's MSC is informed by their past math achievement scores, their peer's math achievement scores, as well as their verbal achievement. Bringing together the three processes into one unified whole can allow for inferences above and beyond what can be explained by each of the individual models separately. Indeed, Marsh, Pekrun et al. (2018) proposed a unified model of ASC formation that integrates the REM, I/E, and BFLPE into a single conceptual and statistical model. In their study, they evaluated relations among math and native-language (German) school grades from the end of primary school (Year 4), measures of math test scores and MSC collected during each of the subsequent five years of secondary school, and school-average measures of math achievement. Their integration highlighted new tests of the robustness, interconnectedness, and complementarity of the three models of ASC formation, but also new theoretical predictions and substantive implications at their intersections. For instance, from the combination of the REM and I/E models, they were able to show that the total effects of math and language achievement from Year 4 achievement (from the end of primary school) over the subsequent five years of secondary school were remarkably consistent in size—positive for math achievement and negative for verbal achievement. It is worth noting here that ASC research has historically created a synergy between the strong theoretical models emphasized in this chapter and robust methodological and statistical models. The Marsh, Pekrun et al. (2018) study is a good example of that. This trend of the creative use of emerging statistical methodology is likely to continue and result in new findings with important substantive and policy-practice implications.

Further to the Marsh, Pekrun et al. (2018) study, Marsh, Parker, Guo, Pekrun, and Basarkod (2020) provided cross-cultural generalizability for the BFLPE and I/E models, as well as the integration of the two, using the extensive PISA 2012 database (485,490 15-year-old students from 68 countries/regions, and 18,292 schools). Data included achievement tests in three content areas (math, verbal, and science), MSC, and many additional backgrounds/demographic variables. In relation to the combination of the BFLPE and I/E models, they found that country-average math achievement was negatively related to MSC. Importantly, in their discussion, the authors emphasized that students did not actually have to compare their achievements with those of students in other countries, but only had to know how their achievement compared to other students in their school and how their school compared to other schools in their country. This study and many others using the meta-analytic framework or large cross-cultural datasets like PISA crucially show the generalizability of the self-concept construct. Owing to the multitudinous research, the evidence-base for self-concept is undeniable and irrefutable.

References

Alicke, M. D., Zell, E., & Bloom, D. L. (2010). Mere categorization and the frog-pond effect. *Psychological Science, 21*, 174–177. https://doi.org/10.1177/0956797609357718

Bandura, A. (1977). Self-efficacy: Toward a unifying theory of behavioral change. *Psychological Review, 84*, 191–215. https://doi.org/10.1037/0033-295X.84.2.191

Bandura, A. (1986). *Social foundations of thought and action: A social cognitive theory.* Prentice-Hall.

Bandura, A. (1989). Human agency in social cognitive theory. *American Psychologist, 44*(9), 1175–1184. https://doi.org/10.1037/0003-066X.44.9.1175

Bandura, A. (1994). Social cognitive theory and exercise of control over HIV infection. In R. J. DiClemente & J. L. Peterson (Eds.), *AIDS prevention and mental health. Preventing AIDS: Theories and methods of behavioral interventions* (pp. 25–59). Sage. https://doi.org/10.1007/978-1-4899-1193-3_3

Bandura, A. (2006). Toward a psychology of human agency. *Perspectives on Psychological Science, 1*, 164–180. https://doi.org/10.1111/j.1745-6916.2006.00011.x

Bandura, A. (2008a). An agentic perspective on positive psychology. In S. Lopez (Ed.), *Positive Psychology: Exploring the best in people* (pp. 167–196). Greenwood Publishing Group.

Bandura, A. (2008b). Toward an agentic theory of the self. In H. W. Marsh, R. G. Craven, & D. M. McInerney (Eds.), *Self-processes, learning, and enabling human potential: Dynamic new approaches. Advances in Self Research* (pp. 15–49). Information Age Publishing, Inc.

Bong, M., & Skaalvik, E. M. (2003). Academic self-concept and self-efficacy: How different are they really? *Educational Psychology Review, 15*, 1–40. https://doi.org/10.1023/A:1021302408382

Branden, N. (1994). *The six pillars of self-esteem.* Bantam Books.

Bruner, J. S. (1996). *The culture of education*: Harvard University Press.

Burnett, P. C., Pillay, H., & Dart, B. C. (2003). The influences of conceptions of learning and learner self-concept on high school students approaches to learning. *School Psychology International, 24*, 54–66. https://doi.org/10.1177/0143034303024001621

Calsyn, R. J., & Kenny, D. A. (1977). Self-concept of ability and perceived evaluation of others: Cause or effect of academic achievement? *Journal of Educational Psychology, 69*, 136–145. https://doi.org/10.1037/0022-0663.69.2.136

Carver, C. S., & Scheier, M. F. (2002). The hopeful optimist. *Psychological Inquiry, 13*, 288–290. https://www.jstor.org/stable/1448869

Chen, S.-K., Yeh, Y.-C., Hwang, F.-M., & Lin, S. S. (2013). The relationship between academic self-concept and achievement: A multicohort–multioccasion study. *Learning and Individual Differences, 23*, 172–178. https://doi.org/10.1016/j.lindif.2012.07.021

Chiu, M. S. (2012). The internal/external frame of reference model, big-fish-little-pond effect, and combined model for mathematics and science. *Journal of Educational Psychology, 104*, 87–107. https://doi.org/10.1037/a0025734

Clark, A. E. (2018). Four decades of the economics of happiness: Where next? *Review of Income and Wealth, 64*, 245–269. https://doi.org/10.1111/roiw.12369

Davis, J. A. (1966). The campus as a frog pond: An application of theory of relative deprivation to career decisions for college men. *American Journal of Sociology, 72*, 17–31. https://doi.org/10.1086/224257

Deci, E. L., & Ryan, R. M. (2012). Self-determination theory. In P. A. M. Van Lange, A. W. Kruglanski, & E. T. Higgins (Eds.), *Handbook of theories of social psychology* (pp. 416–436). Sage. https://doi.org/10.4135/9781446249215.n21

Dicke, T., Marsh, H. W., Parker, P. D., Pekrun, R., Guo, J., & Televantou, I. (2018). Effects of school-average achievement on individual self-concept and achievement: Unmasking phantom effects masquerading as true compositional effects. *Journal of Educational Psychology, 110*(8), 1112. https://doi.org/10.1037/edu0000259

Donahue, E. M., Robins, R. W., Roberts, B. W., & John, O. P. (1993). The divided self: Concurrent and longitudinal effects of psychological adjustment and social roles on self-concept differentiation. *Journal of Personality and Social Psychology, 64*, 834–846. https://doi.org/10.1037/0022-3514.64.5.834

Ehm, J.-H., Hasselhorn, M., & Schmiedek, F. (2019). Analyzing the developmental relation of academic self-concept and achievement in elementary school children: Alternative models point to different results. *Developmental Psychology, 55*, 2336–2351. https://doi.org/10.1037/dev0000796

Elliot, A. J., & Dweck, C. S. (2005). Competence and motivation: Competence as the core of achievement motivation. In A. J. Elliot & C. S. Dweck (Eds.), *Handbook of competence and motivation* (pp. 3–12). Guilford Press.

Fang, J., Huang, X., Zhang, M., Huang, F., Zhe, L., & Yuan, Q. (2018). The big-fish-little-pond effect on academic self-concept: A meta-analysis. *Frontiers in Psychology, 9*, 1569. https://doi.org/10.3389/fpsyg.2018.01569

Fantuzzo, J. W., McDermott, P. A., Manz, P. H., Hampton, V. R., & Burdick, N. A. (1996). The pictorial scale of perceived competence and social acceptance: Does it work with low-income urban children? *Child Development, 67*, 1071–1084. https://doi.org/10.2307/1131880

Festinger, L. (1954). A theory of social comparison processes. *Human Relations, 7*, 117–140. https://doi.org/10.1177/001872675400700202

Greenwald, A. G. (1988). A social-cognitive account of the self's development. In D. K. Lapsley & F. C. Power (Eds.), *Self, ego, and identity: Integrative approaches* (pp. 30–42). Springer. https://doi.org/10.1007/978-1-4615-7834-5_2

Guo, J., Marsh, H. W., Morin, A. J., Parker, P. D., & Kaur, G. (2015). Directionality of the associations of high school expectancy-value, aspirations, and attainment: A longitudinal study. *American Educational Research Journal, 52*, 371–402. https://doi.org/10.3102/0002831214565786

Guo, J., Marsh, H. W., Parker, P. D., & Dicke, T. (2018). Cross-cultural generalizability of social and dimensional comparison effects on reading, math, and science self-concepts for primary school students using the combined PIRLS and TIMSS data. *Learning and Instruction, 58*, 210–219. https://doi.org/10.1016/j.learninstruc.2018.07.007

Guo, J., Parker, P. D., Marsh, H. W., & Morin, A. J. (2015). Achievement, motivation, and educational choices: A longitudinal study of expectancy and value using a multiplicative perspective. *Developmental Psychology, 51*, 1163–1176. https://doi.org/10.1037/a0039440

Harter, S. (1986). Cognitive-developmental processes in the integration of concepts about emotions and the self. *Social cognition, 4*, 119–151. https://doi.org/10.1521/soco.1986.4.2.119

Harter, S. (1990). Processes underlying adolescent self-concept formation. In R. Montemayor, G. R. Adams, & T. P. Gullotta (Eds.), *Advances in adolescent development: An annual book series, Vol. 2. From childhood to adolescence: A transitional period?* (p. 205–239). Sage Publications, Inc.

Harter, S. (1998). The development of self-representations. In W. Damon & N. Eisenberg (Ed.), *Handbook of child psychology: Social, emotional, and personality development* (p. 553–617). John Wiley & Sons Inc.

Harter, S. (2012). *Self-perception profile for adolescents: Manual and questionnaires.* Denver, CO: University of Denver, Department of Psychology. https://doi.org/10.1037/t05703-000

Huang, C. (2011). Self-concept and academic achievement: A meta-analysis of longitudinal relations. *Journal of School Psychology, 49*, 505–528. https://doi.org/10.1016/j.jsp.2011.07.001

James, W. (1963). *The principles of psychology.* Holt, Rinehart & Winston. (Original work published 1890).

Kagan, S. L., Moore, E., & Bredekamp, S. (1998). *Reconsidering children's early development and learning toward common views and vocabulary: National education goals panel.* Diane Publishing.

Luszczynska, A., & Abraham, C. (2012). Reciprocal relationships between three aspects of physical self-concept, vigorous physical activity, and lung function: A longitudinal study among late adolescents. *Psychology of Sport and Exercise, 13*, 640–648. https://doi.org/10.1016/j.psychsport.2012.04.003

Marsh, H. W. (1986). Verbal and math self-concepts: An internal/external frame of reference model. *American Educational Research Journal, 23*, 129–149. https://doi.org/10.3102/00028312023001129

Marsh, H. W. (1987). The big-fish-little-pond effect on academic self-concept. *Journal of Educational Psychology, 79*, 280–295. https://doi.org/10.1037/0022-0663.79.3.280

Marsh, H. W. (1990). Causal ordering of academic self-concept and academic achievement: A multiwave, longitudinal panel analysis. *Journal of Educational Psychology, 82*, 646–656. https://doi.org/10.1037/0022-0663.82.4.646

Marsh, H. W. (1991). Failure of high-ability high schools to deliver academic benefits commensurate with their students' ability levels. *American Educational Research Journal, 28*, 445–480. https://doi.org/10.3102/00028312028002445

Marsh, H. W. (2007). *Self-concept theory, measurement and research into practice: The role of self-concept in educational psychology.* British Psychological Society.

Marsh, H. W., Abduljabbar, A. S., Parker, P. D., Morin, A. J., Abdelfattah, F., Nagengast, B., Möller, J., & Abu-Hilal, M. M. (2015). The internal/external frame of reference model of self-concept and achievement relations: Age-cohort and cross-cultural differences. *American Educational Research Journal, 52*, 168–202. https://doi.org/10.3102/0002831214549453

Marsh, H. W., Chessor, D., Craven, R. G., & Roche, L. (1995). The effects of gifted and talented programs on academic self-concept: The big fish strikes again. *American Educational Research Journal, 32*, 285–319. https://doi.org/10.3102/00028312032002285

Marsh, H. W., & Craven, R. G. (1997). Academic self-concept: Beyond the dustbowl. In G. Phye (Ed.), *Handbook of classroom assessment: Learning, achievement, and adjustment* (pp.131–198). Academic Press. https://doi.org/10.1016/B978-012554155-8/50008-9

Marsh, H. W., & Craven, R. G. (2006). Reciprocal effects of self-concept and performance from a multidimensional perspective: Beyond seductive pleasure and unidimensional perspectives. *Perspectives on Psychological Science, 1*, 133–163. https://doi.org/10.1111/j.1745-6916.2006.00010.x

Marsh, H. W., Debus, R., & Bornholt, L. (2005). Validating young children's self-concept responses: Methodological ways and means to understand their responses. In D. M. Teti (Ed.), *Handbook of research methods in developmental science* (p.138–160). Blackwell Publishing Ltd. https://doi.org/10.1002/9780470756676.ch8

Marsh, H. W., Ellis, L. A., & Craven, R. G. (2002). How do preschool children feel about themselves? Unraveling measurement and multidimensional self-concept structure. *Developmental Psychology, 38*, 376–393. https://doi.org/10.1037/0012-1649.38.3.376

Marsh, H. W., & Hau, K. T. (2004). Explaining paradoxical relations between academic self-concepts and achievements: Cross-cultural generalizability of the internal-external frame of reference predictions across 26 countries. *Journal of Educational Psychology, 96*, 56–67. https://doi.org/10.1037/0022-0663.96.1.56

Marsh, H. W., & O'Mara, A. (2008). Reciprocal effects between academic self-concept, self-esteem, achievement, and attainment over seven adolescent years: Unidimensional and multidimensional perspectives of self-concept. *Personality and Social Psychology Bulletin, 34*, 542–552. https://doi.org/10.1177/0146167207312313

Marsh, H. W., Parada, R. H., Craven, R. G., & Finger, L. (2004). In the looking glass: A reciprocal effects model elucidating the complex nature of bullying, psychological determinants, and the central role of self-concept. In C. E. Sanders & G. D. Phye (Eds.), *Bullying* (pp. 63–106). Academic Press. https://doi.org/10.1016/B978-012617955-2/50009-6

Marsh, H. W., & Parker, J. W. (1984). Determinants of student self-concept: Is it better to be a relatively large fish in a small pond even if you don't learn to swim as well? *Journal of Personality and Social Psychology, 47*, 213–231. https://doi.org/10.1037/0022-3514.47.1.213

Marsh, H. W., Parker, P., Guo, J., Basarkod, G., Niepel, C., & Van Zanden, B. (2020). Illusory gender-equality paradox, math self-concept, and frame-of-reference effects new integrative explanations for multiple paradoxes. *Journal of Personality and Social Psychology*. Advanced online publication. https://doi.org/10.1037/pspp0000306

Marsh, H. W., Parker, P. D., Guo, J., Pekrun, R., & Basarkod, G. (2020). Psychological comparison processes and self-concept in relation to five distinct frame-of-reference effects: Pan-human cross-cultural generalizability over 68 countries. *European Journal of Personality, 34*, 180–202. https://doi.org/10.1002/per.2232

Marsh, H. W., Parker, P. D., & Pekrun, R. (2018). Three paradoxical effects on academic self-concept across countries, schools, and students: Frame-of-reference as a unifying theoretical explanation. *European Psychologist, 24*, 231–242. https://doi.org/10.1027/1016-9040/a000332

Marsh, H. W., Pekrun, R., Murayama, K., Arens, A. K., Parker, P. D., Guo, J., & Dicke, T. (2018). An integrated model of academic self-concept development: Academic self-concept, grades, test scores, and tracking over 6 years. *Developmental Psychology, 54*, 263–280. https://doi.org/10.1037/dev0000393

Marsh, H. W., Pekrun, R., Parker, P. D., Murayama, K., Guo, J., Dicke, T., & Arens, A. K. (2019). The murky distinction between self-concept and self-efficacy: Beware of lurking jingle-jangle fallacies. *Journal of Educational Psychology, 111*, 331–353. https://doi.org/10.1037/edu0000281

Marsh, H. W., & Perry, C. (2005). Self-concept contributes to winning gold medals: Causal ordering of self-concept and elite swimming performance. *Journal of Sport and Exercise Psychology, 27*, 71–91. https://doi.org/10.1123/jsep.27.1.71

Marsh, H. W., Relich, J. D., & Smith, I. D. (1983). Self-concept: The construct validity of interpretations based upon the SDQ. *Journal of Personality and Social Psychology, 45*, 173–187. https://doi.org/10.1037/0022-3514.45.1.173

Marsh, H. W., & Seaton, M. (2015). The big-fish–little-pond effect, competence self-perceptions, and relativity: Substantive advances and methodological innovation. In A. J. Elliot (Ed.), *Advances in motivation science.* (Vol. 2, pp. 127–184). Elsevier. https://doi.org/10.1016/bs.adms.2015.05.002

Marsh, H. W., Seaton, M., Trautwein, U., Lüdtke, O., Hau, K.-T., O'Mara, A. J., & Craven, R. G. (2008). The big-fish–little-pond-effect stands up to critical scrutiny: Implications for theory, methodology, and future research. *Educational Psychology Review, 20*, 319–350. https://doi.org/10.1007/s10648-008-9075-6

Marsh, H. W., & Shavelson, R. (1985). Self-concept: Its multifaceted, hierarchical structure. *Educational Psychologist, 20,* 107–123. https://doi.org/10.1207/s15326985ep2003_1

Marsh, H. W., Trautwein, U., Lüdtke, O., Köller, O., & Baumert, J. (2005). Academic self-concept, interest, grades and standardised test scores: Reciprocal effects models of causal ordering. *Child Development, 76,* 297–416. https://doi.org/10.1111/j.1467-8624.2005.00853.x

Marsh, H. W., Walker, R., & Debus, R. (1991). Subject-specific components of academic self-concept and self-efficacy. *Contemporary Educational Psychology, 16*(4), 331–345. https://doi.org/10.1016/0361-476X(91)90013-B

Marsh, H. W., Xu, M., & Martin, A. J. (2012). Self-concept: A synergy of theory, method, and application. In K. R. Harris, S. Graham, T. Urdan, C. B. McCormick, G. M. Sinatra, & J. Sweller (Eds.), *APA handbooks in psychology. APA educational psychology handbook, Vol. 1. Theories, constructs, and critical issues* (pp. 427–458). American Psychological Association. https://doi.org/10.1037/13273-015

Marsh, H. W., & Yeung, A. S. (1997). Causal effects of academic self-concept on academic achievement: Structural equation models of longitudinal data. *Journal of Educational Psychology, 89,* 41–54. https://doi.org/10.1037/0022-0663.89.1.41

Möller, J., & Marsh, H. W. (2013). Dimensional comparison theory. *Psychological Review, 120,* 544–560. https://doi.org/10.1037/a0032459

Möller, J., Pohlmann, B., Köller, O., & Marsh, H. W. (2009). A meta-analytic path analysis of the internal/external frame of reference model of academic achievement and academic self-concept. *Review of Educational Research, 79,* 1129–1167. https://doi.org/10.3102/0034654309337522

Nagengast, B., & Marsh, H. W. (2012). Big fish in little ponds aspire more: Mediation and cross-cultural generalizability of school-average ability effects on self-concept and career aspirations in science. *Journal of Educational Psychology, 104,* 1033–1053. https://doi.org/10.1037/a0027697

Pajares, F. (2009). Toward a positive psychology of academic motivation: The role of self-efficacy beliefs. *Journal of Educational Research, 95,* 27–35. https://doi.org/10.1080/00220670109598780

Pajares, F., & Schunk, D. (2005). Self-efficacy and self-concept beliefs. In H. Marsh, R. G. Craven, & D. McInerney (Eds.), *New frontiers for self-research Vol. 2, International Advances in self research* (pp. 95–121). Information Age Publishing.

Parker, P. D., Nagy, G., Trautwein, U., & Lüdtke, O. (2014). Predicting career aspirations and university majors from academic ability and self-concept. In I. Schoon (Ed.), *Gender differences in aspirations and attainment: A life course perspective* (pp. 224–246). Cambridge University Press. https://doi.org/10.1017/CBO9781139128933.015

Parker, P. D., Trautwein, U., Marsh, H. W., Basarkod, G., & Dicke, T. (2020). Development in relationship self-concept from high school to university predicts adjustment. Developmental Psychology. Advanced online publication. http://dx.doi.org/10.1037/dev0000992

Ryan, R. M., & Deci, E. L. (2017). *Self-determination theory: Basic psychological needs in motivation, development, and wellness.* Guilford.

Schunk, D. H., & Pajares, F. (2005). Competence perceptions and academic functioning. In A. J. Elliot & C. S. Dweck (Eds.), *Handbook of competence and motivation* (pp. 85– 104). Guilford.

Seaton, M., Marsh, H. W., & Craven, R. G. (2010). Big-fish-little-pond effect: Generalizability and moderation—Two sides of the same coin. *American Educational Research Journal, 47,* 390–433. https://doi.org/10.3102/0002831209350493

Sewasew, D., & Koester, L. S. (2019). The developmental dynamics of students' reading self-concept and reading competence: Examining reciprocal relations and ethnic-background patterns. *Learning and Individual Differences, 73,* 102–111. https://doi.org/10.1016/j.lindif.2019.05.010

Seligman, M., & Csikszentmihalyi, M. (2000). Special issue on happiness, excellence, and optimal human functioning. *American Psychologist, 55,* 5–183. https://doi.org/10.1037/0003-066X.55.1.5

Shavelson, R. J., Hubner, J. J., & Stanton, G. C. (1976). Self-concept: Validation of construct interpretations. *Review of Educational Research, 46,* 407–441. https://doi.org/10.1026/1612-5010.12.4.135

Tietjens, M., Möller, J., & Pohlmann, B. (2005) Leistung und selbstkonzept in verschieden sportarten [Achievement and self-concept in various sports]. *Zeitschrift für Sportpsychologie, 12,* 135–143. https://doi.org/10.1026/1612-5010.12.4.135

Trzesniewski, K. H., Donnellan, M. B., Moffitt, T. E., Robins, R. W., Poulton, R., & Caspi, A. (2006). Low self-esteem during adolescence predicts poor health, criminal behavior, and limited economic prospects during adulthood. *Developmental Psychology, 42,* 381–390. https://doi.org/10.1037/0012-1649.42.2.381

Valentine, J. C., DuBois, D. L., & Cooper, H. (2004). The relation between self-beliefs and academic achievement: A meta-analytic review. *Educational Psychologist, 39,* 111–133. https://doi.org/10.1207/s15326985ep3902_3

PART B

Social Development

14

EMPATHY

A Necessary Ingredient in School-Based Social-Emotional Health and Equity

Aileen Fullchange

Defining Empathy

Although there is common agreement that empathy is a social-emotional construct that is important and even vital in healthy psychosocial development, historically, there has been little universal agreement about a single definition. Compounding this complexity, empathy is often utilized interchangeably with sympathy, perspective-taking, understanding, and compassion. The definition of empathy used in this chapter is, "the ability to understand and share in another's emotional state or context" (Cohen & Strayer, 1996, p. 988). Implied within this definition are the two types of empathy: affective and cognitive. Affective empathy is an emotional reaction that is instinctive and automatic; in contrast, cognitive empathy is the intellectual ability to recognize and understand another's feelings in the context of that person's perspective. Neuroimaging studies seem to support these two distinct types of empathy, with cognitive and affective systems of empathy localized in distinct locations in the brain (Shamay-Tsoory et al., 2009).

Affective empathy is like the mirroring of another's emotional state, both figuratively and literally, as mirror neurons seem to be involved in this process (Praszkier, 2016). Affective empathy exists along a continuum. Overstimulation of the affective empathy system can result in personal distress, where a shared emotional experience results in anxiety (Hoffman, 2000). Personal distress can be a deterrent to prosocial behaviors. One extreme case of this is mothers who abuse their children. Studies have shown that *lack* of care does not cause mothers to abuse their children but, rather, excessive distress in response to their child's distress (de Paúl et al., 2008).

Cognitive empathy, on the other hand, is a purely intellectual ability to recognize and understand the feelings of another in the context of that person's perspective. In other words, there are two components: recognition and understanding. There are a number of ways of that recognizing another's emotional state can be demonstrated, including through the interpretation of facial expressions, changes in tone of voice, and nonverbal body language, just to name a few. This ability to "step" into another's shoes, imagining another's experiences, allows a person to come closer to fully living as if another person. Perhaps this can broaden a person's internal states beyond those to which they have direct knowledge and immediate access.

DOI: 10.4324/9781003013778-18

Measuring Empathy

There are several self-report measures of empathy for use with adults including the Interpersonal Reactivity Index (IRI; Davis, 1980), the Ethnocentric Empathy Scale (Wang et al., 2003), the Basic Empathy Scale (BES; Jolliffe & Farrington, 2006), the Empathy Quotient (EQ; Baron-Cohen & Wheelwright, 2004), and the Multifaceted Empathy Test (MET; Dizobek et al., 2008). All these measures assess cognitive and affective empathy. However, few measures exist that are developed for and normed on youth. Perhaps the most comprehensive of such measures is the BES (Jolliffe & Farrington, 2006), which examines both cognitive and affective empathy via a 20-question self-report. Other youth empathy measures include the Empathy Continuum Scoring Manual (ECM; Strayer, 1993), which measures affective and cognitive empathy via vignettes; the Empathy Questionnaire for Children and Adolescents (EmQue-CA; Overgaauw et al., 2017), measuring affective empathy, cognitive empathy, and intention to comfort; and the Index of Empathy for Children and Adolescents (IECA; Bryant, 1982), which focuses on affective empathy.

Currently, there are no empathy measures for youth that assess both affective and cognitive empathy along with personal distress. The only measure that exists, for any population, that measures all three constructs is the IRI (Davis, 1980). There is support for its validity in adults (Davis, 1980). The psychometric properties of the IRI have been examined with youth in the United States (Hawk et al., 2013).

The Importance of Empathy

Empathy and Prosocial Behaviors

Perhaps the most well-studied positive outcome of empathy is prosocial behaviors, defined as those voluntary behaviors which are "intended to help or benefit another individual or group of individuals" (Eisenberg & Mussen, 1989, p. 3). Eisenberg and Miller (1987) analyzed 10 different studies related to social competence and found, in all of them, a correlation between empathy and prosocial behaviors. This correlation is present in children as young as one to three years old (Knafo et al., 2008) and also holds for elementary students (Trommsdorff et al., 2007), middle school students (Van der Graaff et al., 2018), and adolescents (Yoo et al., 2013) as well as through adulthood (Masten et al., 2011).

Among 10- to 14-year-olds, empathy is correlated with prosocial, assertive, and considerate behaviors toward others (Garaigordobil, 2009). Students who self-report being more empathetic than their peers are rated by teachers as having more prosocial behaviors (McMahon et al., 2006). Further, across the lifespan, empathy is associated with altruistic behaviors (Batson et al., 2015), the subset of prosocial behaviors that not only are intended to benefit others but are also intrinsically motivated (Eisenberg & Mussen, 1989, p. 3). Empathy strongly correlates with the personality trait of friendliness amongst adolescents, and there are also smaller correlations between empathy and energy, conscientiousness, and openness (Del Barrio et al., 2004).

Empathy and Moral Development

The empathic distress response is like a moral red flag, cueing the observer that there may be something wrong occurring. Perspective-taking may increase an observer's sensitivity to these cues, which, in turn, facilitates an affective empathetic response and gives rise to moral actions (Pizarro, 2000). The ventromedial prefrontal cortex is involved in both affective empathy and moral reasoning (Decety & Cowell, 2014). There is also some evidence that empathy is related to moral reasoning through the emotion of guilt. For example, when an individual experiences empathic concern for another's suffering that has been caused by that individual's actions, guilt can be triggered, which then fuels moral responses (Eisenberg, 2000). Further, studies have shown that children's empathic abilities correlate with their morality, even sometimes extending to empathy and morality about nature and the environment (Kahn, 2006).

Empathy and Well-Being

Empathy appears to have an interactional relation to overall emotional and social well-being. Multiple studies have found that empathic individuals tend to have high self-concepts/self-esteem (e.g. Laible et al., 2004). Further, empathy positively correlates with better conflict management and closeness in friendships (Chow et al., 2013). This positive outcome may be a result of healthy attachments. In one study, empathy in adolescents correlated with secure attachment relationships with peers and more prosocial behaviors, which, in turn, predicted higher self-esteem (Carlo & Randall, 2002). The reverse relationship seems to be true as well. That is, the probability of the development of empathy increases in contexts where positive self-concept and feelings of competence are stimulated and decreases when such environmental stimulation is absent (Garaigordobil, 2009).

Empathy and Academic Outcomes

Research has also shown empathy correlates with improved academic performance. Particularly, students with more empathy especially do better in reading, literature, and social studies, perhaps because students who are able to imagine themselves from the perspectives of, say, historical or literary figures are better able to understand these subject matters (Feshbach & Feshbach, 2009). Some studies show that empathy at younger ages can predict spelling and reading outcomes a few years later in elementary school (Feshbach & Feshbach, 2009). Those who exhibit more empathy perhaps show improved academic performance through the mediating factor of social competence (Zorza et al., 2013). That is, teachers perhaps attend to children with more advanced social skills and, therefore, experience them as being easier to teach. There is some evidence for this: teachers give higher prosocial ratings to students who rate themselves as being more empathetic than their peers (McMahon et al., 2006).

Students who receive empathy also tend to have improved learning outcomes, an effect that may have to do with the role of empathy by adults in decreasing disciplinary referrals and, therefore, time away from the classroom (Okonofua et al., 2016). Teachers who exhibit empathy also seem to be more attuned to students' needs, especially those with higher needs (Chang, 2003). Therefore, such teachers are better able to support their students' learning (Lam et al., 2011) as well as create a more harmonious classroom with fewer problematic behaviors (Mishna et al., 2005). Additionally, there may be beneficial social-emotional outcomes for students who receive empathy such that they may develop increased motivation, improved self-concept, higher well-being, and improved emotion regulation strategies (Waxman, 1983), all of which likely support students' learning.

Empathy and Prejudice

Given the rise in hate crimes throughout the United States (Edwards & Rushin, 2018), with the largest portion of such incidents in schools (Southern Poverty Law Center, 2017), it is important to mention the significance of empathy in reducing social prejudice in youth (Abbott & Cameron, 2014). There is evidence that empathy training can result in reduced implicit biases (Herrera et al., 2018). One study showed empathy training for teachers results in reduced biases toward minority students (Whitford & Emerson, 2019). The importance of empathy in combatting prejudice has implications for addressing implicit bias and racial biases in the schools, which perhaps contribute to some of the disproportionate representation of children of color in disciplinary referrals and special education (Losen et al., 2014) and the phenomenon of the school-to-prison pipeline (Togut, 2011).

Youths who exhibit higher empathy levels, especially perspective-taking, also tend to be less prejudiced (Miklikowska, 2018), and interventions that specifically target empathy seem to be effective at reducing prejudice (Beelmann & Heinemann, 2014). In an analysis of over 100 interventions aimed at reducing prejudice and/or promoting positive intergroup attitudes in children and adolescents, Beelmann and Heinemann (2014) found the most effective interventions were based on increasing direct contact between in- and out-groups as well as promoting both affective and cognitive empathy. Such findings give hope to the possibility of combatting the current wave of anti-immigrant and xenophobic sentiments and of addressing racial trauma.

Empathy and Resilience

Research has shown that empathy can be a protective factor for maltreated children, with those with higher cognitive empathy tending to display fewer internalizing and externalizing behaviors (Burack et al., 2006). Additionally, empathy is associated with the ability to self-regulate, resist impulses, and maintain motivation in the face of obstacles (Leontopoulou, 2010). One study that examined the effectiveness of an intervention program in countering violent radicalization and decreasing attitudes toward violence-based ideology and intentions in Muslim teenagers and young adults found that the benefits of such a program were most related to higher empathy levels (Feddes et al., 2015).

Barbara Fredrickson's (2004) Broaden and Build Theory posits that children with resilience-promoting factors tend to attract more resilience-promoting factors, resulting in positive cascades toward resilience. As a positive psychosocial construct and one which is foundational in social interactions, the Broaden and Build Theory may especially apply to empathy. For example, Burack and colleagues' 2006 study on maltreated children found that the resilient children who had higher empathy and fewer internalizing and externalizing behaviors also tended to do better with interpersonal negotiation strategies with new peers. This skill may have led these children to have more opportunities to develop positive relationships and external support systems, further improving such youth's capacities for resilience.

Detrimental Effects of Low Empathy

Just as research has established the benefits of empathy, low levels of empathy correlate with adverse life outcomes and behaviors, with unique outcomes associated with deficits in cognitive versus affective empathy. Deficits in affective empathy are associated with psychopathology, such as narcissistic personality disorder (Ritter et al., 2011), sociopathology (Blair, 2005), bullying perpetration (Jolliffe & Farrington, 2006), and adult criminal behaviors (Jolliffe & Farrington, 2004). On the other hand, deficits in cognitive empathy are associated with aggression (Lovett & Sheffield, 2007), anger (Day et al., 2012), social skills deficits (Pouw et al., 2013), and being a victim of bullying (Woods et al., 2009). Some studies have found that youths with behavioral disorders, bullying, and other displays of anger and aggression tend to have lower overall empathy levels (de Wied et al., 2005).

Can Empathy Be Taught?

Parenting style and resulting attachment style seem to have a significant effect on the development of empathy. The optimal attachment style for developing empathy seems to be a secure attachment. As early as preschool, children who are securely attached exhibit more cognitive empathy than those who are insecurely attached (Knight, 2010), especially for preschoolers who exhibit little self-control in their temperament (Cornell & Frick, 2007). Older children (Thompson & Gullone, 2008), as well as adults, exhibit a similar connection between attachment style and levels of empathy (Teymoori & Shahrazad, 2012). However, the relationship between attachment style and empathy is made complicated by the finding that some adults who have low avoidance and high anxiety have the highest levels of affective empathy (Trusty et al., 2011), perhaps giving hope to the idea that some children who have experienced trauma and unhealthy attachment styles can actually have the protective factor of higher empathy. Furthermore, there is evidence that someone who is a recipient of an empathy-driven action will themselves tend to also display empathy toward others (van Baaren et al., 2009), perhaps indicating that receiving empathy, regardless of one's experiences in their family of origin, can still promote and spread empathy.

Several environmental factors seem to inhibit empathy development in children, including authoritarian and neglectful parenting (Cornell & Frick, 2007) and overexposure to emotional or physical violence (Cohen & Strayer, 1996). Permissive parenting also seems to impede emotional and cognitive empathy, which, in turn, seems to lead to adult antisocial behaviors (Schaffer et al., 2009).

Teaching Cognitive Empathy

Parenting techniques seem to have a significant impact on children's development of cognitive empathy as well. In particular, induction, when a parent refers to the other's perspective, points out their distress and clarifies that the child's action caused this distress, promotes perspective-taking (Hoffman, 2000). Perspective-taking also increases when parents use distancing, in which caregivers question and challenge the child's viewpoint (versus explicitly explaining logic as in induction), thereby promoting consideration of alternative explanations (Peterson & Skevington, 1988). Concerning the framing of perspective-taking questions, Batson and colleagues (1997) found that asking individuals to imagine how others feel was more effective at inducing empathy and reducing personal distress than asking them to imagine how they would feel in the others' situation. The latter condition induced empathy but also induced personal distress.

Further, longitudinal studies have found that when parents make references to feelings in ordinary conversations with children, children's later perspective-taking and affect recognition increase (Youngblade & Dunn, 1995). This parenting behavior is especially effective when caregivers refer to the "why" underlying feelings (Garner et al., 1997), as in when a parent says to a child "You see that your friend is crying. They look sad. Why do you think your friend is sad?" Although most studies examining conversations around feelings have focused on younger children, Bosacki (2013) found similar results with 8- to 12-year-olds, and Marin and colleagues (2008) found that preteens whose family conversations referred to feelings showed improved emotional and behavioral adjustment. Although these studies primarily focused on the family context, it is not difficult to see how such strategies could be extended to school-based contexts and interactions between children and their school-based caregivers.

In terms of studies outside of the family context, there is evidence that role-playing has a positive effect on empathy at all age levels. At the preschool level, one study found that students participating in role-playing of altruistic behaviors had the most substantial increases in perspective-taking compared to control conditions of observing altruistic behavior on TV and watching neutral TV programming (Ahammer & Murray, 1979). Among late elementary-age students, participation in acting classes correlates with higher cognitive empathy (Goldstein & Winner, 2011). Similarly, Goldstein and Winner (2012) found that role-playing in the form of theatrical acting increased cognitive empathy, and, in particular, emotion identification for high school students participating in once-a-week 90-minute acting classes after school. These findings extend to young adulthood (Goldstein, 2011) and even to individuals who are merely passively observing others' role-playing (Clore & Jeffery, 1972).

There is also evidence linking gratitude and empathy (McCullough et al., 2002), gratitude and lower levels of aggression with empathy as a mediator (DeWall et al., 2012), and gratitude and prosocial behaviors (Grant & Gino, 2010). Gratitude is also a positive emotion that, as Fredrickson (2004, p. 149) argues, broadens and builds personal assets such as empathy by increasing an individual's willingness to consider other perspectives. Additionally, there appears to be a correlation between gratitude and decreased personal distress (Shoshani & Steinmetz, 2014). Hence, gratitude may have a double effect of increasing empathy and protecting against overstressing the empathic response system.

Lastly, there is preliminary evidence that mindfulness is associated with higher cognitive empathy levels. Mindfulness activities are intentional, in the present moment, and nonjudgmental (Bishop et al., 2004). There is evidence that such interventions increase empathic accuracy, the ability to infer mental states from facial expressions, a foundation to cognitive empathy (Mascaro et al., 2013). Shapiro and colleagues' (1998) study supports the assertion that mindfulness increases both affective and cognitive components of empathy. However, some studies also show only a positive impact on cognitive empathy (Birnie et al., 2010). In youth, there is support for mindfulness having a positive impact on empathy overall (Schonert-Reichl et al., 2015) as well as for reducing personal distress (Coholic et al., 2012). Such results extend even to younger preschool-age children (Flook et al., 2015).

Teaching Affective Empathy

Familiarity bias, one factor that increases affective empathy (Hoffman, 2000), posits that people intimately connect to those with whom they feel most familiar. For example, people tend to empathize with others whom they are in frequent contact with, who they consider to be in the in-group, who are friends, and who they perceive to be similar as themselves. The familiarity bias may be a factor in creating empathy in group-based activities, such as creating music together (Rabinowitch et al., 2012) or structured cooperative learning activities, such as jigsaws (Aronson, 2002). People also respond more emotionally and empathically to situations that seem more immediate, a phenomenon known as the here-and-now bias (Hoffman, 2000).

In addition to these contextual factors, various interventions seem to contribute to increased affective empathy. For example, priming for secure attachment can result in increased affective empathy and helping behaviors (Mikulincer & Shaver, 2005). Ways to prime for secure attachment might include reading a story in which a fictional character experienced secure attachment, exposure to the names and or images of close relationship partners or caregivers, or explicit directions to imagine one in a safe and secure scenario. Stupica and colleagues (2019) found that priming for secure attachment in elementary-aged children decreased their physiological responses of distress to potentially threatening stimuli. Given that distress can be a hindrance to empathic responsiveness, this study indicates perhaps that not only does priming for attachment seem to increase affective empathy in and of itself but it also seems to decrease barriers to empathy such as distress.

Promoting Prosocial Behaviors

The empathy-altruism hypothesis states that empathy leads to altruism via attachment. That is, an individual's perception of attachment leads to affective sharing of emotions and openness to the perspective of others, which then leads to altruistic behaviors (Batson & Shaw, 1991). However, whether altruistic behaviors more highly correlate with affective versus cognitive empathy is debatable. Generally, studies indicate a stronger correlation between affective empathy and altruism (Persson & Kajonius, 2016) but cognitive empathy nonetheless seems important as a contributor to altruistic behaviors (Carlo et al., 2010).

Further evidence of cognitive empathy correlating with altruism was provided by Underwood's and Moore's (1982) meta-analysis of school-age children, while correlations between affective empathy and altruism were inconclusive and varied widely amongst studies examined. Hence, it seems that cognitive empathy seems to have a consistent but moderate relationship with altruism. However, affective empathy may have the highest potential for the strongest correlation with altruistic behavior. Other factors also influence the interaction between affective empathy and altruism, such as the degree of personal distress, the context of the altruistic behavior, and if there is a reward or fear of punishment associated with the altruistic act.

Peters and Calvo (2014) posited three possible ways to increase prosocial behaviors. One is to address people's attitudes of who deserves compassion. For example, provide accurate psychoeducation about the roots of mental illness, obesity, and poverty, so that the blame for such outcomes does not fall on the individual. Second, they suggest addressing the empathic distress response, which often occurs when people believe that their prosocial behaviors are not connected to meaningful positive impacts. Hence, one way to address this is by explicitly connecting altruistic actions to positive differences in the real world. Another way to address the distress response is through compassion-training practices, such as meditation, which research has shown to increase positive emotions, decrease negative emotions, increase overall well-being, and promote prosocial behaviors. Lastly, there is some evidence for practicing prosocial behaviors leading to more prosocial behaviors.

Evidence-Based and Evidence-Supported School-Based Programs

Most evidence-based interventions for youth address empathy along with various other social-emotional constructs targeted. Malti and colleagues (2016) identified 19 social-emotional learning (SEL) programs that had empirical support, focused on empathy development, and were school-based for children PreK through eighth grade. They also found that programs targeting more empathy components most effectively decreased problematic behaviors and increased positive academic outcomes. Some examples of such programs that address both affective and cognitive components of empathy within a broader SEL program include the Incredible Years School Dinosaur Program (Webster-Stratton et al., 2008), PATHS (Conduct Problems Prevention Research Group, 2010), RULER (Brackett et al., 2012), Second Step (Holsen et al., 2008), and Interpersonal Skills Program (Vaughn et al., 1984).

However, evidence supporting school-based interventions that specifically target empathy is scant. There is one empirically reviewed program, Roots of Empathy, whose mission is to "build caring, peaceful, and civil societies through the development of empathy in children and adults" (http://www.rootsofempathy.org/). Through monthly visits by an infant and their caregiver(s) to classrooms, Roots of Empathy aims to decrease aggression while increasing social-emotional skills and prosocial behaviors for K-8 students. Evaluations of this program have shown teacher-reported decreases in aggressive behaviors and increases in prosocial behaviors, but no changes in empathy, perhaps due to the limitation of the self-report instrument used to measure empathy (Schonert-Reichl et al., 2012).

Another program, HEROES, specifically targets empathy and is designed for use by a broad range of school-based personnel with middle and high school students who display aggression. HEROES consists of several core activities that target mindfulness, gratitude, feelings identification, group cohesion, and perspective-taking via role-playing, direct imagination exercises, and applications of induction and distancing. These activities that can be done individually are as part of an eight-week structured curriculum designed for use in small group settings once a week. The eight-week structured HEROES curriculum has been evaluated in a randomized control trial with a sample of 26 high school students in foster care and/or in an alternative high school in an urban setting. Results showed statistically significant increases in affective empathy with a large effect size as well as a large effect size for increased cognitive empathy.

Other existing programs, such as Seeds of Empathy, an SEL curriculum for three- to five-year-old children, which similarly centers around infant-caregiver visits, and Start Empathy's *Toolkit for Promoting Empathy in Schools*, have not yet been evaluated.

Discussion and Future Directions

During this time in history, when the wealth divide is the greatest it has been since the 1900s (Saez, 2018); when schools are more segregated than during the civil rights era (Strauss, 2013); when hate crimes are increasing, especially in schools (Southern Poverty Law Center, 2017); and when rates of empathy seem to be decreasing (Konrath et al., 2010); it is perhaps more important than ever for societies to bring attention to the importance of empathy and to support efforts at cultivating empathy in youth. Despite research supporting empathy as a vital construct in promoting prosocial behaviors, encouraging moral development, resulting in positive academic outcomes, developing resilience, and reducing prejudice, there are few evidence-based interventions that specifically seek to foster empathy in youth. Although there are several evidence-based interventions that target empathy as part of a broader SEL program, the overall landscape of empathy intervention research seems to indicate a need for more innovation and creation of interventions as well as more research on how to effectively measure the full spectrum of empathy in youth. Furthermore, given the evidence that empathy has a domino effect such that those who experience empathy are likely to pass it forward (van Baaren et al., 2009), perhaps further research should be dedicated to not only increasing empathy in students via interventions targeted at youth but also via interventions targeted at caregivers of youth, such as school staff.

References

Abbott, N., & Cameron, L. (2014). What makes a young assertive bystander? The effect of intergroup contact, empathy, cultural openness, and in-group bias on assertive bystander intervention intentions. *Journal of Social Issues, 70*(1), 167–182. https://doi.org/10.1111/josi.12053

Ahammer, I. M., & Murray, J. P. (1979). Kindness in the kindergarten: The relative influence of role playing and prosocial television in facilitating altruism. *International Journal of Behavioral Development, 2*(2), 133–157. https://doi.org/10.1177/016502547900200203

Aronson, E. (2002). Building empathy, compassion, and achievement in the Jigsaw Classroom. *Improving Academic Achievement*, 209–225. https://doi.org/10.1016/b978–012064455–1/50013–0

Batson, C. D., Early, S., & Salvarani, G. (1997). Perspective taking: Imagining how another feels versus imaging how you would feel. *Personality and Social Psychology Bulletin, 23*, 751–758. https://doi.org/10.1177/0146167297237008

Batson, C. D., Lishner, D. A., & Stocks, E. L. (2015). The empathy–altruism hypothesis. *The Oxford Handbook of Prosocial Behavior*, 259–268. https://doi.org/10.1093/oxfordhb/9780195399813.013.023

Batson, C. D., & Shaw, L. L. (1991). Evidence for altruism: Toward a pluralism of prosocial motives. *Psychological Inquiry, 2*(2), 107–122. https://doi.org/10.1207/s15327965pli0202_1

Beelmann, A., & Heinemann, K. S. (2014). Preventing prejudice and improving intergroup attitudes: A meta-analysis of child and adolescent training programs. *Journal of Applied Developmental Psychology, 35*(1), 10–24. https://doi.org/10.1016/j.appdev.2013.11.002

Birnie, K., Speca, M., & Carlson, L. E. (2010). Exploring self-compassion and empathy in the context of mindfulness-based stress reduction (MBSR). *Stress and Health, 26*, 359–371. https://doi.org/10.1002/smi.1305

Bishop, S. R., Lau, M., Shapiro, S., Carlson, L., Anderson, N. D., Carmody, J., Segal, Z., Abbye, S., Speca, M, Velting, D., & Devins, G. (2004). Mindfulness: A proposed operational definition. *Clinical Psychology: Science and Practice, 11*, 230–241. https://doi.org/10.1093/clipsy.bph077

Blair, R. J. R. (2005). Responding to the emotions of others: Dissociating forms of empathy through the study of typical and psychiatric populations. *Consciousness and Cognition, 14*, 698–718. https://doi.org/10.1016/j.concog.2005.06.004

Bosacki, S. L. (2013). A longitudinal study of children's theory of mind and drawings of play. *World Journal of Education, 3*(5), 13–25. https://doi.org/10.5430/wje.v3n5p13

Brackett, M. A., Rivers, S. E., Reyes, M. R., & Salovey, P. (2012). Enhancing academic performance and social and emotional competence with the RULER feeling words curriculum. *Learning and Individual Differences, 22*(2), 218–224. https://doi.org/10.1016/j.lindif.2010.10.002

Bryant, B. K. (1982). An index of empathy for children and adolescents. *Child Development, 53*(2), 413–425. https://doi.org/10.1037/t01742-000

Burack, J. A., Flanagan, T., Peled, T., Sutton, H. M., Zygmuntowicz, C., & Manly, J. T. (2006). Social perspective-taking skills in maltreated children and adolescents. *Developmental Psychology, 42*(2), 207–217. https://doi.org/10.1037/0012–1649.42.2.207

Carlo, G., Knight, G. P., McGinley, M., Goodvin, R., & Roesch, S. C. (2010). *The developmental relations between perspective taking and prosocial behaviors: A meta-analytic examination of the task-specificity hypothesis.* In B. W. Sokol, U. Müller, J. I. M. Carpendale, A. R. Young, & G. Iarocci (Eds.), *Self and social regulation: Social interaction and the development of social understanding and executive functions* (pp. 234–269). Oxford University Press. https://doi.org/10.1093/acprof:oso/9780195327694.003.0010

Carlo, G., & Randall, B. A. (2002). The development of a measure of prosocial behaviors for late adolescents. *Journal of Youth and Adolescence, 31*, 74–44. https://doi.org/10.1023/A:1014033032440

Chang, L. (2003). Variable effects of children's aggression, social withdrawal, and prosocial leadership as functions of teacher beliefs and behaviors. *Child Development, 70*, 535–538. https://doi.org/10.1111/1467–8624.7402014

Chow, C. M., Ruhl, H., & Buhrmester, D. (2013). The mediating role of interpersonal competence between adolescents' empathy and friendship quality: a dyadic approach. *Journal of Adolescence, 36*(1), 191–200. https://doi.org/10.1016/j.adolescence.2012.10.004

Clore, G. L., & Jeffery, K. M. (1972). Emotional role playing, attitude change, and attraction toward a disabled person. *Journal of Personality and Social Psychology, 23*(1), 105–111. https://doi.org/10.1037/h0032867

Cohen, D., & Strayer, J. (1996). Empathy in conduct-disordered and comparison youth. *Developmental Psychology, 32*, 988–998. https://doi.org/10.1037/0012–1649.32.6.988

Coholic, D., Eys, M., & Lougheed, S. (2012). Investigating the effectiveness of an arts-based and mindfulness-based group program for the improvement of resilience in children in need. *Journal of Child and Family Studies, 21*(5), 833–844. https://doi.org/10.1007/s10826-011-9544-2

Conduct Problems Prevention Research Group. (2010). Fast Track intervention effects on youth arrests and delinquency. *Journal of Experimental Criminology, 6*(2), 131–157. https://doi.org/10.1007/s11292-010-9091-7

Cornell, A. H., & Frick, P. J. (2007). The moderating effects of parenting styles in the association between behavioral inhibition and parent-reported guilt and empathy in preschool children. *Journal of Clinical Child and Adolescent Psychology, 36*, 305–318. https://doi.org/10.1080/15374410701444181

Davis, M. A. (1980). A multidimensional approach to individual differences in empathy. *JSAS Catalog of Selected Documents in Psychology, 10*, 85. Retrieved from https://www.uv.es/friasnav/Davis_1980.pdf.

Day, A., Mohr, P., Howells, K., Gerace, A., & Lim, L. (2012). The role of empathy in anger arousal in violent offenders and university students. *International Journal of Offender Therapy and Comparative Criminology, 56*, 599–613. https://doi.org/10.1177/0306624x11431061

de Paúl, J., Pérez-Albéniz, A., Guibert, M., Asla, N., & Ormaechea, A. (2008). Dispositional empathy in neglectful mothers and mothers at high risk for child physical abuse. *Journal of Interpersonal Violence, 23*(5), 670–684. https://doi.org/10.1177/0886260507313532

de Wied, M., Goudena, P. P., & Matthys, W. (2005). Empathy in boys with disruptive behavior disorders. *Journal of Child Psychology and Psychiatry, 46*, 867–880. https://doi.org/10.1111/j.1469–7610.2004.00389.x

Decety, J., & Cowell, J. M. (2014). The complex relation between morality and empathy. *Trends in Cognitive Sciences, 18*(7), 337–339. https://doi.org/10.1016/j.tics.2014.04.008

Del Barrio, V., Aluja, A., & García, L. F. (2004). Relationship between empathy and the Big Five personality traits in a sample of Spanish adolescents. *Social Behavior and Personality, 32*, 677–682. https://doi.org/10.2224/sbp.2004.32.7.677

DeWall, C. N., Lambert, N. M., Pond, R. S., Kashdan, T. B., & Fincham, F. D. (2012). A grateful heart is a nonviolent heart: Cross-sectional, experience sampling, longitudinal, and experimental evidence. *Social Psychological and Personality Science, 3*(2), 232–240. https://doi.org/10.1177/1948550611416675

Edwards, G. S., & Rushin, S. (2018, January 18). *The effect of President Trump's election on hate crimes.* SSRN. https://papers.ssrn.com/sol3/papers.cfm?abstract_id=3102652.

Eisenberg, N. (2000). Emotion, regulation, and moral development. *Annual Review of Psychology, 51*(1), 665–697. https://doi.org/10.1146/annurev.psych.51.1.665

Eisenberg, N., & Miller, P. A. (1987). The relation of empathy to prosocial and related behaviors. *Psychological Bulletin, 101*, 91–119. https://doi.org/10.1037/0033–2909.101.1.91

Eisenberg, N., Mussen, P. H. (1989). *The Roots of Prosocial Behavior in Children.* Cambridge University Press.

Feddes, A. R., Mann, L., & Doosje, B. (2015). Increasing self-esteem and empathy to prevent violent radicalization: a longitudinal quantitative evaluation of a resilience training focused on adolescents with a dual identity. *Journal of Applied Social Psychology, 45*(7), 400–411. https://doi.org/10.1111/jasp.12307

Feshbach, N. D., & Feshbach, S. (2009). Empathy and education. In J. Decety & W. Ickes (Eds.), *Social neuroscience: The social neuroscience of empathy* (pp. 85–97). MIT Press. https://doi.org/10.7551/mitpress/9780262012973.003.0008

Flook, L., Goldberg, S. B., Pinger, L., & Davidson, R. J. (2015). Promoting prosocial behavior and self-regulatory skills in preschool children through a mindfulness-based kindness curriculum. *Developmental Psychology, 51*(1), 44–51. https://doi.org/10.1037/a0038256

Fredrickson, B. L. (2006). The broaden-and-build theory of positive emotions. In M. Csikszentmihalyi & I. Csikszentmihalyi (Eds.), *A life worth living: Contributions to positive psychology* (pp. 85–103). Oxford University Press.

Fullchange, A. (2017). *Effectiveness of an empathy intervention for youths at-risk.* Doctoral dissertation, University of California Santa Barbara.

Garaigordobil, M. (2009). A comparative analysis of empathy in childhood and adolescence: Gender differences and associated socio-emotional variables. *International Journal of Psychology & Psychological Therapy, 9,* 217–235. Retrieved from https://dialnet.unirioja.es/descarga/articulo/2992452.pdf.

Garner, P. W., Carlson Jones, D., Gaddy, G., & Rennie, K. M. (1997). Low-income mothers' conversations about emotions and their children's emotional competence. *Social Development, 6*(1), 37–52. https://doi.org/10.1111/j.1467–9507.1997.tb00093.x

Goldstein, T. R., & Winner, E. (2011). Engagement in role play, pretense, and acting classes predict advanced theory of mind skill in middle childhood. *Imagination, Cognition and Personality, 30*(3), 249–258. https://doi.org/10.2190/ic.30.3.c

Goldstein, T. R., & Winner, E. (2012). Enhancing empathy and theory of mind. *Journal of Cognition and Development, 13*(1), 19–37. https://doi.org/10.1080/15248372.2011.573514

Grant, A. M., & Gino, F. (2010). A little thanks goes a long way: Explaining why gratitude expressions motivate prosocial behavior. *Journal of Personality and Social Psychology, 98*(6), 946–955. https://doi.org/10.1037/a0017935

Hawk, S. T., Keijsers, L., Branje, S. J., van der Graaff, J., de Wied, M., & Meeus, W. (2013). Examining the Interpersonal Reactivity Index (IRI) among early and late adolescents and their mothers. *Journal of Personality Assessment, 95*, 96–106. https://doi.org/10.1080/00223891.2012.696080

Herrera, F., Bailenson, J., Weisz, E., Ogle, E., & Zaki, J. (2018). Building long-term empathy: A large-scale comparison of traditional and virtual reality perspective-taking. *PloS one, 13*(10), e0204494. https://doi.org/10.1371/journal.pone.0204494

Hoffman, M. L. (2000). *Empathy and moral development: Implications for caring and justice.* Cambridge University Press.

Jolliffe, D., & Farrington, D. P. (2004). Empathy and offending: A systematic review and meta-analysis. *Aggression and Violent Behavior, 9*, 441–476. https://doi.org/10.1016/j.avb.2003.03.001

Jolliffe, D., & Farrington, D. P. (2006). Examining the relationship between low empathy and bullying. *Aggressive Behavior, 32*(6), 540–550. https://doi.org/10.1002/ab.20154

Kahn, P. H., Jr. (2006). Nature and moral development. In M. Killen & J. G. Smetana (Eds.), *Handbook of moral development* (pp. 461–480). Erlbaum.

Knafo, A., Zahn-Waxler, C., Van Hulle, C., Robinson, J. L., & Rhee, S. H. (2008). The developmental origins of a disposition toward empathy: genetic and environmental contributions. *Emotion, 8*(6), 737–752. https://doi.org/10.1037/a0014179

Knight, R. (2010). Attachment theory: In search of a relationship between attachment security and preschool children's level of empathy. *The Plymouth Student Scientist, 4*(1), 240–258. Retrieved from http://bcur.org/journals/index.php/TPSS/article/view/295.

Konrath, S. H., O'Brien, E. H., & Hsing, C. (2011). Changes in dispositional empathy in American college students over time: A meta-analysis. *Personality and Social Psychology Review, 15*(2), 180–198. https://doi.org/10.1177/1088868310377395

Laible, D. J., Carlo, G., & Roesch, S. C. (2004). Pathways to self-esteem in late adolescence: The role of parent and peer attachment, empathy, and social behaviours. *Journal of Adolescence, 27*, 703–716. https://doi.org/10.1016/j.adolescence.2004.05.005

Lam, M. C. T., Kolomitro, K., & Alamparambil, F. C. (2011). Empathy training: Methods, evaluation practices, and validity. *Journal of MultiDisciplinary Evaluation, 7*, 162–200. Retrieved from http://journals.sfu.ca/jmde/index.php/jmde_1/article/download/314/327/0.

Leontopoulou, S. (2010). An exploratory study of altruism in Greek children: Relations with empathy, resilience and classroom climate. *Psychology, 1*(05), 377–385. https://doi.org/10.4236/psych.2010.15047

Losen, D., Hodson, C., Ee, J., & Martinez, T. (2014). Disturbing inequities: Exploring the relationship between racial disparities in special education identification and discipline. *Journal of Applied Research on Children, 5*(2), Article 15. Retrieved from https://files.eric.ed.gov/fulltext/EJ1188495.pdf.

Lovett, B. J., & Sheffield, R. A. (2007). Affective empathy deficits in aggressive children and adolescents: A critical review. *Clinical Psychology Review, 27*, 1–13. https://doi.org/10.1016/j.cpr.2006.03.003

Malti, T., Chaparro, M. P., Zuffianò, A., & Colasante, T. (2016). School-based interventions to promote empathy-related responding in children and adolescents: A developmental analysis. *Journal of Clinical Child & Adolescent Psychology, 45*(6), 718–731. https://doi.org/10.1080/15374416.2015.1121822

Marin, K. A., Bohanek, J. G., & Fivush, R. (2008). Positive effects of talking about the negative: Family narratives of negative experiences and preadolescents' perceived competence. *Journal of Research on Adolescence, 18*(3), 573–593. https://doi.org/10.1111/j.1532-7795.2008.00572.x

Mascaro, J. S., Rilling, J. K., Negi, L. T., & Raison, C. L. (2013). Compassion meditation enhances empathic accuracy and related neural activity. *Social Cognitive and Affective Neuroscience, 8*(1), 48–55. https://doi.org/10.1093/scan/nss095

Masten, C. L., Morelli, S. A., & Eisenberger, N. I. (2011). An fMRI investigation of empathy for 'social pain' and subsequent prosocial behavior. *Neuroimage, 55*(1), 381–388. https://doi.org/10.1016/j.neuroimage.2010.11.060

McCullough, M. E., Emmons, R. A., & Tsang, J.-A. (2002). The grateful disposition: A conceptual and empirical topography. *Journal of Personality and Social Psychology, 82*(1), 112–127. https://doi.org/10.1037/0022-3514.82.1.112

McMahon, S. D., Wernsman, J., & Parnes, A. L. (2006). Understanding prosocial behavior: The impact of empathy and gender among African American adolescents. *Journal of Adolescent Health, 39*, 135–137. https://doi.org/10.1016/j.jadohealth.2005.10.008

Miklikowska, M. (2018). Empathy trumps prejudice: The longitudinal relation between empathy and anti-immigrant attitudes in adolescence. *Developmental Psychology, 54*(4), 703–717. https://doi.org/10.1037/dev0000474

Mishna, F., Scarcello, I., Pepler, D., & Wiener, J. (2005). Teachers' understanding of bullying. *Canadian Journal of Education/Revue canadienne de l'éducation, 28*(4), 718–738.

Okonofua, J. A., Paunesku, D., & Walton, G. M. (2016). Brief intervention to encourage empathic discipline cuts suspension rates in half among adolescents. *Proceedings of the National Academy of Sciences, 113*(19), 5221–5226. https://doi.org/10.1073/pnas.1523698113

Overgaauw, S., Rieffe, C., Broekhof, E., Crone, E. A., & Güroğlu, B. (2017). Assessing empathy across childhood and adolescence: Validation of the Empathy Questionnaire for Children and Adolescents (EmQue-CA). *Frontiers in Psychology, 8*, Article 870. https://doi.org/10.1037/t64516-000

Peters, D., & Calvo, R. (2014). Compassion vs. empathy: designing for resilience. *Interactions, 21*(5), 48–53. https://doi.org/10.1145/2647087

Peterson, C., & Skevington, S. (1988). The relation between young children's cognitive role-taking and mothers' preference for a conflict-inducing childrearing method. *The Journal of Genetic Psychology: Research and Theory on Human Development, 149*, 163–174. https://doi.org/10.1080/00221325.1988.10532150

Pizarro, D. (2000). Nothing more than feelings? The role of emotions in moral judgement. *Journal for the Theory of Social Behaviour, 30*, 355–375. https://doi.org/10.1111/1468-5914.00135

Pouw, L. B. C., Rieffe, C., Oosterveld, P., Huskens, B., & Stockmann, L. (2013). Reactive/proactive aggression and affective/cognitive empathy in children with ASD. *Research in Developmental Disabilities, 34*, 1256–1266. https://doi.org/10.1016/j.ridd.2012.12.022

Praszkier, R. (2016). Empathy, mirror neurons and SYNC. *Mind & Society, 15*(1), 1–25. https://doi.org/10.1007/s11299-014-0160-x

Rabinowitch, T., Cross, I., & Burnard, P. (2012). Musical group interaction, intersubjectivity and merged subjectivity. In Reynolds, D., Reason, M. (Eds.), *Kinesthetic Empathy in Creative and Cultural Practices* (pp. 109–120). Intellect Press.

Ritter, K., Dziobek, I., Preißler, S., Rüter, A., Vater, A., Fydrich, T., Lammers, C., Heekeren, H. & Roepke, S. (2011). Lack of empathy in patients with narcissistic personality disorder. *Psychiatry Research, 187*(1–2), 241–247. https://doi.org/10.1016/j.psychres.2010.09.013

Saez, E. (2018). Striking it richer: The evolution of top incomes in the United States. In D. Grusky & J. Hill (Eds.), *Inequality in the 21st Century* (pp. 39–42). Routledge. https://doi.org/10.4324/9780429499821-8

Schaffer, M., Clark, S., & Jeglic, E. L. (2009). The role of empathy and parenting style in the development of antisocial behaviors. *Crime & Delinquency, 55*(4), 586–599. https://doi.org/10.1177/0011128708321359

Schonert-Reichl, K. A., Oberle, E., Lawlor, M. S., Abbott, D., Thomson, K., Oberlander, T. F., & Diamond, A. (2015). Enhancing cognitive and social-emotional development through a simple-to-administer mindfulness-based school program for elementary school children: A randomized controlled trial. *Developmental Psychology, 51*(1), 52–66. https://doi.org/10.1037/a0038454

Schonert-Reichl, K. A., Smith, V., Zaidman-Zait, A., & Hertzman, C. (2012). Promoting children's prosocial behaviors in school: Impact of the "Roots of Empathy" program on the social and emotional competence of school-aged children. *School Mental Health: A Multidisciplinary Research and Practice Journal, 4*(1), 1–21. https://doi.org/10.1007/s12310-011-9064-7

Shamay-Tsoory, S. G., Aharon-Peretz, J., & Perry, D. (2009). Two systems for empathy: A double dissociation between emotional and cognitive empathy in inferior frontal gyrus versus ventromedial prefrontal lesions. *Brain, 132*(3), 617–627. https://doi.org/10.1093/brain/awn279

Shapiro, S. L., Schwartz, G. E., & Bonner, G. (1998). Effects of mindfulness-based stress reduction on medical and premedical students. *Journal of Behavioral Medicine, 21*(6), 581–599. https://doi.org/10.1023/A:1018700829825

Shoshani, A., & Steinmetz, S. (2014). Positive psychology at school: A school-based intervention to promote adolescents' mental health and well-being. *Journal of Happiness Studies: An Interdisciplinary Forum on Subjective Well-Being, 15*(6), 1289–1311. https://doi.org/10.1007/s10902-013-9476-1

Southern Poverty Law Center. (2017). The Trump effect. Retrieved June 10, 2019 from https://www.splcenter.org/fighting-hate/intelligence-report/2017/trump-effect

Strauss, V. (2013). Report: Public schools more segregated now than 40 years ago. *The Washington Post.* https://www.washingtonpost.com/news/answer-sheet/wp/2013/08/29/report-public-schools-more-segregated-now-than-40-years-ago/

Strayer, J. (1993). Children's concordant emotions and cognitions in response to observed emotions. *Child Development, 64*(1), 188–201. https://doi.org/10.2307/1131445

Stupica, B., Brett, B. E., Woodhouse, S. S., & Cassidy, J. (2019). Attachment security priming decreases children's physiological response to threat. *Child Development, 90*(4), 1254–1271. https://doi.org/10.1111/cdev.13009

Teymoori, A., & Shahrazad, W. (2012). Relationship between mother, father, and peer attachment and empathy with moral authority. *Ethics & Behavior, 22*(1), 16–29. https://doi.org/10.1080/10508422.2012.638820

Thompson, K. L., & Gullone, E. (2008). Prosocial and antisocial behaviors in adolescents: An investigation into associations with attachment and empathy. *Anthrozoos: A Multidisciplinary Journal of the Interactions of People & Animals, 21*(2), 123–137. https://doi.org/10.2752/175303708x305774

Togut, T. D. (2011). The gestalt of the school-to-prison pipeline: The duality of overrepresentation of minorities in special education and racial disparity in school discipline on minorities. *Journal of Gender, Social Policy & the Law, 20*(1), 163–181. Retrieved from https://digitalcommons.wcl.american.edu/cgi/viewcontent.cgi?referer=&httpsredir=1&article=1553&context=jgspl

Trommsdorff, G., Friedlmeier, W., & Mayer, B. (2007). Sympathy, distress, and prosocial behavior of preschool children in four cultures. *International Journal of Behavioral Development, 31*(3), 284–293. https://doi.org/10.1177/0165025407076441

Trusty, J., Ng, K., & Watts, R. (2011). Model of effects of adult attachment on emotional empathy of counseling students. *Journal of Counseling and Development, 83*(1), 66–77. https://doi.org/10.1002/j.1556-6678.2005.tb00581.x

Underwood, B., & Moore, B. (1982). Perspective-taking and altruism. *Psychological Bulletin, 91*(1), 143–173. http://dx.doi.org/10.1037/0033-2909.91.1.143

van Baaren, R., Decety, J., Dijksterhuis, A., van der Leij, A., & van Leeuwen, M. L. (2009). Being imitated: Consequences of nonconsciously showing empathy. In J. Decety & W. Ickes (Eds.), *The social neuroscience of empathy* (pp. 31–42). MIT Press.

Van der Graaff, J., Carlo, G., Crocetti, E., Koot, H. M., & Branje, S. (2018). Prosocial behavior in adolescence: Gender differences in development and links with empathy. *Journal of Youth and Adolescence, 47*(5), 1086–1099. https://doi.org/10.1007/s10964-017-0786-1

Vaughn, S. R., Ridley, C. A., & Bullock, D. D. (1984). Interpersonal problem-solving skills training with aggressive young children. *Journal of Applied Developmental Psychology, 5*(3), 213–223. https://doi.org/10.1016/0193-3973(84)90019-4

Wang, Y., Davidson, M., Yakushko, O., Savoy, H., Tan, J., & Bleier, J. (2003). The scale of ethnocultural empathy: Development, validation, and reliability. *Journal of Counseling Psychology, 50*(2), 221–234. https://doi.org/10.1037/0022-0167.50.2.221

Webster-Stratton, C., Jamila Reid, M., & Stoolmiller, M. (2008). Preventing conduct problems and improving school readiness: evaluation of the incredible years teacher and child training programs in high-risk schools. *Journal of Child Psychology and Psychiatry, 49*(5), 471–488. https://doi.org/10.1111/j.1469-7610.2007.01861.x

Whitford, D. K., & Emerson, A. M. (2019). Empathy intervention to reduce implicit bias in pre-service teachers. *Psychological Reports, 122*(2), 670–688. https://doi.org/10.1177/0033294118767435

Woods, S., Wolke, D., Nowicki, S., & Hall, L. (2009). Emotion recognition abilities and empathy of victims of bullying. *Child Abuse & Neglect, 33*(5), 307–311. https://doi.org/10.1016/j.chiabu.2008.11.002

Yoo, H., Feng, X., & Day, R. D. (2013). Adolescents' empathy and prosocial behavior in the family context: A longitudinal study. *Journal of Youth and Adolescence, 42*(12), 1858–1872. https://doi.org/10.1007/s10964-012-9900-6

Youngblade, L. M., & Dunn, J. (1995). Individual differences in young children's pretend play with mother and sibling: Links to relationships and understanding of other people's feelings and beliefs. *Child Development, 66*(5), 1472–1492. https://doi.org/10.2307/1131658

Zorza, J. P., Marino, J., Lemus, S. D., & Mesas, A. A. (2013). Academic performance and social competence of adolescents: Predictions based on effortful control and empathy. *The Spanish Journal of Psychology, 16*(e87), 1–12. https://doi.org/10.1017/sjp.2013.87

15

INTEGRATING ASSESSMENT INTO SCHOOL ENVIRONMENTS TO PROMOTE STUDENTS' PSYCHOLOGICAL WELL-BEING

Beth Doll

A recurring finding of developmental risk and resilience research is that well-being and life success can be provoked even in the face of extraordinary risk by infusing protective supports into the important contexts where children develop (Masten, 2018). Schools, and particularly classrooms, represent one of the most important developmental contexts for children because that is where they will spend over 15,000 hours during their formative years (Rutter & Maughan, 2002). This chapter addresses the integration of data-based screening and progress monitoring into the facilitation and maintenance of school and classroom environments that support psychological well-being and resilience. Universal screening and progress monitoring are an increasingly common practice in school mental health services (NASP, 2016), and there are some instances of their use in school-wide and class-wide improvement programs (Kettler et al., 2014). Nonetheless, most applications of screening and progress monitoring address instances of disorders, disturbances, or behavior problems (Dowdy et al., 2015; Theron, 2016). Instead, this chapter describes available resources for screening and progress monitoring students' collective psychological well-being and competence in schools and classrooms. It articulates the contributions that such data make to the effectiveness of strength-promoting population-based intervention programs in schools.

Options for data-based assessments of school and classroom learning environments are numerous. However, only a few have evidence attached to them (Fraser, 1998) and assessments appropriate for screening and progress monitoring the psychological well-being of school environments are quite limited (Dowdy et al., 2015; Eklund et al., 2021). This is unfortunate since data-based decision-making is fundamental to school mental health practice and so is essential for interventions that promote well-being and resilience in schools (Doll, 2019). School psychologists' commitment to progress monitoring was prompted by Deno's (1985) use of brief curriculum-based measures (CBMs) to monitor the academic progress of students suspected of having learning disabilities. CBM was the precursor to present-day response to intervention (RtI), which uses progress monitoring measures to determine whether a student's learning or behavior improves in response to interventions. Subsequently, Sugai et al. (2000) merged RtI with a three-tiered prevention continuum to propose school-wide Positive Behavior Supports (PBIS) that use progress monitoring data to make decisions about students' need for intensive behavioral support services. Multitiered systems of support have become central features of comprehensive school psychological services (NASP, 2016).

Universal screening and progress monitoring are defining elements of multitiered systems of support. *Universal screening* is the assessment of the full enrollment of a school, with results used to

DOI: 10.4324/9781003013778-19

prioritize the most urgent needs for intervention and operationally define the purpose or goals for mental health services. Dowdy et al. (2015) describe this as moving:

> ...psychological services from the back of the service delivery system, where students are only provided services after significant symptoms of distress are present, to the front of the service delivery system, where all students are screened and provided access to a range of prevention or early intervention services.

(p. 179)

Progress monitoring is the administration of very brief assessments, repeatedly over time, and analysis of the data series for trends of increasing, decreasing, or unchanging scores. Progress monitoring facilitates schools' efficient focus on intervention strategies that are working. In the past, the primary goal of universal screening and progress monitoring was to identify and intervene with students who are most likely to experience psychological difficulties or behavioral disorders (DiPerna et al., 2014). This chapter extends the purpose of universal screening and progress monitoring to identifying and strengthening systemic supports for students' psychological well-being, moving psychological services even further forward in schools' service delivery system.

This chapter builds on substantial evidence that complete mental health includes both the presence of psychological well-being and the absence of disorders (Dowdy et al., 2015; Provencher & Keyes, 2011; Suldo & Doll, 2021). Maslow (1970) alluded to the importance of psychological well-being when he wrote that psychology had been more successful in revealing people's shortcomings than their potentialities. Subsequently, Seligman and Csikszentmihalyi (2000) dedicated the new century's first issue of the *American Psychologist* to psychological well-being. Since then, evidence has established the importance of psychological well-being to students' mental health and their school success. Examples include evidence that (a) students' subjective well-being predicts their academic grades and standard test scores (Bucker et al., 2018); (b) students' life satisfaction predicts their grades one year later (Ng et al., 2015); and (c) students' positive emotions predict stronger school engagement (Rose et al., 2017). Frameworks for implementing multitiered systems of support using a complete mental health model are articulated in Doll et al. (2021) and Suldo and Romer (2016).

This chapter describes emerging resources for screening and progress monitoring students' collective psychological well-being in school learning environments. It follows the Christ and Nelson (2014) framework for the development of universal screening measures and generalizes this framework to include universal and progress monitoring assessments of psychological well-being. The chapter first grounds the necessary content of such environmental assessments in substantial research on children's resilience, psychological well-being, and school climate. Next, it details requirements for optimal assessments for screening and progress monitoring the psychological attributes of school environments, as derived from standards for technical soundness and pragmatic constraints in school resources. The chapter concludes with descriptions of five assessments of school environments that operationalize this framework.

Implementing screening and progress monitoring assessments to strengthen schools' psychological environments is an effort in its infancy. Much needs to be done. Regardless, responsible practice demands that school resource deployment apply the principles of effective school mental health interventions when working to create positive learning environments.

Necessary Content for Assessing Positive Classroom Environments

A critical first step in any educational assessment development is a well-reasoned description of the measure's content (Christ & Nelson, 2014). The content defines the assessment items' breadth and depth and integrates the assessment with the decisions that might be made and actions that might be taken based on its results. Fortunately, three interlocking lines of research describe the contextual supports that predispose students toward psychological well-being: developmental resilience, psychological well-being, and school climate.

Developmental Resilience

The rich tradition of developmental resilience research rests on an accumulation of multiple large-scale longitudinal studies that meticulously documented the adverse experiences of very young children and then tracked the children's life outcomes as adolescents and adults (Werner, 2013). Results showed that children growing up with three or more significant life adversities were more likely to succumb to social, psychological, or educational distress. By the 1970s, the researchers turned their attention to the phenomenon of resilience—those children growing up with multiple and chronic adversities who, nevertheless, achieved successful adult lives (Masten, 2018). Although the studies were conducted on multiple continents and across decades, their results were remarkably consistent (Garmezy et al., 1984). Recognizing this, Masten (2014) compiled a short list of keystone factors that predispose children to resilience.

Table 15.1's first column describes Masten's (2014) short list. The top three resilience factors on her short list are relationships: (a) close and caring relationships between children and their parents, (b) of children with other important adults, and (c) of children with their peers. Indeed, most developmental resilience researchers recognize effective relationships as the foremost determinant of resilience in children (Theron, 2016; Ungar et al., 2014). The next four factors on Masten's (2014) short list are elements of children's developing human agency:[1] problem-solving skills, self-control and emotional regulation, motivation to succeed, and self-efficacy. The third set of factors describes children's belief that life has meaning, which may be represented through faith-based affiliation, personal hopefulness, and cultural spiritualism.

A compelling insight of developmental researchers is that the phenomenon of resilience is not a characteristic of children as much as a product of the interaction of children with the developmental contexts within which they are nurtured. In the words of Theron (2016), "resilience cannot be reduced to a purely psychological mechanism or to one for which children are primarily accountable. Instead, a social-ecological understanding tasks social systems—including schools—with the responsibility of actively co-enabling resilience processes" (p. 88). Nevertheless, Christmas and Khanlou (2019) have lamented that most contemporary approaches to youth resilience are still focused on individual behaviors, motivations, problems, and pathologies of the child. Luthar and Eisenberg (2017) conclude that the essential task is to minimize toxins and maximize nurturance in the everyday environments where children live and particularly school environments that are malleable and open to intervention.

Psychological Well-Being

In most respects, the factors described by Masten (2014) mirror those that Seligman (2011) identified in his theory of psychological well-being. Seligman's five elements of flourishing are positive emotions, engagement, relationships, meaning, and achievement, and are represented with the acronym PERMA. The second column of Table 15.1 describes Seligman's PERMA elements. Closely related descriptions of positive psychology include Keyes' (2006) description of flourishing, and Diener et al.'s (2009) description of subjective well-being, as indicated by high self-ratings of life satisfaction and more frequent reports of positive affect relative to negative affect. Kern et al.'s work (2015) provides support for the application of the PERMA framework to adolescents' psychological well-being although some subsequent work (Kern et al., 2016) suggests an adaption of this framework that retains most of Seligman's elements while substituting "perseverance" for Seligman's "accomplishment."

Table 15.1 Dimensions of Psychological Well-Being in School Environments

	Developmental Resilience (Masten, 2014)	Flourishing (Seligman, 2011)	Covitality (Furlong et al., 2014)	School/Classroom Climate (Thapa et al., 2013; Zullig et al., 2011)
Relationships	Close relationships with capable adults; close peer friendships	Relationships: people in my life who really care about me	Belief in others: peer support, school support, family coherence	Classroom social climate: peer friendships; peer conflict; teacher-student relationships
Human agency	Elements of human agency—problem-solving, self-control, emotional regulation; motivation to succeed, self-efficacy	Engagement; interest in learning new things Achievement: accomplishment for the sake of accomplishment	Belief in self: self-awareness, self-efficacy, persistence	Classroom achievement climate: interest in and likely success at learning—self-efficacy, academic expectations, mastery goals
Discipline			Emotional competence: emotional regulation, self-control, empathy	Disciplinary climate of classrooms: fair behavioral norms and student behavior consistent with these Safety climate: trust that students and teachers will be safe from harm
Meaning	Faith, hope, and belief that life has meaning	Meaning—what I do is valuable and worthwhile		
Happiness		Positive emotions; happiness and life satisfaction	Engaged living: gratitude, zest, optimism	Physical environment of the school: attractiveness, cleanliness, good repair

Building on the positive psychology research, Furlong and colleagues (2014) proposed a model of adolescent covitality based on four traits of psychological well-being, with three variables underlying each of the traits. In support of their model, they describe a two-stage factor analysis of the Social-Emotional Health Survey, a measure derived from the California Healthy Kids Surveys. The resulting model includes both relationship assets that support the student and internal social-emotional competencies that are students' personal assets. The third column of Table 15.1 describes Furlong's traits and the measured variables underlying each.

These varying definitions of psychological well-being are strongly intercorrelated (Furlong et al., 2014; Suldo & Doll, 2021). Specific to school environments, longitudinal studies have shown that life satisfaction and psychological well-being are positively related to later academic engagement, achievement, and grades (Ciarrochi et al., 2007; Datu & King, 2018; Ng et al., 2015).

A meta-analysis by Allen et al. (2018) affirms the impact that positive emotions and relationships have on students' sense of school belonging and, in turn, the importance of school belonging for students' academic adjustment including grades and scholastic competence.

School Climate

The importance of school climate was evident in the 1960s when researchers began using sociometric procedures to describe networks of social relationships represented in students' reports of classmates they did or did not want to work or play with (Barclay & Doll, 2001). A striking result was that sociometric data gathered in elementary school could be linked to high school graduation several years later. Although the use of sociometric procedures fell into disfavor, interest in school climate contributions to students' academic success did not wane. School climate researchers generally reference the social and psychological environment of a school or classroom as experienced by students or teachers. Subsequent research has linked positive school or classroom climate to higher academic achievement, more effective academic and social attitudes, higher school attendance, fewer behavior problems, and fewer instances of mental illness (Bear, 2011; Fraser, 1998; Zullig et al., 2010). Thapa et al. (2013) document positive school climate's contributions to students' *behavioral success* (e.g., reduced absenteeism and less aggression and harassment); *social success* (e.g., fewer psychological disturbances and less frequent substance abuse); and *academic success* (e.g., enhanced motivation to learn and higher grades).

Three comprehensive research reviews have identified common dimensions emphasized in school and classroom climate research: Thapa et al.'s (2013) review of school climate research; Zullig et al.'s (2010) examination of the assessment of school climate; and the National Research Council and Institute of Medicine's (2004) report on engaging schools. Classrooms' social climate is a prominent dimension in all three reviews. It consists of the social interactions that characterize a learning environment, incorporating peer friendships, peer conflicts, the relationships between students and their teachers, the adult-adult relationships of school staff, and relationships between the school and community. A second important dimension, achievement climate, describes the classrooms' extra-instructional practices that support students' learning: self-efficacy, self-determination, academic expectations, and the use of mastery rather than competitive classroom goals. All three reviews also mention the classroom's safety climate, describing students' and teachers' trust that they will be safe from physical, verbal, and social harm. Some climate measures distinguish a separate disciplinary climate of the classroom, referring to the perceived fairness of class rules and their enforcement. Some school climate measures also include an analysis of schools' physical environment including the attractiveness and adequacy of facilities. Table 15.1 describes these primary dimensions of classroom climate.

It is anomalous that programs promoting positive school and classroom climates are often evaluated by their effectiveness in preventing behavior problems (Bear et al., 2011). Indeed, Cohen et al. (2015) make a compelling case that school climate goals to foster student success must be more comprehensive than the simple prevention of problem behavior. Table 15.1 describes the attributes of safe, supportive, engaging, and flourishing school environments; it illustrates the very striking concordance across all three domains of research: developmental resilience, positive psychology, and school climate. Implications for assessing the psychological environments of schools are clear: items related to students' interpersonal relationships are of central importance for promoting psychological well-being, including teacher–student relationships and peer relationships. Items representing the achievement climate and support for human agency are also necessary to the measures. Two additional topics may be relevant for assessment: meaningfulness that students attach to their school lives, and students' perceptions of the safety of school environments.

Optimal Assessments of School Environments' Resilience

Within Cohen et al.'s (2015) agenda to promote psychologically healthy school environments, assessment serves as a mechanism to engage students, teachers, and families in school improvement efforts and to examine the impact of these efforts. Cohen et al. envision both comprehensive assessments of overall school climate as well as process assessments to mark progress over time, parallel in most respects to the universal screening and progress monitoring assessments that are the focus of this chapter. Similarly, Allen et al. (2018) remark on the urgent need to examine the extent to which interventions are effectively strengthening the key factors underlying school belonging, as a necessary next step toward fostering students' school success. Given the consistent and robust relationship between students' school success and school learning environments, one might anticipate that schools would be eager to examine their students' psychological well-being. It is surprising, then, that a recent national survey found that only 12.6% of 454 schools conducted school-wide screening of their students' emotional and behavioral health (Bruhn et al., 2014). Of the 57 schools that screened students for social, emotional, or behavioral competence, 38% conducted the screening once a year, with an additional 40% conducting the screening twice a year or more often. (The more frequent assessment schedules suggest that a few schools were using these assessments in a progress-monitoring fashion to assess change over time.) When follow-up questions asked why 397 of the schools were not screening, the most frequent reasons were that the schools were unaware that such screening existed, did not have sufficient funds for screening, and did not have access to screening assessments. Schools were also wary of labeling students and the concomitant responsibility for addressing well-being. They were concerned about parental backlash should the questions be seen as intrusive and less relevant to the schools' core academic mission.

Bruhn et al.'s (2014) survey asked schools whether they conducted "universal screening for the emotional and/or behavioral health of all students in the building" (p. 616). Instead, this chapter examines both universal screening and progress monitoring to describe students' collective psychological wellness. These differ in essential ways. Universal screening inevitably relates to the expenditure of resources (Dowdy et al., 2015). When planning for school-wide wellness promotion, universal screening's decision is one of systems-level prioritization: which dimension(s) of the learning environment, if strengthened, is most likely to boost the psychological well-being of students who learn there? Alternatively, in the more familiar universal screening for students' behavioral health, the unit of analysis is the student, and the decision of interest is an individual-level classification: Which students need school mental health services? Eklund et al. (2021) convincingly argue that school mental health systems risk overlooking essential school mental health needs if focusing too narrowly on either the individual students or the system to the exclusion of the other.

The assessments of school environments described in this chapter are student-completed scales, although some researchers prefer teacher-completed assessments or parallel forms from multiple raters (i.e., parents, teachers, and students). DiPerna et al. (2014) point out that teacher judgments of students' academic performance and social behaviors are both reliable and strong. Still, when teachers complete student-focused assessments for every student in a class, teacher fatigue becomes a significant problem that threatens the integrity of the data (Eklund & Dowdy, 2014). Brand et al. (2003) also discourage evaluations in which teachers complete assessments for a randomly selected subset of students because this might mask the degree and types of diversity among students that are essential aspects of climate. An advantage of students as respondents is that it is procedurally easier to collect ratings from a class full of students than for teachers to rate each student separately (Bear et al., 2011). Moreover, students can report internalized experiences that may not be visible to teachers (Eklund et al., 2021), and the student's voice is valuable for intervention planning

(Riley, 2004). Kearney et al. (2016) examined school climate using student completed data because, in their judgment, the definition of school climate implies experiences of the students. Similarly, Bear et al. (2011) constructed the Delaware School Climate Scale using student ratings because these assess the school environment as the students experience it.

One consistent finding is that teacher ratings and student ratings of the same climate almost always differ significantly. Bear et al. (2011) have found student ratings to be generally less favorable than teacher ratings. Similarly, Durlak et al. (2011) found that student self-report assessments of social-emotional learning programs generally yielded smaller effect sizes than parent reports or teacher reports. However, Chapla (2018) asked teachers to predict how their students would describe the classroom learning environment and found that students' perceptions were more positive than their teachers expected.

Which attributes are essential for the utility of universal screening and progress monitoring assessments of students' collective well-being? Christ and Nelson (2014) provide a reasonable response, "Assessments that do not meet the purpose, require too many resources, have limited relevance to student population, or lack technical documentation can be dismissed without further review" (p. 81). Given their purpose, universal screening assessments will need to be comprehensive, assessing the essential content dimensions represented in Table 15.1. Alternatively, progress monitoring assessments must focus on intervention programs' immediate goals and must be of a length and format that facilitates repeated administration and time-series analyses (Dart et al., 2019). Some progress monitoring assessments may be a portion or subscale of a more extensive universal screening assessment. For simplicity, this chapter will discuss the characteristics of learning environment assessments in three parts: the pragmatic requirements for assessment, the preferred item formats, and the technical soundness of assessments.

Pragmatic Requirements for Assessing Learning Environments

In Bruhn et al.'s (2014) survey, 80% of the schools did not believe universal screening was practical to do, reinforcing the importance of designing feasible assessments of classroom learning environments. Bear et al. (2011) used feasibility principles when designing the Delaware School Climate Survey: they constructed the assessment to be brief, easy to administer, requiring no more than 20 minutes of students' time, and available at very low cost to schools. So that trends in data could be compared across grades, they maintained the same assessment format in Grades 3–12. In a similar nod to pragmatics, Brand et al. (2003) examined the readability of the Inventory of School Climate-Student (ISC-S) to ensure that secondary students could read it independently. A readable assessment greatly eases the collection and confidentiality of screening assessments. Dart et al. (2019) explain the critical importance of a measure's face validity. Teachers and students who are fully engaged in designing and carrying out an assessment will find the data to be believable and worth collecting.

Ultimately, the value of an assessment is its utility for making decisions. When a universal screening demonstrates that a particular dimension of the learning environment is already quite positive, priority may be given to the enhancement of other dimensions of support. As one example, universal screening data for an urban middle school showed that teacher-student relationships were remarkably strong, but students' collective efficacy for learning was quite low. Upon reflection, the building team concurred. The team explained that some of their students lived in unheated Quonset huts and when their family's power was turned off, the teachers would tell them, "that's ok, we know that it was too hard for you to get this done." And by saying this, the team realized that they were reinforcing the students' beliefs about what they could not do without helping the students find ways that they *could* do it. The school's goal for the following year was to strengthen supports for their students' efficacy.

Progress monitoring assessments need to align with the purpose of the intervention, be capable of repeated administration, and be brief. Progress monitoring questions of interest are whether, in what direction and to what degree data collected over time show meaningful progress toward healthier well-being among students. Some assessments used for progress monitoring may be a subset of a universal screening assessment. There is no consensus on how often school-wide progress monitoring assessments should be collected. Eklund et al. (2021) describe varying practices from once annually to three times a year when screening to identify students with emotional or behavioral disorders. In Bruhn et al.'s (2014) survey, approximately 40% of the schools that conducted universal screening administered their assessments twice or more annually. In the middle school example, the building team's progress was monitored using only the academic efficacy subscale of their universal screening assessment as a time-saving strategy, administering it three times a year.

Preferred Item Format

Table 15.1 identifies five critical dimensions of school wellness that need to be in place if students are to flourish. Four of these represent attributes of students (students' access to close and caring relationships with teachers and peers; systemic reinforcement of students' developing human agency; the meaningfulness that schooling represents for the students; students' happiness and gratitude). Resilience research reminds us that these are also characteristics of the environment and, in the collective across all students enrolled in a school, could represent the availability of assets and supports for well-being. The fifth dimension underlying school wellness promotion represents attributes of the school management routines (the safety and disciplinary climate that the school provides to ensure order and security).

Is it best, then, that assessments of the school's learning environment include items describing the school or class (class statements) or items describing the students themselves (personal statements)? For example, the 2004 version of the ClassMaps Survey's (Doll et al., 2004) Following Class Rules subscale included four items worded as personal statements (e.g., "I follow the rules in this class") and four items worded as class statements (e.g., "Most kids follow the rules in this class"). Students routinely rated themselves quite positively while rating the class quite poorly, and teacher feedback was that ratings using the class statements were far more accurate. Consequently, the revised version of the subscale used only class statements (Doll et al., 2014). The opposite occurred when Fraser et al. (1995) compared assessments with items worded as "class statements" to parallel items worded as "personal statements." They found that student ratings using the class statements were systematically more favorable. Currently, there is no clear consensus on whether personal statements or class statements are preferable, and many assessments use a combination of these.

Brand et al. (2003) examined the impact of various item formats using the ISC-S, and their results showed that students' responses were more informative using a brief Likert-type scale rather than a *yes/no* response. The ISC-S used a 1- to 5-point scale for some subtests and a 1- to 4-point scale for others. Brand et al. advise that collating assessment data by classroom is quite appropriate for elementary students who spend most of the school day in a single classroom. They recommend collating data by school for middle- and high-school students because those students move from class to class throughout the day.

At the very least, universal screening assessments require parental notice and student assent. Parents should be informed about the purpose of the screening, allowed to review the items upon request, and provided with explanations of how the data will be used (Eklund et al., 2021). More intrusive questions will likely require positive and written parental consent, and so will require significantly more time and resources than screening assessments requiring only parental notice.

Beth Doll

Questions asking about typical school expectations related to learning will generally not require positive parental consent, while those that ask about student or family practices or behaviors unrelated to schooling are more likely to require positive consent under state or national record privacy statutes. In some cases, students complete the assessment anonymously, identified only by grade, gender, and homeroom. Students have reported that they prefer anonymity when completing the ClassMaps Survey, explaining that their responses will be more frank if their privacy is protected (Doll et al., 2014). Anonymous screening simplifies notice, assent, and administration procedures and is appropriate for school-wide or class-wide assessment. However, anonymity limits options for the collection of demographics or student-level outcome data. In this case, the school may not be able to examine group differences in students' experiences of the learning environment. Classroom teachers are also sensitive about the possibility that classroom assessment data might be misused for teacher evaluation decisions. Research using the ClassMaps Survey routinely reports classroom-level data only to the teacher, securing school leadership's advance approval to report only aggregated data to the building leadership team.

Technical Soundness

Since the allocation of scarce resources could be based on assessments of school environments, evidence for the psychometric soundness of these assessments is critical. This chapter applies Christ and Nelson's (2014) multistep framework for the development of universal screening measures extrapolated from classical test theory. Their first step is to use existing research to specify the essential constructs to include in a "blueprint" for the test. Table 15.1 illustrates this vital step; assessments that represent the constructs more accurately and completely will contribute to higher quality decisions.

A necessary next step is field testing the assessment with a sample to examine agreement between the drafted items and assessment "blueprint" (Christ & Nelson, 2014). This requires a careful analysis of the degree to which the construct, as defined, relates to the assessment's internal structure. Most researchers use factor analysis to compare the actual assessment structure to the proposed structure. In optimal designs where sample sizes are sufficiently large, exploratory factor analysis is performed on half of a sample to refine the assessment structure, and the refined assessment structure is analyzed using a confirmatory factor analysis with the remainder of the sample to test its fit to the data. When sample sizes are sufficiently large and diverse, analyses can examine the invariance of the assessment's structure across age, gender, ethnicity, social-economic status, or linguistic subgroups.

In almost every case, researchers report Cronbach's alpha coefficients of the refined assessment as a measure of each subscale's internal consistency reliability. Christ and Nelson (2014) recommend Cronbach's alpha values of 0.70–0.80 for subscales used for screening purposes and higher values (alpha > 0.90) for high stakes decisions. When using a measure for progress monitoring, the subscale reliability must be sufficient to use as brief, stand-alone progress monitoring measures. Agreement between teacher, student, and parent forms of an assessment is sometimes reported but, because adults and children have different experiences of the classroom, the inter-rater agreement is not necessarily expected in school environment assessments.

Subsequent validation of the assessment examines the degree to which the assessment predicts outcomes that the construct is presumed to predict. Ample preexisting evidence has accumulated to show that assessments of schools' psychological environments should predict students' subsequent school engagement and academic achievement. With sufficient numbers of schools represented in a sample, it might be possible to establish descriptive statistics (means and standard deviations) to examine differences among schools. However, because this research is almost always conducted with a volunteer sample, these descriptions are not used to represent normative standards. Instead, some assessments establish criterion-referenced standards for the assessment by convening an expert panel to review the assessment materials. A few assessments demonstrate criterion validity by reporting correlations between the assessment and other measures of classroom learning environments. Examinations of the criterion validity of universal screening and progress monitoring assessments are only useful if there is a well-established criterion measure of the construct (Christ & Nelson, 2016). It is unclear whether this is the case for positive attributes of school learning environments. Still, there are some examples of criterion comparisons for the assessments described in this chapter: Furlong et al. (2014) compared their Social and Emotional Health Survey to the Student Life Satisfaction Scale (Huebner, 1995) and the Positive and Negative Affect Scale for Children (Hughes & Kendall, 2009). Kearney et al. (2016) compared their Classroom Climate Index to the My Classroom Index (Fraser et al., 1982).

One of the best examples of a thorough examination of an assessment's construct validity is Brand et al.'s (2003) meticulous analysis of the Inventory of School Climate-Student[2] form (ISC-S; Felner et al., 1985). Data were available from 185 schools over three or more years and included measures of student success. This is a distinctive sample because of the number of schools they examined; other studies have impressive numbers of students and classrooms but represent relatively few schools. Brand et al. argue that the appropriate unit of analysis for school climate research is the school and not the student, and the best research designs will use a large number of schools as participants. Given their substantial dataset, Brand et al. were able to show that the ISC-S's factor structure remained stable over years. They compared the stability of school-wide climate ratings from one year to the next for 159 schools, reporting a relatively strong correlation ($r = 0.76$), and their results showed significant relationships between school climate and students' academic, behavioral, and socioemotional success in school.

Universal screening and progress monitoring of schools' and classrooms' learning environments are integrated inevitably into systemic change efforts. How might this occur? One example is Woods and Fraser's (1995) five-step process to improve classroom environments. First, students completed a questionnaire about the classroom. Next, the teacher was given feedback from the questionnaire. Third, the teacher then "engaged in private reflection and informal discussion" and decided what to do. Fourth, the teacher introduced a two-month intervention in response to the students' questionnaire. Fifth, the questionnaire was re-administered. Teachers who received the feedback achieved more improvements in the class than a control group who received no feedback. Yarrow et al. (1997) replicated this strategy with preservice education teachers, using the My Classroom Inventory (MCI; Fraser et al., 1982), and reported similarly positive results. The Resilient Classrooms strategy uses a similar process with one additional step: students review the group survey results and suggest possible strategies that teachers might select for improvement (Doll et al., 2014).

Selected Assessments of Positive Learning Environments

Despite a large number of assessments of school learning environments, only a few measures have evidence supporting their use, and fewer still have been peer-reviewed through publication in a professional journal. The situation is not new. Twenty years ago, Fraser (1998) reviewed nine classroom environment instruments and was disappointed to find that there was very little statistical information about them. Fifteen years later, Cohen et al. (2015) reported that most school climate measures were not developed in a scientifically sound manner. Similarly, Zullig et al. (2010) were only able to identify five school climate assessments that were student-reported scales, were consistently used, and addressed five historically common domains of school climate: order, safety, and discipline; academic outcomes; social relationships; school facilities; and school connectedness. Only one of the five assessments was supported by a report of its technical properties in a peer-reviewed journal. This exception was the California School Climate and Safety Survey (Furlong et al., 2005). Two additional assessments were identified by Zullig et al. as reporting some technical data but are no longer readily available (School Development Program survey; Haynes et al., 2001; and Comprehensive Assessment of School Environments; National Association of Secondary School Principals, 1987). Instead, Zullig et al. (2010) report that many school districts were using homemade instruments that are not psychometrically sound. Most recently the Safe and Supportive Learning website (2020) lists 23 approved school climate student surveys, with only six published in peer-reviewed journals.

Table 15.2 describes five assessments that are feasible assessments of the Table 15.1 dimensions with descriptions of their pragmatic assets, item format and content, and technical properties. Three of the assessments are for use with elementary classrooms, four for middle-level classrooms, and three for high schools. The item content of the five assessments overlaps to a greater or lesser extent with the dimensions of psychological well-being articulated in Table 15.1. All five assessments examine the quality of relationships in schools, and three of the five examine the three primary dimensions of relationships, human agency, and discipline/safety. The assessments' proposed structure of scales and subscales have been examined through both exploratory and confirmatory factor analyses. Each assessment's subscales demonstrate sufficient internal consistency to be used independently, as progress monitoring assessments of an intervention's specific goal for improvement. With one exception, the assessments' development and technical properties have been the subject of one or more peer-reviewed journal publications. The exception is the U.S. Department of Education School Climate Surveys (EDSCLS; NCES, 2015) which are supported by an extensive website with information on their structural analysis but have not been the subject of a peer-reviewed journal publication. These practical assessments are brief, low-cost options ranging in length from 21 to 53 items, allowing schools to use their limited resources for administering and responding to the assessments without budgeting for their purchase. Two of the assessments are part of state-supported efforts to promote optimal school learning environments, and one is provided through a national effort. The remaining two assessments represent independent lines of research.

Conclusion

For the past two decades, educational researchers have bemoaned the limited number and quality of surveys assessing school learning environments despite the overwhelming evidence that learning environments contribute in important ways to students' academic engagement, educational success, and mental health. The logistics underlying this research are challenging: the level of analysis for these studies are classrooms and schools, and it is difficult to secure the participation of a sufficiently large number of representative classes to thoroughly examine an assessment's structure and validity. Educators have been similarly critical of schools' decisions to use homemade instruments with little or no technical support and lacking a clear rationale. Such decisions are often born out of the pragmatic constraints of under-resourced schools that lack the funds and the time to implement costly and complicated programs of assessment. This chapter made the case that there are promising assessment options for elementary and secondary schools that incorporate content founded in the science of youth resilience and psychological well-being. The assessments share a commitment to building evidence of the assessments' reliability and validity, are carefully designed to be feasible for schools to adopt, and can support the data-based planning and progress monitoring of school-wide programs to promote the psychological well-being of all students. Nevertheless, these assessments represent primarily regional efforts, except for the federal EDSCLS-S. Sample sizes are small when characterized by the number of schools. While there is a growing consensus on the content that defines effective school learning environments,

Table 15.2 Selected Assessments of Positive Learning Environments

Description	Pragmatic Features	Item Format	Technical Properties
Delaware School Climate Survey (DSCS-S; Bear et al., 2011)			
An assessment of schools' social support and disciplinary climate for Grades 3–12	• Brief • Available at no cost to Delaware schools • Supported by a website describing programs and practices to strengthen climate	29 Likert-type items, worded primarily as school statements; describe teacher–student relationships; student-student relationships; fairness of rules; school safety; liking of school	A series of exploratory and confirmatory factor analysis involving 85 schools and 12,240 surveys confirmed the structure of the scale and its measurement invariance across grade, ethnic groups and gender. Subscale Cronbach's alphas range from 0.70 to 0.88; total scale alpha of 0.94. The DSCS-S correlated significantly with pass rates on standards assessments and school rates of suspensions and expulsions
Social and Emotional Health Survey-Secondary (SEHS-S; Furlong et al., 2014) and (SEHS-S-2020; Furlong et al., under review)			
An assessment of covitality [a composite of positive mental health indicators] for secondary students	• Brief • Available at minimal cost to California schools • Supported by a website describing social emotional health resources	36 Likert-type items, worded primarily as personal statements, describe belief-in-self (self-efficacy; self-awareness; persistence); belief-in-others (peer support, school support, family coherence), emotional competence (emotional regulation, empathy, behavioral regulation), engaged living (gratitude, zest, optimism).	SEHS-S-2020 and its measurement invariance across gender, grade, ethnicity, and Latinx status. Subscale Cronbach's alphas of the SEHS-S-2020 range from 0.59 to 0.65; total scale alpha of 0.68. Scores on the SEHS-S correlated with the Student Life Satisfaction Scale (Huebner, 1995) and the Positive and Negative Affect Scale (Hughes & Kendall, 2009).
Classroom Climate Index (CCI; Kearney et al., 2016)			
A measure of elementary classroom learning environments	• Brief • Available at no cost	21 Likert-type items worded primarily as class statements, describe supportive teacher behavior, supportive peer behavior, and student engagement.	A principal components factor analysis involving 17 elementary classrooms (and 2,340 students) confirmed the three factor structure of the scale. Subscale Cronbach's alphas range from 0.72 to 0.80. Subscale scores correlated ($r = 0.29$–0.56) with respective subscales of the My Classroom Inventory (Sink & Spencer, 2005)

(Continued)

Table 15.2 (Continued)

Description	Pragmatic Features	Item Format	Technical Properties
U.S. Department of Education School Climate Surveys-Student (EDSCLS-S; National Center for Educational Statistics, 2015)			
An adaptable resource for schools to use in collecting and reporting school climate.	• Available at no cost to schools in the United States; • Scores can be compared to results of other schools in the pilot sample; • Administration and analysis are supported by NCES although data are stored locally in school data systems.	63 Likert-type items describe engagement (cultural linguistic, relationships, school participation); safety (emotional, physical, bullying substance abuse); environment (physical, instructional, mental health, disciplinary).	Confirmatory factor analysis involving 92 schools verified the three-domain structure of the scale. Domain and subscale internal consistency reliability ranged from Cronbach's alpha of 0.72–0.91.
ClassMaps Survey (CMS; Doll, Spies, Champion et al., 2010; Doll, Spies, LeClair et al., 2010)			
A screening and progress monitoring survey of resilience-promoting characteristics of second–eighth grade classrooms;	• Available at no cost; • independently readable for fourth grade and higher; • subscales can be used independently for progress monitoring	55 Likert-type items worded primarily as personal statements describe teacher-student relationships; peer friendships; peer conflict; worry about bullying; home-school engagement; academic efficacy; academic self-determination; behavioral self-control	Exploratory and confirmatory factor analyses involving 2 elementary schools (345 students) and 42 middle schools (1,019 students) supported the eight-subscale structure Cronbach's alphas for subscales range from 0.78 to 0.92 for elementary classrooms, and 0.82–0.91 for middle-level classrooms

it is still clear that different assessments are aligned with varying research traditions. The feasibility of school-wide and class-wide universal screening and progress monitoring the well-being of students continues to challenge many schools even though these are critical components of school-wide programs to enhance the learning environments and, ultimately, the success of students.

Notes

1 Human agency is a term made prominent by Bandura (2006), and is defined as "to be an agent is to influence intentionally one's functioning and life circumstances" (p. 164). The term is infrequently used in school mental health contexts. In this chapter, human agency incorporates efficacy (expectations of success), self-management skills, goal setting, and monitoring, as well as self-control and self-regulation.
2 Like many of the classic school climate surveys (Fraser, 1998), the ISC-S is no longer readily available and the research team conducting this work has disbanded.

References

Allen, K. A., Kern, M. L., Vella-Brodrick, D., Hattie, J., & Waters, L. (2018). What schools need to know about fostering school belonging: A meta-analysis. *Educational Psychology Review, 30,* 1–34. https://doi.org/10.1007/s10648-016-9389-8

Bandura, A. (2006). Toward a psychology of human agency. *Perspectives on Psychological Science, 1(2),* 164–180. https://doi.org/10.1111/j.1745-6916.2006.00011.x

Barclay, J. R., & Doll, B. (2001). Early prospective studies of the high school dropout. *School Psychology Quarterly, 16,* 357–369. https://doi.org/10.1521/scpq.16.4.357.19900

Bear, G. G., Gaskinsm C., Blank, J., & Chen, F. F. (2011). Delaware School Climate Survey – Student: Its factor structure, concurrent validity and reliability. *Journal of School Psychology, 49*, 157–174. https://doi.org/10.1016/j.jsp.2011.01.001

Brand, S., Felner, R. D., Shim, M., Seitsinger, A., & Dumas, T. (2003). Middle school improvement and reform: And validation of a school-level assessment of climate, cultural pluralism and school safety. *Journal of Educational Psychology, 95*(3), 570–588. https://doi.org/10.1037/0022-0663.95.3.570

Bruhn, A. L., Woods-Grovers, S., & Huddle, S. (2014). A preliminary investigation of emotional and behavioral screening practices in K-12 schools. *Education and Treatment of Children, 37*(4), 611–634. https://doi.org/10.1353/etc.2014.0039

Bucker, S., Nuraydin, S., Simonsmeier, B. A., Schneider, M., & Luhmann, M. (2018). Subjective well-being and academic achievement: A meta-analysis. *Journal of Research in Personality, 74*, 83–94. https://doi.org/10.1016/j.jrp.2018.02.007

Chapla, B. (2018). *Shared perceptions of the classroom environment and the impact of teacher efficacy.* [Unpublished doctoral dissertation.] University of Nebraska Lincoln.

Christ, T. J., & Nelson, P. M. (2014). Developing and evaluating screening systems: Practical and psychometric considerations. In R. J. Kettler, T. A. Glover, C. A. Albers, & K. A. Feeney-Kettler (Eds.), *Universal screening in educational settings: Evidence-based decision making for schools* (pp. 79–110). American Psychological Association. http://dx.doi.org/10.1037/14316-004

Christmas, C. M., & Khanlou, N. (2019). Defining youth resilience: A scoping review. *International Journal of Mental Health and Addictions, 17*, 731–742. https://doi.org/10.1007/s11469-018-0002-x

Ciarrochi, J., Heaven, P. C., & Davies, F. (2007). The impact of hope, self-esteem and attributional style on adolescents' school grades and emotional well-being: A longitudinal study. *Journal of Research in Personality, 41*(6), 1161–1178. https://doi.org/10.1016/j.jrp.2007.02.001i

Cohen, J., Espelage, D. L., Twemlow, S. W., Berkowitz, M. W., & Comer, J. P. (2015). Rethinking effective bully and violence prevention efforts: Promoting healthy school climates, positive youth development, and preventing bully-victim-bystander behavior. *International Journal of Violence and Schools, 15*, 2–40.

Dart, E. H., Arora, P. G., Collins, T. A, & Doll, B. (2019). Progress monitoring measures for internalizing symptoms: A systematic review of the peer-reviewed literature. *School Mental Health, 11*(2), 265–275. https://doi.org/10.1007/s12310-018-9299-7

Datu, J. A. D., & King, R. B. (2018). Subjective well-being is reciprocally associated with academic engagement: A two-wave longitudinal study. *Journal of School Psychology, 69*, 100–110. https://doi.org/10.1016/j.jsp.2018.05.007

Deno, S. L. (1985). Curriculum-based measurement: the emerging alternative. *Exceptional Children, 52*, 219–232. https://doi.org/10.1177/001440298505200303

Diener, E., Scollon, C. N., & Lucas, R. E. (2009). The evolving concept of subjective well-being: The multifaceted nature of happiness. In E. Diener (Ed.), *Assessing well-being: The collected works of Ed Diener* (pp. 67–100). Springer.

DiPerna, J. C., Bailey, C., & Anthony, C. (2014). Broadband screening of academic and social behavior. In R. J. Kettler, T. A. Glover, C. A. Albers, & K. A. Feeney-Kettler (Eds.), *Universal screening in education settings: Evidence-based decision-making for schools* (pp. 223–248). American Psychological Association. https://doi.org/10.1037/14316-009

Doll, B. (2019). Addressing student internalizing behavior through multi-tiered systems of support: A commentary. *School Mental Health, 11*(2), 290–293. https://doi.org/10.1007/s12310-019-09315-3

Doll, B., Brehm, K., & Zucker, S. (2014). *Resilient classrooms: Creating healthy environments for learning* (2nd ed.). Guilford.

Doll, B., Dart, E. H., Arora, P. G., & Collins, T. A. (2021). Framing school mental health services within a dual factor model of mental health. In P. J. Lazarus, S. Suldo, and B. Doll (Eds.), *Fostering the emotional well-being of our nation's youth: A school based approach* (pp. 40–60). Oxford University Press.

Doll, B., Spies, R. A., Champion, A., Guerrero, C., Dooley, K., & Turner, A. (2010).The ClassMaps Survey: A measure of students' perceptions of classroom resilience. *Journal of Psychoeducational Assessment, 28*, 338–348. https://doi.org/10.1177/0734282910366839

Doll, B., Spies, R. A., LeClair, C., Kurien, S., & Foley, B. P. (2010). Student perceptions of classroom learning environments: Development of the ClassMaps Survey. *School Psychology Review, 39*, 203–218. https://doi.org/10.1080/02796015.2010.12087774

Doll, B., Zucker, S., & Brehm, K. (2004). *Resilient classrooms: Creating healthy environments for learning.* Guilford.

Dowdy, E., Furlong, M., Raines, T. C., Bovery, B., Kauffman, B., Kamphaus, R. W., Dever, B. V., Price, M., & Murdock, J. (2015). Enhancing school-based mental health services with a preventive and promotive approach to universal screening for complete mental health. *Journal of Educational and Psychological Consultation, 25*(2–3), 178–197. https://doi.org/10.1080/10474412.2014.929951

Durlak, J. A., Weissberg, R. P., Dymnicki, A. B., Taylor, R. D., & Schellinger, K. B. (2011). The impact of enhancing students' social and emotional learning: A meta-analysis of school-based universal interventions. *Child Development, 82*(1), 405–432. https://doi.org/10.1111/j.1467-8624.2020.01564.x

Eklund, K., & Dowdy, E. (2014). Screening for behavioral and emotional risk versus traditional school identification methods. *School Mental Health, 6*, 40–49. https://doi.org/10.1007/s12310-013-9109-1

Eklund, K., Kilgus, S. P., Meyer, L., & Barber, A. (2021). Using universal screening to monitor students' social, emotional, and behavioral health. In P. J. Lazarus, S. Suldo, & B. Doll (Eds.), *Fostering the emotional well-being of our nation's youth: A school-based approach* (pp. 484–505). Oxford University Press.

Felner, R. D., Aber, M. S., Cauce, A., & Primavera, J. (1985). Adaptation and vulnerability in high risk adolescents: An examination of environmental mediators. *American Journal of Community Psychology, 13*, 365–380. https://doi.org/10.1007/bf00911214

Fraser, B. J. (1998). Classroom environment instruments: Development, validity and applications. *Learning Environments Research, 1*, 7–33.

Fraser, B. J., Anderson, G. J., & Walberg, H. J. (1982). *Assessment of learning environments: Manual for Learning Environment Inventory and My Class Inventory* (ED223649). ERIC. https://eric.ed.gov/?id=ED223649.pdf

Fraser, B. J., Giddings, G. J., & McRobbie, C. J. (1995). Evolution and validation of a personal form of an instrument for assessing science laboratory classroom environments. *Journal of Research in Science Teaching, 32*, 399–422. https://doi.org/10.1002/tea.3660320408

Furlong, M. J., Greif, J. L., Bates, M. P., Whipple, A. D., Jimenez, T. C., & Morrison, R. (2005). Development of the California School Climate and Safety Survey–Short Form. *Psychology in the Schools, 42*, 137–149. https://doi.org/10.1002/pits.20053

Furlong, M. J., You, J., Renshaw, T. L., Smith, D. C., & O'Malley, M. D. (2014). Preliminary development and validation of the social and emotional health survey for secondary school students. *Social Indicators Research, 117*, 1011–1032. https://doi.org/10.1007/s11205-013-0373-0

Garmezy, N., Masten, A. A., & Tellegen, A. (1984). The study of stress and competence in children: A building block for developmental psychopathology. *Child Development, 55*, 97–111. https://doi.org/10.2307/1129837

Haynes, N. M., Emmons, C., & Ben-Avie, M. (2001). *The School Development Program: Student, staff and parent school climate surveys.* Yale Child Study Center.

Huebner, E. S. (1995). The Students' Life Satisfaction Scale: An assessment of psychometric properties with black and white elementary school students. *Social Indicators Research, 34*, 315–323. https://doi.org/10.1007/BF01078690

Hughes, A. A., & Kendall, P. C. (2009). Psychometric properties of the positive and negative affect scale for children (PANAS-C) in children with anxiety disorders. *Child Psychiatry and Human Development, 40*, 343–352. https://doi.org/10.1007/s10578-009-0130-4

Kearney, W. S., Smith, P. A., & Maika, S. (2016). Asking students their opinions of the learning environment: an empirical analysis of elementary classroom climate. *Educational Psychology in Practice, 32*(3), 310–320. https://dx.doi.org/10.1080/02667363.2016.1173015

Kern, M. L., Benson, L., Steinbert, E. A., & Steinberg, L. (2016). The EPOCH measure of adolescent well-being. *Psychological Assessment, 28*(5), 586–597. https://dx.doi.org/10.1037/pas0000201

Kern, M. L., Waters, L. E. Adler, A., & White, M. A. (2015). A multidimensional approach to measuring well-being in students: Application of the PERNA framework. *The Journal of Positive Psychology, 10*(3), 262–271. https://doi.org/10.1080/17439760.2014.936962

Kettler, R. J., Glover, T. A., Albers, C. A., & Feeney-Kettler, K. A. (2014). *Universal screening in educational settings: Evidence-based decision making for schools.* American Psychological Association.

Keyes, C. L. M. (2006). Mental health in adolescence: Is America's youth flourishing? *American Journal of Orthopsychiatry, 76*, 395–402. https://doi.org/10.1037/0002-9432.76.3.395

Luthar, S. S., & Eisenberg, N. (2017). Resilient adaptation among at-risk children: Harnessing science toward maximizing salutary environments. *Child Development, 88*(2), 337–349. https://doi.org/10.1111/cdev.12737

Maslow, A. H. (1970). *Motivation and personality* (2nd ed.). Harper & Row.

Masten, A. S. (2014). *Ordinary magic: Resilience in development.* Guilford.

Masten, A. S. (2018). Resilience theory and research on children and families: Past, present and promise. *Journal of Family Theory and Review, 10*, 12–31. https://doi.org/10.1111/jftr.12255

National Association of School Psychologists. (2016). *Ensuring high quality, comprehensive, and integrated specialized instructional support services* [Position Statement]. Author.

National Association of Secondary School Principals. (1987). *Comprehensive assessment of school environments.* Author.

National Center for Educational Statistics. (2015, August). *ED school climate surveys (EDSCLS) national benchmark study 2016.* Author. https://files.eric.ed.gov/fulltext/ED577461.pdf

National Research Council and Institute of Medicine. (2004). *Engaging schools: Fostering high school students' motivation to learn.* The National Academies Press. https://doi.org/10.17226/10421

Ng, Z. J., Huebner, E. S., & Hills, K. J. (2015). Life satisfaction and academic performance in early adolescents: Evidence for reciprocal association. *Journal of School Psychology, 53,* 479–491. https://doi.org/10.1016/j.jsp.2015.09.004

Provencher, H. L., & Keyes, C. L. (2011). Complete mental health recovery: Bridging mental illness with positive mental health. *Journal of Public Mental Health, 10,* 57–69. https://doi.org/10.1108/17465721111134556

Riley, A. W. (2004). Evidence that school-age children can self-report on their health. *Ambulatory Pediatrics, 4,* 371–376. https://doi.org/10.1367/a03-178r.1

Rose, T., Lindsey, M. A., Xiao, Y., Finigan-Carr, N. M., & Joe, S. (2017). Mental health and educational experiences among Black youth: A latent class analysis. *Journal of Youth and Adolescence, 46,* 2321–2340. https://doi.org/10.1007/s10964-017-0723-3

Rutter, M., & Maughan, B. (2002). School effectiveness findings, 1979–2002. *Journal of School Psychology, 40,* 451–475. https://doi.org/10.1177/0143034316664391

Seligman, M. E. P. (2011). *Flourish: A visionary new understanding of happiness and well-being.* Simon & Schuster.

Seligman, M. E. P., & Csikszentmihalyi, M. (2000). Positive psychology: An introduction. *American Psychologist, 55*(1), 5–14. https://doi.org/10.1037//0003-066X.55.1.5

Sink, C. A., & Spencer, L. R. (2005). My Class Inventory–Short Form as an accountability tool for elementary school counselors to measure classroom climate. *Professional School Counseling, 9*(1), 37–48. https://doi.org/10.1177/2156759x0500900112

Sugai, G., Horner, R. H., Dunlap, G., Hieneman, M., Lewis, T. J., Nelson, C. M., Scott, T., Liaupsin, C., Sailor, W., Turnbull, A. P., Turnbull, H. R., Wickham, D., Wilcox, B., & Ruef, M. (2000). Applying positive behavior support and functional behavioral assessment in schools. *Journal of Positive Behavior Interventions, 2*(3), 131–143. https://doi.org/10.1177/109830070000200302

Suldo, S., & Doll, B. (2021). Conceptualizing youth mental health through a dual-factor model. In P. J. Lazarus, S. Suldo, and B. Doll (Eds.), *Fostering the emotional well-being of our nation's youth: A school based approach* (pp. 20–39). Oxford University Press.

Suldo, S. M., & Romer, N. (2016). Integrating positive psychology in a multitiered system of support. In S. M. Suldo (Ed.), *Promoting student happiness: Positive psychology interventions in schools* (pp. 146–159). Guilford.

Thapa, A., Cohen, J., Guffey, S., & Higgins-D'Alessandro, A. (2013). A review of school climate research. *Review of Educational Research, 83*(3), 357–385. https://doi.org/10.3102/0034654313483907

Theron, L. C. (2016). The everyday ways that school ecologies facilitate resilience: Implications for school psychologists. *School Psychology International, 37*(2), 87–103. https://doi.org/10.1177/0143034315615937

Ungar, M., Russell, P., & Connelly, G. (2014). School-based interventions to enhance the resilience of students. *Journal of Educational and Developmental Psychology, 4*(1), 66–83. https://doi.org/10.5539/jedp.v4n1p66

Werner, E. E. (2013). What can we learn about resilience from large-scale longitudinal studies? In S. Goldstein & R. B. Brooks (Eds.), *Handbook of resilience in children* (pp. 87–102). Springer.

Woods, J., & Fraser, B. J. (1995, April). *Utilizing feedback data on students' perceptions of teaching style and preferred learning style to enhance teaching effectiveness.* Paper presented at the annual meeting of the National Association for Research in Science Teaching, San Francisco, CA.

Yarrow, A., Millwater, J., & Fraser, B. (1997, March). *Improving university and elementary school classroom environments through preservice teachers' action research.* Paper presented at the annual meeting of the American Educational Research Association, New York.

Zullig, K. J., Koopman, T. M., Patton, J. M., & Ubbes, V. A. (2010). School climate: Historical review, instrument development, and school assessment. *Journal of Psychoeducational Assessment, 28*(2), 139–152. https://doi.org/10.1177/0734282909344205

16

COMING TOGETHER

A Comprehensive Overview of the Transdisciplinary Perspectives of School Belonging

*Kelly-Ann Allen, Kathryn Riley, Annie Gowing, Michelle H. Lim,
Christopher Boyle, Roby Michalangelo Vota, Mark Richardson,
Melissa J. Wolfe, Tegan Cruwys, Mark Stevens, Erin Leif, Syed Marwan,
Rick van Der Zwan and Mark Ammermann*

Introduction

Interdisciplinary collaboration is necessary for the progression and solution of many social problems we face in society. Many research areas in academia are criticized for being siloed but this criticism is not leveled easily at school belonging. Many fields provide input into school belonging: social psychology, economics, design, urban design, architecture, neuroscience, education/school psychology, clinical psychology, inclusive education, behavior analysis, and creative arts education. Each field offers its own set of unique insights that contribute to a nascent collective understanding of what school belonging is, what it should be, and how to improve students' school belonging experience. To date, there is no published work that has encapsulated and integrated the salient work from different disciplines in one body of work. For the first time, this chapter integrates school belonging perspectives to explore commonalities and differences and contribute to the transdisciplinary growth and understanding of school belonging inquiry.

Defining School Belonging

School Belonging as a Sociological Concept

Belonging has a broad conceptual heritage, which partly contributes to definitional challenges (O'Brien & Bowles, 2013). Drawing on sociological theories, belonging has antecedents in the concept of alienation, which is an individual's response to the perceived unequal social structures in which they are situated (Seeman, 1959). Mau (1992) adapted Seeman's conceptualization to the school context by applying the dimensions of powerlessness, meaninglessness, normlessness, and social estrangement. In establishing the lineage between alienation and belonging, the dimension of social estrangement provides some shared ground. Socially estranged students have weak or non-existent links to any peer or friendship group and low participation rates in school activities (Mau, 1992). The concept of school membership emerged as sharing similar components to alienation with

DOI: 10.4324/9781003013778-20

Smerdon (2002) developing a measure of perceived school membership consisting of belonging, commitment to the school institution, and commitment to the school's academic requirements.

School Belonging in the Domain of Psychology

Various psychological perspectives conceptualize school belonging in similar ways, theoretically and empirically (Allen & Kern, 2017, 2019). Several proposed school belonging definitions have been described across the literature that include interchangeable terms (e.g., school connectedness; Lester et al., 2013; McNeely et al., 2002) and in-school practices (Allen et al., 2017a, 2018a). Goodenow and Grady's (1993) widely cited work defined a sense of school belonging as "...the extent to which they [students] feel personally accepted, respected, included, and supported by others—especially teachers and other adults in the school social environment" (p. 60). A qualitative meta-synthesis of students' perspectives on school belonging highlighted the importance of students' "feeling safe and secure in schools" (p. 1,422) and peer-to-peer relationships (Craggs & Kelly, 2018). Several psychological theories have been described across the literature regarding school belonging. These include the belongingness hypothesis (Baumeister & Leary, 1995), Bowlby's attachment theory (Bowlby, 1973), and self-determination theory (Ryan & Deci, 2000). A socioecological framework (Allen et al., 2016, 2018c) of school belonging was also proposed based on Bronfenbrenner's (1979) ecological systems theory. Several measures have been used to assess school belonging among student populations. These include the School Belonging Scale (SBS; Anderman, 2002), the Psychological Sense of School Membership (PSSM; Goodenow, 1993; Hagborg, 1998), and School Belongingness Scale (Arslan & Duru, 2016). Across the literature, there does not appear to be a gold-standard measure to assess school belonging. The variation of measures used to assess may stem from the variations that exist in how school belonging is defined.

Social Psychology and School Belonging

The social identity approach has become a cornerstone framework for social psychology, including for understanding group processes and behavior related to school belonging. The social identity approach combines social identity theory (Tajfel & Turner, 1979) and self-categorization theory (Turner et al., 1987). This perspective's central proposition is that people's sense of who they are originates from their view of themselves as both a unique individual (i.e., as "I" or "me"—their personal identity) and a member of the groups to which they psychologically categorize themselves as members of (i.e., their social identities). Social identities can be broad (e.g., as an Australian or American) or narrower (e.g., as a member of a particular school, university, and club). What is critical is the subjective sense of affiliation and self-definition in terms of group membership.

The social identity approach has made a vital contribution to our understanding of belonging. A large body of research—spanning domains including business and organizations (Van Knippenberg & Van Schie, 2000), health (Steffens et al., 2019), sport and exercise (Stevens et al., 2018, 2020), and, crucially, education (Mavor et al., 2017)—has focused on how the strength of one's social identification impacts a person's behaviors, experiences, and well-being. In education contexts, "school identification" has thus often been adopted as a more specific term for the extent to which students feel, in social identity terms, a sense of belonging at their school.

A Sense of Belonging in Urban Education

From an urban education perspective, a sense of place is emphasized. School belonging has been defined as that sense of being somewhere where a person is confident that they will fit in and be safe in their identity (Riley, 2017), a feeling of being valued (Flewitt, 2017) and at home in a place

(Yuval-Davis, 2006). The urban education perspective emphasizes that belonging is as much relational as it is cultural and geographic. In the global context of "alienation and disengagement, and the possibilities of radicalization," schools need to offer a "safe and secure environment for young people" in which "they can feel they belong" (Riley, 2017, p. 65). Providing this for students is particularly important for communities experiencing high levels of disadvantage or volatility.

Behavior Analysis and School Belonging

Behavior analysis provides a perspective on school belonging not readily visible in the academic literature. Behavior analysis is a pragmatic science devoted to understanding and improving socially significant human behavior that may also shed light on school belonging (Cooper et al., 2007). The field has not yet put forth a unified and conceptually systematic account of a student's sense of school belonging but has demonstrated a long interest in the scientific study of strategies for improving all students' social, behavioral, and academic development (Allen & Bowles, 2014). A sense of school belonging may be conceptualized as a value, a set of behaviors, and/or an outcome in behavior analysis.

The true meaning of school belonging may incorporate the interactions among values, behaviors, and outcomes within a school community. Values without corresponding action by school community members are likely to be ineffective at promoting all students' full inclusion and active participation. Actions not guided by values may fail to produce the type of outcomes deemed meaningful and essential by the school community members. Therefore, this perspective acknowledges that school belonging is *malleable* because it can be enhanced in a school setting through interventions and strategies.

School Belonging in Creative Arts Education

Creative arts education has also long accounted for belonging at school (Chappell et al., 2019) through process-driven and interdisciplinary aesthetic-affective pedagogies (Webster & Wolfe, 2013; Wolfe, 2013) that inherently account for creative and critical openings of affirmative difference and joyous affect. This generalized effect is evidenced by belonging that extends beyond the bell, where students congregate in the art room or the music room at lunchtimes and outside of school hours (see Webster & Wolfe, 2013). Creative, inclusive dialogues, affections, and interdisciplinarity are core creative arts education practices that are transferrable to other learning domains. Aesthetic-affective pedagogies of thinking-feeling (Massumi, 2015) inherent in arts education, account for an aesthetic mobilization of affect that inspires innovative approaches for teachers, students, and researchers to undergo learning (Dewey, 2005) through seeing, doing, and feeling that evokes situational interest (Tsai et al., 2008). Aesthetic and nonverbal communication should be scrutinized in education as both differential and culturally coded (Hickey-Moody, 2017, p. 1084). This understanding enables a potential for creative dialogues that facilitate and foster deep understanding and student belonging at school.

School Belonging and the Economics of Education

The area of *economics of education* may be the closest subject that can help conceptualize school belonging from a financial perspective (Dustmann et al., 2008; Hanushek & Welch, 2006). This field considers education as a form of investment in human capital. In this sense, school belonging can be viewed as an "output" of education investment. Like other forms of investments, this entails "returns on investment" through the productivity of human capital that it sustains. Also considered are the "investment costs" from the perspective of opportunity costs of ineffective educational programs and social costs of diminished school belonging (Dustmann et al., 2008; Lange & Topel, 2006).

Another consideration is the cost associated with a rapid increase in rates of exclusion, alienation, and a sense of *not* belonging in school that contributes to mounting concerns about the mental health, well-being, and life chances of children and young people. This concern is widely accepted and acknowledged across disciplines (Chodkiewicz & Boyle, 2017). The economics of education and the concept of school belonging are indelibly connected. Students with a low sense of school belonging have been shown to fail to thrive on factors such as positive youth development, including trusting others in the community, tolerance of ethnic differences, trust in authorities, and taking on civic responsibilities (O'Connor, 2010, p. 24).

School Belonging in Design Education

Belongingness is a central part of tertiary education in design, but it is often not explicitly termed *belonging*. Schools often describe themselves as a *vibrant, rich, pioneering community of creatives*, or use aggregative terms like *culture* and *social environment*. The membership to these creative social realities is conveyed through expressions such as *joining* or *immersing* in the community (Monash Art Design and Architecture, n.d.; Carnegie Mellon Design, n.d. a). Based on their self-presentations, design academic communities are defined by (a) *common purpose* (e.g., fostering social and environmental good; Parsons School of Design, n.d.); (b) *common practice* (e.g., share interests, discourses, and ways of doing things; RMIT University School of Design, n.d.); and (c) *shared effort* (e.g., we work together to create a social and supportive environment; Umeå Institute of Design, n.d.). In such design communities, a student's sense of belonging is reinforced by a social environment that pays attention to, respects, appreciates, and supports each learner (e.g., "students and staff who'll nurture, challenge and encourage you" [Monash Art Design and Architecture, n.d.]; "candidates are supported and engaged" [RMIT University School of Design, n.d.]; and "classmates who offer encouragement, critiques, and opportunities for collaboration" [Carnegie Mellon Design, n.d. b]).

One of the most explicit and rich vocabularies related to belongingness comes from Harvard University Graduate School of Design (n.d.) that developed the *Diversity, Inclusion, and Belonging* framework to

> be an example of a design community that can hold multiple identities and conflicting perspectives in an engaging and respectful way; one that is thoughtful of diversity and helps people understand how respect and acknowledgement of others allows us to be better design practitioners.
>
> *(p. 1)*

A Neuroscience Perspective of School Belonging

Humans evolved working in extended family groups, where everyone knew everyone and understood the social and functional hierarchies that made their little troop work. To operate effectively in those groups, humans developed brains that run a complex set of processes designed to understand and conduct social functions. Those processes use many different brain regions, including some dedicated to helping us operate in social environments—the social brain (Johnson et al., 2005).

The purpose of the social brain is to help us *read* others' minds (Changizi, 2009): People all signal, unintentionally and unconsciously, what they are thinking, how they are feeling, and what they are most likely to do next. Those signals can be expressions on their face, smell, and movements; and they can be what is said and how it is said. Being able to detect those signals, and interpret them, is essential for normal social functioning. Our social brain provides the tools for doing so unconsciously and automatically. In other words, our social brain allows us, with some degree of certainty, to predict others' future behavior.

People are best at predicting the future in environments where ambiguity and uncertainty are low. In social contexts, this means environments where people know what is expected and what to expect of others. In such environments, people can most easily begin to add value to the group and be recognized for that value. When we detect that recognition, when others signal to us our value to them, belongingness develops.

In that context, school belonging is a microcosm of belonging generally. Schools are communities, and integration into the school community is equivalent to being integrated into an extended troop of known and understood individuals. Shared purpose and predictability allow individuals to feel safe and to belong.

The Value of Belonging to School

The importance of a sense of belonging in school has been well-articulated in the literature across all disciplines. School belonging has high value to multiple fields interested in schools because of its links with academic outcomes, student motivation, and absenteeism (Goodenow & Grady, 1993; Louis et al., 2016). It also has a strong association with other positive social outcomes, such as health and well-being (Arslan et al., 2020; Putnam, 2000). Given the long-term outcomes in the literature associated with adults' psychological functioning, most disciplines value a sense of school belonging in young people (O'Connor, 2010; Steiner et al., 2019). In the field of clinical psychology, a low sense of school belonging is generally explicitly examined in the context of poor mental health and well-being. It is widely acknowledged that a low sense of school belonging is strongly associated with higher levels of depression, anxiety, and suicidal ideation (Allen et al., 2018a; Wyman et al., 2019). These factors alone make school belonging a relevant construct to all disciplines.

Feelings of safety and belonging are closely connected. For example, research in highly disadvantaged communities in Chile identified safety as a nonnegotiable prerequisite for a sense of belonging. Principals argued that children needed to feel visible and valued—and loved (Riley et al., 2017). Recent data from Trends in International Mathematics and Science Study (TIMMS; The International Study in Maths and Science) shows a strong link between children's sense of physical and emotional safety in school—a key aspect of belonging—and their academic performance in math and science (IEA, 2019).

Students' sense of belonging at school continues to be recognized as vital because it enhances student participation and successful trajectories postschool. In the social sciences literature, belonging is also recognized with regard to student engagement (McGarrigle, 2013; Solomonides, 2007); however, there is often less focus on belonging as a teachable entity within the pedagogy and curriculum assigned in the classroom. Dominant conceptions of belonging conceive that belonging pre-existed the student entering school and are derived from a psychoanalytical approach that grapples with fitting a preidentified square-shaped student into a preidentified round hole that is school. The different professions have varying approaches to practicing school belonging effectively.

Creative arts frameworks differ from psychoanalytic approaches, by drawing on the notion of *intra-action* (Barad, 2007, p. 33) with contemporary affect theories (Manning, 2016; Massumi, 2015) where student belonging is not reducible to the individual student. We posit that it is the material-discursive schooling processes as they are encountered that create belonging. New materialist thought accounts for "the unprecedented scale on which contemporary technologies, sciences and eco-crises produce ways of manipulating, living as and being affected by matter" (Tianinen et al., 2015, p. 5).

In design education, the concept of belonging is seen as a collective endeavor rather than something that can be done individually with students. Belonging's importance principally lies in its capacity to support collective creativity, problem-solving, and decision-making (Hennessy & Murphy, 1999; Ledwith & Lynch, 2017; Sanders, 2001). These are necessary to address social or technological problems that are too "wicked" for a singular creative genius. Besides increasing the efficiency and effectiveness of the design process, the sense of belonging to a design team and its design project is potentially relevant to increment design students' engagement and motivation in the project (Garner & Evans, 2015; Kreitler & Casakin, 2009; Reid & Solomonides, 2007), trust in teammates and lecturers (Holland et al., 2007; Watson et al., 2011), engage in collective and mutual learning (Chaves & Bittencourt 2018; Turnbull et al., 2012), and empathetically involve end-users, clients, and other stakeholders in design projects (Brueggemann et al., 2017; Lam & Suen, 2015; McDonagh et al., 2011).

School belonging can be valued in various measures of outcome from an economic perspective as well. In the case of the Development Impact Bond (DIB) Educate Girls program in India, the outcomes were student enrolment and learning, such as literacy rates (Loraque, 2018). There are also cases where investments in education are given monetary or numerical values, either from students' estimated future productivity output or by the estimated savings that the government/public gains from not spending on programs addressing social problems that result from a lack of school belonging. Additionally, there is also a qualitative valuation of outcomes where numerical estimates cannot be used as a form of measure, such as improvement in behavior and attitude (Bloomgarden et al., 2014). These valuations are continuously evolving, especially with the development of impact measurements from mechanisms such as social impact bonds (SIBs) and evidence-based policymaking.

In neuroscience, there is a concept known as the "critical period." These are times of brain development when experiences impact directly, immediately, and permanently on how processes and structures emerge and mature. Positive prosocial experiences are critical for normative development. School belongingness is an important factor for supporting the development of the social brain.

Because schools are communities, transitions between school levels often represent transitions between communities, sometimes and for some students, with little social continuity. Disruption of community, especially chronic disruption of social bonds, presents, at the level of brain functioning, as a threat. The ongoing disruption to feelings of belongingness that can arise after school transitions can impact students like chronic physical threats unless social bonds in the new school form quickly, impacting physical and psychological health and other cognitive functions (Eisenberger & Cole, 2012). In particular, perceived threat impacts creativity, imagination, and attention because in threatening environments, cognitive and attentional resources are given over to monitoring the environment more closely than otherwise is the case. In terms of social processing, cortical regions involved in monitoring the environment for threats also form part of the developing social brain. The potential to negatively impact learning and psychological well-being is clear and explored in several studies (Fu & Chow, 2017; Gold et al., 2015). Importantly, effective signaling of transitioning students' value to the new school community can ameliorate those impacts (Cooks et al., 2012).

Similarly, work with children of primary school age points to the importance of safe, nurturing environments on brain development, particularly for the development of Theories of Mind (ToM) and empathy (Gerdes et al., 2011). In particular, safe social environments are essential for developing both ToM and empathy for children aged 3–12 (Richardson et al., 2018). After 12, more recent brain studies have shown changes in the patterns of activity in parts of the social brain (Blakemore, 2008). Those data suggest that social functioning associated with belongingness remains critical through adolescence and into early adulthood.

The Main Issues of School Belonging from Transdisciplinary Lenses

Adoption of School Belonging

While school belonging is known to deliver multiple benefits to young people ranging from academic success to enhanced well-being (Abdollahi et al., 2020; Craggs & Kelly, 2018), recent sociological readings of belonging challenge an unrestrained embrace of the concept as universally delivering unqualified benefits. School belonging is a subset of broader scholarly theorizing within youth studies—a framing belonging within the context of identity, social change, inclusion, and temporal and spatial dimensions characterized by ambiguity, fluctuations, and precarity (Habib & Ward, 2020). School belonging emerges from these perspectives as interacting with individual and collective desires, dispositions, and discourses, resulting in a nonlinear, volatile, and continuously negotiated process. This understanding of belonging requires school communities to reimagine how they enable this process, particularly for students whose attachments are fragmented. When this does not happen, it can be argued schools failed to adopt practices and policies that maintain or increase students' sense of school belonging.

This potential failure to adopt school belonging practices is also noted through behaviorist disciplines. School-wide positive behavior support (SWPBS) is a practical example of behavior analysis in schools. SWPBS involves applying behavior and learning principles in a school context to minimize or prevent problematic behavior and enhance educational outcomes for all students (Horner & Sugai, 2015). It can also help students build a sense of school belonging through equitable and fair interventions and practices. Many factors hinder the adoption and sustained implementation of SWPBS, which may negatively impact school belonging. The main issue is priorities. The predominate educational climate leans toward a strong emphasis being placed on the academic achievement of students (Greenberg et al., 2003; Hardy & Boyle, 2011) at the detriment of school well-being and the presence of an inclusive and belonging environment (Allen & Boyle, 2018; Boyle & Anderson, 2020).

Supporting Vulnerable Children

For a growing number of young people today, home and community are not fixed, and schools represent one of the few continuity and stability points in their lives. Children from disadvantaged communities are twice as likely as their more advantaged peers to feel they do not belong. For too many young people, school life can be a dispiriting or dislocating experience (Riley & Rustique-Forrester, 2002). This dislocation becomes an economic concern for students from low socioeconomic circumstances who are most at risk (OECD, 2017).

The main issue related to school belonging in economics is arguably how the outcomes are defined and measured (Bloomgarden et al., 2014; Gertler et al., 2014). Another issue is the efficiency of allocating resources for effective programs or policies that address school belonging (Dustmann et al., 2008; Hanushek & Welch, 2006). As the school focus and expenditures emphasize academic results, economic concerns reinforce and sustain low priority funding for positive, effective school belonging programs that could benefit vulnerable students.

Further economic concerns are present for young people who see themselves as outsiders—they do not belong or feel excluded from school. These students are vulnerable to exploitation. Their access to education is limited, and they are more likely to become caught up in crime. The disaffected, excluded students search for belongingness elsewhere, finding it in many ways, including extremism (Roffey & Boyle, 2018), self-harming, and gang membership. Knowledge about what is happening to young people in schools can be separated into several silos: inclusion, exclusion, safety, special needs, well-being, physical and mental health, and cyberbullying. These silos make it difficult to understand the broader picture and the ways in which schools' practices shape young people's sense of belonging or exclusion.

Urban education perspectives suggest that young people's sense of *not* belonging in school is often reinforced by the experience of living in their community. For example, in the U.K. children from low-income families are four times more likely to be excluded than their more affluent peers (The Fair Education Alliance, 2017). These same young people are also more likely to experience the loss of public and relational space and the communities' dismantling.

Social Identity

Relative to other contexts (particularly business and health), research examining the consequences of social identification in school settings remains in its infancy. Nevertheless, initial findings point to its benefits for both students' well-being and academic performance. For example, among almost 700 Australian schoolchildren, Bizumic et al. (2009) found that school identification was positively associated with students' self-esteem and positive affect, and negatively associated with their anxiety and depression. More recent research also speaks to the generalizability of these findings to non-Western cultures, with Tong et al. (2019) finding evidence for correlations between school identification and reduced stress and depressive symptoms in a large sample ($N = 1,369$) of Chinese schoolchildren.

Concerning academic outcomes, recent research found a positive association between school identification and Australian students' objectively assessed writing and numeracy skills (Reynolds et al., 2017). One of the reasons for this link may be that school identification motivates students to engage more deeply with the content itself. In a university student sample, Bliuc et al. (2011) found evidence that people with a stronger sense of student social identification were more likely to engage in "deep" (as opposed to "surface") learning.

Mental Health and Well-Being

From a psychological perspective, one of the main issues related to school belonging is the potential impact on students' mental health and well-being (Allen & McKenzie, 2015). School belonging has been found to predict students' mental ill-health experiences, including anxiety and depression (Arslan, 2020; Arslan et al., 2020; Lester et al., 2013; Pittman & Richmond, 2007). School belonging research shows that disruptions to belonging can have a detrimental impact on short- and long-term well-being with particular implications for students' psychosocial adjustment and transition into adulthood (Steiner et al., 2019). Lester et al. (2013) found a reciprocal relationship between school connectedness and mental ill-health, although school connectedness was a stronger predictor of anxiety and depression. In particular, Arslan (2020) explored the relationship between school belonging constructs (i.e., social inclusion and social exclusion) and mental ill-health and reported feelings of loneliness mediated the relationships. Indeed, higher levels of loneliness are associated with poorer mental health (Matthews et al., 2018; Meltzer et al., 2013). These findings suggest loneliness may be a crucial factor to consider in examining school belongingness and the impact it may have on students' mental health (Arslan, 2020).

Skills and Competencies

As the literature discussed so far suggests, belongingness—being part of a safe and predictable community in which one is valued—is critical for normal social functioning and even more important for normal brain development from neuroscience and psychological perspectives. As such, skills like ToM empathy depend on children engaging in environments that are nonthreatening and are not neglectful. Children must be engaged, have opportunities to test their developing skills, and learn social functioning (Allen et al., 2017b). That means schools must create environments where all students feel valued and safe. Doing so allows the social brain to develop alongside the cognitive skills, typically the focus of learning. Indeed, psychologists, and particularly educational and developmental psychologists in schools, alongside educators, have an important preventative role to play in teaching children social and emotional skills so that they are equipped with the competencies to engage with others and feel a sense of belonging to school (Allen et al., 2018b; Frydenberg et al., 2012).

The Loss of School as We Know It

During COVID-19, students experienced a variety of school disruptions, ranging from near-empty classrooms to full school closures. Children with parents unable to provide home-based learning may have had further disruptions. Still, thousands of vulnerable children rely on school for safety, social support, and even breakfast or meal programs—these children will feel the impact the hardest. While a sense of school belonging is a vital psychological need for all children, school sometimes serves as the only place where the most vulnerable children belong. Their sense of belonging to school may be challenged even by the mere threat of losing access to school, as with the government-enforced school closures. How can we belong to a place to which we have no physical access? Suddenly, schools that usually offer a predictable, universal, and unerring place of belonging give way to uncertainty, undermining the manifest benefits they offer (Wyman et al., 2019). Digital technology (such as Zoom or Teams) has become much more ingrained into direct teaching in schools due to the COVID-19 pandemic. However, the evidence is unclear whether a sense of belonging can be achieved for students using this modality, however, the previous concerns about digital technology and belonging should be questioned following COVID-19 (Allen et al., 2014; Ryan et al., 2017).

Addressing Students Who Do Not Belong

Inclusive Education

In various disciplines, studies in inclusive education have addressed the overlap between inclusion and belonging in schools, with some scholars describing inclusion as a layered and complex form of belonging (Kovač & Vaala, 2019). Students' ongoing exclusion based on some form of difference is the failure of both inclusion and belonging policies and practices in schools (Anderson & Boyle, 2019; Boyle & Anderson, 2020). Addressing these failures requires a back-to-basics evaluation of young people's everyday experiences at school—this should include school-student power-sharing and pedagogical and relational in-class practices that are culturally responsive and respectful (Berryman & Eley, 2019).

Linking Theory to Practice

There are many other ways that the theory and practice of place and belonging can be anchored more firmly in school communities through an urban education perspective.

1   School-level practice: Collaborative research inquiry around the question "Is this school a place where everybody feels they belong? If not, what are we going to do about it?" generates a sense of agency and belonging with student-researchers and teacher-researchers (Riley, 2017).

2   System-level practice: Connecting the dots at a local school system level speeds up the process of change. Influenced by the work of Riley (2013, 2017, 2020), several school systems (e.g., Telford and Wrekin Council in England) are moving away from traditional behavior management approaches (with their overemphasis on rewards and sanctions linked to behavior) toward a humanist, relational, and universally inclusive approach (Telford & Wrekin, 2019).

3   Leadership: Understanding more about how school leaders shape the climate for belonging or exclusion through the lenses of leadership of *place* and *caring leadership* could yield rich rewards.

Leadership of place implies that leadership is a place-making activity, highly dependent on leaders' willingness to activate the physical and emotional spaces within schools, trigger the agency of staff and young people, and harvest the social capital that is too frequently ignored in communities. For leadership of place to be enacted, it requires intentionality and explicit theory of action that recognizes the importance of developing agency and building social capital (Riley, 2020) and it requires compassion (Riley, 2021).

Caring leadership is a dynamic ministry. Principals who demonstrate empathy, caring, and compassion are present. In the busy world of principalship, they are attentive to young people and what is going on in their lives. They ask humble and authentic questions and use their skills to cultivate caring communities (Smylie et al., 2020).

Efforts to develop social identification have already shown benefits in business, health, and sports settings (e.g., Haslam et al., 2017, 2019; Stevens et al., 2019). Although school-based work of this kind is in its infancy, recent research provides clues regarding how to achieve school identification gains. Tong et al.'s (2019) and Reynolds et al.'s (2017) research is especially informative in this regard, with both studies providing evidence for the role of school climate as an antecedent of school identification. Specifically, these studies suggest that schools which (a) adopt fair procedures, (b) foster strong staff-student relations, (c) instill a sense of shared mission, and (d) make academic expectations clear are most likely to imbue students with a strong sense of school identification.

Normal pedagogical practices emphasize that the production of belonging in the classroom is collective and generated in events through affective-aesthetic relations and actions. Educators should scrutinize enacted pedagogies in order not just to accommodate, but positively enact valued difference in classrooms. Pedagogical encounters are always relational and in situ and thus interfere (diffract) with and change affective intensities that can increase students' sense of belonging. Affect is felt, but this is not necessarily cognitive. Instead, it is felt as a sense of dis/comfort, a sense of belonging or even a heart flutter. This illustrates the complexity of the aesthetic dimension as it involves affect, "…emotions, social relationships, doing and undergoing (Dewey, 2005), feedback and further undergoing" (Webster & Wolfe, 2013, p. 32).

From an economics perspective, the recent development on tackling the issue of school belonging can be seen in SIBs and DIBs that seek to improve the accessibility and quality of education (Bloomgarden et al., 2014; Loraque, 2018). SIBs and DIBs are mechanisms that raise capital primarily from the private sector to fund social intervention programs. Returns are then provided to investors based on the achievement of outcomes or social impact. In doing so, there are different measurements of outcomes depending on the nature of the program.

The theory underlying this is arguably the theory of change, which looks at why the desired change is expected to happen from a particular input or particular context (Brook & Akin, 2019; Schindler et al., 2019). A methodology related to this is the social returns on investment (SROI), aiming to provide a consistent quantitative measurement of understanding the program's impact or outcome (Then et al., 2017).

Within design education, interventions that contribute to a student's sense of belonging include physical objects, digital systems, services, media, events, and spaces in the educational environment. These mediate the social interactions between students, lecturers, and other school staff and are typically brought about in one of two ways (but not necessarily mutually exclusive):

1 By design, designers are commissioned to design products, systems, services, and infrastructure that help foster belonging. In this instance, the students and/or learning facilitators are end-users and/or beneficiaries of the design incursions (see, for example, Vota's (2020) group learning experience about collective social intelligence).

2 Through design, designing with people with the express aim of building community and individual agency through collective participation. In this approach, school belonging is supported and incremented during the design process itself, sometimes as a by-product of designing for other goals (see, for example, CoMake Melbourne, n.d.).

Addressing Students with Low to No Belonging

Comprehensive screening of school belonging as part of existing school-based mental health screens has been proposed. These screening efforts seek to identify students at risk of or experiencing a reduced sense of belonging, who could benefit from targeted psychological interventions to improve their mental health and well-being (Moffa et al., 2018). One example program is Youth Mental Health First Aid, which educators can administer. Jorm et al. (2010) conducted a randomized control trial (RCT) to examine the effectiveness of a Youth Mental Health First Aid course for teachers across secondary schools in South Australia. Fourteen schools were assigned randomly into two conditions: (a) those who received the Youth Mental Health First Aid training course or (b) a waitlist group. Researchers found that teachers who engaged with the Youth Mental Health First Aid course reported increased knowledge about mental health difficulties in students and increased confidence in supporting students and colleagues, as well as reductions in elements of stigma. Further, teachers who had completed the course were a better source of information related to mental health for students (Jorm et al., 2010).

Implications for Practice and Research

The malleability of the varied understanding and approaches toward belonging offers schools many opportunities to be cocreators with young people. Working together to shape and create new spaces and places in which multiple possible selves can be welcomed and find connections should be encouraged.

Economic perspectives guide us to consider impact measurement mechanisms to ensure only effective school belonging programs are implemented and allowed to continue. SIB and DIB programs have provided a sound "proof of concept" (Nabers, 2016; OECD, 2016). It allows for an improved response from the government and policymakers, as numerical valuations can be presented for their consideration. What can be changed is the emphasis on innovation in policymaking as well as improvements in stakeholder engagement.

A key contention of the social identity approach is that one's group memberships structure individual psychology (and thus, behavior). This framework provides specific predictions about how school belonging can (and does) shape children's behaviors, while research underpinned by the social identity approach has yielded insights into how such belonging can be facilitated. A comprehensive account of school belonging requires the incorporation of the social identity approach.

Aesthetic-affective pedagogies of belonging should be instigated through creative arts practices across the subject domains as social mediation is created through aesthetic-affective production in situ. Belonging is not a binary term that is the opposite of nonbelonging but can be conceived as a sense of pulsing dis/comfort (Allen, 2020). The slash acts as a conjunction, to emphasize that dis/

comfort (or non/belonging) is not opposite or separate to comfort but integral to it (Wolfe, 2021). Such an approach moves beyond phenomenological and interpretive understandings of belonging to what is felt within classroom encounters as they occur. Nonlinguistic methods in both teaching and research open up possibilities for belonging through a critical dialogical and material processional approach that is making the community with students themselves. Pedagogical encounters are central to identity through intersectional (unspoken and spoken) dialogues. Educators (and their students) are obliged to notify the crafting of what counts and is privileged as a normative student (Wolfe, 2017) in order to encourage a re/affirming entangled difference of bodies, cultures, religions, and sexualities (Hickey-Moody & Willcox, 2019) that is more inclusive. This account necessitates prioritizing the senses, so often excluded in educational research, that assumes the sensuous as nonacademic and in conflict with educational assemblages' conventional rationality (Kenway & Youdell, 2011).

Programs designed to enhance students' sense of school belonging should consider additional training and support. Teachers and other relevant employees schools can receive training "...to identify early warning signs of mental illness, trained in mental health first aid, and informed of the appropriate referral and response pathways for students at risk" (Arslan et al., 2020, p. 12). Controlled studies are needed to evaluate the efficacy of psychological interventions that target improving mental health outcomes (e.g., depression and anxiety), difficulties related to feeling connected at school, or reduced feelings of loneliness amongst students (Arslan, 2019; Arslan et al., 2020). For example. Matthews et al. (2018) suggested that interventions aiming to reduce loneliness should focus on children or adolescents who experience bullying or social isolation from their peers or present with internalizing problems. Some psychological interventions attempt to increase social contact between students by focusing more on the quality of social contacts, not their quantity (Matthews et al., 2018). A meta-analysis of interventions targeting loneliness reported that the most impactful interventions addressed individuals' maladaptive social cognitions (Masi et al., 2011). Slaten et al. (2016) observed that some psychosocial interventions were developed to improve a sense of belonging; nonetheless, there is yet a dearth of research. Future research is required to specifically investigate psychosocial interventions aimed at addressing school belonging to develop an evidence-base toward the types of interventions that may be beneficial in promoting students' sense of belonging in schools to improve students' mental health and well-being. There is a pressing need to bring transdisciplinary theory, research and discourse together under one broad shared narrative—*belonging*. This would enable policymakers, practitioners, and researchers to understand more about the entirety of young peoples' lives. A cross-disciplinary framework that looked at young people's lives through social and relational, cultural and historical, and embodied and geographical dimensions (Cameron & Hauari, 2019) supports this.

Building on a Transdisciplinary Understanding

As sociology scholars continue to theorize about school belonging, the broad-brush understandings of this concept are likely to benefit from greater nuance and a deeper embrace of the multifaceted and malleable nature of what it means to experience belonging in the school setting. Schools can now act on current understandings of the concept that foreground belonging as agentic identity work (Habib & Ward, 2020) with young people storying themselves within their schools' social milieu.

SWPBS offers a framework for building schools' capacity to use evidence-based practices to support all students' social, behavioral, and academic development. However, behavior analysis has taught us that "...organizations do not behave, people behave" (Horner & Sugai, 2015, p. 82). Although SWPBS focuses on the whole school as the context in which intervention occurs, interventions derived from this framework focus on making environmental changes that alter teachers' and students' behavior in meaningful ways. A primary focus is on preventing disengagement (and maximizing school belonging) for all students. A secondary emphasis is on delivering individualized interventions and supports for students at risk for disengagement or who have already disengaged from school. Central to this framework is the adoption of systems (leadership, training, and coaching) to help teachers learn how to select, teach, and richly reinforce prosocial behaviors that may illustrate school belonging. Individualized interventions for students at risk are particularly important in light of research indicating that quality of life variables (e.g., inclusion, friendship, and choices) are less than optimal among students with disabilities and students with social, emotional, and behavioral problems (Huebner & Gilman, 2004; Sacks & Kern, 2008). Overcoming negative attitudes toward managing behavior is important to meet these objectives (Allen & Bowles, 2014).

Evidence from university settings highlights the need for researchers to consider the content of educational identities within efforts to enhance student outcomes by fostering their school identification. Here, research has shown that students' perceptions of other students' normative behaviors (i.e., people with whom they share an educational identity) impact their own behaviors. For instance, Smyth et al. (2015) found that university students' identification as a student in their field of study was associated with greater engagement in deep learning (see also Bliuc et al., 2011). This relationship was attenuated if, and to the extent that, students believed their peers were engaging in surface learning (see Smyth et al., 2017). Similarly, identification with one's student peer group was only positively associated with studying intentions if studying was normative among group members (Cruwys et al., 2017).

These findings align with a fundamental proposition of the social identity approach: categorizing oneself as a group member is associated with a desire to coordinate one's behaviors with those that are normative of other group members (Turner et al., 1987). They further speak to the value of this framework in helping us understand the consequences of belonging in educational contexts.

Artmaking in whatever medium allows for nonverbal and collective expression where students may negotiate differences and acceptance where "...the materiality of making is core to this process of expression" (Hickey-Moody, 2017, p. 1092). Belonging through transmissions of empathy is entangled within the creative arts subjects. It is nurtured through self/world-exploration, experimentation with technique, and the development of affirming risk-taking and critique. Space and time are provided for students to be, express, and to share. Making with material explorations is the language of art (Robinson, 2001). It is central to student belonging in the art classroom where the goal of making should not be the object produced but rather the growth and development of the maker (Garber, 2019) through the experience. Artmaking includes learning to feel-think with the materials of practice as experience (Ingold, 2013).

Design brings unique perspectives to interdisciplinary collaboration, being a form of research valued for its ability to continually and creatively challenge status-quo thinking (Gaver, 2012). Design is generative, speculative, provocative, propositional, ad hoc, risky, and opportunistic, targeting the user to create outcomes which are theories in themselves codified for a specific context (Haynes & Carroll, 2007). Above all, design develops situated solutions that, whether successful or not, help ground theories through artifacts, systems, and services that ultimately help negotiate pathways forward. In this way, design is provisional and occasionally right—instead of being extensible and verifiable. Theory produced by research through design (RtD) tends to be contingent and aspirational (Gaver, 2012), developing solutions that are optimal for current situations and focusing on proposing a preferred state (Zimmerman et al., 2010). With these principles in mind, design offers unique practice-based approaches to developing frameworks for belongingness through research practitioner reflection-in-action collaborative projects (Schön, 1983).

Belonging in schools is critical for well-being as the onset of emerging mental illness often occurs between 7 and 25 years old (Kessler et al., 2007). In an Australian survey examining the prevalence of mental illness in children and adolescents aged 4–17 years, approximately one in seven children and adolescents experienced mental ill-health, for example, anxiety and depression (Lawrence et al., 2015). The report outlined that child or adolescent mental illness appeared to impact slightly more on their family (19.5%) and school (17.6%) relative to their friends (12.4%) or themselves (14.4%). In particular, children and adolescents experiencing depression were associated with more school absenteeism, followed by anxiety disorders (Lawrence et al., 2015). A sense of low belonging may be a signal to monitor and assess for emerging mental illness.

A psychological perspective provides an opportunity to consider students' mental health and well-being (i.e., assessment, diagnosis, and treatment), alongside other factors related to their school environment (e.g., bullying, feeling lonely, or disconnected from peers). There is, however, limited research investigating the potential efficacy of psychological interventions aimed at improving students' sense of belonging at school. Thus, there is a need for future research to understand evidence-based psychological interventions for improving students' sense of belonging in schools.

While there is limited neuroscience research on school belongingness *per se*, there is a vast and growing literature on brain development in school-aged children, neurodiversity (autism and other neurological disorders), social functioning and environments, and stimuli positively and negatively impacting on development. This work provides something of a novel scaffold for understanding and developing new practices and approaches. Understanding how brains function at different stages of development, and what types of stimulation and experiences are critical during development can inform transdisciplinary research in ways that have not yet been explored. However, realizing these opportunities requires a common vocabulary and a shared understanding of what is meant by learning. In that context, there is a real opportunity to advance transdisciplinary programs and projects by beginning to unpack accepted paradigms using that shared vocabulary.

Concluding Comments

School belonging has been fashioned as a unique, crucial niche area of research by various disciplines and fields. Research to date has remained siloed in how school belonging has been discussed, yet, with so many interdisciplinary perspectives on the problem and potential solutions, it is at a detrimental cost to young people if researchers and educators do not work collaboratively. Globally there is a vast number of students who have low school belonging or do not feel like they belong to school. Without a systematic response, we will continue to see this number grow. A major contribution of this chapter was to initiate and build transdisciplinary conversations concerned with school belonging. The authors hope that it is the beginning of new collaboration pathways.

References

Abdollahi, A., Panahipour, S., Tafti, M. A., & Allen, K. A. (2020). Academic hardiness as a mediator for the relationship between school belonging and academic stress. *Psychology in the Schools*. https://doi.org/10.1002/pits.22339

Allen, K. A. (2020). *Psychology of Belonging*. Routledge (Taylor and Francis Group).

Allen, K. A., & Bowles, T. V. (2014). Examining the effects of brief training on the attitudes and future use of behavioral methods by teachers. *Behavioral Interventions*, *29*(1), 62–76. https://doi.org/10.1002/bin.1376

Allen, K. A., & Boyle, C. (2018). The varied pathways to belonging. In K. A. Allen & C. Boyle (Eds.), *Pathways to school belonging: Contemporary research in school belonging* (pp. 1–6). Brill.

Allen, K. A., & Kern, M. L. (2017). *School Belonging in Adolescents: Theory, research, and practice.* Springer Social Sciences. ISBN 978–981-10–5996-4

Allen, K. A., Kern, M. L., Vella-Brodrick, D., & Waters, L. (2018a). Understanding the priorities of Australian secondary schools through an analysis of their mission and vision statements. *Educational Administration Quarterly, 54*(2), 249–274. https://doi.org/10.1177/0013161X18758655

Allen, K. A., Kern, M. L., Vella-Brodrick, D., Hattie, J., & Waters, L. (2018b). What schools need to know about belonging: A meta-analysis. *Educational Psychology Review, 30*(1), 1–34. https://doi.org/10.1007/s10648-016-9389-8

Allen, K. A., & Kern, P. (2019). *Boosting School Belonging in Adolescents: Interventions for teachers and mental health professionals.* Routledge.

Allen, K. A., & McKenzie, V. (2015). Adolescent mental health in an Australian context and future interventions. *International Journal of Mental Health, 44*, 80–93. https://doi.org/10.1080/00207411.2015

Allen, K. A., Ryan, T., Gray, D. L., McInerney, D., & Waters, L. (2014). Social media use and social connectedness in adolescents: The positives and the potential pitfalls. *The Australian Educational and Developmental Psychologist, 31*(1), 18–31.

Allen, K. A., Vella-Brodrick, D., & Waters, L. (2016). Fostering school belonging in secondary schools using a socio-ecological framework. *The Educational and Developmental Psychologist, 33*(1), 97–121. https://doi.org/10.1017/edp.2016.5

Allen, K. A., Kern, M. L., Vella-Brodrick, D., & Waters, L. (2017a). School Values: A comparison of academic motivation, mental health promotion, and school belonging with student achievement. *The Educational and Developmental Psychologist, 34*(1), 31–47. https://doi.org/10.1017/edp.2017.5

Allen, K. A., Vella-Brodrick, D., & Waters, L. (2017b). School belonging and the role of social and emotional competencies in fostering an adolescent's sense of connectedness to their school. In E. Frydenberg, A. J. Martin, & R. J. Collie (Eds.), *Social and emotional learning in Australia and the Asia-Pacific: Perspectives, programs and approaches* (1st ed., pp. 83–99). Springer. https://doi.org/10.1007/978-981-10-3394-0_5

Allen, K. A., Vella-Brodrick, D., & Waters, L. (2018c). Rethinking school belonging: A socio-ecological framework. In K. A. Allen & C. Boyle (Eds.), *Pathways to belonging: Contemporary research in school belonging* (1st ed., pp. 191–218). Brill. https://doi.org/10.1163/9789004386969_011

Anderman, E. M. (2002). School effects on psychological outcomes during adolescence. *Journal of Educational Psychology, 94*(4), 795–809. https://doi.org/10.1037//0022-0663.94.4.795

Anderson, J., & Boyle, C. (2019). Looking in the mirror: reflecting on 25 years of inclusive education in Australia. *International Journal of Inclusive Education, 23*(7–8), 796–810. https://doi.org/10.1080/13603116.2019.1622802

Arslan, G. (2019). School belonging in adolescents: Exploring the associations with school achievement and internalising and externalising problems. *Educational and Child Psychology, 36*(4), 22–33.

Arslan, G. (2020). School belongingness, well-being, and mental health among adolescents: Exploring the role of loneliness. *Australian Journal of Psychology.* https://doi.org/10.1111/ajpy.12274

Arslan, G., Allen, K. A., & Ryan, T. (2020). Exploring the impacts of school belonging on youth wellbeing and mental health among Turkish adolescents. *Child Indicators Research, 13*, 1619–1635. https://doi.org/10.1007/s12187-020-09721-z

Arslan, G., & Duru, E. (2016). Initial development and validation of the School Belongingness Scale. *Child Indicators Research, 10*(4), 1043–1058. https://doi.org/10.1007/s12187-016-9414-y

Barad, K. (2007). *Meeting the universe halfway: Quantum physics and the entanglement of matter and meaning.* Duke University Press.

Baumeister, R. F., & Leary, M. R. (1995). The need to belong: Desire for interpersonal attachments as a fundamental human motivation. *Psychological Bulletin, 117*(3), 497–529. https://doi.org/10.1037/0033-2909.117.3.497

Berryman, M., & Eley, E. (2019). Student belonging: Critical relationships and responsibilities. *International Journal of Inclusive Education, 23*(9), 1–17. https://doi.org/10.1080/13603116.2019.1602365

Bizumic, B., Reynolds, K. J., Turner, J. C., Bromhead, D., & Subasic, E. (2009). The role of the group in individual functioning: School identification and the psychological well-being of staff and students. *Applied Psychology: An International Review, 58*(1), 171–192. https://doi.org/10.1111/j.1464-0597.2008.00387.x

Blakemore, S. J. (2008). Development of the social brain during adolescence. *Quarterly Journal of Experimental Psychology, 61*(1), 40–49. https://doi.org/10.1080/17470210701508715

Bliuc, A. M., Ellis, R. A., Goodyear, P., & Hendres, D. M. (2011). The role of social identification as university student in learning: Relationships between students' social identity, approaches to learning, and academic achievement. *Educational Psychology, 31*(5), 559–574. https://doi.org/10.1080/01443410.2011.585948

Bloomgarden, D., Eddy, M., & Levey, Z. (2014). *Social impact bonds & education in Latin America.* GEMS Education Solutions Ltd. Retrieved from https://www.instiglio.org/wp-content/uploads/2016/05/Eddy-et-al-SIBs-in-Education-in-LatAm-GEMS-White_Paper_FINAL.pdf

Bowlby, J. (1973). *Attachment and loss, volume 2: Separation.* Basic Books.

Boyle, C., & Anderson, J. (2020). Including into what? Reigniting the 'good education' debate in an age of diversity'. In C. Boyle, J. Anderson, A. Page, & S. Mavropoulou (Eds.), *Inclusive education: Global issues & controversies* (pp. 15–34). Brill. https://doi.org/10.1163/9789004431171_002

Bronfenbrenner, U. (1979). *The ecology of human development: Experiments by nature and design.* Harvard University Press.

Brook, J., & Akin, B. (2019). Using theory of change as a framework for examining community context and philanthropic impact. *Evaluation and Program Planning, 77,* 101708. https://doi.org/10.1016/j.evalprogplan.2019.101708

Brueggemann, M. J., Strohmayer, A., Marshall, M., Birbeck, N., & Thomas, V. (2017). Reflexive practices for the future of design education: An exercise in ethno-empathy. *The Design Journal, 20*(sup1), S1260–S1269. https://doi.org/10.1080/14606925.2017.1352655

Cameron, C., & Hauari, H. (2019). *Foster care disruption and belonging.* Institute of Education: Thomas Coram Research Unit.

Carnegie Mellon Design. (n.d. a). *International Network.* CMU. Retrieved from https://www.design.cmu.edu/content/international-network

Carnegie Mellon Design. (n.d. b). *Campus and facilities.* CMU. Retrieved from https://www.design.cmu.edu/content/campus-and-facilities

Changizi, M. (2009). *The vision revolution: How the latest research overturns everything we thought we knew about human vision.* Benbella Books.

Chappell, K., Hetherington, L., Keene, H. R., Wren, H., Alexopoulos, A., Ben-Horin, O., Nikolopoulos, K., Robberstad, J., Sotiriou, S., & Bogner, F. X. (2019). Dialogue and materiality/embodiment in science|arts creative pedagogy: Their role and manifestation. *Thinking Skills and Creativity, 31,* 296–322. https://doi.org/10.1016/j.tsc.2018.12.008

Chaves, I. G., & Bittencourt, J. P. (2018). Collaborative learning by way of human-centered design in design classes. *Strategic Design Research Journal, 11*(1), 27–33. https://doi.org/10.4013/sdrj.2018.111.05

Chodkiewicz, A. R., & Boyle, C. (2017). Positive psychology school-based interventions: A reflection on current success and future directions. *Review of Education, 5*(1), 60–86. https://doi.org/10.1002/rev3.3080

CoMake Melbourne. (n.d.) *CoMake Melbourne.* Retrieved from https://comakemelbourne.wordpress.com/

Cooks, J. E., Purdie-Vaughns, V., Garcia, J., & Cohen, G. L. (2012). Chronic threat and contingent belonging: Protective benefits of values affirmation on identity development. *Journal of Personality and Social Psychology, 102,* 479–496. https://doi.org/10.1037/a0026312

Cooper, J. O., Heron, T. E., & Heward, W. L. (2007). *Applied behavior analysis* (2nd ed.). Pearson.

Craggs, H., & Kelly, C. (2018). Adolescents' experiences of school belonging: A qualitative meta-synthesis. *Journal of Youth Studies, 21*(10), 1411–1425. https://doi.org/10.1080/13676261.2018.1477125

Cruwys, T., Gaffney, A., & Skipper, Y. (2017). Uncertainty in transition: The influence of group cohesion on learning. In K. I. Mavor, M. J. Platow, & B. Bizumic (Eds.), *Self and social identity in educational contexts* (pp. 193–208). Routledge.

Dewey, J. (2005). *Art as experience* (Trade pbk. ed.). Perigee Books.

Dustmann, C., Fitzenberger, B., & Machin, S. (2008). *The economics and training of education.* Springer.

Eisenberger, N. I., & Cole, S. W. (2012). Social neuroscience and health: Neurophysiological mechanisms linking social ties with physical health. *Nature Neuroscience, 15*(5), 669–674. https://doi.org/10.1038/nn.3086

Flewitt, R. S. (2017). Equity and diversity through story: A multimodal perspective. In T. Cremin, R. S. Flewitt, B. Mardell, & J. Swann, J. (Eds.), *Storytelling in early childhood: Enriching language, literacy, and classroom culture* (pp. 150–168). Routledge.

Frydenberg, E., Deans, J., & O'Brien, K. A. (2012). *Developing children's coping in the early years: Strategies for dealing with stress, change and anxiety.* Bloomsbury. ISBN: 9781441161048

Fu, F., & Chow, A. (2017). Traumatic exposure and psychological well-being: The moderating role of cognitive flexibility. *Journal of Loss and Trauma, 22*(1), 24–35. https://doi.org/10.1080/15325024.2016.1161428

Garber, E. (2019). Objects and new materialisms: A journey across making and living with objects. *Studies in Art Education, 60*(1), 7–21. https://doi.org/10.1080/00393541.2018.1557454

Garner, S., & Evans, C. (2015). Fostering motivation in undergraduate design education. In M. M Tovey (Ed.), *Design pedagogy: Developments in art and design education* (pp. 69–81). Ashgate.

Gaver, W. (2012). What should we expect from research through design? In J. A. Konstan, E. Chi, & K. Höök (Eds.), *Proceedings of the SIGCHI conference on human factors in computing systems* (pp. 937–946). ACM Press.

Gerdes, K. E., Segal, E. A., Jackson, K. F., & Mullins J. L. (2011). Teaching empathy: A framework rooted in social cognitive neuroscience and social justice. *Journal of Social Work Education, 47,* 109–131. https://doi.org/10.5175/JSWE.2011.200900085

Gertler, P., Heckman, J., Pinto, R., Zanolini, A., Vermeersch, C., Walker, S., Chang, S. M., & Grantham-Mc-Gregor, S. (2014). Labor market returns to an early childhood stimulation intervention in Jamaica. *Science, 344*(6187), 998–1001. https://doi.org/10.1126/science.1251178

Gold, A. L., Morey, R. A., & McCarthy, G. (2015). Amygdala–Prefrontal Cortex functional connectivity during threat-induced anxiety and goal distraction. *Biological Psychiatry, 77*, 394–403. https://doi.org/10.1016/j.biopsych.2014.03.030

Goodenow, C. (1993). The psychological sense of school membership among adolescents: Scale development and educational correlates. *Psychology in the Schools, 30*(1), 79–90. https://doi.org/10.1002/1520-6807(199301)30:1

Goodenow, C., & Grady, K. E. (1993). The relationship of school belonging and friends' values to academic motivation among urban adolescent students. *The Journal of Experimental Education, 62*(1), 60–71. https://doi.org/10.1080/00220973.1993.9943831

Greenberg, M. T., Weissberg, R. P., O'Brien, M. U., Zins, J. E., Fredericks, L., Resnik, H., & Elias, M. J. (2003). Enhancing school-based prevention and youth development through coordinated social, emotional, and academic learning. *American Psychologist, 58*(6–7), 466–474. https://doi.org/10.1037/0003-066x.58.6-7.466

Habib, S., & Ward, M. R. M. (2020). *Youth, place and theories of belonging.* Routledge.

Hagborg, W. J. (1998). An investigation of a brief measure of school membership. *Adolescence, 33*(130), 461–468.

Hanushek, E. A., & Welch, F. (2006). *Handbook of the economics of education* (Vol. 1). North Holland.

Hardy, I., & Boyle C. (2011). My school? Critiquing the abstraction and quantification of education. *Asia-Pacific Journal of Teacher Education, 39*(3), 211–222. http://dx.doi.org/10.1080/1359866X.2011.588312

Harvard University Graduate School of Design. (n.d.). *Commitment to diversity, inclusion, and belonging.* Harvard University GSD. Retrieved from https://www.gsd.harvard.edu/commitment-to-diversity-inclusion-and-belonging/

Haslam, C., Cruwys, T., Chang, M. X. L., Bentley, S. V., Haslam, S. A., Dingle, G. A., & Jetten, J. (2019). GROUPS 4 HEALTH reduces loneliness and social anxiety in adults with psychological distress: Findings from a randomized controlled trial. *Journal of Consulting and Clinical Psychology, 87*, 787–801. https://doi.org/10.1037/ccp0000427

Haslam, S. A., Steffens, N. K., Peters, K., Boyce, R. A., Mallett, C. J., & Fransen, K. (2017). A social identity approach to leadership development: The 5R program. *Journal of Personnel Psychology, 16*(3), 113–124. https://doi.org/10.1027/1866-5888/a000176

Haynes, S. R., & Carroll, J. M. (2007). Theoretical design science in human–Computer interaction: A practical concern? *Artifact: Journal of Design Practice, 1*(3), 159–171. https://doi.org/10.1080/17493460701872016

Hennessy, S., & Murphy, P. (1999). The potential for collaborative problem solving in design and technology. *International Journal of Technology and Design Education, 9*(1), 1–36. https://doi.org/10.1023/A:1008855526312

Hickey-Moody, A. C. (2017). Arts practice as method, urban spaces and intra-active faiths. *International Journal of Inclusive Education, 21*(11), 1083–1096. https://doi.org/10.1080/13603116.2017.1350317

Hickey-Moody, A., & Willcox, M. (2019). Entanglements of difference as community togetherness: Faith, art and feminism. *Social Sciences, 8*(9), 264. https://doi.org/10.3390/socsci8090264

Holland, R., Kim, B., Kang, B., & Borja de Mozota, B. (2007). Design education for successful cross-functional cooperation in NPD. In *DS 43: Proceedings of E&PDE 2007, the 9th International Conference on Engineering and Product Design Education.* University of Northumbria, Newcastle, UK.

Horner, R. H., & Sugai, G. (2015). School-wide PBIS: An example of applied behavior analysis implemented at a scale of social importance. *Behavior Analysis in Practice, 8*(1), 80–85. https://doi.org/10.1007/s40617-015-0045-4

Huebner, E. S., & Gilman, R. (2004). Perceived quality of life: A neglected component of assessments and intervention plans for students in school settings. *California School Psychologist, 9*, 127–134. https://doi.org/10.1007/BF03340913

IEA (2019). *Trends in International Mathematics and Science Study.* IEA. Retrieved from https://www.iea.nl/studies/iea/timss

Ingold, T. (2013). *Making: Anthropology, archaeology, art and architecture.* Routledge.

Johnson, M. H., Griffin, R., Csibra, G., Halit, H., Farroni, T., de Haan, M., Tucker, L. A., Baron-Cohen, S., & Richards, J. (2005). The emergence of the social brain network: Evidence from typical and atypical development. *Development and Psychopathology, 17*(3), 599–619. https://doi.org/10.1017/S0954579405050297

Jorm, A. F., Kitchener, B. A., Sawyer, M. G., Scales, H., & Cvetkovski, S. (2010). Mental health first aid training for high school teachers: A cluster randomized trial. *BMC Psychiatry, 10*, 1–12. https://doi.org/10.1186/1471-244X-10-51

Kenway, J., & Youdell, D. (2011). The emotional geographies of education: Beginning a conversation. *Emotion, Space and Society, 4*(3), 131–136. https://doi.org/10.1016/j.emospa.2011.07.001

Kessler, R. C., Amminger, G. P., Aguilar-Gaxiola, S., Alonso, J., Lee, S., & Ustun, T. B. (2007). Age of onset of mental disorders: A review of recent literature. *Current Opinion in Psychiatry, 20*(4), 359–364. https://doi.org/10.1097/YCO.0b013e32816ebc8c

Kovač, V. B., & Vaala, B. L. (2019). Educational inclusion and belonging: A conceptual analysis and implications for practice. *International Journal of Inclusive Education*, 1–15. https://doi.org/10.1080/13603116.2019.1603330

Kreitler, S., & Casakin, H. (2009). Motivation for creativity in design students. *Creativity Research Journal, 21*(2–3), 282–293. https://doi.org/10.1080/10400410902861471

Lam, Y. Y., & Suen, B. Y. S. (2015). Experiencing empathy in design education through community engagement. *International Journal of Continuing Education and Lifelong Learning, 7*(2), 53–69.

Lange, F., & Topel, R. (2006). The social value of education and human capital. In K. J. Arrow & M. D. Intriligator (Eds.), *Handbook of the economics of education* (Vol. 1, pp. 459–509). North Holland.

Lawrence, D., Johnson, S., Hafekost J., Boterhoven De Haan, K., Sawyer, M., Ainley, J., & Zubrick, S. R. (2015). *The mental health of children and adolescents: Report on the second Australian Child and Adolescent Survey of Mental Health and Wellbeing*. Department of Health. Retrieved from https://www1.health.gov.au/internet/main/publishing.nsf/Content/9DA8CA21306FE6EDCA257E2700016945/$File/child2.pdf

Ledwith, A., & Lynch, R. (2017). How design education can support collaboration in teams. In DS 88, *Proceedings of the 19th International Conference on Engineering and Product Design Education (E&PDE17), Building Community: Design Education for a Sustainable Future* (pp. 014–019). Oslo, Norway.

Lester, L., Waters, S., & Cross, D. (2013). The relationship between school connectedness and mental health during the transition to secondary school: A path analysis. *Australian Journal of Guidance and Counselling, 23*(2), 157–171. https://doi.org/10.1017/jgc.2013.20

Loraque, J. (2018). Development impact bonds: Bringing innovation to education development financing and delivery. *Childhood Education, 94*(4), 64–68. https://doi.org/10.1080/00094056.2018.1494454

Louis, K. S., Smylie, M., & Murphy, J. (2016). Caring leadership for schools: Findings from exploratory analyses. *Education Administration Quarterly, 52*(2), 310–348. https://doi.org/10.1177/0013161X15627678

Manning, E. (2016). *The minor gesture*. Duke University Press.

Masi, C. M., Chen, H. Y., Hawkley, L. C., & Cacioppo, J. T. (2011). A meta-analysis of interventions to reduce loneliness. *Personality and Social Psychology Review, 15*(3), 219–266. https://doi.org/10.1177/1088868310377394

Massumi, B. (2015). *Politics of affect*. Wiley.

Matthews, T., Danese, A., Caspi, A., Fisher, H. L., Goldman-Mellor, S., Kepa, A., Moffitt, T. E., Odgers, C. L., & Arseneault, L. (2018). Lonely young adults in modern Britain: Findings from an epidemiological cohort study. *Psychological Medicine, 49*, 268–277. https://doi.org/10.1017/

Mau, R. Y. (1992). The validity and devolution of a concept: Student alienation. *Adolescence, 27*(107), 731–741.

Mavor, K. I., Platow, M. J., & Bizumic, B. (2017). *Self and social identity in educational contexts*. Routledge.

McDonagh, D., Thomas, J., & Strickfaden, M. (2011). Empathic design research: Moving towards a new rode of industrial design education. *Design Principles & Practice: An International Journal, 5*(4), 301–313.

McGarrigle, J. (2013). Exploring student engagement and collaborative learning in a community-based module in fine art. *Irish Journal of Academic Practice, 2*(1), 1. https://doi.org/10.21427/D7ZQ6D

McNeely, C. A., Nonnemaker, J. M., & Blum, R. W. (2002). Promoting school connectedness: Evidence from the national longitudinal study of adolescent health. *Journal of School Health, 72*(4), 138–146. https://doi.org/10.1111/j.1746-1561.2002.tb06533.x

Meltzer, H., Bebbington, P., Dennis, M. S., Jenkins, R., McManus, S., & Brugha, T. S. (2013). Feelings of loneliness among adults with mental disorder. *Social Psychiatry and Psychiatric Epidemiology, 48*(1), 5–13. https://doi.org/10.1007/s00127-012-0515-8

Moffa, K., Dowdy, E., & Furlong, M. J. (2018). Does including school belonging measures enhance complete mental health screening in schools? In K. Allen & C. Boyle (Eds.), *Pathways to Belonging: contemporary research in school belonging* (pp. 65–81). Brill.

Monash Art Design and Architecture. (n.d.). *Why study at MADA?* Monash University. Retrieved from https://www.monash.edu/mada/future-students/why-study-at-mada

Nabers, M. S. (2016). *Social impact bonds: New opportunities for public-private partnerships*. Economic Development. Retrieved from http://economicdevelopment.org/2016/02/social-impact-bonds-new-opportunities-for-public-private-partnerships/

O'Brien, K. A., & Bowles, T. V. (2013). The importance of belonging for adolescents in secondary school settings. *The European Journal of Social & Behavioural Sciences, 5*(2), 976–984. http://dx.doi.org/10.15405/ejsbs.72

O'Connor, M. (2010). Life beyond school: The role of school bonding in preparing adolescents for adulthood. *Independence, 35*(1), 24–28.

Organization for Economic Cooperation and Development (OECD). (2016). *Social impact Bonds: State of Play & Lessons Learnt*. OECD. Retrieved from https://www.oecd.org/cfe/leed/SIBs-State-Play-Lessons-Final.pdf

Organization for Economic Cooperation and Development (OECD). (2017). *PISA results 2015* (Volume III). OECD. Retrieved from https://www.oecd-ilibrary.org/education/pisa-2015results-volume-iii_9789264273856-en

Parsons School of Design. (n.d.). *About parsons*. PSD. Retrieved from https://www.newschool.edu/parsons/about/

Pittman, L. D., & Richmond, A. (2007). Academic and psychological functioning in late adolescence: The importance of school belonging. *The Journal of Experimental Education, 75*(4), 270–290. https://doi.org/10.3200/jexe.75.4.270-292

Putnam, R. D. (2000). *Bowling alone: The collapse and revival of American community*. Simon and Schuster.

Reid, A., & Solomonides, I. (2007). Design students' experience of engagement and creativity. *Art, Design & Communication in Higher Education, 6*(1), 27–39. https://doi.org/10.1386/adch.6.1.27_1

Reynolds, K. J., Lee, E., Turner, I., Bromhead, D., & Subasic, E. (2017). How does school climate impact academic achievement? An examination of social identity processes. *School Psychology International, 38*(1), 78–97. https://doi.org/10.1177/0143034316682295

Richardson, H., Lisandrelli, G., Riobueno-Naylor, A., & Saxe, R. (2018). Development of the social brain from age three to twelve years. *Nature Communications, 9*, 1027. https://doi.org/10.1038/s41467-018-03399-2

Riley, K. (2013). *Leadership of place: Stories for schools in the US, UK and South Africa*. Bloomsbury.

Riley, K. (2017). *Place, belonging and school leadership: Researching to make the difference*. Bloomsbury.

Riley, K. (2020). Transforming schools into places of belonging. *International Congress for School Effectiveness and Improvement*. Monograph Series pp. 1–27. Retrieved from www.theartofpossibilities.org.uk

Riley, K. (2021). *Compassionate leadership for school belonging*. UCL Press.

Riley, K., Montecinos, C., & Ahumada, L. (2017). Effective principals serving in high poverty schools in Chile: Managing competing realities. *Procedia-Social and Behavioral Sciences, 237*, 843–849. http://dx.doi.org/10.1016/j.sbspro.2017.02.181

Riley, K., & Rustique-Forrester, E. (2002). *Why children lose interest in school and what we can do about it*. Sage.

RMIT University School of Design. (n.d.). *Master of Design overview*. RMIT. Retrieved from https://www.rmit.edu.au/study-with-us/levels-of-study/research-programs/masters-by-research/master-of-design-mr235

Robinson, K. (2001). *Out of our minds: Learning to be creative*. Wiley.

Roffey, S., & Boyle, C. (2018). Belief, belonging and the role of schools in reducing the risk of home-grown extremism. In K. Allen & C. Boyle (Eds.), *Pathways to school belonging: Contemporary research in school belonging* (pp. 149–166). Brill.

Ryan, R. M., & Deci, E. I. (2000). Self-determination theory and the facilitation of intrinsic motivation, social development, and wellbeing. *American Psychologist, 55*, 68–78. https://doi.org/10.1037//0003-066x.55.1.68

Ryan, T., Allen, K. A., Gray, D. L., & McInerney, D. M. (2017). How social are social media? A review of online social behaviour and connectedness. *Journal of Relationships Research, 8*(e8), 1–8. https://doi.org/10.1017/jrr.2017.13

Sacks, G., & Kern, L. (2008). A comparison of quality of life variables for students with emotional and behavioral disorders and students without disabilities. *Journal of Behavioral Education, 17*, 111–127. https://doi.org/10.1007/s10864-007-9052-z

Sanders, L. (2001). Collective creativity. *Design, 6*(3), 1–6.

Schindler, H. S., McCoy, D. C., Fisher, P. A., & Shonkoff, J. P. (2019). A historical look at theories of change in early childhood education research. *Early Childhood Research Quarterly, 48*, 146–154. https://doi.org/10.1016/j.ecresq.2019.03.004

Schön, D. (1983). *The reflective practitioner*. Basic Books.

Seeman, M. (1959). On the meaning of alienation. *American Sociological Review, 24*(6), 783–791. https://doi.org/10.2307/2088565

Slaten, C. D., Ferguson, J. K., Allen, K. A., Brodrick, D. V., & Waters, L. (2016). School belonging: A review of the history, current trends, and future directions. *The Educational and Developmental Psychologist, 33*(1), 1–15. https://doi.org/10.1017/edp.2016.6

Smerdon, B. A. (2002). Students' perceptions of membership in their high schools. *Sociology of Education, 75*(4), 287–305. https://doi.org/10.2307/3090280

Smylie, M. A., Murphy, J. & Seashore L. K. (2020). *The practice of caring school leadership*. Corwin.

Smyth, L., Mavor, K. I., & Platow, M. J. (2017). Learning behaviour and learning outcomes: The roles for social influence and field of study. *Social Psychology of Education, 20*(1), 69–95. https://doi.org/10.1007/s11218-016-9365-7

Smyth, L., Mavor, K. I., Platow, M. J., Grace, D. M., & Reynolds, K. J. (2015). Discipline social identification, study norms and learning approach in university students. *Educational Psychology, 35*(1), 53–72. https://doi.org/10.1080/01443410.2013.822962

Solomonides, I. (2007). Design students' experience of engagement and creativity. *Art, 6*(1), 27–39. https://doi.org/10.1386/adch.6.1.27_1

Steffens, N. K., LaRue, C. J., Haslam, C., Walter, Z. C., Cruwys, T., Munt, K. A., Haslam, S. A., Jetten, J., & Tarrant, M. (2019). Social identification-building interventions to improve health: A systematic review and meta-analysis. *Health Psychology Review*, 1–28. https://doi.org/10.1080/17437199.2019.1669481

Steiner, R. J., Sheremenko, G., Lesesne, C., Dittus, P. J., Sieving, R. E., & Ethier, K. A. (2019). Adolescent connectedness and adult health outcomes. *Pediatrics, 144*(1), e20183766. https://doi.org/10.1542/peds.2018-3766

Stevens, M., Rees, T., Coffee, P., Steffens, N. K., Haslam, S. A., & Polman, R. (2020). Leading us to be active: A two-wave test of relationships between identity leadership, group identification, and attendance. *Sport, Exercise and Performance Psychology, 9*(1), 128–142. https://doi.org/10.1037/spy0000164

Stevens, M., Rees, T., & Polman, R. (2018). Social identification, exercise participation, and positive exercise experiences: Evidence from parkrun. *Journal of Sports Sciences, 37*(2), 221–228. https://doi.org/10.1080/02640414.2018.1489360

Stevens, M., Rees, T., Steffens, N. K., Haslam, S. A., Coffee, P., & Polman, R. (2019). Leaders' creation of shared identity impacts group members' effort and performance: Evidence from an exercise task. *PLoS ONE, 14*(7), e0218984. https://doi.org/10.1371/journal.pone.0218984

Tajfel, H., & Turner, J. C. (1979). An integrative theory of intergroup conflict. In W. G. Austin & S. Worchel (Eds.), *The social psychology of intergroup relations* (pp. 33–47). Brooks/Cole.

Telford and Wrekin Belonging Strategy (2019). Retrieved from www.telford.gov.uk/download/downloads/id/14959/belonging_strategy.pdf

The Fair Education Alliance. (2017). Report Card 2016/17. Retrieved from https://static1.squarespace.com/static/543e665de4b0fbb2b140b291/t/59af2a4cccc5c50550ff4bd5/1504451878199/FEA+Report+-Card+2016-17.pdf

Then, V., Schober, C., Rauscher, O., & Kehl, K. (2017). *Social return on investment analysis: Measuring the impact of social investment*. Palgrave.

Tianinen, M., Kontturi, K. K., & Hongisto, I. (2015). *Movement, aesthetics, ontology. Cultural Studies Review, 21*(2), 4–13. http://dx.doi.org/10.5130/csr.v21i2.4737

Tong, L., Reynolds, K. J., Lee, E., & Liu, Y. (2019). School relational climate, social identity, and student well-being: New evidence from China on student depression and stress levels. *School Mental Health, 11*(3), 509–521. https://doi.org/10.1007/s12310-018-9293-0

Tsai, Y. M., Kunter, M., Lüdtke, O., Trautwein, U., & Ryan, R. M. (2008). What makes lessons interesting? The role of situational and individual factors in three school subjects. *Journal of Educational Psychology, 100*(2), 460–472. https://doi.org/10.1037/0022-0663.100.2.460

Turnbull, M., Littlejohn, A., & Allan, M. (2012). Preparing graduates for work in the creative industries: a collaborative learning approach for design students. *Industry and Higher Education, 26*(4), 291–300. https://doi.org/10.5367/ihe.2012.0105

Turner, J. C., Hogg, M. A., Oakes, P. J., Reicher, S. D., & Wetherell, M. S. (1987). *Rediscovering the social group: A self-categorization theory*. Blackwell.

Umeå Institute of Design. (n.d.). *What is UID?* UMU. Retrieved from http://www.dh.umu.se/en/about-us/what-is-uid/

Van Knippenberg, D., & Van Schie, E. C. (2000). Foci and correlates of organizational identification. *Journal of Occupational and Organizational Psychology, 73*(2), 137–147.

Vota, R.M. (2020). *GALACSI: Gameful Lab for Collective Social Intelligence*. Retrieved from https://www.collectivesocialintelligence.org/

Watson, K., McIntyre, S., & McArthur, I. (2011). Trust and relationship building: Critical skills for the future of design education in online contexts. *Iridescent, 1*(1), 22–29. https://doi.org/10.1080/19235003.2011.11428486

Webster, R. S., & Wolfe, M. (2013). Incorporating the aesthetic dimension into pedagogy. *Australian Journal of Teacher Education, 38*(10), 21–33. https://doi.org/10.14221/ajte.2013v38n10.2

Wolfe, M. J. (2013). Affective aesthetic pedagogy-interactions between teachers and students. In B. Knight & R. V. D. Zwan (Eds.), *Teaching innovations: Supporting student outcomes in the 21st century* (pp. 116–127). Oxford Global Press.

Wolfe, M. J. (2017). Affective schoolgirl assemblages making school spaces of non/belonging. *Emotion, Space and Society, 25,* 63–70. https://doi.org/10.1016/j.emospa.2017.05.010

Wolfe, M. J. (2021). *Affect and the making of the schoolgirl: A new materialist perspective on gender inequity in schools.* Routledge.

Wyman, P. A., Pickering, T. A., Pisani, A. R., Rulison, K., Schmeelk-Cone, K., Hartley, C., & Brown, C. H. (2019). Peer-adult network structure and suicide attempts in 38 high schools: Implications for network-informed suicide prevention. *Journal of Child Psychology and Psychiatry, 60*(10), 1065–1075. https://doi.org/10.1111/jcpp.13102

Yuval-Davis, N. (2006). Belonging and the politics of belonging. *Patterns of Prejudice, 40*(3), 197–214. https://doi.org/10.1080/00313220600769331

Zimmerman, J., Stolterman, E., & Forlizzi, J. (2010, August). An analysis and critique of Research through Design: Towards a formalization of a research approach. In *Proceedings of the 8th ACM Conference on Designing Interactive Systems* (pp. 310–319). 8th ACM conference on designing interactive systems. https://doi.org/10.1145/1858171.1858228

PART C

Academic Development

17

ACADEMIC SELF-EFFICACY

Dale H. Schunk and Maria K. DiBenedetto

Academic self-efficacy refers to one's perceived capabilities for learning or performing actions at designated levels in academic settings (Schunk & DiBenedetto, 2014). The topic of academic self-efficacy fits well with positive psychology, which investigates the conditions that make for personal agency and thriving (Kristjánsson, 2012). Self-efficacy, which is grounded in Bandura's (1986, 1997) social cognitive theory, includes beliefs about what one can do or learn. Focusing on people's capabilities rather than their deficiencies is stressed by positive psychology. Further, self-efficacy is a key component of a sense of *agency* or the belief that one can exert a large degree of control over significant events in one's life. Research with diverse learners in varied contexts supports the influence of self-efficacy on learning, motivation, and self-regulation (Schunk & DiBenedetto, 2014; Schunk & Usher, 2019; Usher & Schunk, 2018).

Earlier versions of this chapter (Pajares, 2009; Schunk & DiBenedetto, 2014) appeared in prior editions of the *Handbook of Positive Psychology in Schools* (Furlong et al., 2014; Gilman et al., 2009). Pajares (2009) and Schunk and DiBenedetto (2014) explicated Bandura's (1986) social cognitive theory and the conceptual background of self-efficacy theory, along with describing academic self-efficacy research. Although parts of the present chapter are devoted to conceptual grounding, much of it covers recent advances in self-efficacy theory. We also make recommendations for areas requiring further research.

We initially discuss self-efficacy theory and present research evidence that demonstrates the influential role of self-efficacy for both students and teachers. Recommendations for future research include areas that should enhance our understanding of the operation of self-efficacy in academic settings: methodology, sociocultural influences, out-of-school contexts, technology, and impoverished students. We conclude with educational implications or applications to settings involving teaching and learning. A primary goal of this chapter is to expand academic self-efficacy research.

Theoretical Background

Model of Reciprocal Interactions

Self-efficacy is grounded in Bandura's (1977, 1986, 1997) social cognitive theory, which postulates that human functioning results from reciprocal interactions among personal (e.g., cognition, beliefs, skills, and affects), behavioral, and social/environmental influences (Schunk & Usher, 2019).

DOI: 10.4324/9781003013778-22

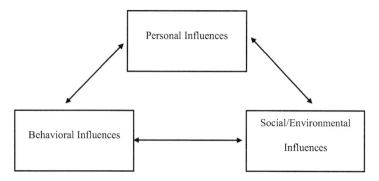

Figure 17.1   Model of Reciprocal Interactions in Bandura's Social Cognitive Theory

For example, self-efficacy (personal factor) influences various achievement behaviors, such as task choice, effort, persistence, and the use of effective learning strategies (Schunk & Usher, 2019). These behaviors reciprocally affect self-efficacy when learners work on tasks and observe their progress, which raises self-efficacy for continued learning (see Figure 17.1).

To illustrate the connection between personal and social/environmental factors, consider that many students with learning disabilities hold low self-efficacy for learning (Klassen, 2010; Major et al., 2013). Persons in their environments may react to them based on common attributes (e.g., low skills) rather than based on their actual capabilities. Social/environmental feedback can raise self-efficacy, as when teachers tell students, "I know you can do this."

Instructional sequences highlight the link between behavioral and social/environmental factors. Social/environmental factors direct behaviors when teachers call students' attention to a display (e.g., "Look at this"), to which students attend without much conscious deliberation. The influence of behavior on the social environment occurs when teachers ask questions, and students' answers convey a lack of understanding. Teachers are likely to reteach the material rather than continue the lesson.

As noted earlier, an underlying premise of Bandura's (1986) social cognitive theory is that people desire to possess a sense of *agency*. Individuals form beliefs that allow them to positively influence their thoughts, feelings, actions, social interactions, and aspects of their environments. They are not merely acted upon by their environments. Instead, they set goals and employ strategies to attain those goals. Students who wish to become skilled violinists set goals and seek out opportunities to improve their skills, such as by studying with master violinists and playing in orchestras.

Characteristics of Self-Efficacy

Self-efficacy has been shown by researchers to influence behaviors and environments and be affected by them (Schunk, 2012; Schunk & Usher, 2019). Students with high self-efficacy for learning are apt to choose to:

1   engage in challenging tasks;
2   expend effort to succeed;
3   persist in the face of difficulties;
4   engage in self-regulated learning (e.g., set goals, use effective learning strategies, monitor their comprehension, and evaluate their goal progress);
5   create effective environments for learning (e.g., eliminate or minimize distractions and find effective study partners); and
6   achieve at higher levels (Schunk & DiBenedetto, 2016).

In turn, self-efficacy is influenced by the outcomes of behaviors such as perceived goal progress and achievement, as well as by feedback from teachers and social comparisons with peers.

People acquire information to gauge their self-efficacy from their performance accomplishments, vicarious (e.g., modeled) experiences, forms of social persuasion, and physiological indexes (Bandura, 1997). Performances provide the most reliable information for assessing self-efficacy because they are tangible indicators of one's capabilities. Successful performances raise self-efficacy, whereas failures lower it, although an occasional failure or success after many successes or failures may not have much impact.

Individuals acquire information about their capabilities through knowledge of how others perform (Bandura, 1997). The similarity to others is a cue for gauging self-efficacy (Schunk, 2012). Observing similar others' success can raise observers' self-efficacy and motivate them to engage in the task because they may believe that if others can succeed, they can as well. However, a vicarious increase in self-efficacy can be negated by subsequent performance failure. Persons who observe similar peers fail may believe they lack the competence to succeed, which may not motivate them to attempt the task.

Individuals also develop self-efficacy from social persuasions they receive from others (e.g., "I know you can do this") (Bandura, 1997; Schunk & Usher, 2019). Social persuasions must be credible to cultivate people's beliefs in their capabilities for successfully attaining outcomes; persuasion not backed up by success is likely to be ineffective. Although positive feedback can raise self-efficacy, the increase will not endure if students subsequently perform poorly (Schunk, 2012). Negative persuasions can lower self-efficacy.

Individuals acquire self-efficacy information from physiological and emotional states such as anxiety and stress (Bandura, 1997). When students experience negative thoughts and fears about their capabilities (e.g., feeling nervous thinking about taking a test), those reactions can lower self-efficacy and trigger additional stress and agitation that help bring about the feared inadequate performances. Learners may feel more efficacious when they perceive that they are less anxious about academic outcomes.

Self-efficacy is important, but it is not the only influence on behavior. No amount of self-efficacy will produce a competent performance when students lack the necessary skills to succeed (Schunk, 2012). Students' *values* (perceptions of importance and utility of learning) can also affect behavior (Wigfield et al., 2016). Students who feel highly efficacious in science may not take science courses that they believe are not germane to their goal of becoming a veterinarian. Also important are *outcome expectations*, or beliefs about the anticipated outcomes of actions (Bandura, 1997). Students typically engage in activities that they believe will result in positive outcomes and avoid actions that they believe may lead to adverse outcomes, even when they feel efficacious about attaining the latter.

Self-efficacy develops a sense of agency when individuals select tasks and activities in which they feel competent and confident and avoid those in which they do not. Unless people believe that their actions will produce the desired consequences, they have little incentive to engage in those actions. Self-efficacy also affects how resilient people are when faced with adversity (Schunk & DiBenedetto, 2016). Students with robust self-efficacy approach difficult tasks as challenges to be mastered rather than as threats to be avoided. They set goals and stay committed to attaining them, heighten and sustain their efforts in the face of failure, and quickly recover their sense of self-efficacy after setbacks. These actions develop perceived agency.

Operation of Self-Efficacy

Self-efficacy is dynamic and subject to many changes while students are engaged in academic activities. To understand this process better, researchers have explored the operation of self-efficacy during learning, including determining the effects of instructional and other classroom processes on self-efficacy (Schunk & DiBenedetto, 2016). This body of research shows that when instructional, social, and environmental factors inform students about their learning, they use this information to assess their self-efficacy for continued learning.

At the outset of a learning activity, students' self-efficacy for learning depends on their prior experiences, personal qualities (e.g., abilities and attitudes), and social supports. The latter include the extent that teachers, parents, and others encourage students to learn, facilitate their access to resources necessary for learning (e.g., materials and facilities), and teach them self-regulatory strategies that enhance skill development.

As students engage in learning activities, they are influenced by personal factors (e.g., goal setting and cognitive information processing) and situational variables (e.g., feedback and social comparisons). These influences provide students with cues about how well they are learning. Their perception of learning progress strengthens their self-efficacy. Slow progress will not necessarily lower self-efficacy if students believe they can perform better, such as by expending more considerable effort or using more effective learning strategies (Schunk, 2012). In turn, self-efficacy enhances their motivation and continued learning.

Types of Self-Efficacy

Researchers have investigated the operation of various types of self-efficacy. For example, *self-efficacy for performance* refers to one's perceived capabilities for performing actions that one already has learned. *Self-efficacy for learning* denotes perceived capabilities for learning new skills. Learning self-efficacy is important because students who hold a sense of self-efficacy for learning display higher motivation and learn more efficiently than those who doubt their capabilities (Schunk, 2012).

Self-efficacy for self-regulated learning refers to one's perceived capabilities for productively engaging in self-regulatory activities while learning. Self-regulated learning (discussed later in this chapter) is critical for learning outside of formal learning contexts.

Collective self-efficacy refers to the perceived capabilities of members of a group for the group's accomplishing given actions. Collective self-efficacy is important in schools. When teachers and administrators feel collectively self-efficacious about improving student learning, they are likely to work together to facilitate positive changes in classrooms and curricula.

Teacher self-efficacy refers to a teacher's sense of self-efficacy for helping students learn. Teachers who hold a sense of self-efficacy are apt to work harder to design activities to help students learn and persist longer with them than will teachers who question their capabilities to improve student learning. *Collective teacher self-efficacy* is the self-efficacy of a group of teachers for improving learning environments and helping students learn.

Distinctions with Other Variables

The term *self-efficacy* is sometimes used interchangeably with other variables that bear conceptual similarity to it (Schunk & Zimmerman, 2006). *Self-concept* refers to one's collective and general self-perceptions formed through experiences with and interpretations of the environment and is influenced by reinforcements and evaluations by others (Shavelson & Bolus, 1982). Self-concept typically is viewed as hierarchically organized with a general self-concept on top and subarea self-concepts below it (Marsh & Shavelson, 1985; Schunk & DiBenedetto, 2016). Self-perceptions of specific competencies influence subarea self-concepts (e.g., subject areas such as history and biology), which in turn combine to form the general self-concept. Because self-efficacy comprises perceived capabilities in specific areas, it should contribute to one's overall general self-concept (Schunk & DiBenedetto, 2016).

Self-esteem is a general affective evaluation that often includes judgments of self-worth (Schunk & DiBenedetto, 2016). Like self-concept, it differs markedly from self-efficacy. Self-efficacy involves questions of *can* (e.g., "Can I write this essay?"), whereas self-esteem reflects questions of *feel* (e.g., "How do I feel about myself as a writer?"). One's beliefs about what one can do may bear little relation to how one feels about oneself. There are, for example, students with high self-efficacy for learning but who have low self-esteem because they are socially unpopular with peers.

Perceived control (or *agency*) also differs from self-efficacy. One's sense of personal agency, or perceived control over significant events in one's life, includes self-efficacy and outcome expectations (discussed earlier). Self-efficacy is a key component of personal agency (Bandura, 1997), but not the only one. For example, a responsive environment is necessary for self-efficacy to exert its effects. Students may believe they can learn yet make no effort to do so because they believe that in their present environment, learning will not be rewarded. Thus, high self-efficacy does not guarantee perceptions of control.

Self-efficacy also differs from *self-confidence*, or a general belief about one's capabilities that often does not specify the object of the belief (e.g., "She is highly self-confident"). Self-efficacy is situated within Bandura's (1986) social cognitive theory and has a clear and specific meaning. Although self-confident individuals often are self-efficacious, there is no automatic relation between these variables. People who know they will fail at a task are highly confident about failing but have low self-efficacy (Bandura, 1997).

The growth of positive psychology in recent years has shifted the focus of learning to characteristics such as well-being, optimism, and perseverance—sometimes referred to as *grit* (Duckworth et al., 2007; Usher et al., 2019). Grit, a trait-personality characteristic, has seen widespread use and is deemed to be able to explain the differences in performance among two individuals of equal ability (Credé et al., 2017). Students who have grit are more likely to have the drive to reach long-term goals and persist when faced with challenges (DiBenedetto & Schunk, 2018). Research has not supported the predictive power of grit on academic achievement. In a recent study of adolescents' reading and math achievement, grit was weakly or unrelated to performance as compared to self-efficacy (Usher et al., 2019). In a meta-analysis of 584 effect sizes for over 65,000 individuals, researchers found that while there was a relationship between grit and academic performance, these effect sizes were modest in comparison to other well-known predictors of academic success (Credé et al., 2017). We should expect that many students with grit are self-efficacious students who set long-term personal goals and persist when faced with challenges (DiBenedetto & Schunk, 2018). However, unlike grit, self-efficacious students set proximal goals directed to long-term goal achievement, and with the use of feedback, they can make necessary adaptations and adjustments to ensure attainment of their final goal.

Self-efficacy differs from a *growth mindset* or the belief that intelligence is malleable and can change (Dweck & Yeager, 2018). Students with a growth mindset believe that intellectual ability can be increased through learning and will persevere when faced with challenges. Students' beliefs about their abilities and intelligence can affect their self-efficacy beliefs (Dweck & Master, 2009). Research has shown, for example, that students with a history of failure, such as is often found with students who have disabilities, tend to have lower levels of self-efficacy (Klassen, 2010; Schunk & DiBenedetto, in press).

In summary, there are a number of constructs that share some similarity with self-efficacy including self-concept, self-esteem, perceived control, self-confidence, grit, and growth mindset. In this section, we discussed points of similarity, as well as how self-efficacy differs. Self-efficacy refers to beliefs about one's capabilities to learn or perform actions at designated levels. Maintaining this distinction with other constructs is important for not only research but also for applications because interventions that are designed to raise self-efficacy should address how persons will improve their perceived capabilities to accomplish specific tasks.

Research Evidence

Researchers have investigated different aspects of academic self-efficacy. The next two chapter sections discuss research evidence with students and teachers pertaining to influences on self-efficacy and its relation to motivation, learning, and achievement.

Students

There is a wealth of self-efficacy research with students that supports the hypothesized operation and prediction of self-efficacy. Notably, there is research evidence with students in different grade levels (e.g., elementary, middle, high, and postsecondary), with diverse abilities (e.g., regular, remedial, and gifted), and in different content areas (e.g., reading, writing, mathematics, and computer applications; Schunk, 2012; Schunk & DiBenedetto, 2016; Schunk & Ertmer, 2000; Schunk & Usher, 2019). In a recent study, for example, children as young as in Grades 1–3 held self-efficacy beliefs that were predictive of reading achievement (Lee & Jonson-Reid, 2016). Some instructional and social processes that raise students' self-efficacy are:

1 setting proximal and specific learning goals,
2 observing models explaining and demonstrating skills,
3 providing students with positive performance and attributional feedback,
4 using effective learning strategies,
5 verbalizing strategies while applying them,
6 linking rewards to learning progress, and
7 monitoring and evaluating learning progress (Schunk & DiBenedetto, 2016; Schunk & Usher, 2019).

These processes differ in many ways, but they all convey information to students about their learning progress, which raises self-efficacy.

Researchers have shown that students' self-efficacy for learning or performance correlates positively and significantly with subsequent achievement on those tasks (Pajares, 1996; Schunk & Usher, 2019). DiBenedetto and Bembenutty (2013) examined changes in science self-efficacy over a semester for 113 college students enrolled in intermediate-level science courses. Findings revealed self-efficacy beliefs at the end of the semester declined and yet were more closely related to final term averages than they were at the start of the semester, suggesting that students' beliefs about their performance became better calibrated as the semester progressed. A recent study examined 273 twelfth-grade students' reading self-efficacy (Dona et al., 2019). Data were collected using two instruments—reading self-efficacy and reading comprehension. Findings showed a significant correlation between self-efficacy and performance. In an examination of the 2003 PISA mathematics results on younger students, self-efficacy was positively correlated with 15-year-old students' performance on mathematics in 30 out of 33 nations, suggesting that self-efficacy is a motivational variable that consistently predicts performance across nations and cultures (Williams & Williams, 2010). In another recent investigation on 881 urban first- to third-graders who were considered at-risk for reading delays, self-efficacy predicted reading achievement and differentiated between self-efficacy and self-concept, suggesting students are developmentally capable of this distinction at a young age (Lee & Jonson-Reid, 2016).

Empirical research also supports the predictive and mediational power of self-efficacy on achievement. Falco and Summers (2019) conducted an intervention study incorporating the four sources of self-efficacy on high school girls' STEM (science, technology, engineering, and mathematics) career self-efficacy beliefs. Ethnically diverse high school girls received nine 50-minute counseling sessions targeted at building students' self-efficacy for making intentional career decisions and for building self-efficacy for careers in STEM. The four sources to build self-efficacy included focusing on performance accomplishments, modeling, strategies for controlling anxiety, and verbal persuasions and encouragement. Results showed positive moderate-to-large effect sizes for the impact of the intervention on both students' career decision-making self-efficacy and self-efficacy for careers in STEM.

Ramdass and Zimmerman (2011) examined the influence of modeling and social feedback on 76 sixth- and seventh-grade students' self-efficacy and mathematical achievement. Students observed coping models with or without social feedback, or mastery models with or without social feedback. Findings revealed that students in the coping model conditions surpassed those in the mastery model conditions on the posttests, and their self-efficacy was better associated with higher mathematics performance.

Researchers have also explored the operation of students' self-efficacy for self-regulated learning. *Self-regulated learning* results from students' self-generated thoughts, feelings, and behaviors systematically directed toward attainment of learning goals (Zimmerman, 2000). Self-regulated learning involves students implementing goal-directed activities, such as focusing on task demands, applying effective strategies to learn, establishing productive social and work environments, assessing learning progress, and making strategic adjustments as needed. Self-efficacy for self-regulated learning motivates students and promotes achievement (Schunk & Usher, 2019).

Zimmerman's (2000) cyclical and recursive model of self-regulated learning comprises forethought, performance, and self-reflection phases. *Forethought* involves processes that students engage in before learning and includes motivational beliefs and task analysis. Fundamental motivational beliefs are self-efficacy, outcome expectancies, intrinsic interest, and goal orientations (reasons why students want to learn). Task analysis includes goal setting (short- and long-term goals) and strategic planning. While researchers have shown that each of these processes is related to achievement, self-efficacy is a strong predictor and affects goal setting and strategic planning (Schunk, 2012; Zimmerman & Bandura, 1994).

During *performance*, students systematically engage in learning. Key self-regulatory processes are self-control and self-observation. Students exert self-control by using strategies such as imagery, self-instruction, and attention focusing (Zimmerman, 2002). Self-observation includes self-monitoring and self-recording learning progress. Students gain progress information from their observations and feedback from others (e.g., teachers, peers, and parents). Students' self-efficacy about their capability to learn sustains their efforts (Pajares, 2008).

Based on monitoring and feedback from others, students form judgments and experience self-reactions during *self-reflection*. Self-judgments include self-evaluations of learning progress and performance attributions (i.e., perceived causes of outcomes; Schunk, 2012). Self-evaluations reflect performance standards that derive from individuals' previous performances, performances by others (e.g., teachers), or absolute criteria (Zimmerman, 2002). Causal attributions may reflect perceived causes that students can control, such as strategy use and effort or uncontrollable ones such as luck or ability (Graham & Taylor, 2016; Weiner, 1985). Students also react to their performances with self-satisfaction and adaptive/defensive responses. Self-satisfaction refers to the level of contentment students feel about their performance relative to a standard or goal. Adaptive/defensive responses include emotional reactions to performances. Students who react defensively exhibit apathy, helplessness, procrastination, and cognitive disengagement for future learning. Students who respond adaptively adjust their self-regulatory behaviors by modifying their motivational beliefs and task analyses.

Self-reflections return learners to the forethought or performance phase, thus forming the recursive loop in the self-regulation cycle. Students who are self-efficacious about their self-regulatory capabilities sustain their efforts and persist even when they form negative evaluations (Schunk, 2012). These students may attribute their progress to strategy use and effort and make adjustments as they plan for subsequent learning.

The development of self-regulatory competence explains how self-efficacy becomes a central motivation process during self-regulated learning (Zimmerman et al., 2015). Schunk and Zimmerman (1997) formulated a four-level model of the development of self-regulatory competence: observation, emulation, self-control, and self-regulation. Initially, social models, such as teachers and peers serve as important sources of self-regulatory behaviors and self-efficacy. At the *observation* level, students observe models perform actions and learn many self-regulated processes such as strategic planning, self-monitoring, and performance adaptations (Zimmerman, 2000). Students may observe models receive rewards such as praise and good grades. These observations serve as vicarious sources of self-efficacy information.

At the *emulation* level, students practice the behaviors previously demonstrated by the model with assistance from the model as needed (Zimmerman, 2000). Students receive reinforcement from the model and their sensory and motoric feedback. Students' self-efficacy is strengthened by the model's feedback, along with their perceptions of their increasing capabilities to apply self-regulatory processes needed to complete a task.

In these first two levels, learners derive information about their self-efficacy primarily from external (social) sources (e.g., vicarious experiences and social persuasions). At the third level of *self-control*, students begin to experience stronger self-efficacy. Schunk and Zimmerman (1997) describe the self-control level as learners using strategies independently of the model. Students have internalized what they have observed and emulated; however, they are still using the representational patterns of the model to perform behaviors. During this level, students begin to experience self-efficacy internally as they reflect on their improved capability to match their work against the standards displayed by the model.

At the *self-regulation* level, learners can systematically adapt their performance to different environmental and personal conditions and are motivated by their self-efficacy (Zimmerman, 2000). They are capable of initiating the use of strategies, making behavioral adjustments based on situational needs, and evaluating performances knowing they can make changes as needed. As students engage in the three cyclical phases of self-regulated learning, they strengthen their self-efficacy and regulate their thoughts, feelings, and behaviors toward goal attainment.

White and DiBenedetto (2015) developed a framework integrating the three phases of self-regulated learning within each of the levels of self-regulated learning competency. Within each level, self-efficacy beliefs develop and strengthen as students have opportunities to observe, emulate, gain self-control, and eventually regulate their learning. Critical to the development of self-regulation competency are efficacy beliefs. In the integrated model, educators *pace* the learning such that self-efficacy beliefs initially develop socially, through vicarious and social persuasive means, and eventually become internalized as students obtain physiological and mastery experiences (Schunk, 1999).

In a study examining achievement on students learning English as a foreign language, Yang and Wu (2012) found that high school students who received a digital storytelling intervention for 20 weeks had higher self-efficacy scores and English achievement than those who received traditional English instruction. Digital storytelling involves using technology to bring stories to life by using a combination of images, music, graphics, and sounds mixed in with the author's story voice (Porter, 2005). In Yang and Wu's study, students were taught how to create digital stories on Chinese festivals using images, music, graphics, and their own voices through a series of scaffolds and steps provided by the instructor. In the comparison group, the instructor lectured in a more traditional way using textbook readings and PowerPoint presentations. These researchers suggest that students experienced transformative changes, leading to increased competency beliefs. Self-efficacious students are likely to be motivated by these beliefs and regulate learning without the need of others (Bembenutty et al., 2016).

Teachers

In contrast to the literature on student self-efficacy, there is less research on *teacher* (or *instructional*) *self-efficacy*, which refers to personal beliefs about one's capabilities to help students learn (Fives & Buehl, 2016; Tschannen-Moran et al., 1998; Woolfolk Hoy et al., 2009). Teacher self-efficacy influences teachers' activities, effort, and persistence. Teachers with low self-efficacy may (a) avoid planning activities they believe exceed their capabilities, (b) not persist with students having difficulties, (c) expend little effort to find materials, and (d) not reteach content in ways students might better understand. Teachers with high self-efficacy are more likely to develop challenging activities, help students succeed, and persist with students who have trouble learning. These teacher behaviors enhance student learning and strengthen teachers' self-efficacy for helping students learn.

Guo et al. (2012) examined the effects of teacher self-efficacy, years of experience, and education on fifth-grade students' literacy outcomes using longitudinal data from the National Institute of Child Health and Human Development Study of Early Child Care and Youth Development. Teachers who held higher self-efficacy beliefs provided a more supportive and positive classroom environment. Teacher self-efficacy beliefs are also related to higher literacy achievement. Perera and John (2020) obtained similar findings in a recent study on teacher efficacy and mathematics achievement on 6,000 fourth-grade students and 450 teachers. Zee and Koomen (2016) examined 165 studies conducted over the past 40 years on teacher efficacy. They found that teacher self-efficacy is positively related to several important characteristics leading to student success, such as teachers' behaviors and practices in the classroom, teachers' sense of personal accomplishments, satisfaction, and commitment, and students' motivation.

Collective teacher self-efficacy represents teachers' beliefs that their capabilities as a group can enhance students' learning (Henson, 2002). Teachers develop collective self-efficacy when they (a) work collaboratively to achieve common goals (performance accomplishments), (b) learn from one another and have mentors who serve as role models (vicarious experiences), (c) receive encouragement and support from administrators (forms of social persuasion), and (d) work together to cope with difficulties and alleviate stress (physiological indexes). As collective self-efficacy becomes stronger, teachers remain motivated to collaborate to improve students' learning. Some research shows that collective self-efficacy positively predicts teachers' job satisfaction (Caprara et al., 2003).

Recommendations for Future Research

Although the academic self-efficacy research literature continues to grow, areas remain in which further research is needed. In this section, we recommend research emphasis on methodology, sociocultural influences, out-of-school contexts, technology, and impoverished students.

Methodology

One recommendation is for continued research in methodological advancements in academic self-efficacy research. Many studies have employed self-report questionnaires of self-efficacy, often administered before and after an intervention. These questionnaires have strengths and weaknesses. Their ease of use and direct assessment of participants' self-efficacy contrast with concerns about participants' accuracy when making judgments pooled across different times and tasks, and especially when questionnaire data are collected only once or twice.

We recommend increased emphasis on real-time self-efficacy assessments that occur as students are engaged in academic activities (Schunk & Greene, 2018). These include interviews, observations, data traces, and microanalytic methods (assessments collected at multiple time points). These assessments better capture the dynamic and fluid nature of self-efficacy as it changes while individuals are engaged in learning. They can also show how self-efficacy responds over time to changes in students' knowledge and skills and contextual variables, such as teacher feedback and peer social comparisons. A better understanding of the operation of self-efficacy over time will advance the research agenda and potentially lead to theoretical revisions and implications for teaching and learning.

Sociocultural Influences

An important direction for future research is to determine how sociocultural variables may influence self-efficacy. *Culture* refers to beliefs and value systems that can influence motivation and learning outcomes (McInerney, 2008). Although self-efficacy theory predicts that the principles apply across cultures, researchers have shown that cultural variables affect students' beliefs to include self-efficacy (McInerney & King, 2018).

For example, an important cultural dimension is individualism-collectivism. Individualistic cultures tend to stress independence and individual initiative; collectivist cultures emphasize group identity and a "we" mindset (Klassen, 2004). It is not unusual for persons from collectivist cultures (e.g., China and Korea) to judge self-efficacy lower than those from individualistic cultures (e.g., the United States and Canada) even when performances are comparable (Klassen, 2004). Further, the lower self-efficacy beliefs are typically better aligned with actual performances, which suggests that collectivist cultures may promote modesty in self-efficacy judgments. These results also raise the issue of whether collective self-efficacy may be a better predictor of performances in these cultures than individual self-efficacy (Klassen, 2004). How individualism and collectivism impact self-efficacy deserve expanded empirical research.

This issue is educationally important given the influx into many countries of students of varied cultural backgrounds. Teachers need to understand what their students' self-efficacy beliefs are to plan effective lessons to promote teaching and learning. Teachers can also effectively differentiate instruction to tailor learning activities to differences in students' self-efficacy.

Out-of-School Contexts

We strongly recommend increased research attention to exploring the operation of self-efficacy in out-of-school contexts. Most researchers have conducted academic self-efficacy research with students in formal settings (e.g., classrooms). However, much learning occurs in other venues such as in homes (e.g., homework), volunteer activities, and during mentoring interactions. Relative to school-based research, much less is known about the development of and operation of self-efficacy in these and other academic settings.

For example, mentoring relationships can enhance the mentees' self-efficacy (Schunk & Mullen, 2013). Mentors are models who show how to complete tasks at required proficiency levels. They demonstrate self-regulation and how to cope with challenges. Through the development of self-regulatory competencies, mentors foster mentees' self-efficacy and help them become independent and self-directed (DiBenedetto & White, 2013). Like self-efficacy, mentoring relationships can undergo many changes, and it is important to determine how changes in these relationships may impact self-efficacy.

Another point is that self-efficacy sources outside of school may conflict with those experienced in school. For example, in school, students develop self-efficacy through performance accomplishments, exposure to competent models, and teacher encouragement, but these same positive sources may not be present outside of school. Students may experience frustration while working on homework, which can negate self-efficacy gains from success in school. A key question is how students reconcile discrepant self-efficacy information. It may prove valuable to provide instruction to parents and others outside of school on how to inculcate positive self-efficacy to foster motivation and learning. Drawing on sources of self-efficacy, for example, parents could be taught how to convey learning progress to students (performance accomplishments), model successful strategies (vicarious information), and provide encouragement (persuasive information).

Technology

Research on the role of technology in developing academic self-efficacy continues to evolve. Evidence shows that self-efficacy developed through students' use of technology (e.g., computer-based learning environments) relates positively to learning outcomes (Moos & Azevedo, 2009). Research must continue given the prevalence of technology use in education. Also, while researchers have explored some forms of technology extensively (e.g., computer-based learning environments), there is much less research on newer forms of technology (e.g., social media).

An area witnessing increased inquiry is game-based learning. Initial research shows that video gaming can increase motivation and interest, and help students make connections to real-life situations (Foster, 2008). Video games capture learners' attention, are fun and exciting to play, often involve cognitive flexibility, and the ability to strategize, are familiar to many learners and can be developed to target learning goals. Good instructional video games can take advantage of learners' attention by allowing them to identify with avatars that represent the players or other characters (e.g., a scientist), which helps boost interest and self-efficacy for learning (Nietfeld, 2018).

We recommend increased research attention on the role that technology may play in the development of self-efficacy, and especially among learners with different cognitive capabilities. The motivational inducements provided by technology may have the desired effect of gaining and holding learners' attention, which can enhance self-efficacy as they experience success. Also, cell phones and other electronic devices may help students with disabilities self-monitor learning progress with alarms for due dates or reminders to be working on school assignments.

Conversely, the extra audio and video features of technology may prove distracting and raise demands on students' working memories (Kalyuga, 2007), which is not desirable for learning, motivation, or self-efficacy. Designing ways to minimize these demands with technology will prove beneficial for learners and especially those who may have problems maintaining attention.

Impoverished Students and Self-Efficacy

Another area where self-efficacy research is needed is among impoverished children or those who are socioeconomically disadvantaged. McLaughlin (2018) examines an afterschool program's effects on students in Cabrini-Green, a notorious public-housing project in one of the most impoverished and violent neighborhoods in Chicago. Thirty years after the students participated in the program, many of them have successful careers and are employed. In the description of the program, McLaughlin highlights the importance of social models and mentoring, teacher expectations in low-income community schools, and the need to provide mastery experiences to build self-efficacy among adolescents.

Gomez and Beachum (2019) conducted a study examining the lack of resources available to fourth- and fifth-grade students in low-income communities regarding their understanding of various careers and their self-efficacy for reaching their career aspirations. Results revealed that while these young students had self-efficacy beliefs to reach their career aspirations, they had a little-to-no understanding of the academic requirements to achieve their desired careers. Findings such as these suggest the need for research on self-efficacy beliefs of the teachers who work in low SES schools and their students, and how to create opportunities that foster self-efficacy for learning and performance.

Educational Applications

There are several positive applications of self-efficacy theory and research (Table 17.1). As Pajares (2009) recommended, teachers play a crucial role in nurturing the academic self-efficacy of their students through the four sources of self-efficacy information. Students need to be taught skills and given opportunities to practice and refine them. As students observe their learning progress, they experience self-efficacy for continued learning.

Teachers can also provide vicarious experiences by modeling successful strategies and pointing out how other similar students have mastered skills. Such encouragement must be realistic. Telling students "You can do this" when they know they lack the skills to succeed is demoralizing and can lower self-efficacy. Teachers can use physiological indicators, such as when they tell students that they are reacting in a less stressful way when completing their assignments.

Teachers routinely assist students so that they can be successful. Assistance often is necessary in the early stages of learning. However, success gained with much help does not build strong self-efficacy, because students are likely to attribute their success to the help they have received. Allowing students to succeed on their own exerts more potent effects on self-efficacy.

We also recommend individualizing instruction where possible. Students do not learn in the same way or at the same rate. When assignments are not individualized, some students will succeed, but others will have difficulty. When those in the latter group socially compare their performances to those of students who have done well, they are apt to doubt their capabilities for learning. Individualizing instruction minimizes opportunities for social comparisons. Teachers can show individual students their learning progress (e.g., "See how much better you're doing on these now?"), and the perception of progress by learners builds self-efficacy.

Students can be encouraged to evaluate their learning. Students are not used to assessing their learning; instead, they rely on teachers to provide these assessments. However, teachers cannot continuously provide learners with progress feedback. Students can learn to gauge their progress. In mathematics, for example, teachers might show students different types of problems and ask them to judge their learning progress on a scale ranging from low to high. Students' assessments can then be used to determine where they need further study and which areas they have mastered. It is possible that teachers' and students' evaluations could conflict (e.g., students judge greater progress than they actually have made), in which case teachers should call attention to students' prior work.

A desirable educational goal is for learners to experience a sense of realistic optimism. The theory and research we summarize in this chapter are designed to do that. Self-efficacy judgments that slightly exceed what they can do can motivate them to expend effort and persist (Bandura, 1997).

Table 17.1 Ways to Increase Student Self-Efficacy

Ways to Increase Student Self-Efficacy
Provide individual instruction where possible and practice opportunities
Model successful strategies
Point out desirable models
Provide positive encouragement
Have students self-evaluate their learning progress

Learners should not have unrealistically high expectations (i.e., where no amount of effort and per-sistence will produce learning) or those that are unrealistically low (i.e., far lower than what they can do). Teachers need to take into account the potential effects of instructional conditions not only on students' learning but also on their self-efficacy. Helping to produce realistically optimistic learners will improve students' motivation and learning and their enjoyment in classrooms.

Conclusion

Self-efficacy reflects positive psychology's focus on well-being. Theory and research support the idea that self-efficacy influences learning, motivation, and self-regulation. From instructional and social/environmental sources, students acquire information that affects their self-efficacy, and in turn, self-efficacy influences various academic behaviors. Teachers should determine how various facets of instruction may affect learning, motivation, and self-efficacy. By helping to produce learners with a sense of realistic optimism, teachers can ensure that students will be successful, find learning enjoyable and be motivated to continue learning outside of school.

References

Bandura, A. (1977). Self-efficacy: Toward a unifying theory of behavioral change. *Psychological Review, 84*, 191–215. doi:10.1037/0033-295X.84.2.191

Bandura, A. (1986). *Social foundations of thought and action: A social cognitive theory*. Prentice Hall.

Bandura, A. (1997). *Self-efficacy: The exercise of control*. Freeman.

Bembenutty, H., White, M. C., & DiBenedetto, M. K. (2016). Applying social cognitive theory in the development of self-regulated competencies throughout K-12 grades. In A. A. Lipnevich, P. Preckel, & R. D. Roberts (Eds.), *Psychological skills and school systems in the 21st century: Theory, research, and applications* (pp. 215–239). Springer.

Caprara, G. V., Barbaranelli, C., Borgogni, L., & Steca, P. (2003). Efficacy beliefs as determinants of teach-ers' job satisfaction. *Journal of Educational Psychology, 95*, 821–832. doi:10.1037/0022-0663.95.4.821

Credé, M., Tynan, M., & Harms, P. (2017). Much ado about grit: A meta-analytic synthesis of the grit liter-ature. *Journal of Personality and Social Psychology, 113*(3), 492–511. doi:10.1037/pspp0000102

DiBenedetto, M., & Bembenutty, H. (2013). Within the pipeline: Self-regulated learning, self-efficacy, and socialization among college students in science courses. *Learning and Individual Differences, 23*(1), 218–224. doi:10.1016/j.lindif.2012.09.015

DiBenedetto, M. K., & Schunk, D. H. (2018). Self-efficacy in education revisited through a sociocultural lens: Current and future directions. In G. A. D. Liem, & D. M. McInerney (Eds.), *Big theories revisited 2* (pp. 117–140). Information Age Press.

DiBenedetto, M. K., & White, M. C. (2013). Applying the model of development of self-regulatory com-petence to mentoring. In H. Bembenutty, T. Cleary, & A. Kitsantas (Eds.), *Applications of self-regulated learning across diverse disciplines* (pp. 445–472). Information Age Publishing.

Dona, R., Dedi, S., & Fernandita, G. (2019). The correlation between reading self-efficacy and reading comprehension. *Journal of English Education and Teaching, 3*(1), 1–13. doi:10.33369/jeet.3.1.1–13

Duckworth, A. L., Peterson, C., Matthews, M. D., & Kelly, R. D. (2007). Grit: Perseverance and passion for long-term goals. *Journal of Personality and Social Psychology, 92*, 1087–1101. doi:10.1037/0022-3514.92.6.1087

Dweck, C., & Master, A. (2009). Self-theories and motivation: Student's beliefs about intelligence. In K. R. Wentzel & A. Wigfield (Eds.), *Handbook of motivation at school* (pp. 123–140). Routledge.

Dweck, C., & Yeager, D. S. (2018). Mindsets change the imagined and actual future. In G. Oettingen, A. T. Sevincer, & P. M. Gollwitzer (Eds.), *The psychology of thinking about the future* (pp. 362–377). Guilford.

Falco, L. D., & Summers, J. J. (2019). Improving career decision self-efficacy and STEM self-efficacy in high school girls: Evaluation of an intervention. *Journal of Career Development, 46*(1), 62–76. https://doi.org/10.1177/0894845317721651

Fives, H., & Buehl, M. M. (2016). Teacher motivation, self-efficacy and goal orientation. In K. R. Wentzel & D. B. Miele (Eds.), *Handbook of motivation at school* (2nd ed., pp. 340–360). Routledge.

Foster, A. (2008). Games and motivation to learn science: Personal identity, applicability, relevance and meaningfulness. *Journal of Interactive Learning Research, 19*, 597–614. Retrieved from https://www.learn-techlib.org/primary/p/24259/

Furlong, M. J., Gilman, R., & Huebner, E. S. (Eds.) (2014). *Handbook of positive psychology in schools* (2nd ed.). Routledge.

Gilman, R., Huebner, E. S., & Furlong, M. J. (Eds). (2009). *Handbook of positive psychology in schools*. Routledge.

Gomez, K., & Beachum, F. D. (2019). The "voice" of children of poverty: Candid insights to their career aspirations and perceptions of self-efficacy. *Urban Review, 51*, 724–747. doi:10.1007/s11256-019-00503-8

Graham, S., & Taylor, A. Z. (2016). Attribution theory and motivation in school. In K. R. Wentzel & D. B. Miele (Eds.), *Handbook of motivation at school* (2nd ed., pp. 11–33). Routledge.

Guo, Y., Connor, C. M., Yang, Y., & Roehrig, A. (2012). The effects of teacher qualification, teacher self-efficacy, and classroom practices on fifth-graders literacy outcomes. *Elementary School Journal, 113*(1), 3–24. doi:10.1086/665816

Henson, R. K. (2002). From adolescent angst to adulthood: Substantive implications and measurement dilemmas in the development of teacher efficacy research. *Educational Psychologist, 37*, 127–150. doi:10.1207/S15326985EP3703_1

Kalyuga, S. (2007). Enhancing instructional efficiency of interactive e-learning environments: A cognitive load perspective. *Educational Psychology Review, 19*, 387–399. doi:10.1007/s10648-007-9051-6

Klassen, R. M. (2004). Optimism and realism: A review of self-efficacy from a cross-cultural perspective. *International Journal of Psychology, 39*, 205–230. doi:10.1080/00207590344000330

Klassen, R. M. (2010). Confidence to manage learning: The self-efficacy for self-regulated learning of early adolescents with learning disabilities. *Learning Disability Quarterly, 33*(1), 19–30. doi:10.1177/073194871003300102

Kristjánsson, K. (2012). Positive psychology and positive education: Old wine in new bottles? *Educational Psychologist, 47*, 86–105. doi:10.1080/00461520.2011.610678

Lee, Y., & Jonson-Reid, M. (2016). The role of self-efficacy in reading achievement of young children in urban schools. *Child & Adolescent Social Work Journal, 33*(1), 79–89. doi:10.1007/s10560-015-0404-6

Major, A., Martinussen, R., & Wiener, J. (2013). Self-efficacy for self-regulated learning in adolescents with and without attention deficit hyperactivity disorder (ADHD). *Learning and Individual Differences, 27*, 149–156. doi:10.1016/j.lindif.2013.06.009

Marsh, H. W., & Shavelson, R. (1985). Self-concept: Its multifaceted, hierarchical structure. *Educational Psychologist, 20*, 107–123. doi:10.1207/s15326985ep2003_1

McInerney, D. M. (2008). The motivational roles of cultural differences and cultural identity in self-regulated learning. In D. H. Schunk & B. J. Zimmerman (Eds.), *Motivation and self-regulated learning: Theory, research, and applications* (pp. 369–400). Erlbaum.

McInerney, D. M., & King, R. (2018). Culture and self-regulation in educational contexts. In D. H. Schunk & J. A. Greene (Eds.), *Handbook of self-regulation of learning and performance* (2nd ed., pp. 485–502). Routledge.

McLaughlin, M. W. (2018). *You can't be what you can't see: The power of opportunity to change young lives*. Harvard Education Press.

Moos, D. C., & Azevedo, R. (2009). Learning with computer-based learning environments: A literature review of computer self-efficacy. *Review of Educational Research, 79*, 576–600. doi:10.1007/s11409-009-9045-5

Nietfeld, J. L. (2018). The role of self-regulated learning in digital games. In D. H. Schunk & J. A. Greene (Eds.), *Handbook of self-regulation of learning and performance* (2nd ed., pp. 271–284). Routledge.

Pajares, F. (1996). Self-efficacy beliefs in achievement settings. *Review of Educational Research, 66*, 543–578. doi:10.3102/00346543066004543

Pajaras, F. (2008). Motivational role of self-efficacy beliefs in self-regulated learning. In D. H. Schunk & B. J. Zimmerman (Eds.), *Motivation and self-regulated learning: Theory, research and applications* (pp. 111–139). Taylor & Francis.

Pajares, F. (2009). Toward a positive psychology of academic motivation: The role of self-efficacy beliefs. In R. Gilman, E. S. Huebner, & M. J. Furlong (Eds.), *Handbook of positive psychology in schools* (pp. 149–160). Routledge.

Perera, H. N., & John, J. E. (2020). Teachers' self-efficacy beliefs for teaching math: Relations with teacher and student outcomes. *Contemporary Educational Psychology*. doi:10.1016/j.cedpsych.2020.101842

Porter, B. (2005). *Digitales: The art of digital stories*. Bernajean Porter Consulting.

Ramdass, D., & Zimmerman, B. J. (2011). The effects of modeling and social feedback on middle-school students' math performance and accuracy judgments. *The International Journal of Educational and Psychological Assessment, 7*(1), 4–23.

Schunk, D. H. (1999). Social-self interaction and achievement behavior. *Educational Psychologist, 34*, 219–227. doi:10.1207/s15326985ep3404_3

Schunk, D. H. (2012). Social cognitive theory. In K. R. Harris, S. Graham, & T. Urdan (Eds.), *APA educational psychology handbook: Vol. 1. Theories, constructs, and critical issues* (pp. 101–123). American Psychological Association.

Schunk, D. H., & DiBenedetto, M. K. (2014). Academic self-efficacy. In M. J. Furlong, R. Gilman, & E. S. Huebner (Eds.), *Handbook of positive psychology in schools* (2nd ed., pp. 115–121). Elsevier.

Schunk, D. H., & DiBenedetto, M. K. (2016). Self-efficacy theory in education. In K. R. Wentzel & D. B. Miele (Eds.), *Handbook of motivation at school* (2nd ed., pp. 34–54). Routledge.

Schunk, D. H., & DiBenedetto, M. K. (in press). Social cognitive theory, self-efficacy, and students with disabilities. In A. J. Martin, R. A. Sperling, & K. J. Newton (Eds.), *Handbook of educational psychology and students with special needs*. Routledge.

Schunk, D. H., & Ertmer, P. A. (2000). Self-regulation and academic learning: Self-efficacy enhancing interventions. In M. Boekaerts, P. R. Pintrich, & M. Zeidner (Eds.), *Handbook of self-regulation* (pp. 631–649). Academic Press.

Schunk, D. H., & Greene, J. A. (Eds.) (2018). *Handbook of self-regulation of learning and performance* (2nd ed.). Routledge.

Schunk, D. H., & Mullen, C. A. (2013). Toward a conceptual model of mentoring research: Integration with self-regulated learning. *Educational Psychology Review, 25*, 361–389. doi:10.1007/s10648-013-9233-3

Schunk, D. H., & Usher, E. L. (2019). Social cognitive theory and motivation. In R. M. Ryan (Ed.), *The Oxford handbook of human motivation* (2nd ed., pp. 11–26). Oxford University Press.

Schunk, D. H., & Zimmerman, B. J. (1997). Social origins of self-regulatory competence. *Educational Psychologist, 32*, 195–208. doi:10.1207/s15326985ep3204_1

Schunk, D. H., & Zimmerman, B. J. (2006). Competence and control beliefs: Distinguishing the means and ends. In P. A. Alexander & P. H. Winne (Eds.), *Handbook of educational psychology* (2nd ed., pp. 349–367). Erlbaum.

Shavelson, R., & Bolus, R. (1982). Self-concept: The interplay of theory and methods. *Journal of Educational Psychology, 74*, 3–17. doi:10.1037/0022–0663.74.1.3

Tschannen-Moran, M., Woolfolk Hoy, A., & Hoy, W. K. (1998). Teacher efficacy: Its meaning and measure. *Review of Educational Research, 68*, 202–248. doi:10.3102/00346543068002202

Usher, E., Li, C., Butz, A., & Rojas, J. (2019). Perseverant grit and self-efficacy: Are both essential for children's academic success? *Journal of Educational Psychology, 111*(5), 877–902. doi:10.1037/edu0000324

Usher, E. L., & Schunk, D. H. (2018). Social cognitive theoretical perspective of self-regulation. In D. H. Schunk & J. A. Greene (Eds.), *Handbook of self-regulation of learning and performance* (2nd ed., pp. 19–35). Routledge.

Weiner, B. (1985). An attributional theory of achievement motivation and emotion. *Psychological Review, 12*, 1–14. doi:10.1037/0033–295X.92.4.548

White, M. C., & DiBenedetto, M. K. (2015). *Self-regulation and the common core: Applications to ELA standards.* Routledge.

Wigfield, A., Tonks, S. M., & Klauda, S. L. (2016). Expectancy-value theory. In K. R. Wentzel & D. B. Miele (Eds.), *Handbook of motivation at school* (2nd ed., pp. 34–54). Routledge.

Williams, T., & Williams, K. (2010). Self-efficacy and performance in mathematics: Reciprocal determinism in 33 nations. *Journal of Educational Psychology, 102*(2), 453–453. doi:10.1037/a0017271

Woolfolk Hoy, A., Hoy, W. K., & Davis, H. A. (2009). Teachers' self-efficacy beliefs. In K. R. Wentzel & A. Wigfield (Eds.), *Handbook of motivation at school* (pp. 627–653). Routledge.

Yang, Y., & Wu, W. (2012). Digital storytelling for enhancing student academic achievement, critical thinking, and learning motivation: A year-long experimental study. *Computers & Education, 59*(2), 339–352. doi:10.1016/j.compedu.2011.12.012

Zee, M., & Koomen, H. (2016). Teacher self-efficacy and its effects on classroom processes, student academic adjustment, and teacher well-being. *Review of Educational Research, 86*(4), 981–1015. doi:10.3102/0034654315626801

Zimmerman, B. J. (2000). Attaining self-regulation: A social cognitive perspective. In M. Boekaerts, P. R. Pintrich, & M. Zeidner (Eds.), *Handbook of self-regulation* (pp. 13–39). Academic Press.

Zimmerman, B. J. (2002). Becoming a self-regulated learner: An overview. *Theory into Practice, 41*, 64–70. doi:10.1207/s15430421tip4102_2

Zimmerman, B. J., & Bandura, A. (1994). Impact of self-regulatory influences on writing course achievement. *American Educational Research Journal, 31*, 845–862. doi:10.3102/00028312031004845

Zimmerman, B. J., Schunk, D. H., & DiBenedetto, M. K. (2015). A personal agency view of self-regulated learning: The role of goal setting. In F. Guay, H. Marsh, D. M. McInerney, & R. G. Craven (Eds.), *Self-concept, motivation, and identity* (pp. 83–114). Information Age Publishing.

18

FLOW IN SCHOOLS REEXAMINED

Cultivating Engagement in Learning from Classrooms to Educational Games

David J. Shernoff and Shalva Twersky

Educational observers and researchers have frequently characterized public schools in terms of pervasive boredom and disengagement among students (Shernoff, 2013; Steinberg et al., 1996). For example, the 2009 High School Survey of Student Engagement found that two-thirds (66%) of students reported being bored at least every day in high school, and approximately one in six students (17%) was bored in every class (Yazzie-Mintz, 2010). Studies have reported that disengagement is strongly related to poor attendance and dropout, substance abuse, and criminal offending (Conner & Pope, 2014; Henry et al., 2011). Chronic disengagement, inattention, and lack of interest are problems nationally and internationally. The Program for International Student Assessment survey of 540,000 15-year-old students from 72 countries found that 27% of them felt disaffected from school; for example, 26% reported skipping at least one class in the two weeks before the survey (Organisation for Economic Co-operation and Development [OECD], 2016).

Schools have historically struggled to provide meaningful and engaging experiences for many youths. Many students in public schools see themselves as passive participants in a mass, anonymous educational system (Larson & Richards, 1991). Accordingly, fostering engagement and enjoyment in learning has become a dominant concern for educators, researchers, policymakers, and other stakeholders of the U.S. public school system. Nevertheless, many students remain apathetic toward school.

With its focus on optimal health and human functioning rather than illness, can Positive Psychology help to foster healthier schools? The concept of optimal experience, or flow, has served as a theoretical cornerstone of Positive Psychology (Seligman & Csikszentmihalyi, 2000). In this chapter, we focus on how optimal learning experiences, as theoretically rooted in the concept of flow, have a direct and meaningful application to student engagement in schools. Our review, guided by multiple studies bearing on this topic in the last 25 years, specifically focuses on the perceptual and environmental factors that can influence student engagement. We close by sharing some new directions in this line of research.

Flow in Learning

By interviewing individuals from diverse backgrounds about their peak experiences, Csikszentmihalyi (1990) and colleagues identified the phenomenological characteristics of the most

DOI: 10.4324/9781003013778-23

meaningful and satisfying moments in people's lives. From rock climbers and chess players to accomplished scientists and artists, optimal experiences in diverse activities were often described in similar terms—intense concentration and absorption in an activity with no psychic energy for distractions, a merging of awareness with action, a feeling of control, loss of self-consciousness, and a contraction of the normal sense of time (i.e., time seems to fly). Csikszentmihalyi subsequently coined the term "flow" to describe experiences when skillful and successful action seems effortless, even when exerting a great deal of physical or mental energy. Subsequent research on flow has found that certain properties of the task enhanced the experience. Specifically, in most flow activities, goals are clear, and feedback on meeting those goals is immediate and forthcoming. The activities also are often *autotelic*, or a goal in and of itself performed for the sheer experience of it—sometimes even in the face of personal risk or danger. Perhaps the most central flow-producing condition is that the challenge of the activity and an individual's skill to meet that challenge are well matched. Typically, the challenge and skill are relatively high and appropriately balanced; individuals stretch their skills to their limits in pursuit of a challenging goal. The various combinations of high or low challenges and skills predict distinct psychological states: (a) *apathy*, resulting from low challenge and low skill; (b) *relaxation*, resulting from high skill but low challenge; (c) *anxiety*, resulting from high challenge but low skill; and (d) *flow*, resulting from high challenge combined with high skill. This model later evolved into one with eight flow channels, including four intermediary or transitional states between these four quadrants (see Strati et al., 2018); however, we discuss only the four quadrants here for simplicity.

Using downhill snow skiing as an example, intermediate-level skiers may find themselves in apathy while waiting at the ski lift before any challenge is present. If the first slope is a bunny trail, the skiers may find that they have more skills than required and feel only relaxation as they take in the scenery. When confronted with a slope that is too steep, bumpy, or icy for their ability, however, anxiety may set in until safely navigating their way down. Only on the slopes that are challenging for their ability, but not excessively so, do they feel themselves enter into an enjoyable, rhythmic peak experience in which time seems to stand still. The exhilaration of the flow experience is typically the main reason skiers invest the time, money, and energy to hit the slopes in the first place (Csikszentmihalyi, 1990).

Flow experiences can involve mental tasks as much as physical ones. Anyone who has been "sucked into" a good novel that one cannot set down implicitly understands the phenomenon. Recent experiments in neuroscience have demonstrated that when a reader is fully engrossed in a novel, the human brain is activated not only in areas responsible for attention; it also dramatically "lights up" in areas controlling affect and emotion (Thompson & Vedantam, 2012). Still, an experienced reader is unlikely to enter flow reading a children's book. A more sophisticated novel not only appeals to one's reading ability but also stimulates a full array of skills: to understand the geographical and historical context, infer the motivations of the characters, or solve the central mystery, for example. Studies in numerous settings have supported the relationship between flow and the balance of challenge and skills (e.g., Csikszentmihalyi & Csikszentmihalyi, 1988).

The theory of flow, then, is inherently related to learning. When learning a new skill, the challenge of even a basic task may exceed one's beginning level of ability, and hence one may feel overwhelmed. Even "Twinkle, Twinkle Little Star" may be too difficult for a beginner pianist. To reach flow, the level of skill must increase to match the challenge. Much like Vygotsky's (1978) *zone of proximal development,* the level in which most learning occurs is just one step beyond the skills one has already mastered. In this case, the pianist may need sufficient practice until the song is mastered. Once the song is played comfortably with relative ease (causing a state of "relaxation"), only one thing can restart a cycle of fresh learning: a new song at a higher level of challenge, causing one's skill to increase yet again. Thus, the pianist may progress through increasingly difficult songs at ever-higher levels of skill. The theory would predict flow to peak at the highest level of challenge and skill, as when a master pianist is playing a Mozart concerto with great poise and fluency. Fullagar and colleagues (2013) found that the balance between the challenge of a passage of music and the skills utilized to play the passage is significantly and consistently correlated with optimal experiences. This balance of challenge and skill increases motivation, enhances competence, fosters growth, and extends the student's capacities (Csikszentmihalyi et al., 2005; Fullagar et al., 2013).

Also applicable to learning is the finding that flow activities tend to be selected and replicated over time because they are so gratifying. This process of *psychological selection* plays a crucial role in the development of specific interests, goals, and talents throughout one's life (Delle Fave & Massimini, 2003). In Csikszentmihalyi and colleagues' (1993) study of talented teenagers, adolescents who developed their talents were those who repeatedly engaged in meaningful and skill-building pursuits during their free time—in the arts, music, science, technology, and other domains. A strong predictor of the propensity to repeatedly engage in such activities was the extent to which these adolescents reported high levels of flow and enjoyment when engaged in them. Thus, individuals appear to select, pay attention to, and repeatedly engage in activities that are enjoyable and psychologically rewarding; and they develop their talents in activities in which they repeatedly engage.

Measuring Flow and Engagement in Learning

In the last 25 years, the study of flow has been pursued mainly through the use of the Experience Sampling Method (or ESM; Hektner et al., 2007). Respondents carry a paging device (traditionally a programmable wristwatch, but more recently smartphones) that signals them at random moments throughout the day. When signaled, they complete a brief questionnaire containing open-ended and scaled questions. Questions include day and time of the signal, the current activity, and the cognitive, affective, and motivational qualities of their experience in the activity. Example items include: "When signaled, did you *enjoy* what you were doing?" "How well were you *concentrating*?" and "Was this activity *interesting*?" Respondents also rate the challenge of the activity and their skill in the activity. The ESM thus solicits repeated "snapshots" of subjective experience, improving upon the problem of recall and estimation errors inherent to one-time surveys and interviews. Multiple studies have provided evidence of the method's reliability and validity; we refer the reader to Hektner and colleagues (2007) and Zirkel and colleagues (2015).

Based on flow theory, we have conceptualized *student engagement* as the simultaneous occurrence of high *concentration, interest,* and *enjoyment* (Shernoff, 2013). *Concentration* or *absorption*, which is central to flow (Csikszentmihalyi, 1990), is related to meaningful learning (Montessori, 1967), including depth of cognitive processing and academic performance (Corno & Mandinach, 1983). *Interest* directs attention, reflects intrinsic motivation, stimulates the desire to continue engagement in an activity, and is related to school achievement (Hidi, 1990; Schiefele et al., 1992). *Enjoyment* is a positive feeling related to the demonstration of competencies, creative accomplishment, and school performance (Csikszentmihalyi et al., 1993; Nakamura, 1988). In this conceptualization, student engagement is highest when all three components are simultaneously stimulated. As flow theory predicts, student engagement was maximized in classroom experiences in which perceived challenge and skill were above average compared to those marked by apathy (i.e., low challenge, low skill), anxiety (i.e., high challenge, low skill), or relaxation (i.e., low challenge, high skill; Shernoff et al., 2003).

What Flow Theory and the ESM Have Taught Us about Student Engagement in Public Schools

Initial ESM research in U.S. public schools has highlighted the rarity with which students experience flow while in school (Csikszentmihalyi & Larson, 1984; Shernoff, 2013). On average, high school students are less engaged in classrooms than in other daily settings, such as at home and in public (e.g., parks, stores, cars, and churches). In fact, the only setting in which intrinsic motivation is as low as school is in paid work settings (Csikszentmihalyi & Larson, 1984). Concentration in the classroom is higher than elsewhere, but classroom interest is low, and enjoyment is especially low compared with nonclassroom activities. Students are also found to be thinking about topics entirely unrelated to academics a full 40% of the time while in classrooms (Shernoff, 2010). Overall, studies suggest that schools need alternative approaches in order to provide what is most lacking: greater enjoyment, motivation, and opportunities for action in the learning process (Bassi & Delle Fave, 2004; Shernoff et al., 2003).

Perceptual and Contextual Factors Influencing Student Engagement

Perceptual Factors Influencing Engagement

Student engagement is significantly enhanced when instruction is perceived as challenging, relevant, and based on meaningful inquiry (Shernoff, 2013). Students also experience greater enjoyment, motivation, self-esteem, and engagement when they perceive themselves to be active, in control, and skilled in the activity or subject at hand. One study of 347 students in the Philippines and Argentina found a direct effect of self-efficacy as well as eustress (i.e., moderate stress interpreted as beneficial by the experiencer) on flow, which, in turn, had a positive effect on student engagement (Mesurado et al., 2016).

Supporting flow theory, studies of high school classrooms have found that secondary students report peak engagement when perceived challenges and skills are both high (Shernoff et al., 2003). However, one study of elementary school instruction found that fifth-graders reported more optimal experience when perceiving skills as high but challenge as low (Chao-Yang et al., 2017). Otherwise, there have been very few studies of flow in elementary school.

The Influence of Classroom Context and the Learning Environment

Student engagement appears to be significantly influenced by contextual and classroom factors, such as instructional format and learning environment. For example, students have more engagement when doing group and individual work than while listening to a lecture or watching TV or a video. Overall, students reported being more engaged during instructional methods that present opportunities for action and demonstration of skills (Shernoff et al., 2000).

More recent studies further qualify the importance of instructional format. One study of seven academic classes in two high schools videotaped classroom interactions across a variety of academic subjects and matched ratings of observation data to ESM data by instructional episode (Shernoff et al., 2011, 2014). In this study, some of the highest levels of engagement were reported during lecture formats, provided that they involved Socratic questioning, while some of the lowest levels of engagement were reported during large-group discussions that featured a high level of discourse. Results support the proposition that specific, distinguishing instructional features, such as rules, goals of the activity, and quality of the learning environment were more operative in influencing student engagement than the main instructional format. Supporting this conclusion in a sample of seven elementary school classes in Taiwan, Chao-Yang and colleagues (2017) found that classroom settings with the highest likelihood of flow experience incorporated activities featuring clear goals, student focus, and autonomous work.

Constructivist classroom principles such as reciprocal instruction, cooperative learning, and a supportive classroom climate can also shape students' experiences (Zhang et al., 2009). Shernoff and colleagues (2016) examined the extent to which the high school classroom learning environment, characterized as a whole, predicted fluctuations in engagement. Motivational characteristics of the learning environment were coded from an observational instrument and synchronously matched to ESM data on student engagement. They found that *environmental complexity*, or the simultaneous combination of environmental challenge and environmental support, predicted engagement and self-esteem. Environmental challenge was characterized by the importance of the instructional activity and goals clarity. Environmental support included support for motivational drives (for example, support of the learner's sense of autonomy or perceived competency), the availability of performance feedback, and positive relationships with teachers and peers. Further findings from Shernoff and colleagues (2017) revealed that environmental support was significantly related to perceived learning, an association that was mediated by student engagement. This mediating relationship was confirmed for two components of environmental support, specifically: motivational supports and supportive relationships. Overall, when students believed that what they were doing was both important and had clear goals, they were more likely to interact within the classroom environment with interest and absorb what was available in the environment. When they were additionally supported to reach those goals, particularly with motivational and relational supports, their engagement increased and enhanced learning.

Another theoretical lens of student engagement in classrooms building on flow theory is the *capabilities-expectations* model proposed by Cavanaugh and colleagues (e.g., Cavanagh, 2015), which conceptualizes the capabilities for student learning in relation to expectations for learning. Both models of *capabilities-expectations* and *environmental complexity* highlight the importance of positive relationships, intrinsic motivation, emotional support, relational support, self-esteem, and self-concept in contributing to student engagement (Cavanagh & Shernoff, 2014). Both models are also suggestive of a unidimensionality among the various properties of engaging classrooms. For example, Shernoff and colleagues (2017) proposed a unidimensional model in testing student engagement as a "general factor" of classroom experience, conceptualized in terms of flow. Examining student experience in the context of college-level accounting classes, they found that the bifactor model using a general factor of student engagement fit the data better than models conceptualizing engagement in terms of several specific, related factors (e.g., intrinsic motivation, self-esteem). Flow was the theoretical framework best suited for interpreting this unifying quality of classroom experience. Results also suggested that student behaviors such as sitting in the front of the classroom, active listening, taking notes, and working on problems given during the lesson increased students' engagement, which, in turn, promoted learning.

Several studies have also investigated the effect of instructional interventions on student engagement and flow (Pino-James et al., 2019). For example, Larson (2014) implemented an instructional intervention called, the *Engagement Model of Academic Literacy for Learning* (EngageALL), by organizing high school biology instruction according to the characteristics of flow and interest development. Using a quasi-experimental design, she found that students receiving the intervention reported higher levels of engagement and conceptual understanding than a schooling-as-usual control group, and their levels of flow increased throughout the instructional unit.

Shernoff and colleagues (2020) implemented an integrated STEAM (i.e., STEM subjects plus the arts) Academy in a participating high school by recruiting an interdisciplinary team of teachers to co-plan integrated STEAM curricula, supported by ongoing Professional Learning Communities (PLCs). They found that students in the integrated STEAM Academy reported significantly higher engagement during instruction than a schooling-as-usual academy. Educational attitudes and future aspirations over the course of the intervention year improved for students in the integrated STEAM Academy in contrast to students in the control academy, whose educational aspirations declined. Findings were consistent with both the previous research on flow and student engagement as well as the young literature on STEAM: when students (a) exercised greater control over their learning (due to freedom to explore), and (b) interacted with peers (enhancing relationships), to (c) solve authentic, real-life problems (increasing meaning and relevance) through integrated STEAM projects, they reported experiencing excitement, motivation, and engagement. Providing opportunities for co-planning and continuing feedback supported teachers' ability to design and implement such projects.

The Teacher's Role in Fostering Engagement

An obvious influence on students' engagement and flow experience is the teacher. Although teaching and learning have traditionally been studied as separate processes, in reality, teachers and students cocreate the pattern of classroom interactions together, which, in turn, impacts both teacher and student motivation (Turner & Warzon, 2009). Turner and Meyer (e.g., Turner & Meyer, 2004; Turner et al., 1998) provided a rich, contextualized picture of how skilled teachers go about achieving optimal levels of challenge and support to create high student engagement. For example, optimally engaging teachers might assign fewer problems to students, but they make these problems sufficiently challenging. Such teachers also provide support for students to solve the problems independently. They also ask questions for higher-order conceptual understanding, combined with providing feedback and emotionally supportive encouragement (e.g., conveying enthusiasm and demonstrating a sense of humor).

Teacher's Flow

Although most engagement research has focused on student engagement, it is also important to study teacher engagement. One significant reason is to reduce teacher attrition. The attrition rate for U.S. public school teachers is approximately 25% (Kaufman & Ring, 2011), with some estimates as high as 50% for new teachers with less than five years of service (Hughes, 2012). Teachers frequently cite job dissatisfaction as the primary reason for leaving (Hughes, 2012). Therefore, it is important to understand the conditions leading to teacher engagement. Another reason for its importance is that teachers who regularly experience flow are those who continually improve their skills to meet the needs of their students (Smith, 2009).

Under what conditions, then, do teachers experience flow? Basom and Frase (2004) reported that teachers frequently claim that they derived their sense of flow from students' engagement, just as students claim that the teachers' engagement and enthusiasm sparked their own flow. In one study, Smith (2009) demonstrated that teachers who applied differentiated instruction (a kind of instruction that requires close and individualized interaction between teacher and student) were more likely to experience higher levels of flow. This was observed especially when teachers assessed students' differences based on their interests and abilities and then accounted for these differences in their instructional approach. Serving each student then became like a puzzle to be solved, instilling flow and a spirit of artistry. Smith concluded that the more teachers take students into account and consider how each student will best learn, the more engaged they become in their teaching.

When in flow, teachers reported feeling connected to their class; they maintained good eye contact and could sense the attentiveness of the class. One study of 178 music teachers and 605 students in 16 different music schools tested the hypothesis that flow experiences can "cross over" from teachers to their students (Bakker, 2005). The study found that students' and teachers' flow were indeed positively related: The more flow the teachers experienced, the more the students experienced. When this occurs, both teachers and students may experience the classroom dynamic as "group flow" (Custodero, 2005). Overall, student and teacher engagement appears to be highly interactive and interrelated.

Conceptual Model of Student Engagement and Optimal Learning Environments

Based on previous ESM studies (Shernoff et al., 2003), there are two processes that describe the formation of meaningful student engagement. The first is *academic intensity,* which refers to heightened concentration and effort in skill-building activities (e.g., taking a test or a quiz, or completing tasks in which students are very challenged and concentrate hard but often do not enjoy the experience). The second is a *positive emotional response,* which refers to spontaneous enjoyment undergirding intrinsic interest and continued motivation (e.g., watching a video, attending an art class, or other activity that students find enjoyable but not necessarily challenging or important). Consistent with the notion of flow as combining both work-like and play-like aspects of engagement, researchers have found that both processes are integral parts of optimal engagement in the learning process, but they seldom operate together during school instruction (Csikszentmihalyi & Schneider, 2000; Rathunde, 1993).

Activities or environments that can combine both aspects of engagement, as is frequently reported during individual work in computer science class and during group lab activities in science class, are of utmost importance because they provide opportunities for *meaningful engagement* (Shernoff et al., 2011). Optimal learning environments thus (a) include activities that are challenging and relevant and yet also allow students to feel confident and in control; (b) exact concentration but also provide enjoyment; (c) are intrinsically satisfying in the short term and also build a foundation of skills and interest for the future; (d) involve both intellect and feeling; and (e) are both work-like and play-like—that is, they foster *meaningful engagement* (Shernoff, 2013). We have characterized learning environments that meaningfully engage students by *environmental complexity,* or the simultaneous combination of environmental challenge and environmental support (Shernoff, 2013; Shernoff et al., 2016).

New Directions in Student Engagement Research

Flow, Educational Games, and Video Games

Because flow involves a challenge, the employment of skills, and deep engagement, certain types of educational games can provide a platform for learning through flow. Wen and colleagues (2019) found that educational board games can engage students in flow during classroom learning. In a small sample of 19 undergraduate students, educational board games improved course performance by arousing flow in learning, as well as narrowing the gap between high- and medium-level students.

The research area on flow and learning that has experienced the most growth in the past several decades has focused on educational video games. Flow theory has been the theoretical base for exploring the implications of learning through immersion or "being enveloped" by a virtual learning environment since the emotional constitution of these experiences resembles flow. This sense of "presence" or "flow" while immersed in virtual-reality interfaces facilitates efficient or deep learning of the content and skills that are integral to successful gameplay (e.g., Abrantes & Gouveia, 2012; Johnson et al., 2005; Liu et al., 2011; Procci et al., 2012; Van Eck, 2006).

Coller and colleagues (2011) examined the impact of applying a video game approach in teaching an undergraduate mechanical engineering course on engagement and learning. The video game developed by Coller, *EduTorcs,* was similar to commercial car racing games, except that student drivers wrote computer programs drawing on principles from mechanical engineering to race the car. The researchers found that students using the video game approach experienced significantly more engagement, intrinsic motivation, and positive affect during their homework and labs, as measured by the ESM, compared to a control group using traditional instructional methods (i.e., solving problem sets from a textbook). Students using the video game approach also made considerably greater learning gains as demonstrated by their course test performance, scoring almost one standard deviation higher on the tests than the control group (Shernoff & Coller, 2013).

Hamari and colleagues (2016) investigated the impact of flow (operationalized as heightened challenge and skill), engagement, and immersion on learning in video game-based learning environments. The study included (a) 140 undergraduates using the game, *Spumone,* for assignments in their undergraduate mechanical engineering classes, and (b) 134 high school students in 11 classrooms across the United States who played the game, *Quantum Spectre,* as part of their physics unit on optics. In support of flow theory, findings from the study suggested that increasing levels of challenge and skills through educational video games can increase immersion and engagement to promote learning.

Business Education and Flow

Several recent studies have focused on the role of flow in business education. In a study by Ro and colleagues (2018), flow was used as a benchmark to assess instructional quality for undergraduate business students. The researchers gave questionnaires to 315 undergraduate students before and after a typical Operations Management (OM) lecture class to understand the impact of flow on the students' experience and learning. They found strong evidence that flow impacts perceived learning, and moderate support for their hypothesis that flow promotes learning performance (as measured by the change in a pre-learning to a postlearning quiz). Flow and students' satisfaction with the lecture were also correlated. The findings suggest that the employment of flow in classroom environments will enhance many aspects of learning in business education (Ro et al., 2018).

Simulation games are another standard method for education and professional development in the business context. In a trial of 167 undergraduate business students, Buil and colleagues (2018) explored the impact of players' flow experience while playing a simulation game as part of their coursework. Students were assigned a fictitious company within the game, and required to make decisions about production, marketing, workforce, and other aspects of management. After each of 10 rounds, students analyzed their strategies and level of success. They then received a debriefing with instructors, as well as a final written debriefing. Goal clarity was not significantly related to flow; however, students reported feeling more flow when the game provided feedback during gameplay. Notably, characteristics of flow—goal clarity, feedback, and challenge-skill balance— were all statistically significant predictors of perceived learning. The study suggested that educators may be able to promote flow and learning in business education by incorporating simulation games which provide an optimal level of challenge and feedback on decision-making throughout gameplay (Buil et al., 2018).

Flow-through simulation games may also be useful in developing leadership and team-building skills. The simulation game, *FLIGBY* (an acronym for "Flow Is Good Business"; see FLIGBY, n.d.) was designed to teach players how to implement management skills that incorporate the concept of flow. The game is intended to be used in college-level courses or professional development workshops addressing management and leadership. Like many serious games, FLIGBY was designed to promote intense engagement in learning through a combination of novel technology use and game features. Within the game, the player takes on the role of the company manager and must enable as many employees as possible to experience flow. The game is played outside of the class setting, with discussions and exercises to take place during instruction. Approximately 10,000 people have played the game, but researchers have not yet performed a formal, systematic evaluation of it on a large sample (Buzady, 2017).

Implications for Promoting Student Engagement

Several implications for practice may be derived from our analysis of flow as it relates to student engagement and learning in schools. Flow is a useful model with which to conceptualize student engagement in classrooms. Although there has not been a great deal of engagement or flow found in U.S. public schools, factors such as student perceptions, instructional formats, the learning environment, and teacher behaviors all influence student engagement. Most available research converges on the observation that an optimal learning environment coalesces environmental challenge and environmental support, a combination necessary for learning to become both playful and challenging, both spontaneous and important (e.g., Rathunde & Csikszentmihalyi, 2005; Shernoff, 2013; Turner & Meyer, 2004). Teachers create optimal learning environments when they support students' autonomy and initiative, as well as provide the opportunity for students to interact with peers and adults promoting a sense of belongingness. In such environments, teachers provide activities that are challenging and relevant and yet also allow students to feel confident and in control—those that exact concentration but also induce enjoyment. However, the opportunity for action and skill-building seems to be the key. The teacher's flow can also be contagious, having the potential to cross over and stimulate students' flow (Bakker, 2005; Basom & Frase, 2004).

Budding research suggests that new technologies can "envelop" the learner in a virtual learning environment and can be extremely flow-inducing to increase learning (Pearce, 2005; Scoresby & Shelton, 2007). Recent research has also found that flow may play a unique role in business education, especially during simulation games that can enhance learning and leadership skills.

Using the flow model, researchers have discovered that creating engaged learners and optimal learning environments requires attention to a variety of contextual, instructional, developmental, and interpersonal factors. Growing research demonstrates that optimal learning environments are complex in combining environmental challenges such as clear goals and relevance, on the one hand, with environmental support in the form of a positive motivational and relational environment, on the other (Shernoff, 2013; Shernoff et al., 2016, 2017). Further research can profitably investigate conditions promoting such *environmental complexity*, as well as which components of learning environments exert the greatest influence on students' flow and engagement in a variety of contexts and settings.

References

Abrantes, S., & Gouveia, L. (2012). Using games for primary school: Assessing its use with flow experience. In M. M. Cruz-Cunha (Ed.), *Handbook of research on serious games* as *educational, business and research tools* (pp. 769–781). Information Science Reference. doi:10.4018/978-1-4666-4502-8.ch049

Bakker, A. B. (2005). Flow among music teachers and their students: The crossover of peak experiences. *Journal of Vocational Behavior, 66*, 26–44. doi:10.1016/j.jvb.2003.11.001

Basom, M. R., & Frase, L. (2004). Creating optimal work environments: Exploring teacher flow experiences. *Mentoring and Tutoring, 12*, 241–258. doi:10.1080/1361126042000239965

Bassi, M., & Delle Fave, A. (2004). Adolescence and the changing context of optimal experience in time: Italy 1986–2000. *Journal of Happiness Studies, 5*, 155–179. doi:10.1023/B:JOHS.0000035914.66037.b5

Buil, I., Catalan, S., & Martines, E. (2018). Exploring students' flow experiences in business simulation games. *Journal of Computer Assisted Learning, 34*(2), 183–192. doi:10.1111/jcal.12237.

Buzady, Z. (2017). Flow, leadership, and serious games—A pedagogical perspective. *World Journal of Science, Technology and Sustainable Development, 14*, 204–217. doi:10.1108/WJSTD-05–2016–0035

Cavanagh, R. F. (2015). A unified model of student engagement in classroom learning and classroom learning environment: One measure and one underlying construct. *Learning Environments Research, 18*(3), 349–361. doi:10.1007/s10984-015-9188-z

Cavanagh, R. F., & Shernoff, D. J. (2014). Positive change and scholastic education. In P. Inghilleri, G. Riva, & E. Riva (Eds.), *Enabling positive change: Flow and complexity in daily experience* (pp. 123–137). De Gruyter Open. doi:10.3140/2.1.4499.1046

Chao-Yang, C. Y., Sherry, Y. L., & Sunny, S. J. (2017). Episodic and individual effects of elementary students' optimal experience: An HLM study. *The Journal of Educational Research, 110*(6), 653–664. doi:10.1080/00220671.2016.1172551

Coller, B. D., Shernoff, D. J., & Strati, A. D. (2011). Measuring engagement as students learn dynamic systems & control with a video game. *Advances in Engineering Education, 2*(3), 1–32.

Conner, J., & Pope, D. (2014). Student engagement in high-performing schools: Relationships to mental and physical health. In D. Shernoff & J. Bempechat (Eds.), *Engaging youth in schools: Evidence-based models to guide future innovations* (pp. 80–100). NSSE Yearbook by Teachers College Record.

Corno, L., & Mandinach, E. B. (1983). The role of cognitive engagement in classroom learning and motivation. *Educational Psychologist, 18*, 88–108. doi:10.1080/00461528309529266

Csikszentmihalyi, M. (1990). *Flow: The psychology of optimal experience.* Harper Perennial.

Csikszentmihalyi, M., Abuhamdeh, S., & Nakamura, J. (2005). Flow. In A. J. Elliott & C. S. Dweck (Eds.), *Handbook of competence and motivation* (pp. 598–608). Guilford.

Csikszentmihalyi, M., & Csikszentmihalyi, I. S. (Eds.). (1988). *Optimal experience: Psychological studies of flow in consciousness.* Cambridge University Press.

Csikszentmihalyi, M., & Larson, R. (1984). *Being adolescent: Conflict and growth in the teenage years.* Basic Books.

Csikszentmihalyi, M., Rathunde, K., & Whalen, S. (1993). *Talented teenagers: The roots of success and failure.* Cambridge University Press.

Csikszentmihalyi, M., & Schneider, B. (2000). *Becoming adult: How teenagers prepare for the world of work.* Basic Books.

Custodero, L. A. (2005). Observable indicators of flow experience: A developmental perspective on musical engagement in young children from infancy to school age. *Music Education Research, 7*, 185–209. doi:10.1080/14613800500169431

Delle Fave, A., & Massimini, F. (2003). Optimal experience in work and leisure among teachers and physicians: Individual and bio-cultural implications. *Leisure Studies, 22*, 323–342. doi:10.1080/0261436031 0001594122

FLIGBY (n.d.). *FLIGBY FAQ.* Retrieved from https://www.fligby.com/faq/

Fullagar, C. J., Knight, P. A., & Sovern, H. S. (2013). Challenge/skill balance, flow, and performance anxiety. *Applied Psychology: An International Review, 62*, 236–259. doi:10.1111/j.1464–0597.2012.00494

Hamari, J., Shernoff, D. J., Rowe E., Coller, B. D., Asbell-Clarke J., & Edwards, T. (2016). Challenging games help students learn: An empirical study on engagement, flow and immersion in game-based learning. *Computers in Human Behavior, 54*, 170–179. doi:10.1016/j.chb.2015.07.045

Hektner, J. M., Schmidt, J. A., & Csikszentmihalyi, M. (2007). *Experience sampling method: Measuring the quality of everyday life.* Sage.

Henry, K. L., Knight, K. E., & Thornberry, T. P. (2011). School disengagement as a predictor of dropout, delinquency, and problem substance use during adolescence and early adulthood. *Journal of Youth and Adolescence, 41*, 156–166. doi:10.1007/s10964–011–9665–3

Hidi, S. (1990). Interest and its contribution as a mental resource for learning. *Review of Educational Research, 60*, 549–571. doi:10.3102/00346543060004549

Hughes, G. D. (2012). Teacher retention: Teacher characteristics, school characteristics, organizational characteristics, and teacher efficacy. *Journal of Educational Research, 105*, 245–255. http://dx.doi.org/10.1080/00220671.2011.584922

Johnson, W. L., Vilhjalmsson, H., & Marsella, S. (2005). Serious games for language learning: How much game, how much AI? In C. Looi & G. McCalla (Eds.), *Proceeding of the 2005 conference on artificial intelligence in education: Supporting learning through intelligent and socially informed technology* (pp. 306–313). IOS Press Amsterdam.

Kaufman, R. C., & Ring, M. (2011). Pathways to leadership and professional development. *Teaching Exceptional Children, 43*, 52–60. doi:10.1177/004005991104300505

Larson, R. W., & Richards, M. H. (1991). Boredom in the middle school years: Blaming schools versus blaming students. *American Journal of Education, 99*, 418–443. https://psycnet.apa.org/doi/10.1086/443992.

Larson, S. (2014). Exploring the roles of the generative vocabulary matrix and academic literacy engagement of ninth-grade biology students. *Literacy Research and Instruction, 53*(4), 287–325. https://doi.org/10.1080/19388071.2014.880974

Liu, C. C., Chen, Y. B., & Huang, C. W. (2011). The effect of simulation games on the learning of computational problem solving. *Computer and Education, 57*, 1907–1918. doi:10.1016/j.compedu.2011.04.002

Mesurado, B., Richaud, M. C., & Mateo, N. J. (2016). Engagement, flow, self-efficacy, and eustress of university students: A cross-national comparison between the Philippines and Argentina. *Journal of Psychology, 150*(3), 281–299. doi:10.1080/00223980.2015.1024595

Montessori, M. (1967). *The absorbent mind* (1st ed.). Holt, Rinehart, and Winston.

Nakamura, J. (1988). Optimal experience and the uses of talent. In M. Csikszentmihalyi & I. S. Csikszentmihalyi (Eds.), *Optimal experience: Psychological studies of flow in consciousness* (pp. 319–326). Cambridge University Press. doi:10.1017/CBO9780511621956.019

OECD. (2016). *PISA 2015 Results: Policies and practices for successful schools—Vol II / Students' wellbeing—Vol III.* Organization for Economic Cooperation and Development.

Pearce, J. M. (2005). *Engaging the learner: How can the flow experience support e-learning?* Paper presented at the E-Learn 2005 Conference, Vancouver, British Columbia, Canada.

Pino-James, N., Shernoff, D. J., Bressler, D. M., Larson, S. C., & Sinha, S. (2019). Instructional interventions that support student engagement: An international perspective. In J. A. Fredricks, A. L. Rechly, & S. L. Christensen (Eds.), *Handbook of student engagement interventions: Working with disengaged youth* (pp. 103–119). Elsevier.

Procci, K., Singer, A. R., Levy, K. R., & Bowers, C. (2012). Measuring the flow experience of gamers: An evaluation of the DFS-2. *Computers in Human Behavior, 28*, 2306–2312. doi:10.1016/j.chb.2012.06.039

Rathunde, K. (1993). Undivided interest and the growth of talent: A longitudinal study of adolescents. *Journal of Youth and Adolescence, 22*, 385–405. doi:10.1007/BF01537720

Rathunde, K., & Csikszentmihalyi, M. (2005). Middle school students, motivation and quality of experience: A comparison of Montessori and traditional school environments. *American Journal of Education, 111*, 341–371. doi:10.1086/428885

Ro, Y. K., Guo, Y. M., & Klein, B. D. (2018). The case of flow and learning revisited. *Journal of Education for Business, 9*, 128–141. https://doi.org/10.1080/08832323.2017.1417229

Schiefele, U., Krapp, A., & Winteler, A. (1992). Interest as a predictor of academic achievement: A meta-analysis of research. In K. A. Renninger, S. Hidi, & A. Krapp (Eds.), *The role of interest in learning and development* (pp. 183–212). Erlbaum.

Scoresby, J., & Shelton, B. E. (2007). *Visual perspectives within educational computer games: Effects on presence and flow within virtual learning environments.* Paper presented at the annual meeting of the American Educational Research Association, Chicago, IL.

Seligman, M. E. P., & Csikszentmihalyi, M. (2000). Positive psychology: An introduction. *American Psychologist, 55*, 5–14. doi:10.1037/0003–066X.55.1.5

Shernoff, D. J. (2010). *The experience of student engagement in high school classrooms: Influences and effects on long-term outcomes.* Lambert Academic.

Shernoff, D. J. (2013). *Optimal learning environments to promote student engagement.* Springer.

Shernoff, D. J., Bressler, D., Massaro, I., & Sinha, S., (2020, April). *The influence of a freshman iSTEAM academy on student engagement and educational attitudes.* Paper presented at the annual meeting of the American Educational Research Association, San Francisco, CA.

Shernoff, D. J., & Coller, B. D. (2013, April). *A quasi-experimental comparison of learning and performance in engineering education via video game versus traditional methods.* Paper presented at the annual meeting of the American Educational Research Association, San Francisco, CA.

Shernoff, D. J., Csikszentmihalyi, M., Schneider, B., & Shernoff, E. S. (2003). Student engagement in high school classrooms from the perspective of flow theory. *School Psychology Quarterly, 18*, 158–176. doi:10.1521/scpq.18.2.158.21860

Shernoff, D. J., Kelly, S., Tonks, S., Anderson, B., Cavanagh, R., Sinha, S., & Abdi, B. (2016). Student engagement as a function of environmental complexity in high school classrooms. *Learning and Instruction, 43*, 52–60. doi:10.1016/j.learninstruc.2015.12.003

Shernoff, D. J., Knauth, S., & Makris, E. (2000). The quality of classroom experiences. In M. Csikszentmihalyi & B. Schneider (Eds.), *Becoming adult: How teenagers prepare for the world of work* (pp. 141–164). Basic Books.

Shernoff, D. J., Ruzek, E. A., Sannella, A. J., Schorr, R., Sanchez-Wall, L., & Bressler, D. M. (2017). Student engagement as a general factor of classroom experience: Associations with classroom practices and educational outcomes in a university gateway course. *Frontiers in Psychology, 15*, 1–22. doi:10.3389/fpsyg.2017.00994

Shernoff, D. J., Ruzek, E. A., & Sinha, S. (2017). The influence of the high school classroom environment on leaning as mediated by student engagement. *School Psychology International, 38*(2), 201–218. doi:10.1177/0143034316666413

Shernoff, D. J., Tonks, S., & Anderson, B. G. (2014). The impact of the learning environment on student engagement in high school classrooms. In D. J. Shernoff & J. Bempechat (Eds.), *Engaging youth in schools: Evidence-based models to guide future innovations.* NSSE Yearbook by Teachers College Record.

Shernoff, D. J., Tonks, S., Anderson, B., & Dortch, C. (2011). *Linking instructional practices with student engagement from moment to moment in high school classrooms.* Paper presented at the Annual Meeting of the American Educational Research Association, New Orleans, LA.

Smith, M. P. (2009). *Differentiated instruction and teacher flow.* Unpublished doctoral dissertation, Saint Mary's University of Minnesota.

Steinberg, L., Brown, B. B., & Dornbusch, S. M. (1996). *Beyond the classroom: Why school reform has failed and what parents need to do.* Simon & Schuster.

Strati, A. D., Shernoff, D. J., & Kackar, H. Z. (2018). Flow. In R. Levesque (Ed.), *Encyclopedia of adolescence, 2nd edition* (Vol. 2, pp. 1440–1453). Springer. doi:10.1007/978-3-319-32132-5_173-2

Thompson, H., & Vedantam, S. (2012). A lively mind: Your brain on Jane Austen. *NPR: National Public Radio Website.* Retrieved from https://www.npr.org/sections/health-shots/2012/10/09/162401053/a-lively-mind-your-brain-on-jane-austen

Turner, J. C., & Meyer, D. K. (2004). A classroom perspective on the principle of moderate challenge in mathematics. *Journal of Educational Research, 97,* 311–318. doi:10.3200/JOER.97.6.311–318

Turner, J. C., Meyer, D. K., Cox, K. E., Logan, C., DiCintio, M., & Thomas, C. T. (1998). Creating contexts for involvement in mathematics. *Journal of Educational Psychology, 90,* 730–745. doi:10.1037/0022–0663.90.4.730

Turner, J. C., & Warzon, K. B. (2009). *Pathways to teacher motivation: The outcomes of teacher–student interaction.* Paper presented at the annual meeting of the American Educational Research Association, San Diego, CA.

Van Eck, R. (2006). Digital game-based learning: It's not just the digital natives who are restless. *Educase Review, 41,* 16–30.

Vygotsky, L. S. (1978). *Mind in society: The development of higher mental processes.* Harvard University Press.

Wen, J. M., Lin, C. H., & Liu, E. Z. F. (2019). Integrating educational board game in Chinese learning environment to enhance students' learning performance and flow experience. *International Journal of Online Pedagogy and Course Design (IJOPCD), 9*(4), 31–43. doi:10.4018/IJOPCD.2019100103

Yazzie-Mintz, E. (2010). *Charting the path from engagement to achievement: A report of the 2009 High School Survey of Student Engagement.* Center for Evaluation & Education Policy.

Zhang, J., Scardamalia, M., Reeve, R., & Messina, R. (2009). Designs for collective cognitive responsibility in knowledge-building communities. *Journal of the Learning Sciences, 18,* 7–44. doi:10.1080/10508400802581676.

Zirkel, S., Garcia, J. A., & Murphy, M. C. (2015). Experience-sampling research methods and their potential for education research. *Educational Researcher, 44,* 7–16. doi:10.3102/0013189x14566879

19

PROMOTING STUDENTS' GROWTH MOTIVATION

Mastery-Structured Classrooms

Helen Patrick and Avi Kaplan

Students' motivation to improve their knowledge and skills leads unequivocally to success at school and well-being. The motivation to improve encompasses several concepts in the motivation literature—growth mindset, incremental theory of intelligence, learning goals, mastery orientation, and growth orientation—that share the same or very similar features; therefore, they are discussed together under the label "growth motivation." Our focus in this chapter is on classroom environments and teacher practices that promote students' growth motivation for academics. First, however, we briefly outline the characteristics of students who are motivated toward growth.

Students' Growth Motivation

Growth-oriented students focus on learning and improvement. Most importantly, this focus is based on students' belief that their ability or intelligence can grow. The belief in the malleability of ability undergirds a broad pattern of engagement that is characterized by mastery-oriented thinking and behavior (Dweck & Sorich, 1999). Growth-oriented students seek out challenges that will stretch and grow their competencies, practice their developing skills to improve performance, monitor their progress, try alternative strategies to master the material, seek out assistance when necessary, and gauge success in terms of their improvement. They also respond positively to challenges and do not interpret making mistakes and taking time to accomplish the task as an indicator that they cannot be successful. Instead, when encountering difficulty or set-backs growth-oriented students remain persistent, effortful, self-regulating, strategic, and optimistic—all responses that lead to greater learning and achievement (Dweck, 2002; Dweck & Leggett, 1988; Dweck & Sorich, 1999; Yeager & Dweck, 2012; Yu & McLellan, 2020). Not surprisingly, therefore, students' growth motivation predicts many positive outcomes, including academic engagement and achievement (Blackwell et al., 2007; Linnenbrink-Garcia et al., 2008; Yu & McLellan, 2020).

Contrasting with the view that intelligence or ability is malleable and grows is a belief that people's intelligence is inherently finite, beyond which failure is inevitable (i.e., fixed mindset or entity theory of intelligence; Dweck, 2002; Dweck & Leggett, 1988; Dweck & Sorich, 1999). Students who view their academic abilities as having fixed limits also tend to engage productively

DOI: 10.4324/9781003013778-24

in academic tasks, but only when they believe they have the ability to be successful. However, when they view success in the task as uncertain, these students tend to engage in classroom activities in maladaptive ways, especially within competitive situations that encourage comparisons of abilities. Students who believe that ability is fixed view time and effort expended to complete an activity as indicators of this inherent ability. Therefore, they consider quick success to signal high intelligence and slow progress or difficulty as a sign of the limits to their intelligence. Consequently, such students typically do not persevere; doing so merely provides evidence of their deficiencies. Instead, they tend to choose easier tasks in which they know they can be successful or, if not possible, they engage in behaviors that hide their perceived limitations. Such maladaptive responses include (a) submitting others' answers or products as their own (e.g., cheating) and (b) providing reasons—real or claimed—for poor performance that do not reflect low ability, such as not trying, feeling sick, or being too engaged in other activities (Dweck, 2002; Dweck & Sorich, 1999; Urdan et al., 2002; Yeager & Dweck, 2012; Yu & McLellan, 2020). Ironically, these behaviors undermine learning and *ensure* that their competence does not increase.

Over time, students with equal initial performance but different levels of growth motivation come to exhibit different trajectories of engagement and achievement that correspond to that motivation. That is, students who believe they can grow their abilities tend to engage with schoolwork more positively and experience greater academic success than those who believe their abilities are fixed (Blackwell et al., 2007; Yu & McLellan, 2020). Importantly, students' fates are not inevitable. In fact, and of particular relevance to this chapter, growth motivation can itself be grown. Specific interventions target changes in students' core beliefs about the malleability of intelligence by teaching them about the elasticity of the brain (Yeager & Dweck, 2012). However, the research also suggests that the effectiveness of these very specific interventions depends on characteristics of the educational context (Walton & Yaeger, 2020). There are comprehensive features of learning environments and teacher practices that can promote or hinder students' growth motivation (Ames, 1992a; Maehr & Midgley, 1996). In the next section, we focus on those contextual features and on how teachers can foster and support students' growth motivation.

Environments that Promote Growth Motivation

Motivation is not only influenced by dispositions and beliefs, but also by achievement-related meanings that are salient in students' environments (e.g., schools, and classrooms). Relevant to growth-oriented motivation, learning environments explicitly and implicitly communicate messages about the purposes of school and schoolwork; the nature of ability and its role in the learning process; the meanings, bases, and implications of success and failure; and the likelihood that different students will succeed (Ames, 1984; Dweck & Leggett, 1988; Maehr, 1984; Nicholls, 1989). As a result, students in different learning environments form different meanings; for example, whether learning calculus is a realistic goal for everyone or is beyond the reach of some people because they lack the necessary ability to learn advanced mathematics. Together, different types of messages cohere into psychological *goal structures*, or networks of assumptions, beliefs, values, and goals about students' learning that manifest in the educational discourse and practices. These structures frame students' own achievement-related beliefs and associated behaviors (Ames, 1984, 1992a, 1992b).

The goal structure that supports students' growth motivation is a *mastery goal structure*. It comprises messages that students' ability can be increased, and that success is based on intentional effort and indicated by learning, personal improvement, and meeting absolute standards (Ames, 1992b). These messages are sufficiently powerful that even students who view intelligence as a fixed capacity can change their beliefs in line with a growth orientation and exhibit mastery-oriented behaviors. In the next section, we describe research on student outcomes associated with mastery-structured classrooms.

Student Engagement in Mastery-Structured Classrooms

In mastery-structured classrooms, students interpret the discourse and practices to mean that everyone can improve; learning takes time; improvement requires deliberate effort and appropriate strategies; challenge and mistakes are normal aspects of learning; deep understanding of content is more important than getting the correct answer to a question; and personal improvement rather than comparisons among students is the basis for achievement and success (Ames, 1992b; Ames & Archer, 1988). These perceptions foster students' growth-oriented beliefs, influencing how they engage with others and with their schoolwork (Ames, 1992a, 1992b).

At all educational levels, mastery-structured classrooms are consistently associated with, and promote, students' growth motivation and adaptive engagement (Bardach et al., 2020). These outcomes include students' growth-oriented beliefs, behaviors, cognitive strategies, emotions, and achievement. For example, classroom mastery structure is associated with students (a) endorsing a growth mindset (Lüftenegger et al., 2017); (b) attributing success to effort (Ames & Archer, 1988; Tapola & Niemivirta, 2008); (c) feeling competent academically and confident about their ability to learn (e.g., Lüftenegger et al., 2014; Murayama & Elliot, 2009; Wolters, 2004); and (d) believing their schoolwork is interesting, enjoyable, useful, and important (Lazarides et al., 2018; Murayama & Elliot, 2009).

Mastery-structured classrooms are also related positively to students' adaptive behaviors. These behaviors include (a) effort, persistence, and attention (e.g., Lau & Nie, 2008; Madjar, 2017; Wolters, 2004); (b) preferring challenging tasks (Ames & Archer, 1988); (c) asking for appropriate help (i.e., explanations but not answers) when it is needed (e.g., Ryan & Shim, 2012); and (d) responding to problems with adaptive coping responses such as trying to figure out what went wrong (Kaplan & Midgley, 1999).

Students' perception of their classroom mastery structure is related positively to adaptive kinds of thinking and learning. These include (a) thinking critically and using deep, effortful learning strategies (e.g., summarizing main points, making connections with what they already know) and (b) using metacognitive and self-regulatory strategies (e.g., planning, monitoring; Bergsmann et al., 2013; Michou et al., 2013; Wolters, 2004).

Because mastery-structured classrooms allow all students to be successful, they are associated with positive learning-related emotions. These emotions include students' (a) satisfaction with their learning (Nolen, 2003); (b) happiness at school (Anderman, 1999; Kaplan & Midgley, 1999); and (c) feelings of belonging to the classroom (Anderman, 2003). Mastery structures also relate positively to students having supportive relationships with teachers and peers and negatively to peer conflict (Polychroni et al., 2012).

Correspondingly, perceived classroom mastery structure is related negatively to students' maladaptive beliefs, behaviors, cognitions, and emotions. These include (a) anxiety (Federici et al., 2015); (b) avoiding asking for help when needed (Linnenbrink, 2005; Ryan et al., 1998); (c) self-handicapping (e.g., purposefully withdrawing effort; Lau & Nie, 2008; Turner et al., 2002; Urdan, 2004); (d) being disruptive (Kaplan et al., 2002); (e) procrastinating (Wolters, 2004); and (f) cheating (Murdock et al., 2001; Tas & Tekkaya, 2010).

Finally, consistent with the array of adaptive beliefs and behaviors just outlined, students' perceptions of a classroom's mastery structure are related to achievement, including grades (e.g., Bergsmann et al., 2013; Urdan, 2004; Urdan & Midgley, 2003; Wolters, 2004) and test scores (Lau & Nie, 2008; Linnenbrink, 2005). Notably, this association has not been found in all studies (Linnenbrink-Garcia et al., 2008). Growth-oriented behaviors such as expending effort, using deep learning and regulatory strategies, and not giving up when experiencing difficulty are only likely to predict achievement when test scores reflect those behaviors. Suppose students can receive high grades or test scores without understanding the content or needing to expend effort. In this case, achievement would not be expected to relate to mastery-structured classroom environments or growth motivation.

Given the evidence that classroom mastery structure is associated with positive and valued outcomes for students in all grade levels and countries, it is important to understand how educators can translate beliefs about the malleability of intelligence and ability, the value of challenge and error, and the goals of learning and self-improvement into discourse and practices that emphasize them to students. We discuss this issue next.

Features of Mastery-Structured Classrooms

Classroom mastery structure is a constellation of related perceptions. It is not an "objective" characteristic, but rather, refers to the ways that individual students comprehensively perceive, make meaning, and experience a particular classroom environment. Because students' personal history and current social positioning frame their experiences, perceptions vary among students in the same classroom; nevertheless, some facets of students' classroom experiences are shared. Moreover, there are differences in mastery structure across classrooms (Ames, 1992b; Bardach et al., 2019).

Teachers are most proximal to students and are most impactful on the classroom environments that students experience. As such, teachers play a central role in creating growth- or mastery-structured classrooms (Ames, 1992b). Although teachers are embedded within political and organizational systems that have policies and requirements that constrain their options (Maehr & Midgley, 1996), teachers can mediate and modify messages to students through their classroom discourse and practices about who can (and cannot) learn the content, how success is manifested, and what students must do to be successful. For example, teachers may communicate whether making mistakes or feeling confused are natural parts of the learning process that can be overcome with effort and practice, or that they imply unsurmountable limitations to learning. Teachers may convey that students' "potential for learning" is indicated by improving on their current competence or that is indicated by them "knowing it" or "getting it" quickly.

Researchers customarily use surveys to measure students' perceptions of their classroom's mastery structure. These perceptions commonly focus on the teacher (e.g., the extent to which the teacher thinks mistakes are okay as long as students are learning) or their classroom (e.g., how important it is in that class for students to try hard or improve; Midgley et al., 1996, 2000). Because students create these perceptions based on their interpretations of classroom norms, rules, routines, and relationships, knowing what teacher practices contribute to students' perceptions is critical for creating mastery-structured classrooms.

Carole Ames (1984, 1990, 1992a, 1992b) was the pioneering researcher who synthesized experimental research and incorporated teaching principles and strategies that emphasize student growth. Ames built on Epstein's (1983) framework of dimensions of the classroom environment to devise a conceptual framework that defines classroom mastery structure. This framework comprises a cohesive set of six separate, but interrelated, dimensions of instructional practices (i.e., Task, Authority, Recognition, Grouping, Evaluation, and Time), represented by the acronym TARGET. Ames noted that teachers create mastery-structured classrooms, not with any single type of practice, but by using practices from many dimensions together to convey a consistent, coherently integrated, and salient message (Ames, 1990, 1992a, 1992b). A seventh category—Social—was added subsequently to form TARGETS; it addresses the role of classroom relational factors in emphasizing or undermining growth motivation (Kaplan & Maehr, 1999; Patrick, 2004).

Early survey measures of classroom mastery structure assessed either perceptions of an overall emphasis on growth or perceptions of some, but not all, TARGET categories (Midgley et al., 1996, 2000). More recent instruments measure the six original dimensions of the classroom environment (Lüftenegger et al., 2014, 2017; Tapola & Niemivirta, 2008). Studies with these newer scales support the contention that the practices in the different growth-promoting dimensions function synergistically. For example, although the items that correspond to each category form distinct scales, they also cohere to form a single higher-order factor representing classroom mastery structure (Lüftenegger et al., 2014, 2017). Similarly, a different set of items corresponding to the TARGET categories was perceived by students as six factors (although only five formed internally consistent scales). The factors represented different emphases in the classroom—Learning, Ability and Evaluation, Autonomy and Choice, Individualistic Work, and Task Variety (Tapola & Niemivirta, 2008). Although these scales included the six categories of practices, each category contributed items to more than one scale. For example, some Evaluation items were part of the Learning scale (e.g., "In evaluation the teacher takes into consideration how I have developed in my schoolwork," p. 311) and others were part of the Ability and Evaluation scale (e.g., "The teacher evaluates students' work publicly," p. 311). Therefore, students' perceptions were grouped according to more holistic systems of meaning instead of by TARGET dimensions. The scales, with the exception of Ability and Evaluation, correlated highly with each other (Tapola & Niemivirta, 2008), which also indicated that the practices were perceived as interconnected.

None of the instruments discussed address the social dimension of the environment—the seventh category of practices that communicate classroom mastery structure. Other studies, however, indicate that students' perceptions of social dimensions of the classroom (e.g., teacher support, mutual respect) are central to their perceptions of the classroom's mastery structure (Patrick et al., 2011; Turner et al., 2013).

Although studies that use self-report surveys to measure classroom mastery structure provide valuable information about its composition, they are less helpful in identifying what teachers actually do and say to communicate a perceived emphasis on mastery and personal growth. Information about teacher mastery-supporting behavior comes predominantly from studies linking students' perceptions to (a) researchers' observations of teacher discourse and behavior (e.g., Anderman et al., 2002, 2011; Patrick et al., 2001, 2003; Urdan, 2004); (b) teacher and student interactions during lessons (e.g., Boden et al., 2020; Turner et al., 2002, 2003); and (c) students' responses to open-ended questions about the basis for their perceptions (Patrick & Ryan, 2008; Urdan, 2004). In the next section, we describe the teacher practices identified in these studies.

Teacher Practices that Create Mastery-Structured Classrooms

In this section, we use the TARGETS framework to organize the classroom and teacher practices that contribute to students' perceptions of the educational environment as emphasizing learning, mastery, and personal growth. Although we discuss practices separately by dimension, it is necessary to remember that they are interconnected, and their instantiation needs to be integrated into a cohesive instructional approach. These connections will be evident in many of the examples we present, where particular instructional practices correspond to more than one dimension.

Tasks

Students make inferences about their teachers' emphasis on growth and mastery from the kinds of learning activities teachers provide for students, the end products, and the expressed rationales and reasons for particular types of tasks and topics. Task-related practices also include teachers' practices of engaging students in academic activities, such as using higher-order questioning, scaffolding, and pressing for understanding (Patrick et al., 2001).

Enthusiasm. Teachers in mastery-structured classrooms portray learning as enjoyable, fascinating, valuable, and worthwhile, and they express their genuine enthusiasm for the content and activity (Anderman et al., 2011). An example from one of the studies is a teacher who related enthusiastically how understanding imagery in literature enables him to deepen his appreciation of movies (Patrick et al., 2003). By contrast, teachers in classrooms with a low emphasis on growth refer to tasks with low enthusiasm and an expectation that students won't want to engage in them; for example, "You may find this boring, and I don't disagree with you" (Patrick et al., 2001, p. 44).

Diversity. Teachers convey a mastery structured, by presenting content in diverse ways and through different kinds of activities. Such presentations increase opportunities for students to connect the content with their previous knowledge, which promotes more meaningful understanding. For example, in another study, a student explained they could tell the teacher wanted them to understand the content because they were "doing all kinds of problems in different forms, not just memorizing how to do one type of problem" (Patrick & Ryan, 2008, p. 108). By contrast, a student in a low mastery-structure classroom recounted that the teacher "give[s] us the same thing over and over and expects us to do it. Then she says we're going to do these worksheets over and over until we get the concept" (Patrick & Ryan, 2008, p. 108). This latter approach may convey that what is important is the procedure rather than their understanding and that if students aren't understanding the content, then the problem is with them.

Relevance. Mastery-focused teachers help students see the relevance of what they are learning beyond being tested on it. For example, a high school science teacher teaching about pH made many connections between concepts and everyday situations, such as how antacids neutralize stomach acids and why changing the soil's pH affects the color of flowers. Similarly, a history teacher connected primary source documents from the past to contemporary events, such as a media celebrity's race-related scandal (Anderman et al., 2011). Other strategies for creating relevance involve encouraging students to make their own connections between the content and their lives and interests (Albrecht & Karabenick, 2018).

High expectations. Communicating a clear expectation that *all* students can learn and improve is a central part of promoting a mastery focus and growth motivation. A teacher expressed this explicitly when telling students emphatically and confidently,

> When you leave sixth grade, … if you don't know how to do anything else, you're going to know how to do MATH, you're going to know how to READ, you're going to be organized, and you're going to write.
>
> *(Patrick et al., 2003, p. 1537)*

In contrast, teachers in low mastery-structured classrooms talk about negative consequences of failure and express expectations that some students will have difficulty or not be successful (Patrick et al., 2003).

Challenge. High expectations are communicated by providing all students with challenging activities that they can learn from; that is, tasks that involve skills or knowledge that students have not mastered completely but can accomplish with instruction and support (Turner et al., 1998, 2002). Assigning tasks that are too easy communicates low expectations for students and does not promote learning because learning has already occurred. On the other hand, activities beyond those in which students can experience success with assistance also offer little learning opportunity. Furthermore, struggling unsuccessfully over time undermines students' confidence in their ability and often leads to feelings of helplessness and a belief that their failure is inevitable (Dweck, 2002).

Support. Challenging tasks must be accompanied by instructional supports that enable student learning. Because these supports assist incremental improvement, they also promote growth motivation. One type of support is scaffolding—a set of practices that explicitly guide the student performing increasingly more challenging tasks and thus developing competence (Meyer & Turner, 2002). High levels of appropriate teacher scaffolding are features of mastery-structured classrooms (Anderman et al., 2011; Turner et al., 2002). With scaffolding, the teacher structures the situation, guiding students to accomplish the task with assistance that gradually diminishes in concert with students' increasingly independent performance while also mediating frustration and providing encouragement (Meyer & Turner, 2002).

Academic press. Academic press is also often evident in mastery-structured classrooms (Anderman et al., 2011). Press refers to a teacher "staying with" a student who either does not know or gives a superficial answer, rather than moving on to ask another student or providing the answer themselves. Teachers probe students' understanding by asking them to explain their thinking and encouraging them to think deeply and persevere. This process occurred when a teacher said: "Now, you had to explain your answer, what did you do to prove that this is a right triangle?" (Boden et al., 2020, p. 1239). This cognitive demand provides challenge, scaffolds more advanced performance, and expresses confidence that students can extend their ability (Middleton & Midgley, 2002).

Authority

Authority refers to the locus of responsibility in the classroom and includes aspects of rules and classroom management. In mastery-structured classrooms, teachers afford students opportunities to share responsibility for their learning and engagement.

Modeling authority in learning. In mastery-structured classrooms, teachers do not position themselves as the sole authority about content but communicate that not knowing something, or making a mistake, does not imply that someone is not intelligent. They establish this understanding by comfortably acknowledging that they are uncertain about some things instead of presenting themselves as knowing all the content. Teachers emphasize growth motivation by modeling problem-solving, sharing how they go about finding new information and encouraging students to look for answers themselves. Teachers may also encourage students to share their expertise or knowledge rather than always appear to know more than their students (Anderman et al., 2011).

By contrast, in a low mastery-structured classroom, teachers who feel uncertain about the content they are teaching typically do not want students to realize it, so they control the lesson and limit students' questioning. Not only does this constrain students' learning, but students miss out on seeing how others go about getting information and witnessing the acceptability of adults—including teachers—not having all the answers. Excessive teacher authority also communicates a lack of confidence in students' ability and undermines interest in learning (Ames, 1992a).

Effective management norms. The clear emphasis on student learning in mastery-structured classrooms is possible because teachers create effective management routines, and therefore rarely spend time dealing with student disruptions. Classrooms, therefore, appear to be "well-oiled machines." Teachers lay the groundwork for effective management at the beginning of the year; they communicate clear routines and rules, provide examples, and ensure that students understand the reasons for rules. Teachers express positive expectations and, importantly, monitor student behavior closely and apply rules consistently and fairly (Anderman et al., 2011; Patrick et al., 2001, 2003).

Promoting student autonomy. Student autonomy contributes to classroom mastery structure and students' growth motivation. Consistent with their positive expectations for students, teachers promote student autonomy by affording them some responsibility for academics. This may involve encouraging students to incorporate their own content into tasks, choose among different tasks or the order for completing tasks, or allowing them to check their answers. Choice is insufficient to create mastery structure; however, it interacts with the types of tasks, the time allowed, and feedback or recognition. Mastery-structured teachers also allow students to show responsibility procedurally, such as by letting them use the bathroom or get up to sharpen a pencil without requiring teacher permission (Anderman et al., 2002; Patrick et al., 2001). These practices also allow lessons to proceed without procedural interruptions.

Recognition and Evaluation

Recognition and evaluation involve assessing and responding to students' engagement and their products. Evaluation, or assessment, may be formal (e.g., tests) or informal (e.g., monitoring students' understanding during lessons), and recognition includes feedback, praise, and awards. Because the two categories are closely related, we group them here. Features relevant to students' growth motivation include what is ostensibly being assessed (e.g., progress, ability), explicated reasons for students' performance (e.g., effort, strategies, ability), and whether and how students can improve their performance. It is also necessary that teachers' practices are consistent with their spoken language—students interpret what teachers value primarily from their practices, rather than their words (Patrick et al., 2003).

Self-referenced improvement. Teachers convey a mastery focus by helping students learn and improve. This requires that they monitor students' progress, perhaps by moving around the room while students are working and assisting when students need help (Anderman et al., 2011). If students are making slow progress, teachers can understand why and respond by adding explanations or examples, changing the task, or providing encouragement; for example: "This may seem difficult, but if you stay with it, you'll learn more than you bargained for!" (Turner et al., 1998, p. 735). Without such close monitoring, teachers often misunderstand why students' progress is slow, such as when a frustrated sixth-grade teacher said, "All of these angles are not drawn properly. ... We're playing. We're not serious about what we're doing" (Patrick et al., 2003, p. 1549).

Teachers' feedback to students sends important messages relevant to mastery and growth. Giving informational feedback, which conveys specifically what students did well, what can be improved, and how they can improve, is crucial. For example, a fifth-grader's journal entry consisted of one very long sentence. In response, the teacher helped to identify the issue ("Have you ever in your life read a book that had a sentence that long?"), suggested where the student could break it into shorter sentences, and asked that it be rewritten. The teacher's feedback was supportive, constructive, mastery-focused, and did not imply that either effort or ability was lacking (Anderman et al., 2002).

Attributions to effort and strategies. Mastery-focused teachers notice students' improvement and attribute it to using effective strategies and effort. Their praise is related to learning and is informational, specific, and contingent. For example, the day after a lesson about using commas, a fifth-grade teacher praised a student for using commas throughout a writing assignment instead of linking words with "and" multiple times, like previously (Patrick et al., 2001). By contrast, an emphasis on following procedures rather than understanding content undermines mastery structure. An example is a teacher who subtracted points if students turned in a paper with "fringe" (i.e., the half-torn edge after a page is pulled from a spiral notebook) (Patrick et al., 2003). Another teacher, when telling fifth graders they did not want them to feel anxious, said grading writing would be based on writing complete sentences, not having complete thoughts. (i.e., if they were grammatically correct rather than making sense) (Anderman et al., 2002).

Mistakes as opportunities for learning. In building a mastery structure, teachers are explicit that mistakes are part of the learning process and do not indicate that students are not intelligent enough to master the knowledge or skills. When asked how they know their teacher thinks mistakes are okay as long as they are learning, one-third of middle-grade students' responses mentioned their teacher's evaluation practices, which included being allowed to re-do homework, quizzes, or tests and grading homework for completion and not correctness (Patrick & Ryan, 2008).

Part of building a mastery structure involves responding to student mistakes in ways that prevent or minimize embarrassment and provides them with information and encouragement. Importantly, teachers' responses do not have to be private; it is not *that* a student has difficulty, but the *meaning* of that difficulty that conveys growth-related messages (Turner et al., 2003). An example is a teacher's response to a student's mistake while measuring angles. The teacher used this as an opportunity for the class to learn from the mistake, saying, "I want to point it out to you here, because it is probably THE MOST common mistake that students make in using a protractor" (Patrick et al., 2003, p. 1548). This constructive practice contrasts with teachers responding to students' mistakes by telling them that they should know to do the math problem because it is in the book (Patrick & Ryan, 2008) or that "half of the class is brain dead" (Turner et al., 2003, p. 372).

Grouping

Grouping involves whether and how teachers require, allow, or encourage students to work together. It includes characteristics of groups and group members, the stability and flexibility of groups, and the rationale for selecting group members.

Malleable grouping. Teachers who emphasize student growth do not assign students to stable groups based on test scores or other presumed indicators of ability. Studies of classroom mastery structures based on qualitative data rarely mention ability-based grouping. One of the few examples is a fifth-grade teacher who said, on the first day of school, "Hopefully there will be only one reading group, but I know better than that. Everyone reads on a different level" (Patrick et al., 2001, p. 48). With this comment, the teacher implied that reading groups were organized by reading ability and that it was not good to have more than one ability-based group.

Mutual help. Teachers in mastery-structured classrooms encourage students to work together and help each other, and observers note that students typically interact with each other about schoolwork, albeit not in defined groups (Anderman et al., 2011; Patrick et al., 2001, 2003). However, it is also notable that when students identified teacher practices that signal a mastery focus, fewer than 1% of responses mentioned working with others (Patrick & Ryan, 2008).

Survey research provides converging evidence that grouping practices are not central to mastery-structured classrooms. Grouping made the smallest contribution of the six subscales to the TARGET Goal Structure scale (Lüftenegger et al., 2017). Furthermore, in Tapola and Niemivirta's (2008) measure of the classroom learning environment, students did not identify a separate factor related to student grouping. Instead, one item ("Students are allowed to work in groups during the lessons," p. 311) was part of the Task Variety scale. A second item ("In group work students are divided into groups on the basis of their ability and skills," p. 311) was perceived similarly to questions about normative evaluation (i.e., comparisons among students' performance).

These results do not mean that student grouping is unimportant. At least in the United States, when ability grouping occurs within classrooms, it is predominantly in the earliest grades. There has been very little research about classroom growth- or mastery-promoting environments in the early grades. In later grades, sorting is more likely at the school level, with students assigned to classrooms according, ostensibly, to their ability. Although students' growth motivation is undoubtedly influenced a great deal by this tracking, such grouping may be more salient within schools (i.e., among classrooms) or across schools, unless teachers refer to a hierarchy of classrooms or schools.

Time

The Time dimension encompasses how the teacher manages time in the classroom. It includes time limits, whether time limits are flexible to match students' needs, and teacher comments about the speed of students' learning or finishing their work.

Time for learning. Teachers in high mastery-structured classrooms allow students enough time to work through problems and ensure they understand the content before moving on. Giving sufficient time communicates to students that learning usually takes time, and is central to the expectation that everyone can learn. That is the message in the following example: after a student said they did not understand the problem, a teacher responded by saying, "You know what? That's why we're going to keep working on it today and tomorrow. You'll get it. Okay? We're just now starting it...so I don't expect you to fully understand it right away" (Turner et al., 2002, p. 93). Observers could not know whether or not the teacher had intended to spend more time on the topic, and students may not have known either, which probably lessens the saliency of teachers' time-related practices when they promote students' learning.

Matching time to students' needs. Teachers' instructional time use may be most noticeable when it does not match students' learning needs. For example, when students have too much time, they are prone to being disruptive, whereas having too little time often results in students' complaints, frustration, or off-task behavior when they do not understand and give up. Although time use that matches students' needs is not easily observed by outsiders, students are aware of it, especially when they have too much or too little time to learn. Of note, when students explained reasons for their view of their classroom's mastery structure, practices involving time were mentioned more often than those involving tasks, authority, grouping, and evaluation (Patrick & Ryan, 2008).

Social

A central feature of mastery-structured classrooms is the students' sense of social security that allows them to concentrate fully on learning and improvement. A sense of psychological safety in relationships with the teacher and other students frames the effect of all other types of practices. Without feeling socially secure, it is unlikely that students will be willing to engage in challenging tasks, where success is uncertain and students are vulnerable to negative reactions from others.

Mutual respect. Teachers are responsible for creating socially safe environments and insisting that students show respect for each other is key. An example is a sixth-grade teacher who told the class emphatically that it is not acceptable for them to treat others disrespectfully. The teacher then promoted empathy by saying, "Don't you think we all have enough problems that we don't need to create them for other people?" (Patrick et al., 2003, p. 1542). However, words alone are insufficient; teachers must monitor students' behavior and ensure that ridicule, teasing, or exclusion does not occur.

Supportive relationships. Teachers who are perceived as encouraging growth motivation also build supportive relationships with their students. They communicate caring about students as individuals and caring about their learning. They show personal caring by viewing students as individuals with unique interests, strengths, and needs; being warm, friendly, responsive, and approachable in their interactions; and listening to students. Teachers demonstrate sensitivity to students' needs by easing stress or anxiety, perhaps by lightening the mood with humor, acknowledging students' emotions, and sharing their concerns. They may also disclose (appropriate) personal information that helps students see commonalities between themselves and teachers (Patrick et al., 2001, 2003; Patrick & Ryan, 2008; Turner et al., 2002).

Open communication. Teachers show they care about students' learning by communicating positive expectations that students will learn and then affording them the opportunities (e.g., through tasks, attention, assistance, feedback, encouragement, time) to ensure that learning occurs. Teachers encourage students to communicate openly about their experiences, challenges, and needs, providing them opportunities to ask questions, and are available to help outside classroom hours. In mastery-structured classrooms, teachers communicate interest in helping students learn, and their effort into preparing and teaching lessons is evident (Anderman et al., 2011; Patrick et al., 2001, 2003; Patrick & Ryan, 2008). Importantly, students often misinterpret teachers' practices. Open communication about the meaning of schooling that allows students to constructively critique instructional practices from their own perspective can both facilitate the perceptions that students' voices are valued and provide important insights to teachers about the practices that would emphasize teachers' focus on growth to students (Thorkildsen & Nicholls, 1991).

Conclusion

This chapter discussed contextual features that promote students' growth motivation. We reviewed research about learning environments characterized as mastery-structured classrooms—also labeled classroom mastery goal structures—that promote students' beliefs that their ability can grow, that their success depends on effort and strategies in pursuing challenging tasks, and that the purpose of school is improvement and deep understanding. We outlined many of the myriad academic, social, and emotional benefits associated with this type of classroom environment. We presented an overview of different dimensions of teacher practices that build a mastery structure. Finally, we provided examples of teachers' mastery-promoting practices that were identified primarily from qualitative classroom research. However, whereas some research has addressed this crucial link between research and educational practice, far too little research investigated how mastery-focused teaching manifests in diverse, authentic classrooms. We hope that this type of research becomes prevalent and that researchers consider a wider range of grade levels, school systems, and cultures.

References

Albrecht, J. R., & Karabenick, S. A. (2018). Relevance for learning and motivation in education. *The Journal of Experimental Education, 86*(1), 1–10. https://doi.org/10.1080/00220973.2017.1380593

Ames, C. (1984). Competitive, cooperative, and individualistic goal structures: A cognitive-motivational analysis. In R. Ames & C. Ames (Eds.), *Research on motivation in education, Volume 1: Student motivation* (pp. 177–207). Academic Press.

Ames, C. (1990, April). *Achievement goals and classroom structure: Developing a learning orientation in students.* Paper presented at the annual meeting of the American Educational Research Association in Boston, MA.

Ames, C. (1992a). Achievement goals and the classroom motivational climate. In D. H. Schunk & J. L. Meece (Eds.), *Student perception in the classroom* (pp. 327–348). Erlbaum. https://doi.org/10.4324/9780203052532-22

Ames, C. (1992b). Classrooms: Goals, structures, and student motivation. *Journal of Educational Psychology, 84*(3), 261–271. https://doi.org/10.1037/0022-0663.84.3.261

Ames, C., & Archer, J. (1988). Achievement goals in the classroom: Students' learning strategies and motivation processes. *Journal of Educational Psychology, 80*(3), 260–267 https://doi.org/10.1037/0022-0663.80.3.260

Anderman, L. H. (1999). Classroom goal orientation, school belonging, and social goals as predictors of students' positive and negative affect following the transition to middle school. *Journal of Research and Development in Education, 32*(2), 89–103.

Anderman, L. H. (2003). Academic and social perceptions as predictors of change in middle school students' sense of school belonging. *The Journal of Experimental Education, 72*(1), 5–22. https://doi.org/10.1080/00220970309600877

Anderman, L. H., Andrzejewski, C. E., & Allen, J. L. (2011). How do teachers support students' motivation and learning in their classrooms? *Teachers College Record, 113*(5), 969–1003.

Anderman, L. H., Patrick, H., Hruda, L. Z., & Linnenbrink, E. A. (2002). Observing classroom goal structures to clarify and expand goal theory. In C. Midgley (Ed.), *Goals, goal structures, and patterns of adaptive learning* (pp. 243–278). Erlbaum. https://doi.org/10.4324/9781410602152-16

Bardach, L., Lüftenegger, M., Yanagida, T., Schober, B., & Spiel, C. (2019). The role of within-class consensus on mastery goal structures in predicting socio-emotional outcomes. *British Journal of Educational Psychology, 89*, 239–258. https://doi.org/10.1037/edu0000419

Bardach, L., Oczlon, S., Pietschnig, J., & Lüftenegger, M. (2020). Has achievement goal theory been right? A meta-analysis of the relation between goal structures and personal achievement goals. *Journal of Educational Psychology, 112*(6), 1197–1220. https://doi.org/10.1037/edu0000419

Bergsmann, E. M., Lüftenegger, M., Jöstl, G., Schober, B., & Spiel, C. (2013). The role of classroom structure in fostering students' school functioning: A comprehensive and application-oriented approach. *Learning and Individual Differences, 26,* 131–138. https://doi.org/10.1016/j.lindif.2013.05.005

Blackwell, L. S., Trzesniewski, K. H., & Dweck, C. S. (2007). Implicit theories of intelligence predict achievement across an adolescent transition: A longitudinal study and an intervention. *Child Development, 78*(1), 246–263. https://doi.org/10.1111/j.1467-8624.2007.00995.x

Boden, K. K., Zepeda, C. D., & Nokes-Malach, T. J. (2020). Achievement goals and conceptual learning: An examination of teacher talk. *Journal of Educational Psychology, 112*(6), 1221–1242. https://doi.org/10.1037/edu0000421

Dweck, C. S. (2002). The development of ability conceptions. In A. Wigfield & J. S. Eccles (Eds.), *Development of achievement motivation* (pp. 57–88). Academic Press. https://doi.org/10.1016/b978-012750053-9/50005-x

Dweck, C. S., & Leggett, E. L. (1988). A social-cognitive approach to motivation and personality. *Psychological Review, 95*(2), 256–273. https://doi.org/10.1037/0033-295x.95.2.256

Dweck, C. S., & Sorich, L. A. (1999). Mastery-oriented thinking. In C. R. Snyder (Ed.), *Coping: The psychology of what works* (pp. 232–251). Oxford University Press. https://doi.org/10.1093/med:psych/9780195119343.003.0011

Epstein, J. L. (1983). Longitudinal effects of family-school-person interactions on student outcomes. *Research in sociology of education and socialization, Volume 4. Personal change over the life course* (pp. 101–127). JAI Press. https://doi.org/10.1093/med:psych/9780195119343.003.0011

Federici, R. A., Skaalvik, E. M., & Tangen, T. N. (2015). Students' perceptions of the goal structure in mathematics classrooms: Relations with goal orientations, mathematics anxiety, and help-seeking behavior. *International Education Studies, 8*(3), 146–158. https://doi.org/10.5539/ies.v8n3p146

Kaplan, A., Gheen, M., & Midgley, C. (2002). The classroom goal structure and student disruptive behavior. *British Journal of Educational Psychology, 72,* 191–211. https://doi.org/10.1348/000709902158847

Kaplan, A., & Maehr, M. L. (1999). Enhancing the motivation of African American students: An achievement goal theory perspective. *Journal of Negro Education, 68*(1), 23–41. https://doi.org/10.2307/2668207

Kaplan, A., & Midgley, C. (1999). The relationship between perceptions of the classroom goal structure and early adolescents' affect in school: The mediating role of coping strategies. *Learning and Individual Differences, 11*(2), 187–212. https://doi.org/10.1016/s1041-6080(00)80005-9

Lau, S., & Nie, Y. (2008). Interplay between personal goals and classroom goal structures in predicting student outcomes: A multilevel analysis of person-context interactions. *Journal of Educational Psychology, 100*(1), 15–29. https://doi.org/10.1037/0022-0663.100.1.15

Lazarides, R., Buchholz, J., & Rubach, C. (2018). Teacher enthusiasm and self-efficacy, student-perceived mastery goal orientation, and student motivation in mathematics classrooms. *Teaching and Teacher Education, 69,* 1–10. https://doi.org/10.1016/j.tate.2017.08.017

Linnenbrink. (2005). The dilemma of performance-approach goals: The use of multiple goal contexts to promote student' motivation and learning. *Journal of Educational Psychology, 97*(2), 197–213. https://doi.org/10.1037/0022-0663.97.2.197

Linnenbrink-Garcia, L., Tysen, D. F., & Patall, E. A. (2008). When are achievement goal orientations beneficial for academic achievement? A closer look at main effects and moderating factors. *Revue Internationale de Psychologie Sociale, 21*(1–2), 19–70.

Lüftenegger, M., Tran, U. S., Bardach, L., Schober, B., & Spiel, C. (2017). Measuring a mastery goal structure using the TARGET framework: Development and validation of a classroom goal structure questionnaire. *Zeitschrift für Psychologie, 225*(1), 64–75. https://doi.org/10.1027/2151-2604/a000277

Lüftenegger, M., van de Schoot, R., Schober, B., Finsterwald, M., & Spiel, C. (2014). Promotion of students' mastery goal orientations: Does TARGET work? *Educational Psychology, 34*(4), 451–469. https://doi.org/10.1080/01443410.2013.814189

Madjar, N. (2017). Stability and change in social goals as related to goal structures and engagement in school. *The Journal of Experimental Education, 85*(2), 259–277. https://doi.org/10.1080/00220973.2016.1148658

Maehr, M. L. (1984). Meaning and motivation: Toward a theory of personal investment. In R. Ames & C. Ames (Eds.), *Research on motivation in education: Student motivation* (Vol. 1, pp. 115–143). Academic Press.

Maehr, M. L., & Midgley, C. (1996). *Transforming school cultures.* Westview Press.

Meyer, D. K., & Turner, J. C. (2002). Using instructional discourse analysis to study the scaffolding of student self-regulation. *Educational Psychologist, 37*(1), 17–25. https://doi.org/10.1207/s15326985ep3701_3

Michou, A., Mouratidis, A., Lens, W., & Vansteenkiste, M. (2013). Personal and contextual antecedents of achievement goals: Their direct and indirect relations to students' learning strategies. *Learning and Individual Differences, 23,* 187–194. https://doi.org/10.1016/j.lindif.2012.09.005

Midgley, C., Maehr, M. L., Hicks, L., Roeser, R., Urdan, T., Anderman, E. M., & Kaplan, A. (1996). *The Patterns of Adaptive Learning Survey* (PALS). University of Michigan.

Midgley, C., Maehr, M. L., Hruda, L. A., Anderman, E., Anderman, L., Gheen, M., Kaplan, A., Kumar, R., Middleton, M. J., Nelson, J., & Urdan, T. (2000). *Manual for the Patterns of Adaptive Learning Scale.* University of Michigan. Retrieved from https://www.researchgate.net/publication/272474856_The_Patterns_of_Adaptive_Learning_Scales_PALS_2000

Middleton, M. J., & Midgley, C. (2002). Beyond motivation: Middle school students' perceptions of press for understanding in math. *Contemporary Educational Psychology, 27,* 373–391. https://doi.org/10.1006/ceps.2001.1101

Murayama, K., & Elliot, A. J. (2009). The joint influence of personal achievement goals and classroom goal structures on achievement-relevant outcomes. *Journal of Educational Psychology, 101*(2), 432–447. https://doi.org/10.1037/a0014221

Murdock, T. B., Hale, N. M., & Weber, M. J. (2001). Predictors of cheating among early adolescents: Academic and social motivations. *Contemporary Educational Psychology, 26,* 96–115. https://doi.org/10.1006/ceps.2000.1046

Nicholls, J. G. (1989). *The competitive ethos and democratic education.* Harvard University Press.

Nolen, S. B. (2003). Learning environment, motivation, and achievement in high school science. *Journal of Research in Science Teaching, 40*(4), 347–368. https://doi.org/10.1002/tea.10080

Patrick, H. (2004). Re-examining classroom mastery goal structure. In P. R. Pintrich & M. L. Maehr (Eds.), *Advances in motivation: Vol. 13. Motivating students, improving schools: The legacy of Carol Midgley* (pp. 233–263). Elsevier JAI Press. https://doi.org/10.1016/s0749-7423(03)13009-9

Patrick, H., Anderman, L. H., Ryan, A. M., Edelin, K., & Midgley, C. (2001). Teachers' communication of goal orientations in four fifth-grade classrooms. *Elementary School Journal, 102*(1), 35–58. https://doi.org/10.1086/499692

Patrick, H., Kaplan, A., & Ryan, A. M. (2011). Positive classroom motivational environments: Convergence between mastery goal structure and the classroom social climate. *Journal of Educational Psychology, 103*(2), 367–382. https://doi.org/10.1037/a0023311

Patrick, H., & Ryan, A., M. (2008). What do students think about when evaluating their classroom's mastery goal structure? An examination of young adolescents' explanations. *The Journal of Experimental Education, 77*(2), 99–123. https://doi.org/10.3200/jexe.77.2.99-124

Patrick, H., Turner, J. C., Meyer, D. K., & Midgley, C. (2003). How teachers establish psychological environments during the first days of school: Associations with avoidance in mathematics. *Teachers College Record, 105*(8), 1521–1558. https://doi.org/10.1111/1467-9620.00299

Polychroni, F., Hatzichristou, C., & Sideridis, G. (2012). The role of goal orientations and goal structures in explaining classroom social and affective characteristics. *Learning and Individual Differences, 22,* 207–217. https://doi.org/10.1016/j.lindif.2011.10.005

Ryan, A. M., Gheen, M., & Midgley, C. (1998). Why do some students avoid asking for help? An examination of the interplay among students' academic efficacy, teacher's social-emotional role and classroom goal structure. *Journal of Educational Psychology, 90*(3), 528–535. https://doi.org/10.1037/0022-0663.90.3.528

Ryan, A. M., & Shim, S. S. (2012). Changes in help seeking from peers during early adolescence: Associations with changes in achievement and perceptions of teachers. *Journal of Educational Psychology, 104*(4), 1122–1134. https://doi.org/10.1037/a0027696

Tapola, A., & Niemivirta, M. (2008). The role of achievement goal orientations in students' perceptions of and preferences for classroom environment. *British Journal of Educational Psychology, 78,* 291–312. https://doi.org/10.1348/000709907x205272

Tas, Y., & Tekkaya, C. (2010). Personal and contextual factors associated with students' cheating in science. *The Journal of Experimental Education, 78*(4), 440–463. https://doi.org/10.1080/00220970903548046

Thorkildsen, T. A., & Nicholls, J. G. (1991). Students' critiques as motivation. *Educational Psychologist, 26*(3–4), 347–368. https://doi.org/10.1080/00461520.1991.9653138

Turner, J. C., Gray, D. L., Anderman, L. H., Dawson, H. S., & Anderman, E. M. (2013). Getting to know my teacher: Does the relation between perceived mastery goal structures and perceived teacher support change across the school year? *Contemporary Educational Psychology, 38,* 316–327. https://doi.org/10.1016/j.cedpsych.2013.06.003

Turner, J. C., Meyer, D. K., Cox, K. E., Logan, C., DiCintio, M., & Thomas, C. T. (1998). Creating contexts for involvement in mathematics. *Journal of Educational Psychology, 90*(4), 730–745. https://doi.org/10.1037/0022-0663.90.4.730

Turner, J. C., Meyer, D. K., Midgley, C., & Patrick, H. (2003). Teachers' discourse and sixth graders' reported affect and achievement behaviors in two high mastery/high performance mathematics classrooms. *The Elementary School Journal, 103*(4), 357–382. https://doi.org/10.1086/499731

Turner, J. C., Midgley, C., Meyer, D. K., Gheen, M., Anderman, E. M., Kang, J., & Patrick, H. (2002). The classroom environment and students' reports of avoidance strategies in mathematics: A multi-method study. *Journal of Educational Psychology, 94*(1), 88–106. https://doi.org/10.1037/0022-0663.94.1.88

Urdan, T. (2004). Using multiple methods to assess students' perceptions of classroom goal structures. *European Psychologist, 9*(4), 222–231. https://doi.org/10.1027/1016-9040.9.4.222

Urdan, T., & Midgley, C. (2003). Changes in the perceived classroom goal structure and pattern of adaptive learning during early adolescence. *Contemporary Educational Psychology, 28*, 524–551. https://doi.org/10.1016/s0361-476x(02)00060-7

Urdan, T., Ryan, A. M., Anderman, E. M., & Gheen, M. H. (2002). Goals, goal structures, and avoidance behavior. In C. Midgley (Ed.), *Goals, goal structures, and patterns of adaptive learning* (pp. 55–83). Erlbaum. https://doi.org/10.4324/9781410602152-10

Walton, G. M., & Yaeger, D. S. (2020). Seed and soil: Psychological affordances in contexts help to explain where wise interventions succeed or fail. *Current Directions in Psychological Science, 29*(3), 219–226. https://doi.org/10.1177/0963721420904453

Wolters, C. A. (2004). Advancing achievement goal theory: Using goal structures and goal orientations to predict students' motivation, cognition, and achievement. *Journal of Educational Psychology, 96*(2), 236–250. https://doi.org/10.1037/0022-0663.96.2.236

Yeager, D. S., & Dweck, C. S. (2012). Mindsets that promote resilience: When students believe that personal characteristics can be developed. *Educational Psychologist, 47*(4), 302–314. https://doi.org/10.1080/00461520.2012.722805

Yu, J., & McLellan, R. (2020). Same mindset, different goals and motivational framework: Profiles of mindset-based meaning systems. *Contemporary Educational Psychology, 62*. https://doi.org/10.1016/j.cedpsych.2020.101901

20

STUDENTS' GROWTH ORIENTATION

Implications for Their Academic Flourishing

Keiko C. P. Bostwick, Andrew J. Martin, Rebecca J. Collie, and Tracy L. Durksen

Research in Positive Psychology is focused on understanding and promoting the components of life that help people to flourish, build positive personal qualities, increase life satisfaction, and enable thriving communities (Seligman & Csikszentmihalyi, 2014). Indeed, in educational settings, research often focuses on constructs and contexts that help to promote students' flourishing—for example, by way of enhanced academic well-being, perseverance, buoyancy, and a sense of belonging in the classroom. Thus, Positive Psychology is reflected (explicitly or implicitly) in much educational research to date. The present chapter applies a Positive Psychology lens to look at students' growth-focused motivation (i.e., growth constructs and growth orientation) and its implications for their flourishing at school.

Previous research has identified that growth constructs, such as growth mindset and growth goals, demonstrate positive associations with key Positive Education outcomes, such as students' well-being at school (e.g., Elliot & McGregor, 2001; Zeng et al., 2016). In particular, an emerging line of research on students' growth orientation (Bostwick et al., 2017) suggests that students' broader inclinations toward academic growth may be particularly relevant to their academic flourishing, as evidenced by enhanced persistence and positive interpersonal relationships with peers and teachers (Bostwick et al., 2021). In this chapter, we begin by providing definitions of distinct growth constructs and underlying growth orientation. Following this, we discuss the relevance of these growth components to students' academic flourishing and Positive Psychology research in education.

Growth Constructs

A primary focus of motivational research in education has been on students' growth constructs and their associations with students' academic outcomes. These constructs include students' growth mindset (Dweck, 2000) and various types of growth-focused academic goals (Elliot et al., 2011, 2015; Martin, 2006; Phan et al., 2016). As described later in this chapter, growth constructs are positively associated with a variety of student outcomes, including those commonly examined in educational settings as part of Positive Psychology research (e.g., well-being). Thus, researchers consider growth constructs to be essential components of students' academic lives, including academic well-being and positive development at school. The following section provides details for two major areas of growth construct research, including growth mindset and growth goals.

DOI: 10.4324/9781003013778-25

Growth Mindset

Growth mindset captures the degree to which students believe their intelligence can change over time (Dweck, 2000). Researchers have referred to the construct by several names, including theories of intelligence or malleable mindsets (e.g., Dweck, 2000), and have proposed varying conceptualizations of such beliefs (Martin et al., 2020). For example, a growth mindset is often conceptualized as a unidimensional continuum, with one end representing students with a fixed mindset (or, entity theory of intelligence) and the other end representing students with a growth mindset (or, incremental theory of intelligence). Students with a fixed mindset are said to believe that intelligence and abilities are relatively immutable and predetermined. In contrast, students with a growth mindset tend to believe that intellect and abilities can develop over time, especially through effort (Dweck, 2000). In other conceptualizations of the growth mindset construct, researchers have proposed a two-factor approach, whereby growth and fixed mindset beliefs are modeled as two separate constructs (e.g., Dupeyrat & Mariné, 2005; Martin, 2015b). Thus, in the two-factor approach, it is possible for students to hold both growth and fixed mindset beliefs simultaneously.

Researchers have demonstrated that students who endorse a high level of growth mindset beliefs (and, in the two-factor approach, a low level on the fixed mindset belief factor) tend to demonstrate more positive academic behaviors and outcomes at school. More precisely, researchers have shown that students with a growth mindset typically demonstrate (a) more persistence through educational challenges (Bettinger et al., 2018; Blackwell et al., 2007; Dweck, 2000; O'Rourke et al., 2014), (b) greater willingness to seek help when needed (Hong et al., 1999; Kim et al., 2018), (c) higher intrinsic interest (Cury et al., 2006), (d) greater school engagement (Zeng et al., 2016), (e) greater adaptability (Martin et al., 2013; Zeng et al., 2016), (f) more positive interpersonal relationships (Zander et al., 2018), and (g) greater well-being (King, 2017; Zeng et al., 2016). There is some debate on the extent to which students' growth mindsets are associated with their academic achievement (e.g., Bahník & Vranka, 2017). Recent meta-analyses, however, report evidence of a robust and reliable (yet relatively small) positive association with academic achievement (Burnette et al., 2013; Sisk et al., 2018). Overall, the evidence suggests that growth mindset beliefs are meaningfully associated with several components of students' academic lives.

Growth Goals

Growth goals refer to students' academic aims focused on self-improvement and personal striving (Martin, 2015a). Research on growth goals stems from the long history of student achievement goal literature (Senko, 2016), which initially recognized two types of goals: mastery goals and performance goals. Mastery goals (sometimes called learning goals or task goals) are academic aims focused on personal learning. In contrast, performance goals (sometimes referred to as ego goals) refer to aims focused on demonstrations of ability, often relative to one's peers (Elliot, 2005). Researchers have found that these goals present different patterns of associations with students' academic behaviors (e.g., persistence through difficult work) and outcomes (e.g., achievement). Students who set mastery goals tend to demonstrate more adaptive behaviors and positive outcomes (Bong, 2009; Elliot & Church, 1997; Elliot & McGregor, 2001; Huang, 2012), whereas students who set performance goals tend to demonstrate some positive and some negative effects (Harackiewicz et al., 2002; Mouratidis et al., 2018).

As the achievement goal literature has developed throughout the years, researchers have further delineated the original mastery and performance goals (Elliot, 2005). For example, researchers have examined the approach (mastery approach and performance approach) and avoidance (mastery avoidance and performance avoidance) dimensions of achievement goals (Elliot, 1999; Elliot & McGregor, 2001). These dimensions indicate that students may set goals that strive toward a particular outcome (e.g., learn all of the course material, be the top-performing student) or set goals to avoid particular outcomes (e.g., not forget course material, not be the lowest-performing student). These new iterations of achievement goals are particularly important because they help researchers to understand why performance goals demonstrated mixed effects with students' achievement. That is, findings suggested that performance-avoidance goals were especially maladaptive for students' academic performance (Harackiewicz et al., 2002; Senko et al., 2011).

Alongside these insights into the mixed effects of performance goals, the expansion of the achievement goal literature also enabled researchers to identify goals aligned with tenets of Positive Psychology. That is, researchers were now able to investigate goals specifically focused on students' striving toward academic growth (i.e., mastery-approach goals), opening the door for research into students' growth goals (Martin, 2015a). Indeed, recent iterations of the achievement goal literature have further specified growth goals into two categories: self-based growth goals and task-based growth goals (Elliot et al., 2011). This further delineation of growth goals more precisely identifies different pathways for students' self-improvement and personal striving and encompasses both intrapersonal growth (i.e., self-based growth) and criteria-focused growth (i.e., task-based growth).

Self-based growth goals are students' academic aims focused on intrapersonal improvement. When students are focused on self-based growth goals, they are said to use their previous performance as a reference point for their current or future performance. Thus, these academic aims are focused on personal growth, rather than performance or growth relative to peers (e.g., performance goals). Examples of self-based growth goals include potential-based goals (Elliot et al., 2015), optimal best goals (Phan et al., 2016), and personal best (PB) goals (Martin, 2006). Of these self-based growth goals, PB goals are perhaps the most widely studied. PB goals are defined as academic aims that are specific, appropriately challenging, and focused on self-improvement (Martin, 2006). These goals can either refer to the process of learning (e.g., trying to study longer this week than last week) or to learning outcomes (e.g., achieving a better mark on a current exam than a previous one).

Task-based growth goals are students' academic aims focused on personal improvement relative to a task (whereas self-based growth goals connote personal improvement relative to self). These aims use the objective task criteria as the reference point for future improvement and thus differ from self-based growth goals that focus on intrapersonal comparisons. Task-based growth goals are commonly seen in the literature as mastery or mastery-approach goals (Elliot & McGregor, 2001), whose operationalizations focus on the learning of course material.

Researchers have found that self-based and task-based growth goals are associated with several student outcomes. For example, both constructs tend to be positively associated with (a) academic engagement (Collie et al., 2016; Elliot & McGregor, 2001; Elliot et al., 2011; Martin et al., 2016; Martin & Liem, 2010), (b) deep learning (Ikeda et al., 2015; Liem et al., 2012; Murayama & Elliot, 2011), (c) academic buoyancy (Liem et al., 2012; Yu & Martin, 2014), (d) positive emotions (Pekrun et al., 2009), and (e) positive interpersonal relationships (Collie et al., 2016; Liem et al., 2012). Researchers have found positive associations between self-based growth goals and achievement (Burns et al., 2018; Martin & Liem, 2010). However, similar to research on growth mindset, there is debate about the extent to which task-based growth goals are positively associated with achievement. Although some studies have found evidence of null associations (Elliot & McGregor, 2001), meta-analyses have found small positive associations between task-based growth goals and achievement (Huang, 2012; Van Yperen et al., 2014).

Importantly, researchers have demonstrated that although self-based and task-based growth goals are positively associated, they are indeed distinct growth constructs. For example, researchers have found evidence of unique factor structures for the goal constructs (Elliot et al., 2011), indicating that they are psychometrically distinct. In addition, there is evidence that the two constructs explain unique variance in a variety of academic outcomes, such as students' engagement, achievement, and academic buoyancy (Martin & Elliot, 2016; Yu & Martin, 2014), and that these goals present different patterns of associations with different outcomes (e.g., task-based growth goals are associated with intrinsic motivation whereas self-based growth goals are not; Elliot et al., 2011). Thus, in research that has compared the relative yields of these growth goals, the evidence suggests that these constructs are related, yet distinct, academic aims focused on personal growth and striving.

Summary of Growth Constructs

Taken together, research on students' distinct growth constructs demonstrates that students' beliefs in (growth mindset) and striving toward (growth goals) personal growth demonstrate positive associations with a variety of academic and nonacademic outcomes, including outcomes related to students' positive educational development (e.g., well-being and positive emotions). Such findings mark these distinct growth constructs as important components of students' positive academic development. However, although extensive work has investigated how these growth constructs are associated with students' outcomes, relatively less work has focused on the potential relationships among the growth constructs themselves, nor the potential educational implications of these interrelationships. Such investigations are essential, as they help researchers to understand how growth constructs may be interrelated and work together to promote students' outcomes at school. As described in the following section of this chapter, emerging work in this area provides evidence of a broader growth factor that underpins each of these distinct growth constructs—namely, students' underlying growth orientation. The evidence further suggests that this broader growth factor has significant implications for students' educational outcomes.

Growth Orientation

Growth orientation is defined as students' broader approach to academic growth. It captures the overlap among students' distinct growth constructs (Bostwick et al., 2019) by encompassing students' beliefs that academic growth is possible (i.e., growth mindset) and students' aims toward both personal and objective growth (i.e., self- and task-based growth goals). However, growth orientation extends beyond the mere sum of these distinct growth constructs. It reflects students' broader tendency to focus on and pursue academic growth. Researchers hypothesize that this tendency helps students identify and act on available opportunities for positive personal development in their educational settings, leading to meaningful gains in their academic outcomes over time (Bostwick et al., 2019). Therefore, students with a high growth orientation are said to hold a system of beliefs that work together to help them to capitalize on positive personal development. As noted, this system of beliefs extends beyond the distinct growth constructs that highlight a specific aspect of growth. Namely, growth orientation captures the multidimensional nature of students' growth-focused beliefs and their broader inclinations for personal academic growth.

Researchers have provided both theoretical and empirical support for the growth orientation construct. For example, a large cross-sectional study of Australian secondary school students found that the distinct growth constructs (i.e., growth mindset and growth goals) were well represented by an underlying growth orientation (Bostwick et al., 2017) and that the measurement of the construct was invariant across several student subpopulations (e.g., gender and socioeconomic status). These findings support the hypothesis that students from many different backgrounds vary on the extent to which they hold broad orientations toward academic growth. In addition, there is evidence that students hold both distinct growth constructs and an underlying growth orientation simultaneously. Using a bifactor exploratory structural equation model, researchers found evidence of both the unique and overlapping components of the factor structure of these growth constructs, suggesting that these components capture different aspects of students' focus and desire for academic growth (Bostwick et al., 2021). Therefore, although there are overlaps among the growth constructs that are captured and represented by an underlying growth orientation, there are also unique components of each distinct growth construct. This evidence suggests that students do not hold growth constructs independently of each other. Rather, there is a complex system of beliefs that underpin students' distinct growth constructs that is captured by their underlying growth orientation.

Growth Orientation and Positive Educational Development

Although research on growth orientation is just emerging, there is evidence of its positive associations with students' academic and nonacademic outcomes. Researchers found that students' growth orientation was positively associated with gains in their mathematics engagement and achievement across one year of secondary school (Bostwick et al., 2019), suggesting that changes in students' growth orientation may be associated with meaningful changes in students' outcomes. As growth orientation is a construct ultimately focused on growth, it is essential to understand the extent to which it is associated with actual growth in students' outcomes (e.g., gains in student engagement).

When comparing the relative yields of growth orientation and distinct growth constructs on students' outcomes, researchers found that different components of growth demonstrated distinct patterns of associations with various outcomes. More precisely, students' growth orientation was significantly and positively associated with a wide range of outcomes, including students' positive interpersonal relationships with peers and teachers, classroom behaviors (e.g., persistence through difficult work), and academic achievement. In contrast, the distinct growth constructs demonstrated varying significant associations with the outcomes, with some associations being relatively strong (e.g., self-based growth goals and homework completion) and others nonexistent (e.g., growth mindset and peer relationships). Such findings highlight that growth orientation may be a reliable predictor of a wide range of outcomes associated with positive educational development, whereas distinct growth constructs may be more strongly associated with specific outcomes. Therefore, it may be necessary for researchers and practitioners to focus on different components of growth (i.e., growth orientation or distinct constructs) depending on the particular outcome they aim to improve for students. It is possible, for example, that students' sense of well-being may be more strongly associated with growth orientation than the other distinct growth constructs. Alongside other areas of potential future research (see the next section of this chapter), investigating such research questions will help researchers to identify reliable pathways to promoting students' positive educational development.

Directions for Future Research

As researchers continue to investigate students' growth constructs and underlying growth orientation, there are several opportunities for future research to delineate their relationships with students' well-being and flourishing at school. For example, although researchers have found that growth orientation is positively associated with several important nonacademic outcomes for students (e.g., interpersonal relationships with peers and teachers; Bostwick et al., 2021), it is also important to understand how this construct may be specifically associated with students' sense of academic well-being, a major aim of Positive Psychology research in education.

Many researchers in education continue to focus on the impact of various motivational and psychological constructs on students' academic and achievement-focused outcomes. Although there is a continuing need for researchers to understand how such constructs affect achievement, researchers should also consider important yet relatively under-studied outcomes relevant to students' academic life. For example, schools in the United States are now incorporating measures of students' well-being and safety at school into accountability programs (Darling-Hammond et al., 2016) to monitor how teachers and school climate may help to increase these nonacademic outcomes for students. Indeed, such outcomes are now even incorporated into many U.S. states' school accountability policies (e.g., Hawaii Department of Education, 2019). Therefore, alongside efforts to understand how growth constructs and growth orientation are associated with academic outcomes, there is a need to precisely understand its relation to students' well-being, or other associated outcomes (e.g., optimism; *Boman & Mergler, THIS BOOK*).

Alongside the examination of growth orientation as a *predictor* of outcomes, it may also be instructive for Positive Psychology researchers to investigate growth orientation as a student *outcome*. Students' broad focus on academic growth aligns with the core aims of Positive Psychology research in education—helping students flourish and develop positive personal qualities. A focus on self-development through self-growth is a personal quality that is likely to carry through to other aspects of students' lives. Therefore, identifying ways to improve students' growth orientation (or other distinct growth constructs) is a valuable research area in students' positive educational development.

One area that may shed light on the development of students' growth orientation is the impact of students' classroom environment. The classroom context could promote or diminish students' growth-focused motivation. For example, researchers who study growth constructs have sought to understand how teachers' distinct growth constructs (e.g., teachers' growth mindset) influence their pedagogical decisions (Gutshall, 2013; Mascret et al., 2017; Patrick et al., 2001; Retelsdorf & Gunther, 2011; Rissanen et al., 2018) or contribute to students' growth constructs and academic and nonacademic outcomes (Canning et al., 2019; Friedel et al., 2007; Park et al., 2016; *Patrick, THIS BOOK*). Teachers' growth constructs may be strongly associated with the classroom climate they cultivate, which may influence a variety of related outcomes, including students' well-being (Friedel et al., 2007) and growth constructs. Thus far, the limited research on classroom growth orientation (Bostwick et al., 2020) suggests that contextual growth orientation factors (i.e., those of the teacher or students' surrounding peers) may influence students' academic outcomes. As researchers continue to investigate how teachers' personal constructs may influence classroom climates and outcomes (e.g., *Zakkrzeski & Eva, THIS BOOK*), more work is needed to understand how such classroom growth constructs and growth orientations are associated with students' academic outcomes, growth orientation, and other positive educational development outcomes.

Finally, growth construct researchers have increasingly focused their attention on the development of educational interventions that target growth constructs and increase positive academic outcomes (Blackwell et al., 2007; Bostwick & Becker-Blease, 2018; Ginns et al., 2018; Martin et al., 2014). For example, interventions targeting growth mindset teach students about the malleability of intelligence, often during times of academic difficulty such as the transition between primary and secondary school (Blackwell et al., 2007). Interventions targeting growth goals embed goal-setting into students' academic activities (Martin et al., 2014). Such interventions urge students to set growth goals that are specific and challenging, which are facets known to make goal-setting more effective (Locke & Latham, 2006). However, researchers have noted that further work is needed to develop psychologically precise interventions that truly target their intended growth constructs (Sisk et al., 2018). As research into growth orientation enables researchers to understand where growth constructs are truly unique and where they overlap, it will also contribute to efforts to build better educational interventions that target these constructs more precisely. Alongside this, researchers must also focus their attention on how such growth construct interventions may benefit students' academic well-being. It is possible, for example, that already-established interventions could have positive effects on students' positive development and function at school (*Proctor, THIS BOOK*), in addition to positive effects on achievement.

Conclusion

Taken together, emerging research on growth orientation and continuing research on students' distinct growth constructs highlight their importance and utility for students' positive academic development in school. Such variables are directly associated with students' academic well-being (e.g., Elliot & McGregor, 2001; Zeng et al., 2016) or are associated with other closely related Positive Psychology variables (e.g., interpersonal relationships; Bostwick et al., 2021), suggesting that they are relevant to research in Positive Psychology in education. There are several promising directions for future research into students' distinct growth constructs and their underlying growth orientation that may help researchers, teachers, and policymakers improve students' positive academic development. As schools and educational policies continue to incorporate students' well-being as relevant outcomes for accountability systems (Darling-Hammond et al., 2016) alongside achievement-focused outcomes, researchers must also consider the extent to which widely studied motivational variables (e.g., growth constructs) contribute to students' academic flourishing, positive educational qualities, and thriving educational communities.

References

Bahník, Š., & Vranka, M. A. (2017). Growth mindset is not associated with scholastic aptitude in a large sample of university applicants. *Personality and Individual Differences, 117*, 139–143. https://doi.org/10.1016/j.paid.2017.05.046

Bettinger, E., Ludvigsen, S., Rege, M., Solli, I. F., & Yeager, D. (2018). Increasing perseverance in math: Evidence from a field experiment in Norway. *Journal of Economic Behavior & Organization, 146*, 1–15. https://doi.org/10.1016/j.jebo.2017.11.032

Blackwell, L. S., Trzesniewski, K. H., & Dweck, C. S. (2007). Implicit theories of intelligence predict achievement across an adolescent transition: A longitudinal study and an intervention. *Child Development, 78*(1), 246–263. https://doi.org/10.1111/j.1467-8624.2007.00995.x

Bong, M. (2009). Age-related differences in achievement goal differentiation. *Journal of Educational Psychology, 101*(4), 879–896. https://doi.org/10.1037/a0015945

Bostwick, K. C. P., & Becker-Blease, K. A. (2018). Quick, easy mindset intervention can boost academic achievement in large introductory psychology classes. *Psychology Learning & Teaching, 17*(2), 177–193. https://doi.org/10.1177/1475725718766426

Bostwick, K. C. P., Burns, E. C., Martin, A. J., Collie, R. J., & Durksen, T. L. (2021). *An integrative network of growth-focused motivation: A bifactor exploratory structural equation model of students' growth mindset, growth goals, and growth orientation*. Manuscirpt under review.

Bostwick, K. C. P., Collie, R. J., Martin, A. J., & Durksen, T. L. (2017). Students' growth mindsets, goals, and academic outcomes in mathematics. *Zeitschrift Fur Psychologie / Journal of Psychology, 225*(2), 107–116. https://doi.org/10.1027/2151-2604/a000287

Bostwick, K. C. P., Collie, R. J., Martin, A. J., & Durksen, T. L. (2020). Teacher, classroom, and student growth orientation in mathematics: A multilevel examination of growth goals, growth mindset, engagement, and achievement. *Teaching and Teacher Education, 94*. https://doi.org/10.1016/j.tate.2020.103100

Bostwick, K. C. P., Martin, A. J., Collie, R. J., & Durksen, T. L. (2019). Growth orientation predicts gains in middle and high school students' mathematics outcomes over time. *Contemporary Educational Psychology, 58*, 213–227. https://doi.org/10.1016/j.cedpsych.2019.03.010

Burnette, J. L., O'Boyle, E. H., VanEpps, E. M., Pollack, J. M., & Finkel, E. J. (2013). Mind-sets matter: A meta-analytic review of implicit theories and self-regulation. *Psychological Bulletin, 139*(3), 655–701. https://doi.org/10.1037/a0029531

Burns, E. C., Martin, A. J., & Collie, R. J. (2018). Adaptability, personal best (PB) goals setting, and gains in students' academic outcomes: A longitudinal examination from a social cognitive perspective. *Contemporary Educational Psychology, 53*, 57–72. https://doi.org/10.1016/j.cedpsych.2018.02.001

Canning, E. A., Muenks, K., Green, D. J., & Murphy, M. C. (2019). STEM faculty who believe ability is fixed have larger racial achievement gaps and inspire less student motivation in their classes. *Science Advances, 5*(2). https://doi.org/10.1126/sciadv.aau4734

Collie, R. J., Martin, A. J., Papworth, B., & Ginns, P. (2016). Students' interpersonal relationships, personal best (PB) goals, and academic engagement. *Learning and Individual Differences, 45*, 65–76. https://doi.org/10.1016/j.lindif.2015.12.002

Cury, F., Elliot, A. J., Da Fonseca, D., & Moller, A. C. (2006). The social-cognitive model of achievement motivation and the 2 x 2 achievement goal framework. *Journal of Personality and Social Psychology, 90*(4), 666–679. https://doi.org/10.1037/0022-3514.90.4.666

Darling-Hammond, L., Bae, S., Cook-Harvey, C. M., Lam, L., Mercer, C., Podolsky, A., & Stosich, E. L. (2016). *Pathways to new accountability through the Every Student Succeeds Act.* Learning Policy Institute. Retrieved from http://learningpolicyinstitute.org/our-work/publications-resources/ pathways-new-accountability-every-student-succeeds-act

Dupeyrat, C., & Mariné, C. (2005). Implicit theories of intelligence, goal orientation, cognitive engagement, and achievement: A test of Dweck's model with returning to school adults. *Contemporary Educational Psychology, 30*(1), 43–59. https://doi.org/10.1016/j.cedpsych.2004.01.007

Dweck, C. S. (2000). *Self-theories: Their role in motivation, personality, and development.* Psychology Press.

Elliot, A. J. (1999). Approach and avoidance motivation and achievement goals. *Educational Psychologist, 34*(3), 169–189. https://doi.org/10.1207/s15326985ep3403

Elliot, A. J. (2005). A conceptual history of the achievement goal construct. In A. J. Elliot & C. S. Dweck (Eds.), *Handbook of competence and motivation* (pp. 52–72). Guilford.

Elliot, A. J., & Church, M. A. (1997). A hierarchical model of approach and avoidance achievement motivation. *Journal of Personality and Social Psychology, 72*(1), 218–232. https://doi.org/10.1037//0022-3514.72.1.218

Elliot, A. J., & McGregor, H. A. (2001). A 2 x 2 achievement goal framework. *Journal of Personality and Social Psychology, 80*(3), 501–519. https://doi.org/10.1037/10022-3514.80.3.501

Elliot, A. J., Murayama, K., Kobeisy, A., & Lichtenfeld, S. (2015). Potential-based achievement goals. *British Journal of Educational Psychology, 85*, 192–206. https://doi.org/10.1111/bjep.12051

Elliot, A. J., Murayama, K., & Pekrun, R. (2011). A 3 x 2 achievement goal model. *Journal of Educational Psychology, 103*(3), 632–648. https://doi.org/10.1037/a0023952

Friedel, J. M., Cortina, K. S., Turner, J. C., & Midgley, C. (2007). Achievement goals, efficacy beliefs and coping strategies in mathematics: The roles of perceived parent and teacher goal emphases. *Contemporary Educational Psychology, 32*, 434–458. https://doi.org/10.1016/j.cedpsych.2006.10.009

Ginns, P., Martin, A. J., Durksen, T. L., Burns, E. C., & Pope, A. (2018). Personal best (PB) goal-setting enhances arithmetical problem-solving. *The Australian Educational Researcher, 45*(4), 533–551. https://doi.org/10.1007/s13384-018-0268-9

Gutshall, C. A. (2013). Teachers' mindsets for students with and without disabilities. *Psychology in the Schools, 50*(10), 1073–1083. https://doi.org/10.1002/pits.21725

Harackiewicz, J. M., Barron, K. E., Pintrich, P. R., Elliot, A. J., & Thrash, T. M. (2002). Revision of achievement goal theory: Necessary and illuminating. *Journal of Educational Psychology, 94*(3), 638–645. https://doi.org/10.1037//0022-0663.94.3.638

Hawaii Department of Education. (2019). *School quality survey statewide summary report.* Retrieved from http://arch.k12.hi.us/PDFs/sqs/2019/SQS2019State.pdf

Hong, Y., Chiu, C., Dweck, C. S., Lin, D. M. S., & Wan, W. (1999). Implicit theories, attributions, and coping: A meaning system approach. *Journal of Personality and Social Psychology, 77*(3), 588–599. https://doi.org/10.1037/0022-3514.77.3.588

Huang, C. (2012). Discriminant and criterion-related validity of achievement goals in predicting academic achievement: A meta-analysis. *Journal of Educational Psychology, 104*(1), 48–73. https://doi.org/10.1037/a0026223

Ikeda, K., Castel, A. D., & Murayama, K. (2015). Mastery-approach goals eliminate retrieval-induced forgetting: The role of achievement goals in memory inhibition. *Personality and Social Psychology Bulletin, 41*(5), 687–695. https://doi.org/10.1177/0146167215575730

Kim, S., Zhang, K., & Park, D. (2018). Don't want to look dumb? The role of theories of intelligence and humanlike features in online help seeking. *Psychological Science, 29*(2), 171–180. https://doi.org/10.1177/0956797617730595

King, R. B. (2017). A fixed mindset leads to negative affect: The relations between implicit theories of intelligence and subjective well-being. *Zeitschrift Fur Psychologie / Journal of Psychology, 225*(2), 137–145. https://doi.org/10.1027/2151-2604/a000290

Liem, G. A. D., Ginns, P., Martin, A. J., Stone, B., & Herrett, M. (2012). Personal best goals and academic and social functioning: A longitudinal perspective. *Learning and Instruction, 22*, 222–230. https://doi.org/10.1016/j.learninstruc.2011.11.003

Locke, E. A., & Latham, G. P. (2006). New directions in goal-setting theory. *Current Directions in Psychological Science, 15*(5), 265–268. https://doi.org/10.1111/j.1467-8721.2006.00449.x

Martin, A. J. (2006). Personal bests (PBs): A proposed multidimensional model and empirical analysis. *British Journal of Educational Psychology, 76*(4), 803–825. https://doi.org/10.1348/000709905X55389

Martin, A. J. (2015a). Growth approaches to academic development: Research into academic trajectories and growth assessment, goals, and mindsets. *British Journal of Educational Psychology, 85*, 133–137. https://doi.org/10.1111/bjep.12071

Martin, A. J. (2015b). Implicit theories about intelligence and growth (personal best) goals: Exploring reciprocal relationships. *British Journal of Educational Psychology, 85*(2), 207–223. https://doi.org/10.1111/bjep.12038

Martin, A. J., Bostwick, K., Collie, R. J., & Tarbetsky, A. L. (2020). Implicit beliefs about intelligence. In V. Zeigler-Hill & T. K. Shackelford (Eds.), *Encyclopedia of personality and individual differences* (pp. 2184–2190). Springer International Publishing. https://doi.org/10.1007/978-3-319-24612-3_301219

Martin, A. J., Collie, R. J., Mok, M. M. C., & Mcinerney, D. M. (2016). Personal best (PB) goal structure, individual PB goals, engagement, and achievement: A study of Chinese- and English-speaking background students in Australian schools. *British Journal of Educational Psychology, 86*(1), 75–91. https://doi.org/10.1111/bjep.12092

Martin, A. J., Durksen, T. L., Williamson, D., Kiss, J., & Ginns, P. (2014). Personal best (PB) goal setting and students' motivation in science: A study of science valuing and aspirations. *Australian Educational & Developmental Psychologist, 31*(2), 85–96. https://doi.org/10.1017/edp.2014.19

Martin, A. J., & Elliot, A. J. (2016). The role of personal best (PB) and dichotomous achievement goals in students' academic motivation and engagement: A longitudinal investigation. *Educational Psychology, 36*(7), 1285–1302. https://doi.org/10.1080/01443410.2015.1093606

Martin, A. J., & Liem, G. A. D. (2010). Academic personal bests (PBs), engagement, and achievement: A cross-lagged panel analysis. *Learning and Individual Differences, 20*, 265–270. https://doi.org/10.1016/j.lindif.2010.01.001

Martin, A. J., Nejad, H. G., Colmar, S., & Liem, G. A. D. (2013). Adaptability: How students' responses to uncertainty and novelty predict their academic and non-academic outcomes. *Journal of Educational Psychology, 105*(3), 728–746. https://doi.org/10.1037/a0032794

Mascret, N., Elliot, A. J., & Cury, F. (2017). The 3 × 2 achievement goal questionnaire for teachers. *Educational Psychology, 37*(3), 346–361. https://doi.org/10.1080/01443410.2015.1096324

Mouratidis, A., Michou, A., Demircioğlu, A. N., & Sayil, M. (2018). Different goals, different pathways to success: Performance-approach goals as direct and mastery-approach goals as indirect predictors of grades in mathematics. *Learning and Individual Differences, 61*, 127–135. https://doi.org/10.1016/j.lindif.2017.11.017

Murayama, K., & Elliot, A. J. (2011). Achievement motivation and memory: Achievement goals differentially influence immediate and delayed remember-know recognition memory. *Personality and Social Psychology Bulletin, 37*(10), 1339–1348. https://doi.org/10.1177/0146167211410575

O'Rourke, E., Haimovitz, K., Ballweber, C., Dweck, C., & Popović, Z. (2014). Brain points: A growth mindset incentive structure boosts persistence in an educational game. CHI '14: Proceedings of the SIGCHI Conference on Human Factors in Computing Systems, 3339–3348. https://doi.org/10.1145/2556288.2557157

Park, D., Gunderson, E. A., Tsukayama, E., Levine, S. C., & Beilock, S. L. (2016). Young children's motivational frameworks and math achievement: Relation to teacher-reported instructional practices, but not teacher theory of intelligence. *Journal of Educational Psychology, 108*(3), 300–313. https://doi.org/10.1037/edu0000064

Patrick, H., Anderman, L. H., Ryan, A. M., Edelin, K. C., & Midgley, C. (2001). Teachers' communication of goal orientations in four fifth-grade classrooms. *The Elementary School Journal, 102*(1), 35–58. https://doi.org/10.1086/499692

Pekrun, R., Elliot, A. J., & Maier, M. A. (2009). Achievement goals and achievement emotions: Testing a model of their joint relations with academic performance. *Journal of Educational Psychology, 101*(1), 115–135. https://doi.org/10.1037/a0013383

Phan, H. P., Ngu, B. H., & Williams, A. (2016). Introducing the concept of optimal best: Theoretical and methodological contributions. *Education, 136*(3), 312–322.

Retelsdorf, J., & Gunther, C. (2011). Achievement goals for teaching and teachers' reference norms: Relations with instructional practices. *Teaching and Teacher Education, 27*(7), 1111–1119. https://doi.org/10.1016/j.tate.2011.05.007

Rissanen, I., Kuusisto, E., Hanhimäki, E., & Tirri, K. (2018). Teachers' implicit meaning systems and their implications for pedagogical thinking and practice: A case study from Finland. *Scandinavian Journal of Educational Research, 62*(4), 487–500. https://doi.org/10.1080/00313831.2016.1258667

Seligman, M. E. P., & Csikszentmihalyi, M. (2014). Positive psychology: An introduction. In *Flow and the foundations of positive psychology: The collected works of Mihaly Csikszentmihalyi* (pp. 279–298). Springer. https://doi.org/10.1007/978-94-017-9088-8

Senko, C. (2016). Achivement goal theory. In K. R. Wentzel & D. B. Miele (Eds.), *Handbook of motivation at school* (2nd ed., pp. 75–95). Routledge.

Senko, C., Hulleman, C. S., & Harackiewicz, J. M. (2011). Achievement Goal Theory at the crossroads: Old controversies, current challenges, and new directions. *Educational Psychologist, 46*(1), 26–47. https://doi.org/10.1080/00461520.2011.538646

Sisk, V. F., Burgoyne, A. P., Sun, J., Butler, J. L., & Macnamara, B. N. (2018). To what extent and under which circumstances are growth mind-sets important to academic achievement? Two meta-analyses. *Psychological Science, 29*(4), 549–571. https://doi.org/10.1177/0956797617739704

Van Yperen, N. W., Blaga, M., & Postmes, T. (2014). A meta-analysis of self-reported achievement goals and nonself-report performance across three achievement domains (work, sports, and education). *PLoS ONE, 9*(4), e93594. https://doi.org/10.1371/journal.pone.0093594

Yu, K., & Martin, A. J. (2014). Personal best (PB) and 'classic' achievement goals in the Chinese context: Their role in predicting academic motivation, engagement and buoyancy. *Educational Psychology, 34*(5), 635–658. https://doi.org/10.1080/01443410.2014.895297

Zander, L., Brouwer, J., Jansen, E., Crayen, C., & Hannover, B. (2018). Academic self-efficacy, growth mindsets, and university students' integration in academic and social support networks. *Learning and Individual Differences, 62*, 98–107. https://doi.org/10.1016/j.lindif.2018.01.012

Zeng, G., Hou, H., & Peng, K. (2016). Effect of growth mindset on school engagement and psychological well-being of Chinese primary and middle school students: The mediating role of resilience. *Frontiers in Psychology, 7*(1873). https://doi.org/10.3389/fpsyg.2016.01873

21

ACHIEVEMENT EMOTIONS

Reinhard Pekrun

Achievement emotions are essential for human learning, development, and performance. This is especially true for positive achievement emotions such as enjoyment of learning, hope for success, or pride in one's accomplishments. Positive emotions help to envision goals and challenges, open the mind to creative problem-solving, lay the groundwork for self-regulation, and protect health by fostering self-esteem and resiliency. Even negative achievement emotions such as anger, anxiety, or shame can sometimes be beneficial. Traditionally, these emotions did not receive much attention from researchers, except for studies on test anxiety (Zeidner, 1998, 2014). During the past 20 years, however, there has been growing recognition that emotions are central to students' academic agency. In this burgeoning research, emotions are considered as critically important for students' learning and achievement (Camacho-Morles et al., 2021; Lajoie et al., 2020; Loderer et al., 2020; Mendzheritskaya & Hansen, 2019; Pekrun & Linnenbrink-Garcia, 2014; Schutz & Pekrun, 2007).

In this chapter, I first discuss the concepts of emotion and achievement emotions. Next, I provide summaries of theories and empirical evidence on achievement emotions. In the subsequent section, issues of diversity, universality, and development are addressed. In conclusion, I discuss approaches to the measurement of achievement emotions and implications for educational practice.

Definition of Emotion and Achievement Emotion

There seems to be consensus that *emotions* are multifaceted phenomena involving sets of coordinated psychological processes, including affective, cognitive, physiological, motivational, and expressive components (Shuman & Scherer, 2014). For example, a students' anxiety before an exam can be comprised of nervous, uneasy feelings (affective); worries about failing the exam (cognitive); increased cardiovascular activation (physiological); impulses to escape the situation (motivation); and anxious facial expression (expressive). As compared to intense emotions, *moods* are of lower intensity and lack a specific referent.

Achievement emotions are emotions related to achievement activities (e.g., studying) or achievement outcomes (success and failure; Pekrun, 2006, 2018, 2021; see Table 21.1). Most emotions pertaining to attending class, doing homework assignments, or taking tests and exams are considered achievement emotions because they relate to activities and outcomes judged according

DOI: 10.4324/9781003013778-26

Table 21.1 A Three-Dimensional Taxonomy of Achievement Emotions

Object Focus	Positive[a]		Negative[b]	
	Activating	Deactivating	Activating	Deactivating
Activity	Enjoyment	Relaxation	Anger Frustration	Boredom
Outcome/Prospective	Hope Joy[c]	Relief[c]	Anxiety	Hopelessness
Outcome/Retrospective	Joy Pride Gratitude	Contentment Relief	Shame Anger	Sadness Disappointment

[a] Positive = pleasant emotion. [b] Negative = unpleasant emotion. [c] Anticipatory joy/relief.

to competency-based standards of quality. However, not all of the emotions experienced in academic settings are achievement emotions. Social emotions are frequently experienced in these same settings, such as empathy for a classmate. Achievement and social emotions can overlap, as in emotions directed toward the achievement of others (e.g., contempt, envy, empathy, or admiration; Weiner, 2007). Furthermore, topic emotions and epistemic emotions also are important for learning. Topic emotions relate to the contents of learning material, such as students' frustration when Pluto was redefined as a dwarf planet (Broughton et al., 2013). Epistemic emotions pertain to the cognitive process of knowledge generation inherent to constructive learning and problem-solving, such as surprise, curiosity, or confusion triggered by cognitive incongruity (D'Mello et al., 2014; Muis et al., 2018; Vogl et al., 2020).

Past research on achievement emotions focused on emotions induced by achievement outcomes, such as hope and pride related to success or anxiety and shame related to failure (Weiner, 1985, 2019; Zeidner, 1998). However, emotions directly pertaining to learning activities are also considered achievement emotions and are of equal relevance to students' achievement strivings. The excitement arising from the commencement of a new class, boredom experienced when performing monotonous assignments, or anger felt when an exam's demands seem unreasonable are examples of activity-related emotions.

Achievement emotions can be organized in a three-dimensional taxonomy (Pekrun, 2006, 2018; Table 21.1). In this taxonomy, the differentiation of activity versus outcome emotions pertains to the *object focus* of these emotions. In addition, like emotions more generally, achievement emotions can be grouped according to their *valence* and the degree of implied *activation*. In terms of valence, positive emotions can be distinguished from negative emotions, such as pleasant enjoyment versus unpleasant anxiety. In terms of activation, physiologically activating emotions (e.g., excitement) can be distinguished from deactivating emotions (e.g., pleasant relaxation). By using the dimensions valence and activation, the taxonomy is consistent with circumplex models that arrange affective states in a two-dimensional (valence × activation) space (Barrett & Russell, 1998).

Theories of Achievement Emotions

Theoretical work on achievement emotions has focused on their origins. Generally, emotions are influenced by numerous factors, including cognitive appraisals, situational perceptions, genetic dispositions, neurohormonal processes, sensory feedback from facial and postural expression, and social environments (Barrett et al., 2016). Among these factors, cognitive appraisals are likely to play a significant role in arousing achievement emotions. As such, most theories of achievement emotions focus on the emotional relevance of self- and task-related appraisals. The following sections outline the basic propositions of these theories. In addition, I consider theoretical work on the functions of emotions for learning and on reciprocal causation and emotion regulation.

Appraisal Theories

Transactional Model of Test Anxiety

Test anxiety is a prospective emotion related to the threat of failure on an upcoming or ongoing evaluation (i.e., test or exam). Therefore, many authors have regarded threat-related appraisals as the main proximal determinants of test anxiety (Zeidner, 2014). For example, from the perspective of Lazarus's and Folkman's (1984) transactional model of stress and negative emotions, test anxiety is based on two kinds of appraisals. The *primary appraisal* pertains to the likelihood and subjective importance of failure. In the *secondary appraisal*, possibilities to cope with the situation are explored cognitively. Depending on the combined result of the two appraisals, different emotions can be aroused. In the case of threat and insufficient perceived control over threatening failure, anxiety is assumed to be instigated.

Attributional Theory

Extending the perspective beyond anxiety, Weiner proposed an attributional approach to the origins of achievement emotions following success and failure (see Weiner, 1985, 2019). In this theory, causal attributions of success and failure are considered the primary determinants of these emotions. More specifically, it is assumed that achievement outcomes are first subjectively evaluated in terms of success or failure. This outcome appraisal immediately leads to attribution-independent emotions that are less cognitively elaborate: happiness after success, and frustration and sadness after failure. Following these immediate emotional reactions, causal ascriptions are sought that lead to differentiated, attribution-dependent emotions.

Three dimensions of causal attributions are assumed to play critical roles in determining attribution-dependent emotions: (a) the perceived *locus of causality* differentiating internal versus external causes of achievement (e.g., effort versus environmental circumstances), (b) their perceived *controllability* (e.g., effort versus uncontrollable ability), and (c) their perceived *stability* (e.g., stable ability versus unstable chance). Weiner (1985) posits that pride should be experienced when success is attributed to internal causes (e.g., ability); shame when failure is attributed to uncontrollable internal causes (e.g., lack of ability); and gratitude and anger when success or failure, respectively, are attributed to external, other-controlled causes. Hopefulness and hopelessness are expected when past success and failure, respectively, are attributed to stable causes (e.g., stable ability). Weiner (2007) further extended his theory by also speculating about the causal attributional antecedents of "moral" emotions like envy, scorn, sympathy, admiration, regret, and "Schadenfreude."

Control-Value Theory

In Pekrun's (2006, 2018, 2021) control-value theory (CVT), propositions of the transactional stress model and attributional theory are revised to explain a wider variety of achievement emotions, including both outcome emotions and activity emotions. The theory posits that achievement emotions are induced when the individual feels in control of, or out of control of, activities and outcomes that are subjectively important—implying that appraisals of control and value are the proximal determinants of these emotions. Control appraisals pertain to the perceived controllability of achievement-related actions and outcomes, as implied by causal expectations (e.g., self-efficacy expectations), causal attributions of achievement, and competence appraisals (e.g., self-concepts of ability). Value appraisals relate to the subjective importance of these activities and outcomes.

Different control and value appraisals are assumed to instigate different achievement emotions (see Table 21.1). Prospective joy and hopelessness are expected to be triggered when there is high perceived control (joy) or a complete lack of perceived control (hopelessness). For example, a student who believes they have the abilities to excel on an exam may feel joyous about the prospect of receiving the exam grade. Prospective hope and anxiety are instigated when there is uncertainty about control, the attentional focus being on anticipated success in the case of hope, and on anticipated failure in the case of anxiety. For example, a student who is unsure about being able to master an important exam may hope for success, fear failure, or both. Pride, shame, gratitude, and anger are seen to be induced by perceptions of the controllability of success and failure, as implied by causal attributions of these achievement outcomes. In addition, all of these outcome-related emotions are thought to depend on the subjective importance of success and failure, implying that they are a joint function of perceived control and value. For instance, a student should feel worried if judging themself to be incapable of preparing for an exam (low controllability) that is important (high value). In contrast, if the student feels able to prepare (high controllability), or is indifferent about the exam (low value), anxiety should be low.

Regarding activity emotions, enjoyment of learning is proposed to depend on positive competence appraisals and positive appraisals of the intrinsic value of learning. For example, a student is expected to enjoy learning when feeling competent to meet task demands and value the learning material. If the student feels incompetent, or is disinterested in the material, studying is not enjoyable. Anger and frustration are aroused when the value of the activity is negative (e.g., when working on a challenging project is perceived as taking too much effort, which is experienced as aversive). Finally, boredom is experienced when the activity lacks any incentive value (Pekrun et al., 2010).

Theories on the Functions of Achievement Emotions

Theoretical work on the functions of emotions has addressed various mechanisms that can impact learning and achievement, such as cognitive resources available for task performance, motivational processes, memory encoding and retrieval, and styles of information processing. Different models address different subsets of these mechanisms; thus, theories on the functions of emotion for learning are fragmented.

Theories of *cognitive resources* have posited that emotions produce task-irrelevant thinking, thereby depleting working memory resources needed for task performance. For example, a student who worries about possibly failing an upcoming exam may experience difficulties focusing on the learning material. By implication, emotions are thought to impair learning and performance on tasks that demand cognitive resources, such as complex cognitive problem-solving. This proposition was part of early interference and attentional deficit models of test anxiety, which assumed that anxiety produces task-irrelevant thinking that reduces on-task attention and interferes with performance on tasks requiring working memory capacity (e.g., Wine, 1971). Resource-oriented theories were later generalized for negative mood (Ellis & Ashbrook, 1988) as well as positive affective states (Meinhardt & Pekrun, 2003; Mikels & Reuter-Lorenz, 2019).

Resource allocation theories posit detrimental effects on both negative and positive emotions. In contrast, theories on *styles of information processing* propose that emotions can facilitate performance, with positive and negative emotions promoting different modes of cognitive problem-solving.

Specifically, in mood-as-information approaches (see Clore & Huntsinger, 2007), it is assumed that positive moods signal that "all is well," whereas negative moods signal that the situation is problematic. "All is well" conditions imply safety and the discretion to creatively explore the environment, broaden one's cognitive horizon, and build new actions, as addressed by Fredrickson's (2001) broaden-and-build model of positive emotion. In contrast, if there are problems threatening well-being and agency, it may be wise to focus on these problems in cognitively cautious ways. Accordingly, positive affective states are thought to promote holistic, creative, and flexible ways of thinking, whereas negative states are expected to facilitate analytical and detail-oriented information processing.

These theories focus on distinguishing between the effects of positive versus negative emotions. However, different emotions within these two categories may serve different functions. In the *cognitive/motivational model of emotion effects* which is part of CVT, an attempt is made to provide a more nuanced theoretical account by taking both the valence and activation dimensions of emotion into account. Doing so renders four broad categories of emotion: positive activating, positive deactivating, negative activating, and negative deactivating (Table 21.1). Emotions from these four categories are posited to influence both cognitive and motivational mechanisms of learning.

Positive activating emotions such as enjoyment of learning are thought to (a) preserve cognitive resources and focus attention on learning tasks; (b) promote interest and intrinsic motivation; (c) facilitate the use of flexible, creative learning strategies such as organization and elaboration of learning material; and (d) positively affect students' self-regulation of learning. The opposite pattern of effects is expected for negative deactivating emotions such as boredom and hopelessness: depletion of cognitive resources (e.g., daydreaming when feeling bored); undermining effects on any kind of motivation to learn; shallow information processing and under-use of any effortful learning strategies. Consequently, positive activating emotions are expected to promote academic performance in most students and under most task conditions, whereas deactivating negative emotions are expected to be generally detrimental.

In contrast, the effects of positive deactivating emotions (e.g., relief and relaxation) and activating negative emotions (e.g., anger, anxiety, or shame) are expected to be more complex. For example, anxiety can distract attention and undermine interest and intrinsic motivation. On the other hand, anxiety can induce strong motivation to invest effort in order to avoid failure, and it can promote detail-oriented ways of learning (e.g., rigid rehearsal) that can be beneficial for academic performance. Therefore, the overall effects of these emotions on students' achievement are thought to be more variable.

Reciprocal Causation and Emotion Regulation

In Lazarus's transactional model (Lazarus & Folkman, 1984) and Pekrun's (2006) CVT, emotions, their antecedents, and their effects are thought to be linked by reciprocal causation. Emotions influence learning and performance, but performance outcomes reciprocally influence antecedent appraisals and environmental factors (Figure 21.1). Positive feedback loops are likely commonplace (e.g., teachers' and students' enjoyment reciprocally reinforcing each other; Frenzel et al., 2018), but negative feedback loops can also be important (e.g., when a student's failure on an exam induces anxiety, and anxiety motivates the student to avoid failing the next exam).

Reciprocal causation has implications for the regulation and treatment of achievement emotions. Since emotions, antecedents, and effects can be reciprocally linked over time, addressing any of the elements involved in these cyclic feedback processes can change emotions. Regulation and treatment can target (a) the emotion itself (*emotion-oriented* regulation and treatment, such

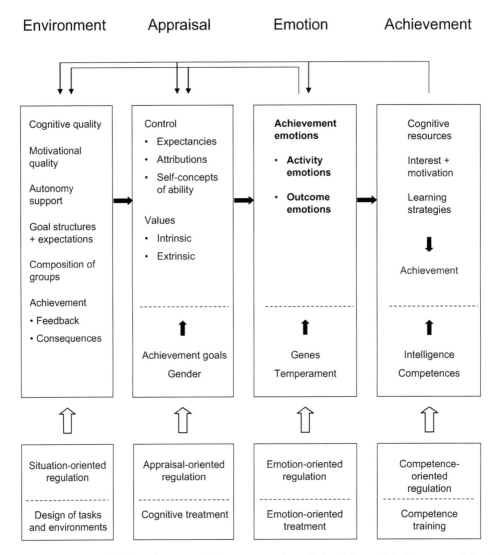

Figure 21.1 Reciprocal linkages between achievement emotions, their origins, and their outcomes (adapted from Pekrun, 2006)

as using relaxation techniques to cope with anxiety or interest-enhancing strategies to reduce boredom); (b) the control and value appraisals underlying emotions (*appraisal-oriented* regulation and treatment; e.g., attributional retraining, Perry et al., 2014); (c) the competences determining students' academic agency (*competence-oriented* regulation and treatment; e.g., training of learning skills); and (d) the learning environment (*situation-oriented regulation*; e.g., designing tasks and environments to enhance students' enjoyment of learning; see also Harley et al., 2019).

Review of Key Research Findings

Due to the focus of researchers' attention on test anxiety, there is cumulative evidence on the origins and functions of students' anxiety. Research on achievement emotions other than anxiety is still relatively scarce. The following sections summarize key findings on the origins, functions, and development of test anxiety and other achievement emotions.

Individual and Social Origins

Appraisals and Achievement Goals

The available empirical evidence is in line with the propositions of appraisal theories. Test anxiety research has shown that test anxiety correlates negatively with variables of perceived control, such as self-concepts of ability and self-efficacy expectations, and positively with students' expectations of failure (Zeidner, 1998, 2014). In attributional studies, retrospective achievement emotions such as pride and shame have been linked to causal attributions of success and failure. Most of these studies used a scenario approach asking students how they might react to success and failure, implying that they asked for participants' subjective theories about links between attributions and emotions. However, there also are experimental and field studies corroborating the validity of attributional assumptions (Weiner, 2019).

Studies testing CVT have found that both perceived control and perceived value are predictive for outcome emotions such as hope and anxiety, and for activity emotions such as enjoyment and boredom (Forsblom et al., 2021; Pekrun & Perry, 2014). Furthermore, a few recent studies have shown that perceived control and value interact in predicting these emotions (see Putwain et al., 2020; Shao et al., 2020). For example, in these studies, enjoyment of achievement activities was high when both control and value related to these activities were high, and low when control, value, or both were low, in line with the propositions of the theory. Overall, the available evidence corroborates that achievement emotions are closely linked to students' achievement-related appraisals.

Students' appraisals are likely to be influenced by their achievement goals. For example, mastery goals can focus attention on the controllability and positive value of achievement activities (Pekrun et al., 2006). Performance-approach goals can facilitate positive appraisals of success, while performance-avoidance goals can sustain appraisals of the uncontrollability and negative value of failure. In line with these considerations, empirical findings show that students' mastery goals relate positively to their enjoyment of learning, performance-approach goals to their hope and pride, and performance-avoidance goals to their anxiety (Pekrun et al., 2006, 2009; see also Huang, 2011).

Classroom Instruction and Test-Taking

Lack of structure and clarity in classroom instruction, as well as excessive task demands, relate positively to students' test anxiety (Zeidner, 2014). Students' appraisals of lack of control and failure expectancies likely mediate the effects of these factors. Lack of structure and transparency regarding exams also contribute to students' anxiety. Furthermore, the format of items has been found to be relevant, with open-ended formats inducing more anxiety than multiple-choice formats. Open-ended formats require more working memory capacity, which may be less available in anxiety because worrying exhausts cognitive resources. This lack of resources induces even more threat and debilitates anxious students' performance.

A few studies have investigated relations between classroom instruction and students' positive emotions. Teacher-centered instruction emphasizing rigid drill and exercise relates negatively to students' positive emotional attitudes toward school (Valeski & Stipek, 2001). In contrast, the cognitive quality of instruction oriented toward creative mental modeling rather than algorithmic routine procedures has been found to correlate positively with students' enjoyment of learning (Pekrun et al., 2007). In addition, support for students' autonomy at learning correlated positively with students' enjoyment in Pekrun et al.'s study. Finally, teachers' enjoyment and enthusiasm during teaching relates positively to students' enjoyment, suggesting transmission of positive emotions from teachers to students (Frenzel et al., 2018).

Social Environments

High achievement expectancies from parents and teachers, negative feedback after achievement, negative consequences of failure, and competition in the classroom correlate positively with students' test anxiety (Zeidner, 2014), likely because these factors reduce perceived control and increase the importance of avoiding failure (see also Murayama et al., 2016). In contrast, positive perceptions of the relationship with teachers were associated with enhanced positive emotions and reduced negative emotions (Goetz et al., 2021). However, parents' and teachers' social support and a cooperative classroom climate sometimes fail to correlate with students' anxiety scores (Hembree, 1988). This surprising lack of correlation may be due to coercive components of efforts to support students, which can counteract the beneficial effects of support per se. A second explanation would be negative feedback loops between support and anxiety, implying that support alleviates anxiety (negative effect of support on anxiety), but that anxiety provokes support in the first place (positive effect of anxiety on demanding support), thus yielding an overall zero correlation.

In addition, it follows from CVT that the composition of student groups is critically important. The ability level of the classroom determines the likelihood of performing well relative to one's classmates. All else being equal, chances for performing well relative to others are reduced when being in a high-achieving class, thus students' perceived control and competence tend to be reduced. In contrast, being in a low-achieving class offers more chances to succeed, enabling a sense of competence. Due to these effects on perceived control, positive emotions such as enjoyment can be reduced, and negative emotions such as anxiety exacerbated when a student is in a high-achieving class ("happy-fish-little-pond effect"; Pekrun et al., 2019).

Functions for Learning and Performance

Positive Emotions

Traditionally, it was often assumed that positive emotions are maladaptive by inducing unrealistic appraisals, fostering superficial information processing, and reducing motivation to pursue challenging goals. As summarized by Aspinwall (1998), traditional approaches to positive emotions imply that "our primary goal is to feel good, and feeling good makes us lazy thinkers who are oblivious to potentially useful negative information and unresponsive to meaningful variations in information and situation" (p. 7). However, experimental mood research has shown that positive mood can enhance divergent thinking and flexible problem solving, thus contradicting views that positive emotions are uniformly detrimental for motivation and performance (Baas et al., 2008; Clore & Huntsinger, 2007).

Evidence on the effects of students' positive emotions supports the view that activating positive emotions can enhance motivation and performance. Specifically, enjoyment of learning, hope, and pride have been found to correlate positively with students' interest, effort, elaboration of learning material, self-regulation of learning, and academic achievement, thus corroborating that these emotions can be beneficial for students' academic agency (Camacho-Morles et al., 2021; Pekrun et al., 2002; Shao et al., 2020). However, in some studies, measures of positive affective states did not correlate with performance indicators (Linnenbrink, 2007; Pekrun et al., 2009). One possible explanation is that the measures used did not clearly differentiate between activating and deactivating variants of positive affect. As such, null correlations may be due to having measured relaxation and task-irrelevant positive affect rather than task-related enjoyment.

Negative Activating Emotions

The effects of achievement anxiety (e.g., test anxiety and math anxiety) have been analyzed in hundreds of studies (Hembree, 1988; Zeidner, 2014; Zhang et al., 2019). Experimental studies have shown that anxiety impairs performance on complex or difficult tasks that demand cognitive resources (e.g., difficult intelligence test items). Performance on easy and less complex tasks need not be reduced, and may even be enhanced. In line with this evidence, field studies have shown that achievement anxiety correlates moderately negatively with students' academic performance. Furthermore, the evidence from a few longitudinal studies suggests that these relations are due to effects of anxiety on achievement over time, in addition to effects of failure and low achievement on the development of anxiety (see Pekrun et al., 2017; Putwain et al., 2020).

A few studies have addressed the effects of students' anger and shame. The findings suggest that students' anger at school correlates positively with task-irrelevant thinking, and negatively with academic self-efficacy, interest, self-regulation of learning, and performance (Boekaerts, 1993; Camacho-Morles et al., 2021; Pekrun et al., 2011). Similarly, students' achievement-related shame shows negative overall correlations with their effort and academic performance (Pekrun et al., 2011). However, as with anxiety, the underlying pattern of functional mechanisms may be complex and imply more than just adverse effects. For example, Turner and Schallert (2001) showed that students experiencing shame following negative exam feedback increased their motivation when they continued to be committed to academic goals and held positive expectancies to reach these goals.

Negative Deactivating Emotions

Negative deactivating emotions (e.g., boredom and hopelessness) are characterized by reduced levels of physiological and cognitive activation. Despite the frequency of boredom experienced by students, this emotion has only recently began to receive attention, as has the less frequent, but devastating emotion of achievement-related hopelessness. Boredom at work was researched early as being induced by monotonous assembly-line work (e.g., Wyatt, 1930), and was discussed as being experienced by gifted students in recent years. In empirical research, boredom was found to correlate negatively with students' attention, motivation to learn, and use of learning strategies, and to be a negative predictor of academic achievement (Camacho-Morles et al., 2021; Pekrun et al., 2010, 2011, 2014; Tze et al., 2016). Similarly, students' achievement-related hopelessness correlates negatively with measures of motivation, study behavior, and achievement (Pekrun et al., 2011).

In sum, the available evidence suggests that emotions exert profound effects on students' motivation, learning, and achievement. Typically, these effects are positive for positive emotions and negative for negative deactivating emotions. The effects of negative activating emotions such as anxiety, anger, and shame are more complex. From an educator's perspective, however, any benefits of these emotions in resilient, highly motivated students are certainly outweighed by their adverse effects on the vast majority of students. Also, beyond effects on academic learning, achievement-related anxiety and shame can have severe consequences for students' long-term psychological well-being, social adaptation, and physical health (Zeidner, 1998).

Diversity, Universality, and Development

Diversity and Universality of Achievement Emotions

The general functional mechanisms of achievement emotions may be bound to universal, species-specific characteristics of our mind. In contrast, the specific contents and reference objects of these emotions, the frequency of their occurrence, and process parameters such as intensity and duration can vary widely between individuals, genders, achievement settings, and sociocultural contexts. Accordingly, the basic structures and causal mechanisms of achievement emotions are expected to follow nomothetic principles, whereas occurrence and phenomenology follow principles of variation and diversity (Pekrun, 2009, 2018).

For example, we found that the relations between girls' and boys' appraisals and their achievement emotions in mathematics were structurally equivalent across the two genders (Goetz et al., 2013). However, perceived control in this domain was substantially lower for girls. As a consequence, girls reported less enjoyment in mathematics, and more anxiety and shame. Concerning settings, we found that students' emotions experienced in mathematics, science, and languages differed in mean levels across subject domains, but showed equivalent internal structures and linkages with academic achievement across domains (Goetz et al., 2007). Similarly, in a cross-cultural comparison of Chinese and German students' achievement emotions, we found that mean levels of emotions differed between cultures, with Chinese students reporting more achievement-related enjoyment, pride, anxiety, and shame, and less anger (Frenzel et al., 2007). Nevertheless, the functional linkages of these emotions with perceived control, important others' expectations, and academic achievement were equivalent across cultures.

This pattern of findings is consistent with findings from the OECD Programme for International Student Assessment (PISA). For example, mean scores for mathematics anxiety differed substantially across countries in the PISA assessments (e.g., OECD, 2013). These mean-level differences notwithstanding, the relations with students' performance were remarkably consistent. For example, in the PISA 2012 assessment, students' anxiety and achievement in math correlated negatively in all of the 64 participating countries, and all of these correlations but one were significant (OECD, 2013). Similarly, in the PISA 2015 assessment, students' schoolwork-related anxiety showed negative correlations with their science performance in 52 of 55 countries participating in the assessment of anxiety, and the relation between students' enjoyment and performance in science was positive in all of the 68 countries for which this relation was examined (OECD, 2016).

Development Across the School Years

Capabilities needed to experience achievement emotions develop early in childhood. Children can express pride and shame when successfully solving tasks or failing to do so at the age of two to three years, suggesting that they are able to differentiate internal versus external causation of success and failure. During the early elementary school years, they additionally acquire capabilities to distinguish between different internal and external causes, such as ability and effort, to develop related causal expectancies, and to cognitively combine expectancies and value-related information. By implication, students develop the cognitive competencies to experience all significant achievement emotions early in their academic careers.

Empirical evidence on the development of these emotions at school is scarce. Again, research on test anxiety is an exception. This research has shown that average scores for test anxiety are low at the beginning of elementary school but increase substantially during the elementary school years (Hembree, 1988; Raccanello et al., 2019). This development is congruent with the decline of academic self-concepts of ability during this period, likely due to increasing realism in academic self-perceptions and the cumulative failure feedback many students receive. After elementary school, average anxiety scores stabilize and remain high throughout middle school, high school, and college (Hembree, 1988; Pekrun et al., 2017). However, stability at the group level notwithstanding, anxiety can change in individual students. One important source for individual dynamics is the change of reference groups implied by transitions between schools and classrooms. As noted, the likelihood of low achievement relative to peers is higher in high-ability classrooms, and lower in low-ability classrooms. Therefore, changing from a low-ability to a high-ability class-room can increase anxiety, while the reverse can happen when entering a low-ability classroom (Pekrun et al., 2019).

Congruent to the increase of average levels of anxiety, positive emotions such as enjoy-ment of learning seem to decrease across the elementary school years (Helmke, 1993; Rac-canello et al., 2019). This decrease of enjoyment can continue through the middle school years (Pekrun et al., 2007), consistent with the decline of average scores for subject-matter interest and general attitudes toward school (Frenzel et al., 2010; Wigfield et al., 2015). Im-portant factors responsible for this development may be an increase of teacher-centered in-struction and academic demands in middle school, the competition between academic and nonacademic interests in adolescence, and the selectivity of subject-matter interest that is part of adolescent identity formation.

Implications for Educational Practice

The evidence summarized above implies that achievement emotions can profoundly influence students' learning and academic performance. Accordingly, educators are well-advised to consider these emotions. However, given the scarcity of knowledge about the influence of education on these emotions, it would be premature to derive firm conclusions for educational practice, with the possible exception of recommendations related to test anxiety. Judging from appraisal theories (see Pekrun, 2006) and test anxiety studies (Zeidner, 1998, 2014), the following factors should be considered by educators to help students develop positive achievement emotions, reduce negative emotions, and productively use the energy provided by negative emotions if they cannot be pre-vented (Figure 21.1; see Linnenbrink et al., 2016; Pekrun, 2014).

Cognitive Quality of Instruction

Well-structured instruction and clear explanations likely contribute to adaptive student emotions by raising students' competencies and feelings of control. By implication, adaptive student emo-tions likely can be fostered, and maladaptive emotions reduced by raising the cognitive quality of instruction.

Motivational Quality of Instruction

Teachers deliver direct messages conveying academic values as well as more indirect messages implied by their behavior. Two ways of inducing values and related emotions may be the most important. First, if learning environments meet the needs of students, positive activity-related emotions are likely fostered. For example, learning environments that support cooperative learning should help students to fulfill needs for social relatedness, thus making learning en-joyable. Second, the enjoyment and enthusiasm teachers experience themselves can facilitate students' adoption of positive emotions by way of emotional contagion and observational learning (Frenzel et al., 2018).

Support for Autonomy and Self-Regulated Learning

Learning environments supporting students' self-regulated learning can be assumed to increase their sense of control and related positive emotions. In addition, such environments can foster positive emotions by meeting students' need for autonomy. However, these beneficial effects likely depend on the match between students' competence and need for academic autonomy, on the one hand, and the affordances of these environments, on the other. In case of a mismatch, loss of control and negative emotions can result. By implication, teachers should attend to matching demands for autonomy to students' competencies and needs.

Goal Structures and Achievement Expectations

Academic achievement can be defined by standards of individual mastery, normative standards based on competitive social comparison, or cooperative group performance standards. These different standards imply individualistic (mastery), competitive (normative performance), and cooperative goal structures in the classroom (Johnson & Johnson, 1974). Goal structures and grading practices determine students' opportunities for experiencing success and perceiving control, thus influencing their emotions. Specifically, competitive goal structures imply, by definition, that some students experience success, whereas others have to experience failure, thus increasing levels of anxiety and hopelessness. Similarly, the demands implied by excessively high achievement expectancies of teachers and parents can lead to lowered control perceptions and related negative emotions. Accordingly, as seen from an emotional perspective, educators should adapt expectancies to students' competencies and refrain from using goal structures that induce individual competition between students.

Composition of Student Groups

The adverse effects of membership in high-achieving classrooms described previously in this chapter pose a conundrum for educators. Placing students in high-ability classes provides them with peers who are role models for cognitive development and can provide cognitive stimulation. However, these possible benefits need to be weighed against the psychosocial costs of such a placement, including the risk of reducing self-confidence, decreasing positive emotions, and increasing negative emotions. Furthermore, it may be that the possible beneficial effects on learning do not even occur. When controlling for measurement error and pre-existing differences, the effects of class-average achievement on individual achievement are small and can even be negative (Becker et al., 2021; Dicke et al., 2018), implying that being in a high-achieving class may neither benefit a student's emotions nor their cognitive learning.

Test-Taking, Feedback, and Consequences of Achievement

Educators can reduce students' test anxiety by increasing the structure and transparency of tests and exams (e.g., providing clear information on demands, materials, and grading practices). In addition, using structured item formats and giving second chances in terms of retaking tests and exams can help reduce test anxiety (Zeidner, 1998). Furthermore, cumulative success and failure feedback is likely a major factor underlying students' achievement emotions (Pekrun et al., 2017). Success experiences can strengthen perceived control and related positive emotions, whereas repeated failure can undermine control and instigate negative emotions. In addition, the perceived consequences of success and failure are important. Positive future-related student emotions can be increased if academic success is seen to produce beneficial long-term outcomes, such as future career opportunities. Negative outcomes of academic failure, on the other hand, can increase students' anxiety and hopelessness. By implication, providing experiences of success, defining mistakes as opportunities to learn rather than as personal failure, linking attainment to beneficial outcomes, and avoiding high-stakes testing involving negative consequences are also important for helping students develop adaptive emotions (Vogl & Pekrun, 2016).

Conclusion

Achievement emotions are among the most frequently experienced and functionally most essential kinds of emotions at school. However, except for studies examining test anxiety which has been a popular construct since the 1950s (Zeidner, 1998), research on achievement emotions is clearly in a nascent stage. Psychological researchers are just beginning to acknowledge the importance of these emotions. The fragmented research efforts in this field need integration. Attention should be given to the functions of achievement emotions not only for performance but also for well-being and health. Of specific importance, little is known to date about regulation, treatment, and design of academic settings targeting achievement emotions other than anxiety (see, e.g., Harley et al., 2019; Loderer et al., in press). However, the success story of test anxiety treatment (Huntley et al., 2019; Putwain & van der Embse, 2020; von der Embse et al., 2013) suggests that future research can be successful in developing ways to shape academic settings to promote adaptive achievement emotions and reduce maladaptive emotions.

References

Aspinwall, L. (1998). Rethinking the role of positive affect in self-regulation. *Motivation and Emotion, 22,* 1–32. doi:10.1023/A:1023080224401

Baas, M., De Dreu, C. K. W., & Nijstad, B. A. (2008). A meta-analysis of 25 years of mood–creativity research: Hedonic tone, activation, or regulatory focus? *Psychological Bulletin, 134,* 779–806. doi:10.1037/a0012815

Barrett, L. F., Lewis, M., & Haviland-Jones, J. M. (Eds.). (2016). *Handbook of emotions* (4th edition). Guilford.

Barrett, L. F., & Russell, J. A. (1998). Independence and bipolarity in the structure of current affect. *Journal of Personality and Social Psychology, 74,* 967–984. doi:10.1037/0022-3514.74.4.967

Becker, M., Kocaj, A., Jansen, M., Dumont, H., & Lüdtke, O. (2021). Class-average achievement and individual achievement development: Testing achievement composition and peer spillover effects using five German longitudinal studies. *Journal of Educational Psychology.* Advance online publication. doi:10.1037/edu0000519

Boekaerts, M. (1993). Anger in relation to school learning. *Learning and Instruction, 3,* 269–280. doi:10.1016/0959-4752(93)90019-V

Broughton, S. H., Sinatra, G. M., & Nussbaum, E. M. (2013). "Pluto has been a planet my whole life!" Emotions, attitudes, and conceptual change in elementary students' learning about Pluto's reclassification. *Research in Science Education, 43,* 529–550. doi:10.1007/s11165-011-9274-x

Camacho-Morles, J., Slemp, G. R., Pekrun, R., Loderer, K., Hou, H., & Oades, L. G. (2021). Activity achievement emotions and academic performance: A meta-analysis. *Educational Psychology Review, 33,* 1051–1095. doi:10.1007/s10648-020-09585-3

Clore, G. L., & Huntsinger, J. R. (2007). How emotions inform judgment and regulate thought. *Trends in Cognitive Sciences, 11,* 393–399. doi:10.1016/j.tics.2007.08.005

Dicke, T., Marsh, H. W., Parker, P. D., Pekrun, R., Guo, J., & Televantou, I. (2018). Effects of school-average achievement on individual self-concept and achievement: Unmasking phantom effects masquerading as true compositional effects. *Journal of Educational Psychology, 110,* 1112–1126. doi:10.1037/edu0000259

D'Mello, S., Lehman, B., Pekrun, R., & Graesser, A. (2014). Confusion can be beneficial for learning. *Learning and Instruction, 29,* 153–170. doi:10.1016/j.learninstruc.2012.05.003

Ellis, H. C., & Ashbrook, P. W. (1988). Resource allocation model of the effect of depressed mood states on memory. In K. Fiedler & J. Forgas (Eds.), *Affect, cognition, and social behavior* (pp. 25–43). Hogrefe International.

Fredrickson, B. L. (2001). The role of positive emotions in positive psychology: The broaden-and-build theory of positive emotions. *American Psychologist, 56,* 218–226. doi:10.1037/0003-066X.56.3.218

Frenzel, A. C., Becker-Kurz, B., Pekrun, R., Goetz, T., & Lüdtke, O. (2018). Emotion transmission in the classroom revisited: A reciprocal effects model of teacher and student enjoyment. *Journal of Educational Psychology, 110,* 628–639. doi:10.1037/edu0000228

Frenzel, A. C., Goetz, T., Pekrun, R., & Watt, H. M. G. (2010). Development of mathematics interest in adolescence: Influences of gender, family, and school context. *Journal of Research on Adolescence, 20,* 507–537. doi:10.1111/j.1532-7795.2010.00645.x

Frenzel, A. C., Thrash, T. M., Pekrun, R., & Goetz, T. (2007). Achievement emotions in Germany and China: A cross-cultural validation of the Academic Emotions Questionnaire-Mathematics (AEQ-M). *Journal of Cross-Cultural Psychology, 38,* 302–309. doi:10.1177/0022022107300276

Goetz, T., Bieg, M., Lüdtke, O., Pekrun, R., & Hall, N. C. (2013). Do girls really experience more anxiety in mathematics? *Psychological Science, 24,* 2079–2087. doi:10.1177/0956797613486989

Goetz, T., Bieleke, M., Gogol, K., van Tartwijk, J., Mainhard, T., Lipnevich, A., & Pekrun, R. (2021). Getting along and feeling good: Reciprocal associations between student-teacher relationship quality and students' emotions. *Learning and Instruction, 71,* Article 101349. doi:10.1016/j.learninstruc.2020.101349

Goetz, T., Frenzel, A. C., Pekrun, R., Hall, N. C., & Lüdtke, O. (2007). Between- and within-domain relations of students' academic emotions. *Journal of Educational Psychology, 99,* 715–733. doi:10.1037/0022–0663.99.4.715

Harley, J. M., Pekrun, R., Taxer, J. L., & Gross, J. J. (2019). Emotion regulation in achievement situations: An integrated model. *Educational Psychologist, 54,* 106–126. doi:10.1080/00461520.2019.1587297

Helmke, A. (1993). Die Entwicklung der Lernfreude vom Kindergarten bis zur 5. Klassenstufe [Development of enjoyment of learning from kindergarten to grade 5]. *Zeitschrift für Pädagogische Psychologie, 7,* 77–86.

Hembree, R. (1988). Correlates, causes, effects, and treatment of test anxiety. *Review of Educational Research, 58,* 47–77. doi:10.3102/00346543058001047

Huang, C. (2011). Achievement goals and achievement emotions: A meta-analysis. *Educational Psychology Review, 23,* 359–388. doi:10.1007/s10648-011-9155-x.

Huntley, C. D., Young, B., Temple, J., Longworth, M., Smith, C. T., Jha, V., & Fisher, P. L. (2019). The efficacy of interventions for test-anxious university students: A meta-analysis of randomized controlled trials. *Journal of Anxiety Disorders, 63,* 36–50. doi:10.1016/j.janxdis.2019.01.007

Johnson, D. W., & Johnson, R. T. (1974). Instructional goal structure: Cooperative, competitive or individualistic. *Review of Educational Research, 4,* 213–240. doi:10.3102/00346543044002213

Lajoie, S. P., Azevedo, R., Pekrun, R., & Leighton, J. (Eds). (2020). Emotions in technology-based learning environments [Special issue]. *Learning and Instruction, 70*(6).

Lazarus, R. S., & Folkman, S. (1984). *Stress, appraisal, and coping.* Springer.

Linnenbrink, E. A. (2007). The role of affect in student learning: A multi-dimensional approach to considering the interaction of affect, motivation, and engagement. In P. A. Schutz, & R. Pekrun (Eds.), *Emotion in education* (pp. 107–124). Academic Press.

Linnenbrink-Garcia, L., Patall, E. A., & Pekrun, R. (2016). Adaptive motivation and emotion in education: Research and principles for instructional design. *Policy Insights from the Behavioral and Brain Sciences, 3*(2), 228–236. doi:/10.1177/2372732216644450

Loderer, K., Pekrun, R., & Lester, J. C. (2020). Beyond cold technology: A systematic review and meta-analysis on emotions in technology-based learning environments. *Learning and Instruction, 70,* Article 101162. doi:10.1016/j.learninstruc.2019.101272

Loderer, K., Pekrun, R., & Plass, J. L. (2019). Emotional foundations of game-based learning. In J. L. Plass, B. D. Homer, & R. E. Mayer (Eds.), *Handbook of game-based learning* (pp. 111–151). MIT Press.

Meinhardt, J., & Pekrun, R. (2003). Attentional resource allocation to emotional events: An ERP study. *Cognition and Emotion, 17,* 477–500. doi:10.1080/02699930244000039

Mendzheritskaya, J., & Hansen, M. (2019). The role of emotions in higher education teaching and learning processes [special issue]. *Studies in Higher Education, 44*(10). doi:10.1080/03075079.2019.1665306

Mikels, J. A., & Reuter-Lorenz, P. A. (2019). Affective working memory: An integrative psychological construct. *Perspectives on Psychological Science, 14,* 543–559. doi:10.1177/1745691619837597

Muis, K. R., Chevrier, M., & Singh, C. A. (2018). The role of epistemic emotions in personal epistemology and self-regulated learning. *Educational Psychologist, 53,* 165–184. doi:10.1080/00461520.2017.1421465

Murayama, K., Pekrun, R., Suzuki, M., Marsh, H. W., & Lichtenfeld, S. (2016). Don't aim too high for your kids: Parental over-aspiration undermines students' learning in mathematics. *Journal of Personality and Social Psychology, 111,* 166–179. doi:10.1037/pspp0000079

Organization for Economic Co-operation and Development. (2013). *PISA 2012 results (Volume 3): Ready to learn. Students' engagement, drive and self-beliefs.* Author.

Organization for Economic Co-operation and Development. (2016). *PISA 2015 results (Volume 1): Excellence and equity in education.* Author.

Pekrun, R. (2006). The control-value theory of achievement emotions: Assumptions, corollaries, and implications for educational research and practice. *Educational Psychology Review, 18,* 315–341. doi:10.1007/s10648-006-9029-9

Pekrun, R. (2014). *Emotions and learning* (Educational Practices Series, Vol. 24). International Academy of Education (IAE) and International Bureau of Education (IBE) of the United Nations Educational, Scientific and Cultural Organization (UNESCO), Geneva, Switzerland.

Pekrun, R. (2018). Control-value theory: A social-cognitive approach to achievement emotions. In G. A. D. Liem & D. M. McInerney (Eds.), *Big theories revisited 2: A volume of research on sociocultural influences on motivation and learning* (pp. 162–190). Information Age Publishing.

Pekrun, R. (2021). Self-appraisals and emotions: A control-value approach. In T. Dicke, F. Guay, H. W. Marsh, R. G. Craven, & D. M. McInerney (Eds). *Self–a multidisciplinary concept* (pp. 1–30). Information Age Publishing.

Pekrun, R. (2009). Global and local perspectives on human affect: Implications of the control-value theory of achievement emotions. In M. Wosnitza, S. A. Karabenick, A. Efklides, & P. Nenniger (Eds.), *Contemporary motivation research: From global to local perspectives* (pp. 97–115). Hogrefe.

Pekrun, R., Elliot, A. J., & Maier, M. A. (2006). Achievement goals and discrete achievement emotions: A theoretical model and prospective test. *Journal of Educational Psychology, 98*, 583–597. doi:10.1037/0022–0663.98.3.583

Pekrun, R., Elliot, A. J., & Maier, M. A. (2009). Achievement goals and achievement emotions: Testing a model of their joint relations with academic performance. *Journal of Educational Psychology, 101*, 115–135. doi:10.1037/a0013383

Pekrun, R., Goetz, T., Daniels, L. M., Stupnisky, R. H., & Perry, R. P. (2010). Boredom in achievement settings: Control-value antecedents and performance outcomes of a neglected emotion. *Journal of Educational Psychology, 102*, 531–549. doi:10.1037/a0019243

Pekrun, R., Goetz, T., Frenzel, A. C., Barchfeld, P., & Perry, R. P. (2011). Measuring emotions in students' learning and performance: The Achievement Emotions Questionnaire (AEQ). *Contemporary Educational Psychology, 36*, 36–48. doi:10.1016/j.cedpsych.2010.10.002

Pekrun, R., Goetz, T., Titz, W., & Perry, R. P. (2002). Academic emotions in students' self-regulated learning and achievement: A program of qualitative and quantitative research. *Educational Psychologist, 37*, 91–106. https://doi.org/10.1207/S15326985EP3702_4

Pekrun, R., Hall, N. C., Goetz, T., & Perry, R. P. (2014). Boredom and academic achievement: Testing a model of reciprocal causation. *Journal of Educational Psychology, 106*, 696–710. doi:10.1037/a0036006

Pekrun, R., Lichtenfeld, S., Marsh, H. W., Murayama, K., & Goetz, T. (2017). Achievement emotions and academic performance: Longitudinal models of reciprocal effects. *Child Development, 88*, 1653–1670. doi:10.1111/cdev.12704

Pekrun, R., & Linnenbrink-Garcia, L. (Eds.). (2014). *International handbook of emotions in education.* Taylor & Francis.

Pekrun, R., Murayama, K., Marsh, H. W., Goetz, T., & Frenzel, A. C. (2019). Happy fish in little ponds: Testing a reference group model of achievement and emotion. *Journal of Personality and Social Psychology, 117*, 166–185. doi:10.1037/pspp0000230

Pekrun, R., & Perry, R. P. (2014). Control-value theory of achievement emotions. In R. Pekrun & L. Linnenbrink-Garcia (Eds.), *International handbook of emotions in education* (pp. 120–141). Taylor & Francis.

Pekrun, R., vom Hofe, R., Blum, W., Frenzel, A. C., Goetz, T., & Wartha, S. (2007). Development of mathematical competencies in adolescence: The PALMA longitudinal study. In M. Prenzel (Ed.), *Studies on the educational quality of schools* (pp. 17–37). Waxmann.

Perry, R. P., Chipperfield, J. G., Hladkyj, S., Pekrun, R., & Hamm, J. M. (2014). Attribution-based treatment interventions in some achievement settings. In S. Karabenick & T. C. Urdan (Eds.), *Advances in motivation and achievement* (Vol. 18, pp. 1–35). Emerald.

Putwain, D. W., Schmitz, E., Wood, P., & Pekrun, R. (2021). The role of achievement emotions in primary school mathematics: Control-value antecedents and achievement outcomes. *British Journal of Educational Psychology, 91*, 347–367. doi:10.1111/ bjep.12367

Putwain, D. W., & von der Embse, N. P. (2021). Cognitive–behavioral intervention for test anxiety in adolescent students: Do benefits extend to school-related wellbeing and clinical anxiety. *Anxiety, Stress, & Coping, 34*, 22–36. doi:10.1080/10615806.2020.1800656

Raccanello, D., Brondino, M., Moè, A., Stupnisky, R. H., & Lichtenfeld, S. (2019). Enjoyment, boredom, anxiety in elementary schools in two domains: Relations with achievement. *The Journal of Experimental Education, 87*, 449–469. doi:10.1080/00220973.2018.1448747

Schutz, P. A., & Pekrun, R. (Eds.). (2007). *Emotion in education.* Academic Press.

Shao, K., Pekrun, R., Marsh, H. W., & Loderer, K. (2020). Control-value appraisals, achievement emotions, and foreign language performance: A latent interaction analysis. *Learning and Instruction, 69*, Article 101356. doi:10.1016/j.learninstruc.2020.101356

Shuman, V., & Scherer, K. R. (2014). Concepts and structure of emotions. In R. Pekrun & L. Linnenbrink-Garcia (Eds.), *International handbook of emotions in education* (pp. 13–35). Taylor & Francis.

Turner, J. E., & Schallert, D. L. (2001). Expectancy-value relationships of shame reactions and shame resiliency. *Journal of Educational Psychology, 93*, 320–329. doi:10.1037/0022–0663.93.2.320

Tze, V. M., Daniels, L. M., & Klassen, R. M. (2016). Evaluating the relationship between boredom and academic outcomes: A meta-analysis. *Educational Psychology Review, 28*, 119–144. doi:10.1007/s10648-015-9301-y

Valeski, T. N., & Stipek, D. J. (2001). Young children's feelings about school. *Child Development, 72*, 1198–1213. doi:10.1111/1467-8624.00342

Vogl, E., & Pekrun, R. (2016). Emotions that matter to achievement: Student feelings about assessment. In G. T. L. Brown & L. R. Harris (Eds.), *Handbook of human and social conditions in assessment* (pp. 111–128). Taylor & Francis / Routledge.

Vogl, E., Pekrun, R., Murayama, K., & Loderer, K. (2020). Surprised – curious – confused: Epistemic emotions and knowledge exploration. *Emotion, 20*, 625–641. doi:10.1037/emo0000578

von der Embse, N., Barterian, J., & Segool, N. (2013). Test anxiety interventions for children and adolescents: A systematic review of treatment studies from 2000–2010. *Psychology in the Schools, 50*, 57–71. doi:10.1002/pits.21660

Weiner, B. (1985). An attributional theory of achievement motivation and emotion. *Psychological Review, 92*, 548–573.

Weiner, B. (2007). Examining emotional diversity in the classroom: An attribution theorist considers the moral emotions. In P. A. Schutz & R. Pekrun (Eds.), *Emotion in education* (pp. 73–88). Academic Press. doi:10.1037/0033-295X.92.4.548

Weiner, B. (2019). The legacy of an attribution approach to motivation and emotion: A no-crisis zone. *Motivation Science, 4*, 4–14. doi:10.1037/mot0000082

Wigfield, A., Eccles, J. S., Fredricks, J., Simpkins, Roeser, R., & Schiefele, U. (2015). Development of achievement motivation and engagement. In R. Lerner (series editor) and M. Lamb (volume editor), *Handbook of child psychology and developmental science* (7th ed., vol. 3, pp. 657–700). Wiley.

Wine, J. D. (1971). Test anxiety and the direction of attention. *Psychological Bulletin, 76*, 92–104. doi:10.1037/h0031332

Wyatt, S. (1930). The problem of monotony and boredom in industrial work. *Industrielle Psychotechnik, 7*, 114–123.

Zeidner, M. (1998). *Test anxiety: The state of the art*. Plenum.

Zeidner, M. (2014). Anxiety in education. In R. Pekrun & L. Linnenbrink-Garcia (Eds.), *International handbook of emotions in education* (pp. 265–288). Taylor & Francis.

Zhang, J., Zhao, N., & Kong, Q. P. (2019). The relationship between math anxiety and math performance: A meta-analytic investigation. *Frontiers in Psychology, 10*, Article 1613. doi:10.3389/fpsyg.2019.01613

22

CREATIVITY IN THE SCHOOLS
Creativity Models and New Directions

James C. Kaufman, Ronald A. Beghetto and Anne M. Roberts

Creativity is a long-recognized, important, yet sometimes neglected educational goal (Al-jughaiman & Mowrer-Reynolds, 2005; Beghetto & Plucker, 2006; Guilford, 1950; Vygotsky, 1967/2004). In recent years, developing young people's creative potential has become a more central goal in schools. Indeed, in the years that have transpired since our earlier versions of this chapter, creativity in education has continued to receive headline attention in popular media outlets (e.g., *The New York Times, Newsweek*, and *Wall Street Journal*), talks given by public intellectuals (e.g., TED talks, blog posts, and podcasts), and various scholarly outlets (e.g., edited books and scholarly and practitioner-based journals).

One reason for this continued interest is that creativity is viewed as necessary for being able to navigate the increasingly complex and unpredictable nature of modern life (Beghetto, 2018; Craft, 2011; Henriksen et al., 2016). Not surprisingly, then, creativity has been featured as a central skill in the national curricula of various countries around the world (Craft, 2007; Mullen, 2020). Concerning the United States, work illustrating the role that creativity can play in the K-12 curriculum has also grown steadily (e.g., Beghetto, 2016, 2020). Further, this focus is evidenced in recent national curricular guidelines that view creativity as a key component to the development of students. For instance, the *Partnership for 21st Century Learning* (now part of Battelle for Kids, 2020) continues to focus on creativity as a core learning skill.

Even though interest in cultivating creativity remains strong, so do challenges regarding the unique constraints placed on schools and classrooms and the potential for such constraints to suppress students' and teachers' creative expression (Beghetto, 2019). Accountability mandates and pressures to perform well on standardized tests continue to be viewed as competing for teachers' and students' attention, often at the cost of efforts aimed at encouraging creative expression (Berliner, 2011). Unless teachers and researchers have a clear understanding of the nature of creativity and how it can coexist in a context of academic accountability, it is unlikely that renewed interest in creativity will lead to substantive changes in classroom practice (see also essays in Beghetto & Kaufman, 2016).

In this chapter, we open with standard creativity definitions and concepts and then discuss the Four C Model of Creativity, which we believe is a comprehensive approach to understanding creativity. Next, we talk about the necessary conditions and student supports for fostering student

DOI: 10.4324/9781003013778-27

creativity development, including conducive educational environments for creativity development. In addition, we will review the importance of teaching students when (and when not) to be creative. We will close with key points from the chapter and provide resources for anyone interested in learning more about creativity in the context of school learning.

What Is Creativity?

Until the 1950s, creativity research was minimal, if barely existent. Less than 0.2% of all entries of *Psychological Abstracts* concentrated on creativity (Guilford, 1950). In a seminal address at the 1950 convention of the American Psychological Association, Guilford persuasively argued for the practical application and scientific merits of creativity research (Kaufman, 2016). Since that influential address, creativity has grown to be a key topic of research studied by numerous scholars, representing varied disciplines (e.g., psychology, sociology, philosophy, the arts, and education) throughout the world.

Most definitions of creativity now comprise two components. First, creative ideas need to represent something unique, new, or innovative. Second, creative ideas must also be task-appropriate. Therefore, creative responses are original and task appropriate as defined in a specific context (Kaufman & Sternberg, 2007; Plucker et al., 2004). One way of exploring how creativity is researched around the world is to focus on *whose* creativity is being studied. For example, the focus of study in creativity depends on whether one is studying internationally famous movie director Steven Spielberg, his plumber (who may creatively fix troublesome leaks), his computer-scientist father and musician mother (both accomplished in their own right), his daughter Mikaela, or her fifth-grade teacher. Thus, the best way to measure creativity may shift according to who creates it. Indeed, one way of distinguishing between creativity and innovation is that the final end product is of more importance in innovation; a creative idea may remain in someone's head, but an innovative idea must be expressed (Kaufman & Beghetto, 2009).

The Four C Model

Big-C Approaches

Most investigations of creativity typically take one of two directions. The first direction focuses on eminent individuals' work—particularly those that are time-honored. Typically, these types of studies and theories are referred to as studying "Big-C" creativity. Examples of studies include those that examine the creative contributions of eminent classical and opera composers whose works have lasted centuries (e.g., Simonton, 1977, 1997) or legendary scientists who create new inventions (Simonton, 2004). Much of the Big-C research uses the historiometric method, which analyzes data taken from biographies or reference sources, thus allowing researchers to examine cross-group patterns in a way that would be impossible to do by individually interviewing each person. Many creativity theories have focused on Big-C concepts. For example, the Propulsion Theory of Creative Contributions (Sternberg et al., 2002; Sternberg & Kaufman, 2012) focuses on how an individual's creative act potentially changes an entire field. The authors outline eight different types of creative contributions, with each representing a different way that a creator can impact a field. The first four contributions all stay within the framework of an existing paradigm. The most basic type of contribution is *replication*, which simply reproduces the past work of others. In comparison, *redefinition* tries to present a different perspective to an established concept, comparable to how a director might re-envision a classic play. The third contribution is *forward incrementation*, which pushes forward a field of study just a little bit. Maybe the creator makes a slight change in what already exists, such as a slight twist on a genre novel. These additions usually are not groundbreaking—it takes the field of study in the same direction it was heading. The final contribution is *advance-forward incrementation*. This contribution pushes the field of study far ahead—and the creator often suffers for being too far ahead of the times. The remaining four creative types discussed in propulsion theory represent attempts to reject and replace the current paradigm. *Redirection* represents an attempt to take a field of study in a new direction. If most of these contribution types represent forward momentum, *reconstruction/redirection* is an attempt to move the field back to where it once was (a reconstruction of the past) so that it may move forward from this point—but in a different direction. Perhaps the most radical of all the creative contributions is *reinitiation*. In *reinitiation*, the creator tries to move the field to a new (as-yet-unreached) starting point, and then progress from there (e.g., Marcel DuChamp entering a urinal in an art exhibit and declaring it art). Finally, the last contribution is *integration*, in which two diverse domains are merged to create a new idea (e.g., the *iPhone*, which combines a handheld computer and a cell phone).

Little-c Approaches

The other predominant approach to creativity focuses on creative activities conducted by everyday people who may not be considered experts or luminaries (e.g., Richards, 2007; Richards et al., 1988). The theories and studies along this line of thinking are usually said to focus on "little-c." Areas of research that focus on little-c creativity may be aimed at developing and warranting the assertion that everyone has creative potential (for reviews of this type of research, see Kaufman & Baer, 2005; Plucker et al., 2004). Some examples of little-c research include investigations of layperson perceptions of creativity (i.e., how a layperson's concept of creativity may differ from how a researcher might define the construct), and cross-cultural comparisons of beliefs about creativity (Lim & Plucker, 2001; Paletz & Peng, 2008).

There are several creativity theories that seem grounded in little-c such as the Investment Theory of Creativity (Sternberg & Lubart, 1995), which argues that the key to being creative is to identify ideas or areas of research that have received only minimal attention, research these ideas, and convince others of how important they might be, and then—when other people have begun to study this topic—move on to another "unpopular" area of research. Sternberg and Lubart list six variables as being essential to creativity: intelligence (i.e., intellectual abilities), knowledge, personality, environment, motivation, and thinking styles. There are, indeed, patterns in these six variables that would describe a creative person. For example, people who are born into environments that value and nurture creativity tend to grow up to be more creative than people who grow up in environments that do not value (and may even punish) creativity. Another theory is Amabile's (1996) Componential Model of Creativity, which contends that three variables are needed for creativity to occur: *domain-relevant skills* (knowledge of a particular field of study having technical skills or talent within that domain); *creativity-relevant skills* (personal characteristics such as tolerance for ambiguity, ability to consider divergent perspectives, having creative metacognition (CMC), being self-disciplined, and willingness to take risks); and *task motivation* (e.g., intrinsic or deep interest in the task).

Beyond Big-C and Little-c

Although the distinction between Big-C and little-c creativity has been useful for helping to clarify different levels of creative magnitude, significant ambiguities remain. There are people who are extremely creative and accomplished, but not at the Big-C level—should they be lumped in with little-c creators? If so, then little-c becomes an extensive category. Furthermore, how are these models applied to K-12 and college-level learning?

Student creative interpretations as they learn a new concept or make a new metaphor are given short shrift in most creativity conceptions. Consider, for example, the above-noted and standard definitions of creativity, which emphasize the combination of novelty and usefulness as defined within a particular sociocultural context (e.g., Plucker et al., 2004). Such definitions highlight the vital role that the sociocultural context (e.g., eighth-grade poetry club versus the Norton Anthology of Poetry) plays in determining what will be considered novel and useful. These core components of creativity (i.e., novelty, usefulness, and social-context) seem most salient to the little-c model. For instance, if an amateur poet shared some poems with a friend, they would not expect a friend to begin a critique by comparing the poems to Robert Frost or T. S. Eliot. Indeed, to reach that level of publishable work usually takes approximately 10 years (Hayes, 1989). The friend would likely evaluate the poems by determining whether there was something new and original about them and make sure that the poems followed some basic conventions of poetry. At the Big-C level, on the other hand, the twin components of novel and usefulness are automatically assumed to be present. An analyst who studies the poetry of Emily Dickenson or W. B. Yeats does not need to begin by asserting that the poems are new or useful. Instead, the larger question rests on how these poets impacted the field and influenced generations of young writers.

Where does this leave the creative insights had by students who are still learning how to write poetry? A student's initial efforts at poetry will not likely be judged as novel or useful. As such, standard (little-c) definitions of creativity are not applicable because the standard definition relies on external judgments of novelty and usefulness. Importantly, however, the student's early poems can still represent work that is personally new and meaningful to *them*. Even though the poem likely will not represent anything new to the field, the very process of learning a field (like writing poetry) presents many opportunities for students to experience creative insights and interpretation.

Big-c and little-c conceptions of creativity are not enough to capture the complex nature of creativity. Kaufman and Beghetto (2009, 2013; Beghetto & Kaufman, 2007), therefore, proposed a Four C Model of Creativity that included two additional categories over what has been previously suggested in existing models: "Pro-c" and "mini-c." Pro-c creativity is expert-level creativity that has not yet attained legendary status: if Jascha Heifitz is a Big-C violinist, then a Pro-c violinist might be the first chair of the Los Angeles Philharmonic. Mini-c creativity constitutes the lowest level of the hierarchy—self-discovering or gleaning personally meaningful insights and interpretations inherent in the learning process (Beghetto & Kaufman, 2007). As one example that distinguishes the little-c from the mini-c, someone who plays violin for a community orchestra would be at the little-c category, while a sixth-grade student starting violin lessons would be at the mini-c category.

Given that mini-c is most applicable to school-aged youth, we focus on that concept here. Mini-c creativity broadens traditional conceptions of creativity to include creative insights and interpretations. Occasionally, such insights and interpretations may develop into little-c (or perhaps even Pro-c) contributions (Beghetto & Kaufman, 2007). In this way, mini-c creativity can also serve as a natural progression to more mature and impactful forms of creativity (little-c, Pro-c, and, in rare instances, Big-C). For example, the invention of Velcro (Big-C creativity) started with George de Mestral's mini-c insight he had after examining the burs that latched onto his clothing while hiking in the Swiss Alps. Of course, the ability to move from such a mini-c insight into the manufacturing of a Big-C product (like Velcro) requires expert knowledge, persistence, resources, and some degree of luck (see Simonton, 1994). Still, it is essential to note that the unambiguous, creative end-product (in this case, Velcro) can overshadow the recognition that the process started with a mini-c (intrapersonal) insight. Although not everyone's insights will lead to innovative and impact products, the genesis of such products (i.e., mini-c insights) occur nearly every day and are available to most anyone (be they world-renowned inventors or grade school children).

The Promise of Smaller C Creativity for Classrooms

The concepts of mini-c and little-c creativity hold great promise for educators interested in supporting creative expression in the classroom. Traditional ways of viewing creativity, which concentrated on eminent creative acts and high productivity levels, made it difficult for any educator who tried to justify spending extensive time on activities that might have a low likelihood of this type of creative act (i.e., revolutionary breakthroughs and high levels of productivity in some domains). In addition, teachers who saw creativity traditionally as only part of the Arts curriculum would not think to foster it in the STEM disciplines, such as with K-12 engineering curriculum as exhibited in the maker movement. Therefore, it is not surprising that if educators hold somewhat narrow views of creativity they may fail to recognize its relevance or importance in their academic curriculum (Beghetto, 2007b; Beghetto & Plucker, 2006).

The marginalization of creativity in schools and classrooms is also sometimes the result of a host of negative stereotypes and perceptions about creative students. These negative beliefs and perceptions are found across cultures and have long histories. For example, some teachers in Western cultures seem to value creative students less than they value bright students, in part, because they associate creativity with nonconformity, impulsivity, and disruptive behavior (e.g., Dawson, 1997; Scott, 1999). Other studies find that teachers feel favorable about creative students (e.g., Runco et al., 1993), although they may not be entirely clear on what creativity means (Aljughaiman & Mowrer-Reynolds, 2005). For example, in one study, teachers reported liking creative students, but then defined creativity with adjectives such as "well-behaved" or "conforming." These perceptions changed for the negative when the researchers switched to descriptors more typically used to describe creative people, such as "impulsive" or "tries to do what others call impossible" to the same teachers (Westby & Dawson, 1995).

Several other investigations have found that teachers' understanding of creativity is often poor. Diakidoy and Phtiaka (2002), for example, discovered that teachers associated creativity primarily with the arts and did not associate "knowledge" as an essential component of creativity (see also Seo et al., 2005). Furthermore, de Souza Fleith (2000) found that although teachers articulated how their attitudes might impact student creativity, they did not consider concepts such as self-evaluation, rewards, or intrinsic motivation as being related to creativity. These negative or misinformed perceptions of creativity can transcend cultures. For example, Tan (2003) reported that student teachers in Singapore favored students who had pleasant dispositions (e.g., kind and friendly) over students who were more creative and risk-taking. Chan and Chan (1999) found that Chinese teachers associated socially undesirable traits with student creativity, arguing that in Chinese cultures, nonconforming or expressive behavior can be interpreted as arrogant or rebellious. Similar findings have been found in Turkish teachers (Günçer & Oral, 1993).

Mini-c and little-c creativity can offer teachers different ways of thinking about student creativity. Indeed, these concepts highlight the creative processes inherent in the development of creative potential. Mini-c and little-c creativity can help teachers recognize that creativity most likely manifested in their classroom will be at a different level and will require more nurturing than what traditional conceptions of creativity would allow. Rather than viewing creativity as something extraordinary (and therefore extracurricular), mini-c and little-c stress that creative insights and interpretations are present in students' everyday learning of core curricular topics. Such smaller levels of creativity are also associated with many dimensions of positive psychology, from broad concepts such as general well-being (Seligman & Csikszentmihalyi, 2000) to specific strengths such as happiness (Csikszentmihalyi, 1990, 1996).

In addition, mini-c creativity serves as a core feature of creative learning (Beghetto, 2016). Creative learning in classrooms refers to the development of new and personally meaningful understandings of academic subject matter for oneself (mini-c) and others (little-c). More specifically, when students are encouraged to make sense of academic subject matter in their own unique and personally meaningful way (mini-c) *and* share their mini-c conceptions with others, then students have an opportunity to develop their understanding and potentially make a creative contribution to the learning of others (little-c). When teachers recognize this, they will be in a better position to encourage the expression and development of student creativity.

Understanding the nuances of the construct of creativity better enables teachers to offer supportive feedback. Indeed, such feedback is a key issue in terms of students' creativity development. Not only does positive feedback seem to support students' confidence beliefs about their creativity, but it also is the primary way that students can develop their mini-c insights and academic understanding into larger-c contributions and learning outcomes (Beghetto, 2006, 2016; Beghetto & Kaufman, 2007). How might this feedback look in the classroom?

Beghetto (2007b) discussed how teachers, once they have internalized these concepts, could encourage movement from mini-c interpretations to little-c expressions by (a) taking the time to listen and attempt to understand how students are interpreting what they are learning; (b) helping students recognize when their contributions are not making sense considering the domain constraints, conventions, and standards of a particular activity or task; and (c) providing multiple opportunities and spaces in the classroom for students to practice developing the skills of a particular domain or task. These suggestions, as well as other practical recommendations (see Beghetto, 2019), provide tangible illustrations of how teachers can recognize the value of students' mini-c and little-c creativity. In addition, it is important to note that Pro-c and Big-C contributions are not possible without the creator's initial mini-c and little-c attempts. Teachers can note the many instances of larger C creativity in the classroom and connect these important outcomes to the roots of smaller creativity that all students can achieve.

Supportive Environments of Creative Expression

The policies, practices, and procedures of schools and classrooms are full of goal-related messages that influence the motivational beliefs and subsequent student achievement behavior (Pintrich & Schunk, 2002). Everything from student–teacher relationships to student-centered classroom practices to student and teacher values displayed in the classroom can lead to student engagement (or nonengagement) in achievement-directed behaviors. For example, if a teacher uses bad student examples as part of classroom practice (rather than having students learning from their mistakes), students might be less likely to volunteer and become actively engaged in classroom activities. Moreover, there is evidence to suggest that how teachers view creativity can play a role in teachers' beliefs about their ability to support student creativity and the kinds of feedback and motivational messages they send to students (Paek & Sumners, 2019).

Motivation researchers traditionally have categorized the messages emphasized by learning environments into two major types: *mastery goal structures* and *performance goal structures* (Anderman & Anderman, 2014). Mastery goal structures have been linked to intrinsic motivation, whereas performance goal structures can trigger extrinsic motivation (Pintrich & Schunk, 2002). Many research studies (Amabile, 1996; Amabile et al., 1986, 1994) report that creativity is typically increased when students have intrinsic task motivation. This is not to say that extrinsic motivation necessarily plays a negative role in student creativity. Indeed, recent research has indicated that extrinsic motivational beliefs can have a positive influence on students' creative confidence; however, intrinsic motivation seems to play a more influential role (see Puente-Díaz & Cavazos-Arroyo, 2017). This work builds on prior research, which has indicated that there may be an "additive pattern" (Barron & Harackiewicz, 2001), which represents a blending of motivational beliefs that have traditionally been considered to be orthogonal. This additive benefit on students' creative self-beliefs seems to occur in cases where more intrinsically oriented beliefs are stronger than extrinsically focused beliefs (Beghetto, 2006; Karwowski & Gralewski, 2011).

In this way, the relationship between motivation and creativity is not a simple dichotomy: intrinsic motivation (good for creativity) versus extrinsic motivation (bad for creativity). Indeed, the very presence of extrinsic rewards for creative work can impact creativity and the desire to be creative in multiple ways. In one study, even with tasks presented in a context that emphasized intrinsic motivation, extrinsic rewards had a negative impact on performance (Cooper et al., 1999). Others argue that rewards can be beneficial if given wisely. For example, neither an individual's intrinsic motivation nor creativity were negatively affected—and could be enhanced—if the researchers delivered the reward (particularly a verbal reward) after the creative activity (Eisenberger & Selbst, 1994). Eisenberger and Shanock (2003) reviewing studies on the harm or benefits of reward concluded that much of the debate involves methodological issues. Specifically, they argued that rewarding creative performance increases both intrinsic motivation and creativity (traditionally measured at the mini-c or little-c level). In contrast, rewarding conventional performance decreases both intrinsic motivation and creativity.

Given the strong connection between the school environment, motivation, and creativity, educators have a responsibility to actively consider how the motivational messages sent by school and classroom policies, practices, and procedures may influence students' willingness to develop and express their creativity. Beghetto (2005) provides several general recommendations for supporting student creativity in educational settings. Those recommendations include: (a) setting challenging but realistic goals for students and focusing on the features of a task that are interesting and personally meaningful (rather than attempting to motivate students to complete tasks simply because they will be graded); (b) supporting creative expression by encouraging the generation of novel ideas and helping students then select the most promising and appropriate ideas for a given task; (c) minimizing the pressures of assessment; (d) helping students recognize that the primary reason for engaging in a task is self-improvement rather than just showing others that they can successfully complete a task; (e) helping students learn from mistakes and recognize that making mistakes is a natural part of learning; and (f) helping students consider the meaning behind their assigned grade, rather than focusing solely on letter grades and test scores (i.e., what they did well and how they might improve in the future).

Teaching Students When (and When Not) to Be Creative

Given the recent attention paid to creativity and the interest on the part of policymakers and business leaders to make creativity a more prominent educational goal in the United States and abroad (Battelle for Kids, 2020; Craft, 2007), the message that may be sent to teachers and students is that they should somehow strive to be creative at all times and in all places. We worry that this would be the wrong message.

Consider how in positive psychology, there are some strengths that can have a dark side, such as resilience (Friedman & Robbins, 2012). There are times to be resilient (such as when trying to succeed in school or help others) and other moments when resiliency may actually cause harm (such as trying to hurt another person). Similarly, part of developing a creative skill-set includes learning when (and when not) to be creative. This knowledge, called CMC (Kaufman & Beghetto, 2013), refers to a combination of creative self-knowledge (i.e., knowing one's creative strengths and limitations, both within a domain and as a general trait) and contextual knowledge (knowing when, where, how, and why to be creative). People can demonstrate CMC even at mini-c levels (e.g., Kaufman, et al., 2016). People tend to show higher CMC when they are more creative (Silvia, 2008), smarter (Karwowski et al., 2020), or are responding to task-specific questions (Pretz & McCollum, 2014). CMC insights can also be used to determine times when reigning in creativity might be best. For example, a student may have a very creative idea about butterflies during a multiplication test, but the best course of action for the student is probably to finish the test first.

A key area of future research is thus to explore how teachers might best encourage students to be creative and, at the same time, teach students how to "read a situation," determining whether and how to express one's creative ideas, insights, and behaviors. One place to start would be in how teachers provide students with specific feedback—highlighting students' creative strengths (what they can already do well) and limitations (where they need to continue to learn and improve). For example, researchers might explore how the use of the *Goldilocks Principle* of feedback (Beghetto & Kaufman, 2007), can support the development of CMC. Specifically, this principle highlights the importance of providing feedback that is not too harsh (stifling students' motivation), yet not too gentle (little attention to real-world standards).

New Avenues for Thought

Many diverse areas could merit future research and, potentially, be applied to the classroom. Providing space, time, and support for creativity in the classroom could, for instance, help teachers bolster their students' and their own creativity. Indeed, establishing small openings in the curriculum can allow students and teachers to meet learning goals in creative ways, which can help them simultaneously develop their and others' understanding and creative competence (Beghetto, 2020). In general, when creativity is seen as an offering (among other benefits) a way to enhance and extend learning and engagement, it is possible to weave creativity into the classroom by integrating it with current tasks designed for learning.

As far as new directions for this line of work, creativity scholars have increased their focus on creativity and positive outcomes, such as finding meaning in life (Kapoor & Kaufman, 2020; Kaufman, 2018) or increased equitable beliefs (Luria & Kaufman, 2017). Related work has focused on how providing students with opportunities to creatively address complex problems in their schools, communities, and beyond might serve as a way to make positive and lasting contributions to the learning and lives of others (Beghetto, 2017, 2018).

Future research along these lines might explore whether focusing on desirable learning, motivational, and practical outcomes related to creative expression would help students, teachers, administrators, and policymakers continue to buy-in on creativity and realize their creative potential. Given the expanding interdisciplinary work in the field of creativity studies and positive psychology, which has helped to clarify the nature of human creativity and the positive role it can play in and beyond schools, it seems likely that this line of work holds much promise for future research and application.

References

Aljughaiman, A., & Mowrer-Reynolds, E. (2005). Teachers' conceptions of creativity and creative students. *Journal of Creative Behavior, 39*, 17–34. doi:10.1002/j.2162–6057.2005.tb01247.x

Amabile, T. M. (1996). *Creativity in context: Update to the social psychology of creativity.* Westview.

Amabile, T. M., Hennessey, B. A., & Grossman, B. S. (1986). Social influences on creativity: The effects of contracted-for reward. *Journal of Personality and Social Psychology, 50*, 14–23. doi:10.1037/0022–3514.50.1.14

Amabile, T. M., Hill, K. G., Hennessey, B. A., & Tighe, E. M. (1994). The work preference inventory: Assessing intrinsic and extrinsic motivational orientations. *Journal of Personality and Social Psychology, 66*, 950–967. doi:10.1037/0022–3514.66.5.950

Anderman, L. H., & Anderman, E. M. (2014). Oriented towards mastery: Promoting positive motivational goals for students. In M. J. Furlong, R. Gilman, & E. S. Huebner (Eds.), *Handbook of positive psychology in schools* (pp. 165–175). Routledge.

Barron, K. E., & Harackiewicz, J. M. (2001). Achievement goals and optimal motivation: Testing multiple goal models. *Journal of Personality and Social Psychology, 80*, 706–722. doi:10.1037/0022–3514.80.5.706

Battelle for Kids (2020). Partnership for 21st century learning: A network of Battelle for kids. Retrieved from https://www.battelleforkids.org/networks/p21

Beghetto, R. A. (2005). Does assessment kill student creativity? *The Educational Forum, 69*, 254–263. doi:10.1080/00131720508984694

Beghetto, R. A. (2006). Creative self-efficacy: Correlates in middle and secondary students. *Creativity Research Journal, 18*, 447–457. doi:10.1207/s15326934crj1804_4

Beghetto, R. A. (2007b). Ideational code-switching: Walking the talk about supporting student creativity in the classroom. *Roeper Review, 29*, 265–270. doi:10.1080/02783190709554421

*Beghetto, R. A. (2016). Creative learning: A fresh look. *Journal of Cognitive Education and Psychology, 15*, 6–23. https://doi.org/10.1891/1945-8959.15.1.6

Beghetto, R. A. (2017). Legacy projects: Helping young people respond productively to the challenges of a changing world, *Roeper Review, 39*, 187–190. http://dx.doi.org/10.1080/02783193.2017.1318998

Beghetto, R. A. (2018). *What if? Building students' problem-solving skills through complex challenges.* ASCD.

Beghetto, R. A. (2019). Creativity in classrooms. In J. C. Kaufman & R. J. Sternberg (Eds.), *The Cambridge handbook of creativity* (pp. 587–606). Cambridge University Press.

Beghetto R. A. (2020). Creative learning and the possible. In V. Glăveanu (Ed.), *The Palgrave encyclopedia of the possible* (p. 2). Palgrave Macmillan.

Beghetto, R. A., & Kaufman, J. C. (2007). Toward a broader conception of creativity: A case for "mini-c" creativity. *Psychology of Aesthetics, Creativity, and the Arts, 1*, 13–79. doi:10.1037/1931–3896.1.2.73

Beghetto, R. A., & Kaufman, J. C. (2016). (Eds.). *Nurturing creativity in the classroom* (2nd ed.). Cambridge University Press.

Beghetto, R. A., & Plucker, J. A. (2006). The relationship among schooling, learning, and creativity: "All roads lead to creativity" or "You can't get there from here?" In J. C. Kaufman & J. Baer (Eds.), *Creativity and reason in cognitive development* (pp. 316–332). Cambridge University Press. doi:10.1017/CB09780511606915.019

Berliner, D. C. (2011). Narrowing curriculum, assessments, and conceptions of what it means to be smart in the U.S. schools: Creaticide by design. In D. Ambrose & R. J. Sternberg (Eds.), *How dogmatic beliefs harm creativity and higher-level thinking* (pp. 79–93). Routledge.

Chan, D. W., & Chan, L. K. (1999). Implicit theories of creativity: Teachers' perception of student characteristics in Hong Kong. *Creativity Research Journal, 12*, 185–195. doi:10.1207/s15326934crj1203_3

Cooper, B. L., Clasen, P., Silva-Jalonen, D. E., & Butler, M. C. (1999). Creative performance on an in-basket exercise: Effects of inoculation against extrinsic reward. *Journal of Managerial Psychology, 14*, 39–56. doi:10.1108/02683949910254747

Craft, A. (2007). Possibility thinking in the early years and primary classroom. In A. G. Tan (Ed.), *Creativity: A handbook for teachers* (pp. 231–249). World Scientific.

Craft, A. (2011). *Creativity and education futures: Learning in a digital age.* Trentham Books.

Csikszentmihalyi, M. (1990). *Flow: The psychology of optimal experience.* New York: Harper & Row.

Csikszentmihalyi, M. (1996). *Creativity: Flow and the psychology of discovery and invention.* New York: HarperCollins.

Dawson, V. L. (1997). In search of the wild bohemian: Challenges in the identification of the creatively gifted. *Roeper Review, 19*, 148–152. doi:10.1080/02783199709553811

de Souza Fleith, D. (2000). Teacher and student perceptions of creativity in the classroom environment. *Roeper Review, 22*, 148–153. doi:10.1080/02783190009554022

Diakidoy, I. N., & Phtiaka, H. (2002). Teachers' beliefs about creativity. In S. P. Shohov (Ed.), *Advances in psychology research* (Vol. 15, pp. 173–188). Nova Science.

Eisenberger, R., & Selbst, M. (1994). Does reward increase or decrease creativity? *Journal of Personality and Social Psychology, 66*, 1116–1127. doi:10.1037/0022–3514.66.6.1116

Eisenberger, R., & Shanock, L. (2003). Rewards, intrinsic motivation, and creativity: A case study of conceptual and methodological isolation. *Creativity Research Journal, 15*, 121–130. doi:10.1207/S15326934CRJ152&3_02

Friedman, H. L., & Robbins, B. D. (2012). The negative shadow cast by positive psychology: Contrasting views and implications of humanistic and positive psychology on resiliency. *The Humanistic Psychologist, 40*, 87–102.

Guilford, J. P. (1950). Creativity. *American Psychologist, 5*, 444–454. doi:10.1037/h0063487

Günçer, B., & Oral, G. (1993). Relationship between creativity and nonconformity to school discipline as perceived by teachers of Turkish elementary school children, by controlling for their grade and sex. *Journal of Instructional Psychology, 20*(3), 208–214.

Hayes, J. R. (1989). *The complete problem solver* (2nd ed.). Erlbaum.

Henriksen, D., Mishra, P., & Fisser, P. (2016). Infusing creativity and technology in 21st century education: A systemic view for change. *Educational Technology & Society, 19*(3), 27–37.

Kapoor, H., & Kaufman, J. C. (2020). Meaning-making through creativity during COVID-19. *Frontiers in Psychology, 11,* 595990.

Karwowski, M., Czerwonka, M., & Kaufman, J. C. (2020). Does intelligence strengthen creative meta-cognition? *Psychology of Aesthetics, Creativity, and the Arts, 14,* 353–360.

Karwowski, M., & Gralewski, J. (2011). Motivated creativity: Motivational synergy of youth's creative attitude, *Chowanna, 2,* 45–58.

★Kaufman, J. C. (2016). *Creativity 101* (2nd ed.). Springer.

Kaufman, J. C. (2018). Finding meaning with creativity in the past, present, and future. *Perspectives on Psychological Science, 13,* 734–749.

Kaufman, J. C., & Baer, J. (Eds). (2005). *Creativity across domains: Faces of the muse.* Erlbaum.

Kaufman, J. C., & Beghetto, R. A. (2009). Beyond big and little: The Four C Model of Creativity. *Review of General Psychology, 13,* 1–12. doi:10.1037/a0013688

★Kaufman, J. C., & Beghetto, R. A. (2013). In praise of Clark Kent: Creative metacognition and the importance of teaching kids when (not) to be creative. *Roeper Review, 35*(3), 155–165. doi:10.1080/02783193.2013.799413

Kaufman, J. C., Beghetto, R A., & Watson, C. (2016). Creative metacognition and self-ratings of creative performance: A 4-C perspective. *Learning and Individual Differences, 51,* 394–399. doi:10.1016/j.lindif.2015.05.004

Kaufman, J. C., & Sternberg, R. J. (2007). Resource review: Creativity. *Change, 39,* 55–58. doi:10.3200/CHNG.39.4.55-C4

Lim, W., & Plucker, J. (2001). Creativity through a lens of social responsibility: Implicit theories of creativity with Korean samples. *Journal of Creative Behavior, 35,* 115–130. doi:10.1002/j.2162–6057.2001.tb01225.x

Luria, S. R., & Kaufman, J. C. (2017). Examining the relationship between creativity and equitable thinking in schools. *Psychology in the Schools, 54,* 1279–1284. https://doi.org/10.1002/pits/22076

Mullen, C. A. (2020). *Revealing creativity: Exploration in transnational education.* Springer.

Paek, S. H., & Sumners, S. E. (2019). The indirect effect of teachers' creative mindsets on teaching creativity. *The Journal of Creative Behavior, 53*(3), 298–311. https://doi.org/10.1002/jocb.180

Paletz, S., & Peng, K. (2008). Implicit theories of creativity across cultures: Novelty and appropriateness in two product domains. *Journal of Cross-Cultural Psychology, 39,* 286–302. doi:10.1177/0022022108315112

Pintrich, P. R., & D. H. Schunk. (2002). *Motivation in education: Theory, research, and applications* (2nd ed.). Prentice Hall.

Plucker, J. A., Beghetto, R. A., & Dow, G. T. (2004). Why isn't creativity more important to educational psychologists? *Educational Psychologist, 39,* 83–96. doi:10.1207/s15326985ep3902_1

Pretz, J. E., & McCollum, V. A. (2014). Self-perceptions of creativity do not always reflect actual creative performance. *Psychology of Aesthetics, Creativity, and the Arts, 8,* 227–236. https://doi.org/10.1037/a0035597

Puente-Díaz, R., & Cavazos-Arroyo, J. (2017). Creative self-efficacy: The role of self-regulation for schoolwork and boredom as antecedents, and divergent thinking as a consequence. *Social Psychology of Education, 20,* 347–359. https://doi.org/10.1007/s11218-017-9376-z

Richards, R. (Ed.). (2007). *Everyday creativity and new views of human nature: Psychological, social, and spiritual perspectives.* American Psychological Association Press. doi:10.1037/11595-000

Richards, R., Kinney, D. K., Benet, M., & Merzel, A. P. (1988). Assessing everyday creativity: Characteristics of the Lifetime Creativity Scales and validation with three large samples. *Journal of Personality and Social Psychology, 54*(3), 476. https://doi.org/10.1037/0022-3514.54.3.476

Runco, M. A., Johnson, D. J., & Bear, P. K. (1993). Parents' and teachers' implicit theories of children's creativity. *Child Study Journal, 23,* 91–113.

Scott, C. L. (1999). Teachers' biases toward creative children. *Creativity Research Journal, 12,* 321–337. doi:10.1207/s15326934crj1204_10

Seligman, M. E. P., & Csikszentmihalyi, M. (2000). Positive psychology: An introduction. *American Psychologist, 55,* 5–14.

Seo, H., Lee, E., & Kim, K. (2005). Korean science teachers' understanding of creativity in gifted education. *Journal of Advanced Academics, 16,* 98–105.

Silvia, P. J. (2008). Discernment and creativity: How well can people identify their most creative ideas? *Psychology of Aesthetics, Creativity, and the Arts, 2,* 139–146. doi:10.1037/1931–3896.2.3.139

Simonton, D. K. (1977). Creative productivity, age, and stress: A biographical time-series analysis of 10 classical composers. *Journal of Personality and Social Psychology, 35,* 791–804. doi:10.1037/0022-3514.35.11.791

Simonton, D. K. (1994). *Greatness: Who makes history and why.* Guilford Press.

Simonton, D. K. (1997). Creative productivity: A predictive and explanatory model of career trajectories and landmarks. *Psychological Review, 104*, 66–89. doi:10.1037/0033–295X.104.1.66

Simonton, D. K. (2004). *Creativity in science: Chance, logic, genius, and zeitgeist.* Cambridge University Press.

Sternberg, R. J., & Kaufman, J. C. (2012). When your race is almost run, but you feel you're not yet done: Application of the Propulsion Theory of Creative Contributions to late-career challenges. *Journal of Creative Behavior, 46*, 66–76. doi:10.1002/jocb.005

Sternberg, R. J., Kaufman, J. C., & Pretz, J. E. (2002). *The creativity conundrum.* Psychology Press.

Sternberg, R. J., & Lubart, T. I. (1995). *Defying the crowd: Cultivating creativity in a culture of conformity.* Free Press.

Tan, A. G. (2003). Student teachers' perceptions of teacher behaviors for fostering creativity: A perspective on the academically low achievers. *Korean Journal of Thinking and Problem Solving, 13*, 59–71.

Vygotsky, L. S. (2004). Imagination and creativity in childhood. (M. E. Sharpe, Inc., Trans.) *Journal of Russian and East European Psychology, 42*, 7–97. (Original work published 1967).

Westby, E. L., & Dawson, V. L. (1995). Creativity: Asset or burden in the classroom? *Creativity Research Journal, 8*, 1–10. doi:10.1207/s15326934crj0801_1

* Suggested core readings.

SECTION III

Whole School Climate and Culture

23

PROSOCIAL APPROACHES TO SCHOOL CLIMATE IMPROVEMENT

Definitions, Measurement, and Improvement Strategies for Thriving Schools

Jonathan Cohen, Philip Brown, Allison Rae Ward-Seidel

Positive Psychology is focused on understanding and promoting individual and community-based strengths that foster our ability to love, work, and play. Mental health professionals have recognized and focused on supporting people's well-being, understanding, and addressing problems that undermine strengths and healthy development for over 100 years (Cohen, 2014). More recently, the empirical study of Positive Psychology focused on what makes life worth living (Peterson, 2008). This approach to studying human thoughts, feelings, and behavior has an essential and explicit focus on strengths instead of weaknesses. That is, building the good in life instead of repairing the bad, and taking the lives of ordinary people up to "great" instead of focusing solely on moving those who are struggling up to "normal" (Peterson, 2008; Snyder & Lopez, 2009).

Positive Psychology overlaps with the growing interest in prosocial educational and well-being-related improvement efforts in K-12 schools (Brown et al., 2012; Furlong et al., 2014). Unlike Positive Psychology, prosocial educational efforts focus explicitly on individual and organizational growth in the context of social realities and challenges with the goal of positive development and learning. Educators and school-based mental health professionals use the term prosocial education to refer to an array of overlapping systemic, instructional, and relational school improvement efforts. These efforts promote "noncognitive" or social, emotional, and civic, as well as academic aspects of learning (Brown et al., 2012). Character education, social-emotional learning (SEL), mental health promotion, and school climate reform represent four of the major traditions and current "camps" in prosocial education. The underlying assumption here is that when all those involved in education intentionally focus on promoting individual and organizational health, schools can create the optimal foundation for children's healthy development and ability to learn (Cohen, 2013; Cohen & Espelage, 2020; Fullan & Rincón-Gallardo, 2020).

Historical Context

Understandings of what matters shape the field of education like all fields. Understandings (and misunderstandings) always shape our goals. Moreover, goals suggest methods, interventions, pedagogies, and a range of strategies education leaders use to actualize goals. Ideally, goals, in

DOI: 10.4324/9781003013778-29

conjunction with any number of contextual factors, drive decisions about which interventions to select. After implementing an intervention, it is a critical yet often neglected step to evaluate the extent to which the method helped reach intended goals and reformulate a new or continuing plan. This problem-solving cycle is addressed later in this chapter.

While societal values drive the goals of education, education has the power to uphold or challenge the status quo (Merriweather, 2012). The values of education in the United States have shifted dramatically over time as we moved from an agrarian society to industrial and postindustrial life. This history of education is not benign. The republic evolved from allowing only a privileged few to access academic preparation, to embrace full citizenship for some, and the idea that education was required to develop those citizens. At the same time, we also maintained "separate but equal" education policies based on race. The attempt to rectify inequities in resources and outcomes led to the *No Child Left Behind* (NCLB) era of strict, standardized testing (Noltemeyer et al., 2012) with limited results. One of the unintended consequences of the NCLB policy was to exacerbate further the false dichotomy between "academic" and "nonacademic" educational aims, sending a message backed by hundreds of millions of dollars that full development of the whole child was not the central focus of schooling. It is essential to periodically revisit our understandings about the purpose of education and societal values driving those goals as we recognize systemic injustice and create change. It is worth noting that education, like many other systems, is rooted in structural racism and inequity (Hayes-Green & Love, 2019; Ross et al., 2020). If our values are that *every* student succeeds, we must explicitly address equity in education as well as surrounding systems (e.g., criminal justice and healthcare). Improving climates of learning for all children, and systems of education on a grander scale provides opportunity and moral responsibility to address whole child development and equity, front and center (Ross et al., 2020). Indeed, the *Every Student Succeeds Act* of 2015 includes a requirement that states use one nonacademic outcome in school quality measures, a policy step in the right direction.

Historically, in the United States and around the world, educational leaders prioritized linguistic, mathematic, and scientific achievement. Over the last two decades, an extraordinary body of empirical research points to a growing appreciation that teaching and learning are always social, emotional, and civic as well as academic. To most effectively promote school and life success, there is a need to support students and school personnel so that they feel culturally recognized, safe, supported, and engaged (Berkowitz, 2011; Berkowitz et al., 2017; Brown et al., 2012; Cohen & Espelage, 2020; Durlak et al., 2016). These interests have contributed to a growing interest in SEL, character education, mental health promotion, and school climate. Furthermore, over the decade, there has been a growing appreciation that we also need to integrate an explicit equity-informed perspective into education in general at the school and state levels (Ross et al., 2020), and prosocial education in particular (Aspen Institute, 2018 & 2019).

Definitions and Educational Traditions

Character education, SEL, mental health promotion, and school climate are conceptually different,[1] and they grow out of somewhat different educational traditions (Cohen, 2006, 2017). For example, conceptually, SEL and character education are focused on teaching and learning. Mental health in schools has generally focused on the individual. School climate, on the other hand, is a concept that is ecologically informed and focused on the school as a whole. Historically, SEL and character education are ideas that the ancient Greeks discussed and deeply valued, for example, "knowing thyself" (Cohen, 1999). John Dewey and ensuing generations of progressive educators highlighted social, emotional, and civic as well as academic education as the foundation for an engaged citizenry in a democracy. Empirical K-12 risk prevention/health promotion researchers in the 1960s, 1970s, and 1980s importantly advanced understandings about effective teaching and learning strategies. For many years, SEL practice leaders focused on skill-based learning in the classroom. Moreover, character education practice leaders focused on didactic approaches to developing a moral compass at the individual level and creating caring school environments. However, over the last 10–15 years, SEL leaders have begun to include a focus on moral or civic educational goals, and character education proponents have focused much more on a broader array of social and emotional as well as moral and civic educational outcomes. More recently, scholars and practitioner-focused organizations have emphasized the need to incorporate SEL and character education with an equity-informed and culturally relevant "lens." An equity approach to SEL means countering "colorblind" SEL that ignores differences in culture and experience in the United States given existing racism and discrimination (Aspen, 2018; Gregory & Fergus, 2017; Jagers et al., 2018). Movements to develop a race-conscious approach to SEL exist and highlight the need to de-center Whiteness in SEL and education (Duchesneau, 2020; Simmons, 2019).

Considering the actual school/district improvement process today, all of these prosocial educational traditions overlap in their ecologically informed focus and on a collaborative effort to promote individual and organizational health as well as addressing challenges: systemically, instructionally, and relationally (Aspen Institute's National Commission on Social-Emotional and Academic Development, 2019; Jones & Kahn, 2017; National School Climate Council, 2015). *Systemically*, they all focus on creating safe, supportive, equitable, and engaging climates for learning and teaching. *Instructionally*, they all invest in promoting social, emotional, and academic learning and teaching in the context of social and civic values. *Relationally,* they all commit to promoting healthy, "connected," and responsible relationships. For example, SEL leaders,[2] now talk about "SEL 2.0" reflecting a focus on systemic as well as instructional improvement efforts (Weissberg et al., 2015). Many character education leaders focus on student learning of virtues and creating caring schools using ecological change models such as the *Eleven Principles of Effective Character Education* (Character.org, 2020; Lickona, 1996; Vincent & Grove, 2012). School-based mental health improvement efforts today are also explicitly attuned to the essential importance of understanding and addressing systemic, instructional, and relational aspects of health in conjunction with an attunement to individual and organizational problems (Weist et al., 2014).

School climate improvement has always represented a comprehensive, ecologically informed perspective that recognizes and seeks to promote individual development, as well as school-wide, and—to a greater or lesser extent—community-wide improvement efforts (Cohen et al., 2009; Thapa et al., 2013). We suggest that there are two primary reasons school climate has garnered growing attention around the world over the last two decades. First, school climate as a concept and school climate improvement as a process have always been ecologically informed with an explicit focus on the interrelationships between individuals, small groups, and larger groups. As noted previously, although individual learning and development historically informed SEL, character education, and mental health efforts, the emphasis has shifted and focus broadened. Second, school climate-informed measurement practices have sought to recognize systemic or large group findings as well as disaggregated or smaller group trends. Disaggregating school climate findings by race, ethnicity, gender, sexual orientation, socioeconomic status, or other lines of identity, particularly in historically marginalized communities, is imperative. Investigating large and small group discrepancies in how different groups experience school climate sheds light on gaps that often reveal essential differences. Understanding these differences then suggests particular important goals that can promote safety, support, and equity for all students.

Measurement in Schools: It's Not Just Academic Anymore

It is well known that what is measured is what is treasured. This sentiment is certainly true in K-12 education as well as many, if not most, worlds of learning and work. Until recently, public education in the United States and around the world has focused on measuring literacy, mathematical, and scientific learning. As noted above, over the last decade this has begun to shift as prosocial-informed empirical research findings have supported the following understanding: Social-emotional and academic instruction in conjunction with systemic efforts to promote even safer, more supportive, and engaging climates for learning foster school and life success (Aspen Institute's National Commission on Social-Emotional and Academic Development, 2019; Brown et al., 2012; Cohen & Espelage, 2020; Furlong et al., 2014; Jones & Kahn, 2017; Weissberg et al., 2015).

Historically, SEL and mental health informed measurement practices have tended to focus on individual skill development and functioning (Cohen et al., 2017). Today, SEL measurement practices are focused on specific learning standards or a "scope and sequence" that support educators considering what students should know and be able to do, by grade level. Character education measures have also tended to focus on individual student characteristics. However, unlike SEL measurement practices character education research and practice standards have also focused on systemic measures or indicators (e.g., school climate surveys) as well as individual learning (Battistich et al., 1997; Person et al., 2009; Vincent & Grove., 2012).

Mental health informed measurement practices have historically focused on individual student functioning. The primary focus has been on student psychopathology and measurement strategies that can help school-based mental health professionals to gauge and "screen" student problems. However, over the last two decades, there has been a growing appreciation that mental health is best understood as the interaction between well-being and psychopathology (Greenspoon & Saklofske, 2001; Moore et al., 2019). The movement to include mental health promotion in schools, particularly at the universal level (e.g., improvement efforts and interventions for *all* students), has been driven by strength-based approaches to human development, such as Social and Emotional Learning, Positive Psychology, educational resilience, and positive youth development. As a result, mental health informed measurement practices have expanded beyond screenings for psychopathology (Furlong et al., 2014). The growing number of states that are adopting SEL standards (or scope and sequence informed guidelines) also support teachers making informed judgments about individual student competencies. These standards can guide specific skill-based interventions and provide a screening tool for early identification of atypical or externalizing behaviors.[3]

School climate measurement tends to focus on school climate surveys that typically recognize student, parent/guardian, and school personnel voice about a range of safety, relationship, teaching and learning, and environmental issues.[4] As prosocial research and practice leaders become more attuned to the challenges of *sustainable* school/district improvement practices as well as important findings from implementation science (Blasé et al., 2013; Bryk et al., 2015; Century & Cassata, 2016; Lyon, 2017) there is a growing interest in three additional school climate-informed measurement concepts and their applications: *Readiness* for engaging in the change process; *Process* measures that illuminate the structure and functioning of the improvement process; and *School-family-community* measures that illuminate and promote these foundationally meaningful partnerships (Cohen et al., 2017; Dymnicki et al., 2017).

For too many years, research, practice, and funding leaders focused only on whether improvement efforts were evidence-based.[5] In the United States, the federal NCLB educational act allocated substantial funding to understand which instructional, and to a much lesser extent, systemically informed improvement efforts were evidence-based. We learned that using evidence-based practices is not enough to create positive and sustainable change in educational systems. Only *one in three* efforts to install new programs was successful (Damschroder et al., 2009). Implementation science in schools suggests that specific kinds of leadership, the supportive organizational climate, and collaborative behaviors from many staff are crucial for sustainable, successful implementation (Locke et al., 2019). The following section outlines a prosocial school improvement process based on existing implementation frameworks and essential guiding principles.

The Prosocial School Improvement Process

To introduce the prosocial improvement process in this chapter, we elucidate common concepts from existing frameworks, present a range of improvement goals, and outline organizing principles that support sustainable improvement.

Five Common Concepts in School Improvement

There are many improvement frameworks to guide K-12 schools or, ideally, districts[6] implementation initiatives to improve educational outcomes. All of these frameworks recognize the foundational importance of changing professional practice and evaluating the improvement process itself as well as the intended outcomes (Blasé et al., 2013; Bryk et al., 2015; Century & Cassata, 2016; Gaglio et al., 2013). Furthermore, they all tend to recognize the following five concepts.

1   *Implementation Stages and the Continuous Problem-Solving Cycle*

There are a range of school improvement models or "road maps" that define these stages in different but very overlapping ways. To a greater or lesser extent, each of these stages is defined by a series of tasks (Cohen & Brown, 2020). Implementation road maps all reflect some version of a continuous and iterative problem-solving cycle (e.g., building on past challenges and successes; evaluating current strengths and challenges, and then using data to develop the next schoolwide, instructional, and/or relational set of improvement goals and strategies). However, well-conceived, schools often do not always follow these "logical" steps. For example, sometimes, schools begin with an intervention in response to a pressing issue. Only later do they evaluate whether the selected intervention is based on an adequate, data-based understanding of the issue and whether critical stakeholders understand the rationale and process for making the decision.

2   *Importance of the Implementation Process and Not Just the Outcomes*

How school leaders and the school community engage in and support the improvement process is almost as important as the outcomes. If we accept the idea that all schools (like all people) have problems and should always be involved with learning and improvement, the implementation process is never-ending. Findings from the relatively new field of implementation science underscore the essential value of paying attention to and evaluating processes as well as outcomes.[7] In prosocial schools, for example, building strong, caring relationships with colleagues and students is as important (if not more so) than any specific, quantifiable goal. How are educators and other school personnel working to foster these kinds of relationships? How are educators and others learning from each other about challenges and opportunities? Fostering and maintaining social trust during the change process is the hard work that will make or break the eventual outcomes that shape the fabric of school culture and success (Bryk & Schneider, 2004).

3   *The Implementation Process Occurs in Complex, Multilevel, Ecological Systems*

Many improvement efforts locate the child at the center of the process, and others place the school as a system at the center (Astor & Benbenishty, 2019). All school climate improvement—by definition—represents a multitiered effort that recognizes individual, small group, and large group learning and development. It is important to consider the influence from and on multiple levels of the ecological model to develop healthy systems (Duchesneau, 2020).

4   *Collaboration on Common Goals is Critical to Sustainability*

Too often, well-intentioned school improvement efforts are not sustained. District-wide improvement efforts that include active collaborations between the district and building leadership dramatically enhance the sustainability of improvement efforts. On the other hand, real change happens at the classroom and school levels, and district leadership needs to be consistent and responsive in managing and supporting change. Placing youth at the center of the improvement process and actively supporting intergenerational school improvement efforts is another incredibly powerful collaborative step. The most effective collaboration should be grounded in the systemic improvement goals (see below).

5   *Embracing Iterative Change Requires Solid, Open-minded, and Strategic Planning*

Be clear about improvement goals, strategies, measurement systems, and the iterative, continuous learning process for improvement. One of the fallacies of the industrial model of education (vestiges of which are still characteristic of many school systems) is that once things are running smoothly and customer complaints are low, an administrator's job is to keep things from ever getting out of hand. In this view, school board meetings, for example, should be occasions for keeping budget, personnel, parent, and taxpayer interests in balance, not for "rocking the boat." In contrast, an attitude embracing iterative change requires solid, open strategic planning processes and adjustments and modifications based on professional judgments as well as formative and summative data.

School Improvement Goals

There are many improvement goals that school leaders can decide to focus on for the next year or three. As noted previously, for many years, school leaders tended to focus almost exclusively on academic instructional goals because that was the focus of measurement practices. Today, there is a growing appreciation of the need to be attuned to positive systemic and relational improvement goals in addition to instructional goals (Jones & Kahn, 2017; National School Climate Council, 2015; Voight & Nation, 2016). The federal educational *Every Student Succeeds Act* (ESSA) mandates that districts measure "nonacademic" aspects of student learning. Realistically, school leaders can and need to use data to decide which systemic, instructional, and relational goals are most important to focus on in the next phase of improvement.

Systemic Improvement Goals

In reviewing existing improvement goals or creating new ones, it is important to pay attention to the degree to which current research informs policy. Unfortunately, there are many relevant district and state policies (e.g., school safety, disciplinary, bully prevention, and school improvement) that do not align with current research-based understandings and recommendations (Cohen & Espelage, 2020). In any case, there are always a range of systems that powerfully create—or undermine—learning as well as a climate of safety, support, and engagement. Here are a number of important examples of systemic improvement goals:

- Cultivate shared vision. Envision a portrait of a graduate that students, parents, and school personnel collectively share and agree to support. This "vision" must be collaboratively developed. This vision is one of many ways that school leaders can engage students, parents, school personnel, and even community members/leaders to be "co-learners" and "co-leaders" of the improvement process. Developing this kind of "shared vision" is one of the essential steps that support sustainable improvement efforts.
- Utilize prosocial measurement systems (e.g., school climate surveys) in conjunction with traditional academics and behavioral measures.
- Develop school/district-wide crisis preparedness plans that recognize social-emotional as well as physical dangers.
- Promote authentic leadership development for students as well as educators.
- Prioritize diverse student representation in decision-making seats for the school/district.
- Support intergenerational school improvement efforts.
- Create alternatives for schools to become service hubs of integrated support for unmet family and student needs.[8]
- Further meaningful school-family-community partnerships. (It is important to note that these partnerships reach outside the school walls to meaningfully engage families and communities who may be traditionally disenfranchised (e.g., people of color and immigrant families) by the education system. Partnerships are bidirectional, meaning families and communities should benefit from the partnership too.)

Instructional Improvement Goals

- Adults—educators and parents—being a helpful living example/role models that support social, emotional, and academic development (SEAD).
- Disciplinary policies that focus on learning and healthy development rather than punishment and discipline practices that rely on the power of school culture and community-building to support prosocial behavior misbehavior (e.g., restorative practices).
- Pedagogic strategies (from conflict resolution and cooperative learning to moral dilemma discussions and more) that support SEAD.
- Curriculum that supports the inclusion of prosocial learning goals, strategies, and measures. This means choosing an evidenced-based curriculum like *Second Steps* and *Facing History and Ourselves* and using a backward design approach when infusing these approaches into existing language arts, social studies/history, and athletics curricula (McTighe & Wiggins, 2004).

Relational Improvement Goals

- Fostering healthy, connected, responsible, and caring relationships between educators and students, students and other students, and educators and educators.
- Creating and nurturing meaningful opportunities for shared leadership and decision-making.
- Fostering effective educator-mental health professional-parent partnerships.
- Offering programs and services based on best practice and sensitivity to local conditions to train staff and meet student needs for trauma-informed instruction and care.
- School leaders cannot address all of these systemic, instructional, and relational goals at once. Most importantly, educational leaders are intentional, strategic, and fundamentally collaborative in their prosocial and school safety improvement efforts.

Intentional, Strategic, and Fundamentally Collaborative: Helpful Organizing Principles that Support Sustainable Improvement

There are many improvement guides (Cohen & Brown, 2020) with a wide range of language being used to support, and sometimes "brand" a given approach to school improvement. We suggest that three foundational principles support sustainable and effective prosocial improvement efforts: (a) being intentional, (b) being strategic, and (c) being fundamentally collaborative. The following section outlines these principles woven throughout the iterative improvement process.

Organizing Principle: Being Intentional

School leaders are explicit about their prosocial school improvement goals. They purposefully set in motion processes that maintain safe, supportive, equitable, and engaging climates for learning; caring, connected, and healthy relationships; and prosocial instruction. School leaders make an effort to learn about the range of factors that undermine students and school personnel feeling safe and supported. They work to address these factors while seeking to optimize prosocial learning environments for both staff and students. Being intentional means that schools:

Healthy Relationships

Build and maintain healthy relationships amongst all stakeholders—students, parents/guardians, school personnel, and community members. Be explicit about this ongoing goal to build community by accepting feedback, scheduling time for listening, and community building.

Iterative and Continuous Process

Plan for an iterative and continuous process of learning and improvement that is responsive to local organizational, cultural, and social context. School improvement is—necessarily—an ongoing process that is always, more or less, "bumpy." There are always challenges! Challenges and failures are the foundation for learning and improvement.[9] Avoid blaming, shaming, and ostracizing groups, which undermines healthy relationships and school improvement efforts. Learn from challenges and failures as well as successes. Plan on adjusting and revising the approach and continuing to improve.

All Students Are Respected and Engaged

Work to ensure that all students are respected as well as engaged in learning. Ensure that students identify as contributing members of the school community. Understanding students feeling respected requires listening to students' opinions (e.g., disaggregated school climate survey data).

Multitiered Systems of Support

Design purposeful multitiered systems of support for coordinated educational, risk prevention as well as social-emotional, and health promotion efforts that support all students and provide identification strategies and targeted support for those who need it.

Equity-Oriented Policy

Review and revise policy (e.g., disciplinary, violence prevention, SEL/character education, safe and supportive/school climate, and youth engagement) to address structural challenges (e.g., racial disproportionality in discipline and achievement gaps) and support helpful, research-based, and sustainable school improvement efforts.

Transparent Communication Plan

Create a communication plan in partnership with district leaders about how to communicate the improvement goals and processes to the school community in a consistent and ongoing manner. Communication should ideally be transparent about the rationale behind any policy changes and the decision-making process, including data derived from school climate or other "nonacademic" measurement practices.

Designate Support

Hire or designate "coordinators" to lead this work at the school level. Allocating resources, such as dedicated time and money (including staff roles and compensation for their time) to school climate improvement, is crucial. If the district cannot or will not provide a coordinator position, school leaders can dedicate staff professional development time or create a committee to drive improvement efforts.

A Proactive Stance

An important first step that supports intentional school improvement is to move from a reactive to a proactive stance. Too often classroom, building, and district leaders feel that they are often on the defensive, reacting to problems ("putting out fires"). When school leaders set in motion conversations with colleagues and even students and their parents about how important it is to foster individual and organizational health proactively, this can be transformational.

Organizing Principle: Being Strategic

School leaders consider past and current efforts to decide on immediate and long-term tasks that support the whole child, every child, and the ongoing SEAD school improvement process. Virtually all schools are involved with a host of educational, risk prevention, and/or health/mental health promotion activities. School leaders need to strategically decide which particular goals are most helpful for their school at different points in the planning and implementation process. Being strategic means that schools:

Commit to Addressing Inequity

Uncover issues that affect the allocation of resources, differential treatment of groups of students (i.e., race, gender, special education status, and English language learners), and individual learning opportunities. Remember, equity means all students get what they need, not necessarily the same support for all students. Addressing inequity includes examining our own implicit biases and leaning into uncomfortable conversations about race and historical, systemic racism (Hayes-Green & Love, 2019). Conversations about historically, systematically oppressed identities require creating conditions of social trust.

Professional Learning Communities

Establish an ongoing planning team with key staff to share leadership and decision-making throughout the school improvement process. Establish professional learning communities (PLCs) that are not just "window dressing." PLCs can provide essential, focused problem-identification and -solving based on identifying student academic, social, and psychological development and needs. PLCs should be structured to provide two-way communication and decision-making between teachers, noninstructional staff, and administrators. PLCs can be engines for change and help make real-time, context-based adjustment to plans as learning and conditions on the ground evolve.

Data-informed Processes and Equity-Oriented Data Interpretation

Create thoughtful, data-informed processes at both the individual and systemic levels to support the school climate improvement process and prosocial development of the whole child. These processes not only use good quality quantitative data from all constituencies about their perceptions of school climate but also using qualitative data. Gather qualitative data (e.g., interviews or focus groups and student-led participatory action research) from diverse perspectives to verify and enhance assumptions made from looking at quantitative findings. We suggest to interpret data from a strength-based and avoid deficit theorizing (Paunesku, 2019).

Iterative Planning, Evaluation, and Celebration

Plan to regularly revisit the school improvement process as a PLC team to evaluate progress on interim goals, celebrate success, and continue with the next steps.

Organizing Principle: Being Fundamentally Collaborative

Fundamentally collaborative school leaders are committed to creating structures for fair and meaningful involvement of all members of the community. Authentic collaboration means the community's diversity is represented on the leadership team and has a seat at the table for decision making. Sustainable school improvement needs to be a community-wide effort. Being collaborative means that schools:

Social Trust

Create conditions of social trust based on caring, respectful relationships, sensitivity to bias, and cultural competence. Dedicate time to developing cultural awareness among all staff. Effective team building is based on mutually beneficial partnerships that are built on respect. Distrust amongst educators is not uncommon and powerfully undermines school improvement efforts.

Fair Process Decision-Making

Guiding a fair process (collective decision-making that values input from all stakeholders) involves the entire school community defining core values that provide the groundwork for shared standards around behavior and support SEAD goals. Ignite the intrinsic motivation of students, parents, school personnel, and community members to learn and work together to meet identified needs and school improvement goals. When the identified needs and goals are born from the community and plans are "co-authored" and "co-led," it fosters engagement and, by definition, a collective effort. Foster engagement on the part of students and families as well as school personnel in the improvement process by "talking with" rather than "talking to."

Student Voice

Commit to amplifying student voice. Provide platforms to gather students' opinions and listen intentionally. Promote student engagement and leadership in intergenerational school improvement efforts. Students will rise to the expectation when leadership opportunities are meaningful.

Recommendations and Implications for Positive Psychology in Schools

Prosocial Education and Positive Psychology focus on creating climates for learning that promote student and organizational well-being (Brown et al., 2012; Shankland & Rosset, 2017). Growing out of the understandings outlined above, we suggest following three recommendations that helpfully shape prosocial—school climate, SEL, character education and mental health—policy and practice improvement efforts and Positive Psychology in schools.

Whole School Approach

Building on a whole-school approach is the most effective way to support school climate, SEL, character education, mental health promotion efforts, or prosocial school improvement efforts. All educators and school personnel, students, and parents need to develop a shared vision about what kind of school community they want. This vision includes actively supporting adult development and working on SEL and character education-informed competencies for educators as well for students (Aspen Institute, 2019). School-wide action plans that support shared goals and address barriers to learning must be iterative, data-driven, and fundamentally collaborative. This process importantly includes diverse representation in school leadership and decision-making that will support ongoing learning and improvement for all students as well as various student subgroups. That said, the whole school approach extends beyond the school walls as well as beyond the education system to include the social systems on which healthy child development depends. Prosocial improvement necessitates a broader shift in values and therefore goals, as mentioned previously.

Focus on Equity

Positive school climate improvement must include an intentional and explicit focus on equity (Ross et al., 2020) as well as safety, support, and engagement (Cohen, & Espelage, 2020). This is accomplished by creating an inclusive, supportive, engaging, and positive school climate; intentionally integrating equity-oriented SEL/character education into rigorous academic instruction; and understanding and addressing the challenges (e.g., bully/victim/bystander behavior) that undermine these efforts. Promoting effective risk prevention and health/mental health promotion efforts is consistent with Positive Psychology principles. Moreover, addressing explicit racial disparities in education is crucial. The global rise in awareness of the need for racial reckoning and resurgent civil rights movement in 2020 underscores the need to address systemic racism. A prosocial school improvement process includes, as a start, examining disaggregated behavioral and academic data to address opportunity gaps, ensuring diverse representation in decision-making spaces and processes, and addressing intrapersonal and broader systemic antiracist ideas and policies.

A Coordinated Approach

Positive school climate, SEL, academic achievement, equity, and violence prevention are interconnected. Longitudinal studies and comprehensive research reviews show that a positive school climate, as well as SEL, can contribute to better mathematics, reading, and literacy outcomes (Durlak et al., 2011). Research suggests that schools that emphasize academics as well as including efforts to improve school climate and prevent violence have increases in academic achievement as well as significant reductions in bullying (Astor & Benbenishty, 2019).

Conclusion

Given the intrinsic human desire to want the best for children, most people would agree that children are—literally—our future. School is an influential factor in most children's experience. Until quite recently, schools have focused on linguistic, mathematical, and scientific learning. As fundamentally important as these competencies are, they are insufficient for students to develop a lifelong learning disposition, social responsibility, effective co-worker/co-leader skills, the capacity to manage conflicts, and lasting friendships. Over the last several decades there has been a growing body of research that shows intentional social, emotional, civic, and academic instruction *in conjunction with* systems that support students feeling safer, more supported, and engaged do, in fact, promote life and school success. School improvement efforts can and need to intentionally promote individual and organizational health on the one hand and develop systems that creatively address challenges and problems on the other hand.

This chapter has summarized research about four overlapping K-12 educational traditions that all share the potential of Positive Psychology to enhance our ability to love, work, and play: SEL, character education, mental health promotion, and school climate improvement. Although these four traditions are historically and conceptually different, they are increasingly similar with regard to the actual school and district improvement process.

Primarily it is important for school leaders to consider and track specific systemic, instructional, and relational improvement goals in intentional, strategic, data-driven, and collaborative ways to further sustainable improvement. Effective and sustainable improvement efforts need to be grounded in a whole school approach; to promote equity, as well as safety and engagement of all stakeholders; and finally to appreciate the complex, multifaceted nature of learning, school life, and the improvement process itself.

Empirical support for the ideas and recommendations in this chapter points to the need to attend to the improvement process as well as address the differentiated needs of various school stakeholders (Berkowitz et al., 2017; Bryk et al., 2015; Durlak et al., 2011; Duchesneau, 2020; Dymnicki et al., 2017). Albeit, there is still a need to learn more about: What specific strategies and practices in given contexts and at different developmental stages promote social, emotional, and academic skill development, understanding, and dispositions for young people and the educators who support them? How can school systems, classrooms, as well as school organizations, structures, and routines adapt for given groups of children to thrive at all levels? Which specific classroom practices are most helpful socially, emotionally, and academically for each child's unique developmental needs and backgrounds? How can professional development and teacher education programs support educators to develop and implement equity-oriented systems? What does it mean for all school communities to be culturally responsive and how can districts support this? How can education realize the goal of closing the opportunity gap? How can school systems, classrooms, pedagogy, and systems that support educators shift toward community responsiveness? What aspect of school experiences are most helpful for given groups of children and why? What kind of preparation and support for adults is needed to further thriving schools? How can district- and state-level policy become more aligned with research findings and support meaningful research-practice partnerships in schools? Contextually grounded research is needed to further these fundamental questions to advance education (Jones et al., 2018).

Today, too many schools in the United States and around the world continue to narrowly focus on academic outcomes as success and physical danger as the alternative. Predictably, this will only sustain the minimum expectations for schools, if even that. The *Thriving Schools* framework introduced in this chapter strives toward an education system that supports academic success, social-emotional development, and civic engagement for all stakeholders including students as well as educators, staff, and families. The guidelines, resources, and recommendations summarized in this chapter can support school leaders on a path to foster thriving schools that promote life as well as school success for school communities.

Notes

1 There is not one agreed-upon definition for character education, SEL, or school climate as we have detailed elsewhere (Cohen & Espelage, 2020). Initially, character education and SEL (like school-based mental health informed interventions) were individually focused, emphasizing learning rather than culture or climate; and, for mental health, diagnosis and treatment, rather than a more developmental approach centering on psychological wellness.

2 In the United States, the Collaborative for Social Emotional and Academic Education (CASEL) has been the leading advocate for SEL and focused on the importance of classroom-based skills instruction in their early years: SEL (1.0).

3 See, for example, The *Devereux Student Strength Assessment*, https://apertureed.com/dessa-system-2/

4 National Center for Safe and Supportive Learning Environments has organized an excellent compendium of school climate surveys here: https://safesupportivelearning.ed.gov/resources/school-climate-survey-compendium.

5 The issue of what constitutes "evidence" is foundational for educational and mental health work. We suggest that there is confusion and too little focus on what constitutes "evidence-based," "empirically validated," and "empirically supported" practices. It is beyond the scope of this paper to detail the scientific and logical strengths and limitations of the "evidence-based" movement (see Wachtel, 2010, for a detailed and thoughtful analysis of these issues).

6 District-level improvement efforts tend to be more sustainable. When school board and central office leaders (superintendents) are involved with improvement efforts, they tend to become (i) multiyear efforts as well as (ii) including important systemic improvements (e.g., district-level policy; measurement practices; leadership development; and the establishment of district themes) that provide the foundation for sustainable improvement efforts.

7 See, for example, Moir, T. (2018, July 25). Why is intervention science important for intervention design and evaluation within educational settings? *Frontiers in Education*. https://www.frontiersin.org/articles/10.3389/feduc.2018.00061/full

8 Communities In Schools is a nationally recognized model, for example; see https://www.communities-inschools.org/

9 In *Learning to improve: How America's schools can get better at getting better* (2015), Bryk and his colleagues detail how educational policy has—inadvertently—undermined school leaders' inclination and ability to be open about challenges and failures. They underscore what all teachers know: confusion and failure are essential foundations for learning.

References

Aspen Institute. (2018). *Pursuing social and emotional development through a racial equity lens: A call to action*. Education & Society Program. Retrieved from https://www.aspeninstitute.org/publications/pursuing-social-and-emotional-development-through-a-racial-equity-lens-a-call-to-action/

Aspen Institute. (2019). *From a national at risk to a nation at hope*. National Commission on Social Emotional and Academic Development. Retrieved from http://nationathope.org

Astor, R. A., & Benbenishty, R. (2019). *Bullying, school violence, and climates in evolving contexts: Culture, organization, and time*. Oxford University Press.

Battistich, V., Solomon, D., Watson, M., & Schaps, E. (1997). Caring school communities. *Educational Psychologist, 32*(3), 137–151. doi:10.1207/s15326985ep3203_1

Berkowitz, M. W. (2011). What works in values education? *International Journal of Educational Research, 50*, 153–158. Retrieved from http://www.sciencedirect.com/science/article/pii/S0883035511000553

Berkowitz, M. W., Bier, M. C., & McCauley, B. (2017). Toward a science of character education: Frameworks for identifying and implementing effective practices. *Journal of Character Education, 13*(1), 33–51. Retrieved from https://irp-cdn.multiscreensite.com/e9b8fc57/files/uploaded/berkowitz_bier_mccauley_jce_2017.pdf

Blasé, K., van Dyke, M., & Fixsen, D. (2013). *Implementation drivers: Assessing best practices.* Adapted with permission by The State Implementation & Scaling-up of Evidence-based Practices Center (SISEP). Based on the work of The National Implementation Research Network (NIRN) Frank Porter Graham Child Development Institute, University of North Carolina Chapel Hill. Retrieved from http://implementation.fpg.unc.edu/resources/implementation-drivers-assessing-best-practices

Brown, P. M., Corrigan, M. W., & Higgins-D'Alessandro, A. (Eds.). (2012). *The handbook of prosocial education.* Rowman & Littlefield.

Bryk, A. S., Gomez, L. M., Grunow, A., & LeMahieu, P/G. (2015). *Leaning to improve: How America's schools can get better at getting better.* Harvard Education Press.

Bryk, A. S., & Schneider, B. (2004). *Trust in schools: A core resource for improvement.* Russell Sage Foundation.

Century, J., & Cassata, A. (2016). Implementation research: Finding common ground on what, how, why, where and who. *Review of Research in Education, 40*(1), 169–215. https://doi.org/10.3102/0091732X16665332

Character.org. (2020). *What we do.* Retrieved from https://www.character.org/what-we-do/

Cohen, J. (1999). Social and emotional learning past and present: A psychoeducational dialogue. In J. Cohen (Ed.), *Educating minds and hearts: Social emotional learning and the passage into adolescence* (pp. 3–23). Teachers College Press and the Association for Supervision and Curriculum Development.

Cohen, J. (2006). Social, emotional, ethical and academic education: Creating a climate for learning, participation in democracy and well-being. *Harvard Educational Review, 76*(2), 201–237. Retrieved from www.hepg.org/her/abstract/8

Cohen, J. (2013). Creating a positive school climate: A foundation for resilience. In S. Goldstein & R. B. Brooks (Eds.), *Handbook of resilience in children* (pp. 411–423).). Springer Science+Business Media. doi:10.1007/978-1-4614-3661-4_24

Cohen, J. (2014). Mental health clinicians and educators learning together: School climate reform and the promotion of effective K-12 risk prevention/health promotion efforts. *Journal of Infant, Child, and Adolescent Psychotherapy, 13*(4), 342–349. doi:10.1080/15289168.2014.951273

Cohen, J. (2017). School climate, social emotional learning, and other prosocial "camps": Similarities and a difference. *Teachers College Record*, September 20, 2017. (ID Number: 22165)

Cohen, J., & Brown, P. (2020). *Compendium of prosocial school improvement models and road maps.* Unpublished paper. Jc273@tc.columbia.edu

Cohen, J., & Espelage, D. (2020). Creating safe, supportive and engaging K-12 schools in the United States. In J. Cohen & D. Espelage (Eds.), *Feeling safe in school: Bullying and violence prevention around the world* (pp. 205–224). Harvard Educational Press.

Cohen, J., McCabe, E. M, Michelli, N. M., & Pickeral, T. (2009). School climate: Research, policy, teacher education and practice. *Teachers College Record, 111*(1), 180–213. Retrieved from www.tcrecord.org/Content.asp?ContentId=15220

Cohen, J., Thapa, A., & Higgins-D'Alessandro, A. (2017). School climate/social emotional learning measurement systems: Trends, contributions, challenges and opportunities. *Journal of Educational Leadership and Policy, 1,* 117–139.

Damschroder, L. J., Aron, D. C., Keith, R. E., Kirsh, S. R., Alexander, J. A., & Lowery, J. C. (2009). Fostering implementation of health services research findings into practice: A consolidated framework for advancing implementation science. *Implementation Science, 4*(1), 50. https://doi.org/10.1186/1748-5908-4-50

Duchesneau, N. (2020). Social, emotional, and academic development through an equity lens. EdTrust.org. Retrieved from https://edtrust.org/social-emotional-and-academic-development-through-an-equity-lens/?utm_medium=email&utm_source=equityexpress&utm_campaign=SEAD&emci=866d-cfc0-25d8-ea11-8b03-00155d0394bb&emdi=1235b16d-cfd8-ea11-8b03-00155d0394bb&ceid=173846

Durlak, J. A., Domitrovich, C. E., Weissberg, R. P., & Gullotta, T. P. (Eds.). (2016). *Handbook of social and emotional learning: Research and practice.* Guildford.

Durlak, J. A., Weissberg, R. P., Dymnicki, A. B., Taylor, R. D., & Schellinger, K. B. (2011). The impact of enhancing students' social and emotional learning: A meta-analysis of school-based universal interventions. *Child Development, 82*(1), 405–432. doi:10.1111/j.1467-8624.2010.01564.x.

Dymnicki, A., Wandersman, A., Osher, D., & Pakstis, A. (2017). Bringing interventions to scale: Implications and challenges for the field of community psychology. In M. Bond, C. B. Keyes, I. Serano-Garcia, & M. Shinn (Eds.), *APA handbook of school psychology* (Vol. II, pp. 297–310). American Psychological Association.

Fullan, M., & Rincón-Gallardo, S. (2020). The integration of learning and well-being as the next frontier in whole-system change. In J. Cohen & D. Espelage (Eds.), *Feeling safe in School: Bullying and violence prevention around the world*. Harvard Educational Press.

Furlong, M. J., Gilmore, R., & Huebner, S. (2014). *Handbook of positive psychology in schools* (2nd ed.). Routledge.

Gaglio, B., Shoup, J. A., & Blagow, R. E. (2013). The RE-AIM framework: A systemic review of use over time. *American Journal of Public Health, 103*, e38_e46. https://doi.org/10.2105/AJPH.2013.301299

Greenspoon, P. J., & Saklofske, D. H. (2001). Toward an integration of subjective well-being and psychopathology. *Social Indicators Research, 54*, 81–108. doi:10.1023/A:1007219227883

Gregory, A., & Fergus, E., (2017). Social and emotional learning and equity in school discipline. *The Future of Children, 27*(1), 117–136. ISBN: 978-0-9857863-7-3

Hayes-Green, D., & Love, B. (2019). *The groundwater approach: Building a practical understanding of structural racism*. Racial Equity Institute.

Jagers, R. J., Rivas-Drake, D., & Borowski, T. (2018). Equity & social and emotional learning: A cultural analysis. CASEL Frameworks Briefs Special Issues Series. Retrieved from https://casel.org/wp-content/uploads/2020/04/equity-and-SEL-.pdf

Jones, S., Farrington, C. A., Jagers, R., Brackett, M., & Kahn, J. (2018). *Social, emotional, and academic development: A research agenda for the next generation*. Aspen Institute, National Commission on Social Emotional and Academic Development. 4/20/2018. Retrieved from http://nationathope.org/wp-content/uploads/aspen_research_final_web_optimized.pdf

Jones, S. M., & Kahn, J. (2017). *The evidence base for how we learn: Supporting students' social, emotional, and academic development*. A consensus statement of evidence from the Council of Distinguished Scientists. The Aspen Institute's National Commission on Social, Emotional and Academic Development.

Lickona, T. (1996). Eleven principles of effective character education. *Journal of Moral Education, 25*(1), 93–100. doi:10.1080/0305724960250110

Locke, J., Lee, K., Cook, C. R., Frederick, L., Vazquez-Colon, C., Ehrhart, M. G., Aarons, G. A., Davis, C., & Lyon, A. R. (2019). Understanding the organizational implementation context of schools: A qualitative study of school district administrators, principals, and teachers. *School Mental Health, 11*, 379–399. doi:10.1007/s12310-018-9292-1

Lyon, A. R. (2017). *Implementation science and practice in the education sector*. Brief prepared for Project AWARE grant recipients. Substance Abuse and Mental Health Services Administration. Retrieved from https://education.uw.edu/sites/default/files/Implementation%20Science%20Issue%20Brief%20072617.pdf

McTighe, J., & Wiggins, G. (2004). *Understanding by design: Professional development workbook*. Association for Supervision & Curriculum Development.

Merriweather, T. R. (2012). Multicultural education is/as/in prosocial education. In P. Brown, M. W. M., Corrigan, & A. Higgins-D'Alessandro (Eds.), *The handbook of prosocial education* (pp. 635–664). Rowman & Littlefield.

Moore, S. A., Dowdy, E., Nylund-Gibson, K., & Furlong, M. J. (2019). A latent transition analysis of the longitudinal stability of dual-factor mental health in adolescence. *Journal of School Psychology, 73*, 56–73. doi:10.1016/j.jsp.2019.03.003

National School Climate Council. (2015). School climate and pro-social educational improvement: Essential goals and processes that support student success for all. *Teachers College Record*, March.

Noltemeyer, A. L., Mujic, J., & McLoughlin, C. S. (2012). The history of inequality in education. In A. L. Noltemeyer & C. S. McLoughlin (Eds.), *Disproportionality in education and special education* (pp. 3–22). Charles C. Thomas.

Paunesku, D. (2019, July 9). The deficit lens of the 'achievement gap' needs to be flipped. Here's how. *Edweek*. Retrieved from https://www.edweek.org/ew/articles/2019/07/10/the-deficit-lens-of-the-achievement-gap.html?cmp=eml-enl-eu-news2&M=58879858&U=1332932&UUID=7a5a250d6c3b344aa829ea733f3fc086

Person, A. E., Moiduddin, E., Hague-Angus, M., & Malone, L. M. (2009). *Survey of outcomes measurement in research on character education programs* (NCEE 2009-006). National Center for Education Evaluation and Regional Assistance, Institute of Education Sciences, U.S. Department of Education. Retrieved from http://ncee.ed.gov

Peterson, C. (2008). What is positive psychology and what is it not? *Psychology Today*, May 16, 2008. Retrieved from https://www.psychologytoday.com/us/blog/the-good-life/200805/what-is-positive-psychology-and-what-is-it-not

Ross, R., Brown, P., & Hamilton Biagas, K. (2020). Creating equitable school climates. *The State Education Standard: The Journal of the National Association of State Boards of Education, 20*(2), 17–22. Retrieved from https://www.nasbe.org/gauging-school-climate/

Shankland, R., & Rosset, E. (2017). Review of brief school-based positive psychological interventions: A taster for teachers and educators. *Educational Psychology Review, 29*(2), 363–392. doi:10.1007/s10648-016-9357-3

Simmons, D. (2019). Why we can't afford whitewashed social-emotional learning. *ASCD Education Update, 61*(4). Retrieved from http://www.ascd.org/publications/newsletters/education_update/apr19/vol61/num04/Why_We_Can%27t_Afford_Whitewashed_Social-Emotional_Learning.aspx

Snyder, C. R., & Lopez, S. J. (2009). *Oxford handbook of positive psychology* (2nd ed.). Oxford University Press.

Thapa, A., Cohen, J., Higgins-D'Alessandro, A., & Guffey, S. (2013). A review of school climate research. *Review of Educational Research, 83*(2), 357–385. doi:10.3102/0034654313483907

Vincent, P., & Grove, D. (2012). Character education: A primer on history, research and effective practices. In P. Brown, M. Corrigan, & H. Higgins D'Alessandro (Eds.), *Handbook of prosocial education* (pp. 115–136). Rowman & Littlefield.

Voight, A., & Nation, M. (2016). Practices for improving secondary school climate: A systematic review of the research literature. *American Journal of Community Psychology, 58*, 174–191. doi:10.1002/ajcp.12074

Wachtel, P. L. (2010). Beyond "ESTs": Problematic assumptions in the pursuit of evidence-based practice. *Psychoanalytic Psychology, 27*(3), 251–272. doi:10.1037/a0020532

Weist, M. D., Lever, N. A., Bradshaw, C. P., & Owens, J. S. (2014). *Handbook of school mental health: Research, training, practice and policy.* Springer.

Weissberg, R. P., Durlak, J. A., Domitrovich, C. E., & Gullotta, T. P. (2015). Social and emotional learning: Past, present and future. In J. A. Durlak, C. E. Domitrovich, R. P. Weissberg, & T. P. Gullotta (Eds.), *Handbook of social and emotional learning: Research and practice* (pp. 3–19). Guildford.

24

POSITIVE PSYCHOLOGY AND SCHOOL DISCIPLINE

George G. Bear, Angela B. Soltys and Fiona H. Lachman

For the past several decades, the developers of multiple new models of school discipline and classroom management have claimed that their models are *positive*. Indeed, two of the most popular models—with over 1 million copies of books sold about each model—have *positive* in their names: *Positive Discipline* (Nelsen et al., 2013) and *Assertive Discipline: Positive Behavior Management for Today's Classroom* (Canter, 2010). Likewise, one of the two most popular general approaches to school-wide discipline and prevention of behavior problems includes *positive* in its title: *Positive Behavioral Interventions and Supports* (PBIS; Sugai et al., 2010; Sugai & Horner, 2009; also see www.pbis.org).

In previous volumes of this handbook (Bear, 2009; Bear & Manning, 2014), this chapter proposed five guiding principles that should apply to models and approaches of school discipline and classroom management for them to be viewed as positive from the perspective of positive psychology. Those principles were applied to Positive Discipline, Assertive Discipline, SWPBIS, and the Social and Emotional Learning (SEL) approach (Collaborative for Academic, Social, and Emotional Learning [CASEL], 2019; Weissberg, et al., 2015). It was argued that beyond advocating that positive reinforcement, or encouragement, and other techniques of prevention should replace punishment, it is unclear how Positive Discipline, Assertive Discipline, and SWPBIS are "positive," or any more positive than most other models and approaches. In this chapter, we update and revise the five guiding principles presented previously while merging two earlier principles and adding a new one that is more specific to school climate. We apply the principles to the SEL and SWPBIS approaches, which are now widely viewed as the two most popular approaches to school discipline and classroom management.

When applied to the school setting, positive psychology has been termed *positive education* and defined as the development of virtues and character strengths that promote academics and enhance emotional well-being, mental health, and happiness (Peterson & Seligman, 2004). Since the onset of American education, the development of virtues and character strengths, especially those associated with self-discipline, has been a primary aim (Bear, 2005). It was not until the early 20th century that children's emotional and mental health joined character development and academic achievement as principal aims (Bear, 2005). Positive psychology differs from earlier mental health movements, however, in emphasizing that character strengths and happiness, rather than the absence of negative behaviors and emotions, should be the foremost target and indicator of mental health and emotional well-being.

DOI: 10.4324/9781003013778-30

Positive education depends on positive, or enabling, institutions, particularly families and schools to be effective (Seligman, 2002). In the context of the school, positive education is seen in teaching techniques, the curriculum, and the overall school climate. We view school discipline broadly and as a major determinant of school climate, while also recognizing that a comprehensive approach to school discipline entails strategies for (a) preventing misbehavior, (b) developing self-discipline, (c) correcting misbehavior, and (d) addressing the needs of students with serious and chronic behavior problems (Bear, 2005, 2010).

Guiding Principles of Positive Psychology Applied to School Discipline

In this section, we discuss five principles of positive psychology that guide positive school discipline. In the following sections, we review the key features of the SEL and SWPBIS approaches and judge the extent to which each approach is viewed as *positive* from the perspective of these principles.

Principle 1. The Primary Aim of Positive School Discipline Is the Development of Virtues and Character Strengths Associated with Self-Discipline

Self-discipline refers to students inhibiting inappropriate behavior and exhibiting prosocial behavior and doing so under their own volition. Self-discipline reflects intrinsic motivation and the internalization of values, standards, beliefs, and attitudes of teachers, peers, parents, and society in general. When used within the context of *school discipline* and positive education, *self-discipline* emphasizes the need for educators to view the development of self-regulated, autonomous behavior as their primary aim. This is contrary to the *use* of external discipline, either with punitive techniques or rewards, by adults to manage, govern, or control student behaviors.

One could argue that each of the six virtues and 24 character strengths identified by Peterson and Seligman (2004) are related to self-discipline. Some character strengths, however, are more clearly and directly related to self-discipline than others, particularly self-regulation, social and emotional intelligence, citizenship, fairness, integrity, persistence, and kindness. Ample research shows that self-discipline is associated with multiple positive outcomes that reflect or are associated with emotional well-being and happiness. Those outcomes include fewer internalizing and externalizing behavior problems (Eisenberg et al., 2010); higher self-esteem and better physical health (e.g., Moffitt et al., 2011); positive interpersonal skills and relationships with others (Boman et al., 2012), and higher academic achievement (Duckworth & Seligman, 2005).

Principle 2. School Discipline Should Help Children Meet Three Basic Human Needs: Competence, Belongingness, and Autonomy

Self-determination theory (Ryan & Deci, 2017) is often presented as a prototypical model of positive psychology theory (e.g., Sheldon & Ryan, 2011). The theory views meeting students' psychological needs for competence, belongingness, and autonomy as critical for intrinsic motivation and academic engagement, as well as for overall subjective well-being and happiness. The need for autonomy is particularly central to self-discipline. Indeed, it is not uncommon for self-discipline and autonomy to be used interchangeably in positive education (e.g., Reeve & Assor, 2011). In the context of school discipline, self-discipline refers to what Kochanska (2002) calls *committed* compliance and Brophy (1996) calls *willing* compliance (in contrast to *situational* or *grudging* compliance). Self-discipline is autonomous behavior, motivated by intrinsic factors, particularly moral emotions and cognitions that underlie virtues and character strengths. Primary among those cognitions and emotions are empathy-based guilt, shame, pride, gratitude, social perspective-taking, and moral reasoning—cognitions and emotions that underlie not only *knowing* and *doing* what is right, but desiring and doing what is right and for the right reasons, and not reasons that are self-centered or hedonistic (e.g., feeling happy because one receives extrinsic rewards or avoids punishment).

Principle 3. Greater Emphasis Should Be Placed on Positive Techniques for Developing Self-Discipline, Preventing Misbehavior, and Meeting Children's Basic Needs than on Punitive Techniques for Correcting Misbehavior

Guiding principles 1 and 2 concern the primary *aims* of school discipline. This principle and those that follow concern the *means* for best attaining the aims set in the first two principles. Positive education emphasizes the use of strategies and techniques for developing and strengthening desired virtues and character strengths and the underlying cognitions and emotions that reflect autonomy/self-discipline, competence, and belongingness. Those strategies and techniques, drawn from theories and research supporting their effectiveness, are implemented at multiple system levels, including the individual, classroom, school, and home. When implemented with fidelity, they substantially reduce the need for the use of discipline.

As emphasized by Seligman et al. (2005), the intent of positive psychology is not merely to replace effective practices for addressing individual weaknesses with effective practices for promoting strengths. Nor is it the intent of positive psychology to necessarily replace reasonable, just, and effective forms of punishment with positive alternatives. Instead, the intent is to minimize the need for punishment and to use it only in a manner that avoids its many limitations. Punitive is not necessarily the opposite of positive, especially when educators use punitive techniques wisely to achieve aims consistent with positive psychology. As such, in light of research on the effectiveness of high behavioral expectations, sanctions, and punishment in deterring misbehavior and promoting safety, learning, and development of self-discipline (Cornell & Mayer, 2010), schools should not forgo the reasonable use of such measures. This guidance is consistent with research on childrearing (Baumrind, 2013) and school discipline (Bear, 2020) that has demonstrated the effectiveness of an authoritative approach to discipline, which is characterized by a balance of social and emotional support, or responsiveness, and structure, or demandingness.

Principle 4. Programs and Techniques for Positive School Discipline Should Be Based on Theory and Empirical Evidence as to Their Effectiveness

In mental health fields, various *positive* therapies and interventions have been implemented with the intended purpose of enhancing personal well-being and happiness but were found to be ineffective (Peterson & Seligman, 2004). The same is true with respect to many positive-oriented educational programs that were designed to develop character strengths, promote happiness and emotional well-being, and prevent behavior problems. Noteworthy among them are values clarification, Kohlberg's moral development approach, and the self-esteem movement. In values clarification (Raths et al., 1966), popular in the 1960s and 1970s, students were taught to identify their personal values and strengths. In Kohlberg's moral development education approach (Kohlberg, 1984), popular in the 1980s, the development of moral reasoning received primary focus. In the self-esteem movement, popular in the early 1990s (California Task Force to Promote Self-Esteem and Personal and Social Responsibility, 1990), it was believed that an emphasis on the promotion of self-esteem led to both greater happiness and academic achievement. Each of these approaches was found to be ineffective or minimally effective in improving emotional well-being and behavior. To prevent positive education from having a similar fate, positive educators argue that strategies and interventions are to be driven by theory and research supporting their effectiveness in enhancing emotional well-being, mental health, and happiness, which include strategies and interventions in the areas of positive emotions, cognitive-behavioral therapy, and positive institutions (Seligman & Csikszentmihalyi, 2000; Seligman et al., 2005).

Principle 5. Building and Maintaining a Positive School Climate Is Critical for Promoting Emotional Well-Being, Developing Self-Discipline, and Fostering Academic Achievement

Positive education recognizes that positive institutions, and especially schools, are of utmost importance in fostering virtues and character strengths, as well as emotional well-being, happiness, and academic achievement. This notion is supported by research in education and psychology linking school climate to multiple highly valued outcomes. School climate consists of four interrelated characteristics of a school (Bear, 2020): (a) *social and emotional support*, as seen in caring and respectful interpersonal relationships and responsiveness to students' basic psychological needs; (b) *structure*, as seen as high behavioral expectations, fair disciplinary practices, and an orderly and safe learning environment; (c) *student engagement*, as seen in students being emotionally, cognitively, and behaviorally engaged in school; and (d) *safety*, as evidenced by students feeling safe in school (including the absence of bullying). Research indicates that the relationship between school climate and valued outcomes is bidirectional. For example, whereas a positive school climate certainly promotes character strengths and emotional well-being, so too do character strengths, and emotional well-being help create a more positive atmosphere for learning and development. However, the strength of the causal relationship tends to be stronger for school climate driving positive outcomes, rather than vice versa (Wang & Degol, 2016).

Popular Approaches to School Discipline

In this section, we present a summary of the defining features of the two most popular approaches to school discipline: SEL and SWPBIS.

Social and Emotional Learning

The SEL approach is grounded in a variety of theories and research that emphasize that how students think (i.e., cognitions) and feel (i.e., emotions) is equally important as their observed behavior, especially for promoting students' mental health, happiness, and educational achievement (Weissberg et al., 2015). The theories and research include the areas of positive youth development, social-cognitive theory, emotional development, moral development, prevention and resilience, and positive psychology. The SEL approach aims not only to promote socially and morally responsible behavior but also the social, cognitive, and emotional processes that underlie such behavior. Five core social and emotional competencies, and the processes underlying them, are typically targeted (Weissberg et al., 2015): (a) responsible decision-making at school, at home, and in the community; (b) relationship skills, (c) self-management of emotions and behavior; (d) social awareness; and (e) self-awareness. These competencies develop within the context of the following basic strategies and features that characterize the SEL approach and are commonly found in SEL programs (Bear, 2020; Jones et al., 2018).

Evidenced-Based Curriculum Lessons

The primary feature of most, if not all, SEL programs are curriculum lessons that are developmentally appropriate, evidence-based, and consistent with the acronym SAFE (Durlak et al., 2011). That is, lessons are *sequenced* (step-by-step lessons taught within and across school years), *active* (students play an active rather than passive role in learning, practicing, and applying skills), *focused* (sufficient time is spent on skill development), and *explicit* (specific skills are defined and targeted and lesson goals are clearly articulated). The most common processes and behaviors targeted in SEL lessons are social skills, identifying feelings of others and empathy, identifying one's own feelings, and coping/relaxation skills (Lawson et al., 2018).

Whole School Approach

SEL is integrated into the everyday life of the classroom and school, including in the general academic curriculum, teaching practices, classroom management, and school-wide discipline. This integration includes infusing SEL lessons into language arts, social studies, health, and other curriculum areas through discussions and projects (Jones & Bouffard, 2012). SEL lessons also are highlighted in assemblies, morning announcements, class meetings, and disciplinary encounters. In order for these additional instructional practices to occur and be effective, ongoing training and professional development is provided to educators, which includes promoting educators' own social and emotional competencies (Jones et al., 2018).

Positive Classroom and School Climates

Emphasis is placed on building and maintaining caring and safe climates that meet students' needs, where students feel good about themselves, feel attached to or connected with others, and are actively engaged in learning. In light of ample research showing the importance of positive teacher-student relationships in developing social and emotional competencies and preventing behavior problems (Williford et al., 2015), these relationships receive primary attention. However, other commonly recognized aspects of school climate and related skills also are targeted, including student-student relationships, school-home relationships, safety, transparent and fair expectations and rules, respect for diversity, and student engagement.

An Authoritative Approach to Discipline

Discipline in the SEL approach is consistent with the two traditional aims of school discipline: the short-term management of student behavior and the long-term development of self-discipline (Bear, 2015). Guided by an evidence-based authoritative approach to discipline (Baumrind, 2013; Brophy, 1996), demandingness (also referred to as structure) and responsiveness (also referred to as support) receive equal emphasis. Thus, a developmentally appropriate school discipline and classroom management system is in place with fair expectations, rules, and consequences (including forms of punishment), and coexists with an emphasis on adults being responsive to students' social and emotional needs and building relationships. Teachers recognize that most discipline problems can be prevented and view disciplinary encounters as opportunities to teach and develop social and emotional competencies.

Ample Opportunities for Students to Apply and Practice SEL Skills

To promote generalization and maintenance of SEL skills, teachers and staff expect students to practice and apply learned skills throughout the school day. This practice and application occurs in the contexts of service-learning, student government, peer-assisted learning, peer mediation, and sports and extracurricular activities. Ideally, opportunities for practice are not limited to the classroom and school setting but also extend into the home and community.

Additional Supportive Systems and Services

School-wide SEL efforts are integrated into multitiered systems of support. It also is recognized that the universal level of implementation is not always sufficient for preventing and correcting behavior problems and developing self-discipline. Thus, additional supports and services, aligned with universal efforts (including SEL), are provided to students at risk for or already experiencing more severe and chronic social, emotional, and behavioral difficulties (Wiley & Siperstein, 2015). Such services include small-group and individual counseling, supplemental lessons and booster sessions from the SEL curriculum, additional social skills or anger management training, consultation to teachers from a mental health specialist, crisis intervention, and supports to parents (Weissberg et al., 2015).

School-wide Positive Behavioral Interventions and Supports

SWPBIS has its roots in behavior modification, and more specifically, in applied behavior analysis (ABA) guiding the choice of behavioral techniques (Sugai & Horner, 2009). During its early years, Rob Horner, one of its developers, noted, "There is no difference in theory or science between positive behavior support and behavior modification. These are the same approach with different names" (Horner, 2000, p. 99). As such, when it first became popular, SWPBIS was simply the school-wide application of behavior modification. Whereas the approach continues to emphasize the application of techniques of behavior modification and ABA (Horner & Sugai, 2015), recently it has been presented as a more general multitiered framework of evidence-based prevention practices and interventions that enhance social and behavioral outcomes for all students (Lee & Gage, 2020; Noltemeyer et al., 2018). Despite changes, and inconsistencies, in definitions and conceptualizations of SWPBIS, four key features of SWPBIS are commonly identified in the literature (Sugai et al., 2010; Sugai & Horner, 2009).

Multitiered System of Prevention, Intervention, and Support

Focusing primarily on behavior concerns, SWPBIS targets three levels of prevention, intervention, and support: tier 1 (universal), tier 2 (targeted), and tier 3 (intensive). Tier 1 interventions and supports are those provided to all students in classrooms and school-wide, with the primary purpose of preventing future behavior problems. Interventions include the direct teaching of school-wide behavioral expectations and rules, as described in the next section of this chapter, and additional behavioral techniques of classroom management with an emphasis on manipulating antecedents to prevent misbehavior (Noltemeyer et al., 2018). Tier 2 builds upon tier 1, providing additional interventions and supports for students at risk for more serious future behavioral problems, and those showing early and frequent signs of behavioral problems. Tier 3 supplements tiers 1 and 2, targeting individual students with critical needs, particularly those who failed to respond favorably to evidence-based interventions implemented previously at tiers 1 and 2. Tier 3 interventions and supports, both academic and behavioral, are more individualized, comprehensive, and intensive than those at tiers 1 and 2 (Sugai & Horner, 2020).

Direct Teaching of Social Skills

Social skills targeted for teaching are observable, measurable, and clearly defined. Teaching includes posting three to five essential school-wide behavioral expectations, modeling the expected behaviors, and systematically reinforcing students with praise and rewards when they exhibit those behaviors (Lee & Gage, 2020; Waasdorp et al., 2012). Rewards often include tokens, such as tickets or coupons, that are exchangeable for tangible rewards or privileges.

Nearly all SWPBIS schools described in research studies have used tokens or tickets to reinforce behavior (e.g., Waasdorp et al., 2012), but recently its developers stated that SWPBIS does not dictate school-wide expectations or how they should be taught (Horner et al., 2017). It is unclear, however, if this means that SWPBIS schools need not use behavioral techniques that have traditionally characterized the SWPBIS approach—ones viewed as a unique feature of the approach (Noltemeyer et al., 2018).

Ongoing Collection and Use of Data for Decision-Making

Since its onset, the SWPBIS approach has emphasized the use of office disciplinary referrals (ODRs) and school suspensions for guiding interventions and evaluating their effectiveness. As such, school teams routinely review the number of ODRs, specific behaviors that led to ODRs, and when and where those behaviors occurred (Sugai et al., 2010). Schools analyze data, especially ODR data, using the principles of functional behavioral assessment applied to the group level. The data guide the development and implementation of evidence-based behavioral interventions that address areas of concern and also serve to systematically monitor program effectiveness. Only recently has SWPBIS included school climate data as a recommended source of data to be used in addition to ODRs (Sprague et al., 2018).

Supportive Systems

SWPBIS emphasizes the importance of team-based selection and implementation of research-validated practices, data-based decision-making, and ongoing administrative and team leadership. Each school is to have a leadership team composed of at least two individuals with expertise and experience in behavioral theory, ABA, function-based behavior intervention planning and support, direct social skills instruction, and principles of reinforcement (Horner et al., 2017; Sugai et al., 2010). SWPBIS also places a priority on staff commitment, communication, and information systems (e.g., website, newsletters, and meetings), adequate supports (e.g., personnel and time, financial resources), and precise guides and tools for implementation.

Are They Positive?

Concerning school discipline, both SEL and SWPBIS are *positive* if one views positive as emphasizing the use of alternatives to punishment, valuing prevention overcorrection, and striving to create safe schools. From the framework of positive psychology, however, those criteria are insufficient. To be judged as positive from the perspective of positive psychology, an approach must be consistent with guiding principles of positive psychology, as presented previously. Those principles are repeated here, with comments as to the extent to which the SEL and SWPBIS approaches are consistent with them.

Principle 1. The Primary Aim of Positive School Discipline Is the Development of Character Strengths and Virtues of Self-Discipline

Consistent with positive psychology, the primary aim of SEL is to develop behaviors, cognitions, and emotions that reflect or underlie character strengths and virtues of self-discipline. These include self-regulation, social and emotional intelligence, citizenship, fairness, integrity, persistence, and kindness. SEL targets behaviors consistent with those character strengths and virtues, but also a variety of cognitive and emotional processes that mediate, support, or enhance self-discipline and prosocial behavior and inhibit antisocial behavior, such as empathy (Berger et al., 2015), social perspective-taking (Berger et al., 2015), and moral reasoning (Malti et al., 2009).

To be sure, responsibility and respect are among the behavioral expectations in many SWPBIS programs. However, when one examines what is taught, it becomes clear that these expectations frequently translate into acts of compliance to the expectations and rules put forth by adults (Lynass et al., 2012; Simonsen & Sugai, 2009). As noted earlier, ODRs and suspensions, which reflect behaviors of compliance with adult rules, have been the primary outcome measures in both practice and research related to SWPBIS.

Principle 2. In Addition to Developing Character Strengths and Virtues, Programs Should Help Children Meet Three Basic Human Needs: The Need for Autonomy, the Need for Belongingness, and the Need for Competence

The SEL approach recognizes the critical importance of the psychological needs of autonomy, belongingness, and competence. Those needs are addressed in SEL by teaching students to be aware of their emotions, self-manage their emotions and behavior, relate well with others, appreciate and respect the perspectives of others, and think and act in a socially responsible manner. Building and maintaining caring relationships and safe climates receive primary emphases.

Unlike in SEL, rarely does one find that an explicit aim of SWPBIS is to meet students' psychological needs of autonomy, belongingness, and competence. To be sure, the behavioral approach offers a range of evidence-based techniques that are useful to help achieve that aim, including those for teaching specific social skills, preventing behavior problems, and providing a safe and supportive learning environment. However, as noted previously, too often, those teacher-centered techniques are used to achieve compliance, which runs the risk of stifling rather than promoting autonomy. This risk is especially true when teacher-centered techniques are not used in combination with student-centered techniques for developing social and emotional competencies, including self-discipline. Likewise, too often, a sense of "belongingness" is simply equated with students demonstrating observable social skills, such as respect, that are consistent with the school's behavioral expectations but have little regard for students feeling liked by others and a sense of community.

Principle 3. Greater Emphasis Should Be Placed on Using Positive Techniques for Developing Self-Discipline, Preventing Misbehavior, and Meeting Children's Basic Needs than on Correcting Misbehavior

SEL and SWPBIS share many of the same positive techniques for preventing behavior problems. For example, both emphasize motivating instruction, teacher-parent communication, and the use of a variety of standard techniques of classroom management for preventing and correcting misbehavior (e.g., redirection, physical proximity, and positive reinforcement). Although both view teacher-student relationships as important, SWPBIS tends to equate a positive teacher-student relationship as one in which teachers disseminate frequent praise and rewards, whereas SEL views a positive teacher-student relationship as one in which students perceive teachers as caring, respectful, and responsive to their psychological needs. Positive perceptions of teachers, irrespective of their use of rewards, are viewed as a primary mechanism for preventing behavior problems and developing self-discipline.

A strength of the SWPBIS approach is that it provides several evidence-based and teacher-centered behavioral strategies that align with the structure, or demandingness, dimension of the authoritative approach to school discipline. As such, SWPBIS addresses a general weakness of positive psychology and the SEL approach with respect to school discipline: a lack of guidance and strategies for correcting and decreasing negative behaviors and establishing order and compliance when needed (Kristjansson, 2012).

The two approaches differ in the systematic and frequent use of praise and rewards, and especially the latter. Whereas rewards are generally effective in teaching new skills and managing behavior, there are many limitations to their use—ones largely ignored by SWPBIS in its systematic use of tokens, tickets, and tangible rewards across all age levels. To be sure, praise and rewards are found in the SEL approach, but educators use them sparingly and strategically. SEL views the frequent and systematic use of rewards as unnecessary for most students, and best for students when self-discipline is lacking.

The systematic and frequent use of tangible rewards has been the focus of considerable criticism in education and psychology, particularly concerning their potential negative impact on intrinsic motivation and moral development. Several studies have shown that under certain conditions (i.e., when rewards are perceived to be controlling, and when social comparisons are highlighted), tangible rewards harm intrinsic motivation and promote extrinsic motivation (Ryan & Deci, 2017). It also is well established that a self-centered and hedonistic focus on gaining rewards and avoiding punishment characterizes the lowest levels of moral development (Kohlberg, 1984) and the most aggressive and antisocial individuals (Stams et al., 2006). Critics of the frequent and systematic use of rewards argue that when schools rely primarily on rewards and punishment to manage student behavior and develop self-discipline, they are encouraging extrinsic motivation and hedonistic moral reasoning (Reeve, 2015). Others argue, however, that most studies that have demonstrated harmful effects of rewards on intrinsic motivation were conducted in controlled laboratory settings and under conditions that do not typically occur in classrooms (Akin-Little & Little, 2009).

In addressing this issue, Bear et al. (2017) examined the impact of the everyday use of praise and rewards on extrinsic and intrinsic motivation, as reported by students, in a sample of over 10,000 students in Grades 5–12. Schools in the study were implementing SWPBIS, but most were doing so in combination with practices consistent with SEL. As predicted, students in schools in which they reported greater use of praise and rewards were found to have higher extrinsic prosocial motivation. However, contrary to the researchers' predictions, the students were *not* lower in intrinsic prosocial motivation. The study also found that punitive consequences had the most harmful effects—they were associated with lower intrinsic prosocial motivation (as well as with greater extrinsic motivation). The authors concluded that most schools, which use a combination of student-centered and teacher-centered techniques, need not worry about the frequent and everyday use of praise and rewards being associated with less intrinsic prosocial motivation.

Principle 4. Programs and Techniques for Positive School Discipline Should Be Based on Theory and Empirical Evidence as to Their Effectiveness

In a comprehensive and often-cited meta-analysis of the research literature (213 studies of universal-level SEL programs and 270,034 students), Durlak and colleagues (2011) reported that SEL programs improved social and emotional skills, including emotion regulation, perspective-taking, and social problem-solving. Additional positive effects of SEL programs included more favorable attitudes toward the self and others, including self-esteem, self-efficacy, self-perceptions of relations with teachers, and liking of school, and increased academic achievement and prosocial behavior. SEL programs also led to fewer conduct problems, including classroom disruption, noncompliance, aggression, and bullying, and less emotional distress. Several other recent meta-analyses of SEL programs have documented similar positive effects on social, emotional, behavioral, and academic skills (e.g., Taylor et al., 2017; Wigelsworth et al., 2016).

As noted earlier, the theoretical foundation of SWPBIS is behaviorism and specifically ABA. A substantial body of research has demonstrated the effectiveness of behavioral techniques in changing a wide range of student behaviors (Landrum & Kauffman, 2006). Much less research exists demonstrating the effectiveness of the SWPBIS approach, especially beyond reducing ODRs and suspensions. Multiple reviews of the research literature have found significant reductions in ODRs and suspensions following the implementation of SWPBIS (e.g., Bradshaw et al., 2010, 2012; Noltemeyer et al., 2018). Although ODRs correlate with behavior problems and serve as a good proxy for such, their limitations as an outcome measure are well known (Bear, 2010). Primary among them is that ODRs and suspensions vary greatly across teachers, schools, and over time and that ODRs and suspensions can be greatly reduced via changes in administrative policies that do not necessarily reflect changes in student behavior.

Despite frequent claims that SWPBIS improves student behavior, increases academic achievement, and promotes a positive school climate (e.g., Sugai & Horner, 2020), evidence supporting those claims is quite weak. Beyond reducing ODRs, to date, the strongest evidence of improving student behavior comes from a longitudinal randomized control group study that included 37 elementary schools. In addition to finding significant reductions in ODRs among students in SWPBIS schools compared to those in non-SWPBIS schools, Bradshaw et al. (2012) found significant decreases in aggressive and disruptive behaviors and concentration problems and increases in emotion regulation and prosocial behavior, as rated by classroom teachers. However, although the effects were statistically significant, the effect sizes were small, ranging from 0.08 to 0.17. Bradshaw et al. found that the effects were strongest among students who were in kindergarten when the approach was first implemented. In another study, and using the same sample, Bradshaw et al. (2015) also found that effects tend to be most significant among those students who are at the highest risk for behavior problems.

Concerning academic achievement, in their comprehensive review of the research literature, and contrary to their hypothesis, Gage et al. (2015) found no evidence that SWPBIS schools have higher academic achievement than non-SWPBIS schools. However, in a recent study, which compared students in SWPBIS and non-SWPBIS schools in Florida, Gage et al. (2017) found statistically significant, yet small, effects for SWPBIS improving mathematics (effect size = 0.10) and reading (effect size = 0.12).

Principle 5. Building and Maintaining a Positive School Climate Is Critical for Emotional Well-Being, Developing Self-Discipline, and Fostering Academic Achievement

The SEL approach aims to produce positive behavioral and academic outcomes for students. However, it also emphasizes creating a positive school climate. Multiple studies support the link between SEL and various dimensions of a positive school climate. For example, studies have shown SEL instruction to be associated with students' perceptions of a positive school climate (Bear et al., 2017), less bullying victimization (Nickerson et al., 2019), and higher student engagement (Yang et al., 2018). Studies also have shown that lesson-based SEL programs improve teacher-student relationships (Rivers et al., 2013), peer relationships (Correia & Marques-Pinto, 2016), and overall school climate (Haymovitz et al., 2018).

Advocates and developers of SWPBIS often assert that improved school climate is an outcome of SWPBIS (e.g., Gage et al., 2019; Horner et al., 2017; Sugai & Horner, 2020), and frequently cite several studies to support that assertion. Most commonly cited is a 2009 randomized control study by Horner et al. In that study, "at least five" teachers and staff members in each SWPBIS school and control school completed the School Safety Survey (SSS; Sprague et al., 1996) at baseline (T1) and at two time points following SWPBIS implementation (T2 and T3). The SSS yields a "risk factor" score and a "protective factor" score. Only scores on the risk factor were reported in this study, as protective factor scores were excluded because they "were consistently high" in both groups (p. 139). Items on the risk factor tap a variety of behavior problems (e.g., gang activity, fights, bullying, truancy, vandalism, and graffiti) but also environmental factors that contribute to those behaviors (e.g., poverty, the physical condition of facilities, "Students adjudicated by the courts").

Contrary to the oft-cited conclusion that this study found that SWPBIS schools improved in school climate, a close examination of the results indicated otherwise. That is, the table of means presented in the article shows that improvements (i.e., decreased risk scores) from T1 and T2 to T3 were higher for the control schools than the SWPBIS schools. The statistical significance of the differences in scores from T1 and T2 to T3 is not reported and the differences are quite small. Risk factor scores improved in SWPBIS schools only from T1 to T2, and those scores also improved significantly in control schools.

Also frequently cited as demonstrating a positive impact of SWPBIS on school climate is a randomized control group study of elementary schools conducted by Bradshaw and colleagues (Bradshaw et al 2008, 2009). Those researchers used the Organizational Health Inventory for

Elementary Schools (OHI; Hoy & Feldman, 1987), a validated measure of staff reports of five dimensions of the school's organizational health. Statistically significant differences in favor of SWPBIS schools were found on two of the five dimensions and in overall OHI scores. Effect sizes were small, ranging from 0.26 to 0.34. The two significant dimensions were resource influence, which assesses the principal's ability to acquire school resources and positively allocate school resources, and staff affiliation, which assesses positive relations among staff. A marginally significant difference was found for academic emphasis, and no significant differences were found for the other two dimensions (i.e., collegial leadership and institutional integrity).

In addition to the studies mentioned in the preceding paragraph not reporting significant differences between SWPBIS schools and control schools on the majority of measures, and using measures that failed to assess dimensions of school climate most commonly found on measures of school climate (e.g., social and emotional support, structure, student engagement, and safety; Bear, 2020; Wang & Degol, 2016), a major shortcoming of both studies was that they failed to evaluate students' perceptions of school climate. Approximately 90% of published studies on school climate evaluate the perceptions of students, not teachers and staff (Wang & Degol, 2016).

Several papers by developers and advocates of the SWPBIS approach (e.g., Sugai & Horner, 2020) have cited two studies of SWPBIS in which students' perceptions of school climate were assessed: a study by Kelm et al. (2014) and another by McIntosh et al. (2011). Whereas the first consisted of a case study of one small elementary school in Canada, the second included 10 additional elementary schools (Grades K–7) in the same school district. In both studies, perceptions of school climate among students in Grades 4 and 7 were assessed using only three items, which examined safety, bullying, and the teaching of behavioral expectations. No means, standard deviations, or statistical tests were reported. Bar graphs showed minimal gains in scores—gains unlikely to be of either statistical or practical significance.

Although the primary bullying outcome decreased, in their study of the effectiveness of SWPBIS, Nese et al. (2014) also examined changes in students' perceptions of school climate. No significant improvements in school climate were found in the three middle schools included in this multiple baseline study. Likewise, using a nonrandomized design that included 28 intervention schools and 20 control schools, Sørlie and Ogden (2015) reported that teachers' perceptions of school climate improved in SWPBIS schools, but students' perceptions did not. In sum, the evidence does not support the claims that SWPBIS improves students' perceptions of school climate.

Conclusion

If a primary aim is to establish structure and elicit situational compliance, SWPBIS should be a chosen approach. However, if a primary aim is the long-term development of self-discipline, then SEL is the preferred approach. Although self-discipline is a primary aim of positive psychology and education, the importance of structure in classroom management and school discipline should not be overlooked. As noted earlier, ample research shows that an authoritative approach to school discipline, characterized by a balance of structure and responsiveness to students' psychological needs, is found in the most effective schools, as well as in schools perceived by students as having positive school climates (Bear, 2020). Structure is especially important in classrooms and schools where self-discipline is lacking. It is for these reasons, and in recognition of both the strengths and weaknesses of each approach (see Bear, 2010), that we recommended that educators desiring a more comprehensive, and authoritative, approach to school discipline should integrate strategies and techniques of SEL and SWPBIS (Bear, 2010; Bear et al., 2015; Bradshaw et al., 2014). Such integration is not uncommon and is supported by research showing that a combination of the two approaches is more effective in reducing behavior problems and improving student mental health than either approach alone (Cook et al., 2015).

References

Akin-Little, A., & Little, S. G. (2009). The true effects of extrinsic reinforcement on "intrinsic" motivation. In A. Akin-Little, S. G. Little, M. A. Bray, & T. J. Kehle (Eds.), *School psychology. Behavioral interventions in schools: Evidence-based positive strategies* (pp. 73–91). American Psychological Association. https://doi.org/10.1037/11886-005

Baumrind, D. (2013). Authoritative parenting revisited: History and current status. In R. E. Larzelere, A. S. Morris, & A. W. Harrist (Eds.), *Authoritative parenting: Synthesizing nurturance and discipline for optimal child development* (pp. 11–34). American Psychological Association.

Bear, G. G. (with A. Cavalier & M. Manning). (2005). *Developing self-discipline and preventing and correcting misbehavior.* Allyn & Bacon.

Bear, G. G. (2009). The positive in positive models of discipline. In R. Gilman, E. S. Huebner & M. J. Furlong (Eds.), *Handbook of positive psychology in schools* (pp. 305–321). Routledge/Taylor & Francis.

Bear, G. G. (2010). *School discipline and self-discipline: A practical guide to promoting prosocial student behavior.* Guilford.

Bear, G. G. (2015). Preventive classroom management. In E. T. Emmer & E. J. Sabornie (Eds.), *Handbook of classroom management* (2nd ed., pp. 15–39). Routledge/Taylor & Francis.

Bear, G. G. (2020). *Improving school climate: Practical strategies to reduce behavior problems and promote social and emotional learning.* Routledge/Taylor & Francis.

Bear, G. G., & Manning, M. A. (2014). Positive psychology and school discipline. In M. J. Furlong, R. Gilman, & E. S. Huebner (Eds.), *Handbook of positive psychology in schools* (2nd ed., pp. 347–364). Routledge/Taylor & Francis.

Bear, G. G., Slaughter, J., Mantz, L., & Farley-Ripple, L. (2017). Rewards, praise, and punitive consequences: Relations with intrinsic and extrinsic motivation. *Teaching and Teacher Education, 65*, 10–20. http://dx.doi.org/10.1016/j.tate.2017.03.001

Bear, G. G., Whitcomb, S., Elias, M., & Blank, J. (2015). SEL and schoolwide positive behavioral interventions and supports. In J. Durlak, T. Gullotta, C. Domitrovich, P. Goren, & R. Weissberg (Eds.), *Handbook of social and emotional learning* (pp. 453–467). Guilford.

Bear, G. G., Yang, C., Mantz, S., & Harris, A. B. (2017). School-wide practices associated with school climate in elementary, middle, and high schools. *Teaching & Teacher Education, 63*, 372–383. https://doi.org.udel.idm.oclc.org/10.1016/j.tate.2017.01.012

Berger, C., Batanova, M., & Cance, J. D. (2015). Aggressive and prosocial? Examining latent profiles of behavior, social status, Machiavellianism, and empathy. *Journal of Youth and Adolescence, 44*(12), 223–2244. http://dx.doi.org/10.1007/s10964-015-0298-9

Boman, J. H., Krohn, M. D., Gibson, C. L., & Stogner, J. M. (2012). Investigating friendship quality: An exploration of self-control and social control theories' friendship hypotheses. *Journal of Youth and Adolescence, 41*(11), 1526–1540. http://dx.doi.org/10.1007/s10964-012-9747-x

Bradshaw, C. P., Bottiani, J., Osher, D., & Sugai, G. (2014). The integration of positive behavioral interventions and supports and social and emotional learning. In M. Weist, N. Lever, C. Bradshaw, & J. Owens (Eds.), *Handbook of school mental health* (pp. 101–118). Springer.

Bradshaw, C. P., Koth, C. W., Bevans, K. B., Ialongo, N., & Leaf, P. J. (2008). The impact of school-wide positive behavioral interventions and supports (PBIS) on the organizational health of elementary schools. *School Psychology Quarterly, 23*(4), 462–473. http://dx.doi.org/10.1037/a0012883

Bradshaw, C. P., Koth, C. W., Thornton, L. A., & Leaf, P. J. (2009). Altering school climate through school-wide positive behavioral interventions and supports: Findings from a group-randomized effectiveness trial. *Prevention Science, 10*(2), 100–115. http://dx.doi.org/10.1007/s11121-008-0114-9

Bradshaw, C. P., Mitchell, M. M., & Leaf, P. J. (2010). Examining the effects of schoolwide positive behavioral interventions and supports on student outcomes: Results from a randomized controlled effectiveness trial in elementary schools. *Journal of Positive Behavior Interventions, 12*(3), 133–148. http://dx.doi.org/10.1177/1098300709334479

Bradshaw, C. P., Waasdorp, T. E., & Leaf, P. J. (2012). Effects of school-wide positive behavioral interventions and supports on child behavior problems. *Pediatrics, 130*(5), e1136–e1145. http://dx.doi.org/10.1542/peds.2012-0243

Bradshaw, C. P., Waasdorp, T. E., & Leaf, P. J. (2015). Examining variation in the impact of school-wide positive behavioral interventions and supports: Findings from a randomized controlled effectiveness trial. *Journal of Educational Psychology, 107*(2), 546–557. http://dx.doi.org/10.1037/a0037630

Brophy, J. E. (1996). *Teaching problem students.* Guilford.

California Task Force to Promote Self-Esteem and Personal and Social Responsibility. (1990). *Toward a state of esteem: The final report of the California Task Force to Promote Self-Esteem and Personal and Social Responsibility.* Author.

Canter, L. (2010). *Assertive discipline: Positive behavior management for today's classroom.* Solution Tree Press.

Collaborative for Academic, Social, and Emotional Learning (2019). *What is SEL?* Retrieved from https://casel.org/what-is-sel/approaches/

Cook, C. R., Frye, M., Slemrod, T., Lyon, A. R., Renshaw, T. L., & Zhang, Y. (2015). An integrated approach to universal prevention: Independent and combined effects of PBIS and SEL on youths' mental health. *School Psychology Quarterly, 30*(2), 166–183. https://doi.org/10.1037/spq0000102

Cornell, D. G., & Mayer, M. J. (2010). Why do school order and safety matter? *Educational Researcher, 39*(1), 7–15. http://dx.doi.org/10.3102/0013189X09357616

Correia, K., & Marques-Pinto, A. (2016). Adaptation in the transition to school: Perspectives of parents, preschool and primary school teachers. *Educational Research, 58*(3), 247–264. http://dx.doi.org/10.1080/00131881.2016.1200255

Duckworth, A. L., & Seligman, M. E. (2005). Self-discipline outdoes IQ in predicting academic performance of adolescents. *Psychological Science, 16*(12), 939–944. http://dx.doi.org/10.1111/j.1467-9280.2005.01641.x

Durlak, J. A., Weissberg, R. P., Dymnicki, A. B., Taylor, R. D., & Schellinger, K. B. (2011). The impact of enhancing students' social and emotional learning: A meta-analysis of school-based universal interventions. *Child Development, 82*(1), 474–501. https://doi.org/10.1111/j.1467–8624.2010.01564.x

Eisenberg, N., Spinrad, T. L., & Eggum, N. D. (2010). Emotion-related self-regulation and its relation to children's maladjustment. *Annual Review of Clinical Psychology, 6,* 495–525. http://dx.doi.org/10.1146/annurev.clinpsy.121208.131208

Gage, N. A., Leite, W., Childs, K., & Kincaid, D. (2017). Average treatment effect of school-wide positive behavioral interventions and supports on school-level academic achievement in Florida. *Journal of Positive Behavior Interventions, 19*(3), 158–167. http://dx.doi.org/10.1177/1098300717693556

Gage, N. A., Rose, C. A., & Kramer II, D. A. (2019). When prevention is not enough: Students' perception of bullying and school-wide positive behavior interventions and supports. *Behavioral Disorders, 45*(1), 29–40. https://doi.org.udel.idm.oclc.org/10.1177/0198742918810761

Gage, N. A., Sugai, G., Lewis, T. J., & Brzozowy, S. (2015). Academic achievement and school-wide positive behavior supports. *Journal of Disability Policy Studies, 25*(4), 199–209. http://dx.doi.org/10.1177/1044207313505647

Haymovitz, E., Houseal-Allport, P., Lee, R. S., & Svistova, J. (2018). Exploring the perceived benefits and limitations of a school-based social–emotional learning program: A concept map evaluation. *Children & Schools, 40*(1), 45–54. http://dx.doi.org/10.1093/cs/cdx029

Horner, R. H. (2000). Positive behavior supports. *Focus on Autism and other Developmental Disabilities,15*(2), 97–105. http://doi.org/10.1177/108835760001500205

Horner, R. H., & Sugai, G. (2015). School-wide PBIS: An example of applied behavior analysis implemented at a scale of social importance. *Behavior Analysis Practice, 8*(1), 80–85. https://doi.org/10.1007/s40617-015-0045-4

Horner, R. H., Sugai, G., & Fixsen, D. L. (2017). Implementing effective educational practices at scales of social importance. *Clinical Child and Family Psychology Review, 20*(1), 25–35. http://dx.doi.org/10.1007/s10567-017-0224-7

Hoy, W. K., & Feldman, J. A. (1987). Organizational health: The concept and its measure. *Journal of Research & Development in Education, 20*(4), 30–37.

Jones, S., Bailey, R., Brush, K., & Kahn, J. (2018). *Preparing for effective SEL implementation.* Harvard Graduate School of Education. Retrieved from https://www.wallacefoundation.org/knowledge-center/Documents/Preparing-for-Effective-SEL-Implementation.pdf

Jones, S. M., & Bouffard, S. M. (2012). Social and emotional learning in schools: From programs to strategies. *Society for Research in Child Development Social Policy Report, 26*(4), 1–33. https://doi.org/10.1002/j.2379-3988.2012.tb00073.x

Kelm, J. L., McIntosh, K., & Cooley, S. (2014). Effects of implementing school-wide positive behavioural interventions and supports on problem behaviour and academic achievement in a Canadian elementary school. *Canadian Journal of School Psychology, 29*(3), 195–212. http://dx.doi.org/10.1177/0829573514540266

Kochanska, G. (2002). Committed compliance, moral self, and internalization: A mediational model. *Developmental Psychology, 38*(3), 339–351. https://doi.org/10.1037/0012–1649.38.3.339

Kohlberg, L. (1984). *Essays on moral development: Vol. 2. The psychology of moral development.* Harper & Row.

Kristjansson, K. (2012). Positive psychology and positive education: Old wine in new bottles? *Educational Psychologist, 47*(2), 86–105. https://doi.org/10.1080/00461520.2011.610678

Landrum, T. J., & Kauffman, J. M. (2006). Behavioral approaches to classroom management. In C. M. Evertson & C. S. Weinstein (Eds.), *Handbook of classroom management: Research, practice, and contemporary issues* (pp. 47–71). Erlbaum.

Lawson, G. M., McKenzie, M. E., Becker, K. D., Selby, L., & Hoover, S. A. (2018). The core components of evidence-based social emotional learning programs. *Prevention Science, 20*(4), 457–467. http://dx.doi.org/10.1007/s11121-018-0953-y

Lee, A., & Gage, N. A. (2020). Updating and expanding systematic reviews and meta-analyses on the effects of school-wide positive behavior interventions and supports. *Psychology in the Schools. First online: January 7, 2020.* http://dx.doi.org/10.1002/pits.22336

Lynass, L., Tsai, S., Richman, T. D., & Cheney, D. (2012). Social expectations and behavioral indicators in school-wide positive behavior supports: A national study of behavior matrices. *Journal of Positive Behavior Interventions, 14*(3), 153–161. http://dx.doi.org/10.1177/1098300711412076

Malti, T., Gasser, L., & Buchmann, M. (2009). Aggressive and prosocial children's emotion attributions and moral reasoning. *Aggressive Behavior, 35*(1), 90–102. http://dx.doi.org/10.1002/ab.20289

McIntosh, K., Bennett, J. L., & Price, K. (2011). Evaluation of social and academic effects of school-wide positive behaviour support in a Canadian school district. *Exceptionality Education International, 21*(1), 46–60.

Moffitt, T. E., Arseneault, L., Belsky, D., Dickenson, N., Hancox, R. J., Harrington, H., Houts, R., Poulton, R., Roberts, B. W., Ross, S., Sears, M. R., Thomson, W. M. T., & Caspi, A. (2011). A gradient of childhood self-control predicts health, wealth, and public safety. *Proceedings of the National Academy of Sciences of the United States of America, 108*(7), 2693–2698. http://dx.doi.org/10.1073/pnas.1010076108

Nese, R. N. T., Horner, R. H., Dickey, C. R., Stiller, B., & Tomlanovich, A. (2014). Decreasing bullying behaviors in middle school: Expect respect. *School Psychology Quarterly, 29*(3), 272–286. http://dx.doi.org/10.1037/spq0000070

Nelsen, J. D., Lott, L., & Glenn, H. S. (2013). *Positive discipline in the classroom: Developing mutual respect, cooperation, and responsibility in your classroom* (4th ed.). Three Rivers.

Nickerson, A. B., Fredrick, S. S., Allen, K. P., & Jenkins, L. N. (2019). Social emotional learning (SEL) practices in schools: Effects on perceptions of bullying victimization. *Journal of School Psychology, 73*, 74–88. http://dx.doi.org/10.1016/j.jsp.2019.03.002

Noltemeyer, A., Palmer, K., James, A. G., & Wiechman, S. (2018). School-wide positive behavioral interventions and supports (SWPIS): A synthesis of existing research. *International Journal of School & Educational Psychology, 7*(4), 253–262. http://dx.doi.org/10.1080/21683603.2018.1425169

Peterson, C., & Seligman, M. E. P. (2004). *Character strengths and virtues: A handbook and classification.* American Psychological Association.

Raths, L., Harmin, M., & Simon, S. (1966). *Values and teaching.* Charles E. Merrill.

Reeve J. (2015). Rewards. In E. T. Emmer & E. J. Sabornie (Eds.), *Handbook of classroom management* (pp. 496–516). Routledge.

Reeve, J., & Assor, A. (2011). Do social institutions necessarily suppress individuals' need for autonomy? The possibility of schools as autonomy-promoting contexts across the globe. In V. I. Chirkov, R. M. Ryan, & K. M. Sheldon (Eds.), *Human autonomy in cross-cultural context: Perspectives on the psychology of agency, freedom, and well-being* (pp. 111–132). Springer.

Rivers, S. E., Brackett, M. A., Reyes, M. R., Elbertson, N. A., & Salovey, P. (2013). Improving the social and emotional climate of classrooms: A clustered randomized controlled trial testing the RULER approach. *Prevention Science, 14*(1), 77–87. http://dx.doi.org/10.1007/s11121-012-0305-2

Ryan, R. M., & Deci, E. L. (2017). *Self-determination theory: Basic psychological needs in motivation, development, and wellness.* Guilford.

Seligman, M. E. P. (2002). *Authentic happiness: Using the new positive psychology to realize your potential for lasting fulfillment.* Free Press.

Seligman, M. E. P., & Csikszentmihalyi, M. (Eds.). (2000). Positive psychology: An introduction. *American Psychologist, 55*(1), 5–14. https://doi.org/10.1037/0003–066X.55.1.5

Seligman, M. E. P., Steen, T. A., Park, N., & Peterson, C. (2005). Positive psychology progress: Empirical validation of interventions. *American Psychologist, 60*(5), 410–421. https://doi.org/10.1037/0003–066X.60.5.410

Sheldon, K. M., & Ryan, R. M. (2011). Positive psychology and self-determination theory: A natural interface. In V. I. Chirkov, R. M. Ryan, & K. M. Sheldon (Eds.), *Human autonomy in cross-cultural context: Perspectives on the psychology of agency, freedom, and well-being (pp. 33–44).* Springer.

Simonsen, B., & Sugai, G. (2009). School-wide positive behavior support: A systems-level application of behavioral principles. In A. Akin-Little, S. G. Little, M. A. Bray, & T. J. Kehle (Eds.), *School Psychology. Behavioral interventions in schools: Evidence-based positive strategies* (p. 125–140). American Psychological Association. https://doi.org/10.1037/11886-008

Sørlie, M. A., & Ogden, T. (2015). School-wide positive behavior support-Norway: Impacts on problem behavior and classroom climate. *International Journal of School & Educational Psychology, 3*(3), 202–217. https://doi.org/10.1080/21683603.2015.1060912

Sprague, J. R., Colvin, G., & Irvin, L. (1996). *The Oregon School Safety Survey*. University of Oregon.

Sprague, J. R., Whitcomb, S. A., & Bear, G. G. (2018). Mechanisms for promoting and integrating school-wide discipline approaches. In M. J. Mayer & S. R. Jimerson (Eds.), *School safety and violence prevention: Science, practice, and policy* (pp. 95–120). American Psychological Association.

Stams, G. J., Brugman, D., Dekovic, M., van Rosmalen, L., van der Laan, P., & Gibbs, J. C. (2006). The moral judgment of juvenile delinquents: A meta-analysis. *Journal of Abnormal Child Psychology, 34*(5), 697–713. http://dx.doi.org/10.1007/s10802-006-9056-5

Sugai, G., & Horner, R. H. (2009). Defining and describing schoolwide positive behavior support. In W. Sailor, G. Dunlap, G. Sugai, & R. Horner (Eds.), *Handbook of positive behavior support* (pp. 307–326). Springer.

Sugai, G., & Horner, R. H. (2020). Sustaining and scaling positive behavioral interventions and supports: Implementation drivers, outcomes, and considerations. *Exceptional Children, 86*(2), 120–136. https://doi.org/10.1177/0014402919855331

Sugai, G., Horner, R. H., Algozzine, R., Barrett, S., Lewis, T., Anderson, C, Bradley, R., Choi, J. H., Dunlap, G., Eber, L., George, H., Kincaid, D., McCart, A., Nelson, M., Newcomer, L., Putnam, R., Riffel, L., Rovins, M., Sailor, W., & Simonsen, B. (2010). *School-wide positive behavior support: Implementers' blueprint and self-assessment*. University of Oregon. Retrieved from www.pbis.org

Taylor, R. D., Oberle, E., Durlak, J. A., & Weissberg, R. P. (2017). Promoting positive youth development through school-based social and emotional learning interventions: A meta-analysis of follow-up effects. *Child Development, 88*(4), 1156–1171. http://dx.doi.org/10.1111/cdev.12864

Waasdorp, T. E., Bradshaw, C. P., & Leaf, P. J. (2012). The impact of schoolwide positive behavioral interventions and supports on bullying and peer rejection: A randomized controlled effectiveness trial. *Archives of Pediatrics & Adolescent Medicine, 166*(2), 149–156. https://doi.org/10.1001/archpediatrics.2011.755

Wang, M., & Degol, J. L. (2016). School climate: A review of the construct, measurement, and impact on student outcomes. *Educational Psychology Review, 28*(2), 315–352. http://dx.doi.org/10.1007/s10648-015-9319-1

Weissberg, R. P., Durlak, J. A., Domitrovich, C. E., & Gullotta, T. P. (Eds.). (2015). Social and emotional learning: Past, present, and future. In J. A. Durlak, C. E. Domitrovich, R. P. Weissberg, & T. P. Gullotta (Eds.), *Handbook of social and emotional learning: Research and practice* (pp. 3–19). Guilford.

Wigelsworth, M., Lendrum, A., Oldfield, J., Scott, A., ten Bokkel, I., Tate, K., & Emery, C. (2016). The impact of trial stage, developer involvement and international transferability on universal social and emotional learning programme outcomes: A meta-analysis. *Cambridge Journal of Education, 46*(3), 347–376. http://dx.doi.org/10.1080/0305764X.2016.1195791

Wiley, A. L., & Siperstein, G. N. (2015). SEL for students with high-incidence disabilities. In J. A. Durlak, C. E. Domitrovich, R. P. Weissberg, & T. P. Gullotta (Eds.), *Handbook for social and emotional learning: Research and practice* (pp. 213–229). Guilford.

Williford, A. P., Wolcott, C. S., Whittaker, J. V., & Locasale-Crouch, J. (2015). Program and teacher characteristics predicting the implementation of banking time with preschoolers who display disruptive behaviors. *Prevention Science, 16*(8), 1054–1063. http://dx.doi.org/10.1007/s11121-015-0544-0

Yang, C., Bear, G. G., & May, H. (2018). Multilevel associations between school-wide social–emotional learning approach and student engagement across elementary, middle, and high schools. *School Psychology Review, 47*(1), 45–61. http://dx.doi.org/10.17105/SPR-2017-0003.V47-1

25

UNDERSTANDING AND PROMOTING SCHOOL SATISFACTION IN CHILDREN AND ADOLESCENTS

Shannon M. Suldo, Hannah L. Gilfix and Myesha M. Morgan

Introduction

Although children spend most of their time outside of the home in school, students' happiness at school garners substantially less attention than academic achievement metrics tied to accountability systems. Nevertheless, students' global satisfaction with life is affected by their experiences in, and satisfaction with, school (Casas et al., 2013). Across nations, children who report the most positive experiences at school in terms of teacher–student relationships, safety, equity, and enjoyment at school are also more likely to experience the highest emotional well-being—more frequent feelings of satisfaction, happiness, and serenity (Minguez, 2020). Noddings (2003) argues, "Happiness and education are, properly, intimately related: Happiness should be an aim of education, and a good education should contribute significantly to personal and collective happiness" (p. 1). In addition to the psychological implications of school satisfaction, it has been reasoned that students learn best when they are happy because they "seize their educational opportunities with delight, and they will contribute to the happiness of others" (Noddings, 2003, p. 261). Accordingly, this chapter summarizes the predictors and outcomes of students' positive appraisals of their schooling and concludes with implications for practice and future research.

Definition and Measurement

In the first edition of this handbook, Baker and Maupin (2009) conveyed that school satisfaction refers to students' subjective cognitive appraisal of their school life quality. School satisfaction is perhaps best understood in the broader context of wellness indicators. In brief, global life satisfaction, a common indicator of happiness, refers to one's cognitive appraisal of the overall quality of their life. When making such overall judgments of personal well-being, individuals vary in which aspects of their lives they value most; for example, some people emphasize financial status while others weigh relationship qualities most heavily. The domains deemed to be most salient to global life satisfaction are mainly a function of one's developmental level. Early investigations of life domains that influence global life satisfaction appraisals among American youth implicated five core domains: family, friendships, living environment, self, and school (Huebner, 1994). Satisfaction in each domain is empirically linked to global life satisfaction (Seligson et al., 2003). Research on the Personal Well-being Index (PWI) among Australian adolescents confirmed that for the School

DOI: 10.4324/9781003013778-31

Children form of the PWI, school is a contributing domain to global life satisfaction (Tomyn & Cummins, 2011). Specifically, Australian adolescents' satisfaction with school predicted their global life satisfaction above and beyond the contributions of the other seven domains of life (e.g., health, safety, achievements, and future security) most commonly assessed with the PWI. A similar finding emerged from Minguez's (2020) study of European nations, as school satisfaction predicted significant variability in children's subjective well-being after accounting for the influence of family, friends, and community among samples from Spain, Germany, England, and Norway.

This chapter summarizes findings from a comprehensive review of published studies of "school satisfaction," "happiness at school," "quality of school life," and "satisfaction with class or school experiences." The studies cited in this descriptive review of the literature on school satisfaction among students at different school levels and from diverse countries and cultures used various student self-report surveys to assess this inherently subjective construct. The Quality of School Life Scale (QSL; Epstein & McPartland, 1976) yielded the earliest multi-item measure of school satisfaction. The QSL includes a five-item Satisfaction with School scale (e.g., "The school and I are like: Good Friends, Friends, Distant Relatives, Strangers, or Enemies"), in addition to two scales assessing students' commitment to classwork and teacher–student relationship quality. A more commonly-used alternative is the eight-item School Satisfaction scale of the Multidimensional Students' Life Satisfaction Scale (MSLSS; Huebner, 1994). Students rate the extent to which they agree with statements like, "I look forward to going to school." The school satisfaction scales of the MSLSS and QSL both have acceptable psychometric properties. Several studies cited in this chapter used the MSLSS (e.g., Coelho & Dell'Aglio, 2019; Moore et al., 2012; Torsheim et al., 2012; Vera et al., 2012; Weber & Huebner, 2015) and a few earlier publications used items from the QSL (e.g., Okun et al., 1990; Verkuyten & Thijs, 2002). In contrast to analyzing composite scores, some researchers have relied on a one-item school satisfaction indicator. Students make a global judgment of their happiness with their schooling experiences. For example, the Brief Multidimensional Students' Life Satisfaction Scale (BMSLSS; Seligson et al., 2003) contains one item that gauges students' satisfaction with school. Students respond to the item "I would describe my satisfaction with my school experience as..." on a seven-point scale from *terrible* to *delighted*. The BMSLSS school item was analyzed to report mean levels of middle school students' school satisfaction by Huebner et al. (2005). In the multinational Health Behavior in School-aged Children (HBSC) survey, students respond to the single item "How do you feel about school at present?" on a four-point scale from *I like it a lot* to *I don't like it at all* (http://www.hbsc.org/). The HBSC is supported by the World Health Organization and administered every four years to adolescents (ages 11–15) in dozens of nations throughout North America and Europe. Studies cited in this chapter that examined the HBSC school satisfaction item include Freeman et al. (2012) and Danielsen et al. (2011). Danielsen and colleagues (2011) provided some support for the construct validity of this single item indicator by finding that it loaded strongly on a factor comprised of several items of the MSLSS School Satisfaction scale. Some HBSC data report analyses on a dichotomized version of the school satisfaction item—high (*like it a lot*) versus low (any of the other three options: *like it a bit, don't like it very much,* or *don't like it at all*). Case in point, Löfstedt and colleagues (2020) examined school satisfaction ratings from students in 32 countries during 2002, 2006, 2010, 2014, and 2018, and concluded that while the proportion of girls reporting high school satisfaction remained steady in half of the countries, for boys the most common trend was an increase in high levels of school satisfaction.

Beyond the MSLSS, QSL, and single-item indicators, some researchers use composite scores of multiple items tapping general school satisfaction. For example, Randolph et al. (2009) developed the six-item Children's Overall Satisfaction with Schooling Scale (COSSS) for Finnish and Dutch children ages 7–12. Four items reflect general school satisfaction (e.g., "I like to go to school") that are conceptually aligned with the QSL Satisfaction with School scale. The other two items pertain to satisfaction with school learning (e.g., "Learning is fun"), akin to the QSL Commitment to Classwork scale. The COSSS was utilized to study intrapersonal and environmental predictors of school satisfaction (Randolph et al., 2010). Using the COSSS, Kangas et al. (2017) found a positive relationship between Finnish and Dutch students' school satisfaction and their satisfaction with the teacher in a playful learning environment that uses bodily actions and gameplay through the use of technology. Other studies with the COSSS identified inverse associations between school satisfaction and social exclusion and stress (Satici, 2020).

Renshaw and colleagues (2015) advanced the 16-item Student Subjective Well-being Questionnaire (SSWQ). The SSWQ includes four subscales that measure school connectedness, academic efficacy, the joy of learning, and educational purpose. These subscales were selected to represent four constructs: school-specific relationships, educational performance and learning behaviors, affective experiences at or about the school, and holistic evaluations of or orientations toward one's school experiences. Renshaw et al. found that the SSWQ had moderate-to-strong positive correlations with two concurrent validity measures, the Student Prosociality Scale and the Academic Perseverance Scale, suggesting the importance of all of these constructs on youth development.

In sum, school satisfaction can be reliably assessed through the use of single-item indicators or multi-item measures that yield a composite score. In terms of practicality, the brevity of many of the aforementioned measures lends to ease of assessment of school satisfaction in research and practice. Of note, studies of school satisfaction that measure the construct indirectly and infer school satisfaction based on conceptually relevant school experiences (e.g., the SSWQ) may yield different findings than studies that use direct questions about students' satisfaction with their school experiences (e.g., the MSLSS, or the HBSC school satisfaction item).

Correlates of School Satisfaction

Factors that contribute to how students judge their school life quality include an array of intrapersonal variables and environmental contexts within and outside of school.

Intrapersonal Factors

The following sections summarize how school satisfaction varies as a function of student factors outside the school's direct realm, including students' cognitive patterns (i.e., perceptions of their abilities and control over their circumstances) and some demographic features such as age and gender. Individual-level variables that have been examined but not associated with school satisfaction include students' socioeconomic circumstances and perceived economic stress (Fang et al., 2016; Huebner et al., 2001).

Age

Throughout the world, school satisfaction appears to decline as students age. Even within elementary school children, younger Finnish and Dutch children reported greater school satisfaction than their older peers (Randolph et al., 2010). Decreasing mean levels of school satisfaction have been observed among cross-sectional samples of American students in Grades 1–8 (Okun et al., 1990) and Grades 6–8 (Elmore & Huebner, 2010); Chinese students in Grades 3–6 (Hui & Sun, 2010) and Grades 4–11 (Liu et al., 2016); Polish students aged 8–12 (Strózik et al., 2016), and Norwegian 13- and 15-year-old boys and girls (Danielsen et al., 2011). Multiyear longitudinal studies are needed to verify which age or grade levels may drive the decreasing trends in school satisfaction that have been observed in groups from different developmental levels, and to rule out potential cohort effects.

Gender

Across developmental levels and countries, girls have generally been found to be happier with school. Concerning children, European girls (median age of 10) from three elementary schools reported greater school satisfaction than their male classmates (Randolph et al., 2010). Adolescent females have also reported slightly higher mean levels of school satisfaction than their same-age male peers in large samples of youth from America (DeSantis King et al., 2006; Huebner et al., 2005), Norway (Danielsen et al., 2009), Ireland (Gilman et al., 2008), China (Liu et al., 2016), and Bangladesh (Hossain et al., 2019). In an examination of two waves of data from the Millennium Cohort Study, which follows a representative sample of children born between 2000 and 2002 in the United Kingdom, Arciuli and Emerson (2020) also observed higher school satisfaction among 11-year-old girls as compared to that of 11-year-old boys. However, at the next follow-up period at age 14, boys reported significantly higher school satisfaction than girls. This potentially age-specific exception to a seemingly robust trend may reflect the higher prevalence of mental health problems such as depression in teenage girls, and a particularly strong inverse link between mental health difficulties and school satisfaction for 14-year-old girls (Arciuli & Emerson, 2020). More research is needed that tracks school satisfaction on an annual basis among sizeable samples of youth from various demographic groups. In one such two-wave study of nearly 6,000 secondary students in Germany, Scharenberg (2016) found higher school satisfaction levels among girls compared to boys during Grades 7 and 8, with significant declines in mean school satisfaction scores across time for both gender groups.

Cognitive Variables

The internal variables that co-occur most strongly with higher school satisfaction are positive self-views: high self-esteem (Vera et al., 2012), confidence in one's academic and social abilities (Briones & Tabernero, 2012), and perception of an internal locus of control (Huebner et al., 2001; Huebner & Gilman, 2006). Stricker et al. (2019) investigated school satisfaction with multiple facets of perfectionism. They found that German high school students who had greater school satisfaction were more likely to report higher personal standards and organization levels, and less likely to report doubts about actions. Higher gratitude levels also predict greater school satisfaction, an association mediated by prosocial behavior (Tian et al., 2014). In research on the relationship between adolescent personality traits and school satisfaction, openness had the strongest positive association with school satisfaction, perhaps because this trait aligned well with opportunities at school to master new things (Weber & Huebner, 2015).

Classroom Context

Aspects of the classroom environment investigated concerning students' school satisfaction include demographic features of the classroom composition and school interpersonal relationships. These contextual variables influence the frequency with which students experience positive emotions during the school day. Early research found that such emotional and social experiences at school were among the strongest correlates of students' school satisfaction (Epstein & McPartland, 1976). Studies with students from China (Tian et al., 2015), Scotland (Karatzias et al., 2002), and the United States (Lewis et al., 2009) have affirmed that students' school satisfaction seems particularly tied to frequency of affective experiences in school. Higher positive affect is related to higher school satisfaction, and negative affect correlates negatively with school satisfaction.

Classroom Composition

There may be a curvilinear relationship between school satisfaction and class size. Randolph et al. (2010) found that elementary school students in classes of around 20 students reported higher school satisfaction than students in classes that were relatively small (i.e., fewer than 15 students) or large (i.e., more than 25 students). Research is mixed as to whether school satisfaction is affected by the demographic features of students in the classroom. Randolph and colleagues (2010) found that the proportion of students in the class of the same gender as the participating student was un-related to school satisfaction for elementary school students. Scharenberg's (2016) study of middle school students' school satisfaction found that classrooms comprised of more students with higher family socioeconomic situations (indicated by parent occupational level) and more immigrant students predicted greater school satisfaction at the end of eighth grade.

Classroom Relationships

Greater perceptions of social support from people at school (i.e., classmates and especially teachers) consistently relate to higher levels of school satisfaction, from teenagers in European countries (Danielsen et al., 2009, 2011) to elementary, middle, and high school students in China (Liu et al., 2016). These supportive relationships likely engender a climate of care that facilitates students' positive appraisals of their schooling experiences. In Baker's (1998) seminal study of intrapersonal and environmental predictors of school satisfaction among low-income, urban, African-American elementary school students, children's perceived quality of their classroom's social climate (in-cluding perceptions of teacher care and fairness) emerged as the strongest correlate of their school satisfaction. Classroom social climate distinguished students with the lowest school satisfaction more than objective indicators of teacher behavior (i.e., the observed frequency of negative or positive teacher–student interactions) or student perceptions of general social support at school (Baker, 1999).

Satisfaction with school is linked explicitly with the student-teacher relationship quality (Whitley et al., 2012), often measured as the students' perceived social support they receive from teachers (Hui & Sun, 2010; Tomyn & Cummins, 2011). Case in point, an analysis of data from over 23,000 students (in Grades 8 and 10) from seven countries found that teacher support was at least twice as strong of a predictor of school satisfaction than classmate support in all contexts, from North American to European countries (Torsheim et al., 2012). A longitudinal study ex-amining different school-related social support sources (i.e., teacher, peer, and family) revealed teacher–student relationships explained the largest amount of variance in American middle school students' school satisfaction (Jiang et al., 2013). In examining sources of school-related social sup-port among a large sample of students from China, teacher support was the greatest predictor of school satisfaction for elementary school students (especially boys) and high school students. For middle school students, classmate support was particularly influential (Liu et al., 2016). Beyond perceived support, teacher characteristics such as promoting student autonomy, personality, and even gender play a role in students' school satisfaction. Regarding autonomy support, teenagers from collectivist and individualistic societies alike reported greater school satisfaction when they perceived their teachers were more receptive to students' points of view and feelings, and afforded students choice and options in class (Ferguson et al., 2010). Among elementary school students in Finland and the Netherlands, greater teacher likeability was the most influential classroom fac-tor associated with school satisfaction (Randolph et al., 2010). Notably, Arens and Morin (2016) found that school satisfaction and perceived teacher support are diminished among students whose teachers report more emotional exhaustion.

Regarding the particular influence of relationships with classmates, students who feel more attached to their peers report greater school satisfaction, even one year later (Elmore & Huebner, 2010). Middle school students who sought social support in response to peer stressors reported greater levels of school satisfaction (Jiang et al., 2019). As aforementioned, classroom support outweighed the importance of teacher support for Chinese middle school students (Liu et al., 2016); in that sample, the positive association between classmate support and school satisfaction was particularly strong for middle school girls. In contrast, peer victimization (i.e., name-calling, social exclusion) has been linked indirectly to lower school satisfaction in Dutch elementary school students (Verkuyten & Thijs, 2002) and Brazilian high school students (Valente & Berry, 2017). In German secondary schools, students who reported liking school a lot were three to ten times *less likely* to be involved in physical bullying (i.e., repeated acts of aggression) or cyberbullying (i.e., bullying using information and communication technologies), either as victims or perpetrators or both, as compared to their peers with moderate to low levels of school satisfaction (Wachs, 2012). Similarly, Moore et al. (2012) reported that school satisfaction was inversely related to the frequency of cyberbullying and victimization among American middle school students.

School Climate

Social relationships in the classroom fall under the broader umbrella of school climate. Multidimensional assessments of school climate among secondary students in Brazil (Coelho & Dell'Aglio, 2019) and the United States (Zullig et al., 2011) indicate that approximately one-third of the variability in school satisfaction levels is explained by adolescents' perceptions of equity, fairness, order, and positive relationships within their school. Multiple aspects of school climate are relevant to school satisfaction. Within a sample of over 2,000 American middle and high school students, school satisfaction was uniquely associated with five dimensions, including student perceptions of academic support, student-teacher relationships, school connectedness, academic satisfaction, and order and discipline (Zullig et al., 2011). Concerning the latter dimension, elementary school children who perceive a more disciplined and academically-oriented classroom environment also experience greater school satisfaction (Verkuyten & Thijs, 2002). Other aspects of school climate that co-occur with greater school satisfaction among high school students include parent involvement in schooling (Suldo et al., 2008) and perceived safety at school (Tomyn & Cummins, 2011).

Environments beyond School

Students' school satisfaction appears influenced not only by the classroom context but also by their relationships with significant others (i.e., family) and the experience of stress in their lives. For example, lower school satisfaction has been observed among students who experience more stressors (chronic strains and acute, significant events) and fewer resources in life areas beyond school, namely family and friends (Huebner et al., 2001). Family relationships, in particular, are among the largest environmental correlates of school satisfaction. For instance, American students who reported greater attachment to their parents reported higher school satisfaction levels concurrently, and one year later (Elmore & Huebner, 2010). Jiang and colleagues' (2013) examination of school-based sources of support in relation to school satisfaction found family support for learning uniquely predicted middle school students' end-of-year school satisfaction even after accounting for initial levels of teacher–student relationships, peer support, and family support. In addition to academic support, aspects of the parent-child relationship co-occur with higher school satisfaction include perceived social support (Danielsen et al., 2009; DeSantis King et al., 2006) and parental promotion of adolescent autonomy (Ferguson et al., 2010). In general, youths who are more satisfied with their family life (for reasons related to or outside of schooling) are also moderately more likely to report satisfaction with school (Vera et al., 2012; Whitley et al., 2012).

Perhaps in part because many stressors pertinent to youth occur in the family context, multiple studies have found that students who experience more frequent stressors also report lower school satisfaction. Case in point, in Baker's (1998) study of urban elementary school children, stress emerged as a greater contributor to students' school satisfaction than other robust correlates, including family satisfaction and social support at school. Correlational studies of American high school students yield moderate, inverse relationships between school satisfaction and perceived stress (Suldo et al., 2019). Similarly, Satici (2020) found that Turkish adolescents reporting greater stress also reported lower school satisfaction, with social isolation contributing to stress and diminished school satisfaction. In sum, stress inside and beyond the family generally contributes to diminished school satisfaction.

A thorough understanding of these intrapersonal and environmental correlates of school satisfaction is, in part, justified by the multiple benefits associated with liking school. As described in the next section, students who are more satisfied with school evidence superior academic adjustment and health.

Educational Outcomes Associated with School Satisfaction

Accumulating evidence suggests that liking school is not synonymous with performing well at school in terms of grades earned or academic skills acquired. The literature reviewed next illustrates null or relatively weak (but generally positive) associations between school satisfaction and objective indicators of academic success and stronger associations with in-school behavior and academic attitudes and motivation that facilitate continued learning.

Academic Achievement

Examinations of American adolescents in middle and high school have identified small but statistically significant, positive correlations between school satisfaction and students' grade point averages (GPA; Lewis et al., 2009; Suldo et al., 2008) or no associations between school satisfaction and either GPA or teacher nomination of a student as at-risk (Suldo et al., 2019; Whitley et al., 2012). Academic performance may be more tied to school satisfaction among children or youth in other countries. This association is seen in moderate, positive correlations between school satisfaction and math skills among Norwegian elementary school students (Cock & Halvari, 1999) and between school satisfaction and performance in language arts and math in Chinese elementary and middle school students (Fang, 2020).

In-School Behavior

Findings from multiple studies demonstrate that school satisfaction is associated with better in-school behavior; that is, compliance with school rules and academic engagement. One study examined the in-class behavior of African American elementary school children deemed at-risk due to high rates of poverty and high school dropout in their community (Baker, 1999). Students with the lowest school satisfaction (a) experienced more negative verbal teacher reprimands about their classroom behavior and (b) self-reported getting in more trouble at school than their peers in the top quartile of school satisfaction. Among Chinese students in Grades 3–5, prosocial behavior in and outside of class predicted subjective well-being in school (school satisfaction and frequency of positive and negative feelings at school), and the two increased one another over time (Liu et al., 2020; Su et al., 2019). Regarding engagement, a longitudinal study found that kindergarten students who reported liking school had greater classroom participation, which, in turn, predicted better achievement (Ladd et al., 2000). Analyses further suggested that gains in achievement were most likely a consequence of high initial school satisfaction, rather than a competing pathway in which high initial participation and achievement would cause children to like school more (Ladd et al., 2000).

These positive associations between school satisfaction and in-school behavior extend beyond the elementary school years. American high school students who were more satisfied with school also reported fewer disruptive behaviors at school, such as cheating, fighting, and skipping class (Suldo et al., 2008). Similarly, greater school satisfaction predicted less frequent misbehavior at school, such as off-task disruptive classroom behaviors, among seventh-grade girls in Hong Kong (Sun, 2016). Australian adolescents with higher school satisfaction levels also reported higher levels of satisfaction with their personal behavior at school, perhaps because engaging with peers and teachers in meaningful ways elicits positive feedback and creates a sense of control over one's schooling experiences (Tomyn & Cummins, 2011). Regarding the lasting benefits of school satisfaction, longitudinal studies have found school satisfaction predicted subsequent behavioral engagement at school. Specifically, American middle school students with greater school satisfaction reported less withdrawal in the classroom, academic resistance, and aggressive classroom behavior one year later (Elmore & Huebner, 2010). Secondary students with higher school satisfaction were more likely to be involved with extracurricular activities (Huebner & Gilman, 2006), including school-based arts programs (e.g., dance, drama, band, and choir; Geagea et al., 2017).

Adaptive Academic Attitudes and Beliefs

Students who experience higher school satisfaction also report substantially greater (a) *intrinsic motivation* for completion of schoolwork (i.e., completing homework and working in class due to enjoyment rather than only to avoid punishment or negative feelings like guilt; Cock & Halvari, 1999); and (b) *academic initiative* (i.e., goal-setting, concentration, and challenge-seeking in one's schoolwork; Danielsen et al., 2011). Danielsen and colleagues found that school satisfaction's facilitative effect on academic initiative was direct and indirect, through positive associations with increased perceived academic competence. Students with higher school satisfaction tend to feel more confident about their academic abilities. This relationship is indicated by mostly moderate correlations between school satisfaction and perceived academic competence among children (Baker, 1998; Huebner, 1994; Verkuyten & Thijs, 2002) and adolescents (Danielsen et al., 2009) from multiple cultures. These research findings, taken together, indicate that school satisfaction is associated with essential beliefs and mindsets that, in turn, are crucial to student willingness to approach academic challenges and utilize self-regulated learning strategies.

Relations with Mental and Physical Health Outcomes

In addition to experiencing an enhanced academic adjustment, students who like school may also evidence superior psychological functioning. Case in point, Huebner and Gilman (2006) compared the outcomes of three groups of American adolescents: students with the lowest 20% of school satisfaction scores, students with the highest 20% of scores, and a comparison sample of students in the average range of school satisfaction (middle 30% of scores). The group with very high school satisfaction reported the highest global life satisfaction and hope, and the lowest clinical levels of psychopathology. The opposite was found for students with very low school satisfaction who reported more anxiety and depression symptoms. Low school satisfaction may be a risk factor for mental health problems, whereas students who like school are generally happier with their lives (Minguez, 2020; Satici, 2020). This pattern is consistent with the theoretical link between school satisfaction and global life satisfaction. Such positive mental health may, in part, reflect resilience factors that co-occur with school satisfaction, including strengths in developmental assets (e.g., social and emotional competence, hopeful thinking; Sun, 2016) and use of effective coping behaviors (e.g., social support seeking; Jiang et al., 2019). Research on students' coping behaviors has yielded evidence to support school satisfaction as both an antecedent and consequence of strategies used to cope with stress. For instance, Jiang and colleagues (2019) found that middle school students who began the school year with higher school satisfaction were more apt to manage social stressors using coping styles that are generally considered more effective and productive (frequent use of social support seeking and problem-solving strategies; infrequent externalizing behaviors in response to peer stress) later in the year. In contrast, Evans et al. (2018) found more support for coping influencing school satisfaction. High school students who responded to school-related stressors by using effective coping strategies like problem-solving reported higher school satisfaction six months later.

In addition to ties with general mental health, studies suggest a positive relationship between school satisfaction and better physical health, as indicated by adaptive health choices such as discussing health-related issues with parents and following medical professionals' health advice (Borup & Holstein, 2006). In contrast, students with low school satisfaction are more likely to engage in health-risk behaviors, including smoking, drinking, regular marijuana use, and sexual activity (Hoff et al., 2010; Takakura et al., 2010). Research has also shown students with disabilities (e.g., learning, memory, physical health, or social impairments) report lower school satisfaction levels than students without disabilities. This association is partially related to individuals with disabilities experiencing more social problems at school, such as less teacher support and more frequent bullying (Arciuli et al., 2019). Studies are needed to determine associations between school satisfaction and linear indicators of physical health such as frequency of illness and physical fitness. Nevertheless, existing research suggests that school satisfaction is linked to better choices that facilitate physical health, in addition to superior academic and psychological well-being.

Variations in School Satisfaction across Countries and Cultural Groups

Studies of youth from multiple continents afford examinations of differences in mean levels and correlates of school satisfaction among students from different countries in North America, Europe, and Asia. For instance, an international report of 14 countries indicated variability in national levels of school satisfaction of 10-year-olds, with over 90% of children in Rwanda, Nepal, Uganda, and Algeria reporting they like going to school compared to around 60% of children in Canada and the United States, and only 43% of students in Israel (Dinisman & Rees, 2014). Despite differences in mean scores at the country level (see also Gilman et al., 2008), there is a remarkable similarity in the predictors of school satisfaction across adolescents from different cultures/countries, likely because most teenagers strive for independence. Thus, mean differences in school satisfaction may reflect differences in how countries provide opportunities for adolescents to experience relatedness, autonomy, and competence. For example, in a study with samples of high school-age students from three countries (Demark, Korea, United States), the lower level of school satisfaction reported by the Korean sample appeared to mainly reflect the lower perceptions of autonomy support offered by parents and particularly teachers in that country (Ferguson et al., 2010). Even among individualistic cultures, greater school satisfaction was evidenced in Denmark, where youth perceived greater parent support for autonomy.

In consideration of the positive link between perceived autonomy support and school satisfaction in Korean students, Ferguson et al. (2010) concluded that their findings contradict the notion that autonomy support is unimportant in collectivistic cultures. Moreover, Tian and colleagues (2014) found that Chinese teenagers' school-related subjective well-being could be reliably predicted by the extent to which youth perceive each of the three basic psychological needs were satisfied at school. Specifically, greater perceptions of autonomy, relatedness, and competence all predicted higher school satisfaction six weeks later, controlling for initial school satisfaction. Regarding the universal importance of basic psychological needs such as relatedness to school satisfaction, research with large samples of teenagers in North America (Canada) and Europe (Norway and Romania) yielded moderate to large correlations between school satisfaction and perceived teacher support and classmate support (Freeman et al., 2012).

Research with different cultural groups within a country suggests that immigrant adolescents' school satisfaction is not necessarily at-risk; rather, immigrant youth may experience particularly positive academic adjustment and outcomes. For example, greater satisfaction with schooling and the learning process was reported by immigrant secondary students in Spain (Briones & Tabernero, 2012) and Chile (Mera-Lemp et al., 2020) in comparison to school satisfaction levels of students native to the country. Among Chinese migrant children and adolescents, Fang (2020) found that students with the highest school satisfaction (and achievement) were highly enculturated while maintaining their original culture. Mera-Lamp et al. (2020) further found that positive beliefs about one's ability to interact successfully with individuals from other cultures predicted higher school satisfaction for both immigrant and native students, underscoring the salience of social relatedness to well-being at school. In sum, fluency in the native culture and respect for different cultures promote school satisfaction, and immigrant students' bicultural experiences may contain more natural opportunities to develop cross-cultural competence.

Educational Applications: Promoting School Satisfaction

Given the modest associations between academic performance and school satisfaction, an exclusive focus on student's academic learning is unlikely to simultaneously influence positive affect pertinent to schooling. Instead, a dual focus on educational achievement and students' emotional experiences at and about school is necessary to ensure academic well-being. Notably, there are no known adverse consequences of considerably high school satisfaction; instead, associations between school satisfaction and desirable outcomes, such as social relationships, increase linearly through the highest level of school satisfaction (Whitley et al., 2012). Thus, attempting to improve students' happiness with their schooling experiences is more likely to enhance functioning than to do harm. The next sections describe logical directions for practices that target identified school satisfaction correlates, and report efficacy of interventions that have been examined in relation to impact on school satisfaction.

Support Adolescents' Strivings for Relatedness, Competence, and Autonomy

The desire for relatedness and competence in the classroom might best be addressed by enhancing students' interpersonal connections at school and providing appropriately challenging and engaging academic and extracurricular experiences. Regarding autonomy, Ferguson and colleagues (2010) summarize that greater well-being follows from perceiving that caregiving adults (including teachers) consider a student's perspective and permit the student as much choice as possible. Students whose academic pursuits are in line with their ideals and desires are likely to experience greater satisfaction with school, including when they are complying with adults' suggestions consistent with their beliefs. Offering multiple curricular and extracurricular opportunities that can potentially align with students' diverse interests and abilities may facilitate needs satisfaction and positive academic outcomes. Indeed, Geagea et al.'s (2017) survey research found that high school students in Australia who participated in extracurricular art activities reported higher levels of school satisfaction as well as a greater reported likelihood of attending university after high school.

As noted earlier in this chapter, most studies find that boys have lower school satisfaction relative to same-age girls (Danielsen et al., 2009; DeSantis King et al., 2006; Hossain et al.,

2019; Liu et al., 2016; Randolph et al., 2010). This phenomenon may be due to expectations for classroom behavior that are a closer match to traditional gender roles that emphasize compliance, or girls' traditional emphasis on relatedness (vs. independence; Randolph et al., 2010). Vera and colleagues (2012) encourage educators to promote experiences particularly likely to enhance boys' school belonging, such as participation in sports teams or clubs that afford leadership opportunities. Creating a classroom context where all students feel free to express themselves and pursue personal goals, feel attached and supported, and have opportunities for mastery experiences is likely to foster high school satisfaction for males and females alike, from diverse cultural groups.

Enhance Students' Interpersonal Connections at Schools

Correlational research suggests fostering a positive classroom climate, complete with strong teacher–student and student–student interpersonal bonds, may hold great potential for facilitating children's school satisfaction. Regarding student-teacher relationships, school administrators may want to consider factors other than teachers' instructional skills and heed Randolph and colleagues' (2010) suggestion to strive to employ teachers who are "nice and likeable" (p. 203). Students themselves can contribute to positive classroom relationships by deliberately initiating and strengthening relationships with peers, teachers, and the community through engaging in service-learning projects, classroom responsibilities, and collaborative learning activities.

At the school-wide level, positive peer relationships can be facilitated through direct teaching of social skills in addition to a proactive, preventative approach to peer victimization. Encouraging school clubs, sports, and other elective afterschool activities may also facilitate bonds between students outside the classroom. Indeed, bullied children (i.e., ages 9–12) who were provided with older peer mentors experienced significant increases in school satisfaction compared to children in a comparison group at the end of the school year. Roach (2014) noted that this result is consistent with the positive effects of participation in any extracurricular school-based activity that typically enhances school belonging and enjoyment. Beyond participation in extracurricular activities, other behavioral engagement indicators at school include on-task, compliant classroom behavior.

As aforementioned, students who misbehave at school are at-risk for experiencing diminished school satisfaction (Elmore & Huebner, 2010; Suldo et al., 2008; Sun, 2016). School administrators might consider promising alternative approaches like school-based Teen Court rather than responding to conduct violations with punishments like school suspensions. Such programs "emphasize adolescent offenders taking responsibility for their transgressions by repairing the harm they have caused to victims and/or the community" (Smokowski et al., 2020, p. 567). An examination of student outcomes in 24 secondary schools randomly assigned to use Teen Court or traditional discipline for students referred for conduct problems (e.g., disruptive classroom behavior, fighting, being out of area) found significant positive effects for high schools (but not middle schools). In particular, students in high schools with Teen Court experienced significant increases in school satisfaction, as well as significant reductions in their number of delinquent friends and a trend for a decrease in bullying victimization (from 23% to 13% of students bullied after two years of intervention, vs. 23% to 18% in control schools). Such findings demonstrate how school-wide programs that emphasize repairing relationships and empowering students to take responsibility for (and improve) misbehavior might alter the trajectory of school satisfaction for the student body.

Cultivate Gratitude and Other Positive Emotions in the Classroom

As noted previously, Tian and colleagues (2014) found that students with higher gratitude experience greater school satisfaction, in part because they display more altruistic and prosocial behavior toward others. Given such observed relationships between variables, it follows that interventions intended to cultivate gratitude may positively impact relationships and school satisfaction. In one such efficacy study, primary school students in the United Kingdom who kept gratitude journals daily for four weeks experienced the expected increases in gratitude, and an increased sense of school belonging not seen among peers in an active control condition (Diebel et al., 2016). Although Diebel et al. did not directly assess school satisfaction, Froh and colleagues (2008) examined the effects of a two-week gratitude intervention on a range of middle school students' outcomes. They found significant positive effects of daily gratitude journaling on the school satisfaction item within the BMSLSS at postintervention and three-week follow-up. Findings from these studies support that prompting students to list three to five things that they were grateful or thankful for since yesterday may be one promising method of improving school satisfaction in elementary and secondary students. Numerous other positive psychology interventions that evoke positive emotions in the classroom are reviewed elsewhere (e.g., Shankland & Rossett, 2017). Although few such positive activities have yet to be examined experimentally concerning school satisfaction changes, their known effect on subjective well-being holds promise given associations between positive affect and school satisfaction (Lewis et al., 2009; Tian et al., 2015).

Consider Children's Contexts Outside of Schools

Students in classrooms come from home circumstances and social networks that vary by stability and stress. Children's stressors range from chronic tension (e.g., family conflict, illness, poverty, and peer victimization) to significant household changes resulting from significant adults' legal, economic, and interpersonal problems. The effects of stress endure beyond a child's daily exit from the home or problematic peer interactions. Given that children who endure more significant stress appear at risk for diminished school satisfaction, educators have an even greater rationale for enacting formal mechanisms to identify students incurring environmental stressors and refer these students for targeted supports. These supports could strengthen coping skills (e.g., increased use of supporting seeking and problem-solving strategies; Evans et al., 2018; Jiang et al., 2019) and relationships such as peer mentoring programs (Roach, 2014). Other supports might be family-based and tailored to helping students and their caregivers who are experiencing a particular stressor. Case in point, Harrison et al. (2017) evaluated the Child-Caregiver-Advocacy Resilience (ChildCARE) intervention, developed for use with students ages 6–17 years old who have at least one biological parent with HIV/AIDS. The goals of ChildCARE are to build students' internal resilience assets such as coping and hope, and external assets such as positive parenting skills and community support. In a sample of 790 students drawn from 30 schools in central China, the child- and parent-focused components of the intervention had a positive effect on students' school satisfaction over an 18-month period, in addition to positive effects on other educational outcomes such as academic achievement and interest in school (Harrison et al., 2017). Such research illustrates that preventative school-based interventions that view students holistically and address stressors stemming from a different setting (e.g., home) can lead to improvements in school satisfaction.

Directions for Future Research

School satisfaction is one of many important academic outcomes to be monitored and fostered. There are multiple brief and reliable measures of school satisfaction that can be used for such purposes, including to evaluate the impact of any school-wide improvement effort. Garcia-Vazquez's (2017) evaluation of Schools for Health (SHE) in secondary schools illustrates a comprehensive approach to outcomes assessment. SHE is a whole-school approach to health promotion through a focus on healthy school policies, school environments conducive to physical activity, building healthy relationships at school, developing students' knowledge and skills relevant to healthy choices, and linking community resources to schools including to provide health services. Compared to students in schools without SHE, a higher percentage of students in schools with SHE reported high school satisfaction in addition to other desirable outcomes more directly associated with intervention goals such as abstinence from alcohol and positive student-teacher relationships (Garcia-Vazquez, 2017). In contrast to, or to complement, the more common deficit-based approaches to monitoring student outcomes which focus on indicators of emotional and behavioral problems, measures of school satisfaction provide a way to assess positive functioning when monitoring the effect of any educational initiative.

The growing body of research on school satisfaction reviewed in this chapter made possible the recommendations for how to systematically improve students' satisfaction with their schooling experiences. In the eight years since the publication of the second edition of this handbook, a few experimental and longitudinal observational studies appeared that began to document which targeted educational interventions resulted in improvements in students' school satisfaction (e.g., Harrison et al., 2017; Smokowski et al., 2020). Much more research is needed to determine if students' school satisfaction changes as a function of the targets described in this manuscript's application section. Further, the mediators of programs and practices that promote school satisfaction need to be identified. For instance, perhaps strengthened interpersonal connections or pride in one's school mediate associations between activity involvement and school satisfaction. Similarly, studies that identify the extent to which changes in school satisfaction covary with academic performance (e.g., student engagement, course grades, academic skills, and persistence in education) would help elucidate the interrelationships between these two crucial student outcomes.

References

Arciuli, J., & Emerson, E. (2020). Type of disability, gender, and age affect school satisfaction: Findings from the UK Millennium Cohort Study. *British Journal of Educational Psychology, 90*(3), 870–885. doi:10.1111/bjep.12344.

Arciuli, J., Emerson, E., & Llewellyn, G. (2019). Adolescents' self-report of school satisfaction: The interaction between disability and gender. *School Psychology, 34*(2), 148–158. http://dx.doi.org/10.1037/spq0000275

Arens, A. K., & Morin, A. J. S. (2016). Relations between teachers' emotional exhaustion and students' educational outcomes. *Journal of Educational Psychology, 108*(6), 800–813. https://doi-org.ezproxy.lib.usf.edu/10.1037/edu0000105.supp

Baker, J. A. (1998). The social context of school satisfaction among urban, low-income, African-American students. *School Psychology Quarterly, 13*, 25–44. doi:10.1037/h0088970

Baker, J. A. (1999). Teacher–student interaction in urban at-risk classrooms: Differential behavior, relationship quality, and student satisfaction with school. *Elementary School Journal, 100*, 57–70. doi:10.1086/461943

Baker, J. A., & Maupin, A. N. (2009). School satisfaction and children's positive school adjustment. In R. Gilman, E. S. Huebner, & M. J. Furlong (Eds.), *Handbook of positive psychology in the schools* (pp. 189–196). Routledge.

Borup, I., & Holstein, B. (2006). Does poor school satisfaction inhibit positive outcome of health promotion at school? A cross-sectional study of schoolchildren's response to health dialogues with school health nurses. *Journal of Adolescent Health, 38*, 758–760. doi:10.1016/j.jadohealth.2005.05.017

Briones, E., & Tabernero, C. (2012). Social cognitive and demographic factors related to adolescents' intrinsic satisfaction with school. *Social Psychology of Education, 15*, 219–232. doi:10.1007/s11218-012-9176-4

Casas, F., Bălțătescu, S., Bertran, I., González, M., & Hatos, A. (2013). School satisfaction among adolescents: Testing different indicators for its measurement and its relationship with overall life satisfaction and subjective well-being in Romania and Spain. *Social Indicators Research, 111*(3), 665–681. doi:10.1007/s11205-012-0025-9

Cock, D., & Halvari, H. (1999). Relations among achievement motives, autonomy, performance in mathematics, and satisfaction of pupils in elementary school. *Psychological Reports, 84*, 983–997. doi:10.2466/PR0.84.3.983–997

Coelho, C. C. D. A., & Dell'Aglio, D. D. (2019). School climate and school satisfaction among high school adolescents. *Psicologia: teoria e prática, 21*(1), 265–281.

Danielsen, A., Breivik, K., & Wold, B. (2011). Do perceived academic competence and school satisfaction mediate the relationships between perceived support provided by teachers and classmates, and academic initiative? *Scandinavian Journal of Educational Research, 55*, 379–401. doi:10.1080/00313831.2011.587322

Danielsen, A., Samdal, O., Hetland, J., & Wold, B. (2009). School-related social support and students' perceived life satisfaction. *Journal of Educational Research, 102*, 303–318. doi:10.3200/JOER.102.4.303–320

DeSantis King, A., Huebner, S., Suldo, S., & Valois, R. (2006). An ecological view of school satisfaction in adolescence: Linkages between social support and behavior problems. *Applied Research in Quality of Life, 1*, 279–295. doi:10.1007/s11482-007-9021-7

Diebel, T., Woodcock, C., Cooper, C., & Brignell, C. (2016). Establishing the effectiveness of a gratitude diary intervention on children's sense of school belonging. *Educational and Child Psychology / Division of Educational and Child Psychology, 2*, 117.

Dinisman, T., & Rees, G. (2014). Findings from the first wave of data collection. *Children's Worlds: International Survey of Children's Well-Being*. Retrieved from https://isciweb.org/wp-content/uploads/2019/12/FirstWaveReport_FINAL2.pdf

Elmore, G., & Huebner, S. (2010). Adolescents' satisfaction with school experiences: Relationships with demographics, attachment relationships, and school engagement behavior. *Psychology in the Schools, 47*, 525–537. doi:10.1002/pits.20488

Epstein, J., & McPartland, J. (1976). The concept and measurement of the quality of school life. *American Educational Research Journal, 13*, 15–30. doi:10.2307/1162551

Evans, P., Martin, A. J., & Ivcevic, Z. (2018). Personality, coping, and school well-being: An investigation of high school students. *Social Psychology of Education, 21*, 1061–1080. doi: 10.1007/s11218-018-9456-8

Fang, L. (2020). Acculturation and academic achievement of rural to urban migrant youth: The role of school satisfaction and family closeness. *International Journal of Intercultural Relations, 74*, 149–160. https://doi-org.ezproxy.lib.usf.edu/10.1016/j.ijintrel.2019.11.006

Fang, L., Sun, R. C., & Yuen, M. (2016). Acculturation, economic stress, social relationships and school satisfaction among migrant children in urban China. *Journal of Happiness Studies, 17*(2), 507–531. https://doi.org/10.1007/s10902-014-9604-6

Ferguson, Y., Kasser, T., & Jahng, S. (2010). Differences in life satisfaction and school satisfaction among adolescents from three nations: The role of perceived autonomy support. *Journal of Research on Adolescence, 21*, 649–661. doi:10.1111/j.1532-7795.2010.00698.x

Freeman, J., Samdal, O., Băban, A., & Bancila, D. (2012). The relationship between school perceptions and psychosomatic complaints: Cross-country differences across Canada, Norway, and Romania. *School Mental Health, 4*, 95–104. doi:10.1007/s12310-011-9070-9

Froh, J. J., Sefick, W. J., & Emmons, R. A. (2008). Counting blessings in early adolescents: An experimental study of gratitude and subjective well-being. *Journal of School Psychology, 46*(2), 213–233. https://doi.org/10.1016/j.jsp.2007.03.005

Garcia-Vazquez, J. (2017). Effects of the School for Health network on students' behaviour in Asturias. *Health Promotion International, 32*, 271–279. doi:10.1093/heapro/dau076

Geagea, A., MacCallum, J., Vernon, L., & Barber, B. L. (2017). Critical links between arts activity participation, school satisfaction and university expectation for Australian high school students. *Australian Journal of Educational & Developmental Psychology, 15*, 53–65. doi:https://files.eric.ed.gov/fulltext/EJ1157110.pdf

Gilman, R., Huebner, S., Tian, L., Park, N., O'Byrne, J., Schiff, M., Sverko, D., & Langknecht, H. (2008). Cross-national adolescent multidimensional life satisfaction report: Analyses of mean scores and response style differences. *Journal of Youth and Adolescence, 37*, 142–154. doi:10.1007/s10964-007-9172-8

Harrison, S. E., Li, X., Zhang, J., Chi, P., Zhao, J., & Zhao, G. (2017). Improving school outcomes for children affected by parental HIV/AIDS: Evaluation of the ChildCARE Intervention at 6-, 12-, and 18-months. *School Psychology International, 38*, 264–286. doi:10.1177/0143034316689589

Hoff, D., Anderson, A., & Holstein, B. (2010). Poor school satisfaction and number of cannabis using peers within school classes as individual risk factors for cannabis use among adolescents. *School Psychology International, 31*, 547–556. doi:10.1177/0143034310382870

Hossain, S., O'Neill, S. C., & Strnadová, I. (2019). What really matters for students' school satisfaction in Bangladesh? *Psychology in the Schools, 56*(5), 670–689. doi:10.1002/pits.22226

Huebner, E. S. (1994). Preliminary development and validation of a multidimensional life satisfaction scale for children. *Psychological Assessment, 6*, 149–158. doi:10.1037/10403590.6.2.149

Huebner, E. S., Ash, C., & Laughlin, J. (2001). Life experiences, locus of control, and school satisfaction in adolescence. *Social Indicators Research, 55*, 167–183. doi:10.1023/A:1010939912548

Huebner, E. S., & Gilman, R. (2006). Students who like and dislike school. *Applied Research in Quality of Life, 1*, 139–150. doi:10.1007/s11482-006-9001-3

393

Huebner, E. S., Valois, R., Paxton, R., & Drane, W. (2005). Middle school students' perceptions of quality of life. *Journal of Happiness Studies, 6*, 15–24. doi:10.1007/s10902-004-1170-x

Hui, E., & Sun, R. (2010). Chinese children's perceived school satisfaction: The role of contextual and intra-personal factors. *Educational Psychology, 30*, 155–172. doi:10.1080/01443410903494452

Jiang, X., Fang, L., & Lyons, M. D. (2019). Does school satisfaction predict coping? A short-term longitudinal examination in early adolescents. *Psychology in the Schools, 56*(4), 582–594. doi:10.1002/pits.22210

Jiang, X., Huebner, E. S., & Sidall, J. (2013). A short-term longitudinal study of differential sources of school-related social support and adolescents' school satisfaction. *Social Indicators Research, 114*(3), 1073–1086. doi: 10.1007/s11205-012-0190-x

Kangas, M., Siklander, P., Randolph, J., & Ruokamo, H. (2017). Teachers' engagement and students' satisfaction with a playful learning environment. *Teaching and Teacher Education, 63*, 274–284. doi: 10.1016/j.tate.2016.12.018

Karatzias, A., Power, K., Flemming, J., Lennan, F., & Swanson, V. (2002). The role of demographics, personality variables and school stress on predicting school satisfaction/dissatisfaction: Review of the literature and research findings. *Educational Psychology, 22*, 33–50. doi: 10.1080/01443410120101233

Ladd, G., Buhs, E., & Seid, M. (2000). Children's initial sentiments about kindergarten: Is school liking an antecedent of early classroom participation and achievement? *Merrill-Palmer Quarterly, 46*, 255–279. Retrieved from https://www.jstor.org/stable/23093716

Lewis, A., Huebner, E. S., Reschly, A., & Valois, R. (2009). The incremental validity of positive emotions in predicting school functioning. *Journal of Psychoeducational Assessment, 27*, 397–408. doi:10.1177/0734282908330571

Liu, W., Mei, J., Tian, L., & Huebner, E. S. (2016). Age and gender differences in the relation between school-related social support and subjective well-being in school among students. *Social Indicators Research, 125*(3), 1065–1083. doi:10.1007/s11205-015-0873-1

Liu, W., Su, T., Tian, L., & Huebner, E. S. (2020). Prosocial behavior and subjective well-being in school among elementary school students: The mediating roles of the satisfaction of relatedness needs at school and self-esteem. *Applied Research in Quality of Life*. Retrieved from https://doi-org.ezproxy.lib.usf.edu/10.1007/s11482-020-09826-1

Löfstedt, P., García-Moya, I., Corell, M., Paniagua, C., Samdal, O., Välimaa, R., Lyyra, M., Currie, D., & Rasmussen, M. (2020). School satisfaction and school pressure in the WHO European Region and North America: An analysis of time trends (2002–2018) and patterns of co-occurrence in 32 countries. *Journal of Adolescent Health, 66*, S59–S69. doi:10.1016/j.jadohealth.2020.03.007

Mera-Lemp, M. J., Bilbao, M., & Basabe, N. (2020). School satisfaction in immigrant and Chilean students: The role of prejudice and cultural self-efficacy. *Frontiers in Psychology, 11*, 613585. doi: 10.3389/fpsyg.2020.613585

Minguez, A. M. (2020). Children's relationships and happiness: The role of family, friends, and the school in four European countries. *Journal of Happiness Studies, 21*, 1859–1878. doi:10.1007/s10902-019-00160-4

Moore, P. M., Huebner, E. S., & Hills, K. J. (2012). Electronic bullying and victimization and life satisfaction in middle school students. *Social Indicators Research, 107*(3), 429–447. https://doi.org/10.1007/s11205-011-9856-z

Noddings, N. (2003). *Happiness and education*. Cambridge University Press.

Okun, M. A., Braver, M. W., & Weir, R. M. (1990). Grade level differences in school satisfaction. *Social Indicators Research, 22*, 419–427. doi:10.1007/BF00303835

Randolph, J. J., Kangas, M., & Ruokamo, H. (2009). The preliminary development of the Children's Overall Satisfaction with Schooling Scale (COSSS). *Child Indicators Research, 2*, 79–93. doi:10.1007/s12187-008-9027-1

Randolph, J. J., Kangas, M., & Ruokamo, H. (2010). Predictors of Dutch and Finnish children's satisfaction with schooling. *Journal of Happiness Studies, 11*, 193–204. doi:10.1007/s10902-008-9131-4

Renshaw, T. L., Long, A. C., & Cook, C. R. (2015). Assessing adolescents' positive psychological functioning at school: Development and validation of the Student Subjective Wellbeing Questionnaire. *School Psychology Quarterly, 30*(4), 534–552. doi:10.1037/spq0000088

Roach, G. (2014). A helping hand? A study into an England-wide peer mentoring program to address bullying behavior. *Mentoring & Tutoring: Partnership in Learning, 22*, 210–223. doi:10.1080/13611267.2014.926663

Satici, B. (2020) Social exclusion and adolescent wellbeing: Stress, school satisfaction, and academic self-efficacy as multiple mediators. *The Educational and Developmental Psychologist, 37*, 67–74. doi:10.1017/edp.2020.7

Scharenberg, K. (2016). The interplay of social and ethnic classroom composition, tracking, and gender on students' school satisfaction. *Journal of Cognitive Education and Psychology, 15*(2), 320–346. doi:10.1891/1945-8959.15.2.320

Seligson, J. L., Huebner, E. S., & Valois, R. F. (2003). Preliminary validation of the Brief Multidimensional Students' Life Satisfaction Scale (BMSLSS). *Social Indicators Research, 61,* 121–145. doi:10.1023/A:1021326822957

Shankland, R., & Rosset, E. (2017). Review of brief school-based positive psychological interventions: A taster for teachers and educators. *Educational Psychology Review, 29*(2), 363–392. doi:10.1007/s10648-016-9357-3

Smokowski, P. R., Evans, C. B. R., Rose, R., & Bacallao, M (2020). A group randomized trial of school-based teen courts to address the school to prison pipeline, reduce aggression and violence, and enhance school safety in middle and high school students. *Journal of School Violence, 19,* 566–578. doi:10.1080/15388220.2020.1780133

Stricker, J., Schneider, M., & Preckel, F. (2019). School satisfaction differentially predicts multidimensional perfectionism one year later. *Personality and Individual Differences, 143,* 30–35. doi:10.1016/j.paid.2019.02.014

Strózik, D., Strózik, T., & Szwarc, K. (2016). The subjective well-being of school children. The first findings from the children's worlds study in Poland. *Child Indicators Research, 9*(1), 39–50. doi:10.1007/s12187-015-9312-8

Suldo, S., Shaffer, E., & Riley, K. (2008). A social-cognitive-behavioral model of academic predictors of adolescents' life satisfaction. *School Psychology Quarterly, 23,* 56–69. doi:10.1037/1045-3830.23.1.56

Suldo, S. M., Storey, E., O'Brennan, L. M., Shaunessy-Dedrick, E., Ferron, J. M., Dedrick, R. F., & Parker, J. S. (2019). Identifying high school freshmen with signs of emotional or academic risk: Screening methods appropriate for students in accelerated courses. *School Mental Health, 11*(2), 210–227. doi:10.1007/s12310-018-9297-9

Su, T., Tian, L., & Huebner, E. S. (2019). The reciprocal relations among prosocial behavior, satisfaction of relatedness needs at school, and subjective well-being in school: A three-wave cross-lagged study among Chinese elementary school students. *Current Psychology: A Journal for Diverse Perspectives on Diverse Psychological Issues.* doi:10.1007/s12144-019-00323-9

Sun, R. C. (2016). Student misbehavior in Hong Kong: The predictive role of positive youth development and school satisfaction. *Applied Research in Quality of Life, 11*(3), 773–789. https://doi.org/10.1007/s11482-015-9395-x

Takakura, M., Wake, N., & Kobayashi, M. (2010). The contextual effect of school satisfaction on health-risk behaviors in Japanese high school students. *Journal of School Health, 80*(11), 544–551. doi:10.1111/j.1746-1561.2010.00540.x

Tian, L., Chen, H., & Huebner, E. S. (2014). The longitudinal relationships between basic psychological needs satisfaction at school and school-related subjective well-being in adolescents. *Social Indicators Research, 119,* 353–372. doi:10.1007/s11205-013-0495-4

Tian, L., Chen, H., & Huebner, E. S. (2015). Development and validation of the brief adolescents' Subjective Well-Being in School Scale (BASWBSS). *Social Indicators Research, 120,* 615–634. doi: 10.1007/s11205-014-0603-0

Tian, L., Chu, S., & Huebner, E. S. (2016). The chain of relationships among gratitude, prosocial behavior and elementary school students' school satisfaction: The role of school affect. *Child Indicators Research, 9*(2), 515–532. doi:10.1007/s12187-015-9318-2

Tomyn, A. J., & Cummins, R. A. (2011). The subjective wellbeing of high-school students: Validating the Personal Wellbeing Index–School Children. *Social Indicators Research, 101,* 405–418. doi:10.1007/s11205-010-9668-6

Torsheim, T., Samdal, O., Rasmussen, M., Freeman, J., Griebler, R., & Dür, W. (2012). Cross-national measurement invariance of the Teacher and Classmate Support Scale. *Social Indicators Research, 105,* 145–160. doi:10.1007/s11205-010-9770-9

Valente, R. R., & Berry, B. J. (2017). Effects of perceived discrimination on the school satisfaction of Brazilian high school graduates. *Brasiliana-Journal for Brazilian Studies, 5*(1), 405–440. Retrieved from https://tidsskrift.dk/bras/article/view/22093

Vera, E. M., Moallem, B. I., Vacek, K. R., Blackmon, S., Coyle, L. D., Gomez, K. L. Lamp, K., Langrehr, K. J., Luginbuhl, P., Mull, M. K., Telander, K. J., & Steele, J. C. (2012). Gender differences in contextual predictors of urban, early adolescents' subjective well-being. *Journal of Multicultural Counseling and Development, 40,* 174–183. doi:10.1002/j.2161-1912.2012.00016.x

Verkuyten, M., & Thijs, J. (2002). School satisfaction of elementary school children: The role of performance, peer relations, ethnicity and gender. *Social Indicators Research, 59,* 203–228. doi:10.1023/A:1016279602893

Wachs, S. (2012). Moral disengagement and emotional and social difficulties in bullying and cyberbullying: Differences by participant role. *Emotional and Behavioural Difficulties, 17*, 347–360. doi:10.1080/1363275 2.2012.704318

Weber, M., & Huebner, E. S. (2015). Early adolescents' personality and life satisfaction: A closer look at global vs. domain-specific satisfaction. *Personality and Individual Differences, 83*, 31–36. https://doi.org/10.1016/j.paid.2015.03.042

Whitley, A. M., Huebner, E. S., Hills, K. J., & Valois, R. F. (2012). Can students be too happy in school? The optimal level of school satisfaction. *Applied Research in Quality of Life, 7*, 337–350. doi:10.1007/s11482-012-9167-9

Zullig, K., Huebner, S., & Patton, J. (2011). Relationships among school climate domains and school satisfaction. *Psychology in the Schools, 48*, 133–145. doi:10.1002/pits.20532

26

STUDENT VOICE

Youth Disrupting Barriers to Achieving the Good Life

Meagan O'Malley, Adam Voight, Regina J. Giraldo-García and Lisa Romero

Introduction

Do youth in schools have the right to define their subjective experience of well-being and to become informed about the sociopolitical forces that boost or constrict their well-being? After becoming conscious of sociopolitical forces that impose limits on their well-being, do youth in schools have the right to organize efforts meant to challenge and dismantle those forces? Is it acceptable for youth to disrupt and reform school policies and practices in order to gain access to resources that promote their well-being? Grappling with the tensions surfaced in these questions is inherent to the work of developing and installing a set of strategies collectively known as *student voice*.

Student voice strategies are organized around the principles that school-aged youth deserve a fundamental role in (a) defining what it means to be well, (b) identifying policies and practices that promote or interfere with their ability to be well, and (c) taking deliberate and meaningful action to influence change in youth-serving systems. Evidence of a mental health crisis among youth gives cause for broadening prevention and intervention approaches to integrate student voice strategies. Over the most recent decade, suicide rates increased 61.7% for high school-aged youth in the United States (i.e., 14–18 years), with suicide now the cause of one out of every three deaths of youth in this age group (Ivey-Stephenson et al., 2020). Among youth with some minoritized identities, prevalence rates are even more dire. 2019 Youth Risk Behavior Survey results show that one in six (15.2%) Black, non-Hispanic youth reported having attempted suicide, a rate that is significantly higher than that of White or Hispanic youth (Ivey-Stephenson et al., 2020). Moreover, nearly half (46.8%) of youth identifying as lesbian, gay, or bisexual had seriously considered attempting suicide, and nearly one in four (23.6%) had attempted suicide (Ivey-Stephenson et al., 2020). Evidence of persistent threats to the psychological well-being of our youth suggests that the time has come to expand traditional mental health promotion and illness prevention efforts, improving access to existing treatments, and evaluating new ones. Student voice strategies are appropriate for consideration in an expanded school-based mental health support framework, given evidence that they confer psychosocial benefits to participating youth and that they help redress systemic inequities affecting students marginalized by forces such as poverty, racism, ableism, and homophobia.

DOI: 10.4324/9781003013778-32

Adopting an *empowerment perspective* on childhood is essential for adopting and implementing student voice strategies (Langhout & Thomas, 2010). The empowerment perspective challenges school adults to expand their outlook on the capacity that school-aged youth possess to reason through complex social problems that influence their psychological well-being and to act as agents in addressing those problems. By seeking to draw out the personal narratives of well-being among young people in schools, student voice strategies complement more traditional approaches to psychological health promotion and intervention. This chapter aims to inspire researchers, mental health practitioners, and educators to integrate student voice into their efforts by (a) orienting readers to the origins and characteristics of student voice strategies, (b) providing a taxonomy of psychological well-being related interventions that include a student voice component, and (c) describing resources for designing, delivering, and monitoring outcomes of student voice interventions.

Philosophical and Theoretical Roots of Student Voice

In the following section, we offer an overview of theories and conceptual frameworks that inform the design and implementation of student voice strategies.

Child Rights

The *United Nations Convention on the Rights of the Child*, currently ratified by over 100 nations, provides an internationally-recognized declaration of the special rights assigned to individuals under the age of 18. By adhering to the convention, nations make a commitment to ensure that youth are "fully prepared to live an individual life in society and be brought up in...the spirit of peace, dignity, tolerance, freedom, equality, and solidarity" (U.N. Commission on Human Rights, 1990, p. 1). Two convention Articles are especially relevant to the topic of student voice as it applies to psychological well-being. Article 13(1) states, "The child shall have the right to freedom of expression; this right shall include freedom to seek, receive and impart information and ideas of all kinds, regardless of frontiers" (p. 5). Article 17 specifies that states shall "...ensure that the child has access to information and material from a diversity of national and international sources, especially those aimed at the promotion of his or her social, spiritual, and moral well-being and physical and mental health" (p. 6). Inspired by these Articles, a child rights framework specifies that young people must be respected as active society members who are expected to partake in the decisions that affect them. To influence those decisions effectively and to develop skills for independence, young people must be provided (a) access to timely and representative information relevant to their lives, (b) opportunities for expressing their needs, and (c) the material resources necessary to be psychologically and physically well.

A child rights framework challenges educators to question the limits of traditional response-to-illness approaches and reorient their practice to the proactive promotion of psychological well-being and the achievement of "self-stewardship" (Hart & Hart, 2014, p. 6). That children have, among other things, the freedom to develop and express their views regarding issues that affect them, including issues impacting psychological well-being, and the right to effective supports for psychological health promotion and disease prevention, are demands of a child rights framework, and are tenets of student voice (Hart & Hart, 2014). Adults facilitating student voice activities acknowledge that youth may encounter influential individuals and alliances that have the power to create and sustain barriers to youths' psychological well-being. Taking social action to challenge those powerful individuals and alliances is consistent with both a child's rights orientation and an empowerment perspective (Berg et al., 2009; Langhout & Thomas, 2010).

Ecological Systems Theory

Student voice strategies support young people as they investigate risks and assets associated with psychological well-being within their environments. When applied in the school setting, they target for action the constraints and opportunities provided within the school environment (Figure 26.1). Ecological systems theory (Bronfenbrenner, 1979) predicts that students in schools engage in ongoing adaptation to innumerable environmental influences. Some of these influences are immediately known to youth and others are not readily identified, but the influences nevertheless shape their thoughts, emotions, and behaviors in the classroom and other school contexts. To improve access to resources that promote psychological well-being, student voice work aims to bring into consciousness the environmental forces in their nested environments that shape students' well-being, to reveal opportunities to act upon their environments, and to provide skills for taking effective individual and collective action.

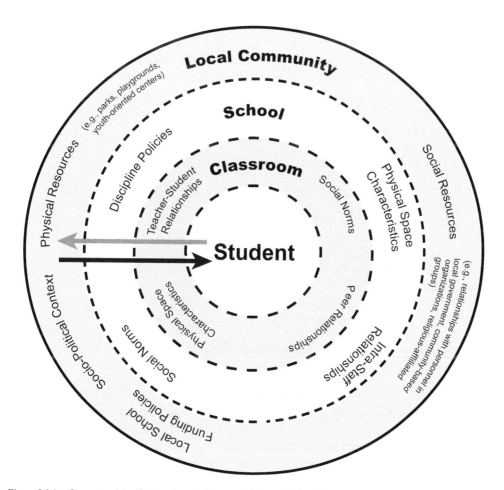

Figure 26.1 Opportunities for Student Influence in Nested School Environments

Critical Theory

Critical theory (Peters et al., 2003) emphasizes subjectivity and first-person accounts for describing one's experience, acknowledges the historical conditions that influence the present reality, and recognizes the influences that power and politics have in determining a person's reality. Critical theory posits that personal realities are constructed and communicated through storytelling to one's self and to others, and that through the process of exchanging these stories, individuals "impose order on experience and it on [them]" (Ladson-Billings & Tate, 2016, p. 21). Informed by critical theory, student voice strategies offer a unique approach to supporting the development of long-term psychological well-being of youth by (a) assisting students as they describe and examine their subjective realities of school and schooling, (b) supporting students as they explore the historical and present-day forces that define their current realities, and then (c) supporting their skills and opportunities for taking action to disrupt the conditions that sustain barriers to well-being.

Characteristics of Student Voice Strategies

As they apply to psychological well-being, student voice strategies exist on a continuum of student discretion and control (Figure 26.2). In their most diluted form, adults determine the parameters of the work, and define narrow roles for students, often as sources of data. Administering a survey with predetermined items measuring student well-being would be considered low on the continuum of student discretion and control. Adults set the parameters in advance, and students may have little say in how data from such surveys are used. Student voice strategies, in their most saturated form, are youth-led—student groups (a) define their decision-making procedures, (b) define the parameters of their work, (c) define their collective goals, (d) examine the school environment for policies and practices that support or interfere with their goals, and (e) take goal-directed collective action. At each stage, one or more adult allies facilitate access to the resources the student group needs to effectively engage in their work (e.g., obtaining meeting space, support access to data sources, such as school discipline data or cross-sectional student survey results, meant to inform decision-making). However, the adult does not weigh in on the value of the students' ideas or plans. When implemented with strong fidelity to its tenets, an example of a saturated student voice activity is youth-led participatory action research (YPAR), described in more detail in later sections of this chapter. Most strategies with a student voice component lie between the two poles, especially when school leaders approve them for implementation in schools.

In general, overly prescriptive, manualized interventions designed by adults and those interventions that *exclusively* target for change constructs internal to the student (e.g., emotion regulation) or student-expressed behavior (e.g., on-task behavior) do not fully cohere with the philosophy of the student voice approach. Instead, student voice strategies must be flexible enough to target for the transaction between students and their contexts as well as the contexts themselves. Student voice strategies give students the opportunity to evaluate the history, purpose, and value of a school's norms, policies, and practices, as well as the impact of those norms, policies, and practices on their psychological well-being. Moreover, student voice strategies cultivate skills for personal and collective action and provide opportunities that empower young people to seek meaningful change in their school environments. The principles of student voice may run contrary to approaches that exclusively ask a student to change her behavior to better adapt to the existing social and behavioral norms, policies, and practices in a school. For this reason, school leaders may

SPECTRUM OF STUDENT VOICE

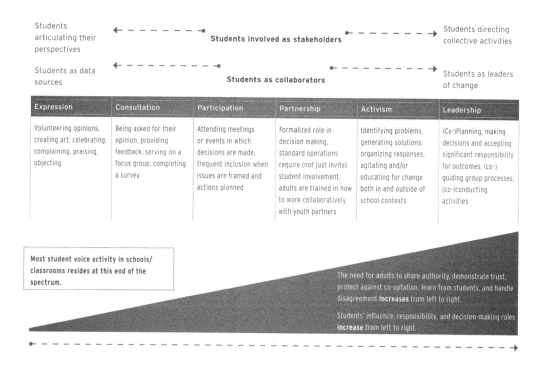

Students articulating their perspectives		Students involved as stakeholders			Students directing collective activities
Students as data sources		Students as collaborators			Students as leaders of change

Expression	Consultation	Participation	Partnership	Activism	Leadership
Volunteering opinions, creating art, celebrating, complaining, praising, objecting	Being asked for their opinion, providing feedback, serving on a focus group, completing a survey	Attending meetings or events in which decisions are made, frequent inclusion when issues are framed and actions planned	Formalized role in decision making, standard operations require (not just invite) student involvement, adults are trained in how to work collaboratively with youth partners	Identifying problems, generating solutions, organizing responses, agitating and/or educating for change both in and outside of school contexts	(Co-)Planning, making decisions and accepting significant responsibility for outcomes, (co-) guiding group processes, (co-)conducting activities

Most student voice activity in schools/classrooms resides at this end of the spectrum.

The need for adults to share authority, demonstrate trust, protect against co-optation, learn from students, and handle disagreement **increases** from left to right.

Students' influence, responsibility, and decision-making roles **increase** from left to right.

SOURCE: Toshalis, Eric & Michael Nakkula. 2012. *Motivation, Engagement, and Student Voice: The Students at the Center Series.* Boston, MA: Jobs for the Future. http://www.studentsatthecenterhub.org/resource/motivation-engagement-and-student-voice.

Figure 26.2   Spectrum of Student Voice

Note: Toshalis, E. & Nakkula, M. (2012). *Motivation, Engagement, and Student Voice: The Students at the Center Series.* Copyright 2014 by Jobs for the Future. Reprinted with permission.

have misgivings about permitting the implementation of highly-saturated student voice strategies on their campuses. Consequently, these strategies may be implemented more successfully in community-organized settings (for review of this issue, see Ozer et al., 2013) or in schools by intermediary organizations (Mitra, 2009a).

Psychosocial Benefits of Student Voice

For the reasons described prior, student voice strategies are primarily nonmanualized; they share philosophical tenets, but do not typically specify treatment protocols. Moreover, implementation of student voice strategies will vary based on the myriad characteristics of the school implementation context (e.g., leadership structure, size, and urbanicity; Kohfeldt et al., 2011). Because modification of the environment is inherent to student voice strategies, confounds exist to using a standard positivist model, wherein researchers attempt to control the environment to test for, and later replicate, treatment effects (Anyon et al., 2018). Furthermore, primarily because of the intensity of the facilitation demands of student voice interventions, many studies using student voice approaches involve small sample sizes for which quantified treatment effects are difficult to discern. Instead, student voice studies often use idiographic designs, such as case studies, and ethnographic methods to describe intervention impacts. Studies seeking nomothetic insights, such as those with group-based experimental designs are harder to locate in the student voice literature, although a few do exist (e.g., Voight & Velez, 2018). Described in the sections below are results from both types of studies across outcomes of interest to school-based professionals, education policymakers, and education researchers.

Psychological Well-Being Outcomes Associated with Student Voice

There are several developmental pathways by which participation in student voice may impact youth mental health and psychological well-being. Ballard and Ozer (2016) explain that involvement in student voice-related activities may confer benefits to mental health through mechanisms such as improving perceived control and psychological empowerment, providing cathartic opportunities for self-expression, encouraging a positive social identity, encouraging social connectedness, and creating meaningful improvements to systems that offer well-being-related supports and resources.

An increasingly robust volume of empirical evidence from various regions of the United States and international sources supports the hypothesis that participation in student voice activities contributes to improvements in psychological well-being of school-aged youth. In the northeastern United States, Berg et al. (2009) used the *Participatory Action Research Curriculum for Empowering Youth* (Institute for Community Research) with three high school-aged youth cohorts. In comparison to controls, participants reported significantly stronger perceptions of collective efficacy for social action and decreased drug use. Using an adaptation of the same curriculum, Ozer and Douglas (2013) used an experimental design to examine treatment effects of a student voice curriculum implemented within a stand-alone semester-long class in four California high schools. Significant but modest treatment effects were found for three dimensions of *psychological empowerment,* measured through a self-report survey: (a) sociopolitical skills (e.g., I can usually figure out how to get an adult to see my point of view, even if they don't agree with me); (b) motivation to influence one's school or community (e.g., I want to have as much say as possible in making decisions in my school); and (c) participatory behavior (e.g., I have spoken with adults in my school about issues that I want to improve at the school). Bertrand (2018) used an ethnographic approach and found that 15 students participating in a YPAR intervention in a K-8 school in Arizona described themselves as having better knowledge and being more able and willing to act in response to bullying associated with race, gender, and/or sexual orientation. Similarly, Halliday et al. (2018) found that among 10 Australian students ages 9–11 years, participation in a six-session YPAR intervention led to meaningful improvements in self-efficacy and engagement. Moreover, in comparison to declines observed in the control group, youth assigned to the YPAR treatment group showed no declines in indicators of well-being over the school year, suggesting that participation in YPAR may have had a prophylactic effect.

Evidence from program evaluations also points to meaningful well-being-related impacts of student voice. In one such evaluation, Chen et al. (2010) instructed approximately 50 high-school-aged females in five locations throughout the United States to use qualitative research methods to study the effects of *Girls Incorporated*, a nonprofit youth empowerment program. Using participatory research methods, the participants, referred to by the authors as "girl researchers," reported improved feelings of connectedness with peers and adults, improved awareness of educational resources and learning opportunities, and improved self-confidence (Chen et al., 2010). Representing perhaps the most direct link between student voice and traditional mental health conceptions is a program evaluation of *Directing Change Program and Student Film Contest*. In this California-based public health initiative, middle and high school-aged youth produce 60-second public service announcements about mental health challenges or suicide prevention (directingchangeca.org; Ghirardelli & Bye, 2016). The evaluators used a cross-sectional survey design with a participant-matched control and found that, compared to controls ($n = 268$), students who participated in *Directing Change* ($n = 131$) reported significantly improved understanding of characteristics of mental health and signs of suicide; improved knowledge of public resources such as crisis hotlines; improved willingness to discuss mental health needs with, and seek help for, themselves and their friends; and significant reductions in negative attitudes toward mental health and those with mental health needs.

This growing body of evidence indicates that participating in student voice activities improves attitudes toward mental health, awareness of mental health support, and willingness to seek help for oneself and one's peers. However, the degree to which participating in student voice activities directly ameliorates traditional mental health pathology indicators, such as anxiety and depression, has yet to be examined. That is, a literature search found no research linking participating in student voice to reduced symptoms of psychological distress. Revealed here is an opportunity for continued exploration of the appropriate use and limits of student voice as it pertains to psychological well-being. Illustrating an initial effort to apply student voice principles to reduce psychological distress, Atkins and Calkins (2020) developed a 14-session YPAR-based curriculum, *Seen and Heard: A School-Based Trauma Informed Student Voice Curriculum*. This curriculum was designed to be used in the postvention process of responding to shared crisis events (i.e., potentially-traumatic events impacting the whole school community), such as natural disasters or, pertinent to the current moment, the COVID-19 pandemic. Of course, this curriculum and others like it must be rigorously evaluated for treatment effects while acknowledging the limits of intervention and avoiding contraindications for vulnerable individuals.

Sociopolitical Outcomes with Student Voice

In addition to mental health and well-being-related benefits to participating in student voice, there is also strong evidence that students benefit in terms of their social and civic development. As described prior, a cluster-randomized experimental study of student voice in four urban California high schools showed that it had a significant effect on participating students' social and political skills, motivation to influence their schools and communities, and civic behavior (Ozer & Douglas, 2013). One study using a regression approach that did not account for selection bias (Holden et al., 2004) and another using qualitative methods (Morsillo & Prilleltensky, 2007) corroborated this latter finding in other samples. Qualitative studies have found that student participants develop an elevated sense of ownership over their school (Voight, 2015), increased agency and power in school decision-making (Giraldo-Garcia & Galletta, 2015; Ozer & Wright, 2012), improved connectedness to school and confidence as scholars (Taines, 2012), and heightened critical consciousness, empathy, trust, and cooperation (Ozer & Douglas, 2013).

Academic Outcomes Associated with Student Voice

Participation in student voice activities confers academic benefits as well. Several studies of student voice have employed experimental and quasi-experimental designs to support its promise in improving student education outcomes, primarily at the secondary level. Voight and Velez (2018) conducted a quasi-experimental study of YPAR as an elective course in six high schools located in a mid-sized school district in California, finding strong evidence for YPAR's beneficial impact on student attendance and mixed evidence for its impact on student's achievement. Investigating a series of Mexican American Studies elective courses using YPAR-infused curricula in four Tucson-area high schools, Cabrera et al. (2014) employed a nonequivalent control group design and found that course participation was associated with an increased likelihood of the students passing the Arizona state standardized test and graduating from high school.

Benefits of Student Voice for Youth from Historically Marginalized Groups

Kirshner and Ginwright (2012) define psychological wellness as a "sense of hope, empowerment, and purpose in life" (p. 12). They explain that student voice strategies are especially well-matched for young people who have experienced the psychological impact of marginalized or oppressed conditions (e.g., youth of color, socioeconomically disadvantaged youth, language-diverse youth, youth with disabilities, LGBTQ+ youth, and those with intersectional identities). This is because more saturated student voice strategies: (a) acknowledge the historical conditions, especially historical conditions of oppression, that impact present-day experience; (b) target for development skills for examining one's experience of the social conditions that impact their lives; and (c) build analytic skills as well as skills for agency and leadership (Anyon et al., 2018; Ozer, 2017). Indeed, a resilience framework predicts that participation in student voice activities is protective in the context of risk; examinations of that hypothesis have started to appear in the empirical literature.

Research examining the utility and impact of student voice participation on racially and ethnically minoritized youth, especially Latinx and Black youth, is flourishing (Gonzalez et al., 2016). Student voice projects have addressed topics relevant to the Latinx youth experience, such as negative stereotypes related to sexuality and childbearing (Gómez et al., 2014; Villaseñor et al., 2013), the school-to-prison pipeline (Irizarry & Raible, 2014), immigration (Cahill, 2010), and juvenile justice and mental health (Haskie-Mendoza et al., 2018). Among Black youth, studies using student voice have tackled myriad social issues, including deficit narratives of Black student achievement (Smith & Hope, 2020); racial discrimination and inequality at school (Hope et al., 2015); self-esteem, body image, and physical activity (Chard et al., 2020); and food access and insecurity (Akom et al., 2016). Later sections of this chapter provide an additional discussion of student voice-related outcomes associated with culturally-adapted interventions.

Student voice activities are often embedded in curricula used by groups organized around a shared minoritized identity, such as Gay-Straight Alliances (GSAs; gsanetwork.org) or Black Student Unions. These organizations use student voice principles, some more saturated than others, to affirm minoritized identities, to empower youth and build self-efficacy, and to give youth tools for social action. Poteat et al. (2018) found that as students participated more often in GSAs, they were more likely to be involved in advocacy-related social action and to report higher levels of personal agency. For students with disabilities, involvement in student voice-based interventions tailored to the Individualized Education Plan (IEP) process holds promise. The IEP process affords a unique opportunity for a young person to inform goals written for their education and to advocate for services and other resources assigned to meet those goals. Based on this premise, Royer (2017) delivered a six-lesson *My IEP* curriculum and found that, among a predominately non-White sample of high-school-aged youth with disabilities, students participating in the *My IEP* curriculum reported increased knowledge about their own IEPs and spoke substantially more during the IEP meeting than students assigned to a comparison group. More recently, Silva and Mihov (2019) designed an eight-week student voice curriculum, *Leading My IEP*, to support high-school-aged youth as they led the development of their transition IEPs. While this curriculum is not yet evaluated, for those students with disabilities who are transitioning to postsecondary life, the student-led IEP model holds promise for developing psychosocial skills necessary for independence, including psychological empowerment, self-advocacy, and self-determination.

School-Based Interventions with a Student Voice Component

Described below are several types of interventions that include a student voice component. Interventions vary in their saturation levels, with some incorporating components involving expression and some, albeit fewer, providing full leadership (Figure 26.1). Developing an exhaustive catalog of interventions is beyond the scope of this chapter; instead, we highlight representative interventions for each category.

Social-emotional Learning Interventions

Student voice strategies reasonably complement other traditionally adult-led approaches to improving psychological well-being, including social and emotional learning (SEL) approaches meant to improve students' ability to regulate internal emotional states, develop self-awareness, and to use communication strategies to prevent and intervene with social conflicts (Greenberg et al., 2003). Some SEL-type approaches include either a student voice component or emphasize constructs associated with student voice. One such program, *Facing History and Ourselves* (facinghistory.org), is intended to be delivered in middle and high school classrooms and focuses on improving students' historical thinking and analysis skills, social and ethical awareness, and civic competencies such as agency (Barr et al., 2015). Results from a randomized controlled trial indicate that, compared to students enrolled in control classrooms, students enrolled in classrooms implementing *Facing History and Ourselves* experienced significant improvements in historical understanding, political tolerance, and civic efficacy (Barr et al., 2015).

Other examples of student-voice infused SEL approaches are those designed to boost psychological assets among youth from subgroups with shared histories and cultures. In a quasi-experimental study of the *Young Empowered Sisters (YES!)* program implemented with ninth- and tenth-grade Black female participants, Thomas et al. (2008) found significant improvements in: (a) ethnic identity (i.e., a sense of membership in an ethnic group and sharing attitudes and feelings with that group), (b) racism awareness (i.e., knowledge of dynamics and nuances of racist and unfair treatment), (c) collectivism (i.e., a cultural orientation in which interdependence and social obligations are given precedence over personal needs), (d) liberatory youth activism (i.e., involvement in social action and community development, and (e) the ability to resist and effectively cope with racism. Similar examples of evidence-based, culturally-adapted social-emotional interventions with a student voice component include *Jóvenes Fuertes* for Latinx middle and high school-aged youth (Castro-Olivo, 2014); adapted *Strong Start* programs for elementary-aged Black boys (Graves et al., 2017) and for kindergarten-aged Latinx dual language learners (Castro-Olivo et al., 2018); *Sisters of Nia* (Aston et al., 2017; Belgrave et al., 2004) and *Brothers of Ujima* (Belgrave et al., 2011) for middle-school-aged Black girls and Black boys, respectively; and *Xinachtli Rites of Passage Curriculum* for adolescent-aged Chicana, Latina, and indigenous girls (Haskie-Mendoza et al., 2018; nationalcompadresnetwork.org).

Pedagogical Practices and Student Governance Structures

Student voice activities have a place at all levels of the school environment. They can be integrated into day-to-day classroom pedagogical decisions to help students surface implicit and culturally-informed values, views, and opinions; to discuss and evaluate those views and opinions with their peers; to think critically about their classroom experience; and to proactively shape the context of their learning. For instance, Langhout et al. (2011) studied the consequences of asking Latinx elementary-aged students to evaluate the benefits and drawbacks of various group decision-making frameworks. Her team found that most youths selected random choice over other options, such as consensus, majority rule, or authoritarian rule. When asked about their reasons, they described a priority on fairness and interpersonal connections. Another strategy, the *Five Whys* method (Kohfeldt & Langhout, 2012), is used during natural times in the school day when a question arises that could be useful for challenging students to think deeply about the context of the problem, rather than to accept reflexive, and often reductive, explanations. In this activity, a question is posed and, instead of giving a single response, students develop five answers drawing on their knowledge and experience (Kohfeldt & Langhout, 2012). The group selects the most reasonable answer, and then that answer is turned into another *why* question. This procedure occurs for four additional revolutions. This type of strategy illuminates the possibility that one's background and history inform answers to a question and that a more in-depth analysis of a question supports creative and divergent problem-solving. When applied to questions of psychological well-being, these types of activities can be useful for challenging culturally-embedded stigma and reducing related barriers to accessing care.

School governance structures are a natural fit for embedding student voice practices. In any school-related environment, there are myriad spaces to provide youth with opportunities to investigate and address issues that affect them. In a case study of one such district-level effort, Cohen et al. (2019) describe high school-aged students in Stockton, California. Students were enrolled in *Peer Leaders Uniting Students* (PLUS; plusprogram.org), a program designed to provide schools with a set of procedures and structures for creating YPAR-based practices to inform school functioning. Students used YPAR methods to inform the school district's high-stakes decisions regarding funding priorities and, relatedly, its accountability plan due to the state's regulatory agency. In their quasi-experimental study of impacts of PLUS in a southern California school district that predominately served youth of color, Voight and Velez (2018) found significant and meaningful effects on student attendance, thereby increasing instructional minutes and educational access for participating youth.

Youth-Led Participatory Action Research

YPAR emphasizes youth leadership and identity, the use of research methods, and the empowerment of young people to address the root causes of problems that affect them (Diemer et al., 2011). According to Langhout and Thomas (2010), YPAR "reconceptualize[s] the research process as an intervention in and of itself, where children learn skills through guided participation and active engagement" (p. 61). YPAR approaches vary, but there are similar phases in two common problem-solving frameworks: (a) problem definition, problem assessment, intervention planning, implementation, and evaluation (Dworski-Riggs & Langhout, 2010) or (b) issue selection, research design and methods, data analysis, and interpretation, and reporting back and taking action for change (Ozer & Piatt, 2017).

YPAR-based approaches help students and school adults avoid the reflex to pathologize individuals. Instead, to comprehend and address the complex circumstances that influence decision-making in schools, students use YPAR methods to move beyond surface-level explanations. If youth in a YPAR-based project initially identify bullying related to race or ethnicity as an issue, they would analyze first a range of causes for the problem (e.g., segregation of students through course tracking, lack of social opportunities for awareness building and bias reduction, and/or poor representation of positive models of diversity throughout the school). Then, they would choose one or more of these structural concerns as the focus of their data collection and analysis. In a recent systematic review of 52 YPAR studies, Anyon et al. (2018) determined that the most common outcomes described were changes to agency and leadership-related outcomes (i.e., self-determination, self-efficacy, confidence, civic engagement, citizenship, voice, empowerment, social responsibility, participatory behavior, identity, and self-awareness). Following these were academic and career outcomes (i.e., organization, time management study skills, goal setting, public speaking, writing, and planning), and then outcomes related to social, interpersonal, critical consciousness, and cognitive categories.

One example of YPAR comes from a public high school in Cleveland, Ohio, where all ninth-grade students partake in a year-long action research project on a social issue of their choosing (Buckley-Marudas & Soltis, 2020). The course is required for all ninth-grade students and meets weekly for approximately two hours. During these meetings, students work with teachers in the school to identify and analyze the root causes of social issues, learn and apply qualitative and quantitative research methods, analyze data, and use the evidence they create to inform change in their school and community. Students present their research at a youth-led research conference held annually at a nearby university, and attendance is open to the public. Participating students have examined myriad topics that concern them, including homelessness, dating violence, mental health, and equitable access to special education resources (Buckley-Marudas & Soltis, 2020).

Implementation Resources and Instruments

During their graduate training, many school-based mental health practitioners, such as school psychologists and school counselors, receive little exposure to the conceptual frameworks that undergird youth voice, and as a consequence youth voice strategies may not come to mind when selecting prevention and intervention approaches for psychological well-being. Even when they are aware of student voice strategies and are eager to adopt them, institutional barriers may feel insurmountable. Furthermore, implementing youth voice strategies, especially saturated youth voice strategies like YPAR, can feel overwhelming such that it is difficult to know where to begin.

Evidence to-date largely supports these concerns. In her examination of student voice projects in 13 urban high schools, Mitra (2009b) found pervasive institutional barriers, including constrictions on time allocations for student voice work, and a tendency to revert to more traditional student and adult roles. As a result of the evident gap between research supporting the utility of student voice and the practical adoption of student voice as a prevention and intervention strategy, researchers have begun to examine ways in which installing student voice can be made easier and more effective. Using an implementation science framework, Giraldo-García et al. (2020) evaluated a large Midwestern school district's effort to form student advisory panels in each of its 22 urban high schools, all of which served predominantly low-income children of color. Those high schools with the strongest implementation adopted a few relatively simple and easy-to-use approaches, such as seeking a representative student roster, rather than selecting from a more narrow group of existing student leaders; meeting regularly with the school principal present, rather than meeting only intermittently and without an adult change-leader present; and undertaking a formal issue-identification process through the analysis of school-level data, rather than using anecdotal and idiosyncratic sources of data (Giraldo-García et al., 2020).

Table 26.1 Organizations Supporting Student Voice

Organization Name	URL
Alliance for Children's Rights	kids-alliance.org
Directing Change	directingchange.org
Educators for Fair Consideration	e4fc.org
Institute for Community Research	icrweb.org
SoundOut	soundout.org
Students at the Center	studentsatthecenterhub.org
Teaching Tolerance	tolerance.org
Up for Learning	upforlearning.org
Voces Y Manos	vocesymanos.org
Youth in Front	youthinfront.org
Youth Participatory Politics Research Network	ypp.dmlcentral.net
YPAR Hub, UC Berkeley	yparhub.berkeley.edu

To support individuals interested in implementing student voice practices in their schools, we provide several accessible, practical resources made available to the public by nonprofit organizations and universities (Table 26.1). Mitra (2009b) recommends finding opportunities to achieve small success early, thereby establishing value to the student voice process. To avoid overtaxing schools and practitioners, consider starting by taking small measures, such as expanding existing student leadership structures to make them more representative of the student body, or infusing just one YPAR-based practice, such as examining existing school data for patterns and developing hypotheses about the root causes of those patterns. Other ways to start small are to weave in just one or two student voice practices into a small group being run with an existing social-emotional learning curriculum, or to use student-led IEP practices with just one or two students with disabilities. For those interested in gauging the effectiveness for their student voice efforts, we have developed a list of instruments designed for measuring well-being-related constructs relevant to the student voice approach (Table 26.2).

Conclusion

Though student voice strategies may not yet be considered mainstream in the traditional medical model of mental illness prevention, they are well aligned with a dual mental health model, which specifies that well-being is defined not just by the absence of pathology, but by the presence of psychological assets. More specifically, student voice strategies hold promise for cultivating the unique psychological assets that are protective for young people with minoritized identities. A growing body of evidence from case studies and quasi-experimental studies examining student voice strategies among predominantly adolescent-aged youth suggests that participation in student voice activities has a positive impact on the psychosocial development of students with diverse identities and histories. Nevertheless, much research remains to be done to examine causal links between participation in student voice and mental health, especially around traditional indicators of mental illness, as well as to identify and rule-out possible contraindications wherein participation in student voice could be ineffective or even harmful. We hope that this chapter will inspire educators and school mental health practitioners to thoughtfully incorporate student voice strategies into their prevention and intervention efforts, and researchers to expand the rigorous study of those efforts.

Table 26.2 Instruments to Measure Constructs Related to Student Voice

Instrument	Construct/Subscale(s)	# Items	Sample Items	Reference(s)
Adapted Social Self-Efficacy Questionnaire for Children	Social-Efficacy	8	• How well can you express your opinions when other classmates disagree with you? • How well can you have a chat with an unfamiliar person? • How well can you work in harmony with your classmates? • How well can you tell other people your age that they are doing something you don't like?	Zullig et al. (2011)
Sociopolitical Control Scale for Youth (SPCS-Y)	Leadership Competence Policy Control	8 9	• I am a leader in groups. • I can usually organize people to get things done.	Lardier et al. (2018) Peterson et al. (2011)
Youth Cognitive Empowerment Scale (Y-CES)	Source of power Nature Instrument of power	12	• Only by working together can teens make a difference. • The only way I can affect community issues is by working with other teens. • Those with power will try to stop teens who challenge them too much. • When teens raise issues, schools and communities ignore the issues they don't agree with.	Speer et al. (2019)
Modified Interracial Climate Scale	Peer Interactions	3	• I talk to students of different ethnic groups only when I have to.	Bellmore et al. (2012)
Psychological Empowerment	Socio-political skills Motivation to Influence Participatory Behavior Perceived Control	8 4 8 6	• I can usually figure out how to get an adult to see my point of view, even if they don't agree with me. • I want to have as much say as possible in making decisions in my school. • I have spoken with other students about issues that I want to improve at school. • Students have a say in what happens at this school.	Ozer & Schotland (2011)

References

Akom, A., Shah, A., Nakai, A., & Cruz, T. (2016). Youth participatory action research (YPAR) 2.0: How technological innovation and digital organizing sparked a food revolution in East Oakland. *International Journal of Qualitative Studies in Education, 29*(10), 1287–1307. http://dx.doi. org/10.1080/09518398.2016.1201609

Anyon, Y., Bender, K., Kennedy, H., & Dechants, J. (2018). A systematic review of youth participatory action research (YPAR) in the United States: Methodologies, youth outcomes, and future directions. *Health Education & Behavior, 45*(6), 865–878. http://dx.doi.org/10.1177/ 1090198118769357

Aston, C., Graves, S., McGoey, K., Lovelace, T., & Tonsend, T. (2017). Promoting sisterhood: The impact of a culturally focused program to address verbally aggressive behaviors in Black girls. *Psychology in the Schools, 55*, 50–62. https://doi.org/10.1002/pits.22089

Atkins, M., & Calkins, A. (2020). *A school-based trauma-informed student voice curriculum.* [Education Specialist Project]. ProQuest.

Ballard, P. J., & Ozer, E. (2016). The implications of youth activism for health and well-being. In J. O. Conner & S. M. Rosen (Eds.), *Contemporary youth activism: Advancing social justice in the United States* (pp. 223–244). Praeger.

Barr, D., Boulay, B., Selman, R., McCormick, R., Lowenstein, E., Gamse, B., Fine, M., & Leonard, M.B. (2015) A randomized controlled trial of professional development for interdisciplinary civic education: Impacts on humanities teachers and their students. *Teacher College Record, 17*(4), 1–52.

Belgrave, F., Allison, K., Wilson, J., & Tademy, R. (2011). *Brothers of Ujima: A cultural enrichment program to empower adolescent African-American males.* Research Press Publishers.

Belgrave, F., Reed, M., Plybon, L., Butler, D., Allison, K., & Davis, T. (2004). An evaluation of Sisters of Nia: A cultural program for African American girls. *Journal of Black Psychology, 30*(3), 329–343. https:// doi.org/10.1177/0095798404266063

Bellmore, A., Nishina, A., You, J. I., & Ma, T. L. (2012). School context protective factors against peer ethnic discrimination across the high school years. *American Journal of Community Psychology, 49*(1–2), 98–111. https://doi.org/10.1007/s10464-011-9443-0

Berg, M., Coman, E., & Schensul, J. J. (2009). Youth action research for prevention: A multi-level intervention designed to increase efficacy and empowerment among urban youth. *American Journal of Community Psychology, 43*(304), 345–359. https://doi.org/10.1007/s10464-009-9231-2

Bertrand, M. (2018). Youth participatory action research and possibilities for student educational leadership. *Educational Administration Quarterly, 54*(3), 366–395. https://doi.org/10.1177/0013161X18761344

Bronfenbrenner, U. (1979). *The ecology of human development: Experiments by nature and design.* Harvard University Press.

Buckley-Marudas, M. F., & Soltis, S. (2020). What youth care about: Exploring topic identification for youth-led research in school. *Urban Review, 52*, 331–350. https://doi.org/10.1007/s11256-019-00530-5

Cabrera, N. L., Milem, J. F., Jaquette, O., & Marx, R. W. (2014). Missing the (student achievement) forest for all the (political) trees: Empiricism and the Mexican American Studies controversy in Tucson. *American Educational Research Journal, 51*(6), 1084–1118. https://doi.org/10.3102/0002831214553705

Cahill, C. (2010). Why do they hate us? Reframing immigration through participatory action research. *Area, 42*(2), 152–161. https://doi.org/10.1111/j.1475-4762.2009.00929.x

Castro-Olivo, S. (2014). Promoting social-emotional learning in adolescent Latino ELLs: A study of the culturally adapted Strong Teens program. *School Psychology Quarterly, 29*(4), 567–577. https://doi. org/10.1037/spq0000055

Castro-Olivo, S., Preciado, J., Le, M., Maricante, M., & Garcia, M. (2018). The effects of culturally adapted version of First Steps to Success for Latino English language learners: Preliminary pilot study. *Psychology in the Schools, 55*(1), 36–49. https://doi.org/10.1002/pits.22092

Chard, C., Nelson, D., Walters, N., Pollard, N., Pollard, N., Gomez, K., Smith, D., Jenkins, N., Muwwakkil, S., Garland, C., Fard, A., & Fields, M. (2020). An inclusive approach to exploring perceptions of body image, self-esteem, and physical activity among Black and African-American girls: Smart Fit Girls Melanin Magic. *The Journal of Park and Recreation Administration.* Advance online publication. https://doi. org/10.18666/JPRA-2019-9710

Chen, P., Weiss, F. L., Nicholson, H. J., & Girls Incorporated (2010). Girls Study Girls, Inc.: Engaging girls in evaluation through participatory action research. *American Journal of Community Psychology, 46*(1–2), 228–237. https://doi.org/10.1007/s10464-010-9328-7

Cohen, A., Ozer, E., Abraczinskas, M., Voight, A., Kirshner, B., & Devinney, M. (2019). Opportunities for youth participatory action research to inform school district decisions. *Evidence & Policy: A Journal of Research, Debate and Practice, 16*(2), 317–329. https://doi.org/10.1332/174426419X15649816542957

Diemer, M. A., Voight, A. M., & Mark, C. (2011). Youth development in traditional and transformational service-learning programs. In T. Stewart & N. Webster (Eds.), *Problematizing service learning: Critical reflections for development and action* (pp. 155–173). Information Age Publishing.

Dworski-Riggs, D., & Langhout, R. D. (2010). Elucidating the power in empowerment and the participation in participatory action research: A story about research team and elementary school change. *American Journal of Community Psychology, 45*, 215–230. https://doi.org/10.1007/s10464-010-9306-0

Ghirardelli, A., & Bye, L. (2016). *California mental health services authority Directing Change Film Contest and program evaluation.* NORC. https://www.directingchangeca.org/wp-content/uploads/CalMHSA%20DC%20Eval%20Report.pdf

Giraldo-Garcia, R., & Galletta, A. (2015). "What happened to our sense of justice?" Tracing agency and critical engagement in a youth participatory action research project. *Journal of Urban Learning, Teaching and Research, 11*, 91–98. ERIC. https://eric.ed.gov/?id=EJ1071569

Giraldo-García, R., Voight, A., & O'Malley, M. (2020). Mandatory voice: Implementation of a district-led student-voice program in urban high schools. *Psychology in the Schools.* Advance online publication. https://doi.org/10.1002/pits.22436

Gómez, C. A., Villaseñor, E., Mann, E. S., Mandic, C. G., Valladares, E. S., Mercado, V., Alcála, M., & Cardona, V. (2014). The new majority: How will Latino youth succeed in the context of low educational expectations and assumptions of sexual irresponsibility? *Sexuality Research and Social Policy, 11*(4), 348–362. https://doi.org/10.1007/s13178-014-0165-6

Gonzalez, T. E., Hernandez-Saca, D. I., & Artiles, A. J. (2016). In search of voice: Theory and methods in K-12 student voice research in the US, 1990–2010. *Educational Review, 69*(4), 451–473. https://doi.org/10.1080/00131911.2016.1231661

Graves, S., Herndon-Sobalvarro, A., Nichols, K., Aston, C., Ryan, A., Blefari, A., Schutte, K., Schachner, A., Victoria, L., & Prier, D. (2017). Examining the effectiveness of a culturally adapted social emotional intervention for African American males in an urban setting. *School Psychology Quarterly, 32*(1), 62–74. https://doi.org/10.1037/spq0000145

Greenberg, M. T., Weissberg, R. P., O'Brien, M. U., Zins, J. E., Fredericks, L., Resnik, H., & Elias, M. (2003). Enhancing school-based prevention and youth development through coordinated social, emotional, and academic learning. *American Psychologist, 58*(6–7), 466–474. https://doi.org/10.1037/0003-066X.58.6-7.466

Halliday, A., Kern, M., Garrett, D., & Turnbull, D. (2018). The student voice in well-being: A case study of participatory action research in positive education, *Educational Action Research, 27*(2), 173–196. https://doi.org/10.1080/09650792.2018.1436079

Hart, S., & Hart, B. (2014). Children's rights and school psychology: Historical perspective and implications for the profession. *School Psychology International, 35*(1), 6–28. https://doi.org/10.1177/0143034313508875

Haskie-Mendoza, S., Tinajero, L., Cervantes, A., Rodriguez, J., & Serrata, J. (2018). Conducting youth participatory action research (YPAR) through a healing-informed approach with system-involved Latinas. *Journal of Family Violence, 33*, 605–612. https://doi.org/10.1007/s10896-018-9996-x

Holden, D. J., Crankshaw, E., Nimsch, C., Hinnant, L. W., & Hund, L. (2004). Quantifying the impact of participation in local tobacco control groups on the psychological empowerment of involved youth. *Health Education and Behavior, 31*(5), 615–628. https://doi.org/10.1177/1090198104268678

Hope, E. C., Skoog, A. B., & Jagers, R. J. (2015). "It'll never be the white kids, it'll always be us": Black high school students' evolving critical analysis of racial discrimination and inequity in schools. *Journal of Adolescent Research, 30*(1), 83–112. http://dx.doi.org/10.1177/0743558414550688

Irizarry, J. G., & Raible, J. (2014). "A hidden part of me": Latino/a students, silencing, and the epidermalization of inferiority. *Equity & Excellence in Education, 47*(4), 430–444. https://doi.org/10.1080/10665684.2014.958970

Ivey-Stephenson, A., Dmissie, Z., Crosby, A., Stone, D., Gaylor, E., Wilkins, N., Lowry, R., & Brown, M. (2020). Suicidal ideation and behaviors among high school students---Youth Risk Behavior Survey, United States, 2019. *MMWR, 69*(1), 47–55. https://doi.org/10.15585/mmwr.su6901a6

Kirshner, B., & Ginwright, S. (2012). Youth organizing as a developmental context for African American and Latino adolescents. *Child Development Perspectives, 6*(3), 288–294. https://doi.org/10.1111/j.1750-8606.2012.00243.x

Kohfeldt, D., Chhun, L., Grace, S., & Langhout, R. D. (2011). Youth empowerment in context: Exploring tensions in school-based yPAR. *American Journal of Community Psychology, 47*(1–2), 28–45. https://doi.org/10.1007/s10464-010-9376-z

Kohfeldt, D., & Langhout, R. (2012). The five whys method: A tool for developing problem definitions in collaboration with children. *Journal of Community and Applied Psychology, 22*(4), 316–329. https://doi.org/10.1002/casp.1114

Ladson-Billings, G., & Tate, W. (2016). Toward a critical race theory of education. In A. Dixson, C. Rousseau Anderson, & J. Donnor (Eds.), *Critical race theory in education: All God's children got a song* (2nd ed., pp. 11–32). Routledge.

Langhout, R., & Thomas, E. (2010). Imagining participation action research in collaboration with children: An introduction. *American Journal of Community Psychology, 46*(1–2), 60–66. https://doi.org/10.1007/s10464-010-9321-1

Langhout, R. D., Kohfeldt, D. M., & Ellison, E. R. (2011). How we became the Schmams: Conceptualizations of fairness in the decision-making process for Latina/o children. *American Journal of Community Psychology, 48*, 296–308. https://doi.org/10.1007/s10464-010-9381-2

Lardier Jr., D.T., Reid, R. J., & Garcia-Reid, P. (2018). Validation of the Brief Sense of Community Scale among youth of color from an underserved urban community. *Journal of Community Psychology, 46*(8), 1062–1074. https://doi.org/10.1002/jcop.22091

Mitra, D. L. (2009a). The role of intermediary organizations in sustaining student voice initiatives. *Teachers College Record, 111*(7), 1834–1868.

Mitra, D. L. (2009b). Strengthening student voice initiatives in high schools: An examination of the supports needed for school-based youth-adult partnerships. *Youth & Society, 40*(3), 311–335. https://doi.org/10.1177/0044118X08316211

Morsillo, J., & Prilleltensky, I. (2007). Social action with youth: Interventions, evaluation, and psychopolitical validity. *Journal of Community Psychology, 35*(6), 1–16. https://doi.org/10.1002/jcop.20175

Ozer, E. J. (2017). Youth-led participatory action research: Overview and potential for enhancing adolescent development. *Child Development Perspectives, 11*(3), 173–177. https://doi.org/10.1111/cdep.12228

Ozer, E. J., & Douglas, L. (2013). The impact of participatory research on urban teens: An experimental evaluation. *American Journal of Community Psychology, 51*(1–2), 66–75. https://doi.org/10.1007/s10464-012-9546-2

Ozer, E. J., Newlan, S., Douglas, L., & Hubbard, E. (2013). Bounded empowerment: Analyzing tensions in the practice of youth-led participatory research in urban public schools. *American Journal of Community Psychology, 52*, 13–26. https://doi.org/10.1007/s10464-013-9573-7

Ozer, E. J., & Piatt, A.A. (2017). *Adolescent participation in research: Innovation, rationale and next steps.* Innocenti Research Briefs 2017, UNICEF Office of Research. https://www.unicef-irc.org/publications/879-adolescent-participation-in-research-

Ozer, E. J., & Schotland, M. (2011). Psychological empowerment among urban youth: Measure development and relationship to psychosocial functioning. *Health Education and Behavior, 38*(4), 348–356. https://doi.org/10.1177/1090198110373734

Ozer, E. J., & Wright, D. (2012). Beyond school spirit: The effects of youth-led participatory action research in two urban high schools. *Journal of Research on Adolescence, 22*(2), 267–283. https://doi.org/10.1111/j.1532-7795.2012.00780.x

Peters, M., Lankshear, C., & Olssen, M. (2003). Introduction: Critical theory and the human condition. In M. Peters, C. Lankshear, & M. Olssen (Eds.), *Critical theory and the human condition: Founders and praxis* (pp. 1–14). Peter Lang.

Peterson, N. A., Peterson, C. H., Agre, L., Christens, B. D., & Morton, C. M. (2011). Measuring youth empowerment: Validation of a sociopolitical control scale for youth in an urban community context. *Journal of Community Psychology, 39*(5), 592–605. https://doi.org/10.1002/jcop.20456

Poteat, V. P., Calzo, J. P., & Yoshikawa, H. (2018). Gay-Straight Alliance involvement and youths' participation in civic engagement, advocacy, and awareness-raising. *Journal of Applied Developmental Psychology, 56*, 13–20. https://doi.org/10.1016/j.appdev. 2018.01.001

Royer, D. J. (2017). My IEP: A student-directed individualized education program model. *Exceptionality, 25*(4), 235–252. https://doi.org/10.1080/09362835.2016.1216850

Silva, A., & Mihov, R. (2019). *Leading my IEP: A student voice curriculum to support student-led transitional IEPs.* [Education Specialist Project] ProQuest. http://hdl.handle.net/10211.3/210195

Smith, C. D., & Hope, E. C. (2020). "We just want to break the stereo-type": Tensions in Black boys' critical social analysis of their suburban school experiences. *Journal of Educational Psychology, 112*(3), 551–566. https://doi.org/10.1037/edu0000435

Speer, P. W., Peterson, N. A., Christens, B. D., & Reid, R. J. (2019). Youth cognitive empowerment: Development and evaluation of an instrument. *American Journal of Community Psychology, 64*(3–4), 528–540. https://doi.org/10.1002/ajcp.12339

Taines, C. (2012). Intervening in alienation: The outcomes for urban youth of participating in school activism. *American Educational Research Journal, 49*(1), 53–86. https://doi.org/10.3102/0002831211411079

Thomas, O., Davidson, W., & McAdoo, H. (2008). An evaluation study of the Young Empowered Sisters (YES!) program: Promoting cultural assets among African American adolescent girls through a culturally relevant school-based intervention. *Journal of Black Psychology, 34*(3), 281–308. https://doi.org/10.1177/0095798408314136

Toshalis, E., & Nakkula, M. J. (2012). The spectrum of student voice oriented activity [graphic]. In *Motivation, Engagement, and Student Voice* (p. 24). Retrieved from https://studentsatthecenterhub.org/resource/motivation-engagement-and-student-voice/

UN Commission on Human Rights. (1990). *Convention on the rights of the child.* https://www.ohchr.org/en/professionalinterest/pages/crc.aspx

Villaseñor, E., Alcalá, M., Valladares, E. S., Torres, M. A., Mercado, V., & Gómez, C. A. (2013). Empower Latino Youth (ELAYO): Leveraging student voice to inform the public debate on pregnancy, parenting and education. *Community Literacy Journal, 8*(1), 21–39. https://doi.org/10.1353/clj.2013.0017

Voight, A. (2015). Student voice for school-climate improvement: A case study of an urban middle school. *Journal of Community & Applied Social Psychology, 25*(4), 310–326. https://doi.org/10.1002/casp.2216

Voight, A., & Velez, V. (2018). Youth participatory action research in the high school curriculum: Education outcomes for student participants in a district-wide initiative. *Journal of Research on Educational Effectiveness, 11*, 433–451. https://doi.org/10.1080/19345747.2018.1431345

Zullig, K. J., Teoli, D. A., & Valois, R. F. (2011). Evaluating a brief measure of social self-efficacy among US adolescents. *Psychological Reports, 109*(3), 907–920. https://doi.org/10.2466/02.09.PR0.109.6.907-920

SECTION IV

Positive Education in Practice

27

USING THEORY OF CHANGE FOR FOSTERING WELL-BEING AND ENGAGEMENT IN LEARNING COMMUNITIES

Tan-Chyuan Chin, Edwina Ricci, Adam Cooper,
Andrea Downie and Dianne Vella-Brodrick

There is a growing demand for learning environments such as schools, arts, sporting, and community youth organizations to nurture and empower young people to build skills, be the best version of themselves, and be well prepared for an uncertain future. In addition to traditional learning and performance metrics, well-being is valued increasingly as a desirable outcome. In Australia, there are several national programs (Be You by Beyond Blue and Headspace; Bounce Back by Toni Noble and Helen McGrath; ReachOut Schools by ReachOut) that specifically aim to promote maintenance or elevation of positive mental well-being and buffer against the loss of mental health. There are also many programs and interventions available for learning communities to include into their pre-existing curriculum (Cilar et al., 2020; Sin & Lyubomirsky, 2009; Waters, 2011). However, there is limited evidence of the sustained efficacy, uptake, suitability, and impact of programs or interventions to adequately meet the well-being needs of the whole learning community. As the core business of learning communities such as schools is to focus on the development, growth, and healthy functioning of young people, it comes as no surprise that most resources are dedicated to student outcomes.

One challenge of implanting effective programs is that a young person is embedded in a dynamic system with different elements. Their family, peers, school, and local services form a "microsystem," which has the most immediate and direct impact on young people. Interactions among the microsystem elements further distinguish a "mesosystem." Finally, the "macrosystem" involves broader cultural and sociopolitical influences (Bronfenbrenner, 1994). A child's development, education, and learning are perhaps best nurtured and supported by a strong mesosystem. This enables young people to carry their knowledge and skills of well-being across the various contexts of their microsystem, providing more opportunities to thrive and flourish in all aspects of their life beyond the classroom or schoolyard. Therefore, an effective way to foster and optimize youth well-being is to engage all stakeholders within young people's learning communities (Slemp et al., 2017). This integrated systems approach enables the creation of sustainable educational systems and practices for optimizing youth well-being. These learning experiences, a common language and shared understanding of well-being, can be reinforced and applied beyond the classroom, throughout the school, in the family, and the broader community (Alford, 2017; Bronfenbrenner, 1994).

DOI: 10.4324/9781003013778-34

The Whole Is Greater than the Sum of Individual Parts

Every system, such as learning communities, has "a set of elements or parts that is coherently organized and interconnected in a pattern or structure that produces a characteristic set of behaviors, often classified as its 'function' or 'purpose'" (Meadows, 2008, p. 188). Senge (1990) succinctly described that

> events [in a system can be] distant in time and space, and yet they are all connected within the same pattern. Each has an influence on the rest, an influence that is usually hidden from view. You can only understand the system…by contemplating the whole, not any individual part of the pattern.
>
> *(p. 7)*

Therefore, a sustainable, scalable approach to building well-being in an interconnected learning community is to view and work in wholes—considering all elements in the relationships—rather than viewing or developing specific or some parts outside of the community's context.

Learning communities have a unique opportunity to work collaboratively with young people, their families, and the organizational staff to assess current and emerging needs, and to understand and optimize well-being for the whole community. Furthermore, researchers have shown that the well-being of school staff and parents/carers, and their relationships with students can positively impact student well-being (e.g., Suldo et al., 2008). This concept is much like the inflight safety instructions regarding the use of the oxygen mask onboard airplanes—for passengers to put on their mask before helping someone else. For staff to positively influence and support student well-being, they first need to be well themselves. A recent study demonstrated that teacher well-being and mental health were associated with students' well-being and psychological distress. If teachers are not faring well, neither are their students (Harding et al., 2019). Other research found that staff well-being was related to students' academic performance in primary and secondary schools (Briner & Dewberry, 2007). There is likely a reciprocal relationship such that elevating teacher well-being may improve students' performance, further improving staff well-being (Roffey, 2012). This evidence highlights that staff members and school climate are vital—organizations should address their well-being needs in strategies, activities, and training.

In addition to significant adults such as school staff, coaches, instructors, and mentors, it is also crucial to engage and work closely with young peoples' parents and carers. Although adolescence can bring changes to the family dynamic, young people seek support from their parents and carers (Paterson et al., 1994). Parents and carers bring a unique perspective on their children's needs and what the school and community can offer to optimize their children's well-being. It is well evidenced that parental mental health influences child mental health (Fatori et al., 2013; Schepman et al., 2011). Similarly, parental well-being (e.g., life satisfaction and optimism) is positively associated with children's well-being and development (Berger & Spiess, 2011; Yu & Ko, 2013). Children learn how to regulate their emotions and manage challenging situations from their parents and carers (Morris et al., 2007). For example, emotionally expressive parents are more likely to have emotionally secure and expressive children, which is related to their children's well-being, including prosocial behavior, social competence, emotional understanding, and positive emotionality (Morris et al., 2007). Similarly, parents with higher emotional competency have children with better emotion regulation skills, peer relationships, physical and psychological health, and academic performance (Gottman et al., 1996; Stocker et al., 2007). Therefore, efforts to improve outcomes for young people also need to consider and actively involve all significant adults in their home and learning environments.

A Theory of Change Approach for Well-Being Initiatives in Learning Communities

We advocate for a whole-system approach to fostering well-being for all members of the learning community—staff, students, and their parents/carers/families. This approach moves beyond the individual school setting to identify broader social and contextual factors that influence individual and collective well-being and the potential consequences of well-being initiatives (Slemp et al., 2017). According to systems science, the elements within a system (e.g., families, schools, and neighborhoods) dynamically interact with one another, producing a whole that is greater than the sum of the parts (Kern et al., 2019). System approaches generally consider three vital aspects: interconnectedness, perspectives, and boundaries (Williams & van't Hof, 2014). They first seek to understand how different elements (or structures) are connected and how they impact each other. Second, they consider the unique perspectives of different groups in the broader systems such as students, staff, and parents/carers. And, third, they attempt to define boundaries such as what kinds of resources are given to whom and for what purpose. Through this process, factors that enable or impede well-being such as policies, resource allocations, community norms/values, and skills/attitudes, can then be adequately targeted (Foster-Fishman et al., 2007).

While each learning community is unique, there are common elements across the various approaches to implementing well-being initiatives. A Theory of Change (ToC) framework can provide a clear process model of how any initiative such as a well-being strategy, intervention, or program, contributes through a chain of early and intermediate outcomes to the intended results (Funnell & Rogers, 2011). It provides a guide of how the various sets of activities carried out by a particular group or organization can lead to a measurable change in outcomes or impacts. These changes can occur within or between individuals or groups over time. For learning communities, three features of ToC's are particularly relevant. First, a ToC is context-specific with the primary goal of implementing a specific initiative, and is less concerned with the generalizability to other settings (Janzen et al., 2012). Second, a ToC is aspirational, focusing on what is anticipated rather than what actually occurred, thereby providing a clear scope for evaluating the anticipated outcomes compared with the results (Janzen et al., 2016). Third, the developmental nature of ToCs provides the scope for an initiative to evolve and develop over time in response to complex and dynamic fluctuations in the broader system (Janzen & Wiebe, 2010). As learning communities contain various levels of stakeholders, this framework is most useful from a systemic perspective, reflecting the complexity of change pathways and processes, as well as the participants, linkages, chains, and learning loops. Therefore, the nonlinear process challenges the common cause and effect understanding or interpretation of initiatives such as single/individual positive psychology interventions or positive education programs and highlights the need for ongoing reflective analysis and practice.

This chapter draws on the collective learnings and insights of the authors across several projects. Two of these projects are presented below as case studies. The shared purpose is to develop a deeper understanding of the common elements across projects, hoping that this will help advance the sustainable implementation of well-being initiatives for learning communities more broadly.

Case Study One: Maroondah Positive Education Network

Background

In 2013, Maroondah City Council (MCC) launched a community-wide consultation where diverse community representatives came together to discuss key community issues. These discussions uncovered a recurring theme of mental ill-health and a desire to build well-being as the priority for their thriving municipality by 2040. Two years later, with a focus on young people, the MCC began an engagement process for its youth strategy. Partnering with local schools and the University of Melbourne (UoM), they undertook consultation about the well-being needs of 5,000 students. Student well-being was measured using the UoM's Well-Being Profiler (Chin, 2017; Slemp et al., 2017). After obtaining these valuable data, the principals declared well-being as a shared priority between their network and with the MCC. Since then, a journey of discovery and collaboration has facilitated a broad range of activities, progressively establishing well-being as a focus across the community. The generative process has reaffirmed underlying principles about building strong relationships and meaningful collaborations to achieve shared desirable outcomes for the community.

Why?

Maroondah's Positive Education Project aims to mobilize a network of 27 government schools toward the goal of raising student, staff, and community well-being, resilience, and achievement. It is a partnership based upon the community-wide implementation of well-being education—extending beyond traditional single school implementation, into a network of schools and the broader community. There is a foundational belief that the interconnectedness between the school system and the broader community provides a robust opportunity to create sustainable positive change to well-being.

Who?

This ambitious collaboration between local schools, the Department of Education and Training (Victoria), MCC, UoM, the Geelong Grammar School's Institute of Positive Education (GGSIPE) and local community groups aims to improve well-being and achievement by influencing the language, behaviors, knowledge, processes, relationships, and environments within and across education and community systems.

How?

Using Collective Impact as a framework for sustained community change, this systems approach aims to:

1   facilitate collaboration between Council, schools, and the broader community to enable well-being;
2   develop a system of sustainable well-being leadership;
3   increase schools' capacity to support student well-being;
4   increase the capacity of parents and caregivers to support their children's and their own well-being; and
5   improve staff and students' ability to build well-being for themselves and others.

Figure 27.1 illustrates the intersection of education and community as a means to build community well-being.

Change Process, Activities, and Anticipated Outcomes

Educational transformation is complex, and while models exist for single school implementation of well-being education, achieving this across multiple schools is considerably more challenging. Simple models rarely work under conditions of complexity where the unpredictable interactions of multiple

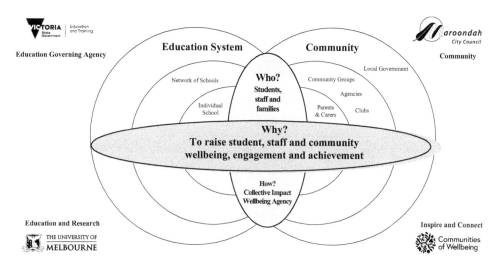

Figure 27.1   Flourishing Individuals, Classrooms, Schools, and Communities

stakeholders affect outcomes (Kania & Kramer, 2013), particularly when this involves multiple systems across a community. A coherent framework was critical to achieving the ambitious plan to raise well-being across an entire community. Collective impact is a model of social change to tackle complex community problems at a systems level (Kania & Kramer, 2011). The framework involves a centralized infrastructure, dedicated staff, and a structured process (a backbone) that establishes a common agenda, shared measurement, continuous communication, and mutually reinforcing activities among a cross-section of community stakeholders. This model has provided a framework for the delivery of project activities, which broadened our focus from implementing positive education in our schools to cultivating well-being literacy across the whole community. *Well-being literacy* shifts thinking from achieving short-term knowledge acquisition through external interventions, to "exploring language mediated cocreated actions which can create ongoing sustained well-being gains" (Oades & Johnston, 2017, p. 2). This relates to the well-known proverb that if you give a person a fish, you feed them for a day, but if you teach them to fish, you feed them for a lifetime.

What?

This is what the project has so far achieved:

1 all school principals naming student well-being as a network priority,
2 all schools provided with expert mentoring from the GGSIPE,
3 substantial funding and engagement from the Victorian Minister for Education,
4 established Heads of Positive Education (HOPE) leaders in each school to lead implementation and share practice,
5 development of formalized annual well-being goals in each school,
6 tailored training for principals and with all staff in every school,
7 90 education, community, and Council staff attending a three-day course in positive education delivered by the GGSIPE,
8 33 education and Council staff completing a professional certificate in positive education delivered by UoM,
9 27 staff learning about contextual well-being provided by Dr. Helen Street,

10 1,000 school staff attending a shared well-being day for the first day of 2019,
11 80 new staff from across the network attending a positive education "induction day" before the 2020 school year, and
12 themed days in schools to celebrate concepts such as gratitude and growth mindsets.

These initial outcomes reflect the adoption of Geelong Grammar School's philosophy of "learn it, live it, teach it, embed it" (Hoare et al., 2017; Norrish et al., 2013) as a crucial initial focus for the project. Building baseline knowledge and experience of positive education concepts, alongside enhancing leadership capacity and capability concerning positive education has been pivotal. The network's HOPE leaders share responsibility for project implementation and have undertaken two key rounds of high-quality training from the GGSIPE and UoM to build their knowledge and capabilities. Armed with this experience, HOPE leaders, in partnership with school leaders, are now coordinating positive change in their school contexts, and across the network. In addition to training, schools were provided a library of resources to foster the more profound personal discovery of positive psychology concepts and research, and other human resources in the form of a project leader to coach and support each school's progress.

At a network level, a community governance group, Maroondah Positive Education Network Steering Committee, was established with key leaders from partner organizations, including students, to bring shared expertise and practice to shape the project's goals and implementation. While formal project structures and activities are central, the most valuable asset for effective project execution has been the positive relationships that have built shared purpose, amplified achievement, and motivated partners toward the common purpose and goals. This has been achieved through mutual support, time and effort, and shared lived experiences of positive psychology practice.

Assessment, Monitoring, and Evaluation of Outcomes

Sustainability requires that well-being and resilience education are not seen as "another thing"—an addition to an already crowded curriculum. It must be integrated with all school and community improvement priorities. It is essential that improvements are measurable and have multiple benefits across domains, or it will not be sustained. Therefore, it is crucial when assessing, designing, and implementing well-being education that one is mindful that the evaluations are honest, reflective, and evolve. The project's HOPE leaders are a valuable resource, and their first-hand experiences need to be captured and understood to ensure the project remains relevant and beneficial. Well-being education will continue to earn its place by demonstrating its impact. All government schools in Victoria, Australia use the Framework for Improving Student Outcomes (FISO; State of Victoria Department of Education and Training, 2020) as the unifying framework for improvement in all the key areas of education (e.g., literacy and numeracy). The FISO uses contemporary school improvement and school effectiveness research to help schools focus their efforts on critical areas known to have the most significant impact on improved student outcomes. Central to this model is "student well-being, engagement and achievement," and the group's work has focused on this.

In the Maroondah Network, 27 schools developed a shared FISO goal of raising the well-being of staff, students, and parents. This is driving priorities in individual schools, throughout the network, and into the community. This shared model has four stages (State of Victoria Department of Education and Training, 2020):

1 *Evaluate and diagnose* the performance successes and challenges around key improvement initiatives and strategies.
2 *Prioritize and set goals* for improvement strategies and initiatives that have the greatest impact on student well-being and learning.

3   *Develop and plan* improvement strategies and initiatives to ensure successful implementation.
4   *Implement and monitor* selected improvement strategies and initiatives and their impact on staff and student well-being and learning outcomes.

Maroondah's HOPE leaders assess contextual needs using data, observations, conversations, and reflections on the previous year's goals. They then develop an action plan with the School Improvement Team (SIT team), which establishes priorities based on the desire to improve engagement, well-being, resilience, and achievement data. Schools publish their Annual Implementation Plans each year, and the goals are laid out alongside other priorities. Most schools extend well-being planning down to individual staff levels where their Personal Development Plans (PDP) also set a personal well-being goal. Having accountability enables well-being to stake its claim in the professional learning calendar. One of the things the group takes pride in is the inclusivity and sharing of their learning experiences. The knowledge, processes, skills, and capabilities are universally relevant, and learners are encouraged to apply them into their personal and professional life. This means that primary, secondary, and alternative educational settings and special development schools can share the same learning experiences with community group leaders. The paradigm shift happens when individuals create a unique understanding and inspire others with their stories of transformation and then translate it to their professional or volunteer settings. The shared journey of discovery also leads to new possibilities and further collaborations.

Key Elements for Sustainability

The success has come from the partners' commitment and the effective collaboration made possible through the use of the Collective Impact Framework with five conditions: backbone organization, common agenda, shared measurement, mutually reinforcing activities, and continuous communication. This systems approach enables the network to turn shared goals into tangible outcomes. While many organizations work in isolation, the network recognizes that only a team of committed partners will realize their vision of a community of well-being and sustain it with a shared language and skillset, equipping everyone to be the best versions of themselves individually and collectively.

Backbone Organization

This is a team dedicated to orchestrating the project, and in this case, the Steering Committee made up of key leaders from each partner agency supports it. The committee guides the vision, strategy, and priorities of the project, supporting aligned activities, monitoring measurement practices, building public support, advancing policy, and mobilizing resources. The Project Manager oversees the day-to-day activities of the project, coaching HOPE leaders, sharing the vision, and implementing the strategic priorities. This role is also the key connector within and beyond the education system to gather like-minded individuals and organizations to build capacity, inspire collaboration, and partner in implementation. In this case, the essential relationship has been between the local government and education systems, and a community-wide approach has been catalyzed through the aligned vision and willingness to collaborate. The MCC's contribution through participation and resources has enabled the project's sustainability for the last five years. Moving forward, the MCC made well-being a core priority, which is critical to a community flourishing together.

Common Agenda

All partners share an aspirational vision for change that includes a common understanding of the problem and a joint commitment to solutions through agreed-upon actions. These shared goals are the unifying purpose behind everyone's involvement.

Mutually Reinforcing Activities

A diverse set of multisector stakeholders coordinates a set of activities through a diverse but mutually reinforcing plan of action tailored to local needs and capabilities. For example, the Professional Certificate of Positive Education was an important ingredient for the network's success. It enabled the HOPE leaders to be guided through the development of whole-school well-being plans. Graduates' projects included staff and leadership training, whole-school immersion on topics such as gratitude and positive relationships (connectedness). Staff well-being and school culture are also featured strongly, which acknowledges the importance of first getting the right environment to enable sustainable change. It is also worth noting that success in student outcomes can only come when staff learn and live the theory before teaching the principles to students and parents and embedding them within policies and procedures.

Shared Measurement

Partners agree on how success will be measured and reported, with a short list of common indicators identified and used for learning and improvement. The network monitors progress using the University of Melbourne's Well-being Profiler, metrics from the Department of Education, and community-wide surveys.

Continuous Communication

Frequent and structured open communication builds trust, assures mutual objectives, and creates common motivation. There are many conversations, official and impromptu, held daily between partners, building strong relationships that are pivotal to the network's success. New ways are established to utilize the collective strengths, demonstrating that the whole is greater than the sum of the parts.

Looking to the future, it is exciting to know that momentum is growing as enthusiasm about well-being education is spreading. Inspiring stories are emerging as HOPE leaders discover staff using their initiative to develop the concepts with their students and parents. Community members and parents are also taking the learnings to their contexts. The network will continue to expand professional learning opportunities and support the ongoing collaboration to grow its impact in the broader community. The network welcomes the opportunity to share and learn from other communities hoping to take a system's approach to raise well-being.

Case Study Two: Geelong Catholic Primary Principals Network

Background

In 2016, Andrea Downie cofounded the purpose-driven organization Project Thrive to "make well-being commonplace" and partnered with the Geelong Catholic Primary Principals Network. This network currently spans 20 schools across the Geelong and surf coast region in Victoria, Australia. Andrea was known to the network through teaching and having served as a leader in one of the network schools. She had a strong endorsement from her former principal, who engaged her to facilitate this project. Trust was therefore established early on in the project. It was important that this journey started with a defined group of stakeholders, in this case, the principals, and that they became the leaders within their communities. In addition to the partnership, 95% of the network schools individually engaged with Project Thrive in different capacities to further personalize their approach and have context-specific and meaningful reach. Stakeholders in the processes included school staff, contractors to the schools (psychologists, councilors, and speech therapists), parish priests, students, parents, school boards, and the wider community. Staff from the Catholic Education Melbourne Western Region Office were also involved and have been supportive.

The schools in this network span different suburbs with varying sociodemographic profiles. Each school has a dedicated well-being leader. A number of the schools were accredited "Kidsmatter" schools, and every classroom teaches social and emotional learning, which is included under the Personal and Social Capabilities national curriculum. Well-being, supported by the Catholic Education directive, is a major priority for all network schools. Additionally, consultation with the principal network conference committee showed that mental health challenges within their communities impacted all principals. A health and well-being survey (Riley, 2017) showed that principal well-being was of increasing concern in Australia.

Mental health challenges continue to escalate and impact all facets of learning and teaching despite more money than ever being spent on well-being. In 2019, Australia was spending $9B a year on mental health, equating to $1M every hour (Australian Institute of Health and Welfare, 2019). In 2016, one in seven children in Australian primary schools and one in four in secondary schools, had a diagnosable mental illness. What was also clear is that many school leaders did not know how to focus on improving well-being, and as a result, those in well-being positions became consumed by welfare, reactive, and intervention tasks. Responding to adverse events is considered to be more urgent than creating positive events; therefore, the confusion between welfare and well-being began.

Change Process, Activities, and Anticipated Outcomes

The goals of the principal network were clear, meaningful, and codesigned. As the process developed, the goals evolved to ensure relevance for all principals, including those new to the group. The group continues to change, but a shared purpose remains. There were eight goals as follows: (a) building principal relationships and collegiality; (b) being intentional about the "why" and developing this with other key stakeholders; (c) enhancing well-being of the principals and their understanding of well-being science; (d) developing systems leadership and enhancing middle leader capability; (e) activating growth systemically by being relevant and effective; (f) empowering engagement by increasing student, staff, and community well-being; (g) taking risks and encouraging growth; and (h) developing a strong understanding of and commitment to a Catholic school.

The goals within the individual schools were also evident, to cocreate a paradigm shift toward becoming well-being ecosystems. This meant schools were not just speaking about their values; they coevolved and cotransformed toward wholeheartedly living them. They were moving from merely "doing more good" to "becoming." Overall, for maximum community benefit, the aim was to move from reactive problem-solving to intentionally cocreating the future. As part of this process, some schools codesigned ways of being and considered the inclusion of all stakeholders. These were about living their values; how they wanted to "show up" every day.

The initial engagement was a two-day conference exploring well-being elements, including relationships, engagement, and success with a focus on principal well-being. After a successful two days working together mostly on culture and relationships, the work began to deepen exploration of the system. Being intentional about the direction and initiatives and increasing capabilities in systems leadership to address complexities in education that exist was a major focus. Using several systems tools and processes provocations like, "What is the purpose of education?", "What assumptions do we make?", "What is my story?", and "How do I contribute to these assumptions?" were explored. The assumption that the education system creates competition, which fuels a fight for reputation, was considered and discussed. It increasingly became apparent that schools are not just in a battle for reputation in education as a whole system, but the struggle was for relevance. Schools need to become more relevant to reflect 21st-century challenges and set young people up with the necessary skills and values to thrive.

Appreciative inquiry (Cooperrider et al., 2011) was used throughout the journey with the network and individual schools. Systems mapping tools such as the iceberg model, causal loop diagrams, and connected circles were frequently used. The network engaged Robert Steele, a leading systems thinker from Compass Education. Shifts of the mind and shifts of relationships are at the core of transforming systems, therefore, mapping our system and connecting to more of ourselves was fundamental.

Perhaps the most important in all the processes was the immersions that took place throughout the journey. Scharmer and Kaufer (2013) explained that we cannot think differently in the same space; therefore, the principals were taken outside of the school setting to focus genuinely on opening minds (to challenge existing assumptions), hearts (being vulnerable and listening to one another), and will (letting go of preset agendas and goals to explore what is possible and needed). Immersions have included Project Thrive facilitated experiences in Bali. In this country, interconnectedness, ritual, nature, self, and others are of the highest priority. Eudaimonia (meaning) is the cornerstone of well-being and, despite Bali having fewer resources, communities are thriving from a well-being point of view. The principal network undertook an overseas week-long immersion in Bali, using processes such as deep spiritual connection and Theory U (Scharmer & Kaufer, 2013). The week was about developing Scharmer's seven essential leadership capacities: holding the space, observing, sensing, presencing, crystallizing, prototyping, and performing. Carefully designed activities took place at the Green School, Bali, Indonesia, to reimagine education that the group deemed eudaimonic. The week was about disrupting their current assumptions and inspiring potentiality of what could be with all principals agreeing that this emerged for them.

The focus led mostly to a shift toward meaning and purpose, the eudaimonic elements of well-being, and the opportunity to activate more learning aligned with purpose. Exploring the difference between hedonic well-being and eudaimonic well-being, some schools mapped all their programs, practices, and initiatives in well-being as being mostly reactive or proactive and hedonic (about pleasure and happiness) or mostly eudaimonic (about meaning, purpose, and authenticity). We believed that knowledge, skills, attitudes, and values cannot be authentically developed through happiness education and lessons. It is through the experiences of authentic learning that they would acquire these skills. Learning that considers a set of systems conditions that enable human flourishing, learning that considers nature, the economy, society, and well-being and, most importantly, is relevant to their local community.

The journey was not about a program or an overarching framework created from the beginning. Facilitator led and group informed, the group and their schools grew together. Constant attention and reflection were dedicated to this (Where are we now and where do we need to be?). The processes included taking responsibility for one's actions and creating aspirations to create a groundswell that the broader education system would notice. The codesign shared purpose and context-specific approach all created the direction. Inspiring leaders to intentionally act rather than be acted upon enabled them to empower staff and students to do the same. There was a mutual understanding that the "well-being of society is a shared destination" (OECD, 2019).

Assessment, Monitoring, and Evaluation of Outcomes

The approach being long-term deliberately avoids quick fixes deemed to be unsustainable. It was acknowledged that many frameworks and initiatives with best intentions do not have the desired impact. This journey also avoided heavy measurement of hedonic well-being (pleasure) and ensured it measured and assessed eudaimonic well-being. Unlike recommendations from Collective Impact Framework (Kania & Kramer, 2011), measurement differed across each school for reasons such as cost, access, and existing requirements. The compass education tool mapped relevance to well-being, society, nature, and the economy—all four deemed fundamental for human flourishing. Existing measures, both internal and external to Catholic Education, were used in some schools to measure culture, trust, staff, student, and parent perceptions, and overall well-being of staff, students, and the wider community. Additionally, internal measurements were designed by staff based on other scales providing a cost-effective and consistent approach.

Qualitative data, such as narratives and reflections, were collected along the way from principals' networks, such as pre- and postimmersions using Survey Monkey® and statements captured during the immersion sessions. Actions for goals were also captured throughout the journey from each principal in the network sessions. In addition, data were collected from the systems mapping exercises. Appreciative inquiry gauged network thinking as a reflective tool to ascertain the level of thought and creativity in their evolving approaches. Reflection has been a constant; discovering what is working, what is not working, and celebrating achievements. Given resources available and the context of the project, elements of the Collective Impact Framework (Kania & Kramer, 2011) were used, including ensuring a common agenda, continuous communication, mutually reinforcing activities, and to some extent, a backbone organization.

Over four years, each of the schools developed substantially. Some developed through their sustainability practices with a heightened awareness that well-being and sustainability are inseparable and provide a pathway. Other schools progressed by redesigning their schools or by redesigning the curriculum by aligning purpose and authentic processes. Still others developed their ways of being or by designing their immersions for staff to have the opportunity to get away and think differently. The impact in this network has been far and wide, and although the inspiration and catalyst came from one journey, it has supported school leaders to value systems leadership. As Senge et al. (2015) say, "knowing that there are no easy answers to truly complex problems, system leaders cultivate the conditions wherein collective wisdom emerges over time through a ripening process that gradually brings about new ways of thinking, acting, and being" (p. 30). How do we know a program has been effective? We wanted our communities to grow together. We wanted to enable collective wisdom and intelligence to emerge, and as demonstrated through constant reflection captured in network meetings, it is emerging. Collective leadership was described by Chinese philosopher Lao Tzu (as cited in Senge et al., 2015, p. 33) as "The great leader is s/he of whom the people say, we did it ourselves." Because of the nature of systems change, it will be difficult to fully capture the long-term impact of this journey and the disruption and innovation it has activated for many.

Key Elements for Sustainability

Throughout all Project Thrive partnerships, a number of key ingredients were found to be critical to the success of creating the desired paradigm shift. It is recognized that to do justice to measuring the approach, a longitudinal study would be required. The three Cs of success were developed for this approach: cocreation, collaboration and contribution, and context-specific.

Cocreation

Commitment and investment of time into the approach need to be *initiated* by those involved, and a *shared purpose* must exist. This was not a sponsored partnership or directed by a higher authority. From the beginning, there was buy-in because the partnership came from the group building upon their codesigned strategic plan. The shared purpose must be continuously reviewed and reflected upon as well as adapted when necessary. The groups who displayed the most growth and positive disruption were led by leaders who wholeheartedly believed in the work or were passionate about it. Trust was established in the facilitator and, therefore, the journey. All stakeholders needed to have open communication lines, including the facilitator (Andrea), who presented to school boards or managed parent/community evenings and staff sessions. Videos were made to bring the experiences from the immersions, preimmersion and postimmersion, back to each principal's wider communities. Even if stakeholders did not initially see the relevance because the idea seemed so unusual, an understanding and appreciation developed over time. Processes to enable cocreation were used and the voice of all stakeholders captured. As educators, we were fully aware and mindful of how much comes and goes with little impact and this we wanted to avoid. The group members were invested.

Collaboration and Contribution

This element is very much about culture. Trust is everything. If principals or schools are in competition, this fuels disconnection. We are wired to be interconnected, and doing deep inner work requires trust to develop connection. Trust needed to be established first to shift people from competing to collaborating and contributing. In other scenarios, it has been found that when trust was not present, there was more resistance among those involved and desired outcomes took longer to achieve.

Context-specific

Successful projects utilize a context-specific process. Knowing the group, understanding their strengths and challenges, and their intentions are crucial. Even within the principal network, what came alive in schools was unique and relevant to its context. The schools involved have been ready for different things at different times. For example, St. Aloysius in Queenscliff implemented experiential and authentic learning processes, and was nominated for state-wide awards in sustainability as a result of the work of their passionate staff and students and the collective leadership of their principal. Lisieux in Torquay, has been highly innovative in the design of their school and dedication to the natural world and complex learning done outside in real-life settings. The connection to one's self, nature, and each other is heightened in this environment. Clairvaux in Belmont is challenging how well-being is empowered with intentional cocreated strategic plans that focus on curriculum design that is not just about happiness education but about learning processes that empower well-being and students as change-makers. Regular network meetings among principals, deputy principals, and well-being leaders allow schools to feed off and inspire each other. Within the principal network, time is dedicated to reorienting strategy so that there is space for creating change, to enable collective intelligence and wisdom to emerge (Senge et al., 2015).

The immersions for the principal network were transformational and took relationships to the next level, deepening spiritual awareness to assist leadership and, for some, getting leaders outside of their comfort zone. Putting aside competitive motives to focus on the ecosystem is paramount. Some schools are used to seeing each other as competitors because, in many respects, the education system encourages it. The current system in place pushes young people to be the best in the world, and get the best grades measured against their peers and the National average instead of making them want to be the best *for* the world. This breeds hyperindividualism, which is counterproductive to building mutually beneficial relationships, interconnectedness, and well-being. Coming together and doing this work does not produce progress if high engagement, mutual trust, and shared purpose are not established from the outset. As Parker Palmer (2004) said,

> We can put the chairs in a circle, but as long as they are occupied by people who have an inner hierarchy, the circle itself will have a divided life, one more form of 'living within the lie': a false community.

(p. 25)

The future for this principal network and these schools is very exciting as they look toward a systems approach that is focused on contribution over the competition.

Considerations for Your Learning Community

As demonstrated in the two case studies, the ToC approach can address four broad categories: strategic planning, monitoring and evaluation, description, and learning (Stein & Valters, 2012). When applied to well-being initiatives in learning communities, strategic planning can be used to identify and map the change process and the expected outcomes. The processes and outcomes can then be monitored and evaluated over time, allowing the learning community to assess the various levels of contribution to change, and revise their ToC. This change process can then be used for communication with the various partners and learning community stakeholders. Explicit descriptions of this process can also facilitate active engagement and learning for the community. The ToC approach is a conscious, collaborative, and iterative exercise that requires dedicated time and resources to develop and evolve with ongoing reflective analysis and practice. Even though each learning community has its own sets of processes and assessment frameworks, there are universal underlying principles that enable well-being initiatives to be sustained over time across different communities. These principles are presented alongside sample activities and outcomes in Figure 27.2 using the four broad categories for ToC. Figure 27.2 provides an overview of four key principles underpinning a sustainable approach to fostering well-being for learning communities. Figure 27.3 provides individual level sample activities and outcomes for the key stakeholder groups of the community. It is not intended to be prescriptive, rather the aspiration is to provide an initial SyInC-ToC guide for learning communities seeking to shift well-being learning and engagement in a systematic manner. The insights, sample activities, and outcomes provide a general scope for discussion when initiating the process for implementing well-being initiatives in a learning community. This SyInC-ToC approach can be useful across different education sectors or organizational structures, ranging from one school with multiple campuses, to multiple schools across a network, to multiple networks across a region. This guide can be used to facilitate discussions to consider place-based needs and clarify knowledge gaps, with the view to develop critical reflection so that well-being learning and engagement practices adapt and mature over time, while taking into account contexts and complexities of the interconnected system. Existing approaches, frameworks, or tools are often complementary to a ToC approach, as demonstrated using the two case studies. Importantly, a ToC approach can be used to support well-being learning for reshaping strategy, understanding the context, strengthening organizational capacity, as well as developing individual and collective capabilities.

SYSTEM LEVEL

	Learning community strategic planning	Monitoring and evaluation through action research	Advocacy and engagement through communication	Learning through ongoing reflective analysis and practice
Principles for focusing on the process — General	• Foundation of strong, trusting relationships and meaningful collaboration to achieve shared outcomes for the community • Shared purpose with a common agenda and joint autonomous commitment to co-design goals and actions • Shared goals of improving well-being for whole of learning community—staff, student and community well-being • Dedicated time and resources for all stages			
Principles for focusing on the process — Categorical	• Use a systems approach framework to facilitate partner collaboration • Integrate well-being with community priorities	• Shared purposeful measurement that captures staff, student and parent/carers' well-being perceptions and experiences • Use place-based needs assessment to maximize fit for context-specific needs and capabilities	• Continuous partner communication • Active engagement with community using suitable forums	• Co-create authentic and inclusive learning experiences relevant to community needs • Build staff capacity, capabilities with deliberate, regular professional learning • Encourage active reflection
System level sample activities	• Involve representatives from each relevant stakeholder group in learning community • Develop partnerships with local agencies • Identify current individual needs across relevant groups • Outline unique contextual characteristics and factors of the learning community • Examine suitability and relevance of existing support and resources to adequately meet current needs • Consider the level of readiness within the learning community to change • Develop strategic plan to create or modify supports and resources • Identify short, intermediate, and long-term outcomes with corresponding time-frame	• Develop shared measurement across relevant groups (e.g., staff, students, parents/carers', campuses, networks) • Allocate adequate resources for assessment, monitoring and evaluation of outcomes • Collect and utilize data from existing and new sources that facilitate assessment of identified outcomes • Collect information about usage, engagement and fidelity of training • Use a variety of data collection methods (e.g., focus group, narratives, experience sampling, self-report survey) • Develop partnerships with external research institutions for independent evaluation	• Use suitable communication channels (e.g., videos, animation, info-graphs, newsletters) for each relevant stakeholder group in learning community • Provide regular updates through internal and external channels • Share learnings through community forums • Share resources and project findings with other learning communities	• Develop cohesive practice of using local data to inform both system and individual level learning and development • Establish working group to share and refine learning practices • Develop a feedback system to collate information regarding ways to optimize processes from relevant groups • Use local data and project learnings to update ToC model for the learning community

Figure 27.2 An Integrated Approach for Tracking System Level Activities and Impacts in Learning Communities Using ToC (SyInC-ToC)

- Planning documents reflect iterative updates based on local data and learnings
- Sustainable working partnerships developed with local agencies
- Adequate supports and resources developed to meet current and emerging individual needs across relevant groups
- Contextual characteristics and factors of the learning community considered in implementation of initiatives

- Increased awareness and participation of shared measurement across relevant groups (e.g., staff, students, parents/carers, campuses, networks)
- Adequate resources established for routine assessment, monitoring and evaluation of short, intermediate and long-term outcomes
- Greater usage and integration of data from existing and new sources that enable assessment of identified outcomes over time
- Using data to influence policy
- Enhanced capacity to triangulate data from various ways of data collection (e.g., qualitative, quantitative)
- Greater contribution to systems-level research for optimizing well-being in learning communities

- Increased awareness and engagement with each relevant stakeholder group in learning community
- Increased opportunities to share well-being initiatives with the broader community (e.g., forums, symposiums, conferences, media or peer-reviewed publications)

- Community of practice established through working groups to routinely use local data to inform both system and individual level learning
- Enhanced capacity to obtain and collate feedback from relevant groups in the learning community
- Greater usage and integration of local data and project learnings to update ToC model for the learning community

System level sample outcomes

431

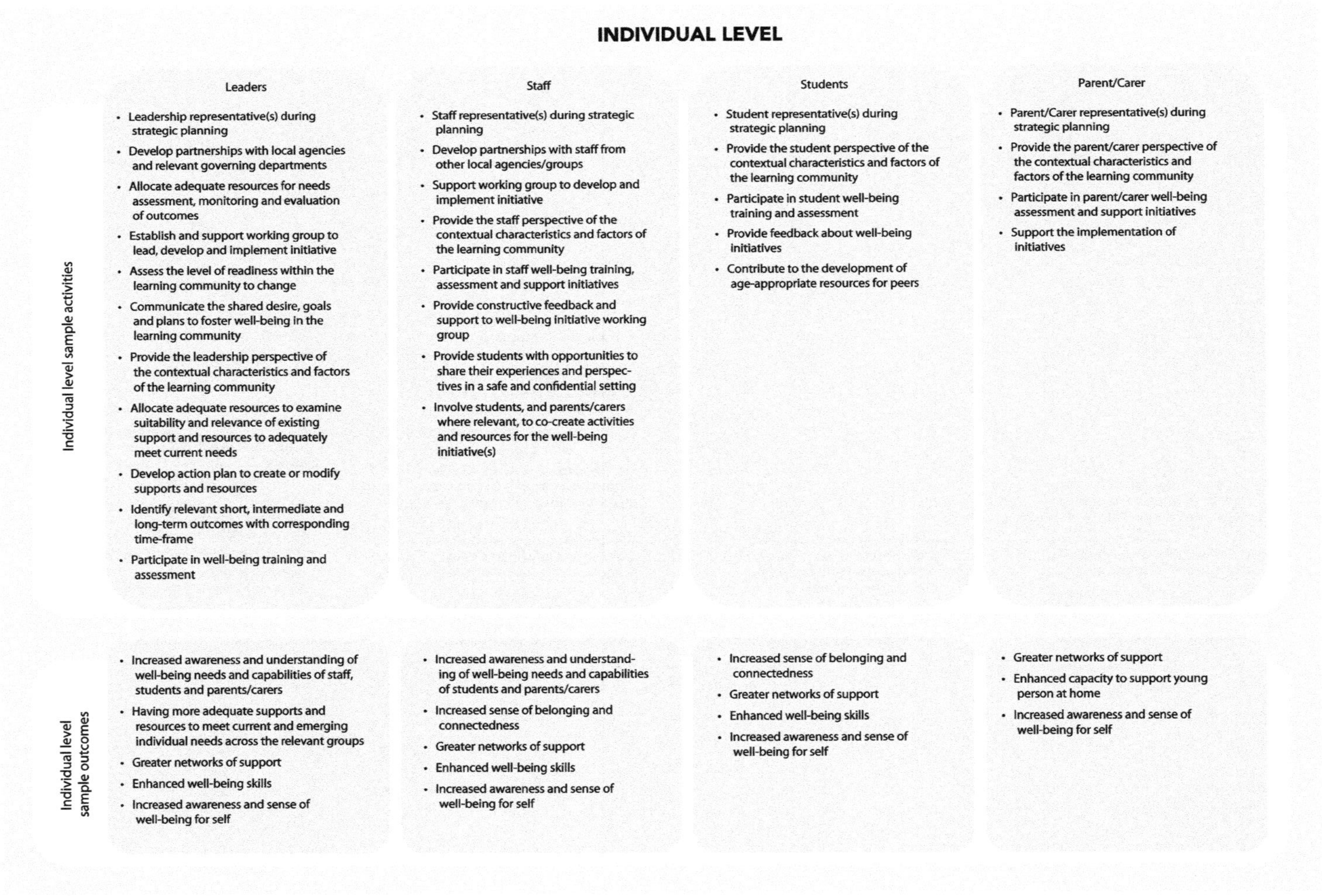

INDIVIDUAL LEVEL

Leaders

- Leadership representative(s) during strategic planning
- Develop partnerships with local agencies and relevant governing departments
- Allocate adequate resources for needs assessment, monitoring and evaluation of outcomes
- Establish and support working group to lead, develop and implement initiative
- Assess the level of readiness within the learning community to change
- Communicate the shared desire, goals and plans to foster well-being in the learning community
- Provide the leadership perspective of the contextual characteristics and factors of the learning community
- Allocate adequate resources to examine suitability and relevance of existing support and resources to adequately meet current needs
- Develop action plan to create or modify supports and resources
- Identify relevant short, intermediate and long-term outcomes with corresponding time-frame
- Participate in well-being training and assessment

Staff

- Staff representative(s) during strategic planning
- Develop partnerships with staff from other local agencies/groups
- Support working group to develop and implement initiative
- Provide the staff perspective of the contextual characteristics and factors of the learning community
- Participate in staff well-being training, assessment and support initiatives
- Provide constructive feedback and support to well-being initiative working group
- Provide students with opportunities to share their experiences and perspectives in a safe and confidential setting
- Involve students, and parents/carers where relevant, to co-create activities and resources for the well-being initiative(s)

Students

- Student representative(s) during strategic planning
- Provide the student perspective of the contextual characteristics and factors of the learning community
- Participate in student well-being training and assessment
- Provide feedback about well-being initiatives
- Contribute to the development of age-appropriate resources for peers

Parent/Carer

- Parent/Carer representative(s) during strategic planning
- Provide the parent/carer perspective of the contextual characteristics and factors of the learning community
- Participate in parent/carer well-being assessment and support initiatives
- Support the implementation of initiatives

Individual level sample activities

Leaders

- Increased awareness and understanding of well-being needs and capabilities of staff, students and parents/carers
- Having more adequate supports and resources to meet current and emerging individual needs across the relevant groups
- Greater networks of support
- Enhanced well-being skills
- Increased awareness and sense of well-being for self

Staff

- Increased awareness and understanding of well-being needs and capabilities of students and parents/carers
- Increased sense of belonging and connectedness
- Greater networks of support
- Enhanced well-being skills
- Increased awareness and sense of well-being for self

Students

- Increased sense of belonging and connectedness
- Greater networks of support
- Enhanced well-being skills
- Increased awareness and sense of well-being for self

Parent/Carer

- Greater networks of support
- Enhanced capacity to support young person at home
- Increased awareness and sense of well-being for self

Individual level sample outcomes

Figure 27.3 An Integrated Approach for Tracking Individual Level Activities and Impacts in Learning Communities Using ToC (SyInC-ToC)

Closing Remarks and Implications for Practice

Creating sustained shifts in well-being across learning communities involves intentional and strategic actions that are based on theory, prior experience and learnings, data, practical boundaries, and available or created resources. Although the specific actions and outcomes are not necessarily consistent across contexts, a template of standard processes that can be applied at the foundational level to achieve widespread, impactful, and sustained community change across a range of community well-being initiatives, seems plausible. This is evident from this chapter's two case examples. There were many overlapping processes relating to shared values, clear and consistent communication, collaboration, and codesign that were pivotal to the success of the initiatives. ToC provides some fundamental insights about significant determinants of achieving these community-wide well-being benefits and sets up realistic thinking around nonlinear processes, complexity, iterations, and timelines, despite encouraging aspirational thinking and goals. The SyInC-ToC framework in Figure 27.2 presents some of these ToC fundamental insights in general terms, such as building quality relationships and meaningful collaboration, having a shared purpose with a codesigned agenda, devising shared goals across the whole learning community, and providing sufficient resources throughout the project. The framework then outlines four categories of general processes: (a) the importance of strategic planning, (b) monitoring and evaluation, (c) advocacy and engagement, and (d) reflective analysis and practice. The framework presents methods for achieving these four processes that are context-specific and hence, varied. Sample activities and outcomes at both the systems level and individual level are provided for each category. For example, the monitoring and evaluation category includes collecting data from existing and new sources (sample activity) and using the data to influence policy (sample outcome).

Future work should focus on adding more detail and refining this SyInC-ToC framework to better understand whether all four principles are equally important for well-being change to occur across varied environments. It would also be helpful to gain insights into which activities are best suited to specific contexts and whether undertaking more activities equates with better outcomes. While we caution against automating the process and being prescriptive, as this is counter to context-specific theories of change, it is incumbent on professionals using systems approaches to promote well-being to create sensible shortcuts based on prior experience and learnings. This is possible if information about principles, activities, and outcomes at both the system and individual level, are routinely collected and summated for specific community contexts (such as learning communities for young people). Future initiatives need to draw on this type of information to enable limited resources to be used to the greatest effect, at least as a starting point. This SyInC-ToC framework is a preliminary attempt at devising such a template for learning communities to apply and also serves to encourage others to refine and add general and categorical principles, as well as systems- and individual-level sample activities and outcomes. A well populated template of this kind can be a valuable tool, guide, and motivator for those about to embark on projects aiming to create community-wide change such as fostering well-being. This call to action expands on this framework, represents joint efforts, and facilitates resourceful collective impact.

Acknowledgments

The authors would like to express their gratitude to the following:

- The Youth and Children's Services team at Maroondah City Council; in particular, Mel Jeffery, Rachelle Jones, Sarah Cullen, and Heather Cummings.
- Communities of Wellbeing Inc, in particular, Peter Feeney, and Maria Allison.
- The Maroondah Principal's Network, in particular, Shaun McClare and Johanna Walker, as well as all of the Principals from The Maroondah Positive Education Network.

- All of the HOPE Leaders and schools from the Maroondah Positive Education Network: Ainsley Parklands PS; Bayswater North PS; Bayswater PS; Bayswater SC; Bayswater South PS; Bayswater West PS; Croydon Community School; Croydon Hills PS; Croydon PS; Croydon SDS; Dorset PS; Eastwood PS; Great Ryrie PS; Heathmont College; Heathmont East PS; Kalinda PS; Marlborough PS; Melba SC; Mullum PS; Norwood SC; Ringwood Heights PS; Ringwood North PS; Ringwood SC; Ruskin Park PS; Tinternvale PS; Warranwood PS; Yarra Road PS.
- The Maroondah Positive Education Network Steering Group, in particular, Anthony Raitman (Department of Education and Training, Victoria) and Grant Meyer (Maroondah City Council).
- All of the Principals between 2016 and 2020 from the Geelong Catholic Primary Principals Network: Basil Flynn, Fiona Dawson, Dr. Susan Ryan, Rachel Holdsworth, Noel Dillon, Peter Brunt, Rhonda Boyd, Paul Cahir, Dena Reddan, Brian Everett, Peter Brunt, Maria Scala, Rod Sims, Natalie Heard, Michael Lane, Annice Lappin, John Grant, Anthony Drill, Jose Blackley, Mark Soldani, Kerryn Sells, Vin Healy, and Sean Kennedy.
- Project Thrive affiliated schools from the Geelong Catholic Primary Principals Network: Clairvaux Catholic Primary, Belmont; St. Aloysius, Queenscliff; Lisieux, Torquay; Holy Family, Bell Park; Holy Spirit, Manifold Heights; Nazareth, Grovedale; St. Margarets, East Geelong; St. Thomas, Drysdale; St. Anthony's, Lara; St. Mary Mackillop, Bannockburn; St. Patrick's, Geelong West; St. Therese, Torquay; St. Thomas Aquinas, Norlane; Our Lady Star of the Sea, Ocean Grove; St. Roberts, Newtown.
- Garry Trainor, Denise Mugavin, Wayne Richard, and Rob Aron from Catholic Education Melbourne, Western Region Office.
- Colleagues at Centre for Wellbeing Science at The University of Melbourne, in particular, Isabelle Stevenson, Rowan Jacques-Hamilton, and Dr. Kent Patrick.

References

Alford, Z. (2017). Positive education: Developing skills for school life and beyond. In M. White, G. R. Slemp, & S. Murray (Eds.), *Future directions in well-being: Education, organizations, and policy* (pp. 7–11). SPC Press.

Australian Institute of Health and Welfare. (2019). *Health expenditure Australia 2017–18*. Cat. no. HWE 077. AIHW.

Berger, E. M., & Spiess, C. K. (2011). Maternal life satisfaction and child outcomes: Are they related? *Journal of Economic Psychology, 32*, 142–158. https://doi.org/10.1016/j.joep.2010.10.001

Briner, R., & Dewberry, C. (2007). *Staff well-being is key to school success*. Worklife Support Ltd/Hamilton House.

Bronfenbrenner, U. (1994). Ecological models of human development. In T. Husen & T. N. Postlethwaite (Eds.), *International encyclopedia of education* (Vol. 3, 2nd ed., pp. 1643–1647). Pergamon.

Chin, T-C. (2017). Keeping up with the times: A considered approach to measuring youth well-being. In M. White, G. R. Slemp, & S. Murray (Eds.), *Future directions in well-being: Education, organizations, and policy* (pp. 47–51). SPC Press.

Cilar, L., Štiglic, G., Kmetec, S., Barr, O., & Pajnkihar, M. (2020). Effectiveness of school-based mental well-being interventions among adolescents: A systematic review. *Journal of Advanced Nursing, 76*, 2023–2045. https://doi.org/10.1111/jan.14408

Cooperrider, D., Whitney, D. D., & Stavros, J. M. (2008). *The appreciative inquiry handbook: For leaders of change* (2nd ed.). Berrett-Koehler.

Fatori, D., Bordin, I. A., Curto, B. M., & de Paula, C. S. (2013). Influence of psychosocial risk factors on the trajectory of mental health problems from childhood to adolescence: A longitudinal study. *BMC Psychiatry, 13*(31). https://doi.org/10.1186/1471-244X-13-31

Foster-Fishman, P. G., Nowell, B., & Yang, H. (2007). Putting the system back into systems change: A framework for understanding and changing organizational and community systems. *American Journal of Community Psychology, 39*(3–4), 197–215. https://doi.org/10.1007/s10464-007-9109-0

Funnell, S. C., & Rogers, P. J. (2011). *Purposeful program theory: Effective use of theories of change and logic models*. Jossey-Bass/Wiley.

Gottman, J. M., Katz, L. F., & Hooven, C. (1996). Parental meta-emotion philosophy and the emotional life of families: Theoretical models and preliminary data. *Journal of Family Psychology, 10*(3), 243–268. https://doi.org/10.1037/0893-3200.10.3.243

Harding, S., Morris, R., Gunnell, D., Ford, T., Hollingworth, W., Tilling, K., … Brockman, R. (2019). Is teachers' mental health and wellbeing associated with students' mental health and wellbeing? *Journal of Affective Disorders, 242*, 180–187. https://doi.org/10.1016/j.jad.2018.08.080

Hoare, E., Bott, D., & Robinson, J. (2017). Learn it, Live it, Teach it, Embed it: Implementing a whole school approach to foster positive mental health and well-being through Positive Education. *International Journal of Wellbeing, 7*(3), 56–71. https://doi.org/10.5502/ijw.v7i3.645

Janzen, R., Ochocka, J., & Stobbe, A. (2016). Towards a theory of change for community-based research projects. *Engaged Scholar Journal, 2*(2), 44–64. https://doi.org/10.15402/esj.v2i2.165

Janzen, R., Seskar-Hencic, D., Dildar, Y., & McFadden, P. (2012). Using evaluation to shape and direct comprehensive community initiatives: Evaluation, reflective practice, and interventions dealing with complexity. *Canadian Journal of Program Evaluation, 25*(2), 61–88.

Janzen, R., & Wiebe, D. (2010). Putting God in the logic model: Developing a national framework for the evaluation of faith-based organizations. *Canadian Journal of Program Evaluation, 25*(1), 1–26.

Kania, J., & Kramer, M. (2011). Collective impact. *Stanford Social Innovation Review, 9*(1), 36–41. https://ssir.org/articles/entry/collective_impact

Kania, J., & Kramer, M. (2013). Embracing emergence: How collective impact addresses complexity. *Stanford Social Innovation Review* (Winter). https://ssir.org/articles/entry/social_progress_through_collective_impact#

Kern, M. L., Williams, P., Spong, C., Colla, R., Sharma, K., Downie, A., Taylor, J. A., Sharp, S., Siokou, C., & Oades, L. G. (2019). Systems informed positive psychology. *The Journal of Positive Psychology*, 1–11. https://doi.org/10.1080/17439760.2019.1639799

Meadows, D. H. (2008). *Thinking in systems*. Earthscan.

Morris, A. S., Silk, J. S., Steinberg, L., Myers, S. S., & Robinson, L. R. (2007). The role of the family context in the development of emotion regulation. *Social Development, 16*(2), 361–388. https://doi.org/10.1111/j.1467-9507.2007.00389.x

Norrish, J. M., Williams, P., O'Connor, M., & Robinson, J. (2013). An applied framework for positive education. *International Journal of Wellbeing, 3*(2), 147–161. https://doi.org/10.5502/ijw.v3i2.2

Oades, L. G., & Johnston, A. L. (2017). Wellbeing literacy. The necessary ingredient in positive education. *Psychology and Behavioural Science International Journal, 3*(5), 5556212. https://doi.org/10.19080/PBSIJ.2017.03.555621

Organisation for Economic Co-operation and Development (OECD). (2019). *Trends shaping education*. OECD Publishing. https://doi.org/10.1787/trends_edu-2019-en

Palmer, P. J. (2004). *A hidden wholeness: The journey toward an undivided life*. Jossey-Bass.

Paterson, J. E., Field, J., & Pryor, J. (1994). Adolescents' perceptions of their attachment relationships with their mothers, fathers, and friends. *Journal of Youth and Adolescence, 23*(5), 579–600. https://doi.org/10.1007/BF01537737

Riley, P. (2017). *The Australian principal occupational health, safety and wellbeing survey: 2016 data*. Australian Catholic University.

Roffey, S. (2012). Pupil wellbeing–Teacher wellbeing: Two sides of the same coin? *Educational and Child Psychology, 29*(4), 8–17.

Scharmer, C. O., & Kaufer, K. (2013). *Leading from the emerging future: From ego-system to eco-system economies*. Berrett-Koehler.

Schepman, K., Collishaw, S., Gardner, F., Maughan, B., Scott, J., & Pickles, A. (2011). Do changes in parent mental health explain trends in youth emotional problems? *Social Science & Medicine, 73*(2), 293–300. https://doi.org/10.1016/j.socscimed.2011.05.015

Senge, P. M. (1990). *The fifth discipline: The art and practice of the learning organization*. Doubleday/Currency.

Senge, P., Hamilton, H., & Kania, J. (2015). The dawn of system leadership. *Stanford Social Innovation Review, 13*(1), 27–33. https://ssir.org/articles/entry/the_dawn_of_system_leadership

Sin, N. L., & Lyubomirsky, S. (2009). Enhancing well-being and alleviating depressive symptoms with positive psychology interventions: A practice-friendly meta-analysis. *Journal of Clinical Psychology, 65*, 467–487.

Slemp, G. R., Chin, T-C., Kern, M. L., Siokou, C., Loton, D., Oades, L. G., Vella-Brodrick, D. A., & Waters, L. (2017). Positive education in Australia: Practice, measurement, and future directions. In E. Frydenberg, A. J. Martin, & R. J. Collie (Eds.), *Social and emotional learning in Australia and the Asia-Pacific: Perspectives, programs and approaches* (pp. 101–122). Springer.

State of Victoria Department of Education and Training. (2020, April 30). *Framework for improving student outcomes (FISO)*. https://www.education.vic.gov.au/school/teachers/management/improvement/Pages/FISO.aspx

Stein, D., & Valters, C. (2012). *Understanding theory of change in international development: A review of existing knowledge* (JSRP Paper 1). JSRP and The Asia Foundation.

Stocker, C. M., Richmond, M. K., Rhoades, G. K., & Kiang, L. (2007). Family emotional processes and adolescents' adjustment. *Social Development, 16*(2), 310–325. https://doi.org/10.1111/j.1467–9507.2007.00386.x

Suldo, S., Shaffer-Hudkins, E., & Riley, K. N. (2008). A social-cognitive-behavioral model of academic predictors of adolescents' life satisfaction. *School Psychology Quarterly, 23*, 56–69. https://doi.org/10.1037/1045–3830.23.1.56

Vella-Brodrick, D. A., Rickard, N. S., & Chin, T-C. (2017). Evaluating positive education: A framework and case study. In N. J. L. Brown, T. Lomas, & F. J. Eiroa-Orosa (Eds.), *The Routledge international handbook of critical positive psychology* (pp. 488–502). Routledge.

Waters, L. (2011). A review of school-based positive psychology interventions. *The Australian Educational and Developmental Psychologist, 28*(2), 75–90. https://doi.org/10.1375/aedp.28.2.75

Williams, B., & van't Hof, S. (2014). *Wicked solutions: A systems approach to complex problems.* Lulu.com.

Yu, J. J., & Ko, Y. K. (2013). Paternal family expressiveness as a mediator between fathers' dispositional optimism and child's dispositional optimism. *Journal of Genetic Psychology, 174*(6), 677–695. https://doi.org/10.1080/00221325.2013.783548

28

TRACKING THE EFFECTS OF POSITIVE EDUCATION AROUND THE WORLD

*Dianne Vella-Brodrick, Jessica Frisina, Tan-Chyuan Chin
and Mohsen Joshanloo*[1]

Education in the 21st century increasingly recognizes the importance of developing well-being skills in addition to improving academic abilities (Elias & Moceri, 2012; Slemp et al., 2017). Positive Education—defined as applying the science of well-being to educational best practices— supports the promotion of student health (Seligman et al., 2009). Positive education practices (PEPs) are diverse. They range from brief and specific activities (Shankland & Rosset, 2017) including documenting one's best possible self or identifying three good things that happened in a day (Liau et al., 2016) to more comprehensive multicomponent programs that include a series of topics such as positive emotions, hope, strengths, meaning, and prosocial behaviors (Tejada-Gallardo et al., 2020). PEPs implemented over an extended period typically exist within a whole-school model, which simultaneously upholds Positive Education through implicit policies and procedures (e.g., Hoare et al., 2017).

School-based PEP models are associated with many advantages. One key advantage is that a large proportion of young people have access to such programs, given that most young people attend school. PEPs provide early intervention by focusing on healthy rather than maladaptive behaviors during critical adolescent developmental stages. In addition to a preventative effect, PEPs can be remedial to students in need. This is especially important since many young people are reluctant to seek professional help (Rickwood et al., 2005). Universal school-based programs also minimize the stigma often associated with seeking "psychological" help; they do not single out individuals as a result of having a "problem". Furthermore, schools can integrate PEPs in the curriculum, which offers a cost advantage to individuals and public health . Despite the advantages of universal PEPs, the conceptualization and application of positive education are often limited to Westernized contexts and ideals that emphasize individualism and self-fulfillment (Becker & Marecek, 2008). Hence, getting an insight into the distribution and effectiveness of PEPs across the globe will help elucidate how generalizable the effects of PEPs are across countries.

This chapter identifies key studies focused on the delivery and evaluation of positive education and critically reviews these study findings concerning their geographic and cultural contexts. The focus is on school-based programs that are delivered universally to students (typically in class groups) rather than specifically to those with poor mental health. A search of several databases, including Scopus, PsycINFO, and ERIC, identified relevant studies and any associated publicly available reports were also included. The search terms included: "positive education", "positive psychology," and "well-being" combined with "student," "education" "train*," "world*," and

DOI: 10.4324/9781003013778-35

"global." Searches were limited to studies published from 2010 onward. The inclusion criteria were based on the PICOS approach (Liberati et al., 2009) and included:

1   a population group of students
2   an explicit positive psychology practice (that covers topics focusing specifically on enhancing positive emotions, engagement and meaning, including gratitude, hope, and strengths identification) conducted in an educational setting including kindergarten, primary, secondary (high school), and higher educational institutions (e.g., universities);
3   an active *or* treatment-as-usual control group;
4   outcomes related to well-being; and
5   experimental and quasi-experimental studies.

In total, 11 studies met the inclusion criteria and were selected for this review. Of these, one study included students from Singapore, one from India, one from Portugal, one from Kuwait, one from North America, two from Israel, and four from Australia. The majority of these studies (seven) were undertaken with high school students, three studies recruited university students while primary school students and preschoolers were recruited for one study each (note: Lambert et al. 2018 included both university and high school students).

Asia

Liau et al. (2016) explored the implementation of a brief PEP in a higher education setting located in Singapore. A total of 191 participants with an average age of 18 years were recruited for the study. Participants formed six groups, half of which were randomly selected for the experimental group and the other half for the active control group. The experimental groups completed the Best Possible Self activity where participants were asked to project themselves into the future and imagine that they have met all their goals in every domain of their life. The control group was asked to write about their past week with a suggested focus on factors they liked and did not like. Both writing tasks comprised two sessions, one month apart. Participants completed measures of positive affect and negative affect pre and post each writing session, totaling four times. They also completed measures of optimism, life satisfaction and depressive symptoms twice; at baseline and at postintervention. The total number of participants completing the posttests was 162 (81 in each condition).

Results indicated that following the first writing session, the experimental group exhibited a more significant decrease of negative affect than the control group, and no significant positive affect changes (Liau et al., 2016). Furthermore, no significant interaction effects were found for optimism, life satisfaction, and depressive symptoms. Analyses of change scores indicated that changes in positive affect, albeit not significant, were related to changes in optimism scores, whereas significant changes in negative affect were related to changes in life satisfaction and depressive symptoms. A strength of this study was the inclusion of an active control group and the use of a relatively brief intervention. Furthermore, the contexts and instructions for both conditions were adequately described. However, there were no details regarding PEP facilitator training or delivery fidelity.

Leventhal and colleagues (2015, 2016) conducted a four-arm randomized controlled trial with 3,560 females with an average age of 13 years in Nihar, a rural location in India. They examined the effects of the Girls First resilience program on emotional, social, physical, and educational well-being. The four study conditions were: (a) Girls First, a combination of the Girls First Resilience Curriculum (RC), which targets social and emotional assets and well-being and the Girls First Health Curriculum (HC), which targets adolescent physical health and well-being; (b) Girls

First RC alone; (c) Girls First HC alone; and (d) a school-as-usual control group (SC). Seventy-six schools were randomly assigned to one of the four study conditions, resulting in 19 schools per condition.

Positive psychology and other fields such as restorative practice and peer support provide the foundation of the comprehensive Girls First program. More specifically, topics in the RC include listening skills, character strengths, goal planning, emotion identification and management, inter-personal communication, forgiveness, self-esteem, and group problem-solving. In total, the full Girls First program (the combination of the RC and HC) comprised 44 hours, delivered weekly in one-hour facilitated peer support group sessions. The separate RC and HC programs were in a similar format but, respectively, comprised 23 hours and 21 hours in total, each taking around half the time as the full Girls First program. Sessions were held at school in groups of 12–15 girls. They combined didactic learning with peer-led discussion and problem-solving. The program facilitators were 74 local women trained specifically by four master trainers to deliver these pro-grams. Training occurred over three or five days, depending on the group to which they were allocated. Facilitators were also provided with a three-day follow-up session mid-way through the intervention. Quality and fidelity were ensured through the guidance of protocols, manuals, and observation forms that were completed monthly by facilitators. In addition, biweekly group meet-ings with all facilitators were conducted throughout the program as were refresher workshops if required. All participants completed the surveys at four times points (average of 92% retention rate) and 99 girls also participated in either interviews or focus groups.

To examine psychosocial assets and well-being outcomes, Leventhal et al. (2015) examined a subset of 2,308 participants from 57 government schools. They compared the results of par-ticipants from the full Girls First or RC programs at baseline and immediate postprogram with those from the SC. As predicted, they found that participants exposed to the resilience programs significantly improved their positive psychological well-being and social well-being, in addition to other psychosocial assets such as self-efficacy, emotional resilience, and social-emotional skills. However, no improvements in depression or anxiety were reported. In sum, this study, along with the broader research program found that the Girls First program can improve social, physical, and emotional well-being for teenage girls from poor communities in India. As the Girls First pro-gram was delivered during school time in place of regular curriculum, the novelty of the program may have bolstered the positive outcomes. Training local women as facilitators was a strength of the study as it indicates that with moderate levels of training nonprofessionals can deliver the pro-gram and achieve favorable outcomes. This is helpful for scaling up program delivery using local resources and keeping costs down.

Australia

In Victoria, Australia, Geelong Grammar School (GGS) is at the forefront of positive education and serves as a model for many schools aiming to enhance student well-being (Slemp et al., 2017). The school-wide GGS model of Positive Education is based on six domains central to well-being—positive emotions, positive engagement, positive accomplishment, positive purpose, pos-itive relationships, and positive health—underpinned by a focus on character strengths (Norrish et al., 2013). These domains are delivered to students using explicit lessons during the school week, and implicitly through policies and procedures. Teacher training is integrated into the GGS model with all staff attending multiday positive education programs to develop their knowledge and application of it to their personal lives and their work at the school. Refresher workshops are provided for teaching and nonteaching staff each term to develop personal understanding and practice. A PEP community was also established and includes initiatives such as staff discussion groups and journal club meetings (Hoare et al., 2017).

In collaboration with the University of Melbourne, a nationally funded Australian Research Council–Linkage grant evaluated the GGS model. Reports by Vella-Brodrick and colleagues (2014, 2015, 2017) concluded that GGS students (n = 383) had a range of advantages through their positive education model across Years 9–11 compared with other best matched independent school students (n = 138) who did not complete a specific PEP but did have some exposure to well-being education in their standard curricula but in much smaller dosages. This comparison group is labeled "well-being-as-usual" (WBAU), as it is not a pure inactive control group per se. In 2013, over four years, the independent evaluation of Year 9 students' well-being was tracked. Several well-being dimensions were assessed in response to positive education over multiple time points using a variety of measurement methods, including self-reports, focus groups, and experience sampling.

Year 9 students live together at the Timbertop campus for an academic school year in a nature-based environment and complete classes aligned to the principles of positive education, in addition to conventional academic lessons and outdoor education. The Year 9 PEP has 10 modules presented for 60 minutes each week over the school year. These modules were: (a) activating event, thoughts and consequence (ATC), (b) Avoiding Thinking Traps, (c) Detecting Icebergs, (d) Energy Management, (e) Problem Solving, (f) Putting it in Perspective, (g) Real-Time Resilience, (h) Character Strengths, (i) Active Constructive Responding, (j) and Hunt the Good Stuff. Compared to WBAU, Year 9 students within the Timbertop PEP experienced significantly improved mental health (decreased depressive and anxiety symptoms) and well-being including life satisfaction, positive emotions, engagement, and meaning (Vella-Brodrick et al., 2014).

Vella-Brodrick et al. (2019) assessed the extent to which the Year 9 PEP met psychological needs such as competence, relationships, and autonomy. These Year 9 Timbertop students (n = 119) were compared with students (n = 79) undertaking well-being as usual from a range of best-matched independent schools. Based on responses to a student intrinsic need scale, the PEP students showed improved competency, relatedness, and autonomy postintervention, compared with WBAU participants.

Data from focus groups (n = 46) support the beneficial effects of the Year 9 Timbertop PEP. Students frequently expressed how they readily and meaningfully applied various components of the program to the social, physical, and emotional challenges they faced at Timbertop. Mobile devices were also used to assess real world, real-time daily experiences of a subset of Year 9 students for a week at the start of the school year before the core PEP classes and assessments were repeated for the following three school terms (four times in total). On several occasions throughout each day during a week, students would be notified via their devices to rate their current emotional state, indicate if they have experienced something significant, either positive or negative since they were last notified, and to select from a range of options any psychological strategies they were using to respond to these significant experiences. Strategies were categorized into positive (e.g., savoring the moment) or negative (e.g., taking negative feelings out on others).

Students whose well-being improved over the year (62% of the cohort) showed a significant decrease in the use of negative strategies in response to negative events. Also, students whose satisfaction with life increased over the year (67% of the cohort) showed a significant increase in the use of positive strategies in response to positive events. Students whose well-being improved attributed their use of positive strategies specifically to their learnings from GGS. This suggests that the Year 9 PEP was being translated into everyday life by increasing positive strategies such as savoring the moment, keeping everything in perspective, trying to relax and using the skill of real-time resilience (challenging counterproductive thoughts in the moment to stay focused and motivated), as well as reducing negative strategies such as avoiding the situation or taking negative feelings out on others. Being able to apply these strategies is related to enhanced levels of well-being and satisfaction with life.

From the same cohort of GGS students, the following year, 162 Year 10 students were compared with 83 WBAU students from other schools (Vella-Brodrick et al., 2015). A comparison of self-reported questionnaires at the beginning of the school year between GGS students and best-matched WBAU students from two other independent schools indicated that GGS students significantly improved on some well-being measures, specifically meaning, hope, social relationships, and physical health. Experience sampling methods identified strategies used by participants who improved in meaning and hope. These strategies included: making the most out of a good situation, changing attitude/thoughts, approaching others, and showing kindness and compassion. Focus groups were conducted with a subset of 33 GGS students to inform researchers about preferred features of the positive education program, which identified engaging teachers, hands-on learning, and relatable concepts (Vella-Brodrick et al., 2015). Changes in school engagement, depression, anxiety, and antisocial behaviors were not significant. Significant positive affects observed at the end of Year 10 were not sustained at 6- and 12-month follow-ups. School-based PEPs may provide limited support as students transition into the often challenging senior years of high school and subsequently experience heightened mental health issues. This study raised questions about how to better address patterns of increasing mental health across the senior years of schooling, pointing to the need for continued well-being training or booster sessions tailored to the specific needs of senior students.

The GGS Positive Education program (GGS PEP) was also applied and evaluated in government schools (Vella-Brodrick et al., 2017). Year 10 classes from two government schools in Melbourne were cluster-randomized into two study groups. A treatment group (*n* = 100) received four lessons (selected from a pool of 16 lessons) of the GGS PEP. A WBAU group (*n* = 182) received usual well-being services (e.g., pastoral care and occasional workshops by external facilitators). Teachers in the treatment group received two days of face-to-face training to prepare them for the program delivery of up to 16 lessons. Teachers and students from the treatment schools rated the PEP components they perceived as most relevant. The top-rated components— how to develop a positive attitude to life, recognizing your positive qualities, using strengths in everything you do and feeling hopeful about the future—were consequently included in the PEP intervention delivered across four lessons throughout the academic year. A comparison of self-reported questionnaire data found a significant improvement in psychological well-being and a decline in the treatment group's psychological ill-health at immediate postintervention, compared with the WBAU group. Changes in other factors such as antisocial behaviors, social engagement, and accomplishment were not significant (Vella-Brodrick et al., 2017). This finding is salient. It demonstrates that only a small number of sessions, particularly if tailored to students' needs, can have a significant impact on student well-being and mental health. Adapting positive education to each school's unique context appears to be an essential aspect of successful implementation.

This study is the first to comprehensively examine effects across the secondary school years. These findings suggest that secondary school students in independent and government schools that employ a school-wide positive education model manage their psychological health better. Qualitative data from student focus groups and novel data collection methods such as the experience sampling method provided insights about improving the program content and delivery, enabling more relevant and youth-friendly future programs. Future studies could use a similar mixed-methods design to add richness to quantitative data and inform changes to enhance the program effectiveness.

Another study conducted in Australia by Burckhardt et al. (2015) examined the mental health and well-being effects of Bite Back, an online school-based positive psychology program. Participants were students from four secondary schools randomly assigned to either the Bite Back program or the control condition based on classroom groups. Bite Back was delivered online for a total of six hours over four to six weeks. The program was designed primarily to help students build resilience and to reach their full potential and live a full and engaged life. Bite Back was highly interactive and included "making gratitude entries, mindfulness meditations, describing personal stories, and a mindfulness exercise involving taking photos" (p. 3). Students posted activities using an anonymous profile or kept their activities private if they preferred. Given the online context of the program, extensive monitoring, safety, and security measures were applied by the researchers to protect participants from any harm. A guide was also developed for students to use alongside the website content and interactive activities. The control condition involved viewing a series of entertainment (nonpsychology) websites such as the *Australian Broadcasting Corporation, World Wildlife Fund, Wikipedia, Internet Movie Database, and World Youth News*. Students read the material, wrote a summary, and answered questions in workbooks.

Participants completed depression, stress, and total symptom assessments as well as life satisfaction and flourishing at two time points: pre- and postintervention. Multilevel modeling found that participants from both groups reported improvements in all mental health outcomes and life satisfaction. Contrary to expectations, only the control participants showed significant improvements in flourishing postintervention. In sum, Bite Back, when administered online in the school context, was ineffective compared to control participants. The authors noted that delivery and progress checks may have been insufficient and that the online program may not be suitable as a structured classroom intervention.

Burckhardt and colleagues (2016) examined the effects of Strong Minds, a school-based mental health program, that blends acceptance commitment therapy with positive psychology. An Australian sample of 267 senior secondary school students (Years 10 and 11) were randomly assigned by their tutor group to either Strong Minds or usual pastoral care. The Strong Minds program involved the delivery of 16 face-to-face, 30-minute sessions, of which nine were primarily on acceptance and commitment therapy and seven on positive psychology. The first author, a qualified psychologist, led the sessions. A research assistant was also present for each session. Broad topics covered in the program included meaning, kindness, social relationships, and healthy lifestyles. Program fidelity was also assessed for the acceptance commitment therapy component. The pastoral care program was of equal duration and addressed issues such as how to manage social media and to engage in voluntary services.

For students participating in the Strong Minds program who had elevated psychopathology symptom scores at the program commencement ($n = 63$), there was evidence of improvements in depression and stress compared with the control participants, with medium and large effect sizes, respectively. From the larger sample of Years 10 and 11 students, only Year 10 students had an increase in well-being for the Strong Mind participants compared with the pastoral care group. While not all measures improved for all groups of students, the results showed that the program could be effective, particularly for students who experience elevated psychopathology symptoms at baseline.

Young et al. (2020) examined the efficacy of a positive psychology well-being intervention with undergraduate students from a university in Queensland, Australia. The intervention that was used across three studies, covered six topics (positive emotions, autonomy, meaning and purpose in life, environmental mastery, positive relations with others, and self-acceptance) and was integrated into the students' psychology classes and included lectures, in-class activities (e.g., best possible self, goal setting, and loving kindness meditation) and take-home activities such as 'three good things' and strengths spotting. A control group was included only for the third study. Hence, only the third study will be detailed in this review. In total, 188 students participated in this study; 105 in the positive psychology condition and 83 in the control group who completed the university subject "The Science of Everyday Thinking." The outcomes measured included well-being and positive and negative affect at two time points; pre and postintervention. Only 113 students completed the assessments at the second time point.

Mixed factorial ANOVAs found a statistically significant interaction between time and group with simple effects of time for each group indicating there was no significant increase in well-being for the intervention group, but rather a significant decrease in well-being for the control group participants. The authors concluded that the positive psychology intervention produced favorable outcomes in that it prevented a decrease in well-being which likely resulted from increased stress typically encountered by students as the semester progresses. Hence, the positive psychology intervention was described as serving a protective function.

The benefits of the positive psychology intervention were that it could be embedded within existing university content (psychology subjects)—which also helped to reduce the attrition rate—and was inexpensive and easy to administer. A major study limit pertains to the comparison condition which adopted different delivery methods and educators to the intervention condition. Ideally, these factors needed to be better matched to enable more accurate comparisons between the conditions.

Europe

The effect of PEPs on teachers and students has been considered by Carvalho et al. (2017) in Lisbon, Portugal. This study implemented the MindUp program, which is a mindfulness program that includes social and emotional learning, neuroscience, and positive psychology. MindUp was delivered by classroom teachers to an intervention group of 223 third- and fourth-grade students with an average age of 8.5 years. A control group included 231 same-aged children. Convenience sampling was adopted to select the schools from four clusters in the Lisbon District that were matched on socioeconomic status. Thirteen teachers also participated in the intervention, and seven teachers were involved as control participants. The MindUp program has 15 lessons taught once per week to students for 45–60 minutes. The mindfulness activities allow children to learn about their brain, understand how feelings and thoughts affect their actions, and learn ways of becoming a caring and altruistic person. The program also includes activities that teachers can embed in their daily teaching activities as well as three-minute formal mindfulness activities that are practiced three times per day. Teachers involved in the intervention were trained over six sessions, totaling 25 hours by an expert who delivered theoretical information about social and emotional learning, mindfulness, neuroscience, and positive psychology. Throughout the training, teachers were able to practice their mindfulness skills and to trial and practice how they would implement each session—this involved a further 25 hours of practice (Carvalho et al., 2017).

A comparison of the intervention group and control group on measures of positive and negative affect, emotional control, self-compassion, and mindful states for children was conducted (Carvalho et al., 2017). The results were generally favorable with approximately 50% of the children who participated in the MindUp program scoring above the control group mean on their ability to regulate emotions, to experience more positive affect, and to be more self-compassionate, and approximately 50% scoring lower than the control group mean in negative affect. Teacher outcomes were more pronounced as analyses found that over 80% of teachers scored above the control group mean in observing, personal accomplishment, and self-kindness (Carvalho et al., 2017). The data suggest there was a particularly substantial intervention effect for teachers compared to students. This is not surprising given the greater time commitment on MindUp for teachers compared with students. Fidelity data were not provided but should be considered in future studies to identify effective teacher training practices when implementing PEPs. Nonrandomization of classes into the intervention and control conditions is also a study limit. Follow-up assessments are also needed to establish the sustainability of any positive program effects. In addition, given MindUp is a multicomponent program, it would be helpful to examine which program components were most effective in enhancing the desired outcomes.

Middle East

A study conducted in Israel considered the long-term effects of PEPs (Shoshani et al., 2016). The study took place over two years and included 2,517 students in Grades 7–9 across six schools. Cluster randomization allocated 1,262 students to the intervention group, "The Maytiv program," which was compared with the control group participants who completed school as usual. The PEP evaluated in this study is based on the well-being determinants as proposed by the PERMA model (Seligman, 2011), including positive emotions, engagement, positive relationships, meaning, and achievement. More specifically, program components included experiencing joy and gratitude, managing negative emotions, cultivating flow activities, engaging in acts of kindness, identifying and pursuing personal strengths, enhancing resilience, and pursuing self-concordant goals. These topics were covered over 15 sessions that lasted 90 minutes and occurred biweekly. Teachers were trained in two 90-minute introductory sessions before the intervention commencement. Additional training sessions occurred before every student lesson to guide the delivery of content via stories, exercises, discussions, and activities (Shoshani et al., 2016).

Measures of subjective well-being, school engagement, and academic achievement were collected four times: time 1 (preintervention), time 2 (immediate postintervention), time 3 (eight months postintervention), and time 4 (one-year postintervention). Results concluded positive intervention effects on positive emotions, peer relations, emotional engagement in school, cognitive engagement, and grade point average scores (*Cohen's d*s = 0.16–0.71). There were significant decreases in positive emotions and cognitive engagement in the control group, and no significant changes in peer relations, emotional engagement, or school achievements. Strengths of the study include the detail provided about the intervention, such as session content, facilitators, and fidelity information. This process information provided a better understanding and interpretation of the study outcomes. Limitations of the results are a lack of information regarding teacher training, the reliance on self-report measures, and a lack of evaluation of teacher outcomes (Shoshani et al., 2016).

The first known study worldwide that implemented a positive psychology intervention for kindergarten aged children was also conducted in Israel (Shoshani & Slone, 2017). Random assignment placed 160 participants, ages 3–6.5 years from 12 preschool classrooms, into the Maytiv program, adapted by the authors to be developmentally appropriate. It had four content areas: positive emotions, engagement, achievement, and positive relationships. The content was combined into a regular classroom routine containing discussions, stories, songs, and games, lasting 32 weeks, with five activities implemented per week. Trained teachers delivered the intervention as in Shoshani et al. (2016). A high level of fidelity was documented with monthly reports evaluating the teachers' adherence to lesson plans (Shoshani & Slone, 2017).

All participants were measured pre- and postintervention on subjective well-being measures, including positive and negative affect, life satisfaction, empathy, and behavioral self-regulation (Shoshani & Slone, 2017). At the same time points, parents reported on the students' positive and negative affect, internalizing and externalizing behavior disorders, and prosocial behaviors. Teachers reported on the student's approaches to learning. Analyses concluded that the intervention improved children's self-reported positive emotions, life satisfaction, and empathy, compared to the control group. However, negative emotions and self-regulation did not show a significant improvement. Similarly, parent reports showed significant increase in positive emotions and prosocial behavior in the intervention group compared with the control group, but not for negative emotions and mental health difficulties. The intervention group improved students' positive learning behaviors and engagement, as reported by teachers, with no similar significant changes in the control group.

This study included data from a variety of stakeholder perspectives and shows that a PEP delivered by trained teachers can increase positive emotions and behavior in preschool-aged children.

A more comprehensive intervention that includes a parent component may be required to observe significant reductions in negative emotions. Exploration of effects on teacher outcomes and a more extended follow-up time point may increase knowledge of conditions that enhance effective PEP implementation in the younger years (Shoshani & Slone, 2017).

Another example of the growing interest in positive psychology in the Middle East comes from Kuwait. The nonprofit Alnowair group, which aims to increase the well-being of youth and adults has undertaken the Bareec Positive Psychology initiative (Lambert et al., 2018). The Bareec is a two-year intervention, trialed over eight weeks, with 15-minute weekly PEPs implemented during class time. A total of 133 university students across four universities and 833 students from 10 secondary schools were assigned to an intervention group. The control group included 77 university students and 237 secondary students. The intervention group participated in activities such as engaging in three good deeds over the week, plan a great day, participating in an engaging family activity, checking limiting beliefs, and physical activity. Teachers delivered the intervention following training similar to that provided by the GGS in Melbourne, Australia, which included instructions on how to implement sessions, plans, scripts, and topical articles to supplement teacher knowledge. Details surrounding the context, frequency and intensity of teacher training or fidelity of the program were not provided (Lambert et al., 2018).

All participants completed three measures, both preintervention and immediately postintervention, to identify changes in flourishing—a state of social psychological prosperity, positive feelings, negative feelings, and satisfaction with life (Lambert et al., 2018). Analyses of the university student data revealed that flourishing was significantly higher in the treatment group postintervention. However, levels of satisfaction with life, positive affect, and negative affect were not significantly different between the groups for the university sample at post-intervention. Similar results of improved flourishing, and positive affect, were found for high school students involved in the intervention compared to the control group. Levels of satisfaction with life and negative affect were also not significantly different between the high school groups at postintervention.

Several limitations exist in the study, including the possibility of contamination from intervention classes to control classes and a disproportionate number of females in the university sample (Lambert et al., 2018). More details about the teacher training and PEP implementation were needed to better understand the program quality and fidelity.

North America

A North American study (Roth et al., 2017) examined the effects of a multicomponent positive psychology program with 42 seventh graders from an urban school in a southeastern U.S. state. Students were randomly assigned to the positive psychology intervention or to a waitlist control group that received the positive psychology intervention in the following school year. Students completed well-being and psychopathology surveys on four occasions: at baseline, immediately after the intervention, and five and seven weeks later. Students in three groups of seven each received the positive psychology intervention. There were 10 weekly sessions of 50 minutes. Two follow-up sessions were provided to students, one and two months after the intervention. The intervention had an average of 10 hours of exposure to the positive psychology program. Each group had a leader and a coleader allocated from the research team that was responsible for overseeing homework tasks, providing materials, and supporting students during the intervention sessions. Leaders also completed fidelity records detailing the level of adherence to the intervention plan. There also was a parent component. Around 67% of the participant's parents attended an information session and all parents received weekly email handouts summarizing each lesson, homework tasks, and application suggestions for their family.

Compared with the waitlist group, Positive Psychology program participants reported improvements in all aspects of well-being (life satisfaction, positive affect, and negative affect); however, the small decreases in psychopathology symptoms were not significant. The benefits were still evident at the seven-week follow-up only for positive affect. The parent component aimed to reinforce student learning. The parent component's full effect is difficult to ascertain as there was no comparison intervention without a parent component. The small sample size comprised of students who are low on life satisfaction at baseline was another limitation. Measuring the level of parental involvement and/or parent perceptions of the intervention in future studies with larger samples is recommended.

When programs have positive affects, it would be helpful to identify the most impactful program components as this would help increase program efficiency, particularly for schools where time and space are especially critical. The use of mixed methods incorporating qualitative methods may provide more rich and descriptive data. Teacher perspectives about how well students received program components would also be valuable. Evaluating long-term effects beyond seven weeks is recommended. This study was thorough in detailing the program content as well as supporting and monitoring the program fidelity as delivered by the team of leaders. The Roth et al. (2017) study provides an excellent example for researchers conducting intervention studies.

Discussion

Despite the growing application of PEPs across the world, further research is needed to determine the features most conducive to the effective implementation of these practices and whether there are elements that are unique to location and culture. Barriers to such conclusions arise from a lack of consistency in the definitions of PEPs and the frameworks that underpin related programs. Consequently, the varying methods and interventions lack robust empirical evidence because of limited replication across different contexts. Other limitations, such as a tendency to report significant findings without a complete representation of nonsignificant findings, bias the current research base. Preregistration of study protocols can help provide a full account of the study questions, hypotheses, and methods. Two of the studies examined in this review were registered before conducting it—the Bite Back evaluation and the Girls First evaluation. Hopefully, these studies will serve to encourage other positive psychology researchers to do the same.

Existing literature indicates PEPs can result in promising outcomes for students; however, small sample sizes and attrition can limit the type of statistical analyses and findings obtained. Although small sample sizes are typical in preliminary or treatment studies that aim to explore the impact of PEPs before investing more resources, it can be difficult to ascertain the impact of other relevant variables for educational research such as school and teacher characteristics. In school-based research where generalizability is important, a variety of schools from government and non-government sectors and facilitators (e.g., teachers) need to be included in the study to determine if the program effects are consistent across all contexts. The data collection tools also need to be appropriate. Many studies relied on self-report questionnaires, which is a common drawback in the literature (Carvalho et al., 2017; Lambert et al., 2018; Leventhal et al., 2016; Liau et al., 2016) and often relies on reading and comprehension skills. Many of the measures are developed for adult samples and are not appropriate for use with children. This may explain why there are less studies examining positive education in younger children at primary or preschool levels. The inclusion of academic grades can provide supplementary objective information to evaluate the impact of PEPs and enhance the understanding of student functionality, as demonstrated by Shoshani et al. (2016). In addition, Shoshani and Slone (2017) included parent and teacher reports of student behaviors to provide a more holistic assessment of well-being, which could be replicated by future studies to enhance the validity of conclusions. Vella-Brodrick and colleagues (2014, 2015, 2017, 2019) extended beyond self-report questionnaires and included focus group and experience sampling data. This varied data provides information about efficacy and real-world effectiveness which can be used to iteratively improve the program for future delivery.

Another limitation of studies evaluating teacher-led PEPs is the scarcity of fidelity data, for example, Carvalho et al. (2017), Lambert et al. (2018), Liau et al. (2016), and Vella-Brodrick et al. (2014, 2015, 2017). In some cases, PEP facilitators record information about the accuracy of lesson plan delivery (Leventhal et al., 2016; Roth et al., 2017; Shoshani & Slone, 2017). Without this feedback regarding PEP implementation, program feasibility is difficult to determine. Furthermore, the teacher training component that often accompanies teacher-led PEPs is rarely described with adequate detail to enable replication or analysis of features that lead to effective outcomes, or otherwise. Researchers could include extended information regarding context, content, frequency, duration, and manuals when describing teacher training in future interventions. Expanding the range of data sources and including qualitative information in future reputable studies could enhance the conclusions and insights derived from research to inform practical recommendations regarding PEPs.

Given the relatively novel development and application of positive education, longitudinal studies on student well-being are limited. The studies presented in this chapter reflect the trend of short follow-up periods with immediate postintervention being typical (Lambert et al., 2018; Leventhal et al., 2016; Liau et al., 2016; Roth et al., 2017; Shoshani & Slone, 2017). However, improvements in student well-being following a PEP have been documented for a school year and up to six years postintervention (e.g., Shoshani et al., 2016; Vella-Brodrick, 2014, 2016, 2017, 2019). These studies justify more long-term evaluative research to determine which PEP mechanisms lead to lasting changes in student well-being and to examine if there are any lagged effects resulting from positive education. The inclusion of multiple stakeholders in PEPs may also enhance the likelihood of long-term positive intervention effects. School-wide processes and involvement of school leaders, teachers, and parents, guided by the PEP principles could be featured in future studies to widen the program reach and effectiveness.

Explicit PEPs implemented in isolation of a clear whole-of-school or systems approach are common (Leventhal et al., 2016; Liau et al., 2016). Fewer PEP programs incorporate teacher and parent components in addition to student learning, such as the MindUp program in Portugal and the GGS PEP program in Victoria, Australia (Hoare et al., 2017; Vella-Brodrick et al., 2014, 2015, 2017, 2019). These comprehensive models enhance the opportunity to understand the impact for multiple stakeholders. Future studies could explore the amount of involvement required for optimal results on measures of student, teacher, parent, and school leader well-being. These findings could uncover specific mechanisms and conditions conducive to the effective implementation of PEPs relative to the target population.

Based on this chapter's review, intervention quality, and training–support appear to be more essential for program success than the country of delivery. Almost all of the studies, irrespective of country, demonstrated some favorable outcomes resulting from the PEPs in comparison to control conditions. However, within each country, there may be unique needs. For example, in the studies by Leventhal and colleagues (2015, 2016) working with students from India (a low and middle income country) where a high number of females do not receive formal education especially compared to males, are involved in forced marriages during childhood and are at high risk of domestic abuse and teenage pregnancy. Hence, considerable attention was placed by these researchers on providing health and well-being education to those with heightened needs such as for girls from poor communities. There are still many cultural barriers to respectfully manage, including attitudes about girls' responsibilities and access to education, poor infrastructure, and limited resources. Leventhal and colleagues focused on building local capacity and saving costs by training local women with a base level of education to be the program facilitators.

Although country and culture may intersect in many instances, there are also examples of countries like Australia that are multicultural and hence, it is difficult to isolate any one culture when sampling the general population from that country. The cultural heterogeneity of the sample, and not just the country, needs to be considered in future work. Most studies reviewed typically included English-speaking participants with enough education to complete standardized well-being scales. Although English versions of scales are translated and back-translated to enable varied cultures to complete the measures, comprehension and cultural relevance are often a concern. Some empirical results cast doubt on the cross-cultural validity and equivalence of the scales widely used to measure positive outcomes (e.g., Oishi, 2018). Hence, it is crucial for future studies in non-Western cultures to pay more attention to cross-cultural differences in teaching and learning practices (e.g., Tweed & Lehman, 2002) and interpretations of positive psychological concepts (Uchida et al., 2008). Liau et al. (2016), for example, found that their Best Possible Self intervention decreased negative affect but not positive affect after the first writing session. As most studies have found the reverse, with improvements in positive affect but not negative affect, they attribute these differences in part to cultural factors. Cross-cultural researchers such as Joshanloo (2014) found that the constituents of happiness vary between Asians and Westerners. In some Asian cultures like Singapore, negative affect holds more significance for well-being than positive affect. Therefore, it may be more important for well-being interventions to decrease negative affect than to elevate positive affect for these populations. This observation is consistent with findings showing that culture can influence the effectiveness of positive psychology interventions (Shin & Lyubomirsky, 2017), and predictors of mental well-being vary according to culture (e.g., Suh & Choi, 2018).

This review identifies that the delivery and evaluation of school-based PEPs using rigorous research designs, is relatively scarce. While this work is occurring across the world and includes non-Western regions such as Asia and the Middle East, it seems that currently Australia is leading the way in this field of work. Although other reviews which include many more studies are emerging, they include a greater range of designs including pilot and correlational studies (e.g., Cilar et al., 2020). Continued research conducted worldwide can help evaluate the outcomes of PEPs and determine their level of validity and robustness across countries and should take into account unique needs and cultural contexts and adapt the program delivery and evaluation accordingly. This chapter's review makes it clear that the broad well-being benefits of positive education for student populations in different educational settings appear to be somewhat consistent despite geographical differences—however, some cultural nuances may impact some of these findings. A fruitful next step is to critically examine the influence of cultural factors using well designed studies with that objective at the forefront.

References

Becker, D., & Marecek, J. (2008). Dreaming the American dream: Individualism and positive psychology. *Social and Personality Psychology Compass, 4*(5), 1767–1780. https://doi.org/10.1111/j.1751-9004.2008.00139.x

Burckhardt R., Manicavasagar V., Batterhamb P. J., & Hadzi-Pavlovic, D. (2016). A randomized controlled trial of strong minds: A school-based mental health program combining acceptance and commitment therapy and positive psychology. *Journal of School Psychology, 57*, 41–52. https://doi.org/10.1016/j.jsp.2016.05.008

Burckhardt R., Manicavasagar V., Batterhamb P. J., Miller L. M., Talbot E., & Lum A. (2015). A web-based adolescent positive psychology program in schools: Randomized controlled trial. *Journal of Medical and Internet Research, 17*(7), e187. https://doi.org/10.2196/jmir.4329

Carvalho, J. S., Pinto, A. M., & Maroco, J. (2017). Results of a mindfulness-based social-emotional learning program on Portuguese elementary students and teachers: A Quasi-experimental study. *Mindfulness, 2*, 337–350. https://doi.org/10.1007/s12671-016-0603-z

Cilar, L., Štiglic, G., Kmetec, S., Barr, O., & Pajnkihar, M. (2020). Effectiveness of school-based mental well-being interventions among adolescents: A systematic review. *Journal of Advanced Nursing, 76*(8), 2023–2045. https://doi.org/10.1111/jan.14408

Elias, M. J., & Moceri, D. C. (2012). Developing social and emotional aspects of learning: The American experience. *Research Papers in Education, 4,* 423–434. https://doi.org/10.1080/02671522.2012.690243

Hoare, E., Bott, D., & Robinson, J. (2017). Learn it, live it, teach it, embed it: Implementing a whole school approach to foster positive mental health and well-being through positive education. *International Journal of Well-being, 7*(3), 56–71. https://doi.org/10.5502/ijw.v7i3.645

Joshanloo, M. (2014). Eastern conceptualizations of happiness: Fundamental differences with western views. *Journal of Happiness Studies, 15*(2), 475–493. https://doi.org/10.1007/s10902-013-9431-1

Lambert, L., Passmore, H., Scull, N., Al Sabah, I., & Hussain, R. (2018). Well-being matters in Kuwait: The Alnowair's Bareec education initiative. *Social Indicators Research, 5*(2), 1–23. https://doi.org/10.1007/s11205-018-1987-z

Leventhal, K. S., DeMaria, L. M., Gillham, J. E., Andrew, G., Peabody, J., & Leventhal, S. M. (2016). A psychosocial resilience curriculum provides the "missing piece" to boost adolescent physical health: A randomized controlled trial of Girls First in India. *Social Science & Medicine, 161,* 37–46. https://doi.org/10.1016/j.socscimed.2016.05.004

Leventhal, K. S., Gillham, J. E., DeMaria, L. M., Andrew, G., Peabody, J., & Leventhal, S. M. (2015). Building psychosocial assets and well-being among adolescent girls: A randomized controlled trial. *Journal of Adolescence, 45,* 284–295. https://doi.org/10.1016/j.adolescence.2015.09.011

Liau, A., Neihart, M., Teo, C., & Lo, C. (2016). Effects of the Best Possible Self activity on subjective well-being and depressive symptoms. *Asia-Pacific Education Researcher, 25*(3), 473–481.

Liberati, A., Altman, D., Tetzlaff, J., Mulrow, C., Gøtzsche, P., Ioannidis, J., Clarke, M., Deveraux, P., Kleijnen, J., & Moher, D. (2009). The PRISMA statement for reporting systematic reviews and meta-analyses of studies that evaluate health care interventions: Explanation and elaboration. *Journal of Clinical Epidemiology, 62*(10), e1–e34. https://doi.org/10.1016/j.jclinepi.2009.06.006

Norrish, J. M., Williams, P. O'Connor, M. & Robinson J. (2013). An applied framework for positive education. *International Journal of Well-being, 3*(2), 147–161, https://doi.org/10.5502/ijw.v3i2.2

Oishi, S. (2018). Culture and subjective well-being: Conceptual and measurement issues. In E. Diener, S. Oishi, & L. Tay (Eds.), *Handbook of well-being.* Salt Lake City, UT: DEF Publishers.

Rickwood, D., Deane, F. P., Wilson, C. J., Ciarrochi, J. (2005). Young people's help-seeking for mental health problems. *Australian E-Journal for the Advancement of Mental Health, 4*(3), 218–251. https://doi.org/10.5172/jamh.4.3.218

Roth, R. A. Suldo, S. M., & Ferron, J. M. (2017). Improving middle school student's subjective well-being: Efficacy of a multicomponent, positive psychology intervention targeting small groups of youth. *School Psychology Review, 46,* 21–41. https://doi.org/10.17105/SPR46-1.21-41

Seligman, M .E. P., Ernst, R. M., Gillham, J., Reivich, K. & Linkins, M. (2009). Positive education: Positive psychology and classroom interventions, *Oxford Review of Education, 35* (3), 293–311, https://doi.org/10.1080/03054980902934563

Seligman, M. E. P. (2011). Flourish: A visionary new understanding of happiness and well-being. Free Press.

Shankland, R., & Rosset, E. (2017). Review of brief school-based positive psychological interventions: A taster for teachers and educators. *Educational Psychology Review. 29*(2), 363–392. https://doi.org/10.1007/s10648-016-9357-3.

Shoshani, A., & Slone, M. (2017). Positive education for young children: Effects of a positive psychology intervention for preschool children on subjective well-being and learning behaviors. *Frontiers in Psychology, 8.* https://doi.org/10.3389/fpsyg.2017.01866

Shoshani, A., Steinmetz, S., & Kanat-Maymon, Y. (2016). Effects of the Maytiv positive psychology school program on early adolescents' well-being, engagement, and achievement. *Journal of School Psychology, 57,* 73–92. https://doi.org/10.1016/j.jsp.2016.05.003

Shin, L. J., & Lyubomirsky, S. (2017). Increasing well-being in independent and interdependent cultures. In S. I. Donaldson & M. A. Warren (Eds.), *Scientific advances in positive psychology* (pp. 11–36). Praeger.

Slemp, G., Chin, T-C., Kern, M., Siokou, C., Loton, D., Oades, L., Vella-Brodrick, D., & Waters, L. (2017). Positive education in Australia: Practice, measurement, and future directions. In E. Frydenberg, A. Martin, A., & R. Collie (Eds.), *Social and emotional learning in Australia and the Asia-Pacific: Perspectives, programs and approaches* (pp. 101–122). Springer.

Suh, E. M., & Choi, S. (2018). Predictors of subjective well-being across cultures. In E. Diener, S. Oishi, & L. Tay (Eds.), *Handbook of well-being.* DEF Publishers. https://www.nobascholar.com/chapters/45/download.pdf

Tejada-Gallardo, C., Blasco-Belled, A., Torrelles-Nadal, C., & Alsinet, C. (2020). Effects of school-based multicomponent positive psychology interventions on well-being and distress in adolescents: A systematic review and meta-analysis. *Journal of Youth and Adolescence, 49(10)*, 1943–1960. https://doi.org/10.1007/s10964-020-01289-9

Tweed, R. G., & Lehman, D. R. (2002). Learning considered within a cultural context: Confucian and Socratic approaches. *American Psychologist, 57(2)*, 89–99. https://doi.org/10.1037/0003-066X.57.2.89

Uchida, Y., Kitayama, S., Mesquita, B., Reyes, J. A. S., & Morling, B. (2008). Is perceived emotional support beneficial? Well-being and health in independent and interdependent cultures. *Personality and Social Psychology Bulletin, 34(6)*, 741–754. https://doi.org/10.1177/0146167208315157

Vella-Brodrick D. A., Chin, T-C., & Rickard, N. S. (2019). Examining the processes and effects of an exemplar school-based well-being approach on student competency, autonomy and relatedness, *Health Promotion International, 35(5)*, 1190–1198. https://doi.org/10.1093/heapro/daz115

Vella-Brodrick, D. A., Rickard, N. S., & Chin, T-C. (2014). An evaluation of positive education at Geelong Grammar School: A snapshot of 2013. Melbourne, Australia: The University of Melbourne. Commissioned by Geelong Grammar School.

Vella-Brodrick, D. A., Rickard, N. S., & Chin, T-C. (2015). An Evaluation of Year 10 Positive Education at Geelong Grammar School: Findings from 2014. Melbourne, Australia: The University of Melbourne. Research funded by Australian Research Council LP130100357.

Vella-Brodrick, D. A., Rickard, N. S., Hattie, J., Cross, D., & Chin, T-C. (2017). Enhancing adolescent mental health through positive education. A longitudinal evaluation of Year 10 Positive Education: Findings from 2014 to 2016. Melbourne, Australia: The University of Melbourne. Research funded by Australian Research Council LP130100357.

Young, T., Macinnes, S., Jarden, A., & Colla, R. (2020). The impact of a wellbeing program imbedded in university classes: The importance of valuing happiness, baseline wellbeing and practice frequency. *Studies in Higher Education*, 1–20. doi: 10.1080/03075079.2020.1793932

29

ENHANCING WELL-BEING IN YOUTH

Positive Psychology Interventions for Education in Britain

Carmel Proctor

In 2007, UNICEF published a groundbreaking study examining the lives of children and adolescents in economically advanced nations (UNICEF, 2007). Results of that initial study were shocking—children in Britain were among the unhappiest, unhealthiest, economically disadvantaged, and least educated in the developed world. During the six years that followed, however, the U.K. moved from being at the bottom of a list of 21 developed nations on five dimensions of child well-being (material, educational, family, and peer relationships, behaviors and risks, subjective well-being) to 16th out of the world's richest 29 countries (UNICEF, 2013).

Over the past 20 years, the U.K. has actively attended to national concerns with regards to the well-being of children and adolescents, which were tragically brought to the forefront by the death of Victoria Climbié in 2000. In 2003, in response to Victoria's death, the U.K. government issued the *Every Child Matters* agenda. Within the *Every Child Matters* agenda is the responsibility of schools to promote students' well-being (Challen et al., 2011). Moreover, in 2004, the U.K. government amended the *Children Act* of 1989, largely a result of the Climbié inquiry. According to the *Children Act* 2004, there is a duty to "[s]afeguard children and young people, improve their life outcomes and general well-being" until they are 19.

Within the U.K., a national children's charity, The Children's Society, issues an annual report, *The Good Childhood Report* focusing exclusively on the well-being of children and adolescents. Since 2005, with support from the University of York, The Children's Society has carried out substantive research examining what improves and what diminishes well-being according to young people. Overall, the society seeks to obtain a national overview of child and adolescent well-being, by asking children themselves.

Despite the 2003 *Every Child Matters* agenda, in 2007, the UNICEF overview of child well-being (UNICEF, 2007) indicated that unacceptable levels of disadvantage, poverty, and lack of education remained. As reported in the last release of this volume, *The Good Childhood Report 2012* (The Children's Society, 2012), although most U.K. children were happy with their lives as a whole, approximately one in 11 (9%) were not—approximately half a million children between the ages of 8 and 15. Moreover, the research suggested that children's overall well-being varied little according to individual or family characteristics, that there were few differences in well-being for boys and girls, for children living in different types of households, and that well-being declines with age—with approximately 4% of children aged eight years having low well-being

DOI: 10.4324/9781003013778-36

compared to 14% of adolescents aged 15 years. These findings are consistent with those reported in the literature (see Gilman & Huebner, 2003; Proctor et al., 2009 for reviews).

According to *The Good Childhood Report 2019* (The Children's Society, 2019), there has been a significant decrease in happiness with life as a whole among 10- to 17-year-old children and adolescents over the past decade. Further, there has been a significant decrease in happiness with friends and school; however, there is no significant change in happiness with family, appearance, or schoolwork.

Data presented were gathered using their *Good Childhood Index*, which includes measurement of overall well-being in 10 key areas: family, home, money and possessions, friendships, school, health, appearance, time use, choice and autonomy, and the future. The reported research findings not only shed light on the state of well-being among Britain's young people but are also in keeping with findings reported in the research literature, suggesting the generalizability of the results. In the paragraphs that follow, results from the *Good Childhood Report* 2012 and 2019 will be summarized, and examples of corresponding research literature presented.

What Effects Children's Well-Being in Britain?

As found in previous years, *The Good Childhood Report 2019* (The Children's Society, 2019) found that children are most satisfied with their relationship with their family and least happy with the school they attend. These findings are in keeping with the literature identifying children's parental relationship as the essential component of well-being, irrespective of family structure. Family structure stability is also of utmost importance (see Proctor et al., 2009 for a review). Youth who experience a change in the family structure were twice as likely to experience low well-being (cf. Brown, 2004; Laursen et al., 2019).

The home environment also plays a critical role with safety, poverty, and frequent moves having an adverse impact on children's well-being (cf. Clair, 2019). Related to these findings, lack of money and possessions also adversely impacts well-being. Children living in the poorest 20% of households having significantly lower well-being than those not in income poverty or without financial strain; above average, there is little difference in levels of well-being (cf. Wilson et al., 1997). Friends also appear to play an important role in well-being, with the number and quality of relationships having an impact. For example, *The Good Childhood Report 2012* (The Children's Society, 2012) reported that 6% of children felt they did not have enough friends, which was linked to lower well-being, and those who experienced bullying were six times more likely to have low well-being than those who had not been bullied at all (cf. Asher & Hopmeyer, 1997; Diener et al., 2010; Flouri & Buchanan, 2002; Rigby, 2000). Satisfaction with school, schoolwork, and safety at school were also important aspects, with 80% reporting that doing well at school was very important and 7% reporting that they felt unsafe at school (cf. Park, 2005; Valois et al., 2006). Children's well-being is also related to their physical health, with those who rate their health as "very bad" being more likely than those who are happy with their health to be living in poor households (cf. Zullig et al., 2005). Satisfaction with appearance was also a factor that increased with age—32% of boys and 56% of girls worry about their appearance by age 15. Children who are unhappy with their appearance are also more likely to be the victims of bullying (cf. Blom-Hoffman et al., 2006; Valois et al., 2003).

In *The Good Childhood Report 2019* (The Children's Society, 2019), more than half of all children viewed seven different aspects of their future—educational grades, going to university, finding a job, having enough money, finding a place to live, and their mental and physical health—as "very important." These views were considered important irrespective of household income; however, children in more impoverished families had less expectation of going to university than other children. Worries across the seven different future aspects increased with age, and 40% of all children were worried about broad environmental and societal issues, such as climate change and crime.

Overall, the 2019 report further highlights the importance of children's experiences on their subjective well-being and happiness (cf. Adverse Childhood Experiences (ACES; Felitti, 2002)). According to this report, a single experience of poverty or financial strain can relate to increased depression and low life satisfaction at age 14, with multiple disadvantages in different areas negatively impacting well-being in general. School emerged as an important focus, with scores associated with happiness with school found to be significantly lower than previously reported. Analyses of connections between poverty and financial strain and well-being suggest that improving children's subjective experience of school may be key to improving their overall subjective happiness. In keeping with the Department of Educations' *Every Child Matters* agenda, schools are, therefore, an ideal place for initiatives to improve overall well-being among children and adolescents.

Promoting Positive Well-Being in Schools

Researchers of positive psychology asked the vital question: "should well-being be taught in school?" (Seligman et al., 2009, p. 294). According to Seligman et al. (2009), the answer is yes, not only because increased well-being is synergistic with better learning but also because increased well-being and happiness are outcomes that parents most want for their children. Moreover, although most young people report that they are happy, it is not necessarily the case that they are flourishing; that is, filled with positive emotion and functioning well psychologically and socially (Diener & Diener, 1996; Huebner et al., 2000). Indeed, parents want more for their children than just the avoidance of negative behaviors (e.g., drug and alcohol abuse, violence, bullying, and depression), they want their children to be happy and to thrive in all domains of life (Moore & Lippman, 2005). Unfortunately, as already noted, there are a significant number of children and adolescents who are unhappy and dissatisfied with life. Healthy psychological states, such as happiness and well-being, are both the cause and consequence of diverse positive personal, behavioral, psychological, and social outcomes (Lyubomirsky et al., 2005; Sheldon & Lyubomirsky, 2019). Hence, it is vital to understand how to boost those who are languishing and unhappy to a more optimal state of functioning (Sin & Lyubomirsky, 2009) while protecting those with positive levels from diminishing.

Schools are an ideal place for well-being initiatives, especially considering that children spend the majority of their weekday in school and much of their day-to-day interactions affecting their well-being occur while at school (Seligman et al., 2009). Indeed, national education strategies, such as the Social and Emotional Aspects of Learning (SEAL), have been implemented, so that emotional and personal well-being can be taught overtly through existing curriculum courses, such as Personal, Social, and Health Education (PSHE). Indeed, driven in part by the positive psychology movement, attention is now turning to how to make schools happy places (Noddings, 2003). Despite nation-wide efforts to promote well-being among young people over the last two decades, reports (e.g., as reviewed above) on the state of well-being within the U.K. suggest that their effectiveness may be in question.

Concerns over the effectiveness of such nation-wide efforts to promote well-being point to many of these initiatives being too prescriptive, with a focus on informing students what to do and what not to do, instead of fostering good character through practicing and modeling moral behavior (Park & Peterson, 2009). A promising alternative to increasing well-being among young people in school is through positive psychology interventions (intentional activities that aim to cultivate positive feelings, behaviors, or cognitions; Sin & Lyubomirsky, 2009). Indeed, exploratory investigations into the teaching of well-being in school through the application of positive psychology interventions and theory has led to significant improvements in students' well-being and life satisfaction (e.g., Proctor et al., 2011; for reviews see Seligman et al., 2009; Waters, 2011).

The remainder of this chapter reviews school-based positive psychology interventions in Britain, which are outside of the context of national well-being strategies implemented by the U.K. government and are not typically associated with positive psychology. Reviewed in the section that follows are nine examples of curriculum-based programs implemented in Britain, including examples of interventions in Scotland and Ireland.

School-Based Positive Psychology Interventions

Positive psychology interventions (PPIs) have been successfully applied in educational settings and resulted in positive behavioral, social, psychological, and academic outcomes among adolescent students. Such interventions and strategies come in various diverse forms and include a wide array of activities. In general, however, PPI interventions can be conceptualized as either single-component PPIs that focus on one key strength, such as gratitude, or multicomponent PPIs that integrate several positive psychology concepts (Green & Norrish, 2013).

Examples of Curriculum-Based Single Component PPIs

Making Listening Special

Making Listening Special is a project at the Milestone School in Gloucestershire. This project is part of the Listening to Young Children Strategy, which is committed to hearing the voices of young children and enabling these voices to shape services. Milestone School is a special school for children aged 2–16 who have a mixture of special needs. The project uses teaching approaches adapted from *Gentle Teaching* (McGee & Menolascino, 1991), an approach to helping those with special needs that have an explicit focus on well-being (Fox Eades et al., 2013). The project recognizes that children learn to be strong and independent from a base of secure relationships and that for children with autism and complex learning difficulties, creating a safe and secure environment is an essential prerequisite to their learning (Thompson, 2009). The class group that took part included six kindergarten children with autism and severe learning difficulties and involved three staff supporting the children at any one time. The project aimed to achieve the following outcomes for the children:

- to feel happy and safe within their new classroom environment—increasing confidence and self-esteem;
- to feel a valued member of the class group—wanting to be with others and feeling relaxed in interactions with others;
- to feel a good sense of self-worth—increasing confidence in participation and cooperation;
- to understand they are special and valued through the response of adults to their individual needs—feeling a sense of companionship, having a close circle of friends and respecting others and being respected by others;
- to feel inner contentment—feeling inner harmony, free from traumatic experiences.
- to have meaningful daily activities—enjoying daily life and having daily activities which incorporate their individual special needs and interests; and
- to begin to experience daily structure—having daily routines and having their individual beliefs and rituals respected by others.

The staff skillfully put the individual strengths and abilities of the students at the heart of student learning and created a personalized curriculum; rather than making the students fit into an imposed curriculum. Assessment of the project involved using a variety of methods, including photographs, observations, discussions with staff and parents, and school assessment procedures. Results indicated that teaching by teacher development enhanced teaching of the following abilities:

- be engaged or "fully present" in all interactions with the children—being there for the children with clarity of mind and fully focused attention;
- be unconditionally accepting—value the children for who they are, which involves giving them space to be themselves;
- "let go"—of assumptions and being open to listening by allocating equal worth to the children and listening with the intent to understand;
- teach not only with mind but also with heart—teaching with love, kindness, and compassion;
- foster a sense of belonging—enabling the children to achieve inner states of harmony and ease;
- provide serenity of approach—giving time for reflection and being sensitive to the inner world of individual children's special needs; and
- believing in the children—grounded in respects and understanding.

To effectively achieve these outcomes in the classroom, the staff recognize the importance of the students as "experts" in their lives and focus on individual preferred activities to increase positive emotions and improve learning (Fox Eades et al., 2013). Areas of difficulty were approached by drawing on individual strengths and by giving students choices. Overall outcomes included positive changes to both the individual classroom and the general school environment.

Mindfulness

Mindfulness is an intentional self-regulated state of attention on the present moment involving an orientation that is characterized by curiosity, openness, and acceptance (Bishop et al., 2004). Mindfulness meditation is a form of meditation that involves acknowledgment and observation of continually changing internal and external stimuli as they arise, thereby allowing one to relate opening with their experience (Bishop et al., 2004). Huppert and Johnson (2010) examined the results of mindfulness training in a classroom setting among adolescent boys from two English private boys' schools. Religious education teachers in both schools were long-standing mindfulness practitioners and keen to participate in the research. Students in the intervention group participated as part of their religious instruction classes and completed four mindfulness lessons over four weeks (Waters, 2011). The intervention group was taught by the teachers who were already long-standing mindfulness practitioners and the control group was made up of classes normally taught by other teachers. Comparison of groups on measures of mindfulness, resilience, and psychological well-being was undertaken. Although differences between the two groups failed to reach significance, among the mindfulness group, there was a significant positive association between outside the classroom individual mindfulness practice and improvements in psychological well-being and mindfulness (Huppert & Johnson, 2010). Overall, most students reported that they enjoyed and benefited from the training, and 74% indicated that they would like to continue to practice mindfulness in the future.

Examples of Curriculum-Based Multicomponent PPIs

Wellington College

Since 2006, Wellington College in Berkshire has been implementing a happiness and well-being course for their fourth and fifth Form students. The course aims to promote flourishing and excellence among young people by educating them on how to capitalize upon their strengths and potentialities (Wellington College, 2012). Six elements of the course serve to promote well-being:

- Physical Health—foundations of well-being and physical health;
- Positive Relationships—relationships with other people;
- Perspective—building resilience and developing thinking skills to overcome adversity;
- Strengths—identifying character strengths and abilities and applying them in daily life;
- World—living sustainably and considering our place in the world; and
- Meaning and Purpose—exploring meaning-making and our response to the questions life asks of us.

Each strand contains examples of dispositions that can be explicitly taught and also reflected across the whole school community (Morris, 2013). During the first three years of school, students receive one hour every other week of well-being instruction. These lessons involve teaching the students skills and cognitive methods they can use to enhance their well-being in life. The students also benefit from a series of lectures from inspiring speakers designed to help them reflect on making the most of their lives. Moreover, mindfulness has been an integral part of the well-being program at Wellington since it began, and short meditations form part of the well-being lessons. Overall, the approach to teaching well-being at Wellington is one of activity or habituation, an approach most closely associated with Aristotle—that is, that happiness arises from doing things well by striving for personal excellence. At Wellington, the staff believe that schools should "educate for happiness"; that is, the formal curriculum should enable children to acquire, develop, and exercise their strengths and talents and foster their decision-making skills, so that they can experience what makes them happy (see Morris, 2014 for a review).

Celebrating Strengths

At the primary school level, *Celebrating Strengths* (Fox Eades, 2008) is an approach that takes a holistic school view of well-being. This approach builds upon the belief that a flourishing classroom requires a flourishing teacher to create the conditions in which students will flourish. This program links the VIA Classification (Peterson & Seligman, 2004) of character strengths and virtues to specific festivals and events throughout the school calendar. It incorporates activities such as the strengths-based classroom (recognizing the strengths of all class members), victory logs (record books noting students' achievements), and celebrations (of "what went well") into the curriculum. The program structure includes three threads: strengths, festivals, and stories, and works at three levels: individual, class, and the whole school. The teaching principles within *Celebrating Strengths* include: using the environment to reinforce and highlight strengths and concepts, linking abstract concepts such as hope to durable traditions, exploring abstract concepts through philosophy for children, directly reinforcing strengths and concepts through exercises, and indirectly reinforcing strengths and concepts through stories. To fully imbed all aspects of the program takes approximately three years. An evaluation of this program has indicated several positive outcomes, including increases in children's self-confidence and motivation to achieve, improved behavior at home and school, and an overall positive impact on cognitive, emotional, and behavioral development (Govindji & Linley, 2008, August).

Strengths Gym

At the middle and secondary school levels, *Strengths Gym* (Proctor & Fox Eades, 2019) is an approach constructed around the character strengths included in the VIA Classification (Peterson & Seligman, 2004). The approach aims to combine a focus on the individual (e.g., through specific strengths-based activities) with a focus on the institution (e.g., by providing classroom lesson plans and applications across the curriculum; Fox Eades et al., 2013). The program involves students completing age-appropriate strengths-based exercises on each of the 24 VIA Classification of character strengths and virtues across a three-level learning process.

The program aims to encourage students to build their strengths, learn new strengths, and to recognize strengths in others. The course is designed for use with children aged 11–14; however, it is adaptable across the student and age range. Student worksheets corresponding to which level and strength students are working on are provided. The student activities begin with a self-identification of each individual's top five strengths. Students are encouraged to create a work-booklet in order to collate and record their work. Each of the three levels of the program include 24 lessons, one for each of the 24 VIA character strengths. Each lesson contains a definition of the character strength and two "Strengths Builder" and one "Strengths Challenge" exercise. The exercises at each level are unique but designed to be equivalent and age-appropriate. The program involves a three-stage learning process: (a) general understanding of strengths and development of a strengths vocabulary, (b) identification of own use of strengths, and (c) recognition and identification of the use of strengths by others. The conclusion of each level provides students with the opportunity to list any strengths they found difficult but persisted in learning. There is space to write about things they are proud of accomplishing, and an opportunity to reevaluate their top five strengths after they have had a chance to learn about all 24 strengths (Proctor & Fox Eades, 2019). The program includes a comprehensive teacher's manual (Proctor & Fox Eades, 2019) containing flexible lesson plans enabling teachers to choose activities that suit the mood and the needs of their class. The manual is designed to provide teachers with as much flexibility as possible and enough material and options to cover all three levels of the course. Each strengths session in the manual contains the following elements: key features, definition, benefits, famous quotes, (philosophical) thinking questions, closing activities, display suggestions, strengths story, and applications across the curriculum. Results of a preliminary research study examining the impact of the program among 319 adolescent students aged 12–14 years by Proctor et al. (2011) revealed that students who participated in the program experienced significantly increased life satisfaction compared with adolescents who did not participate in the program.

The U.K. Resilience Program

The U.K. Resilience Program (UKRP) is the U.K. implementation of the Penn Resiliency Program (PRP). A three-year study of the UKRP began in 2007, led by the London School of Economics. During 2007, members of the PRP research team trained approximately 90 teachers to deliver an adapted version of the PRP curriculum to groups of students in three local authorities (South Tyneside, Hertfordshire, and Manchester; UPenn, 2007). The PRP is an 18-lesson curriculum designed to prevent depression in young people. The primary goal of the PRP curriculum is to increase students' ability to handle daily stressors and adolescent problems (Seligman et al., 2009). The PRP promotes optimism through realistic and flexible thinking techniques and teaches students assertiveness, creative brainstorming, decision-making, relaxation, and coping and problem-solving skills (Seligman et al., 2009). In general, the program is a cognitive-behavioral program developed within the positive psychology framework that helps students understand their thinking styles and how it impacts on how they feel and what they do.

A central element to PRP is Albert Ellis's Activating-Belief-Consequences model—that beliefs (B) about an activating (A) influence the consequent (C) feelings (Challen et al., 2011). Overall, the program aims to provide young people with the skills to be more resilient in dealing with situations in and out of school.

The UKRP was pilot tested with Year 7 students in 22 schools, to build resilience and promote well-being. Teachers attended a five- to eight-day training course on how to teach the program to young people. The nature of the curriculum is such that cognitive behavior therapy skills appropriate for use with adults are required. Thus, during the training, teachers develop resilience skills, appropriate for themselves and other adults, before learning how to teach the program to students. A large-scale evaluation of the program conducted by Challen and colleagues (2011) appears in a report of the findings commissioned by the U.K. Government. The research consisted of both quantitative and qualitative elements. The quantitative results indicated significant improvements in depression and anxiety scores, attendance rates, and attainment in English and math. Overall, the impact varied by student characteristics with a larger impact for students: (a) entitled to free school meals, (b) who had not attained the national targets at key stage 2, and (c) who had worse initial symptoms of depression or anxiety.

The qualitative results indicated that teachers were extremely positive about the ideas underlying the program and the training they had received, with most reporting that they used the skills themselves. The students were positive about the program and interviews for the First Interim Report suggested that students had applied PRP skills in real-life situations, with some interviewees showing a good understanding of elements of the program. Also, return visits to nine of the case study schools in autumn of 2009 revealed that seven of the nine schools were continuing to deliver the UKRP to all Year 7 students.

Overall, the key findings of the UKRP evaluations included: (a) significant short-term improvements in depression symptom scores, school attendance rates, and academic attainment in English; (b) larger improvements with increased participation (e.g., weekly more than biweekly); (c) impacts lasting only as long as participation, with effects fading after one year, and with no impacts at two years; (d) no impacts of workshops on behavior scores or life satisfaction scores; and (e) students reporting generally positive appraisal of the program and that they were using skills in real-life circumstances (L. Bailey, personal communication, November 22, 2012). These findings are similar to those of the PRP, which has been demonstrated to reduce and prevent symptoms of depression in young people (cf. Challeng et al., 2014).

Haberdashers' Aske's Hatcham College

Through a unique partnership with the University of East London, the Haberdashers' Aske's Federation, principally sponsored by the Worshipful Company of Haberdashers, has developed its well-being curriculum devised for Years 1–13 based on the research and theory of positive psychology. This program was implemented at Haberdashers' Aske's Hatcham College in London. The aim in developing this program was to create a comprehensive positive psychology-based well-being curriculum that targets all of the significant predictors and correlates of well-being, using individually tested interventions to enhance learning. In Years 1–9, the emphasis is on positive interventions intended to foster happiness, positive emotions, flow, resilience, achievement, positive relationships, and meaning. In Years 10–11, the emphasis is on positive education, such as enabling young people to reflect upon and make choices about their well-being and development.

The program spans across five different blocks of years (or key stages) of the national curriculum with different outcomes and focuses for each year group. The weekly well-being lessons take the form of informal discussions, group work, practical exercises, and roleplay grounded in the latest positive psychological theory. Examples of the topics covered in Years 1–3 during the primary phase of the program include: happiness, recognizing emotions, joy, just for fun, interest/curiosity, love, being calm and patient, sadness, anger, flow, good memories, savoring, celebrating, play, noticing good things and being thankful, hope, and mood-boosting.

In Years 7–9, students participate in one well-being class per week, which is delivered by the tutor of their year group. Some of the topics covered in this lower secondary phase of the program include essential skills of well-being, measuring happiness, the effects of happiness, optimizing well-being, positive and negative emotions, managing feelings through minimizing negative emotions, enhancing positive emotions, getting on with others, resolving conflict, positive reminiscence, learning to breathe, mindfulness, meditation basics, the power of exercise, nutrition, sleep, and being in charge.

In Years 10–11, students also participate in one well-being class per week delivered by the tutor of their year group. Some of the topics covered in this upper secondary phase of the program include self-awareness and acceptance, personal change, self-evaluation (respect and esteem), feelings, emotions and moods, reasoning, creative thinking, beliefs, courage, and confidence, worrying, security, aliveness, pleasure, learning, and death.

Program effectiveness has been evaluated with standardized questionnaires administered at the beginning and end of each year. These measures assess: self-actualization, global and multidimensional life satisfaction, and affect. A control school where no well-being intervention took place served as a comparison of the initial results. Results from data gathered during the first year of implementation (2008–2009) indicated significant increases in positive affect; satisfaction with friends, self, and family; self-actualization; and global life satisfaction (Popovic, 2017; P. A. Koureas, personal communication, November 28, 2012). There were significant decreases in negative affect in comparison with students who did not receive the program.

Examples of Interventions in Scotland and Ireland

Bounce Back

Bounce Back (N. Miguni, personal communication, November 24, 2012) is an Australian well-being and resilience program sponsored by The Young Foundation that was introduced in 16 schools in Scotland. Bounce Back is based on the following acronyms:

- **B**ad times don't last. Things always get better. Stay optimistic.
- **O**ther people can help if you talk to them. Get a reality check.
- **U**nhelpful thinking makes you feel more upset. Think again.
- **N**obody is perfect—not you and not others.
- **C**oncentrate on the positives, no matter how small, and use laughter.
- **E**verybody experiences sadness, hurt, failure, rejection, and setbacks sometimes, not just you.
- **B**lame fairly—how much was due to you, to others, and to bad luck?
- **A**ccept the things you can't change, but try to change what you can first.
- **C**atastrophizing exaggerates your worries—don't believe the worst possible picture.
- **K**eep things in perspective—it's only one part of your life.

The program includes nine units (i.e., core values, people bouncing back, courage, looking on the bright side, emotions, relationships, humor, no bullying, and success), which repeat in each book (Kindergarten to Grade 8) with age-appropriate activities. It uses children's literature and literacy activities, and integrates the content across subject areas. Activities include circle time, cooperative learning, and educational games. The program is integrated with Social Emotional Learning (SEL) and incorporates both positive psychology and cognitive behavioral therapy techniques. The integrated teaching strategies include literacy activities and games, thinking tools and activities, cooperative strategies, drama, multimedia and art, and numeracy activities. For example, a "blame fairly" activity can utilize the "attribution wheel," whereby students explore their attributional style (i.e., how they explain the bad events in their lives) and learn to improve optimistic thinking.

Evaluation of the program in Scotland included comparing quantitative and qualitative data collected before implementation of the program and at 18-month follow-up. Conclusions from the evaluation are that students:

- reported feeling more connected to their school,
- perceived school as a happier and kinder place where fewer students felt lonely or left out, and more students were now accepted,
- perceived that they had more control over their feelings and actions, and
- felt it increased their sense of confidence and their social skills.

Conclusions from the evaluation are that teachers:

- observed more positive relationships and interactions between students;
- felt more resilient and confident;
- reported more effective skills for dealing with challenging situations in their professional and personal lives, and
- had higher levels of overall well-being.

Overall, results to date are encouraging with the program having a positive impact on both students and teachers (N. Miguni, personal communication, November 24, 2012).

Blackrock College

In Ireland in 2012, an all-boys school, Blackrock College in Dublin, introduced a Leadership Values and Behavior Policy as part of its future strategic development. An integral part of this strategy was a training program in positive psychology for the 72 House Captains (school prefects from second to sixth year inclusive, aged between 13 and 18, approximately). The objective of this Positive Leadership and Well-Being Program was to facilitate a basic understanding and to promote the creation of the necessary skills for positive leadership. Specifically including: self-awareness, character strengths, personal values and virtues, growth mindset, love of learning, true grit and drive, courage and compassion, goals for growth, willpower and intrinsic motivation, self-regulation, self-control, effective decision-making and routine. Skills that aid the creation of authentic self-esteem and healthy confidence necessary for quality leadership.

The aim was optimum engagement through active participation and energetic fun and was both task and team-oriented, involving games and play designed to be challenging and promote creativity. Short videos and illustrations that represent learning through visual senses and humor were utilized to facilitate visual thinking. Forum theatre or roleplay to replicate real school life scenarios were also utilized to ensure ongoing engagement through variety and novelty. A popular session of guest speakers also complemented these scenarios, with fun topics such as "creative problem solving games."

The learning from these multivaried sessions was concretely reinforced by debriefings and both small and full group discussions. In addition, all participants were given preparatory tasks, and ongoing assignments were reviewed and discussed in the next session/workshop. Preparatory tasks included online completion of the VIA-Youth (Peterson & Seligman, 2004) and an assessment of personal meaning. Assignments included prescribing book reviews and listing of top lessons. Positive active interventions were also included, such as: expressing gratitude, cultivation of optimism, committing to your goals, practicing random acts of kindness, learning to forgive, and savoring life's joys. Storyboard posters were also created, displaying particular leadership events within the college, which were displayed on the college campus to enhance leadership awareness.

In sum, the Positive Leadership and Well-being Program is an individual strengths-based and positive culture approach to enhancing leadership and personal potential. Its design enhances the environment and culture where "strength and truth," "fearless and bold," and a "creed of caring" are nurtured and allowed to flourish. Overall, feedback on the program has been positive and encouraging and a solid start for future development at Blackrock College (D. Hevey, personal communication, December 9, 2012).

Applying Positive Psychology Interventions in Schools: Considerations

In considering the application of positive psychology interventions in schools, several points are noteworthy for those wishing to implement or develop well-being programs. Firstly, it is essential to have the support of the headteacher of the school. Headteachers are the most senior teacher of a school and are responsible for leading and implementing learning and managing the school overall.

Secondly, consultants and others working with teachers and schools need to provide them with "positive psychoeducation"; that is, teachers require genuine insight into the techniques they will be implementing in order to maximize success. As noted in Waters' (2011) review of positive education interventions, teachers implement most PPIs, and thus positive education training needs to be delivered to teachers. Indeed, teachers need to understand the positive psychology approach and value it in order to apply it. For example, research on the success of the PRP program indicated that training was essential, with the level of training and supervision that group leaders received being related to variability in effectiveness (Gillham et al., 2007; Seligman et al., 2009).

One of the major stumbling blocks to providing adequate positive psychoeducation, however, is the lack of funding and resources by the majority of schools who need these programs the most (Chodkiewicz & Boyle, 2017). Indeed, impressive positive outcomes of whole school applications appear in the literature (e.g., Morris, 2013; White, 2013); however, schools considered are often privately funded and thus have the ability and resources to implement school-wide programs (e.g., PRP and Strath Haven Positive Psychology Program). Therefore, materials supplied to teachers designed to enable them to implement positive psychology programs where training is not possible need to be informative and user friendly. Furthermore, the job of educational consultants is not to teach teachers how to teach, but to provide them with the tools to implement positive psychology techniques into their teaching. Those working with schools need to consider what they can give that can be applied once they leave. In the school context, very little is "pure" manualized positive psychology—learning is adapted to suit the needs of the institution. Successful application in the school context involves adding positive psychology to existing techniques. For example, art teachers will respond well to creativity applications. Overall, the key is the infusion of positive psychology skills into established school subjects.

Third, school-wide approaches ensure that positive psychology becomes part of the wider school culture (Waters, 2011). In order to achieve this, teachers need to know how to implement the techniques across the curriculum and be provided with ideas and suggestions on how to do this. Moreover, the implementation of programs needs to extend throughout the whole school year. Research has indicated that longer interventions produce greater gains in well-being (Sin & Lyubomirsky, 2009). Unfortunately, however, many look to positive psychology for quick-fix remedies. Schools need to be reminded that PPI programs are a way of being and doing, not a quick remedy for unhappiness. Thus, interventions need to be built into the whole school curriculum throughout the year. Structure and consistency are also necessary for integration and learning to occur among both staff and students.

Finally, research has indicated that a scattered approach, in which individuals practice multiple and varied PPI activities, are more effective than single approaches (Sheldon & Lyubomirsky, 2019; Sin & Lyubomirsky, 2009). Therefore, where possible, schools need programs that include multiple activities and techniques for application across the curriculum. Indeed, a variety of PPIs have been found effective in increasing well-being and could be developed into individual programs. For example, counting blessings and participating in self-guided gratitude exercises (Emmons & McCullough, 2003; Froh et al., 2008), counting one's acts of kindness for one week (Otak et al., 2006), keeping a gratitude journal (Froh et al., 2008), writing down three good things that went well each day and using strengths in a new way every day for one week (Seligman et al., 2005), mindfulness training (Huppert & Johnson, 2010), and meditation (Nidich et al., 2011) to name but a few. Teachers are best placed to adapt these and many more applications into their classrooms.

Conclusion

Within the U.K., there is ongoing concern about the well-being of children and adolescents. Recent reports indicate that despite national strategies to increase well-being among Britain's young people, there has been a significant decrease in life satisfaction and well-being over the last decade (The Children's Society, 2012). A major priority in addressing low levels of well-being among young people is through high-quality education, positive relationships with teachers, and fostering children's ability to have positive views of themselves. Recently, positive psychology interventions are proving to be beneficial in aiding these endeavors, through both independent application and application through existing strategies and curriculum courses. Applied techniques reviewed in this chapter include:

- allowing those with special needs to become experts in their own lives, thereby enabling them to engage in preferred activities to increase positive emotions;
- increasing psychological well-being through mindfulness training and meditation;
- promoting flourishing and excellence through whole school techniques and a community environment that focuses on teaching students how to capitalize on their strengths and potentialities;
- creating the conditions in which young students will flourish by linking personal strengths to festivals and celebrations throughout the year;
- providing lesson plans and activities that enable students to explore and identify with their strengths and learn how to apply these skills in their own lives to increase happiness;
- promoting optimism through realistic and flexible thinking techniques that focus on enabling students to handle daily stressors and problems;
- implementing positive education across the whole school, thereby enabling young people to reflect upon and make choices about their well-being and development; and
- using cognitive and dialectical behavior therapy techniques alongside positive psychology application to facilitate resilience and applying positive leadership to facilitate and promote well-being.

Overall, these applications and interventions provide encouraging support for the continued development and application of positive psychology interventions in education.

Chapter Summary

- Children's perception of their relationship with parents is the most important component of well-being, irrespective of family structure.
- Consistency and stability of family structure is vital to well-being.
- A safe and stable home environment is related to increased well-being.
- Cultivating good friendships along with spending quality time with both friends and family is associated with increased well-being.
- A major priority in addressing low levels of well-being among young people is through high quality education, positive relationships with teachers, and fostering children's ability to have positive views of themselves.
- Teachers need to understand the positive psychology approach to apply it successfully.
- Successful application in the school context involves adding positive psychology to existing techniques.
- School-wide approaches are required in order that positive psychology becomes part of the ethos of the school.
- Interventions need to be applied throughout the whole school year in order for habituation to occur.
- Application of multiple and varied activities and techniques appear to be more effective than focusing on single activities.

References

Asher, S. R., & Hopmeyer, A. (1997). Loneliness in childhood. In G. G. Bear, K. M. Minke, & A. Thomas (Eds.), *Children's needs II: Development, problems and alternatives* (pp. 279–292). National Association of School Psychologists.

Bishop, S. R., Lau, M., Shapiro, S., Carlson, L., Anderson, N. D., Carmody, J., ... Devins, G. (2004). Mindfulness: A proposed operational definition. *Clinical Psychology: Science and Practice, 11*(3), 230–241. https://doi.org/10.1093/clipsy.bph077

Blom-Hoffman, J., Edwards George, J. B., & Franko, D. L. (2006). Childhood overweight. In G. G. Bear & K. M. Minke (Eds.), *Children's needs III: Development, prevention and intervention* (pp. 989–1000). National Association of School Psychologists.

Brown, S. L. (2004). Family structure and child well-being: The significance of parental cohabitation. *Journal of Marriage and Family, 66*(2), 351–367. https://doi.org/10.1111/j.1741–3737.2004.00025.x

Challen, A., Noden, P., West, A., & Machin, S. (2011). *UK Resilience Programme evaluation: Final report.* Retrieved November 20, 2012 from www.education.gov.uk/publications/eOrderingDownload/DFE-RR2097.pdf

Challenge, A. R., Machin, S. J., & Gillham, J. E. (2014). The UK resilience programme: A school-based univeral nonrandomized pragmatic controlled trial. *Journal of Consulting and Clinical Psychology, 82*(1), 75–89. https://doi.org/10.1037/a0034854

★Chodkiewicz, A., & Boyle, C. (2017). Positive psychology school-based interventions: A reflection on current success and future directions. *Educational Review 5*(1), 60–86. https://doi.org/10.1002/rev3.3080

Clair, A. (2019). Housing: An under-explored influence on children's well-being and becoming. *Child Indicators Research, 12*, 609–626. https://doi.org/10.1007/s12187-018-9550-7

Diener, E., & Diener, C. (1996). Most people are happy. *Psychological Science, 7*(3), 181–185. https://doi.org/10.1111/j.1467–9280.1996.tb00354.x

Diener, E., Wirtz, D., Tov, W., Kim-Prieto, C., Choi, D., Oishi, S., & Biswas-Diener, R. (2010). New well-being measures: Short scales to assess flourishing and positive and negative feelings. *Social Indicators Research, 97*(2), 143–156. https://doi.org/10.1007/s11205-009-9493-y

Emmons, R. A., & McCullough, M. E. (2003). Counting blessings versus burdens: An experimental investigation of gratitude and subjective well-being in daily life. *Journal of Personality and Social Psychology, 84*(2), 377–389. https://doi.org/10.1037/0022-3514.84.2.377

Felitti, V. J. (2002). The relation between adverse childhood experiences and adult mental health: Turning gold into lead. *The Permanente Journal, 6*(1), 44–47.

Flouri, E., & Buchanan, A. (2002). Life satisfaction in teenage boys: The moderating role of father involvement and bullying. *Aggressive Behavior, 28*(2), 126–133. https://doi.org/10.1002/ab.90014

Fox Eades, J. M. (2008). *Celebrating strengths: Building strengths-based school.* CAPP Press.

Fox Eades, J. M., Proctor, C., & Ashley, M. (2013). Happiness in the classroom. In S. A. David, I. Boniwell, & A. C. Ayers (Eds.), *Oxford handbook of happiness* (pp. 579–591). Oxford University Press.

Froh, J. J., Sefick, W. J., & Emmons, R. A. (2008). Counting blessings in early adolescents: An experimental study of gratitude and subjective well-being. *Journal of School Psychology, 46*(2), 213–233. https://doi.org/10.1016/j.jsp.2007.03.005

Gillham, J. E., Brunwasser, S. M., & Freres, D. R. (2007). Preventing depression early in adolescence: The Penn Resiliency Program. In J. R. Z. Abela & B. L. Hankin (Eds.), *Hanbook of depression in children and adolescence* (pp. 309–332). Guilford.

Gilman, R., & Huebner, E. S. (2003). A review of life satisfaction research with children and adolescents. *School Psychology Quarterly, 18*(2), 192–205. https://doi.org/10.1521/scpq.18.2.192.21858

Govindji, R., & Linley, P. A. (2008, August). *An evaluation of Celebrating Strengths.* Prepared for North Lincolnshire Local Education Authority. Centre for Applied Positive Psychology: Warwick University.

Green, L. S., & Norrish, J. M. (2013). Enhancing well-being in adolescents: Positive psychology and coaching psychology interventions in schools. In C. Proctor & P. A. Linley (Eds.), *Research, applications and interventions for children and adolescents: A positive psychology perspective* (pp. 211–222). Springer.

Huebner, E. S., Drane, J. W., & Valois, R. F. (2000). Levels and demographic correlates of adolescent life satisfaction reports. *School Psychology International, 21*(3), 281–292. https://doi.org/10.1177/0143034300213005

Huppert, F. A., & Johnson, D. M. (2010). A controlled trial of mindfulness training in schools: The importance of practice for an impact on well-being. *Journal of Positive Psychology, 5*(4), 264–274. https://doi.org/10.1080/17439761003794148

Laursen, L. L., Madsen, K. B., & Obel, C. et al. (2019). Family dissolution and children's social well-being at school: A historic cohort study. *BioMed Central Pediatrics, 19*, 449. https://doi.org/10.1186/s12887-019-1821-z

Lyubomirsky, S., King, L., & Diener, E. (2005). The benefits of frequent positive affect: Does happiness lead to success? *Psychological Bulletin, 131*(6), 803–855. https://doi.org/10.1037/0033–2909.131.6.803

McGee, J., & Menolascino, F. J. (1991). *Beyond gentle teaching: A nonaversive approach to helping those in need.* Plenum.

Moore, K. A., & Lippman, L. H. (2005). Introduction and conceptual framework. In K. A. Moore & L. H. Lippman (Eds.), *What do children need to flourish: Conceptualizing and measuring indicators of positive development* (pp. 1–10). Springer.

Morris, I. (2013). A place for well-being in the classroom? In C. Proctor & P. A. Linley (Eds.), *Research, applications and interventions for children and adolescents: A positive psychology perspective* (pp. 185–198). Springer.

Morris, I. (2013). Going beyond the accidental: Happiness, education, and the Wellington College experience. In S. David, I. Boniwell, & A. C. Ayres (Eds.), *The Oxford handbook of happiness,* (pp. 644–656). Oxford University Press.

Nidich, S., Mjasiri, S., Nidich, R., Rainforth, M., Grant, J., Valosek, L., Change, W., & Zigler, R. (2011). Academic achievement and transcendental meditation: A study with at-risk urban middle school students. *Education, 131*(3), 556–564.

Noddings, N. (2003). *Happiness and education.* Cambridge University Press.

Otake, K., Shimai, S., Tanaka-Matsumi, J., Otsui, K., & Frederickson, B. L. (2006). Happy people become happier through kindness: A counting kindnesses intervention. *Journal of Happiness Studies, 7*(3), 361–375. https://doi.org/10.1007/s10902-005-3650-z

Park, N. (2005). Life satisfaction among Korean children and youth: A developmental perspective. *School Psychology International, 26*(2), 209–223. https://doi.org/10.1177/0143034305052914

Park, N., & Peterson, C. (2009). Strengths of character in schools. In R. Gilman, E. S. Huebner, & M. J. Furlong (Eds.), *Handbook of positive psychology in schools* (pp. 65–76). Routledge.

Peterson, C., & Seligman, M. E. P. (2004). *Character strengths and virtues: A classification and handbook.* American Psychological Association.

Popovic, N. (2017). The happiness of pursuit, not the pursuit of happiness. *The Schools, Students, and Teachers Network, 9*, 41–45.

Proctor, C., & Fox Eades, J. (2019). *Strengths Gym: Build and exercise your strengths!* Positive Psychology Centre.

*Proctor, C., Linley, P. A., & Maltby, J. (2009). Youth life satisfaction: A review of the literature. *Journal of Happiness Studies, 10*(5), 583–630. https://doi.org/10.1007/s10902-008-9110-9

Proctor, C., Tsukayama, E., Wood, A. M., Maltby, J., Fox Eades, J. M., & Linley, P. A. (2011). Strengths Gym: The impact of a character strengths-based intervention on the life satisfaction and well-being of adolescents. *Journal of Positive Psychology, 6*(5), 377–388. https://doi.org/10.1080/17439760.2011.594079

Rigby, K. (2000). Effect of peer victimization in schools and perceived social support on adolescent well-being. *Journal of Adolescence, 23*(1), 57–68. https://doi.org/10.1006/jado.1999.0289

Seligman, M. E. P., Ernst, R. M., Gillham, J., Reivich, K., & Linkins, M. (2009). Positive education: Positive psychology and classroom interventions. *Oxford Review of Education, 35*(3), 293–311. https://doi.org/10.1080/03054980902934563

Seligman, M. E. P., Steen, T. A., Park, N., & Peterson, C. (2005). Positive psychology progress: Empirical validation of interventions. *American Psychologist, 60*(5), 410–421. https://doi.org/10.1037/0003-066X.60.5.410

*Sheldon, K. M., & Lyubomirsky, S. (2019). Revisiting the sustainable happiness model and pie chart: Can happiness be successfully pursued? *Journal of Positve Psychology.* https://doi.org/10.1080/17439760.2019.1689421

Sin, N. L., & Lyubomirsky, S. (2009). Enhancing well-being and alleviating depressive symptoms with positive psychology interventions: A practice-friendly meta-analysis. *Journal of Clinical Psychology, 65*(5), 467–487. https://doi.org/10.1002/jclp.20593

The Children's Society. (2012). *The Good Childhood Report 2012: A review of our children's well-being.* The Children's Society. https://www.childrenssociety.org.uk/sites/default/files/tcs/good_childhood_report_2012_final_0.pdf

The Children's Society. (2019). *The good childhood report 2019.* The Children's Society. http://www.childrenssociety.org.uk/good-childhood-report.

Thompson, J. (2009). *Making listening special.* Unpublished manuscript.

UNICEF. (2007). *An overview of child well-being in rich contries: A comprehensive assessment of the lives and well-being of children and adolescents in the economically advanced nations. Innocenti Report Card 7.* UNICEF Office of Research.

UNICEF. (2013). *Child well-being in rich countries: A comparative overview. Innocenti Report Card 11.* UNICEF Office of Research.

UPenn. (2007). *Resilience research in children.* http://www.ppc.sas.upenn.edu/prpsum.htm

Valois, R. F., Paxton, R. J., Zullig, K. J., & Huebner, E. S. (2006). Life satisfaction and violent behaviors among middle school students. *Journal of Child and Family Studies, 15*(6), 695–707. https://doi.org/10.1007/s10826-006-9043-z

Valois, R. F., Zullig, K. J., Huebner, E. S., & Drane, J. W. (2003). Dieting behaviors, weight perceptions, and life satisfaction among public high school adolescents. *Eating Disorders: The Journal of Treatment & Prevention, 11*(4), 271–288. https://doi.org/10.1080/10640260390242506

*Waters, L. (2011). A review of school-based positive psychology interventions. *The Australian Educational and Developmental Psychologist, 28*(2), 75–90. https://doi.org/10.1375/aedp.28.2.75

Wellington College. (2012). *Well-being.* http://www.wellingtoncollege.org.uk/well-being

White, M. A. (2013). Positive education at Geelong Grammar. In S. David, I. Boniwell, & A. C. Ayres (Eds.), *The Oxford handbook of happiness* (pp. 644–656). Oxford University Press.

Wilson, S. M., Henry, C. S., & Peterson, G. W. (1997). Life satisfaction among low-income rural youth from Appalachia. *Journal of Adolescence, 20*(4), 443–459. https://doi.org/10.1006/jado.1997.0099

Zullig, K. J., Valois, R. F., Huebner, E. S., & Drane, J. W. (2005). Adolescent health-related quality of life and perceived satisfaction with life. *Quality of Life Research, 14*(6), 1573–1584. https://doi.org/10.1007/s11136-004-7707-y

Reference Notes

Information on the UKRP not otherwise referenced was kindly provided by Lucy Bailey from How to Thrive: https://www.thrive-creative.co.uk

Information on Strengths Gym not otherwise included can be found on the Positive Psychology Research Centre website: https://www.pprc.gg/products

All of the information on Haberdashers' Aske's Hatcham College was kindly provided by P. A. Koureas from the Haberdashers' Aske's Federation: http://www.hahc.org.uk

All of the information on the Positive Leadership and Well-Being program at Blackrock College was kindly provided by D. Hevey from P2P Leadership Consulting: http://www.denishevey.ie

30

APPLICATION OF POSITIVE PSYCHOLOGY IN CHINESE SCHOOL CONTEXTS

Chunyan Yang

Application of Positive Psychology in Schools in China

In recent decades, positive psychology has received increased interest and attention among researchers, educators, and school-based practitioners in China. Many positive psychology constructs (e.g., subjective well-being, covitality, and mindfulness) developed and well-studied in Western countries have been studied in the Chinese context. A sizable body of research is developing theoretical frameworks and measurement instruments to assess children's and adolescents' positive characteristics and strengths (e.g., psychological *suzhi*) embodied in native Chinese cultural and educational contexts. This chapter first reviews positive psychology applications in Chinese schools. It also examines research related to the theoretical conceptualization, assessment, and research applications of psychological *suzhi*, subjective well-being, positive youth development (PYD), covitality, and mindfulness. Based on intervention studies' findings, the discussion focuses on applying important positive psychology constructs to character education, mental wellness promotion, mental health intervention, and family education among Chinese school-age youths and their families. Also included is a review of practice development in Mainland China and a research application of positive psychology in Hong Kong.

Psychological *Suzhi*

For many decades, promoting students' cognitive development and academic achievement has been one of the most urgent priorities in the Chinese educational system and Chinese society. In the past 20 years, Chinese researchers and policymakers have made increased efforts to promote school-age youths' positive development across cognitive, psychological, and physical domains through comprehensive quality education. The concepts of psychological *suzhi* and *suzhi education* have guided the Chinese educational system's transition from a pure focus on academic achievement-orientation to a balanced, all-around quality-oriented education (e.g., Zhang, 2012; Zhang et al., 2000). Although psychological *suzhi* is a concept reflecting traditional Chinese culture, its core components align with Western positive psychology constructs, such as self-awareness, self-regulation, and autonomy. Suzhi's emphasis on the combinatorial effects of integrated positive personal assets is similar to covitality, an integrated construct from U.S. positive psychology (e.g., Furlong et al., 2014; Lenzi et al., 2015).

Psychological *suzhi* is a widely applied Chinese construct describing a comprehensive and integrated set of positive psychological qualities of Chinese children and adolescents. The hypothesis

DOI: 10.4324/9781003013778-37

is that it has foundational, derivative, and developmental functions that influence individuals' adjustment, development, and creative behavior (Zhang, 2012; Zhang et al., 2011, 2017). Thirty years of theoretical and empirical studies with Chinese students show that psychological *suzhi* is a hierarchical, multidimensional construct. Suzhi has three interrelated subdimensions: quality of cognition, quality of individuality, and quality of adaptability. Quality of cognition reveals as individual's reflection on objects, involving awareness, metacognition, and associative memory (Zhang et al., 2000). Quality of individuality refers to an individuals' idiosyncratic behavior in treating objects and is reflected in behavior. This construct corresponds to the Western concept of personality and includes emotional characteristics and self-characteristics, and various concepts such as persistence, self-regulation, and self-control (Zhang et al., 2011). Quality of adaptability refers to individuals' ability to have consistency between themselves and the environment by changing themselves or the environment during socialization. This construct includes interpersonal adaptation, societal harmony, and stressful adjustment (Zhang et al., 2000). Several assessments have been developed in the past 10 years to measure students' psychological *suzhi* in elementary (Pan et al., 2017) and secondary schools (Hu et al., 2017). Ample research shows that the overall psychological *suzhi* predicts Chinese adolescents' educational and developmental outcomes, such as higher academic achievements (Nie et al., 2018), higher self-esteem (Liu et al., 2018), lower social anxiety (Wu et al., 2018), and fewer behavioral problems (Liu et al., 2017; Pan et al., 2017). Moreover, psychological *suzhi* was positively associated with school climate (e.g., Dong & Zhang, 2015; Nie et al., 2018) and negatively associated with adolescents' depressive symptoms (e.g., Hu & Zhang, 2015; Ma et al., 2018). Several empirical studies have demonstrated that psychological *suzhi* is a malleable factor that can change over time. For example, in an 18-month (four waves in six-month intervals) longitudinal study with a sample of 403 children in the third grade, Ma et al. (2018) found that children's psychological *suzhi* followed a piecewise linear growth, and its development had a certain level of stability. In another four-wave longitudinal study of 4,077 adolescents, Nie et al. (2020) found that adolescents' psychological suzhi and its three subdimensions demonstrated slow linear growth across two years.

Application of *Psychological Suzhi* in Quality Education in China

Given the significance of psychological *suzhi* supported in the extensive research literature, its educational and policy implications have been recognized nationally. For example, the Chinese Ministry of Education's Guidelines for Mental Health Education in Primary and Secondary Schools (2012) recommended developing a comprehensive school-based framework grounded within the theoretical conceptualization of psychological *suzhi* to promote students', teachers', and parents' educational and mental health outcomes. Following the policy guidance, national psychological *suzhi* scales have been established for elementary, middle, and high school students in mainland China. Moreover, computer programs and case management systems help teachers, administrators, and school-based psychological service providers assess and monitor students' psychological *suzhi* competencies at individual and classroom levels (Wu et al., 2018; Zhang et al., 2017). Also, classroom-based curricula have been developed and implemented in the classroom as part of the character education and mental health prevention and intervention efforts. Awareness of psychological *suzhi* has grown in Chinese schools during the past decade; however, there are few rigorous intervention studies of its efficacy. Moreover, most of the *suzhi* curricula and educational practice applications are in classroom settings. Researchers proposed that it is vital to develop a multi-component intervention model that integrates school, family, and the community in promoting youths' *suzhi* development (Zhang, 2002). These are some of the gaps to be addressed in research and practice related to psychological *suzhi*'s school applications in China.

Application of Subjective Well-Being among School-Age Youths

The research literature on subjective well-being has gained growing interest and research attention from China during economic growth in the past few decades (Wang & Wang, 2016). A recent study based on three-wave national data from the China Household Finance Survey showed a rising level of subjective well-being among Chinese people in the second decade of the 21st century (Clark et al., 2019). Compared to the research of Chinese adults' and college students' subjective well-being, there has been relatively less research on school-age children's subjective well-being. Moreover, more research examines subjective well-being based on the theoretical framework and measurement instruments adapted from Western countries than those initially developed within the native Chinese culture and school contexts. For example, some subjective well-being measures widely used with Chinese students originated in Western countries: the Chinese version of the Satisfaction With Life Scale (SWLS; Jiang, 2018) and the Chinese Version of Multidimensional Students' Life Satisfaction Scale (MSLSS-Chinese; Tian & Liu, 2005). Although limited, a few measures of subjective well-being were initially developed based on the perceptions and experiences of Chinese youths and adolescents, such as the Chinese Adolescent Student's Life Satisfaction Scale (Zhang & Zhang, 2004) and the Subjective Well-being for Senior High School Students measure (Zhao et al., 2011).

Subjective Well-Being in the School Context

Researchers are refining theoretical frameworks and measurement instruments to assess domain-specific subjective well-being in Chinese school contexts to better understand youths' subjective well-being. For example, grounded in Diener's theory of subjective well-being, Tian (2008) proposed a theoretical model of subjective well-being in school, which conceptualizes how students subjectively evaluate and emotionally experience their lives, specifically in the context of school. This model includes a cognitive component and an affective component. The cognitive component is school satisfaction, referring to a student's subjective, cognitive evaluation of school life using their internal standards related to several specific school life subdomains (Tian, 2008). The affective component includes two types of school experience: positive affect and negative affect, referring to the frequency of a student's positive emotions and negative emotions experienced during school (Tian, 2008). Tian and colleagues found that students' perception of subjective well-being in schools, particularly the cognitive component (i.e., school satisfaction), had a significant bidirectional, longitudinal association with the satisfaction of relatedness needs among adolescents in cross-sectional and longitudinal studies (Tian et al., 2014). They also argued that Chinese students tended to place more importance on their relatedness needs due to Chinese society's collectivistic values. Thus, they are more likely to improve their subjective well-being in school by building close relationships with others.

Cross-Cultural Perspective of Subjective Well-Being

To understand subjective well-being among Chinese people, researchers have argued that it is essential to delineate its theoretical implications from the cross-cultural lens when applying a theoretical framework developed from Western countries to China (Lu & Gilmour, 2006). More specifically, Lu and Gilmour (2006) argued that Euro-American subjective well-being theories, based on an individualistic self-concept model, are variously termed *independent self* (Markus & Kitayama, 1991) or *individual-oriented* self (Yang, 2004). This perspective views personhood as bounded, coherent, stable, autonomous, and free. In contrast, in the East Asian culture of collectivism, social customs, institutions, and the media emphasize a relational way of being, emphasizing roles, statuses, and in-group membership (Markus & Kitayama, 1998). Moreover, Asian cultures prioritize collective welfare over personal interests while rewarding self-control, diligent role performance, and rigorous self-cultivation (Lu, 2008). Thus, East Asian cultural conceptions of subjective well-being have a distinct emphasis on role obligations; the foundation of happiness is the fulfillment of social role obligations accomplished through self-cultivation. Adopting this indigenous cross-cultural approach, Chinese researchers have developed a cultur-ally balanced measure, named the Individual--oriented and Socially oriented cultural conceptions of Subjective Well-Being scale (ISSWB; Lu & Gilmour, 2006). Measurement validation across Chinese and American college students and community adults showed that the 51-item ISSWB had good internal consistency, test-retest reliability, convergent validity, and discriminant validity (Lu & Gilmour, 2006). Further analysis showed that the Chinese sample possessed more robust social-oriented subjective well-being than the American sample. In contrast, the American sample possessed more robust individual-oriented subjective well-being than the Chinese sample.

Application of SWB in the Dual-Factor Model of School Mental Health

The dual-factor model (DFM) of mental health emphasizes the importance of assessing positive indicators of wellness (i.e., subjective well-being) and traditional negative indicators of illness (e.g., psychopathology) (Greenspoon & Saklofske, 2001; Suldo & Shaffer, 2008). With the grow-ing attention to positive psychology and PYD in China, the DFM has been applied with Chinese youths, with subjective well-being being the primary positive indicator of mental health (Xiong et al., 2017). For example, Dong et al. (2014) verified the applicability of subjective well-being and psychopathology as indicators of the DFM with a sample of 1,213 Chinese adolescents. Confirma-tory factor analyses indicated that the DFM identified students' mental health status better than a unidimensional model. Moreover, mentally healthy students experienced significantly more re-laxation, less anxiety, and hopelessness in learning, and less academic pressure than the other DFM groups (Dong et al., 2014). These empirical findings verified the benefits of applying the DFM to understand relationships between Chinese adolescents' mental health and psychosocial outcomes.

In a related study on the DFM, Xiong et al. (2017) examined the dynamics of mental health group membership via a two-wave longitudinal study of 531 Chinese students (Grades 7–12). Based on the longitudinal data, the DFM was supported by the identification of its four constit-uent groups, namely: (a) *complete mental health* (high in subjective well-being and low in psycho-pathology), (b) *vulnerable* (low in subjective well-being and low in psychopathology), (c) *troubled* (low in subjective well-being and high in psychopathology), and (d) *symptomatic but content* (high in subjective well-being and high in psychopathology). Significant group differences were found in affective self-regulatory efficacy, academic self-efficacy, and academic emotions. There was a clear differentiation between mentally healthy adolescents and their vulnerable peers and between troubled adolescents and their symptomatic but content peers. Moreover, mentally healthy youth demonstrated the highest stability and troubled youth the lowest. In contrast, vulnerable youth had the highest transition rates into both the complete mental health and troubled groups.

Assessment of Positive Youth Development in China

The strength-based PYD approach aims to capitalize on human plasticity and emphasizes that all youth can gain healthy or positive development when their strengths align with their ecological assets (Lerner et al., 2005). In the past decade, researchers have sought to develop conceptual frameworks and assessment tools to understand Chinese adolescents' PYD in mainland China. Some researchers have directly applied U.S.-based PYD models, such as the Five Cs Model (com-petence, confidence, character, caring, and connection), developed by Lerner et al. (2014) to

Table 30.1 The Operational Definitions of the Four-Factor Model of PYD in Chinese Culture (Chai et al., 2020)

Subscale	Construct Definition
Character	• Benevolence (Ai or 爱, e.g., kindness, filial piety, and patriotism) • Determination (Zhi or 志, e.g., diligence and lofty aspiration) • Trustworthiness (Xin or 信, e.g., honesty and self-discipline) • Perseverance (Yi or 义, e.g., persistence)
Competence	• Academic competence (e.g., reflective capacity, research ability, and critical thinking) • Social-emotional competence (e.g., social skills and emotion regulation) • Living competence (e.g., healthy living ability and physical ability)
Confidence	• Positive self-concept (e.g., positive views about self) • Self-acceptance (e.g., accepting everything about self, especially for shortcomings)
Connection	• Positive bonds with family, school, and community

identify the definitional and structural discrepancies of Chinese PYD (Chen et al., 2018; Wen et al., 2015). A recent study completed in-depth individual and focus group interviews with elementary and middle school students, teachers, parents, community social workers, and experts in developmental and educational science in mainland China. Based on these interviews, the grounded theory approach identified a four-factor Chinese culture PYD model (see summary in Table 30.1). Taking an integrative etic–emic approach, Chai et al. (2020) developed a culturally contextualized PYD scale. This measure shared a theoretical foundation with Lerner's U.S. PYD model and demonstrated a culturally unique definition and manifestation for some PYD indicators.

In the past two decades, researchers have also achieved fruitful research development in assessing PYD among Chinese students in Hong Kong. One representative assessment tool is the Chinese Positive Youth Development Scale (CPYDS) developed by Shek et al. (2007) to measure a multidimensional and integrated set of healthy, holistic, and valuable developmental attributes, assets, and potentials of Chinese youths in Hong Kong. This approach integrated PYD character strengths with Confucian virtues. Table 30.2 shows the 15 CPYDS constructs and their definitions. The CPYDS measure has good psychometric qualities with four dimensions: cognitive-behavioral competencies, positive identity, prosocial attributes, and overall PYD qualities (Shek & Ma, 2010). However, Chai et al. (2020) pointed out that the development of CPYDS followed an etic approach to generate items developed initially for American adolescents, focusing on universal processes that transcend cultural differences (Ho et al., 2014). Lerner et al. (2019) noted that any single Western-developed PYD model might omit or underestimate some potentially unique cultural factors related to youth development in other cultures.

Application of Covitality in China

Covitality is a relatively newer positive psychology construct in China that has received increasing research attention in the past 10 years. Its definition is "the synergist effect of positive mental health resulting from the interplay among multiple positive-psychological building blocks" (Furlong et al., 2013, p. 1013). To assess the covitality construct, Furlong and colleagues developed and validated the Social-Emotional Health Survey (SEHS) for elementary and secondary school students (Furlong et al., 2013, 2014) in the United States and other countries, such as Japan (Ito et al., 2015) and Korea (Lee et al., 2016). Language adaptation has also been made to these two scales to develop the Chinese version of SEHS-Primary and SEHS-Secondary among elementary,

Table 30.2 Chinese Positive Youth Development Scale Core Constructs

Subscale	Construct Definition
Bonding	Development of positive relationship with healthy adults and positive peers
Resilience	Capacity for adapting to change and stressful events in healthy ways
Social competence	Interpersonal skills such as communication and conflict resolution skills
Emotional competence	Skills to recognize feelings in oneself and others and emotional self-management strategies
Cognitive competence	Cognitive skills such as problem-solving and goal setting
Behavioral competence	Behavioral skills such as taking action and provision of reinforcement for effective behavior choices and action patterns
Moral competence	Ability to differentiate right and wrong, respect for rules and standards, and social justice
Self-determination	Sense of autonomy, independent thinking, or self-advocacy
Self-efficacy	Skills for coping and mastery
Spirituality	Sense of purpose and meaning in life, hope, or beliefs in a higher power
Beliefs in the future	Ability to develop future potential goals, choices, or options
Clear and positive identity	Development of healthy identity formation and achievement
Prosocial involvement	Activities and events to make positive contributions to groups
Prosocial norms	Development of clear and explicit standards for prosocial engagement
Recognition for positive behavior	Systems for rewarding, recognizing, or reinforcing positive behavior

middle, and high school students. For example, Wang et al. (2018) noted that the factor structure of SEHS-Primary, found for the original U.S. sample (first-order factors: optimism, gratitude, persistence, zest; second-order factor: covitality) replicated among 653 Chinese children from Grades 4 to 6. The covitality latent trait was associated with fewer depressive symptoms, higher prosocial behaviors, less victimization, less violence perpetration, and predicted higher academic achievement. Moreover, Xie et al. (2019) reported that the original SEHS-Secondary U.S. sample factor structure was replicated with 3,750 Chinese middle and high school students. Moreover, the covitality latent trait was associated with adolescent subjective well-being, depression, anxiety, stress, and self-reported academic performance.

Covitality in School-Based Programs

Based on the development of the Chinese version of the SEHS for research studies among Chinese students, some Chinese researchers have used the covitality theoretical framework to develop school-based programs to promote Chinese students' social-emotional strengths. For example, Pan (2018) developed a group intervention to improve Chinese elementary school students' social and emotional well-being. This program was grounded in the core primary school covitality dimensions (i.e., gratitude, optimism, zest, and persistence) and the transtheoretical model and stages of change (Prochaska et al., 2008). The eight-session group counseling program included four major stages:

1   understanding the conceptualization and core dimensions of covitality (i.e., gratitude, optimism, zest, and persistence) using activities such as role-play, visual stories, and movies;
2   understanding the values of the four core dimensions of covitality using group games and activities;

3   providing feedback and supporting group members to set up goals and an action plan to im-
     prove some specific dimensions of covitality; and
4   providing peer support and promoting a positive group climate to help decrease negative
     emotions that might hinder the growth of covitality.

A quasi-experimental study involving 1,542 elementary students (Grades 3–6) showed that this
group counseling intervention program effectively promoted Chinese elementary school students'
social-emotional well-being across the four covitality domains. Also noted was decreased bullying victimization and increased school belonging during the intervention and at a five-month
follow-up.

Application of Mindfulness Education among Chinese Students

The concept of mindfulness, originally derived from Buddhist philosophy, is described as an awareness of moment-by-moment experience arising from purposeful attention and a nonjudgmental
acceptance of these present-moment experiences (Kabat-Zinn, 2003). In recent years, mindfulness
practice has received increasing research and practical attention in teaching practice and mental
health prevention/intervention in China. A substantial body of mindfulness studies has focused on
Chinese college students. As for its application in Chinese schools, one noticeable area is applying
mindfulness practice to reduce school-age youths' testing anxiety, academic pressure, and learning
difficulties. This popular application area is primarily related to the fact that Chinese students face
high pressure from academic learning and testing due to the "pressure-cooker" exam system. A
few empirical studies have supported mindfulness interventions' effectiveness in reducing testing
anxiety, academic stress, and other negative emotions and mental health symptoms. For example, Meng (2013) showed that a seven-session group-based mindfulness intervention effectively
reduced high school students' test anxiety compared with relaxation. In this intervention study,
this group-based mindfulness intervention had seven components, including (a) introduction to
the mindfulness curriculum, (b) body scan and daily mindful practice, (c) reflection on automated
thinking in testing, (d) mindful breathing, (e) imagination, (f) breathing, and (g) summary. In
another study, Su (2016) found a negative link between mindfulness skills and students' academic
procrastination among middle school students. Moreover, implementing an eight-week mindfulness group intervention effectively reduced procrastination among middle and high school students (Su, 2016). In a more recent study, Liu et al. (2019) showed that an eight-week mindfulness
group intervention effectively reduced negative emotions and mental health symptoms (stress, depression, and anxiety) and improved academic performance among middle school students. Thus
far, most of the mindfulness intervention studies in China have been conducted at the classroom
or small group level; future evaluation studies should employ school-wide intervention designs.

Application of Positive Education Models in Teacher Training

In the past 10 years, one noticeable application of positive psychology in Chinese schools is the
collaborative and societal-level initiatives and efforts of Chinese researchers, educators, and practitioners to translate research knowledge into public knowledge and practical positive psychology
applications in the Chinese society. An important focus of such initiatives is the development
of the Positive Education Model, a comprehensive framework of positive psychology education
integrating theoretical perspectives and applied techniques developed in China and many other
countries, such as the United States and Australia. The Positive Education Model consists of
one higher-order domain and six core subdomains. The character strength system's cultivation
is conceptualized as the higher-order domain and overarching system connecting the six core

Table 30.3 Positive Education Model's Fundamental Theory and Applied Techniques

Domains	Fundamental Guiding Theory	Applied Techniques
Positive self	• Self-esteem theory • Self-efficacy theory • Self-acceptance theory	• Identify character strengths and virtues • Build and improve self-esteem • Self-acceptance and self-care • Successful experience assets
Positive emotion	• Gratitude theory • Savoring • Emotional management theory • Resilience theory • ABC model of emotion	• Focus on the positive: three positive things • Three good things: gratitude journal • Savoring practice: past, present, and future • Internal self-talk • Loving kindness meditation
Positive engagement	• Flow • Self-determination theory	• Learning task flow • Deepening learning interest • Improving autonomy support from teachers and parents
Positive relationships	• Helping others • Forgiveness • Responding theory	• Positive group (e.g., forgiveness and trust) • Helping others with goodwill, gratitude in action • Discovery of others' strengths and responding skills • Active constructive responding • Seven steps to conflict resolution
Positive purpose	• Meaning theory	• Identifying meaning and purpose of learning • Learning from role models (make contributions to others' happiness, county, nation, and science, etc.) • Discovering and pursuing dreams (e.g., dream consultation and dream trip)
Positive accomplishment	• Perseverance • Goal-setting theory • Path-goal theory • Mindset theory • Intensive education • Neuroplasticity	• Perseverance strengthening exercises • Goal-setting instruction • Micro communication model • Learned optimism • Growth mindset training • Intensive education training • Neuroplasticity training
Overall: Cultivation of character strength system	• Character Strengths and Virtues	• Identifying self-strengths • Playing to self-strengths • Identifying others' strengths • Specifying strength-based behaviors

subdomains in the Positive Education Model. Among the six subdomains, five were adapted from Seligman's (2011) PERMA model of flourishing. Psychological well-being is defined in terms of positive emotions (P), engagement (E), relationships (R), meaning (M), and accomplishment (A). The sixth subdomain is positive self, which is a unique and essential addition in the Chinese context. Historically, there has been a lack of self-confidence, self-esteem, self-compassion, self-awareness, and self-acceptance in Chinese school education. Table 30.3 provides a more detailed description of the Positive Education Model's seven domains (Zeng & Zhao, 2018).

Guided by the Positive Education Model, a group of researchers in the Department of Psychology at Tsinghua University have developed the Positive Psychology Instructor Certification Program. This program trains Chinese school teachers and professional instructors in many other fields, such as public health, healthcare, and information technology (Tsinghua University School of Social Science, 2016). The professional program's goal is to promote public awareness of positive psychology applications in Chinese society, particularly in the field of education (Tsinghua University School of Social Science, 2016). In addition to teaching trainees, the foundational theories and applied techniques using the Positive Education Model, the Positive Psychology Instructor Certification Program also supports the trainees to apply positive psychology theories and applied techniques in their daily teaching practice. The continued professional support also emphasizes applying the key theoretical concepts and practical techniques to help build a positive climate at the school level. While innovative theoretical models and instructional support have been developed in the Positive Psychology Instructor Certification Program in Mainland China, there is a lack of rigorous empirical studies to evaluate this certification program's efficacy among school teachers and other professionals. Future evaluation studies and implementation research in this area are needed.

PATHS Program in Hong Kong

The application of positive psychology in Chinese schools is developing rapidly in mainland China. Most of the existing research focuses on understanding the theoretical frameworks and vital positive psychology concepts applicable to the Chinese school contexts and understanding their linkages with Chinese students' school adjustment and developmental outcomes. Some positive psychology concepts, such as *suzhi* and covitality, are being applied in schools. These efforts include classroom mental health assessments and classroom or group-based intervention programs. Other efforts include large-scale applications in school-wide or community-based prevention and intervention programs. On the whole, however, such efforts are yet still rare in mainland China. One notable exception is the Project Positive Adolescent Training through Holistic Social Program (PATHS program) in Hong Kong (Shek & Sun, 2012).

The PATHS program is a PYD program initiated and financially supported by The Hong Kong Jockey Club Charities Trust. Since 2005, the project has gone through several phases, including the initial phase (2005–2012), school-based extension phase (2009–2016), and community-based extension phase (2013–2017). In the initial phase, with the involvement of faculty from five Hong Kong universities, the research team (a) developed youth enhancement programs for junior secondary school students (20 hours per grade), (b) trained the program implementers (20 hours per grade), (c) assisted in the implementation in more than 250 schools, and (d) evaluated the program using multiple evaluation strategies, including a five-year longitudinal experimental study. In the school-based extension phase, the project was implemented for another cycle (2009–2010 and 2011–2012 school years). A six-year longitudinal study was conducted to understand the psychosocial development of Chinese adolescents in Hong Kong. In the community-based extension phase, the programs were administered by social workers in community settings. Extensive evaluation studies with randomized control trials and long-term longitudinal studies showed that the implementation of the PATHS program was linked to reduced risk behaviors among Chinese adolescents, such as delinquency behaviors. The program participants also reported a positive perception of the program, the instructor, and the benefits of the PATHS program.

Moreover, this project was identified by the World Health Organization (INSPIRE) as an effective program for the promotion of life skills in young people, where INSPIRE is an evidence-based resource for everyone committed to preventing and responding to violence against children and adolescents. In recent years, the implementation of the PATHS project has been extended to mainland China. For example, a recent quasi-experimental evaluation study conducted among middle school students in mainland China showed students who participated in the PATHS project demonstrated significant improvement in perceived PYD attributes and a significant decline in perceived delinquency compared to the control group (Zhu & Shek, 2020).

Conclusion

In the past 20 years, with the increasing public awareness of positive psychology in China, many vital positive psychology concepts and theories have been applied in Chinese schools. These efforts' overarching goals are to promote students' and teachers' well-being and happiness, learning and teaching effectiveness, and address mental health challenges. As shown in the review above, significant research advancements in positive psychology have been made in the past two decades in China. While researchers and practitioners are actively exploring and refining culturally contextualized and sensitive approaches to advancing the application of positive psychology in Chinese schools, most of the key constructs and assessment tools have been adapted from Western countries. Moreover, the initial intervention studies have primarily focused at the classroom level; system-level intervention programs and evaluation studies applying the key positive psychology constructs and theories are needed in future research.

References

Chai, X., Wang, J., Li, X., Liu, W., Zhao, G., & Lin., D. (2020). Development and validation of the Chinese Positive Youth Development Scale. *Applied Developmental Science* (online first). https://doi.org/10.1080/1 0888691.2020.1712206

Chen, B.-B., Wiium, N., & Dimitrova, R. (2018). Factor structure of positive youth development: Contributions of exploratory structural equation modeling. *Personality and Individual Differences, 124,* 12–15. https://doi.org/10.1016/j.paid.2017.11.039

Chinese Ministry of Education. (2012). *Guidelines for mental health education in primary and secondary schools.* http://old.moe.gov.cn//publicfiles/business/htmlfiles/moe/s3325/201212/145679.html

Clark W. A. C., Daichun, Y., & Huang, Y. (2019). Subjective well-being in China's changing society. *Proceedings of the National Academy of Sciences of the United States of America, 116* (34), 16799–16804. https://doi.org/10.1073/pnas.1902926116

Dong, W. T., Xiong, J. M., & Wang, Y. H. (2014). An empirical investigation of the dual-factor model of mental health in Chinese senior high school students. *Chinese Journal of Clinical Psychology, 22*(1), 88–91. (in Chinese).

Dong, Z., & Zhang, D. (2015). The relationship between class environment and psychological *suzhi* of minority middle school students in Yunnan. *Cross-Cultural Communication, 11*(11), 118–122. https://doi.org/10.3968/7883

Furlong, M. J., You, S., Renshaw, T. L., O'Malley, M. D., & Rebelez, J. (2013). Preliminary development of the positive experiences at school scale for elementary school children. *Child Indicators Research, 6*(4), 753–775. https://doi.org/10.1007/s12187-013-9193-7

Furlong, M. J., You, S., Renshaw, T. L., Smith, D. C., & O'Malley, M. D. (2014). Preliminary development and validation of the social and emotional health survey for secondary school students. *Social Indicators Research, 117*(3), 1011–1032. https://doi.org/10.1007/s11205-013-0373-0

Greenspoon, P. J., & Saklofske, D. H. (2001). Toward an integration of subjective well-being and psychopathology. *Social Indicators Research, 54*(1), 81–108. https://doi.org/10.1023/A:1007219227883

Hu, T., & Zhang, D. (2015). The relationship between adolescents' psychological *suzhi* and depression: The mediating effect of self-service attribution bias. *Journal of Southwest University (Social Sciences Edition), 41*(6), 104–109. (in Chinese).

Ito, A., Smith, D. C., You, S., Shimoda, Y., & Furlong, M. J. (2015). Validation and utility of the Social Emotional Health Survey–Secondary for Japanese students. *Contemporary School Psychology, 19*(4), 243–252. https://doi.org/10.1007/s40688-015-0068-4

Jiang, X., Fang, L., Stith, B. R., Liu, R.-de, & Huebner, E. S. (2018). A psychometric evaluation of the Chinese version of the students' life satisfaction scale. *Applied Research in Quality of Life, 13*(4), 1081–1095. https://doi.org/10.1007/s11482-017-9576-x

Kabat-Zinn, J. (2003). Mindfulness-based interventions in context: Past, present, and future. *Clinical Psychology: Science and Practice, 10*(2), 144–156. https://doi.org/10.1093/clipsy.bpg016

Lee, S., You, S., & Furlong, M. J. (2016). Validation of the social emotional health survey-secondary for Korean students. *Child Indicators Research, 9*(1), 73–92. https://doi.org/10.1007/s12187-014-9294-y

Lerner, R. M., Lerner, J. V., Almerigi, J. B., Theokas, C., Phelps, E., Gestsdottir, S., Naudeau, S., Jelicic H., Alberts, A., Ma, L., Smith, L., & Bobek, D. L., Richman-Raphael, D., Simpson, I., Christiansen E.

D., & von Eye A. (2005). Positive youth development, participation in community youth development programs, and community contributions of fifth-grade adolescents: Findings from the first wave of the 4-H study of positive youth development. *The Journal of Early Adolescence, 25*(1), 17–71. https://doi.org/10.1177/0272431604272461

Lerner, R. M., Tirrell, J. M., Dowling, E. M., Geldhof, G. J., Gestsdóttir, S., Lerner, J. V., King, P. E., Williams, K., Iraheta G., & Sim, A. T. R. (2019). The end of the beginning: Evidence and absences studying positive youth development in a global context. *Adolescent Research Review, 4*(1), 1–14. https://doi.org/10.1007/s40894-018-0093-4

Lerner, R. M., Wang, J., Chase, P. A., Gutierrez, A. S., Harris, E. M., Rubin, R. O., & Yalin, C. (2014). Using relational developmental systems theory to link program goals, activities, and outcomes: the sample case of the 4-H study of positive youth development. *New Directions for Youth Development, 2014*(144), 17–30. https://doi.org/10.1002/yd.20110

Lenzi, M., Furlong, M. J., Dowdy, E., Sharkey, J., Gini, G., & Altoè, G. (2015). The quantity and variety across domains of psychological and social assets associated with school victimization. *Psychology of Violence, 5*(4), 411–421. https://doi.org/10.1037/a0039696

Liu, G., Pan, Y., Ma, Y., & Zhang, D. (2021). Mediating effect of psychological *suzhi* on the relationship between perceived social support and self-esteem. *Journal of Health Psychology, 26*(3), 378–389. https://doi.org/10.1177/1359105318807962

Liu, G., Zhang, D., Pan, Y., Ma, Y., & Lu, X. (2017). The effect of psychological suzhi on problem behaviors in Chinese adolescents: The mediating role of subjective social status and self-esteem. *Frontiers in Psychology, 8*, 1490–1490. https://doi.org/10.3389/fpsyg.2017.01490

Liu, Y., Zhao, C., Jia, L., Hu, Z., Ai, X., Yang, D., Chen, X., Tang, X., Wang, F., & Zhu, Z. (2019). Effectiveness of mindfulness training on negative emotions and academic performance in junior one students, *33*(09), 661–665. https://doi.org/10.3969/j.issn.1000-6729.2019.09.005 (in Chinese).

Lu, L. (2008). Culture, self, subjective well-being: Cultural psychological and social change perspectives. *Psychologia: An International Journal of Psychology in the Orient, 51*(4), 290–303. https://doi.org/10.2117/psysoc.2008.290

Lu, L., & Gilmour, R. (2006). Individual-oriented and socially oriented cultural conceptions of subjective well-being: Conceptual analysis and scale development. *Asian Journal of Social Psychology, 9*(1), 36–49. https://doi.org/10.1111/j.1467-839X.2006.00183.x

Ma, Y., Su, Z., & Zhang, D. (2018). The application of the theory of "Diathesis-Stress" in childhood: A longitudinal study. *Chinese Journal of Clinical Psychology, 26*(5), 960–965. (in Chinese).

Markus, H. R., & Kitayama, S. (1991). Culture and the self: Implications for cognition, emotion, and motivation. *Psychological Review, 98*(2), 224–253. https://doi.org/10.1037/0033-295X.98.2.224

Meng, X. H. (2013*). An intervention study of middle school students' test anxiety by mindfulness training and relaxation training*. Unpublished master's thesis. Tianjin Normal University. Tianjin, China. (in Chinese).

Nie, Q., Yang, C., Teng, Z., Furlong, M. J., Pan, Y., Guo, C., & Zhang, D. (2020). Longitudinal association between school climate and depressive symptoms: The mediating role of psychological suzhi. *School Psychology, 35*(4), 267–276. https://doi.org/10.1037/spq0000374

Nie, Q., Zhang, D., Teng, Z., Lu, X., & Guo, C. (2018). How students perceived school climate effect on subjective and objective academic achievement: The mediating role of psychological suzhi (in Chinese). *Psychological Development and Education, 34*(6), 715–723.

Pan, D. (2018). *Intervention research on group psychological counseling for pupils' social and emotional health based on stage change model*. Unpublished master's thesis. Hunan Normal University. Changsha, China.

Pan, Y., Hu, Y., Zhang, D., Ran, G., Li, B., Liu, C., Liu, G., Luo, S., & Chen, W. (2017). Parental and peer attachment and adolescents' behaviors: The mediating role of psychological suzhi in a longitudinal study. *Children and Youth Services Review, 83*, 218–225. https://doi.org/10.1016/j.childyouth.2017.10.038

Prochaska, J. O., Redding, C. A., & Evers, K. E. (2008). The transtheoretical model and stages of change. In K. Glanz, B. K. Rimer, & K. Viswanath (Eds.), *Health behavior and health education* (4th ed., pp. 97–121). Jossey-Bass.

Seligman, M. E. P. (2011). *Flourish: A visionary new understanding of happiness and well-being*. Free Press.

Shek, D. T. L., & Ma, C. M. S. (2010). Dimensionality of the Chinese positive youth development scale: Confirmatory factor analyses. *Social Indicators Research, 98*(1), 41–59. https://doi.org/10.1007/s11205-009-9515-9

Shek, D. T. L., Siu, A. M. H., & Yan, T. (2007). The Chinese positive youth development scale: A validation study. *Research on Social Work Practice, 17*(3), 380–391. https://doi.org/10.1177/1049731506296196

Shek, D. T. L., & Sun, R. C. (2012). The project P.A.T.H.S. in Hong Kong—lessons learned and implications for positive youth development programs. *The Scientific World Journal*, 687536. https://doi.org/10.1100/2012/687536

Su, L. P. (2016). *Intervention study of mindfulness training on middle school students' academic procrastination.* Unpublished master's thesis. Chongqing Normal University. Chongqing, China.

Suldo, S. M., Shaffer, E. J., & Riley, K. N. (2008). A social-cognitive-behavioral model of academic predictors of adolescents' life satisfaction. *School Psychology Quarterly, 23*(1), 56–69. https://doi.org/10.1037/1045-3830.23.1.56

Tian, L. (2008). Developing scale for school well-being in adolescents. *Psychological Development and Education, 24,* 100–106. (in Chinese).

Tian, L., Chen, H., & Huebner, E. S. (2014). The longitudinal relationships between basic psychological needs satisfaction at school and school-related subjective well-being in adolescents. *Social Indicators Research, 119*(1), 353–372. https://doi.org/10.1007/s11205-013-0495-4

Tian, L., & Liu, W. (2005). Test of the Chinese version of multidimentional students' life satisfaction scale. *Chinese Mental Health Journal, 19*(5), 302–303. (in Chinese).

Tsinghua University School of Social Science. (2016). *THU Positive Psychology Instructor Certificate Program starts successfully.* http://www.sss.tsinghua.edu.cn/publish/sssen/7920/2016/20160411111849277314455/20160411111849277314455_.html

Wang, F., & Wang, D. (2016). Place, geographical context and subjective well-being: State of art and future directions. In D. Wang & S. He (Eds.), *Mobility, sociability and well-being of urban living* (pp. 189–230). Heidelberg.

Wang, C., Yang, C., Jiang, X., & Furlong, M. J. (2018). Validation of the Chinese version of the social emotional health survey-primary. *International Journal of School & Educational Psychology, 6*(1), 62–74. https://doi.org/10.1080/21683603.2016.1272026

Wen, M., Su, S., Li, X., & Lin, D. (2015). Positive youth development in rural China: The role of parental migration. *Social Science & Medicine, 132,* 261–269. http://doi: 10.1016/j.socscimed.2014.07.051

Wu, L., Zhang, D., Cheng, G., & Hu, T. (2018). Bullying and social anxiety in Chinese children: Moderating roles of trait resilience and psychological suzhi. *Child Abuse & Neglect, 76,* 204–215. https://doi.org/10.1016/j.chiabu.2017.10.021

Xiong, J., Qin, Y., Gao, M., & Hai, M. (2017). Longitudinal study of a dual-factor model of mental health in Chinese youth. *School Psychology International, 38*(3), 287–303. https://doi.org/10.1177/0143034317689970

Xie, J., Liu, J., Wei, Yu., Yang, C., Bear, G. G., & Wang, W. (2019). Validation of the Chinese version of Delaware positive, punitive, and Social-Emotional Learning (SEL) techniques scale–teacher. *Chinese Journal of Clinical Psychology, 28*(4), 701–706. https://doi.org/10.16128/j.cnki.1005-3611.2019.04.012

Yang, K. S. (2004). A theoretical and empirical analysis of the Chinese self from the perspective of social and individual orientation. *Indigenous Psychological Research in Chinese Societies, 22,* 11–80.

Zeng, G., & Zhao, Y. K. (2018). *Science of happiness: Application of positive psychology in education.* Posts & Telecom Press.

Zhang, D. J. (2012). Integrating adolescents' mental health and psychological *suzhi* cultivation. *Journal of Psychological Science, 35*(3), 530–536. https://doi.org/ 10.16719/j.cnki.1671–6981.2012.03.001

Zhang, D. J. (2002) Strengthen mental health education in schools and foster students' psychological *suzhi. Journal of Hebei Normal University (Educational Science) 4*(1), 17–23. https://doi.org/ CNKI:SUN:HSJY.0.2002-01-002

Zhang, D. J., Feng, Z. Z., Guo, C., & Chen, X. (2000). Problems on research of children psychological *suzhi. Journal of Southwest China Normal University (Humanities and Social Sciences Edition), 26,* 56–62. (in Chinese).

Zhang, X., He, L., & Zheng, X. (2004). Adolescent students' life satisfaction: Its construct and scale development. *Psychological Science, 27,* 1257–1260. (in Chinese).

Zhang, D. J., Su, Z., & Wang, X. (2017). Thirty-years study on the psychological suzhi of Chinese children and adolescents: Review and prospect. *Studies of Psychology and Behavior, 15*(1), 3–11. (in Chinese).

Zhang, D. J., Wang, J. L., & Yu, L. (2011). *Methods and implementation strategies on cultivating children's psychological suzhi.* Nova Science.

Zhao, S., Cai, T., Zeng, X., & Chen, Z. (2011). Subjective well-being of senior high school students and its relationship to school-work achievement. *Chinese Journal of Clinical Psychology, 19*(1), 128–129. (in Chinese).

Zhu, X., & Shek, D. T. L. (2020). Impact of a positive youth development program on junior high school students in mainland china: A pioneer study. *Children and Youth Services Review, 114.* https://doi.org/10.1016/j.childyouth.2020.105022

31

APPLICATIONS OF POSITIVE PSYCHOLOGY IN SPAIN

Strengths-Based Interventions in Diverse Spanish School Ecosystems

José A. Piqueras, Juan C. Marzo, Raquel Falcó,
Beatriz Moreno-Amador, Victoria Soto-Sanz,
Tíscar Rodríguez-Jiménez and Maria Rivera-Riquelme

Child and Youth Mental Health

The transitions from childhood to adolescence and from youth to adulthood are crucial developmental stages. According to the World Health Organization (WHO, 2017), every young person has the right to grow up in the most nurturing environment possible to become a healthy and responsible adult, contribute to society, and lead a happy and fulfilling life. Childhood, adolescence, and emerging adulthood involve specific psychosocial and developmental needs, and characteristics that should be addressed within the framework of youth rights. These are also appropriate life stages to develop knowledge and skills, learn how to manage emotions and relationships, and ultimately acquire attributes and abilities essential for enjoying youthful years and preparing to assume adult roles (WHO, 2010).

Among all the life stages, adolescence, the transition between childhood and adulthood, is a particularly vulnerable period for developing mental health problems, with 110 million young people suffering from emotional problems worldwide. However, these disorders are the least identified and most undertreated mental health problems in this population, which places adolescents at risk of developing related problems (Education, Audiovisual and Culture Executive Agency, 2019).

Unfortunately, the above statement contains a meta-problem concerning the implicit definition of mental health problems: it assumes that mental health problems correspond exclusively to the presence of symptoms, psychopathology, or mental disorders; in short, psychological distress. Traditionally, research and practice addressing social and emotional health have used a unidimensional mental health model. Research on these issues has almost exclusively focused on models that explain psychopathology as psychological problems or distress, neglecting other aspects such as personal strengths or well-being, which offer an all-inclusive mental health vision (Ryff & Keyes, 1995). Furthermore, an exclusive focus on problems applies to only 15%–20% of the population (i.e., those presenting symptoms). Overidentifying externalizing symptoms does not provide any information about positive potentials or strengths (Keyes, 2006).

DOI: 10.4324/9781003013778-38

Over the past two decades, converging mental health research has challenged the unidimensional model and provides evidence for a bidimensional model. This bidimensional model conceptualizes distress and well-being as distinct but complementary concepts, which, when considered together, offer a complete and richer understanding of the human condition (Keyes, 2005). This contemporary approach has advantages because it (a) follows a dual-component mental health model; (b) applies to 100% of individuals; and (c) seeks to foster resilient, successful people, instead of solely preventing psychological problems. Moreover, to measure mental health, there is a need to consider the presence of psychopathology and subjective well-being (Keyes, 2006).

Studies focusing on children and youth provide evidence supporting this bidimensional mental health model (Eryilmaz, 2012; Kelly et al., 2012; Suldo et al., 2011). Children with high levels of psychological distress often show low levels of subjective well-being. Psychological distress combined with diminished psychological well-being is associated with low academic functioning. Together they provide a higher predictive value for positive adjustment to a school than each one alone.

Consequently, some authors emphasize "…(a) bidimensional model of mental health suggests that efforts seeking to cultivate positive mental health warrant shared attention with efforts aiming to ameliorate psychological impairment and symptoms" (Furlong et al., 2014b, p. 1012). Consequently, in this chapter, we suggest that mental health promotion programs measure two constructs: subjective distress, understood as present psychopathological symptoms, and subjective well-being, understood as psychological, emotional, and social aspects of well-being.

Adolescents experience numerous issues that require urgent responses. Among these issues are: (a) self-harm and suicidal behavior (WHO, 2014b), (b) (cyber)victimization (WHO, 2015), (c) vulnerable and social minority groups (Miranda-Mendizabal et al., 2017), (d) mental health stigma (Telesia et al., 2020), (e) school failure and its consequences (European Commission, 2017), and (f) lack of healthy lifestyles (Sepúlveda et al., 2020). Other matters of recent concern are pornography-related problems, addictive use of the Internet, and drug use (Eurosurveillance editorial team, 2012; WHO, 2014a). Regarding the burden of youth mental problems and their cost to society, 4.4% of the world's population experienced depression and 3.6% anxiety in 2015 (WHO, 2017), representing 615 million people aged 15 years and older (Chisholm et al., 2016). The incidence for children and adolescents is 2.6% for depression and 6.5% for anxiety (Polanczyk et al., 2015).

In Europe, the Organisation for Economic Co-operation and Development (OECD) reported that one in three Europeans experienced mental health problems. Depression prevalence is approximately 4.5% or 21 million people and at the cost of €118B per year—1% of member states' gross domestic product (Chisholm et al., 2016). In contrast, flourishing emotional well-being, including that of young people, is associated with healthy lifestyles, vigorous physical activity, and appropriate social and family support networks. Healthy youths also acquire social skills, coping skills, and learning strategies that help them to successfully manage adulthood challenges.

Promoting Mental Health and Emotional Well-Being

Until a few years ago in Spain, mental health preventive interventions focused exclusively on screening, detection, identification, and early intervention in psychological problems or difficulties (Vázquez et al., 2009). The Interdisciplinary Research Network for the PROmotion of mental health and wellness EMotional in young people (PROEM network) is a Spanish research network funded by the Spanish Ministry of Economy, Industry and Competitiveness, the European Regional Development Fund, and the State Research Agency (AEI). It aims to achieve a comprehensive description of the assessment and promotion of emotional health and well-being in young people experiencing emotional problems. One of the main objectives is to deliver a roadmap for the early diagnosis of emotional disorders and promote youths' emotional health and well-being. This roadmap guides the efforts of researchers, mental health providers, end-users, the school sector, civil organizations, stakeholders, and policy-makers. Particular consideration addresses the needs of minorities and underrepresented groups, including gender identities. In this sense, the PROEM Network (2018) has identified these gaps and needs in health and emotional well-being associated with children, adolescents, and young people:

- poor health and emotional well-being literacy;
- delay in the identification of mental health problems in schools and unvalidated instruments;
- limited resources and coordination among different stakeholders and regions;
- excessive medicalization of mental health and the associated costs;
- lack of health and emotional well-being policies coupled with an insufficient budget;
- lack of awareness of certain vulnerable and social minority groups; and
- increasing unhealthy lifestyles among youth and abusive use of information and information communication technologies (ICTs).

The PROEM Network (2018) report made recommendations to address mental health service gaps. These recommendations to develop an efficient health network included (a) building mental health literacy, (b) hiring more mental health specialists in schools, (c) training for education and primary healthcare professionals, and (d) increasing the budget for mental health policy implementation. Public policy also supported research to identify risk factors, promote positive mental health, and develop efficient and effective interventions.

The School as the Most Appropriate Setting for Mental Health Interventions

Positive health and well-being during adolescence largely depend on opportunities to develop specific emotional and cognitive abilities that enable the highest possible degree of autonomy and functioning. This development occurs through a well-rounded education and a successful transition to employment, ensuring a lasting network of connections. However, Spain has the second highest early school dropout rate (16%) in the EU, according to 2020 data (Instituto Nacional de Estadística [National Institute of Statistics], 2020).

Education and health are closely related. Schools allow learners to acquire specific cognitive abilities and knowledge while promoting essential emotional, personal, and mental health. School provides an environmental framework that encourages an individual's cognitive, emotional, and social development. Education helps prevent poverty and illness, minimize health risks, promote full development potential, and ward off emotional problems, abusive alcohol and substance consumption, suicide, and death (Davidson et al., 1989).

Adolescents with mental health problems are less likely to achieve excellent academic performance, are at risk for school dropout, and are less likely to enter higher education. Fully aware of the importance of adolescents receiving adequate schooling, a European Commission goal is to reduce the percentage of school dropouts by at least 10% and hopefully see at least 40% tertiary education attainment among 30- to 40-year-olds by 2020 (European Commision, 2017).

The Internet as the Present and Future Setting for Mental Health Promotion

Considering the limitations of traditional research approaches, new methodological frameworks and research designs are evaluating children and youths' mental health interventions (Liverpool et al., 2020). Several studies support the viability of developing approaches to detect mental health problems through the Internet in various school contexts (e.g., Blasco et al., 2017; Piqueras et al., 2017). Other studies highlight technology-support interventions for depression and anxiety in children and adolescents (Christ et al., 2020; Grist et al., 2019). However, despite the growth of research applying new technologies to child and youth clinical psychology, few studies have developed these programs, including routine check-ups for school-based prevention of emotional distress and well-being.

Comprehensive Strengths Assessment Models for School Contexts

Following Pérez-González et al. (2020), in the last 25 years, two approaches to empower personal and environmental factors that favor psychological and social well-being have expanded internationally. On the one hand, the field of health education has evolved from focusing on the causes of disease and disease avoidance (pathogenesis) to an understanding of the conditions and mechanisms that contribute to the promotion and maintenance of health (Antonovsky, 1993; Bauer et al., 2019). This focus includes mental health education as an area of focus for higher education institutions (Furnham & Swami, 2018). On the other hand, another regeneration movement has taken place in the field of psychology. After behaviorism and cognitivism's emotional blackout, an *affective revolution* emerged (Panksepp, 1998)—studying emotions in general and positive emotions in particular. This affective revolution has provoked change through reconsidering the importance of emotions and their scientific research. In this context, more than a quarter of a century ago, the construct of emotional intelligence (EI) emerged, consisting of the exaltation of the value of emotions and distancing from rationalism and cognitivism that had prevailed until then (Mayer et al., 2000). A second regenerative psychology movement includes psychological variables that facilitate well-being (Greene et al., 2016; Seligman & Csikszentmihalyi, 2000). Following these developments, another concept emerged, *covitality*, understood as a set of personal factors (mainly socioemotional skills) that favor psychosocial adjustment and health (Furlong et al., 2014a, 2014b), among which EI is a prominent factor.

In recent decades, researchers have increased attention to positive mental health in young people (e.g., Kirschman et al., 2009), resilience studies (e.g., Masten et al., 2009), positive youth development (e.g., Larson, 2000), empowerment approaches (e.g., Jimerson et al., 2004), and social-emotional learning (SEL) (e.g., Greenberg et al., 2003). Historically, these subfields studied young people's positive mental health within an isolated framework of protective factors. The effects of single indicators (e.g., gratitude; Froh et al., 2010) or several indicators (e.g., social support and school participation; Shekhtmeyster et al., 2011) were studied as predictors of psychosocial adjustment (e.g., academic performance and prosocial behavior). It was less common to conduct positive mental health studies in adolescents within a cumulative protective framework. A composite protective index, composed of several integrated indicators, provided a meta-indicator for predicting mental health and adjustment (e.g., Ostaszewski & Zimmerman, 2006).

Research on SEL has indicated that social-emotional competence is a critical factor in pursuing universal preventive interventions in schools. This is because the competence construct (a) is associated with social, behavioral, and academic adjustment, which are essential for healthy development; (b) predicts adjustment in adult life; (c) can improve with viable, cost-effective interventions; and (d) plays a critical role in the process of behavior change (Domitrovich et al., 2017). Within the large noncognitive skills domain, social-emotional competencies (e.g., self-awareness, self-management, social awareness, social skills, and decision-making) are among those receiving attention by clinical and educational disciplines (Capsada & Ferrer-Esteban, 2016). Data offered by four meta-analyses and three systematic reviews of the literature, in general, indicate positive effects of the programs considered as most programs improve social-emotional skills. However, the meta-analysis also highlights that, even with the increased implementation of SEL programs in various countries such as the United States and the United Kingdom, they lack scientific rigor. Moreover, few longitudinal studies have examined relations between socioemotional skills and health and psychosocial adjustment outcomes in children and youth.

Spanish School-Based Positive Psychology Interventions on Mental Health for Children and Adolescents

At least two comprehensive approaches (emotional education and positive psychology) have recently focused on the presence of distress and risk factors and well-being and protective factors, personal strengths, or resources. Regarding a positive-psychology approach, we reviewed the literature on children and adolescents' mental health interventions (Ivan, 2018). This review of published studies from these databases: MEDLINE-Pubmed, PsycINFO, Scopus, SciELO, Dialnet, and Google Scholar. The following descriptors guided the search in Spanish and English: (adolescents OR children) AND (mental health OR well-being) AND (strength OR positive psychology) AND (program OR interventions OR prevention). The inclusion criteria were:

1   presence of the descriptors in titles and abstracts;
2   studies after 2000, to ensure that publications adapted to the society of the 21st century and its problems;
3   samples composed of participants aged between 4 and 18 years old, belonging to developmental stages of childhood and adolescence, crucial for the formation of self-perception and personality, as these are stages where emotional, attitudinal, and psychological problems related to prevention can be strengthened through positive psychology;
4   experimental designs (with the presence of a control group, randomizing, and control of variables), which included programs supported within the framework of positive psychology; and
5   studies carried out in Spain.

The review yielded 10 studies (see Figure 31.1), highlighting the benefits of positive psychology-based interventions for mental health in children and adolescents. In this sense, the review's recommendation emphasized that preventive interventions should include environmental modifications that reduce stress, thereby allowing youths to develop positive competencies simultaneously within their social environments. Educational contexts that offer rewards and the achievement of realistic goals are more likely to increase motivation and decrease disruptive behaviors in children and adolescents.

School-Based Positive Psychology Interventions in Children and Adolescents

The following section presents a brief description of these 10 studies and their main results. A summary of these prominent school-based programs developed at the Spanish national level appears below.

Pereira and Martínez (2004) applied a program to develop coping strategies to decrease depression indicators in eight institutionalized adolescents aged 15–17. In general, the adolescents developed problem-solving strategies and achieved higher assertiveness and emotional self-control, reaching a balance and adequately managing their anger and stress.

De Benito et al. (2009) proposed an assertiveness and social skills program. They trained infant, primary, and secondary school teachers in attitudes, values, cognitions, emotions, and behaviors to help children and adolescents live together effectively and satisfactorily. The curriculum included a series of social skills activities related to communication, assertiveness, emotions, and positive and challenging interactions. The program's impact was predictably positive because it was designed to promote coexistence, which implies teaching and fostering social skills to promote a good climate of positive relations in all students.

The Aulas Felices program (Arguís et al., 2010), aimed at preschool, primary, and secondary school students, provides resources to work in various curricular areas, promoting transversal

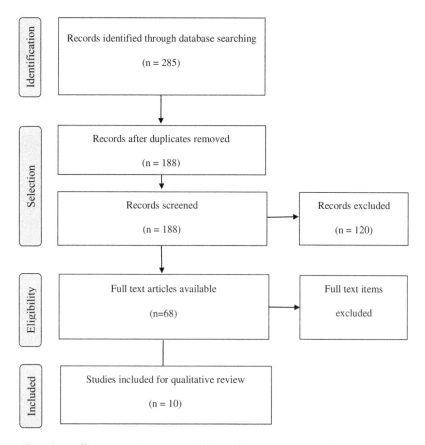

Figure 31.1 Flow chart of literature review process (adapted from PRISMA flow diagram (Moher et al., 2009)

skills, tutorial action, and education in values. This program disseminates the contributions of positive psychology among the educational community. The effectiveness of this program has been positive, generating happier and more self-governing students.

Justicia et al. (2011) examined the Learning to Live Together program's implementation with four- to five-year-old children located in Granada (Spain). This universal antisocial behavior prevention program builds students' social competence through content related to rules, feelings, communication skills, help, cooperation, and conflict resolution. The results showed a reduction of antisocial behaviors and increased social competence in the experimental group participants. In general, the children increased their reflective capacity, improved their emotional reactivity, reduced aggression, and improved cognitive attention.

Reyes-Bossio et al. (2012) presented a psychological training program applied to high-performance volleyball players between 13 and 16 years old and evaluated its effectiveness before and after its application. The results showed statistically significant differences in self-confidence, attention control, and negative energy. The areas of visualization, motivation, positive attitude, and positive energy showed average increases.

Regalado-Cuenca and Fajardo-Caldera (2014), through the Fierabrás Intervention Program, proposed improving the mood and increasing the sense of well-being of adolescents with multiple sclerosis. A case-study design supported the interventions' effectiveness in treating depression and mainly psychological well-being, although it did improve anxiety or depression symptoms.

Lera (2015) coordinated the European project GOLDEN5, a universal school program to increase students' intrinsic motivation while improving their personal development. Although it flexibly considers diversity (students with disabilities and/or at risk of social exclusion), it targets an entire classroom, adapting to primary school settings. Its quantitative results were positive and indicated increased academic performance, sociability, and self-esteem. Qualitative results focused on individual and group changes in the teaching staff. While addressing emerging obstacles, the program continues to be used in many national and international schools (Lera, 2015).

Also noteworthy is Orenes' (2015) work to adapt the Fortius Program (Méndez et al., 2012) for children and preadolescents (4,628 students were recruited, aged from 8 to 11 years). Orenes combined clinical psychology's focus on solving emotional difficulties and positive psychology's emphasis on enhancing personal skills. This program reduced anxiety symptoms in younger adolescents, and reduced depressive symptoms and behavioral problems in females, and improved their perceived state of health.

Mónaco, de la Barrera, and Montoya-Castilla (2017) analyzed the effectiveness of a pilot intervention to develop emotional skills applied to 46 adolescents. The program was beneficial in increasing adolescents' positive affect, cognitive empathy, and emotional vocabulary. The importance of developing this type of program, which effectively increases adolescents' psychosocial adjustment and well-being is noteworthy.

Sarrionandia and Garaigordobil (2017) evaluated the effects of a program that promotes EI in 148 adolescents (13–16 years), emphasizing possible differences according to gender identity. The results showed a significant increase in EI and a decrease in psychosomatic symptoms and emotional instability. However, there were no significant differences found according to gender identity.

Spanish Positive-Psychology-Based and School-Based Mental Health Programs

A recent review by Cobos-Sánchez et al. (2018) on assessment and intervention protocols in emotional education for adolescents in educational contexts observed that social-emotional competencies are essential to the child's healthy development youth population (see Table 31.1). These competencies are protective or salutogenic factors against the development of psychological disorders in adulthood. On the other hand, research from various EI models has shown that emotional competencies predict people's academic and social success. This observation led to the creating of educational center programs because these settings are the context in which a substantial part of children's lives takes place. Education centers provide naturalistic contexts for youths to develop essential competencies. There is an institutional obligation because state and European regulations insist on training students comprehensively as competent citizens in all developmental areas. When examining this recent review, a question arises: What is the empirical evidence for these emotional education programs? The response is that more evidence-based studies supporting this type of intervention are needed.

Covitality Model

Chapter 10 (Paz & Kim, this volume) broadly describes and reviews the covitality model and its Social-Emotional Health Surveys (SEHS). Evaluation of the SEHS in international studies indicates that high covitality predicts subjective well-being and quality of life, including academic performance and school safety (Furlong et al., 2014b). Also, covitality is a predictor of college students' internalizing symptoms, the onset of depressive symptoms, and substance use (Jones et al., 2013). It predicts prosocial behavior, caring relationships, school acceptance, and school rejection in elementary school students (Furlong et al., 2014b). The covitality construct presumes a psychological mindset shaped in early childhood experiences and nurtured through the developmental life span.

Table 31.1 Main Programs Developed in Spain in the Educational Field (Based on Cobos-Sánchez et al., 2018)

Authors	Program Name
Díaz-Aguado (1996)	Program to promote tolerance of diversity in ethnically heterogeneous environments (Autonomous Community of Madrid).
Triánes & Fernández-Figarés (2001)	Learning to be a person and to live together (University of Málaga).
Blasco et al. (2002)	Emotional education. Proposals for tutoring. Secondary education (Valencian Community).
Comas et al. (2002)	Ulysses. Program for learning and developing emotional self-control (Sport and Life Association, Madrid).
Segura-Morales & Pérez-Díaz (2002)	Being a person and relating (University of La Laguna).
Gallego-Gil & Gallego-Alarcón (2004)	Program for the Development of Emotional Intelligence (PRIE, UNED).
Vallés-Arándiga (2007)	Emotional intelligence program for school coexistence (PIECE, University of Alicante).
Grupo Aprendizaje Emocional (2007)	Emotional Education Programs. 1st and 2nd cycles of Compulsory Secondary Education (CSE). Ministry of Education. Generalitat Valenciana.
Gararigordobil (2000) Gararigordobil (2005)	Program for the development of personality and human rights education (University of the Basque Country). Cooperative and creative games for groups of children from 6 to 8 years old.
Giménez-Dasí et al. (2016)	Thinking emotions with full attention. Intervention Program for Primary Education.
Giménez-Dasí et al. (2017)	Thinking emotions with full attention. Intervention Program for Children's Education.
Montoya et al. (2016)	PREDEMA. Emotional Education Program for Adolescents. From emotion to meaning.
Méndez et al. (2012)	FORTIUS program. Psychological strength and prevention of emotional difficulties.
Bisquerra (2013)	Emotional Education. Proposal for educators and families (University of Barcelona).
Arguis Rey (2010)	Happy Classrooms (Zaragoza).
Ruiz Aranda et al. (2013). Cabello, et al. (2016).	INTEMO Program. Guide to improve the emotional intelligence of adolescents (Emotions Lab., University of Malaga). INTEMO + Program. Improving the emotional intelligence of adolescents.

Different research groups in many countries are leading what could be considered a global covitality strategy. The first step that most teams have followed is validating the SEHS measures in their versions. Thus, studies in Australia, Chile, China, Greece, Japan, Korea, Mexico, Turkey, and the United Kingdom, among other countries, have validated the SEHS measures or are in the process of validation for children, adolescents, and transition-age youths (Furlong et al., 2021). Nevertheless, it is also essential to evaluate the impact that covitality studies are having internationally, broadening the use of a construct associated with positive mental health and psychosocial adjustment cross-culturally. The following section provides an overview and illustration of how some positive psychology models are applied to Spain's academic contexts.

Covitality Model's Strengths-Based Assessment in Diverse Spanish School Ecosystems

Until a few years ago, school-based preventive interventions for mental health in Spain focused on detection, identification, and early intervention, targeting, exclusively, the presence of psychological problems or difficulties. Recently, assessment approaches have focused not only on identifying distress and risk factors but also on well-being and protective factors, or personal strengths or resources. The Covitality Project's research team (Proyecto Covitalidad in Spanish; see http://covitalidad.edu.umh.es/) began working from this comprehensive and broad-based approach in 2010 with the DetectaWeb Project study (Piqueras et al., 2017). The DetectaWeb Project developed a procedure for the early detection of children and adolescents' mental health. This project uses a web-based platform for MHC screening, including psychological problems (anxiety, depression, and suicidality) and personal strengths (emotional, cognitive/psychological, and social aspects). Some of this study's results are reported by Garcia-Olcina et al. (2014, 2017), Rivera-Riquelme et al. (2019), and Piqueras et al. (2020, 2021).

Since 2016, the Covitality-Spain team, led by the first author, has carried out psychological assessments based on strengths and difficulties in children, adolescents, and university students. These three related studies illustrate school-based applications for each group. In all cases, the assessments were carried out through online surveys and within the framework of universal prevention, so all students completed the survey. Our study's first common aim was to validate specific instruments to assess covitality (SEHS-Primary, SEHS-Secondary, and SEHS-Higher Education).

Our team has recruited different samples of elementary school children ($N = 800$) aged between 8 and 12 years. These children's social and emotional competencies were assessed using the covitality's SEHS-Primary scale. Other measures considered mental health, health-related quality of life, distress, strengths and difficulties, sociometric status, peer bullying, trait EI, and perfectionism. Some of the main results were that covitality mediated the relationship between suffering bullying and psychosocial adjustment. Furthermore, the protocol, including SEHS-Primary, has been used to assess an intervention's efficacy to reduce bullying focused on observers (Pineda et al., 2017).

Among adolescents, the first study employed 1,042 high school students, including distress and well-being variables. The main results were that the covitality SEHS-Secondary measure was negatively associated with internalizing and externalizing symptoms and peer and parents' relationship problems. Large, positive associations were found with measures of positive covariates (well-being, health-related quality of life, and prosocial behaviors, Piqueras, Rodriguez-Jimenez et al., 2019). A second longitudinal study collected responses from 5,627 secondary and high school students from southeastern Spain (Region of Murcia and Province of Alicante). Distress, well-being, health-related quality of life, psychopathology, and relationship with parents were measured. Although the results obtained are not yet published, the cross-sectional data have been preliminarily analyzed (Piqueras, Marzo et al., 2019). The third study results with a sample of 438 adolescents aged 11–17 reflected that the SEHS-S measure negatively predicted 30% of the presence of internalizing symptoms and 24% of externalizing symptoms. Therefore, covitality acted as a protective variable (Falcó et al., 2020). The main results of studies involving adolescents showed that social-emotional competencies predict psychosocial adjustment and mediate the influence of stressful life events on psychosocial adjustment. The protocol, including SEHS-Secondary, is being used to create group and individual reports (risk warnings, especially in those cases in which adolescents present a risk for suicide or mental health problems).

We have conducted a longitudinal study in three universities in southeastern Spain using the SEHS-Higher Education measure. The cross-sectional sample included 1,511 participants. This study collected data on well-being, EI, self-esteem, suicide, anxiety and depression, psychological difficulties and problems, positive and negative affect, and health-related quality of life. Although the data analyzed have not yet been published, the cross-sectional results of this experience offer the following results: The absence of covitality explains 23% of the presence of internalizing (anxiety and depression) and externalizing (behavioral problems) symptoms. Specifically, regarding internalizing symptoms, the most important are self-control, emotion regulation, and peer support. All these factors are protective factors against suffering symptoms (Soto-Sanz et al., 2018). Simultaneously, the prediction of suicidal behaviors in university youth (18–19 years old) was analyzed through the internalizing symptoms, with covitality as a moderator. In this analysis, it was found that covitality moderated the relationship between suicidal behaviors and internalizing symptoms, explaining 15% of the variance of suicidal behaviors (Soto-Sanz et al., 2019).

The SEHS measures' applications have provided another resource to focus on psychological difficulties and positive aspects of human functioning among Spanish children, adolescents, and emerging adults. Proyecto Covitality's ongoing efforts (see http://covitalidad.edu.umh.es/) have clear implications for improving and expanding Spanish prevention of health programs to foster all youths' well-being, especially vulnerable populations.

Conclusion

This chapter examined studies focusing on interventions based on the positive psychology perspective, designed to improve Spain's child and adolescent mental health. The main findings of this review are presented here.

First, the selected publications' analysis indicated that, regardless of the approach, criteria, or working methodology used to address and implement programs based on positive psychology, the programs offer positive results for well-being, personal growth, and emotional development. This finding is consistent with a recent systematic and meta-analytic review on the effects of school-based positive psychology interventions for adolescents, reporting small effects for subjective well-being ($g = 0.24$), psychological well-being ($g = 0.25$), and depression symptoms ($g = 0.28$). This supports evidence for the efficacy of school-based multicomponent positive psychology interventions in improving mental health in the short and long term (Tejada-Gallardo et al., 2020). It also coincides with the findings of broader, nonchild-focused reviews, such as that by Koydemir et al. (2020), showing an overall effect size (Cohen's d) of 0.23 for general well-being and short- and long-term intervention effects.

Childhood and adolescence are crucial stages for human beings, which is why orienting their learning and experiences during these stages to foster the resilient, proactive, and healthy perspectives proposed by positive psychology is essential and compulsory. The bibliographical review pointed out three ways through which positive psychology has practical usefulness: (a) as a preventive strategy for the strengthening of mental health; (b) as a corrective or therapeutic strategy through the influence of its interventions or programs in the psychosocial adjustment of children and adolescents, key for greater cognitive empathy and emotional well-being; and (c) as an inclusion strategy, providing children and youth with tools for social strengthening, emotional proactivity, and healthy decision-making.

A second observation is the documentation of considerable research on positive psychology and education. This growing Spanish literature shows its relevance as a research theme and as prevention and treatment strategies. It is even an educational tool to nurture prosocial behaviors, accurately perceive reality, and assertively adjust to it.

A third conclusion is that the covitality model's strength-based approach is a promising construct that continues to receive growing interest, contributing to the knowledge of mental health from the viewpoint of positive psychology, emphasizing strengths and resources rather than deficits. Extant research has focused on assessment, but there are yet few studies evaluating interventions focused on increasing social-emotional competencies from the covitality model framework (Naples, 2019)—it is suggested to develop such interventions and test their effectiveness.

The early efforts of the Proyecto Covitalidad indicate that positive psychology offers promising results for the improvement of Spanish children's and youth's well-being, decreasing negative attitudes, and promoting flourishing mental health. This chapter also identified the need for more research and practical positive psychology applications to develop strategies that foster mental health in Spain and worldwide.

References

Antonovsky, A. (1993). The structure and properties of the Sense of Coherence Scale. *Social Science & Medicine, 36*(6), 725–733. https://doi.org/10.1016/0277-9536(93)90033-Z

Arguís, R., Bolsas, A., Hernández, S., & Salvador, M. (2010). *Programa "Aulas Felices". Psicología positiva aplicada a la educación* [Happy Classroom Program. Positive psychology applied to education]. Equipo SATI.

Bauer, G. F., Roy, M., Bakibinga, P., Contu, P., Downe, S., Eriksson, M., Espnes, G. A., Jensen, B. B., Juvinya Canal, D., Lindström, B., Mana, A., Mittelmark, M. B., Morgan, A. R., Pelikan, J. M., Sabiga-Nunes, L., Sagy, S., Shorey, S., Vaandrager, L., & Vinje, H. F. (2020). Future directions for the concept of salutogenesis: A position article. *Health Promotion International, 35*(2), 187–195. https://doi.org/10.1093/heapro/daz057

Blasco, M. J., Castellví, P., Almenara, J., Lagares, C., Roca, M., Sesé, A., Piqueras, J. A., Soto-Sanz, V., Rodríguez-Marín, J., Echeburúa, E., Gabilondo, A., Cebrià, A. I., Miranda-Mendizábal, A., Vilagut, G., Bruffaerts, R., Auerbach, R. P., Kessler, R. C., & Alonso, J. (2016). Predictive models for suicidal thoughts and behaviors among Spanish university students: Rationale and methods of the UNIVERSAL (University & Mental Health) Project. *BMC Psychiatry, 16,* 122. https://doi.org/10.1186/s12888-016-0820-y

Capsada, Q., & Ferrer-Esteban, G. (2016). *¿Son efectivos los programas de educación socioemocional como herramienta para mejorar las competencias del alumnado?* [Are social-emotional education programs effective as a tool to improve students' skills?]. Fundació Jaume Bofill, Ivàlua.

Chisholm, D., Sweeny, K., Sheehan, P., Rasmussen, B., Smit, F., Cuijpers, P., & Saxena, S. (2016). Scaling-up treatment of depression and anxiety: A global return on investment analysis. *The Lancet, 3*(5), 415–424. https://doi.org/10.1016/S2215-0366(16)30024-4

Christ, C., Schouten, M. J., Blankers, M., van Schaik, D. J., Beekman, A. T., Wisman, M. A., Stikkelbroek, Y. A., & Dekker, J. J. (2020). Internet and computer-based cognitive behavioral therapy for anxiety and depression in adolescents and young adults: Systematic review and meta-analysis. *Journal of Medical Internet Research, 22*(9), e17831. https://doi.org/10.2196/17831

Cobos-Sánchez, L., Flujas-Contreras, J. M., & Gómez-Becerra, I. G. (2018). Revisión de protocolos de evaluación e intervención en educación emocional en adolescentes en contextos educativos a nivel grupal [Review of evaluation and intervention protocols in emotional education in adolescents in educational contexts at the group level]. *Revista de Estudios de Juventud, 121,* 151–167.

Davidson, L. E., Rosenberg, M. L., Mercy, J. A., Franklin, J., & Simmons, J. T. (1989). An epidemiologic study of risk factors in two teenage suicide clusters. *JAMA, 262*(19), 2687–2692. https://doi.org/10.1001/jama.1989.03430190071034

De Benito, M. P., Elices, J. A., Francia, M. V., García-Larrauri, B., & Monjas, M. I. (2009). *Cómo promover la convivencia: Programa de Asertividad y Habilidades Sociales (PAHS) (Educación Infantil, Primaria y Secundaria)* [How to promote coexistence: Assertiveness and Social Skills Program (PAHS) (Infant, Primary, and Secondary Education)]. CEPE Ciencias de la Educación Preescolar y Especial.

Domitrovich, C. E., Durlak, J. A., Staley, K. C., & Weissberg, R. P. (2017). Social-motional competence: An essential factor for promoting positive adjustment and reducing risk in school children. *Child Development, 88*(2), 408–416. https://doi.org/10.1111/cdev.12739

Education, Audiovisual and Culture Executive Agency. (2019). *7.5 Mental health* (Spain). https://eacea.ec.europa.eu/national-policies/en/content/youthwiki/75-mental-health-spain

Eryilmaz, A. (2012). A model of subjective well-being for adolescents in high school. *Journal of Happiness Studies, 13,* 275–289. https://doi.org/10.1007/s10902-011-9263-9

European Commision. (2017). *Focus on: Mental health in education: An unspoken issue of our age.* https://eacea.ec.europa.eu/national-policies/eurydice/content/focus-mental-health-education-unspoken-issue-our-age_en

Eurosurveillance Editorial Team. (2012). EMCDDA publishes 2012 report on the state of the drugs problem in Europe. *Eurosurveillance, 17*(46), 20315. https://www.eurosurveillance.org/docserver/fulltext/

eurosurveillance/17/46/art20315-en.pdf?expires=1596110666&id=id&accname=guest&checksum=592949543607CD2383FF6A063C3EE33C

Falcó, R., Marzo, J. C., & Piqueras, J. A. (2020). La covitalidad como factor protector ante problemas interiorizados y exteriorizados en adolescentes españoles [Covitality as a protective factor against internalizing and externalizing problems in Spanish adolescents]. *Behavioral Psychology / Psicología Conductual, 28*(3), 393–413. https://dialnet.unirioja.es/servlet/articulo?codigo=7695389

Froh, J. J., Bono, G., & Emmons, R. (2010). Being grateful is beyond good manners: Gratitude and motivation to contribute to society among early adolescents. *Motivation and Emotion, 34*(2), 144–157. https://doi.org/10.1007/s11031-010-9163-z

Furlong, M. J., Dowdy, E., Carnazzo, K., Bovery, B. L., & Kim, E. (2014). Covitality: Fostering the building blocks of complete mental health. *Communique, 42*(8), 1–28. https://eric.ed.gov/?id=EJ1192977

Furlong, M. J., Dowdy, E., Nylund-Gibson, K., Wagle, R., Carter, D., & Hinton, T. (2021). Enhancement and standardization of a universal social-emotional health measure for students' psychological strengths. *Journal of Well-Being Assessment.* https://doi.org/10.1007/s41543-020-00032-2

Furlong, M. J., You, S., Renshaw, T. L., Smith, D. C., & O'Malley, M. (2014). Preliminary development and validation of the Social and Emotional Health Survey for secondary students. *Social Indicators Research, 117*, 1011–1032. https://doi.org/10.1007/s11205-013-0373-0

Furnham, A., & Swami, V. (2018). Mental health literacy: A review of what it is and why it matters. *International Perspectives in Psychology: Research, Practice, Consultation, 7*(4), 240–257. https://doi.org/10.1037/ipp0000094

García-Olcina, M., Piqueras, J. A., & Martínez-González, A. E. (2014). Datos preliminares de la validación del Cuestionario de Detección vía Web para los trastornos emocionales (DETECTA-WEB) en adolescentes españoles [Preliminary data of validation of the Web-based Screening Questionnaire for Emotional Mental Disorders (DETECTA-WEB) in Spanish adolescents]. *Revista de Psicología Clínica con Niños y Adolescentes, 1*(1), 69–77.

Garcia-Olcina, M., Rivera-Riquelme, M., Canto-Diez, T. J., Tomas-Berenguer, M. R., Bustamante, R., & Piqueras, J. A. (2017). Detección online de trastornos emocionales en población clínica de niños y adolescentes: Escala DetectaWeb-Malestar [Online detection of emotional disorders in the clinical population of children and adolescents: DetectaWeb-Distress Scale]. *Revista de Psicología Clínica con Niños y Adolescentes, 4*(3), 35–45.

Greenberg, M. T., Weissberg, R. P., O'Brien, M. U., Zins, J. E., Fredericks, L., Resnik, H., & Elias, M. J. (2003). Enhancing school-based prevention and youth development through coordinated social, emotional, and academic learning. *American Psychologist, 58*, 466–474. https://doi.org/10.1037/0003-066x.58.6-7.466

Greene, J. D., Morrison, I., & Seligman, M. E. P. (2016). *Positive neuroscience.* Oxford University Press.

Grist, R., Croker, A., Denne, M., & Stallard, P. (2019). Technology delivered interventions for depression and anxiety in children and adolescents: A systematic review and meta-analysis. *Clinical Child and Family Psychology Review, 22*(2), 147–171. https://doi.org/10.1007/s10567-018-0271-8

Instituto Nacional de Estadística. (2018). (INE) [National Institute of Statistics]. http://www.ine.es/

Ivan, F. I. (2018). *Programas de promoción de la salud mental en niños y adolescentes desde la psicología positiva: Una revisión bibliográfica* [Programs for the promotion of mental health in children and adolescents from positive psychology: A literature review]. [Final Degree Project, Miguel Hernandez University, Spain]. http://193.147.134.18/bitstream/11000/6383/1/TFG.%20IZABELA%20IVAN.pdf

Jimerson, S. R., Sharkey, J. D., Nyborg, V., & Furlong, M. J. (2004). Strength-based assessment and school psychology: A summary and synthesis. *The California School Psychologist, 9*, 9–19. https://doi.org/10.1007/BF03340903

Jones, C. N., You, S., & Furlong, M. J. (2013). A preliminary examination of covitality as integrated well-being in college students. *Social Indicators Research, 111*(2), 511–526. https://doi.org/10.1007/s11205-012-0017-9

Justicia, A., Corredor, G. A., Pichardo, M. C., Justicia, F., & Quesada, A. B. (2011). *Efectos del programa aprender a convivir en educación infantil* [Effects of the learning to live together program in early childhood education]. *International Journal of Developmental and Educational Psychology, 3*(1), 39–58. http://infad.eu/RevistaINFAD/2011/n1/volumen3/INFAD_010323_39-50.pdf

Kelly, R. M., Hills, K. J., Huebner, E. S., & McQuillin, S. (2012). The longitudinal stability and dynamics of group membership in the dual-factor model of mental health: Psychosocial predictors of mental health. *Canadian Journal of School Psychology, 27*(4), 337–355. https://doi.org/10.1177/0829573512458505

Keyes, C. L. M. (2005). Mental illness and/or mental health? Investigating axioms of the complete state model of health. *Journal Consulting and Clinical Psychology, 73*(3), 539–548. https://doi.org/10.1037/0022-006X.73.3.539

Keyes, C. L. M. (2006). Mental health in adolescence: Is America's youth flourishing? *American Journal of Orthopsychiatry, 76*(3), 395–402. https://doi.org/10.1037/0002-9432.76.3.395

Kirschman, K. J. B., Johnson, R. J., Bender, J. A., & Roberts, M. C. (2009). Positive psychology for children and adolescents: Development, prevention, and promotion. In S. J. Lopez & C. R. Snyder (Eds.), *The Oxford handbook of positive psychology* (2nd ed., pp. 133–148). Oxford University Press.

Koydemir, S., Sökmez, A. B., & Schütz, A. (2020). A meta-analysis of the effectiveness of randomized controlled positive psychological interventions on subjective and psychological well-being. *Applied Research in Quality of Life*. https://doi.org/10.1007/s11482-019-09788-z

Larson, R. W. (2000). Toward a psychology of positive youth development. *American Psychologist, 55*(1), 170–183. https://doi.org/10.1037/0003-066X.55.1.170

Lera, M. J. (2015). *Programa Golden5: Una mirada positiva al desarrollo del alumnado* [Golden5 Program: A positive look at students' development]. *Convives, 10,* 15–22.

Liverpool, S., Mota, C. P., Sales, C. M., Čuš, A., Carletto, S., Hancheva, C., Sousa, S., Cerón, S. C., Moreno-Peral, P., Pietrabissa, G., Moltrecht, B., Ulberg, R., Ferreira, N., & Edbrooke-Childs, J. (2020). Engaging children and young people in digital mental health interventions: Systematic review of modes of delivery, facilitators, and barriers. *Journal of Medical Internet Research, 22*(6), e16317. https://doi.org/10.2196/16317

Masten, A. S., Cutuli, J. J., Herbers, J. E., & Reed, M. G. (2009). Resilience in development. In S. J. Lopez & C. R. Snyder (Eds.), *The Oxford handbook of positive psychology* (2nd ed., pp. 117–131). Oxford University Press.

Mayer, J. D., Salovey, P., & Caruso, D. R. (2000). Emotional intelligence as zeitgeist, as personality, and as a mental ability. In R. Bar-On & J. D. A. Parker (Eds.), *The handbook of emotional intelligence: Theory, development, assessment, and application at home, school, and in the workplace* (pp. 92–117). Jossey-Bass.

Miranda-Mendizábal, A., Castellví, P., Parés-Badell, O., Almenara, J., Alonso, I., Blasco, M. J., Cebrià, A., Gabilondo, A., Gili, M., Lagares, C., Piqueras, J. A., Roca, M., Rodríguez-Marín, J., Rodríguez-Jiménez, R., Soto-Sanz, V., Vilagut, G., & Alonso, J. (2017). Sexual orientation and suicidal behaviour in adolescents and young adults: Systematic review and meta-analysis. *The British Journal of Psychiatry: The Journal of Mental Science, 211*(2), 77–87. https://doi.org/10.1192/bjp.bp.116.196345

Moher, D., Liberati, A., Tetzlaff, J., Altman, D. G., & Prisma Group. (2009). Preferred reporting items for systematic reviews and meta-analyses: the PRISMA statement. *PLoS medicine, 6*(7), e1000097. https://doi.org/10.1371/journal.pmed.1000097

Mónaco, E., de la Barrera, U., & Montoya-Castilla, I. (2017). Desarrollo de un programa de intervención para mejorar las competencias emocionales, el afecto positivo y la empatía en la adolescencia [Development of an intervention program to improve emotional competencies, positive affect and empathy in adolescence]. *Calidad de Vida y Salud, 10*(1), 41–56.

Naples, L. H. (2019, March). *Neurodivergence in early childhood: Deriving a dual-factor model of educational well-being through a design-based research pilot program.* Dissertation Graduate School fo Education and Human Development of the George Washington University. https://search.proquest.com/openview/487ffe4af4101da676c588e2156960c5/1?pq-origsite=gscholar&cbl=18750&diss=y

Orenes, A. (2015). *Evaluación de la ansiedad por separación y prevención escolar de las dificultades emocionales* [Evaluation of separation anxiety and prevention of emotional difficulties at school]. Doctoral Thesis. Faculty of Psychology. University of Murcia. Spain.

Ostaszewski, K., & Zimmerman, M. A. (2006). The effects of cumulative risks and promotive factors on urban adolescent alcohol and other drug use: A longitudinal study of resiliency. *American Journal of Community Psychology, 38*(3–4), 237–249. https://doi.org/10.1007/s10464-006-9076-x

Panksepp, J. (1998). The quest for long-term health and happiness: To play or not to play, that is the question. *Psychological Inquiry, 9*(1), 56–66. https://doi.org/10.1207/s15327965pli0901_9

Pereira, C., & Martínez, A. (2004). Programa para disminuir indicadores de depresión mediante el desarrollo de estrategias de afrontamiento (Un estudio en adolescentes institucionalizados) [Program to decrease indicators of depression by developing coping strategies (A study of institutionalized adolescents)]. *Ajayu Órgano de Difusión Científica del Departamento de Psicología UCBSP, 2*(1), 54–66.

Pérez-González, J. C., Yáñez, S., Ortega-Navas, M. C., & Piqueras, J. A. (2020). Emotional education in health education: A public health issue. *Clínica y Salud, 31*(3), 127–136. https://doi.org/10.5093/clysa2020a7

Pineda, D., Piqueras, J. A., Martinez, A., Rodriguez-Jimenez, T., Martínez Gonzalez, A. E., Santamaria, P., & Furlong, M. J. (2017, July 5–8). A *new instrument for covitality: The revised Social Emotional Health Survey–Primary in a Spanish sample of children* [Paper presentation]. 14th European Conference on Psychological Assessment, Lisbon, Portugal.

Piqueras, J. A., Garcia-Olcina, M., Rivera-Riquelme, M., Martinez-Gonzalez, A. E., & Cuijpers, P. (2021). DetectaWeb-Distress scale: A global and multidimensional web-based screener for emotional disorder symptoms in children and Adolescents. *Frontiers in Psychology, 12*, 93. https://doi.org/10.3389/fpsyg.2021.627604

Piqueras, J. A., García-Olcina, M., Rivera-Riquelme, M., & Pineda, D. (2020). Evidencia de validez diagnóstica de la Escala DetectaWeb-Malestar [Evidence of diagnostic utility of the DetectaWeb-Distress Scale]. *Revista de Psicopatologia y Psicologia Clínica, 25*(3), 161–174. http://doi.org/10.5944/rppc.28931

Piqueras, J. A., Garcia-Olcina, M., Rivera-Riquelme, M., Rodríguez-Jiménez, T., Martínez-González, A. E., & Cuijpers, P. (2017). DetectaWeb Project: Study protocol of a web-based detection of mental health of children and adolescents. *BMJ Open*, 7:e017218. http://doi.org/10.1136/bmjopen-2017-017218

Piqueras, J. A. Marzo, J. C., Falcó, R., Moreno-Amador, B., Mira, F., Soto-Sanz, V., Rodríguez-Jiménez, T., Martínez-González, A. E., Rivera-Riquelme, M., Maciá, D., Keyes, C., Cuijpers, P., Dowdy, E., & Furlong, M. J. (2019, July 7–10). *Web-based assessment and classification of complete mental health in Spanish adolescents: preliminary results* [Paper presentation]. 15th European Conference on Psychological Assessment, Brussels, Belgium.

Piqueras, J. A., Rodriguez-Jimenez, T., Marzo, J. C., Rivera-Riquelme, M., Martinez-Gonzalez, A. E., Falco, R., & Furlong, M. J. (2019). Social Emotional Health Survey-Secondary (SEHS-S): A universal screening measure of social-emotional strengths for spanish-speaking adolescents. *International Journal of Environmental Research and Public Health, 16*(24), 4982. https://doi.org/10.3390/ijerph16244982

Polanczyk, G. V., Salum, G. A., Sugaya, L. S., Caye, A., & Rohde, L. A. (2015). Annual research review: A meta-analysis of the worldwide prevalence of mental disorders in children and adolescents. *Journal of Child Psychology and Psychiatry, 56*(3), 345–365. https://doi.org/10.1111/jcpp.12381

PROEM Network. (2018). Report and roadmap on the state of the art, needs and recommendations for improving psychological assessment and promoting mental health and emotional well-being in young people. *Report developed by Red PROEM members and partners.* http://redproem.es/wp-content/uploads/2018/06/Informe_encuentro_Red_PROEM_EN.pdf

Regalado-Cuenca, A. B., & Fajardo-Caldera, M. (2014). Eficacia de un programa de psicología positiva en un adolescente con esclerosis múltiple [Effectiveness of a positive psychology program in an adolescent with multiple sclerosis]. *International Journal of Developmental and Educational Psychology, 1*(1), 379–389. https://doi.org/10.17060/ijodaep.2014.n1.v1.383

Reyes-Bossio, M., Raimundi, M. J., & Gomez Correa, L. (2012). Programa de entrenamiento en habilidades psicológicas en jugadoras de voleibol de alto rendimiento [Psychological Skills Training Program in High Performance Volleyball Players]. *Cuadernos de Psicología del Deporte, 12*(1), 9–16.

Rivera-Riquelme, M., Piqueras, J. A., & Cuijpers, P. (2019). The Revised Mental Health Inventory-5 (MHI-5) as an ultra-brief screening measure of bidimensional mental health in children and adolescents. *Psychiatry Research, 274*, 247–253. https://doi.org/10.1016/j.psychres.2019.02.045

Ryff, C. D., & Keyes, C. L. M. (1995). The structure of psychological well-being revisited. *Journal of Personality and Social Psychology, 69*(4), 719–727. https://doi.org/10.1037//0022-3514.69.4.719

Sarrionandia, A., & Garaigordobil, M. (2017). Efectos de un programa de inteligencia emocional en factores socioemocionales y síntomas psicosomáticos [Effects of a program of emotional intelligence on socioemotional factors and psychosomatic symptoms]. *Revista Latinoamericana de Psicología, 49*(2), 110–118. https://doi.org/10.1016/j.rlp.2015.12.001

Seligman, M. E. P., & Csikszentmihalyi, M. (2000). Positive psychology: An introduction. *American Psychologist, 55*(1), 5–14. https://doi.org/10.1037/0003-066X.55.1.5

Sepúlveda, A. R., Solano, S., Blanco, M., Lacruz, T., & Veiga, O. (2020). Feasibility, acceptability, and effectiveness of a multidisciplinary intervention in childhood obesity from primary care: Nutrition, physical activity, emotional regulation, and family. *European Eating Disorders Review, 28*(2), 184–198. https:/doi.org/ 10.1002/erv.2702

Shekhtmeyster, Z., Sharkey, J. D., & You, S. (2011). The influence of multiple ecological assets on substance use patterns of diverse adolescents. *School Psychology Review, 40*(3), 386–404. https://doi.org/10.1080/02796015.2011.12087705

Soto-Sanz V., Marzo-Campos J. C., Rodríguez-Jiménez T., Martínez-González A. E., Rivera-Riquelme M., Piqueras J. A., Falcó R., & Furlong M. J. (2019, November 14–16). *Covitalidad como mediador entre la sintomatología internalizante y el riesgo de suicidio en universitarios* [Covitality as a mediator between internalizing symptoms and suicide risk in university students] [Paper presentation]. 5th International Congress of Clinical and Health Psychology in Children and Adolescents, Oviedo, Spain. http://www.aitanacongress.com/2019/wp-content/uploads/2019/10/Abstracts_2019.pdf

Soto-Sanz V., Mira-López., F., Marzo-Campos J. C., Rivera-Riquelme M., Moreno-Amador, B., Falcó R., Ramos M., & Furlong M. J. (2018, November 15–17). *Sintomatología internalizante y externalizante y la covitalidad como factor protector en estudiantes universitarios* [Internalizing and externalizing symptomatology and covitality as a protective factor in university students] [Paper presentation]. 4th International Congress of Clinical and Health Psychology in Children and Adolescents, Palma de Mallorca, Spain. http://www.aitanacongress.com/documentos/abstracts_cipcna_2018.pdf

Suldo, S., Thalji, A., & Ferron, J. (2011). Longitudinal academic outcomes predicted by early adolescents' subjective well-being, psychopathology, and mental health status yielded from a dual factor model. *The Journal of Positive Psychology, 6*(1), 17–30. https://doi.org/10.1080/17439760.2010.536774

Tejada-Gallardo, C., Blasco-Belled, A., Torrelles-Nadal, C., & Alsinet, C. (2020). Effects of school-based multicomponent positive psychology interventions on well-being and distress in adolescents: A systematic review and meta-analysis. *Journal of Youth and Adolescence, 49*(10), 1943–1960. https://doi.org/10.1007/s10964-020-01289-9

Telesia, L., Kaushik, A., & Kyriakopoulos, M. (2020). The role of stigma in children and adolescents with mental health difficulties. *Current Opinion in Psychiatry, 33*(6), 571–576. https://doi.org/10.1097/YCO.0000000000000644

Vázquez, C., Hervás, G., Rahona, J. J., & Gómez, D. (2009). Bienestar psicológico y salud: Aportaciones desde la Psicología Positiva [Psychological well-being and health: Contributions from Positive Psychology]. *Anuario de Psicología Clínica y de la Salud, 5*(1), 15–28.

World Health Organization. (2010). *Mental health promotion in young people: an investment for the future.* https://www.euro.who.int/__data/assets/pdf_file/0013/121135/E94270.pdf?ua=1

World Health Organization. (2014a). *Global status report on violence prevention 2014.* WHO Press.

World Health Organization. (2014b). *Preventing suicide: A global imperative.* https://apps.who.int/iris/bitstream/handle/10665/131056/9789241564779_eng.pdf?sequence=1

World Health Organization. (2015). *Preventing youth violence: An overview of the evidence.* http://apps.who.int/iris/bitstream/10665/181008/1/9789241509251_eng.pdf

World Health Organization. (2017). *Depression and other common mental disorders: Global health estimates.* https://apps.who.int/iris/bitstream/handle/10665/254610/WHO-MSD-MER-2017.2-eng.pdf;jsessionid=AB8E7AC561A7915A65CBB121B44B1481?sequence=1

32
MEASURING AND PROMOTING RESILIENCE IN YOUTH

Gökmen Arslan

Resilience has been a topic of interest within the burgeoning literature of human strengths and flourishing. It is a popular topic in different disciplines, including psychology, education and sociology, particularly with the emergence of positive psychology. Resilience has received growing attention from scholars and practitioners because of the predictive power of the concept on a range of academic, psychosocial, and behavioral outcomes for young people (Almazan et al., 2018, 2019; Arslan, 2016; Arslan & Balkıs, 2016; Bostan & Duru, 2019; Ding et al., 2017; Kumi-Yeboah, 2020; Lee et al., 2018; Mohammadinia et al., 2019; Rutter, 2013; Sanders et al., 2015; Yildirim, 2019). Resilience is an interactive pattern. Some people have a relatively positive outcome despite experiencing multiple adverse life experiences—with better outcomes than those of other people who experienced the same events (Rutter, 2013). The literature suggests that resilience is an important resource to improve youth positive outcomes and support adjustment despite adversities (Yıldırım & Tanrıverdi, 2020). Nonetheless, resilience research with samples of young people who experience adversities has typically been conducted in developed or Western countries (Ungar & Liebenberg, 2011), which raise generalizability issues to other countries (Kagitcibasi, 2017). Ungar and Liebenberg (2013) suggested a need to move resilience from the *Minority World* to the *Majority World* (i.e., the population outside of Western countries) to provide a more comprehensive understanding on measuring and promoting resilience in young people.

The present chapter considers Western-focused limitations and the role of resilience in positive youth development and well-being. It examines the resilience construct's multidimensional nature, definition, measurement, and promotion strategies for young people. The resilience construct is defined first, followed by a discussion of measures commonly used to assess resilience, specifically among young Turkish people. Then, we briefly review various interventions and programs designed to promote resilience. We conclude the chapter with specific implications and suggestions for the promotion of resilience in young Turkish people. Overall, this chapter emphasizes the importance of measuring resilience for developing interventions and preventions and points out strategies for enhancing resilience to foster young people's psychological adjustment and flourishing in challenging circumstances, again focusing on the Turkish cultural context.

DOI: 10.4324/9781003013778-39

Defining Resilience

Resilience is a complex construct described in various ways in the literature, including the ability to bounce back from adversity, adapt successfully to difficult circumstances, and grow despite these adverse experiences (Southwick et al., 2014; Tusaie & Dyer, 2004). Over the years, the definition of resilience has changed and been refined, focusing on person–context interactions and adaptive processes (Southwick et al., 2014; Ungar & Liebenberg, 2013; Wong & Wong, 2012). For example, resilience was associated with young people's positive developmental outcomes despite serious disadvantages (Masten, 2001; Wong & Wong, 2012; Wright et al., 2013). Connor and Davidson (2003) pointed out that resilience encompasses the personal characteristics that help a person to thrive in adversity. Resilient youths have a high internal locus of control, self-esteem, expectations, self-efficacy, and autonomy despite adverse life events (Garmezy, 1974). Benard (1991) highlighted the importance of school, family, and community protective factors in fostering the resilience of young people and provided a profile of the resilient youth by describing them as socially competent, having good problem-solving skills, high levels of autonomy, and a better sense of purpose and future.

Resilience involves positive adaptation to a new situation or outcome despite dire circumstances and successful coping with these experiences (Zolkoski & Bullock, 2012). Masten (2014a) provided a broad definition of resilience as "…the capacity of a dynamic system to adapt successfully to disturbances that threaten system function, viability, or development" (p. 6). According to Bonanno (2004), resilience is the ability to sustain a stable equilibrium in aversive life circumstances. Some research also emphasizes that resilience is a psychological resource reflecting the ability to "bounce back" after stressors, flexibly adapt to adverse circumstances, and even achieve positive psychological changes in the face of adverse events or circumstances (e.g., Yıldırım et al., 2020; Smith et al., 2008). Ungar (2008) defined of resilience using an ecological perspective with recent resilience literature developments. He describes resilience as a capability to navigate ways to examine personal, social, physical, and cultural resources needed to maintain one's flourishing in the context of exposure to severe adversities and the capacity to negotiate these sources to be experienced in meaningful ways that are culturally specific. Understood this way, this concept embraces the qualities of youth and their social environments' capacity to facilitate adjustment and foster positive development (Ungar & Liebenberg, 2011).

Some researchers have viewed resilience as a trait-like characteristic of an individual. In contrast, others have defined it as the capacity to adapt to adverse situations and the ability to successfully overcome from challenges (Masten, 2018). According to Masten et al.'s (1990) definition, resilience is the process of, capacity for, or outcome of positive adaptation despite adverse experiences. Similarly, Luthar et al. (2000) defined resilience as a dynamic process comprising positive adaptation in the context of significant challenges, while Connor and Davidson (2003) viewed resilience as a set of personal qualities that facilitate an individual to flourish in the face of stressful situations. Considering the definitions of resilience, scholars have highlighted two fundamental judgments required for defining resilience: exposure to adversity and the manifestation of positive outcomes or adaptation despite significant threats (e.g., Luthar & Cicchetti, 2000; Luthar et al., 2000; Masten, 2001). Luthar and Cicchetti (2000) emphasized that adversity refers to undesirable life circumstances associated with adverse outcomes. Alongside this, positive adaptation is identified and assessed in various ways, including performance in age-salient developmental tasks, absence of psychological challenges, subjective well-being, and psychological or social competence (Luthar & Cicchetti, 2000; Masten, 2014; Wright & Masten, 2015). In sum, resilience is considered positive adaptation despite the occurrence of stressful experiences and recovery from trauma. However, there is no single consensus research definition.

Approaches to Resilience

Resilience research has focused on identifying the factors related to better outcomes and adaptation for children and adolescents at risk and exploring processes that underlie its link of adversity with positive outcomes (Masten & Powell, 2002). Three main approaches have guided researchers' understanding and measuring resilience: *person-focused*, *variable-focused*, and *hybrid* models (Masten, 2014). Person-focused approaches of resilience focus on identifying individuals who meet the diagnostic or definitional criteria for resilience (Masten & Powell, 2002) and investigate differences between resilient and nonresilient persons (Climie et al., 2013). A classic example of a person-focused approach is the Kauai Longitudinal Study (Werner, 1993, 2005; Werner & Smith, 2001). The Kauai study followed babies (initially 698) born in 1955 on the Hawaiian island of Kauai over time (at ages 1, 2, 10, 18, 32, and 40 years). The study focused on high-risk children who flourished (e.g., successful in school and healthy psychosocial functioning), emphasizing their differences with troubled children who experienced significant problems (e.g., delinquency and mental health difficulties). The children with resilience had various protective and promotive factors, such as supportive social relationships, higher-quality caregiving, better educational outcomes, greater optimism, internal locus of control, and better cognitive skills. Children and young people who had successful adaptation in adulthood despite significant adversity relied on these individual, family, and community resources that promoted their competencies and provided new opportunities (Werner, 1993).

In contrast to person-focused approaches, variable-focused approaches of resilience explore the associations between adversity, favorable outcomes, and potential protective factors to better understand which aspects of these factors explain positive outcomes despite adverse experiences. For example, compensatory or additive models emphasize that resources, such as intellectual skills, better parenting, or social support, can offset the adverse impacts of negative experiences so that young people have positive outcomes. Therefore, increasing key protective factors could theoretically help to improve the well-being and adjustment of youths at-risk (Masten & Powell, 2002). Resilience research has often used hybrid models that combine the features of person- and variable-focused approaches (Masten, 2014). The Project Competence Longitudinal Study (Masten & Tellegen, 2012) is an important example that combined person—and variable—focused strategies to better understand resilience in the context of adversity. The study showed that more resilient young people reported better cognitive, social, and emotional skills and high-quality social relationships. In contrast, their peers who showed significant problems had fewer protective resources in terms of internal factors (e.g., cognitive skills) and external resources (e.g., positive relationships with caregivers; Masten, 2014). Although these approaches have not been commonly used in past research on resilience, Masten (2014) emphasized that they hold promise for future studies focusing on clarifying different resilience pathways and trajectories among individuals studied over time. Nonetheless, more research is needed that focuses on resilience's complex characteristics, thereby providing a comprehensive perspective of factors that mitigate or moderate the effect of adversity and foster recovery in the face of challenges to youth development, especially in the Turkish context.

Promoting Resilience in Youths

Children and adolescents are vulnerable groups who may experience a variety of dire circumstances and risk factors. Research has shown that children are at risk of deprivation of basic needs, exploitation, maltreatment, antisocial activities, and substance abuse (Alshehri et al., 2020; Yildirim et al., 2020). Research has documented that young people engage in risk-taking behavior more often than adults (Arnett, 1996; Gardner & Steinberg, 2005; Gheorghiu et al., 2015).

They also are more likely to experience various adversities (e.g., peer pressure and violence) than other age groups (Blakemore, 2019; Gheorghiu et al., 2015). Young people are more likely than adults to drive while intoxicated, have unprotected sex, use various illicit substances, and engage in serious antisocial behavior (Arnett, 1992). Specifically, peers play an important role in explaining risk-taking behavior and risky decision-making during adolescence (Gardner & Steinberg, 2005). This stress and complexity takes a toll on their mental health and flourishing (Waters, 2011). In addition to these external challenges, the prevalence rates of mental health disorders, such as depression (Lewinsohn et al., 1993) and anxiety, are high among young people around the world (World Health Organization, 2017), with an estimated 20% of youths experiencing these problems (Kieling et al., 2011; Lewinsohn et al., 1993; Myers & Holland, 2000). A recent study by Alshehri et al. (2020) showed that almost half of adolescents (46%) experience peer problems at the clinical levels, while 21% of adolescents experience clinically significant emotional problems. Therefore, mental health problems are one of the main targets for prevention efforts (Kranzler et al., 2014).

The pattern of mental health problems among Turkish youths (a nearly 20% incidence) is similar to youths from other cultures (Erol & Şimşek, 2000). Üner et al. (2007) conducted a study of 748 Turkish adolescents (ages 10–14 years) and reported that 65% of respondents were identified as being at risk of mental health problems. Unfortunately, the majority of these Turkish youths do not receive appropriate mental health services. Moreover, considering the population of young people in Turkey (nearly 16%; Turkish Statistical Institute, 2019), there is a crucial need to develop prevention and intervention strategies designed to promote young people's mental health and improve overall well-being. Adopting positive psychology principles to cultivate resilience provides a promising approach to alleviate mental health problems in Turkish society.

Measuring Resilience in Youths

Worldwide, adversities that have severe consequences for individuals, families, and societies threaten young peoples' healthy development and functioning (Masten, 2014). The measurement of resilience is an initial and essential step toward understanding the nature of this construct and developing prevention strategies that promote young people's positive development and adjustment in the face of adverse experiences (Arslan, 2015a). However, the complexity of defining resilience creates significant challenges when developing measures (Windle et al., 2011). A review study by Ahern et al. (2006) reported that measures of young peoples' resilience assess successful stress-coping ability, resilience as a positive personality characteristic, resilient coping behavior, protective factors, and central protective resources of health adjustment. Findings from this study also showed that although other scales are available in the extant literature, the Resilience Scale (RS; Wagnild & Young, 1993) has better psychometric properties for use with the youth population compared to others. Although the scale does not operationalize a specific theory, it measures resilience in terms of various empirically derived personal characteristics that improve individual positive adaptation (Ahern et al., 2006). Developed initially to assess resilience among adults, several studies have examined RS's psychometric properties with young people (see Wagnild, 2009). There is no research providing evidence regarding the psychometric adequacy of this scale with young Turkish people.

Several self-report measures have assessed Turkish young people's resilience; however, most of these instruments were developed to measure young people's resilience from Western countries (Ungar & Liebenberg, 2011). For example, the Child and Youth Resilience Measure (CYRM; Ungar & Liebenberg, 2011) is one of the most widely employed self-report instruments used for measuring resilience among young Turkish people. The CYRM was designed based on the social-ecological perspective. The original version used a mixed-methods design in 11 countries with a sample 1,451 young people to assess resilience in diverse socioecological contexts (Ungar & Liebenberg, 2011). The CYRM has 28-items measuring three main domains of resilience: *individual* (personal skills, peer support, and social skills), *relational* (physical caregiving and psychological caregiving), and *contextual* (spirituality, culture, and education). Previous research has indicated both the CYRM-12 and the CYRM-28 have adequate psychometric properties with young Turkish people (Arslan, 2015b, 2015c).

The Resilience and Youth Development Module (RYDM; WestEd, 2001) is another measure commonly used to assess positive youth development and resilience among Turkish young people. The RYDM is a strength-based survey developed based on the youth development framework, as seen in Figure 32.1. Youth development is the process of fostering young people's physical, cognitive, psychosocial, moral, and spiritual development through meeting their basic developmental needs for belonging, safety, respect, love, identity, mastery, power, challenge, and meaning (WestEd, 2008). Resilience has been viewed as a natural wisdom indicator that inherently motivates people to meet their essential human needs (Benard & Slade, 2009; WestEd, 2008), leading to healthy development in the face of adverse life circumstances (Masten, 2014). Resilience is a dynamic construct reflecting the capacity of a person to manage and overcome stressors and to adapt successfully despite these experiences. Thus, the youth development approach conceptualizes resilience as a capacity for positive development innate to all people (WestEd, 2008). Theoretically, the framework emphasizes external assets (e.g., caring relationships and participation in school-based activities) to meet young peoples' fundamental developmental needs. These, in turn, foster the enhancement of internal resources (e.g., problem-solving skills and social competence) that promote healthy development and academic functioning (Furlong et al., 2009).

As shown in the theoretical framework in Figure 32.1, the RYDM measures a variety of external protective factors and internal strengths related to positive youth development and well-being. The module measures external and internal assets associated with school achievement and positive youth development. External assets comprise of prosocial and meaningful bonding to community, family, peers, and school. Internal assets include personal characteristics, such as problem-solving skills and self-efficacy (Hanson & Kim, 2007). Prior research has found that the RYDM provides psychometrically adequate properties for assessing young people's internal and external resilience assets in (Hanson & Kim, 2007; Furlong et al., 2009).

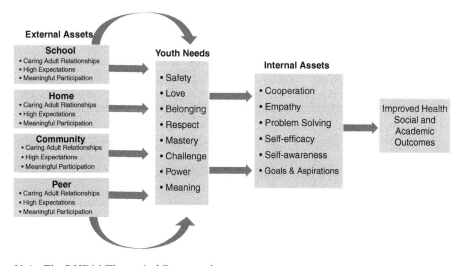

Figure 32.1   The RYDM Theoretical Framework

The Turkish version assesses nine *external protective factors:* (a) meaningful school participation, (b) school caring relationships and high expectations, (c) community meaningful participation, (d) community caring relationships and high expectations, (e) peer high expectations, (f) peer caring relationships, (g) home high expectations, (h) home caring relationships, and (i) home meaningful participation. It also assesses seven *internal strengths* (cooperation and communication, problem-solving, empathy, self-awareness, goals, self-efficacy, and educational aspirations; Gizir & Aydin, 2009). Research showed that the measure had psychometrically adequate properties with young Turkish people (Gizir & Aydın, 2006).

Bulut et al. (2013) developed and validated the 29-item Adolescent Psychological Resilience Scale with Turkish adolescents. This measure has six resilience dimensions: family support, confident-friend support, school support, adjustment, sense of struggle, and empathy. Research provided evidence indicating that the scale was psychometrically adequate for measuring resilience among young Turkish people. However, the measure's psychometric properties were investigated with adolescents who had experienced few adversities or challenges, which could be considered a significant limitation.

The most commonly used resilience measures adapted into Turkish cultures are ones developed initially with adult samples (e.g., Connor-Davidson RS [Connor & Davidson, 2003], Ego-Resiliency Scale [Kremen, 1996], and Brief Resilience Scale [Smith et al., 2008]). However, there are significant differences between adolescents and adults in many aspects, such as cognitive and language development. Such measures' content and language may not be applicable for children and adolescents, which may raise the issues of reliability and validity when investigating samples of young people. To the best of the author's knowledge, there is currently no evidence of how the content of those measures performs with samples of children and adolescents. For example, Karaırmak (2010) investigated the Connor-Davidson RS's psychometric properties with Turkish earthquake survivors and found the scale provided satisfactory psychometric properties with a three-factor solution measuring tenacity and personal competence, tolerance of negative affect, and a tendency toward spirituality.

Although these measures are used to assess Turkish young people's resilience, their psychometric properties have been assessed with only university students or adults. The original authors noted culture-specific issues with the CYRM-28, who suggested that understanding resilience concerning a specific cultural context is essential for measuring and promoting this construct (Ungar & Liebenberg, 2011). Due to the scale's sensitivity to various cultural backgrounds, the scale has yielded different factor solutions for different cultures (e.g., Govender et al., 2017; Jefferies et al., 2019; Sanders et al., 2017). Turkish society has, for instance, a relatively collectivist structure compared with Western societies, and social and family values have a vital role to play in developing young peoples' emotions and behaviors (Kagitcibasi, 2017; Kagitcibasi & Ataca, 2005). Young people from different cultures can respond to items on a scale differently, which may cause different results from a psychometric perspective. For instance, some scale items measure how young people experience and talk with their parents about their feelings and thoughts. However, this may not be an example of resiliency or a protective factor in Turkish culture due to cultural values, specifically in rural areas which do not emphasize the importance of sharing such feelings and thoughts.

Glover and Albers (2007) additionally emphasized that measurement tools should be (a) contextually and developmentally appropriate (e.g., population fit and theoretical and empirical support), (b) usable (e.g., feasibility of administration and acceptability), and (c) have technically adequate norms (e.g., internal consistency reliability and predictive validity). Considering these criteria for evaluating screeners (see Glover & Albers, 2007), very few current tools have psychometrically adequate properties for assessing young peoples' resilience. For example, Arslan (2015c) did not report evidence for validity supporting the psychometric properties of the CYRM-28 and has only examined the factor structure of the measure using confirmatory factor analysis with nonrisk adolescents. Similarly, the RYDM has limited concurrent or predictive validity evidence. Some external and internal scales also have low internal reliability estimates (e.g., cooperation and communication $\alpha = 0.50$ and community meaningful participation $\alpha = 0.55$) with Turkish adolescents (Gizir & Aydın, 2006). Therefore, future research requires developing a usable, technically adequate, contextually appropriate, and culturally sensitive measure for assessing children's and adolescents' resilience.

Resilience-Based Efforts to Promote Mental Health and Flourishing

Programs designed to enhance flourishing and resilience generally utilize one of two approaches: *prevention* and *promotion* (Kranzler et al., 2014). Prevention approaches focus on helping young people by building adaptive coping skills and resilience (e.g., adaptive coping and problem-solving skills) and preparing youths to respond to stressors effectively. Promotion approaches help young people develop and use personal strengths by focusing on increasing positive emotions and positive experiences (Kranzler et al., 2014). Specifically, youths' capacity for positive emotions is an essential resource for improving their problem-solving skills (Fredrickson, 2001). Kranzler et al. (2014) have emphasized that many positive psychology-based programs incorporate elements from both these approaches (e.g., the High School Positive Psychology Curriculum; Seligman et al., 2009). Given these approaches, resilience-based interventions and programs focus on youths' capacity to prevent the negative impacts of adverse experiences and promote protective factors, such as self-efficacy, peer relationships, coping skills, and help-seeking behaviors.

There are several different approaches to building youth resilience. Intervention programs designed to improve resilience among young people generally focus on cultivating strengths, teaching various skills, and fostering a positive school climate and culture (Gillham et al., 2013). The Penn Resiliency Program (PRP) takes a prevention approach and is a promising strengths-based program designed to build resilience by employing cognitive-behavioral techniques among young people. This program's primary aim is to increase young peoples' ability to handle stressors and promote optimism by teaching them to think flexibly and realistically about their problems. Additionally, the curriculum focuses on relaxation, effectiveness, decision making, creative brainstorming, and problem solving and coping skills (Seligman et al., 2009). Research indicates that the PRP is widely used to prevent depressive symptoms among young people (Gillham et al., 2008), effectively reduces depression in children and adolescents, and prevents other depressive symptoms (Brunwasser et al., 2009; Horowitz & Garber, 2006).

The PRP is a 12-session program applicable to young people with a duration ranging between 90 and 120 minutes per session (Bastounis et al., 2016) that focuses on the two primary components of problem-solving and cognitive skills. The program's cognitive component focuses on various skills that help youths think more flexibly about their problems and raise awareness about their emotions. This component centers on Ellis's ABCDE model (Ellis & Dryden, 2007). The problem-solving component teaches various skills that help youths create realistic goals and identify ways to reach them through a five-step problem-solving approach. The program also teaches self-management skills for complex feelings and coping with adverse experiences (see Gillham et al., 2013, for more information).

Gillham et al. (2013) report that the PRP generally fosters the following youth skills and strengths that contribute to improving resilience:

- Emotional competence—being able to determine, label, express emotions, and control feelings when appropriate.

- Self-control—being able to determine and resist impulses that are counterproductive for a given situation or reaching long-term goals.
- Problem-solving and decision-making—particular skills of flexibility (being able to consider a wide range of possible interpretations, to view situations from multiple aspects, and to generate a variety of solutions to problems) and judgment (being able to make informed decisions based on evidence).
- Social awareness—being able to consider others' opinions and empathize with others.
- Social competence—being able to work through challenges in important relationships.
- Self-efficacy and realistic optimism—confidence in one's abilities to achieve goals and determine and implement coping and problem-solving skills suited to a given situation.

Overall, the PRP focuses on skills and strategies that target emotional and cognitive well-being, positive social relationships, and character strengths and aims to teach participants how to apply these skills and strategies in their lives (see Table 32.1). There is also empirical evidence suggesting the effectiveness of this program on improving well-being and reducing of mental health problems (e.g., depression and anxiety; see Seligman, 2018 for a brief review).

Social and emotional learning (SEL) is another prominent example aiming to improve resilience among young people. The SEL programs integrate developmental frameworks and competence promotion to decrease risk factors and increase protective factors, allowing for better mental health and flourishing (Durlak et al., 2011). The SEL is a strengths-based approach fostering young people's skills and their capacity for social connection, empathy, and self-expression, with the ultimate aim of supporting their ability to manage their feelings and work well with others (Durlak et al., 2011; Juvonen et al., 2019; Weissberg et al., 2015). SEL is a staple of several programs designed to foster resilience and mental health in effective ways, such as "I Can Problem Solve," "Promoting Alternative Thinking Strategies," and "Strong Kids" (see Tran et al., 2014 for a review). Bernard and Walton (2011) investigated the effectiveness of an SEL-based resiliency program called "You Can Do It! Education (YCDI)," which focuses on five lessons: organization, confidence, resilience, persistence, and getting along. This study compared youth from six schools where the YCDI program was implemented to a control group of youths from six other schools. Findings from the study showed that students in the YCDI schools had better school functioning (e.g., school connectedness and student motivation), well-being, and lower distress.

The High School Positive Psychology Program (Gillham et al., 2013) emphasizes a health promotion approach designed to enhance resilience and promote positive youth development. This program helps youth identify and use their strengths, develop positive relationships, experience positive feelings, and engage in meaningful school activities. The positive psychology curriculum targets improvements in life satisfaction and reductions in depressive symptoms through increasing engagement, positive emotions, and life meaning (Seligman et al., 2006). The program is based on three units: the *pleasant* life, the *meaningful* life, and the *engaged* life. The pleasant life aims to improve positive emotions, optimism, gratitude, and savoring. The engaged life is the largest unit that encourages young people to identify their strengths (e.g., creativity, kindness, and perseverance) and to use these personal strengths more in their daily life. Finally, the meaningful life is a unit reflecting on the life purpose of young people and encourages them to experience what makes life meaningful (Gillham et al., 2013).

The Meaning-Centered Intervention is the final example of an intervention designed to foster resilience among young people. This intervention reflects an integrative and holistic framework for understanding youth resilience and is based on the interaction between three modules: AB-CDE strategy of resilience, tragic optimism elements, and the PURE principles of meaningful living (Wong & Wong, 2012). The PURE principles include purpose (P), understanding (U), responsible action (R), and enjoyment (E), which are essential for improving resilience and

Table 32.1 Skills and Strategies of Penn Resilience Programs

Skills and Strategies	
Enhance Cognitive-Emotional Well-Being	
Self-talk	Enhance resilience by thinking effectively
Learn optimism	Notice and expect the positive, focus on what you can control, and take purposeful action
Avoid thinking traps	Identify and correct pessimistic patterns in thinking
Detect icebergs	Identify core values and beliefs that drive behavior and out of proportions emotions and reactions
Problem-solving	Fight biases in thinking to accurately identify causes of a problem and generate solutions
Put it in perspective	Stop catastrophic thinking, reduce anxiety, and take purposeful actions
Deliberate breathing	Control your breathing to regulate your thoughts, feelings, and physiology
Mental games	Stop counterproductive thinking to build focus
Real-time resilience	Shut down counterproductive thinking and build focus and confidence
Positive emotions and savoring	Build positive emotions to increase well-being and buffer against stress
Gratitude	Cultivate gratitude by noticing and reflecting on what is good in the world
Rejuvenation	Regulate emotion and energy levels to enable focus and optimal performance
Cultivate Strengths of Character	
Identity and leverage character strengths	Identify top character strengths to enhance resilience and well-being and notice the others' character strengths
Character strengths and leadership	Leverage character strengths to lead authentically
	Identify and leverage character strengths in others to create effective teams
Character strengths and challenges	Leverage character strengths to overcome challenges and enhance success
Use a signature strength in a new way	Identify new ways to use signature strengths to increase well-being and engagement
Character strengths and values	Leverage character strengths to live your values more fully and create the life you want to live
Develop a strength you value	Plan actions that are designed to build a strength you value
Build Strong Relationships	
High-quality connections	Develop connections that are characterized by mutual positive regard, trust, and active engagement
Assertive communication	Build trust and connection when having difficult conservations through the IDEAL model
Joy multiplier	Build trust and connection through sharing in another's joy

Note: Adapted from Seligman's (2018) Penn resilience and well-being programs executive summary. Available at https://www.cns.org/surgeon-well-being/wellness-for-residents-detail/penn-resilience-well-being-programs-executive-summ

flourishing (Wong, 2010). The ABCDE approach, which signifies the components of acceptance, belief, commitment, discovery, and evaluation, mainly focuses on strategies dealing with adversity and threatening life circumstances. This model provides the skills and strategies for young people to overcome suffering and challenges, while the PURE model focuses on meaningful living principles (Wong & Wong, 2012). Tragic optimism is the final component of the module, referring to optimism and sustaining a positive outlook in the face of tragic experiences and adversity (Leung, 2019). Wong and Wong (2012) suggest that a comprehensive meaning-centered program to enhance resilience encompasses the following themes:

1 life goals and purposes;
2 freedom and responsibility;
3 courage to accept internal and external constraints;
4 understanding the self and one's place in the world;
5 right and wrong pathways to happiness;
6 faith and belief in a better future;
7 commitment to growth;
8 positive thinking, attribution, and meaning-management;
9 discovery of hidden dimensions of the self and new frontiers of life; and
10 power of self-transcendence, empathy, compassion, and altruism.

The meaning-centered approach highlights the multidimensional nature of resilience. It suggests that a comprehensive intervention enhancing young people's resilience of needs to incorporate all dimensions (e.g., emotional resilience, cognitive competence, and relational resilience; Wong & Wong, 2012). Consequently, meaning-centered interventions may be useful options for practitioners and researchers to foster flourishing and resilience among young people experiencing adverse life events (Arslan & Yildirim, 2020). Although the programs mentioned earlier have been effectively implemented in Western cultures, mainly the United States and Canada, it is unknown how effective such programs are in non-Western cultures such as Turkey.

Conclusion

Children and adolescents currently face various threatening circumstances and adverse events that may increase the risk of mental health problems and decrease well-being and positive functioning. Measurement is an initial and essential step toward understanding the nature of resilience construct for developing prevention strategies. Although several self-report tools measure Turkish young people's resilience, most of these measures have been developed to assess young people's resilience in Western countries—the Minority World. However, measuring resilience within a specific cultural context is essential for developing culturally sensitive instruments and developing more effective prevention and intervention strategies. Future research needs to define resilience in the sociocultural context to develop a valid, reliable, and culturally sensitive measure to assess Turkish young people's resilience. It is essential to include qualitative studies to understand better and explore the conceptualization and measurement of Turkish youths' resilience. This chapter reviewed the literature on the efficacy of selected intervention curriculums and programs that support adolescent resilience and well-being (e.g., Social and Emotional Learning, Penn Resiliency Program). These programs teach cognitive, emotional, and behavioral skills that help youth cope with daily life stressors. These programs provide practical ways to help young people identify their strengths, build resilience, and experience purpose and meaning (Kranzler et al., 2014). Nonetheless, future research needs to test the effectiveness of these programs with Turkish youth in schools.

Recent research has examined the effectiveness of several approaches (e.g., cognitive behavioral-based intervention) to increase resilience and positive youth functioning among Turkish young people (e.g., Eminoğlu & Erden-Çınar, 2020). Although few studies examine these approaches' role in promoting resilience, they are constrained, and assessing such programs' long-term effectiveness is difficult. Efforts have generally focused on the specific program level, performed in classrooms with small samples. These programs need to move beyond the programs at the classroom level and provide school-wide interventions to improve strategies and skills that contribute to building resilience in young people. With the development of school-based programs, effective preventions and interventions could foster youths' resilience and flourish despite dire circumstances. Considering the latest unprecedented and severe adversities around the world (e.g., global pandemics and warfare), this is the time to build youth resilience and promote flourishing. Specifically, there is a need for intervention programs that provide effective ways to promote resilience and increase the likelihood that young people have the skills and knowledge necessary to overcome these challenges.

References

Ahern, N. R., Kiehl, E. M., Lou Sole, M., & Byers, J. (2006). A review of instruments measuring resilience. *Issues in Comprehensive Pediatric Nursing, 29*(2), 103–125. https://doi.org/10.1080/01460860600677643

Almazan, J. U., Albougami, A. S., Alamri, M. A., Colet, P. C., Adolfo, C. S., Allen, K. A., Gravoso, R., & Boyle, C. (2019). Disaster-related resiliency theory among older adults who survived Typhoon Haiyan. *International Journal of Disaster Risk Reduction, 35*(1), 101070. https://doi.org/10.1016/j.ijdrr.2019.101070

Almazan, J. U., Cruz, J. P., Alamri, M. S., Alotaibi, J. S. M., Albougami, A. S. B., Gravoso, R., Abocajo, F., Allen, K. A., & Bishwajit, G. (2018). Predicting patterns of disaster-related resiliency among older adult typhoon Haiyan survivors. *Geriatric Nursing, 39*(6), 629–634. https://doi.org/10.1016/j.gerinurse.2018.04.015

Alshehri, N., Yildirim, M., & Vostanis, P. (2020). Saudi adolescents' reports of the relationship between parental factors, social support and mental health problems. *Arab Journal of Psychiatry, 31*(2), 130–143. doi:10.12816/0056864

Arnett, J. (1992). Reckless behavior in adolescence: A developmental perspective. *Developmental Review, 12*(4), 339–373.

Arnett, J. J. (1996). Sensation seeking, aggressiveness, and adolescent reckless behavior. *Personality and Individual Differences, 20*(6), 693–702.

Arslan, G. (2015a). Yetişkin Psikolojik Sağlamlık Ölçeği'nin (YPSÖ) psikometrik özellikleri: Geçerlik ve güvenirlik çalışması. [Psychometric Properties of Adult Resilience Measure (CYRM-12): The study of reliability and validity]. *Ege Eğitim Dergisi, 16*(2), 344–357.

Arslan, G. (2015b). Çocuk ve Genç Psikolojik Sağlamlık Ölçeği'nin (ÇGPSÖ) psikometrik özellikleri: Geçerlilik ve güvenirlik çalışması [Psychometric Properties of Child and Youth Resilience Measure (CYRM-12): The study of reliability and validity]. *Ege Eğitim Dergisi, 16*(1), 1–12.

Arslan, G. (2015c). Ergenlerde psikolojik sağlamlık: Bireysel koruyucu faktörlerin rolü [Resilience in Adolescents: The Role of Individual Protective Factors]. *Türk Psikolojik Danışma ve Rehberlik Dergisi, 5*(44), 73–82.

Arslan, G. (2016). Psychological maltreatment, emotional and behavioral problems in adolescents: The mediating role of resilience and self-esteem. *Child Abuse & Neglect, 52*, 200–209. https://doi.org/10.1016/j.chiabu.2015.09.010

Arslan, G., & Balkıs, M. (2016). Ergenlerde duygusal istismar, problem davranışlar, öz-yeterlik ve psikolojik sağlamlık arasındaki ilişki [The relationship between emotional maltreatment, problem behaviors, psychological resilience, and self-efficacy in adolescents]. *Sakarya University Journal of Education, 6*(1), 8–22.

Arslan, G., & Yildirim, M. (2020). Coronavirus stress, meaningful living, optimism, and depressive symptoms: A study of moderated mediation model. *PsyArXiv.* doi:10.31234/osf.io/ykvzn

Bastounis, A., Callaghan, P., Banerjee, A., & Michail, M. (2016). The effectiveness of the Penn Resiliency Programme (PRP) and its adapted versions in reducing depression and anxiety and improving explanatory style: A systematic review and meta-analysis. *Journal of Adolescence, 52*, 37–48. https://doi.org/10.1016/j.adolescence.2016.07.004

Benard, B. (1991). *Fostering resiliency in kids: Protective factors in the family, school, and community.* Western Center for Drug-Free Schools and Communities.

Benard, B., & Slade, S. (2009). Listening to students: Moving from resilience research to youth development practice and school connectedness. In R. Gilma, E. S. Huevner, & M. J. Furlong (Eds.), *Handbook of positive psychology in schools* (pp. 353–369). New York: Routledge/Taylor & Francis.

Bernard, P. M. E., & Walton, K. (2011). The effect of You Can Do It! Education in six schools on student perceptions of well-being, Teaching-learning and relationships. *The Journal of Student Wellbeing, 5*(1), 22–37. https://doi.org/10.21913/jsw.v5i1.679

Blakemore, S. J. (2019). Adolescence and mental health. *Lancet, 393*, 2030–2031. https://doi.org/10.1016/S0140-6736(19)31013-X

Bonanno, G. A. (2004). Loss, trauma, and human resilience: Have we underestimated the human capacity to thrive after extremely aversive events? *American Psychologist, 59*(1), 20–28. https://doi.org/10.1037/0003-066X.59.1.20

Bostan, B. C., & Duru, E. (2019). Ergenlerde algılanan psikolojik istismar ve öznel iyi oluş ilişkisinde psikolojik sağlamlığın ve sosyal bağlılığın rolü [The role of psychological resilience and social connectedness in the relationship between perceived psychological maltreatment and subjective well-being among adolescents]. *Pamukkale Üniversitesi Eğitim Fakültesi Dergisi*, 47, 205–224. https://doi.org/10.9779/pauefd.568123

Brunwasser, S. M., Gillham, J. E., & Kim, E. S. (2009). A meta-analytic review of the Penn Resiliency Program's effect on depressive symptoms. *Journal of Consulting and Clinical Psychology, 77*(6), 1042–1054. https://doi.org/10.1037/a0017671

Bulut, S., Doğan, U., & Altundağ, Y. (2013). Adolescent psychological resilience scale: validity and reliability study. *Contemporary Psychology, Suvremena Psihologija, 16*(1), 21–32.

Climie, E. A., Mastoras, S. M., McCrimmon, A. W., & Schwean, V. L. (2013). Resilience in childhood disorders. In S. Prince-Embury & D. H. Saklofske (Eds.), *The Springer series on human exceptionality. Resilience in children, adolescents, and adults: Translating research into practice* (pp. 113–131). Springer Science + Business Media.

Connor, K. M., & Davidson, J. R. (2003). Development of a new resilience scale: The Connor-Davidson resilience scale (CD-RISC). *Depression and Anxiety, 18*(2), 76–82. https://doi.org/10.1002/da.10113

Ding, H., Han, J., Zhang, M., Wang, K., Gong, J., & Yang, S. (2017). Moderating and mediating effects of resilience between childhood trauma and depressive symptoms in Chinese children. *Journal of Affective Disorders, 211*, 130–135. https://doi.org/10.1016/j.jad.2016.12.056

Durlak, J. A., Weissberg, R. P., Dymnicki, A. B., Taylor, R. D., & Schellinger, K. B. (2011). The impact of enhancing students' social and emotional learning: A meta-analysis of school-based universal interventions. *Child Development, 82*(1), 405–432. https://doi.org/10.1111/j.1467-8624.2010.01564.x

Ellis, A., & Dryden, W. (2007). *The practice of rational emotive behavior therapy*. Springer.

Eminoğlu, Z., & Erden-Çınar, S. (2020). Bilişsel davranışçı temelli psiko-eğitim programının psikolojik dayanıklılık ve duygu düzenleme üzerindeki etkisi [The effect of cognitive behavioral based psychoeducation program on psychological resilience and emotion regulation]. *OPUS Uluslararası Toplum Araştırmaları Dergisi, 15*(21), 555–582. https://doi.org/10.26466/opus.626228

Erol, N., & Şimşek, Z. T. (2000). Mental health of Turkish children: Behavioral and emotional problems reported by parents, teachers, and adolescents. *International Perspectives on Child and Adolescent Mental Health, 1*, 223–247. https://doi.org/10.1016/S1874-5911(00)80014-7

Fredrickson, B. L. (2001). The role of positive emotions in positive psychology: The broaden-and-build theory of positive emotions. *American Psychologist, 56*(3), 218–226. https://doi.org/10.1037/0003-066X.56.3.218

Furlong, M. J., Ritchey, K. M., & O'Brennan, L. M. (2009). Developing norms for the California Resilience Youth Development Module: Internal assets and school resources subscales. *The California School Psychologist, 14*(1), 35–46. https://doi.org/10.1007/BF03340949

Gardner, M., & Steinberg, L. (2005). Peer influence on risk taking, risk preference, and risky decision making in adolescence and adulthood: an experimental study. *Developmental Psychology, 41*(4), 625–635. https://doi.org/10.1037/0012-1649.41.4.625

Garmezy, N. (1974). The study of competence in children at risk for severe psychopathology. In E. J. Anthony & C. Koupernik (Eds.), *The child in his family: Children at psychiatric risk* (pp. 77–97). Wiley.

Gheorghiu, A., Delhomme, P., & Felonneau, M. L. (2015). Peer pressure and risk taking in young drivers' speeding behavior. *Transportation research part F: traffic psychology and behaviour, 35*, 101–111.

Gillham, J. E., Abenavoli, R., Brunwasser, S. M., Linkins, M., Reivich, K., & Seligman, M. E. P. (2013). Resilience education. In S. David, I. Boniwell, & A. Conley Ayers (Eds.), *The Oxford handbook of happiness* (pp. 609–630). Oxford University Press.

Gillham, J. E., Brunwasser, S. M., & Freres, D. R. (2008). Preventing depression in early adolescence: The Penn Resiliency Program. In J. R. Z. Abela & B. L. Hankin (Eds.), *Handbook of depression in children and adolescents* (pp. 309–322). Guilford.

Gizir, C. A., & Aydın, G. (2006). The adaptation of the Resilience and Youth Development Module: Validity and reliability studies. *Turkish Psychological Counseling and Guidance Journal, 26*, 87–100.

Gizir, C., & Aydin, G. (2009). Protective factors contributing to the academic resilience of students living in poverty in Turkey. *Professional School Counseling, 13*(1), 38–49. https://doi.org/10.5330/psc.n.2010-13.38

Glover, T. A., & Albers, C. A. (2007). Considerations for evaluating universal screening assessments. *Journal of School Psychology, 45*(2), 117–135. https://doi.org/10.1016/j.jsp.2006.05.005

Govender, K., Cowden, R. G., Oppong Asante, K., George, G., & Reardon, C. (2017). Validation of the child and youth resilience measure among South African adolescents. *PloS One, 12*(10), e0185815. https://doi.org/10.1371/journal.pone.0185815

Hanson, T. L., & Kim, J. O. (2007). *Measuring resilience and youth development: The psychometric properties of the Healthy Kids Survey.* Issues & answers. Regional Educational Laboratory West.

Horowitz, J. L., & Garber, J. (2006). The prevention of depressive symptoms in children and adolescents: A meta-analytic review. In *Journal of Consulting and Clinical Psychology, 74*(3), 401–415. https://doi.org/10.1037/0022-006X.74.3.401

Jefferies, P., McGarrigle, L., & Ungar, M. (2019). The CYRM-R: A Rasch-validated revision of the child and youth resilience measure. *Journal of Evidence-Based Social Work, 16*(1), 70–92. https://doi.org/10.1080/23761407.2018.1548403

Juvonen, J., Lessard, L. M., Rastogi, R., Schacter, H. L., & Smith, D. S. (2019). Promoting social inclusion in educational settings: Challenges and opportunities. *Educational Psychologist, 54*(4), 250–270. https://doi.org/10.1080/00461520.2019.1655645

Kagitcibasi, C. (2017). *Family, self, and human development across cultures: Theory and applications.* Routledge. https://doi.org/10.4324/9781315205281

Kagitcibasi, C., & Ataca, B. (2005). Value of children and family change: A three-decade portrait from Turkey. *Applied Psychology, 54*(3), 317–337. https://doi.org/10.1111/j.1464-0597.2005.00213.x

Karaırmak, Ö. (2010). Establishing the psychometric qualities of the Connor–Davidson Resilience Scale (CD-RISC) using exploratory and confirmatory factor analysis in a trauma survivor sample. *Psychiatry Research, 179*(3), 350–356.

Kieling, C., Baker-Henningham, H., Belfer, M., Conti, G., Ertem, I., Omigbodun, O., Rohde, L. A., Srinath, S., Ulkuer, N., & Rahman, A. (2011). Child and adolescent mental health worldwide: Evidence for action. *The Lancet, 378*(9801), 1515–1525. https://doi.org/10.1016/S0140-6736(11)60827-1

Kranzler, A., Hoffman, L. J., Parks, A. C., & Gillham, J. E. (2014). Innovative models of dissemination for school-based interventions that promote youth resilience and well-being. In M. J. Furlong, R. Gilman, & E. S. Huebner (Eds.), *Handbook of positive psychology in schools* (2nd ed., pp. 381–397). Routledge/Taylor & Francis.

Kremen, A. M. (1996). IQ and ego-resiliency: Conceptual and empirical connections and separateness. *Journal of Personality and Social Psychology, 70*(2), 349–361.

Kumi-Yeboah, A. (2020). Educational resilience and academic achievement of immigrant students From Ghana in an urban school environment. *Urban Education, 55*(5), 753–782. https://doi.org/10.1177/0042085916660347

Lee, S. W., Bae, G. Y., Rim, H. D., Lee, S. J., Chang, S. M., Kim, B. S., & Won, S. (2018). Mediating effect of resilience on the association between emotional neglect and depressive symptoms. *Psychiatry Investigation, 15*(1), 62–69. https://doi.org/10.4306/pi.2018.15.1.62

Leung, M. M. (2019). Tragic optimism: An integrative meaning-centered approach to trauma treatment. *Counselling Psychology Quarterly, 32*(3–4), 529–547. https://doi.org/10.1080/09515070.2019.1633497

Lewinsohn, P. M., Rohde, P., Seeley, J. R., & Fischer, S. A. (1993). Age-cohort changes in the lifetime occurrence of depression and other mental disorders. *Journal of Abnormal Psychology, 102*(1), 110–120. https://doi.org/10.1037/0021-843X.102.1.110

Luthar, S. S., & Cicchetti, D. (2000). The construct of resilience: Implications for interventions and social policies. *Development and Psychopathology, 12*(4), 857–885. doi:10.1017/s0954579400004156

Luthar, S. S., Cicchetti, D., & Becker, B. (2000). The construct of resilience: A critical evaluation and guidelines for future work. *Child Development, 71*(3), 543–562. https://doi.org/10.1111/1467-8624.00164

Masten, A. S. (2001). Ordinary magic: Resilience processes in development. *American Psychologist, 56*(3), 227–238. https://doi.org/10.1037/0003-066X.56.3.227

Masten, A. S. (2014a). Global perspectives on resilience in children and youth. *Child Development, 85*(1), 6–20. https://doi.org/10.1111/cdev.12205

Masten, A. S. (2014b). *Ordinary magic: Resilience in development.* Guilford.

Masten, A. S. (2018). Resilience theory and research on children and families: Past, present, and promise. *Journal of Family Theory & Review, 10*(1), 12–31. https://doi.org/10.1111/jftr.12255

Masten, A. S., Best, K. M., & Garmezy, N. (1990). Resilience and development: Contributions from the study of children who overcome adversity. *Development and Psychopathology, 2*(4), 425–444. https://doi.org/10.1017/S0954579400005812

Masten, A. S., & Powell, J. L. (2003). *A resilience framework for research, policy, and practice.* In S. S. Luthar (Ed.), *Resilience and vulnerability: Adaptation in the context of childhood adversities* (pp. 1–25). Cambridge University Press.

Masten, A. S., & Tellegen, A. (2012). Resilience in developmental psychopathology: Contributions of the project competence longitudinal study. *Development and Psychopathology, 24*(2), 345–361. https://doi.org/10.1017/S095457941200003X

Mohammadinia, L., Ebadi, A., Malekafzali, H., Allen, K. A., & Nia, H. S. (2019). The design and psychometric evaluation of the Adolescents' Resilience in Disaster Tool (ARDT-Q37): A mixed method study. *Heliyon, 5*(7), e02019. https://doi.org/10.1016/j.heliyon.2019.e02019

Myers, C. L., & Holland, K. L. (2000). Classroom behavioral interventions: Do teachers consider the function of the behavior? *Psychology in the Schools, 37*(3), 271–280. https://doi.org/10.1002/(SICI)1520-6807(200005)37:3<271::AID-PITS7>3.0.CO;2-8

Rutter, M. (2013). Annual research review: Resilience–clinical implications. *Journal of Child Psychology and Psychiatry and Allied Disciplines, 54*(4), 474–487. https://doi.org/10.1111/j.1469-7610.2012.02615.x

Sanders, J., Munford, R., Thimasarn-Anwar, T., & Liebenberg, L. (2017). Validation of the Child and Youth Resilience Measure (CYRM-28) on a sample of at-risk New Zealand youth. *Research on Social Work Practice, 27*(7), 827–840. https://doi.org/10.1177/1049731515614102

Sanders, J., Munford, R., Thimasarn-Anwar, T., Liebenberg, L., & Ungar, M. (2015). The role of positive youth development practices in building resilience and enhancing wellbeing for at-risk youth. *Child Abuse and Neglect, 42*, 432–450. https://doi.org/10.1016/j.chiabu.2015.02.006

Seligman, M. E. P., Ernst, R. M., Gillham, J., Reivich, K., & Linkins, M. (2009). Positive education: Positive psychology and classroom interventions. *Oxford Review of Education, 35*(3), 293–311. https://doi.org/10.1080/03054980902934563

Seligman, M. E. P., Rashid, T., & Parks, A. C. (2006). Positive psychotherapy. *American Psychologist, 61*(8), 774–788. https://doi.org/10.1037/0003-066X.61.8.774

Smith, B. W., Dalen, J., Wiggins, K., Tooley, E., Christopher, P., & Bernard, J. (2008). The brief resilience scale: Assessing the ability to bounce back. *International Journal of Behavioral Medicine, 15*(3), 194–200. https://doi.org/10.1080/10705500802222972

Southwick, S. M., Bonanno, G. A., Masten, A. S., Panter-Brick, C., & Yehuda, R. (2014). Resilience definitions, theory, and challenges: Interdisciplinary perspectives. *European Journal of Psychotraumatology, 5*(1), 1–14. https://doi.org/10.3402/ejpt.v5.25338

Tran, O. K., Gueldner, B. A., & Smith, D. C. (2014). Building resilience in schools through social and emotional learning. In M. J. Furlong, R. Gilman, & E. S. Huebner (Eds.), *Handbook of positive psychology in schools* (chap. 19). Routledge. https://doi.org/10.4324/9780203106525.ch19

Turkish Statistical Institute. (2019). *Turkey's statistics, 2019.* Retrieved from https://biruni.tuik.gov.tr/yayin/views/visitorPages/index.zul

Tusaie, K., & Dyer, J. (2004). Resilience: A historical review of the construct. *Holistic Nursing Practice, 18*(1), 3–8. https://doi.org/10.1097/00004650-200401000-00002

Üner, S., Bağcı, B. T., & Velipaşaoğlu, M. (2007). Ankara'da bulunan iki lisenin öğrencilerinin ruhsal durumlarının GSA-12 ile değerlendirilmesi [Evaluation of the mental status of students via 12-Item GHQ in two high schools in Ankara]. *Toplum Hekimliği Bülteni, 26*(1), 25–31.

Ungar, M. (2008). Resilience across cultures. *British Journal of Social Work, 38*(2), 218–235. https://doi.org/10.1093/bjsw/bcl343

Ungar, M., & Liebenberg, L. (2011). Assessing resilience across cultures using mixed methods: Construction of the child and youth resilience measure. *Journal of Mixed Methods Research, 5*(2), 126–149. https://doi.org/10.1177/1558689811400607

Ungar, M., & Liebenberg, L. (2013). A measure of resilience with contextual sensitivity—The CYRM-28: Exploring the tension between homogeneity and heterogeneity in resilience theory and research. In S. Prince-Embury & D. Saklofske (Eds.), *Resilience in children, adolescents, and adults* (pp. 245–255). Springer. https://doi.org/10.1007/978-1-4614-4939-3_18

Wagnild, G. M., & Young, H. M. (1993). Development and psychometric evaluation of the Resilience Scale. *Journal of Nursing Measurement, 1*(2), 165–178.

Wagnild, G. (2009). A review of the Resilience Scale. *Journal of nursing measurement, 17*(2), 105–113.

Waters, L. (2011). A review of school-based positive psychology interventions. *The Australian Educational and Developmental Psychologist, 28*(2), 75–90. https://doi.org/10.1375/aedp.28.2.75

Weissberg, R. P., Durlak, J. A., Domitrovich, C. E., & Gullotta, T. P. (Eds.). (2015). Social and emotional learning: Past, present, and future. In J. A. Durlak, C. E. Domitrovich, R. P. Weissberg, & T. P. Gullotta (Eds.), *Handbook of social and emotional learning: Research and practice.* (pp. 3–19). Guilford.

Werner, E. (2005). Resilience and recovery: Findings from the Kauai longitudinal study. *Research, Policy, and Practice in Children's Mental Health, 19*(1), 11–14.

Werner, E. E. (1993). Risk, resilience, and recovery: Perspectives from the Kauai Longitudinal Study. *Development and psychopathology, 5*(4), 503–515.

Werner, E. E., & Smith, R. S. (2001). *Journeys from childhood to midlife: Risk, resilience, and recovery.* Ithaca, NY: Cornell University Press.

WestEd. (2001). *Resilience youth development: Key findings.* Author.

WestEd. (2008). *Resilience & youth development.* Retrieved from https://data.calschls.org/resources/rydm_surveycontent.pdf

Windle, G., Bennett, K. M., & Noyes, J. (2011). A methodological review of resilience measurement scales. *Health and Quality of Life Outcomes, 9*(1), 1–188. https://doi.org/10.31234/osf.io/wsr3e

Wong, P. T. P. (2010). The PURE strategy to create lean and excellent organizations. *International Journal of Existential Psychology and Psychotherapy, 3*(2), 1–21.

Wong, P. T. P., & Wong, L. C. J. (2012). A meaning-centered approach to building youth resilience. In *The human quest for meaning: Theories, research, and applications* (2nd ed., pp. 585–617). Routledge/Taylor & Francis Group.

World Health Organization. (2017). *Depression and other common mental disorders: Global health estimates.* WHO Press.

Wright, M. O., & Masten, A. S. (2015). *Pathways to resilience in context.* In L. C. Theron, L. Liebenberg, & M. Ungar (Eds.), *Cross-cultural advancements in positive psychology: Vol. 11. Youth resilience and culture: Commonalities and complexities* (pp. 3–22). Springer Science + Business Media.

Wright, M. O., Masten, A. S., & Narayan, A. J. (2013). Resilience processes in development: Four waves of research on positive adaptation in the context of adversity. In R. B. Goldstein, & S. Brooks (Ed.), *Handbook of resilience in children* (2nd ed., pp. 15–37). Springer Science + Business Media. https://doi.org/10.1007/978-1-4614-3661-4_2

Yildirim, M. (2019). Mediating role of resilience in the relationships between fear of happiness and affect balance, satisfaction with life, and flourishing. *Europe's Journal of Psychology, 15*(2), 183–198. https://doi.org/doi:10.5964/ejop.v15i2.164010.5964/ejop.v15i2.1640

Yıldırım, M., Arslan, G., & Wong, P. (2020). Meaningful living, resilience, affective balance, and psychological health problems among Turkish young adults during coronavirus pandemic. *Current Psychology.* https://doi.org/10.1007/s12144-020-01244-8

Yıldırım, M., Iqbal, N., Khan, M. M., O'Reilly, M., & Vostanis, P. (2020). Psychosocial needs and supports for street children in India: Stakeholder perspectives. *International Journal of Child Development and Mental Health, 8*(2), 19–28. https://he01.tci-thaijo.org/index.php/cdmh/article/view/226740

Yıldırım, M., & Tanrıverdi, F.Ç. (2020). Social support, resilience and subjective well-being in college students. *Journal of Positive School Psychology.* https://journalppw.com/index.php/JPPW/article/view/229

Zolkoski, S. M., & Bullock, L. M. (2012). Resilience in children and youth: A review. *Children and Youth Services Review, 34*(12), 2295–2303. https://doi.org/10.1016/j.childyouth.2012.08.009

SECTION V

Perspective

33

"SMART" TECHNOLOGY HAS AN IMPORTANT ROLE TO PLAY IN MAKING LEARNING ABOUT WELL-BEING IN SCHOOLS ENGAGING AND REAL FOR STUDENTS

Monique West, Dr Kent Patrick and Prof Dianne Vella-Brodrick

The advancement and implementation of digital technologies have had a profound impact on how we live our lives, influencing most aspects of what we do from the way we communicate to the acquisition of knowledge (Organisation for Economic Cooperation and Development [OECD], 2016). The education sector has been a beneficiary of a range of advances that promote positive student outcomes. For example, smartboards, computers, and tablets are now considered mainstream learning tools in many schools. Despite these technological innovations, *transformation of educational practices* has not been widespread. This may be due to factors such as inadequate teacher training and limits with producing appropriate software for students (OECD, 2016). Consequently, there are still numerous unexplored opportunities using new technologies to help engage and motivate young people to learn or change behavior. There is now a range of cost-effective advanced equipment available to the general public (e.g., portable electroencephalography [EEG]) that were previously only used for medicine, science, and business due to prohibitive costs or limited access. Well-being education in secondary schools is an area that could benefit from affordable and user-friendly technological advances. Indeed, the OECD has highlighted that "digital technologies offer a large potential for innovation, growth and greater well-being" (OECD, 2015, p. 14).

There are several reasons to support incorporating technological innovation within educational systems. First, innovation is a priority within many public sectors, including education (OECD, 2016). Second, it is important for the education sector to stay up-to-date with the changing environment, particularly given the rapid and ubiquitous uptake of new technologies by young people (Patton et al., 2016). To engage and motivate students, educators need to be flexible in their approach and remain relevant in the face of rapid change, and this includes using new technology to enhance pedagogical practice. Increasing the capabilities of using new technologies will equip young people for the workforce of tomorrow. Third, the use of innovation in the education sector may lead to improved learning outcomes for students (OECD, 2016) and thus improve the quality of education being delivered. Finally, the use of new technologies not only promotes young peoples' engagement in education but is an effective way of tapping into their world. Indeed, secondary school students are *digital natives*, having grown up with a variety of technologies such as the Internet, mobile devices, and social media.

DOI: 10.4324/9781003013778-41

Technology-Based Programs within Schools

Schools have increasingly adopted technology (Digital Education Advisory Group, 2012). An international survey of 20,000 respondents from more than 100 countries found that 48% of students used desktop computers in class, 42% used smartphones, and 33% of classrooms had smartboards (Global Education Monitoring, 2018). However, merely embedding technology within classrooms does not guarantee effective teaching and improved learning outcomes. Pedagogy is at the core of teaching, and technology needs to be skillfully integrated to leverage the potential of digital formats to enhance learning.

Technology-based educational programs incorporate strategies to increase student motivation and engagement, both of which are critical for learning. Two popular strategies are gamification and immersion. *Serious games* are developed with a purpose beyond pure entertainment. Within the educational context, serious games are typically designed with the primary aim of supporting student learning in key curriculum areas (Victorian State Government, 2017). Serious games incorporate game technology and features, such as challenges, rewards, and point-scoring, to increase student engagement and to promote knowledge attainment and skill development.

Immersion style digital programs include augmented and virtual reality. Immersive technology refers to any technology that extends reality by creating a digital or simulated environment. Schools are integrating immersive technology within their curriculum to expose students to environments or situations that would be impossible or challenging within a classroom setting. Augmented and virtual realties are increasingly used in education (Liu et al., 2017). Augmented reality entails superimposing digital images within the real world. An example is Pokémon Go where users explore their neighborhoods searching for computer-generated images that designers have overlaid on their environment. In contrast, virtual reality allows users to experience a 3D environment through computer-generated simulations. The user can interact with the content or environment in a seemingly real world. Virtual reality has been implemented within multiple contexts. It is often used for training purposes; for example, commercial pilots can undertake virtual flights, and surgeons can perform virtual operations without risking lives. Ethical considerations need to be addressed when implementing immersive technologies. For example, an awareness of individuals' unique needs, life experiences, or cultural norms should be considered. In addition, teachers and students should be aware of potential risks such as cybersickness, or pre-existing health conditions that are affected by an immersive experience.

Technology-based educational programs have the potential to invigorate student learning and revolutionize teaching approaches. Students embrace technology within their social world; therefore, it is not surprising that research suggests they also report positive experiences and outcomes for technology-based educational programs. Serious games with sound learning principles can increase motivation to learn and improve performance (Chen & Hsu, 2019; Gee, 2009; Laamarti et al., 2014). Immersive digital programs enable students to engage more with content (Moro et al., 2017), they increase enjoyment and interest (Lee et al., 2017) and improve learning efficiency (Liang & Xianoming, 2013). However, the introduction of technology-based programs within education is relatively new. As such, there is a need for robust evaluative measures to ascertain program effectiveness and to learn how to leverage the potential that technology has to enhance learning.

Examples of Successful Innovative Technology-Based Educational Programs

We now present three examples of popular technology-based programs that were developed specifically for schools and show promise in promoting learning and increasing engagement.

PhET Interactive Simulations

PhET interactive simulations were designed to help students learn scientific and mathematical concepts in an innovative and engaging way. To date, 158 interactive simulations have been developed and translated into 93 different languages. Students can discover and explore concepts in a range of subjects, including Earth Science, Biology, Chemistry, Physics, and Mathematics (classvr. com, 2020). The animation simulations incorporate gaming features to motivate students and to help them gain a deeper understanding of concepts. A range of teaching resources is also available. Preliminary research suggests that PhET simulations can enhance learning (Ajredini et al., 2014; Ceberio et al., 2016; Perkins et al., 2006). For example, Correia et al. (2019) used one of the PhET Chemistry simulations to teach 114, 12th-grade students about gas behavior. Survey data revealed that the PhET simulation provided a positive learning experience for most students and that having the opportunity to manipulate gas parameters increased knowledge and was an effective learning strategy that students highly valued.

ClassVR

ClassVR is a multiaward winning virtual, augmented, and mixed reality technology program designed exclusively for classroom use to promote engagement and increase students' knowledge retention. The underlying philosophy is that personal experience is a powerful way to enhance information retention. Launched in 2017, ClassVR has scaled rapidly with distribution to more than 60 countries worldwide, with over 800 VR and AR resources available. ClassVR packages include standalone fully integrated headsets, curriculum-aligned educational resources, student-friendly interface with intuitive gesture controls, and a web-based portal for teachers to manage and control devices easily (classvr.com, 2020). ClassVR is pedagogically sound with content that covers a wide range of subjects including Science, Mathematics, Humanities, Literacy and Language, Social Studies, Physical Education, and Creative Arts. Students immerse themselves in 360-degree environments to learn to emulate a first-hand experience. For example, students can wander through the town of Pripyat and experience the aftermath of the Chernobyl nuclear disaster, or they can explore the human heart in 3D comparing blood vessels of someone with anemia with someone with normal hemoglobin levels.

The ClassVR website has many case studies and testimonials from schools worldwide outlining the successful implementation of the program. Considering ClassVR is a new product, there is scarce published literature examining its effectiveness. However, Kurniawati et al. (2019) piloted the ClassVR with 13 students with special educational needs who were between 5 and 20 years old. They found that these students were highly motivated and focused when using ClassVR, and most could complete the task with very little assistance from teachers.

Minecraft: Education Edition

Minecraft: Education Edition (2020) is based on the multiple award-winning 3D video game Minecraft that has a reported 480 million players worldwide (Dent, 2019). The premise of Minecraft is to create and modify environments by discovering and extracting pixilated cubes that represent various materials. Different game modes provide players with fun and challenging experiences. The Minecraft Education Edition was launched in 2016 and has been implemented within school curricula across 115 countries. It combines elements of serious gaming and immersion. A wide range of teaching resources are available, including lesson plans for 25 different subjects that align with the curriculum. For example, students can learn about mathematical concepts such as perimeter and area through creating different buildings or biological and environmental concepts through creating a biome (Minecraft Education Edition, 2020).

Studies examining the effectiveness of Minecraft Education Edition are scarce. However, the literature suggests that Minecraft could be a promising tool to motivate student learning (Kuhn, 2018; Nebel et al., 2016). The constructivist learning principles and collaborative learning approach of Minecraft foster communication skills and improve language acquisition (Kuhn, 2018). Callaghan (2016) conducted a study with 168 secondary school students from Years 7 to 10 to explore how Minecraft can contribute to student learning. Learning outcomes were achieved, and student online feedback surveys and teacher/researcher observations revealed that Minecraft also promoted engagement and collaboration.

These three examples of educational programs highlight the potential for technology to enhance student learning, motivation, and engagement for students, including those with diverse needs. Currently, most technology-based school programs target traditional school assessed subjects. However, many programs now include learning objectives aligned with improving well-being. For example, Minecraft: Education Edition has added an empathy edition focusing on service learning, doing social good, and improving social and emotional health. ClassVR has lesson plans that focus on prosocial behavior and empathy. This aligns with the demand by schools to include both implicit and explicit learning opportunities on the topic of well-being for their students and school community (Slemp et al., 2017).

Well-Being, Positive Psychology, and Innovative Technology

Leveraging technology to promote well-being and optimal functioning is a growing area of interest. This is evident through the continually increasing range of self-help and professional online programs, devices, and apps available that target health and well-being. The field of Positive Psychology has capitalized on technological advances within both research and practice. Digital methods of data collection are providing exciting opportunities to study human interaction and behavior in a way that were previously challenging, if not impossible. For example, online environments such as social media are enabling large-scale studies of social interactions and experiences. Similarly, portable electronic devices within experience sampling methods allow real-time data to be captured easily (Chin et al., 2016). Online positive psychological interventions are becoming widespread (Banos et al., 2017) and, recently, there is an increase in the development and implementation of technology-based interactive positive psychological interventions.

The integration of technological advances and Positive Psychology has resulted in the emergence of two new streams: Positive Technology and Positive Computing. Positive Technology aims to explore how digital technologies can be utilized to foster well-being (Gaggioli et al., 2019). It includes perspectives from Positive Psychology and Human-Computer Interaction with a focus on "the design, development, and validation of novel digital experiences that aims at promoting positive change through pleasure, flow, meaning, competence and positive relationships" (Gaggioli et al., 2019, p. 7). The past decade has seen an increased interest in Positive Technology. A recent edition of *Frontiers in Psychology* (Gaggioli et al., 2019) was dedicated to Positive Technology, highlighting the conceptual frameworks and showcasing the expanding applications, including cognitive enhancement, mental health, sociocognitive skills, multicultural integration, and education.

Positive Computing refers to "the design and development of technology to support well-being and human potential" (Calvo & Peters, 2014). It is a multidisciplinary field that combines research and methods from Psychology, Human–Computer Interaction, Neuroscience, Affective Computing, Behavioural Economics, and Philosophy. The underlying notion of Positive Computing is that well-being should be a key priority during the design process of technologies (Calvo et al., 2016). Moreover, technologies should do more than increase productivity, efficiency, and accuracy; they should improve psychological health and quality of life. Technologists and well-being scientists are increasingly collaborating to combine knowledge and expertise to produce well-being-supportive technologies. This partnership will see the growth of more opportunities to include technology in educational contexts to achieve specific learning and well-being objectives.

Positive Education and Innovative Technology in the School Context

With the rising prevalence of depression and anxiety among young people (Carlisle et al., 2019; Twenge et al., 2019), it is necessary to look for new ways of helping them to improve their mental health and well-being. Young people are often reticent to seek help from health professionals (Rickwood et al., 2005) and much of the anxiety experienced by young people is related to school life (Carlisle et al., 2019). Therefore, schools have a responsibility and are well placed to equip students with well-being skills that go beyond counseling and pastoral care services. Fortunately, many schools are recognizing the potential to help their students to thrive and not just survive. Hence, providing young people with the tools to manage daily stress and anxiety and to live a fulfilling life is an essential goal of schooling that complements academic achievement (Slemp et al., 2017).

Many schools are turning to the science of positive education to achieve this objective and combat the escalating anxiety students face around the perceived or real pressure to perform well. Positive education dovetails a strengths-based framework that focuses on building a range of factors, some of which include: positive emotions, quality social connections, engagement, meaning, and accomplishment with best-practice standards in education to promote student flourishing. Positive education can be implemented explicitly through the curriculum and/or implicitly as part of a school's educational philosophy. Topics typically covered include identifying and using personal strengths, savoring, gratitude, growth mindset, kindness, mindfulness, and community engagement. Notable improvements to student well-being are often reported by schools practicing positive education (Vella-Brodrick et al., 2017, 2020).

A successful example of the intersection between innovative technology and positive education is Smiling Mind, a not-for-profit organization that focuses on teaching mindfulness (Smiling Mind, 2020). They developed a *whole-of-school* program that not only involves more traditional educational practices such as professional development for school staff, in-school student workshops, and resources for student learning, but also an app for smartphone or tablet that encourages the ongoing practice of mindfulness activities. The app can be used as part of classroom teaching in addition to allowing self-directed practice, so is integral to the program both in and out of the classroom (Smiling Mind, 2020). An evaluation of the program in 12 Victorian primary and secondary schools demonstrated positive outcomes for teachers, including improved mental health, concentration and sleep, and students, including improved mental health and reductions in classroom disruption (Smiling Mind, 2016).

Clearly, technological innovation is key to maximizing positive student outcomes. The following section presents a case study of a newly developed program called Bio-Dash that combines well-being science and innovation in technology to transform the way young people learn about well-being.

Case Study—The Bio-Dash Trial within an Australian Secondary School

Overview of the Bio-Dash Program

In 2018, Bio-Dash was founded by Professor Vella-Brodrick from the Centre for Wellbeing Science at the University of Melbourne in Australia. A school-based version was codesigned by a research team from the Centre for Wellbeing Science and Year 10 students from an independent boys school in Australia.

Bio-Dash is an innovative optimal performance and well-being program. It was designed in response to the rising levels of anxiety and depression amongst young people and the increasing expectations for students to perform well across multiple life domains (Carlisle et al., 2019). Bio-Dash equips students with evidence-based strategies to focus, manage stress and anxiety, and thrive in their everyday performance, whether it be in academics, socially, on the sports field, or for artistic pursuits. However, the goal was to make learning about well-being more tangible, engaging, and personalized through improved student buy-in and the integration of dynamic real-time technology such as biofeedback and gaming features. Bio-Dash is a carefully sequenced educational training program based on the latest evidence from health, sport, and well-being science. Figure 33.1 outlines the key components of the Bio-Dash program.

Every evidence-based strategy within the toolkit has been specifically chosen, taking into account its effectiveness and applicability to young peoples' activities and needs. To make the program relevant and engaging for young people, some of the latest innovations in technology involving gamification and biofeedback have been incorporated.

Biofeedback is a process for gaining awareness into ones' physiological functioning (such as skin conductance, brain activity, and respiration) using monitoring sensors, with the goal of learning to control physiological functioning for improved well-being outcomes. Biofeedback devices help young people to receive immediate feedback about how well an activity is working to improve their well-being (e.g., levels of relaxation and focus). It also makes the concept and experience of well-being more tangible and personalized as there are metrics around their physiological responses to stimuli.

Gamification involves applying game mechanics (such as competition, rewards, and point scoring) into a task. This motivates participation and maintains an interest in the activity. Gaming is appealing for a variety of reasons, including receiving instant feedback, applying strategic decision-making, and having the opportunity to pursue and achieve goals. Leveraging the

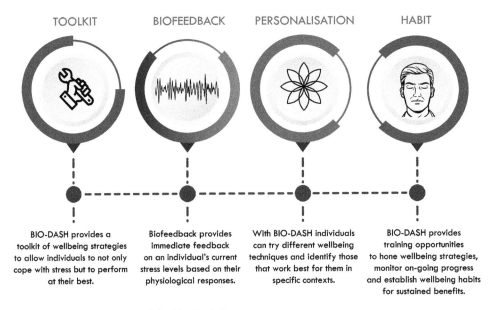

Figure 33.1 Key Components of the Bio-Dash Program

Table 33.1 Sample Bio-Dash Plan

	Relaxation	*Focus*	*Motivation*
Academic	Managing stress before an exams **Progressive muscle relaxation**	Getting homework done **Manage distraction (leaf)**	Doing extra revision before exams
Sporting and Performing Arts	Controlling anxiety before taking a shot at goal **4-4 breathing**	Focus on the game rather than negative thoughts	Going to training regularly Express gratitude
Social	Being more chilled about what other people think of me **Self-compassion**	Get to know Jeo better **Hunting the good stuff**	Organize a social event/activity
Other			Walking my dog more **Mental Imagery**

Note: Bolding signifies the well-being strategies students identified as useful for achieving their goals.

enjoyment of gaming can enhance learning. Bio-Dash incorporates tailor-made games that specifically target situations that are meaningful and important to young people. The games enable students to learn how to relax when in stressful circumstances such as giving a speech at school, kicking a goal, or social situations. Another element of personalization within the Bio-Dash program is the inclusion of the Bio-Dash plan. The plan helps students to set goals they would like to achieve in different life domains such as academic, sporting, performing arts, or social. Students identify the strategies they have learned throughout the program that would be useful in different situations (refer to Table 33.1 for an example). Not all cells need to be completed—only those that are relevant to students' goals.

How Was Bio-Dash for Schools Designed?

Bio-Dash Codesign

To address the challenges of engaging young people with well-being and optimal performance programs delivered in schools, a collaborative, user-focused approach was required. Fifteen Year 10 students (approximately 16 years of age) helped codesign the Bio-Dash program with the research team. The aim was to increase the relevance and impact of the program for young people while ensuring the latest scientific developments were included.

The codesign process involved multiple stages. The student codesigners attended 12 sessions facilitated by Professor Vella-Brodrick, where they provided valuable feedback and insights toward developing and enhancing the effectiveness of the program. Throughout the sessions, students trialed a broad range of evidence-based well-being strategies, used the biofeedback devices, and learnt the science behind the strategies and devices. They also discussed ideas about the pedagogical aspects of delivery and the implementation of Bio-Dash at a systems level. This process encouraged mutual learning and active participation in testing and refining ideas for the program.

The Bio-Dash program evolved throughout the codesign process. It reflected the aspects that appealed and were meaningful to young people. Understanding the perspectives and experiences of young people was a crucial element toward producing a program that is useful, engaging, and relevant. In late 2018, some of the key aspects of the Bio-Dash program were piloted with a Year 9 class who provided feedback to enhance the programs' effectiveness further.

Delivery of the Bio-Dash and General User Experiences

In 2019, the Bio-Dash program was delivered by Professor Vella-Brodrick and her trained staff to all Year 9 students (167 in total) at the original independent boys secondary school where the program was codesigned and trialed. The program was delivered to six classes, two classes per school term. Throughout delivery, numerous adjustments were made and implemented to create a more engaging and effective program for students. Modifications included changing seating arrangements, including more videos and fine-tuning content, to be more interactive and meaningful to young people.

In the final delivery, students received five Bio-Dash sessions that were conducted during scheduled well-being class time and ran for approximately 55 minutes. The Bio-Dash program focused on five core areas: breathing, emotion regulation, mindfulness and focusing, mental imagery, and savoring. Multiple strategies were taught within each core area. Considerable thought was also placed on program sequencing and delivery. The fundamental teaching and learning elements of each session are shown in Table 33.2.

Based on feedback from surveys, students reported feeling connected with the technological aspect of the program; they liked the personalized information gained from biofeedback devices and seeing how their body responded to stress and relaxation. They noted that incorporating technology made learning about well-being more appealing and they enjoyed learning about the various Bio-Dash relaxation techniques.

Peer Coaching

As supported by the Positive Youth Development literature, which advocates for youth initiative and agency (Larson, 2000), learning from peers can heighten the relatability and relevance of a program. Hence, the Year 10 students who helped codesign the Bio-Dash program in 2018 had the opportunity to receive training in foundational coaching from the University of Melbourne staff with the aim of coaching Year 9 students in 2019.

Eight Year 11 students (who had previously codesigned the Bio-Dash program and participated in coaching training) coached 167 Year 9 students who participated in the Bio-Dash program in term 2 of 2019. There were approximately seven Year 9 students in each coaching group. Three coaching sessions were strategically scheduled throughout the term (refer to Table 33.3). Coaches were given a handout that outlined the plan for each coaching session. The plan was useful for prompting and guiding the coaches within each session. It also aided in standardization and consistency of the coaching sessions in terms of the central learning objectives. In addition, each coach shared their knowledge and experiences of the Bio-Dash program with their Year 9 students ("coachees"). Coaches welcomed coachees to share their thoughts and experiences with the group. During these sessions, coaches reinforced how to perform the strategies, and each group brainstormed situations where they may be useful. Coaches also helped coachees to set their personal goals using the Bio-Dash Plan and encouraged them to practice strategies before the next session.

Table 33.2 Fundamental Elements of Bio-Dash Sessions

Clear learning intensions	Clear learning intentions emphasized the learning outcomes for each session
Theoretical component	Scientific theory was taught to encourage deeper level learning and meaningful connections to the content
Active engagement	A variety of interactive methods were employed to promote active learning
Reflection	Students had the opportunity to reflect on the lesson and their level of personal progress

Table 33.3 Bio-Dash Coaching Schedule

Term 2 Sessions	Goal of Lesson
Bio-Dash Session 1	Introduction
Bio-Dash Session 2	Breathing
Coaching Session 1	**Deep Breathing**
Bio-Dash Session 3	Emotion Regulation
Bio-Dash Session 4	Mindfulness and Focus
Coaching Session 2	**Peer Coaching**
Bio-Dash Session 5	Mental Imagery and Savoring
Bio-Dash Session 6	Overview and consolidation
Coaching Session 3	**Peer Coaching**

Encouraging this type of peer to peer learning seems to be highly engaging, and the Year 9 boys responded well to this new learning experience.

Teacher Involvement

In 2019, two Bio-Dash information sessions were conducted for teachers. All staff had the opportunity to attend the first session, which was held mid-year as a professional development option. The other was held in December for the Health and Physical Education staff members. These sessions (a) provided an overview of the Bio-Dash program, (b) allowed teachers to learn some strategies and use the biofeedback devices, and (c) garnered feedback and insights from teachers as to how best to integrate Bio-Dash using a whole-school approach.

Feedback from teachers was encouraging. Many expressed views that this program would be invaluable to students, particularly in a range of academic and sporting contexts. Including school staff in learning about new innovative programs contributes to a whole-school approach which visibly supports and integrates the program activities and learnings in day-to-day school operations.

Technological Elements of Bio-Dash

Technology is a critical element of the Bio-Dash program and plays a pivotal role in each of the program sessions. Every student receives immediate individual physiological feedback from biofeedback devices, which they monitor via an iPad. Three wireless biofeedback devices were used to measure respiration, skin conductance, and brain activity. They are noninvasive and meet global certifications for safety.

Devices

The Spire Stone. To sense physiology, Spire uses proprietary passive sensors to measure the detailed movement of the body as individuals breathe and move. Through the rhythms of expansion and contraction in the torso and diaphragm, the Spire Stone detects periods of breathing, which reflect a tense, focused, or calm state of mind.

The Pip. The Pip detects galvanic skin response (the electrical activity of the sweat glands in the skin). It has gold-plated sensors that help to maximize detection sensitivity. Electrodermal activity increases when stressed—the Pip measures and displays levels of stress while undergoing activities.

The Muse. The Muse is a compact EEG system that detects and reports brain wave data. The Muse uses real-time brain wave information to measure states of focus, relaxation, and mind-wandering.

It is important to note that the primary aim of the program is for students to learn well-being strategies and implement them within their daily lives. Technological devices are tools to help students do this by making learning more fun, tangible, and engaging. They provide an observable indicator of which strategies work well for individuals and feedback on whether students' well-being skills are improving. For example, they received information about how long tasks took them to complete, performance scores, and rewards achieved. The devices used within this program were chosen based on safety, practicality, affordability, and reliability in measuring the specific physiological constructs. As new and improved devices become available, these will be included in the Bio-Dash program, ensuring that it offers some of the best tools to enhance student learning.

Gamification

Gamification is integrated within a range of apps that synced with the biofeedback devices and helped students learn to destress, relax, and focus. Some generalized apps and games are available with each of the devices, but these do not always portray realistic contexts for students. Some examples of the games include changing the color of small dots or picking up speed during a dragon race. Success in these tasks is contingent on the student's ability to relax, as detected by the biofeedback device. In conjunction with a software developing company, Harmonious Productions, the Bio-Dash team developed apps that were tailored specifically to young people. The apps provided relatable everyday contexts (such as on the sporting field, in school settings, and in social situations), for students to practice well-being strategies. Providing students with choices to suit their needs and preferences was important. Within the games, students were able to choose the difficulty level, the Bio-Dash strategies they would like to use, and the context (academic, sporting, or social).

Suggestions for Future Implementation of the Bio-Dash Program within Schools

Trialing the Bio-Dash program within a school was valuable toward identifying how best to deliver the program to maximize outcomes. To gain optimal effects of the Bio-Dash program within school contexts, the following strategies are suggested:

- Integrate Bio-Dash strategies and learnings into everyday school practices and policies.
- Integrate elements of the program across multiple year levels to reinforce the knowledge and skills learned.
- Incorporate periodic booster/refresher sessions.
- Deliver tailor-made content for specific events such as exams, music recitals, or sporting competitions.
- Set up physical Bio-Dash training hubs (e.g., in the library and sports complex) to allow students and staff to practice and monitor their progress.
- Encourage students to practice the strategies outside of school:
  - Set homework tasks and
  - Send mobile messages to students to encourage them to apply specific strategies.
- Deliver the Bio-Dash program to school staff and provide clear delivery instructions and resources to school facilitators. Teaching is one of the most stressful professions (Hartney, 2020), and it is imperative to minimize the burden on teachers of new material and methods. Relevant time for training and transition needs to be provided by school leaders. Teacher training would also enable teachers to have an understanding of the program principles and practices so they can integrate them into their classes and be role models for students. This shared experience may also improve student–teacher relationships.

- Conduct parent information sessions to improve understanding of programs and to assist them in encouraging their children to adopt strategies at home. Parents themselves may benefit from participation and, therefore, may become role models for their children.
- Develop relevant assessment tasks to encourage students to be more engaged and to enable students and teachers to monitor their progress and understanding of the Bio-Dash program content.
- Collaborate with community members to help reinforce the underlying strategies and principles of the program (e.g., appoint ambassadors to talk to students about the program content and how they use it in their own lives).
- Conduct ongoing monitoring and evaluation of the program, including student and staff consultation, to enable continued improvements and updates to be made.

Considerations When Using Technology within Educational Programs

Using technology within classrooms offers many benefits, however, it also presents some challenges. Technology is enticing for young people, especially new gadgets they have not seen or used before. However, it can also be distracting. Hence, facilitators needed to employ tactics to prevent students from playing with technology at inappropriate times. For example, initially when delivering the Bio-Dash program the iPads and biofeedback devices were placed on students' tables as they arrived to class. After recognizing the potential for distraction, facilitators distributed the technology after the learning intentions and theoretical components of the session had been completed. Delaying the distribution of technological devices led to enhanced concentration from students and a better understanding of learning intentions. Another consideration is to provide clear verbal and visual instructions as to when and how to use the technology and associated activities. Clear instructions can reduce instances of students pressing the wrong buttons, using the wrong apps, or being confused as to task instructions.

Recommendations for Integrating Technological Innovations for Enhanced Learning

Technology can be embedded within educational learnings and practices to help create a well-being culture within schools. Following are some useful recommendations to enhance the delivery of technology-based programs:

- Gain buy-in from core school staff who will be involved in supporting and or delivering the program as well as from students, teachers, and parents. Buy-in can be enhanced by educating the school community about the benefits of integrating technology into learning processes and the support available for this to be done.
- Work collaboratively with technology experts to develop purpose-specific devices, software, and serious games to enhance learning objectives while maintaining student safety.
- Involve students in the design, delivery, and assessment of new technological programs. For example, it is recommended that student advisory groups be formed to provide input about some of the latest educational technologies and to give feedback on new school programs integrating technology. Additionally, schools should promote peer-to-peer coaching and learning as an ongoing activity to enhance the relatability and relevance of newly developed programs.
- Regularly monitor the effects of using technology, in terms of user experience and the achievement of learning intentions. Best practice standards need to be implemented to assess

how well new initiatives are working and to gain insights into where improvements can be made for future iterations.

- Provide adequate training to the school community, and not just the students, on the technology being implemented.
- Ensure that health, safety, and privacy standards are at the forefront of innovative technologies.
- Ascribe leaders to facilitate the effective delivery of newly developed technology-based programs. Leaders would be responsible to support and build the capacity to develop a whole-school approach and to guide and monitor the long-term program delivery and outcomes.

Conclusion

There is growing evidence that learning environments can optimize the learning experience and outcomes for students when technological innovations such as serious gaming, apps, and devices (e.g., virtual reality and physiological monitors) are strategically integrated into the curriculum and carefully monitored (Blumberg, 2014; Holliman & Sheehy, 2017). It is important for schools to stay abreast of the latest innovative developments as young people are digital natives who expect to use technology in their everyday lives, including for educational purposes. Provided that technology is used appropriately, is well supported and resourced, is monitored for safety and educational utility, and is accessible to all students, it can enhance the way students learn. Indeed, students are indicating that they welcome these technological advances. It is therefore sensible to capitalize on this enthusiasm, particularly when it comes to learning about well-being where they can adopt practical skills that they can use to manage stress and thrive in life. To facilitate this motivation for learning it is important to engage the students and the technology experts to contribute to these innovative educational programs to promote buy-in, credibility, and a genuine partnership with teachers. A systems approach that involves comprehensive training, communication, collaboration, and monitoring will optimize the success of technology-based school programs, and the benefits students will derive both during their education and beyond, especially when it comes to learning about well-being and managing anxiety. Smart technology can make a world of difference to the way well-being is learned in schools, and most importantly, it can help to make these learnings a habit so that they stick throughout life and in times of most need.

Resources

Vella-Brodrick, D. A. (2019). How technology is boosting our young people's wellbeing. Pursuit, https://pursuit.unimelb.edu.au/articles/how-technology-is-boosting-our-young-people-s-wellbeing.

Vella-Brodrick, D. A. (2019). Deans Lecture: Wellbeing Education that Feels like a TREAT, Rather than a Treatment Plan. University of Melbourne. https://www.youtube.com/watch?v=u-0J8rwCZpus&feature=youtu.be

References

Ajredini, F., Izairi, N., & Zajkov, O. (2014). Real experiments versus PhET simulations for better high-school students' understanding of electrostatic charging. *European Journal of Physics Education, 5*(1), 59–70. Retrieved from https://www.learntechlib.org/p/159229/

Banos, R. M., Etchemendy, E., Mira, A., Riva, G., Gaggioli, A., & Botella, C. (2017). Online positive interventions to promote well-being and resilience in the adolescent population: A narrative review. *Frontiers in Psychiatry, 8*, 1–9. doi:10.3389/fpsyt.2017.00010

Blumberg, F. C. (2014). *Learning by playing: Video gaming in education.* Oxford University Press.

Callaghan, N. (2016). Investigating the role of Minecraft in educational learning environments. *Educational Media International, 53*(4), 244–260. doi:10.1080/09523987.2016.1254877

Calvo, R. A., & Peters, D. (2014). *Positive computing: Technology for well-being and human potential.* The MIT Press.

Calvo, R. A., Vella-Brodrick, D. A., Desmet, P., & Ryan, R. M. (2016). Positive computing: A new partnership between psychology, social sciences and technologists (editorial introduction). *Psychology of Well-Being: Theory, Research and Practice, 6*, 1–6. doi:10.1186/s13612-016-0047-1.

Carlisle, E., Fildes, J., Hall, S., Perrens, B., Perdriau, A., & Plummer, J. (2019), *Youth survey report 2019.* Mission Australia. Retrieved from https://www.missionaustralia.com.au/what-we-do/research-impact-policy-advocacy/youth-survey

Ceberio, M., Almudi, J. S., & Franco, A. (2016). Design and application of interactive simulations in problem solving in university-level physics education. *Journal Science Education and Technology, 25*(4), 590–609. doi:10.1007/s10956-016-9615-7

Chen, H. J., & Hsu, H. L. (2019). The impact of a serious game on vocabulary and content learning. *Computer Assisted Language Learning, 33*, 1–22. doi:10.1080/09588221.2019.1593197

Chin, T. C., Rickard, N. S., & Vella-Brodrick, D. A. (2016). Development and feasibility of a mobile experience sampling application for tracking program implementation in youth well-being programs. *Psychology of Well-being: Theory, Research and Practice, 6*(1), 112. doi:10.1186/s13612-016-0038-2

Classvr.com (2020). *ClassVR update January 2020.* Retrieved from https://www.classvr.com/classvr-update-january-2020/

Correia, A. P., Koehler, N., Thompson, A., & Phye, G. (2019). The application of PhET simulation to teach gas behavior on the submicroscopic level: Secondary school students' perceptions. *Research in Science & Technological Education, 37*(2), 193–217. doi:10.1080/02635143.2018.1487834

Dent, S. (2019). Minecraft player count reaches 480 million. *PCGamesN.com.* Retrieved from https://www.pcgamesn.com/minecraft/minecraft-player-count

Digital Education Advisory Group. (2012). Beyond the classroom: A new digital education young Australians in the 21st century. Retrieved from https://docs.education.gov.au

Gaggioli, A., Villani D., Serino S., Banos, R., & Botella, C. (2019). Editorial: Positive technology: Designing E-experiences for positive change. *Frontiers in Psychology, 10*, 1571. doi:10.3389/fpsyg.2019.01571

Gee, J. P. (2009). Deep learning properties of good digital games: How far can they go? In U. Ritterfield, M., Cody & P. Vorderer (Eds.), *Serious Games: Mechanisms and Effects* (pp. 67–82). Routledge Taylor & Francis Group. doi:10.4324/9780203891650

Global Education Monitoring. (2018). *Global education census report, 2018.* Retrieved from https://www.cambridgeinternational.org/Images/514611-global-education- census-survey-report.pdf

Hartney, E. (2020). Stress management to enhance teaching quality and teaching effectiveness: A professional development framework for teachers. In Information Resources Management Association (Eds.), *Occupational stress: Breakthroughs in research and practice* (pp. 306–331). doi:10.4018/978-1-7998-0954-8

Holliman, A., & Sheehy, K. (2017). *Education and new technologies : Perils and promises for learners.* Routledge. doi:10.4324/9781315644851

Kuhn, J. (2018). Minecraft education edition. *Calico Journal, 35*(2), 213–224. doi:10.1558/cj.34600

Kurniawati, A., Kusumaningsih, A., & Hasan, I. (2019). Class VR: Learning class environment for special educational needs using virtual reality games. *2019 International Conference on Computer Engineering, Network, and Intelligent Multimedia (CENIM)*, Surabaya, Indonesia, pp. 1–5.

Laamarti, F., Eid, M., & Saddik, A. E. (2014). An overview of serious games. *International Journal of Computer Games Technology*, Article number 358152, 1–15. doi:10.1155/2014/358152

Larson, R. (2000). Towards a psychology of positive youth development. *American Psychologist, 55*, 170–183. doi:10.1037/0003–066X.55.1.170

Lee, S. H., Sergueeva, K., Catangui, M., & Kandaurova, M. (2017). Assessing Google cardboard virtual reality as a content delivery system in business classrooms. *Journal of Education for Business, 92*(4), 153–160. doi:10.1080/08832323.2017.1308308

Liang, H., & Xiaoming, B. (2013). Application research of virtual reality technology in electronic technique teaching. *Intelligence Computation and Evolutionary Computation, 180*, 153–159. https://doi.org/10.1007/978-3-642-31656-2_22

Liu, D., Bhagat, K. K., Gao, Y., Chang, T. W., & Huang, R. (2017). The potentials and trends of virtual reality in education. In D. Li, C. Dede, R. Huang, & J., Richards (Eds.), *Virtual, augmented, and mixed realities in education. Smart computing and intelligence* (pp. 1–16). Springer.

Minecraft: Education Edition. (2020). *Minecraft education edition.* Retrieved from https://education.minecraft.net/

Moro, C., Åtromberga, Z., Raikos, A., & Stirling, A. (2017). The effectiveness of virtual and augmented reality in health sciences and medical anatomy. *Anatomical Sciences Education, 10*, 549–559. doi:10.1002/ase.1696

Nebel, S., Schneider S., & Rey, G. D. (2016). Mining learning and crafting scientific experiments: A literature review on the use of Minecraft in education and research. *Journal of Educational Technology & Society,*
19, 355–366. Retrieved from www.jstor.org/stable/jeductechsoci.19.2.355

Organisation for Economic Cooperation and Development (OECD). (2015), *OECD Digital Economy Outlook*
2015. Paris: OECD Publishing. https://doi.org/10.1787/9789264232440-en.

Organisation for Economic Cooperation and Development (OECD). (2016). *Innovating education and ed-*
ucating for innovation: The power of digital technologies and skills. OECD Publishing. http://dx.doi.
org/10.1787/9789264265097-en

Patton, G. C., Sawyer, S. M., Santelli, J. S., Ross, D. A., Afifi, R., Allen, N. B., . . . Bonell, C. (2016).
Our future: A Lancet commission on adolescent health and well-being. *The Lancet, 387,* 2423–2478.
doi:10.1016/S0140–6736(16)00579-1

Perkins, K., Adam, W., Dubson, M., Finkelstein, N., Reid, S., Wieman, C., & Lemaster, R. (2006).
Phet: Interactive simulations for teaching and learning physics. *The Physics Teacher, 44,* 18–23.
doi:10.1119/1.2150754

Rickwood, D., Deane, F. P., Wilson, C. J., & Ciarrochi, J. (2005). Young people's help-seeking for mental health problems. *Australian E-Journal for the Advancement of Mental Health, 4,* 218–251. doi:10.5172/
jamh.4.3218

Slemp, G., Kern, P., Chin, T. C., Soukous, C., Loton, D., Oades, L., Vella-Brodrick, D. A., & Waters, L.
(2017). Positive education in Australia. In E. Frydenberg, A. Martin, & R. Collie (Eds.), *Social emotional*
learning in the Australasian context (pp. 83–99). Springer Social and Behavioural Sciences.

Smiling Mind. (2016). *Establishing an evidence base for the Smiling Mind education program.* Deakin University &
InsightSRC. Retrieved from https://www.smilingmind.com.au/education

Smiling Mind. (2020). *We make it easy for educators to improve student well-being.* Retrieved from https://www.
smilingmind.com.au/education#anchor-whole-school-approach

Twenge, J, M., Cooper, A. B., Joiner, T. E., Duffy, M. E., & S. G. Binau. (2019). Age, period, and cohort
trends in mood disorder indicators and suicide-related outcomes in a nationally representative dataset,
2005–2017. *Journal of Abnormal Psychology, 128*(3). doi:10.1037/abn0000410

Vella-Brodrick, D. A., Chin, T. C., & Rickard, N. S. (2020). Examining the effects of an exemplar school-
based well-being approach on student competency, autonomy and relatedness. *Health Promotion Interna-*
tional. doi.org/10.1093/heapro/daz115

Vella-Brodrick, D. A., Rickard, N., Hattie, J., Cross, D. & Chin, T. (2017). Enhancing adolescent mental
health through positive education. A longitudinal evaluation of Year 10 positive education: Findings
from 2014 to 2016. The University of Melbourne.

Victorian State Government. (2017). *Serious games.* Retrieved from https://www.education.vic.gov.au/
about/programs/learningdev/Pages/expired/techgames.aspx

34

USING EXPERIENCE SAMPLING METHODS TO UNDERSTAND HOW VARIOUS LIFE AND SCHOOL EXPERIENCES AFFECT STUDENT WELL-BEING

Rowan Jacques-Hamilton, Tan-Chyuan Chin and Dianne Vella-Brodrick

Introduction

Psychological well-being is a valued outcome of formal education, as demonstrated by the rising prominence of positive education in school systems across the world (see Vella-Brodrick et al., Chapter 29 of this book). Well-being is not only a valued outcome in its own right, but research indicates that it also supports the more traditional outcome of schooling, namely, academic performance (Dix et al., 2012; Suldo et al., 2011). For example, more exceptional academic performance has been observed in students higher in aspects of well-being such as hope (Marques et al., 2017), emotion regulation (Trentacosta & Izard, 2007), and life satisfaction (Gilman & Huebner, 2006). See Section II, Part C of this handbook for a more detailed discussion of how well-being supports and enhances student learning and academic performance.

Positive affect (PA) is one aspect of well-being that is particularly relevant in the educational context. Affects are subjective experiences, including feelings and emotions, which theories describe with two dimensions: (a) valence (pleasant versus unpleasant) and (b) arousal (activation versus deactivation or sleepiness; Barrett & Russell, 1999). PA includes affects that are characterized by both positive valence and high arousal, such as excitement, interest, enthusiasm, and elation (Watson & Tellegen, 1985). PA is core to many prominent conceptions of well-being such as subjective well-being (Diener et al., 1999) and PERMA (Seligman, 2018). Broaden and build theory (Fredrickson, 2004) describes how PA is highly relevant to educational contexts. This theory draws on research findings showing how positive emotions *broaden* the array of thoughts and behaviors. The consequence of this broadening is that individuals develop an urge to play and explore, which in turn *builds* physical, psychological, and social resources, ultimately improving resilience and the ability to cope with challenging situations (Fredrickson, 2004, 2013). Having increased interest and broadened thought patterns are beneficial for learning and performance (Lyubomirsky et al., 2005; Mega et al., 2014; Pekrun et al., 2002), hence the importance of PA in education.

Given the significance of well-being for learning, furthering our understanding of the factors that impact well-being of school students is imperative. Much research in positive education has to date used traditional techniques and approaches, such as delivering programs or brief interventions

DOI: 10.4324/9781003013778-42

and using self-report questionnaires before and after the intervention to ascertain if changes in the intended outcomes have occurred. There is, however, an opportunity to further understanding of student well-being by using new technologies and tools.

Experience Sampling Methodology (ESM, also known as EMA, or Ambulatory Assessment) is one such tool that was developed by Larson and Csikszentmihalyi (1983). ESM is a method that typically uses mobile devices to gather information on multiple occasions about people's experiences in daily life, including how they are feeling, what they are doing and their environmental context. Contemporary methods of data gathering using ESM involve delivering short surveys, monitoring passive phone sensor data (e.g., activity and phone usage), and continuous physiological measurement. Unlike traditional psychological questionnaires, which ask people to retrospect and summarize their experience, ESM gathers information about experiences and events as they unfold in real-time or very shortly after.

Csikszentmihalyi and colleagues (Csikszentmihalyi, 1990; Nakamura & Csikszentmihalyi, 2002) have used ESM in research examining the circumstances in which people report optimal experiences and flow and found that the best moments arise when individuals voluntarily engage in activities that extend them physically or psychologically to achieve something challenging and meaningful (Hunter & Csikszentmihalyi, 2003). ESM has been used successfully to study young people. For example, ESM was used to identify adolescents with different levels of interest in their everyday life in a study that found that there was a positive association between adolescents' interest level and well-being (Hunter & Csikszentmihalyi, 2003). Adolescents wore a wristwatch, which prompted participants to respond to questions such as their activity, location, and mood on eight occasions per day over one week. There were over 28,000 ESM responses from 806 adolescents, which provided extensive detail about their real-time experiences of school, work, play, and home time. ESM has also been used successfully in several other fields such as organizational research (Beal, 2015), physical activity research (Dunton, 2017), behavioral medicine (Smyth & Stone, 2003), and clinical psychology (Shiffman et al., 2008; Trull & Ebner-Priemer, 2013).

A significant advantage of ESM is that it can reduce the impact of biases associated with retrospective reports. For example, because retrospective reports are more distant from actual experiences, they are more likely to be distorted by recent events, semantic knowledge, and beliefs (Robinson & Clore, 2002). Therefore, data from ESM provide a type of evidence that potentially has greater ecological validity. A particularly salient point is that ESM is also well-suited to studying processes that unfold over short periods, such as emotion dynamics (Bolger & Laurenceau, 2013). However, ESM also has drawbacks, such as increased participant burden and increased complexity of data analysis. Participating in an ESM protocol may itself impact well-being, for example, by causing participants to pay more attention to their mood states (Bolger & Laurenceau, 2013). Furthermore, there are circumstances in which retrospective reports are better predictors than momentary reports for future behavior (Conner & Barrett, 2012; Redelmeier et al., 2003). For example, Wirtz et al., (2003) found that students retrospective reports of feelings during a vacation, relative to momentary reports of those feelings, better predicted whether those students intended to repeat the trip in the future. Therefore, evidence from ESM and retrospective surveys can often be seen as complementary, with both techniques gaining valuable information using different approaches, each with particular strengths and limitations.

In summary, using ESM for well-being research in schools could have a range of benefits, such as the ability to investigate research questions with increased ecological validity. ESM also could address new types of research questions that are not well suited to pen-and-paper surveys. However, there has been little uptake of ESM in positive education, so there has been a need for more studies using this technique in this field of research.

This Study

We employed ESM to investigate how different aspects of situational context can impact well-being in school students. We collected data about a large variety of social situations and environments and investigated how these situations relate to two important variables: PA and feelings of control. Feelings of control are viewed as an important precursor to well-being (Peterson, 1999) and it closely aligns with the concept of autonomy from Self-Determination Theory (Ryan & Deci, 2017), which is associated with positive academic and learning outcomes (Vansteenkiste et al., 2004). We had several specific research questions about the relationship between well-being and situational context.

First of all, we were interested in whether the degree of control students felt in their present situation was associated with their levels of PA, which would support the notion that feelings of personal control are essential for well-being (Peterson, 1999).

Secondly, we investigated how well-being was related to being in different social contexts. Adolescence is a time of significant change in social relationships (Brown, 2004; Larson et al., 2013), and it is argued that relationships are vital for healthy functioning in young people (Chu et al., 2010; Gadermann et al., 2016; Goswami, 2012). We investigated this relationship by comparing levels of PA between situations when students were with others versus when they were alone. If social relationships are indeed crucial for well-being, we expected that PA would be higher when with other people.

Furthermore, there remains some uncertainty regarding the relative importance of quality and quantity of social interactions (Lucas & Dyrenforth, 2006; Pinquart & Sörensen, 2000; Sun et al., 2019). There is substantial evidence that the *quantity* of social relationships is related to well-being (e.g., Lucas & Dyrenforth, 2006; Rohrer et al., 2018; Watson et al., 1992), whereas there is less evidence that the *quality* of those relationships is essential. A critical aspect of relationship quality is closeness. Some research indicates that having social interactions with close friends is associated with higher PA than spending time with those more distant, due to feeling greater confidence of experiencing social approval and authenticity in closer interactions (Venaglia & Lemay, 2017). However, other research appears to contradict this finding. For example, Dunn and colleagues (2007) found that people experienced just as much well-being during a short experimental task when spending time with a stranger relative to their romantic partner. Therefore, our third question asked whether students felt higher levels of PA when with closer friends compared with more distant friends and peers.

Our fourth research question asked whether students' levels of PA differed when they spent time indoors versus outdoors. We predicted that spending time outdoors would be related to higher well-being for several reasons. Exposure to nature is more likely to occur outdoors and several theories predict that nature exposure benefits well-being (Bratman et al., 2012), such as Attention Restoration Theory (Kaplan, 1995), Stress-Reduction Theory (Ulrich et al., 1991), and biophilia (Kellert & Wilson, 1993; Wilson, 1984). Furthermore when outdoors, people are more likely to be physically active and less likely to be sedentary (Cooper et al., 2010; Dumith et al., 2012; Sterdt et al., 2014), which is associated with higher levels of psychological well-being (Biddle & Asare, 2011; Costigan et al., 2013).

Finally, we explored whether different school contexts were supportive or detrimental to well-being. We focused on four main categories of school context: academic class, cocurricular activities (i.e., school-based sport, music, and performing arts), study/preparation time, and leisure time. This exploratory research question provided new insights, particularly with the use of real-time, real-world data provided by using ESM.

Method

Participants and Procedure

Participants were Year 10 students from three independent schools in Victoria, Australia. These schools were part of a more extensive study examining the effects of positive education on well-being, and data were gathered in 2016. All Year 10 students in these schools (n = 355) were invited to participate through their school, and 100 students received parental consent and signed up to the study (age range 15–16 years; 66% male). All of these students completed the study, but one student was excluded from the study due to having nonsensible ESM responses (i.e., all questions answered with a response of 7), resulting in an analyzed sample of 99 students.

All participants attended an introductory session at school, during which they were provided with necessary instructions and research iPods, which contained the ESM application "Wuzzup" (Chin et al., 2016). This app was programmed to send short surveys to students about their current levels of affect and their situational context (see Figure 34.1 for an example of how questions are displayed) four times per day for seven days. When a survey was available, a notification message was sent, after which students were asked to respond to the survey within 30 minutes, if possible. However, to minimize disruptions, students were informed that if the survey came at an inconvenient time, it could be completed at a later more appropriate time by pressing a button in the app. Eighty-two percent of all ESM reports were submitted using this option. Students were able to set the time frame during which they received the prompts, as long as two prompts were in the morning, and two were in the afternoon. Most students selected the time range of 8 am–5 pm. Surveys could be delivered before school, during school hours, or after school. On average, students completed 24.1 out of 28 ESM reports (median = 28, range = 2–28), which is a relatively high compliance rate; other studies of high school students commonly report compliance rates in the region of 70%–75% (Csikszentmihalyi & Larson, 1987; Hunter & Csikszentmihalyi, 2003). Students were compensated $30 for participating.

 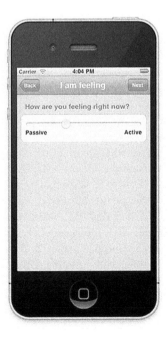

Figure 34.1   Example 7-point Sliding Scale ESM Questions, as Appears in the Wuzzup Application

Positive Affect and Control

In every momentary survey, students were asked to report on their current levels of valence and activation on a 7-point scale. This is consistent with the Circumplex model which identifies valence and arousal emotional dimensions (Russell, 1980) which have been employed by other scholars in their ESM (e.g., Rickard et al., 2016). Valence was measured on a 7-point sliding scale with anchors 1 = *Unpleasant*, and 7 = *Pleasant*. Activation was measured on a 7-point sliding scale with anchors 1 = *Passive*, and 7 = *Active*. We then created a positive affect score, which was a composite of activation and valence scores (see Figure 34.2). This score was created following the logic of (Barrett & Russell, 1999) and (Watson & Tellegen, 1985) who define high levels of PA as simultaneously containing high levels of activation and valence, and low levels of PA as containing both low valence and low activation. States that did not lie along this diagonal were not given a score for PA and were treated as missing data (marked as NA in Figure 34.2). Precisely, 27.6% of cases had missing values for PA scores. We also created a binary score for PA, whereby affective states with scores of 5 or higher on valence and 5 or higher on activation were coded as 1 (PA), and any other affective state was coded as 0 (not PA). This alternative scoring yielded qualitatively similar results and is not displayed. Levels of personal control were also reported on a 7-point sliding scale, ranging from 1 = *Helpless* to 7 = *In control*. Descriptive statistics for affect and control outcome variables are shown in Table 34.1.

The grid in Figure 34.2 shows different possible combinations of scores on valence and activation that could be provided in any given ESM survey. Numbers within the grid show how those valence and activation values are combined into a PA score. PA scores range from −3 to +3. ESM surveys with both higher valence and higher activation were given higher scores for PA, and surveys with lower valence combined with lower activation were given lower scores for PA. ESM reports in the neutral range of both the valence and the activation scales were also given a neutral PA score of 0.

Situational Context

Two multiple-choice questions were used to measure the situational context; "who are you with?" (social context) and "where are you?" (environment). Students were instructed to select the response option that best described their current situation. Lists of all possible response options and response frequencies are shown for the social context in Table 34.2, and the environment in Table 34.3.

Table 34.1 Descriptive Statistics for Affect and Personal Control Variables

Variable	Mean	SD (between-person)	SD (within-person)	n
Valence	5.13	0.80	1.24	2,389
Activation	4.07	0.98	1.56	2,389
Positive affect	4.55	0.74	1.13	1,730
Control	5.20	0.93	1.17	2,389

Note: Mean is calculated by taking a mean score for every individual and then taking the mean of these aggregates. SD (between-person) is calculated by averaging scores across every individual and then taking the standard deviation of these aggregates. SD within-person calculates a standard deviation for each individual and then taking the mean of these standard deviations. *n* is smaller for PA due to the missing values that are created when computing this composite score

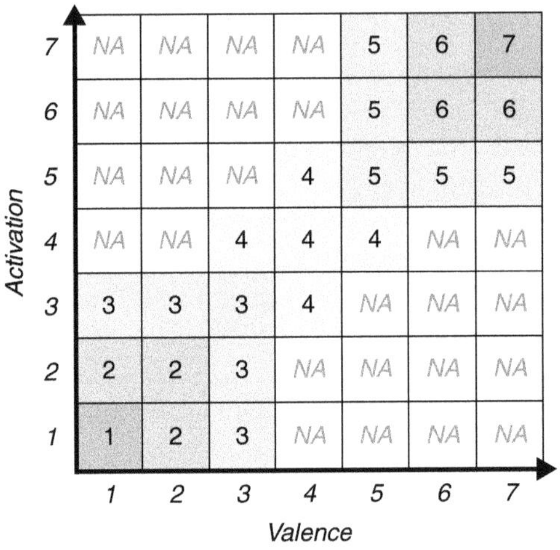

Figure 34.2 Coding for the Composite Positive Affect (PA) Score Used in this Study. Squares Marked NA (not available) Represent States That Are Orthogonal to a PA Score, and Are Treated as Missing Data. Figures Should Use Grey Tones

Table 34.2 Frequency with Which Students Reported Being in Different Social Contexts

Social Context	n ESM Reports (%)	n *Students Reporting This Context at Least Once (%)*	Mean *PA in This Context [95% CI]*	Mean *Control in This Context [95% CI]*
Alone	968 (40.5%)	95 (96.0%)	4.59 [4.42, 4.75]	5.16 [4.97, 5.35]
With others (all combined)	1421 (59.5%)	96 (97.0%)	4.78 [4.63, 4.94]	5.28 [5.10, 5.46]
Best friend(s)	51 (2.1%)	28 (28.3%)	4.81 [4.45, 5.16]	5.41 [5.03, 5.78]
Romantic friend	7 (0.3%)	6 (6.1%)	5.07 [4.57, 5.58]	5.21 [4.57, 5.85]
Peer(s)/classmate(s)	13 (0.5%)	11 (11.1%)	4.26 [3.17, 5.36]	5.29 [4.31, 6.27]
Other friend(s)	33 (1.4%)	24 (24.2%)	4.30 [3.66, 4.94]	4.57 [3.98, 5.17]
Sibling(s)	48 (2.0%)	24 (24.2%)	4.76 [4.09, 5.43]	5.11 [4.53, 5.69]
Parent(s)	331 (13.9%)	79 (79.8%)	4.84 [4.64, 5.04]	5.39 [5.18, 5.60]
Teacher(s)	322 (13.5%)	79 (79.8%)	4.89 [4.68, 5.10]	5.21 [4.99, 5.43]
Coach/tutor	366 (15.3%)	80 (80.8%)	4.81 [4.61, 5.01]	5.35 [5.13, 5.57]
Other family	77 (3.2%)	35 (35.4%)	4.66 [4.39, 4.92]	5.34 [5.06, 5.62]
Someone else	173 (7.2%)	50 (50.5%)	4.57 [4.34, 4.80]	5.23 [5.00, 5.47]

Statistical Analyses

Due to the nested structure of the data, with longitudinal observations nested within participants, we used multilevel models to analyze these data. The *lme4* (Bates et al., 2015), *lmerTest* (Kuznetsova et al., 2017), and *emmeans* (Length, 2019) packages in R were used to fit multilevel models, calculate estimated group means, and to run post hoc comparisons with Tukey *p*-value adjustments. We tested if gender was an important predictor in each of these models by first including gender as a covariate, and then subsequently including an interaction between gender and situational context. There were no significant main effects of gender nor interaction effects of gender by the situational context in any model, so gender was not included in these statistical models.

Table 34.3 Frequency with Which Students Reported Being in Different Environments

Environment	n ESM Reports (%)	n *Students Reporting This Context at Least Once during (%)*	Mean *PA in This Context [95% CI]*	Mean *Control in This Context [95% CI]*
At home	682 (28.5%)	79 (79.8%)	4.51 [4.33, 4.68]	5.20 [5.01, 5.40]
Indoors	188 (7.9%)	58 (58.6%)	4.66 [4.41, 4.92]	5.27 [5.01, 5.52]
Outdoors	147 (6.2%)	58 (58.6%)	5.29 [5.04, 5.55]	5.46 [5.19, 5.73]
School—academic class	122 (5.1%)	54 (54.5%)	5.15 [4.87, 5.43]	5.27 [4.98, 5.56]
School—prep/homework	469 (19.6%)	87 (87.9%)	4.57 [4.37, 4.76]	5.20 [4.99, 5.40]
School—cocurricular activity	138 (5.8%)	61 (61.6%)	4.53 [4.25, 4.81]	5.02 [4.74, 5.29]
School—leisure time	474 (19.8%)	81 (81.8%)	4.84 [4.65, 5.03]	5.28 [5.08, 5.50]
Traveling	169 (7.1%)	60 (60.6%)	4.67 [4.42, 4.91]	5.18 [4.92, 5.44]

Results and Discussion

Are Feelings of Control Related to Positive Affect?

We explored several research questions using ESM in this sample of high school students. First, we investigated whether feelings of control were associated with PA. To test this, we used a random-slope multilevel model with PA as the response variable and control as the predictor variable, clustered by individual to account for multiple measurements from each participant. Control was person-centered following recommendations for centering when investigating within-person processes (Bolger & Laurenceau, 2013). Modeling results showed a significant and strong relationship between PA and control, $b_{control}$ = 0.59, SE = 0.03, df = 71.69, t = 18.13, $p < 0.001$; that is, when students reported higher levels of control on ESM surveys, they also tended to report higher levels of PA. This finding aligns with theoretical predictions that feelings of personal control (Peterson, 1999) and autonomy (Ryan & Deci, 2017) are important precursors for well-being. However, given that our analyses are correlational, we cannot rule out other causal explanations for this relationship, for example, that feeling higher levels of PA cause people to experience greater perceived control.

Is Spending Time with Others Associated with Levels of Positive Affect?

To investigate whether spending time with others was associated with higher levels of PA relative to spending time alone, we created two multilevel models. Social context (alone or with others) was modeled as the predictor variable in both models, and either PA or control were the response variable, with random intercepts to account for repeated observations from each participant. Response variables were standardized to yield regression coefficients (β) that provide a more interpretable indicator of effect size (analogous to Cohen's *d*). We found that when students reported being with others, relative to being alone, they tended to report significantly higher levels of PA, β = 0.14, SE = 0.05, df = 1720.7, t = 3.09, p = 0.002, and significantly higher levels of control, $\beta = 0.08$, $SE = 0.04$, $df = 2362.5$, $t = 2.11$, $p = 0.035$ (Figure 34.3). Therefore, these findings support the notion that social relationships are generally important for well-being in adolescents.

To investigate whether closer relationships were more beneficial for well-being, we compared students' levels of PA when they spent time with closer friends versus more distant peers. We used the same modeling approach as for the previous question, but included a type of friend (romantic friend, best friend, other friend[s], or peer[s]/classmate[s]) as the predictor variable, instead of "alone" versus "with someone." Furthermore, due to heterogeneity of variance among levels of friend type, we included parameters in the model to account for unequal variances using the nlme package in R (Pinheiro et al., 2019), following Pinheiro and Bates (2000). Specific comparisons between groups were drawn using post hoc comparisons with a Tukey p-value adjustment (see Table 34.3). As shown in Figure 34.4 and Table 34.4, we found that mean levels of PA were generally higher in socially close relationships (i.e., with romantic friends and best friends), compared to more distant friends (other friends and peers/classmates). This finding aligns with the idea that interactions with closer social partners are more beneficial to well-being. However, interpret these differences with caution because they were not statistically significant. It is emphasized that students infrequently reported being with friends and peers; students reported being in one of these contexts in only 4.3% of all ESM reports. Consequently, there was a small sample size for this comparison, making it difficult to draw conclusions from these data.

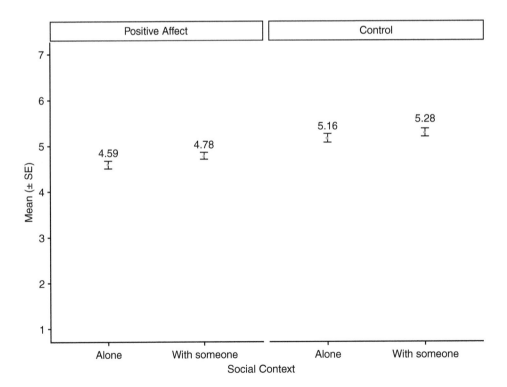

Figure 34.3 Mean Levels of Positive Affect and Control Reported by Students When with Others or When Alone

Note: Points represent mean values as estimated by the statistical model, and error bars show ± standard error.

Table 34.4 Pairwise Comparisons for Levels of PA and Control Reported by Students When Spending Time with Different Types of Friends

Comparison	β	SE	df	t	p
Positive affect					
Best friend(s)—Romantic friend	−0.19	0.27	31	−0.70	0.895
Best friend(s)—Other friend(s)	0.31	0.29	31	1.07	0.710
Best friend(s)—Peer(s)/classmate(s)	0.39	0.38	31	1.05	0.724
Romantic friend—Other friend(s)	0.50	0.35	31	1.45	0.479
Romantic friend—Peer(s)/classmate(s)	0.59	0.41	31	1.42	0.498
Other friend(s)—Peer(s)/classmate(s)	0.08	0.43	31	0.19	0.997
Control					
Best friend(s)—Romantic friend	0.17	0.26	45	0.65	0.915
Best friend(s)—Other friend(s)	0.53	0.24	45	2.19	0.142
Best friend(s)—Peer(s)/classmate(s)	0.10	0.32	45	0.31	0.990
Romantic friend—Other friend(s)	0.36	0.32	45	1.15	0.663
Romantic friend—Peer(s)/classmate(s)	−0.07	0.37	45	−0.20	0.997
Other friend(s)—Peer(s)/classmate(s)	−0.44	0.36	45	−1.21	0.626

Note: β = regression coefficient with response variable standardized, representing the difference in PA or control between a pair of situations (analogous to Cohen's *d*). *SE* = standard error. *p* = *p* value with Tukey adjustment applied mean values as estimated by the statistical model, and error bars show ± standard error.

Are There Differences in Well-Being When in Different Environments?

Indoors or Outdoors

We examined whether students reported higher levels of well-being and control outdoors compared to indoors. The mean levels of PA and control estimated in each environment are shown in Figure 34.5. Again, we used multilevel models to test for differences between these two contexts, this time using environmental context (outdoors or indoors) as the predictor variable, and again standardizing the dependent variables PA and control, and clustering by individual. Overall, we found that students tended to report higher levels of PA when outdoors compared to indoors, $\beta = 0.42$, $SE = 0.13$, $df = 242.1$, $t = 3.32$, $p = 0.001$, but there were no differences in feelings of control, $\beta = 0.14$, $SE = 0.10$, $df = 329.7$, $t = 1.32$, $p = 0.189$. Students reported statistically significantly higher levels of PA when outdoors compared to any other environment except academic class (statistical output not shown). This finding supports the idea that spending more time outdoors is beneficial to well-being. It also is consistent with the theoretical perspective that increased exposure to nature (Bratman et al., 2012), increased physical activity, and reduced sedentary activity (Biddle & Asare, 2011; Costigan et al., 2013) benefit well-being.

However, this conclusion has some limitations. We do not have detailed information about the specific outdoors and indoor environments that students reported being in when they made their responses, so it is not possible to conclude which processes account for the observation of higher well-being in outdoors environments. The "outdoors" selection likely represents a variety of different contexts, which makes the results the consequence of several blended causal processes. For example, students could have reported being outdoors if they were sitting down in a nature reserve, or if they were playing basketball on a concrete court with little visible nature, and each environment could impact well-being in quite different ways. Furthermore, there might be biases

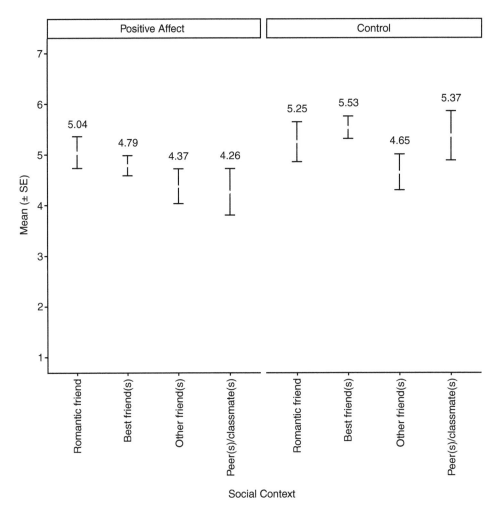

Figure 34.4 Levels of Positive Affect and Control Reported by Students When with Different Types of Friends

Note: Points represent mean values as estimated by the statistical model, and error bars show ± standard error.

in these responses such as missing prompts due to being physically active and not responding within the 30-minute timeframe. Further research would need to specifically target assessments of indoor and outdoor environments in more depth, rather than assessing a broad array of situations with less depth to overcome such limitations

Different School Contexts

We examined how much PA and control students experienced in several different school contexts, including in-class, cocurricular activities, homework/preparation time, or leisure time (Figure 34.4). We used the same multilevel modeling approach, as has been described previously, using post hoc comparisons. We found that there were statistically significant differences among these school contexts in PA but not feelings of control (Table 34.5).

Specifically, students tended to have higher levels of PA in academic class than in cocurricular activities or in homework/preparation time. The finding that cocurricular activities elicited less

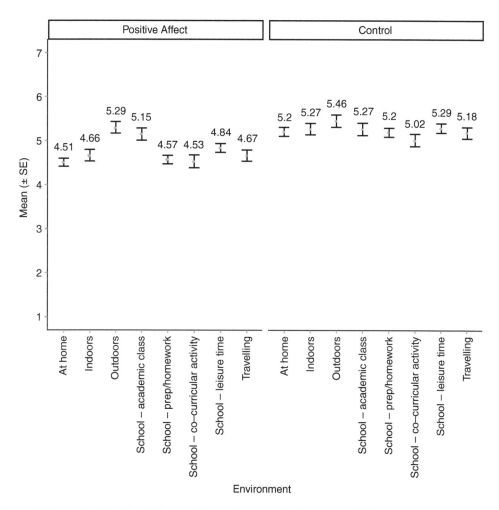

Figure 34.5 Levels of Positive Affect and Control Reported by Students in Different Environments
Note: Points represent mean values as estimated by the statistical model, and error bars show ± standard error.

PA than did academic classes was unexpected, particularly if students could select cocurricular activities and undertake them when desired. However, cocurricular activities are compulsory in the schools participating in this study, with sports training often occurring before or after school and competition occurring on the weekend. Choice in the activities to be undertaken may also be limited and may not always align with the students' preferences. A further finding was that students also tended to report higher levels of PA during their leisure time than in homework/preparation time. This finding is not surprising given that there is more freedom to exercise volition and engage in activities that are of personal interest during leisure time than during homework time.

Practical Implications

Our results show that feeling a sense of control is associated with higher levels of well-being, suggesting that learning practices enabling students to feel a sense of control and autonomy, may facilitate well-being and learning. This aligns well with other findings showing that autonomy is central to aspects of student well-being such as student engagement (Hafen et al., 2012). The

Table 34.5 Pairwise Comparisons for Levels of PA and Control Reported by Students in Different School Environments

Comparison	β	SE	df	t	p
Positive affect					
Academic class—Prep/homework	**0.42**	**0.11**	**850**	**3.97**	**0.001**
Academic class—Cocurricular activity	**0.43**	**0.13**	**837**	**3.29**	**0.006**
Academic class—Leisure time	0.21	0.11	846	2.00	0.191
Prep/homework—Cocurricular activity	0.01	0.11	837	0.09	1.000
Prep/homework—Leisure time	**−0.21**	**0.07**	**855**	**−2.89**	**0.020**
Cocurricular activity—Leisure time	−0.22	0.10	826	−2.10	0.153
Control					
Academic class—Prep/homework	0.03	0.09	1178	0.32	0.989
Academic class—Cocurricular activity	0.13	0.11	1158	1.16	0.651
Academic class—Leisure time	−0.04	0.09	1175	−0.48	0.964
Prep/homework—Cocurricular activity	0.10	0.09	1163	1.13	0.670
Prep/homework—Leisure time	−0.07	0.06	1187	−1.19	0.632
Cocurricular activity—Leisure time	−0.17	0.09	1151	−2.02	0.182

Note: β = regression coefficient with response variable standardized, representing the difference in PA or control between a pair of situations (analogous to Cohen's *d*). *SE* = standard error. *p* = *p* value with Tukey adjustment applied. Significant effects are given in bold.

principles of Self-Determination Theory suggest that to best foster student motivation and engagement, choices should be relevant and meaningful to the student, enhance feelings of competence, and provide the right amount of choice, not too much or too little (Evans & Boucher, 2015).

Our results also suggest that being outdoors is related to higher levels of student well-being, suggesting that schools could enhance well-being by increasing outdoor time into students' lives, especially exposure to nature. This link between nature and well-being is also prominent in research that suggests benefits to well-being of increasing access to green space for children at schools (e.g., McCormick, 2017), such as spending time in outdoor classrooms and learning environments (e.g., Largo-Wight et al., 2018; Mirrahmi et al., 2011) and having gardens at school (Dyg & Wistoft, 2018). These approaches to increase exposure to nature are a philosophy underlying Forest and Nature Schools (Cumming & Nash, 2015; O'Brien, 2009).

Finally, our findings show that students enjoyed academic class, reflected by their reports of high levels of PA in this context. We speculate that this may be due to the use of pedagogical techniques that engage students in interactive learning and colearning (e.g., flipped classrooms). For example, Shernoff and Csikszentmihalyi (2009) found that student engagement is best when students perceive their learning environment as challenging, cooperative, and interactive. Findings of high levels of PA during leisure time also suggest that it is important to protect time for leisure.

Limitations and Future Research

An important limitation of this research is that the sample consisted of students from three independent schools in Australia. Therefore, it is uncertain to what degree these results may apply to public schools or different cultural contexts. For example, levels of academic engagement may differ in independent schools, so the relatively high levels of PA we observed in academic classes may not translate to public schools. This positive finding differs from the work by Csikszentmihalyi and Larson, (1984) and Larson and Kleiber (1993) which found that students in high school report low levels of student engagement when in class and high levels of engagement when they are participating in organized activities outside of school. Youth report more positive states when they are involved in voluntary structured activities that provide challenge and foster involvement and feelings of control and competence especially in contrast to being in a classroom where they are passive learners (Larson, 2000; Shernoff & Csikszentmihalyi, 2009).

Our findings warrant deeper investigations into the experiences and effects of indoor and outdoor experiences, or social experiences, on adolescents' well-being. ESM studies could be complemented by focus groups or interviews to understand findings in more detail and from the perspectives of the students.

Young people are digital natives who are familiar with technology, and they are likely to engage in research using this type of technology as long as they are not overburdened. It is challenging to know the ideal number of times to prompt young people during a day, and a trade-off exists between the amount of data collected from each student and their compliance with the study protocol. Prior consultation with young people and school staff about this before launching a research project is beneficial to ensure what we are asking of them is feasible, especially in the school context where there might be restrictions about accessing mobile devices and responding during class times. There is often also a trade-off between collecting more data from fewer individuals, versus gaining less data from a greater number of individuals. Researchers should consider this trade-off in the context of their research question, considering factors such as the frequency of the experiences of interest, and whether they are primarily interested in within-person processes, or between-person processes.

Future research should consider using newer mobile assessment techniques such as passive phone sensors and physiological monitoring. These devices provide an array of data that can investigate relevant experiences that impact well-being, such as sleep, activity levels, and physiological stress, often with minimal effort on the part of the individual. Researchers should also consider the implementation of reactive mobile interventions, or "just-in-time" interventions, which are enabled by this technology. These protocols trigger interventions on peoples' devices in real-time, based on their current experience or situation. For example, prompts with intervention materials can be delivered to people after long periods of inactivity, after specific responses to survey questions (e.g., after reporting low well-being), when in certain physical locations using GPS technology (e.g., extended periods at home in isolation), or when physiological stress indicators increase beyond some critical threshold. These interventions can also be combined with machine learning algorithms to tailor the delivery to each user (*Just-in-time adaptive interventions*; Nahum-Shani et al., 2018). These innovations can enhance lifestyle and physiological awareness, complement evaluations of well-being educational programs, or enhance student experiences within well-being education programs.

ESM also has the potential to increase the benefits reaped for research participants by providing them with feedback. For example, Bakker and Rickard (2018) provide participants with a portal allowing participants to track their mood over time. The app delivers both ESM surveys and longer retrospective surveys according to a researcher-specified timeline. It breaks up longer surveys into shorter modules that participants can complete at their convenience. This increased reward and flexibility in data collection shows promise for improving engagement with the research.

With the development and use of smart methods to collect real-time, real-world data, alongside personalized options that concurrently benefit research participants, well-being awareness can be heightened, and positive behaviors encouraged. This transfer of knowledge into relevant contexts is critical for improved well-being outcomes and is often the ultimate incentive for conducting applied research. Hence, researchers are encouraged to consider how they can use new technologies with valuable methods such as ESM, to optimize participant engagement and improve the quality of data collected. Well-being research with young people is highly suited to these opportunities.

References

Bakker, D., & Rickard, N. (2018). Engagement in mobile phone app for self-monitoring of emotional well-being predicts changes in mental health: MoodPrism. *Journal of Affective Disorders, 227*, 432–442. https://doi.org/10.1016/j.jad.2017.11.016

Barrett, L. F., & Russell, J. A. (1999). The structure of current affect: Controversies and emerging consensus. *Current Directions in Psychological Science, 8*(1), 10–14. https://doi.org/10.1111/1467-8721.00003

Bates, D., Maechler, M., Bolker, B., & Walker, S. (2015). Fitting linear mixed-effects models using lme4. *Journal of Statistical Software, 67*(1), 1–48. https://doi.org/10.18637/jss.v067.i01

Beal, D. J. (2015). ESM 2.0: State of the art and future potential of experience sampling methods in organizational research. *Annual Review of Organizational Psychology and Organizational Behavior, 2*(1), 383–407. https://doi.org/10.1146/annurev-orgpsych-032414-111335

Biddle, S. J. H., & Asare, M. (2011). Physical activity and mental health in children and adolescents: A review of reviews. *British Journal of Sports Medicine, 45*(11), 886–895. https://doi.org/10.1136/bjsports-2011-090185

Bolger, N., & Laurenceau, J.-P. (2013). *Intensive longitudinal methods: An introduction to diary and experience sampling research*. Guilford.

Bratman, G. N., Hamilton, J. P., & Daily, G. C. (2012). The impacts of nature experience on human cognitive function and mental health. *Annals of the New York Academy of Sciences, 1249*(1), 118–136. https://doi.org/10.1111/j.1749-6632.2011.06400.x

Brown, B. B. (2004). Adolescents' relationships with peers. In R. M. Lerner & L. Steinberg (Eds.), *Handbook of adolescent psychology* (2nd ed., pp. 363–394). Wiley. https://doi.org/10.1002/9780471726746

Chin, T. C., Rickard, N. S., & Vella-Brodrick, D. A. (2016). Development and feasibility of a mobile experience sampling application for tracking program implementation in youth well-being programs. *Psychology of Well-Being, 6*(1). https://doi.org/10.1186/s13612-016-0038-2

Chu, P. S., Saucier, D. A., & Hafner, E. (2010). Meta-analysis of the relationships between social support and well-being in children and adolescents. *Journal of Social and Clinical Psychology, 29*(6), 624–645. https://doi.org/10.1521/jscp.2010.29.6.624

Conner, T. S., & Barrett, L. F. (2012). Trends in ambulatory self-report: The role of momentary experience in psychosomatic medicine. *Psychosomatic Medicine, 74*(4), 327–337. https://doi.org/10.1097/PSY.0b013e3182546f18

Cooper, A. R., Page, A. S., Wheeler, B. W., Hillsdon, M., Griew, P., & Jago, R. (2010). Patterns of GPS measured time outdoors after school and objective physical activity in English children: The PEACH project. *International Journal of Behavioral Nutrition and Physical Activity, 7*, 1–9. https://doi.org/10.1186/1479-5868-7-31

Costigan, S. A., Barnett, L., Plotnikoff, R. C., & Lubans, D. R. (2013). The health indicators associated with screen-based sedentary behavior among adolescent girls: A systematic review. *Journal of Adolescent Health, 52*(4), 382–392. https://doi.org/10.1016/j.jadohealth.2012.07.018

Csikszentmihalyi, M. (1990). *Flow: The psychology of optimal experience*. Harper and Row.

Csikszentmihalyi, M., & Larson, R. (1984). *Being adolescent: Conflict and growth in the teenage years*. Basic Books.

Csikszentmihalyi, M., & Larson, R. (1987). Validity and reliability of the experience-sampling method. *Journal of Nervous and Mental Disease, 175*(9), 526–536. https://doi.org/10.1097/00005053-198709000-00004

Cumming, F., & Nash, M. (2015). An Australian perspective of a forest school: Shaping a sense of place to support learning. *Journal of Adventure Education and Outdoor Learning, 15*(4), 296–309. https://doi.org/10.1080/14729679.2015.1010071

Diener, E., Suh, E. M., Lucas, R. E., & Smith, H. L. (1999). Subjective well-being: Three decades of progress. *Psychological Bulletin, 125*(2), 276–302. https://doi.org/10.1037/0033-2909.125.2.276

Dix, K. L., Slee, P. T., Lawson, M. J., & Keeves, J. P. (2012). Implementation quality of whole-school mental health promotion and students' academic performance. *Child and Adolescent Mental Health, 17*(1), 45–51. https://doi.org/10.1111/j.1475-3588.2011.00608.x

Dumith, S. C., Gigante, D. P., Domingues, M. R., Hallal, P. C., Menezes, A. M. B., & Kohl, H. W. (2012). Predictors of physical activity change during adolescence: A 3.5-year follow-up. *Public Health Nutrition, 15*(12), 2237–2245. https://doi.org/10.1017/S1368980012000948

Dunn, E. W., Biesanz, J. C., Human, L. J., & Finn, S. (2007). Misunderstanding the affective consequences of everyday social interactions: The hidden benefits of putting one's best face forward. *Journal of Personality and Social Psychology, 92*(6), 990–1005. https://doi.org/10.1037/0022-3514.92.6.990

Dunton, G. F. (2017). Ecological momentary assessment in physical activity research. *Exercise and Sport Sciences Reviews, 45*(1), 48–54. https://doi.org/10.1249/JES.0000000000000092

Dyg, P. M., & Wistoft, K. (2018). Wellbeing in school gardens–The case of the Gardens for Bellies food and environmental education program. *Environmental Education Research, 24*(8), 1177–1191. https://doi.org/10.1080/13504622.2018.1434869

Evans, M., & Boucher, A. R. (2015). Optimizing the power of choice: Supporting student autonomy to foster motivation and engagement in learning. *Mind, Brain, and Education, 9*(2), 87–91. https://doi.org/10.1111/mbe.12073

Fredrickson, B. L. (2004). The broaden-and-build theory of positive emotions. *Philosophical Transactions of the Royal Society B: Biological Sciences, 359*(1449), 1367–1377. https://doi.org/10.1098/rstb.2004.1512

Fredrickson, B. L. (2013). Positive emotions broaden and build. *Advances in Experimental Social Psychology, 47*, 1–53. https://doi.org/10.1016/B978-0-12-407236-7.00001-2

Gadermann, A. M., Guhn, M., Schonert-Reichl, K. A., Hymel, S., Thomson, K., & Hertzman, C. (2016). A population-based study of children's well-being and health: The relative importance of social relationships, health-related activities, and income. *Journal of Happiness Studies, 17*(5), 1847–1872. https://doi.org/10.1007/s10902-015-9673-1

Gilman, R., & Huebner, E. S. (2006). Characteristics of adolescents who report very high life satisfaction. *Journal of Youth and Adolescence, 35*(3), 293–301. https://doi.org/10.1007/s10964-006-9036-7

Goswami, H. (2012). Social relationships and children's subjective well-being. *Social Indicators Research, 107*(3), 575–588. https://doi.org/10.1007/s11205-011-9864-z

Hafen, C. A., Allen, J. P., Mikami, A. Y., Gregory, A., Hamre, B., & Pianta, R. C. (2012). The pivotal role of adolescent autonomy in secondary school classrooms. *Journal of Youth and Adolescence, 41*(3), 245–255. https://doi.org/10.1007/s10964-011-9739-2

Hunter, J. P., & Csikszentmihalyi, M. (2003). The positive psychology of interested adolescents. *Journal of Youth and Adolescence, 32*(1), 27–35. https://doi.org/10.1023/A:1021028306392

Kaplan, S. (1995). The restorative benefits of nature. *Journal of Environmental Psychology, 15*, 169–182. https://doi.org/10.1016/0272-4944(95)90001-2

Kellert, R. K., & Wilson, E. O. (1993). *The biophilia hypothesis*. Island Press. https://doi.org/https://doi.org/10.1177/027046769501500125

Kuznetsova, A., Brockhoff, P. B., & Christensen, R. H. B. (2017). lmerTest package: Tests in linear mixed effects models. *Journal of Statistical Software, 82*(13). https://doi.org/10.18637/jss.v082.i13

Largo-Wight, E., Guardino, C., Wludyka, P. S., Hall, K. W., Wight, J. T., & Merten, J. W. (2018). Nature contact at school: The impact of an outdoor classroom on children's well-being. *International Journal of Environmental Health Research, 28*(6), 653–666. https://doi.org/10.1080/09603123.2018.1502415

Larson, R. W. (2000). Toward a psychology of positive youth development. *American Psychologist, 55*, 170–183.

Larson, R. W., & Kleiber, D. (1993). Daily experiences of adolescents. In P. H. Tolan & B. J. Cohler (Eds.), *Handbook of clinical research and practice with adolescents* (pp. 125–145). John Wiley & Sons.

Larson, R., & Csikszentmihalyi, M. (1983). The experience sampling method. *New Directions for Methodology of Social and Behavioral Sciences, 15*, 41–56. https://doi.org/10.1007/978-94-017-9088-8

Larson, R., Moneta, G., Richards, M. H., & Holmbeck, G. (2013). Changes in adolescents' daily interactions with their families from ages 10 to 18: Disengagement and transformation. *Adolescents and Their Families: Structure, Function, and Parent-Youth Relations, 32*(4), 118–128. https://doi.org/10.1037//0012-1649.32.4.744

Length, R. (2019). emmeans: Estimated Marginal Means, aka Least-Squares Means. R package version 1.4.3.01. Retrieved from https://CRAN.R-project.org/package=emmeans

Lucas, R. E., & Dyrenforth, P. S. (2006). Does the existence of social relationships matter for subjective well-being? In K. D. Vohs & E. J. Finkel (Eds.), *Self and relationships: Connecting intrapersonal and interpersonal processes* (pp. 254–273). Guilford.

Lyubomirsky, S., King, L., & Diener, E. (2005). The benefits of frequent positive affect: Does happiness lead to success? *Psychological Bulletin, 131*(6), 803–855. https://doi.org/10.1037/0033-2909.131.6.803

Marques, S. C., Gallagher, M. W., & Lopez, S. J. (2017). Hope- and academic-related outcomes: A meta-analysis. *School Mental Health, 9*(3), 250–262. https://doi.org/10.1007/s12310-017-9212-9

McCormick, R. (2017). Does access to green space impact the mental well-being of children: A systematic review. *Journal of Pediatric Nursing, 37*, 3–7. https://doi.org/10.1016/j.pedn.2017.08.027

Mega, C., Ronconi, L., & De Beni, R. (2014). What makes a good student? How emotions, self-regulated learning, and motivation contribute to academic Achievement. *Journal of Educational Psychology, 106*(1), 121–131. https://doi.org/10.1037/a0033546

Mirrahmi, S. Z., Tawil, N. M., Abdullah, N. A. G., Surat, M., & Usman, I. M. S. (2011). Developing conducive sustainable outdoor learning: The impact of natural environment on learning, social and emotional intelligence. *Procedia Engineering, 20*, 389–396. https://doi.org/10.1016/j.proeng.2011.11.181

Nahum-Shani, I., Smith, S. N., Spring, B. J., Collins, L. M., Witkiewitz, K., Tewari, A., & Murphy, S. A. (2018). Just-in-time adaptive interventions (JITAIs) in mobile health: Key components and design principles for ongoing health behavior support. *Annals of Behavioral Medicine, 52*(6), 446–462. https://doi.org/10.1007/s12160-016-9830-8

Nakamura, J., & Csikszentmihalyi, M. (2002). The concept of flow. In C. R. Snyder & J. Lopez (Eds.), *Handbook of positive psychology* (pp. 89–105). Oxford University Press.

O'Brien, L. (2009). Learning outdoors: The forest school approach. *Education 3–13, 37*(1), 45–60. https://doi.org/10.1080/03004270802291798

Pekrun, R., Goetz, T., Titz, W., & Perry, R. P. (2002). Academic emotions in students' self-regulated learning and achievement: A program of qualitative and quantitative research. *Educational Psychologist, 37*(2), 91–105. https://doi.org/10.1207/S15326985EP3702_4

Peterson, C. (1999). Personal control and well-being. In D. Kahneman, E. Diener, & N. Schwarz (Eds.), *Well-being: Foundations of hedonic psychology* (pp. 288–301). Russell Sage Foundation.

Pinheiro, J., & Bates, D. (2000). *Mixed-effects models in S and S-Plus.* Springer.

Pinheiro, J., Bates, D., DebRoy, S., Sarkar, D., & Team, R. C. (2019). *nlme: Linear and nonlinear mixed effects models. R package version 3.1–140.* Retrieved from https://CRAN.R-project.org/package=nlme

Pinquart, M., & Sörensen, S. (2000). Influences of socioeconomic status, social network, and competence on subjective well-being in later life: A meta-analysis. *Psychology and Aging, 15*(2), 187–224. https://doi.org/10.1037/0882-7974.15.2.187

Redelmeier, D. A., Katz, J., & Kahneman, D. (2003). Memories of colonoscopy: A randomized trial. *Pain, 104*(1–2), 187–194. https://doi.org/10.1016/S0304-3959(03)00003-4

Rickard, N., Arjmand, H. A., Bakker, D., & Seabrook, E. (2016). Development of a mobile phone app to support self-monitoring of emotional well-being: A mental health digital innovation. *JMIR Mental Health, 3*(4), e49. https://doi.org/10.2196/mental.6202

Robinson, M. D., & Clore, G. L. (2002). Episodic and semantic knowledge in emotional self-report: Evidence for two judgment processes. *Journal of Personality and Social Psychology, 83*(1), 198–215. https://doi.org/10.1037/0022-3514.83.1.198

Rohrer, J. M., Richter, D., Brümmer, M., Wagner, G. G., & Schmukle, S. C. (2018). Successfully striving for happiness: Socially engaged pursuits predict increases in life satisfaction. *Psychological Science, 29*(8), 1291–1298. https://doi.org/10.1177/0956797618761660

Russell, J. (1980). A circumplex model of affect. *Journal of Personality and Social Psychology, 39*(6), 1161–1178. doi:10.1037/h0077714.

Ryan, R. M., & Deci, E. L. (2017). *Self-determination theory: Basic psychological needs in motivation, development, and wellness.* Guilford.

Seligman, M. E. P. (2018). PERMA and the building blocks of well-being. *Journal of Positive Psychology, 13*(4), 333–335. https://doi.org/10.1080/17439760.2018.1437466

Shernoff, D. J., & Csikszentmihalyi, M. (2009). Flow in schools: Cultivating engaged learners and optimal learning environments. In R. Gilman, E. S. Huebner, & M. J. Furlong (Eds.). *Handbook of positive psychology in schools* (pp. 131–146). Routledge.

Shiffman, S., Stone, A. A., & Hufford, M. R. (2008). Ecological momentary assessment. *Annual Review of Clinical Psychology, 4*(1), 1–32. https://doi.org/10.1146/annurev.clinpsy.3.022806.091415

Smyth, J., & Stone, A. A. (2003). Ecological momentary assessment research in behavioral medicine. *Journal of Happiness Studies, 4*, 35–52. https://doi.org/10.1023/A:1023657221954

Sterdt, E., Liersch, S., & Walter, U. (2014). Correlates of physical activity of children and adolescents: A systematic review of reviews. *Health Education Journal, 73*(1), 72–89. https://doi.org/10.1177/0017896912469578

Suldo, S., Thalji, A., & Ferron, J. (2011). Longitudinal academic outcomes predicted by early adolescents' subjective well-being, psychopathology, and mental health status yielded from a dual factor model. *Journal of Positive Psychology, 6*(1), 17–30. https://doi.org/10.1080/17439760.2010.536774

Sun, J., Harris, K., & Vazire, S. (2019). Is well-being associated with the quantity and quality of social interactions? *Journal of Personality and Social Psychology.* Advance online publication. https://doi.org/10.1037/pspp0000272

Trentacosta, C. J., & Izard, C. E. (2007). Kindergarten children's emotion competence as a predictor of their academic competence in first grade. *Emotion, 7*(1), 77–88. https://doi.org/10.1037/1528-3542.7.1.77

Trull, T. J., & Ebner-Priemer, U. (2013). Ambulatory assessment. *Annual Review of Clinical Psychology, 9*(1), 151–176. https://doi.org/10.1146/annurev-clinpsy-050212-185510

Ulrich, R. S., Simons, R. F., Losito, B. D., Fiorito, E., Miles, M. A., & Zelson, M. (1991). Stress recovery during exposure to natural and urban environments. *Journal of Environmental Psychology, 11*(3), 201–230. https://doi.org/10.1016/S0272-4944(05)80184-7

Vansteenkiste, M., Simons, J., Lens, W., Sheldon, K. M., & Deci, E. L. (2004). Motivating learning, performance, and persistence: The synergistic effects of intrinsic goal contents and autonomy-supportive contexts. *Journal of Personality and Social Psychology, 87*(2), 246–260. https://doi.org/10.1037/0022-3514.87.2.246

Venaglia, R. B., & Lemay, E. P. (2017). Hedonic benefits of close and distant interaction partners: The mediating roles of social approval and authenticity. *Personality and Social Psychology Bulletin, 43*(9), 1255–1267. https://doi.org/10.1177/0146167217711917

Watson, D., Clark, L. A., McIntyre, C. W., & Hamaker, S. (1992). Affect, personality, and social activity. *Journal of Personality and Social Psychology, 63*(6), 1011–1025. https://doi.org/10.1037/0022-3514.63.6.1011

Watson, D., & Tellegen, A. (1985). Toward a consensual structure of mood. *Psychological Bulletin, 98*(2), 219–235. https://doi.org/10.1037/0033-2909.98.2.219

Wilson, E. O. (1984). *Biophilia*. Harvard University Press.

Wirtz, D., Kruger, J., Scollon, C. N., & Diener, E. (2003). What to do on spring break? The role of predicted, on-line, and remembered experience in future choice. *Psychological Science, 14*(5), 520–524. https://doi.org/10.1111/1467-9280.03455

35

THE USE OF POSITIVE PSYCHOLOGY INTERVENTION TO FOSTER TEACHER WELL-BEING

Duyen T. Vo, Kelly-Ann Allen and Margaret L. Kern

It is widely recognized that teachers play a critical role in society. Teachers often have a significant, enduring social and emotional connection with their students, making a lasting impression on young peoples' lives. Additionally, amongst the range of educational factors that occur within a school, teachers often have the most significant influence on student learning (Hattie, 2003; Zee & Koomen, 2016). Indeed, research suggests that teachers' influence goes beyond the classroom, affecting students' lives not only during their time at school but also well into adulthood. According to a recent analysis of social media data, when people were asked what they remember about their teachers, Allen and colleagues (2020) found that most respondents were grateful for their teachers' ability to inspire, encourage, and provide kindness.

Despite the vital role that teachers play, their workload can take a toll. This is partly due to the highly emotional aspects of the profession, which requires teachers to manage their feelings so that they can manage others effectively (Hochschild, 1983). Research also suggests the cumulative effect of day-to-day alertness and vigilance is a primary source of teacher stress (Kyriacou, 1987). These pressures inherent to the discipline have existed for decades. Nevertheless, the demands facing teachers have expanded in the 21st century. Increasing workload (AEU, 2016; Education Support, 2019), pressure on schools to "perform" on national and international standardized testing (Baker et al., 2010; Gonzalez et al., 2016; Thompson, 2013), and the learners' changing profiles (including the rise of mental health issues, see Haidt & Lukianoff, 2019; Headspace, 2020; OECD, 2018) contribute to teacher stress and strain.

This chapter highlights the potential benefits of incorporating positive psychology interventions (PPIs) in education to better support teacher well-being. The chapter first points to the key issues that need to be addressed—the mental health and well-being challenges teachers face and their impact. PPIs are introduced, and their use in education and related areas are reviewed, providing a case for their implementation and practice in teacher well-being. Recent positive psychology (PP) approaches to enhance teacher well-being are described, highlighting school-based PPI's value and potential. In combination, this chapter provides schools, educators, policymakers, and other stakeholders practical insights into the elements and practices that may contribute to effective PPIs that foster teacher well-being.

DOI: 10.4324/9781003013778-43

Teacher Stress and Burnout

Teacher stress and burnout have consistently been identified as areas of concern worldwide (Hastings & Agrawal, 2015; Organisation of Economic Cooperation and Development [OECD], 2018). For example, a survey of 2,444 Australian teachers found that 19% felt unsafe at work (Heffernan et al., 2019). Many teachers reported concerns about the health impacts of ongoing stress, the emotional toll of teaching, and their lack of work/life balance. Consequently, 58% of those teachers intended to leave the profession. Another study reported that nearly 82% of the 166 teachers surveyed met the criteria for moderate to severe anxiety (Stapleton, 2019).

Stress in and of itself is not necessarily a bad thing (Carver & Conner-Smith, 2010; Lazarus & Folkman, 1984; The Wellbeing Lab, 2020), and is inherent to most work and professions. Experiences of stress motivate action and focus. For instance, a student might experience stress over a spelling test, motivating them to study the words and subsequently perform well. Similarly, teaching a new topic can create feelings of tension, which motivates the educator to prepare the lesson well. Short-term, acute experiences of stress can help individuals develop healthy ways of coping and managing challenges. However, stress can become problematic as demands and experiences overwhelm a person's resources and capacity to manage the stressors (Bakker & Demerouti, 2007). The stress then becomes chronic (Shernoff et al., 2011). Extended periods of chronic stress can lead to burnout, characterized by emotional exhaustion, decreased feelings of personal accomplishment, and increased cynicism (Maslach & Jackson, 1981).

Teacher stress and burnout can lead to absenteeism, high attrition rates, and low productivity through depersonalization of the job (Darr & Johns, 2008; OECD, 2018). Burnout increases the risk for several physical and mental health problems, including heart disease (Melamed et al., 2006), depression, and anxiety (Iacovides et al., 2003; Maslach & Leiter, 2016; Mousavi et al., 2017), which can negatively impact social relationships (Maslach & Leiter, 2016). According to a Gallup poll exploring employee engagement, 70% of U.S. teachers were disengaged in their work due to poor health (Hastings & Agrawal, 2015). As a result, it was estimated that this group would miss a collective 2.3 million more workdays over their careers than teachers who were engaged in their jobs (Hastings & Agrawal, 2015). Another international study by the OECD (2018) showed that, on average, teachers who reported experiencing significant stress in their work were twice as likely (compared to their colleagues with lower levels of stress) to stop working within the next five years.

For teachers from minority groups, the personal impacts of stress are further exacerbated. For example, research has shown that a hostile racial school climate significantly increased the stress teachers of color experienced in urban schools in the United States (Kholi, 2018). Similarly, in South Korea, racial discrimination from parents, colleagues, and administrators at schools, and workplace bullying added to the levels of stress and burnout of foreign black education professionals (Dos Santos, 2020).

Teachers working in disadvantaged school settings are also under additional pressure due to the unique challenges of their context (Perry et al., 2015; Wessels & Wood, 2019). The challenges of attending to increased levels of student truancy, behavior management issues in the classroom, bullying, and alcohol and substance abuse all add to teachers' work and their mental and emotional load (Thomson, 2017).

Ultimately, teachers' health and well-being affect the quality of education they are able to provide and the academic performance of their students (Zee & Koomen, 2016). In the United Kingdom, a recent study found 77% of the 775 teachers surveyed felt that their poor mental health had a detrimental effect on their students' progress (Glazzard & Rose, 2019). Many teachers indicated that the quality of their lesson planning and the delivery of lessons were adversely affected by their mental health. Importantly, teacher stress negatively affects students' behavior in the classroom, straining the vital student-teacher relationships at the heart of learning and a student's sense of belonging to school (Allen et al., 2018; Howard et al., 2020).

Recent studies have shown a clear link between teachers' mental health and student academic outcomes. One study revealed that students of teachers who reported more depressive symptoms made weaker gains in math achievement than those with teachers who reported fewer symptoms (McLean & McDonald Connor, 2015). Another study explored how teacher stress, burnout, coping, and self-efficacy relate to student behavior and academic outcomes (Herman et al., 2018). The researchers found that highly stressed teachers with low coping skills were associated with the poorest student outcomes and disruptive behavior.

These concerning statistics on the personal impacts of stress and burnout on teachers and their potential effect on student outcomes demonstrate the critical need to focus on teachers' mental health and well-being. While some efforts exist to address the problems (e.g., Parker et al., 2011; Richards, 2012), these efforts are often reactive, treating symptoms well after breakdown and illness occur. For instance, a burned-out teacher might be offered a period of sick leave, struggling educators are referred to an employee assistance program, or the school might offer professional development approaches to manage stress. Importantly, there is a need to explore how to better equip teachers with the skills and mindsets that proactively improve their mental health and well-being *before* reaching their breaking point. Motivated and enthusiastic teachers with the emotional and mental resources to address the profession's challenges are critical for providing quality education to students.

Arguably, given the current spotlight on student well-being (Humphrey et al., 2010; Mahoney et al., 2020; WHO, 2003), it is more important than ever to ensure that teachers maintain their positive mental health. Indeed, extensive studies have concluded that teachers need assurance of their own well-being to support children with their mental health and educational endeavors (Cherkowski & Walker, 2018; McCallum & Price, 2010; Zins, 2004). Enhanced teacher well-being prepares instructors to fulfill their role as encouraging, caring, and inspiring teachers (Allen et al., 2020; Jennings & Greenberg, 2009), and model well-being practices and strategies to students (McCallum & Price, 2010).

Understanding Well-Being

Previous research into approaches to support teachers' mental well-being has been informative in understanding the sources of stress and burnout, and potential strategies to help teachers cope with the profession's demands (e.g., Parker et al., 2011; Richards, 2012; Roeser et al., 2013). The studies aim to support teachers in recognizing their stressors and provide suggestions on how to minimize detrimental effects. While understanding coping strategies is necessary, arguably there is a need to complement current understandings of stress with a comprehensive approach to well-being that also promotes a sense of thriving, productive functioning, workplace engagement, and job satisfaction. Notably, there has been a recent and growing interest in supporting teachers' well-being in this more holistic way (Kern et al., 2014; McCallum, 2021; Taylor, 2018; Wessels & Wood, 2019). This body of work encourages a shift from merely managing stress to approaches that enable teachers to flourish and thrive; a notion embraced and promoted by the field of PP. PP is an area that focuses on understanding and building well-being and supporting optimal functioning in individuals, groups, organizations, and communities (Kern et al., 2020; Seligman & Csikszentmihalyi, 2000). PP provides promising opportunities to complement typical reactive and deficit-focused approaches, proactively enhancing positive factors and strengths of teachers to contribute to teacher effectiveness, and help buffer against adversity (Duckworth et al., 2009).

The World Health Organization (WHO) defines mental health as "a state of well-being in which individuals realize their abilities, can cope with the normal stresses of life, can work productively and fruitfully, and can make a contribution to his or her community" (WHO, 2015, p. 10). PP focuses on emotional, psychological, and social aspects of well-being, with an emphasis on subjective experiences of well-being rather than objective conditions that allow or hinder well-being (e.g., poverty, crime, inequity, and corruption). Scholars working within the PP area have argued that models and frameworks of subjective well-being are best organized as a profile of factors across multiple domains (Kern et al., 2014; Pollard & Lee, 2003; Seligman, 2011). In other words, well-being is best understood and measured as a multidimensional construct (Kern et al., 2020; Waters, 2011).

For example, Seligman (2011) suggested one such multidimensional model, known as PERMA, where teacher well-being is comprised of five components. *Positive emotions* refer to teachers' experiences demonstrating a positive approach to all aspects of their work (Seligman, 2011). This includes feelings of joy, enthusiasm, hope, and optimism (Kern et al., 2014). *Engagement* is an experience of "flow" where there is a strong "focus of attention, intense absorption, and high energy" toward teachers' work-related tasks (Rothbard & Patil, 2011, p. 1). *Positive relationships* can be described as high-quality connections developed with coworkers, students, and others in the school community (Stephens et al., 2011). *Meaning* refers to a sense of purpose derived from belonging to and serving something greater than oneself (Seligman, 2011). When teachers feel that what they are doing is valuable, they function at their optimal best (Steger, 2012). *Accomplishment* can be considered an experience that contributes to well-being when teachers feel a sense of mastery or achievement over their work-related skills (Wessels & Wood, 2019). Other well-being models have included dimensions such as environmental mastery, purpose, autonomy, competence, and satisfaction with life and with one's work (e.g., Deci & Ryan, 2002; Diener et al., 1985; Fisher, 2010; Ryff & Keyes, 1995).

A vital contribution to applying a multifaceted approach to understand well-being in schools highlights the association between different well-being aspects and employee outcomes. Using Seligman's multidimensional PERMA model, Kern and colleagues (2014) analyzed the association between multiple aspects of well-being and three specific employee outcomes: physical health, life satisfaction, and professional thriving. The researchers found that the dimensions of positive emotion, meaning, and accomplishment were strongly connected to life satisfaction and health, while engagement and relationships related strongly to job satisfaction and organizational commitment. In other words, when school staff flourish in multiple aspects of well-being, there is a positive effect on their commitment to the school and individual satisfaction with life, health, and jobs.

Positive Psychology Interventions

Models and frameworks of well-being are an important starting point, as they provide specific focal areas (Kern et al., 2020). Interventions can then target one or more areas to more robustly support and cultivate well-being. PPIs have been defined as "programs, practices, treatment methods or activities aimed at cultivating well-being through positive feelings, positive behaviors and positive cognition" (Sin & Lyubomirsky, 2009, p. 467). PPIs range from simple one-off activities (e.g., writing a gratitude letter to a friend or engaging in a kind act) to comprehensive programs that incorporate multiple positive activities repeated over time, attempting to build positive habits and behaviors, mindsets, and response patterns. Research on PPIs shows promising outcomes in diverse areas, including clinical settings (Hoffman et al., 2010; Rashid, 2009; Seligman, 2006), education (Adler, 2015; Vella-Brodrick et al., 2014), workplaces (Donaldson et al., 2019), and communities (Cooper, 2019).

For example, mindfulness and gratitude are two forms of single-focus PPIs that have received considerable attention (Chan, 2013; Hwang et al., 2017; Wood et al., 2010). Mindfulness is a mental state in which people pay attention to the present moment, on purpose, and without judgment (Kabat-Zinn, 1994). Numerous activities and programs have been developed to train people to be more mindful, with the most extensive program being the eight-week Mindfulness-Based Stress Reduction program (Kabat-Zinn, 1994). Studies using random controlled trials reveal that mindfulness programs can improve mental and physical health (Ludwig & Kabatt-Zinn, 2008), and cognitive, affective, and interpersonal outcomes (Brown et al., 2015).

Gratitude is defined as a sense of thankfulness toward someone or something, creating positive emotions in people's lives (Schueller & Parks, 2014). Various gratitude interventions have been developed and tested, such as a daily listing of things that one is grateful for, grateful contemplation, and behavioral expressions (Wood et al., 2010). Studies find many positive outcomes of gratitude interventions, including reducing excessive worrying (Geraghty et al., 2010), improving functioning in people with neuromuscular diseases (Emmons & McCullough, 2003), improving sleep quality (Wood et al., 2009), and building positive relationships (Waters & Stokes, 2015).

Other single-focus PPIs include engaging in random acts of kindness (Pressman et al., 2015), savoring (Jose et al., 2012), identifying and using one's character strengths (Peterson & Seligman, 2004), recognizing and regulating emotions, connecting with others, spending time in nature, and physical activity. Intervention efforts, especially within schools, combine multiple activities, training individuals around multiple strategies to support well-being. This has the benefit of providing choice, and some activities resonate with some people better than others (Lyubomirsky & Layous, 2013; Schueller, 2012).

Several reviews have reported on the effectiveness of PPIs (e.g., Bolier et al., 2013; Donaldson et al., 2019; Lyubomirsky et al., 2005; Meyers et al., 2013; Sin & Lyubomirsky, 2009; White et al., 2019). In general, these reviews have found positive effects associated with PPIs. For instance, in a meta-analysis of 51 interventions with 4,266 individuals, Sin and Lyubomirsky (2009) showed that PPIs were significantly more effective than comparison groups for enhancing well-being and decreasing depression symptoms in clinical patients. Similarly, evaluating PPIs in the workplace, Donaldson and colleagues' (2019) systematic review and meta-analysis found that PPIs significantly improved well-being, engagement, and other important work outcomes such as workplace trust. Although the review did not discuss other factors that could affect organizational interventions, the results provide encouraging possibilities. In these reviews, effect sizes are often small; studies typically use small, selective samples with varying attrition rates; and study quality varies (White et al., 2019). Nonetheless, as a whole, PPIs appear promising, but there is a need to improve our understanding of which PPIs work best for whom, under what conditions and for what duration (Kern et al., 2020).

Notably, PPIs have shown efficacy for a range of minority groups, including ethnic and racial groups (Boehm et al., 2011; Fung et al., 2016), lesbian, gay, bisexual, and queer individuals (Nadav et al., 2021), indigenous (Kraus et al., 2016), and religious groups (Al-Seheel & Noor, 2016). These findings suggest that PPIs may have specific implications for teachers of marginalized groups given their unique experiences of stress and burnout.

Positive Psychology Interventions in Schools

School-based positive psychology interventions (SB-PPIs) can play an important preventative role within schools (Chodkiewicz & Boyle, 2017; Dray et al., 2015; Waters, 2011). In recent years, a large body of evidence has emerged in the area of student well-being, due in part to the 21st-century learning aims of equipping students with the skills and character they need to succeed in the rapidly changing world (Ananiadou & Claro, 2009; Saavedra & Opfer, 2012). In addition, the rising mental health concerns of young people have highlighted the pressing need to make student well-being a priority (Education Services Australia, 2020; Haidt & Lukianoff, 2019), with the hope that by proactively equipping young people with essential skills, mindsets, and behaviors, they will be more resilient and less likely to experience severe mental illness in the future.

Most SB-PPIs studies have tested the impact of combining multiple PPIs into comprehensive programs. The blending of these components included consideration of (a) the *taught* curriculum (i.e., lessons on well-being taught to students) and (b) the *caught* curriculum (i.e., indirect ways of learning well-being skills, such as through modeling by teachers, the visual environment, and behavioral management strategies; White & Kern, 2018).

Several reviews have explored the effectiveness of SB-PPIs to enhance student well-being. Waters (2011) systematically evaluated 12 interventions. Using PERMA as a framework (Seligman, 2011), she found that PP programs significantly related to student well-being and academic performance. In a second review, Dray et al. (2017) assessed the effects of "universal" resilience interventions (implemented across entire student groups) targeting child and adolescent health in the school setting relative to a comparison group. Overall, there was a significant intervention effect for depressive symptoms and anxiety symptoms (Dray et al., 2017).

Fewer studies have directly examined the impact of SB-PPIs on teachers. However, many of the capabilities developed through SB-PPIs for students—such as adaptive coping skills, social and emotional regulation, and strategies to reduce negative emotions and increase positive emotions—are helpful for both children and adults. Further, SB-PPIs are often facilitated by the teachers themselves (rather than relying on outside expertise), with studies suggesting that implementation may be more effective when the teachers first learn about and experience the interventions, before facilitating the activities with their students (e.g., Shankland & Rosset, 2017; Waters, 2011).

Positive Psychology Interventions for Teacher Well-Being

Considering the long and lasting impact that teachers have on their students, the likelihood that student wellbeing initiatives most likely will be implemented by teachers, and concerns over the stresses and mental health pressures that teachers face, further prioritizing PPIs for educators as part of the professional development and support of staff within the school is critical. Professional learning in schools has traditionally focused on refining knowledge, skills, and practice related to teaching and learning (Australian Institute for Teaching and School Leadership, 2017), rather than on the mental health and well-being development of teachers. In the same way that the prioritization of the development of the "whole student" is starting to demonstrate benefits for students (Allen et al., 2017, 2018; Waters, 2011), it is helpful to consider further how PPIs can best support the "whole educator."

The last few decades have seen a growing body of research, interventions, and programs explicitly focusing on enhancing teachers' mental health (Chan, 2013; Cook, Miller et al., 2017; Cooper & Woods, 2017; McCallum et al., 2017). This body of work demonstrates that there are multiple ways that schools can incorporate training around PPIs to support teachers. For instance, schools might offer onsite professional development on PP concepts and interventions, challenging teachers to learn about and use the interventions in their own lives before considering how those interventions might be useful for their students. Training delivered in schools can provide a meaningful and practical context for training, with educators encouraged to directly consider how PPIs fit specifically within their classroom context. In addition, schools have also provided training and development beyond the school context through engaging external providers or utilizing online interfaces.

PPIs often focus on strategies that teachers can engage in individually. Research suggests that an individual's personal qualities and capabilities are key factors that contribute to well-being (Jennings & Greenberg, 2009; Ross et al., 2012; Seligman, 2011). Thus, many of these strategies aim to build teachers' positive capabilities be resilient to challenges and feel and function better. For example, in Hong Kong, an online interface was used to foster teachers' subjective well-being through an eight-week gratitude intervention (Chan, 2013). Participants randomly assigned to the gratitude condition were asked to reflect on the good things or events they experienced during the working week using an online journal (Chan, 2013). Comparing pre- and postintervention measurements with a group of teachers who focused on their misfortunes, the study showed that the grateful-reflecting teachers experienced significantly increased life satisfaction (Chan, 2013).

Cooper and Woods (2017) evaluated a U.K. program aimed explicitly at headteachers, drawing on a strengths-based development tool, the *Realise2 Introductory Profile*. Strengths can be defined as "pre-existing personality qualities that arise naturally, feel authentic, are intrinsically motivating to use, and energizing" (Brdar & Kashdan, 2010, p. 151). Research has shown that identifying and applying character strengths can contribute to a fulfilling life, helping people flourish (Harzer, 2020). Assessing teachers' strengths and facilitating debrief sessions, conducted at a local authority (government service), the mixed-methods study found that headteachers experienced increased self-awareness, motivation, and commitment to using self-reflection core practice (Cooper & Woods, 2017).

In the United States, McCullough's (2015) study with elementary school teachers provided preliminary support for the feasibility, acceptability, and efficacy of a character strengths intervention that utilized the Values in Action (VIA) framework. Teachers completed the VIA Strengths Survey online, then planned to use a signature strength in new ways in the classroom. In three subsequent coaching meetings, teachers reflected on the use of character strengths at work and planned for use of different strengths. Using a concurrent multiple baseline single-case design, results of masked visual analysis and hierarchical linear modeling indicated significant gains in teachers' subjective well-being, work satisfaction, and flourishing, as well as reductions in stress and burnout (McCullough, 2015).

Other interventions have incorporated mindfulness, meditation, or other contemplative practices to help teachers manage and reduce stress. One example is the CARE (Cultivating Awareness and Resilience Education) program in the United States, a mindfulness-based professional development program designed to improve teachers' social and emotional awareness, enhancing both teacher and classroom outcomes (Schussler et al., 2016). Similarly, the ACHIEVER Resilience Curriculum (ARC) aims to incorporate several practices, including mindfulness, gratitude, and sleep hygiene, into a single professional development series (Cook, Miller et al., 2017). Both programs reported positive outcomes, including greater self-awareness and self-efficacy, and job-related stress reduction (Cook et al., 2017; Schussler et al., 2016).

While training and development beyond the school context can provide depth and insight to learning about PP concepts for motivated educators, translating the learning back to the school context may be difficult (Luk-Fong, 2009). Interventions provided at the school level mean all employees can access well-being programs' positive impacts, not just those who are considered "at-risk'" (Giga et al., 2003). Moreover, the provision of school-based interventions may have a flow-on effect—teachers are allowed to build on their practices in a purposeful context with colleagues over the long term (Fredrickson, 2001; Hwang et al., 2019).

Helping to guide strategies for implementing SB-PPIs with educators in the future, Vo and Allen (2020) conducted a systematic literature review, providing a summary about the elements, practices, and values of PPIs to foster teacher well-being. The research aimed to investigate how SB-PPIs are delivered and identify the types of interventions and common core features. The authors developed three inclusion criteria for the review: (a) the study aimed to build strengths and positive psychological well-being, (b) the intervention was implemented with in-service teachers at schools, and (c) the study used valid and reliable measures assessed through quality appraisal tools. Using the PERMA framework (Seligman, 2011), a search examined four electronic databases (ERIC, A+ Education, Scopus, and PsycINFO) using key terms (e.g., teacher/s well-being/wellness and intervention/s) and keywords associated with PP (e.g., mindfulness, resilience, gratitude, character strengths, and flourishing). After a rigorous two-stage screening process, 10 international studies were identified and included in the review. Thematic analysis was utilized to order the extracted data into central themes and subthemes (Braun & Clarke, 2006).

The systematic review found that most SB-PPIs were mindfulness-based interventions, followed by multimodal programs and gratitude interventions. Many of the studies drew on the Mindfulness-Based Stress Reduction (MBSR) program developed by Kabat-Zinn (1994) in the late 1970s; however, adjustments were made specifically for teachers, considering both practical and contextual factors. For example, in some studies, adaptions included shorter periods of practice and lessons on applying simple practices to the classroom (Frank et al., 2015; Harris et al., 2016).

All mindfulness-based studies have reported positive outcomes via pre- and posttest subjective measures (e.g., self-reports) and physiological indicators (e.g., blood pressure and salivary cortisol assessments). In some studies, interventions enhanced teachers' well-being by reducing perceived stress and symptoms of occupational burnout (Frank et al., 2015; Hwang et al., 2019; Roeser et al., 2013), while in others, teachers reported increased self-compassion, emotion regulation, and self-efficacy (Frank et al., 2015; Reiser & McCarthy, 2018; Tarrasch et al., 2020). Notably, the interventions enhanced the individual teacher's well-being and resulted in increased well-being from an organizational perspective. For example, teachers reported strengthened relationships with colleagues, compassion for others (colleagues and students), and improved efficacy in the classroom (Harris et al., 2016; Tarrasch et al., 2020).

Other studies involved multimodal programs that incorporate a variety of approaches (Taylor, 2018). One example is the CALMERSS intervention (Taylor, 2018), which included approaches such as psychoeducation (understanding the nervous system and its role in stress), physical exercise, conflict resolution, character strengths, and the importance of sleep. Two of the three multimodal programs explicitly referred to PP, incorporating activities in the program design not covered by other studies in the review. For instance, character strengths exercises were featured in one (Taylor, 2018), whereas another involved "acts of kindness" activities (Wessels & Wood, 2019), which is similar to the single-focused "three good things" gratitude intervention (Critchley & Gibbs, 2012). Across these studies, teachers reported reduced psychological strain (e.g., depression, anxiety, and irritability) and increased resilience, motivation, and self-efficacy (see Fernandes et al., 2019; Taylor, 2018). Themes derived from qualitative measures demonstrated an improvement in relationships with colleagues and enabled teachers to "take action" to sustain their well-being experiences (Critchley & Gibbs, 2012; Wessels & Wood, 2019).

Implementing SB-PPIs to Foster Teacher Well-Being

As a whole, Vo and Allen's (2020) review supports the benefit of continuing to identify best practice approaches for incorporating SB-PPIs focused on educators. The question becomes how to implement SB-PPIs in ways that will best support teacher well-being. The authors' research revealed six uniting elements in their review findings that may contribute to an effective SB-PPI design, regardless of the category. For schools, educators, and policymakers, these elements and practices could be considered to optimize SB-PPI's potential to support teacher well-being.

Supporting Autonomy: Voluntary Participation and Multiple Methods

First, intervention effectiveness increases when it supports participant autonomy, whether through voluntary participation and/or providing choice in terms of the activities and interventions. Most of the participants in the interventions reviewed were volunteers. Recruitment methods included advertising to teachers (flyers, brochures, and meetings) via district or local authorities and headteachers. Other PPIs studies similarly have identified the importance of participants being motivated to improve their well-being, rather than a program being forced upon them (Schueller &

Parks, 2014). Across the behavior change literature, motivation is consistently identified as a core contributor to the extent to which efforts are successful (Neves de Jesus & Lens, 2005; Ololube, 2006). While extrinsic motivators (e.g., rewards and punishments for specific behaviors) drive some change, behavior change tends to be more successful when there is some degree of intrinsic motivation that drives the person forward (Deci & Ryan, 1981).

Second, it is important to incorporate multiple methods, whether in terms of the number of interventions or how interventions are practiced. For instance, participants might be taught various mindfulness techniques for a mindfulness-based intervention, such as awareness of the breath, yoga, mindful eating, a walking meditation, or using a phone-based application. Different approaches will work better with different individuals, and it may be more about fit with the individual rather than the specific approach used (Schueller, 2012). Similarly, a program might introduce a range of interventions, allowing participants to choose what fits well with their strengths, personality, and interests (Kern, 2021; Lyubomirsky & Layous, 2013).

Giving teachers a choice to participate and activities that they engage in presents an interesting common finding across the interventions reviewed, aligned to well-being and motivation theories (Deci & Ryan, 2002; Rogers, 1963). Extensive research shows that choice or autonomy is a critical factor in promoting intrinsic motivation and engagement (Brooks & Young, 2011; Deci & Ryan, 1981; Evans & Boucher, 2015; Patall et al., 2008). Teachers' motivation for growth and development is supported by providing them options to access development opportunities, engage in learning, and utilize strategies to practice in multiple ways. These opportunities, in turn, can promote their well-being.

Context Specificity

A third common feature involves the context-specific design of interventions, where a majority were explicitly designed to suit teachers or the specific school context. For instance, in addition to the mindfulness-based interventions adapted to suit teachers (Frank et al., 2015; Reiser & McCarthy, 2018), the *Call to Care—Israel for Teachers* program (Tarrasch et al., 2020) addressed a unique context. Recognizing that many mindfulness-based programs to support teacher well-being have been studied in and adapted for teachers in the United States, this program aimed to address Israeli education's challenges. In another example, using a participatory action learning and action research approach, Wessels and Wood (2019) developed an exceptional context-specific design. The entire intervention—developing a plan, identifying well-being needs, selecting well-being tools and themes for evaluation—was continuously adapted with input from teachers to suit their specific requirements in a disadvantaged school in rural South Africa.

It could be argued that this common core feature demonstrates the importance of "personalizing" and "contextualizing" learning. This instructional approach emphasizes that learners are more motivated to learn concepts and skills that are relevant and applicable to their lives (Bates, 2014). Accordingly, through context-specific design and appropriate adaptations, SB-PPIs are tailored to meet teachers' and schools' needs and circumstances. This design feature is likely to result in teachers' increased motivation to learn the skills and mindsets needed to support their well-being.

Group Format

Fourth, all 10 studies pointed to the benefit of the group-based intervention. Groups of teachers in the interventions reviewed ranged from five (Taylor, 2018) to 118 teachers (Roeser et al., 2013). Four studies specifically emphasized the importance of group and community (Harris et al., 2016; Reiser & McCarthy, 2018, Tarrasch et al., 2020; Wessels & Wood, 2019). Qualitative data generated in the studies highlight the importance of the group setting. Participants in one intervention noted they "enjoyed fostering and strengthening relationships with colleagues during the group and experienced a sense of belonging and acceptance" (Reiser & McCarthy, 2018, p. 24). In another study, teachers reported that their "sense of belonging, the improved relationships, the shared positive emotions and shared personal problems, contributed to their experiences of well-being" (Wessels & Wood, 2019, p. 7).

A group format offers some benefits compared to individual-based interventions. Groups can provide a sense of psychological safety, promoting change and growth (Yalom & Crouch, 1990). A group format promotes shared experiences and mutual support, as members encourage one another, share their own experiences with an intervention, and hold each other accountable for enacting interventions. As teachers connect, it also supports a basic psychological need for relatedness (Deci & Ryan, 2002; Maslow, 1998).

Professional Knowledge and Weekly Meetings

Fifth, many of the interventions involved professional instructors with specific forms of expertise who met regularly (often weekly over a specified period) with participants. The instructors' experiences ranged from certified mindfulness training facilitators to yoga instructors, educational psychologists, to teacher training professionals. Five of the instructors were directly involved in the curriculum design of the interventions. Even though the instructors were not officially qualified or trained in PP, they had professional knowledge and experience in well-being science and education.

Notably, the use of outside facilitators contrasts with student SB-PPIs, in which teachers often implement the program (Waters, 2011). For students, teacher-delivered programs have the advantage of greater scale (e.g., using a train-the-trainer approach, a small group of educators can be trained in a program, and then deliver that program across a large number of students). Teachers are more attuned to their students' specific needs and contexts, allowing materials to be adjusted in ways that best fit their students' needs. Nevertheless, Vo and Allen's (2020) review suggests that teachers find outside expertise valuable. For instance, it is well established that the quality of theoretical and experiential understanding of an instructor is of paramount importance to a mindfulness-based intervention (Hwang et al., 2017; Kabat-Zinn, 1994; Segal et al., 2002).

The interventions' duration varied greatly, from three weeks (Critchley & Gibbs, 2012) to an entire year (Tarrasch et al., 2020). Similarly, the lessons ranged from 20 minutes to two and a half hours. Regardless of the program duration or time, regular weekly meetings were a sixth common feature. The regular schedule may have helped reinforce learning and build relationships between the instructor and participants and among participants. Furthermore, scheduling to suit teachers' busy schedules is critical to the effectiveness of the intervention. The weekly format also allows the PPIs to become ingrained positive habits, much like regularly going to the gym allows physical activity to be a person's life habit.

Intervention Content and Structure

Finally, embedding PP methods into the content and the intervention structure helps form a comprehensive approach that effectively and proactively supports teacher well-being. Content describes the "what" of interventions: the knowledge, mindset, and skills taught and instilled through the intervention. Critical to the content is building upon concepts and interventions developed within the PP literature that have positive effects on well-being. For example, mindfulness, resilience, gratitude, acts of kindness, and character strengths are featured in many programs, and all of these have been related to better mental well-being (Dray et al., 2015; Ludwig & Kabatt-Zinn, 2008; Wood et al., 2010). Content focuses on proactively developing capabilities to manage challenges well, empowering teachers to proactively care for their own and others' well-being.

Structure refers to the "how" of the intervention. As described above, several structural components appear critical: (a) supporting autonomy and choice through voluntary participation and the incorporation of multiple methods, (b) supporting relatedness through group-based learning, and (c) building competence through regular sessions facilitated by appropriate professionals. SB-PPIs benefit from supporting teachers' basic psychological needs (Deci & Ryan, 2002). It is also essential to consider the school's context and how it is or is not supportive of the intervention. Merely providing training to teachers within a toxic school environment can render the training ineffective, undermine teachers' motivation to change, blame individuals for broader organizational issues, and do more harm than good (Kern et al., 2020; Williams et al., 2016).

Conclusions

A teacher's role is recognized as one of the most influential in students' lives. Importantly, the ability to inspire, encourage, and develop students' social and emotional capabilities may be more valued than advancing intellectual aptitude. Yet, while society acknowledges this crucial role, many teachers are exhausted and stressed. This stress manifests itself in many ways, including teacher burnout, absenteeism, high attrition rates, and ultimately, affecting the quality of education and student outcomes.

While research and practice to support teachers' well-being is not an entirely new area, recently, there has been a shift from focusing on deficits to recognizing strengths, a notion captured by the field of PP. In particular, the outcomes of PPIs show encouraging possibilities, especially in school settings. SB-PPIs potentially provide a meaningful and practical context to enhance teacher well-being holistically. Supporting such efforts, Vo and Allen's (2020) review points to several common elements of SB-PPIs for teachers: voluntary participation, the use of multiple methods, group-based formats, delivery by a professional, regular (often weekly) meetings, and careful consideration of the content and structure included. The context should be considered when thinking about the design of interventions, tailoring the SB-PPI to teachers and schools' needs and circumstances. This design feature is likely to increase motivation to learn the skills and mindsets needed to support teachers' well-being. Together, these elements support teachers' innate need for autonomy, relatedness, and competence, promoting growth, development, and well-being (Deci & Ryan, 2006).

Overall, there is convincing evidence for the practice of school-based PPIs to foster teacher well-being, promoting a holistic approach by shifting the focus from coping to thriving. Further development in this area of research would support the significant idea of looking after teachers to ultimately better look after themselves and their students.

References

Adler, B. (2015, August 13). *The teacher turned manager: Transitioning into a management role* [Video file]. SIT. Retrieved from https://digitalcollections.sit.edu/sandanona/summer2015/thursdayaugust13/3/

AEU (Australian Education Union). (2016). *School staff workload study*. Retrieved from https://www.aeuvic.asn.au/school-staff-workload-study

Allen, K. A., Grove, C., May, S. F., & Gamble, N. (2020). I wouldn't be who I am today without these incredible teachers: A social media analysis of the #ThankYourTeacher campaign. *World Teachers' Day Report*. Monash University. 30 p.

Allen, K. A., Kern, M. L., Vella-Brodrick, D., & Waters, L. (2017). School values: A comparison of academic motivation, mental health promotion, and school belonging with student achievement. *The Educational and Developmental Psychologist, 34*(1), 31–47. doi:10.1017/edp.2017.5

Allen, K. A., Kern, M. L., Vella-Brodrick, D., Waters, L., & Hattie, J. (2018). What schools need to know about belonging: A meta-analysis. *Educational Psychology Review, 30*(1), 1–34. https://doi.org/10.1007/s10648-016-9389-8

Al-Seheel, A. Y., & Noor, M. N. (2016). Effects of an Islamic-based gratitude strategy on Muslim students' level of happiness. *Mental Health, Religion & Culture, 19*(7), 686–703. http://dx.doi.org/10.1080/136746 76.2016.1229287

Ananiadou, K., & Claro, M. (2009). 21st century skills and competences for new millennium learners in OECD countries, *OECD Education Working Papers,* No. 41, OECD Publishing. http://dx.doi. org/10.1787/218525261154

Australian Institute for Teaching and School Leadership. (2017). Improving teacher professional learning. Retrieved from https://www.aitsl.edu.au/teach/improve-practice/improving-teacher-professional-learning

Baker, E. L., Barton, E. P., Darling-Hammond, L., Haertel, E., Ladd, H. F., Linn, R. L., Ravitch, D., Rothstein, R., Shavelson, R. J., & Shepard, L. A. (2010) Problems with the use of student test scores to evaluate teachers. *EPI Briefing Paper #278.* Retrieved from https://eric.ed.gov/?id=ED516803

Bakker, A. B., & Demerouti, E. (2007). The job demands-resources model: State of the art. *Journal of Managerial Psychology, 22*(3), 309–328. https://doi.org/10.1108/02683940710733115

Bates, A. (2014). Instructional design for distance learning. In S. Dijkstra, F. Schott, N. Seel, R. & D. Tennyson (Eds.), *Instructional design: International perspectives II: Volume I: Theory, Research, and Models: Volume II: Solving Instructional Design Problems* (p. 369). Routledge.

Boehm, J. K., Lyubomirsky, S., & Sheldon, K. M. (2011). A longitudinal experimental study comparing the effectiveness of happiness-enhancing strategies in Anglo Americans and Asian Americans, *Cognition & Emotion, 25*(7), 1263–1272. doi:10.1080/02699931.2010.541227

Boiler, L., Haverman, M., Westerhof, G. J., Riper, H., Smit, F., & Bohlmeijer, E. (2013). Positive psychology interventions: A meta-analysis of randomized controlled studies. *Public Health, 13,* 119. doi:10.1186/1471–2458-13–119

Braun, V., & Clarke, V. (2006). Using thematic analysis in psychology. *Qualitative Research in Psychology, 3*(2), 77–101. doi:10.1191/1478088706qp063oa

Brdar, I., & Kashdan, T. B. (2010). Character strengths and well-being in Croatia: An empirical investigation of structure and correlates. *Journal of Research in Personality, 44*(1), 151–154. doi:10.1016/j.jrp.2009.12.001.

Brooks, C. F., & Young, S. L. (2011). Are choice-making opportunities needed in the classroom? Using self-determination theory to consider student motivation and learner empowerment. *International Journal of Teaching and Learning in Higher Education, 23*(1), 48–59.

Brown, D. B., Bravo, A. J., Roos, C. R., & Pearson, M. R. (2015). Five facets of mindfulness and psychological health: Evaluating a psychological model of the mechanisms of mindfulness. *Mindfulness, 6*(5), 1021–1032. doi:10.1007/s12671-014-0349-4

Carver, C. S., & Connor-Smith, J. (2010) Personality and coping. *Annual Review of Personality, 61,* 679–704. https://doi.org/10.1146/annurev.psych.093008.100352

Chan, L. C. (2013). Mindfulness to enhance teaching and learning. In D. Salter (Ed.), *Cases on quality teaching practices in higher education* (pp. 119–130). IGI Global.

Cherkowski, S., & Walker, K. (2018) *Teacher wellbeing: Noticing, nurturing, sustaining and flourishing in schools.* Word & Deed.

Chodkiewicz, A. R., & Boyle, C. (2016). Promoting positive learning in Australian students aged 10-to 12-years-old using attribution retraining and cognitive behavioral therapy: A pilot study. *School Psychology International, 37*(5), 519–535. doi:10.1177/0143034316667114

Chodkiewicz, A. R., & Boyle, C. (2017). Positive psychology school-based interventions: A reflection on current success and future directions. *Review of Education, 5*(1), 60–86. doi:10.1002/rev3.3080

Cook, C., Miller, F., Fiat, A., Renshaw, T., Frye, M., Joseph, G., & DeCano, P. (2017). Promoting secondary teachers' well-being and intentions to implement evidence-based practices: Randomized evaluation of the ACHIEVER Resilience Curriculum. *Psychology in the Schools, 54,* 13–28. doi:10.1002/pits.21980

Cook, C. R., Grady, E. A., Long, A. C., Renshaw, A. C., Codding, T., Fiat, R. S., & Larson, M. (2017). Evaluating the impact of increasing general education teachers' ratio of positive-to-negative interactions on students' classroom behavior. *Journal of Positive Behavior Interventions, 19*(2), 67–77. doi:10.1177/1098300716679137

Cooper, A. (2019, July 20). *Power in numbers: How well-being measurement mobilised a community* [Conference 6th presentation]. World Congress on Positive Psychology 2019, Melbourne, Australia.

Cooper, L., & Woods, K. (2017). Evaluating the use of a strengths-based development tool with head teachers. *Educational Psychology in Practice, 33*(1), 31–49. doi:10.1080/02667363.2016.1220924

Critchley, H., & Gibbs, S. (2012). The effects of positive psychology on the efficacy beliefs of school staff. *Educational and Child Psychology, 29*(4), 64–76.

Darr, W., & Johns, G. (2008). Work, strain, health and absenteeism: A meta-analysis. *Journal of Occupational Health Psychology, 13,* 293–318. doi:10.1037/a0012639

Deci, E. L., & Ryan, R. M. (1981). Curiosity and self-directed learning: The role of motivation in education. In L. G. Katz (Ed.), *Current topics in early childhood education* (vol. 4, pp. 71–86). Ablex.

Deci, E. L., & Ryan, R. M. (2002) *Handbook of self-determination research*. University of Rochester Press.

Deci, E. L., & Ryan, R. M., (2006). Self-regulation and the problem of human autonomy: Does psychology need choice, self-determination, and will? *Journal of Personality, 74*(6), 1557–1586. doi:10.1111/j.1467-6494.2006.00420.x

Diener, E. D., Emmons, R. A., Larsen, R. J., & Griffin, S. (1985). The satisfaction with life scale. *Journal of Personality Assessment, 49*(1), 71–75. doi: 10.1207/s15327752jpa4901_13

Department of Education and Training Victoria. (2019). *Practice principles for excellence in teaching and learning*. Retrieved from https://www.education.vic.gov.au/school/teachers/teachingresources/practice/improve/Pages/principlesexcellence.aspx

Donaldson, S.I., Lee, J.Y., & Donaldson, S.I. (2019). Evaluating positive psychology Interventions at work: A systematic review and meta-analysis. *International Journal of Applied Positive Psychology. 4*, 113–134. https://doi.org/10.1007/s41042-019-00021-8

Dos Santos, Luis. (2020). Stress, burnout, and turnover issues of black expatriate education professionals in South Korea: Social biases, discrimination, and workplace bullying. *International Journal of Environmental Research and Public Health, 17*(11), 3851. doi:10.3390/ijerph17113851.

Dray, J., Bowman, J., Wolfenden, L., Campbell, E., Freund, M., Hodder, R., & Wiggers, J. (2015). Systematic review of universal resilience interventions targeting child and adolescent mental health in the school setting: Review protocol. *Systematic Reviews, 4*(1), 1–8. doi:10.1186/s13643-015-0172-6

Dray, J., Bowman, J., Wolfenden, L., Campbell, E., Fruend, M., Hodder, R., & Wiggers, J. (2017). Systematic review of universal resilience-focused interventions targeting child and adolescent mental health in the school setting. *Journal of the American Academy of Child & Adolescent Psychiatry, 56*(10), 813–824. doi:10.1016/j.jaac.2017.07.780

Duckworth, A. L., Quinn, P. D., & Seligman, M. E. (2009). Positive predictors of teacher effectiveness. *The Journal of Positive Psychology, 4*(6), 540–547. doi:10.1080/17439760903157232

Education Services Australia. (2020). *National framework for student wellbeing*. Retrieved from https://studentwellbeinghub.edu.au/educators/framework/

Education Support. (2019). *Teacher wellbeing index 2019*. Retrieved from https://www.educationsupport.org.uk/resources/research-reports/teacher-wellbeing-index-2019

Emmons, R. A., & McCullough, M. E. (2003). Counting blessings versus burden: An experimental investigation of gratitude and subjective well-being in daily life. *Journal of Personality and Social Psychology, 84*, 377–389. doi:10.1037/0022-3514.84.2.377

Evans, M., & Boucher, A. R. (2015). Optimizing the power of choice: Supporting student autonomy to foster motivation and engagement in learning. *Mind, Brain, and Education, 9*(2), 87–91. doi:10.1111/mbe.12073

Fernandes, L., Peixoto, F., Gouveia, M. J., Silva, J. C., & Wosnitza, M. (2019). Fostering teachers' resilience and well-being through professional learning: Effects from a training programme. *The Australian Educational Researcher, 46*(4), 681–698. https://doi.org/10.1007/s13384-019-00344-0

Fisher, C. D. (2010). Happiness at work. *International Journal of Management Reviews, 12*(4), 384–412. http://dx.doi.org/10.1111/j.1468-2370.2009.00270.x

Frank, J. L., Reibel, D., Broderick, P., Cantrell, T., & Metz, S. (2015). The effectiveness of mindfulness-based stress reduction on educator stress and well-being: Results from a pilot study. *Mindfulness, 6*, 208–216. doi:10.1007/s12671-013-0246-2

Fredrickson, B. L. (2001). The role of positive emotions in positive psychology: The broaden-and-build theory of positive emotions. *American Psychologist, 56*(3), 218–226. https://doi.org/10.1037/0003-066X.56.3.218

Fung, J., Guo, S., Jin, J., Bear, L., & Lau, A. (2016). A pilot randomized trial evaluating a school-based mindfulness intervention for ethnic minority youth. *Mindfulness, 7*, 819–828. doi:10.1007/s12671-016-0519-7

Geraghty, A. W., Wood, A. M., & Hyland, M. E. (2010). Attrition from self-directed interventions: Investigating the relationship between psychological predictors, intervention content and dropout from a body dissatisfaction intervention. *Social Science & Medicine, 71*(1), 30–37. doi:10.1016/j.socscimed.2010.03.007

Giga, S. L., Cooper, C. L., & Faragher, B. (2003). The development of a framework for a comprehensive approach to stress management interventions at work. *International Journal of Stress Management, 10*, 280–296. doi:10.1037/1072-5245.10.4.280

Glazzard, J., & Rose, A. (2019). The impact of teacher well-being and mental health on pupil progress in primary schools. *Journal of Public Mental Health, 19*(4), 349–357. doi:10.1108/JPMH-02-2019-0023

Gonzalez, A., Peters, M., Orange, A., & Grigsby, B. (2016). The influence of high-stakes testing on teacher self-efficacy and job-related stress. *Cambridge Journal of Education, 47*(4), 1–19. doi:10.1080/0305764X.2016.1214237

Haidt, J., & Lukianoff, G. (2019) *The coddling of the American mind: How good intentions and bad ideas are setting up a generation for failure.* Penguin Press.

Harris, A. R., Jennings, P. A., Katz, D. A., Abenavoli, R. M., & Greenberg, M. T. (2016). Promoting stress management and well-being in educators: Feasibility and efficacy of a school-based yoga and mindfulness intervention. *Mindfulness, 7,* 143–154. doi:10.1007/s12671-015-0451-2

Harzer, C. (2020) Fostering character strengths to promote thriving and flourishing in organizations. *Organisationsberatung, Supervision, Coaching, 27,* 37–50. https://doi.org/10.1007/s11613-020-00636-w

Hastings, M., & Agrawal, S. (2015). *Lack of teacher engagement linked to 2.3 million missed workdays.* Retrieved from https://news.gallup.com/poll/180455/lack-teacher-engagement-linked-million-missed-workdays.aspx

Hattie, J. (2003). Teachers make a difference: What is the research evidence? *Australian Council for Educational Research: Annual Conference on Building Teacher Quality.* Melbourne. Retrieved from http://research.acer.edu.au/research_conference_2003/4/

Headspace. (2020). *Mental health statistics and health report.* Retrieved from https://headspace.org.au/health-professionals/what-does-the-evidence-say-mental-health-statistics-and-reports/

Heffernan, A., Longmuir, F., Bright, D., & Kim, M. (2019). *Perceptions of teachers and teaching in Australia.* Monash University. Retrieved from https://www.monash.edu/education/teachspace/articles/how-do-australias-teachers-feel-about-their-work

Herman, K., Hickmon-Rosa, J., & Reinke, W. (2018). Empirically derived profiles of teacher stress, burnout, self-efficacy, and coping and associated student outcomes. *Journal of Positive Behavior Interventions, 20*(6). doi:10.1177/1098300717732066.

Hochschild, A. R. (1983). *The managed heart: Commercialization of human feeling.* University of California Press.

Hoffman, E., Starobin, S., Laanan, F. S., & Rivera, M. (2010). Role of community colleges in STEM education: Thoughts on implications for policy, practice, and future research. *Journal of Women and Minorities in Science and Engineering, 16*(1), 85–96. doi:10.1615/JWomenMinorScienEng.v16.i1.60.

Howard, J. R., Milner-McCall, T., & Howard, T. C. (2020). *No more teaching without positive relationships.* Heinemann.

Humphrey, N., & Symes, W. (2010). Perceptions of social support and experience of bullying among pupils with autistic spectrum disorders in mainstream secondary schools. *European Journal of Special Needs Education, 25*(1), 77–91. doi:10.1080/08856250903450855

Hwang, K., Kwon, A., & Hong, C. (2017). A preliminary study of new positive psychology interventions: Neurofeedback-aided meditation therapy and modified positive psychotherapy. *Current Psychology, 36*(3), 683–695. doi:10.1007/s12144-016-9538-8

Hwang, Y. S., Noh, J. E., Medvedev, O. N., & Singh, N. N. (2019). Effects of a mindfulness-based program for teachers on teacher wellbeing and person-centered teaching practices. *Mindfulness, 10*(11), 2385–2402. doi:10.1007/s12671-019-01236-1

Iacovides, A., Fountoulakis, K. N., Kaprinis, S., & Kaprinis, G. (2003). The relationship between job stress, burnout and clinical depression. *Journal of Affective Disorders, 75*(3), 209–221. doi:10.1016/S0165-0327(02)00101-5

Jennings, P. A., & Greenberg, M. T. (2009). The prosocial classroom: Teacher social and emotional competence in relation to student and classroom outcomes. *Review of Educational Research, 79*(1), 491–525. doi:10.3102/0034654308325693

Jose, P. E., Lim, B. T., & Bryant, F. B. (2012) Does savoring increase happiness? A daily diary study. *The Journal of Positive Psychology, 7*(3), 176–187. doi:10.1080/17439760.2012.671345

Kabatt-Zinn, J. (1994). *Wherever you go, there you are: Mindfulness meditation in everyday life.* Hyperion.

Kern, M. L. (2021). PERMAH: A useful model for focusing on well-being in schools. In K. A. Allen, M. J. Furlong, S. M. Suldo, & D. A. Vella-Brodrick (Eds.), *The handbook of positive psychology in schools* (3rd ed.). Taylor and Francis.

Kern, M. L., Waters, L., Adler, A., & White, M. (2014). Assessing employee wellbeing in schools using a multifaceted approach: Associations with physical health, life satisfaction, and professional thriving. *Psychology, 5,* 500–513. http://dx.doi.org/10.4236/psych.2014.56060

Kern, M. L., Williams, P., Spong, C., Colla, R., Sharma, K., Downie, A., Taylor, J. A., Sharp, S., Siokou, C., & Oades, L. G. (2020). Systems informed positive psychology. *Journal of Positive Psychology, 15*(6), 705–715, doi:10.1080/17439760.2019.1639799

Kholi, R. (2018). Behind school doors: The impact of hostile racial climates on Urban Teachers of Color. *Urban Education, 53*(3), 307–333, doi:10.1177/0042085916636653

Kraus, C., Bartgis, J., Lahiff, M., & Auerswald, C. L. (2016). The gathering of native americans intervention: Cultivating hope and meaningful relationships for urban American Indian adolescents in California. *Journal of Adolescent Health, 60*(2), S1–S1. https://doi.org/10.1016/j.jadohealth.2016.10.024

Kyriacou, C. (1987). Teacher stress and burnout: An international review. *Educational Research, 29*(2), 146–152. doi:10.1080/0013188870290207

Lazarus, R. S., & Folkman, S. (1984). *Stress, appraisal, and coping.* Springer.

Ludwig, D. S., & Kabat-Zinn, J. (2008). Mindfulness in medicine. *JAMA, 300*(11), 1350–1352. doi:10.1001/jama.300.11.1350

Luk-Fong, P. Y. Y. (2009). Teachers' stress and a teachers' development course in Hong Kong: Turning 'deficits' into 'opportunities'. *Professional Development in Education, 35*(4), 613–634. Retrieved from https://doi-org.ezproxy.lib.monash.edu.au/10.1080/19415250903017341

Lyubomirsky, S., King, L., & Diener, E. (2005). The benefits of frequent positive affect: Does happiness lead to success? *Psychological Bulletin, 131*(6), 803–855. http://dx.doi.org/10.1037/0033-2909.131.6.803

Lyubomirsky, S., & Layous, K. (2013). How do simple positive activities increase well-being? *Current Directions in Psychological Science, 22*(1), 57–62. doi:10.1177/0963721412469809

Mahoney, J. L., Weissberg, R. P., Greenberg, M. T., Dusenbury, L., Jagers, R. J., Niemi, K., Schlinger, M., Schlund, J., Shriver, T. P., VanAusdal, K., & Yoder, N. (2020). Systemic social and emotional learning: Promoting educational success for all preschool to high school students. *American Psychologist.* Advance online publication. http://dx.doi.org/10.1037/amp0000701

Maslach, C., & Jackson, S. E. (1981). The measurement of experienced burnout. *Journal of Organizational Behaviour, 2,* 99–113. https://doi.org/10.1002/job.4030020205

Maslach, C., & Leiter, M. P. (2016). Understanding the burnout experience: Recent research and its implications for psychiatry. *World Psychiatry, 15*(2), 103–111. doi:10.1002/wps.20311

Maslow, A. H. (1998). *Toward a psychology of being* (3rd ed.).Wiley.

McCallum, F. (2021). Teacher and staff wellbeing: Understanding the experiences of school staff. In M. L. Kern & M. L. Wehmeyer (Eds.), *Palgrave handbook on positive education.* Palgrave Macmillan.

McCallum, F., & Price, D. (2010). Well teachers, well students. *The Journal of Student Wellbeing, 4*(1), 19–34. doi:10.21913/JSW.v4i1.599

McCallum, F., Price, D., Graham, A., & Morrison, A. (2017) *Teacher wellbeing: A review of the literature.* Association of Independent Schools NSW. Retrieved from https://apo.org.au/node/201816

McCullough, M. (2015). *Improving elementary teachers' well-being through a strengths-based intervention: A multiple baseline single-case design* [Unpublished master's thesis]. University of South Florida. Retrieved from ProQuest Dissertations & Theses Global. (Order no. 1749001781)

McLean, L., & McDonald Connor, C. (2015). Depressive symptoms in third-grade teachers: Relations to classroom quality and student achievement. *Child Development, 86*(3), 945–954. doi:10.1111/cdev.12344.

Melamed, S., Shirom, A., Toker, S., Berliner, S., & Shapira, I. (2006). Burnout and risk of cardiovascular disease: Evidence, possible causal paths, and promising research directions. *Psychological Bulletin, 132*(3), 327–353. doi:10.1037/0033–2909.132.3.327

Meyers, M. C., van Woerkom, M., & Bakker, A. B. (2013). The added value of the positive: A literature review of positive psychology interventions in organizations. *European Journal of Work and Organizational Psychology, 22*(5), 618–632. doi:10.1080/1359432X.2012.694689

Mousavi, S. V., Ramezani, M., Salehi, I., Hossein Khanzadeh, A. A., & Sheikholeslami, F. (2017). The relationship between burnout dimensions and psychological symptoms (depression, anxiety and stress) among nurses. *Journal of Holistic Nursing and Midwifery, 27*(2), 37–43. Retrieved from http://hnmj.gums.ac.ir/browse.php?a_id=882&sid=1&slc_lang=en&html=1

Nadav, A. G., Friedman, A. A. & Schrimshaw, E. W. (2021) Character strengths and their associations with well-being and mental distress among lesbian, gay, bisexual, and queer individuals. *Journal of Gay & Lesbian Social Services, 33*(2), 157–179. doi:10.1080/10538720.2020.1859424

Neves de Jesus, S., & Lens, W. (2005). An integrated model for the study of teacher motivation. *Applied Psychology, 54*(1), 119–134. doi:10.1111/j.1464–0597.2005.00199.x

OECD. (2018). *Children & young people's mental health in the digital age: Shaping the future.* Retrieved from https://www.oecd.org/els/health-systems/mental-health.htm

Ololube, N. P. (2006). Teachers job satisfaction and motivation for school effectiveness: An assessment. *Essays in Education, 18*(1), 9. Retrieved from https://openriver.winona.edu/eie/vol18/iss1/9

Parker, P. D., Martin, A. J., Colmar, S., & Liem, G. A. (2011). Teachers' workplace well-being: Exploring a process model of goal orientation, coping behavior, engagement and burnout. *Teaching and Teacher Education, 28,* 503–513. doi:10.1016/j.tate.2012.01.001

Patall, E. A., Cooper, H., & Robinson, J. C. (2008). The effects of choice on intrinsic motivation and related outcomes: A meta-analysis of research findings. *Psychological Bulletin, 134*(2), 270–300. https://doi.org/10.1037/0033-2909.134.2.270

Perry, N., Brenner, C., Collie, J.R., & Hofer, G. (2015). Thriving on challenge: Examining one teacher's view on sources of support for motivation and well-being. *Exceptionality Education International, 25*(1), 6–34; Retrieved from https://ir.lib.uwo.ca/eei/vol25/iss1/2

Peterson, C., & Seligman, M. (2004) *Character strengths and virtues.* Oxford University Press.

Pollard, E. L., & Lee, P. D. (2003). Child well-being: A systematic review of the literature. *Social Indicators Research, 61*(1), 59–78. doi:10.1023/A:1021284215801

Pressman, S. D., Kraft, T. L., & Cross, M. P. (2015). It's good to do good and receive good: The impact of a 'pay it forward' style kindness intervention on giver and receiver well-being. *The Journal of Positive Psychology, 10*(4), 293–302. doi:10.1080/17439760.2014.965269

Rashid, T. (2009). Positive interventions in clinical practice. *Journal of Clinical Psychology, 65*(5), 461–466. doi:10.1002/jclp.20588

Reiser, J. E., & McCarthy, C. J. (2018). Preliminary investigation of a stress prevention and mindfulness group for teachers. *The Journal for Specialists in Group Work, 43*(1), 2–34. doi:10.1080/01933922.2017.1338811

Richards, J. (2012, July). Teacher stress and coping strategies: A national snapshot. *The Educational Forum, 76*(3), 299–316. doi:10.1080/00131725.2012.682837

Roeser, R. W., Schonert-Reichl, K. A., Jha, A., Cullen, M., Wallace, L., Wilensky, R., Oberle, E., Thomson, K., Taylor, C., & Harrison, J. (2013). Mindfulness training and reductions in teacher stress and burnout: Results from two randomized, waitlist-control field trials. *Journal of Educational Psychology, 105*(3), 787–804. doi:10.1037/a0032093

Rogers, C. R. (1963) The concept of the fully functioning person. *Psychotherapy: Therapy, Research & Practice, 1*(1), 17–26. doi:10.1007/BF01769775

Ross, S. W., Romer, N., & Horner, R. H. (2012). Teacher well-being and the implementation of school-wide positive behavior interventions and supports. *Journal of Positive Behavior Interventions, 14*(2), 118–128. doi:10.1177/1098300711413820

Rothbard, N. P., & Patil, S. V. (2011). Being there: Work engagement and positive organizational scholarship. In G. M. Spreitzer & K. S. Cameron (Eds.), *The Oxford handbook of positive organizational scholarship* (pp. 1–25). Oxford University Press.

Ryff, C. D., & Keyes, C. L. M. (1995). The structure of psychological well-being revisited. *Journal of Personality and Social Psychology, 69*(4), 719. https://doi.org/10.1037/0022-3514.69.4.719

Saavedra, A. R., & Opfer V. D. (2012). Learning 21st-century skills requires 21st-century teaching. *Phi Delta Kappan, 94*(2), 8–13. doi:10.1177/003172171209400203

Schueller, S. (2012). Personality fit and positive interventions: Extraverted and introverted individuals benefit from different happiness increasing strategies. *Psychology, 3*, 1166–1173. doi:10.4236/psych.2012.312A172

Schueller, S. M., & Parks, A. C. (2014). The science of self-help. *European Psychologist, 19*(2), 145–155. http://dx.doi.org/10.1027/1016-9040/a000181

Schussler, D. L., Jennings, P. A., Sharp, J. E., & Frank, J. L. (2016). Improving teacher awareness and well-being through CARE: A qualitative analysis of the underlying mechanisms. *Mindfulness, 7*(1), 130–142. doi:10.1007/s12671-015-0422-7

Segal, Z. V., Teasdale, J. D., Williams, J. M., & Gemar, M. C. (2002). The mindfulness-based cognitive therapy adherence scale: Inter-rater reliability, adherence to protocol and treatment distinctiveness. *Clinical Psychology & Psychotherapy, 9*(2), 131–138. doi:10.1002/cpp.320

Seligman, M. E. P. (2006). *Learned optimism: How to change your mind and your life.* Vintage.

Seligman, M. E. P. (2011). *Flourish.* Simon & Schuster.

Seligman, M. E. P., & Csikszentmihalyi, M. (2000). Positive psychology: An introduction. *American Psychologist, 55*(1), 5–14. https://doi.org/10.1037/0003-066X.55.1.5

Shankland, R., & Rosset, E. (2017). Review of school-based positive psychological interventions: A taster for teachers and educators. *Educational Psychological Review, 29*, 363–392. doi:10.1007/s10648-016-9357-3

Shernoff, E. S., Mehta, T. G., Atkins, M. S., Torf, R., & Spencer, J. (2011). A qualitative study of the sources and impact of stress among urban teachers. *School Mental Health, 3*(2), 59–69. doi:10.1007/s12310-011-9051-z

Sin, N. L., & Lyubomirsky, S. (2009). Enhancing well-being and alleviating depressive symptoms with positive psychology interventions: A practice-friendly meta-analysis. *Journal of Clinical Psychology, 65*(5), 467–487. doi:10.1002/jclp.20593

Stapleton, P. (2019). *Teachers are more depressed and anxious than the average Australian.* Retrieved from https://theconversation.com/teachers-are-more-depressed-and-anxious-than-the-average-australian-117267

Steger, M. F. (2012). Experiencing meaning in life: Optimal functioning at the nexus of spirituality, psychopathology, and well-being. In P. T. P Wong (Ed.), *The human quest for meaning* (2nd ed., pp. 165–184). Routledge.

Stephens, P. J., Greenman, C. D., Fu, B., Yang, F., Bignell, G. R., Mudie, L. J., Pleasance, E. D., Lau, K. W., Beare, D., Stebbings, L. A., McLaren, S., Lin, M. L., McBride, D. J., Varela, I., Nik-Zainal, S., Leroy, C., Jia, M., Menzies, A., Butler, A. P., Teague, J. W., Quail, M. A., Burton, J., Swerdlow, H., Carter, N. P., Morsberger, L. A., Iacobuzio-Donahue, C., Follows, G. A., Green, A. R., Flanagan, A. M., Stratton, M. R., Futreal, P. A., Campbell, P. J., & McLaren, S. (2011). Massive genomic rearrangement acquired in a single catastrophic event during cancer development. *Cell, 144*(1), 27–40. doi:10.1016/j.cell.2010.11.055

Tarrasch, R., Berger, R., & Grossman, D. (2020). Mindfulness and compassion as key factors in improving teacher's well-being. *Mindfulness, 11*, 1049–1061. doi:10.1007/s12671-020-01304-x

Taylor, M. J. (2018). Using CALMERSS to enhance teacher well-being: A pilot study. *International Journal of Disability, Development and Education, 65*(3), 243–261. doi:10.1080/1034912X.2017.1394985

The Wellbeing Lab. (2020?). *The wellbeing lab 2020 workplace report.* Retrieved from https://www.michellemcquaid.com/thewellbeinglab/

Thomson, S. (2017). The effects of inequity in Australian schools. Professional Voice, *12*(1). Australian Education Union. Retrieved from https://www.aeuvic.asn.au/effects-inequity-australian-schools

Thompson, G. (2013). NAPLAN, MySchool and accountability: Teacher perceptions of the effects of testing. *International Education Journal: Comparative Perspectives, 12*(2), 62–84. Retrieved from http://openjournals.library.usyd.edu.au/index.php/IEJ

Vella-Brodrick, D. A., Rickard, N. S., & Chin, T. C. (2014). *An evaluation of positive education at Geelong Grammar School: A snapshot of 2013.* The University of Melbourne. Retrieved from https://findanexpert.unimelb.edu.au/scholarlywork/913722-an-evaluation-of-positive-education-at-geelong-grammar-school--a-snapshot-of-2013

Vo, D. T., & Allen, K. A. (2020). *A systematic review of school-based positive psychology interventions to foster teacher wellbeing* [Manuscript submitted for publication]. Faculty of Education, Monash University.

Waters, L. (2011). A review of school-based positive psychology interventions. *The Educational and Developmental Psychologist, 28*(2), 75–90. doi:10.1375/aedp.28.2.75

Waters, L., & Stokes, H. (2015). Positive education for school leaders: Exploring the effects of emotion-gratitude and action-gratitude. *The Educational and Developmental Psychologist, 32*(1), 1–22. doi:10.1017/edp.2015.1

Wessels, E., & Wood, L. (2019). Fostering teachers' experiences of well-being: A participatory action learning and action research approach. *South African Journal of Education, 39*(1), doi:10.15700/saje.v39n1a1619

White, C. A., Uttl, B., & Holder, M. D. (2019). Meta-analyses of positive psychology interventions: The effects are much smaller than previously reported. *PLoS ONE, 14*(5), e0216588. https://doi.org/10.1371/journal.pone.0216588

White, M., & Kern, M. (2018). Positive education: Learning and teaching for wellbeing and academic mastery. *International Journal of Wellbeing, 8*(1), 1–17. doi:10.5502/ijw.v8i1.588

Williams, P., Kern, M. L., & Waters, L. (2016). Inside-out-outside-in: A dual approach process model to developing work happiness. *International Journal of Wellbeing, 6*(2), 30–56. doi:10.5502/ijw.v6i2.3

WHO (World Health Organization). (2003). *Creating an environment for emotional and social well-being: An important responsibility of a Health Promoting and Child Friendly School.* Retrieved from https://www.who.int/school_youth_health/resources/information_series/en/

WHO (World Health Organization). (2015). *Promoting mental health: Concepts, emerging evidence, practice (Summary Report).* World Health Organization. Retrieved from https://apps.who.int/iris/handle/10665/42940

Wood, A. M., Froh, J. J., & Geraghty, A. W. (2010). Gratitude and well-being: A review and theoretical integration. *Clinical Psychology Review, 30*(7), 890–905. doi:10.1016/j.cpr.2010.03.005

Wood, A. M., Joseph, S., Lloyd, J., & Atkins, S. (2009). Gratitude influences sleep through the mechanism of pre-sleep cognitions. *Journal of Psychosomatic Research, 66*(1), 43–48. doi:10.1016/j.jpsychores.2008.09.002

Yalom, I. D., & Crouch, E. C. (1990). The theory and practice of group psychotherapy. *The British Journal of Psychiatry, 157*(2), 304–306. doi:10.1192/S0007125000062723

Zee, M., & Koomen, M. Y. (2016). Teacher self-efficacy and its effects on classroom processes, student academic adjustment and teacher well-being: A synthesis of 40 years of research. *Review of Educational Research, 86*(4), 981–1015. doi:10.3102/0034654315626801

Zins, J. E. (Ed.). (2004). *Building academic success on social and emotional learning: What does the research say?* Teachers College Press.

INDEX

Note: **Bold** page numbers refer to tables, *Italic* page numbers refer to figures and page number followed by "n" refer to end notes.

symptom proportion 61
system approaches 419
systemic improvement goals 354–355
systems approach 522

Tan, A. G. 339
TARGET Goal Structure scale 303
TARGETS framework; *see also* teacher practices
task motivation 337
teachability 29
teacher-centered instruction 325
teacher-completed assessments 235
teacher-led program 158
teacher practices: authority 301; evaluation 302–
303; grouping 303; recognition 302–303; social
304–305; tasks 299–301; time 303–304
teachers: academic self-efficacy 276; of academic
subjects 29; autonomy-supportive behaviors 174;
beliefs and behavior 111; competence support 28;
emotional support from 30; express enthusiasm
28; feedback to students 302; GiveThx App 125,
127; involvement 519; and learner 98; personal
change and growth 163–164; positive feedback
28; self-efficacy 271; stress management skills
139; well-being 98
teacher–student relationships 234, 236
teacher training 472–474
teacher well-being 542; PPIs (*see* positive
psychology interventions (PPIs)); stress and
burnout 543–544; understanding well-being
544–545
teaching mental health programs 111
technical soundness 238–239
technology-based programs, schools 512
technology role: academic self-efficacy 278
test anxiety transactional model 321
Thapa, A. 234
theory of change (ToC) 417, 419, **430–432**, 433
"theory of mind" 184
Theron, L. C. 232
Thomas, E. 406
"thought–emotion link" 192
Tian, L. 123, 388, 390, 468
Tong, L. 253, 255
topic emotions 320
*Toward an Integration of Subjective Well-Being and
Psychopathology* (Greenspoon and Saklofske) 56
tragic optimism 502
trait mindfulness assessment tools 140–141
transactional stress model 321
transaction model 323
transdisciplinary lenses 251–254; mental health
and well-being 253; school belonging adoption
252–253; skills and competencies 253; social
identity 253; understanding 257–259
transparent communication plan 357
Trends in International Mathematics and Science
Study (TIMSS) 208, 209, 250

Troubled and Complete Mental Health groups 62
troubled mental health 469
Trzesniewski, K. H. 203
Tudge, J. R. 129
Turkish youths: assessing resilience 498, 502;
mental health problems 496
Turner, J. C. 288, 327
Tvedt, M. S. 30
Tyson, O. 111

The U.K. Resilience Program (UKRP) 457–458
UN Convention on the Rights of the Child 182
undergraduate students study 106
Underwood, B. 223
Üner, S. 496
Ungar, M. 493, 494
UNICEF 451
United Nations Convention on the Rights of the
Child 398
United States Institute of Education Sciences 57
universality 27
universal school-based programs 437
universal school wellness screening 78–79
universal screening 230
University of Melbourne (UoM) 420, 422
University of Melbourne Human Ethics Research
Committee 186
urban education 247–248, 253, 254
U.S. Department of Education Institute of
Education Sciences (IES) 42
U.S. Department of Education School Climate
Surveys (EDSCLS) 240
U.S. public school system 283, 285

Valentine, J. C. 205, 206
Values in Action (VIA) 22
variable-focused approaches 495
Veit, C. T. 56
Velez, V. 404
Vella-Brodrick, D. A. 440, 446, 515–518
victimization 75
video games 289–290
virtual reality 512
visual narrative analysis (VNA) 185
Vo, D. T. 549, 551
"voice," sense of 28
Voight, A. 404
vulnerable mental health 469
Vygotsky, L. S. 157, 158

"Walls of Well-being" (WOWs) 183
Walton, K. 500
Wang, C. 42
Ware, J. E. 56
Waters, L. 461, 547
weekly meetings 551
Weiner, B. 105, 321
Weiner's theory 105